WYATT AND DASHWOOD'S

EUROPEAN UNION LAW

FOURTH EDITION

By

ANTHONY ARNULL
B.A. (Sussex), Ph.D. (Leicester)
Solicitor of the Supreme Court of England and Wales
Professor of European Law and
Director of the Institute of European Law
University of Birmingham

ALAN DASHWOOD
B.A. (Rhodes), M.A. (Oxon)
Of the Inner Temple, Barrister
Director in the Legal Service of the Council
of the European Communities
Visiting Professor of Law in the University of Leicester

MALCOLM ROSS
LL.B., M.Phil
Professor of European Law
University of Sussex

and

DERRICK WYATT, Q.C.
M.A., LL.B. (Cantab.), J.D. (Chicago)
Of Lincoln's Inn, Barrister
Fellow of St. Edmund Hall, Oxford
and Professor of Law, University of Oxford

LONDON
SWEET & MAXWELL
2000

First Edition 1980
Second Impression 1981
Third Impression 1986
Second Edition 1987
Second Impression 1990
Third Impression 1991
Third Edition 1993
Second Impression 1993
Third Impression 1994
Fourth Edition 2000

Published in 2000 by
Sweet & Maxwell Limited of
100 Avenue Road, London NW3 3PF
(http://www.sweetandmaxwell.co.uk)
Typeset by Dataword Services Limited, Chilcompton
Printed in England by Clays Ltd, St Ives plc

A CIP catalogue record for this book
is available from the British Library

ISBN 0421 680 407

PREFACE

The aim of the fourth edition of this book is essentially the same as that of its predecessor; to produce a work that could stand on its own as a textbook for general university courses on European Union Law, while also providing in-depth analysis of the main topics of European economic and social law explored in more specialised courses. We hope, too, that practitioners will find it useful to have the discussion of substantive legal issues placed in the context of the constitutional principles and institutional arrangements of the Communities and of the Union, and we are encouraged in this hope by references to previous editions in the arguments of counsel in litigation, and in judicial decisions.

The scheme of this edition is similar to that of the last edition, although we have omitted the chapter on social security for migrants, in order to allow for a more detailed and extensive exposition and critical analysis of what we regard as core subject matter relating to the internal market (covering the free movement of goods, persons and services, and the legislative mechanisms for completing the internal market). There is more detailed treatment in this edition of the judicial architecture of the Communities, and of the jurisdiction of the Community courts. We also address the Amsterdam Treaty's arrangements for "flexibility" (successor to what is described in the older literature as "variable geometry"), and provide more detailed exposition of the principles of subsidiarity and proportionality. There is a new chapter on Economic and Monetary Union. Chapters on competition law, state aids, sex discrimination, and education and vocational training have been revised and/or rewritten to deal with the changes which have taken place as the result of new and amended legislation, and the case law of the Community courts. The increased size of the present edition— more than one hundred pages longer than the third edition—reflects the scale and complexity of the evolution that has taken place in recent years.

This book has remained a team effort, and the members of the team have co-operated as equal partners in the exercise of producing this fourth edition of "Wyatt and Dashwood". Anthony Arnull wrote Chapters 9–11 (Jurisdiction of the Community Courts), and 27 and 28 (Aspects of Social Law and Policy, comprising Sex Discrimination, and Education and Vocational Training). Alan Dashwood wrote Chapters 1–3 (History, Institutions, and Legal Process); 7 (Conservatory Principles) and 18 (European Community and European Union); 17 (Completing the Internal Market) and 18 (Economic and Monetary Union). Malcolm Ross wrote Chapters 19–26 (Competition Policy, including Restrictive Practices, Abuse of a Dominant Position, Mergers, State Aids and Public Undertakings). Derrick Wyatt wrote Chapters 4–6 (The Community Legal Order), and 12–16 (Customs Duties and Discriminatory Internal Taxation,

Quantitative Restrictions and Measures having Equivalent Effect, Free Movement of Workers, the Right of Establishment and Freedom to provide Services, Residuary of Movement and Residence and Citizenship of the European Union).

We have given the Articles of the E.C. Treaty and the TEU their new numbering with the old number in brackets. However, occasionally, when referring to a historical situation, we have used the old numbering, so as (we hope!) to avoid confusion, and we have generally done the same where quoting from documents using the old numbering, such as judgments of the Community courts.

To those who have encouraged and supported us, we extend our thanks.

Anthony Arnull
Alan Dashwood
Malcolm Ross
Derrick Wyatt

August 2000

CONTENTS

PART I: HISTORICAL INTRODUCTION

PART II: INSTITUTIONS AND LEGISLATIVE PROCESS

PART III: THE LEGAL ORDER

PART IV: JURISDICTION OF THE COURT OF JUSTICE AND THE COURT OF FIRST INSTANCE

PART V: THE INTERNAL MARKET AND ECONOMIC AND MONETARY UNION

PART VI: COMPETITION POLICY

PART VII: ASPECTS OF SOCIAL LAW AND POLICY

TABLE OF CASES (ALPHABETICAL)

TABLE OF CASES (EUROPEAN COURT OF JUSTICE)

TABLE OF CASES (EUROPEAN COURT OF FIRST INSTANCE)

E.C. COMMISSION DECISIONS

NATIONAL CASES

INTERNATIONAL TRIBUNAL CASES

E.C. TREATIES AND CONVENTIONS

Note. For convenience, all references to sections of the 1957 EEC and 1992 E.C. Treaties are tabled under the 1957 EEC Treaty only.

REGULATIONS

DIRECTIVES

COUNCIL DECISIONS

RULES OF PROCEDURE (OF THE EUROPEAN COURT OF JUSTICE AND COURT OF FIRST INSTANCE)

U.K. LEGISLATION

INTERNATIONAL TREATIES AND CONVENTIONS

PART I: HISTORICAL INTRODUCTION

CHAPTER 1

FROM THE FOUNDING TREATIES TO THE TREATY ON EUROPEAN UNION

The Schuman Plan and the establishment of the ECSC

Although there was a certain ideological groundswell in favour of a "United Europe" shortly after the Second World War[1]—as evidenced by the call of the 1948 Hague Congress for Western European economic and political union—the first concrete steps towards integration were prompted by the spectre of Soviet expansion. Within days of the signature by France and the United Kingdom of the Dunkirk Treaty, providing for mutual assistance in the event of a renewal of hostilities with Germany, the breakdown of the Moscow Conference over the future of occupied Germany was to set the pattern for future strained relations between the U.S.S.R. on the one side, and the United States, Great Britain and France on the other. Despite the indispensable United States defence commitment affirmed in the North Atlantic Treaty, Western Europe stood divided and vulnerable in the face of a Soviet Union whose wartime military potential had been scarcely diminished by demobilisation, and whose political influence had been enhanced by successful Communist Party coups in Bulgaria, Rumania, Poland and Czechoslovakia.[2] It was in this context that Mr Robert Schuman, the French Foreign Minister, made an historic proposal to a ministerial meeting in London on May 9, 1950.[3] His proposal was for nothing less than the fusion of the coal and steel industries of France and Germany, and any other countries wishing to participate, under a supranational High Authority. Not only would such a pooling of production make future conflict between France and Germany impossible, it would provide a sound basis for economic expansion. The implications of the scheme were clearly far-reaching, constituting, as Mr Schuman explained, "the first concrete foundation for a European Federation which is indispensable for the preservation of peace."

The Schuman Plan was enthusiastically endorsed by the Benelux countries, France, Germany and Italy, but the United Kingdom declined to participate, refusing to accept the supranational role of the projected High Authority. The Treaty Establishing the European Coal and Steel Community (or ECSC) was signed in Paris on April 18, 1951, and came into force on July 20 of the following

---

[1] On the historical context, see A. S. Milward, *The Reconstruction of Western Europe 1945–51* (1984). On the early history of the European Communities, see Michael Palmer *et al.*, *European Unity* (1968), Introduction; Gladwyn, *The European Idea* (1967), Chap. 4; A. H. Robertson, *European Institutions* (3rd ed., 1973), pp. 5–17; D. Urwin, *The Community of Europe: A History of European Integration* (2nd ed., 1995).

[2] *NATO—Facts and Figures* (1971, Brussels), Chap. 1.

[3] For the French text, see *Documents on International Affairs* (1949–50), pp. 315–317. An English translation (from which the quotations in the text are extracted) appears in 22 Department of State Bulletin at pp. 936, 937.

year. It was concluded for a period of 50 years from that date and is, therefore, due to expire in July 2002.[4]

The strategy of the Treaty, inspired by the Schuman Declaration, was to set limited and specific economic objectives as steps towards the long-term political objective of European unity. The preamble to the Treaty announced that Europe was to be built "through practical achievements which will first of all create real solidarity, and through the establishment of common bases for economic development." The economic community created pursuant to the Treaty was to constitute "the basis for a broader and deeper community among peoples long divided by bloody conflicts" and the foundations were to be laid "for institutions which will give direction to a destiny henceforward shared."

The central economic mechanism of the ECSC is a common market for coal and steel.[5] A definition of this mechanism, from a negative point of view, is given by Article 4 of the Treaty, which provides that the following are recognised as incompatible with the common market for coal and steel and shall accordingly be abolished and prohibited within the Community:

(a) import and export duties, or charges having equivalent effect, and quantitative restrictions on the movement of products;
(b) measures or practices which discriminate between producers, between purchasers or between consumers, especially in prices and delivery terms or transport rates and conditions; and measures or practices which interfere with the purchaser's free choice of supplier;
(c) subsidies or aids granted by States, or special charges imposed by States, in any form whatsoever;
(d) restrictive practices which tend towards the sharing or exploiting of markets.

Article 4 thus envisages a Community-wide market for coal and steel free from interference by the Member States or by economic operators tending to impede the flow of trade or to distort the play of competition. The Community is empowered to carry out its task under the Treaty "with a limited measure of intervention," *inter alia* by placing financial resources at the disposal of undertakings for investment and by bearing part of the cost of readaptation.[6] Only when circumstances so require it is authorised to exert direct influence upon production or upon the market, for instance by imposing production quotas.[7]

The EDC and EPC—a false dawn

Significant as the founding of the ECSC may have been, it contributed little of itself to the increasingly pressing problem of incorporating West Germany into the defence network established by the Brussels and North Atlantic Treaties.

---

[4] Art. 97 ECSC. If no steps are taken to renew the ECSC Treaty (and there is no plan to do so) the coal and steel sectors will come within the purview of the E.C. Treaty.
[5] Art. 1 ECSC proclaims that the Community is "founded upon a common market, common objectives and common institutions."
[6] Art. 5 ECSC.
[7] *ibid.* second sub-para., third indent.

While the United States was enthusiastic for German participation, France was naturally chary of seeing her recently vanquished enemy so soon rearmed. At the instigation of Sir Winston Churchill and Mr Paul Reynaud[8] the Consultative Assembly of the Council of Europe[9] called for the "immediate creation of a unified European Army, under the authority of a European Minister of Defence, subject to proper European democratic control and acting in full co-operation with the United States and Canada."[10]

After a French initiative known as the "Pleven Plan," the Treaty Establishing the European Defence Community (EDC) was signed—subject to ratification—by the Benelux countries, France, Germany and Italy.[11] Once again the United Kingdom held aloof. If the ECSC had been calculated to bind Germany to France industrially, the European Defence Community was to provide the framework for German rearmament.

The projected Defence Community had two significant characteristics. First, it was to be endowed with a supranational institutional structure not unlike that of the Coal and Steel Community. Secondly, its statute assumed that it would be of a transitional nature, and would give way to some more comprehensive form of federal or confederal European Union.

The EDC Treaty provided for a European Army, composed of units placed at the disposal of the Council of Ministers by the Member States. A Common Budget would be drawn up, and an executive body, the "Commissariat," would lay down common programmes in the field of armaments, provisioning and military infrastructure. The objects of the Community were to be purely defensive, within the context of the North Atlantic Treaty.

The transitional nature of the proposed Community was evidenced by the terms of Article 8(2), which provided that the institutional structure laid down in the Treaty would remain in force until displaced by the establishment of the federal or confederal organisation envisaged by Article 38.

This latter Article required the Assembly of the EDC to make proposals to the Governments of the Member States on the establishment of a directly elected Assembly, and the powers it should exercise. Particular regard was to be had to the principle that such a modified Parliamentary body should be able to constitute one of the elements in a subsequent federal or confederal structure.

These proposals were to be presented to the Governments of the Six after the Assembly of the EDC assumed its functions, but within days of the signature of the Treaty the Consultative Assembly of the Council of Europe

---

[8] Robertson, *op. cit.*, note 1, *supra*, p. 18.

[9] The Council of Europe is an inter-governmental organisation established in 1949. Its aim is to achieve greater unity among its members, and to this end it seeks agreement on common action "in economic, social, cultural, scientific, legal and administrative matters and in the maintenance and further realisation of human rights and fundamental freedoms". See Bowett, *The Law of International Institutions* (4th ed., 1982), p. 168; Robertson, *op. cit.* p. 36.

[10] Resolution of the Consultative Assembly of the Council of Europe, August 11, 1950; *Documents on International Affairs* (1949–50), p. 331. As is clear from the quotation cited in the text, the Council at times interprets the terms of its statute with some liberality. Robertson, *op. cit.* note 1, *supra*, p. 19.

[11] May 27, 1952. See *Documents on International Affairs* (1952), pp. 116–162. See also E. Furdson, *The European Defence Community: A History* (1979).

resolved that it would be "of great advantage if the basic principles of a European supranational political authority and the nature and limits of its powers were defined within the next few months, without waiting for the entry into force of the Treaty instituting the European Defence Community."[12] Despite the fact that the Assembly provided for in Article 38 of the EDC Treaty was not yet in existence, and that the Article only referred to the constitution of a future Parliamentary body, the Foreign Ministers of the Member States of the Coal and Steel Community requested the Members of the Coal and Steel Community Assembly to co-opt additional Members, reorganise the distribution of seats laid down in the Paris Treaty in accordance with that prescribed for the Assembly of the proposed EDC, and draw up a draft Treaty for a European Political Community (EPC). On March 10, 1953, the "Ad Hoc Assembly" presented the requested draft.[13]

The "European Community" proposed by the Ad Hoc Assembly provided for the extensive political and economic integration of its Members. Its aims were as follows:

— to contribute towards the protection of human rights and fundamental freedoms in Member States;
— to co-operate with the other free nations in ensuring the security of Member States against all aggression;
— to ensure the co-ordination of the foreign policy of Member States in questions likely to involve the existence, the security or the prosperity of the Community;
— to promote . . . the development of employment and the improvement of the standard of living in Member States, by means, in particular, of the progressive establishment of a common market. . . .

To ensure the protection of human rights in the proposed Community, provision was made for the application—as part of the Community Statute—of the provisions of section I of the European Convention on Human Rights, along with the first Protocol to that Convention, signed in Paris on March 20, 1952.

The Institutions of the EPC were to comprise a bicameral legislature, a European Executive Council, a Council of National Ministers, Court of Justice, and an Economic and Social Council. Financial resources would be derived from a combination of Community taxation and contributions from the Member States.

The hopes of those who saw the future of Western Europe in immediate federation were dashed when the French Parliament voted against ratification of the EDC Treaty. A change of Government in France, and an easing of tension

---

[12] Resolution of May 30, 1952. Texts Adopted (1952), and see *Report on the Constitutional Committee instituted to work out a Draft Treaty setting up a European Political Community* (Paris, December 20, 1952), p. 6.
[13] See *Information and Official Documents of the Constitutional Committee of the Ad Hoc Assembly* (Paris, 1953), pp. 53 *et seq.* For a brief but informative account of the events surrounding the preparation of the draft Treaty and its ultimate demise, see Richard T. Griffiths, "Europe's First Constitution: The European Political Community, 1952–1954" in S. Martin (ed.) *The Construction of Europe* (1994).

between East and West,[14] contributed to the rejection of the Treaty by the combined votes of Gaullists, Communists, Socialists and Radicals.[15]

In the event, Germany's participation in the defence of Western Europe was achieved by other means. The Paris Agreements of October 23, 1954 provided for the recognition of the Federal Republic of Germany as a sovereign state, and for its subsequent accession to the North Atlantic Treaty.[16]

The Spaak Report and the two Treaties of Rome

Despite the setback represented by the rejection of the EDC Treaty, the Six were still convinced of the need for closer integration. At a Conference held in the Sicilian city of Messina in 1955, the Foreign Ministers of the ECSC countries expressed the belief that the time had come to make "a fresh advance towards the building of Europe," but that this must be achieved "first of all, in the economic field."[17] The two objectives were agreed of developing atomic energy for peaceful purposes, and establishing a European common market. An intergovernmental committee under the Chairmanship of the Belgian Foreign Minister, Mr Paul-Henri Spaak, was entrusted with the task of making proposals to this end. The United Kingdom was invited to participate in the work of the committee, but although a Board of Trade official was initially dispatched, he was recalled after a few weeks.

The Spaak Report was published in April 1956.[18] In the light of its conclusions two new Treaties were negotiated, one providing for the establishment of a European Economic Community (EEC) and the other for the establishment of a European Atomic Energy Community (Euratom). The EEC and Euratom Treaties were signed in Rome on March 25, 1957 and came into force on January 1, 1958.

The preamble to the EEC Treaty expresses the determination of the High Contracting Parties "to lay the foundation of an ever closer union among the peoples of Europe," and, from 1958, it has been that Treaty which has provided the main framework of the continuing process of European integration. As we shall see, successive amendments to the Treaty have greatly extended the range and variety of the governmental activities falling within its scope. This reached a point where it was thought appropriate to drop the adjective "Economic" from the name of the Community: it is now known simply as "the European Community" (or E.C.).[19] To avoid confusion, from here on we refer to the Community by that name, and to the Treaty as "the E.C. Treaty". When making

---

[14] Robertson, *op. cit.* n.1, *supra*, p. 21.

[15] Palmer, *loc. cit.* n.1, *supra*.

[16] *NATO—Facts and Figures* (Brussels, 1971), p. 35. For the Protocol to the North Atlantic Treaty on the Accession of the Federal Republic of Germany, and the texts known collectively as the "Paris Agreements," see Apps. 9 and 10.

[17] *Documents on International Affairs* (1955), p. 163; Cmnd. 9525.

[18] *Rapport des chefs de délégation aux ministres des affaires étrangères* (Brussels), April 21, 1956. A summarised translation of Part I of the Spaak Report—"The Common Market" was published by Political and Economic Planning as Broadsheet No. 405 of December 17, 1956.

[19] The change of name was effected by the TEU (see below).

an historical point, as in the present Chapter, we refer to "the original EEC Treaty".

The central mechanism of the E.C. was, and is, a common market covering all economic sectors other than those falling within the purview of the ECSC or Euratom Treaties.[20] The aim is to create, on a Community scale, economic conditions similar to those on the market of a single state.[21] This involved the establishment of a customs union, through the elimination of all customs duties and quantitative restrictions (or quotas) in trade between the Member States and the erection of a common customs tariff (C.C.T.), as well as the removal of barriers to the free movement of "the factors of production"—labour, business and capital. In addition, the Treaty contains rules designed to prevent competition from being restricted by arrangements between private operators, or by government subsidies or the activities of state monopolies. Legal machinery was provided for the harmonisation of national legislation that may have a bearing on the well-functioning of the common market. Other primordial features of the system are the common agricultural policy and the common transport policy, relating to sectors where a completely free market was thought impracticable; and provisions relating to the Community's external trade and the possibility of creating an "association" with a third country or an international organisation.[22]

A single set of institutions

The ECSC Treaty created four main institutions—a High Authority, a Special Council of Ministers, a Common Assembly and a Court of Justice. In accordance with the Schuman Plan, the leading role in the implementation of the Treaty was given to a supranational High Authority, whose members were under a duty to act with complete independence, in the Community interest.[23] The High Authority was empowered to take legally binding decisions[24] and was authorised, *inter alia*, to procure funds,[25] to fix maximum and minimum prices for certain products[26] and to fine undertakings in breach of the ECSC's rules on competition.[27] The Special Council of Ministers, a body composed of representatives of the Member States, was given the function of harmonising "the action of the High Authority and that of Governments, which are responsible for the general economic policies of their countries."[28] With limited exceptions, the role of the Council in the institutional system of the ECSC is confined to consultation with the High Authority and the giving (or withholding) of its assent (*avis conforme*) to actions which the latter is proposing to take.

---

[20] See Art. 305 (ex 232) E.C.
[21] See the description of the common market in Case 15/81 *Schul v. Inspecteur de Invoerrechten en Accijnzen* [1982] E.C.R. 1409 at 1431–1432; [1981] 3 C.M.L.R. 229.
[22] As to the extension of the scope of the E.C. Treaty by the SEA, the TEU and the T.A., see below.
[23] Art. 9 ECSC, replaced by Merger Treaty, Art. 10.
[24] Art. 14 ECSC.
[25] Art. 49 ECSC.
[26] Art. 61 ECSC.
[27] Arts 65 and 66 ECSC.
[28] Art. 26 ECSC.

According to the E.C. and Euratom Treaties, the two later Communities were each to have, in their turn, four main institutions—an Assembly, a Council, a Commission and a Court of Justice—but, to avoid unnecessary proliferation, a Convention was signed contemporaneously with the Treaties of Rome providing for there to be a single Assembly (now the European Parliament) and a single Court to carry out the functions assigned to those institutions under the three Community Treaties.[29] For some years after 1957, however, in addition to the High Authority and the Special Council of Ministers of the ECSC, there was a separate E.C. Council and Commission and a separate Euratom Council and Commission. That situation was brought to an end by the Treaty establishing a Single Council and a Single Commission of the European Communities (known as the "Merger Treaty") which was signed in April 1965 and came into force in July 1967.[30] From that time, the ECSC, the E.C. and Euratom have been served by the same set of institutions whose powers vary depending on the Treaty under which they act for a given purpose.

As will be seen in Chapters 2 and 3, below, in the institutional structure of the Rome Treaties, and particularly of the E.C. Treaty, decision-making power is concentrated in the hands of the Council, and the role of the Commission is principally that of the initiator, and subsequently the executant, of Council decisions.[31] This difference, as compared with the institutional structure of the ECSC, is explained by the fact that, whereas the rules applicable to the coal and steel sectors are spelt out in considerable detail in the ECSC Treaty itself, in many areas of E.C. competence the Treaty merely establishes a framework for common action, leaving fundamental political choices to be made by the Community institutions. It was inevitable that the final say in respect of such choices be left to the Council, the institution in which Member States are directly represented.

Enlargement—from six to fifteen

Largely in response to the creation of the E.C., Austria, Denmark, Norway, Sweden, Switzerland, Portugal and the United Kingdom signed the Stockholm Convention on January 4, 1960, and the European Free Trade Association (or EFTA) came into being in May of that year. The primary object of the "Outer Seven" was to offset any detrimental effects to their trade resulting from the progressive elimination of tariffs inside the Community by a similar reduction within EFTA.

To a certain extent, EFTA was regarded as a stepping stone to possible future Community membership. As the White Paper that was published in July 1971 setting out the terms agreed, and the case for, United Kingdom membership of the Communities explained: "From the outset . . . it was recognised that some

---

[29] Convention on certain Institutions Common to the European Communities, March 25, 1957; see Sweet & Maxwell's *Encyclopedia of European Comunity Law, European Community Treaties*, Vol. I, Pt. B8, B8–029.

[30] Treaty Establishing a Single Council and a Single Commission of the European Communities; see Sweet & Maxwell's *Encyclopedia*, B8–034.

[31] The Commission is also "guardian of the Treaties," with powers to ensure that the Member States and other Community institutions comply with their obligations: see, in particular, Art. 211 (ex 155) E.C., first indent and Arts 226 (ex 169), 230 (ex 173) and 232 (ex 175) E.C.

members of the EFTA might eventually wish to join, and others to seek closer trading arrangements with, the European Communities."[32] Indeed, barely 14 months after the Stockholm Convention entered into force, the Macmillan Government applied for E.C. membership. This was to be the first of two applications thwarted by the opposition of President de Gaulle of France. After lengthy negotiations had taken place with the Six, the French President made it clear, in January 1963, that he would not consent to British accession.

Applications in 1967 by the United Kingdom, Denmark, Ireland and Norway met with a similar rebuff. Nevertheless, these four countries left their applications "lying on the table," and at the Hague Summit Conference of the Six in December 1969, summoned on the initiative of the new President of France, Mr Pompidou, it was agreed that "The entry of other countries of the continent to the Communities . . . could undoubtedly help the Communities to grow to dimensions more in conformity with the present state of world economy and technology. . . . In so far as the applicant States accept the Treaties and their political objective . . . the Heads of State or Government have indicated their agreement to the opening of negotiations between the Community on the one hand and the applicant States on the other."[33]

Negotiations between the applicant States and the Six formally opened on June 30, 1970, and a Treaty of Accession was eventually signed on January 22, 1972. The provisions of the Treaty, and the detailed adaptations contained in the Act of Accession annexed to it, have served as a model, *mutatis mutandis*, for later enlargements. The only institutional changes required were those resulting from the need to accommodate the additional Member States. The elimination of customs duties and quotas between the prospective Member and the Six, and the adoption of the Common External Tariff, were to be phased in between April 1973 and July 1977. A transitional period was also to be allowed for the adoption of the Common Agricultural Policy, and for the build up of contributions to the Community budget. Although the United Kingdom would be compelled to forego Commonwealth preference as such, special arrangements were agreed for the access of New Zealand diary products and lamb, and the importation of sugar from Commonwealth suppliers. It was understood that association arrangements comparable with those already accorded to developing countries enjoying traditional relations with the original Six would be made with developing countries in the Commonwealth.[34]

On January 1, 1973, the Treaty of Accession entered into force, and Denmark, Ireland and the United Kingdom became Members of the three Communities. Norway, which had signed the Treaty on January 22, 1972, did not proceed to ratification, following an adverse result in a national referendum held on the issue of membership.

---

[32] See *The United Kingdom and the European Communities*, Cmnd. 4715. After the accession of Denmark, Ireland and the United Kingdom of the European Communities, Austria, Finland, Norway, Portugal, Sweden and Switzerland entered into free trade agreements within the Nine. See *Seventh General Report on the Activities of the European Communities* (1973), p. 400.

[33] *Third General Report on the Activities of the Communities* (1969) Annex—Documents on the Summit Conference, pp. 497, 489.

[34] See [1973] O.J. L2/1.

British membership of the Communities was briefly put in doubt by the election in February 1974 of a Labour Government. Although the membership negotiations which were brought to a successful conclusion by the Conservative administration had been set in train by their predecessors, Labour in opposition declared themselves unable to accept the terms of entry finally agreed. When Labour returned to power, the Government of Mr Harold Wilson set out to "renegotiate" the agreed terms in respect of agriculture, contributions to the Community Budget, economic and monetary union, state aids to industry, movement of capital, the Commonwealth and developing countries, and value added tax, and on January 23, 1975 it was announced that a national referendum would be held on the results of the renegotiation. The Government declared itself satisfied with those results and felt able to recommend to the British people that they cast their votes in favour of continued membership of the European Communities.[35] This view was endorsed by an overwhelming majority of the votes in the referendum which followed on June 5, 1975.[36]

The transitional period for the accession of the three new Member States was barely half spent when a further application for membership was received from Greece. Negotiations commended on July 27, 1976. The instruments relating to Greece's accession were signed in Athens on May 28, 1979 and Greece became the tenth Member State on January 1, 1981.[37]

Meanwhile, Spain and Portugal had also applied for membership. After long and sometimes difficult negotiations, the instruments of accession were signed in Madrid and Libson on June 12, 1985 and Spain and Portugal joined the Communities on January 1, 1986.[38]

The latest enlargement, which took place on January 1, 1995, brought into the European Union (or "E.U."), as it had by then become (see below), three States which had formerly belonged to EFTA—Austria, Finland and Sweden.[39] Norway had also applied for membership, and had taken part in the negotiations and signed the accession instruments; however, once again as in 1972, the referendum in that country on the ratification of the Treaty of Accession produced a negative result. So, at the time of writing, the original Six had become the Fifteen, comprising all the European States that escaped the imposition of Communist regimes protected by Soviet military power in the aftermath of the Second World War, with the exception of Iceland, Norway, Lichtenstein and Switzerland.

The collapse of those Communist regimes, which was symbolised by the dismantling of the Berlin Wall in 1989, and given concrete reality by the withdrawal of the Red Army behind the borders of what was once more to become Russia, has opened up the perspective of a new and even more challenging enlargement of the E.U. So-called "Europe Agreements" have been concluded with a large number of central and eastern European countries (or "CEECs")—Bulgaria, the Czech Republic, Hungary, Poland, Romania, Slovakia

---

[35] See, *Membership of the European Community*, Cmnd. 5999; *Report on Renegotiation*, Cmnd. 6003.
[36] See R. E. M. Irving, "The United Kingdom Referendum" (1975–76) 1 E.L.Rev. 1.
[37] [1979] O.J. L291.
[38] [1985] O.J. L302.
[39] [1994] O.J. C241/10. See also Council Dec. 95/1/E.C. Euratom, ECJC, [1995] O.J. L1/1, adjusting the instruments of accession in the light of Norway's failure to ratify.

and Slovenia, together with the three Baltic Republics that were formerly part of the Soviet Union, Estonia, Latvia and Lithuania. The Agreements establish a close "association" between the E.U. and each of those countries, and explicitly hold out the prospect of eventual accession. They have been bolstered by the adoption of pre-accession strategies to help each of the countries concerned prepare for membership, *inter alia*, by providing technical assistance on the harmonisation of their legislation and administrative structures and practices with those of the Union. Other candidates for membership of the Union are Cyprus, Malta and Turkey, with which the E.C. has longstanding association agreements.[40]

The European Council held in Luxembourg in December 1997 decided that accession negotiations should formally be opened with five of the CEECs, namely the Czech Republic, Estonia, Hungary, Poland and Slovenia, as well as with Cyprus. The other seven candidate countries were not, however, to remain out in the cold for long. The Helsinki European Council in December 1999 reaffirmed "the inclusive nature of the accession process, which now comprises 13 candidate States within a single framework". Those States, it was said, "are participating in the accession process on an equal footing". Clearly, though, not all of the candidates will fulfil the political and economic criteria for membership of the Union at the same time. The Helsinki Conclusions state that "the Union should be in a position to welcome new Member States from the end of 2002 as soon as they have demonstrated their ability to assume the oblgiations of membership and once the negotiating process has been successfully completed".[41]

Amendments and development of the founding Treaties

Apart from the amendments contained in the Merger Treaty and in successive Accession Treaties, the texts of the three founding Treaties have been amended or developed over the years by a series of Treaties, Decisions or Acts, the most significant of which are identified below.

The Budgetary Treaties of 1970 and 1975

These two Treaties, which were signed, respectively, on April 22, 1970 and on July 22, 1975, replaced the original budgetary procedure of the Communities with a new one giving important powers to the European Parliament.[42] The different roles in that procedure of the Council, which has the last word in respect of so-called "compulsory expenditure," and the Parliament, which has the last word in respect of "non-compulsory expenditure," are analysed in the next chapter. The 1975 Treaty also created a new body, the Court of Auditors, to act as a financial watchdog for the Communities.

---

[40] "Association" is a form of relationship involving "special, privileged links with a non-member country": Case 12/86 *Demirel* [1987] E.C.R. 3719, para. 9.

[41] See Presidency Conclusions, paras 3 to 13.

[42] The text of the 1970 Treaty is published at [1971] O.J. L2/1 and that of the 1975 Treaty at [1977] O.J. L359/1.

Own resources decisions

In the early years of the EEC and Euratom, the Communities' revenue came from direct financial contributions by the Member States, according to scales that were laid down by the Treaties. However, Article 269 (ex 201) EEC and Article 173 Euratom looked forward to the replacement of financial contributions by a system giving the Communities their "own resources."[43] A legislative procedure was provided for the establishment of such a system by a unanimous decision of the Council, acting on the basis of proposals by the Commission and after consulting the European Parliament, with the additional step that the Council decision be recommended to the Member States for adopting in accordance with their respective national requirements. That especially solemn procedure gives the decisions to which it applies a legal status only slightly inferior to the Treaties themselves.

A first own resources Decision was adopted in 1970.[44] This has been replaced by a series of Decisions, the latest one due to take effect from 2002 as part of the "Agenda 2000" financial package (see Chapter 2, below).[45]

Under present arrangements, revenue from the following sources constitutes own resources entered in the budget of the Communities:

— levies and other charges imposed in respect of trade in agricultural products under the rules of the common agricultural policy;
— customs duties levied under the C.C.C. on imports from third countries;
— the application of a uniform rate[46] to a uniform VAT assessment base determined in a uniform manner for Member States in accordance with Community rules;
— the application of a rate (variable from year to year, depending on the amount of additional revenue needed to balance the budget) to the sum of all the Member States' G.N.P.[47]

Of those four categories of own resources, only agricultural levies and customs duties (often referred to as "traditional own resources") have the true character of Community taxes. They are collected on behalf of the Communities by the Member States which have the right to retain, by way of collection costs, 10 per cent of the amounts paid.[48] The VAT own resource does not give the Communities a fixed share of Member States' *actual* VAT receipts, since the prescribed rate is applied to an artificially constructed assessment basis. As for the G.N.P. own resource, its purpose is, in part, to redress the economically regressive effect of the VAT resource, which, because it is related to consumption, falls more heavily on the less prosperous Member States, by shifting the burden towards those that are more prosperous. The G.N.P. rate is fixed each year under the budgetary procedure, to cover the amount needed to balance the budget, after account has been taken of revenue from the other three resources.

---

[43] The relevant provision of the E.C. Treaty, Art. 200, was deleted as being obsolete by the T.A. Different financial arrangements apply under the ECSC Treaty: see Arts 49 ECSC *et seq.*
[44] Council Dec. 70/243 [1970] O.J. L94/19.
[45] At the time of writing the new Decision had been approved in principle by the Council but was still awaiting formal adoption.
[46] Dec. Art. 2(1)(c) and (4).
[47] 1999 Decision, Art. 2(1)(d).
[48] 1999 Decision, Art. 2(3), applicable from 2001.

It may be added that, from 1985 onwards, own resources Decisions have included a mechanism for the correction, in favour of the United Kingdom of so-called "budgetary imbalances," *i.e.* the difference between payments to, and receipts from, the Community budget.[49]

A directly elected European Parliament

Article 190(4) (ex 138(3)) EEC and the corresponding provisions of the other Treaties[50] lay down a solemn procedure for the enactment of rules for direct elections to the European Parliament. Under that procedure, an Act concerning the election of the representatives of the European Parliament by direct universal suffrage was approved by the Council in September 1976 and recommended to the Member States for adoption in accordance with their respective constitutional requirements.[51] The first elections were held in June 1979 and these have been followed by elections in 1984, 1989, 1994 and 1999. Further discussion of these developments is found in the section relating to the European Parliament in the next Chapter.

The Single European Act

The Single European Act (SEA) was signed on February 17, 1986 and entered into force on July 1, 1987.[52] Its odd-seeming title is explained by the fact that, within a single legal instrument, there were juxtaposed provisions amending the three European Community Treaties and provisions organising co-operation in the inter-governmental sphere of foreign policy.

The amendments to the Treaties contained in Title II of the SEA were the most extensive adopted up to that time. They included the introduction of a new "co-operation procedure" giving the European Parliament a significantly enhanced role in the legislative process, which is discussed in Chapter 3. One of the principal objectives of the SEA was to ensure the completion of the E.C.'s internal market by the end of 1992: in Chapter 17 we consider the special legal machinery provided in order to achieve this, and how it has functioned in practice.[53] The SEA also inserted into the E.C. Treaty a number of specific new legal bases for Community action, for example on economic and social cohesion,[54] on research and technological development[55] and on the protection of the environment.[56]

Title III of the SEA contained the Treaty provisions on European Co-operation in the sphere of foreign policy, known more shortly as "European Political Co-operation" (or EPC). Those provisions have been superseded by Title V of the Treaty on European Union, which constitutes the legal basis for the common foreign and security policy (see below).

---

[49] See Chap. 2.
[50] Art. 21(3) ECSC; Art. 108(3) Euratom.
[51] Council Dec. 76/787 [1976] O.J. L278/1.
[52] The SEA is published at [1987] O.J. L169/1.
[53] See, in particular, Art. 14 (ex 7a) and Art. 95 (ex 100a).
[54] Arts 158 to 162 (ex 130a to 130e).
[55] Arts 163 to 173 (ex 130f to 130p).
[56] Arts 174 to 176 (ex 130r to 130t).

The Treaty on European Union (TEU)

The Treaty on European Union[57] (often referred to by the name of the Dutch city, Maastricht, where it was signed in February 1992) entered into force on November 1, 1993.

The Treaty brought into being a new legal and political entity, the European Union. Article 1 (ex A) TEU says that "[t]he Union shall be founded on the European Communities, supplemented by the policies and forms of co-operation established by this Treaty". That wording brings out the complex character of the Union and the preponderant influence of the three Communities (E.C., ECSC and Euratom) within it. The clumsy phrase, "policies and forms of co-operation", refers to the legal arrangements provided by Title V and Title VI of the TEU, which organise the activity of the common institutions in two fields of activity the Member States could not agree to bring within the purview of the E.C. Treaty. Title V concerns the common foreign and security policy (or CFSP). Broadly speaking, that covers the *political* aspect of external relations (diplomatic contacts, election monitoring and other forms of political assistance to third countries, security activities such as peace-keeping and peace-making, prospectively even defence), to be distinguished from external *economic* relations (such as trade, development co-operation and emergency aid) which are within the competence of the E.C. The two branches of the European Union's external relations competence require delicate consideration. In the TEU as originally concluded, Title VI grouped together, under the heading "Co-operation in the fields of justice and home affairs" (or JHA), a variety of matters concerning the treatment of third country nationals and aspects of law enforcement and the maintenance of public order. These included: aspects of the free movement of persons, such as asylum policy, the control of the Union's external frontiers, and immigration policy; combating drug addition and international fraud; and co-operation between the Member States' judicial, customs and police authorities. As we shall see, certain of those matters have now been transferred to the E.C. Treaty, pursuant to the Treaty of Amsterdam (T.A.).

The image of a Greek temple façade, with three pillars joined by a pediment, is commonly used to illustrate the constitutional structure that was created by the TEU. The difference between the "First Pillar" (comprising the three Communities) and the "Second and Third Pillars" (respectively, Titles V and VI of the TEU) lies in the much lesser degree to which, in respect of the latter, the sovereign powers of the Member States have been curtailed. The "pediment" consists of the elements common to the three components of the Union, notably that they are served by a single institutional framework,[58] and that there is common machinery for the amendment of the Treaties[59] and for enlargement.[60] The relationship between the E.C. and the E.U. is further explored in Chapter 8, below.[61]

---

[57] [1992] O.J. C191/1. Note that the numbering of the TEU, like that of the E.C. Treaty, was altered by the Treaty of Amsterdam.

[58] Art. 3 (ex C) TEU.

[59] Art. 48 (ex N) TEU.

[60] Art. 49 (ex O) TEU.

[61] The structure created by the TEU has been much criticised. See, in particular, Everling, "Reflections on the Structure of the Union" (1992) 29 C.M.L.Rev. 1053; Curtin, "The Constitutional Structure of the Union: a Europe of Bits and Pieces" (1993) 30 C.M.L.Rev. 17.

Besides establishing the Union structure, the TEU effected a number of significant reforms within the European Community system (the First Pillar), two of which may briefly be noticed here. First, an effort was made to tackle the problem of the "democratic deficit" in the system, by changing the rules on the appointment of the Commission and by introducing a new legislative procedure, commonly referred to as "co-decision", both measures being designed to enhance the role of the European Parliament: these are matters considered in Chapter 2 and 3, below. Secondly, the Treaty contains detailed provisions on the organisation of economic and monetary union (EMU), and a timetable for its realisation in three stages. It was specifically provided that the third stage, involving the introduction of a single currency, must start, at the latest, on January 1, 1999; and so, in the event, it did, with the introduction on that date of the "euro" as the currency of 11 out of the 15 Member States. EMU is the subject of Chapter 18, below.

The ratification process of the TEU was thrown off course by the negative outcome of the referendum that was held in Denmark in June 1992. Subsequent referenda in Ireland in June, and in France in September 1992, brought votes in favour of ratification, although in the latter case by a narrow margin. Political and economic uncertainty increased as a result of turbulence in the international money markets during the period immediately preceding and following the French referendum, and this led to the suspension by Italy and the United Kingdom of their membership of the exchange rate mechanism of the European Monetary System and to the reintroduction of exchange rate controls by Spain and Ireland. However, at an extraordinary meeting of the European Council at Birmingham on October 16, 1992, the Heads of State or Government reaffirmed their commitment to the TEU. It was agreed that the Community must develop together, on the basis of the TEU, while respecting, as the Treaty did, the identity and diversity of the Member States.[62]

That positive development was confirmed by the European Council held in Edinburgh on December 11 and 12, 1992. Agreement was reached in Edinburgh on texts establishing interpretations of various provisions of the TEU which the Danish authorities announced would make it possible to hold a second referendum, with a good prospect that Denmark would be in a position to ratify the Treaty. The European Council also approved texts on the application by the Council of the principle of subsidiarity (see Chapter 7, below) and on greater "openness" in the legislative process. Finally, there was agreement on the financial arrangements that were applied for the seven-year period to 1999 ("the Delors II package"[63]), and this, in turn, opened the way for the launching, early in 1993, of negotiations with the EFTA applicants for Community membership.[64]

There were more alarms and delays during 1993. Ratification of the TEU by the Parliament of the United Kingdom was achieved by the narrowest of margins; and in Germany the Treaty was the subject of a legal challenge before

---

[62] See Presidency Conclusions, Birmingham, October 1992, to which the text of the "Birmingham Declaration" is annexed.

[63] See the discussion, in Chap. 2, of the financial arrangements under which relative peace has been preserved between the Council and the European Parliament in budgetary matters, since 1988.

[64] See Presidency Conclusions, Edinburgh, December 1992.

the Constitutional Court.[65] Thus, it was only on January 1, 1993, towards the end of the Belgian Presidency, that the TEU finally entered into force, and the European Union appeared as a new player on the international stage.

The Treaty of Amsterdam (T.A.)

To some of those who had been involved in the Intergovernmental Conference (IGC) on the TEU, the institutional reforms that were agreed seemed disappointing; and provision was made in Article N(2) of the Treaty (since deleted by the T.A.) for a new IGC to be convened as early as 1996, in order to consider further changes. However, the ambition to press ahead with further "deepening" of European integration was overtaken by other aims which became the primary focus of the 1996 IGC: to counteract the alienation of public opinion from the whole European Union enterprise, which had become painfully apparent during the process of ratifying the TEU; and to effect the changes in the composition and functioning of the institutions of the Union, necessary in order to pave the way for an enlargement, by then perceived as politically ineluctable, that would bring in many (and eventually perhaps all) the countries of central and eastern Europe, as well as other applicants from the Mediterranean area.[66]

The IGC on the Treaty of Amsterdam completed its work in June 1997, and the Treaty was signed in October of that year. The ratification process went more smoothly than that of the TEU, and the T.A. entered into force on May 1, 1999.[67]

A major achievement of the Treaty was the reform of the Community legislative process, in ways that are considered in detail in Chapter 3, below. As previously mentioned, the T.A. also brought about a significant shift of matters relating to the treatment of third country nationals from the Third Pillar to the First Pillar: there is a new Title IV of Part Three of the E.C. Treaty on "Visas, asylum, immigration and other policies related to free movement of persons", which also includes provisions relating to judicial co-operation in civil matters. The reorganised Third Pillar is now focused on "Police and judicial co-operation in criminal matters", where the scope of Union powers has been notably extended. Another reform, which will be examined in Chapter 7 below, was the adoption of the principle of "closer co-operation" (or flexibility). The idea behind the principle is that it should be possible for a limited number of Member States to establish, within the institutional framework of the Union, rules in relation to a certain matter, which will apply only to themselves, and not to the non-participating Member States.

There were, however, two important issues, regarded as relevant to the impending enlargement of the Union, on which the IGC on the Treaty of Amsterdam was unable to reach agreement: the size and composition of the Commission; and the distribution of votes between the Member States when the

---

[65] See Bundesvervassungsgericht, judgment of October 12, 1993, 2 BvR 2134 and 2 BvR 2153/92 [1994] 1 C.M.L.R. 57. Noted by Crossland at (1994) 19 E.L.Rev. 206 *et seq.*

[66] On the task of the IGC, see Dashwood (ed.), *Reviewing Maastricht Issues for the 1996 IGC* (Sweet and Maxwell, London, 1996).

[67] On the T.A. in general, see Duff, *The Treaty of Amsterdam* (Sweet and Maxwell, London, 1997); Langrish, "The Treaty of Amsterdam: Selected Highlights" (1998) 23 E.L.Rev. 3.

Council[68] acts by a qualified majority (the so-called "weighting" of votes in the Council). Those matters, together with a possible extension of the policy areas in which the Council is empowered to act by a qualified majority (rather than by unanimity), are on the agenda of a new IGC which, at the time of writing, was on the point of being convened, and which is expected to complete its work by December 2000.[69]

The process of structural reform that was set in motion by the SEA has thus continued, almost without interruption, into the new century.

---

[68] The political and legal link established between those two matters is dicussed in Chap. 2, below.
[69] See Presidency Conclusions, Helsinki, December 1999, para. 15.

PART II: INSTITUTIONS AND LEGISLATIVE PROCESS

CHAPTER 2

THE INSTITUTIONS OF THE EUROPEAN UNION

Article 7 (ex 4) of the E.C. Treaty

According to Article 7 (ex 4) E.C. the tasks entrusted to the Community are to be carried out by five institutions—a European Parliament, a Council, a Commission, a Court of Justice and a Court of Auditors.[1] It is expressly provided that each of the institutions "shall act within the limits of the powers conferred on it by this Treaty." Thus the institutional system is founded on the idea of the "attribution of powers."[2] The Community institutions have only the powers given to them expressly or impliedly by the Treaties.

The founding Treaties endowed each of the European Communities with separate institutions. However, as we have seen, a Convention on certain Institutions common to the European Communities, which came into force at the same time as the E.C. and Euratom Treaties, provided for there to be a single Assembly and a single Court of Justice exercising the various powers attributed to those institutions by the three Treaties. This was followed by the establishment, from July 1967, of a single Council of the European Communities, replacing the Special Council of Ministers of the ECSC, and the E.C. and Euratom Councils, and a Commission of the European Communities, replacing the High Authority of the ECSC, and the E.C. and Euratom Commissions.[3] The unity of the institutions will be maintained by the provision in Article 3 (ex C), first paragraph of the TEU that the Union shall be served by a single institutional framework.[4]

Besides the five Community institutions listed in its first paragraph, Article 7 mentions, in its second paragraph, the Economic and Social Committee and the Committee of the Regions. The role of these two bodies is to assist the Council and the Commission by giving advisory opinions. The Economic and Social Committee, which has been in existence since the establishment of the E.C. and Euratom, consists of representatives of the different categories of economic and social life and of the general interest, while the Committee of the Regions, which was created by the Treaty on European Union, consists of representatives of regional and local bodies.[5] Power to appoint the members of these Committees is given to the Council acting unanimously on the basis of lists of names put forward by each of the Member States. The decision to establish a Committee of the Regions represents a response to political demands in certain Member

---

[1] The three Community Treaties contain identical sets of provisions on the main institutions. References in this Chapter are to the E.C. Treaty.
[2] As to this, and the other "conservatory principles" of the constitutional order, see Chap. 7, *infra*.
[3] The Treaty Establishing a Single Council and a Single Commission of the European Communities was signed on April 8, 1965 and entered into force on July 13, 1967. See Chap. 1, *supra*.
[4] See the discussion of the structure of European Union in Chap. 8.
[5] On the Economic and Social Committee, see Arts 257 to 262 (ex 193 to 198) E.C. On the Committee of the Regions, see Arts 263 to 265 (ex 198a to 198c) E.C.

States, particularly those with a federal structure, that regional and local interests be given a direct line of communication to the Community institutions. It remains to be seen whether the new Committee will become a significant political force.

The Court of Auditors was created by the Financial Treaty of 1975, replacing the former Audit Board. The TEU "promoted" the Court of Auditors to paragraph (1) of Article 7, thus giving it the full status of a Community institution: previously it was mentioned in a separate paragraph (3). Under powers which have been spelt out in progressively greater detail in the TEU and the T.A., the Court of Auditors is required to examine the accounts of all Community revenue and expenditure and ensure their reliability, and the legality and regularity of the underlying transactions. Its annual report, and the replies of the institutions under audit to its observations, are essential elements in the exercise of giving a discharge to the Commission in respect of the implementation of the budget, and it may also, at any time, submit observations on specific questions and deliver opinions at the request of one of the Community institutions.[6]

The remainder of the present chapter will be devoted to a closer examination of the Communities' three main *political* institutions—the Council, the Commission and the European Parliament. However, before turning to those institutions, it is necessary to consider a body which, although not an institution in the sense of Article 7(1), may be regarded as the supreme political authority of the Union—the European Council.

The European Council[7]

It was at the summit meeting of European Community leaders in Paris in December 1974 that the decision was taken to hold regular meetings at the highest political level, within a "European Council." The first European Council was held in Dublin in March 1975, and the series of meetings continued on an informal basis for some years. A legal basis for the activity of the European Council is now to be found in Article 4 (ex D) of the TEU.

According to that Article, the European Council brings together the Heads of State or Government of the Member States and the President of the Commission, who are assisted by Ministers of Foreign Affairs and by a member of the Commission. The formula "Heads of State or Government" is designed to accommodate the constitutional position of the French President. Meetings are chaired by the Head of State or Government of the Member State holding the Presidency of the Council for the time being. At least two meetings must be held per year, *i.e.* one in each six-monthly Presidency. However, it is common for additional meetings to be called on an ad hoc basis.

The role of the European Council which the years has become increasingly significant, is essentially a political one. This is emphasised by Article 4 of the

---

[6] As to the composition and powers of the Court of Auditors, see Arts 246 to 248 (ex 188a to 188c) E.C. As to its role in the discharge of the Budget, see Art. 276 (ex 206) E.C.

[7] See J. Werts, *The European Council* (1992, North-Holland). See also A. H. Lauwaars (1977) C.M.L.Rev. 25.

TEU which states in its first paragraph: "The European Council shall provide the Union with the necessary impetus for its development and shall define the general political guidelines thereof." To demonstrate the contribution European Councils have made to the strategic development of the Communities, it is enough to recall: the meeting in Bremen in July 1978 when the foundations of the European monetary system were laid; the meeting in Fontainebleau in June 1984 when work was set in train which eventually bore fruit in the institutional reforms of the SEA; the meeting in Hanover in June 1988 when the project of establishing an economic and monetary union was relaunched; and the series of meetings at which the criteria for, and the modalities of, the accession to the Union of the countries of central and eastern Europe have been laid down, from Copenhagen in June 1993 to Helsinki in December 1999. The Fontainebleau meeting illustrates another function of the European Council—that of unravelling knotty political problems which have defeated the efforts of the institutions. It was at that meeting that a solution was found to the long-running dispute about the level of the United Kingdom's net contribution to the Community budget.[8] European Councils also provide an opportunity for reviewing foreign policy questions, both those falling within the Communities' external competence and those which are the subject of the common foreign and security policy.

Does the existence of the European Council, unforeseen by the original Treaties, distort the institutional structure of the Communities? The question is a legitimate one, since the task of leading the Member States along the road towards the ever closer union referred to in the preamble to the E.C. Treaty and in Article 1 (ex A) TEU might be thought to belong more particularly to the Commission. Experience, however, has shown that a strongly led Commission has nothing to fear and everything to gain from working in close partnership with the European Council to achieve its medium term objectives. Thus political support from successive European Councils was an important factor in the implementation of the White Paper of 1985 on completing the internal market and in the realisation of plans for economic and monetary union with the introduction of the euro in January 1999.

The Council[9]

The first paragraph of Article 203 (ex 146) E.C. provides: "The Council shall consist of a representative of each Member State *at ministerial level*, authorised to commit the government of that Member State" (emphasis added). That

---

[8] The solution consisted of providing for a "correction" of the amount payable by the United Kingdom under the rules for the calculation of the "own resources" which constitute the Communities' revenue. Provision has been made for this correction in successive Council Decisions on own resources. The advantage from the United Kingdom's point of view, of the solution devised at Fontainbleau is that unanimity is required for the adoption of own resources decisions: see Art. 269 (ex 210) E.C.

[9] See Dashwood, "The Role of the Council of the European Union" in Curtis and Heukels (eds), *Institutional Dynamics of European Integration*, Vol. II (1994), p. 117; Dashwood, "The Council of the European Union in the Era of the Amsterdam Treaty", in Heukels, Blokker and Brus (eds), *The European Union after Amsterdam* (1998), p. 117.

wording allows Member States with a devolved structure to be represented, when the Council is dealing with matters falling within the competence of regional authorities, by a member of one of those authorities rather than by a minister in the central government.[10] In such a case, the regional minister concerned would have to be authorised to act on behalf of the Member State as a whole, so that his agreement to a matter on the Council agenda would bind that Member State both legally and politically. At all events, it is clear that a representative within the meaning of Article 203 must be a person holding political office, *i.e.* not a civil servant.

In law, the Council is a unitary institution: in other words, it is the same institution with the same powers under the Treaties, whatever the particular national responsibilities of the ministers attending a given meeting. However, the Council customarily meets in certain formations, determined in accordance with the matters on the agenda. The General Affairs Council, which brings together Foreign Ministers, deals with external relations and with broad institutional and policy issues, providing a measure of co-ordination of the Council's multifarious activities. It also has the task of preparing European Councils. Another Council with a wide remit is the Economic and Financial Affairs (or Ecofin) Council which, like the General Affairs Council, meets, in principle, monthly except in August. The Ecofin Council is responsible for, *inter alia*, tax harmonisation and, generally, for the co-ordination of the economic policies of Member States. More specialised Council formations in which important legislative business is regularly transacted include the Agriculture, Internal Market, Environment and Transport Councils. There are also Councils which handle specific business at certain times of the year, such as the Budget Council, which normally meets in July to establish the draft general budget of the Communities and in November to give the draft budget a second reading. Other Councils meet more sporadically, depending on the priorities of different Presidencies. The Helsinki European Council in December 1999 decided that, to ensure coherence and consistency, the number of Council formations should be reduced to a maximum of 15.

Recent procedural changes have put the principle of the unicity of the Council under some strain. Article 121 (ex 109j) E.C., which was introduced into the Treaty by the TEU, provides for certain decisions connected with the transition to the third stage of EMU and the establishment of a single currency to be taken by the Council "meeting in the composition of the Heads of State or Government" on the basis of recommendations put to it by the Council meeting in one of its ordinary formations (in practice, the Ecofin Council). It is a constitutional innovation that powers should be expressly reserved for the Council in a particular formation and that the basis for the exercise of those powers should consist of recommendations from the same institution meeting in a different formation. Another example is the procedure of Article 11 E.C. for the authorisation of closer co-operation initiatives, which was brought in by the T.A. (as closer to co-operation or "flexibility", see Chapter 7). A qualified majority decision by the Council, acting in the formation determined by the subject-matter of the proposed co-operation, can be blocked by a Member State for "important

---

[10] The United Kingdom could, for instance, be represented by a member of the Scottish Executive.

and stated reasons of national policy". If that happens, the Council may request that the matter be referred to the Council meeting in the composition of Heads of State or Government. An important point to note in this context is that there is a clear distinction in law between the 15 Heads of State or Government taking decisions as a formation of the Council in the sense of Article 203 E.C.—which will be the case here—and the same leaders meeting as the European Council, with the President of the Commission as a sixteenth member.

Article 3 of the Council's Rules of Procedure[11] allows a member of the Council (*i.e.* a minister) unable to be present at a meeting, or part of it, to arrange to be represented. His place will usually be taken by the Permanent Representative or the Deputy Permanent Representative of the Member State concerned. Since the latter are civil servants, they cannot, strictly speaking, cast their minister's vote: Article 9(3) of the Rules of Procedure provides that delegation of the right to vote can only be made to another member of the Council. In practice, however, non-ministerial representatives vote in accordance with the instructions of their Governments, theoretically under the "cover" of one of the ministers present. Article 9(3) of the Rules of Procedure must be read together with Article 206 (ex 150) E.C. which provides that, where a vote is taken, a Council member may act on behalf of not more than one other member. The combined effect of the two provisions, now spelled out in Article 9(4) of the Rules of Procedure, is that a majority of the members of the Council entitled to vote on a given matter must be present, to enable a vote to be taken.

The Presidency of the Council is held in turn by the Member States for periods of six months, following the order laid down by the Council pursuant to Article 203, second paragraph of the Treaty.[12] The duties of the Presidency include, besides taking the chair at Council meetings, the convening of meetings[13] and the establishment of the provisional agenda, which must be circulated to other members of the Council at least a fortnight in advance and must contain an indication of the items on which a vote may be taken.[14] The Presidency has come to play an active role in managing the progress of Commission proposals through the Council. Negotiations between national delegations within the Council take place in relation to a series of compromise texts devised by the Presidency with a view to securing the necessary majority or unanimity for the adoption of the measure in question. A Presidency is expected to show objectivity in furthering proposals, without undue regard to its specific national interests. A certain rivalry has developed between Presidencies in seeking to achieve an impressive "score" of measures adopted, and this has undoubtedly been a factor in the acceleration of the legislative process in recent years.

---

[11] The Rules were first published in 1979: see [1979] O.J. L268/1. The latest version is to be found at [1999] O.J. L147/13.

[12] See Council Dec. 95/2/E.C., Euratom, ECSC, fixing the following order, as from January 1995, [1995] O.J. L1/220: France, Spain, Italy, Ireland, Netherlands, Luxembourg, United Kingdom, Austria, Germany, Finland, Portugal, France, Sweden, Belgium, Spain, Denmark, Greece.

[13] Rules of Procedure, Art. 1(1).

[14] Rules of Procedure, Art. 2(1) and (2). The items on which a vote may be taken are indicated on the draft agenda by an asterisk. If no such indication is given, a matter cannot be put to the vote under Art. 9 of the Rules of Procedure, except by unanimous agreement of the Council.

The work of the Council is prepared by a Committee of Permanent Representatives (COREPER) who are senior national officials based in Brussels. The legal basis of COREPER's activities is Article 207(1) (ex 151(1)) E.C. The Committee operates at two levels, that of COREPER II, composed of the Permanent Representatives, who are of ambassadorial rank, and that of COREPER I, composed of the Deputy Permanent Representatives. The distribution of files between the two parts of COREPER is intended to reflect the more political nature of those given to COREPER II (for example, external relations), and the more technical nature of those given to COREPER I (for example, internal market legislation), but in practice even technical-seeming matters, such as the organisation of veterinary checks, may have political implications for some Member States. COREPER does not concern itself with matters relating to agricultural market organisations: the task of preparing the work of the Agriculture Council on these matters has been effectively delegated to the Special Committee on Agriculture. In addition, with the extension of European Union activity into new fields, the need was felt for the creation of bodies capable of providing the Council with specialised back-up. The relationship between COREPER and bodies such as the Economic and Financial Committee, the Political Committee (concerned with the CFSP) and the Co-ordinating Committee (concerned with police and judicial co-operation in criminal matters) is inevitably somewhat delicate. The Committees' contribution to the preparation of Council business is, however, stated by the relevant Treaty provisions to be "without prejudice to Article 207," thereby preserving the position of COREPER as the filter through which such business must pass.[15] The principle is important because, with so many different formations of the Council, there is a danger political coherence may be lost: COREPER is the only Council body able to take a horizontal view of the development of Community policies.

The business that comes to COREPER will have been prepared, in turn, by specialised working groups made up of national officials. In addition to the numerous standing groups, COREPER from time to time establishes *ad hoc* groups to deal with matters requiring specific expertise.

The Council, COREPER and working groups are assisted by an independent body of civil servants, the General Secretariat. This has Article 207(2) (ex 151(2)) E.C. as the legal basis for its activities. The T.A. enhanced the status of the Secretary General of the Council by combining the office with that of "High Representative for the CFSP" (see also Article 26 TEU). The day-to-day running of the General Secretariat has been entrusted to the Deputy Secretary General.

Council agendas are divided into a Part A and a Part B.[16] Items listed in Part A (known as A-points) are those which COREPER has agreed may be adopted by the Council without discussion, which does not exclude the possibility for a delegation to have a statement or a negative vote recorded in the minutes. Any member of the Council, or the Commission, may ask for an item to be taken

---

[15] See, respectively, E.C. Treaty, Art. 114(2) (ex 109c(2)) and TEU Arts 25 (ex Art. J.15) and 36 (ex Art. K8).
[16] Rules of Procedure, Art. 2(7).

off the list of A-points, in which case the item will be held over for a later Council, unless a simple majority of Council members decides that it should remain on the agenda.[17] In the latter event, the item cannot be voted on unless the A-point list on which it appears was circulated within the 14-day time limit.[18] The A-point procedure is often used for the formal adoption of texts which have been agreed in principle at an earlier Council.

Turning from the composition and organisation of the Council to its powers, these are described in the first two indents of Article 202 (ex 145) in an oddly cursory way. The first indent says the Council is to "ensure co-ordination of the general economic policies of the Member States" and the second indent that it is to "have power to make decisions."[19]

The Council's function of economic policy co-ordination is now carried out under the arrangements of the E.C. Treaty relating to Economic and Monetary Union (EMU). The guiding principles, stated in Article 4 (ex 3a) of the Treaty, and reiterated in Article 98 (ex 102a), are those of "an open market economy with free competition, favouring an efficient allocation of resources". Among other things, the Member States have put themselves under a legal duty to avoid excessive government deficits, and the Council (in practice, Ecofin) has been empowered to intervene actively, to ensure compliance.[20] The arrangements are examined more fully in Chapter 18, below.

The reference in the second indent of Article 202 to the Council's "power to take decision" highlights its essential role in the system of the E.C. and Euratom Treaties—that of the institution that has to decide for or against measures developing or extending the body of primary rules contained in the Treaties.[21] The system of the ECSC Treaty is different: powers of decision are given under that Treaty not so much for the creation of new primary rules as for the implementation of the rules laid down by the Treaty itself; the Commission is the natural recipient of such a power, its exercise being subject, however, to the assent of the Council in certain cases.[22] We return to the subject of decision-making by the Council, including the once vexed question of majority voting, in the next chapter.

Consistently with its central role in the creation of law in the internal Community sphere, the Council has to agree to the acceptance by the E.C. of new obligations in international law resulting from the conclusion of agreements

---

[17] Rules of Procedure, Art. 2(8).

[18] Rules of Procedure, Art. 2(2). In theory, the members of the Council might decide *unanimously* that the item be put to the vote.

[19] The third indent of Art. 202 which concerns implementing powers, is discussed *infra* in connection with the powers of the Commission.

[20] See Art. 104 (ex 104c) E.C. and Protocol (No. 5) on the excessive deficit procedure.

[21] In the "co-decision" procedure, which is discussed in the next Chapter, the Council acts jointly with the European Parliament.

[22] The Commission is given an independent power of decision on certain matters where, unusually, basic rules limiting the discretion of the legislator are found in the E.C. Treaty itself: *e.g.* under the (now obsolete) provisions for the completion of the customs union during the E.C.'s transitional period, for which a detailed timetable was provided by the Treaty. As noted in Chap. 18, *infra*, the European Central Bank, too, will have law-making powers on aspects of monetary policy: see E.C. Treaty, as amended, Art. 110 (ex 108a).

with third countries.[23] It is the Commission which negotiates with third countries on behalf of the Community, but Council authorisation is required for opening negotiations, and it is the Council that takes the decision to conclude agreements. In some important cases the assent (*avis conforme*) of the European Parliament also has to be obtained.

Another area in which the Council has important powers is that of the adoption of the Community budget. The Council and the European Parliament together constitute the budgetary authority of the Communities which has the annual task of elaborating and adopting the general budget, as well as any supplementary and amending budgets that may prove necessary in the course of the financial year.[24] The division of powers between the Council and the European Parliament in the budgetary procedure is further examined below.

The Commission

Unlike the Council, whose members directly represent the interests of their Governments, the Commission has a vocation to further the interests of the Community as a whole. The members of the Commission are required to be persons "whose independence is beyond doubt,"[25] and the Treaty provides that they "shall, in the general interest of the Community, be completely independent in the performance of their duties."[26] They may not seek or take instructions from any government or other body, and each Member State has undertaken to respect that principle and not to seek to influence Commissioners in the performance of their tasks.[27] The rule that the Commission acts by a majority of its members[28] provides a further guarantee that its decisions will not reflect, even inadvertently, particular national viewpoints.

At the time of accession of Austria, Finland and Sweden to the European Union, the number of Members of the Commission was fixed at 20.[29] The convention, followed since the creation of a single Commission by the Merger Treaty, that one Commissioner be appointed from each of the smaller Member States, and two from each of the larger (currently, Germany, France, Italy, Spain and the United Kingdom), was thus maintained for the time being. However, it is generally accepted that a reduction to a maximum of one Commissioner per Member State is necessary, to prevent the institution from becoming unwieldy after the next enlargement of the Union.[30] A proposal to that effect was discussed by the Intergovernmental Conference that resulted in the T.A. but could not be agreed. There was, however, agreement on a "Protocol on the

---

[23] The procedure for the negotiation and conclusion of agreements is found in E.C. Treaty, Art. 300 (ex 228).

[24] The budgetary procedure is laid down by Art. 272 (ex 203).

[25] E.C. Treaty, Art. 213(1) (ex Art. 157(1)).

[26] E.C. Treaty, Art. 213(2) (ex Art. 157(2)).

[27] *ibid.*

[28] E.C. Treaty, Art. 219 (ex Art. 163).

[29] Art. 213(1) (ex 157(1)).

[30] On the pros and cons, see Justus Lipsius, "The 1996 Intergovernmental Conference" (1995) 20 E.L.Rev. 265; Dashwood, *Reviewing Maastricht: Issues for the 1996 IGC* (Sweet & Maxwell, 1996), pp. 152 *et seq.*

institutions with the prospect of enlargement of the European Union", which provides, in its Article 1: "At the date of entry into force of the first enlargement of the Union . . . the Commission shall comprise one national of each of the Member States, provided that, by that date, the weighting of the votes in the Council has been modified . . .". The proviso represents a *quid pro quo* for the larger Member States: their loss of a Commissioner would be compensated by an adjustment of the qualified majority voting system (as to which, see Chapter 3, below), to correct somewhat the present numerical bias in favour of the smaller Member States. Those two prospective changes, now indissolubly linked politically as well as legally, are on the agenda of the new Intergovernmental Conference which is due to conclude its work before the end of the year 2000.[31]

The procedure for the appointment of the President and Members of the Commission is found in Article 216 (ex 158) E.C.[32] Amendments introduced by the TEU and the T.A. have both enhanced the role of the European Parliament in the selection process, and given the President-designate a greater say in the composition of his "team". The first step in the procedure is the nomination, by the governments of the Member States, of the person they intend to appoint as President: they do this by "common accord", a stricter voting rule than unanimity as defined by Article 205(3) (ex 148(3)) of the E.C. Treaty, since it does not allow abstentions. The nomination requires approval by the Parliament. Those to be appointed as Members of the Commission are then nominated by common accord between the governments and the President-designate, which means the latter effectively has a veto. The whole slate of Commissioners is subject to a vote of approval by the Parliament; and the final step in the procedure is the appointment of the President and Members by common accord of the governments.

The amended procedure is designed to ensure both a more coherent Commission, and one more politically accountable to the European Parliament. To the latter end, the term of the Commission (five years, renewable) has been aligned on that of the Parliament: each new College of Commissioners will be vetted by MEP's newly elected in the previous June.

The number and method of appointment of the Commission's Vice-Presidents was also changed by the TEU. Instead of six Vice-Presidents, there are now one, or at most two, no longer appointed by common accord of the Member States but by the Commission itself.[33]

When a new Commission comes into office its members are assigned portfolios giving them responsibility for different policy areas. However, the Commission acts as a collegiate body, either by decisions taken at its weekly meetings (normally on Wednesdays) or by a written procedure. It is assisted by a staff of permanent officials under a Secretary General, who are organised into Directorates General and various other services, and, in addition, each Commissioner has a small personal staff (or *cabinet*) composed partly of political associates and seconded national officials and partly of seconded Community officials. Meetings

---

[31] Presidency Conclusions, Helsinki, paras 15 and 16.
[32] See R. Gonsalbo Bono, "The Commission after Amsterdam" in Heukels, Blokker & Brus (eds), *The European Union after Amsterdam* (1998), p. 69.
[33] Art. 217 (ex 161) E.C.

of the heads of these personal staffs (the *Chefs de Cabinet*) prepare the weekly meetings of the Commission.

The various elements that define the complex role of the Commission are described in Article 211 (ex 155) E.C. in the following terms:

> "In order to ensure the proper functioning and development of the common market, the Commission shall:
> — ensure that the provisions of this Treaty and the measures taken by the institutions pursuant thereto are applied;
> — formulate recommendations or deliver opinions on matters dealt with in this Treaty, if it expressly so provides or if the Commission considers it necessary;
> — have its own power of decision and participate in the shaping of measures taken by the Council and by the European Parliament in the manner provided for in this Treaty;
> — exercise the powers conferred on it by the Council for the implementation of the rules laid down by the latter."

In the present section we consider two aspects of the Commission's role—as the initiator of decisions and as the institution that sees to their implementation once they have been adopted, whether by the Council or by the Commission iself. Another important role, that of "guardian of the Treaties," is associated with the Commission's right to invoke against the Council or against a Member State judicial remedies which are discussed in Chapter 10.

The Treaties contain no general rule reserving to the Commission the right to put forward proposals for Community acts. The Commission's right of initiative is, accordingly, nothing but an inference drawn from the numerous Treaty provisions that empower the Council to act "on a proposal from the Commission." That form of words, or a similar one, is used by the E.C. Treaty in almost every case where the Council is given power to make new Community law. Thus the Council is usually able to exercise its legislative powers only in relation to a text which has been formulated by the institution with a duty to act independently of specific national interests. The way in which the Commission's right of initiative, and its right to amend its own proposals at any time before their adoption by the Council, interacts with the right of the Council to amend those proposals, is discussed in Chapter 3.

One of the defining features of decision-making under Titles V and VI of the TEU (the so-called "Second and Third Pillars") is that, in contrast to the Community system, the Commission does not enjoy an exclusive right of initiative. Thus Article 22 (ex Article J.12) TEU provides: "Any Member State or the Commission may refer to the Council any question relating to the common foreign and security policy and may submit proposals to the Council". As regards police and judicial co-operation in criminal matters, the Council is empowered to take the various kinds of measure provided for by Article 34(2) (ex Article K.6) TEU "on the initiative of any Member State or of the Commission".[34]

---

[34] See Chap. 8, *infra*.

The feature of a shared right of initiative is retained, for decision-making on the matters which have been transferred by the T.A. from Title VI TEU to the new Title IV of the E.C. Treaty on "Visas, asylum, immigration and other policies related to free movement of persons". Article 67(1) E.C. provides that, during a transitional period of five years, the Council is to act, under the various legal bases found in the new Treaty Title, "on a proposal from the Commission or on the initiative of a Member State . . .". The deviation from the Community norm will thus only be temporary: at the end of the five-year period the Commission will automatically regain its monopoly of the initiative.

The Commission is sometimes described as the "executive" of the Communities but this is misleading. It implies that the Commissionis like a government, with inherent or residual power to implement legislation, whereas Article 7(1) (ex 4(1)), second sub-paragraph of the E.C. Treaty makes clear that it has only those powers of implementation that have been conferred on it either directly by the Treaties or by acts of the Council. In this respect, there is a clear contrast between the ECSC and E.C. Treaties: in ECSC matters the Commission, as successor to the High Authority, enjoys wide direct powers, whereas under the E.C. Treaty, although directly empowered to act for certain purposes, for example the establishment of the customs union and the supervision of State aids to industry, the Commission derives the bulk of its powers from legislation enacted by the Council. A change introduced by the SEA was the insertion into Article 202 (ex 145) E.C. of a third indent establishing, as a general rule, that power to implement acts of the Council be conferred on the Commission: the Council is allowed to reserve implementing power for itself in specific cases but the Court of Justice has said, "it must state in detail the grounds for such a decision."[35] The Court has also stipulated that the essential elements of matters to be dealt with by the Commission under derived powers must be determined by the Council act directly based on the Treaty.[36] It would be a breach of the Treaty for the Commission to be given a discretion co-extensive with that which the Council is required under the Treaty to exercise in accordance with a prescribed procedure.

The grant of powers to the Commission may cover, besides the management of the policy in question, the development, by subordinate legislation, of the rules contained in the basic Council act. This is most notably the case with the common agricultural policy where the Commission is responsible both for establishing the regulatory framework within which the competent national authorities are required to act and for the day-to-day management of agricultural markets, in close collaboration with those authorities. Competition policy provides another instructive example: this is an area where, unusually, the Commission has been given, pursuant to Regulation 17,[37] administrative and coercive powers which can be used against individual undertakings; in addition, it has been empowered, under a series of Council measures, to adopt regulations

---

[35] Case 16/88, *Commission v. Council* [1989] E.C.R. 3457 at 3485.
[36] Case 25/70, *Köster* (1970) E.C.R. 1161 at 1170; [1972] C.M.L.R. 255. The same principle applies where the Council reserves for itself power to adopt implementing acts by a simpler procedure than the one prescribed by the Treaty for the basic act.
[37] [1959–62] O.J. Spec. Ed. 87.

exempting certain categories of restrictive agreements and practices from the automatic prohibition to which they would otherwise be subject under the rules of Article 81 E.C.[38] Other areas in which the Commission has acquired, more recently, an enhanced administrative role are those of research, where it implements the specific programmes developed within the various activities envisaged by the multi-annual framework programme, and economic and social cohesion where, in partnership with beneficiary Member States, it manages the resources made available through the structural funds.

The exercise by the Commission of powers of implementation which it has been granted under acts of the Council is frequently subjected to procedural requirements. Article 202, third indent, expressly preserves the Council's right to impose such requirements, while providing that the latter "must be consonant with principles and rules to be laid down in advance." A closed catalogue of forms of procedure has accordingly been laid down by what is known as the Council's "Comitology" Decision because the different procedures all involve the submission of the Commission's draft implementing measures to a committee composed of national officials.[39] The degree of constraint placed on the Commission varies from one procedure to another: for instance, under the "advisory committee" procedure the Commission is required to take the utmost account of the opinion delivered by the Committee, but is not bound by it[40]; whereas, under the "management committee" procedure, in the event of a negative opinion by the committee, the matter is referred to the Council which may, within a prescribed time limit, substitute its own decision for that of the Commission.[41] It is for the Council, when it adopts an act conferring implementing power on the Commission, to determine which, if any, procedure should be attached to the exercise of that power. The Court of Justice has rejected the argument that, where implementation does not involve adopting subordinate legislation but simply applying rules to individual cases, only the advisory committee procedure is legally acceptable.[42]

The European Parliament[43]

The European Parliament has undergone more fundamental changes in its history than any of the other Community institutions. First, as to its name: it was called the "Assembly" in the founding Treaties, and continued to be referred to as such in Council acts until its change of name was officially recognised by the

---

[38] See Chap. 20, *infra*.

[39] The current version of the Comitology Decision is Council Dec. 1999/468/E.C. [1999] O.J. L184/23. This replaced, from July 8, 1999, the original Council Dec. 87/373, [1987] O.J. L197/33.

[40] See, respectively, Arts 3 and 4 of the Decision. In addition, there is provision for a "regulatory procedure" (Art. 5) and a "safeguard procedure" (Art. 6). Provisions designed to improve the transparency of comitology procedures are laid down by Art. 7; *inter alia*, the principles and conditions on public access to documents now apply to the various committees. Art. 8 allows intervention by the European Parliament if it considers that a draft implementing measure based on an instrument adopted by co-decision (see Chap. 3) would exceed the powers thereby conferred.

[41] Criteria for the guidance of the Council have been provided by the new Comitology Decisions.

[42] Case 16/88, *loc. cit.* n.35, *supra*.

[43] See F. Jacobs and R. Corbett, *The European Parliament* (1990, Longman).

SEA.[44] Secondly, as to its composition: originally a nominated body, its members drawn from the parliamentary institutions of the Member States, the European Parliament was transformed into a body of representatives directly elected by universal suffrage in June 1979 when the first elections were held under rules which had been laid down by an Act annexed to a Council decision of 1976.[45] Thirdly, as to its powers, described in the founding Treaties as exercising "advisory and supervisory powers," the European Parliament has received significant new powers, in the budgetary sphere, under the Treaties of 1970 and 1975 and, in the legislative sphere, through the introduction of the co-operation procedure by the SEA and of the co-decision procedure by the TEU, and through the further development of the latter by the T.A.

The Act of 1976 was approved by the Council under the procedure prescribed by Article 190(4) (ex 138(3)) E.C. That procedure requires a proposal to be drawn up by the European Parliament "for elections by direct universal suffrage in accordance with a uniform procedure in all Member States" and empowers the Council, acting unanimously, after obtaining the assent of the Parliament, to lay down the appropriate provisions, which must then be recommended to the Member States for adoption in accordance with their respective constitutional requirements. It did not prove possible in 1976 to agree a uniform electoral procedure and Article 7(2) of the Act, accordingly, states that, pending the entry into force of such a procedure (and subject to specific provisions of the Act, such as those relating to the timing of elections and the counting of votes), "the electoral procedure shall be governed in each Member State by its national provisions." The elections so far held (in 1979, 1984, 1994 and 1999) have therefore been organised under national electoral laws, all of them based on variants of proportional representation, including now in the United Kningdom. The requirement of Parliamentary "assent" (which was added to Art. 190(4) by the TEU) means that the Council is no longer in a position simply to impose its own conception of an appropriate electoral system. Thus the European Parliament will have to give its formal approval to any uniform electoral system that may be adopted in the future.

The number of members of the European Parliament (or MEPs) is currently fixed at 626, divided up as follows: 99 from Germany; 87 each from France, Italy and the United Kingdom; 64 from Spain; 31 from the Netherlands; 25 each from Belgium, Greece and Portugal; 16 from Denmark and Finland; 15 from Ireland; six from Luxembourg.[46] Like the qualified majority as defined by Article 148(2), the number of seats given to the various Member States reflects, in a rough and ready way, differences in their populations. An upper limit of 700 MEPs has been set by the second paragraph of Article 189 (ex 137), which was inserted by the T.A.

The MEPs are organised in cross-national political groups, broadly following the ideological divisions that are familiar in national politics. Thus the two largest groups are the Socialist Group, to which the British Labour Members belong,

---

[44] SEA, Art. 3(1) speaks, rather coyly, of the instutitions "henceforth designated as referred to hereafter," and goes onto refer to "the European Parliament" in subsequent provisions.

[45] Dec. 76/787, [1976] O.J. L278/1.

[46] Art. 190(2) (ex 138(2)).

and the Group of the European People's Party, composed in the main of Christian Democrats from Continental Member States, who were joined in 1992 by the British Conservatives. Article 191 (ex 138a) of the TEU emphasises the importance of political parties at European level as a factor for integration within the Union.

Article 3(1) of the Act of 1976 provides for a fixed parliamentary term of five years.[47] This can be varied by up to a month either way, if the Council, acting unanimously after consulting the European Parliament, decides that elections are to be held during a period not exactly corresponding to the period chosen for the first elections in 1979, *i.e.*, June 7 to 10.[48]

The increase in the powers of the European Parliament under successive Treaties, was remarked on at the beginning of this section. The formal powers of the Parliament are broadly of three kinds: it participates in various ways, depending on the legal basis of the act in question, in the law-making process of the Communities; together with the Council, it constitutes the budgetary authority of the Communities; and it exercises political supervision over the performance by the Commission of its tasks. Besides these formal powers, the European Parliament evidently considers that it is entitled, as the collective voice of the Community electorate, to express reactions to political events both within the Communities and in the wider world. It does not have an independent right of initiative but brings its influence to bear on the Commission and, so far as it is able, on the Council, to provoke any action by those institutions that it considers necessary. For that purpose, the position of the European Parliament has been strengthened by the second paragraph of Article 192 (ex 138b) E.C. an amendment introduced by the TEU, which provides that it may "acting by a majority of its members, request the Commission to submit any appropriate proposal on matters on which it considers that a Community act is required for the purpose of implementing this Treaty."[49]

The participation of the European Parliament in the law-making process will be discussed in Chapter 3. In the present chapter we confine our attention to the budgetary powers of the Parliament and to its role as political watchdog of the Commission.

In the budgetary sphere, as a result of the Treaties of 1970 and 1975, the European Parliament has become an equal partner of the Council. Their respective powers are determined by the distinction between "compulsory expenditure" (usually referred to by its French acronym, DO) and "non-compulsory expenditure" (or DNO). DO has been defined as "such expenditure as the budgetary authority is obliged to enter in the budget by virtue of a legal undertaking entered into under the Treaties or acts adopted by virtue of the said Treaties."[50] The Council has the last word on DO, which consists almost entirely of expenditure on the common agricultural policy, while the Parliament has the

---

[47] See also Art. 190(3) E.C.

[48] See Act, Art. 10(2).

[49] *cf.*, the Council's rarely used right under Art. 200 (ex 152) E.C. to request the Commission to undertake studies and to submit to it any appropriate proposals.

[50] See Inter-institutional Agreement of May 6, 1999, para. 30 [1999] O.J. C172/1. The quoted definition replaces one in the Joint Declaration of June 30, 1982 [1982] O.J. C194/1.

last word on DNO, which includes expenditure on the structural funds, on research and on aid to non-Community countries. At one time DNO accounted for only a small proportion of Community expenditure, but that proportion has risen very significantly with the doubling of expenditure on the structural funds between 1988 and 1993 and the high level of financial support for Central and Eastern European countries and the former Soviet Union. The increase not only in the amount but also in the political importance of DNO has reinforced the bargaining power of the European Parliament in financial matters.

The different roles assigned to the Council and the European Parliament in the budgetary procedure laid down by Article 272 (ex 203) reflect the division of competence between them. On the basis of a provisional draft budget proposed by the Commission, the Council establishes the draft budget, which it is required to submit to the European Parliament before October 5 in the year preceding the one in which the budget is to be implemented.[51] At its first reading of the draft budget, the Parliament has the right to propose modifications of items classified as DO and to amend items classified as DNO.[52] The draft budget then returns to the Council for a second reading. Proposed modifications to DO which are not explicitly accepted by the Council stand as rejected (except for those involving no increase in total expenditure whose rejection requires a positive decision by the Council) and the Council may also modify any of the amendments to DNO adopted by the Parliament.[53] All Council decisions connected with the budgetary procedure are taken by a qualified majority. At its second reading of the draft budget, the Parliament may, acting by a majority of its members and three-fifths of the votes case, amend or reject any of the modifications made by the Council to its amendments to DNO, but it no longer has any right to touch DO.[54] The procedure concludes with the formal declaration by the President of the European Parliament that the budget has been finally adopted.[55] However, the Parliament may "for important reasons," decide, by a majority of its members and two-thirds of the votes cast, to reject the budget as a whole and ask for a new draft to be submitted to it.[56] Drastic as that power may seem, it has been used by the Parliament on three occasions, in respect of the general budgets for 1980 and 1985 and a supplementary and amending budget in 1982.

A complex mechanism to prevent DNO from increasing excessively from one year to another is provided by Article 272(9). A "maximum rate of increase" is fixed by the Commission, through the mechanical application of a set of economic criteria; and the rate can only be altered if there is consensus between the two branches of the budgetary authority. The functioning of that mechanism was the subject of frequent disputes between the Council and the European Parliament, one of them, in respect of the 1986 budget, leading to proceedings before the Court of Justice and the annulment by the Court of the act of the President of the Parliament declaring the budget to have been finally adopted.[57]

---

[51] Art. 272(4).
[52] *ibid.*
[53] Art. 272(5).
[54] Art. 272(6).
[55] Art. 272(7).
[56] Art. 272(8).
[57] Case 34/86, *Council v. European Parliament* [1986] E.C.R. 2155; [1986] 3 C.M.L.R. 94.

In 1988, however, the package of financial measures (known as the "Delors I" package) was adopted, with the aim of ensuring adequate resources to achieve the objectives of the SEA, within a framework of budgetary discipline. The measures included an Inter-Institutional Agreement (or I.I.A.) between the European Parliament, the Council and the Commission containing "financial perspectives" by which annual ceilings were fixed for various categories of expenditure over the period 1988 to 1992. There have since been two further I.I.A.'s, covering respectively the periods of the financial packages known as "Delors II" (1993 to 1999) and "Agenda 2000" (2000 to 2006).[58] The financial perspectives have provided a basis for the orderly development of expenditure in accordance with agreed priorities. Thanks to the series of I.I.A.'s, relative peace has reigned between the two branches of the budgetary authority since 1987, and this in spite of the fact that unforeseen events, notably in Central and Eastern Europe and the former Soviet Union, have made it necessary for some of the ceilings of the financial perspectives to be raised.

The recourse to I.I.A.'s is interesting not only as a technique of budgetary policy but also from a legal point of view. An I.I.A. is not an agreement in international law, since the parties—Community institutions—do not have international legal personality. It should rather be regarded as a pact between equal partners in a constitutional order about the way in which they will exercise co-ordinate powers. In fact, this kind of arrangement between institutions seems to be characteristic of the Community order: other examples are the Joint Declaration of 1975 on the institution of a conciliation procedure[59] and the Joint Declaration of 1982 on various measures to improve the budgetary procedure, now replaced by Part II of the 1999 I.I.A.[60] Whether such arrangements create legal or purely political obligations is a matter which, ultimately, only the Court of Justice can decide. Perhaps they may be found to constitute a concrete expression of the obligation of loyal co-operation between the institutions. At all events, the parties to the series of I.I.A.'s have consistently behaved as if they expected their terms to be observed in good faith.

Detailed supervision by the European Parliament over the activities of the Commission is made possible by the regular attendance of members of the Commission at part-sessions of the Parliament, and of Commissioners or their officials at meetings of Parliamentary committees. There is an express Treaty obligation on members of the Commission to reply to written and oral questions[61] and, following the first enlargement of the Communities in 1973, a question time, clearly influenced by the British model, was introduced. The Treaty also requires the Commission to submit an annual general report to the Parliament,[62] and the practice has developed of publishing, in conjunction with that report, other reports of a more specialised character relating, for instance, to

---

[58] For the text of the current I.I.A., see [1999] O.J. C172/1. The I.I.A. replaces a range of texts relating to different aspects of co-operation between the institutions involved in the budgetary procedure.

[59] [1975] O.J. C89/1.

[60] See note 50, *supra*.

[61] Art. 197 (ex 140) E.C., third para.

[62] Art. 200 (ex 143) E.C.

the agricultural situation in the Community or to competition policy, which are an important source of information.

Although not obliged by the Treaty to do so, the Council replies to written questions from the European Parliament and, through the President or any other member of the Council, to oral questions. Council Presidents are invited to appear before Committees of the Parliament and they attend part-sessions to represent the views of the Council or to give an account of their management of Council business. Before Parliamentary Committees, the Council may be represented by the Secretary-General, the Deputy Secretary-General or other senior officials, acting on instructions from the Presidency.[63]

The supervisory powers of the European Parliament were reinforced by the TEU in three ways. First, the Parliament was given the right, under Article 193 (ex 138c), to set up temporary Committees of Inquiry to investigate "alleged contraventions or maladministrations in the implementation of Community law," except where the matter is *sub judice*. It is interesting to note that the text does not explicitly limit the scope of such investigations to contraventions or maladministration for which Community institutions or bodies are allegedly responsible. Secondly, Article 194 (ex 138d) confirms an established practice by giving any citizen of the Union or any resident of a Member State the right to petition the European Parliament on a matter within Community competence which affects him directly. Thirdly, under Article 195 (ex 138e), the European Parliament appoints an Ombudsman who is empowered to receive complaints concerning instances of maladministration in the activities of Community institutions or bodies (other than the Court of Justice or the Court of First Instance acting judicially). If the Ombudsman establishes a case of maladministration, he must give the institution concerned three months in which to inform him of its views and then forwards a report to the European Parliament and to the instition, while also informing the complainant of the outcome. The Ombudsman is appointed after each election for the duration of the newly elected Parliament's term of office.

The effectiveness of the European Parliament's supervision of the Commission does not depend only on the moral authority of its democratic mandate: Article 201 (ex 144) E.C. puts into the hands of the Parliament the supreme political weapon of a motion of censure by which it can force the resignation of the College of Commissioners. If a motion of censure is tabled, three days must elapse before a vote is taken; and, for the motion to be carried, there must be a two-thirds majority of the votes cast, representing a majority of the members of the Parliament. In the past it was sometimes claimed that the power to dismiss the Commission by a vote of censure was too powerful a weapon ever to be used; and, even if the Commission could be forced to resign in this way, it would immediately be reappointed by common accord of the Governments of the Member States. If that claim was ever plausible, the events of March 1999, when the Commission presided over by Jacques Santer resigned in a body, following an adverse report by a Committee of Experts which had been appointed to investigate claims of fraud, mismanagement and nepotism, showed that it is no

---

[63] As to all this, see Art. 23 (ex 140) E.C., fourth para. and Rules of Procedure of the Council.

longer so. The resignation was evidently precipitated by pressure from the European Parliament, where it had become clear that a motion of censure would otherwise, in all likelihood, be adopted. The episode, it has been said, marked the coming of age politically of the Parliament.[64]

---

[64] See Editorial Comment, 36 C.M.L. Rev. (1999), p. 270.

CHAPTER 3

THE LEGISLATIVE PROCESS

Legislative procedures

The E.C. Treaty provides the constitutional framework for a very large volume of legislative activity by the political institutions of the European Union. Legislation can also be enacted under the ECSC and Euratom Treaties but this, for the most part, is only of concern to the specific economic sectors of coal, steel and atomic energy. In addition, under Titles V and VI of the TEU, there are special procedures for adopting the legally binding instruments available for pursuing the objectives of the common foreign and security policy and of police and judicial co-operation in criminal matters: the salient points of difference between second and third Pillar decision-making, and that under the first Pillar, are considered in Chapter 8, below. The present Chapter is solely concerned with the legislative process of the European Community.

There is no single institution that constitutes the Community's legislature. The different institutions—Council, Commission and European Parliament (together with the consultative bodies, the Economic and Social Committee and the Committee of the Regions)—are assigned their respective roles in more or less elaborate law-making procedures. The technique used in the E.C. Treaty is to specify in the particular provision authorising action by the Community for a given purpose, which is known as the "legal basis", the precise procedural steps to be followed in taking such action.

As was noted in the previous chapter, it is a hallmark of the Community system that the legislative process almost always requires a formal Commission proposal to set it in motion.[1] There is thus an inbuilt bias towards a text formulated (in principle) independently of particular national or sectoral interests, to further the wider interests of the Community as a whole. Another constant feature is the Council's power of final decision: no primary legislation can be enacted without receiving the positive approval (expressed according to the voting rule prescribed by the Treaty) of the institution that comprises representatives of the Member States. This gives concrete reality to the claim that the latter have "pooled" their sovereignty, rather than surrendering it. Also, the participation, in the definitive phase of decision-making, of those who will ultimately be responsible for the implementation of Community law on the ground (the E.C. institutions themselves having no coercive machinery), is a guarantee of the effectiveness of the system.[2]

The difference between legislative procedures is marked by the role given to the European Parliament. In the simplest procedure of all, that prescribed by

---

[1] We draw attention there to the important, but temporary, exception to this principle under Title IV of Part Three of the E.C. Treaty, which relates to matters transferred to the first Pillar from the third Pillar.

[2] See Dashwood, "The Role of the Council of the European Union" in Curtin and Heukels (eds), *Institutional Dynamics of European Integration*, p. 117.

Article 133 (ex 113) of the E.C. Treaty for legislating on the common commercial policy, the Parliament is not legally required to play any part at all: the Council acts by a qualified majority on a proposal from the Commission.[3] Usually, however, in the Community order at its present stage of development, the power-conferring provisions of the Treaty provide for the adoption of law-making acts either by the procedure known as "consultation" or by that known as "co-decision". The two procedures, in the form in which they apply under the E.C. Treaty as amended most recently by the T.A. will be examined in detailed below. Briefer consideration will be given to other procedures which are either more limited in their application or are now mainly of historical interest.[4]

The consultation procedure

In the original EEC Treaty, this was the only procedure giving the European Parliament a guaranteed role in the enactment of legislation. Under the procedure, a piece of legislation is proposed by the Commission, the European Parliament is consulted on the proposal and the Council takes the final decision, acting by a qualified majority or unanimity, as laid down by the relevant provision of the Treaty (and depending on whether the Council exercises its power of amendment, as to which, see below).

Although it has been, to a significant degree, superseded by co-decision, the consultation procedure continues to be used under the E.C. Treaty for legislation in several important policy areas, including the common agricultural policy,[5] harmonisation of indirect taxation,[6] certain aspects of the protection of the environment,[7] and matters connected with the establishment and functioning of EMU.[8]

As we shall see, co-decision was the procedure prescribed by the T.A. under most of the new legal bases in the E.C. Treaty which it created. An important exception is Article 67 E.C., laying down the procedure for enacting legislation under the Treaty Title on "Visas, asylum, immigration and other policies related to free movement of persons", which has brought into the Community sphere a range of matters formerly covered by Title VI of the TEU (the third Pillar). For an initial period of five years, a variant of the consultation procedure will apply— the variation being that the Member States share the right of initiative with the Commission.[9] After the end of the five-year period, not only will the Commission recover its monopoly of the initiative but the Council will have power to

---

[3] The European Parliament may, however, be consulted on an optional basis, see below. The common commercial policy is concerned with the regulation of trade between the E.C. and third countries.

[4] For an historical perspective, see Dashwood "Community Legislative Procedures in the Era of the TEU" (1994) 19 E.L.Rev. 343; brought up to date in "European Community Legislative Procedures after Amsterdam" (1998) 1 C.Y.E.L.S. 25. See also Boyron, "Maastricht and the Co-decision Procedure: a success story" (1996) 45 I.C.L.Q. 293.

[5] Art. 37 (ex 43) E.C.

[6] Art. 93 (ex 99) E.C.

[7] Art. 175 (ex 130s) E.C. The matters in question comprise: provisions primarily of a fiscal nature; town and country planning, land use with the exception of waste management and measures of a general nature, and management of water resources; measures significantly affecting a Member State's choice between different energy sources and the general structure of its energy supply.

[8] *e.g.* Art. 104(14) (ex 104c(14) E.C. (excessive deficit procedure). See Chap. 18, *infra*.

[9] The point was noticed in Chap. 2, above, p. 18.

substitute co-decision for consultation in respect of "all or parts of the areas covered by this Title".[10]

Where the Treaty provides for the consultation of the European Parliament, that requirement must be strictly complied with. In practice, work on a Commission proposal begins immediately within Council bodies, without waiting for the Parliament's Opinion: the Court of Justice has found that practice to be lawful, so long as the Council does not determine its position definitively before the Opinion of the Parliament is received.[11] The reason why the Council must normally await the Opinion before taking its final decision was explained by the Court in the *Isoglucose* case:

> "The consultation provided for in the third sub-paragraph of Article 43(2), as in other similar provisions of the Treaty, is the means which allows the Parliament to play an actual part in the legislative process of the Community. Such power represents an essential factor in the institutional balance intended by the Treaty. Although limited, it reflects at Community level the fundamental democratic principle that the peoples should take part in the exercise of power through the intermediary of a representative assembly. Due consultation of the Parliament in the cases provided for by the Treaty therefore constitutes an essential formality disregard of which means that the measure concerned is void."[12]

In that case the Court annulled a Regulation which the Council had adopted on the basis of Article 43(2) without having received the opinion of the Parliament which had been requested some months previously. The Court rejected the Council's argument that the Parliament, by its own conduct in failing to give an opinion on a measure it knew to be urgent, had made compliance with the consultation requirement impossible. The judgment laid emphasis on the fact that the Council had not formally invoked the emergency procedure for which the Parliament's own rules provide, nor had it taken advantage of its right, under Article 196 (ex 139) of the Treaty, to request an extraordinary session of the Parliament: the implication seemed to be that, if the Council had exhausted all the procedural possibilities open to it, the adoption of the regulation, without waiting any longer for the Opinion, might well have been justified.

That was confirmed, some 15 years later, in a case relating to the Council Regulation laying down the arrangements for granting generalised trade preferences to developing countries during the year 1993.[13] The regulation had to be adopted before the end of 1992, to avoid disrupting trade with the countries concerned. On that occasion, the Council had requested the application of the European Parliament's urgency procedure and, when an Opinion was still not forthcoming, suggested that an extraordinary session be held in late December; having received a negative reply from the Office of the President of the Parliament, the Council proceeded without more ado to adopt the regulation.

---

[10] See Art. 67(2), second indent.
[11] Case C–417/93 *European Parliament v. Council* [1995] E.C.R. I–1185; [1995] 2 C.M.L.R. 829.
[12] Case 138/79 *Roquette Frères v. Council* [1980] E.C.R. 3333 at 3360.
[13] Case C–65/93 *European Parliament v. Council* [1995] E.C.R. I–643; [1996] 1 C.M.L.R. 4.

The action brought by the Parliament for the annulment of the regulation was rejected by the Court of Justice, on the ground that the failure punctually to render an Opinion amounted, in the circumstances, to an infringement of the duty of loyal co-operation which binds the institutions, by analogy with the duty of the Member States under Article 10 (ex 5) E.C.

The consultation of the European Parliament takes place in relation to the Commission's original proposal. If the Commission amends its proposal, or the Council intends to exercise its power of amendment, and this means that, considered as a whole, the substance of the text which was the subject of the first consultation will be altered, there is a duty to consult the Parliament a second time.[14] Reconsultation is not required if the change is one of method rather than of substance (for example, the substitution, in a draft regulation relating to officials' pay, of updated exchange rates); nor if the change goes in the direction of wishes expressed by the Parliament itself in its Opinion.[15] A new case for reconsultation, acknowledged in the practice of the Council since the introduction of the co-operation procedure by the SEA, is where the Council is minded to amend the legal basis proposed by the Commission, and the effect of this will be to substitute simple consultation for one of the procedures that give the Parliament a more significant legislative role.

Reconsultation, which is a legal requirement in certain circumstances, must not be confused with the conciliation procedure instituted by a Joint Declaration of the European Parliament, the Council and the Commission in 1975.[16] This was designed to provide an opportunity, through a face-to-face meeting within a Conciliation Committee, for the European Parliament and the Council to find common ground in certain cases where the Council intends to depart from the Opinion adopted by the Parliament. The act in question must be one of "general application" (this would cover all acts of a normative character, including, by definition, all regulations) and it must have "appreciable financial implications."[17] Acts whose adoption is required pursuant to existing legislation are excluded, because such legislation could itself have been the subject of conciliation. There are also procedural requirements: the Commission must indicate, in submitting its proposal, whether the act in question is a suitable subject for the procedure; and the European Parliament's request for conciliation must be made when it gives its Opinion. Conciliation should normally be completed within three months, or within an appropriate time limit, to be fixed by the Council, if the matter is urgent.[18] It must be stressed that the aim is to *seek* an agreement between the Parliament and the Council: if there is a

---

[14] Case 41/69 *ACF Chemiefarma v. Commission* [1970] E.C.R. 661 at 702; Case 1253/79 *Battaglia v. Commission* [1982] E.C.R. 297; Case C–65/90 *European Parliament v. Council* [1992] E.C.R. I–4593. See also Opinion of Advocate General Mancini in Case 20/85 *Roviello* [1988] E.C.R. 2805 at 2838 *et seq.*; Opinion of Advocate General Darmon in Case 65/90 *European Parliament v. Council, supra.*

[15] Case 1253/79 *Battaglia, supra.*

[16] [1975] O.J. C89. The procedure laid down by the Joint Declaration is in practice resorted to only where the legislative role of the Parliament is restricted to that of being consulted. It must be distinguished from the mandatory conciliation provided for as an element of the co-decision procedure.

[17] Joint Decl., point 2.

[18] Joint Decl., point 6.

sufficient *rapprochement*, the Parliament may give a fresh Opinion and the Council then proceeds to take definitive action[19]; however, even in the absence of agreement, the Council retains its legal right to adopt, according to the applicable voting procedure, the measure it considers appropriate. For the European Parliament, the advantage of the procedure is that it allows influence to be exerted in the final phase of decision-making, and this has been done with some effect, for example in respect of the amendments to the Financial Regulation that were adopted in 1988.[20]

It should finally be noted that there is nothing to prevent the Council from consulting the European Parliament, and it often does so, where this is not required by the Treaty. In such a case, if the Parliament fails, for some reason, to give an Opinion, the Council is free to withdraw the request, but, it is thought, reasonable notice should be given to the Parliament before such withdrawal.

The co-decision procedure

Under this procedure, first introduced into the E.C. Treaty by the TEU, and refined and streamlined by the T.A., the European Parliament is treated, from a formal point of view at least, as the equal legislative partner of the Council. The Commission submits its proposal to both institutions at the same time,[21] and the final "product" of the law-making process is a joint act of the Parliament and the Council, which the President of each institution is required to sign.[22] The unofficial designation "co-decision" is meant to underline that partnership: it is in common use, but is not found in the text of the Treaty which speaks, awkwardly, of "the procedure referred to in Article 251".

The procedure entails successive "readings" of a proposal for legislation, offering a series of opportunities for interaction between the three main political institutions, and designed to channel the European Parliament and the Council towards approval of a joint text. The various possible stages are outlined below, and are also illustrated by the diagram on page 44. We say "possible" stages, because the procedure does not have ro run its full course, if agreement between the co-legislators can be reached earlier. Some of the amendments effected by the T.A. were intended precisely to facilitate such an outcome.[23]

The first reading commences with the submission of the Commission's proposal to the European Parliament and the Council. The Parliament renders an opinion, which may or may not contain amendments. The Council then has a choice, to be exercised by qualified majority decision: it may definitively adopt the proposed act in conformity with the opinion (*i.e.* incorporating the Parliament's amendments, if any); or, if it does not approve all of the amendments contained in the opinion, or wishes to make others, it may adopt a "common position", which must be communicated to the Parliament with a full explanation

---

[19] Joint Decl., point 7.
[20] Council Reg. 610/90 [1990] O.J. L70/1.
[21] Art. 251(2) (ex 189b(2)) E.C.
[22] Art. 254(1) (ex 191(1)) E.C.
[23] See amendments to paras (2) and (3) of Art. 251, enabling a definitive decision to be taken at an early stage in the procedure, as described below.

CO-DECISION PROCEDURE
(Article 251 E.C.)

Commission

FIRST READING: Submits *proposal*

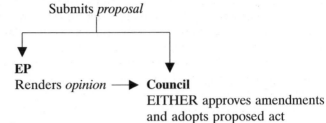

EP
Renders *opinion* ⟶ **Council**
EITHER approves amendments
and adopts proposed act

OR adopts *common position*

SECOND READING: **EP**

EITHER approves *common position*, and
proposed act is deemed to have been adopted

OR rejects *common position* and, proposed act is
deemed not to have been adopted

OR proposes amendments

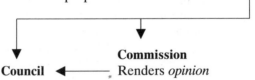

Commission
Council ⟵ Renders *opinion*

EITHER approves all amendments, and proposed
act is deemed to have been adopted

OR does not approve all amendments

Conciliation Committee
CONCILIATION: EITHER approves *joint text*

OR fails to approve *joint text*, and
proposed act falls

EP   EITHER both adopt   **Council**

OR act is deemed
not to have been adopted

of the underlying reasons. The Commission, too, must inform the Parliament fully of its position.[24]

At second reading, the common position of the Council replaces the Commission's proposal as the text which is the object of the interaction between the co-legislative institutions. The choice is now for the European Parliament between: (a) expressly approving the common position (or doing so tacitly by taking no decision within the prescribed period of three months); or (b) rejecting the common position (this requires an absolute majority of MEPs, not merely of those voting); or (c) proposing amendments to the common position (by the same majority).[25] Approval or rejection by the Parliament at this stage has the effect of concluding the procedure one way or the other: the act in question is deemed to have been adopted in accordance with the common position; or, as the case may be, not to have been adopted. In the (more likely) eventuality that amendments are proposed, these must be forwarded to the Council, as well as to the Commission which is required to deliver an opinion on them. The ball is then, once again, in the Council's court. It may, within three months, approve all of the proposed amendments (by a qualified majority, or by unanimity in respect on those on which the Commission has delivered a negative opinion), in which case the act will be deemed to have been adopted in the form of the common position as amended. Otherwise, the President of the Council, in agreement with the President of the Parliament, must, within six weeks, convene a meeting of the Conciliation Committee provided for by paragraph (4) of Article 251.[26]

The procedure of the first and second readings involves interaction between the Council and the European Parliament at arm's length. As described in the preceding paragraphs, they will have had three separate opportunities for reaching agreement, but if they fail to do so Article 251 provides the remedy of direct negotiation within the Conciliation Committee, to break the deadlock. The Committee is composed of the members of the Council or their representatives (normally, the appropriate COREPER, depending on the subject-matter of the act in question) and an equal number of representatives of the European Parliament. Its task is, within six weeks, to reach agreement on a joint text, by a qualified majority on the Council side and by a majority on the Parliament side. The Commission has a role in the proceedings as honest broker. The negotiations within the Committee take place in relation to the common position, which must be addressed on the basis of the amendments proposed by the Parliament. The parties are thus required to focus on the texts formally established by each of them during the earlier phases of the procedure.[27]

---

[24] Art. 251(2), first sub-para. An early example of a measure adopted at first reading was Dir. 1999/103 of the European Parliament and the Council amending Council Dir. 80/181 on the approximation of the laws of the Member States relating to units of measurement, [2000] O.J. L34/17. The Directive, proposed by the Commission on February 5, 1999, was definitively adopted in a little over 10 months, on January 24, 2000.

[25] Art. 251(2), second sub-para. For an example of a measure deemed to have been adopted pursuant to point (a) of the sub-para., following approval by the Parliament of the Council's common position, see Reg. 141/2000 of the European Parliament and of the Council on orphan medicinal products, [2000] O.J. L18/1.

[26] Art. 251(3). The T.A. substituted the six-week time limit for the less precise obligation to convene a meeting of the Conciliation Committee "forthwith".

[27] The last sentence of Art. 251(4) was added by the T.A. It is understood there had been occasions when there was disagreement between the two sides, as to the parameters of the discussion within the Committee.

If conciliation is successful, the joint text agreed by the Committee is submitted to the co-legislators, who have a further six weeks in which formally to adopt the act in question, in accordance with that text. Should either of them fail to do so, the act will fall.[28] That will also be the result, if the Conciliation Committee is unable to agree a joint text within the six-week deadline.[29]

The various time limits prescribed by Article 25 are very important, to prevent the legislative process from becoming too lengthy, and to avoid a loss of political momentum. There is, however, provision in paragraph (7) of the Article for the periods of three months to be extended by a maximum of one month, and those of six weeks by a maximum of a fortnight, at the initiative of either the European Parliament or the Council.

Co-decision was originally prescribed by the E.C. Treaty as amended by the TEU, for enacting legislation relating to the internal market,[30] where it replaced the co-operation procedure (as to which, see below). It was also provided for under several of the legal bases created by the TEU, in policy areas where specific authorisation for action by the Community was previously lacking.[31] The T.A. took matters still further: all of the provisions of the E.C. Treaty prescribing co-operation (with the exception of those found in the Treaty Title on "Economic and Monetary Policy") were amended,[32] by substituting co-decision; and the procedure was substituted for consultation in certain cases.[33] Co-decision was, moreover, the legislative procedure chosen by the authors of the T.A. for almost

---

[28] Art. 251(5).

[29] Art. 251(6). Under the co-decision procedure as provided for by the TEU, if the Conciliation Committee failed to approve a joint text, it remained possible for the Council to confirm unilaterally the common position it had agreed prior to conciliation, with the option of including some or all of the European Parliament's amendments; the measure would then become law, unless it was rejected, within six weeks, by a majority of MEPs. By abolishing this so-called "third reading", the T.A. has formally placed the Parliament on an equal footing with the Council, both being required to give their positive approval to legislation. In a case where the Council sought to exercise its former power at third reading, relating to a proposed directive on open network provision (ONP) for voice telephony, the European Parliament imposed its veto by an overwhelming majority.

[30] Notably, under the general power of approximation conferred by Art. 95 (ex 100a) E.C.

[31] See Art. 152(4) (ex 129(4)) E.C. on public health; Art. 153(4) (ex 129a(2)) E.C. on consumer protection; Art. 156 (ex 129d) E.C. on trans-European networks. See also Art. 15(5) (ex 128(5)), first indent E.C. on culture; and Art. 166(1) (ex 130i(1)) E.C. on the multiannual framework programmes for research. Under both of the latter, as provided for by the TEU, the Council was required to act by unanimity (see *infra*). Another legal basis into which co-decision was introduced by the TEU was Art. 175(3) (ex 130s) E.C. on general action programmes setting out priority objectives for policy on the environment.

[32] Co-decision is substituted for co-operation in the following provisions: Art. 12 (ex 6) second para. E.C. on discrimination on grounds of nationality; Art. 71(1) (ex 75(1)) E.C. on the common transport policy; Art. 80 (ex 84) E.C. on sea and air transport; Art. 137(2) E.C. (ex Art. 2(2) of the Agreement annexed to the Social Protocol) on conditions of employment; Art. 148 (ex 125) E.C. on implementation of the European Social Fund; Art. 150(4) (ex 127(4)) E.C. on vocational training; Art. 162, first para. (ex 130e) E.C. on implementing decisions for the purposes of the European Regional Development Fund; Art. 172, second para. (ex 130o) E.C. on the implementation of the research framework programme; Art. 175(1) (ex 130s) E.C. on the environment; Art. 179 (ex 130n) E.C. on development co-operation.

[33] Art. 42 (ex 51) E.C. on socials ecurity for migrant workers; Art. 46(2) (ex 56(2)) E.C. on the co-ordination of national provisions derogating, on grounds of public policy, public sector or public health, from the right of establishment and the freedom to supply services; Art. 47(2) (ex 57(2)) E.C. on the co-ordination of provisions governing certain aspects of the taking up and pursuant of self-employed activities.

all the new legal bases established pursuant to that Treaty, including in areas of considerable political sensitivity.[34] The trend is towards the recognition of co-decision as the standard procedure for enacting Community measures which are genuinely legislative in character. If that could be achieved, it would be a great constitutional gain, in terms both of simplifying and helping to legitimate the process of Community law-making.

Unfortunately, in a few matters the extension of co-decision has been purchased at the price of requiring the Council to act, throughout the procedure, by unanimity instead of by a qualified majority.[35] That is liable to distort the process of decision-making, and to diminish the ability of the European Parliament to influence the final outcome, since at second reading the Council may be found less willing than normally to shift from its common position, which would have had to accommodate the particular viewpoints of all delegations.[36]

Other procedures

Brief mention must be made of the co-operation procedure (officially, "the procedure referred to in Article 252"), because of its historical significance.[37] The introduction of the procedure by the SEA was the first step towards enhancing the legislative role of the European Parliament beyond the simple consultation provided for by the original EEC Treaty. In the SEA, co-operation was closely associated with the project of completing the internal market by the end of 1992. As we have seen, internal market measures were brought within the scope of co-decision by the TEU, but co-operation survived under the regime of that Treaty for enacting E.C. legislation on, among other things, transport, aspects of environment policy, and development co-operation. Now it has been superseded in those policy areas too: it was allowed by the T.A. to survive only in a few provisions relating to economic and monetary policy (regarded, seemingly for political reasons, as untouchable by the IGC which

---

[34] Art. 129 E.C. on incentive measures in the field of employment; Art. 141(3) E.C. on equal opportunities and equal treatment for men and women in matters of employment and occupation; Art. 152(4) on various public health measures; Art. 255 E.C. on access to documents; Art. 280(4) E.C. on countering fraud against the financial interests of the Community; Art. 285(1) E.C., on the production of Community statistics; Art. 285(2) E.C. on data protection. The glaring exception is legislation for the purposes of the new Treaty Title on "Visas, Asylum, Immigration and other Policies Related to Free Movement of Persons", as to which see above.

[35] See Art. 42 (ex 51) E.C. and Art. 47(2) (ex 52(2)) E.C. The legal basis for action by the Community in the field of culture, Art. 151(5) (ex 128(5)) E.C., which was enacted by the TEU, retains the requirement of unanimity in the context of the co-decision procedure. A similar requirement in Art. 166(1) (ex 130i(1)) E.C. on the adoption of the multinational framework programme for research, has been dropped by the T.A.

[36] For a positive assessment of the way in which the co-decision procedure (in the version provided for by the TEU) has functioned in practice, see Boyron, *op. cit.* note 4, above; and, by the same author, "The co-decision procedure: rethinking the constitutional fundamentals", in Craig and Harlow, *Lawmaking in the European Union* (1998, Kluwer), p. 147.

[37] For a fuller treatment of the co-operation procedure, see Dashwood, "Community Legislative Procedures in the Era of the TEU", *loc. cit.* n.4, above. See also the discussion of the procedure in De Ruyt, *L'Acte unique européen* (1987, Editions de l'Universite de Bruxelles), pp. 124 *et seq.* On the application of the procedure to internal market legislation, see Schwarze (ed.), *Legislation for Europe 1992* (1989, Nomos).

negotiated that Treaty).[38] Like co-decision, of which it was the forerunner, the co-operation procedure involves two readings: the main differences are that it contains no procedure for compulsory conciliation; and, at the end of the day, the Council cannot be prevented from adopting a text that ignores the Parliament's wishes, although it may be required, in so doing, to act by unanimity.[39]

Under the assent procedure, the Council acts on a proposal by the Commission, after obtaining the assent (*avis conforme*) of the European Parliament. This is a form of co-decision, since the act in question can only pass into law if the Council and the Parliament give their positive approval. The difference, as compared with the co-decision of Article 251, is that there is no series of formal interactions between the two institutions: a common orientation is reached within the Council, and this is presented to the Parliament, effectively, on a take-it-or-leave-it basis.

The procedure is, therefore, unsuitable for enacting complex legislative measures. It was replaced, pursuant to the T.A. by co-decision in the legal basis for adopting provisions with a view to facilitating the exercise of E.U. citizens' right to move and reside freely in the territory of the Member States,[40] but not, unfortunately, in the legal basis for the enactment of basic legislation on the Structural Funds, under which resources are transferred to the less prosperous regions of the Community.[41] On the other hand, the retention of assent as the method prescribed by Article 190(4) (ex 138(3)), for deciding on the electoral system of the European Parliament, does not appear objectionable, since here it is the Parliament itself which initiates the process by drawing up a proposal for the Council, so that a measure of interaction does take place. In addition, the procedure is, of course, perfectly suitable for deciding on matters that only require a "yes" or "no" answer from the Parliament, such as the accession of new Member States,[42] or the conclusion of especially important international agreements.[43]

In giving its assent on the electoral procedure and on applications for membership the European Parliament is required, by the relevant legal bases, to act by an absolute majority of its component members; and on other matters by the majority of votes cast. For the Council, the voting rule prescribed in connection with the assent procedure is normally unanimity, but a qualified majority will be sufficient for deciding on some of the international agreements to which Article 300(3) (ex 228(3)) applies.[44]

---

[38] Provisions in which co-operation will, for the time being, survive are: Art. 102(2) (ex 104a(2)) E.C.; Art. 103(2) (ex 104b(2)) E.C.; and Art. 106(2) (ex 105a(2)) E.C.

[39] Unanimity is required in two situations: where the Parliament has formally rejected the common position (Art. 252(c), second para.); or where the Commission, having re-examined its proposal by taking into account the Parliament's amendments, forwards to the Council a text which the latter is unwilling to adopt without amendment (Art. 252(d) and (e)).

[40] Art. 18(2) (ex 8a(2)) E.C.

[41] Art. 161 (ex 130d) E.C.

[42] Art. 49 (ex 0) TEU.

[43] Art, 300(3) (ex 225(3)), second sub-para. E.C.

[44] *e.g.* "agreements establishing a specific institutional framework by organising co-operation procedures" or "agreements having important budgetary implications for the Community" in a field where unanimity is not required for the adoption of internal rules: para. (3) of Art. 228, read together with para. (1), second sub-paragraph and para. (2), second sentence.

What may be termed the "organic law" procedure appears as a variant of either the consultation or the assent procedures. Its unique feature is that the Council, acting unanimously on a proposal from the Commission, and after consulting or, as the case may be, with the assent of, the European Parliament, takes a decision which it then recommends to the Member States for adoption in accordance with their respective constitutional requirements. Such a relatively "heavy" procedure (with what amounts to national ratification of a Community act) can only be justified for the purposes of decisions which are structural in character, just falling short of amendments to the Treaty. For the use of the organic law procedure with consultation, see Article 22 (ex 8e) on provisions to strengthen or add to the rights of European Union citizens as laid down by Part Two of the E.C. Treaty and Article 269 (ex 201), second paragraph, on own resources; for its use with assent, see Article 190(4) (ex 138(3)) on provisions relating to the system of European Parliamentary elections.

Concluding on the legislative procedures, it may be noted that, besides the main ones mentioned here, there are multiple variants in the Treaty, taking the total to above 20. This is an unsatisfactory situation, making the system unintelligible to the average Union citizen. However, a start was made by the T.A. towards simplifying and rationalising the legislative process, through the virtual abolition of co-operation, and the extension of co-decision that was remarked on above.

Majority decisions by the Council

The general voting procedure, laid down by Article 205(1) (ex 148(1)) E.C., is that, save as otherwise provided by the Treaty, the Council shall act by a majority of its members. However, there are few cases where the Treaty confers powers on the Council without specifically providing that acts shall be adopted either by a qualified majority or by unanimity. In the Community of 15, a qualified majority consists of 62 votes out of 87, the allocation of votes to the various Member States being weighted so as to correspond, very roughly, to differences in size of population.[45] In the rather rare cases where the Council may act without a proposal from the Commission, a qualified majority decision requires, in addition, the positive votes of at least 10 Member States. Where the Treaty provides for the Council to act by unanimity, abstentions by the Member States do not prevent the act in question from being adopted[46]; in other words, "unanimity" connotes the absence of negative votes. By contrast, to obtain a qualified majority, 62 positive votes are needed, so any purported abstention will contribute to a blocking minority.

The E.C. Treaty provides for special qualified majorities in certain cases, more particularly in connection with decisions that have to be taken within the context of economic and monetary union. For example, when the Council takes steps

---

[45] Germany, France, Italy and the United Kingdom have 10 votes each; Spain has eight votes; Belgium, Greece, the Netherlands and Portugal have five votes; Austria and Sweden have four votes; Denmark, Ireland and Finland have three votes; Luxembourg has two votes.
[46] Art. 205(3) (ex 148(3)).

under Article 104 (ex 104c) against a Member State found to be running an excessive government deficit, the Member State concerned will not be entitled to vote, and the qualified majority will consist of two thirds of the weighted votes of the other members of the Council. Similarly, only the Member States participating in the single currency have a right to vote on matters connected with its establishment and management, and two thirds of the weighted votes of those Member States constitute a qualified majority.[47]

Since the end of the second stage of the E.C.'s transitional period (December 31, 1965), the qualified majority has been the voting procedure prescribed in the core areas of Community competence—those of the common market and the common policies in agriculture and transport. The range of matters that could be decided by a qualified majority was extended by the SEA, most notably in the case of Article 95 (ex 100a), the legal basis for adopting measures for the approximation of national provisions where such measures have as their object the establishment and functioning of the internal market. With the further extension of qualified majority decisions by the TEU and the T.A., the rule of unanimity has been confined to certain matters of special political sensitivity, such as the harmonisation of indirect taxation,[48] and to decisions of a fundamental character, such as the exercise of the residual power of action given by Article 308 (ex 235).[49]

Despite the opportunities for majority voting offered by the E.C. Treaty, until the early 1980s the Council only regularly took decisions in this way on budgetary and staff matters, acting by consensus in other cases. The tedious process of negotiating a compromise acceptable to all delegations represented an impediment to progress in the development of the E.C. in the decade following the end of the transitional period. That has now changed and it has become the normal practice for the Council to act by a qualified or simple majority where the Treaty allows.[50] The change in practice reflected a new political climate, influenced by the perception that rapid progress towards completing the internal market was necessary to enable the Community to deal on equal terms with its main international competitors. The trend towards majority voting predated the entry into force of the SEA,[51] but it certainly received a fresh impetus from the introduction of new legal bases providing for majority decisions.

In connection with majority voting, something must be said about the so-called "Luxembourg Compromise." This was an "agreement to disagree," reached at a special meeting of the Council in January 1966, to resolve a political crisis precipitated in part because of the shift to decision-making by qualified majority which was foreseen under the EEC Treaty from the

---

[47] E.C. Treaty, Art. 1225 (ex 109k(5)). On these matters, see Chap. 18 *infra.*

[48] Art. 93 (ex 99) E.C.

[49] Other typical examples are Art. 269 (ex 201) (own resources) and Art. 279 (ex 209) (financial legislation).

[50] See J.-L. Dewost in Capotorti *et al.* (eds), *Du droit international au droit communautaire Liber amicorum Pierre Pescatore* (1988, Nomos), pp. 167 *et seq.*; Dashwood in Schwarze (ed.) *Legislation for Europe 1992* (1989, Nomos), pp. 79 *et seq.*

[51] Evidence of the trend can be found in Council answers to Written Questions of the European Parliament: see., *e.g.* the answers to Written Questions No. 1121/86 (Elles) [1986] O.J. C306/42; Written Questions No. 2126/86 (Fontaine), [1987] O.J. C82/43.

beginning of the final stage of the transitional period. The text of the Luxembourg Compromise[52] included a provision to the effect that when, in case of a decision that can be taken by a majority vote, very important interests of a Member State are at stake, the Council will attempt, within a reasonable time, to reach a solution acceptable to all its members. It was noted that, in the view of the French delegation, the discussion in such cases must continue until unanimous agreement is reached, a view not shared by the other delegations. This arrangement left the Council's legal powers fully intact, while influencing its practice. In assessing that influence, it is useful to draw a distinction between the encouragement that was undoubtedly given to the search for consensus within the Council, and formal invocation of the Compromise by a Member State to prevent a vote from being taken on a particular occasion.[53] In fact, Member States have formally invoked the Compromise only about a dozen times, and the political price for doing so is considered to be high. The outcome may also be uncertain: thus in 1982, when the United Kingdom sought to block the adoption of the agricultural price package in order to put pressure on the other Member States to agree a reduction of the British contribution to the Community budget, its purported "veto" was swept aside and a vote was taken[54]; whereas in 1985 Germany successfully invoked the Compromise to forestall a decision on the reduction of cereal prices. Whether the Luxembourg Compromise can be said still to "exist" is not a question to which a legal answer can be given: it all depends on whether, in a concrete case, enough of the Member States to constitute a blocking minority can be persuaded, by the Member State claiming a vital interest, to refrain from voting. However, such cases, if they occur at all in future, will be very rare; more importantly, the Compromise has ceased to influence the Council towards acting by consensus, since, as we have seen, voting, if legally permissible, is now the normal practice.

Concern may, nevertheless, be felt about a procedural mechanism, introduced by the T.A. into both the E.C. Treaty and the TEU, which appears to be a variant of the Luxembourg Compromise. The mechanism occurs in three places: in Article 11 (ex 5a) E.C. on the procedure for authorising initiatives on closer co-operation in the Comunity sphere; in article 40 (ex K.12) TEU, the corresponding provision on closer co-operation under the third Pillar[55]; and in Article 23(2) (ex J.13(2)) TEU, which allows qualified majority decisions to be taken in certain circumstances where the Council is acting for the purposes of the common foreign and security policy. Under each of those provisions, a Council member can prevent a matter from being put to the vote by declaring its opposition to this, "for important and stated reasons of national policy". The Council may then, by a qualified majority, request that the matter be referred, for decision by unanimity, to the Council meeting in the composition

---

[52] The full text of the Luxembourg compromise is published in Bulletin of the EEC, March 1966, pp. 8–10.

[53] Dashwood, op. cit. note 51, supra, pp. 82–83.

[54] A lesson from that episode is that the very important interest which is claimed must be directly linked to the particular measure under consideration. The United Kingdom had indicated that it was invoking the Luxembourg Compromise, not to protect important interests threatened by the price package, but as a purley tactical move.

[55] On "closer co-operation" (or "flexibility"), see Chap. 7, below.

of Heads of State or Government (or, in the case of Articles 23(2) and 40 TEU, to the European Council). Causes of concern are that the new mechanism may, perhaps, be seen as legitimating the Luxembourg Compromise, thereby giving it a new lease of life; or that it will be seized on too readily as an easy solution, when there is controversy in the future about the extension of qualified majority voting.

The interaction between the institutions

The Commission's right to alter or withdraw its proposal

The Commission is expressly empowered, as long as the Council has not acted, to alter its proposal at any time during the procedures leading to the adoption of a Community act.[56] There are various reasons why it may choose to do so.

In the first place, the Commission may independently form the view that the proposal needs to be improved or completed: or perhaps to be updated, in order to keep abreast of scientific developments, especially if it has been lying on the Council's table for some time. Or account may have to be taken of changes in the legal situation: for instance, after the entry into force of the SEA, the Commission substituted the then Article 100a (now Article 95) as the legal basis of a large number of proposals originally based on other provisions of the Treaty.

Secondly, the Commission may respond to an Opinion rendered by the European Parliament under the consultation procedure, or at first reading under the co-decision procedure, by incorporating into its proposal some or all of the amendments put forward by the Parliament. At second reading under the co-decision procedure, the Commission indicates its acceptance, or otherwise, of the Parliament's amendments, not by amending its own proposal, but by delivering an opinion, as required pursuant to Article 151(2)(c).[57]

Thirdly, the Commission may alter, its proposal in order to facilitate decision-making within the Council. Decisions are reached by the Council through negotiations between national delegations in working groups, in COREPER and at ministerial level. These negotiations involve progressive adaptation of the Commission's proposal in order to take account of Member States' particular interests and difficulties. The process is managed by the Presidency, aided by the General Secretariat of the Council, with the aim of achieving a balanced compromise text, commanding the qualified majority or unanimity required for the adoption of the measure in question. The Commission is represented at meetings of Council bodies where its proposals are under discussion,[58] and it may play a vital part in the development of the Presidency compromise, both by providing technical assistance and by indicating amendments it is able to accept. In some cases, final amendments to the proposal are made orally by the Commissioner attending the Council meeting where a measure is adopted, who

---

[56] Art. 250(2) (ex 189a(2)) E.C.

[57] Art. 250(2), as the more general provision, must be read consistently with the specific requirements of the co-decision procedure.

[58] Art. 4(3) of the Council's Rules of Procedure provides: "The Commission shall be invited to take part in meetings of the Council. . . . The Council may, however, decide to deliberate without the presence of the Commission. . . ."

will have been mandated by the College of Commissioners to act within a certain margin of manoeuvre. The Court of Justice has confirmed the legality of the practice of oral amendment, provided that the Commissioner concerned acts within the scope of this mandate.

There is no explicit provision of the Treaty enabling the Commission to withdraw a proposal which it has submitted to the Council. However, it is generally agreed that, within certain limits, the Commission has such a power.[59] One view is that withdrawal may be regarded as the extreme case of amendment, but the better view is, perhaps, that both amendment and withdrawal are corollaries of the right of initiative: the latter would be incomplete, if the Commission, having put forward a proposal which it no longer considered appropriate, were unable to remedy the situation. At the same time, the power of withdrawal must not be used to prevent other institutions from performing the roles the Treaty has given them in the legislative procedure. Thus it would be an abuse of power for the Commission to withdraw a proposal which is on the point of being adopted by the Council, in order to prevent that institution from exercising its own power of amendment (as to which, see below). Similarly, it is submitted, under the co-decision procedure the Commission has no right to withdraw its proposal once the Council has adopted its common position. This seems to follow from the clear terms in which the Treaty specifies the options open to the European Parliament and the Council at second reading, and the legal consequences that ineluctably follow from the course of action chosen.

The Council's power of amendment

The Council has a general power to amend proposals of the Commission, when acting definitively under the consultation procedure or adopting a common position at first reading under the co-decision procedure but, in so doing, it must act unanimously.[60] The rule requiring unanimity for the amendment of Commission proposals was of limited practical significance during the period when the Council habitually acted by consensus; now, however, with the extension of the range of matters that can be decided by a qualified majority, and with majority decisions being taken as a matter of course where the Treaty permits, the rule has come into its own as a pivotal element of the Council/Commission relationship. This is because, if the Council is unwilling to adopt a proposal without making certain changes, the only way of avoiding the unanimity rule is for a compromise to be negotiated that the Commission can makes its own; the compromise will then have the legal status of an amended Commission proposal and be capable of being enacted by a qualified majority. The Commission is thus able to maintain direct influence over the progress of its proposal, right up to the final outcome of the negotiations within the Council.

The right of the Council to amend the Commission's proposal by unanimity does not extend to the substitution of an entirely new proposal, since that would

---

[59] See Mégret *et al.*, *Le droit de la CEE* (1979, Editions de l'Université de Bruxelles), Vol. 9, pp. 135–136.
[60] Art. 20(1) (ex 189a(1)) E.C.

be to usurp the right of initiative.[61] It is submitted that Council amendments, however radical, will not be *ultra vires*, as long as the subject-matter of the measure in question remains the same. For instance, in a draft directive concerning animal welfare, the Council may decide to establish different criteria of welfare from those proposed by the Commission; but it would not be entitled to transform the directive into one fixing quality standards for fresh meat.

The requirement of unanimity for the amendment of Commission *proposals* does not extend to cases where the decision-making process is initiated by the submission to the Council of a *recommendation* by the Commission.[62] That is the case, for example, where the Commission seeks authorisation to negotiate an international agreement with a non-Member country. The Commission makes a recommendation to the Council which decides whether to authorise the opening of negotiations and, if so, whether any negotiating directives should be issued to the Commission; in so doing, the Council is free to act by a qualified majority, even if it departs from the Commission's recommendation as to what the parameters of the negotiations should be.

That model was followed in the case of various key decisions, in relation to the establishment and functioning of EMU. These include, notably, decisions in connection with the excessive deficit procedure (as to the existence of an excessive deficit in a Member State; recommendations for bringing such a deficit to an end; measures for deficit reduction; the imposition of sanctions)[63] and the transition to the third stage of EMU (fulfilment of the conversion criteria[64]; grant of derogations).[65] Such an increase in the number of cases where the Council acts on a simple recommendation by the Commission might seem to represent a significant rebalancing of powers, to the Commission's disadvantage. However, it should be noted that the Council decisions in question are essentially executive in character: where *legislative* acts have to be adopted for the purposes of EMU (for example for the further elaboration of the excessive deficit procedure[66] or for the irrevocable fixing of exchange rates),[67] the Council will act in the traditional way, on the basis of a Commission proposal.

The general rule requiring unanimity for the amendment of a Commission proposal is subject to an express exception in respect of Article 251(4) and (5) of the E.C. Treaty. The exception relates to decisions adopted by the Council in accordance with a joint text agreed with the European Parliament in the Conciliation Committee provided for under the co-decision. The Council under the co-decision procedure is thus able to adopt by a qualified majority a text representing the result of a successful conciliation, regardless of whether the Commission has altered its proposal accordingly: indeed, from the end of the first

---

[61] Mégret, *op. cit.* note 68, *supra*, p. 133.

[62] This follows from the wording of Art. 250(1) (ex 189), which says "Where, in pursuance of this Treaty, the Council acts *on a proposal from the Commission* . . ." (emphasis added). See Art. 133(3) (ex 113(3)) E.C. on agreements in the field of the common commercial policy, and Art. 300(1) (ex 228(1)) E.C. on international agreements in general.

[63] Art. 104 (ex 104) E.C. See paras 7–9, 11, 12 and 13.

[64] Art. 121(2) (ex 109j(2)) E.C.

[65] Art. 122(1) (ex 109k(1)) E.C.

[66] Art. 104(14) (ex 104c(14)) E.C.

[67] Art. 123(4) (ex 109e(4)) E.C.

reading, the Commission's proposal ceases to be relevant to the final outcome of the procedure.

The European Parliament's participation

There is a great difference between the ability of the European Parliament to influence the final shape of a measure enacted under the consultation procedure, and its influence where the prescribed legislative procedure is co-decision. We have seen that, where consultation of the European Parliament is required by the legal basis of a proposal, the Council must be formally seized of the Opinion rendered by the Parliament before proceeding to the adoption of the act in question (apart from urgent cases, where all procedural possibilities for obtaining the Opinion have been tried unsuccessfully); and that, if either the Commission or the Council is minded to amend a proposal in a way that would alter the substance of the text on which the Parliament has been consulted, adoption may have to be postponed pending reconsultation. However, the Council, having considered the Parliament's Opinion, is under no *legal* obligation to follow it. In practice, the most effective way for the European Parliament to influence the final shape of legislation on a matter for which the consultation procedure is prescribed is by putting political pressure on the Commission to incorporate elements of the Opinion into an amended proposal. If the Commission responds favourably, the Council will then be faced with a text which it will only be able to amend further by unanimity.[68]

At first reading under the co-decision procedure, the traditional interplay between the Commission and the Council, based on the former's monopoly of the initiative and the two institutions' respective powers of amendment, still predominates. The main task of the Council Presidency is to negotiate a compromise text that commands a qualified majority among the delegations, and to which the Commission will rally, amending its proposal so that recourse to the adoption of a common position by unanimity can be avoided. However, through informal contacts, and through the Opinion rendered at first reading, the Presidency and the Council will be aware of the major concerns of the European Parliament, which will have to be accommodated, if the act in question is ultimately to receive the approval of the co-legislators; and due account will already be taken of those concerns in the negotiations within Council bodies. All three institutions will, moreover, be alert to any possibility of securing a first reading adoption.[69]

From the begining of the second reading, we have seen, the Commission's proposal is effectively spent, and the politically significant interaction is that between the European Parliament and the Council, in relation to the common position. As amended by the Treaty of Amsterdam, the co-decision procedure no longer gives the Council even the theoretical possibility of acting unilaterally: if it wishes to see a measure adopted, it simply has to take into the common position the amendments that represent the Parliament's "bottom line". On the other hand, it is a fact of life for the Parliament that, once a political deal has been

---

[68] Under the rule in Art. 250(1), considered above.
[69] As in the case of the Directive referred to in n.24, above.

negotiated within the Council at first reading, the scope for securing amendments will be limited. Experience to date provides reason for optimism that the necessary give-and-take will be forthcoming between the co-legislators, to enable the procedure to function effectively.[70]

---

[70] See n.36, above.

PART III: THE LEGAL ORDER

CHAPTER 4

SOURCES, SUPREMACY AND DIRECT EFFECT OF COMMUNITY LAW

THE SOURCES OF COMMUNITY LAW

The title of this part of the book and of this chapter refer to *Community law,* rather than *Union* law, and the reason for this is that the law capable of being invoked by individuals before the national courts of the Member States and the European Court, is predominantly that part of the law of the European Union which comprises the law of the European Communities. This follows in part from the subject matter of European Community law, which includes in particular the law of the single market, of social policy, and of competition policy. And it follows in part from the legal provisions which define the jurisdiction of the European Court of Justice, the most significant of which are to be found in the Treaties establishing the European Communities.[1] The term European *Community* law is used here simply because it is more specific than the all embracing term European *Union* law.

The sources of Community law are as follows:

— The Treaties establishing the three Communities, as supplemented and amended from time to time, and the secondary legislation made thereunder.
— Related treaties concluded between Member States.[2]
— International agreements concluded between the Community and third countries.[3]
— Measures emanating from bodies which have been established by an international agreement between the Community and third countries, and which have been entrusted with responsibility for its implementation.[4]
— International treaties binding upon all the Member States, where the responsibilities of the latter have been assumed by the Community.[5]
— Decisions of the Member States having legal effect within the sphere of operation of the Treaties.[6]

---

[1] Art. 46 (ex L) TEU indicates the limited extent to which the provisions of the Treaties of the E.C., Euratom and ECSC concerning the jurisdiction of the Court of Justice apply to the TEU.

[2] International agreements which are not based on the Treaties establishing the Communities do not fall within the scope of Art. 234 (ex 177) E.C. or Art. 150 of the Euratom Treaty, see Case 44/84 *Hurd v. Jones* [1986] E.C.R. 29 at 76, para. 20.

[3] Appropriately worded provisions of such agreements may be invoked before the courts of Member States, see, *e.g.* Case 104/81 *Kupferberg* [1982] E.C.R. 3641, and generally, *infra*, p. 104.

[4] Case C–192/89 *S.Z. Sevince v. Staatssecretaris van Justitie* [1990] E.C.R. I–3461; [1992] 2 C.M.L.R. 57, para. 10.

[5] Joined Cases 21–24/72 *International Fruit* [1972] E.C.R. 1219.

[6] *e.g.* the "acceleration" decisions of May 12, 1960, J.O. 1217/60 and May 15, 1962, J.O. 1284/62 See Case 22/70 *E.R.T.A.* [1971] E.C.R. 263.

— Judgments of the European Court of Justice and the European Court of First Instance.[7]
— General principles of law, and the fundamental rights upon which the constitutional laws of the Member States are based.[8]
— Recommendations adopted on the basis of the E.C. Treaty inasmuch as they may cast light on the interpretation of national law or Community law,[9] and certain other non-binding acts (*e.g.* joint declarations of the Commission and Council recorded in the minutes of a session at which a Community act was adopted,[10] or recommendations of a Joint Committee entrusted with the administration and implementation of an international agreement between the Community and third countries[11]) which may similarly be held to cast light on the interpretation of national law or Community law.

For the purposes of simplicity, where consideration of the above mentioned sources requires reference to the Treaties and to the secondary legislation made thereunder, discussion will limited to the legal effects of the Treaty establishing the European Community, and the secondary legislation—regulations, directives and decisions—made thereunder.

LEGAL EFFECTS OF THE TREATY AND SECONDARY LEGISLATION—IN GENERAL

Member States are bound to carry out the obligations imposed by the E.C. Treaty and secondary legislation made thereunder. Breach of these obligations may give rise to an action before the Court of Justice at the suit of either the Commission, or another Member State.[12]

The legal impact of Community law in the Member States, however, springs from its capacity, indeed its tendency, to give rise to rights in individuals which national courts are bound to safeguard. The position is complicated, at least at first sight, by a rather confusing terminology, which describes provisions of Community law as being either "directly applicable" or "directly effective." The latter expression describes a provision which is clear and unconditional and bestows a legal right on a natural or legal person, exercisable against another natural legal person, or against the authorities of a Member State. Establishing

---

[7] Decisions of the Court under Art. 234 E.C. are binding on the referring Court; see Case 29/68 *Milchkontor* [1969] E.C.R. 165; Case 52/76 *Benedetti* [1977] E.C.R. 163. *Stare decisis* applies in the United Kingdom as regards both the European Court and the Court of First Instance by virtue of s.3(1) of the European Communities Act 1972. A ruling of the Court under Art. 234 E.C. on the invalidity of a Community act is binding *erga omnes;* see Case 66/80 *International Chemical Corporation* [1981] E.C.R. 1191. Prior decisions of the Court of Justice may extinguish the duty to refer under Art. 234(3), see Case 283/81 *CILFIT* [1982] E.C.R. 3415.
[8] See *infra* Chap. 6, pp. 131 *et seq.*
[9] Case 113/75 *Frecassetti* [1976] E.C.R. 983; Case 90/76 *Van Ameyde* [1977] E.C.R. 1091; Case C–322/88, *Grimaldi* [1989] E.C.R. 4407; [1991] 2 C.M.L.R. 265.
[10] Case C–310/90 *Nationale Raad van de Orde van Architecten v. Ulrich Egle* [1992] E.C.R. I–177; [1992] 2 C.M.L.R. 113. But see Case C–292/89 *Antonissen* [1991] E.C.R. I–773; [1991] 2 C.M.L.R. 373.
[11] Case C–188/91 *Deutsche Shell AG v. Hauptzollamt Hamburg-Harburg* [1993] E.C.R. I–363.
[12] Arts 226 and 227 (ex. 169 and 170) E.C.

direct effect is a matter of interpretation, and it is clear that specific provisions of the Treaty, as well as specific provisions of regulations, directives or decisions, may be endowed with this quality. It has been argued that direct effect, in the sense of practical operation for all concerned, is to be presumed unless established to the contrary.[13] Direct applicability, on the other hand, is that attribute of a regulation which ensures its access, in its entirety, to the national legal order, without the need for specific incorporation.[14] Reproduction of the text of a regulation in the text of national legislation is not only unnecessary, but in principle impermissible, and the status of a regulation as direct Community legislation allows it to pre-empt national legislative competence.

It should be noted that Member States are obliged to implement directives by legislative measures,[15] notwithstanding the fact that in the absence of such implementation, the provisions concerned would be directly effective. The direct effect of a directive is a consequence of the failure of a Member State properly to implement, or transpose, the directive, by ensuring that its provisions are given full force and effect through the medium of binding national rules, and national judicial recognition of direct effect does not remedy the Member State's failure to adopt appropriate legislative measures. By way of contrast, the direct effect of a regulation is not a consequence of the default of the Member State, but the corollary of the direct applicability of regulations, and of the specific text and context of particular provisions of the regulation.

Provisions of the E.C. Treaty may have direct effect, and it does not seem that there is a general and invariable duty to adopt national rules to implement Treaty provisions, as there is for directives. But the direct effect of Treaty provisions has been said by the Court of Justice to be but a minimum guarantee, and not to be itself sufficient to ensure the full and complete implementation of the Treaty.[16] The Court has held (in the context of compliance with Treaty provisions) that the principles of legal certainty and protection of individuals requires that, in areas covered by Community law, the Member States' legal rules should be worded unequivocally so as to the give the persons concerned a clear and precise understanding of their rights and obligations and to enable national courts to ensure that those rights and obligations are observed.[17] And the Court has further held that Member States are obliged to repeal national legislation incompatible with the Treaty, on the ground that it creates an ambiguous state of affairs and leaves interested parties in a state of uncertainty as to their rights.[18] While there may not be a general duty in principle to implement Treaty provisions by national legislation, the duty to repeal inconsistent national legislation appears to bring about a similar position in practice. But the

---

[13] Pescatore, "The Doctrine of 'Direct Effect': An Infant Disease of Community Law" (1983) 8 E.L. Rev. 155.

[14] Art. 249(2) (ex 189) E.C., "A regulation . . . shall be directly applicable and binding in its entirety."

[15] See *infra*, p. 89.

[16] Case 72/85 *Commission v. Netherlands* [1986] E.C.R. 1219; Case 168/85 *Commission v. Italy* [1986] E.C.R. 2945; [1988] 1 C.M.L.R. 135, at para. 11.

[17] Case 257/86 *Commission v. Italy* [1988] E.C.R. 3249; [1990] 3 C.M.L.R. 718; Case 120/88 *Commission v. Italy* [1991] E.C.R. I–621; [1993] 1 C.M.L.R. 41.

[18] Case 159/78 *Commission v. Italy* [1979] E.C.R. 3247; [1980] 3 C.M.L.R. 446; Case 168/85 *Commission v. Italy* [1986] E.C.R. I–2945; [1988] 1 C.M.L.R. 580.

difference in *principle* between the nature of the duty to implement the Treaty on the one hand, and the nature of the duty to implement directives on the other, may retain theoretical significance as regards the respective scope of direct effect in each case. Treaty provisions may have horizontal direct effect (that is to say, certain Treaty provisions may be invoked against private parties as well as against emanations of Member States)[19], but the provisions of directives have only vertical effect—they may only be invoked against authorities of the Member States.[20] It is possible to attribute the rationale of this distinction to the proposition that the direct effect of a directive is the result of the failure of the Member State to implement it by binding national rules, which in turn has the consequence that such direct effect may only be invoked against the Member State in default, and not against private parties, who are not emanations of that Member State, and cannot be held responsible for the latter's failure to implement the directive. No such considerations apply to the Treaty itself, appropriately drafted provisions of which are inherently capable of binding national authorities and private parties alike.

A degree of terminological confusion could be said to arise because the expressions "directly applicable" and "directly effective" are sometimes used interchangeably, even by the Court.[21] While specific provisions of the Treaty, and of directives and decisions, may be directly effective, these instruments as a whole lack the unque pre-emptive quality of regulations,[22] and are not "directly applicable" in the same sense as regulations are described as "directly applicable" by the Treaty. That said, it would be pedantic to do more than note the point, and no misunderstanding is in practice likely to arise, since the context will invariably make clear what is meant.

NATURE OF THE COMMUNITY LEGAL ORDER

The European Community is a developed form of international organisation which displays characteristics of an embryonic federation. Analysis of the nature of the Community legal system is of intrinsic interest, and may facilitate the solution of practical problems. The debt owed by Community law to public international law is considerable, and usually understated.[23] Underpinning the Community legal system are the doctrines of (i) direct applicability/direct effect, and (ii) the supremacy of Community law. Both doctrines are derived from international law.[24] Equally, however, the relationship between Community law and national law clearly lends itself to comparison with the relationship between

---

[19] See *infra*, at p. 77.

[20] See *infra*, at p. 98.

[21] See the ruling in Case 2/74 *Reyners* [1974] E.C.R. 631, to the effect that Art. 43 (ex 52) of the Treaty is directly applicable. In similar vein, see Case 17/81 *Pabst* [1982] E.C.R. 1331; Case 104/81 *Kupferberg* [1982] E.C.R. 3641; [1983] 1 C.M.L.R. 1.

[22] As to which, see *infra*, p. 88.

[23] Wyatt, "New Legal Order or Old?" (1982) 7 E.L.Rev. 147; De Witte, "Retour a 'Costa': La primauté du droit communautaire à la lumière du droit international" (1984) 20 R.T.D.E. 425.

[24] For direct applicability, see "*Jurisdiction of the Courts of Danzig*" (1928) P.C.I.J. Ser. B., No. 15. For the principle that treaty obligations take priority over national law, see Vienna Convention on the Law of Treaties, Art. 27: "*Treatment of Polish Nationals in Danzig*" (1932) P.C.I.J. Rep.Ser. A/B, No. 44, p. 24.

state and federal law in a federal system. In the *Simmenthal* case the Court of Justice held that Community law was competent to "preclude the valid adoption"[25] of inconsistent national legislation. This is a controversial formulation, and seems to equate the relationship between Community law and national law to a constitutional relationship, thereby distancing Community law from international law, which does not determine the validity of provisions of national law. As an eminent international lawyer has put it: "International tribunals cannot declare the internal invalidity of rules of national law since the international legal order must respect the reserved domain of domestic jurisdiction."[26] In the *IN.Co.GE.'90 Srl* case,[27] however, the Court of Justice qualifies the *Simmenthal* formulation to the effect that Community law precludes the "valid adoption" of subsequent inconsistent national legislation. While a national court faced with a conflict between Community law and a provision of subsequently adopted national legislation is obliged to "disapply" the incompatible provision of national law, it cannot "be inferred from the judgment in *Simmenthal* that the incompatibility with Community law of a subsequently adopted rule of national law has the effect of rendering that rule of national law non-existent."[28]

The European Court has contrasted the EEC Treaty with "ordinary international treaties",[29] and even before the establishment of the EEC, Advocate General Lagrange, in the *Fédéchar* case,[30] involving the Coal and Steel Community Treaty, had floated the argument that the Court of Justice was not "an international court but the court of a Community created by six States as a model which is more closely related to a federal than to an international organisation," though he then dismissed the international court versus federal court argument as an "academic discussion". The Court of Justice referred in the event to a "rule of interpretation generally accepted in both international and national law."[31] More significantly, in *Commission v. Luxembourg & Belgium*[32] the Court rejected an argument based on international law, that a default by the Commission in its obligations to a Member State had the effect of suspending the reciprocal obligations of the latter.[33] The Court has subsequently rejected the proposition that a default by one Member State suspends the reciprocal obligations of other Member States.[34] Yet this conclusion is perfectly consistent with the public international law basis of the Community legal system; the International Court of Justice has similarly held that the regime established by the Vienna Convention

---

[25] Case 106/77 [1978] E.C.R. 629 at 643, para. 17.

[26] Brownlie, *Principles of Public International Law*, (5th ed., Clarendon Press, Oxford, 1998), p. 40, citing *"Interpretation of the Statute of the Memel Territory"* P.C.I.J. Ser. A/B, No. 49, p. 236.

[27] Joined Cases C-10/97—22/97 [1998] E.C.R. I–6307.

[28] *ibid.*, para. 21

[29] Case 6/64 *Costa v. ENEL* [1964] E.C.R. 585; [1964] C.M.L.R. 425.

[30] Case 8/55 [1956] E.C.R. 245.

[31] [1956] E.C.R. 292 at 299. For consideration of internationalist, federalist, and functionalist theories of the Community legal order, see Dagtoglou, *"The legal nature of the European Community"* in *Thirty Years of Community Law* (E.C. Publication, 1983) Chap. II.

[32] Joined Cases 90–91/63, [1964] E.C.R. 625; [1965] C.M.L.R. 58.

[33] For the doctrine in international law, see *Tacna-Arica Arbitration* (1925) 2 R.I.A.A. 921; *US-France Air Services Arbitration* 54 I.L.R. 303; Vienna Convention on the Law of Treaties, Art. 60.

[34] Case 232/78 *Commission v. France* [1979] E.C.R. 2729; [1980] 1 C.M.L.R. 418, para. 9; see also Case C–5/94 *Hedley Lomas* [1996] E.C.R. I–2553; [1996]2 C.M.L.R. 391, para. 20; and Case 14/96 *Paul Denuit* [1997] E.C.R. I–2785; [1997] 3 C.M.L.R. 943.

on Diplomatic Relations, which provides "the necessary means of defence against, and sanction for, illicit activities by members of diplomatic missions" excludes measures of self-help in the event of alleged illicit activities by such persons.[35] The principle affirmed by the International Court of Justice is that the provision of procedures capable of providing a remedy for the breach of an international obligation may be held to oust the customary law right of self-help.

The truth is that there are certain legal characteristics of the Community legal order which may be encountered both in international organisations established by "ordinary" international treaties, and in federal systems. Thus the principles of direct applicability/direct effect, the supremacy of Community law, and the predominance of judicial remedies over self-help—all of which are features of the Community system—support analysis of the Community both as a highly developed order of public international law, and as an incipient federal constitutional system. Perhaps the Community at its present stage should be seen in this light. But the "federalism" of the Community system must at the present time be qualifed as incipient, or undeveloped. A federal state is normally characterised, *inter alia*, by the central government's legal monopoly over foreign relations. In the Community there is no real equivalent of the "central government", and the Commission and Council certainly enjoy no such monopoly, though the Community enjoys substantial competence in the field of external relations.[36] The Community is based upon international treaties concluded between States, and the efficacy of Community law is in some Member States still dependent upon its status as international law.[37] In a federal system, state courts resolve conflicts exclusively upon the basis of federal supremacy rules. In the Community, national courts resolve conflicts between national law and Community law upon the basis both of national law and of Community law. Community law is thus applied to the extent that it has been incorporated into national law in accordance with national constitutional requirements. Nevertheless, it has been said with some force that the European Court "has sought to 'constitutionalize' the Treaty, that is to fashion a constitutional framework for a federal type structure in Europe."[38] Consistently with this approach the Court itself has said that: "The EEC Treaty, albeit concluded in the form of an international agreement, none the less constitutes the constitutional charter of a Community based on the rule of law."[39] It is unexciting but accurate to conclude that the Community and Union comprise a hybrid, and as such different elements in this unique institutional and legal order can be expected to reflect different traditions and inspirations. Citizenship of the Union, comprising a bundle of rights exercisable by all those holding the nationality of a Member State, clearly draws

---

[35] *US v. Iran (Hostages)* (1980) I.C.J. Rep. at 28, paras. 83–90. The Court acknowledges that brief arrest or detention of a diplomat caught committing an offence would be permissible, see para. 87.

[36] See in particular the Common Commercial Policy.

[37] For example, in France the supremacy of Community law appears to be based upon the status accorded to treaties by Art. 55 of the French Constitution, see P. Manin, "The *Nicolo* case of the Conseil d'Etat: French constitutional law and the Supreme Administrative Court's acceptance of the Primacy of Community law over subsequent national statute law" (1991) 28 C.M.L. Rev. 499.

[38] G.F. Mancini, "The making of a Constitution for Europe" (1989) 26 C.M.L. Rev. 595 at 596; and see K. Lenaerts, "Fundamental Rights to be included in a Community Catalogue" (1991) 16 E.L. Rev. 367.

[39] Opinion 1/91 *on Draft Agreement between EEC and EFTA* [1991] E.C.R. I–6079, para. 21.

its inspiration from the federal ideal.[40] By way of contrast, the provisions in the Treaty on European Union and the E.C. Treaty, for the suspension of the rights of a Member State, including its voting rights in the Council, if it is found to be guilty of a serious and persistent breach of such fundamental principles as respect for human rights and the rule of law,[41] are reminiscent of provisions to be found in the charters of international organisations for the suspension or expulsion of recalcitrant members.[42] Even participation in European Monetary Union (which is almost certainly the most federalising aspect of European union to date) is subject to conditions, which must be satisfied by Member States prior to entry, while some Member States remain undecided as to the desirability of joining.

THE SUPREMACY OF COMMUNITY LAW

International law by its nature binds the State in its executive, legislative and judicial activities, and no international tribunal would permit a respondent State to plead provisions of its law or constitution as a defence to an alleged infringement of an international obligation.[43] The same is true of European Community law, "over which no appeal to provisions of internal law of any kind whatever can prevail,"[44] and the Court of Justice has always declined to accept a plea of *force majeure* where a Member State has attempted to comply with Community obligations, but failed as a result of delays in the legislative process. The Court's judgment in *Commission v. Belgium* is illustrative.[45] Belgian indirect taxation of home grown and imported timber discriminated against the latter, contrary to Article 90 (ex 95) E.C. In its defence to an action by the Commission under Article 226 (ex 169) E.C., the Belgian Government argued that it had introduced draft legislation to the Chamber of Representatives two years previously, to remedy the situation, but that it had yet to be passed. Under the principle of the separation of powers prevailing in Belgium, pointed out the Government, it could do no more. The Court was unmoved. "The obligations arising from Article 95 of the Treaty," it observed, "devolve upon States as such and the liability of a Member State under Article 169 arises whatever the agency of the State whose action or inaction is the cause of the failure to fulfil its obligations, even in the case of a constitutionally independent institution."[46] Similarly, the Court has consistently held that a Member State may not plead provisions, practices or circumstances existing in its internal legal order to justify a failure to comply with the obligations and time limits laid down in a directive.[47]

---

[40] Part Two of the E.C. Treaty, Arts 17–22 (ex 8, 8a-e).

[41] Art. 7 TEU; Art. 309 E.C.

[42] See *e.g.*, Arts 5 and 6 of the U.N. Charter.

[43] Treatment of Polish Nationals in Danzig (1932) P.C.I.J.Rep., Ser. A/B, No. 44, at p. 24. Vienna Convention on the Law of Treaties 1969, Art. 27.

[44] Case 48/71 *Commission v. Italy* [1972] E.C.R. 527 at 535; [1972] C.M.L.R. 699.

[45] Case 77/69 [1970] E.C.R. 237; [1974] 1 C.M.L.R. 203. The Court has taken the same position in a consistent line of cases, see, *e.g.* Case 254/83 *Commission v. Italy* [1984] E.C.R. 3395.

[46] [1970] E.C.R. 237 at 243, para. 15.

[47] See, *e.g.*, Case C–303/92 *Commission v. Netherlands* [1993] E.C.R. I–4739, para. 9; Case C–298/97-*Commission v. Spain* [1998] E.C.R. I–3301, para. 14.

The duty of Member States to take all appropriate measures to ensure the fulfilment of obligations arising under the Treaty or secondary legislation is laid down explicitly in Article 10 (ex 5) E.C., and this duty devolves directly upon national courts where directly effective provisions of Community law are involved.[48] This factor was emphasised in *Costa v. ENEL*,[49] in which it was argued that the Court's ruling would be irrelevant to the outcome of the national proceedings, since the national tribunal which had made the reference would be bound to apply national law in any event. The Court responded with an analysis of the Community legal system, and an affirmation of its supremacy over national law:

> "By contrast with ordinary international treaties, the EEC Treaty has created its own legal system which, on the entry into force of the Treaty, became an integral part of the legal systems of the Member States and which their courts are bound to apply.
>
> By creating a Community of unlimited duration, having . . . powers stemming from a limitation of sovereignty, or a transfer of powers from the States to the Community, the Member States have limited their sovereign rights, albeit within limited fields, and have thus created a body of law which binds both their nationals and themselves."[50]

As the Court acknowledged in *Costa*, the supremacy of Community regulations is implicit in the legal characteristics attributed to them in Article 249 (ex 189) E.C.[51] Not only does direct applicability require their access to the national legal order without the favour of specific incorporation, but they have the capacity to pre-empt national legislative competence, that is to say, to create a legal regime whose rules and aims national legislation is bound to respect.[52] Their very nature precludes their modication by inconsistent measures of national law.

That the duty of national courts to give precedence to Community law over national law extends to national legislation adopted after the incorporation of the relevant Community rules into the national legal order was made clear in *Simmenthal*[53]:

> "Furthermore, in accordance with the principle of the precedence of Community law, the relationship between provisions of the Treaty and directly applicable measures of the institutions on the one hand and the national law of the Member States on the other is such that those provisions and measures not only by their entry into force render automatically inapplicable any conflicting provision of current national law but—in so far as they are integral part of, and take precedence in, the legal order applicable in the territory of each of the Member States—also preclude the valid adoption of new national measures to the extent to which they would be incompatible with Community provisions

---

[48] See, *e.g.*, Case 45/76 *Comet* [1976] E.C.R. 2043 at 2053, para. 12; [1977] 1 C.M.L.R. 533.
[49] Case 6/64 [1964] E.C.R. 585; and see Case 17/67 *Neumann* [1967] E.C.R. 441 at 453.
[50] [1964] E.C.R. 585 at 593.
[51] "The precedence of Community law is confirmed by Art. 189, whereby a regulation 'shall be binding' and 'directly applicable in all Member States.' " [1964] E.C.R. 585 at 594.
[52] *infra*, at p. 88.
[53] Case 106/77 [1978] E.C.R. 629 at 643, 644.

... It follows from the foregoing that every national court must, in a case within its jurisdiction, apply Community law in its entirety and protect rights which the latter confers on individuals and must accordingly set aside any provision of national law which may conflict with it, whether prior or subsequent to the Community rule."

In *IN.CO.GE.Srl*[54] the Commission relied upon the above passage to argue that a Member State had no power whatsoever to adopt a fiscal provision that is incompatible with Community law, with the result that such a provision and the corresponding fiscal obligation must be treated as non-existent. But the Court rejected this argument, saying:

"In *Simmenthal*, the issue facing the Court related in particular to the consequences of the direct applicability of a provision of Community law where that provision was incompatible with a subsequently adopted provison of national law ... It cannot ... be inferred from the judgment in *Simmenthal* that the incompatibility with Community law of a subsequently adopted rule of national law has the effect of rendering that rule of national law non-existent. Faced with such a situation, the national court is, however, obliged to disapply that rule, provided always that this obligation does not restrict the power of the competent national courts to apply, from among the various procedures available under national law, those which are appropriate for protecting the individual rights conferred by Community law ... "[55]

The principle of the supremacy of Community law, well established as it is in the jurisprudence of the Court of Justice, may in practice be denied full effect by national courts or tribunals. Although as a matter of Community law it is impermissible to condition the effects of its provisions on the requirements of national law, however fundamental,[56] the possibility cannot be ruled out that national courts may nevertheless feel constrained to temper the rigour of the Treaty's requirements, for national courts are established pursuant to national law, and are entrusted first and foremost with maintaining the integrity of the national legal order.

In the United Kingdom, section 2(1) of the European Communities Act 1972 provides for the recognition of all directly enforceable Community law. In *Factortame v. Secretary of State for Transport*,[57] the House of Lords expressed the view that section 2(1) of the 1972 Act has precisely the same effect as if a section were incorporated in an Act of 1988 which in terms enacted that the latter Act was to be without prejudice to the directly enforceable rights of nationals of any Member State of the Community.[58] The *Factortame* litigation[59] makes it clear that an Act of Parliament subsequent to the 1972 European Communities Act

---

[54] Joined Cases C–10–22/97, [1998] E.C.R. I–6907.
[55] Paras 20 and 21.
[56] Case 11/70 *Internationale Handelsgesellschaft* [1970] E.C.R. 1125; [1972] C.M.L.R. 255.
[57] [1990] 2 A.C. 85.
[58] [1990] 2 A.C. 85 at 140, *per* Lord Bridge.
[59] *Factortame*, nn.57 and 58 above, and *Factortame (No. 2)* [1991] 1 A.C. 603. For a view on the constitutional implications of these cases, see Craig, "Supremacy of the United Kingdom Parliament after Factortame", (1991) 11 Y.E.L. 221.

may be subject to judicial review if it contravenes the directly enforceable Community rights of the applicant, and that the doctrine of implied repeal has no application to the 1972 Act, nor to directly enforceable Community rights taking effect thereunder. This was surely a landmark in the evolution of our constitutional system. Express repeal of, or derogation from, section 2(1) of the European Communities Act, would, however, be likely to be given effect by courts in the United Kingdom, since such a step would remove or amend *pro tanto* the constitutional basis for the application of Community law n the United Kingdom.

THE LEGAL EFFECT OF TREATY PROVISIONS

Implementing Treaty provisions by national legislation

It has already been noted that the European Court considers that the E.C. Treaty has created its own legal system which, on its entry into force, became an integral part of the legal systems of the Member States and which their courts are bound to apply.[60] It follows that Member States are bound to introduce constitutional amendments and/or legislation which recognise the full force and effect of Community law, including in particular its supremacy and direct effect. Where provisions of the E.C. Treaty are not directly effective, Member States are clearly obliged to adopt legislative measures of implementation where this is necessary to achieve compliance with the Treaty. But where Treaty provisions are directly effective, and are recognised and enforceable as such under national law, is there any further obligation to adopt national measures of implementation? The answer to this question appears to be that it will be necessary to adopt such measures where otherwise the full and complete implementation of the Treaty would not be achieved. For example, it appears from a case initiated by the Commission against the Republic of France that a Member State may be required to repeal provisions of national law which discriminate on grounds of nationality, notwithstanding the fact that Article 39 (ex 48) E.C. prohibiting discrimination on grounds of nationality as regards access to employment, and the provisions of Regulation 1612/68 having the same effect, are directly applicable. This is because the ambiguous state of affairs resulting from the maintenance in force of the national legislation in question itself comprises a "secondary" obstacle to equal access to employment which itself contravenes Article 39.[61] In a subsequent case against the Republic of Italy alleging that Italian rules restricting access to foreign nationals to certain occupations in the field of tourism infringed Community law, the Court said:

> "It must be observed in that regard that directly applicable provisions of the Treaty are binding on all the authorities of the Member States and they must therefore comply with them without its being necessary to adopt national

---

[60] Above, p. 66. Case 6/64 *Costa v. ENEL* [1964] E.C.R. 585; [1964] C.M.L.R. 425.

[61] Case 167/73 *Commission v. France* [1974] E.C.R. 359; [1974] 2 C.M.L.R. 216. The Court relied upon Case 167/73 and adopted similar reasoning, in Case 159/78 *Commission v. Italy* [1979] E.C.R. 3247; [1980] 3 C.M.L.R. 446.

implementing provisions. However, as the Court held in its judgment . . . in Case 72/85 (*Commission v. Netherlands* . . .), the right of individuals to rely on directly applicable provisions of the Treaty before national courts is only a minimum guarantee and is not sufficient in itself to ensure the full and complete implementation of the Treaty . . ."[62]

The reference in the above quotation to *Commission v. Netherlands*[63] is curious since the latter case concerns an action brought against the Netherlands for failing to take the necessary measures to ensure the implementation of E.C. staff *regulations* providing for the co-ordination of national pension schemes with the Community pension scheme as regards Community officials. As has been noted above,[64] and is explained further below,[65] in principle, regulations are directly applicable and binding in their entirety, and national legislative implementation is both unnecessary and impermissible. That is the position in principle, but in the case in point, the staff regulations (despite their direct applicability) could not have full force and effect unless national implementing rules were adopted to provide for the actual transfer of pension rights accrued under national law to the Community scheme. It was in this context that the Court stated that the right of individuals to rely upon the staff regulations before their national courts represented only a minimum guarantee which was not sufficient in itself to ensure the full and complete implementation of the regulations. In a subsequent *Commission v. Italy*[66] case the Court of Justice considered an allegation by the Commission that an exemption from value added tax for domestic goods under Italian legislation was not extended to imports, contrary to Article 90 (ex 95) E.C. In the course of its judgment, the Court stated:

". . . the Court has consistently held (see *inter alia* the judgment . . . in Case 143/83 *Commission v. Denmark* [1985] E.C.R. 427) that the principles of legal certainty and the protection of individuals require, in areas covered by Community law, that the Member States' legal rules should be worded unequivocally so as to give the persons concerned a clear and precise understanding of their rights and obligations and enable national courts to ensure that those rights and obligations are observed."[67]

The case cited above by the Court—*Commission v. Denmark*, in fact concerned the failure to adopt unambiguous legislation implementing a *directive*, and it seems that at least in certain circumstances a Member State will be under a duty to implement a Treaty provision by national measures in a way which seems analogous to implementing a directive. In later proceedings against Italy, once more alleging that certain features of the Italian value added tax system were being applied in such a way as to infringe Article 90 (ex 95) E.C. the Court referred both to the principle that reliance upon the direct applicability of Article 95 represented only a minimum guarantee and was not sufficient in itself to

---

[62] Case 168/85 *Commission v. Italy* [1986] E.C.R. 2945, at para. 11; [1988] 1 C.M.L.R. 580.
[63] Case 72/85 [1986] E.C.R. 1219.
[64] See p. 61.
[65] See p. 86.
[66] Case 257/86 [1988] E.C.R. 3249.
[67] *ibid.* at para. 12.

ensure the full and complete implementation of the Treaty, and to the principle that in areas covered by Community law, national legal rules should be worded unequivocally so as to give the persons concerned a clear and precise understanding of their rights and obligations.[68] It followed that compliance with the directly applicable provision in question required the Italian authorities to enact national rules specifying the rights of importers as regards value added tax which flowed from the terms of Article 90 (ex 95) E.C. In the latter case the duty to enact the national rules in question amounted to a duty to *disapply* national rules which were incompatible with the Treaty. But the duty to implement the Treaty by adopting national measures is not confined in all cases to a duty to *disapply* inconsistent national rules, it may on occasion amount to a further duty to adopt positive rules and procedures to ensure that individuals can exercise the rights contemplated by the Treaty; the case of *Commission v. Spain* is illustrative.[69] In this case the Commission brought an action under Article 226 (ex 169) E.C. for, *inter alia*, a declaration that, by failing to establish a procedure for examining qualifications acquired by a Community national in another Member State as a tourist guide and comparing them with those required by Spain in order to enable the diploma issued by that other Member State to be recognised, the Kingdom of Spain had failed to comply with, in particular Articles 39 (ex 48) and 43 (ex 52). Advocate General Lenz referred to the case law of the Court of Justice to the effect that a Member State which receives a request to admit a person to a profession to which access, under national law, depends upon the possession of a diploma or a professional qualification, must take into consideration the diplomas and other evidence of qualifications which the person concerned has acquired in order to exercise the same profession in another Member State by making a comparison between the specialised knowledge and abilities certified by those diplomas and the knowledge and qualifications required by the national rules. He went on:

> "With regard to the adjustment of national law to those principles, the Commission implicitly assumes that the defendant Member State must incorporate those principles in the provisions concerning the profession of tourist guide by means of express rules.
>
> That view is correct. The principles of legal certainty and the protection of individuals require that, in areas covered by Community law, the Member States' legal rules should be worded unequivocally so as to give the persons concerned a clear and precise understanding of their rights and obligations and to enable national courts to ensure that those rights and obligations are observed."[70]

The Court held that by failing to establish a procedure for examining qualifications acquired by a Community national who holds a diploma as tourist guide issued in another Member State and comparing them with those required by

---

[68] Case C–120/88 *Commission v. Italy* [1991] E.C.R. 621, paras 10 and 11; [1993] 1 C.M.L.R. 41.

[69] Case C–375/92 [1994] E.C.R. I–923. See also to similar effect in the context of a regulation, Case 72/85 *Commission v. Netherlands* [1986] E.C.R. 1219; see text to n.63, above.

[70] Paras 26 and 27 of Mr Lenz's Opinion. He refers to Case C–120/88, n.68 above.

Spain, the Spanish State had failed to fulfil its obligations under Article 39 (ex 48) E.C., Article 43 (ex 52) E.C. and Article 49 (ex 59) E.C.

It follows that Member States are obliged to adopt national rules to implement provisions of the Treaty which are not directly applicable, where necessary, and to adopt national rules to implement directly applicable provisions of the Treaty in those cases where direct applicability will not secure the full and complete implementation of the Treaty provision in question. Member States must moreover repeal national rules which contradict directly applicable Treaty provisions, since the maintenance in force of such contradictory provisions gives rise to a state of uncertainty which prejudices the exercise by individuals of the rights which they derive directly from the Treaty. It is possible, however, that where a ruling of a superior court has made it clear that the direct applicability of the Treaty has the effect of disapplying a particular provision of national law, this will in itself ensure the full and complete implementation of the Treaty provision in question, without the need for national legislative confirmation of the position.[71]

Interpreting national legal provisions so that they are consistent with Treaty provisions

As has been mentioned, certain non-binding acts may cast light on the interpretation of national law or Community law.[72] And as will be explained below, national courts are under a duty to interpret national law in accordance with relevant provisions of relevant directives, as far as it is possible for them to do so.[73] But to what extent are national courts obliged by Community law to interpret national law in accordance with provisions of the *Treaty*? It has been explained above that the national authorities of Member States are under a duty to repeal national legislation which is incompatible with the Treaty, and are obliged to remove any ambiguities or uncertainties which leave individuals in doubt as to the scope of their rights under the Treaty. Furthermore, the meaning and scope of national legislation is a matter for national courts and tribunals, and this has been recognised by the Court of Justice.[74] And it is established that national courts are under a duty pursuant to Article 10 (ex 5) E.C. "to ensure fulfilment of the obligations arising out of" the Treaty.[75] It would seem to follow that if it is possible under national law for a national court to resolve an ambiguity in national law in such a way as to ensure that the national law in question is consistent with, rather than incompatible with, a provision of the Treaty, the national court is obliged to interpret the national law in this way. The Court's case-law indeed supports this view. In *Murphy v. An Bord Telecom Eireann*, a case involving the interpretation of Article 141 (ex 119), the Court

---

[71] The Court has said that the scope of national laws must be assessed in the light of the interpretation given to them by national courts, see Case C–382/92 *Commission v. United Kingdom* [1994] E.C.R. I–2495, para. 4; [1995] 1 C.M.L.R. 345; Case C–300/95 *Commission v. United Kingdom* [1997] E.C.R. I–2649, para. 37; [1997] 3 C.M.L.R. 923.

[72] nn.9, 10 and 11 above, and text thereto.

[73] See below, p. 92.

[74] n.71 above.

[75] See generally Chap. 5, below.

regarded the duty to set aside national rules incompatible with the direct applicability of the latter article as only arising if it proved impossible to construe national rules in a way which accorded with the requirements of the provision in question.[76] But it seems that the duty of consistent interpretation of the Treaty only arises in a case in which failure to interpret the national rules in accordance with Community law will actually lead to a breach of the Treaty. In *Imperial Chemical Industries plc (ICI) v. Kenneth Hall Colmer (Her Majesty's Inspector of Taxes)*,[77] a taxpayer alleged that a provision of national tax law would in certain circumstances hinder the right of establishment of nationals of Member States, contrary to Article 43 (ex 52) E.C., unless interpreted in the way favoured by the taxpayer. However, it was accepted on all sides that in the circumstances of the case in point no hindrance to the right of establishment of nationals of Member States could arise. Advocate General Tesauro said that the duty of a national court to interpret national law consistently with Community law is irrelevant where the subject matter is covered by a directly effective provision of the Treaty.[78] The Court, having noted that the situation in issue lay outside the scope of Community law, states:

"Accordingly, when deciding an issue concerning a situation which lies outside the scope of Community law, the national court is not required, under Community law, either to interpret its legislation in a way conforming with Community law or to disapply that legislation. Where a particular provision must be disapplied in a situation covered by Community law, but that same provision could remain applicable to a situation not so covered, it is for the competent body of the State concerned to remove that legal uncertainty in so far as it might affect rights deriving from Community rules."[79]

Direct applicability of Treaty provisions

Invoking Treaty Provisions against Member States (vertical direct effect)

The judicial source of the principle that certain provisions of the Treaty may be invoked by individuals in national courts is the judgment in *NV Algemene Transport- en Expeditie Onderneming Van Gend & Loos v. Netherlands Inland Revenue Administration*.[80] Dutch importers challenged the rate of import duty charged on a chemical product imported from the Federal Republic of Germany, alleging that reclassifying it under a different heading of the Dutch customs tariff had resulted in an increase in duty prohibited under the then applicable text of Article 25 (ex 12) E.C., which provided that "Member States shall refrain from introducing between themselves any new customs duties on

---

[76] Case 157/86 [1988] E.C.R. 673, para. 11; [1988] 1 C.M.L.R. 879; Case C–165/91 *Munster* [1994] E.C.R. I–4661, below, at 385.
[77] Case C–264/96, [1998] E.C.R. I–4695.
[78] Para. 32 of Opinion.
[79] Para. 34 of judgment.
[80] Case 26/62 [1963] E.C.R. 1; [1964] C.M.L.R. 29.

imports . . . or any charges having equivalent effect, and from increasing those which they already apply in their trade with each other." The Tariefcommisie, an administrative tribunal having final jurisdiction in cases involving such customs duties, asked the Court of Justice whether the Article in question had "direct application within the territory of a Member State, in other words, whether nationals of such a State can, on the basis of the Article in question, lay claim to individual rights which the courts must protect." The Netherlands Government, in its submissions to the Court, argued that an infringement of the Treaty by a Member State could be submitted to the Court only under the procedure laid down by Articles 226 and 227 (ex 169 and 170), *i.e.*, at the suit of the Commission or another Member State.[81] This general argument, to the effect that the provisions of the Treaty simply give rise to rights and obligations between Member States in international law, was rejected by Advocate General Roemer, who argued that anyone "familiar with Community law" knew that "in fact it does not just consist of contractual relations between a number of States considered as subjects of the law of nations."[82] This followed from the fact that the Community was authorised to make rules of law capable of bestowing rights and obligations on private individuals as well as on Member States.[83] The Court, in a judgment which was to prove of considerable importance for the development of Community law, stated:

"The objective of the EEC Treaty, which is to establish a Common Market, the functioning of which is of direct concern to interested parties in the Community, implies that this Treaty is more than an agreement which merely creates mutual obligations between the contracting states. The task assigned to the Court of Justice under Article 177 [now 234], the object of which is to ensure uniform interpretation of the Treaty by national courts and tribunals, confirms that the States have acknowledged that Community law has an authority which can be invoked by their nationals before those courts and tribunals.

The conclusion to be drawn from this is that the Community constitutes a new legal order of international law for the benefit of which the States have limited their sovereign rights, albeit within limited fields, and the subjects of which comprise not only Member States but also their nationals. Independently of the legislation of Member States, Community law therefore not only imposes obligations on individuals but is also intended to confer upon them rights which become part of their legal heritage. These rights arise not only where they are expressly granted by the Treaty, but also by reason of obligations which the Treaty imposes in a clearly defined way upon individuals as well as upon the Member States and the institutions of the Community."[84]

---

[81] [1963] E.C.R. 1 at 6; [1965] C.M.L.R. 109.

[82] [1963] E.C.R. 1 at 20; [1965] C.M.L.R. 109.

[83] The Advocate General cited in support of this proposition Arts 244, 249, 254 and 256 (ex 187, 189, 191 and 192) of the Treaty.

[84] [1963] E.C.R. 1 at 12; [1965] C.M.L.R. 109.

This reasoning has been criticised for deducing the direct applicability of Treaty provisions "essentially without any legal basis in the Treaty".[85] The above passage of the Court certainly appears to rely more upon rhetoric than tight legal reasoning to persuade the reader. But it would be wrong to consider that the approach of the Court in *Van Gend en Loos* amounted to an improper exercise of its judicial powers. In the view of the present writer, the strongest argument in favour of the Court's approach is to be found in its reference to the task assigned to the Court of Justice under what was then Article 177 of the Treaty. In relevant part this latter Article provides for the Court of Justice to give preliminary rulings on *inter alia* the interpretation of the Treaty, in response to requests from national courts which find that such an interpretation is necessary to enable them to give judgment in the national proceedings. This Article at the very least leaves open the possibility that Treaty provisions might have some legal consequences when pleaded before national courts. The possibility that those legal consequences might have been held to be limited in certain respects, *e.g.* to providing guidance to national courts on the interpretation of national rules meant to implement the provisions of the Treaty, does not render illegitimate the Court's actual conclusion, namely, that provisions of the Treaty could give rise to rights in individuals which they could invoke in national courts. Furthermore, the rhetorical style of the above passage should not be allowed to detract from the underlying soundness of its analysis. The Treaty did set up institutions endowed with legislative powers which could bind individuals, and the Treaty did contemplate issues of Community law being invoked before national courts, which are empowered and in certain cases required to refer questions of Community law to the European Court for decision. Whatever else the Treaty of Rome was, it was not an ordinary international treaty, and the Court of Justice should not be accused of judicial alchemy for acknowledging the fact.

Since *Van Gend en Loos* was a point of departure for so much that followed in the development of the Community legal order, it merits a little further attention. Although the Advocate General had taken the view that certain Treaty provisions were "clearly intended to be incorporated into national law and to modify or supplement it,"[86] he had not numbered among them Article 25 (ex 12), since its application required the resolution of complex issues of interpretation. To hold such a provision directly applicable, he pointed out, would create uncertainties in the law: enterprises would be far more likely to rely upon national customs legislation than upon the text of the Treaty. The Court's approach was less cautious:

---

[85] Hjalte Rasmussen, *European Court of Justice*, (Gadjura, Copenhagen, 1998), at p. 78. For "sceptical" assessments of the role of the Court of Justice in developing *inter alia* the direct effect doctrine, see Sir Patrick Neill, Q.C., *The European Court of Justice: A Case study in Judicial Activism*, evidence submitted to the House of Lords Select Committee on the European Communities, Sub-committee on the 1996 Inter-Governmental Conference, *1996 Inter-Governmental Conference, Minutes of Evidence, House of Lords, Session 1994–95,* 18th Report, p. 218; T. Hartley, "The European Court, Judicial Objectivity and the Constitution of the European Union," (1996) 112 L.Q.R. 95. For a well considered assessment from a somewhat different perspective, see Tridimas, "The Court of Justice and Judicial Activism" (1996) 21 E.L. Rev. 199.

[86] He cited Arts 81, 82, 84, 234, and 256 (ex 85, 86, 88, 177 and 192).

"The wording of Article 12 [now 25] contains a clear and unconditional prohibition which is not a positive but a negative obligation. This obligation, moreover, is not qualified by any reservation on the part of States which would make its implementation conditional upon a positive legislative measure enacted under national law. The very nature of this prohibition makes it ideally adapted to product direct effects in the legal relationship between Member States and their subjects."[87]

The *Van Gend en Loos* judgment affirms the existence of the "new legal order" in which individuals, as well as Member States, may have rights and obligations, and it lays down the criteria to be applied in deciding whether or not a particular provision may be invoked by individuals in national courts. These criteria were to be applied subsequently in numerous cases,[88] and were summed up as follows by Advocate General Mayras in *Reyners v. Belgian State*:

— the provision in question must be sufficiently clear and precise for judicial application[89];
— it must establish an unconditional obligation[90];
— the obligation must be complete and legally perfect, and its implementation must not depend on measures being subsequently taken by Community institutions or Member States with discretionary power in the matter.[91]

The second requirement, that the obligation be unconditional, was of considerable importance during the transitional period (1958-1970), during which period national restrictions on the free movement of goods, persons and services were to be progressively abolished.[92] These conditional prohibitions in the Treaty became unconditional on the expiry of the transitional period, and national measures in force when the Treaty came into effect could be challenged in national courts.[93]

---

[87] [1963] E.C.R. 1 at 13; [1965] C.M.L.R. 109.
[88] *e.g.*, provisions of the Treaty were held directly effective in the following cases: Case 6/64 *Costa* [1964] E.C.R. 585; [1964] C.M.L.R. 425 (repealed Article (formerly Article 53) and Art. 31 (ex 37(2))); Case 57/65 *Lutticke* [1966] E.C.R. 205; [1971] C.M.L.R. 674 (Art. 90(1) (ex 95(1)) and repealed Article (formerly Article 95(3))); Case 28/67 *Molkerei-Zentrale* [1968] E.C.R. 143; [1968] C.M.L.R. 187 (Art. 90(1) (ex 95(1))); Case 27/67 *Fink-Frucht* [1968] E.C.R. 223; [1968] C.M.L.R. 187 (Art. 90(2) (ex 95(2))); Case 13/68 *Salgoil*; [1969] C.M.L.R. 181; [1968] E.C.R. 453 (repealed Arts (formerly 31 and 32(1))); Case 33/70 *SACE* [1970] E.C.R. 1213; [1971] C.M.L.R. 123 (repealed Article (formerly Article 13(2))); Case 18/71 *Eunomia* [1971] E.C.R. 811; [1972] C.M.L.R. 4 (repealed Article (formerly Article 16)); Case 127/73 *SABAM* [1974] E.C.R. 51 (Arts 81 and 82 (ex 85 and 86)).
[89] See *e.g.*, Case 26/62 *Van Gend en Loos*, see n.80; Case 6/64 *Costa*; Case 33/70 *SACE*; Case 18/71 *Eunomia*; for references, see n.88; Case 41/74 *Van Duyn* [1974] E.C.R. 1337; [1975] 1 C.M.L.R. 1 (Article 39 (ex 48)).
[90] See *e.g.*, Case 26/62 *Van Gend en Loos*; Case 6/64 *Costa*; Case 57/65 *Lutticke*; for references, see n.88.
[91] See *e.g.*, Case 26/62 *Van Gend en Loos*; Case 57/65 *Lutticke*; Case 33/70 *SACE*; Case 18/71 *Eunomia*; for references, see n.88; Case 41/74 *Van Duyn*, see n.89.
[92] See, *e.g.*, Arts 7 (repealed), 13(1) and (2) (repealed); Arts 30 (text prior to Amsterdam amendment) and 32(1) (repealed); Art. 48(1) (text prior to Amsterdam amendment); Art. 52(1) (text prior to Amsterdam amendment); Art. 59(1) (text prior to Amsterdam amendment).
[93] Ranbow, "The End of the Transitional Period" (1969) 6 C.M.L. Rev. 434. For obligations directly effective as of the end of the transitional period, see *e.g.*, Case 77/72 *Capolongo* [1973] E.C.R. 611; [1974] C.M.L.R. 230 (Art. 13(2) (repealed)); Case 74/76 *Ianelli & Volpi* [1977] E.C.R. 557; [1977] 2

The first and third requirements, that a legal provision be clear and precise, and be independent of measures to be taken subsequently by the Community institutions or the Member States, may be illustrated by reference to *Salgoil v. Italian Ministry for Foreign Trade*,[94] in which the Court denied direct effect to Article 32(1), last sentence (the Article is now repealed), and Article 33 (now repealed), of the Treaty. These provisions required Member States to phase out quantitative restrictions on imports, by converting bilateral quotas into global quotas, and by progressively increasing their total value. The rate of liberalisation was prescribed for products where "the global quotas amounted to less than 3 per cent. of the national production of the State concerned." The Court conceded that these provisions laid down obligations which were not subject to the adoption of measures by the institutions of the Community, but pointed out that: "Some discretion does fall to be exercised by the Member States from the obligation to 'convert any bilateral quotas . . . into global quotas' and from the concepts of 'total value' and 'national production.' In fact, since the Treaty gives no indication as to the data . . . or as to the methods applicable, several solutions may be envisaged."[95] It followed, in the Court's view, that the provisions in question were insufficiently precise to be considered directly effective.

It must be emphasised that the fact that provisions of Community law may require the appreciation of complex issues does not preclude their being directly effective, providing the requisite conditions are satisfied. Thus Article 90(1) (ex 95(1)) E.C. prohibits the imposition "on the products of other Member States" of "any internal taxation of any kind in excess of that imposed directly or indirectly on similar domestic products." The second paragraph of that Article adds that: "no Member State shall impose on the products of other Member States any internal taxation of such a nature as to afford indirect protection to other products." In *Fink-Frucht v. Hauptzollamt Munchen*,[96] the Court considered whether or not this latter provision was directly effective. It decided that it was, in face of the arguments of the Federal Republic of Germany that the paragraph was "vague and incomplete" and that the "value-judgments" it required should not be forced on national courts.[97] In the Court's view, the provision contained a straightforward prohibition against protection; "it established an unconditional obligation, and no action was required on the part of the institutions of the Community or the Member States for its implementation." "Although this provision involves the evaluation of economic factors," observed the Court, "this does not exclude the right and the duty of national courts to ensure that the rules of the Treaty are observed whenever they can ascertain . . . that the conditions necessary for the application of the Article are fulfilled."[98]

C.M.L.R. 688 (Art. 28 (ex 30)); Case 59/75 *Manghera* [1976] E.C.R. 91; [1976] 1 C.M.L.R. 557 (Art. 31(1) (ex 37(1))); Case 41/74 *Van Duyn* [1974] E.C.R. 1337; [1975] 1 C.M.L.R. 1 (Art. 39 (ex 48)); Case 2/74 *Reyners* [1974] E.C.R. 631; [1974] 2 C.M.L.R. 305 (Art. 43 (ex 52)); Case 33/74 *Van Binsbergen* [1974] E.C.R. 1299; [1975] 1 C.M.L.R. 277 (Art. 49 (ex 59))).
[94] Case 33/68 [1968] E.C.R. 453; [1968] C.M.L.R. 181.
[95] [1968] E.C.R. 453 at 461; [1968] C.M.L.R. 181.
[96] Case 27/67 [1968] E.C.R. 223; [1968] C.M.L.R. 187.
[97] [1968] E.C.R. 223 at 229; [1968] C.M.L.R. 187.
[98] [1968] E.C.R. 223 at 232; [1968] C.M.L.R. 187.

Invoking Treaty Provisions against private individuals and companies (horizontal direct effect)

In the cases discussed above, the Court of Justice was called upon to consider whether or not a provision of the Treaty had modified the legal position of an individual *vis-à-vis* the State. Beginning with the judgment in *Belgische Radio en Televisie v. SABAM*,[99] we see a new development; the acknowledgment that provisions of the Treaty are capable of modifying the rights of private parties (individuals or companies) *inter se*. Thus in *SABAM* the Court observed that the prohibitions of Articles 81(1) (ex 85(1)) and 82 (ex 86) E.C. "tend by their very nature to produce direct effects in relations between individuals," and "create direct rights in respect of the individuals concerned which the national courts must safeguard."[1] It might have been arguable that Articles 81 and 82 (ex 85 and 86), being explicitly concerned with private action, could be treated as special cases, but the Court's later decision in *Walrave & Koch v. Association Union Cycliste Internationale*,[2] suggested a more general principle. Motorcyclists who earned their living "pacing" pedal cyclists in international events asked a Netherlands court for a declaration that certain rules of the defendant association infringed the Treaty's prohibition of discrimination on grounds of nationality. The national court sought a preliminary ruling. Doubts were expressed by the Commission[3] in argument as to whether the prohibition in question applied to private action, as opposed to State action, and the Court addressed itself to the question as follows:

"It has been alleged that the prohibition in these Articles refer only to restrictions which have their origin in acts of an authority and not to those resulting from legal acts of persons or associations who do not come under public law.

Articles 7, 48, 59 [now 12, 39, 49] have in common the prohibition, in their respective spheres of application, of any discrimination on grounds of nationality.

Prohibition of such discrimination does not only apply to the acts of public authorities, but extends likewise to rules of any other nature aimed at regulating in a collective manner gainful employment and the provision of services."[4]

It followed, in the Court's view, that the provisions of the Articles in question could be taken into account by a national court in judging the validity and the effects of the rules of a sporting association.

The extent to which the Treaty may impose obigations on individuals was once again raised in *Defrenne v. Sabena*,[5] a reference from a Belgian court. The

---

[99] Case 127/73 [1974] E.C.R. 51; [1974] C.M.L.R. 251.

[1] [1974] E.C.R. 51 at 62; [1974] C.M.L.R. 251.

[2] Case 36/74 [1974] E.C.R. 1405; [1975] 1 C.M.L.R. 320.

[3] [1974] E.C.R. 1405 at 1410; [1975] 1 C.M.L.R. 320.

[4] [1974] E.C.R. 1405 at 1418, paras 15, 16 and 17; 1 C.M.L.R. 320.

[5] Case 43/75 [1976] E.C.R. 455; [1976] 2 C.M.L.R. 98. The judgment provoked a great deal of discussion at the time, see Wyatt (1975-76) 1 E.L. Rev. 399–402, 418, 419; Crisham (1977) 14 C.M.L. Rev. 102, and the references cited at pp. 108, 109, n.1; Allott [1977] C.L.J. 7.

national proceedings were initiated by a former air hostess against her former employer, Sabena, and in these proceedings she alleged infringement of Article 141 (ex 119) E.C. The text of the latter Article provided at the time that during the first stage "Each Member State shall . . . ensure that subsequently maintain the application of the principle that men and women should receive equal pay for equal work." The original six Member States had not complied with this obligation by January 1, 1973, nor had the then new Member States (Denmark Ireland and the United Kingdom) been in a position to do so when they acceded on that date. The Belgian court asked the Court of Justice whether the Article in question entitled workers to undertake proceedings before national courts in order to ensure its observance. The Court replied in the affirmative; even though the complete implementation of the equal pay principles could not be achieved without legislative elaboration at the Community or national level, the requirement was nevertheless apt for national judicial application in cases of "direct and overt discrimination which may be identified solely with the aid of the criteria based on equal work and equal pay referred to by the Article in question."[6] It might be thought that the greatest obstacle in the way to finding that the equal pay principle in the Treaty could impose a direct obligation on employers was that it was framed in terms of an obligation imposed on Member States. But the Court reasons to the effect that the reference to "Member States" is a reference which is not confined to national legislative authorities, and the term "cannot be interpreted as excluding the intervention of the courts in the direct application of the Treaty."[7] Thus the duty of the Member States to ensure and subsequently maintain the application of the principle of equal pay includes the duty of the courts of Member States to enforce the principle of equal pay in the cases which come before them. This approach paradoxically draws upon traditional principles of State responsibility in international law (to the effect that all acts of the legislative, executive and judicial organs of the State may in principle be attributed to the State) to produce a result which is far from traditional, and which is rather, in this writer's view, intellectually attractive. "In fact," went on the Court, "since Article 119 is mandatory in nature, the prohibition on discrimination between men and women applies not only to the action of public authorities, but also extends to all agreements which are intended to regulate paid labour collectively, as well as to contracts between individuals."[8] The Treaty's prohibition on discrimination on grounds of nationality for individuals exercising their right of free movement, and its guarantee of equal pay for equal work without discrimination on grounds of sex, were thus held enforceable in national courts against natural and legal persons, as well as against Member States.

The Exceptional Case—the Prospective Effect of a ruling on the interpretation of a directly effective Treaty provision

Although the Court in *Defrenne* held that Article 141 (ex 119) E.C. was directly applicable—at least in part—it also held that the Article could not be relied upon

---

[6] [1976] E.C.R. 455 at 473, para. 18; [1976] 2 C.M.L.R. 98, *e.g.*, discrimination in national legislation or in collective labour agreements, which could be detected on the basis of a purely legal analysis of the situation [1976] E.C.R. 455, at 473, para. 21; [1976] 2 C.M.L.R. 98.

[7] [1976] E.C.R. 455 at 475, para. 37; [1976] 2 C.M.L.R. 98.

[8] [1976] E.C.R. 455 at 476, para. 39; [1976] 2 C.M.L.R. 98.

to support claims in respect of pay periods prior to the date of its judgment, except as regards workers who had already brought legal proceedings or made equivalent claims. This was a step of some considerable significance. In normal circumstances a judicial decision defines the meaning and scope of the rule in issue as it should have been understood and applied from the time the rule came into force, and the rule as so interpreted is applicable to legal relationships arising and established prior to the judgment in question. But in *Defrenne* the Court seems to have been moved by the pleas of Ireland and the United Kingdom that if claims to back pay based on Article 119 could be made they would have disastrous economic effects in these countries. It responded as follows:

> "Although the practical consequences of any judicial decision must be carefully taken into account, it would be impossible to go so far as to diminish the objectivity of the law and compromise its future application on the ground of the possible repercussions which might result, as regards the past, from such a judicial decision.
>
> However, in the light of the conduct of several of the Member States and the views adopted by the Commission and repeatedly brought to the notice of the circles concerned, it is appropriate to take exceptionally into account the fact that, over a prolonged period, the parties concerned have been led to continue with practices which were contrary to Article 119, although not yet prohibited under their national law.
>
> The fact that, in spite of the warnings given, the Commission did not initiated proceedings under Article 169 against the Member States concerned on grounds of failure to fulfil and obligation was likely to consolidate the incorrect impression as to the effects of Article 119.
>
> In these circumstances, it is appropriate to determine that, as the general level at which pay would have been fixed cannot be known, important considerations of legal certainty affecting all the interests involved, both public and private, make it impossible to re-open the question as regards the past."[9]

In other words, the *unexpectedness* of the Court's ruling militated against its retrospective application.The legal basis of the decision is the principle of "legal certainty" which holds that parties acting reasonably on the basis of the law as it stands ought to be able to do so in the confidence that their legal position will be changed retrospectively.[10] Analogous principles have been applied by the Supreme Court of the United States, which has declared in certain cases that constitutional rulings will have only prospective effect.[11]

The subsequent case law of the Court of Justice confirms that derogation from the normal principle whereby a ruling on the interpretation of Community law is binding as regards the past as well as the future is permissible only in quite

---

[9] [1976] E.C.R. 455 at 480, 481, paras 71–74; [1976] 2 C.M.L.R. 98.

[10] For legal certainty and legitimate expectations see below, p. 137.

[11] In so doing, it has emphasised three criteria: (i) the purpose to be served by the new rule; (ii) the extent of reliance by law enforcement authorities on the old rule; and (iii) the effect on the administration of justice of a retrospective application of the new rule. See, *e.g. Stovall v. Denno* 388 U.S. 293 at 297; L.Ed. 2d. 1199; 87 S.Ct. 1967.

exceptional circumstances, where the Court considers that compliance with it breaches the principle of legal certainty.[12] In considering whether that principle necessitates the imposition of a temporal limit on the effects of ruling on a request for interpretation, the Court must ascertain (a) whether there is a risk of economic repercussions owing in particular to the large number of legal relationships entered into in good faith on the basis of national rules considered to be validly in force and (b) whether individuals and national authorities have been prompted to adopt practices which do not comply with Community law by reason of "objective significant uncertainty regarding the precise scope of the rule of Community law interpreted by the Court; if it finds that the attitude adopted by other Member States or the Commission contributed to that uncertainty, that will have a particular bearing on its assessment of the matter in that regard."[13]

The Court has limited the temporal effects of a judgment on the meaning of a Treaty provision in only a handful of cases. In *Blaizot*[14] the Court was called upon to rule for the first time whether or not university education in could be regarded as constituting vocational training for the purposes of the application of the principle that there be no discrimination on grounds of nationality as regards enrolment fees for access to vocational training courses. The Court admitted that in so holding it was recognising developments in the Community's vocational training policy, and noted that the conduct of the Commission "might reasonably have led the authorities concerned in Belgium to consider that the relevant Belgian legislation was in conformity with Community law." The Court concluded that in such circumstances, pressing considerations of legal certainty precluded any reopening of the question of past legal relationships where that would retroactively throw the financing of university education into confusion and might have unforeseeable consequences for the proper functioning of universities. It followed that the direct effect of Article 12 (ex 6) E.C. could not be relied on in support of claims regarding supplementary enrolment fees improperly charged prior to the date of this judgment, except in respect of students who brought legal proceedings or submitted an equivalent claim before that date. The circumstances are similar to those in *Defrenne*, in that the Court's judgment broke new ground, and the conduct of the Commission had contributed to a mistaken view of the law on the part of national authorities.

The Court had reason to limit the temporal effects of yet another judgment on the interpretation of Article 141 (ex 119) E.C. on equal pay in *Barber v. Guardian Royal Exchange Assurance Group*.[15] In that case the Court held that the Treaty's guarantee of equal pay applied with direct effect to pensions paid under "contracted out" pension schemes, *i.e.*, schemes recognised in the United Kingdom in substitution for the earnings-related part of the State pension.

---

[12] For a helpful general statement of the law see Advocate General Cosmas in Joined Cases C–197/94 and C–252/94 *Société Bautiaa v. Directeur des Services Fiscaux* [1996] E.C.R. 505 at paras 40–41 of his Opinion.

[13] Advocate General Cosmas, at para. 41 of his Opinion in *Bautiaa*, n.12 above.

[14] Case 24/86 *Vincent Blaizot v. University of Liège and others* [1988] E.C.R. 379; [1989] 1 C.M.L.R. 57.

[15] Case C–262/88 *Barber v. Guardian Royal Exchange Assurance Group* [1990] E.C.R. I–1889; [1990] 2 C.M.L.R. 513.

Nevertheless, the Court limited the temporal effects of its judgment. It was not this time the conduct of the Commission which contributed to a mistaken view of the law on the part of national authorities and private parties, but provisions of Council directives which in certain respects authorised Member States to defer the compulsory implementation of the principle of equal treatment as regards occupational social security schemes and contracted-out schemes such as the one in issue. In the light of these provisions the Court considered that the Member States and the parties concerned were reasonably entitled to consider that the Treaty's guarantee of equal pay did not apply to pensions paid under contracted-out schemes and that derogations from the principle of equality between men and women were still permitted in that sphere.

In *Legros*[16] the Court of Justice held that a charge levied on goods originating in one Member State and imported into a region of another Member State from the metropolitan territory of that State constituted a charge having equivalent effect to a customs duty prohibited *inter alia* by Article 23 and 25 (ex 9 and 12) E.C., despite the fact such a charge was also levied on goods originating in the metropolitan territory of that State. The facts involved French rules on trade between France and Réunion. The Court acceded to requests made by Réunion during the proceedings to limit the temporal effects of its judgment on the grounds that the particular characteristics of the charges in issue and the specific identity of the French overseas departments had created a situation of uncertainty regarding the legality of the charges under Community law. That uncertainty was reflected in the conduct of the Community institutions, in particular the adoption of a Council Decision authorising maintenance of the charges on a temporary basis. Those circumstances "could have led the French Republic and the local authorities in the French overseas departments reasonably to consider that the applicable national legislation was in conformity with Community law."[17]

In *Bosman* the Court considered the compatibility of rules of national sporting associations for the transfer of players between clubs and held that Article 39 (ex 48) E.C. precluded the application of rules laid down by sporting associations, under which a professional footballer who is a national of one Member State may not, on the expiry of his contract with a club, be employed by a club of another Member State unless the latter club has paid to the former club a transfer, training or development fee. But the court limited the temporal effects of its judgment, because, the specific features of the rules laid down by the sporting associations for transfers of players between clubs of different Member States, together with the fact that the same or similar rules applied to transfers both between clubs belonging to the same national association and between clubs belonging to different national associations within the same Member State, may have caused uncertainty as to whether those rules were compatible with Community law.[18]

---

[16] Case C–163/90 *Administration des Douanes et Droits Indirects v. Léopold Legros and others* [1992] E.C.R. I–4625.

[17] See paras 28–34 of the Court's judgment. The limited temporal effects of this judgment were also held to apply to similar charges imposed on the import of goods into the Dodecanese group of islands both from other Member States and from other regions of Greece; Cases C–485/93 and C–486/93 *Maria Simitzi v. Dimos Kos* [1995] E.C.R. I–2655.

[18] Case C–415/93 *Union royale belge des sociétés de football association ASBL v. Jean-Marc Bosman* [1995] E.C.R. I–4921, paras. 139–145; [1996] 1 C.M.L.R. 645.

But in numerous cases the Court of Justice has refused to limit the temporal effects of a judgment, whether on the interpretation of a Treaty provision, or of secondary legislation, on the grounds that the conditions referred to above as justifying such an exceptional course of action were not satisfied.[19]

Direct application of rules of the Treaty which do not give rise to rights in individuals

The law is not exclusively concerned with bestowing rights, or imposing obligations, on individuals, or public authorities. It may, for instance, authorise public authorities to take action which they would not otherwise be authorised to take. Treaty provisions which fall into this category are not "directly applicable" or "directly effective," in the sense that those expressions have been used to describe the case law of the court discussed in the previous sections of this chapter, but they may nevertheless be susceptible to direct application in national courts. It may be recalled that the Advocate General in *Van Gend en Loos* referred to Treaty provisions being "clearly intended to be incorporated into national law and to modify or supplement it,"[20] and this approach is echoed in the words of the Court of Justice in *Costa v. ENEL* to the effect that the "EEC Treaty has created its own legal system which, on the entry into force of the force of the Treaty, became an integral part of the legal systems of the Member States and which their courts are bound to apply."[21]

Whether or not a Treaty provision is to be applied by a national court, independently of national implementation, depends on the interpretation of the provision in question. If, on its proper construction, it is intended to have legal effect, then English courts are bound to give it such, under the appropriately worded text of section 2(1) of the European Communities Act 1972. For example, Article 234 (ex 177) E.C. directly bestows on national courts the competence to refer questions to the Court of Justice for a preliminary ruling. National rules may establish the relevant details of procedure,[22] but they neither create, nor may they condition, the capacity to make the reference. The provision is not directly effective, in the sense that it does not give rise to rights in individuals which national courts are bound to safeguard (apart, perhaps, in circumstances where the third paragraph of Article 234 imposes a duty on

---

[19] See, *e.g.*, Case 69/80 *Susan Jane Worringham and Margaret Humphreys v. Lloyds Bank Limited* [1981] E.C.R. 767; [1981] 2 C.M.L.R. 1 (Art. 141 (ex 119) E.C.); Joined Cases 142–143/80 *Amministrazione delle Finanze dello Stato v. Essevi SpA and Carlo Salengo* [1981] E.C.R. 1413 (Art. 90 (Art. 95) E.C.); Case C–200/90 *Dansk Denkavit ApS and P. Poulsen Trading ApS, supported by Monsanto-Searle A/S v. Skatteministeriet* [1992] E.C.R. I–2217; [1994] 2 C.M.L.R. 377, (Art. 33 of Sixth VAT Directive); Cases C-367/93 to C-377/93 *F. G. Roders BV and Others v. Inspecteur der Invoerrechten en Accijnzen* [1995] E.C.R. I–2229 (Art. 90 (ex 95) E.C.); Case C–137/94 *R v. Secretary of State for Health, ex parte Cyril Richardson* [1995] E.C.R. I–3407; [1995] 3 C.M.L.R. 376 (Arts 3(1) and 7(1)(a) of Dir. 79/7); Case C–126/95 *A. Hallouzi-Choho v. Bestuur van de Sociale Verzekeringsbank* [1996] E.C.R. I–4807 (Art. 41(1) of the Co-operation Agreement between the European Economic Community and the Kingdom of Morocco); Case C–35/97 *Commission v. France* [1998] E.C.R. I–5325 (Art. 39 (ex 48) E.C.).

[20] [1963] E.C.R. 1 at 20.

[21] [1964] E.C.R. 585 at 593; and see Case 17/67 *Neumann* [1967] E.C.R. 441 at 453.

[22] See, *e.g.* RSC, Ord. 114, Schedule 1 to the Civil Procedure Rules.

national courts to make a reference), but it is nevertheless directly applicable, in the sense that it has direct application in the national legal order.

A similar point may be made concerning *principles* derived from the Treaty which have legal effects as regards the application of national law by national courts, without those principles comprising rights in themselves which can be invoked by individuals. The extent to which national courts are under a duty to interpret national rules as far as possible in accordance with Treaty provisions has been examined earlier in this chapter.[23] There is no doubt that national courts are under a duty to interpret national rules in accordance with the provisions of the E.C. Treaty,[24] and of directives if it is possible for them to do so.[25] And certain non-binding acts may be held to cast light on the interpretation of national law or Community law.[26] The responsibility of national courts and tribunals to respect such principles in the exercise of their responsibilities under national law cannot on the face of it be attributed solely or even mainly to the direct effect of substantive provisions of the Treaty or secondary legislation. The duty to interpret national rules in light of the provisions of directives is a duty which more often than not arises in a context in which direct effect for relevant provisions of a directive is excluded because the provisions are invoked against a private individual or other non-State party. Similarly, where the interpretative effects of non-binding acts on national law are concerned, there can again be no question of attributing the legal basis of the duty of national courts to directly effective provisions of Community law. The explanation for the foregoing is that these obligations of national courts and tribunals are derived from the general obligation in Article 10 (ex 5) E.C. "to ensure fulfillment of the obligations" arising out of the Treaty. It seems impossible to avoid the conclusion that that provision is directly effective as regards the duty of national courts to interpret national rules in accordance with non-directly effective provisions of Community law.

THE LEGAL EFFECTS OF COMMUNITY ACTS

One of the most striking characteristics of the legal order established by the Treaty is the competence vested in the Community institutions to enact legislation for the purpose of carrying out the objectives of the Treaty. Article 249 (ex 189) E.C. states:

"In order to carry out their tasks and in accordance with the provisions of this Treaty, the European Parliament acting jointly with the Council, the Council and the Commission shall make regulations and issue directives, take decisions, make recommendations or deliver opinions."

Since regulations and directives are of particular significance as general measures of legislation, they will be examined in detail in the following sections of this chapter.

---

[23] See above, p. 71.
[24] *ibid.*
[25] See below, p. 92.
[26] See above, p. 60.

REGULATIONS

The Legal character of Regulations

Article 249 (ex 189) E.C. states:

"A regulation shall have general application. It shall be binding in its entirety and directly applicable in all Member States."

At first sight, this description of regulations appears to attribute to them the characteristics of those Treaty provisions capable of giving rise to rights in individuals which national courts are bound to safeguard. Even a cursory scrutiny of the Official Journal, however, reveals that each and every provision of each and every regulation does not give rise to rights in individuals against other individuals or against Member States. Various explanations have been offered for this unsurprising phenomenon. On the one hand, it has been suggested[27] that since characterisation of an instrument as a regulation or not is a matter of substance, not form,[28] the provisions of a regulation which do not satisfy the conditions for direct applicability are not regulations in the true sense at all. "In such an instance," the argument runs, "the merely formal regulations could be denied direct application."[29] This view is not without difficulty. It seems to rule out the possibility that Community law may empower national courts to respect as law rules which do not actually bestow rights on individuals. Again, it leads to the conclusion that if the Treaty authorised the competent Community institutions to legislate on certain matters by regulation and regulation only, each and every provision of such a regulation must give rise to rights in individuals which national courts are bound to safeguard; any such provision which does not have this quality is not part of the regulation, in law, is unauthorised by the Treaty Article in question and therefore invalid.[30]

Another view[31] is that the reference to direct applicability in Article 249 concerns the process of incorporation of regulations into the national legal order. This description emphasises that national courts must take cognisance of regulations as legal instruments whose validity and recognition by national courts must not be conditioned on national procedures of incorporation into the national legal order. Whether or not particular provisions of such an instrument in fact give rise to rights in individuals which national courts must safeguard is a matter of interpretation of the provisions concerned, in light of the criteria established by the Court of Justice with respect to the direct application of provisions of the Treaty. This is the better view, and is quite consistent with the decided cases, though the Court has not gone out of its way to clarify the matter.

---

[27] Bebr, [1970] I.C.L.Q. 257 at 290 *et seq.*

[28] Joined Cases 16, 17, 19–22/62 *Confédération Nationale* [1962] E.C.R. 471; [1963] C.M.L.R. 160; Case 30/67 *Industria Molitoria* [1968] E.C.R. 115; Case 6/68 *Zuckerfabrik* [1968] E.C.R. 409; [1969] C.M.L.R. 26.

[29] [1970] I.C.L.Q. 257 at 290.

[30] Art. 89 (ex 94) E.C. on state aids authorises only regulations.

[31] J.A. Winter, (1972) 9 C.M.L. Rev 425. An article which still repays study. For an interesting recent jurisprudential analysis of Winter, see Eleftheriadis, (1996) 16 Y.E.L. at 206 *et seq.*

Thus in *Politi S.A.S. v. Italian Ministry of Finance*,[32] an Italian court asked the Court of Justice whether certain provisions of an agricultural regulation were (i) directly applicable, and (ii) if so, whether they created rights for individuals which national courts were bound to safeguard. The question presented to the Court reflects neatly the distinction indicated above; the Court's response did not; "Under the terms of the second paragraph of Article 189," it declared, "regulations 'shall have general application' and 'shall be . . . directly applicable in all Member State.' Therefore, by reason of their nature and their function in the system of the sources of Community law, regulations have direct effect and are as such capable of creating individual rights which national courts must protect."[33] Similar reasoning appears in *Leonesio v. Italian Ministry of Agriculture and Forestry*,[34] in which an Italian court posed questions which again separated the issue of direct applicability and rights for individuals. The Court ruled that: "A Community regulation has direct effect and is, as such capable of creating individual rights which national courts must protect." Advocate General Roemer, on the other hand, pointed out that simply to acknowledge the status of the instrument in question did not solve the problem before the Court, *i.e.*, whether certain of its provisions bestowed enforceable rights on individual farmers as against the Italian State "wherefore an answer to the question of the legal effects," he argued, "depends on the questions whether an area of discretion was left to the national authorities in the matter of implementation and in what manner the national provisions were to supplement the measures adopted."[35] The circumstances in which national provisions might properly supplement a Community regulation are addressed below.[36]

Although the Court of Justice has not explicitly acknowledged that the direct applicability of regulations does not require the automatic effect of their provisions at the suit of individuals, such is clearly the case, and it is likely that the Court's reticence results from the conviction that the distinction is either obvious, or has been of no practical importance in the cases which have arisen before it. If the question were raised before the Court that on its true construction a particular provision of a regulation was incapable of giving rise to rights in individuals because it was conditional on national implementing measures being adopted, the Court would no doubt construe the provision in question, to see if it were apt for judicial enforcement. Thus, in *Caisse commune D'Assurances "la prevoyance sociale" v. Bertholet*,[37] the Court was asked whether Article 52 of Regulation 3 on social security was applicable in national courts before the bilateral agreements referred to therein had been concluded between the Member States concerned. The Court answered in the affirmative, on the grounds that the first paragraph of that article was couched unequivocal terms, while its provisions were clear and could be applied without difficulty. Obviously the mere status of the instrument in which the provision

---

[32] Case 43/71 [1971] E.C.R. 1039; [1973] C.M.L.R. 60.
[33] [1971] E.C.R. 1039 at 1048, para. 9.
[34] Case 93/71 [1972] E.C.R. 287; [1973] C.M.L.R. 343.
[35] [1972] E.C.R. 287 at 300; [1973] C.M.L.R. 343.
[36] See below, p. 86.
[37] Case 31/64 [1965] E.C.R. 81; [1966] C.M.L.R. 191.

was found could not determine a question dependent on the true construction of the provision itself.

The permissible scope for implementation of Regulations by National rules

A corollary of the proposition that regulations must be recognised as legal instruments without the need for their terms to be transposed into national law by national implementing rules, is that such transposition, unless authorised in a particular case,[38] is impermissible, inasmuch as it tends to disguise from those subject to the law the Community source of their rights and obligations. That the legislative duplication of regulations might in itself be inconsistent with Community law was made clear in *Commission v. Italy*,[39] in which the Italian Government had failed to implement certain EEC Regulations concerning slaughter premia and the withholding of milk supplied from the market, resulting in an action by the Commission under Article 226 (ex 169) E.C. Not only did the Commission complain of the delay of the Italian Government in instituting the scheme, but also of the technique of reproducing the texts of regulations in Italian legislation. This, said the Court, itself constituted a default, since by adopting this procedure, the Italian Government had brought into doubt both the legal nature of the applicable provisions and the date of their coming into force. The Court reiterated its position in *Fratelli Variola v. Italian Finance Ministry*. "No procedure is permissible," it emphasised, "whereby the Community nature of a legal rule is concealed from those subject to it."[40]

It is to be noted that what the Court of Justice found legally objectionable in the foregoing cases was the legislative duplication in national implementing rules of the texts of Community regulations. It does not follow, and it is not the case, that regulations do not ever require supplementary national rules to be adopted to ensure the effective application of regulations in the various Member States. Reference has already been made to *Commission v. Netherlands*,[41] in which the Court held that the Netherlands was in breach of its obligations for failing to take the necessary measures to ensure the implementation of E.C. staff *regulations* providing for the for co-ordination of national pension schemes with the Community pension scheme for Community officials. In the circumstances, the staff regulations (despite their direct applicability) could not have full force and effect unless national implementing rules were adopted to provide for the actual transfer of pension rights accrued under national law to the Community scheme. In this context the Court held that the right of individuals to rely upon the staff regulations before their national courts represented only a minimum guarantee which was not sufficient in itself to ensure the full and complete implementation of the regulations. Furthermore, the Court has acknowledged that where Community regulations require implementation by national measures, the incorporation of the texts of such regulations may be justified for the sake of

---

[38] Case 31/78 *Bussone* [1978] E.C.R. 2429; [1979] 3 C.M.L.R. 18; Case 230/78 *Zuccheri* [1979] E.C.R. 2749.
[39] Case 39/72 [1973] E.C.R. 101; [1973] C.M.L.R. 439.
[40] Case 34/73 [1973] E.C.R. 981 at 991, para. 11.
[41] Case 72/85 [1986] E.C.R. 1219, above p. 69.

coherence and in order to make them comprehensible to the persons to whom they apply.[42] It is not uncommon for Community regulations to be supplemented by quite extensive national rules designed to ensure that the Community rules and national rules can be applied in an effective and comprehensible way. For example, the adoption of Council Regulation 2137/85 on the European Economic Interest Grouping (EEIG)[43] was followed in the United Kingdom by a statutory instrument which, amongst other things, laid down the detailed rules which under the Regulation were to be left to Member States to adopt, and specified how relevant provisions of domestic Company Law and Insolvency Law applied to the EEIG.[44] The Finance Act 1990 made necessary provision for the taxation of the members of an EEIG.[45] The authorities in the United Kingdom are certainly conscious of the peculiar characteristics of E.C. regulations. In Department of the Environment Circular 13/94 on the application of Council Regulation 259/93 on the supervision and control of shipments of waste within, into and out of the European Community, the Department states "The Waste shipment Regulation is directly applicable—that is, *most of its provisions do not require transposition*[46] into national legislation. There are some matters, however, which require national legislation *to give full effect to the provisions of the Regulation*.[47] In the United Kingdom, the legislation in question comprises a Statutory Instrument, The Transfrontier Shipment of Waste Regulations 1995."[48] Giving full effect to the provisions of a Community regulation may require the imposition of penalties to secure enforcement of breaches of the regulation. In this connection the Court of Justice has held:

". . . where a Community regulation does not specifically provide any penalty for an infringement or refers for that purpose to national laws, regulations and administrative provisions, Article 5 of the E.C. Treaty [now 10] requires the Member States to take all measures necessary to guarantee the application and effectiveness of Community law. For that purpose, while the choice of penalties remains within their discretion, they must ensure in particular that infringements of Community law are penalised under conditions, both procedural and substantive, which are analogous to those applicable to infringement of national law of a similar nature and importance and which, in any event, make the penalty effective, proportionate and dissuasive . . ."[49]

---

[42] Case 272/83 *Commission v. Italy* [1985] E.C.R. 1057 at 1074, para. 27; [1987] 2 C.M.L.R. 426.
[43] [1985] O.J. L199/1.
[44] The European Economic Interest Grouping Regulations 1989, S.I. 1989 No. 638.
[45] s.69 and Sched. 11.
[46] Emphasis added. The passage appears to contemplate though that some provisions at least will actually require transposition. In principle they should not require *transposition*, though supplementary national rules may be necessary to ensure that the aims of the regulation are fully achieved.
[47] Emphasis added.
[48] S.I. 1994 No. 1137. See para. 2 of Circular 13/94.
[49] Case C–177/95 *Ebony Maritime SA, Loten Navigation Co. Ltd v. Prefetto della Provincia di Brindisi and Others* [1997] E.C.R. I–1111; [1997] 2 C.M.L.R. 24, citing Case 68/88 *Commission v. Greece* [1989] E.C.R. 2965; [1989] 1 C.M.L.R. 31; Case C–326/88 *Anklagemyndigheden v. Hansen* [1990] E.C.R. I–2911; and Case C–36/94 *Siesse v. Director da Alfândega de Alcântara* [1995] E.C.R. I–3573.

The above formulation has been interpreted by the court as meaning that when Member States are fulfilling such responsibilities as indicated above, they are required to comply with the general principles of Community law, in particular the principle of proportionality.[50]

Regulations may have vertical and horizontal effect and pre-empt national legislative competence

Since regulations constitute direct legislation by the Community, which are binding in their entirety, not only may individuals rely on specific provisions against other individuals and Member States, but they may also invoke the general objective and purpose of the legal regime established by a regulation to challenge the application of conflicting national legal provisions. This pre-emptive quality of regulations has become most obviously apparent in the context of the common agricultural policy, where the Court has ruled on several occasions that national measures have been incompatible with the legal regime established by a Community regulation (as opposed to incompatible with specific provisions vesting rights in individuals).[51] Thus national measures which hinder agricultural producers from selling on the market at a price equal to the target price may be challenged by individuals concerned in the national courts, although producers have no "right" to sell at that price. They may nevertheless invoke the encroachment by national legislation on a Community legal regime from which they are entitled to benefit.[52] As the Court explained in *Amsterdam Bulb BV v. Produktschap voor Siergewassen*:

"From the moment that the Community adopts regulations under Article 40 of the Treaty [now 34] establishing a common organisation of the market in a specific sector the Member States are under a duty not to take any measure which might create exemptions from them or affect them adversely.

The compatibility with the Community regulations of the provisions referred to by the national court must be considered in the light not only of the express provisions of the regulations *but also of their aims and objectives*"[53] (emphasis added).

In certain cases, the terms of a regulation may preclude the enactment of national legislation entirely in the field in question. Thus in *Hauptzollamt Bremen-Freihafen v. Waren-Import-Gesellschaft Krohn & Co.*, the Court declared: "In so far as the Member States have conferred on the Community legislative powers in tariff matters, in order to ensure the proper functioning of the common market in agriculture, they no longer have the power to issue independent provisions in this field."[54]

---

[50] Case C–2/97 *Società Italiana Petroli SpA (IP) v. Borsana Srl* [1998] E.C.R. I–8597, at para. 49, [1998] 1 C.M.L.R. 331, referring to identical wording in Case C–326/88 *Hansen*, n.49.

[51] See, *e.g.* Case 60/75 *Russo v. AIMA* [1976] E.C.R. 45; Case 77/76 *Entreprise Fratelli Cucchi v. Avez Spa* [1977] E.C.R. 987; Wyatt [1977] C.L.J. 216 at 217.

[52] Case 77/76 *Fratelli Cucchi, etc.* n.51.

[53] Case 50/76 *Amsterdam Bulb, etc.* [1977] E.C.R. 137 at 147, para. 8; [1977] 2 C.M.L.R. 218.

[54] Case 74/69 [1970] E.C.R. 451 at 458, [1970] C.M.L.R. 466; and see Case 40/69 *Hauptzollamt Hamburg-Oberelbe v. Firma Paul G. Bollmann* [1979] E.C.R. 69 at 79; [1970] C.M.L.R. 141.

Regulations, in short, are to be treated as "law" in every sense of the word. National courts must take judicial notice of them in their entirety; specific provisions contained therein may bestow on individuals rights against other individuals, or companies, or national authorities; and their effect in a particular area may be to pre-empt national legislative competence.

DIRECTIVES

The duty to implement directives by binding national rules

Article 249 (ex 189) E.C. states:

"A directive shall be binding, as to the result to be achieved, upon each Member State to which it is addressed, but shall leave to the national authorities the choice of form and methods."

The choice left to Member States of the "form and methods" for the implementation of directives allows a Member State to choose the legislative format which it considers appropriate.[55] Thus the legislation adopted to implement a directive need not use the same words as the directive itself.[56] National implementing rules should however give persons concerned a clear and precise understanding of their rights and obligations and enable national courts to ensure that those rights and obligations are observed.[57] As the Court of Justice put it in *Commission v. Greece*:

". . . the Court has consistently held that it is particularly important, in order to satisfy the requirement of legal certainty, that individuals should have the benefit of a clear and precise legal situation enabling them to ascertain the full extent of their rights and, where appropriate, to rely on them before the national courts."[58]

Implementation of a directive requires the transposition of the requirements of the directive by binding measures of national law; neither the adoption of administrative practices, which by their nature may be altered at the whim of the authorities and lack the appropriate publicity, nor the publication of administrative circulars, which do not have binding effects, will be enough to satisfy the

---

[55] Case 163/82 *Commission v. Italy* [1983] E.C.R. 3723 at 3286, 3287; [1984] 3 C.M.L.R. 169.

[56] Case 247/85 *Commission v. Belgium* [1987] E.C.R. 3029 at 3060, para. 9; Case 262/85 *Commission v. Italy* [1987] E.C.R. 3073, at 3097, para. 9; Case 252/85 *Commission v. France* [1988] E.C.R. 2243 at 2263, para. 5.

[57] Case 257/86 *Commission v. Italy* [1988] E.C.R. 3249 at 3267; [1990] 3 C.M.L.R. 718.

[58] Case C–236/95 [1996] E.C.R. I–4459, citing prior case-law. The Court holds a Greek Presidential Decree inadequate to implement a directive, because its general wording does not specifically bestow the relevant rights on the relevent parties, despite case-law of the Council of State interpreting the Presidential Decree in conformity with the directive. But the Court has said that the scope of national laws must be assessed in the light of the interpretation given to them by national courts, see Case C–382/92 *Commission v. United Kingdom* [1994] E.C.R. I–2495, at para. 4; Case C–300/95 *Commission v. United Kingdom* [1997] E.C.R. I–2649, para. 37. Case C–236/95 must be taken to turn on its special facts. Provisions of Community law are on occasion too vague to be capable of confident interpretation without the benefit of the Court's case law, and it is the intervention of the latter which ensures legal certainty, as witnessed, *e.g.* by the doctrine of prospective effect, as to which, see above, p. 78.

requirements of Article 249 (ex 189) E.C.[59] Despite the consistent case-law, Member States have persisted until recently with the argument that transposition by means of administrative circulars was enough.[60] Such national measures must be adopted within the time-limit specified in the Directive. Problems at the national level, such as an overcrowded legislative timetable, cannot justify failure to meet this deadline. The Court has held on numerous occasions that "a Member State may not plead provisions, practices or circumstances existing in its internal legal system in order to justify a failure to comply with the obligations and time-limits laid down in a directive . . ."[61] However, the Court has held that directives do not require legislative implementation where there exist general principles of constitutional or administrative law which render specific legislation superfluous, provided that those principles guarantee the application of the directive, are clear and precise, are made known to those subject to the law, and are capable of being invoked before the courts.[62] It follows that legislation is also superfluous where national legislative provisions in force afford similar guarantees that a directive will be effectively implemented. In the United Kingdom Directive 76/207 on equal treatment for men and women as regards access to employment, vocational training and promotion, and working conditions,[63] is implemented by a prior piece of legislation, the Sex Discrimination Act 1975. On occasions a directive will require that legislative measures of transposition refer to the underlying directive, and in such a case, failure to include a reference to the directive in national implementing legislation will amount to a distinct breach of Community law.[64] In addition to transposing the substantive obligations of a directive Member States are bound to introduce enforcement mechanisms to secure compliance, such as provisions for private law remedies or penalties. Even if a directive makes no express provision for such enforcement mechanisms Member States are nevertheless obliged under Article 10 (ex 5) E.C. and Article 249 (ex 189) E.C. to take all measures necessary to guarantee the application and effectiveness of Community law.[65] Furthermore, both in general terms, and in the context of enforcement mechanisms adopted to secure the implementation of directives, the court has held that Member States must, "in order to secure the full implementation of directives in law and not only in fact, establish a specific legal framework in the area in question."[66] The Court has fiurther held that in adopting national measures to implement a directive,

---

[59] Case 102/79 *Commission v. Belgium* [1980] E.C.R. 1473; [1997] 1 C.M.L.R. 1029; Case 96/81 *Commission v. Netherlands* [1982] E.C.R. 1791; Case 145/82 *Commission v. Italy* [1983] E.C.R. 711; [1984] 1 C.M.L.R. 148.

[60] In Case C–262/95 *Commission v. Germany* [1996] E.C.R. I–5729, Germany initially argued that certain notices circulars and administrative provisions amounted to transposition, but abandoned its argument in light of the court's case-law, see paras 7 and 15 of judgment.

[61] Case C–298/95 *Commission v. Germany* [1996] E.C.R. I–6747, citing previous case-law.

[62] Case 29/84 *Commission v. Germany* [1986] E.C.R. 1661; [1986] 3 C.M.L.R. 579.

[63] [1976] O.J. L39/40.

[64] Case C–360/95 *Commission v. Spain* [1997] E.C.R. I–7337.

[65] Case C–5/94 *R. v. Ministry of Agriculture, fisheries and Food, ex parte Hedley Lomas (Ireland) Ltd* [1996] E.C.R. I–2553, at para. 19; [1996] 2 C.M.L.R. 391.

[66] Case C–340/96 *Commission v. United Kingdom* [1999] E.C.R. I–2023, at paras 27–30 (system of undertakings established to enforce drinking water quality standards inadequate to the extent that implementing legislation did not set out such a specific legal framework as contemplated by the court's case law).

Member States are required to comply with the general principles of Community law, in particular the principles of proportionality.[67]

Implementation of directives in the United Kingdom is achieved either by primary or secondary legislation, the latter normally pursuant to section 2(2) of the European Communities Act 1972. Initially, there was a tendency to transpose directives by translating their requirements, to greater or lesser extent, into the legal language which it was believed would have been used had they been "home grown." An example is the transposition of the product liability directive,[68] which is implemented in Part I of the Consumer Protection Act 1987, which in part substitutes for the language of the directive the language of the Parliamentary draftsman.[69] But transposing directives by adopting the language and techniques of English law to ensure the fulfilment of requirements formulated by the European institutions in a distinctly different style has its pitfalls. It might be said that those subject to the law are better able to understand their legal position by having their rights and obligations set out in the manner characteristic of domestic legislation. If such domestic legislation could be regarded as definitive as regards the rights and obligations of those subject to the law, this proposition would have considerable force. But that is not the legal position. As will be explained below,[70] national rules implementing a directive are to be interpreted as far as possible so as to be consistent with the terms of the relevant directive, while if a Member State fails properly to implement a directive, an individual may invoke against the national authorities of that State those provisions of the directive which are unconditional and sufficiently precise for judicial implementation.[71] The effect of the foregoing is that the rights and obligations of natural and legal persons, and of authorities of Member States, cannot be said with certainty to be definitively stated by national transposing rules which reformulate the requirements of Community law into the language of the national draftsman. No prudent legal adviser would in all cases feel confident that he or she could interpret such national implementing rules without taking account of relevant terms of the relevant directive. Litigation on the scope of the national implementing rules would be likely to involve consideration not only of the terms of those rules, but also the terms of the relevant directive, and of any case-law of the European Court on those terms. In short, translating the requirements of directives into national legal language does not in all cases guarantee improved legal certainty for individuals. It may simply present all concerned with two legal texts to interpret instead of one. It is these considerations, amongst others, which have led to increased use of a technique of transposition sometimes called "copy-out", but which the present writer prefers, in the interests of precision, to describe as "selective word for word incorporation." A further consideration

---

[67] Case C–2/97 *Società Italiana Petroli SpA (IP) v. Borsana Srl* [1998] E.C.R. I–8597, at para. 49; [1998] 1 C.M.L.R. 331.

[68] Dir. 85/374 on the approximation of the laws, etc. of the Member States concerning liability for defective products [1985] O.J. L210/29.

[69] The Commission unsuccessfully challenged a certain aspect of this implementation—as regards the so-called "state of the art" defence, in Case C–300/95 *Commission v. United Kingdom* [1997] E.C.R. I–2649; [1997] 3 C.M.L.R. 923.

[70] Below, p. 92.

[71] Below, p. 95.

which has led to increased use of word for word incorporation is that the drafting techniques of the Community institutions do on occasion lead to texts the precise meaning of which cannot be determined with sufficient precision to enable confident reformulation into national legal language of a Member State. Transposition by the incorporation, word for word, of key provisions of the directive, presents those subject to the law, and national courts, with a single text comprising both European law and national law. This presents a simpler interpretative task than that which results from the consideration of two differently worded texts—the relevant provision of the directive, and the relevant provision of the national transposing legislation. Word for word incorporation may also mean that a reference from an English court on the meaning of the directive will provide a ruling on the meaning of the national implementing provisions. A good example of selective word for word incorporation is to be found in the transposition of the amended waste framework directive, Directive 75/442,[72] as amended by Directive 91/156,[73] which was implemented by the Waste Management Licensing Regulations 1994.[74] While it is not suggested that transposition could or should be entirely achieved by word for word incorporation, the apparent readiness of government to adopt this approach on a selective basis is to be welcomed.

The period available for Member States to adopt necessary measures of implementation is specified in the directive in question. Since the purpose of such a period is to give Member States the necessary time to adopt transposition measures, they cannot be faulted for not having transposed the directive into their internal legal order before expiry of that period.[75] Nevertheless, it follows from Article 10 (ex 5) E.C. and Article 249 (ex 189) E.C. and from the directive itself that during the latter period Member States are required to refrain from adopting measures liable seriously to compromise the result prescribed.[76]

The duty of national courts to construe national rules in accordance with relevant directives

Even before the European Court indicated that there was any *obligation* upon national courts to seek to construe national legislation in accordance with directives, examples could be found of national courts seeking preliminary rulings on the meaning of directives in order to give an appropriate construction to

---

[72] [1975] O.J. L194/47.

[73] [1991] O.J. L78/32.

[74] S.I. 1994 No. 1056. The 1994 Regulations introduce into domestic environmental law the concept of "Directive waste", which is defined by reference to the definition in the directive and to the potentially waste substances listed in Annex I of the directive, which is reproduced as Part II of Sched. 4 to the Regulations. The concepts in the directive of "disposal" and "recovery" are defined by reference to Schedule 4 of the Regulations, which reproduces Annexes IIA (disposal) and IIB (recovery) of the directive. For other examples of transposition of environmental directives by selective word for word incorporation, see Wyatt, "Litigating Community Environmental Law," 10 J.E.L. 9, especially at 9–14.

[75] Case C–129/96 *Inter-environnment Wallonie ASBL v. Région Wallonne* [1997] E.C.R. I–7411, para. 43; [1998] 1 C.M.L.R. 1057.

[76] Case C–129/96 at para. 50; [1998] 1 C.M.L.R. 1057.

national implementing rules.[77] It was in *Von Colson*,[78] and *Harz*,[79] that the Court first referred to the principle that national courts were under an obligation so to interpret national law. It did so in the context of national implementation of Directive 76/207 on equal treatment for men and women in employment. The Court stated:

". . . the Member States' obligation arising from a directive to achieve the result envisaged by the directive and their duty under article 5 of the treaty to take all appropriate measures , whether general or particular, to ensure the fulfillment of that obligation, is binding on all the authorities of Member States including, for matters within their jurisdiction, the courts. It follows that, in applying the national law and in particular the provisions of a national law specifically introduced in order to implement Directive no 76/207, national courts are required to interpret their national law in the light of the wording and the purpose of the directive in order to achieve the result referred to in the third paragraph of article 189."[80]

The Court qualified this statement two paragraphs later in its judgment:

"it is for the national court to interpret and apply the legislation adopted for the implementation of the directive in conformity with the requirements of community law, *in so far as it is given discretion to do so under national law*" (emphasis added).[81]

The Court subsequently explained that the obligation of the national court to refer to the content of the directive when interpreting the relevant rules of its national law was limited by the general principles of law which formed part of Community law, and in particular the principles of legal-certainty and non-retroactivity; thus a directive could not, of itself and independently of a national law adopted by a Member State for its implementation, have the effect of determining or aggravating the liability in criminal law of persons who act in contravention of the provisions of that directive.[82] In *Marleasing SA v. La Comercial Internacional de Alimentacion SA*,[83] the Court of Justice, although it referred to the *von Colson* case and stated that national courts were bound to interpret national law *as far as possible* in the light of the wording and purpose of a relevant directive, went on to describe the duty of national courts to interpret

---

[77] Case 32/74 *Friedrich Haaga GmbH* [1974] E.C.R. 1201; [1975] 1 C.M.L.R. 32; Case 111/75 *Impresa Costruzioni comm. Quirino Mazzalai v. Ferrovia del Renon* [1976] E.C.R. 657; [1977] 1 C.M.L.R. 105.

[78] Case 14/83 *Sabine von Colson and Elisabeth Kamann v. Land Nordrhein-Westfalen* [1984] E.C.R. 1891; [1986] 2 C.M.L.R. 430.

[79] Case 79/83 *Dorit Harz v. Deutsche Tradax GmbH* [1984] E.C.R. 1921.

[80] *Von Colson* at 1909, para. 26. *Harz* at p. 1942, para. 26.

[81] *Von Colson* at para. 28; *Harz* at para. 28.

[82] Case 80/86 *Criminal proceedings against Kolpinghuis Nijmegen BV.*[1987] E.C.R. 3969 at para. 13; [1989] 2 C.M.L.R. 18. And the direct effect of a directive cannot impose obligations upon individuals, see below, p. 98. See also *El Corte Inglés SA v. Cristina Blasquez Rivero* [1996] E.C.R. I–1281; [1996] 2 C.M.L.R. 507; Case C–168/95 *Criminal proceedings against Luciano Arcaro* [1996] E.C.R. I–4705; [1997] 1 C.M.L.R. 179; and Joined Cases C–74 & 129/95 *Criminal Proceedings against X* [1996] E.C.R. I–6609.

[83] Case 106/89 [1990] E.C.R. 4135; [1992] 1 C.M.L.R. 305.

national law in accordance with directives in a way which made the duty indistinguishable from a duty to give effect to the directive. The question which the national court asked in *Marleasing* was as follows: "Is Article 11 of Council Directive 68/151/EEC of March 9, 1968, which has not been implemented in national law, directly applicable so as to preclude a declaration of nullity of a public limited company on a ground other than those set out in the said article?" The Court referred to *Von Colson*, but then went on:

> "It follows that the requirement that national law *must* be interpreted in conformity with Article 11 of Directive 68/151 *precludes the interpretation of provisions of national law relating to public limited companies in such a manner that the nullity of a public limited company may be ordered on grounds other than those exhaustively listed in Article 11 of the directive in question* (emphasis added)."[84]

To require national law to be interpreted in a particular way irrespective of its terms cannot properly be described as an interpretative duty at all. In the present writer's view, this statement is incorrect, and subsequent judgments of the Court support this view. Before turning to this latter case-law, mention should be made of another aspect of the judgment in *Marleasing*. The Court made it clear that the duty of consistent interpretation applied "whether the provisions in question were adopted before or after the directive." In *Wagner Miret*,[85] the Court endorsed the view that the duty of national courts to interpret national rules in accordance with a relevant directive applied whether the provisions in question were adopted before or after the directive. The Court added that the "principle of interpretation in conformity with directives must be followed in particular where a national court considers, as in the present case, that the pre-existing provisions of its national law satisfy the requirements of the directive concerned."[86] *Marleasing* is cited by the Court in *Wagner Miret*, but the duty of the national court is described as a duty to interpret national law *as far as possible* in accordance with the directive, and the Court notes that it appears from the order for reference that in the instant case this is not possible,[87] though the Court adds that it follows that the Member State will incur liability in damages in accordance with the *Francovich* judgment of the Court.[88] There is similar recognition that it might not be possible to construe national law in accordance with a directive in the *Faccini Dori* case, and a similar indication of the consequences in terms of state liability.[89] It is clear that the duty of a national court is to interpret national

---

[84] Case 106/89 at para. 9.
[85] Case C–334/92 *Teodoro Wagner Miret* v. *Fondo de Garantía Salarial* [1993] E.C.R. I–6911; [1995] 2 C.M.L.R. 49.
[86] *ibid.*, at para. 21; [1995] 2 C.M.L.R. 49.
[87] Para. 22.
[88] As to which see p. 124 below.
[89] Case C–91/92 *Paola Faccini Dori* v. *Recreb Srl* [1994] E.C.R. I–3325; [1994] 1 C.M.L.R. 665; Case C–192/94 *El Corte Inglés SA* v. *Cristina Blasquez Rivero* [1996] E.C.R. I–1281, at para. 22 is in similar vein. In *Faccini Dori* there was some discussion at the oral hearing between the advocates for the Commission, and for Italy, and Judge Mancini, as to whether the Italian law in issue might be construed so as to give effect to the directive. The advocate for the Commission argued that the duty of consistent interpretation did not oblige the national judge to construe national legislation *contra legem*.

law as far as possible in light of the wording and purpose of a directive, but not to distort any reasonable meaning of the words, and that it might not be possible in a particular case so to interpret national law.[90] It is equally clear that English courts will strive to do everything possible to secure the interpretation of national legislation in a way which ensures the implementation of a relevant directive, even if at first sight such an interpretation might appear to distort the meaning of a statute.[91]

The vertical direct effect of directives

By "vertical" direct effect is meant the capacity of a provision of a directive to be invoked by private individuals or companies against authorities of a Member State (but not against other individuals or companies). It was initially considered that directives gave rise exclusively to rights and obligations as between the Member States and the Community institutions.[92] Yet the Court gave an early indication that directives might be capable of direct effect when in *Grad v. Finanzamt Traunstein*[93] it indicated that decisions addressed to Member States might have such effects. Since decisions, like directives, are binding on those to whom they are addressed, the Court's reasoning seemed applicable both to decisions and to directives. In *Grad* the Court said that it did not follow from the fact that by virtue of Article 249 (ex 189) regulations were directly applicable and therefore by their nature capable of producing direct effects, that other categories of legal measures mentioned in that Article could never produce similar effects. "In particular," said the Court, "the provision according to which decisions are binding in their entirety on those to whom they are addressed enables the question to be put whether the obligation created by the decisions can only be invoked by the Community institutions against the addressee or whether such a right may possibly be exercised by all those who have an interest in the fulfilment of this obligation."[94] In the Court's view to adopt the alternative solution would call in question the binding nature of decisions, and diminish their useful effect. While the effects of a decision might not be identical to those of a provision contained in a regulation, this difference did not preclude the

---

[90] See recently Case C–131/97 *Annalisa Carbonari and Others v. Univerità degli Studi di Bologna* [1999] E.C.R. I–1103.

[91] In *Webb v. EMO Air Cargo (UK) Ltd* [1992] 2 All E.R. 32 the Court of Appeal indicated that a construction of the Sex Discrimination Act argued to be required by the duty to construe that Act consistently with Dir. 76/207 on equal treatment for men and women in employment would have involved a distortion of the meaning of the Act if the directive were given the meaning contended for. The House of Lords, after a reference to the Court of Justice and a judgment of that Court to the effect that the directive was to be construed as contended for, were nevertheless able so to construe the 1975 Act, see [1995] 4 All E.R. 577; and see Arnull, in Andenas, *English Public Law and the Common Law of Europe* (Key Haven Publications PLC, London 1998), especially at pp. 112–115.

[92] See, *e.g. Joseph Aim* [1972] C.M.L.R. 901 (Cour d'Appel de Paris); *Firma Baer Getreide GmbH* [1972] C.M.L.R. 539 (Hessischer Verwaltunggerichtschof); and even after the development of the European Court's case law, *Cohn-Bendit* [1979] Dalloz Jur. 155 (Conseil d'Etat); and *Kloppenburg*, Judgment of April 25, 1985 (Bundesfinanzhof), see (1985) 10 E.L. Rev. 303.

[93] Case 9/70 [1970] E.C.R. 825; see also Case 20/70 *Transports Lesage* [1970] E.C.R. 861; [1971] C.M.L.R. 1; and Case 23/70 *Haselhorst* [1970] E.C.R. 881; [1971] C.M.L.R. 1.

[94] [1970] E.C.R. 825 at 837, para. 5.

possibility that the end result, namely the right of the individual to invoke the measure before the courts, might be the same as that of a directly applicable provision of a regulation. In the Court's view this conclusion was reinforced by the wording of Article 234 (ex 177) of the Treaty, pursuant to which national courts were empowered to refer to the Court of Justice all questions regarding the validity and interpretation of all acts of the institutions without distinction; this implied that individuals could invoke such acts before national courts. In each particular case, it must be ascertained whether the nature, background and wording of the provision in question were capable of producing direct effects in the legal relationships between the addressee of the act and third parties.These principles were to provide the basis for the Court's later case law on the direct effect of directives, starting with its judgment in *Yvonne van Duyn v. Home Office*.[95] This case concerned a provision of a directive allowing *inter alia* the deportation of a worker of another Member State on public policy grounds based exclusively on the personal conduct of the individual concerned. The Court noted *inter alia* that the provision laid down an obligation which is not subject to any exception or condition and which, by its very nature, did not require the intervention of any act on the part either of the institutions of the Community or of Member States, and concluded that the provision conferred on individuals rights which were enforceable by them in the courts of a Member State and which the national courts were bound to protect.[96] Similar reasoning was adopted in later cases.[97] Individual discretionary decisions of the national authorities, as well as legislative provisions, could be challenged by individuals relying upon the direct effect of provisions of directives.[98] In the *Ratti* case, the Court added a further reason for appropriately worded provisions of directives being held to be directly effective; a Member State which had not adopted the implementing measures required by the directive in the prescribed period could not rely upon its own failure to perform the obligations which the directive entailed.[99] This was a kind of estoppel argument and it paved the way for the Court's later rulings excluding reliance upon directives against private individuals.[1] The Court confirmed its jurisprudence on the direct effect of directives in a consistent case law.[2] The current formulation of the test for direct effect applied by the European Court appears as follows in *Cooperativa Agricola Zootecnica S. Antonio and Others v. Amministrazione delle finanze dello Stato*:

---

[95] Case 41/74 [1974] E.C.R. 1337.

[96] Paras 13–15.

[97] See *e.g.* Case 36/75 *Roland Rutili v. Ministre de l'Intérieur* [1975] E.C.R. 1219; [1976] 1 C.M.L.R. 140; Case 51/76 *Verbond van Nederlandse Ondernemingen v. Inspecteur der Invoerrechten en Accijnzen* [1977] E.C.R. 113; Case 38/77 *Enka BV v. Inspecteur der Invoerrechten en Accijnzen Arnhem.* [1977] E.C.R. 2203.

[98] Case 41/74 *Yvonne van Duyn*, n.95; Case 36/75 *Roland Rutili*, n.97.

[99] Case 148/78 *Criminal proceedings against Tullio Ratti* [1979] E.C.R. 1629; [1980] 1 C.M.L.R. 96. This ground appears in subsequent case law as a feature in the Court's reasoning in support of the direct effect of directives.

[1] See below, p. 98.

[2] Case 8/81 *Ursula Becker v. Finanzamt Münster-Innenstadt.* [1982] E.C.R. 53; [1982] 1 C.M.L.R. 499; Case 255/81 *R.A. Grendel GmbH v. Finanzamt für Körperschaften de Hambourg* [1982] E.C.R. 2301; [1983] 1 C.M.L.R. 379; Case 5/84 *Direct Cosmetics Ltd v. Commissioners of Customs and Excise* [1985] E.C.R. 617; [1985] 2 C.M.L.R. 145; Case 152/84 *M. H. Marshall v. Southampton and South-West Hampshire Area Health Authority (Teaching)* [1986] E.C.R. 723; [1986] 1 C.M.L.R. 688.

"The Court has consistently held . . . that, whenever the provisions of a directive appear, as far as their subject-matter is concerned, to be unconditional and sufficiently precise, those provisions may be relied upon before the national courts by an individual against the State where that State has failed to implement the directive in national law by the end of the period prescribed or where it has failed to implement the directive correctly.

A Community provision is unconditional where it sets forth an obligation which is not qualified by any condition, or subject, in its implementation or effects, to the taking of any measure either by the Community institutions or by the Member States . . . .

Moreover, a provision is sufficiently precise to be relied on by an individual and applied by a national court where it sets out an obligation in unequivocal terms . . ."[3]

The second condition laid down above, which includes the requirement that a Community provision not be subject, in its implementation of effect, to the taking of any measure either by the Community institutions *or by the Member States*, may mean that a provision of a directive becomes directly effective because a Member State has partially implemented the directive in question, thereby removing what would otherwise have been a bar to the direct effect of that provision. Thus a directive may not be directly effective as regards any particular remedy, such as reinstatment for dismissal contrary to its terms; but if a Member State chooses to make the remedy of damages available, the directive may be relied upon to set aside a provision of national law which prevents the remedy of damages under national law from being effective.[4] Even if the above conditions appear to be satisfied, it must be added that a provision of a directive will not be enforceable by a national *judicial* authority if intended by the legislator to be given effect by national administrative authorities.[5] Nevertheless, a provision of a directive which satisfies the conditions for direct effect, and has not been implemented by national law, is binding on all the organs of the administration, including decentralised authorities and municipalities,[6] and other bodies which, irrespective of their legal form, have been given responsibility by the public authorities and under their supervision for providing a public service.[7]

It is to be noted that a provision of a directive may only be relied upon by individuals before national courts where the Member State has failed properly to implement that provision within the period prescribed for that purpose.[8] Where a directive has been properly implemented by national measures, its effects extend

---

[3] Cases C-246/94, etc. [1996] E.C.R. I–4373.
[4] Case 14/83 *Sabine Von Colson and Elisabeth Kamann v. Land Nordrhein-Westfalen* [1984] E.C.R. 1891; [1986] 2 C.M.L.R. 430; Case 79/83 *Dorit Harz v. Deutsche Tradax GmbH* [1984] E.C.R. 1921; Case C–271/91 *M. Helen Marshall v. Southampton and South-West Hampshire Area Health Authority* [1993] E.C.R. I–4367; [1993] 3 C.M.L.R. 293.
[5] Case 815/79 *Cremonini and Vrankovich* [1980] E.C.R. 3583; [1981] 3 C.M.L.R. 49.
[6] Case 103/88 *Fratelli Constanzo v. Commune di Milano* [1989] E.C.R. 1839 at paras 31 and 32; [1990] 3 C.M.L.R. 239.
[7] Case C–188/89 *Foster and Others v. British Gas* [1990] E.C.R. I–3313, para. 19; [1990] 2 C.M.L.R. 833; Cases C–253–258/97 *Helmut Kampelmann and Others, etc.* [1997] E.C.R. I–6907.
[8] Case 148/78 *Ratti*, above at n.99; Case 8/81 *Becker*, above at n.2; Case 126/82 *D.J. Smit* [1983] E.C.R. 73; [1983] 3 C.M.L.R. 106.

to individuals through the medium of those implementing measures.[9] And where a directive has been properly implemented by national measures, it is not open to the litigant to side-step the appropriate provisions of national law and rely upon the direct effect of the provisions of the directive.[10]

No horizontal direct effect for directives

The Court has held that while directives may be invoked against the State (vertical direct effect), they can never be invoked against private individuals (horizontal direct effect).[11] The legal effects of directives (and presumably decisions addressed to Member States) thus differ from those of both Treaty provisions and regulations, and the reasons for this merit consideration.

Before the judgment in the *Ratti* case,[12] there was nothing in the Court's case law to suggest that the legal effects of a directly effective provision in a directive would be any different from those of a directly effective Treaty provision. Since the court had held that Treaty provisions were capable of binding individuals, as well as States,[13] it would have followed that directives could have similar effects. There were several arguments, however, which could be made against this conclusion.[14] First, since there was no legal requirement to publish directives, it might seem to be implied that directives could only bind those to whom they were addressed. Secondly, it was arguable that to allow directives to be pleaded against individuals would assimilate directives to regulations, which would run counter to Article 249 (ex 189) of the Treaty. Thirdly, there was the argument that to allow directives to be pleaded against individuals would be contrary to the principle of legal certainty, since those subject to obligations contained in directives might be unsure whether to rely upon national implementing legislation, or upon the underlying directives. While none of these arguments were conclusive, there was a further argument, of a political, rather than a legal, nature: the courts in some Member States were having difficulty in accepting that directives could have direct effect at all;[15] for the European Court to go even further and attribute horizontal direct effect to directives might further diminish the credibility of the Court of Justice in such Member States, and lead to the uneven enforceability of directives in the Community.

The Court laid the conceptual foundations for its later compromise solution in 1979, in the *Ratti* case, in which the Court declared that:

"a Member State which has not adopted the implementing measures required by the directive in the prescribed period *may not rely, as against individuals, on its own failure to perform the obligations which the directive entails* (emphasis added)."[16]

---

[9] Case 102/79 *Commission v. Belgium* [1980] E.C.R. 1473; [1981] 1 C.M.L.R. 282; Case 8/81 *Becker*, above at n.2.

[10] Case 270/81 *Felicitas* [1982] E.C.R. 2771; [1982] 3 C.M.L.R. 447.

[11] Case 152/84 *M. H. Marshall v. Southampton and South-West Hampshire Area Health Authority (Teaching)* [1986] E.C.R. 723; [1986] 1 C.M.L.R. 688.

[12] Case 148/78 above at n.99.

[13] See above, p. 77.

[14] See, in general, Easson (1979) 4 E.L. Rev. 67 at 70–73; and Craig (1997) 22 E.L. Rev. 519, at 519–524.

[15] Pescatore, (1983) 8 E.L. Rev. 155 at 70–73.

[16] See n.99, [1979] E.C.R. 1629, para. 22.

The italicised words indicated that the legal basis for the direct effect of directives was that a State could not rely upon its own wrong as a defence to an action based upon a directive before its own courts. This doctrine seemed to restrict the application of directives by national courts to actions against defaulting Member States, and to rule out actions against individuals. The Court's case law following *Ratti* incorporated the above mentioned formulation.[17]

The Court's judgment in *Marshall*[18] seemed to lay speculation to rest. The appellant in the national proceedings, Miss Marshall, was an employee of an Area Health Authority in the United Kingdom. She had been dismissed at the age of 62, since she had passed "the normal retirement age" (of 60) applied by the Authority to female employees. An exception had in fact been made for Miss Marshall to work until the age of 62. The normal retiring age for male employees was 65.

Miss Marshall instituted proceedings against the Authority alleging sex discrimination contrary to the principle of equality of treatment laid down in Directive 76/207.[19] The Area Health Authority argued before the Court of Justice: (1) that the directive could not be relied upon against individuals; and (2) that the Authority, although a public authority emanating from central government, had acted, not in its capacity as a state authority, in dismissing Miss Marshall, but in its capacity as employer. The Court held that since a directive under Article 249 (ex 189) was binding only upon "each Member State to which it was addressed," it could not of itself impose obligations upon an individual. However, this did not preclude an individual relying upon a directive against the State, regardless of the capacity in which the latter was acting, whether as an employer or as a public authority. The United Kingdom had argued that the possibility of relying on provisions of the directive against the Authority would give rise to arbitrary and unfair distinctions between the rights of state employees and those of private employees. The Court of Justice did not find this argument convincing. On the contrary, such a distinction might easily be avoided if the Member State concerned implemented the directive in national law.

The *Marshall* decision allows the invocation of "private law" directives against the State, but rules out such actions against private parties. While the compromise may be justifiable on policy grounds, the Court's reasoning seems plausible rather than compelling. The Court says that directives bind the State, and therefore cannot be invoked against individuals. Yet this very argument failed in *Defrenne*[20] to prevent Article 141 (ex 119) being held to bind private parties as well as the State. What is true of the Treaty should also, it is thought, be true of directives, for the obligation to comply with a directive is itself a Treaty obligation, and the Court has held that directives have an effect no less binding than that of any other rule of Community law.[21]

That is not to say that the Court's ruling in *Marshall* could not be justified on legal grounds; on the contrary, there has always been a case to be made against

---

[17] See *e.g.* Case 8/81 *Becker* [1982] E.C.R. 53; [1982] 1 C.M.L.R. 499. And see above p. 62.

[18] Case 152/84 *M. H. Marshall v. Southampton and South-West Hampshire Area Health Authority (Teaching)* [1986] E.C.R. 723; [1986] 1 C.M.L.R. 688.

[19] [1976] O.J. L39/40.

[20] Case 43/75 *Defrenne v. Sabena* [1976] E.C.R. 455; [1976] 2 C.M.L.R. 98. Above, p. 77.

[21] Case 79/72 *Commission v. Italy* [1972] E.C.R. 667; [1973] C.M.L.R. 773; Case 52/75 *Commission v. Italy* [1976] E.C.R. 277.

the horizontal effect of directives based on the principle of legal certainty. Private individuals should clearly not be placed in unreasonable doubt as to their obligations by requiring the scrutiny of overlapping texts at both the national and Community level as a prerequisite to a complete appreciation of the law. The fact that individuals may be bound by Treaty provisions and by regulations does not give rise to the same risk of uncertainty. The Treaty is a single document with a limited number of provisions which may directly bind individuals; the threat to legal certainty is insignificant. As for regulations, it has always been clear that they constitute direct Community legislation; they are as capable of binding individuals as any provisions of national law, and are only subject to national implementation where they so provide. In this latter respect, regulations may be distinguished from directives, and decisions addressed to Member States, which must always be implemented by national legislation, resulting in the duplication of the substance of Community texts, and possible legal uncertainty for individuals. By way of contrast, the principle of legal certainty cannot properly be invoked by a national authority as a ground for denying the legal effects of a directive, irrespective of the capacity in which the authority is alleged to be bound. National authorities exercise power derived from the Member States, and the Member States are in a position to take appropriate measures to ensure legal certainty from their point of view, either in the course of the legislative process in which they participate, or through an action for annulment if they consider that the vagueness of a directive prejudices its legality.

A disadvantage of the Court's approach in *Marshall* however, is that it rules out horizontal effect even in cases where such effect could not prejudice the legal security of individuals, for example in cases where the direct effect of provisions of a "private law" directive have already been established in proceedings against the authorities of a Member State. An alternative approach would have been a case by case approach, allowing the possibility of horizontal direct effect, but also allowing the principle of legal certainty to be pleaded as a complete defence to private individuals in some cases, and as justifying prospective effect for the Court's rulings in others.

While the Court of Justice ruled out horizontal direct effect for directives, it nevertheless adopted a broad view of the concept of "Member State" for the purpose of the principle in *Marshall* that directives might be invoked against the Member States but not against individuals. In *Foster v. British Gas* the Court held that:

> ". . . a body, whatever its legal form, which has been made responsible, pursuant to a measure adopted by the state, for providing a public service under the control of the state and which has for that purpose special powers beyond those which result from the normal rules applicable in relations between individuals is included in any event among the bodies against which the provisions of a directive capable of having direct effect may be relied upon."[22]

---

[22] See Case C–188/89 [1990] E.C.R. I–3313, para. 20; [1990] 2 C.M.L.R. 833. The court pointed out that its previous case law indicated that directives could be relied upon against tax authorities (*e.g.* Case 8/81 *Becker* [1982] E.C.R. 53; [1982] 1 C.M.L.R. 499), local or regional authorities (Case 103/88 *Constanzo* [1989] E.C.R. 1839; [1990] 3 C.M.L.R. 239), and constitutionally independent authorities responsible for the maintenance of public order and safety (Case 222/84 *Johnston v. RUC* [1986] E.C.R. 1651; [1986] 3 C.M.L.R. 240), see para. 19 of judgment.

The ruling in *Marshall* did not prevent continued debate on the question of horizontal direct effect for directives. After the Court in *Marleasing* expressed the duty of national courts to interpret national law consistently with directives in a way which seemed indistinguishable from according horizontal direct effect to directives[23] two Advocates General indicated in Opinions that they favoured horizontal direct effect for directives.[24] In *Paola Faccini Dori v. Recreb Srl*[25] the Court once again considered this controversial question. The national proceedings arose from a contract for an English language correspondence course concluded off business premises at Milan Central Railway Station by Miss Faccini Dori. She later thought better of the transaction, and wrote purporting to cancel the contract, indicating that she relied *inter alia* on the right of cancellation provided under Directive 85/577.[26] This directive had not been transposed into Italian law at the material time, and an Italian court asked for a preliminary ruling on the question whether the directive was nevertheless capable of taking effect as between individuals. In addition to the parties, seven Member States and the Commission made written and/or oral observations in the proceedings before the European Court. All the Member States except Greece argued against horizontal direct effect; as did the Commission. Advocate General Lenz's Opinion pronounced in favour of horizontal direct effect, but only for the future. He pointed out that under the EEC Treaty the publication of directives was not mandatory, and argued that the "basic condition for a burden imposed on the citizen by legislative measures is their *constitutive publication* in an official organ."[27] But in the case of directives adopted following the entry into force of the Maastricht Treaty on November 1, 1993, he thought that the situation was fundamentally different, since Article 254 (ex 191) required directives to be published in the Official Journal of the Community. No objection based on the absence of publication could thereafter be raised against horizontal direct effect.

The Court of Justice confirmed its judgment in *Marshall* that a directive cannot of itself impose obligations on an individual and could not therefore be relied upon as such against an individual. The basis for the Court's case law on the vertical direct effect of directives was that a directive was binding under Article 229 (ex 189) only in relation "to each Member State to which it is addressed". That case law sought to prevent "the State from taking advantage of its own failure to comply with Community law."[28] But, in the view of the Court of Justice:

"The effect of extending that case-law to the sphere of relations between individuals would be to recognise a power in the Community to enact obligations for individuals with immediate effect, whereas it has competence to do only where it is empowered to adopt regulations.

---

[23] See above, p. 93.
[24] Advocate General Van Gerven in Case C–271/91 *M. Helen Marshall v. Southampton and South-West Hampshire Area Health Authority* [1993] E.C.R. I–4367; Advocate General Jacobs in Case C–316/93 *Nicole Vaneetveld v. Le Foyer SA and Le Foyer SA v. Fédération des Mutualités Socialistes et Syndicales de la Province de Liège*.[1994] E.C.R. I–763, paras 18 *et seq.* of Opinion; [1994] 2 C.M.L.R. 852.
[25] Case C–91/92 [1994] E.C.R. I–3325; [1994] 1 C.M.L.R. 665.
[26] [1985] O.J. L372/31.
[27] Para. 64 of Opinion.
[28] Para. 22 of the Court's judgment.

It follows that, in the absence of measures transposing the directive within the prescribed time-limit, consumers cannot derive from the directive itself a right of cancellation as against traders with whom they have concluded a contract or enforce such a right in a national court."[29]

Thus the Court accepted the legal analyses pressed upon it by half a dozen Member States, and by the Commission. These arguments were essentially to the effect that the Court's clear and recent judgment in *Marshall* was correct, and should be adhered to. While the Court endorsed *Marshall*, it also emphasised the duty of a national court to interpret national law, whether adopted before or after a relevant directive, as far as possible in accordance with the directive.[30] Where the result prescribed by the directive could not be achieved by way of interpretation, the Court recalled the duty of Member States to make good the damage caused to individuals through failure to transpose a directive, where the requisite conditions for such liability were fulfilled; as they were in the case before it.[31]

"Triangular" direct effect for directives[32]

While the Court has repeatedly emphasised that a directive cannot of itself impose obligations on an individual, it seems that an individual may be prevented from relying upon or deriving rights from a national legislative or administrative measure which conflicts with the directly effective provisions of a directive. Thus an undertaking which tenders for a public contract and has its tender rejected on grounds inconsistent with the directly effective provision of a directive may rely upon the directive to challenge the rejection of its tender, and it seems that this is the case even if the public contract has been awarded to a third party.[33] The Court has found that certain provisions of a council directive requiring Member States notify to the Commission technical standards likely to impede the free movement of goods[34] are to be interpreted as meaning that individuals may rely upon them before a national court which must decline to apply a national technical regulation which has not been notified in accordance with the directive.[35] The effect of the direct effect of a directive on the position of third parties is well illustrated by the *Medicines Control Agency* case.[36] This case involved the judicial review of a decision of the Medicines Control Agency granting a marketing authorisation to a company in respect of a proprietary medicinal product. The judicial review was initiated by competing undertaking

---

[29] Paras 24 and 25 of the Court's judgment.
[30] See above, p. 92.
[31] See below pp. 124 *et seq.* No question had been referred to the Court on state liability.
[32] See, *e.g.* Lackhoff and Nyssens (1998) 23 E.L. Rev. 397.
[33] Case 103/88 *Fratelli Costanzo SpA v. Comune di Milano* [1989] E.C.R. 1839; [1990] 3 C.M.L.R. 239. It does not necessarily follow that no account should be taken of the legitimate expectations of the third party.
[34] Council Directive 83/189 [1983] O.J. L109/8, as amended.
[35] Case C–194/94 *CIA Security International SA v. Signalson SA and Securitel SPRL* [1996] E.C.R. I–2201; [1996] 2 C.M.L.R. 781. But see Case C–226/97 *Criminal proceedings against Johannes Martinus Lemmens* [1998] E.C.R. I–3711; [1998] 3 C.M.L.R. 261.
[36] Case C–201/94 *R. v. The Medicines Control Agency, ex parte Smith & Nephew Pharmaceuticals Ltd* and *Primecrown Ltd v. The Medicine Control Agency* [1996] E.C.R. I–5819; [1997] 1 C.M.L.R. 812.

which held an original marketing authorisation for a proprietary medicinal product being the same name, alleging that the authorisation had been granted by the Agency contrary to the provisions of the EEC Directive[37] regulating the grant of marketing authorisations of proprietary medicinal products. The Court of Justice held that the holder of the original marketing authorisation could rely upon the relevant provision of the directive in question in proceedings before a national court in order to challenge the validity of an authorisation issued by the competent national authority to one of its competitors. Cases such as the foregoing raise difficulties of principle which the Court has surmounted without troubling to address. While it is established that an individual can rely upon a directive against a public authority to challenge the application to that individual of national legislative or administrative measures, it cannot really be said to follow inexorably that that public authority should be obliged to disapply national legislative or administrative measures which bestow rights on third parties *vis-à-vis* those third parties. In the *Constanzo* case, in which the Court appears to contemplate a tenderer relying upon a directive to challenge its exclusion from the tendering process, notwithstanding the award of the contract to a third party, the Court appears to consider that public authorities can rely upon a directive to cancel a contract awarded to an individual or company, even in the absence of an order of a national court resulting from proceedings initiated by a private party.[38] Yet surely it is also clear law that public authorities cannot rely upon unimplemented directives to impose obligations upon individuals, and it is artificial to deny that relying upon an unimplemented directive to, *e.g.* cancel a contract, or a licence, or a marketing authorisation, which is otherwise valid effective and enforceable, amounts to imposing an obligation on individuals. The strict logic of the limitations ostensibly placed by the Court on the direct effect of directives (to the effect that a directive cannot of itself impose obligations on individuals) would suggest that individuals could rely upon directives to preclude the application to them of national legislative or administrative measures found to be contrary to the directly effective provisions of a directive, without prejudice to the rights of private individuals or companies deriving rights from such measures. But the Court's case law does not support such a proposition. The question nevertheless arises of the extent to which Community law recognises that individuals who have ostensibly derived rights under national law from legislative or administrative measures which have been adopted in contravention of the terms of a directive may have legitimate expectations which may or must be respected by national courts and other authorities which are subsequently called upon to disapply the national measure in question. It is to be noted that in exceptional circumstances Community law recognises a legitimate expectation to retain state subsidies granted contrary to the terms of a directly effective provision of the Treaty.[39] Furthermore, the Treaty recognises the competence of

---

[37] Council Directive 65/65 [1965–66] O.J. Spec. Ed., as amended in particular by Council Directive 87/21 [1987] O.J. L15/36.

[38] Case 103/88 *Fratelli Costanzo SpA v. Comune di Milano* [1989] E.C.R. 1839, paras 31–33; [1990] 3 C.M.L.R. 239.

[39] Art. 88(3) (ex 93(3) E.C.; Case 39/94 *Syndicat Français de l'Express International (SFEI) and Others v. La Poste and Others* [1996] E.C.R. I–3547, para. 70; [1996] 3 C.M.L.R. 369.

the Court of Justice to give definitive effects to Community acts which it annuls; by this means the Court safeguards the legitimate expectations of third parties even in circumstances where a Community act has violated important principles of the Community legal order.[40] In light of the foregoing it would seem to be possible, in principle, and in appropriate circumstances, for a third party to rely upon the principle of legitimate expectations in the somewhat more meritorious context of the triangular direct effect of directive.

THE LEGAL EFFECTS OF INTERNATIONAL AGREEMENTS BETWEEN THE E.C. AND THIRD COUNTRIES

The E.C. Treaty makes provision for the conclusion of agreements between the Community and third countries.[41] The stage has long been reached when it could be said that:

"As far as the Community is concerned, an agreement concluded by the Council with a non-member country in accordance with the provisions of the E.C. Treaty is an act of a Community institution, and the provisions of such an agreement form an integral part of Community law."[42]

Equally, decisions of a Council of Association adopted to give effect to the international agreement under which it was established, are regarded as an integral part of the Community legal system.[43] The Court has also held that if an international agreement to which the Community is party provides for an international court to settle disputes between the Community and third countries, the decisions of that court would bind the Court of Justice when it was called upon to rule, by way of preliminary ruling or in a direct action, on the interpretation of the international agreement as part of the Community legal order.[44]

Appropriately worded provisions of an international agreement between the Community and a third country may have direct effect:

"The Court has consistently held that a provision of an agreement concluded by the Community with third countries must be regarded as directly effective when, having regard to its wording and the purpose and nature of the

---

[40] Art. 231 (ex 174) E.C. See, *e.g.* Case C–106/96 *United Kingdom v. Commission* [1998] E.C.R. I–2729; [1998] 2 C.M.L.R. 981. The Court annulled a decision of the Commission as being outside the Commission's competence. It nevertheless declared that the annulment of the decision should not affect the validity of payments made or undertakings given under the contracts in issue. The Court relied upon Art. 231 (ex 174) by analogy and "important considerations of legal certainty"; see para. 41 of the Court's judgment.

[41] See in particular Arts 133 (ex 113), Art. 300 (ex 228) and Art. 310 (ex 238). The Community may also conclude agreements pursuant to powers implied from its internal competence.

[42] Case C–162/96 *Racke GmbH & Co. v. Hauptzollamt Mainz* [1998] E.C.R. I–3655, para. 41, [1998] 3 C.M.L.R. 219, citing Case 12/86 *Demirel v. Stadt Schwäbisch Gmünd* [1987] E.C.R. 3719, para. 14; [1989] 1 C.M.L.R. 421.

[43] Case 30/88 *Greece v. Commission* [1989] E.C.R. 3711, para. 12; Case C–192/89 *S. Z. Sevince v. Staatssecretaris van Justitie* [1990] E.C.R. I–3461, para. 9; [1992] 2 C.M.L.R. 57.

[44] Opinion 1/91 on E.C.–EFTA Agreement [1991] E.C.R. I–6079, paras 39 and 40.

agreement itself, the provisions contains a clear and precise obligation which is not subject, in its implementation or effects, to the adoption of any subsequent measure . . ."[45]

The Court has held provisions of various agreements between the Community and third countries to be directly effective.[46] This conclusion was not inevitable from a legal point of view and in the opinion of the present writer was unfortunate in policy terms, since it may place Community traders at a disadvantage compared with competitors in third countries. While the latter may invoke provisions of international agreements in their favour before the courts of the Member States, Community traders might be unable to do likewise in the States which refused to recognise that such international agreements have direct effect. It should be recognised that the management of international trading agreements between the Community and third countries raises political as well as legal questions, and in the view of the present writer, such agreements should only have direct effect where provision for such effect is made in the Community act adopting the agreement in question, or in secondary legislation implementing the agreement.

Perhaps for reasons such as those referred to above the Court of Justice denied direct effect to provisions of the General Agreement on Tariffs and Trade (GATT 1947). The Court regarded GATT 1947 as binding on the Community, taking the view that under the EEC Treaty the Community assumed the powers previously exercised by Member States with respect to GATT 1947.[47] But the Court rejected arguments that direct effect could be attributed to GATT 1947 as regards Article II, Article XI, the Protocols concluded within the framework of the GATT, and those provisions of the GATT which determined the effect of those Protocols.[48] The World Trade Organisation Agreement of 1994 included agreements on services (GATS) and Trade Related Intellectual Property Rights (TRIPS), in addition to GATT 1994 on goods. Council Decision 94/800,[49] by which the Community approved the agreements reached in the Uruguay Round multilateral negotiations, states in the eleventh recital to its preamble that "the

---

[45] Case C–416/96 *Nour Eddline El-Yassini* v. *Secretary of State for Home Department* [1999] E.C.R. I–1209; [1999] 2 C.M.L.R. 32, citing Case 12/86 *Demirel*, n.42, para. 14; Case C–18/90 *ONEM v. Kziber* [1991] E.C.R. I–199, para. 15; and Case C–162/96 *Racke*, n.42, para. 31; [1998] 3 C.M.L.R. 219.

[46] See *e.g.* Case 87/75 *Conceria Daniele Bresciani v. Amministrazione Italiana delle Finanze* [1976] E.C.R. 129 (Art. 2(1) of the Yaoundé Convention); Case 17/81 *Pabst & Richarz KG v. Hauptzollamt Oldenburg* [1982] E.C.R. 1331; [1983] 3 C.M.L.R. 11, (Art. 53(1) of the EEC-Greece Association Agreement); Case 104/81 *Hauptzollamt Mainz v. C.A. Kupferberg & Cie KG a.A.* [1982] E.C.R. 3641; [1983] 1 C.M.L.R. 1, (Art. 21 of the EEC-Portuguese Association Agreement); Case 12/86 *Demirel*, n.42 (Art. 12 of the EEC-Turkey Association Agreement); Case C–192/89 *S. Z. Sevince v. Staatssecretaris van Justitie* [1990] E.C.R. I–3461 (certain provisions of certain decisions of the Association Council); Case C–126/95 *A. Hallouzi-Choho* v. *Bestuur van de Sociale Verzekeringsbank.* [1996] E.C.R. I–4807 (Art. 41(1) of the EEC-Morocco Cooperation Agreement); Case C–416/96 *Nour Eddline El-Yassini* v. *Secretary of State for Home Department* [1999] E.C.R. I–1209 (Art. 40(1) of the EEC-Morocco Co-operation Agreement); [1999] 2 C.M.L.R. 32.

[47] Joined Cases 21–24/72 *International Fruit Company v. Produktschap voor Groenten en Fruit* [1972] E.C.R. 1219; [1975] 2 C.M.L.R. 1; Case 9/73 *Schlüter v. Hauptzollamt Lörrach* [1973] E.C.R. 1135; Joined Cases 267–269/81 *Societa Petrolifera Italiana* [1983] E.C.R. 801; [1984] 1 C.M.L.R. 354; Cases 290–291/81 *Compagnia Singer* [1983] E.C.R. 847.

[48] n.47.

[49] [1994] O.J. L336/1.

Agreement establishing the World Trade Organisation, including the Annexes thereto, is not susceptible to being directly invoked in Community or Member State courts". While a reference in the preamble, unaccompanied by any indication to similar effect in the text of the decision, cannot be of determinative legal significance, the preamble is certainly consistent with the view that neither the Community nor the Member States had any intention of establishing an international legal regime having direct effects.[50] As regards GATS it is to be noted that in their Schedule of Commitments the Community and its Member States have excluded direct effect.[51] It has been suggested that the language of the TRIPS agreement lends itself to direct effect,[52] and in *Hermès* Advocate General Tesauro considered that the WTO agreement could be given direct effect on the basis of reciprocity and that Article 50(6) of TRIPS had direct effect.[53] In the view of the present writer it is not possible in practice for courts to establish with any degree of certainty the existence of reciprocity on the part of courts in third countries, and in the absence of any compelling legal argument for the direct effect of the WTO agreement, direct effect should not be accorded to GATT 1994, to GATS, or to TRIPS. This would most likely accord with the expectations of the Member States and the Community institutions, and would enable both national and Community authorities to maintain an appropriate degree of control over the application of these agreements.

A potential difficulty in regarding international agreements between the Community and third countries as part of the Community legal order is that while some such agreements fall within the competence of the Community and the Community alone, others fall partly within Community competence and partly within national competence, and are concluded by both the Community and the Member States. The latter are described as "mixed" agreements. In *Demirel*[54] the Court considered the scope of a "mixed" agreement—the EEC/Turkey Association Agreement. Germany and the United Kingdom objected to the jurisdiction of the Court to interpret the provisions on freedom of movement for workers, since granting freedom of movement to nationals of third countries fell with national competence rather than Community competence. The Court rejected this argument on the ground that freedom of movement for workers fell

---

[50] See the Opinion of Advocate General Cosmas in Case C–183/95 *Affish* [1997] E.C.R. I–4315, para. 127 (reference in preamble not determinative but the learned Advocate General appears to think it has some weight), and the Opinion of Advocate General Elmer in Cases C-364/95 and C-365/95 *T. Port GmbH & Co. v. Hauptzollamt Hamburg-Jonas*.[1998] E.C.R. I–1023 (the learned Advocate General appears to think the recital has at least some weight). Advocate General Tesauro in Case C–53/96 *Hermès International (société en commandite par actions) v. FHT Marketing Choice BV* [1998] E.C.R. I–3603 states at para. 24 of his Opinion that "the statement in question appears only in the preamble to the Council Decision approving the WTO Agreements, not in the operative part of the Decision, and this significantly reduces its effect, in legal terms, of course."

[51] The Introductory Note to the Schedule states that "The rights and obligations arising from the GATS, including the schedule of commitments, shall have no self-executing effect and thus confer no rights directly to individual natural persons or juridical persons." See Eeckhout C.M.L. Rev. 1997 11, 34.

[52] Eeckhout, n.51, p. 33.

[53] See n.50, esp. paras 34 to 37 of his Opinion. The learned Advocate General considered that in the absence of reciprocity Community traders would be placed at a disadvantage compared with their foreign competitors; see para. 31 of his Opinion.

[54] Case 12/86 *Demirel v. Stadt Schwäbisch Gmünd* [1987] E.C.R. 3719; [1989] 1 C.M.L.R. 421.

within Community competence,[55] and the fact that it also involved the exercise of national competence did not exclude its jurisdiction to interpret the provisions in question. There must be a real question as to the competence of the Court of Justice to interpret provisions of a mixed agreement falling solely within national competence.[56] In *Hermès* the Court of Justice received a request for a preliminary ruling on the meaning of Article 50 of TRIPS (a mixed agreement).[57] The Court held that it had jurisdiction to interpret this provision on the ground that national courts would be obliged to take account of it when ensuring the protection of rights arising under the Community trade mark.[58] The question of principle was left unresolved.

Provisions of an international agreement which do not have direct effect may nevertheless have legal effects where Community legislation expressly or impliedly so provides. Thus the Court held in *Fediol* that reference in a regulation to an "illicit commercial practice" in the context of international trade relations requires account to be taken of the terms of GATT 1947.[59] Again, in *Nakajima*, the Court held that where the Community adopts legislation in order to comply with the international obligations of the Community, such as GATT 1947 and its Anti-Dumping Code, the Court will regard provisions of that legislation which are inconsistent with those international obligations as being covered by the words "infringement of this Treaty or of any rule of law relating to its application" which appear as a ground if annulment in Article 230 (ex 173) E.C.[60] In the so-called "bananas" litigation, the Court of Justice confirmed that since GATT 1947 lacked direct effect, it was only if the Community intended to implement a particular obligation entered into within the framework of GATT, or if the Community act expressly referred to specific provisions of GATT, that the Court could review the legality of the Community act in question from the point of view of the GATT rules.[61] But it is to be noted that provisions of international agreements, such as GATT 1947, which are not directly effective,

---

[55] Para. 9 of the Court's judgment. An unconvincing argument, since the provisions of the Treaty on the free movement of workers apply only to nationals of Member States.

[56] For an interesting discussion see Advocate General Tesauro in Case C–53/96 *Hermès International (société en commandite par actions) v. FHT Marketing Choice BV* [1998] E.C.R. I–3603, at paras. 10 to 21 of his Opinion; a discussion of the position as regards TRIPS, but one which raises more general issues of principle.

[57] Opinion 1/94 on WTO Agreement [1994] E.C.R. I–5267.

[58] Para. 28. The Court at para. 32 noted that where a provision can apply both to situations falling within the scope of National law and to situations falling within the scope of Community law, it is in the Community interest that, in order to forestall future differences of interpretation, that provision should be interpreted uniformly, whatever the circumstances in which it is to apply, citing Case C–130/95 *Giloy v. Hauptzollamt Frankfurt am Main-Ost* [1997] E.C.R. I–4291, para. 28, and Case C–28/95 *Leur-Bloem v. Inspecteur der Belastingdienst/Ondermingen* [1997] E.C.R. I–4161, para. 34.

[59] Case 70/87 *Fédération de l'industrie de l'huilerie de la CEE (Fediol) v. Commission of the European Communities* [1989] E.C.R. 1781, paras 19 and 20; [1991] 2 C.M.L.R. 489.

[60] Case C–69/89 *Nakajima All Precision Co. Ltd v. Council of the European Communities* [1991] E.C.R. I–2069, paras 29–31.

[61] Case C–280/93 *Federal Republic of Germany v. Council of the European Union.* [1994] E.C.R. I–4973, para. 111; [1993] 5 C.M.L.R. 201.

may be taken into account in interpreting relevant provisions of Community legislation.[62]

In recent years the Court has had recourse to general principles of public international law as a ground for interpreting, and assessing the validity of Community acts. In *Poulsen* the Court considered the terms of an EEC regulation laying down technical measures on the conservation of fishery resources, noting that:

> "As a preliminary point, it must be observed, first, that the European Community must respect international law in the exercise of its powers and that, consequently, Article 6 abovementioned must be interpreted, and its scope limited, in the light of the relevant rules of the international law of the sea."[63]

That the Court meant by this only that Community secondary legislation should be interpreted in light of international law appeared to be confirmed by its later judgment in *Commission v. Germany*, to the effect that:

> ". . . the primacy of international agreements concluded by the Community over provisions of secondary Community legislation means that such provisions must, so far as is possible, be interpreted in a manner that is consistent with those agreements."[64]

In *Racke* the approach taken by the Court in *Nakajima*[65] was extended to principles of public international law[66] The plaintiff in the national proceedings challenged the validity of an EEC regulation suspending trade concessions under the EEC-Yugoslavia Cooperation Agreement on the ground that such suspension was inconsistent with relevant provisions of the Vienna Convention on the Law of Treaties. These provisions referred to the doctrine of *rebus sic stantibus*, whereby a party may unilaterally terminate a treaty in the event of fundamental change of circumstances. It appeared from the preamble to the suspension regulation that it was based on the conviction of the Council that a radical change in circumstances had occurred. The Court of Justice, purporting to apply *Nakajima* by analogy, denied that the case concerned the direct effect of rules of international law, and emphasised that the case concerned a regulation which had been taken pursuant to the relevant rules of international law, and could thus

---

[62] Case 92/71 *Interfood GmbH v. Hauptzollamt Hamburg-Ericus* [1972] E.C.R. 231, para. 6; [1972] C.M.L.R. 562; (GATT agreements relevant to interpretation of common external tariff); Case C-79/89 *Brown Boveri & Cie AG v. Hauptzollamt Mannheim* [1991] E.C.R. I-1853, paras. 15-19; [1993] 1 C.M.L.R. 814 (decision of GATT Committee on Customs Valuation relevant to interpretation of EEC Regulation on customs value); Case C-70/94 *Fritz Werner Industrie-Ausrüstungen GmbH v. Federal Republic of Germany* [1995] E.C.R. I-3819, para. 23, and Case C-83/94 *Criminal proceedings against Peter Leifer, Reinhold Otto Krauskopf and Otto Holzer* [1995] E.C.R. I-3231, para. 24 (interpretation of E.C. Export Regulation under Common Commercial Policy in light of GATT).

[63] Case C-286/90 *Anklagemyndigheden v. Peter Michael Poulsen and Diva Navigation Corp.* [1992] E.C.R. I-6019, para. 9.

[64] Case 61/94 [1996] E.C.R. I-3989, para. 52; [1997] 1 C.M.L.R. 281.

[65] Case C-69/89 *Nakajima All Precision Co. Ltd v. Council of the European Communities* [1991] E.C.R. I-2069.

[66] Case C-162/96 *A. Racke GmbH & Co. v. Hauptzollamt Mainz* [1998] E.C.R. I-3655; [1998] 3 C.M.L.R. 219.

be challenged if the Council made manifest errors of assessment concerning the conditions for applying those rules; the Court concluded that no such manifest errors had been made. The present writer considers that *Racke* stretches the principles applied by the Court in *Fediol* and *Nakajima* too far. Those cases can best be justified on the basis of the proposition that non directly effective provisions of international agreements may nevertheless govern the scope of Community legislation where that legislation expressly or impliedly so provides. The reference to radical change of circumstances in the preamble to the regulation is not of itself a convincing indication of a legislative intention to condition the efficacy of the regulation on its compatibility with international law.

CHAPTER 5

RIGHTS AND REMEDIES

INTRODUCTION

While the significance of the European Courts and Institutions should not be underestimated in facilitating the application of Community law in the Member States, it must be noted that the Community legal system is in large part administered by national authorities, with the result that national agencies, courts and tribunals are entrusted with the application of sometimes subtle combinations of Community law and national law, based on variations of the following:

— rules of Community law incapable of direct application incorporated into national law in discharge of Community obligations, and enforced by the application of appropriate national procedures, remedies or penalties;
— rules of Community law incapable of direct application which have not been incorporated into national law, but which are taken into account in interpreting national rules and enforcing national remedies or penalties, or which are enforced by an action for damages under Community law, in accordance with appropriate national rules relating to damage actions against the State;
— directly applicable rules of Community law, supplemented by directly applicable Community procedural rules, (and perhaps further supplemented by national procedural rules and national remedies);
— directly applicable rules of Community law, supplemented by national procedural rules and national remedies.

RULES OF COMMUNITY LAW INCAPABLE OF DIRECT APPLICATION

Where non-directly applicable rules of Community law are incorporated into national law, the Community inspiration for the national rules in question may be relevant for the purposes of interpreting and giving effect to relevant national legal rules.[1] In appropriate circumstances, the failure of a Member State to incorporate non-directly applicable rules of Community law into national law will give rise to an action in damages by an individual in accordance with Community law and appropriate provisions of national procedural and remedial law.[2] It may be that a provision of Community law bestows legal competence directly upon a national agency, court or tribunal, without giving any individual a specific right to call upon the agency court or tribunal to take advantage of that competence.

---

[1] See above, p. 71 and p. 92.
[2] See below, p. 124.

Article 234 (ex 177) falls into this category, empowering national courts and tribunals to make references for preliminary ruling to the European Court.[3] Although this provision may be implemented by national procedural rules,[4] the European Court has never suggested that the admissibility of a reference from a national court depended upon anything other than compliance with the terms of the Article in question. Article 234 can properly be described as a provision of Community law which has direct application, in the sense that the competence it bestows upon national courts is not dependant on the enactment of national implementing rules. But Member States would seem in principle to be obliged to repeal any national procedural rules which might directly or indirectly impede recourse by national courts or tribunals to the preliminary ruling procedure,[5] and to be free to adopt appropriate national rules governing the procedure for making a reference. It is clear that in the absence of such national procedural rules national courts or tribunals are free to make references in reliance directly upon the Treaty, and that the Court of Justice may make "practice directions" on the form of such references.[6]

DIRECTLY APPLICABLE PROVISIONS OF COMMUNITY LAW SUPPLEMENTED BY DIRECTLY APPLICABLE COMMUNITY PROCEDURAL RULES

Community Regulations may not only vest rights in individuals as against national authorities; they may also provide detailed procedural rules for the enjoyment of those rights[7], including rules specifying the standard and burden of proof necessary to sustain a claim to the payment of money.[8] Directly applicable Community rules prohibit agreements which restrict competition and affect inter-State trade, and the abuse of a dominant position,[9] and E.C. Regulations provide for the imposition of penalties[10] by the Commission on undertakings which carry on such activities, and lay down procedural rules concerning such matters as

---

[3] Though individuals would seem to have the right to call upon national courts or tribunals to take appropriate account of Art. 234 in the course of proceedings to which they are party, and the third para. of Art. 234 would seem to give a right to parties to a proceeding to call upon a national court from which no judicial remedy lies to make a reference to the Court of Justice.

[4] See, *e.g.* RSC, Ord. 114; Schedule to the Civil Procedure Rules.

[5] On the general duty of Member States to implement Treaty obligations, see above pp. 00.

[6] See Proceedings of the Court of Justice and the Court of First Instance of the European Communities of December 9, 1996, No. 34/96, Notice—Note for Guidance on References by National Courts for Preliminary Rulings.

[7] See, *e.g.* for the buying-in of cereals by intervention agencies, and procedural conditions for the exercise by individuals of the right to sell to intervention agencies, Council Reg. No. 1766/92 on the common organisation of the market in cereals, [1992] O.J. L181/21, Art. 4; and Commission Reg. No. 689/92 fixing the procedure and conditions for the taking-over of cereals by intervention agencies, [1992] O.J. L74.

[8] See, *e.g.*, Commission Reg. No. 3719/88 laying down common detailed rules for the application of the system of import and export licences and advance fixing certificates for agricultural products, [1988] O.J. L331/1, and Commission Reg. No. 1162/95 laying down special detailed rules for the application of the system of import and export licences for cereals and rice, [1995] O.J. L117/2.

[9] Arts 81 and 82 (ex 85 and 86) and Reg. 17, [1959–62] O.J. Spec.Ed. 87.

[10] Reg. 17, Arts 15 and 16.

hearings[11] and time limits,[12] relating to the imposition of such penalties. Procedures and a time limitation period have been laid down in connection with the application of Article 88 (ex 93) E.C.[13]

It is important to establish whether or not an E.C. Regulation lays down comprehensive procedural rules in a specific area, since if it does not, the national authorities may be free to supplement Community law with the rules of the forum.[14] For the sake of the uniform application of Community law, however, resort to provisions of national law is permissible only to the extent necessary to give effect to the Regulation in question.[15]

DIRECTLY APPLICABLE COMMUNITY LAW SUPPLEMENTED BY NATIONAL PROCEDURAL RULES AND REMEDIES—THE GENERAL PRINCIPLES

While E.C. Regulations may, and sometimes do, provide procedural rules for the enforcement of Community rights, Community law more often than not vests rights in individuals (either against the State, or against other individuals or companies), without prescribing explicitly the procedural rules applicable in national courts or tribunals, or the remedies for infringement of these rights. In a consistent case-law, the European Court has laid down down two principles to be applied where individuals derive rights from the direct effect of Community law, but Community law does not prescribe procedural or remedial rules for the enjoyment of such rights. The first principle is that of equivalence—the procedural rules applying to enforcement of Community right must be no less favourable than those which apply to similar domestic actions. The second principle is that of effectiveness,—the application of national procedural rules must not make the enforcement of Community rights virtually impossible or excessively difficult.The Court summarised its case-law as follows in *Peterbroeck, Van Campenhout SCS & Cie v. Belgian State*:[16]

". . . the Court has consistently held that, under the principle of co-operation laid down in Article 5 [now 10] of the Treaty, it is for the Member States to ensure the legal protection which individuals derive from the direct effect of Community law. In the absence of Community rules governing a matter, it is for the domestic legal system of each Member State to designate the courts and tribunals having jurisdiction and to lay down the detailed procedural rules governing actions for safeguarding rights which individuals derive from the

---

[11] Reg. 99/63 on the hearing provided for in Art. 19(1) and (2) of Reg. 17, [1963] O.J. Spec.Ed. 2268.
[12] Reg. No. 2988/74 concerning limitation periods in proceedings and the enforcement of sanctions under the rules of the European Economic Community relating to transport and competition, [1974] O.J. L319/1.
[13] Council Reg. No. 659/1999 laying down detailed rules for the application of Art. 93 of the E.C. Treaty, [1999] O.J. L83/1.
[14] Case 31/69 *Commission of the European Communities v. Italian Republic* [1970] E.C.R. 25, [1970] C.M.L.R. 175.
[15] Case 39/70 *Norddeutsches Vieh- und Fleischkontor GmbH v. Hauptzollamt Hamburg-St. Annen* [1971] E.C.R. 49; [1971] C.M.L.R. 281.
[16] Case C–312/93 [1995] E.C.R. I–4599 at para. 12; [1996] 1 C.M.L.R. 793; [1996] All E.R. (E.C.) 242.

direct effect of Community law. However, such rules must not be less favourable than those governing similar domestic actions nor render virtually impossible or excessively difficult the exercise of rights conferred by Community law . . ."[17]

The Court went on to indicate, in very general terms, the factors to be taken into account in determining the extent to which the application of national procedural rules could be regarded as compatible with Community law:

"For the purposes of applying those principles, each case which raises the question whether a national procedural provision renders application of Community law impossible or excessively difficult must be analysed by reference to the role of that provision in the procedure, its progress and its special features, viewed as a whole, before the various national instances. In the light of that analysis the basic principles of the domestic judicial system, such as protection of the rights of the defence, the principle of legal certainty and the proper conduct of procedure, must, where appropriate, be taken into consideration."[18]

In principle, it is for the national courts to ascertain whether the procedural rules intended to ensure that the rights derived by individuals from Community law are safeguarded under national law comply with the principle of equivalence.[19] However, the Court of Justice can provide a national court with guidance as to the interpretation of Community law in this regard, which may be of use to it in undertaking the assessment in question, and in this connection the Court has stated that the principle of equivalence requires that the national rule at issue be applied without distinction, whether the infringement alleged is of Community law or national law, where the purpose and cause of action are similar.[20] This does not mean, however, that, for example, a Member State must extend its most favourable rule in the field of employment law to an action for equal pay; the national court must consider both the purpose and the essential

---

[17] At para. 12; the Court referred to the following cases: Case 33/76 *Rewe v. Landwirtschaftskammer für das Saarland* [1976] E.C.R. 1989, para. 5; [1997] 1 C.M.L.R. 533. Case 45/76 *Comet v. Produktschap voor Siergewassen* [1976] E.C.R. 2043, paras 12 to 16; [1977] 1 C.M.L.R. 533; Case 68/79 *Hans Just v. Danish Ministry for Fiscal Affairs* [1980] E.C.R. 501, para. 25; [1981] 2 C.M.L.R. 714; Case 199/82 *Amministrazione delle Finanze dello Stato v. San Giorgio* [1983] E.C.R. 3595, para. 14, Joined Cases 331, 376 and 378/85 *Bianco and Girard v. Directeur Général des Douanes des Droits Indirects* [1988] E.C.R. 1099, para. 12; [1989] 3 C.M.L.R. 36; Case 104/86 *Commission v. Italy* [1988] E.C.R. 1799, para. 7; [1989] 3 C.M.L.R. 25; Joined Cases 123 and 330/87 *Jeunehomme and EGI v. Belgian State* [1988] E.C.R. 4517, para. 17; Case C–96/91 *Commission v. Spain* [1992] E.C.R. I–3789, para. 12; and Joined Cases C6 and 9/90 *Francovich and Others v. Italian Republic* [1991] E.C.R. I–5357, para. 43; [1993] 2 C.M.L.R. 66. The same passage as that cited in the text appeared in a judgment delivered the same day as *Peterbroeck*, Joined Cases C430–431/93 *Jeroen van Schijndel and Johannes Nicolaas Cornelis van Veen v. Stichting Pensioenfonds voor Fysiotherapeuten* [1995] E.C.R. I–4705, para.17; [1996] 1 C.M.L.R. 801; [1996] All E.R. (E.C.) 259.

[18] *Peterbroeck*, para. 14; *van Schijndel*, para. 19. Application of the foregoing principle in *Peterbroeck* led to the conclusion that application of a domestic procedural rule was in the circumstances contrary to Community law. The reasoning of the Court of Justice is obscure and the case must be regarded as turning on its own facts.

[19] Case C–326/96 *B.S. Levez v. T.H. Jennings (Harlow Pools) Ltd* [1998] E.C.R. I–7835, para. 39; [1999] 2 C.M.L.R. 363.

[20] *ibid.*, para. 41.

characteristics of allegedly similar domestic actions in order to reach its conclusion.[21]

There can be no doubt that it is for national law to specify the appropriate court, and the appropriate remedy, to enable an individual or company to enforce rights under Community law, but this principle cannot preclude a national court from applying directly effective rules of Community law in all cases falling within its jurisdiction. The problem arose in stark form in the *Simmenthal* case.[22] Should an Italian court refuse to apply national legislation already held by the European Court to be incompatible with Community law, or should the Italian court only do so after referring the question to the Italian Constitutional Court? The Court of Justice ruled that:

"A national court which is called upon, within the limits of its jurisdiction, to apply provisions of Community law is under a duty to give full effect to those provisions, if necessary refusing of its own motion to apply any conflicting provisions of national legislation, even if adopted subsequently, and it is not necessary for the court to request or await the prior setting aside of such provisions by legislative or other constitutional means."[23]

It follows that if a national tribunal is acting within its subject-matter jurisdiction (for example, tax, sex discrimination), it must give effect to Community rights affecting that subject-matter even if its jurisdiction under national law is limited to rights specified under certain national enactments.[24]

The scope of the duty of a national court in a particular case to give effect to Community law will be deducible in principle from the proposition referred to in *Peterbroeck* above—namely, that the national court may apply national procedural rules providing they are no less favourable than those governing similar domestic actions and that they do not render virtually impossible or excessively difficult the exercise of rights conferred by Community law. The latter proviso imposes a duty on national courts and tribunals to ensure the effective protection of Community rights, even if this means applying procedural standards more favourable to those enforcing Community rights than those enforcing rights of purely domestic origin. Indeed, the Court has stated that the existence of effective judicial protection is a general principle of Community law.[25] Thus the Court has held that it is a corollary of the direct effect of the Treaty that an authority of one Member taking a decision on the right of a national of another Member State to access to employment in that State must give reasons for its

---

[21] *ibid.*, para. 43.

[22] Case 106/77 *Amministrazione delle Finanze dello Stato v. Simmenthal SpA.* [1978] E.C.R. 629; [1978] 3 C.M.L.R. 263.

[23] Para. 24

[24] By way of example, direct claims under Art. 141 (ex 119) E.C. may be made before Industrial Tribunals in the United Kingdom, see, *e.g. Pickstone v. Freemans* [1987] 3 All E.R. 756 at 777; *Greater Glasgow Health Board v. Wright and Hannah* [1991] I.R.L.R. 187; *McKechnie v. UBM Building Supplies Ltd* [1991] I.R.L.R. 283; *Livingston v. Hepworth Refractories Plc* [1992] I.R.L.R. 63.

[25] Case 222/86 *Union nationale des entraîneurs et cadres techniques professionnels du football (Unectef) v. Georges Heylens and others* [1987] E.C.R. 4097, para. 14; [1989] 1 C.M.L.R. 901; and Case 222/84 *Johnston v. RUC* [1986] E.C.R. 1651 at 1663; [1986] 3 C.M.L.R. 240.

decision, and that the latter decision be subject to judicial review to assess its compatibility with Community law.[26] It is true that in one case the Court stated that it was incumbent upon national courts to make available national remedies to secure the implementation of Community law, but added that they were not obliged to create *new* remedies for this purpose.[27] One would expect this to be correct, since the creation of new legal remedies would require legislative, rather than judicial action, but the proposition is contradicted by the judicial development of the principle of State liability for breach of Community law.[28] Even to regard the foregoing proposition as the general rule understates the extent to which Community law is capable of modifying the application of national procedures and remedies. For example, a national rule which subjects the availability of a national remedy to a condition which is incompatible with Community law, must be set aside,[29] and in such a case, the practical effect is to make available a remedy which, if not new, is at any rate something of a hybrid. This is all the more so when the conditions for making available such a remedy are governed in part by national law, and in part by principles of Community law, which are in turn derived in part by analogy with the rules and principles to be applied in direct actions before the Court of Justice.[30]

The principle of effectiveness, referred to above, will not require a national court to substitute its own judgment for that of a national authority where the national authority applying Community law is called upon to make complex assessments, and has a wide measure of discretion. In such a case judicial review may be restricted to verifying that the action taken by the national authority is not vitiated by a manifest error or a misuse of powers and that the authority has not clearly exceeded the bounds of its discretion.[31]

The consequences in individual cases of the principle of effectiveness may extend to all national procedural and remedial rules, including the standard and burden of proof. The principal Treaty basis for this principle is Article 10 (ex 5) E.C.[32] which requires Member States to take all "appropriate" measures to ensure the fulfilment of the obligations arising out of the Treaty or resulting from action taken by the Institutions of the Community. Although the Court has suggested on occasion that what is "appropriate" is for the Member State in question to decide,[33] this would render the obligation nugatory, and an objective

---

[26] Case 222/86 *Union nationale des entraîneurs et cadres techniques professionnels du football (Unectef) v. Georges Heylens and others* [1987] E.C.R. 4097; [1989] 1 C.M.L.R. 901; see also Case C–70/95 *Sodemare SA, Anni Azzurri Holding SpA and Anni Azzurri Rezzato Srl v. Regione Lombardia* [1997] E.C.R. I–3395, at paras 17–20; [1997] 3 C.M.L.R. 591, (the duty to give reasons does not extend to national measures of general scope).

[27] Case 158/80 *Rewe-Handelsgesellschaft Nord v. Hauptzollamt Kiel* [1981] E.C.R. 1805; [1982] 1 C.M.L.R. 449.

[28] See below, p. 124.

[29] Case 199/82 *Amministrazione delle Finanze dello Stato v. SpA San Giorgio* [1983] E.C.R. 3595; Case C–213/89 *R. v. Secretary of State for Transport, ex p. Factortame Ltd and others* [1990] E.C.R. I–2433; [1990] 3 C.M.L.R. 375.

[30] See below, in particular as regards injunctive relief.

[31] Case C–120/97 *Upjohn Ltd v. The Licensing Authority established by the Medicines Act 1968 and Others* [1999] E.C.R. I–223; [1999] 1 C.M.L.R. 825.

[32] See, *Peterbroeck*, above at text to n.15.

[33] Case 50/76 *Amsterdam Bulb* [1977] E.C.R. 137 at para. 32; [1977] 2 C.M.L.R. 218.

interpretation is more in accordance with principle.[34] It follows that all national procedural and remedial rules are subject in principle to Community minimum standards, and support for this may be found in *Rheinmühlen-Dusseldorf v. Evst*,[35] in which the Court of Justice acknowledged the competence of national authorities to adopt the standard of proof they thought fit for the purpose of assessing claims for export refunds, but added that complete reliance on shipment without a Community transit document as proof of exportation might nevertheless constitute an abuse of their discretion.

Whether or not Community law provides implicit procedural rules may be difficult to establish without the benefit of a reference to the Court of Justice. In certain cases the Court of Justice has interpreted Community law as implicitly placing the burden of proof on one party or the other in national proceedings. Thus, the Court has held that it is for the national authorities of a Member State to prove that national trading rules inhibiting imports may be justified under Article 30 (ex 36) E.C.[36] Again, in the context of equal pay, the Court has held that if an employer applies a system of pay which is totally lacking in transparency, it is for the employer to prove that this practice in the matter of wages is not discriminatory, if a female worker establishes, in relation to a relatively large number of employees, that the average pay for women is less than that for men.[37] It seems that Community law may mitigate the burden of proof normally incumbent upon one party to adversarial proceedings where the other party is better placed to collect and verify the data which will determine the outcome of the proceedings in question.[38]

Against the background of the foregoing, consideration will be given to the effect of the principles to which reference has been made in certain specific contexts; national rules governing time-limits, injunctive relief, and the recovery of money levied without lawful authority. In these cases, national procedures and remedies are made available under conditions derived from national law but subject to modification, and sometimes significant modification, as a result of the application of the principle of effectiveness. State liability for breach of Community law will also be examined. It is not really possible to explain the development of State liability for breach of Community law in terms of the principle that national remedies must be made available, but in a form which ensures the effective protection of Community rights; the reality is not of a national remedy modified by a principle of Community law, but of a remedy derived from Community law, to be made available under procedural conditions derived from national law. Finally, mention will made of cases in which Community legislation has sought to harmonise the national procedural and

---

[34] The Court has held that although the "choice of form and methods" in implementing directives is left to the Member States, they are nevertheless obliged to choose the most appropriate form and method to ensure the effective functioning of directives, account being taken of their aims; Case 48/75 *Royer* [1976] E.C.R. 497 at para. 73; [1976] 2 C.M.L.R. 619.

[35] Case 6/71 [1971] E.C.R. 823; [1972] C.M.L.R. 401.

[36] See below, p. 351.

[37] Case 109/88 *Handels-og Kontorfunktionaerernes Forbund* [1989] E.C.R. 3199; [1991] 1 C.M.L.R. 8; see also, *e.g.* Case 170/84 *Bilka v. Weber* [1986] E.C.R. 1607; [1986] 2 C.M.L.R. 701.

[38] Case 28/94 *Netherlands v. Commission* [1999] E.C.R. I–1973, para. 41 (clearance of EAGGF accounts).

remedial rules which govern the enforcement before national courts and tribunals of rights derived from Community law.

DIRECTLY APPLICABLE COMMUNITY LAW AND NATIONAL TIME LIMITS

The principles applicable to the application of national time limits in proceedings to enforce Community law are the general principles referred to above;[39] that is to say, the principle of equivalence, and of effectiveness. It is in principle for the national court to decide whether a national time-limit complies with the principle of equivalence, in accordance with interpretative guidance from the Court of Justice.[40]

Reasonable national time-limits are consistent with the principle of effective judicial protection. This is confirmed in *Denkavit* by Advocate General Jacobs, as follows:

"The imposition by a Member State of a reasonable time-limit for taking legal proceedings to challenge a decision cannot be considered to make reliance on Community law virtually impossible or excessively difficult. Such time-limits are an application of the principle of legal certainty protecting both individuals and administrations."[41]

It will be rare for a national time limit complying with the principle of equivalence to fall foul of Community law on grounds of effectiveness. The procedural rule in issue in the national proceedings in one of the seminal cases establishing the principle of effectiveness—the *Comet* case[42]—was a 30-day time-limit, and there is no indication in the Court's judgment that this period was inadequate.[43]

In *Emmott*,[44] a case concerning Directive 79/7 on the progessive implementation of the principle of equal treatment for men and women in matters of social security,[45] the Court held that, owing to the particular nature of directives, "until

---

[39] Above, p. 112.

[40] Case C–326/96 *B.S. Levez v. T.H. Jennings (Harlow Pools) Ltd* [1998] E.C.R. I–7835, at paras 39–53, [1999] 2 C.M.L.R. 363, in which considerable guidance is given to the Employment Appeal Tribunal on the application of the principle of equivalence in the context of the rule limiting a claimant's entitlement to arrears of remuneration or damages for breach of the principle of equal pay.

[41] Case C–2/94 *Denkavit Internationaal BV and Others v. Kamer van Koophandel en Fabrieken voor Midden-gelderland and Others* [1996] E.C.R. I–2827, *per* Advocate General Jacobs, at para. 64, citing Case 33/76 *Rewe v. Landwirtschaftskammer Saarland* [1976] E.C.R. 1989, para. 5; [1977] 1 C.M.L.R. 533; Case 45/76 *Comet v. Produktschap voor Siergewassen* [1976] E.C.R. 2043, para. 17; [1977] 1 C.M.L.R. 533; Case 199/82 *Amministrazione delle Finanze dello Stato v. San Giorgio* [1983] E.C.R. 3595, para. 12.

[42] n.41.

[43] Advocate General Jacobs notes in *Denkavit*, n.41 above, at para. 68 of his Opinion, that "In upholding the right of Member States to lay down reasonable time-limits the Court did not suggest that the time-limit was too short. Such a short time-limit is in any event no more restrictive than the one-month time-limit laid down by Art. 33 of the ECSC Treaty for actions against decisions or recommendations of the Commission".

[44] Case C–208/90 *Emmott v. Minister for Social Welfare and the Attorney General* [1991] E.C.R. I–4269; [1991] 3 C.M.L.R. 894.

[45] [1979] O.J. L6/4.

such time as a directive has been properly transposed, a defaulting Member State may not rely on an individual's delay in initiating proceedings against it in order to protect rights conferred upon him by the provisions of the directive and that a period laid down by national law within which proceedings must be initiated cannot begin to run before that time."[46] It was always difficult to see the precise justification for this broad proposition, and it was no surprise that the Court distinguished it in subsequent cases.[47] In the *Johnson* case[48] the Court stated that it was clear "that the solution adopted in *Emmott* was justified by the particular circumstances of that case, in which a time-bar had the result of depriving the applicant of any opportunity whatever to rely on her right to equal treatment under the directive."[49] The point was explained by Jacobs A.G. as follows in *Denkavit*:[50]

"It seems to me that the judgment in *Emmott*, notwithstanding its more general language, must be read as establishing the principle that a Member State may not rely on a limitation period where a Member State is in default both in failing to implement a directive and in obstructing the exercise of a judicial remedy in reliance upon it, or perhaps where the delay in exercising the remedy—and hence the failure to meet the time-limit—is in some other way due to the conduct of the national authorities. Seen in those terms the *Emmott* judgment may be regarded as an application of the well established principle that the exercise of Community rights must not be rendered 'excessively difficult'. . ."

This is certainly a satisfactory explanation to be attributed to the *Emmott* ruling, not least because it brings the case within the well-established principle of effectiveness, which is a principle which applies whether or not the right relied upon before a national court is derived from a directive or from another source of Community rights. In this regard *Levez*[51] is instructive. In this case the Court held that a national rule applicable in an equal pay claim under which entitlement to arrears of remuneration is restricted to the two years preceding the date on which the proceedings were instituted was not in itself open to criticism.[52] However, the order for reference indicated that the claimant in the national proceedings (who alleged that she had been paid less than her male predecessor) was late in bringing her claim because of inaccurate information provided by her employer regarding the level of remuneration received by her

---

[46] Para. 23.
[47] See *e.g.*, Case C–338/91 *Steenhorst-Neerings v. Bestuur van de Bedrijfsvereniging voor Detailhandel, Ambachten en Huisvrouwen* [1993] E.C.R. I 5475; [1994] 1 C.M.L.R. 773; [1995] 3 C.M.L.R. 323; and Case C–410/92 *Elsie Rita Johnson v. Chief Adjudication Officer* [1994] E.C.R. I–5483; [1994] 1 C.M.L.R. 725; Case C–188/95 *Fantask A/S e.a.* v. *Industriministeriet (Erhvervministeriet)* [1997] E.C.R. I–6783, para. 51; [1998] 1 C.M.L.R. 473; Case C–231/96 *Edilizia Industriale Siderurgica Srl (Edis) v. Ministero delle Finanze.* [1998] E.C.R. I–4951, paras 41–49; [1999] 2 C.M.L.R. 995.
[48] Case C–410/92, n.47.
[49] Para. 26.
[50] Case C–2/94 *Denkavit Internationaal BV and Others v. Kamer van Koophandel en Fabrieken voor Midden-gelderland and Others* [1996] E.C.R. I–2827; [1996] 3 C.M.L.R. 504.
[51] Case C–326/96 *B.S. Levez v. T.H. Jennings (Harlow Pools) Ltd* [1998] E.C.R. I–7835; [1999] 2 C.M.L.R. 363.
[52] Para. 20

male predecessor. The Court of Justice considered that to allow an employer to rely on a national rule such as that in issue would in the circumstances of the case before the national court, be "manifestly incompatible with the principle of effectiveness".[53]

DIRECTLY APPLICABLE COMMUNITY LAW AND INTERIM RELIEF

There can be no doubt that the principle of effectiveness can have the effect of requiring national courts and tribunals to adapt national remedies in order to secure the effective enforcement of Community rights. This is illustrated by the judgment of the Court of Justice in the *Factortame* case.[54] The House of Lords asked whether Community law either obliged or authorised a national court to grant interim relief against a national measure pending a judgment of the Court of Justice under Article 234 (ex 177) E.C. on the compatibility of such a measure with Community law. The House of Lords specified circumstances in which *inter alia* the national court had no power to give interim protection to the rights claimed by suspending the application of a national measure.[55] The question thus asked directly whether Community law could authorise or require the provision of a remedy which could not be granted under national law. The Court of Justice subtly reformulated the issue as follows:

". . . the House of Lords seek essentially to ascertain whether a national court which, in a case before it concerning Community law, considers that the sole obstacle which precludes it from granting interim relief is a rule of national law, must disapply that rule."[56]

Thus the Court of Justice presented the issue as not so much involving the capacity of Community law to create judicial remedies, as the limits on the capacity of national law to impede the application of Community law. The Court of Justice, referring to the principle of the supremacy of Community law, and to the duty of national courts to ensure the legal protection which individuals derive from the direct effect of provisions of Community law, continued:

"The Court has also held that any provision of a national legal system and any legislative, administrative or judicial practice, which might impair the effectiveness of Community law by withholding from the national courts having jurisdiction to apply such law the power to do everything necessary at the moment of its application to set aside national legislative provisions which might prevent, even temporarily, Community rules from having full force and effect are incompatible with those requirements, which are the very essence of Community law . . . Consequently, the reply to the question raised should be that Community law must be interpreted as meaning that a national court

---

[53] See paras 27 to 34. Also see Case C–78/98 *Preston,* judgment of May 16, 2000.
[54] Case C–213/89 *R. v. Secretary of State for Transport, ex p. Factortame Ltd and others* [1990] E.C.R. I–2433; [1990] 3 C.M.L.R. 375.
[55] The House of Lords proceeded on the basis that no injunctive relief could be made available under English law, but see *M. v. Home Office* [1994] 1 A.C. 377; [1993] 3 All E.R. 537, HL.
[56] [1990] E.C.R. I–2433 at para. 17; [1990] 3 C.M.L.R. 375.

which, in a case before it concerning Community law, considers that the sole obstacle which precludes it from granting interim relief is a rule of national law must set aside that rule."[57]

This judgment confirms the principle that national remedies must be made available in order to secure the effective enforcement of Community rights, and that any qualifying rules of national law which render those remedies inadequate in the judgment of the national court seised of the case must be set aside. The result is a hybrid remedy, based on national law, but taking on Community characteristics in certain categories of case.

The Court of Justice in *Factortame* did not address the question of the *criteria* to be applied in granting or withholding interim injunctive relief, although the second question referred by the House of Lords asked what those criteria were. The Court perhaps proceeded on the basis that since the sole ground for the House of Lords refusing relief appeared to be the provision of English law precluding such relief against the Crown, addressing the question of the criteria to be applied in granting or withholding relief would have been superfluous. Later case-law of the Court of Justice indicates that Community law does lay down criteria for the grant of interim relief in cases where individuals rely before national courts on Community law to challenge national or Community administrative or legislative acts. The leading cases—*Zuckerfabrik*[58] and *Atlanta*[59] arose in the context of challenges to national measures which give effect to Community acts, thereby amounting to challenges to the underlying Community acts. It will be recalled that in *Foto-Frost*[60] the Court of Justice held that while a national court did not have jurisdiction to invalidate a Community act (such jurisdiction being reserved to the Court of Justice), different considerations applied if an applicant sought to suspend a Community act pending a ruling on invalidity by the European Court. In that case the Court had not specified with precision the circumstances in which a national court could suspend a Community act, and had not indicated whether those circumstances were defined by Community law or by national law. It might be said that such a question could be left entirely to national law, subject to the principles of equivalence, and effectiveness. But the consequence of this might be the *over*protection of the rights of individuals, at the expense of the uniform application of Community law; in Member States in which interim relief could and would be readily granted against the administration, the practical consequence might be the paralysis of a Community legal regime as a result of the suspension of the relevant Community legislation.

Community law does of course make provision for interim relief in *direct* actions before the Court of Justice for the judicial review of Community acts,

---

[57] *ibid.*, paras 20 and 23. Interestingly, the Court made no reference to cases such as Case 45/76 *Comet*, n.36 above, on the principle of effectiveness, but instead relied upon its judgment in Case 106/77 *Simmenthal v. Amministrazione dello Stato* [1978] E.C.R. 629; [1978] 3 C.M.L.R. 263, on the supremacy and direct effect of Community law, see above, p. 66.

[58] Joined Cases C–143/88 and 92/89 *Zuckerfabrik Süderdithmarschen and Zuckerfabrik Soest* [1991] E.C.R. I–415; [1993] 3 C.M.L.R. 1.

[59] Case C–465/93 *Atlanta Fruchthandelsgesellschaft mbH and others v. Bundesamt für Ernährung und Forstwirtschaft.* [1995] E.C.R. I–3761; [1996] 1 C.M.L.R. 575; [1996] All E.R. (E.C.) 31.

[60] Case 314/85 *Foto-Frost v. Hauptzollamt Lubeck-Ost* [1987] E.C.R. 4199, below, p. 274.

pursuant to Articles 230, 242 and 243 (ex 173, 185 and 186) E.C. In such actions the Court of Justice (or the Court of First Instance)[61] will suspend the act in question where there is a *prima facie* case, and urgency resulting from the likelihood of irreparable damage to the applicant. Where these conditions are satisfied, the urgency is balanced against the possibility of irreparable damage to the Community should the act be suspended but the applicant's case fail. The requirement of a *prima facie* case is not in principle onerous. The question posed is whether it can reasonably be asserted that the plea is without foundation. If the answer is "no", there is a *prima facie* case, and the Court moves on to urgency and balancing.[62]

In *Zuckerfabrik* and *Atlanta*, the Court, in specifying the criteria to be applied by national courts when considering whether to suspend national measures implementing Community rules, draws an analogy with the test under Articles 242 and 243 (ex 185 and 186) E.C. for interim relief in direct actions before the Court. But it substitutes a somewhat different preliminary hurdle. Instead of the *prima facie* case requirement, as that requirement is understood in the context of applications for interim relief in direct actions, the Court holds that a national court must be satisfied that *serious doubts* exist as to the validity of the Community act in question. This approach appears to require the national court to go somewhat further by way of preliminary assessment of the merits than do the Community Courts, which in analogous circumstances consider whether factors have been established which are likely to cast doubt on the conclusions reached by the Community authority.[63] In *Atlanta*, as regards the balancing stage, the Court of Justice stresses the Community interest, and the need for the national court to take into account the cumulative effect which would arise if a large number of courts were also to adopt interim measures for similar reasons. While these principles are derived from those developed by the Court of Justice in direct actions, they also appear adapted to erect hurdles slightly more difficult for the litigant before the national court to clear than for the litigant before the Community Courts. This no doubt reflects concern by the Court of Justice that the over-hasty grant of interim measures by national courts might prejudice the uniform application of Community law. But the criteria referred to above also amount to a minimum standard of protection for those defending the application of *national* measures challenged on the grounds that they infringe Community law. In *Zuckerfabrik* and *Atlanta*, the Court of Justice, referring to *Factortame*, stated that the interim legal protection which Community law ensures for

---

[61] Decisions on interim measures are taken by the President or referred to the Court, or Court of First Instance, as the case may be; Rules of Procedure of the Court of Justice, [1999] O.J. C65/1 (consolidated text), Art. 85; Rules of the CFI, [1991] O.J. L136/1, as amended, Art. 106.

[62] Case T–29/92R *SPO v. Commission* [1992] E.C.R. II—2161, para. 34; Joined Cases C–239 and 240/96R *United Kingdom v. Commission* [1996] E.C.R. I–4475, at paras 51–3 and 61; [1997] 2 C.M.L.R. 123. While the test for prima facie case is not onerous, it seems that some account may be taken of the strength of the applicant's case, see Joined Cases C–239 and 240/96R, above, at para. 70.

[63] Case T–29/92R, n.57, para. 34, "Whilst the judge hearing the application for interim measures cannot make a close examination of all the pleas and arguments in the main action . . . he must nevertheless consider the arguments put forward by the applicants in their application for interim measures and at the hearing, in order to determine whether there is any evidence to cast doubt on the conclusions reached by the Commission."

individuals before national courts must remain the same, irrespective of whether they contest the compatibility of national legal provisions with Community law or the validity of secondary Community law, in view of the fact that the dispute in both cases is based on Community law itself.[64] There can be no doubt that national courts granting injunctive relief in accordance with the foregoing rules are making available hybrid remedies, derived in part from national law, and in part from Community law.

The propensity of the Court to extrapolate principles applicable in direct actions to the context of national proceedings for the enforcement of Community law makes it possible to contemplate novel forms of interim relief being made available before national courts as a consequence of the development of similar principles by the Community courts in direct actions. In *Antonissen*[65] the President refused to rule out the possibility that a request for an advance payment of compensation might amount to a proper subject of an interim application.[66]

RECOVERY OF CHARGES AND TAXES LEVIED CONTRARY TO COMMUNITY LAW

When a charge is imposed contrary to Community law, the question arises of the extent to which an action for recovery is governed by national law, or Community law. In this context, once again, the dominant principles are those of equivalence and effectiveness.[67] Entitlement to the repayment of charges levied by a Member State contrary to Community law is a consequence of, and an adjunct to, the rights conferred on individuals by the Community provisions prohibiting such charges. The Member State is therefore in principle required to repay charges levied in breach of Community law.[68] In the leading case in this area of the law, *San Giorgio*,[69] the Court of Justice considered a national rule which precluded the payment of duties or taxes unduly paid where such duties or taxes had been passed on to third parties. Under the national rule in question, duties or taxes were presumed to have been passed on whenever the goods in respect of which a charge had been levied had been transferred to third parties, in the absence of documentary proof to the contrary. The Court of Justice

---

[64] Joined Cases C–143/88 and 92/89 *Zuckerfabrik Süderdithmarschen and Zuckerfabrik Soest* [1991] E.C.R. I–415, para. 20; [1993] 3 C.M.L.R. 1; Case C–465/93 *Atlanta Fruchthandelsgesellschaft mbH and others v. Bundesamt für Ernährung und Forstwirtschaft* [1995] E.C.R. I–3761, para. 24; [1996] 1 C.M.L.R. 575; [1996] All E.R. (E.C.) 31. The approach of the Court of Justice is not far distant from that of the House of Lords in *Factortame* when the reference came back after the ruling of the European Court. Lord Goff says, at [1991] 1 All E.R. 107 at 120h, "[T]he court should not restrain a public authority by interim injunction from enforcing an apparently authentic law unless it is satisfied, having regard to all the circumstances, that the challenge to the validity of the law is, prima facie, so firmly based as to justify so execeptional a course being taken."
[65] Case C–393/96 P(R) *J. Antonissen v. Council* [1997] EECR I–441; [1997] 1 C.M.L.R. 783.
[66] Paras 35–41, referring to *Factortame, Zuckerfabrik,* and *Atlanta.*
[67] As to which, see above, p. 112.
[68] Joined Cases C–192–218/95 *Comateb and Others* [1997] E.C.R. I–165, para. 20.
[69] Case 199/82 *Amministrazione delle Finanze dello Stato v. SpA San Giorgio* [1983] E.C.R. 3595. See also Joined Cases 331, 376 and 378/85 *Bianco and Girard v. Directeur Général des Douanes et Droits Indirects* [1988] E.C.R. 1099; [1989] 3 C.M.L.R. 36.

confirmed that national courts might legitimately take into account the fact that unduly levied charges had been incorporated into the price of goods and thus passed on to purchasers. However, any requirement of proof which has the effect of making it "virtually impossible or excessively difficult" to secure the repayment of charges levied contrary to Community law would be incompatible with Community law. That was particularly so in the case of presumptions or rules of evidence placing upon the taxpayer the burden of establishing that the charges had not been passed on to other persons, or in the case of special limitations concerning the form of evidence to be adduced, such as the exclusion of any kind of evidence other than documentary evidence. Once it was established that the levying of the charge was incompatible with Community law, the national court must be free to decide whether or not the burden of the charge had been passed on, wholly or in part, to other persons. Furthermore, the Court emphasised that national rules rendering recovery virtually impossible could not be justified on the basis that they were not discriminatory, in as much as recovery of taxes unduly paid under national law was also virtually impossible, as follows:

> "It must be pointed out in that regard that the requirement of non-discrimination laid down by the Court cannot be construed as justifying legislative measures intended to render any repayment of charges levied contrary to Community law virtually impossible, even if the same treatment is extended to taxpayers who have similar claims arising from an infringement of national tax law. The fact that rules of evidence which have been found to be incompatible with the rules of Community law are extended, by law, to a substantial number of national taxes, charges and duties or even to all of them is not therefore a reason for withholding the repayment of charges levied contrary to Community law."[70]

In *Comateb*[71] the question arose once more of the extent to which national rules could be regarded a establishing a presumption that charges unduly paid had been passed on to third parties, thereby providing national authorities with a defence in an action for recovery. The Court stated that the exception to the right to recover charges unduly levied, referred to in *San Giorgio*, which applied in cases where the charge had been passed on to other persons, applied only in a case in which the national court determined, in the light of the facts of the case, that the burden of the charge had been transferred in whole or in part by the trader to other persons, and that reimbursement to the trader would amount to unjust enrichment.[72] There could be no presumption that the charges had been passed on and that it was for the taxpayer to prove the contrary.[73] The fact that there was a legal obligation to incorporate the charge in the cost price of the product concerned did not mean that national authorities could rely upon a presumption to the effect that the entire charge had been passed on, even if the obligation to incorporate the charge in the cost

---

[70] Para. 17.
[71] Joined Cases C–192–218/95 *Comateb and Others* [1997] E.C.R. I–165.
[72] Paras 21–29.
[73] Para. 25.

price carried a penalty.[74] Furthermore, If the burden of the charge was passed on only in part, it was for the national authorities to reimburse the trader the amount passed on.[75]

National procedural conditions which may lawfully be taken into account in relation to the repayment of charges and taxes levied contrary to Community law include time-limits[76]; unjust enrichment resulting from taxes or charges being passed on to third parties[77]; damage to the trade of taxpayers resulting from the imposition of the unlawful charge[78]; and any benefits accruing to a person paying unlawful taxes or charges by virtue of the payment.[79] If national authorities exact money payments in contravention of Community law, the question whether interest in payable on repayment is one for national, not Community law.[80] A Member State may not however adopt provisions making repayment of a tax held to be contrary to Community law by a judgment of the Court, or whose incompatibility with Community law is apparent from such a judgment, subject to conditions relating specifically to that tax which are less favourable than those which would otherwise be applied to repayment of the tax in question.[81]

DAMAGES AS A REMEDY FOR BREACH OF COMMUNITY LAW

There were early suggestions in the Court's case-law that breach of Community law by a Member State might give rise to liability in damages.[82] In *Francovich*[83] the Court delivered a judgment which caused a minor legal earthquake, perhaps comparable to that caused by the ruling of the House of Lords in *Donogue v. Stevenson*.[84] The case concerned a directive on the protection

---

[74] Para. 26.

[75] Para. 28

[76] See, *e.g.* Case C–343/96 *Dilexport Srl v. Amministrazione delle finanze dello Stato* [1999] E.C.R. I–579. But the principle of equivalence does not mean that a Member State is obliged to extend its most favourable rules govening reimbursement to all actions for repayment of charges or dues levied in breach of Community law, *ibid.*, para. 27.

[77] See above. Loss of the unjust enrichment is also a relevant factor when national authorities seek recovery of subsidies paid contrary to Community law, see Case C–298/96 *Oelmühle Hamburg AG and Jb. Schmidt Söhne GmbH & Co. KG v. Bundesanstalt für Landwirtschaft und Ernährung* [1998] E.C.R. I–4767; [1999] 2 C.M.L.R. 492.

[78] Case 68/79 *Just v. Ministry for Fiscal Affairs* [1980] E.C.R. 501, para. 26; [1981] 2 C.M.L.R. 714; Joined Cases C–192–218/95 *Comateb and Others* [1997] E.C.R. I–165, paras 29–34. Damage to traders resulting from the unlawful imposition of national taxes or charges might also give rise to an action for damages: *Comateb*, para. 34.

[79] Case 177/78 *Pigs and Bacon Commission v. McCarren* [1979] E.C.R. 2161; [1979] 3 C.M.L.R. 389.

[80] Case 26/74 *Roquette Frères v. Commission* [1976] E.C.R. 677, paras 11 and 12; Joined Cases C–279, 280 and 281/96 *Ansaldo Energia SpA v. Amministrazione delle Finanze dello Stato, Amministrazione delle Finanze dello Stato v. Marine Insurance Consultants Srl and GMB Srl and Others v. Amministrazione delle Finanze dello Stato* [1998] E.C.R. I–5025, para. 28. But an action in damages might lie for loss arising from non-payment of interest, *cf. R. v. Secretary of State for Social Security, ex p. Eunice Sutton* [1997] E.C.R. I–2613, paras 34, 35.

[81] Case 240/87 *Deville v. Administration des Impôts* [1988] E.C.R. 3513; [1989] 3 C.M.L.R. 611; Case C–231/96 *Edis v. Ministero delle Finanze* [1998] E.C.R. I–4951; [1999] 2 C.M.L.R. 995.

[82] Case 6/60 *Humblet* [1960] E.C.R. 559; Case 60/75 *Russo v. AIMA* [1976] E.C.R. 45 at 47.

[83] Joined Cases C–6 and 9/90 *Andrea Francovich and Danila Bonifaci and others v. Italian Republic* [1991] E.C.R. I–5357; [1993] 2 C.M.L.R. 66.

[84] Wyatt, "Injunctions and Damages against the State for Breach of Community Law—a Legitimate Judicial Development" in *European Community Law in the English Courts* edited by Andenas and Jacobs, Clarendon Press, Oxford 1998, 87 at 93.

of employees in the event of the insolvency of their employer,[85] which had not been implemented by Italy within the time limit specified; a default which had been established by the Court in infraction proceedings.[86] The Court held the principle of State liability for harm caused to individuals by breaches of Community law for which the State can be held responsible is inherent in the scheme of the Treaty. The Court stated in succinct terms the conditions for liability in a case such as that in issue:

> "Although State liability is thus required by Community law, the conditions under which that liability gives rise to a right to reparation depend on the nature of the breach of Community law giving rise to the loss and damage. Where, as in this case, a Member State fails to fulfil its obligation under the third paragraph of Article 189 [ex 249] of the Treaty to take all the measures necessary to achieve the result prescribed by a directive, the full effectiveness of that rule of Community law requires that there should be a right to reparation provided that three conditions are fulfilled. The first of those conditions is that the result prescribed by the directive should entail the grant of rights to individuals. The second condition is that it should be possible to identify the content of those rights on the basis of the provisions of the directive. Finally, the third condition is the existence of a causal link between the breach of the State's obligation and the loss and damage suffered by the injured parties. Those conditions are sufficient to give rise to a right on the part of individuals to obtain reparation, a right founded directly on Community law."[87]

It is to be noted that the above conditions are, as the Court states, required by Community law, but the Court goes on to state that "it is in accordance with the rules of national law on liability that the State must make reparation for the consequences of the harm caused."[88] In the case in point the Court held the conditions referred to above as to liability were satisfied, and the Court concluded that the national court must, "in accordance with the rules of national law on liability, uphold the right of employees to obtain compensation for harm caused to them as a result of the failure to transpose the directive."[89] However, the Court emphasised that the substantive and procedural conditions laid down by national law were subject to the principles of equivalence and effectiveness.[90] In a subsequent case concerning Italian legislation designed to facilitate damages actions pursuant to the *Francovich* ruling, the Court held that a one-year time-limit for such actions was consistent with Community law from the point of view of effectiveness, provided it met the requirement of equivalence.[91]

The judgment was undoubtedly a bold development of the law, and a significant development. The principle of State liability which it propounded

---

[85] Council Dir. 80/987, [1980] O.J. L283/23.
[86] Case 22/87 *Commission v. Italy* [1989] E.C.R. 143.
[87] Paras 38–41.
[88] Para. 42.
[89] Para. 45.
[90] Paras 42, 43. For the principles of equivalence and effectiveness, see above at pp.112–116.
[91] Case C–261/95 *Rosalba Palmisani v. Istituto nazionale della previdenza sociale (INPS)*.[1997] E.C.R. I–4025; [1997] 3 C.M.L.R. 1356.

could not be explained as a corollary or "adjunct" of the direct effect of a provision of Community law, as *e.g.* the right in principle to recover sums of money levied contrary to Community law had been explained.[92] The principle could not be so explained because the provision of the directive relied upon by the plaintiff in *Francovich* was held by the Court in that case not to be directly effective. The liability was thus based not on the breach of a directly applicable Community right, but the failure to bring into existence an enforceable right in national law by way of transposition of the directive. The failure in question nevertheless gave rise to enforceable rights in individuals. One question which arose after *Francovich* was whether, in cases of breach of Community law other than those involving the failure to transpose a directive, liability would follow automatically from breach, or would be conditional on the existence of fault of one kind or another. Another was whether *Francovich* liability was actually confined to breach of the duty to implement non-directly effective norms.

Authoritative guidance on the scope of the principle of State liability for breach of Community law came as a result of the requests for preliminary rulings in *Factortame III and Brasserie du Pêcheur*. Proceedings in the former case arose from the adoption of United Kingdom rules which had sought to reserve the British flag for vessels owned by British nationals. That these rules amounted to an infringement of the right of establishment of Spanish fishermen under Article 43 (ex 52) had later been established by a judgment of the Court of Justice.[93] The fishermen had from the start claimed damages for the losses they had sustained. The *Brasserie du Pêcheur* proceedings resulted from the application of German rules which had had the effect of excluding from the German market beer produced other than in accordance with German "pure beer" requirements. The German rules were held by the Court to be contrary to Article 28 (ex 30) E.C. in infraction proceedings.[94] A French brewery sought compensation for alleged loss of profits which would have been made on exports to Germany but for the exclusionary effects of the Germany rules. These proceedings were if anything more controversial than the judgment in *Francovich*. The German Government argued before the Court of Justice that "an extension of Community law by judge-made law going beyond the bounds of the legitimate closure of lacunae would be incompatible with the division of competence between the Community institutions and the Member States laid down by the Treaty, and with the principle of the maintenance of institutional balance."[95] This comes close to arguing that the Court would exceed its competence if it developed Community law in the way in which, in the event, it did.

The national courts asked the Court of Justice to specify the conditions under which a right to reparation of loss or damage caused to individuals by breaches of Community law attributable to a Member State was guaranteed by Community law. In its response, the Court drew a parallel between liability of the State, and liability of the Community under Article 288(2) (ex 215(2))

---

[92] See above, p. 122.
[93] Case C–221/89 *Factortame II* [1991] E.C.R. I–3905; [1991] 3 C.M.L.R. 589.
[94] Case 178/84 *Commission v. Germany* [1987] E.C.R. 1227; [1988] 1 C.M.L.R. 780.
[95] Report for the Hearing, para. 32.

E.C.[96] Where the Community acted in a legislative context characterised by the exercise of a wide discretion, the Community only incurred liability if the institution concerned manifestly and gravely disregarded the limits on its powers. This strict approach was justified by the need to ensure that the legislative process was not unduly hindered by the prospect of damages actions. The Court noted that when a Member State was bound to implement a directive—as in the *Francovich* case—Community law imposed upon it obligations which reduced its margin of discretion to a substantial degree. But where national authorities had a wide discretion, said the Court, comparable to that of the Community in implementing Community policies, the conditions under which the State might incur liability must in principle be the same as for the Community. The Court considered as regards the proceedings in issue that both the United Kingdom and Germany had a wide discretion in adopting the national rules in question, and accordingly they would be liable only if three conditions were satisfied:

— The rule of law relied upon must be intended to confer rights on individuals;
— The breach must be sufficiently serious;
— There must be a direct causal link between breach and damages.

As regards the question whether the breach was sufficiently serious, the Court said that the test for liability was whether the Member State (or the Community in the case of Community liability) had "manifestly and gravely disregarded the limits on its discretion".[97] The Court went on to indicate the factors which should be taken into consideration by a national court in determining whether a breach of Community law was to be regarded as sufficiently serious to ground liability.

"The factors which the competent court may take into consideration include the clarity and precision of the rule breached, the measure of discretion left by that rule to the national or Community authorities, whether the infringement and the damage caused was intentional or involuntary, whether any error of law was excusable or inexcusable, the fact that the position taken by a Community institution may have contributed towards the omission, and the adoption or retention of national measures or practices contrary to Community law. On any view, a breach of Community law will clearly be sufficiently serious if it has persisted despite a judgment finding the infringement in question to be established, or a preliminary ruling or settled case-law of the Court on the matter from which it is clear that the conduct in question constituted an infringement."[98]

While in principle it was the national court, which had "sole jurisdiction to find the facts in the main proceedings and decide how to characterise the breaches of

---

[96] For Community liability under Art. 288(2), see pp.253–263 below. Such an analogy had been widely canvassed in academic literature and in arguments in the proceedings in question. And as early as 1985 the Court of Appeal had drawn a parallel between Community liability under Art. 215(2) and State liability for breach of directly applicable Treaty provisions (*in casu* Art. 30), *Bourgoin v. MAFF* [1985] 3 All E.R. 585.
[97] Para. 55.
[98] Paras 56 and 57.

Community law at issue", the Court added that it would be "helpful" to indicate a number of circumstances which the national courts might take into account., and this it proceeded to do.[99]

The national courts in *Factortame III/Brasserie du Pêcheur* also asked the Court of Justice to identify the criteria for determining the extent of the reparation due by a Member State responsible for breach. The Court's response endorsed the application of a mix of Community law and national law. The starting point was the following principle of Community law:

"Reparation for loss or damage caused to individuals as a result of breaches of Community law must be commensurate with the loss or damage sustained so as to ensure the effective protection for their rights."[1]

That said, in the absence of relevant Community provisions, it was for the domestic legal system of each Member State to set the criteria for determining the extent of reparation, subject to the Community principles of equivalence and effectiveness.[2] In this connection, the Court noted that the national court may enquire whether the injured person showed reasonable diligence in order to avoid the loss or damage or limit its extent and whether, in particular, "he availed himself in time of all the legal remedies available to him".[3]

As regards the extent of reparation, the German referring court had asked whether national legislation might generally limit the obligation to make reparation for damage done to certain, specifically protected individual interests, for example property, or whether it should also cover loss of profit by the claimants. The Court stated:

"Total exclusion of loss of profit as a head of damage for which reparation may be awarded in the case of a breach of Community law cannot be accepted. Especially in the context of economic or commercial litigation, such a total exclusion of loss of profit would be such as to make reparation of damage practically impossible."[4]

What is slightly curious about this formulation is the use of the word "total", which seems to imply that some exclusion of loss of profit is permissible. Yet the principle that compensation be commensurate with loss or damage sustained would seem to rule out exclusion of loss of profit caused by the breach in question.[5]

---

[99] Para. 58. The Court leaves little doubt that it regarded certain breaches as not being sufficiently serious, and certain others sufficiently serious. The House of Lords held that the breach involving direct discrimination was sufficiently serious, see [1999] 4 All E.R. 906.

[1] Para. 82.

[2] See above, p. 112.

[3] Para. 84.

[4] Para. 87.

[5] *cf.* Case C–271/91 *M. Helen Marshall v. Southampton and South-West Hampshire Area Health Authority* [1993] E.C.R. I–4367; [1993] 3 C.M.L.R. 293, which precludes a limit on compensation for loss sustained as a result of sex discrimination. For the duty to make adequate reparation see also Joined Cases C–94 and 95/95 *Danila Bonifaci and others and Wanda Berto and others v. Istituto nazionale della previdenza sociale (INPS).* [1997] E.C.R. I–3969, para. 53; [1998] 1 C.M.L.R. 257; Case C–373/95 *Federica Maso and others and Graziano Gazzetta and others v. Istituto nazionale della previdenza sociale (INPS) and Repubblica Italiana* [1997] E.C.R. I–4051, para. 41; [1997] 3 C.M.L.R. 1244; Case C–261/95 *Rosalba Palmisani v. Istituto nazionale della previdenza sociale (INPS)* [1997] E.C.R. I–4025, para. 35; [1997] 3 C.M.L.R. 1356.

The Court in *Francovich* said that the conditions under which State liability gives rise to a right to compensation would depend on the nature of the breach of Community law giving rise to the breach. In *Francovich* the breach had been the failure to implement a directive within the specified time limit, and in *Dillenkofer*[6] the Court made it clear that where a Member State fails "to take any of the measures necessary to achieve the result prescribed by a directive within the period it lays down, that Member State manifestly and gravely disregards the limits on its discretion".[7] But what if a Member State transposed a directive, but made an error of interpretation as regards one of its provisions? Would liability automatically follow, or would it be necessary to establish that the breach was "sufficiently serious"? The answer came in *BT*.[8] The United Kingdom had implemented a directive with national rules which in a certain respect failed properly to give effect to the directive. The Court does not say that a Member State enjoys a discretion in implementing a directive, and indeed, a Member State does not enjoy a discretion in bringing about a result which is different from that required as a result of misinterpretation of the directive. What the Court does is to refer to its reasoning in *Factortame III/Brasserie du Pêcheur*, and to the conditions applicable in circumstances where Member States enjoy a discretion in legislative decisions, and then concludes that "Those same conditions must be applicable to the situation, taken as its hypothesis by the national court, in which a Member State incorrectly transposes a Community directive into national law".[9] The Court declares that a restrictive approach to State liability is justified to avoid the prospect of damages actions hindering the exercise of legislative functions when the general interest requires the Member States to adopt measures which might adversely affect individual interests. While the Court acknowledges that in principle it is for the national courts to verify whether or not the conditions governing State liability for a breach of Community law are fulfilled, in the present case the Court declares that it has all the necessary information to assess whether the facts amounted to a sufficiently serious breach of Community law.[10] It goes on to note that factors which the competent court may take into consideration include the clarity and precision of the rule breached,[11] and exonerates the United Kingdom from liability in the case before it, since the provision in issue was "imprecisely worded and was

---

[6] Joined Cases C–178, 179, and 188-190/94 *Erich Dillenkofer, Christian Erdmann, Hans-Jürgen Schulte, Anke Heuer, Werner, Ursula and Trosten Knor v. Bundesrepublik Deutschland* [1996] E.C.R. I–4845.

[7] Para. 26.

[8] Case C–392/93 *R. v. H.M. Treasury, ex p. British Telecommunications plc* [1996] E.C.R. I–1631; [1996] 2 C.M.L.R. 217; [1996] All E.R. (E.C.) 411.

[9] Para. 40

[10] If the Court has all the necessary information it may decide whether a breach is sufficiently serious and whether there is a direct causal link between the breach of Community law and the damage allegedly suffered, see Case C–319/96 *Brinkmann Tabakfabriken GmbH v. Skatteministeriet* [1998] E.C.R. I–5255, paras 26–32; [1998] 3 C.M.L.R. 673. Since it is in principle for the national court to decide whether a breach is sufficiently serious a national court referring questions to the European Court in connection with a damages claim may retain the question of assessment of the breach for itself; see Case C–302/97 *Klaus Konle v. Republik Österreich* [1999] E.C.R. I–3099.

[11] Para. 42; for reference to the clarity and precision of the provision breached, see also Joined Cases C–283, 291 and 292/94 *Denkavit International BV, VITIC Amsterdam BV and Voormeer BV v. Bundesamt für Finanzen* [1996] E.C.R. I–5063, para. 50.

reasonably capable of bearing, as well as the construction applied to it by the Court in this judgment, the interpretation given to it by the United Kingdom in good faith and on the basis of arguments which are not entirely devoid of substance . . . "[12] It seems that an excusable error of law is a good defence to an action for damages when a Member State misimplements a directive, despite the lack of discretion as regards the implementation in question, with the rationale being that a Member State has no choice but to do the best it can to implement the Directive, even if its terms are less than crystal clear. Where however the discretion of a Member State has been considerably reduced by an E.C. Directive harmonising the field in question, and where the Member State in question is not called upon to make legislative choices, any breach of Community law may be sufficiently serious to establish liability.[13]

HARMONISATION OF PROCEDURAL RULES AND REMEDIES

The foregoing sections of this chapter have been concerned with modifications to the scheme of procedures and remedies normally applicable as a consequence of general principles derived from the E.C. Treaty. But in certain cases the Community legislator has intervened to bring about more systematic alignment of national procedures and remedies. Examples are as follows. It has been noted that the Court of Justice has held that the Treaty's guarantee of equal pay for equal work may affect the burden of proof in national legal proceedings.[14] Council Directive 97/80 now lays down harmonised rules on the burden of proof in cases of discrimination based on sex.[15] In the field of procurement, two directives[16] harmonise the remedies available at national level when proceedings are taken to review the decisions of contracting authorities/entities on the ground that such decisions have infringed Community law in the field of procurement or national rules implementing that law. The harmonised rules cover *inter alia* interim relief and damages.

---

[12] Para. 43.

[13] Case C–5/94 *R. v. Ministry of Agriculture, Fisheries and Food, ex p. Hedley Lomas (Ireland) Ltd* [1996] E.C.R. I—2553; [1996] 2 C.M.L.R. 391; [1996] All E.R. (E.C.) 493; (damages liability for export ban on live animals where recourse to Art. 36 was excluded by a directive harmonising the field). This case is not entirely satisfactory. It may be that an excusable error by a Member State that it retains discretion where a harmonising measure has removed or considerably reduced ought generally to be a defence in cases of State liability. In *Lomas* the Advocate General took the view that the harmonisation measure was a measure of partial harmonization and that recourse to Art. 30 (ex 36) was not excluded (paras 12–21), though he considered that Art. 30 (ex 36) did not in any event justify the export ban (paras 22 *et seq.*).

[14] Above at p. 116.

[15] [1998] O.J. L14/6. Extended to the United Kingdom by Dir. 98/52/EC [1998] O.J. L205/66.

[16] Council Dir. 89/66 (review procedures for award of public supply and public works contracts) [1989] O.J. L395/33; Council Dir. 92/13 (procurement procedures of entities operating in the water, energy, transport and telecommunications sectors) [1992] O.J. L76/14.

CHAPTER 6

GENERAL PRINCIPLES OF COMMUNITY LAW

SOURCES OF GENERAL PRINCIPLES

The E.C. Treaty has from the outset expressly laid down certain general legal principles, such as the duty of co-operation which binds both Member States and the Institutions in ensuring fulfilment of the obligations arising from the Treaty[1]; and the principle of non-discrimination on grounds of nationality.[2] Some general principles, such as proportionality, equality, and legitimate expectation, are wholly or mainly the product of judicial development, though the principle of proportionality is now expressly recognised in the Treaty as a constitutional principle of the Community legal order. Fundamental rights travelled a similar road to proportionality; first recognised by the Court's case-law, then endorsed by declarations of the Institutions, and finally written into the fundamental law of the European Union. General principles such as these have important legal effects. They place limits on the administrative and legislative competence of the Community institutions, and they govern the interpretation of provisions of Community law.[3]

The Court can hardly be said to have exceeded its jurisdiction by its recourse to the general principles of law. No Treaty regime, let alone the "new legal order" of the Community, could be interpreted and applied in a legal vacuum. International tribunals have long been regarded as competent to draw upon the general principles of municipal law as a source of international law,[4] and the competence of the Court of Justice in the interpretation and application of Community law could surely have been intended to be no less. The Treaty might be said to imply as much. Article 220 (ex 164) E.C. provides that "The Court of Justice shall ensure that in the interpretation and application of this Treaty the law is observed." While this formulation implies commitment to the rule of law, it has been argued that this implies a *corpus juris* outwith the express Treaty texts.[5] Other provisions are consistent with the proposition that the general principles of law constitute a source of Community law. Article 230 (ex 173) E.C. includes among the grounds of invalidity of Community acts infringement of "any rule of law" relating to the Treaty's application, an expression wide enough to encompass the principles under consideration. Furthermore, Article 288(2) (ex 215(2)) E.C. provides that the non-contractual liability of the Community shall

---

[1] Art. 10 (ex 5), E.C. see below.
[2] Art. 12 (ex 6), E.C. see below.
[3] Case 316/86 *Hauptzollamt Hamburg-Jonas v. Krucken* [1988] E.C.R. 2213, para. 22; Joined Cases 201–202/85 *Klensch* [1986] E.C.R. 3466, para. 10; [1988] 1 C.M.L.R. 151; Joined Cases C–90 and 91/90 *Neu and Others v. Secrétaire d'Etat à l'Agriculture* [1991] E.C.R. I–3617, para. 12.
[4] See Wyatt, "New Legal Order, or Old?" (1982) 7 E.L. Rev. 147 at 157. *cf.* Art. 38 of the Statute of the International Court of Justice, which lists as a source of international law, "the general principles of law recognised by civilised nations."
[5] See Pescatore, "Fundamental Rights and Freedom in the System of the European Communities" [1970] A.J.I.L. 343, at p. 348.

be determined "in accordance with the general principles common to the laws of the Member States", which amounts to express recognition of the role of the general principles of Community law. In the sections of this Chapter which follow, particular principles will be examined.

THE GENERAL PRINCIPLE OF SINCERE CO-OPERATION

Article 10 (ex 5) E.C. provides that Member States shall take all appropriate measures, whether general or particular, to ensure fulfilment of the obligations arising out of the Treaty or resulting from action taken by the institutions of the Community. They are obliged to facilitate the achievement of the Community's tasks, and to abstain from any measure which could jeopardise the attainment of the objectives of the Treaty. This provision is worthy of remark in this context, since it has been developed as a general principle binding upon the Community institutions as well as the Member States. In *Hilmar Kellinghusen* the Court stated:

> "As to Article 5 of the Treaty, it should be born in mind that, according to the case-law of the Court, the relations between the Member States and the Community institutions are governed, under that provision, by a principle of sincere co-operation. That principle not only requires the Member States to take all the measures necessary to guarantee the application and effectiveness of Community law, but also imposes on the Community institutions reciprocal duties of sincere co-operation with the Member States."[6]

The principle of sincere co-operation inherent in Article 10 of the Treaty requires the Community institutions, and above all the Commission, which is entrusted with the task of ensuring application of the provisions of the Treaty, to give active assistance to any national judicial authority dealing with an infringement of Community rules. That assistance, which takes various forms, may, where appropriate, consist in disclosing to the national courts documents acquired by the institutions in the discharge of their duties.[7] The Commission is obliged to respond as quickly as possible to requests from national courts.[8]

SUBSIDIARITY AS A GENERAL PRINCIPLE

In areas which do not fall within its exclusive competence, the Community shall take action, in accordance with the principle of subsidiarity, only if and insofar as the objectives of the proposed action cannot be sufficiently achieved by the Member States and can therefore, by reason of the scale or effects of the proposed action, be better achieved by the Community. This text is dealt with in

---

[6] Joined Cases C–36–37/97 *Hilmar Kellinghusen v. Amt für Land- und Wasserwirtschaft Kiel* and *Ernst-Detlef Ketelsen v. Amt für Land- und Wasserwirtschaft Husum* [1998] E.C.R. I–6337, para. 31.
[7] Case C–2/88 Imm. *J.J. Zwartveld and Others* [1990] E.C.R. I–3365, para. 17; [1990] 3 C.M.L.R. 457; Case T–353/94 *Postbank NV v. Commission* [1996] E.C.R. I–921, para. 64; [1995] 4 C.M.L.R. 150.
[8] Case C–39/94 *Syndicat Français de l'Express International (SFEI) and Others v. La Poste and Others* [1996] E.C.R. I–3547, at para. 50; [1996] All E.R. (E.C.) 685.

the following chapter, and is considered here for the sake of completeness. Since subsidiarity would seem to provide guidance to condition the exercise of competence which the Community possesses, rather than to indicate subject matter over which the Community has no competence, could it be argued that even a manifest error as regards the application of the principle would not justify annulment by the Court of the measure in question? Certain passages in the Protocol on Subsidiarity and Proportionality might seem to support such an approach:

> "The principle of subsidiarity does not call into question the powers conferred on the European Community by the Treaty, as interpreted by the Court of Justice . . . The principle of subsidiarity provides a guide as to how those powers are to be exercised at Community level. Subsidiarity is a dynamic concept and should be applied in the light of the objectives set out in the Treaty."[9]

It would be wrong however to conclude from this that subsidiarity comprises *mere guidelines*, and that subsidiarity amounts to a kind of non-justiciable constitutional convention. The Final point in the Protocol states "Compliance with the principle of subsidiarity shall be reviewed in accordance with the rules laid down by the Treaty," and this is clearly correct in principle. But in what circumstances might such review be exercised in practice? It would certainly be difficult to sustain a challenge to a Community act simply on the broad basis that, nothwithstanding the fact that the act fell within Community competence, the Community institutions had nevertheless so clearly exceeded their discretion in concluding that the objectives of the proposed action could not sufficiently achieved by the Member States that the Court should intervene and annul the act. But more precise legal objections based on failure to respect the requirements of subsidiarity might well have more success. The text of Article 5, and the Protocol on the application of the principles of subsidiarity and proportionality, indicate that the Community institutions are bound to address a number of legal and factual matters before exercising or purporting to exercise their powers under the Treaty.[10] If the Institutions make an error of law or fact,[11] or fail to address an essential matter,[12] this would on the face of it and in accordance with the general principles of judicial review of Community acts appear to provide the basis for an action for annulment, making full allowance for the fact that the Community institutions enjoy wide discretionary powers which correspond with their political responsibilities, and that the European Court would not intervene

---

[9] Point (3), first sentence.

[10] The relevant matters of law and fact were set out in some detail in the the Edinburgh guidelines, E.C. Bull 12, 1992 pp. 9 *et seq.*; and are currently given the force of law by the Protocol on Subsidiarity and Proportionality.

[11] On these general principles of judicial review. see *e.g.*, Case 201/87 *Cargill* [1989] E.C.R. 489; Cases 106 and 107/63 *Töpfer* [1965] E.C.R. 405; [1966] C.M.L.R. 111; Case 62/70 *Bock* [1971] E.C.R. 897; [1972] C.M.L.R. 160; Case 131/77 *Milac* [1978] E.C.R. 1041; [1979] 2 C.M.L.R. 257; Case C–331/88 *Fedesa* [1990] E.C.R. I–4023; [1991] 1 C.M.L.R. 507.

[12] For the duty to take into consideration essential matters, see Case 191/82 *EEC Seed Crushers' and Oil Processors' Federation (FEDIOL) v. Commission* [1983] E.C.R. 2913, at para. 30; [1984] 3 C.M.L.R. 244.

unless any errors were manifest.[13] Furthermore, lack of reasoning as regards subsidiarity could in an appropriate case provide grounds for annulment, even though an express reference to subsidiarity cannot be required.[14]

In principle, subsidiarity might seem relevant to the interpretation of Community acts; at any rate Community acts adopted after the principle took effect within the Community legal order.[15] Since the Community institutions take account of the principle in framing Community legislation, it would seem logical to apply the principle in interpreting that legislation. Furthermore, if two interpretations are possible, one consistent with subsidiarity, and the other not, one would expect the Court to prefer the former—that is the normal approach of the Court where there is a risk of conflict between a provision of a Community act and a general principle of law.[16] In *Fantask* Advocate General Jacobs appears to reject in principle the argument that a directive should be interpreted in light of this principle, as follows:

"In that regard the Danish Government's reference to the principle of subsidiarity in Article 3b of the Treaty, inserted by Article G(5) of the Treaty on European Union, is inapposite. Notwithstanding that provision, where the Community has chosen to adopt a directive in an area not falling within its exclusive competence the Court must interpret it in accordance with its wording and aims and in a manner which will ensure that it is effective."[17]

This observation might suggest that subsidiarity is only concerned with the decision whether or not to adopt a directive in the first place, though it might be possible that a provision of a directive could be capable of more than one interpretation, each in accordance with its wording and aims, but with one possible interpretation being more conducive to respect for the principle of subsidiarity than the other or others. Advocate General Alber in *SPAR Österreichische Warenhandels AG* implies that subsidiarity is relevant to the interpretation of the directive under consideration.[18] It seems that the Commission takes into account subsidiarity along with the other circumstances of the case when deciding whether to dismiss a complaint for want of sufficient Community interest; this is surely correct in principle.[19]

---

[13] Where the Community institutions enjoy a wide discretion, the Court will not intervene unless an error is manifest, see, *e.g.* Case 11/82 *S.A. Piraiki-Patraiki and others v. Comission* [1985] E.C.R. 207 at para. 40; [1985] 2 C.M.L.R. 4. See Wyatt "Subsidiarity and Judicial Review," in *Judicial Review in European Union Law* (2000) Vol. I, p. 505 (O'Keeffe ed., Kluwer, The Hague).

[14] Case C–233/94 *Federal Republic of Germany v. European Parliament and Council of the European Union* [1997] E.C.R. I–2405, para. 28; [1997] 3 C.M.L.R. 1375.

[15] Art. 5 (ex 3b) E.C. cannot have retroactive effect, see Joined Cases C–36–37/97 *Hilmar Kellinghusen v. Amt für Land- und Wasserwirtschaft Kiel* and *Ernst-Detlef Ketelsen v. Amt für Land- und Wasserwirtschaft Husum* [1998] E.C.R. I–6337, para. 35.

[16] See above, p. 131.

[17] Case C–188/95 *Fantask A/S e.a. v. Industriministeriet (Erhvervministeriet)*. [1997] E.C.R. I–6783, at para. 28 of the Opinion; [1998] 1 C.M.L.R. 473. The directive in any event predated the incorporation of subsidiarity into the Community legal order.

[18] Case C–318/96 *SPAR Österreichische Warenhandels AG v. Finanzlandesdirektion für Salzburg* [1998] E.C.R. I–785, at para. 59 of his Opinion.

[19] Case T–5/93 *Roger Tremblay and François Lucazeau and Harry Kestenberg v. Commission of the European Communities* [1995] E.C.R. II–185, para. 61; [1996] 4 C.M.L.R. 305.

PROPORTIONALITY

The principle of proportionality, shortly stated, holds that "the individual should not have his freedom of action limited beyond the degree necessary for the public interest".[20] With the entry into force of the Maastricht Treaty, proportionality, long recognised by the case-law of the Court as a general principle of Community law, was incorporated in an express provision of the E.C. Treaty. Article 5 (ex 3b), which states that the Community shall take action in accordance with the principle of subsidiarity, adds that: "Any action by the Community shall not go beyond what is necessary to achieve the objectives of this Treaty." Even prior to this the principle found some expression in the express words of the Treaty, but only in specific contexts. Thus, for example, the Treaty has always provided, in connection with the establishment of a common organisation of agricultural markets, that such common organisation may include all measures *required* to attain the objectives specified by the Treaty[21]; and the provision made for the harmonisation of indirect taxation is provision for "such harmonisation as is *necessary* to ensure the establishment and the functioning of the internal market . . .".[22] The principle has been expressed in more than one way by the Court. One more or less standard formulation is as follows:

"In order to establish whether a provision of Community law is consonant with the principle of proportionality it is necessary to establish, in the first place, whether the means it employs to achieve the aim correspond to the importance of the aim, and, in the second place, whether they are necessary for its achievement."[23]

A somewhat fuller formulation of the principle is to the effect that:

". . . the principle of proportionality, which is one of the general principles of Community law, requires that measures adopted by Community institutions do not exceed the limits of what is appropriate and necessary in order to attain the objectives legitimately pursued by the legislation in question; when there is a choice between several appropriate measures recourse must be had to the least onerous, and the disadvantages caused must not be disproportionate to the aims pursued . . ."[24]

The principle has operated *inter alia* to invalidate a provision of a regulation providing for the forfeiture of a security for any failure to perform a

---

[20] Case 11/70 *Internationale Handelsgesellschaft* [1970] E.C.R. 1125 at 1127; [1972] C.M.L.R. 255, *per* Advocate General Dutheillet de Lamothe.

[21] Art. 40(3) now Art. 34(2) E.C.

[22] Art. 93 (ex 99) E.C.

[23] Case 66/82 *Fromancais* [1983] E.C.R. 395, at para. 8; [1983] 3 C.M.L.R. 453; Case C–369/95 *Somalfruit SpA, Camar SpA v. Ministero delle Finanze, Ministerio del Commercio con l'Estero* [1997] E.C.R. I–6619.

[24] Case C–157/96 *R. v. Minister of Agriculture, Fisheries and Food and Another ex p. National Farmers' Union and Others* [1998] E.C.R. I–2211, para. 60; [1998] 2 C.M.L.R. 1125; Case C–375/96 *Galileo Zaninotto v. Ispettorato Centrale Repressione Frodi—Ufficio di Conegliano—Ministero delle Risorse Agricole, Alimentari e Forestali* [1998] E.C.R. I–6629, para. 63.

contractual undertaking, irrespective of the gravity of the breach.[25] The Court held that the:

> "Absolute nature . . . of the above-mentioned regulation is contrary to the principle of proportionality in that it does not permit the penalty for which it provides to be made commensurate with the degree of failure to implement the contractual obligations or with the seriousness of the breach of those obligations."[26]

Thus where Community legislation makes a distinction between a primary obligation (such as the export of a commodity from the Community), compliance with which is necessary in order to attain the objective sought, and a secondary obligation (such as the duty to apply for an export licence), essentially of an administrative nature, it cannot, without breaching the principle of proportionality, penalise failure to comply with the secondary obligation as severely as failure to comply with the primary obligation.[27] Penalties imposed to secure compliance with formalities relating to establishing a right of residence under Community law,[28] or providing evidence of entitlement to drive based on recognition of a valid driving licence issued in another Member State,[29] are also subject to scrutiny under the principle of proportionality.[30]

Where a Community Institution has a wide discretionary power, *e.g.* in the context of the common agricultural policy, the Court of Justice will only interfere if a measure is manifestly inappropriate having regard to the objective which the competent institution is seeking to pursue.[31]

As well as constituting a constraint upon Community legislative activities, the principle is resorted to in assessing the legitimacy of State action taken pursuant to Community rules. The principle applies in particular to State action in the context of those Treaty provisions allowing limited derogation from basic Treaty rules, such as Articles 30 (ex 36), 39(3) and (4) (ex 48(3) and (4)), 45 and 46 (ex 55 and 56).

Reference has been made to the Protocol on the application of the principles of subsidiarity and proportionality. Point 1 states that each institution shall ensure "compliance with the principle of proportionality, according to which action by the Community shall not go beyond what is necessary to achieve the objectives of the Treaty". Application of this principle to determine whether the scale of Community action contemplated is necessary to achieve the purpose of

---

[25] Case 240/78 *Atalanta* [1979] E.C.R. 2137.

[26] [1979] E.C.R. 2137 at 2151.

[27] Case 181/84 *R. v. Intervention Board for Sugar, ex p. Man (Sugar)* [1985] E.C.R. 2889, para. 20; [1985] 3 C.M.L.R. 759; Case 21/85 *Maas v. Bundesanstalt für Landwirtschaftliche Marktordnung* [1986] E.C.R. 3537, para. 15; [1987] 3 C.M.L.R. 794; Case C–161/96 *Südzucker Mannheim/Ochsenfurt AG v. Hauptzollamt Mannheim* [1998] E.C.R. I–281, para. 31.

[28] Case C–265/88 *Messner* [1989] E.C.R. 4209; [1991] 2 C.M.L.R. 545.

[29] Case C–193/94 *Criminal proceedings against Sofia Skanavi and Konstantin Chryssanthakopoulos* [1996] E.C.R. I–929, paras 35–38; [1996] 2 C.M.L.R. 372; [1996] All E.R. (E.C.) 435.

[30] See also Case C–29/95 *Pastoors* [1997] E.C.R. I–285; [1997] 2 C.M.L.R. 457 (higher penalty for non-resident permissible in principle but must not be disproportionately higher).

[31] Case 265/87 *Schrader* [1989] E.C.R. 2237, at paras 21, 22; Case 331/88 *ex p. Fedesa* [1990] E.C.R. I–4023, para. 14; Case C–375/96 *Galileo Zaninotto v. Ispettorato Centrale Repressione Frodi—Ufficio di Conegliano—Ministero delle risorse agricole, alimentari e forestali* [1998] E.C.R. I–6629, para. 64.

the draft legislation under consideration could in principle rule out the legislation in question, or have a significant limiting effect on its content, and provide the possibility of annulment if the Community legislator overstepped the mark. The point may be illustrated, hypothetically, by reference to the unfair contract terms directive.[32] The directive is an internal market measure based on Article 95 (ex 100a). The directive harmonises the laws of Member States as regards unfair terms in consumer contracts. The preamble indicates that one of the problems caused for the single market by the existence of different national rules on unfair consumer contracts is that consumers from one Member State may be deterred from purchasing goods and services in another Member State because they may be unaware of the rules of other Member States. If the foregoing—adverse effect on direct cross-border purchases—were regarded as the *only* mischief identified as flowing from the disparities between national rules referred to it, it might be said that the directive was disproportionate in regulating *all* consumer transactions, and that the aim of the directive could be achieved by laying down harmonised rules for cross-border transactions. While such questions involve large elements of policy, and a wide measure of discretion, it is not impossible to envisage the Court of Justice intervening in a case where there is a clear lack of proportion between the wide scope of Community legislation, and the relatively narrow ambit of the aim identified in the preamble of the measure in question.

LEGAL CERTAINTY AND LEGITIMATE EXPECTATION

The principle of legal certainty requires that those subject to the law should not be placed in a situation of uncertainty as to their rights and obligations. The related concept of legitimate expectation constitutes what has been described as a corollary[33] to this principle: those who act in good faith on the basis of the law as it is or as it seems to be should not be frustrated in their expectations.

The principle of legal certainty requires that Community rules must enable those concerned to know precisely the extent of the obligations which are imposed upon them.[34] In one case the Court appears to say that the latter principle requires that the Commission adhere to the interpretation of an E.C. Regulation which is dictated by the normal meaning of the words used, but it is certainly not an invariable principle of interpretation that the normal meaning be attributed to the words in a text.[35] Nevertheless, the Court of Justice in a consistent case-law has held that ambiguity or lack of clarity in measures alleged to impose charges should be resolved in favour of the taxpayer. In *Gondrand Frères* the Court declared:

---

[32] [1993] O.J. L95/29.

[33] Case C–63/93 *Duff and Others v. Minister for Agriculture and Food, Ireland, and the Attorney-General* [1996] E.C.R. I–569, para. 20; Case T–73/95 *Estabelecimentos Isidoro M. Oliveira SA v. Commission* [1997] E.C.R. II–381, para. 29.

[34] Case C–233/96 *Kingdom of Denmark v. Commission* [1998] E.C.R. I–5759, para. 38.

[35] *ibid.* In interpreting a provision of Community law it is necessary to consider not only its wording but also, where appropriate, the context in which it occurs and the objects of the rules of which it is part , see, in particular, Case C–340/94 *De Jaeck v. Staatssecretaris van Financiën* [1997] E.C.R. I–461, para. 17); [1997] 2 C.M.L.R. 779.

"The principle of legal certainty requires that rules imposing charges on the taxpayer must be clear and precise so that he may know without ambiguity what are his rights and obligations and may take steps accordingly."[36]

It seems, however, that rules may present some difficulties of interpretation, without thereby infringing the principle of legal certainty, at any rate where the difficulties result from the complexity of the subject matter, and where a careful reading of the rules in question by one professionally involved in the area allows the sense of the rules to be grasped.[37] The failure of the Commission to amend a regulation concerning tariff nomenclature where it was required to do so, and which resulted in uncertainty on the part of individuals as to their legal obligations, had the consequence that the regulation could not thereafter be applied.[38] The principle is capable of operating in favour of Member States, and a provision laying down a time-limit, particularly one which may have the effect of depriving a Member State of the payment of financial aid, its application for which has been approved and on the basis of which it has already incurred considerable expenditure, should be clearly and precisely drafted so that the Member States may be made fully aware of the importance of complying with the time-limit.[39]

The principle of legal certainty also applies when Member States adopt rules when required or authorised to do so pursuant to Community law. Thus Member States are bound to implement directives in a way which meets the requirements of clarity and certainty, by enacting appropriate national rules, and mere administrative practices will be inadequate for this purpose.[40] In *Raija-Liisa Jokela*, a case involving Finnish legislation adopted in accordance with an E.C. Regulation, the Court described the principle of legal certainty as requiring that "legal rules be clear and precise, and aims to ensure that situations and legal relationships governed by Community law remain foreseeable".[41]

The principle of legal certainty militates against administrative and legislative measures taking effect without adequate notice to persons concerned. As the Court declared in *Racke*:

"A fundamental principle in the Community legal order requires that a measure adopted by the public authorities shall not be applicable to those concerned before they have the opportunity to make themselves acquainted with it."[42]

---

[36] Case 169/80 [1981] E.C.R. 1931 at 1942. See also Case C–143/93 *Gebroeders van Es Douane Agenten BV v. Inspecteur der Invoerrechten en Accijnzen* [1996] E.C.R. I–431, para. 27; Case C–177/96 *Belgian State v. Banque Indosuez and Others and European Community* [1997] E.C.R. I–5659, para. 27; [1998] 1 C.M.L.R. 653. But where a regulation authorises the total or partial suspension of imports, a power to impose charges, as a less drastic measure, may be implied: Case 77/86 *ex p. National Dried Fruit Association* [1988] E.C.R. 757; [1988] 2 C.M.L.R. 195.

[37] Case C–354/95 *R. v. Minister of Agriculture, Fisheries and Food, ex p. National Farmers' Union and Others* [1997] E.C.R. I–4559, para. 57; [1998] 1 C.M.L.R. 195.

[38] C–143/93 *Gebroeders van Es Douane Agenten BV v. Inspecteur der Invoerrechten en Accijnzen* [1996] E.C.R. I–431.

[39] Case 44/81 *Commission v. Germany* [1982] E.C.R. 1855; [1983] 2 C.M.L.R. 656.

[40] Case 102/79 *Commission v. Belgium* [1980] E.C.R. 1473 at 1486; [1981] 1 C.M.L.R. 282. And see above, p. 89.

[41] Joined Cases C–9 and 118/97 [1998] E.C.R. I–6267, para. 48.

[42] Case 98/78 [1979] E.C.R. 69 at 84. And see Case 84/81 *Staple Dairy Products* [1982] E.C.R. 1763 at

This principle argues against the retroactive application of Community measures, and this is indeed the general principle, but it is not invariable. As the Court explained in *Decker*:

"Although in general the principle of legal certainty precludes a Community measure from taking effect from a point in time before its publication, it may exceptionally be otherwise where the purpose to be achieved so demands and where the legitimate expectations of those concerned are duly respected."[43]

Thus a public statement of intention to alter monetary compensatory amounts justifies a later regulation altering the rate retrospectively to the earlier date.[44]

The principle of legitimate expectation, which may be invoked as against Community rules only to the extent that the Community has previously created a situation which can give rise to a legitimate expectation,[45] operates in particular to protect individuals where they have acted in reliance upon measures taken by the Community institutions, as the *Mulder* case illustrates. In order to stabilise milk production, Community rules provided for dairy farmers to enter into non-marketing agreements for a period of five years, in return for which they received a money payment. In 1984 milk quotas were introduced, whereby milk producers would pay a super levy on milk produced in excess of a quota determined by reference to their production during the 1983 marketing year. No provision was made for the grant of quota to those who did not produce during 1983 because of the existence of a non-marketing agreement! Having been urged to suspend milk production under Community rules, farmers were then excluded from milk production when their non-marketing period came to an end. One such farmer challenged the regulations in this regard. The Court of Justice held that the relevant regulation was invalid to the extent that no provision for allocation of quota was made in such cases. The basis of the ruling was the principle of legitimate expectation. As the Court explained:

"where such a producer, as in the present case, has been encouraged by a Community measure to suspend marketing for a limited period in the general interest and against payment of a premium he may legitimately expect not to be subject, upon the expiry of his undertaking, to restrictions which specifically affect him because he availed himself of the possibilities offered by the Community provisions."[46]

1777; [1984] 1 C.M.L.R. 238; Case 108/81 *Amylum* [1982] E.C.R. 3107 at 3130. Case 77/71 *Gervais-Danone* [1971] E.C.R. 1127; [1973] C.M.L.R. 415; Case 158/78 *Biegi* [1979] E.C.R. 1103; Case 196/80 *Ango-Irish Meat* [1981] E.C.R. 2263. A regulation is deemd to be published throughout the Community on the date appearing on the issue of the *Official Journal* containing the text of the regulation, unless the date actual issue was later, Case C–337/88 *SAFA* [1990] E.C.R. I–1.

[43] Case 99/78 [1979] E.C.R. 101 at 111. See also Case 276/80 *Padana* [1982] E.C.R. 517 at 541; Case 258/80 *Runi* [1982] E.C.R. 487 at 503. Procedural rules are generally held to apply to all proceedings pending at the time when they enter into force, while substantive rules are usually interpreted as applying to situations existing before their entry into force only insofar as it clearly follows from the terms, objectives or general scheme that such an effect must be given to them: Joined Cases C212–217/80 *Salumi* [1981] E.C.R. 2735.

[44] Case 338/85 *Pardini* [1988] E.C.R. 2041 at paras 24–26.

[45] Case C–375/96 *Galileo Zaninotto v. Ispettorato Centrale Repressione Frodi—Ufficio di Conegliano—Ministero delle risorse agricole, alimentari e forestali* [1998] E.C.R. I–6629, para. 50.

[46] Case 120/86 [1988] E.C.R. 2321, para. 24; [1989] 2 C.M.L.R. 1. For a survey of the case-law of the Court see Sharpston, "Legitimate Expectation and Economic Reality" (1990) 15 E.L. Rev. 103.

On the basis of the same principle, if an undertaking purchases grain for denaturing with a view to qualifying for a Community subsidy, it is not permissible to discontinue or reduce the subsidy without giving the interested party a reasonable opportunity of denaturing the grain in question at the old rate.[47] Again, if the Community induces prudent traders to omit to cover their transactions against exchange risk, by establishing a system of compensatory amounts which in practice eliminate such risks, it must not withdraw such payments with immediate effect, without providing appropriate transitional measures.[48] Similar reasoning protected certain former Community officials in receipt of pensions which had increased in value over a number of years as a result of the Council's failure to adjust the exchange rates used to calculate the amounts due. The Council sought to rectify the situation and phase out the advantages which had accrued, over a ten month period. The Court held that respect for the legitimate expectations of those concerned required a transitional period twice as long as that laid down by the Council.[49] And if the Commission brings about a situation of uncertainty for an individual, and the individual in consequence does not comply with certain requirements, the Commission may be precluded from relying upon those requirements without notifying the individual and clarifying the situation.[50]

Considerations of both legal certainty and legitimate expectation may argue in favour of modifying the temporal effects of judicial and administrative decisions which would normally apply with retroactive effect. It has already been note that in exceptional circumstances considerations of legal certainty may preclude the retroactive effect of a judgment of the Court of Justice concerning the direct effect of a provision of Community law.[51] Similar considerations explain Article 231 (ex 174) E.C., which allows the Court of Justice to determine which of the legal effects of a regulation declared to be void by the Court shall nevertheless be considered as definitive. The Court applies Article 231 by analogy to acts other than regulations and in preliminary rulings on invalidity under Article 234 (ex 177) E.C., denying retroactivity in appropriate cases to ensure legal certainty and respect for legitimate expectations. Thus in the *Simmenthal* case the Court annulled a Commission decision fixing the minimum selling prices for frozen beef put up for sale by intervention agencies. However, "for reasons of legal certainty and taking special account of the established rights of the participants in the invitation to tender whose tenders have been accepted" the Court ruled that the annulment must be restricted to the specific decision to reject the applicant's

---

[47] Case 78/74 *Deuka* [1975] E.C.R. 421; [1975] 2 C.M.L.R. 28; Case 5/75 *Deuka* [1975] E.C.R. 759.
[48] Case 74/74 *CNTA* [1975] E.C.R. 533; [1977] 1 C.M.L.R. 171; and prudent traders are deemed to know the contents of the *Official Journal*, see Case C–174/89 *Hoche* [1990] E.C.R. I–2681, at para. 35; [1991] 3 C.M.L.R. 343. But an overriding public interest may preclude transitional measures from being adopted in respect of situations which arose before the new rules came into force but which are still subject to change, Case 74/74 para. 44; Case 152/88 *Sofrimport* [1990] E.C.R. I–2477, paras 16 and 19; [1992] E.C.R. I–153.
[49] Case 127/80 *Grogan* [1982] E.C.R. 869; Case 164/80 *De Pasquale* [1982] E.C.R. 909; Case 167/80 *Curtis* [1982] E.C.R. 931.
[50] Case T–81/95 *Interhotel—Sociedade Internacional de Hotéis SARL v. Commission of the European Communities.* [1997] E.C.R. II–1265, paras 49–58.
[51] Above at p. 78.

tender which stemmed from the decision in question.[52] It is established that any Community institution which finds that a measure which it has just adopted is tainted by illegality has the right to withdraw it within a reasonable period, with retroactive effect, but that right may be restricted by the need to fulfil the legitimate expectations of a beneficiary of the measure, who has been led to rely on its legality.[53]

Respect for vested rights is itself an aspect of the principles of certainty and legitimate expectations. In *Rossi* the Court stressed that:

"The Community rules could not, in the absence of an express exception consistent with the aims of the Treaty, be applied in such as way as to deprive a migrant worker or his dependents of the benefit of a part of the legislation of a Member State."[54]

Yet traders may not rely upon legitimate expectations to insulate them from changes in legal regimes subject to constant adjustments. As the Court explained in *Eridania*, in the context of the common agricultural policy:

". . . an undertaking cannot claim a vested right to the maintenance of an advantage which is obtained from the establishment of a common organisation of the market and which it enjoyed at a given time."[55]

The Court has said on numerous occasions that a wrongful act on the part of the Commission or its officials, and likewise a practice of a Member State which does not conform with community rules, is not capable of giving rise to legitimate expectations on the part of an economic operator who benefits from the situation thereby created.[56] But it is possible that the broad scope of this proposition may be limited by the conclusion which is often drawn from it in the case-law to the effect that it follows that the principle of the protection of legitimate expectations cannot be relied upon against a *precise*[57] provision of Community law, or an *unambiguous*[58] provision of Community law. Another limitation on recourse to the principle of legitimate expectation is to the effect that "the principle of the protection of legitimate expectations may not be

---

[52] Case 92/78 [1979] E.C.R. 777, esp. 811; [1980] 1 C.M.L.R. 25.

[53] Case C–90/95P *Henri de Compte v. European Parliament* [1997] E.C.R. I–1999, at para. 35, and cases there cited.

[54] Case 100/78 [1979] E.C.R. 831 at 844; [1979] 3 C.M.L.R. 544.

[55] Case 230/78 [1979] E.C.R. 2749 at 2768. See also Case C–375/96 *Galileo Zaninotto v. Ispettorato Centrale Repressione Frodi—Ufficio di Conegliano—Ministero delle risorse agricole, alimentari e forestali* [1998] E.C.R. I–6629, para. 50 (common agricultural policy). The same principle has been stated in the context of the common commercial policy; Case C–284/94 *Kingdom of Spain v. Council* [1998] E.C.R. I–7309 at para. 43.

[56] Case 188/82 *Thyssen* [1983] E.C.R. 3721; Case 5/82 *Maizena* [1982] E.C.R. 4601 at 4615; Case 316/86 *Hauptzollamt Hamburg-Jonas v. Firma P. Krücken* [1988] E.C.R. 2213, at 2239; Joined Cases C–31/91 to C–44/91 *SpA Alois Lageder and others v. Amministrazione delle Finanze dello Stato* [1993] E.C.R. I–1761, para. 34; Case T– 336/94 *Efisol SA v. Commission* [1996] E.C.R. II–1343, para. 36; [1997] 3 C.M.L.R. 298.

[57] Case 316/86 *Firma P. Krücken*, n.33.

[58] Joined Cases C31–44/91 *SpA Alois Lageder and others*, n.33, at para. 35.

relied upon by an undertaking which has committed a manifest infringement of the rules in force".[59]

Where Community or national subsidies are paid to undertakings in contravention of Community law, the principle of legitimate expectation may preclude recovery.[60] This will not be the case, however, where a beneficiary was in a position to appreciate that state aid was paid contrary to mandatory provisions of Community law.[61] Circumstances in which legitimate expectations may preclude recovery of state aid include long delay on the part of the Commission in taking a decision, and aid comprising measures which do not self-evidently constitute state aid and which could not readily be identified as such by the beneficiary.[62]

NON-DISCRIMINATION

A further principle binding upon the Community in its administrative and legislative activities is that prohibiting discrimination, whereby comparable situations must not be treated differently, and different situations must not be treated in the same way, unless such treatment is objectively justified.[63]

The principle is applied in the relationships between the Community institutions and its officials. As the Court stated in the *Ferrario* case:

"According to the Court's consistent case-law the general principle of equality is one of the fundamental principles of the law of the Community civil service."[64]

On this basis in *Sabbatini* and *Airola* the Court invalidated differentiation between Community officials on grounds of sex in the payment of expatriation allowances.[65] And in *Noonan* the Court said that it would only be lawful to treat candidates with a university qualification differently to those who had none where there were essential differences between the situations in law and in fact of the two categories.[66] However, the Community cannot be called to account for inequality in the treatment of its officials for which it is not itself responsible. In *Sorasio* it was alleged that a Community dependent child tax allowance paid only

---

[59] Case 67/84 *Sideradria v. Commission* [1985] E.C.R. 3983, para. 21; Joined Cases T–551/93, 231/94, 233–234/94 *Industria Pesdquera Campos and Others* v. *Commission* [1996] E.C.R. II–247, para. 76; Case T–73/95 *Estabelecimentos Isidoro M. Oliveira SA v. Commission* [1997] E.C.R. II–381, para 28.

[60] Joined Cases C205–215/82 *Deutsche Milchkontor GmbH and others v. Federal Republic of Germany* [1983] E.C.R. 2633, paras 30–33; [1984] 3 C.M.L.R. 586; Case 5/89 *Commission* v *Federal Republic of Germany* [1990] E.C.R. I–3437, paras 13–16; [1992] 1 C.M.L.R. 117.

[61] Case 5/89 *Germany*, n.58.

[62] Case 223/85 *Rijn-Schelde-Verolme (RSV) Machinefabrieken en Scheepswerven NV v. Commission* [1987] E.C.R. 4617; [1989] 2 C.M.L.R. 259; Case C–39/94 *Syndicat Français de l'Express International (SFEI) and Others v. La Poste and Others* [1996] E.C.R. I–3547, at para. 70, and paras 73–77 of the Advocate General's Opinion; [1996] 3 C.M.L.R. 369.

[63] Case 106/83 *Sermide* [1984] E.C.R. 4209 at para. 28; and a consistent case-law, see, *e.g.* Case C–354/95 *R. v. Minister for Agriculture, Fisheries and Food, ex p. National Farmers' Union and Others* [1997] E.C.R. I–4559 at para. 61; [1998] 1 C.M.L.R. 195.

[64] Joined Cases 152 etc. 81 [1983] E.C.R. 2357 at 2367.

[65] Case 20/71 *Sabbatini* [1972] E.C.R. 345; [1972] C.M.L.R. 945; Case 21/74 *Airola* [1972] E.C.R. 221; see also *Razzouk and Beydoun* [1984] E.C.R. 1509; [1984] 3 C.M.L.R. 470.

[66] Case T–60/92 *Noonan v. Commission* [1996] E.C.R. II–215, para. 32.

once in respect of each child, even where both parents were employed by the Community, was contrary to the principle of equality, since it did not take into account tax allowances which might be claimed by a spouse who did not work for the Community, under national law. The Court rejected this argument:

"The principle of equality does not require account to be taken of possible inequalities which may become apparent because the Community and national systems overlap."[67]

The principle of non-discrimination provides a basis for the judicial review of measures adopted by the Community in all it various activities. Thus the Court has invalidated a Regulation which provided substantially more severe criteria for the determination of the origin of cotton yarn than for the determination of the origin of cloth and fabrics.[68] The Court has also required consistency in the Commission's policy of imposing fines upon undertakings for the infringement of production quotas for steel.[69]

The principle of non-discrimination has been held to add a gloss to Article 34(2) (ex 40(3)) E.C., which provides that the common organisations of the agricultural markets "shall exclude any discrimination between producers or consumers within the Community". In *Codorniu* the Court held the foregoing principle includes the prohibition of discrimination on grounds of nationality laid down in the first paragraph of Article 12 (ex 6) E.C.,[70] which states that "[w]ithin the scope of application of this Treaty, and without prejudice to any special provisions contained therein, any discrimination on grounds of nationality shall be prohibited."[71] In *Ruckdeschel*[72] and *Moulins*[73] proceedings arose from challenges in national courts to the validity of the Council's action in abolishing production refunds on maize used to make quellmehl and gritz, while continuing to pay refunds on maize used to make starch, a product in competition with both quellmehl and gritz. Producers of the latter product argued that they had been placed at a competitive disadvantage by the Council's discriminatory, and hence unlawful, action. Their pleas were upheld. Referring to Article 40(3) (now 34(2)) E.C., the Court observed:

"While this wording undoubtedly prohibits any discrimination between producers of the same product it does not refer in such clear terms to the relationship between different industrial or trade sectors in the sphere of

---

[67] [1980] E.C.R. 3557 at 3572.

[68] Case 162/82 *Cousin* [1983] E.C.R. 1101.

[69] Case 234/82 *Ferriere di roe Volciano* [1983] E.C.R. 3921.

[70] Case C–309/89 *Codorníu SA v. Council of the European Union* [1994] E.C.R. I–1853, para. 26; [1995] 2 C.M.L.R. 561.

[71] The reference to "without prejudice to any special provisions contained therein" refers particularly to other provisions of the Treaty in which the application of the general principle of non-discrimination on grounds of nationality is given concrete form in respect of specific situations, such as free movement of workers, the right of establishment and the freedom to provide services, see Case C–186/87 *Cowan v. Trésor public* [1989] E.C.R. 195 at para. 14; [1990] 2 C.M.L.R. 613. Art. 12 (ex 6) E.C. "applies independently only to situations governed by Community law in regard to which the Treaty lays down no specific prohibition of discrimination," see Case 305/87 *Commission v. Greece* [1989] E.C.R. 1461 at para. 13; [1991] 1 C.M.L.R. 611.

[72] Cases 117/76 and 16/77 [1977] E.C.R. 1753; [1979] 2 C.M.L.R. 445.

[73] Cases 124/76 and 20/77 [1977] E.C.R. 1795; [1979] 2 C.M.L.R. 445.

processed agricultural products. This does not alter the fact that the prohibition of discrimination laid down in the aforesaid provision is merely a specific enunciation of the general principle of equality which is one of the fundamental principles of Community law. This principle requires that similar situations shall not be treated differently unless differentiation is objectively justified."[74]

The *Wagner* case[75] affords a helpful illustration of objective criteria justifying differentiation between apparently similar situations. Community rules provided for reimbursement of storage costs in respect of sugar in transit between two approved warehouses situated in the same Member State, but not in respect of sugar in transit between two approved warehouses in different Member States. The Court rejected the argument that this was discriminatory, since the difference in treatment was based on requirements of supervision which could be objectively justified. The Court's ruling is a reminder that the principle of non-discrimination is only infringed by differences in treatment where the Community legislator treats *comparable* situations in different ways.[76] It follows that an allegation of discrimination cannot be based on differences in treatment of products subject to different market organisations which are not in competition with each other.[77]

The principle whereby Community rules may treat differently apparently similar situations where objective justification exists for such differentiation allows a challenge to the validity of the rules in question once the circumstances constituting objective justification have ceased to obtain.[78] Pending such challenge the Community institutions are bound to continue to apply the measure in question.[79] But it would seem to follow that even in the absence of a challenge, the Community institutions are bound to take steps to amend the rules in question.

The principle of non-discrimination has also been invoked in the budgetary context,[80] and the "equality of states" has been resorted to as a general principle of the interpretation of the Treaties.[81]

FUNDAMENTAL RIGHTS

Unlike the abortive Treaty for the establishment of a European Political Community, which provided explicitly for the application of Section I of the

---

[74] [1977] E.C.R. 1753 at 1769; [1977] E.C.R. 1795 at 1811. And see Case 300/86 *Landschoot v. Mera* [1988] E.C.R. 3443; Case C–37/89 *Weiser* [1990] E.C.R. I–2395; Case C–2/92 *Bostock* [1994] E.C.R. I–955, para. 23; [1994] 3 C.M.L.R. 547. The principle applies as between identical or comparable situations, Case T–48/89 *Beltrante* [1990] E.C.R. II–493 at para. 34.

[75] Case 8/82 [1983] E.C.R. 371.

[76] See, *e.g.* Case 6/71 *Rheinmühlen Düsseldorf* [1971] E.C.R. 823; [1972] C.M.L.R. 401; Case 283/83 *Racke* [1984] E.C.R. 3791.

[77] Joined Cases 292–293/81 *Jean Lion* [1982] E.C.R. 3887.

[78] Joined Case T–177 and 377/94 *Henk Altmann and Margaret Casson v. Commission* [1996] E.C.R. II–2041, paras 121–123.

[79] *ibid.*

[80] Case 265/78 *Ferwerda* [1980] E.C.R. 617; [1980] 3 C.M.L.R. 737.

[81] Case 128/78 *Commission v. United Kingdom* [1979] E.C.R. 419; [1979] 2 C.M.L.R. 45; Case 231/78 *Commission v. United Kingdom* [1979] E.C.R. 1447 at 1462; [1979] 2 C.M.L.R. 427.

European Convention on Human Rights,[82] the EEC Treaty made no provision for the protection of human rights as such. Nevertheless, the Court of Justice soon made it clear that fundamental rights were implicitly recognised by Community law, and that they were capable of limiting the competence of the Community. Thus in *Stauder v. City of Ulm*[83] the Court was asked by a German court whether a Commission Decision which conditioned the distribution of butter at reduced prices on the disclosure of the name of the recipient was compatible "with the general principles of Community law in force". The Court replied that on its true construction the Decision in question did not require the disclosure of the names of beneficiaries to retailers, and added that: "Interpreted in this way the provision at issue contains nothing capable of prejudicing the fundamental rights . . . protected by the Court."[84] The existence of fundamental rights as general principles of Community law was confirmed in the *Internationale Handelsgesellschaft* case, in which the Court stated:

"In fact, respect for fundamental rights forms an integral part of the general principles of law protected by the Court of Justice. The protection of such rights, whilst inspired by the constitutional traditions common to the Member States, must be ensured within the framework of the structure and objectives of the Community."[85]

If *Stauder* confirmed the existence of fundamental rights in Community law, and *International Handelsgesellschaft* identified their primary source as the national constitutional traditions of the Member States, *Nold v. Commission* introduced a further source which was to prove of crucial importance: "international treaties for the protection of human rights on which the Member States have collaborated or of which they are signatories".[86] It was always clear that of the treaties referred to the European Convention on Human Rights was of special significance in this respect, and the Court has said as much in a consistent case-law.[87]

The Court's case-law was endorsed by the Parliament, the Council and the Commission in their Joint Declaration of April 5, 1977.[88] Treaty endorsement came later. Article F(2) of the Treaty on European Union provided that the Union shall respect fundamental rights, as guaranteed by the European Convention and as they result from the constitutional traditions common to the Member States, as general principles of Community law. The latter provision appeared in Title I of the Union Treaty and under Article L it therefore did not fall within the jurisdiction of the Court of Justice. The Amsterdam amendments to the

---

[82] One of the initiatives which predated the EEC Treaty but which failed to secure the support of all potential signatories.

[83] Case 29/69 [1969] E.C.R. 419; [1970] C.M.L.R. 112.

[84] Para. 7.

[85] Case 11/70 [1970] E.C.R. 1125 at para. 4; [1972] C.M.L.R. 255.

[86] Case 4/73 [1974] E.C.R. 491, para. 13; [1974] 2 C.M.L.R. 338.

[87] Case 222/84 *Johnston v. Royal Ulster Constabulary* [1986] E.C.R. 1651, para. 18; [1986] 3 C.M.L.R. 240; Case C–260/89 *Elliniki Radiophonia Tiléorassi AE (ERT) v. Dimotiki Etairia Pliroforissis and others* [1991] E.C.R. I–2925, para. 41; [1994] 4 C.M.L.R. 540; Opinion 2/94 [1996] E.C.R. I–1759, para. 33; Case C–299/95 *Kremzow v. Austria* [1997] E.C.R. I–2629, para. 14; [1997] 3 C.M.L.R. 1289.

[88] [1977] O.J. C103/1.

Treaty on European Union came into effect on May 1, 1999. Article 6(2) is in identical terms to Article F(2). And Article 46, which replaces Article L, provides that the Court's jurisdiction extends to "Article 6(2) with regard to action of the institutions, insofar as the Court has jurisdiction under the Treaties establishing the European Communities and under this Treaty".

It was in any event established from the protection accorded by the Court for fundamental rights that respect for such rights is a condition of the legality of Community acts,[89] and that fundamental rights must also be respected by Member States when they implement Community measures.[90]

The Court has referred to specific provisions of the European Convention on Human Rights (or its First Protocol) in a number of judgments. In *Hauer*[91] the Court held that the right to property is guaranteed in the Community legal order in accordance with the ideas common to the constitutions of the Member States, which are reflected in the First Protocol to the European Convention on Human Rights. However, the Court upheld a Community-imposed restriction on the planting of vines as constituting a legitimate exception to the principle of a type recognised in the constitutional systems of the Member States.[92] The Court has denied that a guarantee afforded to the ownership of property can be extended to protect commercial interests, the uncertainties of which are part of the very essence of economic activity.[93] In *National Panasonic*[94] the Court relied upon an exception to the guarantee of respect for private and family life to be found in Article 8 of the European Convention on Human Rights, in considering the scope of the investigative powers of the Commission under Regulation 17.[95] In *Dow Benelux* the Court held that Article 8 of the Convention applied in Community law to protect the private dwellings of natural persons rather than the premises of undertakings. Nevertheless, investigative powers of the Commission were subject to the principle of proportionality.[96] In *Kirk* the Court held that the retroactivity of a Community regulation could not have the effect of validating after the event national measures of a penal nature which imposed penalties for an act which was not punishable at the time it was committed. The Court declared:

"The principle that penal provisions may not have retroactive effect is one which is common to all the legal orders of the Member States and is enshrined in Article 7 of the European Convention . . . as a fundamental right; it takes its place among the general principles of law whose observance is ensured by the Court of Justice."[97]

---

[89] Opinion 2/94, n.88, para. 34.
[90] Case 5/88 *Wachauf* [1989] E.C.R. 2609, para. 19; [1991] 1 C.M.L.R. 328; Case C–351/92 *Manfred Graff v. Hauptzollamt Köln Rheinau* [1994] E.C.R. I–3361, para. 17.
[91] Case 44/79 [1979] E.C.R. 3727; [1980] 3 C.M.L.R. 42.
[92] [1979] E.C.R. 3727 at 3747.
[93] Case 4/73 *Nold* [1974] E.C.R. 491; [1974] 2 C.M.L.R. 338; Cases 154 etc. 78, and 39 etc. 79 *Valsabbia* [1980] E.C.R. 907; [1981] 1 C.M.L.R. 613.
[94] Case 136/79 [1980] E.C.R. 2033 at 2057; [1980] 3 C.M.L.R. 169.
[95] As to which see below, p. 626.
[96] Case 85/87 [1989] E.C.R. 3137 at paras 28–30.
[97] [1984] E.C.R. 2689 at 2718.

Article 6(1) of the European Convention on Human Rights provides that in the determination of his civil rights and obligations or of any criminal charge against him, everyone is entitled to a fair and public hearing within a reasonable time by an independent and impartial tribunal established by law. Whether this provision is as such applicable to administrative proceedings before the Commission relating to competition policy or not, it is a general principle of Community law that the Commission must act within a reasonable time in adopting decisions following administrative proceedings relating to competition policy and state aids.[98] A similar principle governs the proceedings of the Court of First Instance when it reviews decisions of the Commission on competition matters, and the Court of Justice will secure enforcement of this principle through the appeals procedure. As the Court explained in *Baustahlgewebe GmbH v. Commission*, having referred to Article 6(1) of the European Convention:

"The general principle of Community law that everyone is entitled to fair legal process, which is inspired by those fundamental rights . . . and in particular the right to legal process within a reasonable period, is applicable in the context of proceedings brought against a Commission decision imposing fines on an undertaking for infringement of competition law. It is thus for the Court of Justice, in an appeal, to consider pleas on such matters concerning the proceedings before the Court of First Instance."[99]

The duration of the proceedings being considered by the Court of Justice was approximately five years and six months.[1] The Court noted that such a duration was, at first sight considerable, but added that the reasonableness of such a period must be appraised in the light of the circumstances specific to each case and, in particular, the importance of the case for the person concerned, its complexity and the conduct of the applicant and of the competent authorities; these criteria were derived from judgments of the European Court of Human Rights, to which the Court referred by way of analogy.[2] The Court noted in particular: that the appellant had not contributed in any significant way to the protraction of the proceedings[3]; that about 32 months had elapsed between the end of the written procedure and the decision to open the oral procedure; and that about 22 months had elapsed between the close of the oral procedure and the delivery of the judgment of the Court of First Instance.[4] The Court of Justice held that the proceedings before the Court of First Instance did not satisfy the requirements concerning completion within a reasonable time[4] Having regard to all the circumstances of the case, the Court held that a sum of ECU 50,000 constituted reasonable satisfaction for the excessive duration of the proceedings, and the latter sum was deducted from the ECU 3,000,000 fine determined

---

[98] Joined Cases T–213/95 and 18/96 *SCK, FNK v. Commission* [1997] E.C.R. II–1739, para. 56; [1998] 4 C.M.L.R. 259.

[99] Case C–185/95P [1998] E.C.R. I–8417, paras 20–22; [1995] 5 C.M.L.R. 239.

[1] Para. 28.

[2] Para. 29.

[3] Para. 40.

[4] Para. 45.

[5] Para. 47.

by the Court of First Instance.[6] This judgment amounts to a public reprimand of the Court of First Instance and sends a strong signal that the European Court has no intention of allowing the Community Courts in future to fall short of the standards which they are charged with upholding.

It has already been noted that fundamental rights must be respected by the Member States when they implement Community measures. Thus, for example, measures taken by Member States in reliance upon the derogations to be found in Article 30 (ex 36) E.C. on the free movement of goods,[7] Article 39(3) (ex 48(3)) E.C. on the free movement of workers,[8] and Articles 46 (ex 56) and 55 (ex 66), on freedom to provide services,[9] must comply with fundamental rights. An instructive example of the applicability of general principles of Community law to national authorities when they implement Community rules is to be found in the *Wachauf* case.[10] Under Community regulations concerned with milk quotas it was provided that the milk quota should be transferred when the holding to which the quota related was transferred. A producer acquired a quota in the first place by virtue of his having produced milk during the applicable reference year. The issue in *Wachauf* was whether a transfer of quota from lessee to lessor on the expiry of the lease in accordance with the applicable regulation would be consistent with the general principles of Community law where it had been the lessee's milk production which had secured entitlement to the milk quota. The Court of Justice referred to the *Hauer* case to support applicability of fundamental rights in the Community system, subject to such proportionate restrictions as might be imposed in the general interest. The Court stated:

> "Having regard to those criteria, it must be observed that Community rules which, upon the expiry of the lease, had the effect of depriving the lessee, without compensation, of the fruits of his labour and of his investments in the tenanted holding would be incompatible with the requirements of the protection of fundamental rights in the Community legal order. Since those requirements are also binding on the Member States when they implement Community rules, the Member States must, as far as possible, apply those rules in accordance with those requirements."[11]

OTHER GENERAL PRINCIPLES

The Court of Justice has developed a number of other general principles of law and the categories of general principle do not appear to be closed. In

---

[6] Para. 141.

[7] Case C–368/95 *Vereinigte Familiapress Zeitungsverlags- und vertriebs GmbH v. Heinrich Bauer Verlag* [1997] E.C.R. I–3689, para. 24; [1997] 3 C.M.L.R. 1329.

[8] Case 36/75 *Rutili v. French Minister of the Interior* [1975] E.C.R. 1219; [1976] 1 C.M.L.R. 140.

[9] Case C–260/89 *Elliniki Radiophonia Tiléorassi AE (ERT) v. Dimotiki Etairia Pliroforissis and Others* [1991] E.C.R. I–2925, para. 42; [1994] 4 C.M.L.R. 540.

[10] Case 5/88 [1989] E.C.R. 2609; [1991] 1 C.M.L.R. 328.

[11] [1989] E.C.R. 2609, para. 19. See also Case C–2/92 *Bostock* [1994] E.C.R. I–955; [1994] 3 C.M.L.R. 547; and Case C–351/92 *Manfred Graff v. Hauptzollamt Köln Rheinau* [1994] E.C.R. I–3361.

Transocean Marine Paint[12] the Court invoked the general principle that a person whose interests are affected by a decision taken by a public authority must be given an opportunity to make his point of view known. In *Eyckeler & Malt AG* the Court of First Instance referred to respect for the rights of the defence as a fundamental principle of Community law which must be guaranteed, even in the absence of any rules governing the procedure in question, and held that the principle required not only that the person concerned should be placed in a position in which he may effectively make known his views on the relevant circumstances, but also that he should at least be able to put his own case on the documents taken into account by the decision-making authority.[13] Not all determinations are subject to these principles however. Thus the right to a fair hearing does not extend to the work of a Medical Committee engaged in the medical appraisal of an individual.[14]

The right to be assisted by counsel has been recognised by the Court as a general principle of law. In *Demont*,[15] a staff case, the Court held that the refusal of the Commission to allow the applicant's counsel, as well as the applicant, access to the disciplinary file in the course of proceedings which resulted in a disciplinary measure being taken, amounted to a breach of a fundamental legal principle which the Court would uphold. The Court emphasised that respect for the rights of the defence was all the more important when the disciplinary proceedings were likely to result in particularly severe disciplinary measures.[16]

In its famous *A.M.& S* ruling the Court held that Article 14 of Regulation 17,[17] empowering the Commission to require the production of the business records of an undertaking, was subject to the principle that the confidentiality of certain communications between a lawyer and his client was to be protected.[18] In the *Orkem* case, however, the Court refused to accept that the right normally recognised in a natural person not to incriminate himself extends to a legal person in relation to infringements of competition law.[19]

The Court has recognised that the right to exercise an economic activity is one of the general principles of Community law, subject to those limitations on the exercise of that right which may be justified in the general interest.[20]

---

[12] Case 17/74 [1974] E.C.R. 1063; [1974] 2 C.M.L.R. 459. See also Case 264/82 *Timex* [1985] E.C.R. 849; [1985] 3 C.M.L.R. 550; Case 85/87 *Dow Benelux* [1989] E.C.R. 3137; Case C–49/88 *Al-Jubail Fertiliser* [1991] E.C.R. I–3187; [1991] 3 C.M.L.R. 377. The principle may be invoked by a Member State as well as by an individual, see Case 259/85 *France v. Commission* [1987] E.C.R. 4393; [1989] 2 C.M.L.R. 30.

[13] Case T–42/96 [1998] E.C.R. II–401, paras 76–80. But there is no right to be heard in a legislative process, see Case T–521/93 *Atlanta AG and Others* [1996] E.C.R. II–1707, para. 70.

[14] Case T–154/89 *Vidrányi* [1990] E.C.R. II–455.

[15] Case 115/80 [1981] E.C.R. 3147.

[16] [1981] E.C.R. 3147 at 3158.

[17] Reg. 17 deals with the power of the Commission to establish violations of Arts 81 and 82 E.C. (ex. 85 and 86), see below, p. 626.

[18] Communications between a lawyer and his client are protected providing they are made for the purposes of and in the interests of the client's rights of defence, and that they emanate from independent lawyers, that is, lawyers who are not bound to the client by a relationship of employment.

[19] Case 374/87 [1989] E.C.R. 3283 at paras 28, 29.

[20] Case 234/85 *Keller* [1986] E.C.R. 2897; [1987] 1 C.M.L.R. 875; Case C–370/88 *Marshall* [1990] E.C.R. I–4071; [1991] 1 C.M.L.R. 419; Case T–521/93 *Atlanta AG and Others* [1996] E.C.R. II–1707, para. 62.

The principle of "good administration" or "sound administration" is often invoked before and by the Courts. On one occasion the Court has referred to the duty to allow a person the right to be heard as "a general principle of good administration",[21] but the principle does more than describe other principles. For example, in the *Lucchini* case the Court stigmatised the failure to respond to a communication as a "neglect of the rules of good administration" and reduced a fine accordingly.[22] In the context of a procedure to investigate the compatibility of a proposed state aid with the common market, the Court of First Instance said that "the interests of legal certainty and sound administration require the Commission to be aware, as far as possible, of the particular circumstances of every trader who considers himself injured by the grant of aid proposed."[23]

A further principle which has been invoked by the Court as a guide to the construction of secondary legislation is that of Community preference.[24]

---

[21] Joined Cases 33 and 75/79 *Kuhner* [1980] E.C.R. 1677 at 1698.
[22] Case 179/82 [1983] E.C.R. 3083 at 3095.
[23] Case T–11/95 *BP Chemicals Limited v. Commission* [1998] E.C.R. II–1707, para. 75.
[24] Case 6/78 *Union Française* [1978] E.C.R. 1675.

CHAPTER 7

CONSERVATORY PRINCIPLES

A constitutional order of States

The preceding chapters have explored the principles, worked out by the Court of Justice in its case-law since *Van Gend en Loos*,[1] which establish the constitutional character of the order brought into being by the European Union Treaties.[2] Those "constitutionalising" principles comprise, notably, the direct effect of many of the provisions of Community law and their primacy over conflicting national law. In adhering to the new legal order resulting from the Treaties, the Member States have, in the words of the Court, "limited their sovereign rights in ever wider fields".[3] They have accepted that, in a whole range of policy areas central to a modern political economy, they may or must act together through the common institutions, according to the procedures and with the legal consequences which the Treaties prescribe.

At the same time, it is a central feature of the E.U. system that the constituent entities of the Union retain the quality of states, in both the legal and the political senses. Thus the continuing status of E.U. Members as full subjects of public international law is unquestioned; and, for their own peoples, they remain the principal focus of collective loyalty and the principal forum of democratic political activity. Moreover, the TEU expressly provides in Article 6(3) (ex Article F(1)) that "[t]he Union shall respect the national identities of its Member States". Accordingly, it seems appropriate to describe the unique polity created by the Treaties as "a constitutional order of states".[4]

The paradoxical fact that belonging to the E.U. in no way casts doubt on Members' existence as States, is due to the delicate checks and balances built into the system. One important factor is the role of the Council at the heart of the legislative process. As we have seen in Chapter 3, whether under the simple consultation procedure or the more complex (and more democratic) co-decision procedure, new law that builds on the primary rules of the Treaties cannot normally be enacted without receiving the positive approval of the institution composed of representatives of the Member States.[5] Another factor is the Union's lack of coercive powers exercisable in relation to individuals and businesses. The great exception is competition policy where, as will be shown in Chapter 22, the Commission is able, among other things, to send its officials on "dawn raids" against undertakings suspected of breaking the rules, and to punish infringements with swingeing fines. In the main, however, the law made in

---

[1] Case 26/62 [1963] E.C.R. 1, at 12.
[2] See Mancini, "The Making of a Constitution for Europe", 26 C.M.L. Rev. (1989), 595.
[3] Opinion 1/91 *EEA Agreement* [1991] E.C.R. I–6079, para. 21.
[4] The description was first used in Dashwood (ed.), *Reviewing Maastricht: Issues for the 1996 IGC*, p. 7.
[5] We say "normally", to cover the few cases where the E.C. Treaty gives the Commission an independent power of decision: see Chap. 2, n.22.

Brussels and Strasbourg is implemented on the ground in the Member States by officials wearing national hats (and thus accountable through the national political process). The monopoly of coercion, one of the hallmarks of statehood, has thus been left by the Treaties almost completely undisturbed.[6]

In addition, an *acquis* of the TEU, confirmed by the T.A., has been the legal reinforcement of the position of the Member States, through Treaty amendments enacting certain "conservatory principles" (as they are here called) which provide a counterweight to the constitutionalising principles developed by the Court. These are the subject of the present chapter.

Article 5 E.C.

Article 5 (ex 3b) provides:

"The Community shall act within the limits of the powers conferred on it by this Treaty and of the objectives assigned to it therein.

　　In areas which do not fall within its exclusive competence, the Community shall take action, in accordance with the principle of subsidiarity, only if and insofar as the objectives of the proposed action cannot be sufficiently achieved by the Member States and can therefore, by reason of the scale or effects of the proposed action, be better achieved by the Community.

　　Any action taken by the Community shall not go beyond what is necessary to achieve the objectives of this Treaty."

The principles enshrined in the three paragraphs of the Article are known as, respectively, those of the attribution of powers (or of conferred powers),[7] of subsidiarity and of proportionality. They have always been immanent in the constitutional order, but were erected into express organising principles through the insertion of Article 5 into the E.C. Treaty by the TEU.

An interpretation of the Article 5 principles was agreed by the European Council at its Edinburgh meeting in December 1992, as one of the measures designed to secure the final ratification of the TEU, after the period of uncertainty that had followed the negative outcome of the first referendum in Denmark.[8] The Edinburgh text was a purely political document, describing the "overall approach" to be taken by the Council.[9] It was supplemented in October 1993 by another such text, the Interinstitutional Agreement between the European Parliament, the Council and the Commission on procedure for implementing the principle of subsidiarity.[10] More recently, a "Protocol on the application of the principles of subsidiarity and proportionality", giving legal force to the main elements of the earlier texts, has been annexed to the E.C. Treaty by the T.A.[11]

---

[6] For a fuller treatment, see Dashwood, "States in the European Union", 23 E.L. Rev. (1998), 201. Reprinted in Rider (ed.), *Law at the Centre*, pp. 235 *et seq.*

[7] This was how the Court of Justice referrd to the principle in Opinion 2/94 [1996] E.C.R. I–1759, para. 24.

[8] The crisis surrounding the ratification of the TEU is described in Chap. 1, at p. 16, above.

[9] See Annex 1 to Part A of the Presidency Conclusions: Bull E.C. 12–1992, p. 13, Hereinafter, "the Edinburgh text".

[10] Bull. E.C. 10–1993, p. 128.

[11] Protocol No. 7 to the Final Act of the T.A. Hereinafter, "the Amsterdam Protocol".

The principle of the attribution of powers[12]

Article 7 E.C., which identifies the main institutions of the Community, has always included a sub-paragraph providing: "Each institution shall act within the limits of the powers conferred upon it by this Treaty."[13] The addition to the Treaty of Article 5, first paragraph, made explicitly clear that the principle of the attribution of powers applies not only to the institutions but to the Community as such. The paragraph means, as the Court of Justice put it bluntly in Opinion 2/94, that the Community "has only those powers which have been conferred on it".[14] Or, in the crude but telling language of the Edinburgh text, "national powers are the rule and the Community's the exception".[15] To make the point another way, the Community order is not a self-authenticating one: new powers cannot be generated within the order itself, above and beyond those conferred by the constitution-making authority, acting in accordance with the procedure provided for by Article 48 (ex N) TEU.[16]

Subject to what is said below about the "default mechanism" in Article 308 (ex 235) the technique of attribution employed in the E.C. Treaty is highly specific.[17] Article 2 of the Treaty identifies the "tasks" of the Community, and Articles 3 and 4[18] its "activities"; but they contain no power-conferring provision, and so cannot be used as legal bases for enacting particular measures. The characteristic approach is for provisions giving the institutions law-making powers to be included with the group of substantive provisions that define, in more or less detail, the action the Community is authorised to take in a given area of policy: the powers thus conferred are exercisable, under the conditions specified, in that particular area and not elsewhere.[19] The relevant legal basis will lay down the procedure to be followed for enacting measures (this will normally be consultation or co-decision); and it may also prescribe a measure of a certain kind (*e.g.* only harmonisation or, conversely, no harmonisation), and the form(s) of legal instrument that may be used (*e.g.* only directives).

The scope of the authorisations the Community has received vary significantly under the legal bases applicable to different areas of governmental activity. There is, for instance, a wide legislative discretion to develop common policies in the fields of agriculture,[20] transport,[21] and international trade,[22] but this is exceptional. In contrast, legislation on internal market matters is by way of approximation

---

[12] For an extensive treatment of the attribution principle in the E.C. Treaty, see Dashwood, "The Limits of European Community Powers", 21 E.L. Rev. (1996), 113.

[13] See Art. 7(I) (ex Art. 4(I)), second sub-para.

[14] *loc. cit.* n.7, above, at para. 23.

[15] *loc.* cit. n.9, above, at para. 1.15.

[16] Because it is not a state, the Community lacks what German scholars call *Kompetenz Kompetenz*, the ability to pull itself up legally by its own bootstraps.

[17] Opinion 2/94, *loc. cit.,* n.7, above, at para. 25.

[18] Arts 2 and 3 retain their original numbering. Art. 4 is ex Art. 3a.

[19] The contrasting attribution technique adopted under Titles V and VI TEU is considered in Chap. 8, below.

[20] Art. 37 (ex 43) E.C. This is also the legal basis for legislation on the common fisheries policy.

[21] Art. 71 (ex 75).

[22] Art. 133 (ex 113).

measures only.[23] Such measures must be designed either to iron out existing differences in the applicable law or to prevent differences from arising in the future: there is no power under the relevant legal basis, Article 95 (ex 100a), to do things the Member States cannot do, such as creating a new E.C. form of intellectual property.[24] Even more constraining are the express provisions of the legal bases for Community action on matters such as employment, education, vocational training, culture, public health and consumer protection.[25] For example, Article 149 (ex 126) makes clear that the Community's contribution "to the development of quality education" is ancillary to the powers of the Member States: it may consist of "encouraging co-operation" between the latter and, *if necessary*, of "supporting and supplementing" national action, but must fully respect "the responsibility of the Member States for the content of teaching and the organisation of education systems and their cultural and legal diversity"; and action is only authorised in the form of "incentive measures" (such as the Socrates Programme),[26] with an express prohibition against harmonisation of Member States' laws or regulations.

Given the multiplicity of legal bases in the E.C. Treaty, disputes are liable to arise from time to time as to which is the appropriate Article to use for the adoption of a proposed measure. In the early 1990's, for example, there was a series of cases in which the Council found itself at odds with the Commission and/ or the European Parliament over the correct legal basis for various Community measures regulating the disposal of industrial waste: should the basis be Article 95, since disparities between national provisions could result in different levels of costs for industry in the different Member States, thus distorting competition on the internal market; or should it be Article 175 (ex 130s), which confers law-making powers for the protection of the environment?[27] The Court of Justice has stressed that, in such cases, the choice of Treaty Article cannot be a matter for the discretion of the enacting institution: it must be made in accordance with objective factors, in particular the aim and content of the proposed measure, which are susceptible to judicial control.[28] The main practical significance of such choice is that it may affect the legislative procedure to be applied: for instance, one of the Articles may prescribe co-decision and the other consultation. With the progressive extension of co-decision, however, this is becoming less problematic.[29]

---

[23] Art. 95 authorises the adoption of "measures for the approximation of the provisions laid down by law, regulation or administrative action in the Member States which have as their object the establishment or functioning of the internal market". The scope and significance of Art. 95 is further considered in Chap. 17 below. The Art. derogates, in matters relating to the well-functioning of the internal market, from the more general approximation powers which are found in Art. 94 (ex 100), and which are expressed to be exercisable only by means of directives.

[24] In the absence of a specific legal basis for creating new intellectual property forms, recourse has been had to Art. 308 (ex 235). See, *e.g.* Council Reg. 40/94, on the Community trade mark, [1994] O.J. L11/10.

[25] See, respectively, Art. 129, 149 (ex 126) E.C., Art. 150 (ex 127) E.C., Art. 151 (ex 128) E.C., Art. 152 (ex 129) E.C. and Art. 153 (ex 129a) E.C.

[26] [1995] O.J. L87/10.

[27] See, *e.g.* Case C–300/89, *Commission v. Council* [1991] E.C.R. 2867. *cf.* Case C–155/91, *Commission v. Council* [1993] E.C.R. I–939; Case C–187/93 *European Parliament v. Council* [1994] E.C.R. I–2857; [1995] 2 C.M.L.R. 309. See Chap. 17, below.

[28] *ibid.*

[29] Thus, following the amendment of the E.C. Treaty by the T.A., the legislative procedure for both internal market and environmental measures is now, for most purposes, co-decision.

As noted above, the E.C. Treaty has, in Article 308 (ex 235), a "default mechanism" enabling action to be taken in certain circumstances where a specific legal basis is lacking. Article 308 provides:

"If action by the Community should prove necessary to attain, in the course of the operation of the common market, one of the objectives of the Community and this Treaty has not provided the necessary powers, the Council shall, acting unanimously on a proposal from the Commission and after consulting the European Parliament, take the appropriate measures."

It would tend to undermine the principle of the attribution of powers if the Article were available as a legal basis of last resort for taking any measure that could be seen as appropriate, in some way, to further one of the Community's objectives. The Court of Justice has stressed that the Article "cannot be used as a basis for the adoption of provisions whose effect could, in substance, be to amend the Treaty . . .".[30] That was in Opinion 2/94, where the Court had been asked whether the Community was competent to accede to the European Convention for the Protection of Human Rights and Fundamental Freedoms ("the European Convention"). It was found that "[n]o Treaty provision confers on the Community institutions any general power to enact rules on human rights or to conclude international conventions in this field".[31] Was it, then, possible to fall back on Article 308? The Court held that it was not, because accession to the European Convention would entail entry into "a distinct international institutional system", with fundamental implications for both the Community and the Member States; such a modification of the E.C. system of human rights protection would be "of constitutional significance", and thus could be brought about only by way of Treaty amendment.[32]

While the emphasis in the Court's reasoning was on institutional considerations, the Opinion contains a hint as to the substantive limits of the default mechanism in Article 308. The Article, the Court said, "cannot serve as a basis for widening the scope of Community powers beyond the general framework created by the provisions of the Treaty as a whole and, in particular, by those that define the tasks and the activities of the Community".[33] We take that to mean that a proposed measure is unlikely to qualify for adoption under Article 308 unless it relates to matters which, although not specifically authorised, fall broadly within the purview of the activities referred to in Articles 3 and 4 of the Treaty, interpreted in the light of the different elements constituting the task of the Community, as defined by Article 2.

Historically, there has been a marked tendency for new legal bases to be introduced, through amendment of the E.C. Treaty, in areas where the first steps

---

[30] Opinion 2/94, *loc. cit.* n.7, above, para. 30. The same view has been firmly taken by the German Budesvervassungsgericht (Federal Constitutional Court). The Court indicated in its *Brunner* judgment that a measure based on Art. 308 which exceeded the scope of the democratic authorisation given in respect of the transfer of legislative competence to the Community would not be considered binding in Germany: see [1994] 1 C.M.L.R. 57.

[31] *ibid.* para. 27.

[32] *ibid.* paras 34 and 35.

[33] *ibid.* para. 30.

in constructing a set of Community instruments have been taken under Article 308. The E.C.'s regional, environmental and development co-operation policies were all initiated in this way, and subsequently equipped with specific power-conferring provisions.[34] Future Treaty amendments may thus, perhaps, make it no longer necessary to rely on Article 308 for the creation of intellectual property forms, and for providing technical assistance to countries other than developing countries.[35]

The principle of subsidiarity[36]

Three uses of subsidiarity

The broad idea underlying the principle of subsidiarity is a simple one: that public powers should normally be located at the lowest tier of government where they can be exercised effectively.[37]

In constitutional texts like the TEU and the E.C. Treaty, the principle can be used in a variety of ways.[38] It may, for instance, serve as a general political value permeating the constitutional order: that is the significance of the reference in Article 1 (ex A), second paragraph of the TEU, to the union in the course of being created among the peoples of Europe, as one "in which decisions are taken . . . as closely as possible to the citizen." The principle may also guide the hand of the constitution-maker in allocating powers within a complex order, between the central authorities and the component entities. Examples in the E.C. Treaty would be the field of social policy, where Article 137 (ex 118) makes explicitly clear that the leading role belongs to the Member States, that of the Community being merely to "support and complement" their activities; and also the legal bases on employment, education and other matters, where the limited and supplementary character of Community action has already been noted.[39] Finally, the principle may organise the exercise of concurrent powers: its effect here is to require that, in matters where the constitution allows action to be taken either by

---

[34] See, respectively, Part Three, Title XVII (Economic and Social Cohesion) and Title XIX (Environment), which date from the amendment of the Treaty by the SEA; and Title XX (Development Cooperation), dating from the amendment by the TEU.

[35] The unsuitability of Art. 308 as a legal basis for the latter category of measures is due to the difficulty of demonstrating a connection with "the course of operation of the Common Market".

[36] There is an extensive literature on the principle of subsidiarity, much of it now overtaken by events. For a selection of views, see Constantinesco, "Who's afraid of Subsidiarity?" (1991) 11 Y.E.L. 33; Emiliou, "Subsidiarity—An Effective Barrier against the Enterprises of Ambition?" (1992) 17 E.L. Rev, 383; Toth, "The Principle of Subsidiarity in the Maastricht Treaty" (1992) 29 C.M.L. Rev. 1079; Cass, "The Word that Saves Maastricht? The Principle of Subsidiarity and the Division of Powers within the European Community" (1992) 29 C.M.L. Rev. 1107; Mattina, "Subsidiarité, Démocratie et Transparence" (1992) 4 R.M.U.E. 203; Gonzalez, "The Principle of Subsidiarity" (1995) 20 E.L. Rev. 355.

[37] See the famous formulation of the principle by Pope Pius XI in his Encyclical of 1931, *Quadragesimo Anno*, where he wrote, ". . . it is an injustice, a grave evil and a disturbance of the right order, for a larger and higher association to arrogate to itself functions which can be performed efficiently by smaller and lower societies" (London, Catholic Truth Society, 1936). On the historical background, see Emiliou, *op. cit.* n.36, above.

[38] See the analysis of van Gerven, "Les Principes de 'Subsidiarité, Proportionnalité et Coopération' en Droit Communautaire Européen", a paper delivered in the author's capacity as President of the Académie royale des sciences, lettres et beaux-arts de Belgique, at the general meeting of the Academy on December 21, 1991.

[39] See the legal bases identified in n.25, above.

the central authorities or by component entities, the choice should, other things being equal, fall on the latter.

That last-mentioned function of the subsidiarity principle is the one provided for by the second paragraph of Article 5 E.C. As there formulated, the principle is designed to direct choice, in cases where the Treaty leaves the matter open, in favour of action by the Member States, unless the need for acting at Community level can be demonstrated.

The limitation to areas of exclusive Community competence

The principle encapsulated in Article 5, second paragraph is expressly limited to "areas falling within [the Community's] exclusive competence". The limitation thus placed on the subsidiarity principle is of great practical significance because, where it applies, there is no obligation on the institutions to show that the test prescribed by the paragraph, to establish the need for action at Community level, is satisfied. Unfortunately, the scope of the limitation is unclear, because it seems to be based on a false conception as to the way in which powers are allocated under the Treaty, between the Community and the Member States.

There are, in fact, very few "areas" (in the sense of a discreet range of governmental activities, defined by their subject-matter) where power has passed definitively to the Community, and the Member States no longer have the right to act autonomously for any purpose. The only examples of "pre-emptive exclusivity" (as we call it), which bear the imprimatur of the Court of Justice, are those of the common commercial policy[40] and of fisheries conservation;[41] to which, it is thought, monetary policy should be added, as regards the Member States participating in the single currency. In those areas, if a Member State acts at all, it can only be as a trustee of the Community interest, with the authorisation and under the control of the Institutions.[42] To apply the subsidiarity principle in such cases would be pointless, since the option of leaving it to the Member States to pursue the objectives in question has been specifically disallowed by the Treaty.

However, the normal approach of the Treaty, rather than pre-empt whole policy areas for the Community, is to confer on it the power, which may be coupled with a duty, to pursue specified objectives or to carry out specified tasks.[43] The mere existence of such Community powers does not automatically fetter action by the Member States in respect of the substantive matters to which they apply. National powers can still be exercised, subject of course to the primacy of Community law in any matters which are made the subject of legislation enacted under the Treaty.[44]

---

[40] Opinion 1/75, *Local Cost Standard* [1975] E.C.R. 1255.

[41] Joined Cases 3, 4 and 6/76 *Kramer* [1976] E.C.R. 1279; [1976] 2 C.M.L.R. 440; Case C–25/94 *Commission v. Council (FAO)* [1996] E.C.R. I–1469.

[42] Case 804/79 *Commission v. United Kingdom* [1981] E.C.R. 1045; [1982] 1 C.M.L.R. 543.

[43] See Ehlermann, "Quelques réflexions sur la communication de la Commission relative au principe de subsidiarité", *Revue du Marché Unique Européen* 4/1992, p. 15.

[44] For the corresponding "*AETR* principle", in respect of competence in the field of external relations, see Case 22/70, *Commission v. Council* [1971] E.C.R. 263; [1971] C.M.L.R. 335.

For example, Article 47(2) (ex 57(2)) E.C. provides for the adoption of directives for the co-ordination of the provisions laid down by law, regulation or administrative action in the Member States concerning the taking-up and pursuit of activities as self-employed persons". The effect of that provision is not to deprive the Member States of all right to regulate such activities: they may (and do) continue to legislate in this "area", while being required to comply with any measures of co-ordination which have been taken by the Community.

If, therefore, the regulation of business and professional activities is not to be regarded as an "area" of exclusive Community competence, does it follow that the institutions are required to ask themselves the subsidiarity question every time they exercise their powers under Article 47(2)? Advocate General Léger has taken the view that they do not. In a case concerning the validity of a Directive on deposit-guarantee schemes, he pointed out that the task of co-ordinating the relevant national legislation had been entrusted by Article 47(2) to the Community, with no indication that responsibility for attaining that objective was to be shared by the Member States.[45] This showed "that, *from the very outset*, the authors of the Treaty considered that, as regards the taking up and pursuit of activities of self-employed persons, co-ordination was better achieved at Community rather than national level".[46] The Community was thus exclusively competent, within the meaning of Article 5, second paragraph, not as to the general regulation of self-employed activities, but in the specific matter of the *co-ordination* of the relevant national provisions.

We respectfully adopt that analysis. In our submission, the limitation contained in the opening words of Article 5, second paragraph must be understood as extending to all cases where a duty to perform a certain task has been imposed on the Community alone. It makes no more sense to apply the subsidiarity principle to the performance of such "reserved tasks", than it does in the areas of pre-emptive exclusivity: in both cases, the issue of the need for action at Community level has been settled by the Treaty itself. The logic is the same where the particular means prescribed by the Treaty for attaining certain objectives is something only the Community can do, such as the establishment of a common organisation of national agricultural markets.

In the light of the foregoing, a tentative list of the main "areas" of exclusive Community competence, in the special sense of Article 5 E.C., may be offered:

— actions (whether by way of the approximation of national legislation or otherwise) prescribed by the Treaty for the purpose of removing barriers to free movement within the internal market, as required by Article 14 (ex 7a) E.C.;

— the implementation of the rules on competition laid down by Articles 81 and 82 (ex 85 and 86) E.C.;

— the common organisation of agricultural markets;

— the conservation of fisheries resources;

---

[45] Case C–233/94 *Germany v. European Parliament and Council* [1997] E.C.R. I–2405; [1997] 3 C.M.L.R. 1379.
[46] *ibid.* at I–2426, para. 82.

— the regulation of international transport, and of so-called *"cabotage"*, as provided for, respectively, by sub-paragraphs (a) and (b) of Article 71(1) (ex 75(1)) E.C.;
— the common commercial policy;
— monetary policy (for the Member States participating in the single currency);
— the matters in respect of which action is required to be taken within a five-year transitional period, under the new Treaty Title on "Visas, asylum, immigration and other policies related to the free movement of persons."

In all other matters, Community competence is non-exclusive, and in particular:

— the facilitation of the functioning of the internal market (as distinct from removing barriers to free movement);
— structural actions in the agricultural and fisheries sectors;
— general aspects of transport policy;
— harmonisation of intellectual property law, and the creation of new property forms;
— employment and social policy;
— economic and social cohesion;
— research and technological development;
— protection of the environment;
— development co-operation.

It is worth recalling that, by the express terms of Article 300 (ex 235), the necessity of action by the Community must be demonstrated, as a condition of activating the default mechanism which is there provided for.

The classification that we offer very largely corresponds to indications given by the Commission.[47] Everything turns, however, on the precise wording of the legal basis under which action by the Community is proposed, and the dividing line will often be a fine one. In our submission, the spirit of Article 5, and more generally of the E.C. Treaty since its amendment by the TEU, requires that, in case of doubt, a proposal should be treated as falling into the non-exclusive category, and the principle of subsidiarity be, accordingly, applied to it.

The Article 5 test of subsidiarity

The test of subsidiarity prescribed by Article 5, second paragraph, is that "the objectives of the proposed action cannot be sufficiently achieved by the Member States and can therefore, by reason of the scale or effects of the proposed action, be better achieved by the Community." The test, therefore, has a dual aspect: the impossibility of attaining the objectives in question by action at Member State level; and the superior efficacy of action at Community level. Using "qualitative or, wherever possible, quantitative indicators", it must be shown that both aspects of the test are satisfied, in order to justify action by the Community.[48] The following guidelines have been provided by the Amsterdam Protocol:

---

[47] See the Communication entitled, "The principle of subsidiarity", SEC (92) 1990 final.
[48] Amsterdam Protocol, Arts (4) and (5), read together.

"— the issue under consideration has transnational aspects which cannot be satisfactorily regulated by action by Member States;

— action by Member States alone or lack of Community action would conflict with the requirements of the Treaty (such as the need to correct distortion of competition or avoid disguised restrictions on trade or strengthen economic and social cohesion) or would otherwise significantly damage Member States' interests;

— action at Community level would produce clear benefits by reason of its scale or effects compared with action at the level of the Member States".[49]

Another point emphasised in the Protocol is that subsidiarity is a dynamic concept, allowing action by the Community "to be expanded where circumstances so require, and conversely, to be restricted or discontinued where it is no longer justified".[50] Thus the principle must not be applied crudely as a brake on the exercise of Community powers. Events such as the BSE crisis and the discovery of dioxins in certain foodstuffs may, for instance, point to the need for a new programme of food safety measures.[51] On the other hand, existing proposals should be withdrawn, and legislation repealed, where these are found no longer to meet the test in Article 5, second paragraph.[52]

Implementation of the principle

Primary responsibility for ensuring the effective application of the subsidiarity principle falls on the Commission, the Council and the European Parliament, as the institutions with the leading roles in the Community's legislative process. When putting forward a proposal on a matter for which the Community is not exclusively competent, the Commission must provide a justification as regards subsidiarity, in the accompanying Explanatory Memorandum.[53] The issue of the compliance with Article 5 generally (*i.e.* the attribution and proportionality principles, as well as subsidiarity) of Commission proposals, and of any amendments to them, must be specifically addressed by the Council and the European Parliament in the ordinary course of the relevant procedures[54]; and, in the case of co-decision, there is a formal requirement that the Parliament be informed of the Council's views as to the application of Article 5, by way of the statement of reasons communicated, at the end of the first reading, along with its common position.[55] Last but not least, reasons demonstrating the compliance of a measure with the principles of subsidiarity and proportionality must be given in its preamble.[56] An express reference to the principles is not, however, required.[57]

---

[49] *ibid.*

[50] Amsterdam Protocol, Art. (3).

[51] See the Commission's Report, "Better Lawmaking 1999", COM (1999) 562 final, p. 2.

[52] An extensive review of existing proposals and legislation was initiated by the Commission in 1994: see COM (94) 533 final, pp. 15 *et seq.*

[53] Amsterdam Protocol, Art. 9, second indent.

[54] *ibid.*, Art. (11).

[55] *ibid.*, Art. (12).

[56] *ibid.*, Art. (4).

[57] Case C–233/94 *Germany v. European Parliament and Council* [1997] E.C.R. at I–2453, para. 28; [1997] 3 C.M.L.R. 1379; Case C–150/94 *United Kingdom v. Council* [1998] E.C.R. I–7235; [1999] 1 C.M.L.R. 367.

The Edinburgh text called for the Commission to submit, to the European Council and the European Parliament, an annual report on the application of Article 5; and this was transformed into a binding obligation by the Amsterdam Protocol.[58] From 1995 onwards, the report has been expanded to cover all action aimed at improving Community law-making.[59] The series of reports provides evidence, including statistical evidence, of the seriousness of the efforts being made by the political institutions, in particular the Commission, to give concrete substance to the Article 5 principles.[60]

It was hotly debated, in the early days following the insertion of Article 5 into the E.C. Treaty by the TEU, whether the principle of subsidiarity was justiciable.[61] As an eminent commentator pointed out, there is nothing in the text of Article 5 to suggest the contrary, nor that the Court of Justice does not have power to interpret the provisions of the Article.[62] Any doubts should by now have been dissipated, since the case-law (such as it is) contains no hint of a refusal of jurisdiction in principle.[63]

An issue of pure law would be whether a given measure falls within an area of exclusive Community competence: a wrong characterisation, leading to the non-application of the subsidiarity test, would clearly provide grounds for challenging the measure's validity. Another orthodox ground for challenge would be the failure of the law-making institutions to provide, in the preamble to an instrument adopted under non-exclusive powers, an adequate explanation of why it was considered necessary. Advocate General Léger has noted "how useful . . . it could be, for the purpose of ensuring proper application of the principle of subsidiarity for the obligation to state reasons laid down in Article 190 of the Treaty to be enforced with particular rigour whenever the Community legislature takes action to lay down new rules".[64] He went on to conclude: "All measures adopted by the Community should thus indicate, either implicitly or explicitly, but in any event clearly, on what basis the authority concerned is acting—even if only to state, where this is the case, that the principle of subsidiarity does not come into play."[65] Unfortunately, the Court appears to be rather more easily satisfied.[66] Previously, in a case on the validity of the Council Directive concerning certain aspects of the organisation of working time,[67] it accepted, as

---

[58] See Art. 9, fourth indent.

[59] The reports are, accordingly, entitled "Better Lawmaking".

[60] See, e.g. "Better Lawmaking 1999", COM (1999) 562 final.

[61] See the literature mentioned above, and also Toth, "Is subsidiarity justiciable?", 19 E.L. Rev. (1994), 268.

[62] Lord Mackenzie-Stuart, "Subsidiarity—A Busted Flush?" in Curtin and O'Keefe, *Constitutional Adjudication in European and National Law: Essays for the Hon. Mr Justice T. F. O'Higgins*, p. 19.

[63] See Case C–84/94 *United Kingdom v. Council (Working Time)* [1996] E.C.R. I–5793; [1996] 3 C.M.L.R. 671; Case C–233/94, *Germany v. European Parliament and Council* [1997] E.C.R. I–2404; Joined Cases C–36–37/97, *Kellinghusen and Ketelsen* [1998] E.C.R. I–6337. See also Arnull, *The European Union and its Court of Justice* (Oxford, 1999), at pp. 551–552, where the justiciability of the subsidiarity principle is treated as a *fait accompli*.

[64] Case C–233/94 *Germany v. European Parliament and Council* [1997] E.C.R. at I–2427, para. 87; [1997] 3 C.M.L.R. 1379.

[65] *ibid.*, at I–2428, para. 90.

[66] The judgment in Case C–233/94 goes out of its way to stress that there is no need for the subsidiarity principle to be referred to expressly. The relevant passage reads like a rebuttal of the Advocate General: see [1997] E.C.R., at I–2453, para. 28.

[67] Dir. 93/104, [1993] O.J. L307/18.

justification for Community-wide action, the fact that "the Council has found that it is necessary to improve the existing level of protection as regards the health and safety of workers and to harmonise the conditions in this area while maintaining the improvements made . . .".[68] That seems hardly sufficient, given that the relevant Treaty provisions[69] clearly contemplate the possibility of pursuing those same objectives through action at Member State level.

Litigants have been wary of raising directly the substantive issue of compliance with the dual test in Article 5, second paragraph[70]—and understandably so. The Court of Justice is certain to allow the political institutions wide discretion in weighing up the pros and cons as to whether action should be taken at Community or at national level. Judicial review is likely to be confined to examining whether the assessment reached by the responsible institution has been vitiated by manifest error or abuse of powers, or whether the institution has manifestly exceeded the limits of its discretion.[71]

The principle of proportionality

Long before its importation into the third paragraph of Article 5, the principle of proportionality had become a familiar tool of judicial review in the field of the Community's "administrative law". In that field, as we have seen,[72] the principle has been used mainly for two purposes: controlling the extent to which measures, adopted by the Community authorities in furtherance of objectives of the Treaty, are permitted to override the interests of particular individuals; and limiting the leeway Member States have been given to protect important public interests, through derogations from certain fundamental rules of the Community system. The case-law establishes that, in applying the principle of proportionality, it must be ascertained, first, whether the means employed by the competent authority are suitable for the purpose of achieving the desired objective and, secondly, whether they do not go beyond what is necessary to achieve that objective.[73]

In the context of Article 5, the logic of the proportionality principle remains the same, though it is here operating on the constitutional plane. It provides an answer to the question: "What should be the intensity or nature of the Community's action?".[74] The answer, in effect, guides the legislator towards choosing the form of Community action which, while being well designed to achieve its objective, will intrude, to the smallest praticable extent, on the powers of the Member States.

---

[68] Case C–84/94 *United Kingdom v. Council* [1996] E.C.R. at I–5808 to I–5809, para. 47; [1996] 3 C.M.L.R. 671.

[69] See Arts 136 and 137 (ex 117 and 118) E.C.

[70] In *Working Time*, for example, the United Kingdom did not rely on the infringement of Art. 5 as a separate plea but sought (unsuccessfully) to use the principle of subsidiarity as a tool for the interpretation of the relevant legal basis: see the remarks of Advocate General Léger at [1996] E.C.R., at I–5783, para. 124; and of the Court itself, *ibid.*, at I–5808, para. 46.

[71] This was the approach adopted by the Court in *Working Time*, with respect to the principle of proportionality: [1996] E.C.R., at I–5811, para. 58. See Arnull, *op. cit.* n.63, above, at p. 551.

[72] See the discussion in Chap. 6, above.

[73] See, *e.g.* Joined Cases 279, 280, 285 and 286/84, *Rau v. Commission* [1987] E.C.R. 1069, para. 34; [1988] 2 C.M.L.R. 704; Cited with reference to Art. 5 E.C. in Case 426/93 *Germany v. Council* [1995] E.C.R. I–3723, para. 42.

[74] See Edinburgh text, Bull. E.C. 12–1992, point I.15.

The Edinburgh text went into some detail in describing the elements relevant to an evaluation of proportionality for the purposes of Article 5, third paragraph,[75] and many of these figure in the Amsterdam Protocol, from which they derive legal force. Among other things, it is stated that "[t]he form of Community action must be as simple as possible, consistent with the satisfactory achievement of the objective of the measure and the need for effective enforcement . . . Other things being equal, directives should be preferred to regulations and framework directives to detailed measures." Care must be taken "to respect well established national arrangements and the organisation and working of Member States' legal systems".[76] Examples of the steps taken by the political institutions in adapting their legislative practicᶒ to these requirements can be found in the Commission's annual "Better Lawmaking" Reports.[77]

As one of the instruments deployed by Article 5 E.C. to help preserve the balance between the Community and its Member States, the principle of proportionality has a stronger political flavour than in its usual administrative law setting. Not surprisingly, therefore, when the principle was invoked by the United Kingdom in the *Working Time* case, the Court of Justice saw fit to adopt the technique of "marginal review"[78] (for manifest error, misuse of powers or manifest excess of jurisdiction) which, we have suggested, would be similarly appropriate in dealing with issues of subsidiarity.[79] Applying the two traditional aspects of the proportionality principle, the Court found that, with one exception (the specification of Sunday as a rest day), the measures on the organisation of working time contained in the Directive were apt for the purpose of enhancing workers' health and safety; and that the Council did not commit any manifest error in concluding that the objectives of the Treaty could not have been achieved by less restrictive forms of Community action.[80]

Flexibility [81]

A new organising principle

A development complementing the articulation in Article 5 E.C. of the three conservatory principles just discussed, has been the formal acceptance of the

---

[75] *ibid.*, point I.19.

[76] See Amsterdam Protocol, Arts (6) and (7).

[77] See, *e.g.* "Better Lawmaking 1999", pp. 4–5.

[78] This term is used by Schermers and Waelbroek, *Judicial Protection in the European Communities* (5th ed., Kluwer, 1992), when discussing the use of the technique in the judicial control of decisions based on broad economic assessments.

[79] See n.71, above.

[80] The Court's reasoning is found at [1996] E.C.R., I–5811 to I–5813, paras 59–66.

[81] For an analysis in depth of the flexibility principle, from a political science perspective, see Edwards and Philippart, *Flexibility and the Treaty of Amsterdam: Europe's New Byzantium?*, CELS Occasional Paper No. 3 (1997). See also Dashwood, *op. cit.* n.4, above, at pp. 158–164, 195–201; Stubb, "A Categorisation of Differentiated Integration", 34 J.C.M.S. (1996), 238; Kortenberg, "Closer Cooperation in the Treaty of Amsterdam", 35 C.M.L. Rev., 833; Gaja, "How Flexible is Flexibility under the Amsterdam Treaty?", 35 C.M.L. Rev. (1998), 855; Usher, "Flexibility and Enhanced Cooperation "in Heukels, Blokker and Brus (eds), *The European Union After Amsterdam*, p. 253; Hederman-Robinson, "The Area of Freedom, Security and Justice with Regard to the U.K., Ireland and Denmark: the 'Opt-in Opt-outs' under the Treaty of Amsterdam", in O'Keefe and Twomey (eds.), *Legal Issues of the Amsterdam Treaty*, p. 289.

principle of flexibility as part of the constitutional machinery of the European Union. We use the term "flexibility" in this chapter to designate legal arrangements under which it is recognised that one or more of the Member States may, in principle, remain permanently outside certain activities or practices being pursued within the single institutional framework of the Union, either because they choose to do so or because they do not meet the criteria for participation.[82]

So defined, flexibility is to be distinguished from the long established practice of allowing a transitional period before new Member States are required to apply the whole body of E.U. law; or that of prescribing differential periods for the implementation of new legislation, taking account of the fact that a particular Member State may face special difficulties of adjustment.[83] Such derogations from the rules generally aplicable under the Treaties differ from the flexibility principle, in applying only on a temporary basis, and being accorded in recognition of objective socio-economic factors, not merely the political preferences of the State concerned.[84]

The legitimation of flexibility as an organising principle of the constitutional order was achieved by the TEU; and the vital role the principle will be called upon to play in an increasingly complex and differentiated Union has since been underlined by the T.A. Nevertheless, care must be taken to ensure that, in seeking to accommodate the ambitions of those Member States wishing to push the integration process forward, with the tendency of others to hold back, no irreparable harm is done to the legal fabric of the Union, or to the well functioning of its institutions.

Primary flexibility

In cases of what we call "primary flexibility", the relevant legal arrangements are to be found in Treaty provisions. Thus the policy areas in which flexibility may operate, the decision-making procedures to be followed and the Member States that may benefit from "opt-outs", will all have been determined at the level of the Union's constitutional authority: in other words, the matter will have been specifically negotiated within an Intergovernmental Conference, and ratified in accordance with the Member States' constitutional requirements, as part of an accession or amendment exercise.[85]

The earliest examples of primary flexibility date from the TEU. One such consisted of the Protocol and Agreement on Social Policy, which the TEU annexed to the E.C. Treaty.[86] Their combined effect was to enable the Member States, with the exception of the United Kingdom, to have recourse to the institutions, procedures and mechanisms of the E.C. Treaty, for the purpose of exercising certain powers going beyond those provided for in the Social Provisions Chapter of the Treaty itself. That is now history, since the change of government in the United Kingdom in 1997 brought the abandonment of the

---

[82] The term "variable geometry" is also found, especially in the older literature, in the sense of "flexibility" used here.

[83] cf. Art. 15 (ex 7c) E.C.

[84] See the distinctions drawn in Dashwood, op. cit. n.4, above, at pp. 41–43.

[85] Thus on the basis of either Art. 48 (ex N) or Art. 49 (ex O) TEU.

[86] See Protocol No. 14 to the Final Act of the TEU.

"opt-out", so that the relevant provisions could be incorporated into the E.C. Treaty by the T.A.[87] Of more lasting significance are the arrangements which excuse two classes of Member States from participation in the single currency, following the (otherwise obligatory) transition to the third stage of EMU at the beginning of 1999.[88] One class comprises "Member States with a derogation", *i.e.* those which do not yet fulfil the conditions for the adoption of a single currency.[89] The other class comprises Denmark and the United Kingdom, whose respective positions are governed by separate Protocols[90]: Denmark was given the right, if it notified the Council that it would not be taking part in the third stage, to treatment corresponding, for most purposes, to that of Member States with a derogation; while it was expressly recognised "that the United Kingdom shall not be obliged or committed to move to the third stage of economic and monetary union without a separate decision to do so by its government and Parliament".[91]

Another very important case of primary flexibility has been established by the T.A. We have noted that the T.A.introduced into Part Three of the E.C. Treaty a Title IV on "Visas, asylum, immigration and other policies related to free movement of persons", which covers, among other things, aspects of the treatment of third country nationals previously dealt with under Title VI TEU (the Third Pillar). There is also a Protocol, annexed to the TEU and the E.C. Treaty by the T.A.,[92] which provides for the incorporation into the E.U. framework of the so-called "Schengen *acquis*". That consists of the body of law derived from an Agreement ("the Schengen Agreement") originally signed in 1985 by France, Germany and the Benelux countries, but to which, by the time of the T.A., all of the Member States except Ireland and the United Kingdom had become signatories.[93] The Schengen Agreement represented an attempt to proceed, more rapidly than seemed possible by acting through the Community institutions, to the complete abolition of checks on persons crossing the borders between the countries concerned. Pursuant to the T.A., the different elements of the Schengen *acquis* have been brought within the compass of either the E.C. Treaty (in particular, Title IV of Part Three) or Title VI TEU, depending on their subject-matter.[94] The significance of all this for present purposes lies in the

---

[87] They are now found in the E.C. Treaty, Chap. 1 of Title XI of Part Three.

[88] See the account of the transition, as it occurred, in Chap. 18, below.

[89] Art. 122 (ex 109k) E.C. Greece was such a Member State, at the time of the transition. Sweden, it seems, was allowed to deem itself to be similarly unqualified.

[90] Respectively, Protocols Nos 11 and 12 to the Final Act of the TEU. Hereinafter, "U.K. Protocol" and "Danish Protocol".

[91] U.K. Protocol, opening recital.

[92] Protocol No. 2 to the Final Act of the T.A. Hereinafter "the Schengen Protocol".

[93] The Schengen *acquis* is defined in an Annex to the Schengen protocol as comprising: the Schengen Agreement itself, of 1985; the Implementing Convention, signed in 1990; the series of Accession Protocols and Agreements with eight other Member States of the E.U.; and decisions and declarations adopted by the Schengen Executive Committee, as well as acts of the organs on which the Committee has conferred decision-making powers. Iceland and Norway are also associated with the implementation of the Schengen *acquis*; see Schengen Protocol, Art. 6.

[94] The Council was given the task of assigning appropriate legal bases to the provisions and decisions included in the *acquis*: Schengen Protocol, Art. 2. See Council Dec 1999/435/EC concerning the definition of the Schengen *acquis*, [1999] O.J. L176/1; Council Dec. 1999/436/EC determining . . . the legal basis for each of the provisions or decisions which constitute the Schengen *acquis*, [1999] O.J. L176/17.

flexibility arrangements made for the benefit of Ireland and the United Kingdom; and also for Denmark, even though it is a party to Schengen. As for Ireland and the United Kingdom, they are bound neither by the consequences of the Schengen incorporation nor by the new Title IV, unless they are willing and able to take advantage of the complex provisions on opting in (which, in the case of the Schengen *acquis*, requires the unanimous agreement of the Council composed of the participating Member States).[95] As for Denmark, its legal position, in respect of the elements of the Schengen *acquis* which have been given a legal basis in Title IV is to remain unchanged: the relevant provisions and decisions do not, in other words, acquire (for it) the quality of E.C. law.[96] Nor will Denmark take part in the adoption of measures under Title IV; and if it decides to implement any such measures in its national law, this will give rise, *vis-à-vis* the participating Member States, to an international obligation, not an E.C. one.[97] The unsatisfactory result is that the same set of rules will apply within the four walls of the Community order to 12 Member States (plus Ireland and/or the United Kingdom, if they opt in), but to Denmark with the entirely different character of rules of international law.[98]

Secondary flexibility (closer co-operation)

"Secondary flexibility" was an innovation of the T.A., in the form of the mechanism there referred to as "closer co-operation". The novelty of the mechanism is that it allows flexibility arrangements to be established by internal legislative procedures, and therefore not in policy areas which have been pre-selected for such treatment at Treaty level.

A general enabling provision has been inserted into the TEU,[99] which is complemented by legal bases relating more particularly to action under the E.C. Treaty[1] and under the Third Pillar.[2] Pursuant to those provisions, the Council may authorise a group of Member States to establish closer co-operation, provided that specified conditions are met.

There is a set of general conditions laid down by Article 43(1) (ex K.151(1)) TEU. These require, among other things: that closer co-operation be used only as a last resort, where Treaty objectives could not be attained by applying the normal procedures; that at least a majority of the Member States be involved; that the *acquis communautaire* not be affected; that the co-operation must not affect the competences, rights, obligations and interests of non-participating Member States; and that it be open to non-participants to opt in at any time, provided that they comply with the basic decision and any implementing decisions.

For authorising closer co-operation in Community matters, a further set of severely constraining conditions is laid down by Article 11(1) (ex 5a(1)) E.C. These require that closer co-operation:

---

[95] Schengen Protocol, Arts 4 and 5. The provisions relating to the opt-out from Title IV of Part Three, E.C. Treaty, are found in Protocol No. 4 to the Final Act of the T.A.

[96] Schengen Protocol, Art. 3.

[97] Protocol No. 5 to the Final Act of the TA.

[98] For a full analysis, see de Zwaan; "Opting Out and Opting In", I.C.Y.E.L.S. (1998), 107.

[99] See Arts 43–45 TEU (ex K.15–K.17).

[1] Art. 11 (ex 5a) E.C.

[2] Art. 40 (ex K.12) E.C.

"(a) does not concern areas which fall within the exclusive competence of the Community;

(b) does not affect Community policies, actions or programmes;

(c) does not concern the citizenship of the Union or discriminate between nationals of Member States;

(d) remains within the limits of the powers conferred upon the Community by this Treaty; and

(e) does not constitute a discrimination or a restriction of trade between Member States and does not distort the conditions of competition between the latter."

Recourse is again had, in sub-paragraph (a), to the imprecise concept of "areas which fall within the exclusive competence of the Community". However, it is by no means certain that the meaning is the same here as in Article 5, second paragraph.[3] Sub-paragraph (d) may be noted, since it preserves the attribution principle, by preventing the close co-operation mechanism from being used to enlarge the scope of application of the E.C. Treaty. In effect, an existing legal basis will have to be found for any closer co-operation proposal.

The procedure for obtaining authorisation to undertake closer co-operation in a given E.C. matter is found in Article 11(2) (ex 5a(2)). The Member States concerned must address a request to the Commission, which may or may not make a proposal to the Council. If it does so, the Council will decide by a qualified majority and after consulting the European Parliament, whether to grant authorisation. However, the variant of the Luxembourg Compromise procedure, already remarked on in Chapter 3,[4] applies here. By opposing the authorisation "for important and stated reasons of national policy", a Member State can prevent a vote from being taken, with the possibility of the issue's being referred to the Council, meeting in the composition of the Heads of State or Government, for decision by unanimity. It seems particularly unfortunate to have such a rule inserted into the E.C. Treaty itself.

The authorisation of a co-operation proposal opens the way for its implementation by the enactment of measures destined to apply only between the participating Member States. The procedure prescribed by Article 44 (ex K.16) is similar in its essentials to that generally provided for in cases of primary flexibility.[5] While all the Member States may contribute to the Council's deliberations, only those participating in the co-operation have a right to vote. The qualified majority threshold represents the proportion of the weighted votes of the participating Member States corresponding to the threshold fixed by Article 205(2) (ex 148(2)) E.C. Unanimity is constituted by the absence of negative votes only of those Member States.

The procedure to be followed by a non-participating Member State wishing to opt into an existing measure of closer co-operation, has the look of a compromise cobbled together in the final phase of the Amsterdam negotiations, with

---

[3] See the discussion of the subsidiarity principle, above.

[4] See pp. 51–52, above, and the critisim by Dashwood, *op. cit.* n.6, above, at p. 215.

[5] See, as regards EMU, Art. 122(5) (ex 109k) E.C., which fixes the qualified majority threshold as two thirds of the weighted votes of Member States without a derogation. See also U.K. Protocol, Art. 7. Pursuant to Art. 2 of the Danish Protocol, Denmark counts as a Member State with a derogation.

insufficient attention to detail.[6] The aspiring Member State must give notice of its intention to the Council and the Commission. Within three months, the Commission must give an opinion to the Council, and it then has a further month to decide on the notification, and on any specific arrangements it may deem necessary, seemingly with no further reference to the Council.

The Schengen Protocol presents itself as an instance of "applied" closer co-operation, as provided for pursuant to the T.A.,[7] but that seems misconceived. Such assimilation disguises the constitutional significance of the difference between primary and secondary flexibility. Nor can it be said that all the conditions for closer co-operation are fulfilled in the case of the Schengen Protocol. In particular, the requirement of a unanimous decision to admit Ireland or the United Kingdom to some or all of the *acquis*, flouts the condition of Article 43(1)(g) TEU that a given co-operation must be open to all Member States and must allow all of them to become parties at any time.

There is, though, a generally applicable lesson that can be learned from the experience of Schengen. It is that, if a sufficiently large group of Member States is determined to proceed with closer co-operation in a certain field, and cannot do so within the Union order, they will act outside it, storing up legal complexities for the future. Sensibly and sparingly used, the Amsterdam mechanism (where applicable) seems a better alternative.

---

[6] Art. 11(3) (ex 5a(3)) E.C.
[7] See Schengen Protocol, sixth recital and Arts 1 and 5(1), second sub-para.

CHAPTER 8

EUROPEAN COMMUNITY AND EUROPEAN UNION

The Union architecture

The European Union came into being with the entry into force of the TEU on November 1, 1993.[1]

It has been pointed out that the term "European Union" has long been in use as a generic description of a (possible) ulterior stage of the integration process, transcending the Community model.[2] However, the historic entity that is the E.U. owes its existence, more mundanely, to the course of the negotiations that culminated in agreement on the text of the TEU, at the Maastricht meeting of Heads of State or Government in December 1991.[3] During the negotiations, it became an issue whether certain policy areas to be covered by the Treaty should be brought within the compass of the E.C.; and, to the extent that they were not, what the relationship should be between those policy areas and the Community order. The four areas principally in question were citizenship, economic and monetary union, foreign and security policy and justice and home affairs. The solution eventually adopted was that the powers relating to citizenship and to economic and monetary union should be integrated into the E.C. Treaty, while those on the common foreign and security policy (CFSP) and on co-operation in the fields of justice and home affairs (JHA) should be placed in separate Titles (respectively, Titles V and VI) of the TEU; at the same time, the three Communities would be linked to each other, as well as to the CFSP and JHA, in a new overarching structure, the European Union. Within that structure, the same group of institutions would operate with differing powers under differing procedures, and with differing legal consequences, depending on the substantive policies being pursued.[4]

---

[1] For early, critical reactions, see Everling, "Reflections on the Structure of the Union", 29 C.M.L. Rev. (1992) 1053; Noël "Reflections on the Maastricht Treaty", 27 *Government and Opposition* (1992), 148; Curtin, "The Constitutional Structure of the Union: a Europe of Bits and Pieces", 30 C.M.L. Rev. (1993), 17. A more measured response is that of Weiler, "Neither Unity nor Three Pillars—The Trinity Structure of the Treaty on European Union" in Monar, Ungerer and Wessels (eds), *The Maastricht Treaty on European Union* (1993), p. 49. See also Curtin and Dekker, "The EU as a 'Layered' International Organisation: Institutional Unity in Disguise", in Craig and de Búrca (eds), *The Evolution of EU Law* (1999), 83.

[2] By de Witte, "The Pillar Structure and the Nature of the European Union: Greek Temple or French Gothic Cathedral?", in Heukels, Blokker and Brus (eds) *The European Union after Amsterdam* (1998) 51, at 57. He cites Toth, *The Oxford Encyclopedia of European Community Law*, Vol. I, Institutional Law (1990), at p. 248.

[3] The TEU, in its final form, brought together two texts that were negotiated separately by parallel conferences. One text, relating to what was known as "political union" was negotiated by personal representatives of the Foreign Ministers of the Member States under the auspices of the General Affairs Council, while the other text, relating exclusively to economic and monetary union, was negotiated by personal representatives of Finance Ministers under the auspices of the Economic and Financial Affairs Council.

[4] On the political union negotiations and their outcome, see P. de Schoutheete de Tervarent in J. V. Louis (ed.), *L'Union européenne après Maastricht* (journée d'études Bruxelles, February 21, 1922),

The structure was preserved, indeed strengthened, by the T.A., though it was modified in an important respect.[5] As we have noted in previous chapters, the T.A. caused a large part of the subject-matter of the former JHA (in effect, everything to do with the control of Member States' external frontiers and the treatment of third country nationals, as well as judicial co-operation in civil matters) to be transferred from Title VI TEU to the new Title IV of Part Three of the E.C. Treaty. Title VI TEU, as amended, is now devoted entirely to police and judicial co-operation in criminal matters (PJCCM). The material scope of the Title has thus been curtailed, but in that narrower field the common institutions have been given powers that are more concrete and far-reaching than originally under the TEU.

The general character of the relationship between the E.U. and the European Communities, and that of the various component elements of the Union *inter se*, can be gathered from Article 1 (ex A), third paragraph of the TEU, which provides:

"The Union shall be founded on the European Communities, supplemented by the policies and forms of co-operation established by this Treaty. Its task shall be to organise, in a manner demonstrating consistency and solidarity, relations between the Member States and between their peoples".

The three Communities pre-date the E.U. by many years: the ECSC came into being in July 1952, and the E.C. and Euratom in January 1958. Until November 1993, they were formally distinct, each resting on its own free-standing Treaty. The description of the Union as being "founded" on the Communities indicates that the latter must now be regarded as having been subsumed into the former; but also that they constitute overwhelmingly its most important component, the CFSP and PJCCM providing complementary elements.

The foundational quality of the Communities, and more particularly the E.C., *vis-à-vis* the Union can be seen as both substantive and ideological. Thus the great bulk of European Union activity (covering the fields of economic and social policy, in their internal and external aspects, and much besides) falls within the scope of application of the E.C. Treaty. At the same time, the Community model of European integration has been taken over as standard for the Union as a whole, though not (or not yet) applicable in all its parts. An explicit objective of the Union is "to maintain in full the *acquis communautaire* and build on it with a view to considering to what extent the policies and forms of co-operation introduced by this Treaty may need to be revised with the aim of ensuring the effectiveness of the mechanisms and the institutions of the Community".[6] The

---

p. 17; C. Timmermans, *ibid.* p. 49. For a commentary on the "political union" aspect of the Treaty in the draft put forward by the Luxembourg Presidency to the European Council in June 1991, see D. Vignes, (1991) R.M.C., p. 504. The Addendum on the TEU in de Cockborne *et al.*, *Commentaire Mégret* (2nd ed.), Vol. 1 (1992, Editions de l'Université de Bruxelles) contains at pp. 369 *et seq.*, a commentary on the Preamble and Common Provisions of the TEU.

[5] On the Union structure post-Amsterdam, see de Witte, *op. cit.*, n.2, above; and, for a more negative reaction, Gormley, "Reflections on the Architecture of the European Union after the Treaty of Amsterdam", in O'Keefe and Twomey (eds), *Legal Issues of the Amsterdam Treaty*, 57. See also Curtin and Dekker, *op. cit.* n.1, above.

[6] Art. 2 (ex B), first para., fifth indent.

internal dynamic of the Union, therefore, operates in one direction only—towards alignment on, and further development of, the Community model: the first results of this were found in the T.A., most conspicuously in the transfer of matters from Title VI TEU to the E.C. Treaty, but also in some of the changes in the arrangements under Titles V and VI themselves, which are considered below.

Moreover, it is stated, by Article 47 (ex M) TEU, that, subject to the provisions amending the Community Treaties (found in Titles II to IV TEU), and to the Final Provisions (in Title VIII), "nothing in this Treaty shall affect the Treaties establishing the European Communities or the subsequent Treaties and Acts modifying or supplementing them." Article 47 is one of the provisions of the TEU which the Court of Justice has jurisdiction to apply. The Court has thus been given the role of policing the frontier between the E.C., on the one hand, and the CFSP and PJCCM, on the other. For example, in Case C–170/96, *Commission v. Council*[7] the issue was whether a measure on the granting of airport transit visas to third country nationals ought to have been given a legal basis in the E.C. Treaty, rather than in Title VI TEU. In rejecting an objection to the admissibility of the action, the Court said it had to ensure that acts which, in the Council's view, fell within the scope of Title VI, did not encroach upon the powers conferred by the E.C. Treaty on the Community.

The second sentence of Article 1, third paragraph of the TEU speaks of the Union's task as being "to organise, in a manner demonstrating consistency and solidarity, relations between the Member States and between their peoples". Two organisational values are there highlighted: "consistency", presumably as between activities carried on under the different institutional arrangements that may be applicable;[8] and "solidarity", implying a commitment in principle to systematic co-operation and common action, wherever possible and appropriate.

There are commentators on the TEU who have argued that the Treaty did not give rise to any kind of new legal order: the so-called "Union" was simply a framework for enhanced intergovernmental co-operation in the fields of activity covered by Titles V and VI, as Title III of the SEA had been in respect of the former EPC.[9] We do not share that conception of the Union. It seems clear to us that the intention of the Treaty is to create a complex order, in which powers have been allocated among the common institutions, and as between those institutions and the Member States, under arrangements—found respectively in the Community Treaties and in Titles V and VI TEU—which are sufficiently differentiated to be regarded as three distinct sub-orders.[10] That follows from the operative language of Article 1, first paragraph TEU, which is identical to that of

---

[7] Case C–170/96 *Commission v. Council* [1998] E.C.R. I–2763; [1998] 2 C.M.L.R. 1092. See paras 12–18 of the judgments.

[8] See also Art. 3 (ex Art. C) on the single institutional framework, which is considered below.

[9] The thesis is vigorously propounded by Koenig and Pechstein, *Die Europaische Union* (1995). For an opposite view, see Von Bogdandy and Netterheim, "Ex pluribus unum: Fusion of the Euorpean Communities into the European Union", 2 E.L.J. (1996), 267; "Die Europäische Union: Ein einheitlicher Verband mit eigener Rechtsordnung", 31 *Europarecht* (1996), 3; and Von Bogdandy, "The legal case for unity: the European Union as a single organisation with a single legal system", 36 C.M.L. Rev. (1999), 887.

[10] Our conception is close to that of de Witte, *op. cit.*, n.2, above.

Article 1 E.C.,[11] from the definition of the Union just considered, and from the provisions organising the "complementary" sub-orders internally, and the principles that govern their relationship with the Community sub-order, which are analysed below.

The image of a Greek temple façade, conventionally used to illustrate the structure of the Union, was mentioned in the discussion of the TEU in Chapter 1, above. In that image, the "first pillar" represents the Communities, the "second pillar", the CFSP as provided for by Title V TEU, and the "third pillar", PJCCM as now provided for by Title VI TEU; while the pediment represents the various legal elements that link those three together as components of the Union. There has been criticism of the image,[12] and it is evidently defective: likening the Union's component orders to pillars, exaggerates the separation between them,[13] and makes it hard to convey the idea that the structure is "founded" on the European Communities. Nevertheless, "pillar talk" is pervasive and inescapable; and the image, if not pressed too far, provides a rough but helpful guide to understanding. Our version of it presents the first pillar as being situated in the middle, and also as much more solid than the other two.

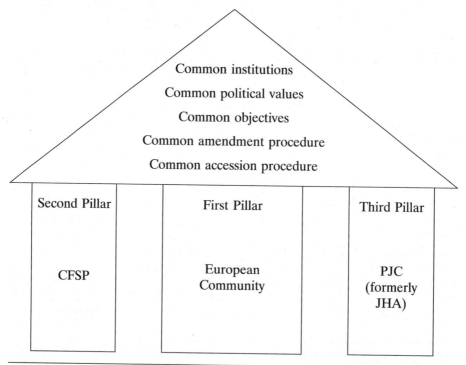

---

[11] "By this Treaty, the HIGH CONTRACTING PARTIES *establish* among themselves a EURO-PEAN UNION . . ." (emphasis added).

[12] By de Witte, *op. cit.* n.2, above, at pp. 52–53; Gormley, *op. cit.*, n.5, above, at pp. 57–58. Suggested alternatives have been a gothic cathedral (see de Witte, *op. cit.*, at pp. 64–65; Kapteyn and VerLoren van Themaat, (ed. Gormley), *Introduction to the Law of the European Communities* (3rd ed., 1998), at p. 47); and a "Trinity . . . in which 'oneness' and 'separateness' co-exist simultaneously" (see Weiler, *op. cit.* n.1, above, at p. 62).

[13] We return to this point when discussing the single institutional framework, below.

In the remainder of this chapter, we examine, first, the "pillars" (*i.e.* what it is that differentiates the European Communities legally from the CFSP and PJCCM) and, secondly, the unifying elements that constitute the "pediment" of the Greek façade; and we conclude with some remarks on the legal personality and capacity of the Communities and the Union.

The three pillars

It has rightly been said by de Witte:

"The *essence* of the pillar structure is the variation in the allocation of powers among the institutions. The Member States consider that primary responsibility for certain matters should remain in the hands of the national executives meeting in the Council."[14]

Nevertheless, we believe that the epithet "intergovernmental", still commonly applied to the institutional and procedural arrangements of the CFSP and PJCCM, is misleading. As we shall see, under those arrangements, especially since they were reformed by the T.A., the first tentative steps have been taken towards Member States' acceptance of the discipline of acting in common; though their sovereign rights are, and are likely to remain, much less severely curtailed than under the first pillar.[15]

The main difference between the first pillar and the second and third pillars follows from their respective Treaty bases. The location of the CFSP and PJCCM in Titles of the TEU, and not in the E.C. Treaty, sets them apart from the new legal order, the principles of which the Court of Justice has been working out in the remarkable series of judgments that began with *Van Gend en Loos*. The "essential characteristics" of that legal order, as we have seen, "are in particular its primacy over the law of the Member States and the direct effect of a whole series of provisions which are applicable to their nationals and to the Member States themselves".[16] Those, and the other constitutionalising principles of the Community order, became automatically applicable in the new policy areas integrated by the TEU and the T.A. into the E.C. Treaty (even where, as in the case of EMU and Title IV on visas etc., the institutional arrangements have unusual features), but not so in respect of the CFSP or JHA (now PJCCM).

A second major difference lies in the rules governing the interaction between the political institutions. The Council has a more than usually dominant role under the second and third pillars; this leaves the other institutions correspondingly reduced opportunities for influencing the development of policy and making their mark on the measures finally adopted, although there was an adjustment of the balance in their favour by the T.A. The Commission must be "fully associated" with the work carried out in the fields of the CFSP and PJCCM;[17] and it has a right of initiative, but not the exclusive right it enjoys for

---

[14] *Op. cit.*, n.2, above, at p. 66.

[15] In Opinion 1/91, the Court said that, for the benefit of the new legal order established by the Community Treaties, "the States have limited their sovereign rights, *in ever wider fields* ..." (emphasis added): [1991] E.C.R. I–6079, at para. 21.

[16] *ibid.*

[17] Art. 27 and Art. 36(2) TEU.

most purposes under the E.C. Treaty.[18] Member States also have a right of initiative, which in practice is normally exercised by the Council's Presidency. It is also the Presidency that has been entrusted with implementing decisions taken under Title V TEU, assisted by the Secretary General of the Council in the capacity of "High Representative for the CFSP", and again in association with the Commission;[19] in Title VI matters, it seems, implementation remains entirely in the hands of the Member States. As for the European Parliament, it must be consulted by the Presidency "on the main aspects and the basic choices" of the CFSP, and have its views "duly taken into consideration", as well as being kept regularly informed of developments;[20] however, it is not directly involved in decision-making on specific matters That is in contrast to the position under Title VI TEU, as amended by the T.A., where the Council is required to consult the Parliament before adopting most kinds of measure; though here, too, there is a difference as compared with the consultation procedure of the E.C. Treaty, since the Council has power to impose a time-limit of not less than three months for the delivery of the Parliament's opinion, after which it may act.[21] The Parliament also has the right to be regularly informed of discussions in the areas covered by Title VI, and to ask questions of the Council or make recommendations to it; and there must be an annual Parliamentary debate on progress made in those areas.[22]

Thirdly, both Title V and Title VI TEU equip the institutions with a different set of legal instruments from those available under Article 249 (ex 189) E.C. The binding instruments provided by Article 12 (ex J.2) TEU for pursuing the objectives of the CFSP are common strategies (decided on by the European Council), and joint actions and positions (adopted by the Council): their function is to give formal expression to policy positions, rather than to lay down rules. For the purposes of PJCCM, the Council has the following at its disposal:

(a) "common positions defining the approach of the Union to a particular matter";

(b) "framework decisions for the purpose of approximation of the laws and regulations of the Member States", of which it is said, as in the case of Community directives, that they "shall be binding upon the Member States as to the result to be achieved but shall leave to the national authorities the choice of form and methods";

(c) "decisions", which can be used for any purpose consistent with the objectives of Title VI, other than approximation; and

(d) "conventions which [the Council] shall recommend to the Member States for adoption in accordance with their respective constitutional requirements".[23]

---

[18] Art. 22(1) and Art. 34(2) TEU. Under the former Art. K.3(2) TEU there were certain matters where the Member States had an exclusive right of initiative.

[19] Art. 18 TEU.

[20] Art. 21 TEU.

[21] Art. 39 TEU.

[22] *ibid.*

[23] Art. 34(2) TEU. *Cf.* the more meagre armoury provided by the original Art. K.3(2) TEU.

There is thus no PJCCM instrument equivalent to a Community regulation, that could be used to enact legislation directly applicable in all of the Member States, in the sense of neither requiring nor permitting implementation by the national authorities.[24] It is also stated expressly, as regards both framework decisions and the residual category of decisions, that they "shall not entail direct effect".[25]

A fourth difference is found in the Council's voting rules. Whereas, under the E.C. Treaty, the trend is towards extending qualified majority voting to an ever wider range of matters,[26] in principle decisions under Titles V and VI TEU are taken by the Council acting unanimously.[27] Here too, however, the T.A. brought changes. In CFSP matters, the Council may act by a qualified majority when *implementing* a common strategy, a joint action or a common position (the basic instrument in each case requiring unanimity).[28] As to PJCCM, there is provision in Article 34(2)(c) for measures implementing, "at the level of the Union", decisions other than framework decisions, to be taken by the Council acting by a qualified majority; while Article 34(2)(d) says that "[m]easures implementing conventions shall be adopted within the Council by a majority of two-thirds of the Contracting Parties". The reference in the latter case to adoption "within", rather than by, the Council, indicates that the measures in question are acts, not of the institution itself, but of the representatives of the governments of the Contracting States; accordingly they have the legal quality of international agreements in simplified form.

Finally, and of great significance because case-law has been so influential in shaping and developing the Community order, the Court of Justice has no jurisdiction under the second pillar, and only a limited one under the third pillar.[29] The latter jurisdiction was conferred on the Court by the T.A.[30] That step, though as we shall see it falls short of establishing the rule of law in Title VI matters at the level of the Union, provides a clear example of the communitarising dynamic referred to above.

Pursuant to Article 35(1) TEU, the Court of Justice has jurisdiction to give preliminary rulings on the validity and interpretation of framework decisions and of decisions, on the interpretation of Title VI conventions, and on the validity and interpretation of the measures implementing them; but only where questions are referred to it by the courts or tribunals of Member States which have made a declaration signifying their acceptance of this jurisdiction.[31] In making such a declaration, a Member State must specify whether the possibility of requesting preliminary rulings is to be restricted to courts or tribunals of final resort, or to be available throughout the judicial hierarchy[32]; in either case, the Treaty does

---

[24] See the discussion in Chap. 4, above.

[25] A belt and braces provision, given that Title VI TEU is outside the Community order.

[26] See the discussion in Ch. 3, above.

[27] Art. 23(1) and Art. 34(2) TEU.

[28] The derogations from the unanimity rule in Art. 23(2) TEU are subject to the variant of the Luxembourg compromise discussed at pp. 51–52, above. Nor do they apply to decisions which have military or defence implications.

[29] See Art. 46 TEU.

[30] For a full discussion of this jurisdiction, see Arnull, "Taming the Beast? The Treaty of Amsterdam and the Court of Justice", in O'Keeffe and Twomey (eds), *Legal Issues of the Amsterdam Treaty*, 109, at 117–120.

[31] Art. 35(2).

[32] Art. 35(30).

not itself place courts or tribunals of final resort under a duty corresponding to that imposed by the third paragraph of Article 234 E.C., but there was a Declaration by the Amsterdam Conference noting that Member States could reserve the right to provide for such a duty in their national law.[33]

It must be possible for the Court of Justice, in giving preliminary rulings on the validity, or as the case may be the interpretation, of the secondary Title VI measures referred to in Article 35(1) TEU, to interpret any relevant provisions contained in the Title itself. However, from the wording of the paragraph, the Court does not seem to have been empowered to respond to requests from national courts, for preliminary rulings relating directly to those primary provisions.

Paragraph (5) of Article 35 TEU provides:

> "The Court of Justice shall not have jurisdiction to review the validity or proportionality of operations carried out by the police or other law enforce-ment services of a Member State or the exercise of the responsibilities incumbent upon Member States with regard to the maintenance of law and order and the safeguarding of internal security."

That appears to be stating the obvious: no jurisdiction "to review the validity or proportionality" of Member State measures of any kind is given by Article 35(1). If it were asked to conduct such a review the Court would doubtless follow its longstanding practice in cases under Article 234 E.C.,[34] and confine itself to an abstract ruling on the applicable Title VI measures, leaving any appropriate conclusions, in respect of actions taken by the national authorities, to be drawn in the main proceedings. Paragraph (5) does not say, and there are no good reasons for interpreting it as meaning, that jurisdiction under Article 35(1) must be refused, wherever it appears from the order for reference that the proceedings for the purposes of which a ruling by the Court is being sought, are concerned with the legality of police or other internal security operations.[35]

Courts in Member States which have chosen not to make a declaration under Article 35(2) TEU accepting the Court's jurisdiction, are not themselves able to request preliminary rulings on the interpretation or validity of Title VI measures; but there is no legal impediment to their recognising the persuasive authority of such rulings in cases that have come to the Court from other Member States, and they are likely in practice to do so.[36] That likelihood is tacitly recognised by Article 35(4), which allows statements of case or written observations to be

---

[33] Declaration No. 10.

[34] See Chap. 11, above.

[35] *Cf.* Art. 68(2) E.C., which excludes the Court's Art. 234 jurisdiction in respect of Council measures taken with a view to ensuring the absence of controls on persons crossing internal borders, where these relate to "the maintenance of law and order and the safeguarding of internal security". The difference of wording is noted by Arnull, *loc. cit.*, n.28, above.

[36] *Cf.* the Protocol on the opt-out for the United Kingdom and Ireland from Title IV of Part Three of the E.C. Treaty (Protocol No. 4 to the Final Act of the Amsterdam Conference). Art. 2 of the Protocol provides that, *inter alia*, no decision of the Court of Justice interpreting any provision of Title IV or any measure adopted under it "shall be binding upon or applicable in the United Kingdom or Ireland"; or "shall in any way affect the competitiveness, rights and obligations of those States"; or "shall in any way affect the *acquis communautaire* nor form part of Community law as they apply to the United Kingdom or Ireland".

submitted in proceedings arising under the Article by any Member State, whether or not it has made a declaration pursuant to paragraph (2).

Besides the optional preliminary rulings procedure, there are two other heads of jurisdiction for the Court of Justice provided by Article 35 TEU. Paragraph (6) enables the Court to review the legality of framework decisions and decisions, in actions brought by a Member State or the Commission, on similar grounds to those that apply under Article 230 E.C., and subject to the same two-month time limit: that natural and legal persons have not been given *locus standi* is unsurprising, since both kinds of instrument in question are expressly stated not to entail direct effect.[37] Under paragraph (7), the Court may rule on a dispute between Member States regarding the interpretation or the application of Title VI instruments, which the Council has been unable to settle within six months of having the matter referred to it; and it also has jurisdiction in disputes between Member States and the Commission regarding the interpretation or application of conventions established under Article 35(2)(d). The paragraph (7) jurisdiction thus gives pride of place to the political resolution of inter-Member State disputes, with recourse to the Court only if this fails. Taking the two paragraphs together, the Commission can be seen as the junior partner of the Member States in preserving legality under Title VI (in contrast with its role as guardian of the E.C. Treaty).[38]

The pediment

The main unifying elements, represented by the pediment of the Greek temple image, are: the single institutional framework within which all Union activities are carried on; a set of fundamental political and constitutional values, and machinery (first provided by the T.A.) to help ensure that these are upheld by all the Member States; common objectives, stated in a way that implies an "interpillar" approach; and common procedures for the amendment of the founding Treaties (the three Community Treaties and the TEU), and for accessions to the Union.

(i) The single institutional framework

Prior to the TEU, co-operation in the matters that would be brought within the second and third pillars was carried on outside the Community institutions (as they then were). European Political Cooperation (or "EPC"), the forerunner of the CFSP, was organised on the basis of Title III of the SEA.[39] The partners to EPC were described as "High Contracting Parties", not Member States; and their Foreign Ministers, when discussing EPC matters, did not constitute "the Council" (though such discussions might take place "on the occasion of meetings of the Council").[40] A Secretariat was established in Brussels to assist in preparing and implementing EPC activities and in administrative matters,[41] but was kept

---

[37] It is hard to see how, in the absence of direct effect, the criterion of direct and individual concern, applicable under Art. 230 E.C., could be satisfied.

[38] Art. 211 (ex 155) E.C., first indent.

[39] Title III SEA was repealed by Art. P(2) TEU.

[40] See the former Art. 30(3)(a) SEA.

[41] See the former Art. 30(10)(g) SEA.

strictly apart from the Council's General Secretariat, and staffed by national officials on secondment from the various Foreign Ministries. As for the matters which came to be grouped under the JHA rubric of the third pillar, structured co-operation had for some time been taking place in a range of intergovernmental working parties, but without a Treaty basis.

Article 3 (ex C) TEU states, in its first paragraph, that "[t]he Union shall be served by a single institutional framework which shall ensure the consistency and the continuity of the activities carried out in order to attain its objectives while respecting and building upon the *acquis communautaire*". The second paragraph of Article 3 lays particular emphasis on "the consistency of the Union's external activities as a whole in the context of its external relations, security, economic and development policies". There must, in other words, be a coherent overall approach to the aspects of a complex international situation (as in Bosnia and subsequently in Kosovo) that belong to the domain of the CFSP, and those aspects falling within the external relations competence of the E.C. Responsibility for ensuring the necessary consistency is placed on the Council and the Commission, which "shall co-operate to this end",[42] to ensuring the implementation of the policies mentioned in the paragraph, "each in accordance with its respective powers".

From the two following Articles of the TEU, the "single institutional framework" can be seen to comprehend the European Council and the five main institutions identified by Article 7 (ex 4) E.C.

A Treaty basis for the European Council was first provided by Article 2 of the SEA. That provision was replaced by Article 4 (ex D) TEU, which defines the role and composition of the European Council, fixes the rhythm of its meetings and imposes upon it reporting obligations to the European Parliament. The reference in the first paragraph of the Article to the "Union", must be interpreted in the sense of Article 1, third paragraph: it follows that the European Council has been entrusted with providing "the necessary impetus", and "defining the general political guidelines" for the development of the E.C. no less than of the CFSP and PJCCM; and Presidency Conclusions from successive European Councils show that is exactly how the latter have understood their task.[43]

According to Article 5 (ex E) TEU: "[t]he European Parliament, the Council, the Commission, the Court of Justice and the Court of Auditors shall exercise their powers under the conditions and for the purposes provided for, on the one hand, by the provisions of the Treaties establishing the European Communities and of the subsequent Treaties and Acts modifying and supplementing them and, on the other hand, by the other provisions of this Treaty." The grammatical construction of the provision ("on the one hand, . . . and, on the other hand") places the powers derived by the five institutions from the TEU on an equal

---

[42] The duty of cooperation was an addition to Art. 3 by the T.A., after friction between the two institutions experienced in the early years of the CFSP.

[43] See, *e.g.* Part III of the December 1999 Helsinki Conclusions. A similar point is made by de Witte, *op. cit.* n.2, above, at p. 60. See also Glaesner, "The European Council", in Curtin and Henkels (eds), *The Institutional Dynamics of European Integration—Essays in Honour of Henry G. Schermers*, 101 at 112–115.

footing with those derived from the Community Treaties. For that reason, the view (which has been widely held,[44] and which the authors of this work once shared),[45] that the institutions retain their Community character and are merely "borrowed" by the Union, seems mistaken. A metaphor that reflects, more accurately than that of "borrowing", the text of Article 5 and the institutional reality, would be that institutions born under the Community Treaties, as amended, have been "legally adopted" by the Union.[46]

We have seen that the respective powers, and the mutual interaction, of the institutions differ significantly between the three pillars. The implications of the creation of a single institutional framework serving the Union as a whole are, nevertheless, profound, in both formal and substantial terms. This is especially clear in relation to the Council, because of its central role in decision-making on the CFSP and PJCCM, as well as in the Community sphere.

Broadly speaking, the Council's mode of operation, as defined by the Treaties and its own Rules of Procedure, and elaborated in its working practices, is the same across the whole spectrum of Union activities. Thus draft measures, whether based on first, second or third pillar powers, undergo technical examination in the appropriate Council working party, and then proceed by way of the Committee of Permanent Representatives (COREPER) to the ministerial level, for political consideration, where necessary, and formal adoption. The same Council agenda may contain items for discussion (so-called "B-points") belonging to different pillars: for instance, CFSP matters, and trade or development co-operation matters falling within the E.C.'s external relations competence, appear alongside each other on agendas of the General Affairs Council. Similarly, A-point lists may contain items for adoption without discussion from all three pillars, regardless of the particular formation in which the Council may be meeting.[47]

There are specialised committees composed of senior national officials—the Political Committee and the Coordinating Committee—which, among their other tasks, contribute to the preparation of Council decisions under the second and third pillars, respectively:[48] that, however, is without prejudice to the role of COREPER as the body with general responsibility for the final preparation and presentation of all agenda items to the Council.[49] As the Helsinki European Council noted:

---

[44] See, among others, Timmermans in J. V. Louis (ed.) *L'Union européenne après Maastricht* (Journée d'études Bruxelles, February 21, 1992) 49, at 51; Constantinesco, "La structure du Traité instituant l'Union européenne", 29 C.D.E. (1993), 251, at 267–268; Everling, *op. cit.*, n.1, above, at p. 1061; Heukels and De Zwaan, "The Configuration of the European Union: Community Dimensions of Institutional Interaction", in Curtin and Heukels (eds.), *op. cit.* n.40, above, 195, at 227.

[45] 3rd ed., at p. 657.

[46] de Witte, *op. cit.* n.2, above, at pp. 58 *et seq.*, though he does not use the suggested metaphor, expresses a similar view. The Council has acknowledged its adoption by the Union through rechristening itself "Council of the European Union": see Council Dec. 93/591, [1993] O.J. L281/18. This, despite the fact that Art. 1 of the Merger Treaty continues to refer to "[a] Council of the European Communities"; as does Art. 9 of the same Treaty, to "[a] Commission of the European Communities". The justification for the Council's change of name lies in reading Art. 1 of the Merger Treaty together with Arts 3 and 5 TEU.

[47] See de Witte, *ibid.* at p. 61. On the organisation of the Council's agenda, see Chap. 2, above.

[48] See, respectively, Art. 25 and Art. 36(1) TEU.

[49] Art. 207(1) (ex 151(1)) E.C.

"For any dossiers where substantive preparation is undertaken in other fora, COREPER must in any case be in a position to verify that the following principles and rules are respected:

(i) the principle of legality in the light of Community law, including the principles of subsidiarity, proportionality and of providing reasons for acts;
(ii) the powers of Union institutions;
(iii) budgetary provisions;
(iv) rules on procedure, transparency and the quality of drafting of legislation;
(v) consistency with other Union policies and measures."[50]

Moreover, the standing invitation for the Commission to take part in meetings of the Council applies irrespective of the legal basis of the matter being discussed.[51] Commission representatives will, therefore, regularly be present at all levels of Council decision-making on CFSP or PJCCM measures, and may contribute actively to the debate.

A last point on the single institutional framework is that it has brought matters covered by Titles V and VI TEU within the field of responsibility of the Council's General Secretariat. The national officials and Ministers dealing with such matters in Council bodies, accordingly, have the benefit of independent advice and assistance from the same corps of permanent civil servants with which they are accustomed to working in the European Community context.

(ii) Fundamental values and principles

Article 6 (ex 8) TEU provides:

"(1) The Union is founded on the principles of liberty, democracy, respect for human rights and fundamental freedoms, and the rule of law, principles which are common to the Member States.
(2) The Union shall respect fundamental rights, as guaranteed by the European Convention for the Protection of Human Rights and Fundamental Freedoms signed in Rome on November 4, 1950 and as they result from the constitutional traditions common to the Member States, as general principles of Community law.
(3) The Union shall respect the national identities of its Member States.
(4) The Union shall provide itself with the means necessary to attain its objectives and carry through its policies."

The principles that encapsulate the fundamental political values of the European Union are stated in paragraph (1) of the Article. The paragraph was added by the T.A.: in the version of the Article found in the original TEU, there was only an oblique reference to the fact that Member States' "systems of government are founded on the principle of democracy".

---

[50] Helsinki Conclusions, Annex III, point 23.
[51] Rules of Procedure, Art. 4(3).

That change has an echo in Article 49 (ex O) TEU, where respect for the principles set out in Article 6(1) has been made a condition which States applying for membership of the Union must fulfil. With the prospect of an enlargement which is likely to bring into the Union some countries where democracy and the rule of law are recent and fragile growths, it may have seemed wise to spell out in black and white that commitment to those principles is, for an applicant, a qualification as indispensable as being "European".

In Article 7 TEU, the T.A., moreover, provided machinery allowing steps to be taken against a Member State guilty of a "serious and persistent breach" of the Article 6(1) principles. The determination that such a breach exists is made by the Council, meeting in the composition of the Heads of State or Government, and acting unanimously on a proposal by a third of the Member States or by the Commission, after obtaining the assent of the European Parliament. The government of the Member State concerned must have been invited to submit its observations. Following such a determination, the Council may, by qualified majority decision, suspend certain of the rights enjoyed by that Member State under the TEU and the E.C. Treaty, including its voting rights (though its obligations must be left intact). Due consideration must be given to the consequences such suspensions may have for the legal situation of individuals. The Council may decide subsequently, again by a qualified majority, to vary or revoke any suspension measures it has taken, in response to changes in the situation. For the purposes of the relevant Council decisions, the vote of the representative of the targeted Member State will not be taken into account.

Scepticism may be felt as to the practical value of that machinery. The unanimity necessary at the level of the Heads of State or Government (excepting only the Member State in the dock) for a determination as to the existence of a serious and persistent breach, seems most unlikely to be achieved—the less so, the larger the Union becomes. The essential thing is that a candidate country be only accepted into the Union once its credentials as a fully functioning democracy have been established. The introduction of the suspension machinery is unfortunate in principle, too: it detracts from the *sui generis* nature of the Union, making it appear like just another international organisation.

We have seen that the fundamental human rights, guaranteed by the European Convention and by the constitutional traditions common to the Member States, have been recognised by the Court of Justice as applying within the European Community order, with the force of general principles of law.[52] The effect of Article 6(2) TEU is to render the obligation to respect fundamental rights applicable to all Union activities, and therefore also to those that take place under the second and third pillars. However, pursuant to Article 46(d) TEU, the jurisdiction of the Court only extends to Article 6(2) "with regard to action of the institutions, insofar as the Court has jurisdiction under the Treaties establishing the European Communities and under this Treaty". The limitation on the justiciability of human rights infringements calls for two comments.

---

[52] See the statement of principle in Opinion 2/94, [1996] E.C.R. I–1759.

First, the reference in Article 46(d) to "action of the institutions" must not be interpreted as purporting to override the case-law that requires respect for fundamental rights on the part of the authorities of the Member States, when they are acting as executants of Community policies or taking advantage of derogations allowed by the E.C. Treaty.[53] Such an interpretation would be incompatible with Article 47, since Article 6(2) is found among the Common Provisions in Title I of the TEU, against the effects of which the Community Treaties are protected.[54]

Secondly, the Court's lack of jurisdiction under the second pillar, though it manifestly weakens the effect of Article 6(2) in respect of actions taken for the purposes of the CFSP, does not render the provision nugatory. The legal obligation of the Union to respect human rights is a factor likely to be invoked in Council debates, and which may influence their outcome; as may have been the case, for example, when it was decided that the powers granted to the E.U. Administrator of the city of Mostar in Bosnia-Herzegovina, should be made subject to a form of judicial review, by a specially appointed Ombudsman.[55]

The two remaining paragraphs of Article 6 require only brief notice. The obligation in paragraph (3) for the Union to "respect the national identities of its Member States" was mentioned in Chapter 7: it applies equally under all three pillars. Paragraph (4) puts the Union under an obligation to provide itself with the means necessary to attain its objectives and carry through its policies. This will come into play as a political makeweight in discussions about the level of "own resources" to be made available to the Union under the financial packages which are agreed periodically.[56]

(iii) Common objectives

According to Article 2 (ex B) TEU, the Union is to set itself the following objectives.

> "— to promote economic and social progress and a high level of employ-
> ment and to achieve balanced and sustainable development, in particu-
> lar through the creation of an area without internal frontiers, through
> the strengthening of economic and social cohesion and through the
> establishment of economic and monetary union, ultimately including a
> single currency in accordance with the provisions of this Treaty;
> — to assert its identity on the international scene, in particular through the
> implementation of a common foreign and security policy including the
> progressive framing of a common defence policy, which might lead to a
> common defence, in accordance with the provisions of Article 17;

---

[53] Case 5/88 *Wachauf* [1989] E.C.R. 2609; [1991] 1 C.M.L.R. 328; Case C–260/89 *ERT* [1991] E.C.R. I–2925; Case C–159/90, *SPUC v. Grogan* [1991] E.C.R. I–4685; [1991] 3 C.M.L.R. 849.

[54] As distinct from Titles II, III and IV which contain the provisions amending the three Community Treaties, and Title VII the TEU's Final Provisions: these are excluded from the saving effect of Art. 47.

[55] See Council Dec. 94/976, [1994] O.J. L312/34.

[56] On the current "Agenda 2000" package, see Chaps 1 and 2, above.

— to strengthen the protection of the rights and interests of the nationals of its Member States through the introduction of a citizenship of the Union;

— to maintain and develop the Union as an area of freedom, security and justice, in which the free movement of persons is assured in conjunction with appropriate measures with respect to external border controls, asylum, immigration and the prevention and combating of crime;

— to maintain in full the acquis communautaire and build on it with a view to considering to what extent the policies and forms of co-operation introduced by this Treaty may need to be revised with the aim of ensuring the effectiveness of the mechanisms and the institutions of the Community."

The second paragraph of the Article imposes a requirement on the Union, in the course of attaining its objectives in conformity with the conditions and the timetable provided for, to respect the principle of subsidiarity as defined in Article 5 E.C.

A first point to note about the statement of objectives in Article 2 TEU is its completeness. The first four indents contain succinct summaries of the concrete activities that can be carried on under all three pillars. This is the clearest possible refutation of the conception of the Union as a mere organising framework for co-operation on Title V and VI matters. It confirms the conception of a comprehensive Union order.

Secondly, the objectives mentioned in the second and fourth indents are ones that presuppose interpillar activity. Although the second indent places particular emphasis on the CFSP, for the Union "to assert its identity on the international scene" calls for the co-ordinated exercise of the full range of external relations powers conferred by the Treaties, as Article 3 TEU goes on to make clear. Similarly, the measures referred to in the fourth indent, "to maintain and develop the Union as an area of freedom, security and justice . . .", are ones that will entail action under both Title IV of Part Three of the E.C. Treaty and Title VI TEU.[57]

The obligation stated in the fifth indent, to maintain in full, and to build on, the *acquis communautaire*, which confirms the centrality of the Community pillar in the Union architecture, was considered earlier in this chapter.

(iv) Common amendment and accession procedures

Prior to the TEU, there were separate procedures under each of the three European Community Treaties, for the amendment of the Treaty[58] and for the accession of new Member States to the Community in question.[59] The relevant provisions were repealed by the TEU, and replaced by standard procedures "for the amendment of the Treaties on which the Union is founded", and for the admission of States to membership of the Union.

---

[57] See, for confirmation, the explicit references to third pillar measures in Art. 61 E.C.
[58] Respectively, the former Art. 98 ECSC, Art. 236 E.C. and Art. 204 Euratom.
[59] Respectively, the former Art. 98 ECSC, Art. 237 E.C. and Art. 205 Euratom.

The common amendment procedure is found in Article 48 (ex O) TEU. Proposals for amendment may come from any Member State or from the Commission, and must be submitted to the Council. After consulting the European Parliament, the Commission (if not itself the initiator of the proposal) and the European Central Bank (in case of institutional changes in the monetary area), the Council may decide (by a simple majority, presumably, since no voting rule is specified)[60] to deliver an opinion in favour of calling an intergovernmental conference (IGC). If it does so, the IGC is convened by the President. The amendments to be made to the Treaties are determined by common accord, and enter into force after being ratified by all Member States in accordance with their respective constitutional requirements.

Article 49 (ex O) TEU lays down the common accession procedure. Applications for membership of the Union must be addressed to the Council, which acts by unanimity, after consulting the Commission and receiving the assent of the European Parliament. The conditions of admission, and any necessary adjustment to the Treaties, have to be agreed between the Member States and the applicant; and the agreement is then submitted for ratification by all the contracting States. In practice, the Council exercises its powers in respect of membership applications, in two phases: there is, first, a decision on the principle of admission, which allows negotiations to be set in train; and, once these have been completed successfully, and the accession instruments are ready for signature, a formal decision is taken,[61] accepting the application.

Legal personality and capacity

Under the present heading, we consider the status of the Communities and the Union in the domestic legal orders of the Member States, on the one hand, and in public international law, on the other. These are interesting issues, but it is important to be clear that they have no particular relevance to the public powers of legislation, administration and adjudication exercisable by the common institutions within the Union's own order.

Each of the European Communities is expressly declared, by its respective founding Treaty, to have legal personality.[62] There is also an explicit statement as to the legal capacity of the Community in the national orders:

"In each of the Member States, the Community shall enjoy the most extensive legal capacity accorded to legal persons under their laws; it may, in particular, acquire or dispose of movable and immovable property and may be a party to legal proceedings . . .".[63]

---

[60] Cf. Art. 205(1) (ex 148(1)) E.C. It is suggested that rule would apply by analogy, since the qualified majority voting rule applicable under the TEU is that of Art. 205(2).

[61] In the case of the accession of Austria, Finland and Sweden it was necessary to adjust the accession instruments to take account of Norway's failure to ratify the Accession Treaty.

[62] Art. 281 (ex 210) E.C.; Art. 6, first para. ECSC; Art. 184 Euratom.

[63] Art. 282 (ex 211) E.C. Art. 185 Euratom is in identical terms. Art. 6, third para. ECSC is similar in substance.

In addition, the Euratom Treaty, like the ECSC Treaty before it,[64] acknowledges the capacity of the Community to act in the international order. Article 101, first paragraph Euratom provides:

"The Community may, within the limits of its powers and jurisdiction, enter into obligations by concluding agreements or contracts with a third State, an international organisation or a national of a third State."

Curiously, the E.C. Treaty contains no equivalent provision expressly recognising the external capacity of the Community. However, the Court of Justice has chosen, with some audacity, to interpret the bare reference in Article 281 to the legal personality of the E.C. as meaning "that in its external relations the Community enjoys the capacity to establish contractual links with third countries over the whole field of objectives defined in Part One of the Treaty . . .".[65] The Court's reasoning was that the generality of the grant of legal personality, evidenced by the position of Article 281 at the head of Part Six of the Treaty devoted to General and Final Provisions, must entail acknowledgement of the external capacity of the E.U. in all policy areas falling within its competence. Effectively, therefore, the position of the E.C. as a subject of international law, has been assimilated by the Court to that of Euratom.

Of course, neither Article 281 E.C., nor the more explicit provisions of the ECSC and Euratom Treaties, could actually have given the Communities international legal personality and capacity: the existence of the former, and the extent of the latter, are matters for international law itself to determine. However, the intentions of the States which have formed the entity in question, as manifested in the foundational instrument, weigh heavily in such a determination; and these can be gathered not only from texts like Article 101, first paragraph Euratom but also, and more particularly, from the goals the entity has been set, and from the nature and scope of the powers conferred on its institutions.[66] The Communities manifestly fulfil the criteria for possession of legal personality that were laid down by the International Court of Justice in the *Reparations for Injuries* case; and recognition of their capacity to pursue their objectives on the international plane has been confirmed by decades of practice.

The TEU contains no provision stating that the Union established pursuant to the Treaty shall have legal personality. Two proposals for the insertion of such a provision into the Treaty were considered at different moments by the IGC

---

[64] See Art. 6, second para. ECSC.

[65] Case 22/70 *Commission v. Council (AETR)* [1971] E.C.R. 263, at para. 14; [1971] C.M.L.R. 335. For a full discussion of this and other aspects of the famous *AETR* case, see Dashwood, "Implied External Competence of the EC", in Koskennienni (ed.), *International Law Aspects of the European Union* (1998), 113.

[66] The leading case is the Advisory Opinion of the International Court of Justice on *Reparation for Injuries suffered in the Service of the United Nations* I.C.J. Reports, 1949, p. 174 (hereinafter "the *Reparation for Injuries*" case). The Opinion draws a distinction between attribution of legal personality in principle, and the scope of the capacity enjoyed by a given international organisation: see, in particular, *ibid.* at pp. 178–184. The criteria of legal personality for international organisations have been summarised by Brownlie as follows: (1) a permanent association of states, with lawful objects, equipped with organs; (2) a distinction between the organisation and its member states; (3) the existence of legal powers exercisable on the international plane and not solely within the national systems of one or more states (see *Principles of Public International Law* (4th ed., 1990) pp. 680–683).

negotiating the future T.A.: one idea was that the Union be given legal personality which would be juxtaposed with the existing personalities of the Communities;[67] while the more radical suggestion (of the Dutch Presidency) was for a single legal personality of the Union as a whole, into which those of the Communities would be assimilated. In the event, however, neither proposal won acceptance.

On the other hand, the T.A. did introduce a Council procedure which may (though it need not) be used when an international agreement, on a matter falling within Title V or Title VI of the TEU, is called for. Article 24 TEU provides:

"When it is necessary to conclude an agreement with one or more States or international organisations in implementation of this Title, the Council, acting unanimously, may authorise the Presidency, assisted by the Commission as appropriate, to open negotiations to that effect. Such agreements shall be concluded by the Council acting unanimously on a recommendation from the Presidency. No agreement shall be binding on a Member State whose representative in the Council states that it has to comply with the requirements of its own constitutional procedure; the other members of the Council may agree that the agreement shall apply provisionally to them.

The provisions of this Article shall also apply to matters falling under Title VI."

There are two possible ways of interpreting that provision.[68] One interpretation would be that the Article merely establishes a simplified procedure, enabling the institutional machinery of the Treaty to be used for the purpose of negotiating and concluding, on behalf of the Member States, international agreements to which they, and not the Union, will be parties. The reference, in the second sentence, to national ratification procedures, and to the possibility of provisional application in respect of "the other members of the Council", would tend to support that construction. The other possibility is that Article 24 TEU acknowledges the capacity of the Union as such to enter into international agreements relating to Title V or Title VI matters. In favour of that interpretation would be the fact that the power to authorise the opening of negotiations and to conclude any agreement, is expressed to belong to the Council, and not to the representatives of the governments of the Member States meeting within the Council.

Practice will show which of those interpretations is the right one. If agreements in the fields of the CFSP and PJCCM are negotiated and concluded in the name of the Union, it will be clear that the Member States and their international partners have accepted that the Union is endowed with external capacity, and necessarily therefore legal personality, at least for the purposes of Titles V and VI TEU. That seems to us the likely outcome. Indeed, applying the criteria of

---

[67] This was part of a rather elaborate draft provision, under the heading "Endowing the Union with legal personality", included in the text which was submitted by the Irish Presidency to the European Council in Dublin in December 1996; see CONF 2500/96, pp. 87–89.

[68] See Dashwood, "External Relations Provisions of the Amsterdam Treaty", 35 C.M.L. Rev. (1998), 1019, at 1038–1041. Reprinted in O'Keeffe and Twomey (eds), *Legal Issues of the Amsterdam Treaty*, 201, at 218–221.

the *Reparation for Injuries* judgment, a good case can be made, independently of Article 24, for the Union's possession of international legal personality, in view of its objectives, which manifestly have an external dimension, as well as its single institutional framework. Support for this analysis can be found in the fact that ambassadors from third countries are now regularly accredited to the Union, rather than to the Communities.[69]

In the result, despite the silence, or at best the equivocation, of the TEU, we take the view that the Union can be recognised as possessing international legal personality and capacity, and that any lingering doubts in this matter will be removed by the developing practice. It is no impediment to such recognition that the Communities, which constitute the major component of the Union, each have their own personality. After all, within the legal order created by the E.C. Treaty, there are, besides the Community, two entities endowed with legal personality, namely the European Central Bank[70] and the European Investment Bank.[71] Complex though the Community's relationship with each of the Banks may be, their co-existence as legal persons is not seen as problematic in itself.[72]

The Union has not been given legal capacity within the domestic orders of the Member States, but that is unlikely to be felt as more than a minor inconvenience. In the private law relationships that call for such capacity (*e.g.* procurement contracts or the acquisition or disposal of real property) the interests of the Union and of the Community will normally be indistinguishable.

---

[69] There is, moreover, a tendency for CFSP instruments to refer to the Union as if it were an international actor with rights and obligations: see, *e.g.* the Joint Action on the participation of the Union in the implementing structures of the peace plan for Bosnia-Herzegovina, [1995] O.J. L309/2.

[70] Art. 266 (ex 198d), first para. E.C.

[71] Art. 107(2) (ex 106(2)) E.C.

[72] As to the EIB, see Case 85/86 *Commission v. Governors of the EIB* [1988] E.C.R. 1281. On the relationship between the ECB and the European Community, see Zilioli and Solmayr, "The European Central Bank: an Independent Specialised Organisation of Community Law", 37 C.M.L. Rev. (2000), p. 591.

PART IV: JURISDICTION OF THE COURT OF JUSTICE AND THE COURT OF FIRST INSTANCE

CHAPTER 9

JUDICIAL ARCHITECTURE AND JUDICIAL METHOD

The Court of Justice of the European Communities in the form in which we know it today was established under the 1957 Convention on Certain Institutions Common to the European Communities.[1] That Convention established a single Court with jurisdiction under the ECSC, EEC and Euratom Treaties, which had each made provision for separate courts. Since 1989 some of the powers conferred on the Court of Justice have been exercised by the Court of First Instance of the European Communities (CFI). The Court of Justice and the CFI are sometimes referred to collectively as the Community judicature or the Community Courts. Both Community Courts sit in Luxembourg. The CFI is considered in more detail below.

⸏The Court of Justice plays a central role in the system created by the Treaties and has made a vital contribution to the Community's development.[2] Some of the concepts which are fundamental to the way in which the Community functions are to be found, not in the Treaties themselves, but in the case-law of the Court. The approach taken by the Court to the discharge of its responsibilities has not escaped criticism. In a paper published in January 1995 entitled "The European Court of Justice: A Case Study in Judicial Activism", Sir Patrick Neill Q.C. suggested that many of the Court's decisions were "logically flawed or skewed by doctrinal or idiosyncratic policy considerations". Sir Patrick Neill's views were considered by the House of Lords Select Committee on the European Communities in the course of its enquiry into the 1996 intergovernmental conference (IGC). Many of those who gave evidence to the Select Committee took a more positive view of the Court's role and the Neill thesis was comprehensively rejected by the Select Committee itself,[3] which observed:

"A strong and independent Court of Justice is an essential part of the structure of the European Union. We agree with those witnesses who stressed the important role of the Court in the consolidation of democratic structures and upholding the rule of law in the European Community. We note the criticisms of 'judicial activism' which have been levelled against the Court but these appear to be based mainly on cases where the Court has made Community law effective against defaulting Member States at the instance of individuals

---

[1] Although sometimes referred to as "the European Court" (see, *e.g.* the European Communities Act 1972), the Court of Justice should not be confused with the European Court of Human Rights, which sits in Strasbourg, France, and is not an institution of the European Union.

[2] See further Arnull, *The European Union and its Court of Justice* (1999); Dehousse, *The European Court of Justice* (1998).

[3] See *1996 Inter-Governmental Conference* (Session 1994–95, 21st Report, HL Paper 105), para. 256. Sir Patrick Neill's paper is published in the Minutes of Evidence taken before the Select Committee (Session 1994–95, 18th Report, HL Paper 88), p. 218. It was also published as a pamphlet by the European Policy Forum in August 1995. Sir Patrick Neill was not without supporters. See, *e.g.* Hartley, "The European Court, Judicial Objectivity and the Constitution of the European Union" (1996) 112 L.Q.R. 95. For an earlier analysis of the Court from a similar perspective, see Rasmussen, *On Law and Policy in the European Court of Justice* (1986).

seeking to enforce their rights. We accept that enforceable remedies are essential to the application of Community legal obligations, with a high degree of uniformity throughout the Member States."

The main rules relating to the Court of Justice are to be found in the Treaties themselves and the Statutes of the Court, which are annexed as protocols to each of them. Detailed effect is given to the Statutes[4] by the Rules of Procedure of the Court (the Rules). The Rules are adopted by the Court itself but they require the unanimous approval of the Council.[5] The CFI has its own Rules of Procedure, which it establishes in agreement with the Court of Justice. The CFI's Rules also require the unanimous approval of the Council.[6] In a discussion paper entitled "The Future of the Judicial System of the European Union" issued in the spring of 1999, the Community Courts pointed out that, in an enlarged Union, the maintenance of that requirement could have the effect of paralysing the process of amending the Rules of Procedure. The Courts therefore advocated that the Treaties be changed to allow them to adopt their own Rules of Procedure or, at the very least, to allow the Council to approve proposed changes by qualified majority. At the time of writing, that suggestion had yet to be implemented.

THE ORGANISATION OF THE COURT

The members

The Court of Justice consists of 15 Judges[7] and is assisted by nine Advocates General.[8] The Judges and Advocates General are sometimes referred to collectively as the members of the Court. The general function of a Judge needs no further explanation here. The distinctive role played by the Advocate General in proceedings before the Court is considered below. The Court sits either as the full Court (for which the quorum is nine) or in chambers of three or five Judges, according to the importance or difficulty of the case.[9] The Treaty used to require cases brought by a Member State or by a Community institution to be heard by the full Court. That requirement was abolished at Maastricht, although the Member States and the Institutions are entitled to require the Court in sit in plenary session in proceedings to which they are parties.[10] In practice limited use is made of that entitlement.

---

[4] References hereafter are to the E.C. Statute.

[5] Art. 245 (ex 188) E.C.

[6] Art. 225(4) E.C.

[7] Art. 221 (ex 165) E.C.

[8] Art. 222 (ex 166) E.C. At the time of writing the ninth post is vacant. The number of Advocates General will fall to eight on October 7, 2000. See below.

[9] A power to create chambers of seven Judges conferred on the Court at Maastricht has yet to be exercised: see Art. 221 (ex 165) E.C.

[10] A Member State or an institution is treated as a "party" for these purposes where it is a party to or an intervener in a direct action or has submitted written observations in a reference for a preliminary ruling: Rules, Art. 95(2). On the distinction between direct actions and references for preliminary rulings, see Chaps. 10 and 11.

Unlike the Commission,[11] there is nothing in the Treaties about the national composition of the Court. In practice, however, one Judge is appointed from each Member State. A party may not apply for a change in the composition of the Court or of one of its chambers on the ground of the nationality of a Judge or the absence of a Judge of the nationality of that party.[12] There is always one Advocate General from each of the five largest Member States.[13] At present, Italy is entitled to a second Advocate General, but that entitlement will lapse on the expiry of a single mandate.[14] The remaining posts rotate among the other Member States.

The accession of a significant number of new Member States in the foreseeable future may cause practical problems for the Court if each new State is accorded the right to nominate a Judge. In a report on the application of the Treaty on European Union published as part of the preparations for the 1996 IGC,[15] the Court observed that "any significant increase in the number of judges might mean that the plenary session of the Court would cross the invisible boundary between a collegiate court and a deliberative assembly. Moreover, as the great majority of cases would be heard by chambers, this increase could pose a threat to the consistency of the case-law." The Court acknowledged, however, that "the presence of members from all the national legal systems on the Court is undoubtedly conducive to harmonious development of Community case-law, taking into account concepts regarded as fundamental in the various Member States and thus enhancing the acceptability of the solutions arrived at. It may also be considered that the presence of a Judge from each Member State enhances the legitimacy of the Court."[16] Those considerations seem compelling enough to outweigh the managerial problems which a big rise in the number of Judges would cause.

Judges and Advocates General "rank equally in precedence according to their seniority in office."[17] The rules relating to their appointment are the same. Thus, according to Article 223 (ex 167) E.C., they must be "persons whose independence is beyond doubt and who possess the qualifications required for appointment to the highest judicial offices in their respective countries or who are jurisconsults of recognised competence." In practice, the members of the Court have come from a variety of backgrounds, including the national judiciary, the civil service, the Bar and universities. It has been suggested[18] that a member's

---

[11] See Art. 213(1) (ex 157(1)) E.C.

[12] Statute, Art. 16.

[13] France, Germany, Italy, Spain and the United Kingdom.

[14] See further Tridimas, "The role of the Advocate General in the development of Community law: some reflections" (1997) 34 C.M.L. Rev 1349, 1351, n.6.

[15] See "The Proceedings of the Court of Justice and Court of First Instance of the European Communities", May 22–26, 1995, No. 15/95.

[16] Para. 16.

[17] Rules, Art. 6. Where there is equal seniority in office, precedence is determined by age. Advocates General have sometimes become Judges (*e.g.* F. Mancini, Sir Gordon Slynn, C. Gulmann) and Judges have sometimes become Advocates General (*e.g.* A. Trabucchi, F. Capotorti). A. La Pergola began his career at the Court as a Judge, then became an Advocate General and subsequently reverted to being a Judge. Only Judges take part in the election of the Court's President, who directs the judicial business and administration of the Court and presides at hearings of the full Court. The President must be a Judge.

[18] By a former President of the Court, Judge O. Due of Denmark, in an interview broadcast on BBC Radio in 1990.

professional background can have at least as significant an influence on his approach to a case as his national origin. British critics sometimes object to the appointment of members without judicial experience. It may be noted, however, that under the ECSC Treaty no legal qualifications whatsoever were required for appointment and two of the original members of the Coal and Steel Court did not possess any. It has also been pointed out that "in all the original six Member States the holder of a University chair of law may be translated to the bench, sometimes at the highest levels."[19] In its report on the 1996 IGC,[20] the House of Lords Select Committee on the European Communities said that "a Treaty amendment which would exclude professors or administrators would narrow the range of professional experience available to the Court and would be seen as trying to impose on other Member States a particularly British view of the best background for senior judicial office."

According to Article 223 (ex 167) E.C., the members of the Court are appointed "by common accord of the Governments of the Member States for a term of six years", which is renewable. It is worth emphasising that the Members are not appointed by the Council of Ministers or by any single Member State. This means that a Member's appointment can in theory be blocked by any of the Member States. It is sometimes suggested that members should instead be chosen from a list of national nominees by a Judicial Appointments Board composed of very senior members of the judiciaries of the Member States.[21] The advantage of such a system is said to be that it would distance the selection of members from the domestic political process. However, the House of Lords Select Committee said in its report on the 1996 IGC: "We do . . . have considerable doubts as to whether senior judges within one judicial system are in fact well qualified to pronounce on the relative merits of candidates from another. The task would add considerably to their responsibilities and they would in practice be likely to depend on confidential assessments of competence and character supplied by their own governments."[22]

In a resolution on the functioning of the TEU adopted on May 17, 1995 as part of the preparations for the 1996 IGC,[23] the European Parliament argued that its assent should be required to nominations to the Court. In its own report on the functioning of the TEU, the Court expressed opposition to the introduction of any such procedure on the ground that prospective appointees would be unable to respond to questions without prejudging issues they might have to decide in the exercise of their judicial functions. The Court's view that such a procedure would be unacceptable was shared by the House of Lords Select Committee.[24] The Parliament's suggestion was not taken up by the Member States.

---

[19] Brown and Kennedy, *Brown and Jacobs' The Court of Justice of the European Communities* (4th ed., 1994), p. 46.

[20] Para. 260.

[21] See Koopmans, "The future of the Court of Justice of the European Communities" (1991) 11 Y.E.L. 15 at 26; Dashwood, evidence to the House of Lords Sub-Committee on the 1996 IGC (Session 1994–95, 18th Report, HL Paper 88), p. 259.

[22] Para. 260.

[23] See [1995] O.J. C151/56, point 23(ii).

[24] See para. 261 of its report on the 1996 IGC.

The role of the Advocate General

One Advocate General is assigned to each case the Court is called upon to decide. After the parties have concluded their submissions, and before the Judges begin their deliberations, the Advocate General presents an independent and impartial Opinion on the case. The Opinion is fully reasoned in the manner of a reserved judgment in the higher English courts. It sets out any relevant facts and legislation, discusses the issues that have been raised, situating them in the evolving pattern of the Court's case-law, and recommends a decision to the Judges.

The office of Advocate General is thought to have been modelled on that of the *commissaire du gouvernement* in the French Conseil d'Etat, although it has now developed in such a way that it is better to regard it as *sui generis*. Because the Advocate General has no counterpart in the English legal system, those whose background is in the common law sometimes search for analogies to elucidate his role. A popular analogy is with a judge of first instance, but that comparison is useful only because of its inappropriateness. First, the Advocate General does not sit alone but hears the case with the Judges. Secondly, the Opinion only contains a recommendation: it is the Judges who actually decide the case. Thirdly, since the Opinion constitutes the last stage in the oral part of the procedure,[25] the parties are not entitled to comment on the views expressed by the Advocate General. The inability of the parties to respond to issues addressed in the Opinion, even those which have not been raised in argument, is consistent with the continental principle that a court is deemed to know the law.[26] According to that view, the task of a court is to apply the relevant legal rules to the facts presented by the parties and if necessary it will engage in its own legal research.[27] The Court is sometimes willing to reopen the oral procedure pursuant to Article 61 of the Rules where a party wishes to respond to the Advocate General's Opinion,[28] but has rejected the view that closing the oral procedure after the Advocate General has delivered his Opinion involves an infringement of the right to a fair trial enshrined in Article 6(1) of the European Convention on Human Rights.[29]

There is good reason to believe that a persuasive Opinion will strongly influence the subsequent deliberation. Lord Slynn, who served as an Advocate General and later as a Judge at the Court, has written[30]: "As an Advocate

---

[25] Rules, Art. 59.

[26] "Jura novit curia" or "curia novit legem".

[27] See Advocate General Jacobs in Joined Cases C–430 and 431/93 *van Schijndel and van Veen v. SPF* [1995] E.C.R. I–4705 at 4717–4718; [1996] 1 C.M.L.R. 801; [1996] All E.R. (E.C.) 259.

[28] See, *e.g.* Case C–35/98, *Staatssecretaris van Financiën v. Verkooijen*, Order of September 17, 1999. The Advocate General delivered a second Opinion on December 14, 1999. *cf.* Case C–163/90 *Administration des Douanes et Droits Indirects v. Legros and Others* [1992] E.C.R. I–4625.

[29] Case C–17/98 *Emesa Sugar (Free Zone) NV v. Aruba*, Order of February 4, 2000; Joined Cases C–270/97 and C–271/97 *Deutsche Post A.G. v. Sievers and Schrage*, judgment of February 10, 2000.

[30] *Introducing a European Legal Order* (1992), pp. 157–158. See also the remarks of Judge Robert Lecourt, a former President of the Court, in a speech delivered on October 9, 1973 on the occasion of the retirement of Advocate General Roemer: "Pour avoir une idée vraie du rôle des conclusions, c'est au délibéré qu'il faut avoir accès. On y decouvrirait l'intérêt de cet ultime répit entre le débat de l'audience et la médiation du juge et l'utile décantation de conflit judiciare qui en résulte. On y apprécierait qu'une voix autorisée et libre, s'élevant au-dessus des parties, ait pu

General, one always hoped that the function had some utility; as a judge I now know that it is very valuable in this kind of court to have a detailed first-round assessment on which the judges can work. The research, the analysis of fact and law, the direction indicated by the Advocate General—even if not followed—are of considerable help." In the majority of cases, the judgment and its rationale follow the Advocate General's Opinion fairly closely. Indeed, in a change from its previous practice, the Court now often refers expressly to the Opinion of the Advocate General where it agrees with it, sometimes without even adding any reasons of its own.[31] However, it is an important safeguard that, even where the Court of Justice sits as a court of first and last resort, its decisions are in effect judicially considered twice over.

The impact of an Opinion is not limited to the case in which it is given. It will be published alongside the judgment in the European Court Reports and may be cited as authority by counsel or Advocates General in future cases, or in legal literature. The value of the Opinion to users of the Court was underlined during the enquiry into the establishment of the CFI by the House of Lords Select Committee on the European Communities.[32] The Court had proposed that there should not be any Advocates General in the new tribunal, but a number of those who gave evidence to the Select Committee expressed the hope that the CFI would be assisted by Advocates General. In the event, the CFI was given the right to call upon one of its Members to perform the function of Advocate General where "the legal difficulty or the factual complexity of the case so requires".[33]

Language

Cases may be conducted in Danish, Dutch, English, Finnish, French, German, Greek, Irish, Italian, Portuguese, Spanish or Swedish.[34] In direct actions,[35] the general rule is that the choice of language lies with the applicant. However, where the defendant is a Member State or a natural or legal person having the nationality of a Member State, the language of the case is the official language of that State. In references for preliminary rulings,[36] which constitute an interlude in proceedings which start and finish in a national court, the language of the case is that of the referring court. The submissions of the parties, both written and oral, must be made in the language of the case. The

---

analyser avec le recul nécessaire l'argumentation de chacune et pris le risque de porter sur le litige un premier jugement. On relèverait, enfin, l'importance de cette tension de l'ésprit que provoque, en chaque juge, des orientations qui alimenteront les éventuelles confrontations du délibéré, en l'absence de votre personne, mais non dans le silence de votre voix."

[31] See, *e.g.* Case C–59/92 *Hauptzollamt Hamburg-St Annen v. Ebbe Sönnichsen* [1993] E.C.R. I–2193, para. 4; Case C–36/92 P *SEP v. Commission* [1994] E.C.R. I–1911, para. 21; [1992] 4 C.M.L.R. 434; Case C–119/97 P *Union Française de l'Express v. Commission*, judgment of March 4, 1999, para. 81; Case C–456/98 *Centrosteel v. Adipol*, judgment of July 13, 2000, para. 12. In Case T–14/98 *Hautala v. Council*, judgment of July 19, 1999, para. 20, the CFI quoted from the Opinion of the Advocate General in another case.

[32] See *A European Court of First Instance* (Session 1987–88, 5th Report, HL Paper 20).

[33] See Art. 18, CFI Rules.

[34] Rules, Art. 29(1). Irish is not in practice used.

[35] *i.e.* actions which start and finish before the Court. See Chap. 10.

[36] See Chap. 11.

Member States may use their own official languages when intervening in a case or taking part in a reference for a preliminary ruling. The Registar of the Court arranges for translation into the language of the case. Inside the Court itself French is the working language, although English is also used a good deal. At hearings, members of the Court are entitled to put questions to the parties in any of the Court's procedural languages. The Advocates General draft their Opinions in their own languages.

Deliberation and judgment

Once the Advocate General has delivered his opinion, the Court begins its deliberations. The process of reaching a decision is usually conducted in French. The authentic version of the judgment in the language of the case, if it is one other than French, will therefore be a translation. An attempt is usually made to reach a consensus on the outcome. Every Judge taking part in the deliberations is obliged to give his view and the reasons for it and to cast a vote. The final decision on a case is, if necessary, taken by majority vote, but all the Judges who took part in the deliberations are required to sign the judgment. There are no dissenting judgments. Moreover, under Article 32 of the Statute, the deliberations of the Court take place in secret. Only the Judges taking part attend. The collegiate character of the Court's judgments helps to protect the Judges from the various forms of political pressure to which they might otherwise be subject. However, the resulting judgment may perhaps have the look of a "committee" document, lacking in elegance and sometimes even in coherence.

JUDICIAL METHOD

Methods of interpretation

The Court of Justice has become well-known for interpreting provisions of Community law by reference, not just—or even principally—by reference to their wording, but also by reference to their spirit and the general scheme of the instrument of which they form part. In *CILFIT v. Ministry of Health*,[37] the Court sought to explain its approach to the interpretation of Community provisions by reference to "the characteristic features of Community law and the particular difficulties to which its interpretation gives rise". The features underlined by the Court in that case included: (a) the fact that the different language versions of a Community provision are all equally authentic and may have to be compared; and (b) the need to place every provision of Community law in its context and to interpret it in the light of Community law as a whole, having regard to the objectives of Community law and its present state of development.

---

[37] Case 283/81 [1982] E.C.R. 3415, paras 17–20; [1983] 1 C.M.L.R. 472.

This does not mean that the Court takes no account of the wording of the provision it is called upon to interpret. Sometimes the Court will conclude that the ordinary meaning of the words used can be applied,[38] but there are two reasons why the wording cannot always be treated as decisive. One, mentioned by the Court in *CILFIT*, is the multi-lingual nature of Community law.[39] In *Regina v. Bouchereau*, that factor was overlooked by the United Kingdom Government when it sought to rely on the use of the same term in the English text of separate provisions of a Community directive. The Court observed[40]: "A comparison of the different language versions of the provisions in question shows that with the exception of the Italian text all the other versions use different terms in each of the two articles, with the result that no legal consequences can be based on the terminology used." The Court treats all the language versions as having the same weight, regardless of the size of the Member States where they are spoken.[41] Another reason why a literal approach is often inappropriate concerns the way in which many Community provisions are drafted. Bingham J. explained in *Customs and Excise v. ApS Samex* that[42] "[t]he interpretation of Community instruments involves very often not the process familiar to common lawyers of laboriously extracting the meaning from words used but the more creative process of applying flesh to a spare and loosely constructed skeleton."

Thus, depending on the circumstances, the Court may give priority to factors other than language, such as the objectives of the provision concerned (so-called "teleological interpretation") and its legal context. These factors were treated as decisive in *Bouchereau*,[43] where the Court declared: "The different language versions of a Community text must be given a uniform interpretation and hence in the case of divergence between the versions the provision in question must be interpreted by reference to the purpose and general scheme of the rules of which it forms a part." The Court has made extensive use of the teleological and contextual approaches, not only to resolve divergences between different

---

[38] See, *e.g.* Case 152/84 *Marshall v. Southampton and South-West Hampshire Area Health Authority* [1986] E.C.R. 723; [1986] 1 C.M.L.R. 688; Case 59/85 *Netherlands v. Reed* [1986] E.C.R. 1283; [1987] 2 C.M.L.R. 448.

[39] See Van Calster, "The EU's tower of babel—the interpretation by the European Court of Justice of equally authentic texts drafted in more than one official language" (1997) 17 Y.E.L. 363.

[40] Case 30/77 [1977] E.C.R. 1999, para 13; [1977] 2 C.M.L.R. 800. *cf.* Case 29/69 *Stauder v. Ulm* [1969] E.C.R. 419; [1970] C.M.L.R. 112; Case 9/79 *Koschniske v. Raad van Arbeid* [1979] E.C.R. 2717; [1989] 1 C.M.L.R. 87; Case C–298/94, *Henke v. Gemeinde Schierke and Verwaltungsgemeinschaft Brocken* [1996] E.C.R. I–4989; [1997] 1 C.M.L.R. 373; Joined Cases C–283, 291 and 292, *Denkavit Internationaal and Others v. Bundesamt für Finanzen* [1996] E.C.R. I–5063; Case C–64/95 *Lubella v. Hauptzollamt Cottbus* [1996] E.C.R. I–5105; [1995] 4 C.M.L.R. 696; Case C–72/95 *Kraaijeveld and Others v. Gedeputeerde Staten van Zuid-Holland* [1996] E.C.R. I–5403; [1997] 3 C.M.L.R. 1; Joined Cases C–267 and 268/95, *Merck and Others v. Primecrown and Others* and *Beecham v. Europharm* [1996] E.C.R. I–6285; [1997] 1 C.M.L.R. 83.

[41] See Case C–296/95, *The Queen v. Commissioners of Customs & Excise, ex p. EMU Tabac* [1998] E.C.R. I–1605, para. 36; [1998] 2 C.M.L.R. 1205.

[42] [1983] 1 All E.R. 1042 at 1056. See also Lord Denning in *Bulmer Ltd v. Bollinger SA* [1974] Ch. 401 at 425.

[43] *Supra,* para. 14. See also *Primecrown, supra,* para. 22; Case C–375/97, *General Motors v. Yplon,* judgment of September 14, 1999, paras 20–23; Case C–231/97 *van Rooij v. Dagelijks bestuur van het waterschap de Dommel,* judgment of September 29, 1999, paras 24–29; [1999] 2 C.M.L.R. 1452; Case C–6/98 *ARD v. PBO Sieben Media AG,* judgment of October 28, 1999, para. 27; Case C–434/97 *Commission v. France,* judgment of February 24, 2000.

language versions but also to confirm interpretations suggested by the wording,[44] to clarify ambiguity and to fill in gaps in the legal framework.[45]

The Court has traditionally made little use of *travaux préparatoires* (preparatory documents) as an aid to discovering the intentions of the authors of the Treaty, although this is a popular method of interpretation in international law.[46] The main reason for the Court's reticence is that the *travaux préparatoires* of the original Treaties were not made public. However, it is possible that this approach will in future be modified. The Court is willing to look at *travaux préparatoires* in cases concerning the interpretation of Community acts.[47] Increasing pressure for transparency[48] and the development of the Internet have now brought some *travaux préparatoires* concerning subsequent amendments to the Treaties themselves into the public domain. This was particularly noticeable during the IGC which resulted in the Treaty of Amsterdam and continued with the 2000 *IGC*. Indications given by *travaux préparatoires* would, however, have to be particularly compelling in order for them to be given precedence over the purpose and general scheme of the Treaty.

In principle the Court's approach to the interpretation of Community acts is similar to the one it takes in interpreting the Treaty. However, the Court may give less emphasis to the objective of a provision and to its legal context where there is a detailed legislative scheme, such as those that have been laid down in the fields of social security and agriculture.[49] Indeed, where the legislature has made its intentions clear through the use of detailed provisions, the Court may feel bound to acknowledge the results, even if they render the act concerned unlawful.[50] Where legislation is less precise, its objectives and context will naturally assume greater prominence.[51] The Court sometimes also has recourse to the comparative analysis of the laws of the Member States on a given problem in order to find the solution which is best adapted to the needs of the Community. An example is *A M & S Europe Ltd v. Commission*.[52] There, having examined the position in the

---

[44] See, *e.g.* Case C–260/90, *Leplat* [1992] E.C.R. I–643; [1992] 2 C.M.L.R. 512; Case C–84/95 *Bosphorus Hava Yollari AS v. Minister for Transport, Energy and Communications, Ireland* [1996] E.C.R. I–3953; [1996] 3 C.M.L.R. 257.

[45] See, *e.g.* Case 26/62 *Van Gend en Loos v. Nederlandse Administratie der Belastingen* [1963] E.C.R. 1; [1963] C.M.L.R. 105. *Cf.* Case 314/85 *Foto-Frost v. Hauptzollamt Lübeck-Ost* [1987] E.C.R. 4199, paras 16 and 17; [1988] 3 C.M.L.R. 57.

[46] See Art. 32 of the Vienna Convention on the Law of Treaties.

[47] See Joined Cases C–68/94 and 30/95, *France and Others v. Commission* [1998] E.C.R. I–1375, para. 167; [1998] 5 C.M.L.R. 136; Case 15/60 *Simon v. Court* [1961] E.C.R. 115 at 125. *Cf.* Case C–321/96 *Mecklenburg v. Kreis Pinneberg—Der Landrat* [1998] E.C.R. I–3809, para. 28; [1999] 2 C.M.L.R. 418.

[48] See, *e.g.* Arts 207(3) (ex 151) and 255 (ex 191a) E.C.; Case C–58/94, *Netherlands v. Council* [1996] E.C.R. I–2169; [1996] 2 C.M.L.R. 996. The pressure has grown since the accession of Sweden, where the law on access to documents is highly developed. See Österdahl, "Openness v. secrecy: public access to documents in Sweden and the European Union" (1998) 23 E.L. Rev. 336.

[49] By contrast, the Court has relied extensively on the teleological and contextual methods in interpreting the Community's detailed VAT legislation: see Farmer and Lyal, *E.C. Tax Law* (1994), pp. 89-90.

[50] See Advocate General Jacobs in Case C–85/90, *Dowling* [1992] E.C.R. I–5305 at 5320–5322; [1993] 1 C.M.L.R. 288.

[51] See, *e.g.* Case C–13/94 *P v. S and Cornwall County Council* [1996] E.C.R. I–2143; [1996] 2 C.M.L.R. 247; [1996] All E.R. (E.C.) 397. *Cf.* Case 184/83 *Hofmann v. Barmer Ersatzkasse* [1984] E.C.R. 3047; [1986] 1 C.M.L.R. 242. Both cases are discussed in Chap. 27.

[52] Case 155/79 [1982] E.C.R. 1575; [1982] 2 C.M.L.R. 264. See also Case 374/87 *Orkem v. Commission* [1989] E.C.R. 3283.

Member States, the Court accepted that a limited doctrine of legal professional privilege applied in E.C. competition cases, notwithstanding the silence of the relevant provisions on the matter. On occasion Member States or Community institutions[53] make statements, which may be recorded in the Council minutes, when a measure is adopted about what they consider its scope to be. Whether or not they are made public, the Court has made it clear that such statements cannot affect the objective meaning of the measure.[54]

In addition to these maxims, there are certain more precise principles which should be mentioned for the sake of completeness. The first is that derogations from general provisions are normally interpreted strictly. This principle has been applied not only to provisions of the Treaty, such as Articles 30 (ex 36)[55] and 39(3) (ex 48(3)),[56] but also to those contained in Community acts.[57] Secondly, the Court has said[58]: "When the wording of secondary Community legislation is open to more than one interpretation, preference should be given as far as possible to the interpretation which renders the provision consistent with the Treaty. Likewise, an implementing regulation must, if possible, be given an interpretation consistent with the basic regulation . . . Similarly, the primacy of international agreements concluded by the Community over provisions of secondary Community legislation means that such provisions must, so far as is possible, be interpreted in a manner that is consistent with those agreements." Finally, it may be noted that "procedural rules are generally held to apply to all proceedings pending at the time when they enter into force, whereas substantive rules are usually interpreted as not applying to situations existing before their entry into force."[59] However, amending legislation applies, unless otherwise stated, to the future consequences of situations which arose under the legislation previously in force.[60]

Precedent

The Court of Justice is not bound by its previous decisions but in practice it does not often depart from them. The Court's approach is epitomised by the extent of the freedom enjoyed by the national courts of the Member States to request preliminary rulings from the Court of Justice under Article 234 (ex 177) E.C. Since the Court of Justice is not bound by its own previous decisions, the

[53] See, *e.g.* the accompanying statements entered in the minutes of the Council when Reg. 4064/89 on merger control (discussed in Chap. 23) was adopted, [1990] 4 C.M.L.R. 314.

[54] Case C–292/89, *Antonissen* [1991] E.C.R. I–745; [1991] 2 C.M.L.R. 373. See also Case C–25/94 *Commission v. Council* [1996] E.C.R. I–1469, para. 38; Joined Cases C–283, 291–292/94, *Denkavit and Others v. Bundesamt für Finanzen* [1996] E.C.R. I–5063, para. 29; Hartley, "Five forms of uncertainty in European Community law" [1996] C.L.J. 265 at 274–278.

[55] See, *e.g.* Case 95/81 *Commission v. Italy* [1982] E.C.R. 2187, para. 27; *Merck v. Primecrown, supra,* para. 23.

[56] See, *e.g.* Case 30/77 *Regina v. Bouchereau* [1977] E.C.R. 1999, paras 31–35; [1977] 2 C.M.L.R. 800.

[57] See, *e.g.* Case 222/84 *Johnston v. Chief Constable of the RUC* [1986] E.C.R. 1651, para. 36; [1986] 3 C.M.L.R. 240; Case C–450/93, *Kalanke* [1995] E.C.R. I–3051, para. 21; [1996] 1 C.M.L.R. 175; [1996] All E.R. (E.C.) 66.

[58] Case C–61/94, *Commission v. Germany* [1996] E.C.R. I–3989, para. 52. See also Case C–135/93, *Spain v. Commission* [1995] E.C.R. I–1651, para. 37; [1997] 1 C.M.L.R. 281.

[59] Case C–61/98, *De Haan Beheer v. Inspecteur der Invoerrechten en Accijnzen* [1999] 3 C.M.L.R. 211, para. 13; [1999] 3 C.M.L.R. 211.

[60] See Case C–60/98, *Butterfly Music Srl v. CEMED*, judgment of June 29, 1999, para. 24.

national courts are not precluded from taking that step merely because the point of Community law at issue has already been dealt with by the Court of Justice.[61] A corollary of the absence of a doctrine of binding precedent in Community law is that the distinction between the *ratio decidendi* of a judgment of the Court and its *obiter dicta* loses much of its significance.[62] The distinction is important in the common law because it is only the *ratio* of a case which is capable of binding other courts in the future. However, in principle everything that is said in a judgment of the Court of Justice expresses the Court's opinion and is therefore capable of having the same persuasive force.[63] Occasionally, however, the Court seeks to distinguish a case on which a party has sought to rely. In order to perform this exercise, the Court has to establish what the previous case, properly construed, in fact decided. This process is analogous to that of identifying the *ratio* of a judgment given by a common law court.[64]

Of course, like all courts the Court of Justice tries to be consistent in the decisions it reaches. Thus, in proceedings under Article 234 E.C. in which the Court is asked to rule on a point it has already dealt with, it will, in the absence of any suggestion that the previous case was wrongly decided, simply repeat its earlier ruling.[65] Indeed, where a question referred to the Court for a preliminary ruling is "manifestly identical to a question on which the Court has already ruled", the Court is empowered by Article 104(3) of the Rules to give its decision by reasoned order in which reference is made to its previous judgment.

The practice of the Court has been strongly influenced by its civil law origins. In the civilian tradition, judicial decisions are not considered a formal source of law and judges do not feel compelled to analyse or reconcile earlier judgments in the manner of the common law judge.[66] As a result, the Court for many years rarely referred in its judgments to its previous decisions, even when repeating a passage verbatim. In due course references to its previous decisions became commonplace, but the analysis of them remained superficial and selective by the standards of English courts. The reader of the Court's judgments will be struck by the fact that previous decisions are often only cited by the Court where they support its argument. Authorities which point the other way are sometimes not

---

[61] See Joined Cases 28–30/62 *Da Costa v. Nederlandse Belastingadministratie* [1963] E.C.R. 31; [1963] C.M.L.R. 224; Case 66/80 *International Chemical Corporation v. Amministrazione delle Finanze dello Stato* [1981] E.C.R. 1191, para. 14; [1983] 2 C.M.L.R. 593; *CILFIT v. Ministry of Health, supra,* paras 14 and 15; Case C–91/92 *Faccini Dori v. Recreb* [1994] E.C.R. I–3325; [1994] 1 C.M.L.R. 665.

[62] See further Toth, "The authority of judgments of the European Court of Justice: binding force and legal effects" (1984) 4 Y.E.L. 1 at 36–42; Cross and Harris, *Precedent in English Law* (4th ed., 1991), pp. 17-18. *cf.* Koopmans, "*Stare decisis* in European Law" in O'Keeffe and Schermers (eds), *Essays in European Law and Integration* (1982), 11 at 22–24.

[63] Thus, the Court's ruling in Case 152/84 *Marshall v. Southampton and South-West Hampshire Area Health Authority* [1986] E.C.R. 723; [1986] 1 C.M.L.R. 688 that directives could not have horizontal direct effect was reached in proceedings in which the respondent was a public authority. See Advocate General Roemer in Case 9/61 *Netherlands v. High Authority* [1962] E.C.R. 213 at 242; [1962] C.M.L.R. 59. *Cf.* Advocate General Warner in Case 112/76 *Manzoni v. FNROM,* [1977] E.C.R. 1647 at 1661–1663.

[64] A good example is Case C–313/90 *CIRFS v. Commission* [1993] E.C.R. I–2557.

[65] See, *e.g.* Case C–350/89 *Sheptonhurst Ltd v. Newham Borough Council* [1991] E.C.R. I–2387; [1991] 3 C.M.L.R. 463, where the Court repeated its ruling in Case C–23/89 *Quietlynn Ltd v. Southend Borough Council* [1990] E.C.R. I–3059; [1990] 3 C.M.L.R. 55. *Cf.* Joined Cases C–418/93 etc. *Semeraro Casa Uno and Others* [1996] E.C.R. I–2975.

[66] See Brown and Kennedy, *op. cit.,* pp. 343–344.

mentioned at all, sometimes presented as if they support the line the Court has chosen to take.[67]

Perhaps as a consequence of the growing influence of the common law, there are signs in some more recent decisions of greater willingness on the part of the Court to confront the implications of earlier case-law. In *HAG II*,[68] the Court for the first time expressly overruled one of its own previous decisions. Following the advice of Advocate General Jacobs, the Court in that case abandoned the much-criticised doctrine of common origin laid down in *HAG I*,[69] which limited the circumstances in which the owner of a trade mark in one Member State could restrain imports of products legally bearing the mark in another Member State. The Court said that it was "necessary to reconsider the interpretation given in [*HAG I*]"[70] and went on to make it clear that the doctrine of common origin no longer formed any part of the case-law on intellectual property. In a subsequent case concerning the scope of Article 28 (ex 30) E.C, *Keck and Mithouard*,[71] the Court also departed from previous case-law, but it did so less candidly. The Court stated that it considered it "necessary to re-examine and clarify its case-law on this matter" and concluded, "contrary to what has previously been decided", that certain types of national legislation which might appear to hinder imports were none the less compatible with the Treaty. Unlike *HAG II*, however, the Court did not make clear precisely what it was overruling. The effect of its judgment was therefore to leave the status of its previous decisions on the matter unclear. This aspect in particular of the *Keck* ruling attracted criticism,[72] which seemed to produce an effect. In *Cabanis-Issarte*,[73] a social security case, the Court made it clear that an earlier ruling[74] was to be regarded as confined to its facts and that a series of specified later cases based on it were no longer good law.[75] By contrast, in *Merck and Others v. Primecrown and Others* and *Beecham v. Europharm*,[76] the Court refused to depart from the rule laid down in a previous case, *Merck v. Stephar and Exler*,[77] on the circumstances in which patent rights were to be considered exhausted. The Court undertook a detailed examination of the arguments for reconsidering the rule in *Merck v. Stephar*, but concluded that it had struck the right balance in that case between the principle of the free movement of goods and the interests of patentees.

---

[67] See, *e.g.* Case C–368/95 *Familiapress v. Bauer Verlag* [1997] E.C.R. I–3689; [1997] 3 C.M.L.R. 1329; Case C–358/89 *Extramet Industrie v. Council* [1991] E.C.R. I–2501; [1993] 2 C.M.L.R. 619; Case C–70/88, *Parliament v. Council ("Chernobyl")* [1990] E.C.R. I–2041; [1991] E.C.R. I–4529; [1992] 1 C.M.L.R. 91.

[68] Case C–10/89, *CNL-Sucal v. HAG GF* [1990] E.C.R. I–3711; [1990] 3 C.M.L.R. 571.

[69] Case 192/73 *Van Zuylen v. HAG* [1974] E.C.R. 731; [1976] 2 C.M.L.R. 127.

[70] At para. 10.

[71] Joined Cases C–267–268/91 [1993] E.C.R. I–6097; [1995] 1 C.M.L.R. 101.

[72] See, *e.g.* Gormley, "Reasoning renounced? The remarkable judgment in *Keck and Mithouard*" (1994) E.B.L.R. 63 at 66; Reich, "The November revolution of the European Court of Justice: *Keck, Meng* and *Audi* revisited" (1994) 31 C.M.L. Rev 459 at 471.

[73] Case C–308/93 [1996] 2 C.M.L.R. 729.

[74] Case 40/76 *Kermaschek v. Bundesanstalt für Arbeit* [1976] E.C.R. 1669.

[75] See also Case C–394/96 *Brown v. Rentokil* [1998] E.C.R. I–4185; [1998] 2 C.M.L.R. 1049, where the Court expressly overruled its decision in Case C–400/95 *Larsson v. Føtex Supermarked* [1997] E.C.R. I–2757; [1997] 2 C.M.L.R. 915. See further Chap. 27.

[76] Joined Cases C–267–268/95 [1996] E.C.R. I–6285; [1997] 1 C.M.L.R. 83.

[77] Case 187/80 [1981] E.C.R. 2063; [1981] 3 C.M.L.R. 463.

THE COURT OF FIRST INSTANCE

The establishment of the Court of First Instance

The Single European Act introduced a provision into the E.C. Treaty, Article 225 (ex 168a),[78] which conferred on the Council a power to attach to the Court of Justice a court of first instance with jurisdiction to deal with certain cases, subject to a right of appeal to the Court itself on points of law. That power was exercised on October 24, 1988 with the adoption of Decision 88/591 establishing a Court of First Instance of the European Communities.[79] The new Court commenced operations on October 31, 1989.[80] The purpose of establishing the CFI was essentially twofold. First, it was intended to reduce the case load of the Court of Justice and thereby to reduce the amount of time taken by that Court to dispose of cases. The burgeoning case load of the Court of Justice had been giving rise to concern for a number of years. The number of cases brought before the Court had risen from 279 in 1980 to 373 in 1988. Although the Court's productivity had also increased over that period, the increase was not enough to keep pace with the growing number of new cases being brought. Thus, in 1980 there were 328 cases pending at the end of the year, but that figure had risen to 605 by the end of 1988. The Court's case-load was having a serious effect on the average duration of proceedings: in 1980, it took the Court nine months on average to deal with a reference for a preliminary ruling and 18 months to dispose of a direct action. The corresponding figures for 1988 were 18 months for a preliminary ruling and 24 months for a direct action. The CFI was also intended to improve the administration of justice by engaging in more detailed investigation of factual matters.[81] The fact-finding procedures of the Court of Justice had been widely criticised[82] and it was hoped that the CFI would develop into a specialised fact-finding tribunal with particular expertise in cases concerning the economic effects of complex factual issues. To that end, the CFI was given extensive investigatory powers in its Rules of Procedure, which it soon began to exercise with gusto.[83]

The jurisdiction of the Court of First Instance

The establishment of the CFI did not result in the creation of new heads of jurisdiction, but simply in a redistribution of responsibility for dealing at first instance with certain cases brought under the existing heads. Under Article 3(1) of the Council's Decision, as subsequently amended, the CFI now has jurisdiction

---

[78] Corresponding provisions were added to the ECSC and Euratom Treaties: see Arts 32d and 140a respectively.

[79] The version of that decision which was originally published contained a number of errors. A corrected version was published in [1989] O.J. C215/1 and [1989] 3 C.M.L.R. 458.

[80] Since then, the numbers of cases decided by the Court of Justice have borne the prefix "C", those decided by the CFI the prefix "T" (for the French word *tribunal*).

[81] See the fourth recital to the Council's decision.

[82] See, *e.g.* House of Lords Select Committee on the European Communities, *A European Court of First Instance* (Session 1987–88, 5th Report, HL Paper 20), paras 35–36 and 63–65.

[83] See Vesterdorf, "The Court of First Instance of the european communities after Two Full years in operation" (1992) 29 C.M.L. Rev 897.

in all direct actions brought by natural and legal persons. Thus, actions brought by private applicants against the Community or its institutions for annulment, failure to act and damages commence in the CFI. The CFI is also responsible for dealing with challenges to decisions of the Boards of Appeal established under the Community trade mark regulation,[84] which creates a Community trade mark existing alongside national trade marks but having equal effect throughout the Community. Responsibility for implementing the regulation belongs to OHIM, the Office for Harmonisation in the Internal Market (Trade Marks and Designs), which is based in Alicante, Spain. Appeal against decisions of the examiners and the various divisions of OHIM lies to independent Boards of Appeal within OHIM. Decisions of the Boards of Appeal are in turn amenable to judicial review before the CFI. Such cases are expected to be voluminous and will place heavy pressure on the CFI.[85] References for preliminary rulings under Article 234 E.C. continue to go directly to the Court of Justice, being excluded by Article 225 from the jurisdiction of the CFI. This is essentially because they are concerned only with questions of law, the application of the law to the facts being a matter for the national court. The uniform application of Community law, properly construed, is of fundamental importance to the proper functioning of the Community and can only be ensured by the Court itself. Were jurisdiction to give preliminary rulings to be conferred on the CFI, it would not be feasible to allow for an appeal to the Court, which would therefore be deprived of the opportunity to supervise the way in which that jurisdiction was exercised.

Article 225 originally excluded actions brought by Member States or by Community institutions from the jurisdiction of the CFI as well, but that exclusion was removed at Maastricht. At the time of writing, however, the Council had not exercised its power to transfer any such cases to the CFI. The result is that the same issue may be raised simultaneously before both Courts in separate proceedings brought by applicants of different status. To avoid difficulties of co-ordination, Article 47 of the Statute entitles either Court to stay the proceedings in such circumstances,[86] but the consequences of recourse to that provision may not be entirely satisfactory. One drawback is that, if the CFI stays a challenge to a Community act brought by a private applicant, that applicant will not be entitled to take part in the parallel proceedings before the Court of Justice.[87] In late 1998 the Court therefore submitted a formal request to the Council for the CFI to be given jurisdiction to hear annulment actions brought by Member States within certain defined fields where there is a serious risk of parallel proceedings or detailed examination of complex facts is likely to be required.[88] The Court excluded from its request actions by Member States against acts of general application and those which are liable to raise institutional questions.[89]

---

[84] Reg. 40/94 [1994] O.J. L11/1.

[85] The first such action was Case T–163/98 *Proctor & Gamble v. OHIM* [1999] 2 C.M.L.R. 1442.

[86] Where the Court of Justice decides to stay the proceedings, the proceedings before the CFI must continue.

[87] See Statute, Art. 37. For others, see (1999) 24 E.L. Rev. 213.

[88] See House of Lords Select Committee on the European Communities, *Enlarging the Jurisdiction of the Court of First Instance* (Session 1998–99, 13th Report, HL Paper 82).

[89] The most significant category of case which would be affected by the Court's request is probably that of actions by Member States for the annulment of Commission decisions in the field of State aid. See further Chap. 24.

The members of the Court of First Instance

The CFI currently consists of 15 members.[90] The qualifications for appointment are laid down in Article 225(3) E.C., according to which the members of the CFI must be "chosen from persons whose independence is beyond doubt and who possess the ability required for appointment to judicial office". Like the members of the Court of Justice, they are appointed by common accord of the Governments of the Member States for renewable terms of six years. The Treaty and the Council's Decision are silent on the question of the nationality of the members, but there is currently one Judge from each Member State.

The CFI has the right to sit in plenary session but in practice it hardly ever does so, normally sitting in Chambers of five or three Judges. Like the Court of Justice, the CFI delivers a single collegiate judgment signed by all the Judges who took part in the case. There are no dissenting judgments. Certain cases assigned to a three-Judge chamber may now be dealt with by a single Judge[91] "where, having regard to the lack of difficulty of the questions of law or fact raised, to the limited importance of the case and to the absence of other special circumstances, they are suitable for being so heard . . ."[92] The decision to delegate a case to a single Judge is taken by the Chamber before which the case is pending acting unanimously after hearing the parties.[93] Delegation to a single Judge is expressly excluded "in cases which raise issues as to the legality of an act of general application" and in certain areas of substantive law.[94]

As a rule, each member of the CFI performs the function of Judge.[95] As mentioned above, there are no full-time Advocates General in the CFI, but any of the Members (with the exception of the President) may be called upon to perform the function of Advocate General.[96] When the CFI sits in plenary session, it must be assisted by an Advocate General, who is designated by the President. A chamber of the CFI "may be assisted by an Advocate-General if it is considered that the legal difficulty or the factual complexity of the case so

---

[90] Council Dec., Art. 2.

[91] See Dec. 1999/291 amending Dec. 88/591 to enable the CFI to give decisions in cases when constituted by a single Judge, [1999] O.J. L114/52. The approach embodied in Dec. 1999/291 represented something of an innovation and had proved controversial. See further the House of Lords Select Committee on the European Communities, *The Court of First Instance: Single Judge* (Session 1997–98, 25th Report, HL Paper 114). The first decision given by a single Judge was Case T–180/98, *Cotrim v. CEDEFOP*, judgment of October 28, 1999. That case was decided about six months earlier than might otherwise have been expected.

[92] CFI Rules, Art. 14(2)(1). Actions for annulment, failure to act and damages must, in order to be eligible for delegation, "raise only questions already clarified by established case law" or "form part of a series of cases in which the same relief is sought and of which one has already been finally decided".

[93] A case must be maintained before the chamber concerned where a Member State or a Community institution which is a party to the proceedings objects to its delegation to a single Judge: CFI Rules, Art. 51(2).

[94] Such as competition, merger control, State aid, trade protection (*e.g.* anti-dumping), the common organisation of agricultural markets (with the exception of cases that form part of a series in which the same relief is sought and one of which has already been decided) and the Community trade mark regulation: CFI Rules, Art. 14(2)(2).

[95] See Art. 2, CFI Rules.

[96] For an example, see Case T–51/89 *Tetra Pak Rausing v. Commission* [1990] E.C.R. II–309; [1992] 4 C.M.L.R. 334.

requires."[97] A Member who is called upon to act as Advocate General in a case may not then take part in deciding that case,[98] although he can of course perform the function of Judge in other cases where the same issues arise. In practice, Advocates General have to date been appointed relatively rarely by the CFI.

Appeals to the Court of Justice

By virtue of Article 225(1) E.C., decisions of the CFI are "subject to a right of appeal to the Court of Justice on points of law only . . .". That provision is expanded by the first paragraph of Article 51 of the Statute, which provides: "An appeal to the Court of Justice shall be limited to points of law. It shall lie on the grounds of lack of competence of the Court of First Instance, a breach of procedure before it which adversely affects the interests of the appellant as well as the infringement of Community law by the Court of First instance." An appeal can only be justified by an interest in having the operative part (as opposed to the reasoning) of the CFI's decision altered.[99] No appeal lies against certain procedural matters, such as decisions on the amount of costs or the party ordered to pay them[1] or on whether to grant legal aid.[2] A party may not put forward for the first time in an appeal a plea which it has not raised before the CFI, since that would mean "allowing that party to bring before the Court, whose jurisdiction in appeals is limited, a case of wider ambit than that which came before the Court of First Instance."[3]

The distinction between questions of law and questions of fact can be difficult to draw.[4] The Court of Justice is wary of attempts to expand the former category at the expense of the latter, for otherwise the right to appeal against decisions of the CFI would become virtually unlimited. In *Antillean Rice Mills and Others v. Commission*,[5] the Court of Justice held that the CFI "has exclusive jurisdiction to find the facts, save where a substantive inaccuracy is attributable to the documents submitted to it, and to appraise those facts. That appraisal does not, save where the clear sense of the evidence has been distorted, constitute a point of law which is subject, as such, to review by the Court of Justice . . ." In competition cases, the Court will not interfere on grounds of fairness with the amount of any fine fixed by the CFI.[6] However, the Court will review the CFI's

---

[97] Art. 18, CFI Rules.

[98] Council Dec., Art. 2(3).

[99] Case C–49/92P, *Commission v. Anic*, judgment of July 8, 1999, para. 168. See also Case C–265/97 P *VBA,* judgment of March 30, 2000, para. 121. The operative part is the passage in bold type at the end of a judgment formally giving the outcome of the case.

[1] Statute, Art. 51.

[2] CFI Rules, Art. 94(2).

[3] Case C–51/92 P, *Hercules Chemicals v. Commission*, judgment of July 8, 1999, para. 58. (The suffix "P" after the number of the case stands for the French word *pourvoi* and denotes a decision given by the Court of Justice on appeal from the CFI.)

[4] See further Advocate General Jacobs in Case C–53/92P, *Hilti v. Commission* [1994] E.C.R. I–667; [1994] 4 C.M.L.R. 614.

[5] Case C–390/95P, judgment of February 11, 1999, para. 29.

[6] *Hercules Chemicals v. Commission, supra,* para. 109.

determination of the legal consequences which ensue from the facts it has established.[7]

Appeals must be brought within two months of the notification of the contested decision. They may be lodged by any party which has been unsuccessful, in whole or in part, in its submissions. Interveners, other than the Member States and the Community institutions, may bring an appeal only where the decision of the CFI directly affects them. Except in staff cases, an appeal may also be brought by Member States and institutions which did not take part in the proceedings at first instance.[8] Where an appeal to the Court of Justice is successful, the decision of the CFI has to be quashed. The Court of Justice may then proceed to give final judgment in the matter, where the state of the proceedings so permits, or it may refer the case back to the CFI for judgment, in which case the CFI is bound by the decision of the Court of Justice on points of law.[9]

Precedent in the Court of First Instance

The establishment of the CFI raised two new questions about the status of judicial precedents in Community law: (a) is the CFI bound by its own previous decisions; and (b) is it bound by the decisions of the Court of Justice? The answer to the first question is that, like the Court of Justice itself, the CFI is not strictly bound by its own decisions but that it endeavours to be consistent. As for the second question, the CFI makes extensive reference to the Court's case-law in its judgments and normally follows it. However, where the CFI believes it is liable to produce adverse results, it has not hesitated to look for ways of avoiding it.

One of the clearest statements of the attitude of the CFI to the case-law of the Court of Justice is to be found in *NMB France and Others v. Commission* (*NMB II*),[10] where the CFI declared[11]: "the Court of First Instance is only bound by the judgments of the Court of Justice, first, in the circumstances laid down in the second paragraph of Article 54 of the Statute of the Court of Justice of the European Community, and, secondly, pursuant to the principle of *res judicata*." As we have seen, Article 54 of the Statute is concerned with the consequences where an appeal to the Court against a decision of the CFI is upheld. In the

---

[7] Case C–136/92 P *Commission v. Brazzelli Lualdi and Others* [1994] E.C.R. I–1981, para. 49. In Case C–73/97 P, *Comafrica and Dole Fresh Fruit v. Commission* [1999] 2 C.M.L.R. 87 at 91, Advocate General Mischo said that the question whether an applicant in annulment proceedings was directly and individually concerned was "undoubtedly a point of law": [1999] 2 C.M.L.R. 87 at 91. See generally Sonelli, "Appeal on points of law in the Community system" (1998) 35 C.M.L. Rev 871.

[8] Statute, Art. 49. That right was exercised by a Member State (France) for the first time in *Comafrica and Dole Fresh Fruit v. Commission, supra*. See also *Commission v. Anic, supra*, paras 171–172.

[9] See Statute, Art. 54. Where a successful appeal is brought by a Member State or Community institution which did not take part in the proceedings at first instance, the Court of Justice may state which, if any, of the effects of the decision of the Court of First Instance which has been quashed are to be considered definitive as between the parties.

[10] Case T–162/94 [1996] E.C.R. II–427 (Second Chamber, Extended Composition).

[11] Para 36. See also Joined Cases T–177/94 and T–377/94 *Altmann and Others v. Commission* [1996] E.C.R. II-2041, para. 80.

interests of completeness, the CFI might also have mentioned the second paragraph of Article 47 of the Statute. According to that provision, where the Court finds that an action which has been brought before it falls within the jurisdiction of the CFI, it must refer the action to the CFI, which "may not decline jurisdiction". In other words, the CFI is bound by the finding of the Court of Justice that the CFI has jurisdiction to hear the action. Neither Article 47 nor Article 54 of the Statute was relevant in the circumstances of *NMB II*, so the CFI went on to consider whether the status as *res judicata*[12] of a judgment of the Court of Justice, *NMB I*,[13] rendered the present action inadmissible. The CFI observed: "It is settled case-law that this can be the case only if the proceedings disposed of by the judgment in [*NMB I*] were between the same parties, had the same purpose and were based on the same submissions as the present case . . . those conditions necessarily being cumulative."[14] Since those conditions were not satisfied, the CFI concluded that the judgment in *NMB I* could not affect the admissibility of *NMB II*. The judgment in the latter case confirms indications given by earlier cases that, while the CFI treats decisions of the Court of Justice as persuasive, it does not consider itself bound by them except in certain exceptional and clearly defined circumstances.

REFORMING THE JUDICIAL ARCHITECTURE OF THE EUROPEAN UNION

In some respects, the CFI has been a great success. The quality of its judgments is on the whole high and there is no doubt that it has had the desired effect of improving judicial scrutiny of complex facts. Unfortunately, it has not succeeded in reducing the length of proceedings in the Court of Justice. In 1998, it took the Court an average of 21.4 months to deal with a reference for a preliminary ruling, 21 months to deal with a direct action and 20.3 months to deal with an appeal. At the same time, the workload of the CFI itself is now giving cause for concern.[15] In 1998 the CFI managed to dispose of 348 cases but was left with a backlog of 1,008 pending cases. Staff cases (disputes between Community officials and the institutions employing them)[16] took an average of 16.7 months to dispose of, other cases an average of 20 months. The position is expected to become much worse when OHIM is fully operational. It is anticipated that between 200 and 400 decisions of the Boards of Appeal set up under the trade mark regulation will be challenged annually before the CFI. That would have a knock-on effect on the number of appeals to the Court of Justice, currently brought in about 25 per cent of the cases decided by the CFI. In April 1999 the Community Courts therefore asked for the appointment of six extra

---

[12] See further Toth, *The Oxford Encyclopaedia of European Community Law*, Vol. I (1990), pp. 464–467.
[13] Case C–188/88 *NMB and Others v. Commission* [1992] E.C.R. I–1689; [1992] 3 C.M.L.R. 80.
[14] Para 37 of judgment in *NMB II*.
[15] Indeed, in Case C–185/95 P *Baustahlgewebe v. Commission* [1998] 4 C.M.L.R. 1203; [1999] 4 C.M.L.R. 1203; the Court of Justice quashed a decision of the CFI by reason of the duration of the procedure.
[16] See Art. 236 (ex 179) E.C.

Judges in the CFI to permit the formation of two additional three-Judge chambers.[17]

The Community Courts followed up their request for extra Judges in the CFI with a wide-ranging discussion paper entitled "The Future of the Judicial System of the European Union", which was sent to the Council on May 10, 1999.[18] Among the more striking proposals put forward by the Courts in that document was the introduction of a requirement that, in certain types of case,[19] the leave of the Court should be required before an appeal against a decision of the CFI could be brought. The Courts also canvassed a range of devices for reducing the number of references for preliminary rulings which the Court of Justice is called upon to determine. These included: (a) limiting the national courts which are permitted to make use of the preliminary rulings procedure; (b) introducing a filtering system to enable the Court to decide which questions needed to be answered having regard to their novelty, complexity or importance; (c) giving the CFI a preliminary rulings jurisdiction; and (d) designating in each Member State decentralised judicial bodies with responsibility for dealing with references from courts within their area of territorial jurisdiction. A Presidency report[20] drawn up for the meeting of the European Council in Helsinki on December 10 and 11, 1999 noted that there was broad support for the forthcoming IGC to consider whether the Treaty provisions concerning the Community Courts should be amended to make decision-making and procedures more flexible.

---

[17] See "Proposals submitted by the Court of Justice and the Court of First Instance with regard to the new intellectual property cases" (April 27, 1999). Additional supporting staff were also requested.

[18] See http://europa.eu.int/cj/en/pres/aveng.pdf; Arnull, "Judicial architecture or judicial folly? The challenge facing the European Union" (1999) 24 E.L. Rev. 516. Proposals for certain consequential changes to the Rules were made on July 1, 1999. See http://europa.eu.int/cj/en/txts/txt5a.pdf.

[19] e.g. Community trade mark proceedings and staff cases, which the Court suggested should be dealt with initially by interinstitutional tribunals and assessors. The decisions of such tribunals would be subject to challenge before the CFI, with any appeal to the Court being subject to "a very strict filtering procedure".

[20] "Efficient institutions after enlargement: options for the intergovernmental conference", http://ue.eu.int/newsroom/main.cfm?LANG=1.

CHAPTER 10

DIRECT ACTIONS

The Court of Justice is required by Article 220 (ex 164) E.C. to "ensure that in the interpretation and application of this Treaty the law is observed". The Treaty proceeds to equip the Court with a series of specific powers in order to enable it to comply with that duty. The proceedings which may be brought before the Court fall broadly speaking into two categories. *Direct actions* are proceedings which start and finish in Luxembourg. Some are considered only by the Court of Justice; some, depending on the status of the applicant, commence in the Court of First Instance (CFI) and may proceed on appeal to the Court of Justice. However, since the CFI does not strictly speaking constitute a separate institution, being "attached" to the Court of Justice according to Article 225(1) (ex 168a(1)) E.C., it may be said that the only court with jurisdiction to deal with direct actions is the Court of Justice. By contrast, *references for preliminary rulings* represent an episode in proceedings which will have begun in one of the national courts of the Member States. Where the national judge encounters a question of European law which needs to be resolved before judgment can be given, provision is made for the question to be referred to the Court of Justice for an answer known as a preliminary ruling. When the ruling has been given, it is for the national court to apply it to the facts of the case. Some national courts are obliged to seek preliminary rulings on questions of European law they are called upon to decide. The CFI has no jurisdiction at present to give such rulings. This chapter is concerned with the jurisdiction of the Community Courts in some of the most important types of direct action. Discussion of the preliminary rulings procedure is postponed until Chapter 11.

The creation by the Member States at Maastricht of a European Union with stronger intergovernmental features than the original Communities led to the insertion in the TEU of a provision limiting the scope of the powers of the Court of Justice. Article L of the TEU made it clear that the powers conferred on the Court by the three Community Treaties did not extend to Title V of the TEU on the common foreign and security policy, the so-called second pillar of the Union, or (except in limited circumstances)[1] to Title VI of the TEU, the so-called third pillar of the Union, which was concerned at the outset with co-operation in the fields of justice and home affairs. The conduct of foreign policy is an area in which many national courts are reluctant to interfere, but the Court's exclusion from Title VI was more controversial because of the potential of measures taken under that Title to affect the rights of individuals. At Amsterdam, Title VI of the

---

[1] Art. K.3 TEU made provision for conventions drawn up by the Member States in the areas referred to in Art. K.1 to "stipulate that the Court of Justice shall have jurisdiction to interpret their provisions and to rule on any disputes regarding their application, in accordance with such arrangements as they may lay down." The Member States made extensive use of that possibility: see, *e.g.* the protocol on the interpretation by the Court of Justice of the Convention on Jurisdiction and the Recognition and Enforcement of Judgments in Matrimonial Matters ("Brussels II"), [1998] O.J. C221/20.

TEU was renamed "Provisions on police and judicial co-operation in criminal matters" and its scope extended. The Court of Justice was given important new powers to rule on disputes concerning its application and Article L (now 46) was amended accordingly.

ENFORCEMENT ACTIONS AGAINST MEMBER STATES

One of the novel features of the Community legal order is the power given to the Commission to supervise compliance by the Member States with their obligations under the Treaties.[2] As far as the E.C. Treaty is concerned, that power derives principally from Article 226 (ex 169),[3] which provides as follows:

"If the Commission considers that a Member State has failed to fulfil an obligation under this Treaty, it shall deliver a reasoned opinion on the matter after giving the State concerned the opportunity to submit its observations.

If the State concerned does not comply with the opinion within the period laid down by the Commission, the latter may bring the matter before the Court of Justice."

Article 226 may be contrasted with Article 88 ECSC, which gives the Commission the power to record in a binding decision the failure of the State concerned to fulfil its obligations. That State may then challenge the Commission's decision before the Court.

Article 226 is complemented by Article 227 (ex 170) E.C., the first paragraph of which provides that "[a] Member State which considers that another Member State has failed to fulfil an obligation under this Treaty may bring the matter before the Court of Justice." A Member State wishing to institute proceedings under Article 227 must first bring the matter before the Commission, which is required to give each of the States concerned the opportunity to submit its own case and its observations on the other party's case, both in writing and orally. The Commission must then deliver a reasoned opinion on the matter. Whether or not the respondent State complies with the reasoned opinion, the applicant State then has the right to refer the matter to the Court. The latter State may also bring the matter before the Court if the Commission does not deliver an opinion within three months of the date on which the matter was brought before it. In practice, the Member States have shown a marked reluctance to commence proceedings under Article 227, only two cases having proceeded to judgment under that provision at the time of writing.[4] The Member States evidently prefer to rely on the Commission to act under Article 226, sometimes intervening in its support when the matter is brought before the Court.[5]

---

[2] See Audretsch, *Supervision in European Community Law* (2nd ed., 1986); Dashwood and White, "Enforcement Actions under Arts 169 and 170 EEC" (1989) 14 E.L.Rev. 388.

[3] An expedited procedure is applicable in the context of State aid under the second para. of Art. 88(2) (ex 93(2)) E.C.

[4] Case 141/78 *France v. United Kingdom* [1979] E.C.R. 2923; [1980] 1 C.M.L.R. 6; Case C–388/95 *Belgium v. Spain*, judgment of May 16, 2000.

[5] Intervention involves taking part voluntarily in proceedings before one of the Community Courts in support of the relief sought by one of the parties. See Statute, Art. 37; Rules, Art. 93; CFI Rules, Arts 115–116.

The procedure laid down in Article 226 falls into two distinct phases, the administrative phase (or pre-litigation procedure, as it is sometimes called in the Court's decisions) and the judicial phase.

The administrative phase

The administrative phase corresponds to the first paragraph of Article 226, which requires the Commission to take two steps: it must give the State concerned "the opportunity to submit its observations" and then, if it is still not satisfied, it must consider whether to "deliver a reasoned opinion on the matter". The purpose of this phase of the procedure "is, in the first place, to give the Member State an opportunity to justify its position and, as the case may be, to enable the Commission to persuade the Member State to comply of its own accord with the requirements of the Treaty. If this attempt to reach a settlement is unsuccessful, the function of the reasoned opinion is to define the subject-matter of the dispute."[6]

The Commission may become aware of a possible breach by a Member State of its obligations under the Treaty either through its own monitoring of the application of Community law or as a result of a complaint by a private party. The Commission relies to a considerable extent on such complaints in detecting possible infringements. When a complaint is received it is registered by the Commission, which acknowledges receipt and informs the complainant of the procedure to be followed. The Commission also provides the complainant with information about the role of the national courts in ensuring the proper application of Community law. The complainant will subsequently be told what action has been taken in response to the complaint and notified of representations made to the national authorities concerned. The complainant will also be told whether or not infringement proceedings are to be instituted and if other proceedings on the same issue are already underway. A decision to close the file without taking any further action or to institute proceedings is taken within one year of the date on which the complaint was registered, except in special cases the reasons for which are stated. Delays in processing complaints are often caused by the need to discuss the matter with the national authorities concerned.

The way in which the Commission deals with complaints by private parties about infringements by Member States of their obligations under the Treaty was the subject of several complaints to the European Ombudsman who, in April 1997, began an enquiry into the matter under Article 195 (ex 138e) E.C.[7] The Ombudsman found no maladministration, but the Commission agreed to extend to all cases a practice, previously applied in some cases only, of informing the

---

[6] Joined Cases 142–143/80 *Amministrazione delle Finanze dello Stato v. Essevi and Salengo* [1981] E.C.R. 1413, para. 15. See also Case C–207/96 *Commission v. Italy* [1997] E.C.R. I–6869, paras 17–18. The Commission is entitled to refuse the public access to documents connected with proceedings under Art. 226 where disclosure might jeopardise the chances of a settlement: see Case T–105/95 *WWF U.K. v. Commission* [1997] E.C.R. II-313; Case T–309/97 *Bavarian Lager Co. v. Commission* [1999] 3 C.M.L.R. 544.

[7] See the European Ombudsman's Annual Report for 1997 at pp. 270–274, where a detailed account of the Commission's procedure for handling complaints is set out. See also Rawlings, "Engaged élites: citizen action and institutional attitudes in Commission enforcement" (2000) 6 E.L.J. 4.

complainant when it was minded to close a file and indicating its reasons for finding that Community law had not been infringed (except where a complaint was manifestly unfounded or the complainant appeared to have lost interest in the matter). This offers the complainant the opportunity to submit observations before the Commission comes to a definitive conclusion. The Ombudsman also suggested that, when acknowledging receipt of a complaint, the Commission should where appropriate provide information about extra-judicial mechanisms, such as national ombudsmen, for providing redress to aggrieved citizens.

When the Commission becomes aware of a possible breach of Community law by a Member State, it will first raise the matter on an informal basis through the Permanent Representative of the State concerned in Brussels. If the Commission is not satisfied that Community law is being respected, it may decide to send to the Member State a letter of formal notice. That letter represents the first formal step in the procedure laid down in Article 226. It gives the Member State the opportunity to submit its observations on the matter, although the Member State is not obliged to avail itself of that opportunity.[8] The letter of formal notice defines the subject-matter of the dispute and indicates to the Member State the essence of the Commission's case. It constitutes "an essential formal requirement of the procedure under Article 169 [now 226]."[9] The Commission is required to allow the Member State a reasonable period in which to reply to the letter of formal notice. What is reasonable depends on the circumstances of the case, but very short periods may sometimes be justified, particularly where there is an urgent need to remedy a breach or where the Member State concerned was aware of the Commission's view before the procedure started.[10]

The letter of formal notice may lead to a further round of discussions between the Commission and the Member State concerned in an attempt to reach a settlement. If this does not prove possible, the Commission may decide to deliver a reasoned opinion on the matter. Although the Treaty uses the word "shall" in this context, it seems that the Commission is not obliged to take this step. In the first place, the Commission may only deliver a reasoned opinion where it "considers" that a Member State is in breach of Community law, which involves an essentially discretionary assessment. Secondly, the second paragraph of Article 226 makes it clear that, even if the Member State concerned fails to comply with the reasoned opinion, the Commission is not obliged, but merely empowered, to bring the matter before the Court.[11] There would therefore have been little point in imposing on the Commission an obligation to deliver a reasoned opinion whenever it took the view that a Member State was in breach of its obligations under the Treaty.[12]

The reasoned opinion should contain "a coherent statement of the reasons which led the Commission to believe that the State in question has failed to fulfil

---

[8] See Case 211/81 *Commission v. Denmark* [1982] E.C.R. 4547, para. 9; [1984] 1 C.M.L.R. 278.
[9] *ibid.*, paras 8 and 9.
[10] Case 293/85 *Commission v. Belgium* [1988] E.C.R. 305, para. 14; [1989] 2 C.M.L.R. 527.
[11] See Case 247/87 *Star Fruit v. Commission* [1989] E.C.R. 291, paras 11 and 12; [1990] 1 C.M.L.R. 733.
[12] See further Evans, "The enforcement procedure of Art. 169 EEC: Commission discretion" (1979) 4 E.L. Rev. 442; Dashwood and White, *op. cit.,* pp. 398–399.

an obligation under the Treaty".[13] Since the reasoned opinion defines the scope of the proceedings, any subsequent application by the Commission to the Court must be founded on the same grounds and submissions. The Court will not consider a complaint that was not formulated in the reasoned opinion.[14] Although the reasoned opinion must be preceded by a letter inviting the Member State concerned to submit its observations, it need not simply repeat the contents of that letter. The Court has said that "there is nothing to prevent the Commission from setting out in detail in the reasoned opinion the complaints which it has already made more generally in its initial letter. Indeed, the reply to that letter may give rise to a fresh consideration of those complaints."[15]

The Commission is not required to indicate in the reasoned opinion the steps which need to be taken to eliminate the alleged infringement. However, if the Commission intends to make failure to adopt a certain measure the subject of the action, it must specifically indicate to the Member State concerned that it needs to adopt that measure.[16] It must also lay down a deadline for compliance by the Member State.[17] That deadline determines the relevant date for the purposes of any subsequent proceedings before the Court,[18] for compliance with its obligations by the Member State concerned after the deadline has passed does not prevent the Commission from bringing the matter before the Court. The Court has said that the Commission retains an interest in continuing with a case in these circumstances, since a judgment of the Court "may be of substantive interest as establishing the basis of a responsibility that a Member State can incur as a result of its default, as regards other Member States, the Community or private parties".[19]

As in the case of the letter of formal notice, the Commission must allow the Member State concerned a reasonable period in which to comply with the reasoned opinion. The Court does not have the power to substitute a different period for that laid down by the Commission,[20] but if it considers the period allowed too short, it may dismiss any subsequent application to the Court as inadmissible. In *Commission v. Belgium*,[21] for example, Belgium was given eight days to reply to the letter of formal notice and 15 days to comply with the reasoned opinion. The Court ruled the Commission's application inadmissible. By contrast, in *Commission v. Ireland*,[22] Ireland was given five days to amend legislation which had been on the statute book for over 40 years. The Court made it clear that it disapproved of so short a deadline, but declined to rule the

---

[13] Case 325/82 *Commission v. Germany* [1984] E.C.R. 777, para. 8; [1985] 2 C.M.L.R. 719.

[14] See, *e.g.* Case 186/85 *Commission v. Belgium* [1987] E.C.R. 2029, para. 13; [1988] 2 C.M.L.R. 759.

[15] Case 74/82 *Commission v. Ireland* [1984] E.C.R. 317, para. 20. See also Case C–365/97 *Commission v. Italy,* judgment of November 9, 1999, para. 26.

[16] Case C–328/96 *Commission v. Austria* judgment of October 28, 1999, para. 39.

[17] See the second para. of Art. 226.

[18] See, *e.g.* Case C–362/90 *Commission v. Italy* [1992] E.C.R. I–2353; [1994] 3 C.M.L.R. 1.

[19] See Case 39/72 *Commission v. Italy* [1973] E.C.R. 101, para. 11; [1973] C.M.L.R. 439; Case C–29/90, *Commission v. Greece* [1992] E.C.R. I–1917, para. 12; [1994] 3 C.M.L.R. 675. On the liability of Member States to private parties for breaches of Community law, see Chap. 5.

[20] Case 28/81 *Commission v. Italy* [1981] E.C.R. 2577, para. 6; Case 29/81 *Commission v. Italy* [1981] E.C.R. 2585, para. 6.

[21] Case 293/85 [1988] E.C.R. 305; [1989] 2 C.M.L.R. 527.

[22] Case 74/82 [1984] E.C.R. 317.

application inadmissible. Member States are usually allowed a month or two to take the necessary steps. In *Commission v. Belgium,*[23] the Court said that "very short periods may be justified in particular circumstances, especially where there is an urgent need to remedy a breach or where the Member State concerned is fully aware of the Commission's views long before the procedure starts."

None of the measures taken by the Commission during the administrative phase of the procedure under Article 226 has binding force. Such measures may not therefore be the subject of annulment proceedings under Article 230 (ex 173) E.C.[24] The legality of those measures may be reviewed only in the context of a subsequent application by the Commission to the Court under Article 226.[25] Moreover, as the CFI explained in *SDDDA v. Commission,*[26] "[t]he Commission is not bound to initiate an infringement procedure against a Member State; on the contrary, it has a discretionary power of assessment, which rules out any right for individuals to require it to adopt a particular position." No action for failure to act under Article 232 (ex 175) E.C. therefore lies against it should it decline to do so.[27] It is not for the Court to decide whether the Commission's discretion was wisely exercised.[28]

The Court has been willing to allow the Commission a degree of flexibility in the internal procedure it follows in deciding whether proceedings should be brought. In *Commission v. Germany,*[29] it was argued that the proceedings were inadmissible because the issue of the reasoned opinion and the decision to commence proceedings before the Court had been delegated to a single Commissioner instead of having been the subject of a decision by the Commission acting as a college. The Commission explained that, because of the number of infringement proceedings, Commissioners did not have before them draft reasoned opinions when they decided to issue such measures. However, they did have available to them the facts of each case and details of the provisions of Community law which the Commission's services considered to have been breached. The decision to issue the reasoned opinion and to commence proceedings before the Court was therefore taken in full knowledge of the essential facts. Drafting of the reasoned opinion then took place at administrative level under the responsibility of the competent Commissioner. The Court ruled that this procedure was acceptable. It was true that the functioning of the Commission was governed by the principle of collegiate responsibility. It followed[30] "that both the Commission's decision to issue a reasoned opinion and its decision to bring an action for a declaration of failure to fulfil obligations must

---

[23] *Supra,* para. 14. See also *Commission v. Austria, supra,* paras 51–56.
[24] Case 48/65 *Lütticke v. Commission* [1966] E.C.R. 19; [1966] C.M.L.R. 378. The action for annulment is discussed below.
[25] *cf.* Joined Cases 76 and 11/69 *Commission v. France* [1969] E.C.R. 523, para. 36; [1970] C.M.L.R. 43.
[26] Case T–47/96 [1996] E.C.R. II-1559, para. 42.
[27] Case 247/87 *Star Fruit v. Commission* [1989] E.C.R. 291; [1990] 1 C.M.L.R. 733. The action for failure to act is discussed below.
[28] Case C–200/88 *Commission v. Greece* [1990] E.C.R. I–4299, para. 9; [1992] 2 C.M.L.R. 151.
[29] Case C–191/95 [1998] E.C.R. I–5449; [1999] 2 C.M.L.R. 1265. See also Case C–272/97 *Commission v. Germany,* judgment of April 22, 1999; Case C–198/97 *Commission v. Germany,* judgment of June 8, 1999; [1997] 5 C.M.L.R. 420.
[30] Para 48.

be the subject of collective deliberation by the college of Commissioners. The information on which those decisions are based must therefore be available to the members of the college. It is not, however, necessary for the college itself formally to decide on the wording of the acts which give effect to those decisions and put them in final form."

The judicial phase

If the Member State fails to comply with the reasoned opinion within the deadline laid down in it, the Commission has the power to bring the matter before the Court of Justice. The Commission is not obliged to do so within any specific period. In *Commission v. Germany*,[31] the Commission brought proceedings against Germany for failure to comply with various Council directives on waste. All had been substantially amended or repealed during the administrative or judicial phases of the proceedings. The Court said that it was "somewhat surprising[,] that the Commission brought its action more than six years after the entry into force of the basic German legislation on the shipment of waste, and did so at a time when the Community had in fact changed its policy in that field along the same lines as those followed by that legislation".[32] However, the Court ruled that the Commission was entitled to decide when it was appropriate to bring an action. It was not for the Court to review the exercise of that discretion. The Court therefore concluded that the action was admissible.

In *Commission v. Italy*, Advocate General Mischo suggested that, in a case of an isolated failure by a Member State to apply a directive correctly, the Commission should only bring proceedings under Article 226 where the situation is particularly flagrant and a sustained effort to induce the State concerned to act has proved unsuccessful.[33] That suggestion was not taken up by the Court. It should be noted that the Commission's attitude to whether or not to bring proceedings does not affect the substance of the Member State's obligations under the Treaty or the rights which individuals may derive from them.[34]

If the Commission decides to make an application to the Court, it will be required to prove its allegation that the obligation in question has not been fulfilled. The burden on the Commission is not easy to discharge. The Court requires the Commission to indicate not merely the legal basis of its complaint but also to give details of the facts and circumstances which are said to give rise to the alleged failure by the State concerned to comply with its obligations.[35] Where a Member State is required by a directive to inform the Commission of the steps taken to comply with it, failure to satisfy that requirement may itself

---

[31] Case C–422/92 [1995] E.C.R. I–1097; [1996] 1 C.M.L.R. 383. See also Case C–96/84 *Commission v. Netherlands* [1991] E.C.R. I–2461; Case C–187/98 *Commission v. Greece,* judgment of October 28, 1999. The Court recognised in those cases that, where the duration of the pre-litigation procedure is excessive, the rights of the defence might be infringed.

[32] Para. 18.

[33] Case C–365/97, judgment of November 9, 1999. See para. 64 of the Opinion.

[34] See Joined Cases 142–143/80 *Amministrazione delle Finanze dello Stato v. Essevi and Salengo* [1981] E.C.R. 1413, paras 16–18.

[35] See, *e.g.* Case C–347/88 *Commission v. Greece* [1990] E.C.R. I–4747; Case C–52/90 *Commission v. Denmark* [1992] E.C.R. I–2187; [1994] 2 C.M.L.R. 885.

amount to a breach of Community law, but it will not entitle the Commission to assume that no implementing measures have in fact been adopted.[36] Moreover, the mere existence in a Member State of a situation which is inconsistent with a directive does not in itself entitle the Commission to conclude that the directive concerned has not been properly implemented. However, the persistence of such a situation may indicate a failure by the State concerned to comply with its obligations.[37]

If the Commission's application to the Court is successful, the Court will declare that the Member State in question has failed to fulfil its obligations under the Treaty. The Court will specify the act or omission giving rise to the failure, but it has no power to tell the Member State what it must do to remedy the breach or to quash any national measure which it may have found unlawful. The Member State is required by Article 228(1) (ex 171(1)) E.C. "to take the necessary measures to comply with the judgment of the Court of Justice". If it fails to do so, it exposes itself to further proceedings under Article 228(2), which may result in the imposition of a financial penalty. This is discussed below.

The effect of the Court's ruling

Action to comply with the Court's judgment must be commenced as soon as it is delivered and completed as soon as possible.[38] The effect produced by a ruling of the Court of Justice under Article 226 in the legal order of the Member State concerned was considered in *Procureur de la République v. Waterkeyn*,[39] where it was held that: "if the Court finds in proceedings under Articles 169 [now 226] to 171 [now 228] of the EEC Treaty that a Member State's legislation is incompatible with the obligations which it has under the Treaty the courts of that State are bound by virtue of Article 171 to draw the necessary inferences from the judgment of the Court. However, it should be understood that the rights accruing to individuals derive, not from that judgment, but from the actual provisions of Community law having direct effect in the internal legal order."

This means that a judgment of the Court under Article 226 does not in itself confer rights on individuals. Such a judgment merely establishes whether or not a given course of conduct by a Member State is compatible with Community law. However, where the Court decides that the Member State is in breach of its obligations under a provision of Community law which produces direct effect, the national courts must draw the appropriate consequences and protect rights claimed by individuals under that provision. The ruling of the Court of Justice under Article 226 establishes conclusively that the provision in question has been breached. Moreover, the Court's ruling in *Francovich and Others*[40] makes it clear that a ruling of the Court under Article 226 establishing that a Member State has failed to comply with a provision of Community law, even one that does not have

---

[36] See Case 96/81 *Commission v. Netherlands* [1982] E.C.R. 1791, paras 4–6.
[37] See Case C–365/97 *Commission v. Italy,* judgment of November 9, 1999, para. 68.
[38] See, *e.g.* Joined Cases 227–230/85 *Commission v. Belgium* [1988] E.C.R. 1, para. 11; [1989] 2 C.M.L.R. 797.
[39] Joined Cases 314–316/81 and 83/82 [1982] E.C.R. 4337; [1983] 2 C.M.L.R. 145.
[40] Joined Cases C–6 and 9/90 [1991] E.C.R. I–5357; [1993] 2 C.M.L.R. 66.

direct effect, may render the State concerned liable to pay compensation to anyone who has thereby suffered loss.

Interim measures

Although the Court has no power under Article 226 to order the State concerned to pursue or refrain from pursuing a particular course of conduct, somewhat anomalously such an order may be made in the context of an application for interim measures[41] under Article 243 (ex 186) E.C.[42] Interim measures are not, however, available in proceedings against a Member State for failure to take the steps necessary to comply with a previous ruling of the Court under Article 226 where the measures sought would merely repeat the substance of the Court's earlier ruling.[43] Moreover, according to the second paragraph of Article 83(1) of the Court's Rules of Procedure, an application for interim measures under Article 243 E.C. "shall be admissible only if it is made by a party to a case before the Court and relates to that case". The result is that, in proceedings under Article 226, no such application may be made before the Commission has brought the matter before the Court (although both steps may be taken simultaneously).[44] In particular, no application for interim measures can be made when the letter of formal notice is dispatched. Article 226 does not therefore permit rapid intervention by the Commission in urgent cases. It has been remarked that "a strengthening of the Commission's guardian role in the Community interest by a rapid intervention mechanism is not merely desirable but also essential".[45]

Defences

One of the most promising types of defence open to a Member State in proceedings against it under Article 226 is that the Commission has failed to respect the procedural requirements imposed on it by the Treaty. Thus, it may be said that the period within which the Member State was asked to respond to the letter of formal notice or to comply with the reasoned opinion was unreasonably short, or that the Commission's application to the Court introduces complaints that were not formulated in the reasoned opinion. If such an argument succeeds, the Commission's application will be found inadmissible, either wholly or in part.

It is also open to a Member State to argue that the Commission's view of what Community law requires, or its understanding of national law or of what the State concerned has actually done, is incorrect. The Court will not rule on the meaning of ambiguous provisions of national law which have not yet been the

---

[41] Effectively an interlocutory injunction.

[42] See Case 61/77 R *Commission v. Ireland* [1977] E.C.R. 937 and 1411 (note in particular the remarks of Advocate General Reischl at pp. 953–954); Case 246/89 R *Commission v. United Kingdom* [1989] E.C.R. 3125; [1989] 3 C.M.L.R. 601. (The suffix "R" stands for the French word *référé* and denotes a decision concerning interim measures.).

[43] Joined Cases 24 and 97/80 R *Commission v. France* [1980] E.C.R. 1319.

[44] See, *e.g.* Case 246/89 R *Commission v. United Kingdom, supra.*

[45] See Gormley (ed.), *Kapteyn and VerLoren van Themaat's Introduction to the Law of the European Communities* (3rd ed., 1998), p. 454.

subject of decisions by the competent national courts. In *Commission v. United Kingdom*,[46] the Commission argued that the British Consumer Protection Act 1987 failed to give effect properly to a directive on liability for defective products. The United Kingdom pointed out that section 1(1) of the Act made it clear that its purpose was to give effect to the directive and required it to be construed accordingly. It maintained that the contested provision of the Act, section 4(1)(e), was capable of being interpreted consistently with the directive. The Court held that the Commission had not succeeded in refuting that argument: ". . . the Court has consistently held that the scope of national laws, regulations or administrative provisions must be assessed in the light of the interpretation given to them by national courts . . . Yet in this case the Commission has not referred in support of its application to any national judicial decision which, in its view, interprets the domestic provision at issue inconsistently with the Directive." The British courts have a good record in interpreting national provisions consistently with directives they are designed to implement[47] and this provided a further ground for rejecting the Commission's application: ". . . there is nothing in the material produced to the Court to suggest that the courts in the United Kingdom, if called upon to interpret section 4(1)(e), would not do so in the light of the wording and the purpose of the Directive so as to achieve the result which it has in view and thereby comply with the third paragraph of Article 189 [now 249] of the Treaty . . . Moreover, section 1(1) of the Act expressly imposes such an obligation on the national courts."

The Court has, however, been steadfast in refusing to allow Member States to rely on more subjective factors, making it clear that "an action based on Article 226 E.C. requires only an objective finding of a failure by a Member State to fulfil its obligations and not proof of any inertia or opposition on the part of the Member State concerned."[48] Thus, it is no defence that national legislation, although technically incompatible with Community law, is in practice applied in accordance with the requirements of the Treaty. The Court has said that the mere maintenance in force of such legislation "gives rise to an ambiguous state of affairs by maintaining, as regards those subject to the law who are concerned, a state of uncertainty as to the possibilities available to them of relying on Community law."[49] The need to avoid this type of uncertainty has also led the Court to refuse to allow Member States to rely on the fact that the provisions of Community law which have been breached are directly effective and may therefore be relied on in the national courts, which must accord them precedence over inconsistent provisions of national law. The Court has stated that "the primacy and direct effect of the provisions of Community law do not release Member States from their obligation to remove from their domestic legal order any provisions incompatible with Community law . . ."[50] Nor can Member States

---

[46] Case C-300/95 [1997] E.C.R. I-2649. See also Case C-80/92 *Commission v. Belgium* [1994] E.C.R. I-1019, para. 7. *cf.* Case C-392/96 *Commission v. Ireland*, judgment of September 21, 1999.

[47] See generally Arnull, "Interpretation and precedent in English and Community law: evidence of cross-fertilisation?" in Andenas (ed.), *English Public Law and the Common Law of Europe* (1998), Chap. 6.

[48] Case C-215/98 *Commission v. Greece*, judgment of July 8, 1999, para. 15.

[49] Case 167/73 *Commission v. French Republic* [1974] E.C.R. 359, para. 41; [1974] 2 C.M.L.R. 216. See also Case C-58/90 *Commission v. Italy* [1991] E.C.R. I-4193, para. 12.

[50] Case 104/86 *Commission v. Italy* [1988] E.C.R. 1799, para. 12; [1989] 3 C.M.L.R. 25.

rely on a failure by the Community institutions to comply with their own obligations under the Treaty. In *Commission v. Luxembourg and Belgium*,[51] the Court said that "the Treaty is not limited to creating reciprocal obligations between the different natural and legal persons to whom it is applicable . . . [E]xcept where otherwise expressly provided, the basic concept of the Treaty requires that the Member States shall not take the law into their own hands. Therefore the fact that the Council failed to carry out its obligations cannot relieve the defendants from carrying out theirs." The appropriate remedy for a Member State in such circumstances would be a direct action against the institution in question.

Similarly, a Member State may not justify a breach of Community law on the ground that its object was to correct the effects of such a breach by another Member State. The Court made it clear in *Commission v. France*[52] that "[a] Member State cannot under any circumstances unilaterally adopt, on its own authority, corrective measures or measures to protect trade designed to prevent[53] any failure on the part of another Member State to comply with the rules laid down by the Treaty." The Court pointed out that a Member State which considers the action of another Member State incompatible with Community law can take action at the political level, invite the Commission to bring proceedings against that State under Article 226 or take action itself under Article 227. Moreover, reservations or statements made by the Member State concerned in the course of the procedure leading to the adoption of an act which is alleged to have been breached will not be taken into account by the Court, since "the objective scope of rules laid down by the common institutions cannot be modified by reservations or objections which Member States have made at the time the rules were being formulated."[54]

As the Court pointed out in *Commission v. Ireland*,[55] "[i]t is well established in the case-law of the Court . . . that a Member State may not plead internal circumstances in order to justify a failure to comply with obligations and time-limits resulting from Community law. Moreover, it has been held on several occasions . . . that practical difficulties which appear at the stage when a Community measure is put into effect cannot permit a Member State unilaterally to opt out of fulfilling its obligations." In particular, the Court has made it clear that the obligations arising from the Treaty "devolve upon States as such and the liability of a Member State under Article 169 [now 226] arises whatever the agency of the State whose action or inaction is the cause of the failure to fulfil its obligations, even in the case of a constitutionally independent institution."[56] Thus, it is no defence that draft legislation intended to give effect to the

---

[51] Joined Cases 90–91/63 [1964] E.C.R. 625 at 631; [1965] C.M.L.R. 58.
[52] Case 232/78 [1979] E.C.R. 2729, para. 9; [1980] 1 C.M.L.R. 418. See also Case C–5/94 *The Queen v. MAFF, ex p. Hedley Lomas* [1996] E.C.R. I–2553, para. 20; [1996] 2 C.M.L.R. 391; [1996] All E.R. (E.C.) 493; Case C–265/95, *Commission v. France* [1997] E.C.R. I–6959, para. 63.
[53] *Sic.* The French text reads ". . . destinées à obvier à une méconnaissance éventuelle, par un Etat membre, des règles du traité".
[54] Case 39/72 *Commission v. Italy* [1973] E.C.R. 101, para. 22; [1973] C.M.L.R. 439. See also Case 38/69 *Commission v. Italy* [1970] E.C.R. 47, para. 12; [1970] C.M.L.R. 77.
[55] Case C–39/88 [1990] E.C.R. I–4271, para. 11; [1991] 2 C.M.L.R. 876.
[56] Case 77/69 *Commission v. Belgium* [1970] E.C.R. 237, para. 15; [1974] 1 C.M.L.R. 203.

requirements of Community law lapsed due to the dissolution of the national parliament.[57] It appears to follow that proceedings under Article 226 could in theory be brought against a Member State if its courts failed to comply with their obligations under the Treaty.[58] It seems clear, however, that an isolated failure by a national court to apply Community law correctly would not give rise to a right of action. Only a deliberate refusal by a national court to comply with its obligations under the Treaty[59] could have this result. Even then, proceedings under Article 226 might not be desirable.[60]

A Member State may even incur liability under Article 226 as a result of the actions of private individuals if the Court takes the view that it has not taken appropriate steps to prevent such actions from interfering with the proper functioning of the common market. This was established in *Commission v. France*,[61] where the Commission argued that France had breached its Treaty obligations by failing to take effective action to prevent imports of fruit and vegetables from other Member States from being disrupted by acts of violence committed by farmers. The Court held that the Treaty required the Member States to take all necessary and appropriate measures to ensure that the fundamental principle of the free movement of goods was respected on their territory. Although the Member States had a margin of discretion in determining what measures were most appropriate to eliminate barriers to imports in a given situation, it was the responsibility of the Court to ensure that that margin had not been exceeded. The Court concluded that "in the present case the French Government has manifestly and persistently abstained from adopting appropriate and adequate measures to put an end to the acts of vandalism which jeopardise the free movement on its territory of certain agricultural products originating in other Member States and to prevent the recurrence of such acts."[62]

The effectiveness of enforcement proceedings under Article 226

Of the cases in which the Commission sends a letter of formal notice under Article 226, the vast majority are settled following receipt of that letter by the State concerned or following the dispatch by the Commission of the reasoned opinion. In practice, the Commission is even willing to settle some cases after the expiry of the deadline laid down in the reasoned opinion, so that only a small proportion of the cases in which proceedings are instituted proceed to judgment.[63] This suggests that, in many cases, the threat of proceedings under Article 226 is enough to bring recalcitrant Member States to heel.

---

[57] *ibid.* See also, *e.g.* Case 91/79 *Commission v. Italy* [1980] E.C.R. 1099; [1981] 1 C.M.L.R. 331.

[58] See Advocate General Warner in Case 9/75 *Meyer-Burckhardt v. Commission* [1975] E.C.R. 1171 at 1187.

[59] *e.g.* a refusal by a national court against whose decisions there is no judicial remedy under national law to comply with the obligation imposed on it by the third para. of Art. 234 (ex 177) E.C. See further Chap. 11.

[60] See Dashwood and White, *op. cit.,* p. 391 and the materials cited there.

[61] Case C–265/95 [1997] E.C.R. I–6959.

[62] Para. 65. The Court's decision led to the adoption of Reg. 2679/98 on the functioning of the internal market in relation to the free movement of goods among the Member States, [1998] O.J. L337/8.

[63] See Dashwood and White, *op. cit.,* pp. 411–413 and the materials cited there.

Of the cases which result in a ruling of the Court adverse to the Member State concerned, most are in due course complied with, although sometimes only after considerable delay. However, the 1980s saw a marked increase in the number of rulings given by the Court against Member States for breach of Article 228.[64] In order to give Member States an added incentive to comply with rulings against them under Article 226, a new second paragraph was added to Article 228 at Maastricht giving the Court the power to impose financial sanctions on Member States which fail to do so. Article 228(2) provides that the Commission, if it considers that the State concerned has not taken the measures necessary to comply with the Court's judgment,

". . . shall, after giving that State the opportunity to submit its observations, issue a reasoned opinion specifying the points on which the Member State concerned has not complied with the judgment of the Court of Justice.

If the Member State concerned fails to take the necessary measures to comply with the Court's judgment within the time-limit laid down by the Commission, the latter may bring the case before the Court of Justice. In so doing it shall specify the amount of the lump sum or penalty payment to be paid by the Member State concerned which it considers appropriate in the circumstances.

If the Court of Justice finds that the Member State concerned has not complied with its judgment it may impose a lump sum or penalty payment on it.

This procedure shall be without prejudice to Article 227."

One drawback of this procedure is that the Commission may not ask for the imposition of a financial penalty in its initial application to the Court under Article 226. Moreover, no further penalties are envisaged if a Member State refuses to pay a sanction imposed on it.[65] On the other hand, although the Commission is required to follow an administrative procedure which corresponds to that laid down in Article 226, involving an opportunity for the State concerned to submit its observations and the issue of a reasoned opinion, it is not required to specify the amount of any sanction it considers appropriate until it brings the case before the Court. It will also be noted that the Treaty does not set any limit to the amount of the penalty which the Court may impose.

By the time the Maastricht Treaty was signed on February 7, 1992, the Court of Justice had held in the famous *Francovich* case,[66] decided the previous November, that there was a principle "inherent in the system of the Treaty" that Member States were liable to compensate individuals for damage caused by

---

[64] The explanation for this development may lie partly in the increased vigour with which the Commission, between the late 1970s and the early 1990s, pursued Member States which failed to comply with their Treaty obligations. See Dashwood and White, *op. cit.,* pp. 399–400; Gormley (ed.), *op. cit.,* p. 454.

[65] *cf.* Art. 88 ECSC, which provides that, where a Member State's failure to comply with its Treaty obligations has been established, the High Authority may, with the assent of the Council acting by a two-thirds majority, (a) suspend the payment of any sums which it may be liable to pay to the State in question under the Treaty, and (b) take measures, or authorise the other Member States to take measures, which would otherwise be prohibited as incompatible with the common market for coal and steel in order to correct the effects of the infringement. These apparently draconian sanctions have never been imposed.

[66] Joined Cases C–6 and 9/90 [1991] E.C.R. I–5357; [1993] 2 C.M.L.R. 66. See Chap. 5.

breaches of Community law for which they were responsible. That principle deprived Article 228(2) of much of its significance, but there remain some situations where the principle of State liability is unlikely to have much practical effect. The conditions laid down in *Francovich* and the Court's later case-law on the principle of State liability may not be satisfied. The loss suffered by a potential plaintiff may be too small to justify the cost of bringing proceedings; causation may be hard to prove. In some cases, it may be undesirable to leave matters until a willing litigant emerges. In circumstances such as these, the imposition of a financial sanction under Article 228(2) may be particularly apt.

In the summer of 1996 the Commission issued a "Memorandum on applying Article 171 [now 228] of the E.C. Treaty"[67] in which it set out its views on how the second paragraph of that article might be applied. The Commission observed that the penalty payment, rather than the lump sum, was the "most appropriate instrument" for achieving the objective of the infringement procedure, which was "to secure compliance as rapidly as possible". The Commission stated that the amount of the penalty would be calculated on the basis of three criteria: (a) the seriousness of the infringement, (b) its duration and (c) the need to deter further infringements. The Commission acknowledged that failure to comply with a judgment of the Court is always a serious matter, but said that it would also take account of the effects of the underlying infringement and the importance of the rules which had been infringed. In January 1997 the Commission issued further guidance on how it proposed to calculate the appropriate penalty in particular cases. It announced[68] that the amount of any penalty payments proposed to the Court would be calculated by multiplying coefficients reflecting the gravity and duration of the infringement by an "invariable factor" based on the gross domestic product of the Member State concerned and the weighting of votes in the Council.

There is evidence that the threat of a financial penalty is sometimes enough to induce Member States to comply with their obligations. In an answer dated November 30, 1998[69] to a written question posed by a Member of the European Parliament, the Commission stated that, as of that date, there had been 12 instances where it had proposed the imposition of a financial penalty on a Member State. In six of them the States involved were prompted to conform with the requirements of the Treaty and the disputes were settled before the applications were submitted to the Court. In one case, a settlement was in the process of being reached. In two cases, the Commission submitted applications to the Court but the States concerned complied before the Court gave a decision. In three of the 12 cases, applications had been submitted and the Court's ruling was pending.[70]

THE ACTION FOR ANNULMENT

The extensive legislative authority conferred on the Community institutions by the E.C. Treaty made it essential to create a system for reviewing the legality of

---

[67] [1996] O.J. C242/6.
[68] See [1997] O.J. C63/2.
[69] See [1999] O.J. C135/182.
[70] The first to be decided by the Court was Case C–387/97 *Commission v. Greece,* judgment of July 4, 2000. The court imposed a penalty of Euros 20,000 for each day of delay in taking the measures necessary, with effect from delivery of its judgment.

the way in which that authority was exercised. The principal device for achieving that objective is Article 230 (ex 173) E.C., under which direct actions for the annulment of Community acts may be brought before the Community Courts. It may also be possible to challenge the validity of Community acts in proceedings before the courts of the Member States, which must, where there is a serious doubt about the validity of the act in question, ask the Court of Justice for a preliminary ruling on the matter under Article 234 (ex 177) E.C.[71] The preliminary rulings procedure is discussed in the following chapter.

Article 230 E.C., as amended as Maastricht and Amsterdam, provides as follows:

> "The Court of Justice shall review the legality of acts adopted jointly by the European Parliament and the Council, of acts of the Council, of the Commission, and of the ECB other than recommendations or opinions, and of acts of the European Parliament intended to produce legal effects *vis-à-vis* third parties.
>
> It shall for this purpose have jurisdiction in actions brought by a Member State, the Council or the Commission on grounds of lack of competence, infringement of an essential procedural requirement, infringement of this Treaty or of any rule of law relating to its application, or misuse of powers.
>
> The Court shall have jurisdiction under the same conditions in actions brought by the European Parliament, by the Court of Auditors and by the ECB for the purpose of protecting their prerogatives.
>
> Any natural or legal person may, under the same conditions, institute proceedings against a decision addressed to that person or against a decision which, although in the form of a regulation or a decision addressed to another person, is of direct and individual concern to the former.
>
> The proceedings provided for in this Article shall be instituted within two months of the publication of the measure, or of its notification to the plaintiff, or, in the absence thereof, of the day on which it came to the knowledge of the latter, as the case may be."

As explained in Chapter 19, jurisdiction in annulment proceedings brought by natural and legal persons is now exercised by the CFI, from which appeal lies to the Court of Justice on points of law. Annulment actions brought by the Institutions and the Member States for the time being commence in the Court of Justice, although the Court has proposed that certain categories of such action brought by Member States should be transferred to the CFI.[72]

Reviewable acts

Under the first paragraph of Article 230, proceedings may be brought against "acts adopted jointly by the European Parliament and the Council, of acts of the Council, of the Commission, and of the ECB other than recommendations or opinions . . .". According to Article 249 (ex 189) E.C., the last two categories of

---

[71] See Case 314/85 *Foto-Frost v. Hauptzollamt Lübeck-Ost* [1987] E.C.R. 4199.
[72] See Chap. 9.

act "have no binding force".[73] The other categories of act mentioned in Article 249 (regulations, directives and decisions) do have binding force and are in principle susceptible to review under Article 230.

The question whether Article 230 can be used to challenge measures adopted by the Community institutions which produce legal effects, but which do not take the form of any of the binding acts referred to in Article 249, was considered in 'ERTA'.[74] In that case, the Commission sought the annulment of Council proceedings concerning the negotiation and conclusion by the Member States of a European road transport agreement. The Court stated that "Article 173 [now 230] treats as acts open to review by the Court all measures adopted by the institutions which are intended to have legal force." The Court said that it would be inconsistent with the purpose of Article 230, which was to ensure that the law was observed in accordance with Article 220 (ex 164) E.C., "to limit the availability of this procedure merely to the categories of measures referred to by Article 189 [now 249]". It concluded that "[a]n action for annulment must therefore be available in the case of all measures adopted by the institutions, whatever their nature or form, which are intended to have legal effects." Similarly, in *Les Verts v. Parliament*[75] a French political grouping sought the annulment of two measures adopted by the European Parliament. At the material time, the Parliament was not mentioned in the first paragraph of what was then Article 173, but the Court held that it would be inconsistent with the spirit of the Treaty for measures adopted by the Parliament which produced legal effects *vis-à-vis* third parties to be excluded from the scope of the action for annulment.

In the "Airport Transit Visas" case,[76] the applicant sought the annulment pursuant to Article 230 of a joint action adopted by the Council under Article K.3(2) of the Maastricht version of the TEU. The Court rejected the argument of the United Kingdom Government that it had no jurisdiction since the contested act had been adopted outside the framework of the E.C. Treaty. Article 47 (ex M) of the TEU, which the Court had jurisdiction to apply by virtue of Article 46 (ex L), made it clear that measures such as the contested joint action were not intended to affect the E.C. Treaty. The Court declared: "It is therefore the task of the Court to ensure that acts which, according to the Council, fall within the scope of Article K.3(2) of the Treaty on European Union, do not encroach upon the powers conferred by the E.C. Treaty on the Community."[77] The decision was essential to prevent the Member States from using the TEU to avoid the decision-making processes laid down in the E.C. Treaty in fields which should properly be regarded as falling within the scope of the latter.

---

[73] Recommendations are not, however, entirely devoid of legal significance: see Case C–322/88 *Grimaldi v. Fonds des Maladies Professionnelles* [1989] E.C.R. 4407.

[74] Case 22/70 *Commission v. Council* [1971] E.C.R. 263, paras 39–42; [1971] C.M.L.R. 335. See also Case C–366/88 *France v. Commission* [1990] E.C.R. I–3571; [1992] 1 C.M.L.R. 205.

[75] Case 294/83 [1986] E.C.R. 1339; [1987] 2 C.M.L.R. 343. See also Case 34/86 *Council v. Parliament* [1986] E.C.R. 2155; [1986] 3 C.M.L.R. 94; Case C–57/95 *France v. Commission* [1997] E.C.R. I–1627; [1997] 2 C.M.L.R. 935.

[76] Case C–170/96, *Commission v. Council* [1998] E.C.R. I–2763; [1998] 2 C.M.L.R. 1092.

[77] Para 16. *cf.* Case T–174/95 *Svenska Journalistförbundet v. Council* [1998] E.C.R. II–2289, paras 81–86; Case T–14/98 *Hautala v. Council,* judgment of July 19, 1999, paras 41–42.

It should, however, be noted that a provisional measure intended to pave the way for the final decision in a procedure involving several stages cannot be challenged: only the final act definitively laying down the adopting body's position is susceptible to review under Article 230.[78] Nor can proceedings be brought against a measure which merely confirms a previous measure which has not been challenged within the time-limit laid down in the last paragraph of Article 230.[79] Moreover, the preamble to a Community act is not susceptible to review where it is not necessary to support the operative part and does not in itself produce any legal effects.[80]

Grounds of review

In order to succeed in an action for the annulment of a Community act, the applicant must establish that the contested act was unlawful. The second paragraph of Article 230 mentions four grounds, derived from French administrative law,[81] on which this may be done. In practice, those grounds overlap to a considerable extent and the Court does not distinguish rigidly between them.

A measure may be annulled by the Court for *lack of competence* if the adopting institution lacked the authority to adopt it. This typically arises where the enabling provision under which the adopting institution purported to act is found by the Court not to be wide enough to cover the contested measure.[82]

An example of a *breach of an essential procedural requirement* is failure to consult the Parliament prior to the adoption of an act where consultation is required by the Treaty.[83] Another example is failure to hear the views of interested parties before a decision which directly affects them is adopted.[84] In *Lisrestal and Others v. Commission*,[85] an application for the annulment of a decision reducing financial assistance initially granted under the European Social Fund, the CFI stated:

"... it is settled law that respect for the rights of the defence in all proceedings which are initiated against a person and are liable to culminate in a measure adversely affecting that person is a fundamental principle of Community law which must be guaranteed, even in the absence of any specific rules concerning

---

[78] Case 60/81 *IBM v. Commission* [1981] E.C.R. 2639; [1981] 3 C.M.L.R. 635.

[79] See, *e.g.* Joined Cases 166 and 220/86 *Irish Cement Ltd v. Commission* [1988] E.C.R. 6473, para. 16; [1989] 2 C.M.L.R. 57; Case T–275/94 *CB v. Commission* [1995] E.C.R. II–2169, para. 27; [1995] 5 C.M.L.R. 410; [1995] All E.R. (E.C.) 717.

[80] See Joined Cases T–125/97 and T–127/97 *The Coca-Cola Company and Another v. Commission,* judgment of March 22, 2000; T–138/89 *Nederlandse Bankiersvereniging and Nederlandse Vereniging van Banken v. Commission* [1992] E.C.R. II–2181; [1993] 5 C.M.L.R. 436.

[81] See Advocate General Lagrange in Case 3/54 *ASSIDER v. High Authority* [1954 to 1956] E.C.R. 63, a case decided under the ECSC Treaty.

[82] See, *e.g.* Joined Cases 281, 283–285 and 287/85 *Germany, France, Netherlands, Denmark and United Kingdom v. Commission* [1987] E.C.R. 3203; [1988] 1 C.M.L.R. 111; Case 264/86 *France v. Commission* [1988] E.C.R. 973; [1989] 1 C.M.L.R. 13. *cf.* Case 45/86 *Commission v. Council* [1987] E.C.R. 1493; [1988] 2 C.M.L.R. 131.

[83] Case 138/79 *Roquette Frères v. Council* [1980] E.C.R. 3333.

[84] See *e.g.* Case 17/74 *Transocean Marine Paint Association v. Commission* [1974] E.C.R. 1063; [1974] 2 C.M.L.R. 459; Case C–49/88 *Al-Jubail Fertilizer Company v. Council* [1991] E.C.R. I–3187; [1991] 3 C.M.L.R. 377.

[85] Case T–450/93 [1994] E.C.R. II–1177, para. 42.

the proceedings in question . . . That principle requires that any person who may be adversely affected by the adoption of a decision should be placed in a position in which he may effectively make known his views on the evidence against him which the Commission has taken as the basis for the decision at issue."

Thus, a person must be heard if administrative proceedings have been brought against him. However, that requirement does not apply in the context of a decision-making process leading to the adoption of legislation of general application. In that context, the only obligations of consultation which the Community legislature must respect are those laid down in the legal basis of the contested act.[86]

Another important example of an essential procedural requirement is contained in Article 253 (ex 190) E.C., which requires Community acts to contain an adequate statement of the reasons on which they are based. That requirement is regarded as involving a matter of public policy which the Community Courts must raise of their own motion if it is not raised by the applicant.[86a] The amount of detail required by Article 253 depends on the nature of the act and the context in which it is intended to operate. In *Belgium v. Commission*,[87] the Court summarised the effect of the article as follows: "According to settled case-law, the statement of reasons required by Article 190 [now 253] of the Treaty must be appropriate to the nature of the measure in question. It must show clearly and unequivocally the reasoning of the institution which adopted the measure so as to inform the persons concerned of the justification for the measure adopted and to enable the Court to exercise its powers of review. It is also apparent from the case-law that the statement of reasons for a measure is not required to specify the matters of fact or of law dealt with, provided that it falls within the general scheme of the body of measures of which it forms part . . ." In that case, the Court found the reasoning of the contested acts adequate to satisfy the requirements of the Treaty.

The third ground, *infringement of the Treaty or of any rule of law relating to its application*, is the widest one and is capable of subsuming the other three. In particular, a measure may be declared void on this ground if it contravenes a general principle of law recognised by the Court, such as the principles of legal certainty, proportionality, equality and respect for fundamental rights. The general principles of Community law are discussed in Chapter 6.

The last ground of invalidity mentioned in Article 230 is *misuse of powers*. In *Crispoltoni*,[88] the Court stated that ". . . a measure may amount to a misuse of powers only if it appears, on the basis of objective, relevant and consistent factors, to have been taken with the exclusive purpose, or at any rate the main

---

[86] See Case T–521/93 *Atlanta and Others v. European Community* [1996] E.C.R. II–1707, paras 70–74 (endorsed by the Court of Justice on appeal: Case C–104/97 P, judgment of October 14, 1999, paras 37–38).

[86a] By contrast, a plea going to the substantive legality of the contested act can be examined by the Community Courts only if it is raised by the applicant. See, *e.g.* Case C–367/95 P *Commission v. Sytraval and Brink's France* [1998] E.C.R. I–1719, para. 67.

[87] Joined Cases C–71, 155 and 271/95 [1997] E.C.R. I–687, para. 53; [1995] 5 C.M.L.R. 6.

[88] Joined Cases C–133, 300 and 362/93 [1994] E.C.R. I–4863, para. 27.

purpose, of achieving an end other than that stated or evading a procedure specifically prescribed by the Treaty for dealing with the circumstances of the case". This ground is particularly difficult to establish because it requires the applicant to establish that the intentions of the defendant institution were different from those stated in the contested measure. In *Crispoltoni*, the Court found that the alleged misuse of powers had not been substantiated.

Time limits

Under the fifth paragraph of Article 230, proceedings must be instituted "within two months of the publication of the measure, or of its notification to the plaintiff, or, in the absence thereof, of the day on which it came to the notice of the latter". Article 254 (ex 191) of the Treaty requires regulations, directives and decisions adopted in accordance with the procedure referred to in Article 251 (ex 189b) to be published in the Official Journal of the Community, along with regulations of the Council and of the Commission and directives of those institutions which are addressed to all the Member States. Other directives and decisions are only required to be notified to those to whom they are addressed, but may in practice also be published in the Official Journal.

Where a measure is published in the Official Journal, the date of publication is that on which the issue concerned actually becomes available, which may not be the same as the date on the cover. This is so whether or not publication was compulsory and whether or not the measure came to the knowledge of the applicant before it was published. In *Germany v. Council*,[89] the Court said that the wording of the fifth paragraph of Article 230 made it clear "that the criterion of the day on which a measure came to the knowledge of an applicant, as the starting point of the period prescribed for instituting proceedings, is subsidiary to the criteria of publication or notification of the measure".

Where a measure has not been published in the Official Journal and the time-limit runs from notification, it will be important to know precisely what the term "notification" entails. In *Commission v. Socurte and Others*,[90] the Court said that notification for these purposes "necessarily involves the communication of a detailed account of the contents of the measure notified and of the reasons on which it is based. In the absence of such an account, the third party concerned would be denied precise knowledge of the contents of the act in question and of the reasons for which it was adopted, which would enable him to bring proceedings effectively against that decision." That requirement could only be satisfied by sending the applicant the text of the measure in issue, not a brief summary of its contents. However, once a party is aware of the existence of a measure concerning it, it will be expected to request the text of the measure within a reasonable period. Once that period has expired, time will start running against the party concerned.[91]

The fifth paragraph of Article 230 must be read in the light of the Rules of Procedure of the Community Courts. Under Article 80(1)(a) of the Court's

---

[89] Case C–122/95 [1998] E.C.R. I–973, para. 35; [1998] 3 C.M.L.R. 570. See also Case T–14/96 *BAI v. Commission*, judgment of January 28, 1999, paras 32–37.
[90] Case C–143/95 P [1997] E.C.R. I–1, para. 31.
[91] See Case T–155/95 *LPN and GEOTA v. Commission* [1998] E.C.R. II–2751.

Rules and Article 101(1)(a) of the CFI's Rules, the day on which an event occurs is not counted as falling within the prescribed period of time. Furthermore, by virtue of Article 81(1) of the Court's Rules and Article 102(1) of the CFI's Rules, where the period of time allowed for commencing proceedings runs from publication of the contested measure, the period is calculated "from the end of the 14th day after publication thereof in the *Official Journal of the European Communities*". Moreover, in accordance with Article 81(2) of the Court's Rules, extensions of the prescribed time-limits are laid down on account of the distance between the Court and the place where the applicant is habitually resident. Those extensions also apply to the CFI by virtue of Article 102(2) of its own Rules.[92]

In *Mutual Aid Administration Services NV v. Commission*,[93] the CFI said: "It is settled case-law that the time-limit prescribed for bringing actions under Article 173 [now 230] of the Treaty is a matter of public policy and is not subject to the discretion of the parties or the Court, since it was established in order to ensure that legal positions are clear and certain and to avoid any discrimination or arbitrary treatment in the administration of justice . . ." Failure to observe the time limit therefore constituted "an absolute bar"[94] to the admissibility of an application.

The effects of annulment

According to the first paragraph of Article 231 (ex 174) E.C., where the Court of Justice finds an action under Article 230 well founded, it "shall declare the act concerned to be void". The Courts have no power to order the institution concerned to take any particular steps,[95] but the institution is required by the first paragraph of Article 233 (ex 176) E.C. to take the measures necessary to comply with the Court's judgment.[96]

The scope of the defendant institution's obligations under the first paragraph of Article 233 was considered in *Commission v. AssiDomän Kraft Products and Others*. That case was a sequel to the ruling of the Court of Justice in the so-called "Wood Pulp" case,[97] a competition proceeding in which the Court partially annulled a decision of the Commission. In the contested decision, the Commission found that 43 undertakings, including the seven applicants in *AssiDomän* ("the Swedish addressees"), had infringed one of the competition provisions of the Treaty.[98] The Commission imposed fines on almost all the addressees of the decision.[99] In annulment proceedings brought against the decision by 26 of its

---

[92] The period laid down for the United Kingdom and Ireland is 10 days.

[93] Joined Cases T–121 and 151/96 [1997] E.C.R. II–1355, para. 38.

[94] Para. 39.

[95] See, *e.g.* Case 15/85 *Consorzio Cooperative d'Abruzzo v. Commission* [1987] E.C.R. 1005, para. 18; [1988] 1 C.M.L.R. 841; Case C–5/93 P *DSM v. Commission*, judgment of July 8, 1999, para. 36; [1993] 4 C.M.L.R. 289.

[96] See Toth, "The authority of judgments of the European Court of Justice: binding force and legal effects" (1984) 4 Y.E.L. 1.

[97] Joined Cases C–89, 104, 114, 116, 117 and 125/85–129/85 *Ahlström Osakeyhtiö and Others v. Commission* [1993] E.C.R. I–1307; [1993] 4 C.M.L.R. 407.

[98] Art. 81(1) (ex 85(1)): see Chap. 20.

[99] The Commission's power to impose fines on undertakings which infringe the Treaty competition rules is discussed in Chap. 22.

addressees, the Court quashed provisions finding that there had been an infringement of the Treaty and annulled or reduced the fines imposed on the applicants. The Swedish addressees had not sought the annulment of the decision and had paid the fines imposed on them. After the Court had given judgment, they asked the Commission to refund the fines they had paid in respect of findings which had now been quashed by the Court. The Commission refused on the basis that the Court had only annulled or reduced the fines imposed on the applicants in "Wood Pulp" and that the decision was unaffected in so far as it concerned the Swedish addressees.

After a ruling by the CFI in favour of the applicants,[1] an appeal by the Commission was upheld by the Court of Justice.[2] Although drafted and published in the form of a single act, the CFI had treated the contested decision as a bundle of individual decisions affecting each of its addressees. The Court did not dissent from that approach. It made it clear that, although Article 233 required the defendant institution to ensure that any act intended to replace the act annulled was not vitiated by the same defects, it did not mean that the institution was required to "re-examine identical or similar decisions allegedly affected by the same irregularity, addressed to addressees other than the applicant".[3] A decision which had not been challenged by its addressee within the time-limit laid down in Article 230 became definitive as against that addressee. The purpose of that time-limit was "to ensure legal certainty by preventing Community measures which produce legal effects from being called in question indefinitely . . .".[4] The Court explained that "[w]here a number of similar individual decisions imposing fines have [sic] been adopted pursuant to a common procedure and only some addressees have taken legal action against the decisions concerning them and obtained their annulment, the principle of legal certainty . . . precludes any necessity for the institution which adopted the decisions to re-examine, at the request of other addressees, in the light of the grounds of the annulling judgment, the legality of the unchallenged decisions and to determine, on the basis of that examination, whether the fines paid must be refunded."[5]

Where Article 233 requires the adoption of a new measure to replace the one declared void by the Court, the principle of legal certainty will generally mean that the new measure cannot be made retrospective. However, in exceptional cases this is permitted "where the purpose to be achieved so demands and where the legitimate expectations of those concerned are duly respected".[6] The Court's ruling may also lead to a claim for compensation against the Community in accordance with Article 235 (ex 178) and the second paragraph of Article 288 (ex 215) of the Treaty.[7]

In principle, a declaration by the Court under Article 230 that an act is void takes effect *erga omnes* and *ex tunc*, that is, with regard to the whole world and

---

[1] Case T–227/95 [1997] E.C.R. II–1185. See also Case T–220/97 *H & R Ecroyd Holdings Ltd v. Commission,* judgment of May 20, 1999, discussed in Chap. 11.

[2] Case C–310/97 P, [1999] 5 C.M.L.R. 1253.

[3] Para. 56.

[4] Para. 61.

[5] Para. 63.

[6] See, *e.g.* Case 108/81 *Amylum v. Council* [1982] E.C.R. 3107.

[7] See the second para. of Art. 233 (ex 176) E.C. The second para. of Art. 288 is discussed below.

with retrospective effect. The second paragraph of Article 231 states: "In the case of a regulation, however, the Court of Justice shall, if it considers this necessary, state which of the effects of the regulation which it has declared void shall be considered as definitive." This enables the Court to minimise any disruption which might be caused by the gap left by the disappearance of the measure which has been quashed. For example, in a case in which the Court declared void certain provisions of a regulation relating to the remuneration of Community officials, it declared that those provisions should continue to have effect until they were replaced "to avoid discontinuity in the system of remuneration".[8] In *Timex v. Council*, the Court declared void a provision in a regulation imposing an anti-dumping duty. The aim of the action had been to have the rate of the duty increased and to secure the imposition of a duty on a wider range of products. The Court therefore ruled that the provision in question should remain in force until it had been replaced.[9] The Court has applied the power conferred on it by the second paragraph of Article 231 by analogy in a case in which a directive was quashed. This the Court said was justified by "important reasons of legal certainty, comparable to those which operate in cases where certain regulations are annulled".[10]

Capacity to bring proceedings

In order to bring proceedings under Article 230, an applicant must show that he satisfies the conditions regarding standing, or *locus standi*, laid down in the Treaty. Article 230 draws a distinction in this respect between three categories of applicant: (a) the Member States, the Council and the Commission; (b) the European Parliament, the Court of Auditors and the ECB; and (c) natural and legal persons.

Applicants falling within the first category automatically have standing to bring proceedings and do not have to establish any particular interest.[11] To put the point another way, such applicants are presumed to have an interest in the legality of all Community acts. For this reason, they are sometimes referred to as "privileged applicants". Where a Member State seeks the annulment of a measure adopted by the Council, its right to bring proceedings is not affected by whether or not it voted for the measure when it was adopted.[12] The term "Member State" in this context means the governments of the Member States and does not include the governments of regions or autonomous communities, whatever their powers might be under national law. The Court has said that "[i]t is not possible for the European Communities to comprise a greater number of Member States than the number of States between which they were established."[13] Regional governments constitute legal persons for the purposes of

---

[8] Case 81/72 *Commission v. Council* [1973] E.C.R. 575, para. 15; [1973] C.M.L.R. 639.

[9] Case 264/82 [1985] E.C.R. 849, para. 32; [1985] 3 C.M.L.R. 550.

[10] Case C–295/90 *Parliament v. Council* [1992] E.C.R. I–4193, para. 26; [1991] E.C.R. I–5299. This case is discussed in more detail in Chap. 28.

[11] See Case 45/86 *Commission v. Council* [1987] E.C.R. 1493, para. 3; [1988] 2 C.M.L.R. 131.

[12] Case 166/78 *Italy v. Council* [1979] E.C.R. 2575, para. 6.

[13] See Case C–95/97 *Région Wallonne v. Commission* [1997] E.C.R. I–1787, para. 6; Case C–180/97 *Regione Toscana v. Commission* [1997] E.C.R. I–5245, para. 6.

Article 230 and may only bring proceedings where the conditions set out in the fourth paragraph of that article are satisfied.[14]

The European Parliament, the Court of Auditors and the ECB may be described as "semi-privileged applicants". Before it was amended at Maastricht, Article 173 (as it then was) conferred no right of action on the European Parliament, but the Court held in the "Chernobyl" case[15] that the Parliament had the right to seek the annulment of acts adopted by the Council or by the Commission where the purpose of the proceedings was to protect the Parliament's prerogatives, that is, its right to participate to the extent envisaged by the Treaty in the legislative process leading to the adoption of a Community act.[16] Thus, even in the absence in Article 173 of any reference to the European Parliament, that institution could both institute annulment proceedings and be the defendant in such proceedings.[17] The Court's case-law on the status of the Parliament in annulment proceedings is now enshrined in the text of Article 230.

The standing of natural and legal persons to institute annulment proceedings is limited and for this reason they are sometimes referred to as "non-privileged applicants". A natural person is an individual. According to the CFI, "an applicant is a legal person if, at the latest by the expiry of the period prescribed for proceedings to be instituted, it has acquired legal personality in accordance with the law governing its constitution . . . or if it has been treated as an independent legal entity by the Community institutions."[18] The fourth paragraph of Article 230 suggests that an applicant falling within this category[19] may only bring proceedings against three types of act, namely: (i) a decision addressed to him; (ii) a decision in the form of a regulation which is of direct and individual concern to him; (iii) a decision addressed to another person[20] which is of direct and individual concern to the applicant. The Treaty seems to imply that regulations cannot be challenged by private applicants. However, by talking about a "decision in the form of a regulation", the Treaty makes it clear that it is not the label attached to a measure but its substance which counts.[21] So if an applicant can show that a measure called a regulation is really a decision in disguise, he can clearly challenge its validity. This principle cuts both ways, so that a measure entitled a decision may be treated *as if it were a regulation* if it is

---

[14] See, *e.g.* Case T–288/97 *Regione Autonoma Friuli-Venezia Giulia v. Commission,* judgment of June 15, 1999. The conditions laid down in the fourth para. of Art. 230 are considered below.

[15] Case C–70/88 *Parliament v. Council* [1990] E.C.R. I–2041; [1992] 1 C.M.L.R. 91.

[16] The Court made it clear that such proceedings were not brought under Art. 173, but under a right of action created by the Court to ensure respect for the institutional balance established by the Treaties. Indeed, the Court had held less than two years previously that the Parliament had no right of action under Art. 173: see Case 302/87 *Parliament v. Council* ("Comitology") [1988] E.C.R. 5615. The Court followed that ruling on this point in the "Chernobyl" case.

[17] See *Les Verts v. Parliament, supra.*

[18] Case T–161/94 *Sinochem Heilongjiang v. Council* [1996] E.C.R. II–695, para. 31; [1997] 3 C.M.L.R. 214.

[19] Which extends to all natural and legal persons, regardless of their nationality or place of residence.

[20] For the purposes of the fourth para. of Art. 230, this expression includes the Member States: Case 25/62 *Plaumann v. Commission* [1963] E.C.R. 95; [1964] C.M.L.R. 29.

[21] See Joined Cases 16–17/62 *Producteurs de Fruits v. Council* [1962] E.C.R. 471 at 478; [1963] C.M.L.R. 160.

does not have the characteristics of a real decision.[22] The apparent wish of the authors of the Treaty to exclude measures having the characteristics of true regulations from review at the suit of private applicants has produced some rather unsatisfactory results. The Court has therefore allowed private applicants to challenge such measures in certain circumstances. The question whether those circumstances should be widened is a matter of continuing controversy.

It is now necessary to look in more detail at three questions in particular: the distinction between regulations and decisions, the meaning of direct concern and the meaning of individual concern. The discussion is to some extent historical, because recent developments in the case-law can only properly be understood by reference to the position which prevailed previously.

The distinction between regulations and decisions

According to Article 249 (ex 189), "[a] regulation shall have general application. It shall be binding in its entirety and directly applicable in all Member States." The same article provides that "[a] decision shall be binding in its entirety upon those to whom it is addressed." In *Producteurs de Fruits v. Council*,[23] the Court deduced from the terms of that article that "[t]he criterion for the distinction [between regulations and decisions] must be sought in the general 'application' or otherwise of the measure in question." Thus, regulations were said to be essentially legislative in nature and to apply to "categories of persons viewed abstractly and in their entirety".[24] By contrast, the Court said in *Plaumann v. Commission*[25] that "decisions are characterised by the limited number of persons to whom they are addressed. In order to determine whether or not a measure constitutes a decision one must enquire whether that measure concerns specific persons."

The difficulty of satisfying the requirement of a decision may be illustrated by *Calpak v. Commission*.[26] In that case, the Court dismissed as inadmissible a challenge by two Italian companies to a regulation restricting the amount of aid payable to processors of Williams pears preserved in syrup. There were only 38 processors of Williams pears in the Community, 15 in France and 23 in Italy. Nonetheless, the Court said that the contested regulation was "by nature a measure of general application within the meaning of Article 189 [now 249] of the Treaty. In fact the measure applies to objectively determined situations and produces legal effects with regard to categories of persons described in a generalised and abstract manner. The nature of the measure as a regulation is not called in question by the mere fact that it is possible to determine the number or even the identity of the producers to be granted the aid which is limited thereby."[27] The strictness of this approach was somewhat mitigated by

---

[22] See Joined Cases T–480 and 483/93 *Antillean Rice Mills and Others v. Commission* [1995] E.C.R. II–2305, para. 65 (appeal dismissed: Case C–390/95 P, [1999] E.C.R. I–769).

[23] *supra.*

[24] *supra.*

[25] *supra.*

[26] *supra.*

[27] Para. 9.

the Court's acceptance that, where the annulment of only some of the provisions of an act was sought, it was the proper classification of those provisions, and not that of the act as a whole, that was important. The Court was prepared to accept that a true regulation might contain provisions which amounted in substance to decisions and which could therefore be challenged by private applicants under Article 230.[28] This was not, however, a conclusion that the Court would be willing to reach where the provisions in question were an "integral part" of a "legislative whole".[29]

Direct concern

The Court stated in *Les Verts v. Parliament*[30] that a measure was of direct concern to an applicant where it constituted "a complete set of rules which are sufficient in themselves and which require no implementing provisions", since in such circumstances the application of the measure "is automatic and leaves no room for any discretion". Thus, in order to establish direct concern, an applicant must be able to show that, at the time the contested act was adopted, the effect it would produce on him could be foreseen with a reasonable degree of certainty. Where the applicant is only affected by a measure because of the way a third party has exercised a discretion conferred on him and it was not possible to say in advance how he would do so, the applicant will not be able to establish direct concern. In *Alcan v. Commission*,[31] for example, a decision addressed to two Member States refusing to grant them import quotas was held not to be of direct concern to an applicant where the allocation of any quota would have been a matter for the discretion of the Member States concerned.

A measure requiring implementation by a third party may be of direct concern to an applicant if the third party has no discretion in the matter.[32] Similarly, an applicant may be able to establish direct concern if, at the time the contested measure was adopted, there was no real doubt how any discretion left to a third party would be exercised. In *Piraiki-Patraiki v. Commission*,[33] for example, the applicants sought the annulment of a Commission decision authorising France to impose a quota system restricting imports of cotton yarn from Greece during a specific period. The Commission argued that the applicants were not directly concerned by the contested decision, since it required implementation by the French authorities, which were free not to make use of the authorisation. That argument was rejected by the Court, since the contested decision had been adopted in response to a request from the French authorities for permission to impose an even stricter quota system. In those circumstances, the Court concluded that "the possibility that the French Republic might decide not to make use of the authorisation granted to it by the Commission decision was

---

[28] See *Producteurs de Fruits v. Council, supra*, p. 479.
[29] Joined Cases 103–109/78 *Société des Usines de Beauport v. Council* [1979] E.C.R. 17, para. 16; [1979] 3 C.M.L.R. 1.
[30] *supra*, para 31.
[31] Case 69/69 [1970] E.C.R. 385; [1970] C.M.L.R. 337.
[32] See, *e.g.* Case 113/77 *NTN Toyo Bearing Company v. Council* [1979] E.C.R. 1185; [1979] 2 C.M.L.R. 257.
[33] Case 11/82 [1985] E.C.R. 207; [1985] 2 C.M.L.R. 4.

entirely theoretical, since there could be no doubt as to the intention of the French authorities to apply the decision."[34]

Individual concern

This requirement is closely related to the requirement of a decision and in practice has proved particularly difficult to establish. The Court has stated that "[i]n order for a measure to be of individual concern to the persons to whom it applies, it must affect their legal position because of a factual situation which differentiates them from all other persons and distinguishes them individually in the same way as a person to whom it is addressed."[35] Where an applicant can show that he was affected by the contested measure because he was a member of a class which was closed, both in theory and in practice, at the time the measure was adopted, he will have a strong case for being considered individually concerned. In *International Fruit Company v. Commission*, for example, the question arose whether a provision contained in a regulation concerning requests for import licences made in a particular week prior to its adoption was of individual concern to the applicants. The Court pointed out that, when the contested regulation was adopted, the number of applications which could be affected by it was fixed and that no new applications could be added. The Court concluded that the contested provision "must be regarded as a conglomeration of individual decisions taken by the Commission under the guise of a regulation . . . each of which decisions affects the legal position of each author of an application for a licence". Those decisions were therefore held to be of individual concern to the applicants.[36]

However, where the class of persons affected by a measure is an open one, it is much more difficult for a member of that class to establish individual concern, as *Deutsche Lebensmittelwerke v. Commission*[37] illustrates. As part of an initiative to reduce the Community's stocks of butter, the Commission addressed to the Federal Republic of Germany a decision on the promotion of sales of butter in West Berlin. The applicants, who supplied a substantial proportion of the margarine sold there, sought the annulment of the Commission's decision, but their application was held inadmissible. The Court declared[38]:

"the contested decision does not apply to a closed circle of persons who were known at the time of its adoption and whose rights the Commission intended to regulate. Although the contested decision affects the applicants, that is only because of the effects it produces on their position on the market. In that

---

[34] Para. 9 of the judgment.

[35] Case 26/86 *Deutz und Geldermann v. Council* [1987] E.C.R. 941, para. 9; [1988] 1 C.M.L.R. 668. See also, *e.g. Plaumann v. Commission, supra*, p. 107; Case 100/74 *CAM v. Commission* [1975] E.C.R. 1393, para. 19.

[36] Joined Cases 41–44/70 [1971] E.C.R. 411, paras 21 and 22; [1975] 2 C.M.L.R. 515. *cf.* Case 38/64 *Getreide-Import v. Commission* [1965] E.C.R. 203; [1965] C.M.L.R. 276; Joined Cases 106–107/63 *Toepfer v. Commission* [1965] ECR 405; [1966] C.M.L.R. 111; Case 62/70 *Bock v. Commission* [1971] E.C.R. 897; [1972] C.M.L.R. 160; *CAM v. Commission, supra*; Case 88/76 *Exportation des Sucres v. Commission* [1977] E.C.R. 709.

[37] Case 97/85 [1987] E.C.R. 2265. See also Case 1/64 *Glucoseries Réunies v. Commission* [1964] ECR 413; [1964] C.M.L.R. 596.

[38] Para. 11.

regard, the decision is of concern to the applicants just as it was to any other person supplying margarine on the West Berlin market while the contested operation was in progress, and it is not therefore of individual concern to them . . ."

There were admittedly some cases where the Court appeared to demonstrate a more liberal approach to the question of individual concern, but they were characterised by a variety of special features which cast doubt on their wider application. For example, in *Piraiki-Patraiki v. Commission,*[39] which was decided more than two years before *Deutsche Lebensmittelwerke,* the Court held that the contested decision was of individual concern to those of the applicants which, prior to its adoption, had entered into contracts to be performed while it was in force, in so far as the execution of those contracts was wholly or partly prevented by its adoption. The Court ruled that the Commission had been in a position to discover the existence of contracts to be performed during the period of application of the contested decision. However, the Court attached significance to the fact that Article 130 of the Greek Act of Accession required the Commission to take account of the likely effect the measures it was proposing to authorise would have on such traders. That factor left the implications of the case in other contexts unclear. Indeed, the Court later held that the reasoning in *Piraiki* did not apply where the defendant institution was not required to enquire into the effect of its action on pre-existing contractual arrangements.[40]

The wider significance of the Court's ruling on individual concern in *Les Verts v. Parliament*[41] was also doubtful. The applicant in that case sought the annulment of two measures adopted by the European Parliament, in 1982 and 1983 respectively, concerning the reimbursement of election expenses incurred by political groupings taking part in the 1984 European elections. The contested measures affected all groupings participating in those elections, whether or not they were already represented in the Parliament. However, groupings which were already represented took part in the procedure leading to the adoption of the contested measures. The applicant, which was not represented in the Parliament at the time the contested measures were adopted but which intended to contest the 1984 elections, alleged that the measures discriminated in favour of groupings which were already represented and sought the annulment of those measures under what was then Article 173. Not only did the applicant have to establish that measures adopted by the European Parliament could be challenged under that article, it also had to establish that it was individually concerned by the contested measures. On the basis of the Court's existing case-law, this might have seemed an impossible task, since at the time the contested measures were adopted, political groupings which were not represented in the Parliament but which might wish to contest the 1984 elections, and which would therefore be affected by the measures, could not be identified. In other words, the class to which the applicant belonged was an open one. The only class whose members

---

[39] *Supra.*
[40] See Case C–209/94 P *Buralux and Others v. Council* [1996] E.C.R. I–615. *cf.* Case C–390/95 P *Antillean Rice Mills and Others v. Commission,* judgment of February 11, 1999, paras 25–28.
[41] *Supra.*

could be identified at the time the measures were adopted were groupings which were already represented, but they had no interest in mounting a challenge.

Having accepted, as we have seen, that measures adopted by the European Parliament were in principle susceptible to review under Article 173 (now 230), the Court turned to the question of individual concern. It noted the unprecedented circumstances of the action and said that, because the main measure being challenged concerned "the allocation of public funds for the purpose of preparing for elections and it is alleged that those funds were allocated unequally, it cannot be considered that only groupings which were represented and which were therefore identifiable at the date of the adoption of the contested measure are individually concerned by it." The Court concluded that "the applicant association, which was in existence at the time when the 1982 Decision was adopted and which was able to present candidates at the 1984 elections, is individually concerned by the contested measures."[42]

There were also certain particular situations in which the Court had for a number of years been more willing to allow annulment proceedings to be brought by natural and legal persons. These situations all involved quasi-judicial measures taken at the end of a procedure in the course of which interested parties were entitled to express their views. Such procedures, which may begin with the receipt of a complaint, are particularly prominent in three fields[43]: competition,[44] State aid[45] and dumping.[46] The case-law on standing in these contexts was difficult to reconcile with the dominant trend of the case-law on individual concern, for the admissibility of the actions often seemed to have been based, not on the effect produced on the applicants by the contested measure, but on the part they had played in the procedure leading to its adoption. The very difficulty of accommodating these cases within the general body of the case-law might therefore have suggested that there was a need for the Court's approach to be modified.[47]

Lowering the drawbridge?

In order to enlarge significantly the right of private applicants to bring annulment proceedings, the requirement of a decision as well as that of individual concern would have to be relaxed. In practice, the Court had sometimes appeared to overlook the former requirement. In *Extramet Industrie v. Council*,[48] a dumping case, Advocate General Jacobs said that "the Court should

---

[42] Paras 35 and 37 of the judgment. The Court went on the annul the contested measures.

[43] See generally Arnull, "Private applicants and the action for annulment under Art. 173 of the E.C. Treaty" (1995) 32 C.M.L. Rev 7 at 30–33; Hartley, *The Foundations of European Community Law* (4th ed., 1998), pp. 364–369.

[44] See Chaps. 20 and 21.

[45] See Chap. 24.

[46] Dumping takes place when a product is imported into the Community from a non-member country at a price which is lower than its normal value in that country and the result is to cause injury to a Community industry. Dumped products may be the subject of anti-dumping duties. See Reg. 384/96 on protection against dumped imports from countries not members of the European Community, [1996] O.J. L56/1.

[47] See Greaves, "Locus standi under Art. 173 when seeking annulment of a regulation" (1986) 11 E.L. Rev. 119.

[48] Case C–358/89 [1991] E.C.R. I–2501; [1993] 2 C.M.L.R. 619. *cf. CAM v. Commission, supra*; Case C–152/88 *Sofrimport v. Commission* [1990] E.C.R. I–2477.

in my view make clear what is already implicit in the prevailing trend of its case-law, namely that the requirement of a decision does not exist independently of the requirement of individual concern." The judgment of the Court was less explicit, but it did acknowledge that a measure might, without losing its character as a regulation, be of individual concern to certain undertakings, which would as a result have standing to seek its annulment.[49] The Court also took a strikingly relaxed approach to the question of individual concern, effectively concluding that that requirement was met because the applicant happened to carry on a particular commercial activity. Did the case perhaps presage a general relaxation in the standing requirements which had to be satisfied by private applicants?

It remained possible to argue that the approach adopted in *Extramet* was confined to dumping cases,[50] but that argument appeared to be fatally under-mined by the ruling in *Codorniu v. Council*,[51] which concerned the validity of a regulation on the description and presentation of sparkling wines. There the Court accepted that true regulations could in principle be challenged by non-privileged applicants if they could establish individual concern.[52] It went on to rule that the applicant was indeed individually concerned, because the contested regulation prevented it from using a term which it had registered as a trade mark in 1924 and had traditionally used both before and after that date. That factor, according to the Court, was enough to distinguish the applicant from all other traders affected by the regulation.

Codorniu was the last important ruling to be delivered by the Court of Justice on the standing of private applicants under Article 230 before jurisdiction in such cases was transferred to the CFI. It soon became apparent that the CFI was in no hurry to build on the foundations apparently laid by the Court of Justice in *Codorniu*. In a series of cases, annulment proceedings brought by private applicants were dismissed as inadmissible by the CFI on the basis of the conventional test of standing.[53] Moreover, the Court itself showed no inclination to reinforce the message apparently given in *Codorniu*. In *Asocarne v. Council*,[54] the Second Chamber of the Court endorsed the CFI's view that a measure of general application could only be of individual concern to those affected by it where their "specific rights" were adversely affected. This was true of the applicant in *Codorniu* because the contested regulation prevented it from using its trade mark. It was not true of the applicant in *Asocarne* because in the Court's view it was affected only because it was active in the sector covered by the contested act. The Court also took a restrictive approach in *Buralux and Others v.*

---

[49] See also Case C–49/88 *Al-Jubail Fertilizer v. Council* [1991] E.C.R. I–3187, para. 15; [1991] 3 C.M.L.R. 377, where the Court recognised that anti-dumping regulations, "despite their general scope, may directly and individually affect the undertakings concerned and entail adverse consequences for them".

[50] See Joined Cases C–15 and 108/91 *Buckl and Others v. Commission* [1992] E.C.R. I–6061.

[51] Case C–309/89 [1994] E.C.R. I–1853; [1995] 2 C.M.L.R. 561. See Waelbroeck and Fosselard (1995) 32 C.M.L. Rev 257; Usher (1994) 19 E.L. Rev. 636.

[52] Direct concern was not at issue in the case.

[53] See Arnull, "Challenging Community acts—an introduction" in Micklitz and Reich (eds), *Public Interest Litigation before European Courts* (1996), 39 at 47–51.

[54] Case C–10/95 P [1995] E.C.R. I–4149.

Council,[55] where the Court upheld an Order of the CFI dismissing as inadmissible an application for the annulment of a regulation restricting movements of waste within the Community. The applicants were undertakings engaged in the transport of waste from Germany to France. Although the contested regulation appeared to have been aimed at them and had particularly serious consequences for their business, the Court concluded that they were affected by it "only in their objective capacity as economic operators in the business of waste transfer between Member States, in the same way as any other operator in that business . . .".[56] The CFI had therefore been right to hold that they were not individually concerned.

The unwillingness of the Community Courts to sanction any further relaxation in the standing rules applicable to private applicants was confirmed in *Greenpeace and Others v. Commission*. In that case the applicants, several individuals and three associations concerned with the protection of the environment, sought the annulment of a Commission decision granting Spain financial assistance towards the construction of two electric power stations in the Canary Islands. The applicants specifically invited the CFI to take a liberal approach on the question of admissibility and to accept that standing could derive not only from purely economic considerations but also from a concern for the protection of the environment. The applicants claimed that in each Member State associations set up for the protection of the environment which were sufficiently representative of the interests of their members, or which satisfied certain formalities, were entitled to challenge administrative decisions alleged to breach rules on environmental protection.[57] The CFI refused to accept that the standing of the applicants should be assessed by reference to criteria other than those laid down in the case-law.[58] It concluded that the individual applicants were affected by the contested measure in the same way as anyone living, working or visiting the area concerned and that they could not therefore be considered individually concerned. The same was true of the applicant associations, since they had been unable to establish any interest of their own distinct from that of their members, whose position was no different from that of the individual applicants. On appeal to the Court,[59] Advocate General Cosmas observed, citing *Buralux*, that[60] "[t]he significance and extent of mitigation by the Court, in *Extramet* and *Codorniu*, of the rigour of the case-law should not . . . be overstated." His advice that the appeal should be dismissed was followed by the Court, which declared that the approach taken by the CFI was "consonant with the settled case-law of the Court of Justice".[61]

---

[55] Case C–209/94 P [1996] E.C.R. I–615. *cf.* Joined Cases T–125 and 152/96 *BI Vetmedica and Another v. Council and Commission,* judgment of December 1, 1999, where the CFI accepted that a private applicant had standing to challenge a true regulation.

[56] Para. 28.

[57] In England, see *e.g. R. v. Inspectorate of Pollution, ex p. Greenpeace* [1994] 4 All E.R. 329 and 352.

[58] Case T–585/93 [1995] E.C.R. II–2205. See also Case T–219/95 R *Danielsson and Others v. Commission* [1995] E.C.R. II–3051.

[59] Case C–321/95 P [1998] E.C.R. I–1651.

[60] See p. I–1689.

[61] Para 27. *cf.* Case C–73/97 P *France v. Comafrica and Dole Fresh Fruit* [1999] 2 C.M.L.R. 87, where the Court quashed a finding by the CFI that the applicant companies had standing to challenge a Commission regulation.

The standing of representative bodies

One of the issues raised in the *Greenpeace* case was the circumstances in which representative bodies have standing to seek the annulment of Community acts. The CFI provided a helpful summary of the position in *Federolio v. Commission*,[62] in which a trade organisation representing undertakings active on the market for edible vegetable oils challenged a Commission regulation. The CFI explained:

"As regards, more specifically, actions brought by associations, these have been held to be admissible in at least three types of situation, namely:

(a) where a legal provision expressly grants trade associations a series of procedural rights . . .;

(b) where the association represents the interests of undertakings which would be entitled to bring proceedings in their own right . . .;

(c) where the association is differentiated because its own interests as an association are affected, in particular because its position as negotiator is affected by the measure which it seeks to have annulled . . .

In those three situations, the Court of Justice and the Court of First Instance have also taken into account the participation of the associations in question in the procedure."

The fact that a representative body has standing to challenge a Community act does not mean that all its members also have standing. Whether an individual member has standing will depend on its own particular circumstances.[63] Indeed, the *Federolio* case shows that representative bodies may sometimes be accorded standing even where none of their members is directly and individually concerned by the contested act. However, this occurs only exceptionally: in that case, the CFI found that the requirements laid down by the case-law were not met and dismissed the action as inadmissible. In his Opinion in the *Greenpeace* case, Advocate General Cosmas counselled against treating environmental associations as a special case. Otherwise, he observed, "[n]atural persons without *locus standi* under the fourth paragraph of Article 173 [now 230] of the Treaty could circumvent that procedural impediment by setting up an environmental association." Moreover, he said, "the number of environmental associations capable of being created is, at least in theory, infinite."[64]

Interest in bringing proceedings

Quite apart from any question of direct and individual concern, the defendant institution may argue that the applicant has no interest in challenging an act because annulment will not affect his rights or interests. For example, the

---

[62] Case T–122/96 [1997] E.C.R. II–1559, paras 60–61. *cf.* Joined Cases T–447–449/93 *Associazione Italiana Tecnico Economica del Cemento (AITEC) and Others v. Commission* [1995] E.C.R. II–1971, paras 58–62. See also Case T–114/92 *BEMIM v. Commission* [1995] E.C.R. II–147, paras 28–30; [1996] 4 C.M.L.R. 305. Where a number of applicants (*e.g.* an association and some of its members) make a single application, it will be treated as admissible if one of the applicants fulfils the conditions laid down in Art. 230: see Case C–313/90 *CIRFS and Others v. Commission* [1993] E.C.R. I–1125; para. 31; *AITEC*, para. 82.

[63] Case C–70/97 P *Kruidvat v. Commission* [1999] 4 C.M.L.R. 68.

[64] [1998] E.C.R. I–1651, 1699.

contested act may already have been repealed or implemented. It does not, however, follow that an applicant has no interest in seeking the annulment of such an act. The position was helpfully summarised by the CFI in *Antillean Rice Mills and Others v. Commission*[65]:

> "It is settled law that a claim for annulment is not admissible unless the applicant has an interest in seeing the contested measure annulled . . . Such an interest can be present only if the annulment of the measure is of itself capable of having legal consequences . . .
>
> In that regard, it must be borne in mind that, under Article 176 [now 233] of the Treaty, an institution whose act has been declared void is required to take the necessary measures to comply with the judgment. Those measures do not concern the elimination of the act as such from the Community legal order, since that is the very essence of its annulment by the Court. They involve, rather, the removal of the effects of the illegalities found in the judgment annulling the act. The annulment of an act which has already been implemented or which has in the mean time been repealed from a certain date is thus still capable of having legal consequences. Such annulment places a duty on the institution concerned to take the necessary measures to comply with the judgment. The institution may thus be required to take adequate steps to restore the applicant to its original situation or to avoid the adoption of an identical measure . . ."

That case may be compared with *Proderec v. Commission*,[66] where the CFI held that the applicant had no interest in seeking the annulment of the contested act since it had by then been withdrawn with retroactive effect.[67]

Can non-privileged applicants challenge directives?

Another gap in the system of judicial review established by Article 230 is the absence of any provision for private applicants to seek the annulment of directives. This is a significant weakness, not least because bodies which do not constitute Member States for the purposes of the second paragraph of Article 230, such as regional governments, may be bound directly by directives under the doctrine of vertical direct effect. In *Gibraltar v. Council*,[68] the applicant sought to challenge a provision which, although contained in a directive, was alleged to constitute a decision of direct and individual concern to it. The Court stated that, in the circumstances, the contested provision "cannot be regarded as constituting a decision . . . but on the contrary is of the same general nature as that directive".[69] The application was therefore dismissed as inadmissible. The

---

[65] Joined Cases T–480 and 483/93 [1995] E.C.R. II–2305, paras 59–60. See also Case T–102/96 *Gencor Ltd v. Commission* [1999] 4 C.M.L.R. 971, paras 40–41; Case T–82/96 *ARAP and Others v. Commission,* judgment of June 17, 1999, paras 35–37; *BI Vetmedica, supra,* paras 158–160.

[66] Case T–145/95 [1997] E.C.R. II–823.

[67] The CFI reached the same conclusion in Case T–26/97 *Antillean Rice Mills v. Commission* [1997] E.C.R. II–1347.

[68] Case C–298/89 [1993] E.C.R. I–3605; [1994] 3 C.M.L.R. 425.

[69] Para. 23.

judgment clearly implies, however, that in principle a private applicant does have standing to challenge a directive (or a provision contained in a directive) if he can establish that it constitutes a decision of direct and individual concern to him. This possibility was also left open by the Court in *Asocarne v. Council*[70] and (more pregnantly) in *Eurotunnel and Others v. SeaFrance*.[71] In *UEAPME v. Council*,[72] the CFI went so far as to accept that a private applicant could challenge a true directive if direct and individual concern could be established. However, these cases were exceptional. In *Asocarne,* the CFI said that "in the case of directives, the judicial protection of individuals is duly and sufficiently assured by the national courts, which review the transposition of directives into the domestic law of the various Member States."[73]

Title VI of the Treaty on European Union

Notwithstanding a widely held view that the standing rules which private applicants have to satisfy under Article 230 are unduly strict,[74] the only change made to the article by the Treaty of Amsterdam was the addition of the Court of Auditors to the class of semi-privileged applicants. The Court was, however, given an annulment jurisdiction in respect of certain measures adopted under the amended Title VI of the TEU, now renamed "Provisions on police and judicial co-operation in criminal matters". Article 35(6) TEU gives the Court a power to review the legality of "framework decisions and decisions" adopted under Title VI, but only in actions brought by a Member State or the Commission. The failure to confer on individuals standing to bring proceedings may, in the case of framework decisions, be thought justified by the nature of that type of act, which resembles the E.C. directive except that it is expressly provided that framework decisions "shall not entail direct effect".[75] Since, as we have seen, individuals do not normally have standing to challenge directives under Article 230 E.C., it would have been inconsistent to give them the right to challenge framework decisions. The failure to grant individuals standing to challenge decisions adopted under Title VI is harder to justify. Article 34(2)(c) empowers the Council to adopt such acts for *any purpose* consistent with the objectives of Title VI other than that of approximating national laws. Decisions of this type are binding, although it is again provided that they "shall not entail direct effect". The Council is empowered to "adopt measures necessary to implement those

---

[70] Case C–10/95 P [1995] E.C.R. I–4149, para. 32.

[71] Case C–408/95 [1997] E.C.R. I–6315, paras 29–30; [1998] 2 C.M.L.R. 293.

[72] Case T–135/96 [1998] E.C.R. II–2335. See also Joined Cases T–172/98 and T–175/98 to T–177/98 *Salamander AG and Others v. Parliament and Council,* judgment of June 27, 2000.

[73] Case T–99/94 *Asocarne v. Council* [1994] E.C.R. II–871, para. 17; [1995] 3 C.M.L.R. 458 (application manifestly inadmissible).

[74] See generally Arnull, "Private applicants and the action for annulment under Art. 173 of the E.C. Treaty" (1995) 32 C.M.L.Rev 7; Neuwahl, "Art. 173, para. 4 E.C.: past, present and possible future" (1996) 21 E.L.Rev. 17; Vandersanden, "Pour un élargissement du droit des particuliers d'agir en annulation contre des actes autres que les décisions qui leur sont adressées" (1995) 31 C.D.E. 535; Waelbroeck and Verheyden, "Les conditions de recevabilité des recours en annulation des particuliers contre les actes normatifs communautaires" (1995) 31 C.D.E. 399. For some arguments in favour of the present position, see Gormley, *op. cit.,* p. 488; Dashwood (ed.), *Reviewing Maastricht: Issues for the 1996 IGC* (1996), pp. 308–311.

[75] Art. 34(2)(b) TEU.

decisions at the level of the Union". The manifest potential of such decisions, and of measures implementing them, to affect the rights and obligations of individuals makes the failure of Article 35(6) to confer on individuals standing to challenge their legality hard to reconcile with the rule of law, one of the principles on which the Union is now said to be founded.[76]

THE ACTION FOR FAILURE TO ACT

The action for annulment is complemented by the action for failure to act, for which provision is made in Article 232 (ex 175) E.C. That article is in the following terms:

"Should the European Parliament, the Council or the Commission, in infringement of this Treaty, fail to act, the Member States and the other institutions of the Community may bring an action before the Court of Justice to have the infringement established.

The action shall be admissible only if the institution concerned has first been called upon to act. If, within two months of being so called upon, the institution concerned has not defined its position, the action may be brought within a further period of two months.

Any natural or legal person may, under the conditions laid down in the preceding paragraphs, complain to the Court of Justice that an institution of the Community has failed to address to that person any act other than a recommendation or an opinion.

The Court of Justice shall have jurisdiction, under the same conditions, in actions or proceedings brought by the ECB in the areas falling within the latter's field of competence and in actions or proceedings brought against the latter."

The Court has occasionally emphasised the parallel between the action for failure to act and the action for annulment. In *Chevalley v. Commission*,[77] for example, it said that Articles 230 and 232 "merely prescribe one and the same method of recourse". Similarly, in the "Transport" case[78] the Court emphasised that "in the system of legal remedies provided for by the Treaty there is a close relationship between the right of action given in Article 173 [now 230] . . . and that based on Article 175 [now 232] . . ." The analogy between the two articles should not, however, be pushed too far. In particular, the Court has accepted that the right to bring proceedings under Article 232 should not always be confined to failure to adopt an act having legal effects which could be challenged in annulment proceedings.

This emerges from the Court's treatment of failure to adopt preparatory acts which, although not open to review under Article 230 themselves,[79] constitute an

---

[76] See Art. 6(1) TEU. *cf.* the conclusions of the Tampere European Council (October 15–16, 1999), point 1.

[77] Case 15/70 [1970] E.C.R. 975, para. 6. See also Case C–68/95 *T Port v. Bundesanstalt für Landwirtschaft und Ernährung* [1996] E.C.R. I–6065, para. 59.

[78] Case 13/83 *Parliament v. Council* [1985] E.C.R. 1513, para. 36; [1986] 1 C.M.L.R. 138.

[79] See Case 60/81 *IBM v. Commission* [1981] E.C.R. 2639; [1981] 3 C.M.L.R. 635.

essential step in the process leading to another act which itself produces legal effects. In the "Comitology" case,[80] for example, the Court observed that "[t]here is no necessary link between the action for annulment and the action for failure to act." It pointed out that the Parliament could bring proceedings against the Council under Article 232 if it failed to present a draft budget within the deadline laid down in Article 272(4) (ex 203(4)) E.C. The Court noted that, as a preparatory measure, the draft budget could not, once established, be challenged under Article 230. If the Court had held that the Parliament had no right of action under Article 232 in these circumstances, it would be unable to challenge an unlawful failure by the Council to establish a draft budget, without which the Parliament could not exercise the power conferred on it by the Treaty to adopt the budget.

In *Asia Motor France and Others v. Commission*,[81] the Court held that, where the Commission declined to pursue a complaint by a natural or legal person that the Treaty competition rules had been infringed, the complainant could bring an action for failure to act if it had not been informed beforehand of the Commission's reasons and given the opportunity to submit further comments. The Commission was required to take that step by Article 6 of Regulation 99/63,[82] but where it did so the notification concerned could not be challenged under Article 230 because it was only a provisional measure intended to pave the way for the final decision.[83] However, that final decision could not be adopted in the absence of a notification under Regulation 99/63. If a complainant could not challenge an unlawful failure to issue such a notification, it might not be able to challenge a failure by the Commission to adopt the final decision because the Commission could say that, in the absence of the notification, it had no power to adopt such a decision.[84]

It may also be noted that, although a national court can use the preliminary rulings procedure to obtain a ruling from the Court of Justice that a Community act is invalid,[85] it cannot be used to obtain a ruling that a Community institution has failed to act. As the Court explained in *T Port*,[86] national courts therefore "have no jurisdiction to order interim measures pending action on the part of the institution. Judicial review of alleged failure to act can be exercised only by the Community judicature." The Court pointed out[87] that the Community Courts have the power under Article 243 (ex 186) E.C. to adopt interim measures in the framework of proceedings for failure to act.

---

[80] Case 302/87 *Parliament v. Council* [1988] E.C.R. 5615, para. 16.

[81] Case T–28/90 [1992] E.C.R. II–2285, paras 29–30. *cf.* Case T–127/98 *UPS Europe v. Commission*, judgment of September 9, 1999.

[82] [1963-1964] O.J., English Spec.Ed., p. 47. See now Art. 6 of Reg. 2842/98, [1998] O.J. L354/18, which replaced Reg. 99/63 with effect from February 1, 1999; Chap. 22, *post*.

[83] See Case C–282/95P, *Guérin Automobiles v. Commission* [1997] E.C.R. I–1503, paras 33–38; [1997] 5 C.M.L.R. 447. A definitive decision rejecting a complaint may be the subject of an action for annulment. Moreover, if the Commission fails to adopt such a decision within a reasonable time, the complainant may bring proceedings against it for failure to act. That is so even if he has already brought such proceedings in order to obtain the notification provided for by Art. 6 of Reg. 2842/98.

[84] Hartley, *op. cit.*, p. 388.

[85] See Chap. 11.

[86] *supra*, para. 53.

[87] Para. 60.

In the "Transport" case,[88] the Court stated that an action under Article 232 would only lie in respect of "failure to take measures the scope of which can be sufficiently defined for them to be identified individually and adopted in compliance with the Court's judgment . . .". In that case, the Parliament brought proceedings for a declaration that the Council had infringed the Treaty by failing to introduce, before the end of the transitional period, a common policy for transport dealing (among other things) with "the conditions under which non-resident carriers may operate transport services within a Member State".[89] The application was successful in part only. The Court made it clear that it was irrelevant how difficult it might be for the institution concerned to comply with its obligations, but found that under the Treaty the Council enjoyed a discretion with regard to the implementation of the common transport policy. Although that discretion was subject to certain limits, the Court said that it was for the Council to determine "the aims of and means for implementing a common transport policy".[90] The Court concluded that the absence of such a policy "does not in itself necessarily constitute a failure to act sufficiently specific in nature to form the subject of an action under Article 175 [now 232]".[91] The Commission, which intervened in support of the Parliament, argued, however, that the common transport policy envisaged by the Treaty contained one element which was sufficiently well-defined to be regarded as imposing on the Council a specific obligation, namely a requirement to ensure freedom to provide services. The scope of that requirement could be determined by reference to the Treaty rules on services and the relevant directives and case-law.[92] That argument found favour with the Court, which ruled that, in so far as the obligations laid down in the Treaty related to freedom to provide services, they were sufficiently well-defined to be the subject of a finding of failure to act.

Standing

The distinction between privileged and non-privileged applicants which we encountered in the context of Article 230 is reproduced in Article 232, the Member States and the Community institutions enjoying broader rights than natural and legal persons to institute proceedings for failure to act. Unlike Article 230, however, Article 232 places the European Parliament on the same footing as the Member States, the Council and the Commission. This was confirmed in the "Transport" case,[93] where the Court emphasised that, in referring to "the other institutions of the Community", the first paragraph of Article 232 gave the same right of action to all the Community Institutions, including the Parliament. The Court declared that "[i]t is not possible to restrict the exercise of that right by one of them without adversely affecting its status as an institution under the Treaty, in particular Article 4(1) [now 7(1)]." It would

---

[88] *supra.*
[89] See Art. 71(1)(b) (ex 75(1)(b)) E.C.
[90] Para. 49 of the judgment.
[91] Para. 53.
[92] See Chap. 15.
[93] *supra,* para. 17.

seem to follow that the Court of Auditors, which was elevated to the status of an Institution under Article 7(1) at Maastricht, is also entitled to bring proceedings under Article 232.

Under the third paragraph of Article 232, any natural or legal person may complain to the Court "that an institution of the Community has failed to address to that person any act other than a recommendation or an opinion". Thus, in *Chevalley v. Commission*[94] the Court held that a definition of the Commission's position on a question, which would have amounted in substance to an opinion within the meaning of Article 249 (ex 189) E.C., was not capable of forming the subject-matter of an action under the third paragraph of Article 232. However, the decision in *Guérin Automobiles v. Commission*[95] shows that a non-privileged applicant may bring proceedings under Article 232 where an institution fails to take a step which, although it could not itself have been challenged in annulment proceedings, constitutes a prerequisite for the adoption of an act which could.

Article 232 appears to require a non-privileged applicant to show that the act he alleges should have been adopted would have been addressed to him. If that requirement were applied strictly, however, there would be a gap in the system of remedies established by the Treaty: a natural or legal person would be unable to challenge a failure to adopt a measure which would have been of direct and individual concern to him had it been adopted and which he would therefore have been able to challenge under Article 230. The Court has avoided that result by a flexible interpretation of the word "address". In *T Port v. Bundesanstalt für Landwirtschaft und Ernährung*,[96] the Court explained: ". . . just as the fourth paragraph of Article 173 [now 230] allows individuals to bring an action for annulment against a measure of an institution not addressed to them provided that the measure is of direct and individual concern to them, the third paragraph of Article 175 [now 232] must be interpreted as also entitling them to bring an action for failure to act against an institution which they claim has failed to adopt a measure which would have concerned them in the same way. The possibility for individuals to assert their rights should not depend upon whether the institution concerned has acted or failed to act." Notwithstanding earlier case-law to the contrary,[97] it would seem to follow that a natural or legal person may challenge a failure to adopt a regulation, or indeed a directive, if he can establish that he would have been directly and individually concerned by it, even though regulations are not addressed to anyone and directives can only be addressed to Member States. This would be consistent with the position under Article 230.

---

[94] Case 15/70 [1970] E.C.R. 975.

[95] *supra.*

[96] *supra,* para. 59. See also Case T–17/96 *TFI v. Commission,* judgment of June 3, 1999, paras 26–36; Case C–107/91 *ENU v. Commission* [1993] E.C.R. I–599, para. 17; Advocate General Darmon in Case C–41/92R *Liberal Democrats v. Parliament* [1993] E.C.R. I–3153, 3172; Advocate General Dutheillet de Lamothe in Case 15/71 *Mackprang v. Commission* [1971] E.C.R. 797 at 807–808; [1972] C.M.L.R. 52.

[97] See, *e.g.* Case 134/73 *Holtz v. Council* [1974] E.C.R. 1, para. 5; Case 90/78 *Granaria v. Council and Commission* [1979] E.C.R. 1081, para. 14 (from the final sentence of which the word "not" has inadvertently been omitted in the English version); Case 60/79 *Producteurs de Vins de Table et Vins de Pays v. Commission* [1979] E.C.R. 2429.

Procedural aspects

Article 232 does not specify how soon proceedings must be instituted after the alleged failure to act has come to light. In a case decided under Article 35 ECSC, the counterpart of Article 232 E.C., the Court held that proceedings for failure to act must be instituted within a reasonable period once it has become clear that the institution concerned has decided to take no action.[98] In the "Transport" case, however, the Court partially upheld an application made under Article 232 in January 1983 in respect of a failure to discharge an obligation which should have been fulfilled by the end of 1969, by which time the applicant was fully aware of the failure concerned. These cases may perhaps be distinguished on the ground that in the former the defendant had made it clear that it had decided not to take any action, whereas in the latter the defendant accepted the need for it to take further steps. It seems that it is only in the former type of case that proceedings must be brought within a reasonable period of the alleged failure to act having come to light.

According to the second paragraph of Article 232, the institution concerned must first be "called upon to act". In the "Transport" case, the Council argued that that requirement had not been met. The Court disagreed, since the President of the Parliament had sent a letter to the Council which referred to Article 232 (then 175) and which stated that the Parliament was calling on the Council to act pursuant to that provision. Moreover, annexed to the letter was a list of the steps which the Parliament considered necessary to remedy the failure.[98a] If the institution concerned has not "defined its position" within two months of having been called upon to act, an application may be made to the Court within a further period of two months. Thus, where the institution does define its position in time, it is not possible to bring the matter before the Court under Article 232. In the "Transport" case the Court declined to treat as a definition of its position the Council's reply to the letter from the Parliament calling upon it to act. The Court observed[99] that the Council's reply "was confined to setting out what action it had already taken in relation to transport without commenting 'on the legal aspects' of the correspondence initiated by the Parliament. The reply neither denied nor confirmed the alleged failure to act nor gave any indication of the Council's views as to the measures which, according to the Parliament, remained to be taken."

The applicant will not normally be able to seek the annulment of the act by which the institution defines its position unless he would have had standing to challenge the measure requested under Article 230 had it been adopted. In *Nordgetreide v. Commission*[1] the applicant, a private undertaking, sought the annulment of a refusal by the Commission to adopt an act which would have taken the form of a regulation. Since the measure requested "would have

---

[98] Case 59/70 *Netherlands v. Commission* [1971] E.C.R. 639.

[98a] *cf. TFI v. Commission, supra,* paras 41–44.

[99] Para. 25 of judgment.

[1] Case 42/71 [1972] E.C.R. 105; [1973] C.M.L.R. 177. See also Joined Cases C–15 and 108/91, *Buckl and Others v. Commission* [1992] E.C.R. I–6061; Case 48/65 *Lütticke v. Commission* [1966] E.C.R. 19; [1966] C.M.L.R. 378.

affected the applicant only in so far as it belongs to a category viewed in the abstract and in its entirety", it could not have been challenged by the applicant under Article 230. The application was therefore declared inadmissible. However, the CFI takes a more liberal approach where an institution is requested to act but refuses to do so under a procedure laid down by regulation which requires it to rule on such requests. In those circumstances, the nature of the act requested seems to be irrelevant.[2]

Some of the Court's case-law[3] suggests that the defendant institution may define its position for the purposes of Article 232 simply by refusing to adopt the act requested by the applicant. However, the Court took a more relaxed stance in the "Comitology" case,[4] where it considered the question whether the Parliament had the right to institute annulment proceedings under Article 173 EEC, which did not at the material time expressly give it any such right. One of the arguments put forward by the Parliament was that, in the absence of any power to institute annulment proceedings, it would be unable to challenge an express refusal to act issued by the Council or the Commission after the Parliament had called upon them to act under Article 175 (now 232). The Court replied: "that argument is based on a false premise. A refusal to act, however explicit it may be, can be brought before the Court under Article 175 since it does not put an end to the failure to act."[5] It is possible that the Court's statement in "Comitology" is limited to cases where the applicant would otherwise be deprived of a remedy because he is unable to challenge an express refusal to act under Article 230.[6] Since the Parliament remains unable to seek the annulment of an act which does not affect its prerogatives, it would seem to follow that it would not be prevented from pursuing an action for failure to act by a refusal by the defendant institution to adopt such an act.[7] However, Article 232 cannot be used to challenge a refusal by an institution to revoke a Community act which has not been challenged within the deadline laid down in Article 230, since this would provide applicants "with a method of recourse parallel to that of Article 173 [now 230], which would not be subject to the conditions laid down by the Treaty".[8]

Where the failure is remedied within two months of the institution concerned having been called upon to act, no action may be brought before the Court. The steps taken need not be the same as those requested by the applicant, for "Article 175 [now 232] refers to failure to act in the sense of failure to take a decision or to define a position, and not the adoption of a measure different from that desired or considered necessary by the persons concerned."[9] Thus, an

---

[2] See Case T–120/96 *Lilly Industries v. Commission* [1998] E.C.R. II–2571, paras 61–63; *cf.* Joined Cases T–125 and 152/96 *BI Vetmedica and Another v. Council and Commission,* judgment of December 1, 1999, paras 166–169.

[3] See, *e.g.* the *Nordgetreide* case, *supra*.

[4] Case 302/87 [1988] E.C.R. 5615.

[5] Para. 17 of judgment. *cf.* the Opinion of Advocate General Darmon at 5630–5631.

[6] See Due, "Legal remedies for the failure of European Community Institutions to act in conformity with EEC Treaty provisions" (1990-91) 14 Fordham International Law Journal 341 at 356; Hartley, *op. cit.,* p. 383.

[7] See Hartley, *op. cit.,* p. 383.

[8] Joined Cases 10 and 18/68 *Eridania v. Commission* [1969] E.C.R. 459, para. 17.

[9] Joined Cases 166 and 220/86 *Irish Cement Ltd v. Commission* [1988] E.C.R. 6473, para. 17; [1989] 2 C.M.L.R. 57; see also *Buckl, supra,* paras 16–17.

institution which proposes a particular legal basis for a measure cannot use Article 232 to challenge the choice of a different legal basis by the adopting institution.[10]

Where the defendant institution takes the steps requested over two months after being called upon to do so but before judgment is given, the Court will decline to give a ruling on the basis that "the subject-matter of the action has ceased to exist".[11] This is so even though, according to the second paragraph of Article 233, a ruling by the Court under Article 232 is without prejudice to the liability of the institution concerned in damages under the second paragraph of Article 288 (ex 215) E.C.[12] As the Court explained in *Buckl and Others v. Commission*,[13] "where the act whose absence constitutes the subject-matter of the proceedings was adopted after the action was brought but before judgment, a declaration by the Court to the effect that the initial failure to act is unlawful can no longer bring about the consequences prescribed by Article 176 [now 233]. It follows that in such a case, as in cases where the defendant institution has responded within the period of two months after being called upon to act, the subject-matter of the action has ceased to exist . . ." The Court's approach may be contrasted with its attitude in proceedings brought by the Commission under Article 226 where the Member State complies with its obligations after the expiry of the deadline laid down in the reasoned opinion.[14] Such cases are allowed to continue unless withdrawn by the Commission.

Where an application under Article 232 is upheld, the Court declares that the failure of the institution concerned to act is contrary to the Treaty. The Court cannot remedy the failure itself or order the institution concerned to take any particular steps, but the institution is required by the first paragraph of Article 233 (ex 176) E.C. "to take the necessary measures to comply with the judgment of the Court of Justice". The Court has said that those measures must be taken within a reasonable period of the judgment.[15]

THE PLEA OF ILLEGALITY AND NON-EXISTENT ACTS

The strict time limits and rules on standing laid down in Article 230 (ex 173) E.C. are to some extent mitigated by the so-called plea of illegality, for which provision is made in Article 241 (ex 184) E.C. That article provides as follows:

"Notwithstanding the expiry of the period laid down in the fifth paragraph of Article 230, any party may, in proceedings in which a regulation adopted jointly by the European Parliament and the Council, or a regulation of the Council, of the Commission, or of the ECB is at issue, plead the grounds specified in the second paragraph of Article 230, in order to invoke before the Court of Justice the inapplicability of that regulation."

---

[10] See Case C–70/88 *Parliament v. Council* ("Chernobyl") [1990] E.C.R. I–2041; [1991] E.C.R. I–4529; [1992] 1 C.M.L.R. 91.
[11] See Case 377/87 *Parliament v. Council* [1988] E.C.R. 4017.
[12] See below.
[13] *supra,* para. 15.
[14] See, *e.g.* Case 39/72 *Commission v. Italy* [1973] E.C.R. 101; [1973] C.M.L.R. 439.
[15] See the "Transport" case, *supra*, para. 69.

Article 241 allows the illegality of an act to be pleaded indirectly in proceedings which are pending before the Community Courts under some other provision.[16] Where, for example, a natural or legal person seeks the annulment of a decision addressed to him which is based on a regulation, he may contest the validity of that regulation even if he could not have challenged it directly under Article 230. The CFI has explained that, "[s]ince the legality of the individual measure contested must be assessed on the basis of the elements of fact and of law existing at the time when the measure was adopted ... the legality of the legislative measure which forms its legal basis must also be assessed at that time rather than at the time of its own adoption."[17]

The plea of illegality therefore represents a compromise between the principle of legal certainty, which would rule out a challenge to a Community act once the deadline laid down in Article 230 had expired, and the principle of legality, which would preclude reliance on unlawful acts. It is important to emphasise, however, that Article 241 does not give rise to a separate remedy. As the CFI explained in *CSF and CSME v. Commission*,[18] "[t]he possibility afforded by Article 184 [now 241] E.C. of pleading the inapplicability of a measure of general application forming the legal basis of the contested decision does not constitute an independent right of action and recourse may be had to it only as an incidental plea. More specifically, Article 184 [now 241] may not be invoked in the absence of an independent right of action ..." Since Article 241 applies only in proceedings before the Community Courts,[19] it does not affect the circumstances in which the validity of Community acts may be contested in the national courts. It seems, however, that a declaration of inapplicability made by the Court of Justice under Article 241 in a previous case would enable a national court to treat the act in question as invalid without referring the matter to the Court of Justice under Article 234 (ex 177).[20]

Although Article 241 only refers to regulations, the Court said in *Simmenthal v. Commission*[21] that:

"Article 184 of the EEC Treaty [now Article 241 E.C.] gives expression to a general principle conferring upon any party to proceedings the right to challenge, for the purpose of obtaining the annulment of a decision of direct and individual concern to that party, the validity of previous acts of the institutions which form the legal basis of the decision which is being attacked, if that party was not entitled under Article 173 [now 230] of the Treaty to bring a direct action challenging those acts [and] by which it was thus affected without having been in a position to ask that they be declared void."

The Court concluded that Article 241 extended to "acts of the institutions which, although they are not in the form of a regulation, nevertheless produce similar

---

[16] See Joined Cases 31 and 33/62 *Wöhrmann v. Commission* [1962] E.C.R. 501; [1963] C.M.L.R. 152.
[17] Joined Cases T–177 and 377/94 *Altmann and Others v. Commission* [1996] E.C.R. II–2041, para. 119.
[18] Case T–154/94 [1996] E.C.R. II–1377, para. 16.
[19] See *Wöhrmann v. Commission, supra*, 507.
[20] See Case 314/85 *Foto-Frost v. Hauptzollamt Lübeck-Ost* [1987] E.C.R. 4199, para. 16, where the Court refers to Art. 241 (ex 184). The *Foto-Frost* case is discussed in Chap. 11.
[21] Case 92/78 [1979] E.C.R. 777, para. 39; [1980] 1 C.M.L.R. 25.

effects and on those grounds may not be challenged under Article 173 [now 230] by natural or legal persons other than Community institutions and Member States".[22] It seems to follow from *Simmenthal* that the plea of illegality may be invoked in relation to any act producing legal effects which natural and legal persons are unable to challenge directly under Article 230, for example, a decision addressed to a third party which is not of direct and individual concern to the person wishing to contest its validity. Conversely, in *TWD Textilwerke Deggendorf*,[23] it was held that the validity of a Community act may not be challenged in a national court by an applicant who would undoubtedly have had standing to contest its validity in a direct action under Article 230 but who failed to do so in time. In *TWD v. Commission*,[24] the CFI said that, as a result, "[t]he objection of illegality provided for by Article 184 [now 241] of the Treaty cannot be raised by a legal or natural person who could have brought proceedings under the second paragraph of Article 173 [now 230] but who did not do so within the period prescribed therein . . ."

It would seem that Article 241 is not confined to the general principle which the Court in *Simmenthal* said it embodied. According to its express terms, the plea of illegality may be invoked by "any party", an expression which is clearly broad enough to cover Member States, the Council and the Commission notwithstanding their privileged status for the purpose of annulment proceedings. The case-law suggests that a Member State may challenge the validity of a regulation indirectly in proceedings under both Articles 230[25] and 226.[26] The rationale seems to be that "defects appertaining to a general regulation often do not clearly emerge until the regulation is applied to a particular case."[27] That rationale does not apply to acts addressed to a Member State and it is well established that a Member State may not challenge the validity of a decision addressed to it once the deadline laid down in Article 230 has expired.[28] It is submitted that the Council and the Commission are in principle in the same position, *mutatis mutandis*, as the Member States. Applicants who are semi-privileged for the purposes of annulment proceedings should be entitled, in accordance with the judgment in *Simmenthal*, to invoke the plea of illegality in relation to any act which does not in itself infringe their prerogatives and which they could not therefore have challenged in an action under Article 230.

Where a plea of illegality is successful, the Court does not formally annul the measure in question, but simply declares it inapplicable. This has the effect of depriving any act adopted under it of its legal basis. Nevertheless, although the Court's ruling in relation to the first measure is technically limited to the case in which it is made, it is tantamount in practical terms to a declaration of invalidity,

---

[22] Para. 40 of the judgment. Thus, the Court held that Art. 241 could be invoked in relation to notices of invitation to tender.

[23] Case C–188/92 [1994] E.C.R. I–833; [1995] 2 C.M.L.R. 145. See Chap. 11.

[24] Joined Cases T–244 and 486/93 [1995] E.C.R. II–2265, para. 103; [1996] 1 C.M.L.R. 332 (appeal dismissed: see Case C–355/95 P [1997] E.C.R. I–2549); [1998] 1 C.M.L.R. 234.

[25] See Case 32/65 *Italy v. Council and Commission* [1966] E.C.R. 389; [1969] C.M.L.R. 39.

[26] See Case 116/82 *Commission v. Germany* [1986] E.C.R. 2519.

[27] See Advocate General Roemer in Case 32/65 *supra*, at 414.

[28] See, *e.g.* Case C–183/91 *Commission v. Greece* [1993] E.C.R. I–3131, para. 10.

for the institutions will immediately cease to apply the measure and the Community Courts will henceforth treat it as invalid.

Where the plea of illegality cannot be invoked and the deadline for bringing annulment proceedings has expired, any party may nevertheless argue that an act, regardless of its nature, is vitiated by such fundamental defects that it should be considered non-existent[29] and incapable of producing any legal effects.[30] This test is extremely difficult to satisfy, as the Court's judgment in *Commission v. BASF and Others*[31] makes clear. That case was an appeal by the Commission against a ruling of the CFI[32] that a Commission decision on the application of the Treaty competition rules was "vitiated by particularly serious and manifest defects" and was to be considered non-existent. The CFI had taken the view that the defects in question made it impossible to be certain of the exact date on which the contested measure took effect, the precise terms of the statement of reasons it was required by the Treaty to contain, the extent of the obligations it imposed on its addressees, the identity of those addressees or that of the authority which issued the definitive version of the act. The Court took a more lenient approach, observing[33]:

"It should be remembered that acts of the Community institutions are in principle presumed to be lawful and accordingly produce legal effects, even if they are tainted by irregularities, until such time as they are annulled or withdrawn.

However, by way of exception to that principle, acts tainted by an irregularity whose gravity is so obvious that it cannot be tolerated by the Community legal order must be treated as having no legal effect, even provisional, that is to say that they must be regarded as legally non-existent. The purpose of this exception is to maintain a balance between two fundamental, but sometimes conflicting, requirements with which a legal order must comply, namely stability of legal relations and respect for legality.

From the gravity of the consequences attaching to a finding that an act of a Community institution is non-existent it is self-evident that, for reasons of legal certainty, such a finding is reserved for quite extreme situations."

The Court concluded that the irregularities identified by the CFI were not serious enough to render the contested decision non-existent, although it went on to annul it. Unlike the ruling of the CFI, the judgment of the Court therefore had no implications for the validity of earlier decisions suffering from similar defects, in respect of which any challenge under Article 230 would by then have been out of time.

---

[29] Case 226/87 *Commission v. Greece* [1988] E.C.R. 3611, para. 16.

[30] See Case 15/85 *Consorzio Cooperative d'Abruzzo v. Commission* [1987] E.C.R. 1005, para. 10; [1988] 1 C.M.L.R. 841.

[31] Case C–137/92 P [1994] E.C.R. I–2555; [1994] 5 C.M.L.R. 140. See also Case C–199/92 P *Hüls v. Commission,* judgment of July 8, 1999; Case C–227/92 P *Hoechst v. Commission,* judgment of July 8, 1999; Case C–234/92 P *Shell International Chemical Company v. Commission,* judgment of July 8, 1999; Case C–235/92 P *Montecatini v. Commission,* judgment of July 8, 1999; Case C–245/92 P *Chemie Linz v. Commission,* judgment of July 8, 1999.

[32] Joined Cases T–79/89 etc., *BASF and Others v. Commission* [1992] E.C.R. II–315; [1992] 4 C.M.L.R. 357.

[33] See paras 48–50 of judgment.

NON-CONTRACTUAL LIABILITY

Article 235 (ex 178) E.C. gives the Court of Justice jurisdiction in actions for damages brought under the second paragraph of Article 288 (ex 215) E.C.,[34] which provides: "In the case of non-contractual liability, the Community shall, in accordance with the general principles common to the laws of the Member States, make good any damage caused by its institutions or by its servants in the performance of their duties". At Maastricht, a new third paragraph was inserted in Article 288 stating that the second paragraph also applies "to damage caused by the ECB or by its servants in the performance of their duties." That addition may not have been strictly necessary, for the Court held in *SGEEM and Etroy v. EIB*[35] that the term "institutions" in the second paragraph of the article was not confined to the institutions listed in Article 7(1) (ex 4(1)) E.C., but extended to any Community body "established by the Treaty and authorised to act in its name and on its behalf".[36]

According to the Treaty, it is the Community as a whole whose liability is in issue in proceedings under the second paragraph of Article 288. However, in *Werhahn v. Council* the Court said that, "where Community liability is involved by reason of the act of one of its institutions, it should be represented before the Court by the institution or institutions against which the matter giving rise to liability is alleged."[37] Where the action relates to a legislative measure adopted by the Council on a proposal from the Commission, proceedings may be brought against both institutions jointly.[38]

The reference to the general principles common to the laws of the Member States in the second paragraph of Article 288 does not mean that the Community Courts must search in cases on non-contractual liability for a solution favoured by a majority of the Member States, still less that they have to apply the lowest common denominator. It means simply that the Community Courts must look to the national systems for inspiration in devising a regime of non-contractual liability adapted to the specific circumstances of the Community.[39] The principles applied by the Community Courts are in fact relatively strict, with the result that the number of successful claims which have been brought against the Community is fairly small. The case-law has assumed increased practical importance, however, since the Court of Justice acknowledged, in *Brasserie du Pêcheur and Factortame*,[40] that "the conditions under which the State may incur liability for damage caused to individuals by a breach of Community law cannot, in the absence of particular justification, differ from those governing the liability of the Community in like circumstances. The protection of the rights which individuals

---

[34] See generally Heukels and McDonnell (eds), *The Action for Damages in Community Law* (1997).

[35] Case C–370/89 [1992] E.C.R. I–6211.

[36] Para. 15. It therefore covered the European Investment Bank (on which see Arts 266–267 (ex 198d–198e) E.C.).

[37] Joined Cases 63–69/72 [1973] E.C.R. 1229, para. 7.

[38] *ibid.*, para. 8.

[39] See Advocate General Gand in Case 9/69 *Sayag v. Leduc* [1969] E.C.R. 329, 339–340; Advocate General Roemer in Case 5/71 *Zuckerfabrik Schöppenstedt v. Council* [1971] E.C.R. 975, 989.

[40] Joined Cases C–46 and 48/93 [1996] E.C.R. I–1029, para. 42; [1996] 1 C.M.L.R. 889. See Chap. 5.

derive from Community law cannot vary depending on whether a national authority or a Community authority is responsible for the damage."

It is now established that the action for damages constitutes an independent or autonomous form of action. Its purpose is different from that of proceedings for annulment or failure to act and it is not necessary to have recourse to such proceedings before commencing an action under the second paragraph of Article 288.[41] That paragraph may normally be used as a means of challenging indirectly the legality of an act or a failure to act which has not been contested directly under Articles 230 (ex 173) or 232 (ex 175) or where proceedings under those articles have been dismissed as inadmissible. However, a claim for damages will not be entertained where its purpose is to secure exactly the same result as an action for annulment which has been found inadmissible.[42] In *Cobrecaf and Others v. Commission*,[43] for example, the CFI dismissed as inadmissible both an application for annulment and a claim for damages. It found that "the actual purpose of the applicants' alternative claim for damages is to secure payment of a sum corresponding exactly to the amount denied to it by reason of the disputed decision and that it is therefore designed to secure indirectly annulment of the individual decision rejecting the applicants' request for financial aid."[44]

Damage caused by servants of the Community in the performance of their duties

Where the applicant relies on an act performed by a Community official in the performance of his duties, the Court applies a strict, perhaps unduly strict, test. In *Sayag v. Leduc*,[45] a case concerning the corresponding provision of the Euratom Treaty,[46] the Court held that the Community was not liable for an accident caused by a servant while using his private car during the performance of his duties. The Court said that "[o]nly in the case of *force majeure* or in exceptional circumstances of such overriding importance that without the servant's using private means of transport the Community would have been unable to carry out the tasks entrusted to it, could such use be considered to form part of the servant's performance of his duties . . ."

Damage caused by an institution of the Community

Of greater practical importance is the Community's potential liability for loss caused by acts adopted by its institutions. The general conditions which must normally be satisfied if a claim is to be successful were summarised in *New Europe*

---

[41] See, *e.g.* Case 4/69 *Lütticke v. Commission* [1971] E.C.R. 325; Case 5/71 *Zuckerfabrik Schöppenstedt v. Council* [1971] E.C.R. 975.
[42] See Case 25/62 *Plaumann v. Commission* [1963] E.C.R. 95; [1964] C.M.L.R. 29; Case 175/84 *Krohn v. Commission* [1986] E.C.R. 753; [1987] 1 C.M.L.R. 745.
[43] Case T–514/93 [1995] E.C.R. II–621.
[44] Para. 60.
[45] Case 9/69 [1969] E.C.R. 329.
[46] The second para. of Art. 188.

Consulting v. Commission,[47] where the CFI explained that "the conduct of the Community institutions in question must be unlawful; there must be real and certain damage; and a direct causal link must exist between the conduct of the institution concerned and the alleged damage . . ." The Community may also incur liability as a result of an omission, but only where the institution concerned had a legal obligation to act under a provision of Community law.[48] Thus, a failure by the Commission to bring proceedings against a Member State under Article 226 E.C. is not capable of fixing the Community with liability in damages because the Commission is not under any obligation to initiate such proceedings.[49]

The Stanley Adams saga provides a striking example of a successful claim against the Community arising out of both an act and an omission on the part of the Commission.[50] Stanley Adams was an employee of the Swiss pharmaceutical company, Hoffmann-La Roche. He believed that some of the company's practices were incompatible with the competition rules laid down in the E.C. Treaty. He therefore alerted the Commission and supplied it with copies of a number of internal company documents. The Commission subsequently commenced an investigation into the company's activities, in the course of which it handed over to the company edited copies of some of the documents supplied by Adams. The Commission ultimately adopted a decision imposing a substantial fine on the company for breach of Article 82 (ex 86) E.C.[51]

In the meantime, the company, realising the Commission must have had an informant, attempted to discover his identity. The company's lawyer told the Commission that it was considering taking criminal proceedings against the informant for economic espionage under the Swiss Penal Code. The company eventually succeeded in identifying Adams from the copies of its own documents which had been handed to it by the Commission. Adams had by then left the company and moved to Italy, but he was arrested by the Swiss authorities as he attempted to enter Switzerland on a visit. While he was being held in custody, his wife committed suicide. He was subsequently released on bail, but was in due course found guilty of economic espionage and sentenced in his absence to a suspended term of one year's imprisonment. His conviction damaged his creditworthiness and led to the failure of a business he had established after leaving the company.

In proceedings against the Commission under the second paragraph of Article 288,[52] the Court found that two aspects of the Commission's conduct gave rise to liability: first, the disclosure to the company of the documents which enabled Adams to be identified; secondly, the failure to warn Adams of the risk that he

---

[47] Case T–231/97 [1999] 2 C.M.L.R. 1452, para. 29. See also Case C–358/90, *Compagnia Italiana Alcool v. Commission* [1992] E.C.R. I–2457, para. 46; [1992] 2 C.M.L.R. 876; Case C–55/90 *Cato v. Commission* [1992] ECR I–2533, para. 18; [1992] 2 C.M.L.R. 459.

[48] See, *e.g.* Case C–146/91 *KYDEP v. Council and Commission* [1994] E.C.R. I–4199, para. 58; [1995] 2 C.M.L.R. 540.

[49] Case C–72/90 *Asia Motor France v. Commission* [1990] E.C.R. I–2181, para. 13.

[50] The story is recounted by Stanley Adams in *Roche versus Adams* (1984). See also Hunnings, "The Stanley Adams affair or the biter bit" (1987) 24 C.M.L.Rev 65.

[51] The essence of the Commission's decision was upheld by the Court in Case 85/76 *Hoffmann-La Roche v. Commission* [1979] E.C.R. 461; [1979] 3 C.M.L.R. 211.

[52] Case 145/83 *Adams v. Commission* [1985] E.C.R. 3539; [1986] 1 C.M.L.R. 506.

would be prosecuted if he returned to Switzerland, a risk of which the Commission should have been aware following its discussions with the company's lawyer. However, the Court took the view that Adams was partly to blame for his misfortunes: he had not, for example, warned the Commission that he could be identified from the documents he had supplied and he had returned to Switzerland without enquiring as to the risks involved in doing so. The Court therefore decided that responsibility for the damage he had suffered should be apportioned equally between Adams and the Commission.

The act and the omission which gave rise to liability in the *Adams* case may be described as administrative, in the sense that they did not have general application. In such cases it will be enough for the applicant to establish illegality, damage and causation. Measures having general application may also give rise to non-contractual liability on the part of the Community. Where such measures involve choices of economic policy, however, a particularly stringent test of unlawfulness is applied.[53] That test was laid down in *Zuckerfabrik Schöppenstedt v. Council*,[54] where the Court stated: "Where legislative action involving measures of economic policy is concerned, the Community does not incur non-contractual liability for damage suffered by individuals as a consequence of that action . . . unless a sufficiently flagrant violation of a superior rule of law for the protection of the individual has occurred." Since nearly all Community legislation of a type liable to give rise to a claim in damages is concerned in some way with economic policy, the test laid down in the *Schöppenstedt* case is potentially broad in scope. It also applies in the case of an unlawful failure to adopt a legislative act.[55]

What constitutes "legislative action" for these purposes? First, the term does not cover instruments of primary Community law, such as treaties concerning the accession of new Member States[56] or the Single European Act[57]. These are agreements concluded by the Member States, not acts of the institutions. Secondly, the CFI made it clear in *Schröder and Others v. Commission*[58] that "the concept of legislative measure within the meaning of the case-law may apply to all the measures referred to by Article 189 [now 249] and not only to regulations." As in actions for annulment, the decisive question is not what the disputed act is called but whether it is of general application. In *Schröder*, the CFI concluded that the contested measures, even though they took the form of decisions, produced "with regard to the applicants effects which are those of a measure of general application, in the same way as a regulation . . ."[59] The

---

[53] See Case 50/86 *Grands Moulins de Paris v. Council and Commission* [1987] E.C.R. 4833, paras 7–8; Advocate General van Gerven in Joined Cases C–104/89 and 37/90 *Mulder v. Council and Commission* [1992] E.C.R. I–3061 at 3103. It is not enough to establish liability that the measure in question has previously been declared void by the Court: see, *e.g.* Joined Cases 83 and 94/76, 4, 15 and 40/77 *HNL v. Council and Commission* [1978] E.C.R. 1209, para. 4; [1978] 3 C.M.L.R. 566.

[54] Case 5/71 [1971] E.C.R. 975, para. 11.

[55] See Case T–113/96 *Dubois et Fils v. Council and Commission* [1998] E.C.R. II–125, para. 60.

[56] See Joined Cases 31 and 35/86 *Laisa v. Council* [1988] E.C.R. 2285.

[57] See *Dubois, supra*, para. 41.

[58] Case T–390/94 [1997] E.C.R. II–501, para. 54.

[59] Para. 56. See also Case C–390/95 P, *Antillean Rice Mills and Others v. Commission*, judgment of February 11, 1999, para. 60; Joined Cases T–481 and 484/93 *Exporteurs in Levende Varkens and Others v. Commission* [1995] E.C.R. II–2941.

Schöppenstedt test was therefore applicable. The Court has also applied that test in a claim for loss allegedly caused by a directive.[60] Conversely, the *Schöppenstedt* test will not apply where the contested act, although labelled a regulation, is not in fact a legislative measure of general application.[61] Because the action for damages and the action for annulment are independent remedies, the nature of a measure for the purposes of the former action is not affected by whether or not the applicant has standing to challenge it for the purposes of the latter action. Thus, in *Antillean Rice Mills and Others v. Commission*,[62] a decision which had been found to be of direct and individual concern to the applicants for the purposes of Article 230 was treated as a legislative measure in the context of a parallel claim for damages.

A superior rule of law for the protection of individuals may include a provision of the Treaty, such as Article 34(2) (ex 40(3)) E.C. prohibiting discrimination between producers and consumers in the Community in the context of the common organisation of agricultural markets,[63] or a provision contained in a regulation.[64] It seems that an applicant need only show that the rule in question was for the protection of individuals generally, not that it was for the protection of a particular class of which he was a member.[65] Thus, the category has been held to include general principles of law, such as proportionality, equal treatment, the protection of legitimate expectations and the right to be heard. Misuse of powers by an institution is also covered.[66] However, an inadequacy in the statement of the reasons on which a measure of general application is based is not sufficient to render the Community liable,[67] nor is failure to respect the institutional balance laid down in the Treaties. The Court does not regard the division of powers among the institutions as intended to protect individuals.[68]

In order to suceed, the applicant must show that the superior rule of law in question has been breached in a manner that is sufficiently serious to fix the Community with liability. In *HNL v. Council and Commission*,[69] the Court said

---

[60] See Case C–63/89 *Assurances du Crédit v. Council and Commission* [1991] E.C.R. I–1799; [1991] 2 C.M.L.R. 737.

[61] See Case C–119/88 *Aerpo and Others v. Commission* [1990] E.C.R. I–2189; Case T–472/93 *Campo Ebro and Others v. Council* [1995] E.C.R. II–421; [1996] 1 C.M.L.R. 1038 (appeal dismissed: see Case C–138/95 P [1997] E.C.R. I–2027).

[62] *supra*, para. 62. See also Case C–152/88 *Sofrimport v. Commission* [1990] E.C.R. I–2477.

[63] See, *e.g.* Joined Cases 83 and 94/76, 4, 15 and 40/77 *HNL v. Council and Commission* [1978] ECR 1209, para. 5; [1978] 3 C.M.L.R. 566; Case 238/78 *Ireks-Arkady v. Council and Commission* [1979] E.C.R. 2955, para. 11.

[64] See Case 74/74 *CNTA v. Commission* [1975] E.C.R. 533; [1977] 1 C.M.L.R. 171; Case C–152/88 *Sofrimport v. Commission* [1990] E.C.R. I–2477.

[65] See Joined Cases 5, 7 and 13–24/66 *Kampffmeyer v. Commission* [1967] E.C.R. 245, 262–263.

[66] See Joined Cases T–481 and 484/93 *Exporteurs in Levende Varkens and Others v. Commission* [1995] E.C.R. II–2941, para. 102, with references to earlier case-law. See also Case T–489/93 *Unifruit Hellas v. Commission* [1994] E.C.R. II–1201, para. 42; [1996] 1 C.M.L.R. 267 (appeal dismissed: see Case C–51/95 P [1997] E.C.R. I–727); [1995] C.M.L.R. 686.

[67] Case 106/81 *Kind v. EEC* [1982] E.C.R. 2885, para. 14. However, such an inadequacy may be enough where the measure is not one of general application and the *Schöppenstedt* test does not therefore apply: see Case C–358/90 *Compagnia Italiana Alcool v. Commission* [1992] E.C.R. I–2457, para. 47; [1992] 2 C.M.L.R. 876.

[68] Case C–282/90 *Vreugdenhil v. Commission* [1992] E.C.R. I–1937, paras 20–21.

[69] *supra*, para. 6.

that, in a legislative field which involved the exercise of a wide discretion, such as that of the Common Agricultural Policy, the Community did not incur non-contractual liability "unless the institution concerned has manifestly and gravely disregarded the limits on the exercise of its powers". Where the applicant is unable to show that such conduct has occurred, it will not be possible to establish a sufficiently serious breach of a superior rule of law.[70] The Court went even further in *Amylum v. Council and Commission*,[71] where it stated that a legal situation resulting from legislative measures involving choices of economic policy would only be sufficient to fix the Community with liability if the conduct of the institutions concerned "was verging on the arbitrary".

A consequence of that extremely strict test was that actions in respect of legislative measures conferring discretionary powers on the institutions were rarely successful. The Court seemed to regard the strictness of its approach as justified by two factors. The first was that, if liability were too easy to establish, the institutions would be unduly hampered in the performance of the tasks conferred on them by the Treaty.[72] The second was that an individual who considered himself injured by a Community act which had been implemented by the national authorities could challenge the act's validity before the national courts, who could make a reference to the Court of Justice under Article 234 (ex 177). According to the Court, "[t]he existence of such an action is by itself of such a nature as to ensure the efficient protection of the individuals concerned."[73]

There are signs in more recent case-law of a slight relaxation in the Court's approach. Thus, in *Commission v. Stahlwerke Peine-Salzgitter*,[74] the Court acknowledged that it was not necessary to establish "conduct verging on the arbitrary" where the Community's liability for unlawful legislative acts was in issue. In *Mulder v. Council and Commission* (*Mulder II*),[75] the Court upheld claims arising out of unlawful legislative acts even though the consequence was to expose the Community to liability to large numbers of other claimants in a position similar to that of the applicants.[76] The case is a particularly striking one because it arose within the framework of the Common Agricultural Policy, where the institutions enjoy wide discretionary powers.

At the origin of *Mulder II* lay the Community's efforts to limit milk production. A Council regulation adopted in 1977 introduced a system of "non-marketing premiums" which were paid to producers who undertook not to market milk and milk products for a specified period. The system did not prove sufficiently

---

[70] See Case C–390/95 P *Antillean Rice Mills and Others v. Commission,* judgment of February 11, 1999, paras 64–70.

[71] Joined Cases 116 and 124/77 [1979] E.C.R. 3497, para. 19; [1982] 2 C.M.L.R. 590.

[72] See, *e.g.* the *HNL* case, *supra*, para. 5.

[73] See the *Amylum* case, *supra*, para. 14.

[74] Case C–220/91 P [1993] E.C.R. I–2393, para. 51.

[75] Joined Cases C–104/89 and 37/90 [1992] E.C.R. I–3061. See also Case C–152/88 *Sofrimport v. Commission* [1990] E.C.R. I–2477; [1992] E.C.R. I–153.

[76] Because of the number of those affected by the Court's judgment, the Council adopted a regulation to facilitate the settlement of claims: see Reg. 2187/93 providing for an offer of compensation to certain producers of milk and milk products temporarily prevented from carrying on their trade, [1993] O.J. L196/6.

effective in curbing milk production, so in 1984 the Council adopted further regulations imposing a levy on quantities of milk delivered in excess of a reference quantity (or quota) calculated by reference to the amount delivered by the producer concerned during a particular calendar year. A producer who did not deliver any milk during that reference year because he had entered into a non-marketing undertaking under the 1977 regulation could not be certain that he would obtain a reference quantity under the levy system. In *Mulder I*,[77] which was referred to the Court under Article 234 (ex 177), the Court held that the regulations concerning the levy on milk were invalid because they infringed the principle of the protection of legitimate expectations. The Court observed that where a producer "has been encouraged by a Community measure to suspend marketing for a limited period in the general interest and against payment of a premium he may legitimately expect not to be subject, upon the expiry of his undertaking, to restrictions which specifically affect him precisely because he availed himself of the possibilities offered by the Community provisions".[78]

In its judgment in *Mulder I*,[79] the Court accepted that a producer who had voluntarily ceased production for a given period could not legitimately expect to be able to resume production under conditions identical to those which previously prevailed. The Council therefore sought a way of accommodating the legitimate expectations of producers who had given non-marketing undertakings within the framework of the levy system. Accordingly, in 1989 it adopted a further regulation providing essentially that producers who had not, pursuant to a non-marketing undertaking given under the 1977 regulation, delivered any milk during the relevant reference year were to receive a special reference quantity equal to 60 per cent of the quantity of milk delivered during the 12 months preceding the month in which the application for the non-marketing premium was made. In *Spagl*,[80] also a reference for a preliminary ruling, the Court found that the reduction of 40 per cent applied to producers who had entered into non-marketing undertakings substantially exceeded the rates of reduction applicable to producers whose reference quantities were fixed on the basis of milk deliveries actually made during the relevant reference year. The application of such a high rate of reduction therefore amounted to a restriction which specifically affected producers in the former category precisely because of the undertakings they had given under the 1977 regulation. The Court concluded that "the contested 60% rule likewise infringes the legitimate expectations which the producers concerned were entitled to entertain as to the limited nature of their undertakings."[81] The contested provision was therefore declared void.

These cases produced a flood of claims against the Community under the second paragraph of Article 288. The first to be decided were those brought by

---

[77] Case 120/86 *Mulder v. Minister van Landbouw en Visserij* [1988] E.C.R. 2321; [1989] 2 C.M.L.R. 1.
[78] Para. 24. See also Case 170/86 *von Deetzen v. Hauptzollamt Hamburg-Jonas* [1988] E.C.R. 2355; [1989] 2 C.M.L.R. 327. cf. Case C–63/93 *Duff and Others v. Minister for Agriculture and Food* [1996] E.C.R. I–569.
[79] Para. 23.
[80] Case C–189/89 [1990] E.C.R. I–4539; see also Case C–217/89 *Pastätter* [1990] E.C.R. I–4585; Case C–44/89 *von Deetzen II* [1991] E.C.R. I–5119; [1994] 2 C.M.L.R. 487.
[81] Para. 29.

the applicants in *Mulder II*,[82] where the claims were in part upheld. The Court observed[83]:

> "in so far as it failed completely, without invoking any higher public interest, to take account of the specific situation of a clearly defined group of economic agents . . . the Community legislature manifestly and gravely disregarded the limits of its discretionary power, thereby committing a sufficiently serious breach of a superior rule of law.
>
> That breach is all the more serious because the total and permanent exclusion of the producers concerned from the allocation of a reference quantity, which in fact prevented them from resuming the marketing of milk when their non-marketing . . . undertaking expired, cannot be regarded as being foreseeable or as falling within the bounds of the normal economic risks inherent in the activities of a milk producer."

By contrast, the Court held that the introduction of the 60 per cent rule did not give rise to non-contractual liability because the breach of the principle of the protection of legitimate expectations found in *Spagl* was not sufficiently serious to produce that result. Unlike the 1984 rules, it could not be said that the Council had failed to take account of the situation of producers who had given non-marketing undertakings when it introduced the 60 per cent rule. In adopting the 1989 regulation following the rulings in *Mulder I* and *von Deetzen*, the Court said that "the Community legislature made an economic policy choice with regard to the manner in which it was necessary to implement the principles set out in those judgments."[84] The 60 per cent rule represented an attempt by the Council to preserve the fragile stability which had been achieved in the milk products sector while at the same time to strike a balance between all the producers concerned. "Accordingly", the Court observed, "the Council took account of a higher public interest, without gravely and manifestly disregarding the limits of its discretionary power in this area."[85]

Liability without fault

Under the laws of some Member States, the administration may incur liability in damages for loss caused by acts which are lawful. The idea, enshrined in the French doctrine of "égalité devant les charges publiques" and the German doctrine of "Sonderopfer", is that it is unfair to make a limited group of individuals bear the financial burden of measures taken in the general interest.[86] Although the Community Courts generally describe unlawfulness as a condition of the Community's liability under the second paragraph of Article 288, the case-

---

[82] Joined Cases C–104/89 and 37/90 *Mulder and Others v. Council and Commission* [1992] E.C.R. I–3061. See Heukels (1993) 30 C.M.L. Rev 368; van Gerven, "Non-contractual liability of Member States, Community institutions and individuals for breaches of Community law with a view to a common law for Europe" (1994) 1 M.J. 6 at 25–32.

[83] Paras 16–17.

[84] Para 21.

[85] *ibid.*

[86] See Bronkhorst, "The valid legislative act as a cause of liability of the Communities" in Heukels and McDonnell, *op. cit.,* Chap. 8, p. 156.

law does not exclude the possibility that the Community might in exceptional cases incur liability in damages for a lawful act. In *Dorsch Consult v. Council and Commission*,[87] the CFI observed, having reviewed the case-law of the Court of Justice, that:

"in the event of the principle of Community liability for a lawful act being recognised in Community law, such liability can be incurred only if the damage alleged, if deemed to constitute a 'still subsisting injury', affects a particular circle of economic operators in a disproportionate manner by comparison with others (special damage) and exceeds the limits of the economic risks inherent in operating in the sector concerned (unusual damage), without the legislative measure that gave rise to the alleged damage being justified by a general economic interest . . ."

The CFI found that, in the circumstances, those conditions were not satisfied.

Concurrent liability of the Community and the Member States

Under the system established by the Treaties, it is common for Community legislation to require implementation by the national authorities of the Member States. If a person suffers damage as a result of such implementation, the question may arise whether he should commence proceedings against the competent national authorities in the national courts (which might have to ask the Court of Justice for a preliminary ruling), or against the Community under the second paragraph of Article 288. It has been persuasively argued[88] that a claimant should in these circumstances have the right to choose whether to bring proceedings in the national courts or the Community Courts, but that solution would involve a departure from the case-law.

The Court has held that, in some cases, proceedings under the second paragraph of Article 288 will only be admissible if the applicant has exhausted any cause of action he might have against the national authorities in the domestic forum.[89] It seems that such a cause of action must be pursued first where the actions of the national authorities, although based on Community legislation, are a more direct cause of the damage suffered by the applicant.[90] However, where the conduct in question is in fact the responsibility of a Community institution (for example, where the national body was acting under its instructions), it is the Community Courts which have jurisdiction.[91] In any event, it is not necessary to exhaust any national rights of action that may be available where they are not

---

[87] Case T–184/95 [1998] E.C.R. II–667, para. 80 (appeal dismissed: Case C–237/98 P, judgment of June 15, 2000). See also *Dubois, supra*, para. 42.

[88] See Wils, "Concurrent liability of the Community and a Member State" (1992) 17 E.L.Rev. 191 at 204–206.

[89] See, *e.g.* Case 175/84 *Krohn v. Commission* [1986] E.C.R. 753, para. 27; [1987] 1 C.M.L.R. 745.

[90] See, *e.g.* Case 133/79 *Sucrimex v. Commission* [1980] E.C.R. 1299; [1981] 2 C.M.L.R. 479; Case C–282/90 *Vreugdenhil v. Commission* [1992] E.C.R. I–1937.

[91] See, *e.g. Krohn v. Commission, supra*.

capable of providing an effective means of protection for the applicant and compensating him for the damage he claims to have suffered.[92]

Damage

In proceedings under the second paragraph of Article 288, an applicant may in principle recover actual financial loss[93] as well as loss of profits.[94] In order to succeed, the applicant must either quantify the loss which it claims to have suffered or point to evidence on the basis of which its nature and extent can be assessed.[95] It is also possible to recover damages for non-material injury, such as the effect on the applicant's integrity and reputation of defamatory remarks made by the defendant.[96] In staff cases, small amounts have been awarded for shock, disturbance and uneasiness.[97] Moreover, the Court has acknowledged that it may be asked "to declare the Community liable for imminent damage foreseeable with sufficient certainty even if the damage cannot yet be precisely assessed."[98] However, the applicant must take reasonable steps to mitigate any damage[99] and will not be able to recover compensation where he could have passed the loss on to his customers.[1] The applicant must also show that the damage he has suffered "exceeds the limits of the economic risks inherent in operating in the sector concerned".[2]

Where a claim under the second paragraph of Article 288 is successful, the Court does not normally make a specific award of damages. Instead, the judgment will usually establish the acts or omissions giving rise to liability and, if appropriate, make an award of interest. It will then order the parties to attempt to reach an agreement, within a specified period, on the amount of compensation payable. The judgment will require the parties to transmit to the Court a statement of their views, with supporting figures, if they are unable to reach agreement.[3]

---

[92] *Krohn v. Commission, supra*, para. 27; Case 20/88 *Roquette Frères v. Commission* [1989] E.C.R. 1553, para. 15; [1991] 2 C.M.L.R. 6.

[93] See Joined Cases 5, 7 and 13–24/66 *Kampffmeyer v. Commission* [1967] E.C.R. 245; Case 74/74 *CNTA v. Commission* [1975] E.C.R. 533; [1977] 1 C.M.L.R. 171.

[94] See, *e.g. Kampffmeyer, supra. cf.* Joined Cases 54–60/76 *Compagnie Industrielle du Comité de Loheac v. Council and Commission* [1977] E.C.R. 645.

[95] See Case T–277/97 *Ismeri Europa Srl v. Court of Auditors,* judgment of June 15, 1999, para. 67.

[96] See, *e.g. Ismeri Europa, supra,* paras 80–94.

[97] See, *e.g.* Joined Cases 7/56 and 3–7/57 *Algera v. Common Assembly* [1957 and 1958] E.C.R. 39, 66–67.

[98] Joined Cases 56–60/74 *Kampffmeyer v. Commission and Council* [1976] E.C.R. 711, para. 6. *cf.* Case T–230/95 *BAI v. Commission,* judgment of January 28 1999.

[99] See Case 120/83R *Raznoimport v. Commission* [1983] E.C.R. 2573, para. 14. *cf.* Case C–284/98 P *European Parliament v. Bieber,* judgment of March 16, 2000, paras 56–57.

[1] See Joined Cases 64 and 113/76, 167 and 239/78, 27, 28 and 45/79 *Dumortier Frères v. Council* [1979] E.C.R. 3091, para. 15; Case 238/78 *Ireks-Arkady v. Council and Commission* [1979] E.C.R. 2955, para. 14; Joined Cases 241, 242 and 245–250/78 *DGV v. Council and Commission* [1979] E.C.R. 3017, para. 15; Joined Cases 261–262/78, *Interquell Stärke v. Council and Commission* [1979] E.C.R. 3045, para. 17 (the so-called "Gritz and Quellmehl" cases, after the products with which they were concerned). See Rudden and Bishop, "Gritz and quellmehl: pass it on" (1981) 6 E.L.Rev. 243.

[2] Case 59/83 *Biovilac v. EEC* [1984] E.C.R. 4057, para. 28; [1987] 2 C.M.L.R. 881.

[3] See, *e.g.* the "Gritz and Quellmehl" cases, *supra;* Case 145/83 *Adams v. Commission* [1985] E.C.R. 3539; [1986] 1 C.M.L.R. 506. *cf.* Case C–308/87 *Grifoni v. EAEC* [1994] E.C.R. I–341. Joined Cases C–104/89 and C–37/90 *Mulder and Others v. Council and Commission,* judgment of January 27, 2000 where the parties were unable to reach agreement and the Court had to quantify the precise amount of compensation to which the applicant was entitled.

Causation

The Court has said that the second paragraph of Article 288 does not require the Community "to make good every harmful consequence, even a remote one, of unlawful legislation."[100] The applicant must therefore establish that the damage is a "sufficiently direct consequence of the unlawful conduct".[101] In *Compagnia Italiana Alcool v. Commission*,[102] the Court said that there was no causal link between the damage allegedly suffered by the applicant and a deficiency in the statement of reasons contained in a Commission decision. As the Court explained, "[i]f that deficiency had not existed, the damage allegedly suffered by [the applicant] would have been the same." The chain of causation may be broken by, for example, the actions of national authorities or by the behaviour of the applicant himself. In this respect, traders are expected to behave in a prudent manner and to apprise themselves of the conditions on the markets in which they operate. If they fall short of this standard, the Community will not be held responsible for any loss that ensues.[103]

Limitation

Article 43 of the Statute of the Court provides that "[p]roceedings against the Community in matters arising from non-contractual liability shall be barred after a period of five years from the occurrence of the event giving rise thereto." That period is suspended if the aggrieved party brings proceedings for annulment or failure to act against the institution concerned.[104] The limitation period does not start to run "before all the requirements governing an obligation to provide compensation for damage are satisfied and in particular before the damage to be made good has materialised".[105] Thus, where the liability of the Community derives from a legislative measure, the limitation period does not begin "before the injurious effects of that measure have been produced".[106] Where the cause of the damage suffered by the applicant is an administrative act or omission, the limitation period does not start to run until he becomes aware of it.[107]

---

[100] *Dumortier Frères v. Council, supra*, para. 21.

[101] *ibid.*

[102] Case C–358/90 [1992] E.C.R. I–2457, para. 47; [1992] 2 C.M.L.R. 876.

[103] See Case 169/73 *Compagnie Continentale v. Council* [1975] E.C.R. 117, paras 22–32; [1975] 1 C.M.L.R. 578; Case 26/81 *Oleifici Mediterranei v. EEC* [1982] E.C.R. 3057, paras 22–24.

[104] See Joined Cases 5, 7 and 13–24/66 *Kampffmeyer v. Commission* [1967] E.C.R. 245, 260.

[105] Joined Cases 256, 257 and 267/80 and 5/81, *Birra Wührer v. Council and Commission* [1982] ECR 85, para. 10; [1983] 3 C.M.L.R. 176; Case 51/81 *De Franceschi v. Council and Commission* [1982] E.C.R. 117, para. 10.

[106] *ibid.*

[107] See Case 145/83 *Adams v. Commission* [1985] E.C.R. 3539, paras 50–51; [1986] 1 C.M.L.R. 506.

CHAPTER 11

PRELIMINARY RULINGS

INTRODUCTION

The responsibility for giving effect to Community law cast by the Treaties on the national courts gave rise to a danger that equivalent provisions would not be interpreted and applied in the same way in different Member States. Such a situation would be inimical to the proper functioning of the common market. In an attempt to safeguard the uniform application of Community law,[1] the authors of the Community Treaties established a procedure which enables national courts to seek the guidance of the Court of Justice on points of Community law they are called on to decide.[2] That procedure has been described by the Court as "the veritable cornerstone of the operation of the internal market, since it plays a fundamental role in ensurng that the law established by the Treaties retains its Community character with a view to guaranteeing that the law has the same effect in all circumstances in all the Member States of the European Union".[3] The growing importance of Community law to litigants and the national courts of the Member States is reflected in the increasing number of references being made to the Court of Justice. This rose by about 10 per cent in 1998 compared with the previous year and by more than 85 per cent compared with 1990. References for preliminary rulings accounted in 1998 for more than half the new cases brought before the Court, 264 out of a total of 485.[4]

The main provision of the E.C. Treaty dealing with preliminary rulings is Article 234 (ex 177) E.C. which provides as follows:

"The Court of Justice shall have jurisdiction to give preliminary rulings concerning:

(a) the interpretation of this Treaty;
(b) the validity and interpretation of acts of the institutions of the Community and of the ECB;
(c) the interpretation of the statutes of bodies established by an act of the Couil, where those statutes so provide.

Where such a question is raised before any court or tribunal of a Member States, that court or tribunal may, if it considers that a decision on the question is necessary to enable it to give judgment, request the Court of Justice to give a ruling thereon.

---

[1] See Case 166/73 *Rheinmühlen v. Einfuhr- und Vorratsstelle Getreide* [1974] E.C.R. 33; [1974] 1 C.M.L.R. 523.
[2] See generally Anderson, *References to the European Court* (1995).
[3] See the Court's report on the application of the TEU in "The Proceedings of the Court of Justice and Court of First Instance of the European Communities", May 22–26, 1995 (No. 15/95), para. 11.
[4] See "The Future of the Judicial System of the European Union", published by the Community Courts in the spring of 1999, p. 5; Chap. 9, *supra*.

Where any such question is raised in a case pending before a court or tribunal of a Member State, against whose decisions there is no judicial remedy under national law, that court or tribunal shall bring the matter before the Court of Justice."

As we shall see, a reference to the Court of Justice under Article 234 may in principle be made at any stage in the proceedings pending before the national court. The ruling of the Court of Justice is interlocutory in that it constitutes a step in the proceedings before the national court, which must apply the ruling to the facts of the case. It is in this sense that the ruling of the Court of Justice is preliminary. Thus, the national court must be in a position to take account of the ruling of the Court of Justice when giving judgment. The Court of Justice has no jurisdiction to give a preliminary ruling if the proceedings before the referring court have already been terminated.[5]

The Court of Justice enjoys similar jurisdiction under the ECSC Treaty[6] and under the Euratom Treaty.[7] Provision for the Court of Justice to give preliminary rulings has also been made in relation to a number of conventions drawn up between the Member States. Examples are the 1968 Brussels Convention on jurisdiction and the enforcement of judgments in civil and commercial matters[8] and the 1980 Rome Convention on the law applicable to contractual obligations,[9] although the preliminary rulings mechanisms under those conventions do not operate in exactly the same way as Article 234 E.C. In particular, while under Article 234 a reference may be made by any national court of tribunal, under the Brussels and Rome Conventions that facility is available only to superior national courts and other courts when sitting in an appellate capacity. The model offered by the Brussels and Rome Conventions was followed by the Member States at Amsterdam, when a new Title IV entitled "Visas, asylum, immigrattion and other policies related to the free movement of persons" was added to the E.C. Treaty. Within the framework of that Title, Article 234 applies in a modified form by virtue of Article 68 (ex 73p) E.C. Article 68 is considered in more detail below.

QUESTIONS WHICH MAY BE REFERRED

Article 234 enables any question of E.C. law to be referred to the Court of Justice for a preliminary ruling by any national court or tribunal which considers a decision on the question "necessary to enable it to give judgment". The question may be raised either by one of the parties or by the judge of his own motion.[10] A decision is "necessary" for these purposes if the national court sees it

---

[5] Case 338/85 *Pardini v. Ministero del Commercio con l'Estero* [1988] E.C.R. 2041, para. 11. *cf.* Case C–3/90 *Bernini* [1992] E.C.R. I–1071; *Magnavision v. General Optical Council* [1987] 2 C.M.L.R. 262, DC.

[6] See Art. 41 ECSC, as interpreted by the Court of Justice in Case C–221/88 *ECSS v. Busseni* [1990] E.C.R. I–495.

[7] See Art. 150.

[8] See [1998] O.J. C27/1.

[9] See [1998] O.J. C27/34.

[10] Case 166/73 *Rheinmühlen Einfuhr- und Vorratsstelle Getreide* [1974] E.C.R. 33; [1974] 1 C.M.L.R. 523. See also Joined Cases C–87–89/90 *Verholen and Others* [1991] E.C.R. I–3757; [1994] 1 C.M.L.R. 157.

as a step, which need not be the final one, in its strategy for disposing of the case. The Community point need not be conclusive.[11] Questions which may be the subject of a reference include, as well as questions on the interpretation of the E.C. Treaty itself, questions on one of the amending Treaties or on one of the Treaties of Accession, and questions on the validity and interpretation of acts of the Community institutions, such as regulations, directives and decisions of the Council or Commission and non-binding measures such as recommendations.[12] Acts of the European Parliament may also be the subject of references to the Court of Justice.[13] Cases may be referred on the interpretation of an agreement concluded by the Community with a third State, since such an agreement constitutes, as far as the Community is concerned, an act of one of the institutions.[14] References may also be made on whether a provision of Community law produces direct effect, that is, whether it confers rights on individuals which national courts are bound to protect. However, the Court has no jurisdiction under Article 234 to give preliminary rulings on provisions of the TEU other than those which are specifically mentioned in Article 46 (ex L).[15]

In *Dzodzi v. Belgium*,[16] the Court of Justice held that it has jurisdiction under Article 234 to give preliminary rulings on the effect of provisions of Community law which are applicable in the action pending before the national court only because their scope has been extended by national law. The Court took the view that the proper functioning of the Community legal order made it imperative that provisions of Community law be given a uniform interpretation regardless of the circumstances in which they fell to be applied. It proceeded to deal with the substance of the questions which had been put to it.[17] The Court seems to have been concerned that, had it declined jurisdiction to give preliminary rulings in these circumstances, parallel lines of national case-law might have developed, one concerning the interpretation of provisions of Community law applicable in their own right, the other concerning the interpretation of the same provisions when applicable solely by virtue of national law. The possibility that cases in the second category might have influenced cases in the first could in principle have jeopardised the uniform application of Community law.

Doubt was cast on the continued applicability of the *Dzodzi* approach by *Kleinwort Benson v. City of Glasgow District Council*.[18] In that case, the English

---

[11] See, *e.g.* Case C–315/92 *Verband Sozialer Wettbewerb v. Clinique Laboratories and Estée Lauder* [1994] E.C.R. I–317; Joined Cases 36 and 71/80 *Irish Creamery Milk Suppliers Association v. Ireland* [1981] E.C.R. 735; *Polydor Ltd v. Harlequin Record Shops Ltd* [1980] 2 C.M.L.R. 413, CA.

[12] See, *e.g.* Case C–322/88 *Grimaldi v. Fonds des Maladies Professionnelles* [1989] E.C.R. 4407.

[13] See, *e.g.* Case 208/80 *Lord Bruce of Donington* [1981] E.C.R. 2205; [1981] 3 C.M.L.R. 506.

[14] See Case 181/73 *Haegeman v. Belgium* [1974] E.C.R. 449; [1975] 1 C.M.L.R. 515; Opinion 1/76 [1977] E.C.R. 741; Case C–321/97 *Andersson and Another v. Swedish State*, judgment of June 15, 1999. The Court has no jurisdiction under Art. 234 to rule on the interpretation of the EEA Agreement as regards its application in the EFTA States, only to situations which come within the Community legal order.

[15] See Case C–167/94, *Grau Gomis* [1995] E.C.R. I–1023; [1996] 2 C.M.L.R. 129; [1995] All E.R. (E.C.) 668.

[16] Joined Cases C–297/88 and 197/89 [1990] E.C.R. I–3763, followed in Case C–231/89 *Gmurzynska-Bscher v. Oberfinanzdirektion Köln* [1990] E.C.R. I–4003.

[17] Which concerned the rules on the free movement of persons.

[18] Case C–346/93 [1995] E.C.R. I–615; [1995] All E.R. (E.C.) 514.

Court of Appeal made a reference on the interpretation of the Brussels Convention.[19] In the United Kingdom, rules based on the Brussels Convention had been laid down by Act of Parliament (the Civil Jurisdiction and Judgments Act 1982) to provide for the allocation of civil jurisdiction between England and Wales, Scotland and Northern Ireland. In *Kleinwort Benson*, the Court of Appeal asked the Court of Justice for guidance on the meaning of the Convention so that it could decide whether, under the 1982 Act, the dispute between the parties fell within the jurisdiction of the English or Scottish courts. The Court of Justice said it had no jurisdiction to answer. The national court had made the reference to enable it to apply, not the Convention, but its national law. Moreover, the relevant Act, although modelled on the Convention, did not wholly reproduce its terms. The Court concluded that the Act did not render the Convention applicable as such to cases which fell outside its scope. Moreover, the Act did not require United Kingdom courts to follow the interpretation of the Convention supplied by the Court of Justice, but merely to have regard to it when applying its national law. The Protocol did not in the Court's view envisage that it should give purely advisory rulings which lacked binding effect.

In two subsequent cases, however, the Court made it clear that *Kleinwort Benson* was confined to situations where a Member State had adapted a solution applied under Community law to suit its own internal requirements. The *Dzodzi* approach continued to apply where a Member State had chosen to align its domestic legislation with Community law so as to apply the same treatment to purely internal situations as that accorded to situations governed by Community law. The cases in question[20] involved domestic rules on the imposition of tax. The Court explained that "where in regulating internal situations, domestic legislation adopts the same solutions as those adopted in Community law so as to provide for one single procedure in comparable situations, it is clearly in the Community interest that, in order to forestall future differences of interpretation, provisions or concepts taken from Community law should be interpreted uniformly, irrespective of the circumstances in which they are to apply . . ."[21]

COURTS AND TRIBUNALS OF THE MEMBER STATES

The power to make a reference under Article 234 belongs to "any court or tribunal of a Member State". That notion has been interpreted broadly by the Court of Justice. In *Dorsch Consult Ingenieurgesellschaft v. Bundesbaugesellschaft Berlin*,[22] the Court said: "In order to determine whether a body making a reference is a court or tribunal for the purposes of Article 177 [now 234] of the Treaty, which is a question governed by Community law alone, the Court takes

---

[19] The reference was not made under Art. 234 of the Treaty but under a special Protocol on the interpretation of the Convention by the Court of Justice (see [1998] O.J. C27/28). However, this has no bearing on the following discussion.

[20] Case C–28/95 *Leur-Bloem v. Inspecteur der Belastingdienst/Ondernemingen Amsterdam 2* [1997] E.C.R. I–4161; Case C–130/95 *Giloy v. Hauptzollamt Frankfurt am Main-Ost* [1997] E.C.R. I–4291.

[21] *Leur-Bloem*, para. 32, *Giloy*, para. 28. The Court's conclusion was reached against the advice of Advocate General Jacobs: see in particular pp. I–4180 and I–4187 of his Opinion.

[22] Case C–54/96 [1997] E.C.R. I–4961, para. 23; [1998] 2 C.M.L.R.

account of a number of factors, such as whether the body is established by law, whether it is permanent, whether its jurisdiction is compulsory, whether its procedure is *inter partes*, whether it applies rules of law and whether it is independent . . ." Thus, in *Vaassen v. Beamtenfonds Mijnbedrijf*,[23] a Dutch social security tribunal which gave "non-binding opinions" and which did not consider itself a court or tribunal under Dutch law was held to be a court or tribunal of a Member State for the purposes of Article 234. The Court reached that conclusion because the members of the tribunal were appointed, its chairman designated and its rules of procedure laid down by the responsible minister. Moreover, the tribunal was a permanent body which heard disputes according to an adversarial procedure and it was bound to apply rules of law. By contrast, in *Corbiau v. Administration des Contributions*,[24] the Court held that the notion of a court or tribunal for the purposes of Article 234 was confined to authorities which had no connection with the body which had adopted the measure being challenged in the main action. In that case, the reference had been made by the Luxembourg *directeur des contributions*, who was linked organically with the national tax authorities, one of the parties to the action. He was therefore held not to be a court or tribunal within the meaning of Article 234 and the reference was dismissed as inadmissible.

A body may only make use of the facility for which Article 234 provides if its functions are judicial rather than administrative in nature, in other words, if it is responsible for settling disputes through the application of rules of law.[25] Where a body exercises both judicial and administrative functions, it may not request a preliminary ruling when performing its administrative tasks.[26] Moreover, a body will not be considered a "court or tribunal of a Member State" within the meaning of Article 234 unless it is closely linked to "the organisation of legal remedies through the courts in the Member State in question". That requirement was laid down in *Nordsee v. Reederei Mond*,[27] where an arbitrator appointed under a private contract was held not to be entitled to make a reference. The public authorities of the Member State concerned had not been involved in the decision by the parties to the contract to opt for arbitration, nor were those authorities automatically called upon to intervene in the proceedings before the arbitrator. However, the Court made it clear that a court or tribunal hearing an appeal against an arbitrator's award was entitled to make a reference under Article 234.[28]

---

[23] Case 61/65 [1966] E.C.R. 261; [1996] C.M.L.R. 508.
[24] Case C–24/92 [1993] E.C.R. I–1277. *cf.* Joined Cases C–110/98 to C–147/98 *Gabalfrisa SL and Others v. AEAT,* judgment of March 21, 2000.
[25] See, *e.g.* Case C–111/94 *Job Centre* [1995] E.C.R. I–3361, paras 9–11; Case 138/80 *Borker* [1980] E.C.R. 1975, para. 4; [1980] 3 C.M.L.R. 638.
[26] See Case C–192/98 *Ministero dei Lavori Pubblici and Another,* Order of November 26, 1999; Case C–440/98 *RAI,* Order of November 26, 1999. *cf.* Case 14/86 *Pretore di Salò v. Persons Unknown* [1987] E.C.R. 2545; [1989] 1 C.M.L.R. 71.
[27] Case 102/81 [1982] E.C.R. 1095. See para. 13.
[28] See also Case C–393/92 *Almelo* [1994] E.C.R. I–1477. *cf.* Case C–126/97 *Eco Swiss China Time v. Benetton International,* [1999] 5 C.M.L.R. 570.

THE DIALOGUE BETWEEN THE COURT OF JUSTICE AND THE NATIONAL COURT

The relationship between the national court and the Court of Justice in proceedings under Article 234 is co-operative rather than hierarchical in nature. Both courts have distinct but complementary roles to play in finding a solution to the case which is in conformity with the requirements of Community law. A reference to the Court of Justice is not in any sense an appeal against the decision of the national court. There are technically no parties to the proceedings before the Court of Justice,[29] which may be regarded as a form of dialogue between that court and the referring court. The parties to the action before the referring court have the right, along with the Member States and the Commission, to submit written and oral observations to the Court of Justice in accordance with Article 20 of the Statute of the Court. That right is also extended to the Council or European Central Bank, where the validity of interpretation of an act of one of those bodies is in issue, and to the European Parliament and the Council where the validity or interpretation of an act adopted jointly by those institutions is in issue. In order to enable them to exercise that right, Article 20 requires the Court to notify those entitled to submit observations on the reference. However, they only receive the reference itself, not any accompanying documents. The national court's order for reference should therefore be self-contained and self-explanatory.

The Court of Justice will not, in the context of a reference for a preliminary ruling, entertain a challenge to the jurisdiction of the referring court based on national law or to the facts set out by that court in its order for reference.[30] Nor will the Court of Justice rule on the application of the law to the facts or the compatibility of national law with the requirements of Community law.[31] These are matters within the exclusive jurisdiction of the national court in proceedings under Article 234. The questions referred should be couched in terms which pose a general question of Community law rather than the concrete issue as it falls to be decided in the instant case. If they are not, the Court of Justice may reformulate them. Questions may also be reformulated if the Court of Justice considers this necessary to furnish the national court with all the elements of Community law which it requires to give judgment.[32] The Court will not, at the request of one of the parties to the main proceedings, examine questions which have not been submitted to it by the national court.[33]

---

[29] See Case 69/85 *Wünsche v. Germany* [1986] E.C.R. 947, para. 14.

[30] See Case C–435/97 *WWF and Others v. Autonome Provinz Bozen and Others*, judgment of September 16, 1999, paras 28–29.

[31] See, *e.g.* Joined Cases C–332–333/92 and 335/92 *Eurico Italia and Others* [1994] E.C.R. I–711; [1994] 2 C.M.L.R. 580; Case C–295/97 *Piaggio v. IFITALIA and Others*, judgment of June 17, 1999.

[32] See, *e.g.* Case 28/85 *Deghillage v. Caisse Primaire d'Assurance Maladie* [1986] E.C.R. 991, para. 13; [1987] 2 C.M.L.R. 812; Case C–221/89 *The Queen v. Secretary of State for Transport, ex p. Factortame* [1991] E.C.R. I–3905; [1991] 3 C.M.L.R. 589.

[33] See Case C–189/95 *Franzén* [1997] E.C.R. I–5909, para. 79; [1998] 1 C.M.L.R. 1231, *WWF and Others v. Autonome Provinz Bozen and Others, supra,* paras 28–29.

THE DISCRETION CONFERRED BY THE SECOND PARAGRAPH OF ARTICLE 234

Under the second paragraph of Article 234, courts and tribunals in the Member States whose decisions are subject to a judicial remedy under national law enjoy a discretion in deciding whether or not to ask for a preliminary ruling on points of Community law they are called on to decide. The proper functioning of the preliminary rulings procedure depends to a large extent on the way in which that discretion is exercised. Since the scope of the discretion enjoyed by national courts depends on the correct interpretation of Article 234, only the Court of Justice is competent to make authoritative pronouncements on the matter. Nonetheless, some national courts have purported to lay down guidelines on the matter. An early attempt to do so was made by Lord Denning in *HP Bulmer Ltd v. J Bollinger SA*.[34] Lord Denning's guidelines had a considerable influence on the practice of the English courts, but they attracted a certain amount of academic criticism because of their tendency to discourage references.[35] A more positive emphasis was given by Sir Thomas Bingham MR in the more recent case of *R v. Stock Exchange, ex parte Else (1982) Ltd*.[36] In that case, the Master of the Rolls declared:

". . . I understand the correct approach in principle of a national court (other than a final court of appeal) to be quite clear: if the facts have been found and the Community law issue is critical to the court's final decision, the appropriate course is ordinarily to refer the issue to the Court of Justice unless the national court can with complete confidence resolve the issue itself. In considering whether it can with complete confidence resolve the issue itself the national court must be fully mindful of the differences between national and Community legislation, of the pitfalls which face a national court venturing into what may be an unfamiliar field, of the need for uniform interpretation throughout the Community and of the great advantages enjoyed by the Court of Justice in construing Community instruments. If the national court has any real doubt, it should ordinarily refer."

It is well established in the case-law of the Court of Justice that the national court is in principle the sole judge of whether a preliminary ruling is necessary and of the relevance of the questions referred.[37] "Consequently, where the questions submitted concern the interpretation of Community law, the Court of Justice is, in principle, bound to give a ruling."[38] Moreover, the Court of Justice made it clear in *Rheinmühlen*[39] that a national court cannot be deprived of its power to make a reference by the rulings of superior national courts. The Treaty does not preclude a decision to refer from remaining subject to the remedies

---

[34] [1974] Ch. 401.
[35] See, *e.g.* Dashwood and Arnull, "English courts and Art. 177 of the EEC Treaty" (1984) 4 Y.E.L. 255, 263.
[36] [1993] 2 W.L.R. 70 at 76; [1993] 1 All E.R. 420 at 426, CA.
[37] See, *e.g. Dzodzi v. Belgium, supra.*
[38] Case C–256/97 *DMT*, [1999] 3 C.M.L.R. 1, para. 10.
[39] Case 166/73 [1974] E.C.R. 33, paras 3–4; [1974] 1 C.M.L.R. 523.

normally available under national law, but the Court will act on the decision to refer until it has been formally revoked.[40]

The Court of Justice may refuse a request for a preliminary ruling made by a national court "only where it is quite obvious that the interpretation of Community law sought bears no relation to the actual facts of the main proceedings or their purpose, or where it does not have before it the factual or legal material necessary to give a useful answer to the questions submitted".[41] This represents a retreat from the more liberal attitude originally taken by the Court. The retreat began in *Foglia v. Novello*,[42] where the Court refused to entertain a reference made in the context of a collusive action brought in one Member State by parties who are not really in dispute with each other with the intention of challenging the law of another Member State as contrary to Community law. The Court's ruling in that case was heavily criticised[43] and was for many years applied with considerable restraint. However, it was given a new lease of life by the ruling in *Telemarsicabruzzo v. Circostel*.[44] In that case, the Vice Pretore di Frascati referred two questions on the compatibility with the E.C. Treaty, and in particular the competition rules laid down in it, of provisions of Italian law restricting the right of private sector television channels to use certain frequencies. The orders for reference contained very little information about the factual background to the cases or the relevant provisions of Italian law. The Court emphasised that the need to give a useful ruling in proceedings under Article 234 made it essential for the national judge to define the factual and legislative background to the case, or at least the factual hypotheses on which the questions referred were based. These requirements were particularly important in the field of competition, characterised as it was by complex legal and factual situations. The Court pointed out that the orders for reference in the present cases contained no information on these matters. The information the Court had been able to glean during the course of the proceedings was not adequate to enable it to interpret the Treaty competition rules in the light of the circumstances of the case pursuant to the referring court's invitation. In those circumstances, the Court concluded that there were no grounds for ruling on the questions submitted by the Vice Pretore.

The judgment in *Telemarsicabruzzo* was delivered by the full Court and was clearly intended to emphasise that, if the background to the case is not clearly set out by the referring court, the Court will decline to give a ruling. That message was subsequently reinforced in a series of cases in which inadequately-explained

---

[40] See Case 146/73 *Rheinmühlen-Düsseldorf v. Einfuhr- und Vorratsstelle Getreide* [1974] E.C.R. 139, para. 3; [1974] 1 C.M.L.R. 523.

[41] Case C–60/98 *Butterfly Music Srl v. CEMED*, judgment of June 29, 1999, para. 13. See also Case C–421/97 *Tarantik v. Directeur des Services Fiscaux de Seine-et-Marne*, [1999] 2 C.M.L.R. 1083, para. 33; Case C–415/93 *URBSFA and Others v. Bosman and Others* [1995] E.C.R. I–4921, para. 61; [1996] 1 C.M.L.R. 645; [1996] All E.R. (E.C.) 97.

[42] Case 104/79 [1980] E.C.R. 745; [1981] 1 C.M.L.R. 45.

[43] See, *e.g.* Barav, "Preliminary censorship? The judgment of the European Court in *Foglia* v. *Novello*" (1980) 5 E.L.Rev. 443; Bebr, "The existence of a genuine dispute: an indispensable precondition for the jurisdiction of the Court under Art. 177 EEC?" (1980) 17 C.M.L.Rev 525 and "The possible implications of *Foglia v. Novello II*" (1982) 19 C.M.L. Rev 421.

[44] Joined Cases C–320–322/90 [1993] E.C.R. I–393. See also Case C–83/91 *Meilicke v. ADV/ORGA* [1992] E.C.R. I–4871.

references were dismissed by reasoned order as manifestly inadmissible under the abbreviated procedure for which provision is made in Article 92(1) of its Rules of Procedure.[45] In one case, the Court even refused to give a ruling when it thought the reference should have been withdrawn by the national court in the light of developments since it was made.[46] However, there are some recent cases where it has been willing to deal with questions it might have been expected to reject. In *Vaneetveld*,[47] for example, the order for reference contained no information about the facts of the case. Nonetheless, following the advice of Advocate General Jacobs, the Court observed[48]: "It is true that the Court has held that the need to arrive at an interpretation of Community law which is useful for the national court requires that court to define the factual and legislative context of the questions, or at least to explain the factual hypotheses on which they are based . . . None the less, that requirement is less pressing where the questions relate to specific technical points and enable the Court to give a useful reply even where the national court has not given an exhaustive description of the legal and factual situation." The Court concluded that it had enough information to enable it to give a useful answer.

The modern case-law therefore suggests that, where the referring court sets out clearly what the case is about and gives a plausible explanation of why it needs an answer to the questions it has referred, the Court will normally proceed to answer them. However, it will not generally spend time trying to identify what a case is about when this has not been properly explained by the national court, nor will it answer questions which are manifestly irrelevant. The Court is clearly entitled to expect national judges to play their part in defining the issues on which preliminary rulings may properly be sought, particularly in view of its ever-increasing workload. Be that as it may, some national courts remain reluctant on occasion to seek the Court's guidance, even where it is plainly desirable for that step to be taken.[49] The Court needs to be alert to the danger of discouraging references in cases where its guidance is genuinely needed.[50]

---

[45] See, *e.g.* Case C–157/92 *Banchero I* [1993] E.C.R. I–1085; Case C–386/92 *Monin Automobiles I* [1993] E.C.R. I–2049. For the sequel to these cases, see Case C–428/93 *Monin Automobiles II* [1994] E.C.R. I–1707; Case C–387/93 *Banchero II* [1995] E.C.R. I–4663; [1996] 1 C.M.L.R. 829.

[46] See Joined Cases C–422–424/93 *Zabala Erasun and Others* [1995] E.C.R. I–1567; [1996] 1 C.M.L.R. 861; [1995] All E.R. (E.C.) 758.

[47] Case C–316/93 [1994] E.C.R. I–763 [1994] 2 C.M.L.R. 852. See also Case C–412/93 *Leclerc-Siplec v. TF1 Publicité and M6 Publicité* [1995] E.C.R. I–179; [1995] 3 C.M.L.R. 422; Case C–415/93 *URBSFA and Others v. Bosman and Others* [1995] E.C.R. I–4921; [1996] 1 C.M.L.R. 645; [1996] All E.R. (E.C.) 97; Case C–295/97 *Piaggio v. IFITALIA and Others*, judgment of June 17, 1999; Case C–355/97 *Landesgrundverkehrsreferent der Tiroler Landesregierung v. Beck and Another*, judgment of September 7, 1999; Case C–67/96 *Albany International v. Stichting Bedrijfspensioenfonds Textiel–industrie*, [2000] 4 C.M.L.R. 446; Joined Cases C–115–117/97 *Brentjens v. Stichting Bedrijfspensioenfonds voor de Handel in Bouwmaterialen*, [2000] 4 C.M.L.R. 566; Joined Cases C–51/96 and C–191/97 *Deliège v. LFJ and Others*, judgment of April 11, 2000.

[48] Para. 13.

[49] For an example from the United Kingdom, see the decision of the House of Lords in *Freight Transport Association Ltd and Others v. London Boroughs Transport Committee* [1991] 3 All E.R. 915, [1992] 3 C.M.L.R. 915, criticised by Weatherill, "Regulating the internal market: result orientation in the House of Lords" (1992) 17 E.L.Rev. 299 and by Greenwood, *All England Law Reports Annual Review* (1991), 141 at 146–148.

[50] See generally Barnard and Sharpston, "The changing face of Art. 177 references" (1997) 34 C.M.L.Rev. 1113; O'Keeffe, "Is the spirit of Art. 177 under attack? Preliminary references and admissibility" (1998) 23 E.L.Rev. 509.

In a Note for Guidance on References by National Courts for Preliminary Rulings issued in late 1996,[51] the Court summarised its case-law and offered advice on what references should contain. The Note also contains guidance on the point in the proceedings at which references should be made. It states: "A national court or tribunal may refer a question to the Court of Justice as soon as it finds that a ruling on the point or points of interpretation or validity is necessary to enable it to give judgment." The Court stresses, however, that, because it cannot decide issues of fact or of national law, "a decision to refer should not be taken until the national proceedings have reached a stage where the national court is able to define, if only as a working hypothesis, the factual and legal context of the question; on any view, the administration of justice is likely to be best served if the reference is not made until both sides have been heard." National courts which do not follow the advice contained in the Note run a serious risk of having their references dismissed as inadmissible.

PRELIMINARY RULINGS ON VALIDITY

Under the first paragraph of Article 234, the Court of Justice may be asked for a preliminary ruling not only on the interpretation of acts of the Community institutions but also on their validity. The jurisdiction of the Court of Justice to rule on the validity of Community provisions under Article 234 complements its jurisdiction to review the legality of Community acts under Article 230.[52] The former jurisdiction typically arises where a national measure, purportedly based on a Community act, is challenged in a national court on the ground that the Community act is itself invalid. This means that a person affected by a Community act may sometimes challenge its validity independently of the direct action which may be available before the Court of Justice under Article 230. However, the Court has imposed limits on the circumstances in which the validity of Community acts may be challenged in the national courts. The effect of the Court's decision in *TWD Textilwerke Deggendorf*[53] is that a natural or legal person who fails to challenge a Community act under Article 230, even though he clearly has standing to do so, may not subsequently contest the validity of that act in proceedings before a national court. The *TWD* case concerned the Treaty rules on State aid and there was initially some doubt about whether it was confined to that context. The Court made it clear that this was not so in *Wiljo v. Belgian State*,[54] where it applied the *TWD* approach in a different context.[55]

---

[51] [1997] 1 C.M.L.R. 78, (1997) 22 E.L.Rev. 55, (1997) 34 C.M.L.Rev 1319, [1997] All E.R. (E.C.) 1. See also the Practice Direction issued by the Lord Chief Justice of England and Wales on January 14, 1999 on references by the Court of Appeal and the High Court, [1999] 2 C.M.L.R. 799.

[52] See Chap. 10.

[53] Case C–188/92 [1994] E.C.R. I–833; [1995] 2 C.M.L.R. 145.

[54] Case C–178/95 [1997] E.C.R. I–585, [1997] 1 C.M.L.R. 627. See also Case C–408/95 *Eurotunnel and Others v. SeaFrance* [1997] E.C.R. I–6315, [1998] 2 C.M.L.R. 293. *cf.* Case C–241/95 *The Queen v. Intervention Board for Agricultural Produce, ex p. Accrington Beef and Others* [1996] E.C.R. I–6699, [1997] 1 C.M.L.R. 675.

[55] The *TWD* ruling was not well received in some quarters. See, *e.g.* Wyatt, "The relationship between actions for annulment and references on validity after *TWD Deggendorf*" in Lonbay and Biondi (eds.), *Remedies for Breach of E.C. Law* (1997), Chap. 6; Advocate General Tesauro in the

The Treaty appears to confer on national courts (other than those of last resort) the same discretion whether the question of Community law raised is one of interpretation or one of validity. However, in the controversial case of *Foto-Frost v. Hauptzollamt Lübeck-Ost*[56] the Court of Justice held that, while national courts were entitled to find that acts adopted by the institutions of the Community were valid, they had no power to declare such acts invalid. This was because "[d]ivergences between courts in the Member States as to the validity of Community acts would be liable to place in jeopardy the very unity of the Community legal order and detract from the fundamental requirement of legal certainty." The Court also pointed out that, if the matter were referred to it, the institution which adopted the contested act would be able to participate in the proceedings. This will rarely, if ever, be possible in proceedings before a national court. The result is that, where a real and substantial doubt is raised in a national court on the validity of a Community measure, and where it is clear that a decision on the validity of the measure is necessary for the resolution of the case, then the issue must be referred. This is so even where similar provisions have been declared void by the Court of Justice in other cases[57] and even where the national court is not one of last resort. Some commentators[58] have objected to the ruling in *Foto-Frost* on the basis that it is incompatible with the terms of Article 234, but the reasoning underlying the conclusion reached by the Court seems compelling.

The Court's judgment in *Foto-Frost* suggested[59] that national courts might have jurisdiction to declare Community acts invalid in interlocutory proceedings, where the urgency of the case might render it impractical to wait for a ruling from the Court of Justice. The powers of national courts in such proceedings were considered in more detail in *Zuckerfabrik Süderditmarschen v. Hauptzollamt Itzehoe*.[60] The essential point at issue in that case was whether, and if so in what circumstances, a national court could suspend the operation of a Community regulation which was alleged to be invalid but on which a national measure had been based. The Court of Justice observed that the rights of individuals to challenge regulations in the national courts would be compromised if they could not be suspended pending a ruling on their validity from the Court of Justice,

---

Eurotunnel case, *supra*, at I–6328. *cf.* Tesauro, "The effectiveness of judicial protection and co-operation between the Court of Justice and the national courts" (1993) 13 Y.E.L. 1, 15–16. However, the preliminary rulings procedure is in several respects a less satisfactory mechanism for reviewing the legality of Community acts than the action for annulment. See Advocate General Jacobs in *TWD* at I–840–844 and Case C–358/89, *Extramet Industrie v. Council* [1991] E.C.R. I–2501 at 2523–2525; [1993] 2 C.M.L.R. 619; Waelbroeck and Verheyden, "Les conditions de recevabilité des recours en annulation des particuliers contre les actes normatifs communautaires" (1995) 31 C.D.E. 399, 433–436.

[56] Case 314/85 [1987] E.C.R. 4199. See Bebr, "The reinforcement of the constitutional review of Community acts under Art. 177 EEC Treaty" (1988) 25 C.M.L.Rev. 667.

[57] *cf. R. v. Intervention Board for Agricultural Produce, ex p. ED and F Man (Sugar) Ltd* [1986] 2 All E.R. 126, QBD; *R v. Minister of Agriculture, ex p. Fédération Européenne de la Santé Animale* [1988] 3 C.M.L.R. 207 and 661, DC.

[58] See, *e.g.* Hartley, *Constitutional Problems of the European Union* (1999), pp. 34–35.

[59] See para. 19 of judgment.

[60] Joined Cases C–143/88 and 92/89 [1991] E.C.R. I–415; [1993] 3 C.M.L.R. 1. *cf.* Case C–6/99 *Greenpeace and Others v. Ministère de l'Agriculture et de la Pêche and Others,* judgment of March 21, 2000.

which had exclusive jurisdiction to adjudicate on that question.[61] A request for a preliminary ruling was one of the means provided by the Treaty for reviewing the validity of Community acts. Another means was the action for annulment brought directly before the Court of Justice under Article 230 (ex 173) E.C.[62] In such an action, the Court had the power under Article 242 (ex 185) E.C. to order the suspension of the contested act. As a result, "[t]he coherence of the system of interim legal protection therefore requires that national courts should also be able to order suspension of enforcement of a national administrative measure based on a Community regulation, the legality of which is contested."[63]

The Court observed that the suspension of administrative measures based on a Community regulation, whilst governed by national rules of procedure, had to be subject to conditions which were uniform throughout the Community so far as the granting of interim relief was concerned.[64] Since the power of the national courts to suspend administrative measures in these circumstances corresponded to the jurisdiction of the Court of Justice to grant interim measures in actions for annulment, the national courts could only be permitted to grant such relief "on the conditions which must be satisfied for the Court of Justice to allow an application to it for interim measures."[65] The Court concluded that[66]:

"suspension of enforcement of a national measure adopted in implementation of a Community regulation may be granted by a national court only:

(i) if that court entertains serious doubts as to the validity of the Community measure and, should the question of the validity of the contested measure not already have been brought before the Court, itself refers that question to the Court;

(ii) if there is urgency and a threat of serious and irreparable damage to the applicant;

(iii) and if the national court takes due account of the Community's interests."

In *Krüger v. Hauptzollamt Hamburg-Jonas*,[67] the Commission argued that, when considering the Community interest, a national court which was minded to grant interim relief must give the Community institution which adopted the contested act an opportunity to express its views. The Court was not prepared to impose such a requirement on the national courts, simply observing that it was for the national court to decide on the most appropriate way of obtaining all the information it needed to assess the Community interest.

In *Atlanta Fruchthandelsgesellschaft v. Federal Republic of Germany*,[68] the Court offered further clarification of the conditions laid down in *Zuckerfabrik*. Where a

---

[61] See *Foto-Frost, supra.*
[62] See Chap. 10.
[63] Para. 18.
[64] Para. 26.
[65] Para. 27.
[66] Para. 33. See also Case C–17/98 *Emesa Sugar (Free Zone) NV v. Aruba,* judgment of February 8, 2000.
[67] Case C–334/95 [1997] E.C.R. I–4517; [1998] 1 C.M.L.R. 520.
[68] Case C–465/93 [1995] E.C.R. I–3761. *cf.* Case C–68/95 *T Port v. Bundesanstalt für Landwirtschaft und Ernährung* [1996] E.C.R. I–6065; [1997] 1 C.M.L.R. 1.

national court had serious doubts about the validity of a Community act and made a reference to the Court of Justice on that issue, it had to explain why it thought the act in question might be invalid. If the Court had already dismissed as unfounded an action for the annulment of the contested act, or previously held in proceedings under Article 234 that no doubt had been cast on the act's validity, the national court was not entitled to grant interim measures, and any such measures which had already been granted would have to be revoked, unless the new grounds of illegality put forward differed from those which had been rejected by the Court. The same applied, *mutatis mutandis*, where a challenge to the validity of an act had been dismissed by the Court of First Instance in a ruling which had become final and binding.

DECIDING THE POINT WITHOUT A REFERENCE

The mere existence of the right to ask the Court of Justice for a preliminary ruling does not deprive inferior national courts and tribunals of the right to reach their own conclusions on questions of the interpretation of Community law it may be necessary for them to decide.[69] Indeed, where the point raised is reasonably clear or it is possible to deduce from the case-law of the Court of Justice a clear general approach to a particular question, it may be preferable for such a national court to decide the point itself.[70] However, where it seems likely that a reference will be made at some stage in the proceedings, it is sensible for that step to be taken sooner rather than later, for an early reference saves time and costs.[71] Moreover, as Bingham J acknowledged in *Commissioners of Customs and Excise v. Samex ApS*,[72] the Court of Justice is far better equipped than national courts to resolve issues of Community law:

"Sitting as a judge in a national court, asked to decide questions of Community law, I am very conscious of the advantages enjoyed by the Court of Justice. It has a panoramic view of the Community and its institutions, a detailed knowledge of the Treaties and of much subordinate legislation made under them, and an intimate familiarity with the functioning of the Community market which no national judge denied the collective experience of the Court of Justice could hope to achieve. Where questions of administrative intention and practice arise the Court of Justice can receive submissions from the Community institutions, as also where relations between the Community and non-Member States are in issue. Where the interests of Member States are affected they can intervene to make their views known . . . Where comparison falls to be made between Community texts in different languages, all texts being equally authentic, the multi-national Court of Justice is equipped to carry out the task in a way which no national judge, whatever his linguistic skills, could rival. The interpretation of Community instruments involves very

---

[69] See Slade L.J. in *J Rothschild Holdings plc v. Commissioners of Inland Revenue* [1989] 2 C.M.L.R. 621 at 645, CA.

[70] See *Pickstone v. Freemans plc* [1987] 2 C.M.L.R. 572 at 591, CA *per* Purchas L.J.

[71] This was acknowledged by Kerr L.J. in *R. v. Pharmaceutical Society of Great Britain, ex p. The Association of Pharmaceutical Importers* [1987] 3 C.M.L.R. 951 at 972.

[72] [1983] 3 C.M.L.R. 194 at 210–211, HC.

often not the process familiar to common lawyers of laboriously extracting the meaning from words used but the more creative process of applying flesh to a spare and loosely constructed skeleton. The choice between alternative submissions may turn not on purely legal considerations, but on a broader view of what the orderly development of the Community requires. These are matters which the Court of Justice is very much better placed to assess and determine than a national court".

MANDATORY REFERENCES

Where a question of Community law, within the meaning of the first paragraph of Article 234, is raised in a case pending before a court or tribunal of a Member State against whose decisions there is no judicial remedy under national law, that court or tribunal is obliged, under the third paragraph of the article, to refer the question to the Court of Justice. That paragraph is not confined to courts whose decisions are always final, such as the House of Lords. It covers any court, even if not the highest court, against whose decision there is no judicial remedy in the instant case.[73]

In the English legal system, a potential difficulty arises at the level of an appeal from the Court of Appeal to the House of Lords. Such an appeal can only be brought with the leave of the Court of Appeal or the House of Lords. If either of them grants leave, there is no problem, but what is the position if the Court of Appeal refuses to grant leave? In *Chiron Corporation v. Murex Diagnostics*,[74] the Court of Appeal held that, where it refuses leave to appeal and the House of Lords is presented with an application for leave to appeal, then before refusing leave it should consider whether it needed to resolve an issue of Community law. If it decided that it did and that the answer to the question was unclear, it could either make a reference at that stage or grant leave and consider at a later stage whether to make a reference. The Court of Appeal thought that the possibility of making an application to the House of Lords for leave to appeal constituted a "judicial remedy" within the meaning of the third paragraph of Article 234. The Court of Appeal could not therefore be considered a court of last resort itself for the purposes of that provision. Nor did it have jurisdiction to make a reference if the House of Lords refused leave, since by that stage it was *functus officio*.

Although the third paragraph of Article 234 states that a reference is obligatory "where any such question is raised", this does not mean that the obligation arises wherever a party contends that a question of Community law needs to be decided. In *CILFIT v. Ministry of Health*,[75] the Court of Justice held that final courts are in the same position as other national courts in deciding whether they need to resolve a question of Community law before giving judgment. A final court is not therefore obliged to ask for a preliminary ruling

---

[73] Case 6/64 *Costa v. ENEL* [1964] E.C.R. 585; [1964] C.M.L.R. 425. See also Case 107/76 *Hoffmann-La Roche v. Centrafarm* [1977] E.C.R. 957; [1977] 2 C.M.L.R. 334 and Joined Cases 35–36/82 *Morson and Jhanjan v. Netherlands* [1982] E.C.R. 3723; [1983] 2 C.M.L.R. 221. *cf.* Case C–337/95 *Parfums Christian Dior v. Evora* [1997] E.C.R. I–6013; [1998] 1 C.M.L.R. 737.

[74] [1995] All E.R. (E.C.) 88, [1995] F.S.R. 309. See Demetriou (1995) 20 E.L.Rev. 628. *cf. R. v. Secretary of State, ex p. Duddridge* [1996] 2 C.M.L.R. 361.

[75] Case 283/81 [1982] E.C.R. 3415; [1983] 1 C.M.L.R. 472.

where the answer to the question raised cannot affect the outcome of the case. Even where a question of Community law is relevant, however, the Court of Justice went on to hold in that case that a final court is under no obligation to refer if: (a) "previous decisions of the Court have already dealt with the point of law in question"[76] (although in that event the national court remains free to refer if it wishes the Court of Justice to reconsider its earlier ruling)[77]; or (b) the correct application of Community law is so obvious as to leave no scope for any reasonable doubt as to the manner in which the question raised is to be resolved. This is known as "acte clair". However, before the national court reaches this conclusion, it must be convinced that the matter would be equally obvious to the courts of the other Member States and to the Court of Justice. In that regard, it must take account of the characteristic features of Community law and the particular difficulties to which its interpretation gives rise.[78]

The criteria set out by the Court of Justice in the *CILFIT* case are also relevant where courts which are not covered by the third paragraph of Article 234 are called upon to interpret Community law. This is because, where those criteria are satisfied, such courts may properly decline, in the exercise of their discretion, to make a reference. However, it follows from the decision of the Court of Justice in the *Foto-Frost* case, discussed above, where it was held that no national court is competent to declare a Community act invalid, that the considerations laid down in *CILFIT* apply only where the question of Community law raised before the national court is one of interpretation. Accordingly, where there is a real possibility in proceedings before a national court, whether or not it is of last resort, that a Community measure is invalid, the matter must be referred to the Court of Justice.

Some commentators take the view that the *CILFIT* criteria are too strict. The authors of a report entitled *The Role and Future of the European Court of Justice*, published by the British Institute of International and Comparative Law in 1996, observed[79]: "Compliance with these requirements for *acte clair* is virtually impossible. In practice this test is completely unworkable." In one English case, the criteria were even described as "intimidating".[80] That view perhaps gives insufficient weight to the Court's acceptance that the Treaty imposed no obligation to refer where the Court had already dealt in previous decisions with the point at issue. In a development of previous case-law,[81] the Court made it clear that this was so "irrespective of the nature of the proceedings which led to those decisions, even though the questions at issue are not strictly identical".[82] In circumstances such as these, there is no need to invoke the *acte clair* doctrine. The obligation laid down by the third paragraph of Article 234 helps to maintain

---

[76] Para. 14.

[77] This applies *a fortiori* "when the question raised is substantially the same as a question which has already been the subject of a preliminary ruling in the same national proceedings": *Dior v. Evora*, *supra*, para. 29.

[78] See further Chap. 9.

[79] Page 76.

[80] Hodgson J. in *R. v. Secretary of State for Transport, ex p. Factortame* [1989] 2 C.M.L.R. 353 at 379.

[81] See Joined Cases 28–30/62 *Da Costa v. Nederlandse Belastingadministratie* [1963] E.C.R. 31; [1963] C.M.L.R. 224.

[82] Para. 14.

uniformity by providing a safeguard against the incorrect application of Community law by national courts. It is submitted that any relaxation of the obligation beyond that enshrined in the *CILFIT* test could only be contemplated if there were some protection against abuse by national courts or misunderstanding on their part of the circumstances in which a reference ought to be made. Such protection might be afforded by extending to the entire E.C. Treaty Article 68(3), which was introduced at Amsterdam and is currently confined to Title IV. It provides: "The Council, the Commission or a Member State may request the Court of Justice to give a ruling on a question of interpretation of this Title or of acts of the institutions of the Community based on this Title. The ruling given by the Court of Justice in response to such a request shall not apply to judgments of courts or tribunals of the Member States which have become res judicata."[83] Article 68 is considered in more detail below.

It was held in *Hoffmann-La Roche v. Centrafarm* that a national court is not required to refer to the Court a question of interpretation which is raised in interlocutory proceedings for an interim order, provided that each of the parties is entitled to institute proceedings (or to require proceedings to be instituted) on the substance of the case, and that during such proceedings the question provisionally decided at the interlocutory stage may be re-examined and referred to the Court of Justice.[84] This is so even where the criteria laid down in the *CILFIT* case are not satisfied and no judicial remedy is available against the interlocutory decision itself.

THE EFFECTS OF THE RULING OF THE COURT OF JUSTICE

A ruling on interpretation given by the Court of Justice under Article 234 "is binding on the national court as to the interpretation of the Community provisions and acts in question".[85] The referring court is under a duty to give full effect to the provisions of Community law as interpreted by the Court of Justice. This may require it to refuse to apply conflicting provisions of national law, even if adopted subsequently.[86] Moreover, other courts are entitled to treat the ruling of the Court of Justice as authoritative and as thereby obviating the need for the same points to be referred to the Court of Justice again.[87]

---

[83] In other words, such rulings do not affect cases which have already been decided but apply only for the future. *cf.* the protocols on the interpretation of the Brussels and Rome Conventions, mentioned above.

[84] Case 107/76 *Hoffmann-La Roche v. Centrafarm* [1977] E.C.R. 957; [1977] 2 C.M.L.R. 334. The *Hoffmann-La Roche* judgment also refers to questions of validity, but must be considered superseded on that point by *Foto-Frost*: see Advocate General Lenz in *Zuckerfabrik Süderditmarschen*, [1991] E.C.R. I–415 at 483–489.

[85] Case 52/76 *Benedetti v. Munari* [1977] E.C.R. 163, para. 26. This obligation is reinforced for courts in the United Kingdom by s.3(1) of the European Communities Act 1972. For a detailed discussion of the effects of rulings given by the Court of Justice under Art. 177, see Toth, "The authority of judgments of the European Court of Justice: binding force and legal effects" (1984) 4 Y.E.L. 1.

[86] See, *e.g.* Case 106/77 *Amministrazione delle Finanze dello Stato v. Simmenthal* [1978] E.C.R. 629; [1978] 3 C.M.L.R. 263; Case 170/88 *Ford España v. Estado Español* [1989] E.C.R. 2305.

[87] See Joined Cases 28–30/62 *da Costa en Schaake* [1963] E.C.R. 31; [1963] C.M.L.R. 224; Case 283/81 *CILFIT v. Ministry of Health* [1982] E.C.R. 3415; [1983] 1 C.M.L.R. 472.

A ruling by the Court under Article 234 declaring an act of one of the institutions void is also binding on the referring court.[88] Moreover, such a ruling "is sufficient reason for any other national court to regard that act as void . . ."[89] The consequences for the institutions of a preliminary ruling declaring a Community act void were considered by the CFI in *H & R Ecroyd Holdings Ltd v. Commission*.[90] The CFI observed[91]:

". . . when the Court of Justice rules in proceedings under Article 234 E.C. . . . that an act adopted by the Community legislature is invalid, its decision has the legal effect of requiring the competent Community institutions to adopt the measures necessary to remedy that illegality . . . In those circumstances, they are to take the measures that are required in order to comply with the judgment containing the ruling in the same way as they are, under Article 233 [ex 176] E.C., in the case of a judgment annulling a measure or declaring that the failure of a Community institution to act is unlawful . . . [W]hen a Community measure is held to be invalid by a preliminary ruling, the obligation laid down by Article 233 E.C. applies by analogy."

This may mean that the institution concerned must not only adopt the legislative or administrative measures necessary to give effect to the Court's judgment but also consider whether the unlawful measure caused those affected by it damage which has to be made good. On the other hand, where the Court in proceedings under Article 234 rejects a challenge to the validity of a measure, it will rule that consideration of the questions raised has disclosed no factor of such a kind as to affect the validity of the contested act.[92] The national court is not of course entitled to declare the act invalid on the grounds rejected by the Court, but the effect of the ruling is to leave open the possibility of a subsequent challenge on other grounds.

It is important to emphasise, however, that national courts remain free to bring matters of Community law before the Court of Justice under Article 234 whenever they feel it necessary to do so: they are not precluded from doing so by the fact that the point in question seems already to have been settled by the Court.[93] Indeed, a national court may if it wishes make more than one reference in the same proceedings. This was acknowledged in *Pretore di Salò v. Persons Unknown*,[94] where the Court said that a second reference "may be justified when the national court encounters difficulties in understanding or applying the judgment, when it refers a fresh question of law to the Court, or again when it submits new considerations which might lead the Court to give a different answer

---

[88] Case 66/80 *International Chemical Corporation v. Amministrazione delle Finanze dello Stato* [1981] E.C.R. 1191; [1983] 2 C.M.L.R. 593.

[89] *ibid.*, para. 13.

[90] Case T–220/97, judgment of May 20, 1999.

[91] Para. 49.

[92] See, *e.g.* Case C–323/88 *Sermes* [1990] E.C.R. I–3027; [1992] 2 C.M.L.R. 632.

[93] See *International Chemical Corporation*, para. 14; *CILFIT*, para. 15.

[94] Case 14/86 [1987] E.C.R. 2545; [1989] 1 C.M.L.R. 71.

to a question submitted earlier". In practice more than one reference in the same case happens only exceptionally.[95]

A ruling on interpretation, or a declaration that a measure is invalid, will normally relate back to the facts of the case. A preliminary ruling on the interpretation of a rule of Community law "clarifies and defines where necessary the meaning and scope of that rule as it must be or ought to have been understood and applied from the time of its coming into force. It follows that the rule as thus interpreted may, and must, be applied by the [national] courts even to legal relationships arising and established before the judgment ruling on the request for interpretation . . ."[96] Very exceptionally the Court of Justice may, in the interests of legal certainty, be led to limit the effects on past transactions of preliminary rulings on questions of both interpretation and validity.[97] Any such limitation will always be laid down in the ruling itself.[98]

PRELIMINARY RULINGS AFTER THE TREATY OF AMSTERDAM

As mentioned above, the Treaty of Amsterdam inserted into the E.C. Treaty a new Title IV entitled "Visas, asylum, immigration and other policies related to free movement of persons". Although that title is located in the E.C. Treaty, the extent to which it is subject to oversight by the Court of Justice is limited by Article 68 E.C.[99] It should be noted that, by virtue of special protocols annexed to the TEU and the E.C. Treaty, Title IV does not apply to the United Kingdom, Ireland or Denmark unless they decide to "opt in". In the absence of such a decision, cases decided by the Courts of those countries will not be affected by Title IV and they will therefore have no need to avail themselves of Article 68.

Article 68 requires national courts of last resort to seek preliminary rulings on the interpretation of Title IV and the validity and interpretation of acts of the institutions based on it. Moreover, as already explained, the Council, the Commission and the Member States are entitled to ask the Court for a ruling on how the provisions of the Title and acts adopted under it should be interpreted.

---

[95] For examples, see Case 117/77 *Pierik*,[1978] E.C.R. 825; [1978] 3 C.M.L.R. 343 and Case 182/78 [1979] E.C.R. 1977; [1980] 2 C.M.L.R. 88; Case 104/79 *Foglia v. Novello*, [1980] E.C.R. 745; [1981] 1 C.M.L.R. 45 and Case 244/80 [1981] E.C.R. 3045; [1982] 1 C.M.L.R. 585; Case 283/81 *CILFIT* [1982] E.C.R. 3415; [1983] 1 C.M.L.R. 472 and Case 77/83 [1984] E.C.R. 1257; Joined Cases C–6/90 and 9/90 *Francovich* [1991] E.C.R. I–5357, [1993] 2 C.M.L.R. 66 and Case C–479/93 [1995] E.C.R. I–3843; Case C–213/89 *Factortame* [1990] E.C.R. I–2433, [1990] 3 C.M.L.R. 375; Case C–221/89 [1991] E.C.R. I–3905 [1991] 3 C.M.L.R. 589 and Joined Cases C–46 and 48/93 [1996] E.C.R. I–1029; [1996] 1 C.M.L.R. 889; [1996] All E.R. (E.C.) 301.

[96] Case 61/79 *Amministrazione delle Finanze dello Stato v. Denkavit Italiana* [1980] E.C.R. 1205, para. 16; [1981] 3 C.M.L.R. 694.

[97] See, *e.g.* Case 43/75 *Defrenne v. SABENA* [1976] E.C.R. 455; [1976] 2 C.M.L.R. 98; Case 41/84 *Pinna v. Caisse d'Allocations Familiales de la Savoie* [1986] E.C.R. 1; [1988] 1 C.M.L.R. 350; Case 24/86 *Blaizot v. University of Liège* [1988] E.C.R. 379; [1989] 1 C.M.L.R. 57; Case C–262/88 *Barber* [1990] E.C.R. I–1889; [1990] 2 C.M.L.R. 513. See further Chap. 4.

[98] See *Denkavit Italiana, supra.*

[99] But see Art. 67(2) E.C., which requires the Council to consider "adapting the provisions relating to the powers of the Court of Justice" five years after the entry into force of the Treaty of Amsterdam.

However, lower national courts have no power to ask the Court for preliminary rulings in cases covered by the new Title.

The Member States were justifiably concerned about the possibility that the Court would be inundated by references in the large number of immigration and asylum cases which come before national courts and Article 68, where applicable, will undoubtedly have the effect of reducing the number of references. However, the procedure will inevitably be less effective in ensuring uniform application and the effective protection of individual rights. Many of those involved in immigration and asylum cases will not have the resources to pursue them as far as courts of last resort.[1] By contrast, some cases will be taken to such courts purely in order to secure a reference to the Court of Justice.[2]

Under Article 68(2), the Court does not have jurisdiction to rule on Council measures connected with the removal of controls on the movement of persons across internal borders "relating to the maintenance of law and order and the safeguarding of internal security."[3] This provision seems to be applicable only to cases covered by Article 68(1). The Court's other powers, notably those it possesses under Article 230 E.C., are accordingly unaffected by it. As a result, Council measures taken under Title IV remain fully susceptible to review in annulment proceedings.

It is submitted that the *Foto-Frost* principle does not apply to cases covered by Title IV. It would be intolerable if parties to national proceedings could not challenge the validity of acts adopted under Title IV without taking their case to a court of last resort. Even then, the Court of Justice could not be asked to rule on the validity of a measure falling within the scope of Article 68(2). The conclusion must therefore be that national courts are free to declare invalid acts adopted under Title IV (including those covered by Article 68(2)).

Alongside Title IV of the E.C. Treaty go the revised provisions of Title VI of the TEU, which is renamed "Provisions on police and judicial co-operation in criminal matters". Article 35(1) TEU gives the Court of Justice a preliminary rulings jurisdiction in relation to a range of measures adopted under Title VI, although only at the request of national courts situated in Member States which have declared that they accept the involvement of the Court.[4] There is no provision for such declarations to be revoked once they have been made and they may not be limited to specific instruments.[5]

Under Article 35(3), Member States may either confine the right to refer to courts and tribunals of last resort or extend it to any court or tribunal.[6] In neither

---

[1] See JUSTICE, "The jurisdiction of the European Court of Justice in respect of asylum and immigration matters" (May 1997), p. 7.

[2] A point made by the Community Courts in their discussion paper entitled "The Future of the Judicial System of the European Union", p. 24.

[3] *cf.* Art. 2(1), third indent, of the Protocol integrating the Schengen Acquis into the framework of the E.U., which is annexed to the TEU and the E.C. Treaty.

[4] See Art. 35(2). *cf.* the Protocol on the interpretation by the Court of Justice of the Convention on the establishment of a European Police Office ("Europol"), [1996] O.J. C299/1.

[5] Under Art. 35(4), any Member State, whether or not it has made a declaration accepting the Court's jurisdiction, has the right to submit observations in cases referred under Art. 35(1). There is no equivalent provision in Art. 68 E.C., but the same is presumably true under that provision also because it does no more than modify Art. 234 E.C. to the extent specified: see Art. 68(1).

[6] For the position on the entry into force of the Treaty of Amsterdam, see [1999] O.J. C120/24.

case does the Treaty impose an obligation to refer on courts of last resort, but a declaration (No. 10) adopted at Amsterdam notes that Member States may impose such an obligation as a matter of national law. It will therefore be for national law to determine the scope of any such obligation. It follows that the decision of the Court in the *CILFIT* case will apply only to the extent (if any) laid down by national law.[7]

Even where a reference is made from a Member State which has accepted the jurisdiction of the Court, Article 35(5) prevents the Court from reviewing the validity or proportionality of national police operations or national measures concerned with "the maintenance of law and order and the safeguarding of internal security". Like its counterpart in Title IV of the E.C. Treaty, Article 68(2), Article 35(5) TEU poses a potential threat to the uniform application of the law. However, it will be for the Court to define the precise scope of these provisions.

As with Article 68 E.C., the question arises whether the *Foto-Frost* principle applies in the context of Article 35 TEU. The answer once again seems to be that it does not. It is obvious that it could not apply in a Member State which had not accepted the jurisdiction of the Court. For the reasons given above, the *Foto-Frost* principle could not apply either in cases falling within the scope of Article 35(5) or in Member States which have restricted to national courts of last resort the right to refer questions to the Court of Justice. Even in a case brought in a Member State which has extended to all its courts the right to refer, the *Foto-Frost* principle would not be capable of ensuring the uniform application of the law.

---

[7] By contrast, it is submitted that the *CILFIT* decision does apply to Art. 68(1) E.C., since that provision is a specific application of Art. 234.

PART V: THE INTERNAL MARKET AND ECONOMIC AND MONETARY UNION

CHAPTER 12

CUSTOMS DUTIES AND DISCRIMINATORY INTERNAL TAXATION

ESTABLISHMENT OF A CUSTOMS UNION

Whereas a free trade area comprises a group of customs territories in which duties are eliminated on trade in goods originating in such territories, a customs union represents a further step in economic integration, since a common tariff is adopted in trade relations with the outside world.

Article 23(1) (ex 9(1)) E.C. provides that:

"The Community shall be based upon a customs union which shall cover all trade in goods and which shall involve the prohibition between Member States of customs duties on imports and exports and of all charges having equivalent effect, and the adoption of a common customs tariff in their relations with third countries."[1]

The "goods" referred to include all products which have a monetary value and may be the object of commercial transactions. In *Commission v. Italy* the Court rejected an argument adduced by the Italian Government that the free movement provisions of the Treaty could have no application to a charge levied on the export of goods of historic or artistic interest. The products covered by the Italian law in issue, said the Court, regardless of any other qualities which might distinguish them from other commercial goods, resembled such goods in that they had a monetary value and could constitute the object of commercial transactions—indeed, the Italian law recognised as much by fixing the charge in relation to the value of the object in question.[2] Coins may constitute "goods" if they do not constitute a means of payment in the Member States,[3] and substances or objects which comprise waste, whether recyclable or not, and whether they have a commercial value or not, also comprise "goods" for these purposes.[4]

The abolition as between the Member States of customs duties and charges having equivalent effect constitutes a fundamental principle of the common market applicable to all products and goods with the result that any exception, which in any event must be strictly interpreted, must be clearly laid down.[5]

---

[1] Former Art. 9 was held to be directly applicable in conjunction with other Treaty Articles; see, *e.g.*, Cases 2 and 3/69 *Sociaal Fonds, etc. v. Brachfeld and Chougol Diamond Co.* [1969] E.C.R. 211; [1969] C.M.L.R. 335, (former Arts 9 and 12); Case 33/70 *SACE v. Italian Ministry of Finance* [1970] E.C.R. 1213; [1971] C.M.L.R. 123, (former Arts 9 and 13(2)); Case 18/71 *Eunomia v. Italian Ministry of Education* [1971] E.C.R. 811 (former Arts 9 and 16).

[2] Case 7/68 [1968] E.C.R. 423; [1969] C.M.L.R. 1.

[3] Case 7/78 *R. v. Johnson* [1978] E.C.R. 2247; [1979] 1 C.M.L.R. 47.

[4] Case C–2/90 *Commission v. Belgium* [1992] E.C.R. I–4431; [1993] 1 C.M.L.R. 365.

[5] Joined Cases 90 and 91/63 *Commission v. Luxembourg and Belgium* [1964] E.C.R. 625; Joi 80–81/77 *Commissionaires Réunis and Another v. Receveur des Douanes* [1978] E.C.R. 92' Case C–272/95 *Bundesantalt für Landwirtschaft und Ernährung v. Deutsches Milch-Ko* [1997] E.C.R. I–1905, para. 36.

The abolition of customs duties between the constituent territories of a free trade area is normally restricted to goods originating in such territories, because otherwise member countries of the area maintaining high tariffs against non-Member countries would find their markets open to imports from such countries via the territories of lower tariff member countries of the area (a phenomenon known as trade deflection). The problem is avoided if all members adopt the same tariffs in their trade with third countries. And this is indeed the solution adopted in a customs union, such as the European Community. Thus the E.C. Treaty makes provision in Article 26 (ex 28) E.C. for a Common Customs Tariff, and provides in Article 23(2) (ex 9(2)) that its free movement provisions—Articles 25 (ex 12) and Articles 28–31 (ex 30, 34, 36 and 37)—apply not only to goods originating in Member States, but also to products coming from third countries which are in free circulation in the Member States.

Article 24 (ex 10) E.C. thus provides that:

"Products coming from a third country shall be considered to be in free circulation in a Member State if the import formalities have been complied with and any customs duties or charges having equivalent effect which are payable have been levied in that Member State, and if they have not benefited from a total or partial drawback of such duties or charges."

The "drawback" referred to in Article 24 is possible in the case of inward processing, when goods are imported for the purposes of processing followed by re-export.[6] In *Houben* the Court said of the latter Article:

"That article draws no distinction between goods imported from a non-member country in circulation in the Member State where the import formalities were completed and the various duties paid and those which, after due completion of the import formalities and payment of the various duties in one Member State, are subsequently imported into another Member State."[7]

The Court has also made it clear, as regards the free movement of goods within the Community, that products which are in free circulation are "definitively and wholly assimilated to products originating in Member States".[8]

CUSTOMS DUTIES ON IMPORTS AND EXPORTS ARE PROHIBITED

Relevant provisions of the E.C. Treaty prior to the amendments which came into force on May 1, 1999 were as follows. Article 12 prohibited new customs duties on imports and exports and new charges having equivalent effect, and prohibited any increases in such duties or charges. Article 13 stated that customs duties on imports were to be abolished by the end of the transitional period

---

[6] See Reg. 2913/92, [1992] O.J. L302/1, Arts 114 *et seq.*
[7] Case C–83/89 *Openbaar Ministerie and the Minister for Finance v. Vincent Houben.* [1990] E.C.R. I–1161, para. 10; [1991] 2 C.M.L.R. 321.
[8] Case C–130/92 *OTO SpA v. Minstero delle Finanze* [1994] E.C.R. I–3281, para. 16; [1995] 1 ̄.M.L.R. 84.

(December 31, 1969), as were charges having equivalent effect. Article 16 provided that Member States should abolish between themselves customs duties on exports and charges having equivalent effect by the end of the first stage (December 31, 1961). It is to be noted that in certain respects the drafting of the foregoing provisions represented the situation at the time the original Treaty came into force, and to this extent no longer served a useful purpose. The provisions referred to were replaced by the current Article 25 E.C., which states:

"Customs duties on imports and exports and charges having equivalent effect shall be prohibited between Member States. This prohibition shall also apply to customs duties of a fiscal nature."

Customs duties on imports and exports are thus prohibited, and it is proposed to deal first with these. This prohibition is directly applicable. The Court's case-law indicates that former Articles 12,[9] 13 and 16 were directly applicable,[10] and it follows that the equivalent prohibitions now contained in Article 25 are equally directly applicable. The Court of Justice emphasised the "essential nature" and the "importance" of the prohibition of customs duties and similar charges, contained in former Articles 9 and 12 (now Articles 23 and 25), in *Commission v. Luxembourg and Belgium*, basing its view on the respective provisions of these Articles in the scheme of the Treaty, Article 9 being placed at the beginning of the title relating to "Free Movement of Goods", and Article 12 at the beginning of the section dealing with the "Elimination of Customs Duties".[11] This reasoning loses none of its force as regards the current text and context of Articles 23 and 25. The Court in *Luxembourg and Belgium* went on to say that any exception to such an essential rule would require to be clearly stated, and would receive a narrow construction.[12] Thus, to the extent that a Council Regulation concerning the common organisation of the market in wine authorised Member States to impose charges on intra-Community trade, it was held to be invalid by the Court of Justice in *Commissionaires Réunis and Another v. Receveur des Douanes*.[13] The Court's rigorous approach is reflected in a consistent case-law. In *Sociaal Fonds voor de Diamantarbeiders v. S.A. Ch. Brachfeld & Sons and Chougol Diamond Co.* the Court was faced with a reference from an Antwerp magistrate, concerning a levy imposed under Belgian law on

---

[9] Applicable equally to agricultural goods, see Cases 90–91/63 *Commission v. Luxembourg and Belgium* [1964] E.C.R. 625; [1965] C.M.L.R. 58. As of the end of the transitional period, trade in agricultural products in sectors lacking a common organisation of the market became subject to the free movement of goods provisions of the Treaty, see, *e.g.* Case 48/74 *Charmasson v. Minister for Economic Affairs and Finance* [1974] E.C.R. 1383; [1975] 2 C.M.L.R. 208.

[10] Case 26/62 *Van Gend en Loos v. Nederlandse Administratie der Belastingen* [1963] E.C.R. 1; [1963] C.M.L.R. 105 (former Art. 12); Joined Cases 2–3/69 *Sociaal Fonds etc v. Brachfeld and Chougol Diamond Co.* [1969] E.C.R. 211; [1969] C.M.L.R. 335 (former Art. 12); Case C–17/91 *Georges Lornoy en Zonen NV and others v. Belgian State* [1992] E.C.R. I–6523 (former Arts 12 and 13); Case 18/71 *Eunomia di Porro & Co. v. Italian Ministry of Education* [1971] E.C.R. 811; [1972] C.M.L.R. 4 (former Art. 16 directly applicable in conjunction with former Art. 9); Case C–114/91 *Criminal proceedings against Gérard Jerôme Claeys.* [1992] E.C.R. I–6559 (former Arts 12 and 13).

[11] Cases 2 and 3/62 [1962] E.C.R. 425 at 431; [1963] C.M.L.R. 199.

[12] Former Art. 115 E.C. (now Art. 134) permitted unilateral derogation from the free movement provisions of the Treaty, in cases of urgency, during the transitional period, but subsequently, it has been necessary to secure a Commission authorisation.

[13] Joined Cases 80–81/77 [1978] E.C.R. 927.

imported diamonds. The Belgian Government argued that the levy could not be regarded as infringing (former) Articles 9 and 12, since it was devoid of protectionist purpose; in the first place, Belgium did not even produce diamonds, and in the second place, the purpose of the levy was to provide social security benefits for workers in the diamond industry. The following statement of the Court emphasised that the achievement of a single market between Member States requires more than the elimination of protection:

> "In prohibiting the imposition of customs duties, the Treaty does not distinguish between goods according to whether or not they enter into competition with the products of the importing country. Thus, the purpose of the abolition of customs barriers is not merely to eliminate their protective nature, as the Treaty sought on the contrary to give general scope and effect to the rule on elimination of customs duties and charges having equivalent effect in order to ensure the free movement of goods. It follows from the system as a whole and from the general and absolute nature of the prohibition of any customs duty applicable to goods moving between Member States that customs duties are prohibited independently of any consideration of the purpose for which they were introduced and the destination of the revenue obtained therefrom. The justification for this prohibition is based on the fact that any pecuniary charge—however small—imposed on goods by reason of the fact that they cross a frontier constitutes an obstacle to the movement of such goods."[14]

The fact that the achievement of a single market between Member States is dependent on more than the suppression of measures calculated to protect domestic industry is well illustrated by the prohibition of customs duties on exports as well as imports. As Advocate General Gand pointed out in *Commission v. Italy*:

> "What distinguishes customs duties on exports is not that they protect the national industry but that they increase the price of goods and thus tend to hinder their exportation and, without prohibiting trade in goods, to make it more difficult."[15]

CHARGES HAVING EQUIVALENT EFFECT ON IMPORTS AND EXPORTS ARE PROHIBITED

As noted above, Article 25 E.C. prohibits charges having an effect equivalent to customs duties on imports and exports, and is directly applicable. The abolition of charges having an effect equivalent to customs duties on imports has been described by the Court of Justice as the "logical and necessary complement" to the elimination of customs duties proper.[16] Similar logic applies to

---

[14] Joined Cases 2–3/69 [1969] E.C.R. 211; [1969] C.M.L.R. 335.
[15] Case 7/68 [1968] E.C.R. 423 at 434; [1969] C.M.L.R. 1.
[16] Joined Cases 52 and 55/65 *Germany v. Commission* [1966] E.C.R. 159; [1966] C.M.L.R. 22 (former Art. 13(2)); and see, *e.g.* Joined Cases 2–3/69 *Chougol Diamond* [1969] E.C.R. 211; [1969] C.M.L.R. 335; Case 24/68 *Commission v. Italy* [1969] E.C.R. 193.

charges having an equivalent effect on exports. The prohibition of charges having equivalent effect, like the prohibition of customs duties, constitutes a basic Treaty norm, and any exceptions must be clearly and unambiguously provided for.[17]

The concept of charges having equivalent effect must be interpreted in the light of the objects and purposes of the Treaty, in particular the provisions dealing with the free movement of goods,[18] and the Court described such charges on imports or exports in the following terms in *Commission v. Italy*:

"Consequently, any pecuniary charge, however small and whatever its designation and mode of application, which is imposed unilaterally on domestic or foreign goods by reason of the fact that they cross a frontier, and which is not a customs duty in the strict sense, constitutes a charge having equivalent effect within the meaning of Articles 9, 12, 13 and 16 of the Treaty, even if it is not imposed for the benefit of the State, is not discriminatory or protective in effect and if the product on which the charge is imposed is not in competition with any domestic product."[19]

The prohibition of such charges also applies if a Member State engages a private contractor to carry out customs procedures in connection with the transit of goods between Member States. Thus a transit charge paid under a private contract between such a contractor and a road haulier in respect of the above services will amount to a charge having equivalent effect prohibited by Community law.[20]

In *Legros* the Court held that the foregoing description of charges having equivalent effect covered dock dues (comprising *ad valorem* duties on goods) imposed on the import of goods from into the Réunion region of France from another Member State, even though the dock dues in question also applied to goods entering Réunion from Metropolitan France. The Court stated:

"A charge levied at a regional frontier by reason of the introduction of products into a region of a Member State constitutes an obstacle to the free movement of goods which is at least as serious as a charge levied at the national frontier by reason of the introduction of the products into the whole territory of a Member State."[21]

The same system of dock dues as was in issue in *Legros* was the subject of a preliminary ruling in *Lancry*, but this time the question posed was whether the imposition of the dues on goods from the same Member State, France, also amounted to charges having equivalent effect prohibited by the E.C. Treaty. The

---

[17] Joined Cases 52 and 55/65, n.16.
[18] See, *e.g.* Joined Cases 2–3/69 *Chougol Diamond* [1969] E.C.R. 211; [1969] C.M.L.R. 335.
[19] Case 24/68 [1969] E.C.R. 193 at 201; Case 158/82 *Commission v. Denmark* [1983] E.C.R. 3573, para. 18; [1984] 3 C.M.L.R. 658; Case 340/87 *Commission v. Italy* [1989] E.C.R. 1483; Case C–45/94 *Cámara de Comercio, Industria y Navegación, Ceuta v. Municipality of Ceuta* [1995] E.C.R. I–4385, para. 28.
[20] Case C–16/94 *Édouard Dubois et Fils SA and Général Cargo Services SA v. Garoner Exploitation SA* [1995] E.C.R. I–2421; [1995] 2 C.M.L.R. 771; [1995] All E.R. (E.C.) 821.
[21] Case 163/90 *Administration des Douanes et Droits Indirects v. Léopold Legros and others* [1992] E.C.R. I—4625, para. 16; see also Joined Cases C–485–486/93 *Maria Simitzi v. Dimos Kos* [1995] E.C.R. I–2655, para. 17.

Court, perhaps surprisingly, rejected the argument of the Council of the European Union to the effect that the Treaty's prohibition on charges having equivalent effect to customs duties did not apply to charges internal to a Member State, as follows:

> "The unity of the Community customs territory is undermined by the establishment of a regional customs frontier just the same, whether the products on which a charge is levied by reason of the fact that they cross a frontier are domestic products or come from other Member States.
>
> Furthermore, the obstacle to the free movement of goods created by the imposition on domestic products of a charge levied by reason of their crossing that frontier is no less serious than that created by the collection of a charge of the same kind on products from another Member State.
>
> Since the very principle of a customs union covers all trade in goods, as provided for by Article 9 of the Treaty, it requires the free movement of goods generally, as opposed to inter-State trade alone, to be ensured within the union. Although Article 9 *et seq.* makes express reference only to trade between Member States, that is because it was assumed that there were no charges exhibiting the features of a customs duty in existence within the Member States. Since the absence of such charges is an essential precondition for the attainment of a customs union covering all trade in goods, it follows that they are likewise prohibited by Article 9 *et seq.*"[22]

Similarly, in *Simitzi* the Court held that charges imposed on goods despatched from one region of a Member State to another region of that same Member State amounted to charges having equivalent effect to customs duties on exports.[23]

However, a charge may escape prohibition as a charge having equivalent effect "if the charge in question is the consideration for a service actually rendered to the importer and is of an amount commensurate with that service . . ."[24] The Court has usually rejected the "consideration for services" argument in the case of unilateral measures, either because the services in question were rendered in the general interest (for example health inspections), rather than in the interests of traders themselves, or, if the services did benefit traders, because they benefited them as a class in a way which was impossible to quantify in a particular case (for example, compilation of statistical data).[25] The position is

---

[22] Joined Cases C–363/93, etc. *René Lancry SA v. Direction Générale des Souanes etc.* [1994] E.C.R. I–3957, esp. paras 27–29. See also Joined Cases C–485–486/93 *Maria Simitzi v. Dimos Kos* [1995] E.C.R. I–2655, para. 27.

[23] Joined Cases C–485–486/93 *Maria Simitzi v. Dimos Kos.* [1995] E.C.R. I–2655, paras 26 and 27.

[24] Case 132/82 *Commission v. Belgium* [1983] E.C.R. 1649; [1983] 3 C.M.L.R. 600. An *ad valorem* will not meet the requirement that the charge be commensurate with the service, Case 170/88 *Ford Espana* [1989] E.C.R. 2305.

[25] Joined Cases 52 and 55/65 *Germany v. Commission* [1966] E.C.R. 159; [1966] C.M.L.R. 22 (charge by national intervention agency for import licences); Case 24/68 *Commission v. Italy* [1969] E.C.R. 193 at 201 (fee to defray the costs of compiling statistical data); Case 39/73 *Rewe-Zentralfinanz v. Landwirtschaftskammer* [1973] E.C.R. 1039; [1997] 1 C.M.L.R. 630, Case 87/75 *Bresciani v. Italian Finance Administration* [1976] E.C.R. 129, Case 35/76 *Simmenthal v. Italian Minister of Finance* [1976] E.C.R. 1871; [1977] 2 C.M.L.R. 1, Case 251/78 *Firma Denkavit Futtermittel Gmbh v. Minister for Food* [1979] E.C.R. 3369; [1980] 3 C.M.L.R. 513 (fees to offset the costs of compulsory and sanitary inspections).

rather different if charges are imposed to cover the cost of procedures (such as inspections) provided for by Community measures. Such charges will not amount to charges having equivalent effect prohibited by Community law;[26] at any rate where the Community measures reduce obstacles to intra-Community trade which would otherwise result from divergent national measures, where the fee charged does not exceed the actual cost of the operations involved,[27] and where there is a direct link between the amount of the fee and the cost of the actual inspection in respect of which the fee was charged.[28] Measures taken by a Member State under an international treaty to which all Member States are parties, and which encourage the free movement of goods, may be assimilated to Community measures, and fees covering costs may be charged accordingly.[29]

A case neatly illustrating the difficulties of establishing whether or not national charges may be regarded as charges having equivalent effect was *Commission v. Belgium*.[30] The development of Community transit procedures enabled importers to convey their goods from the frontier to public warehouses situated in the interior of the country without paying duties and taxes. In these warehouses, importers could have customs clearance operations carried out, and they also had the opportunity of placing their goods in temporary storage, pending their consignment to a particular customs procedure. The Belgian Government levied storage charges on goods deposited in such public warehouses in the interior of the Community. The Court held that these charges were charges having equivalent effect when they were imposed solely in connection with the completion of customs formalities, but that they were justified in cases where the trader elected to place his goods in storage. In the latter case, the Court accepted that the storage represented a service rendered to traders. A decision to deposit the goods could only be taken at the request of the trader concerned, and ensured storage of the goods without payment of duties. The Belgian Government argued that also in the former case—where the goods were cleared through customs without storage—a service was rendered to the importer. It was always open to the latter to avoid payment by choosing to have his goods cleared through customs at the frontier, where such a procedure was free of charge. By using a public warehouse, the importer could have the goods declared through customs near the places for which his products were bound. The Court acknowledged that the use of a public warehouse in the interior of the country offered certain advantages, but noted that such advantages were linked solely with the completion of customs formalities which, whatever the place, was always compulsory. Furthermore, the advantages in question resulted from the scheme of Community transit, not in the interest of individual traders, but in order to encourage the free movement of goods and facilitate transport in the Community. "There can therefore,"

---

[26] Case 46/76 *Bauhuis v. Netherlands* [1977] E.C.R. 5; Case 18/87 *Commission v. Germany* [1988] E.C.R. 5427; Case C–130/93 *Lamaire v. NDALTP* [1994] E.C.R. I–3215, para. 19.

[27] Case C–209/89 *Commission of the European Communities v. Italian Republic.* [1991] E.C.R. I–1575, para. 10; [1993] 1 C.M.L.R. 155.

[28] *ibid.*

[29] Case 89/76 *Commission v. Netherlands* [1977] E.C.R. 1355; [1978] 3 C.M.L.R. 630.

[30] Case 132/82 [1983] E.C.R. 1649; [1983] 3 C.M.L.R. 600.

concluded the Court, "be no question of levying charges for customs clearance facilities accorded in the interests of the Common Market."

It was noted above that Member States could charge for procedures for which provision is made by Community law,[31] while in the foregoing case it is said that no charges could be made for customs clearance facilities provided for by Community law. What is the dividing line between the Community procedures for which a charge might be made, and those customs clearance facilities which cannot be charged for? The case-law is less than completely clear in this respect. In *Commission v. Italy* in 1991 the Court, citing one of its previous rulings authorising charges for procedures provided for by Community law,[32] referred to "the compatibility with the Treaty rules of fees charged in connection with the completion of customs formalities, on condition that their amount does not exceed the actual cost of the operations in respect of which they are charged".[33] In *Dubois* in 1995 the Court, referring to *Commission v. Belgium*, stated that:

"Articles 9 and 12 of the Treaty require Member States to bear the cost of the controls and formalities carried out in connection with the movement of goods across frontiers."[34]

The explanation for this apparent contradiction is that a distinction is to be drawn between, on the one hand, the customs formalities applicable to all goods in transit pursuant to Community law, for which no charge may be made, and, on the other hand, any additional requirements applicable in the case of certain goods, such as inspections of goods, or any additional facilities provided for by the authorities of a Member State. It is to be noted that the case referred to by the Court in *Commission v. Italy* (1991), as authority for the above proposition concerning charges for "the completion of customs formalities" was a case concerning phytosanitary inspections,[35] while the action by the Commission against Italy in the case itself involved a system of charges payable by undertakings where customs formalities were completed outside the customs area or outside normal office hours. The Commission did not allege that the charges amounted in themselves to charges having equivalent effect to customs duties; only that they amounted to such charges because they were disproportionate to the service rendered in certain cases.[36]

As regards charges having equivalent effect on exports, the Court has held that an internal duty which falls more heavily on exports than on domestic sales amounts to a charge having equivalent effect to a customs duty.[37] Fees for inspections of plants charged only in respect of exported products, and not in respect of those intended for the home market, constitute charges which have an equivalent effect on exports, even if those inspections are applicable to all products, and are carried out to meet the requirements of international

---

[31] n.25 and text to which it relates.

[32] Case 89/76 *Commission v. Netherlands* [1977] E.C.R. 1355, at para. 16; [1978] 3 C.M.L.R. 630.

[33] Case C–209/89 [1991] E.C.R. 1991 at I–1575, para. 10; [1993] 1 C.M.L.R. 155.

[34] Case C–16/94 *Édouard Dubois et Fils SA and Général Cargo Services SA v. Garoner Exploitation SA* [1995] E.C.R. I–2421; [1995] 2 C.M.L.R. 721; [1995] All E.R. (E.C.) 821.

[35] Case 89/76 *Commission v. Netherlands* [1977] E.C.R. 1355; [1978] 3 C.M.L.R. 630.

[36] The action was successful in this respect.

[37] Joined Cases 36 and 71/80 *Irish Creamery Milk Suppliers Assn v. Govt. of Ireland* [1981] E.C.R. 735.

conventions affecting only exported products. The contrary would be true only if it were established that the products intended for the home market derived no benefit from the inspections.[38]

TRANSIT CHARGES PROHIBITED

The E.C. Treaty has been interpreted as prohibiting in the widest possible terms charges on goods originating in the E.C. or in free circulation, even when such charges are imposed on goods of one Member State introduced in another region of that same Member State.[39] But the Treaty does not expressly prohibit transit charges on third country goods which are not in free circulation in the Community. In *SIOT*[40] an Italian undertaking challenged before an Italian court charges imposed upon oil landed at Trieste for consignment via the transalpine oil pipe-line to Germany. The Italian court asked the Court of Justice whether such transit charges were compatible with Community law. The Court held that it was a necessary consequence of the Customs Union and the mutual interest of the Member States that there be recognised a general principle of freedom of transit of goods within the Community. The imposition of transit charges was incompatible with this principle, unless the charges in question represented the costs of transportation or of other services connected with transit, including general benefit derived form the use of harbour works or installations, for the navigability and maintenance of which public authorities were responsible. The Court's conclusion is unremarkable as regards goods originating in Member States or as regards third country goods in free circulation. But it is to be noted that the oil in question did not originate in a Member State, and it is not clear that it was in free circulation in a Member State.[41] While the Treaty states that the elimination of customs duties and quantitative restrictions applies to products originating in Member States and to products coming from third countries which are in free circulation in Member States, the *SIOT* case implies that the above-mentioned provisions apply by analogy to third country goods which are not in free circulation where such goods are in lawful transit in one Member State and destined for another. In the *Richardt* case[42] goods of third country origin in free circulation in France were mistakenly consigned via the community transit procedure applicable to third country goods not in free circulation (the external transit procedure) to Luxembourg for export to the Soviet Union. The Court of Justice confirmed the principle of freedom of transit without stating in so many words that the principle applied to goods in external community transit as well as to goods in free circulation. But the implication is that goods in external community transit or which would be so conveyed unless exempted from that procedure are subject to the application by analogy of the provisions of the

---

[38] Case C–111/89 *Hillegom* [1990] E.C.R. I–1735; [1990] 3 C.M.L.R. 119.
[39] See above, p. 292.
[40] Case 266/81 [1983] E.C.R. 731.
[41] The reference by the Trieste Port Authority to external Community transit suggests that the goods were not in free circulation, [1988] E.C.R. 731 at 752.
[42] Case C–367/89 [1991] E.C.R. I–4621; [1992] 1 C.M.L.R. 61.

Treaty prohibiting customs duties and charges having equivalent effect, and indeed quantitative restrictions and measures having equivalent effect.

DISCRIMINATORY INTERNAL TAXATION PROHIBITED

Article 90 (ex 95)

The first paragraph of Article 90 (ex 95) E.C. provides that no Member State shall impose, directly or indirectly, on the product of any other Member State any internal taxation of any kind in excess of that imposed directly or indirectly on similar domestic products. Paragraph 2 adds that Member States shall furthermore impose no taxation of such a kind as to afford indirect protection to other products. The first paragraph is concerned with imports having such a close competitive relationship with similar domestic products as to merit the same tax treatment as that applicable to those products. The second paragraph contemplates imports which are not in such a close competitive relationship with relevant domestic products as to merit the same tax treatment, but which are nevertheless sufficiently interchangeable from the point of view of consumers to merit tax treatment which is even-handed and free of any protective effect in favour of such domestic products. Although Article 90 (ex 95) refers to products "of other Member States", this has been held to include products from third countries which are in free circulation in Member States.[43] Furthermore, once a product has been imported from another Member State and placed on the market, it becomes a domestic product for the purposes of comparison of its tax position with an import from another Member State under Article 90 (ex 95).[44]

THE PURPOSE OF ARTICLE 90 (EX 95)

The Court has stated that the Article is calculated to close any loopholes which internal taxation might open in the prohibition on customs duties and charges having equivalent effect.[45] The purpose of the Article has been explained as follows in a consistent line of cases:

". . . Article 95 supplements the provisions on the abolition of customs duties and charges having equivalent effect. Its aim is to ensure free movement of goods between the Member States in normal conditions of competition by the elimination of all forms of protection which may result from the application of internal taxation that discriminates against products from other Member States. Thus Article 95 must guarantee the complete neutrality of internal taxation as regards competition between domestic products and imported products."[46]

---

[43] Case 193/85 *Co-Frutta* [1987] E.C.R. 2085 at para. 25.

[44] Case C–47/88 *Commission v. Denmark* [1990] E.C.R. I–4509, para. 17.

[45] Joined Cases 2–3/62 *Commission v. Belgium and Luxembourg* [1962] E.C.R. 425 at 431; [1963] C.M.L.R. 199.

[46] Case 252/86 *Bergandi* [1988] E.C.R. 1343, at para. 24; [1989] 2 C.M.L.R. 933; Case C–45/94 *Cámara de Comercio, Industria y Navegación, Ceuta v. Municipality of Ceuta* [1995] E.C.R. I–4385, para. 29.

The rule prohibiting discriminatory internal taxation on imported goods constitutes an essential basic principle of the common market,[47] and is directly applicable.[48]

Member States free under Article 90(1) (ex 95(1)) to choose system of internal taxation, providing its advantages are extended to imported products

Article 90, first paragraph, prohibits discrimination against similar imported products, with respect to the rate of taxation, basis of assessment,[49] or detailed rules.[50] By way of example, in *Commission v. Greece*,[51] the detailed rules for calculating the taxable value of imported used cars for the purposes of application of a consumer tax were held to be discriminatory and contrary to Article 90 (ex 95), while in *Commission v. France* disproportionately higher penalties for VAT offences regarding import transactions than for such offences regarding domestic transactions were held to contravene Article 90 (ex 95).[52]

Article 90 leaves each Member State free to establish the system of taxation which it considers the most suitable in relation to each product, provided that the system is treated as a point of reference for determining whether the tax applied to a similar product of another Member State complies with the requirements of the first paragraph of that Article.[53] It matters not that tax concessions for domestic products rest, not directly upon national law, but on administrative instructions to the authorities.[54]

A system of taxation can be considered compatible with Article 90 (ex 95) E.C. only if it is proved to be so structured as to exclude any possibility of imported products being taxed more heavily than domestic products, so that it cannot in any circumstances have discriminatory effect.[55] It follows that all manner of tax concessions or advantages available in respect of domestic products must be extended to similar imported products.

---

[47] Case 57/65 *Lütticke* [1966] E.C.R. 205 at 214; [1971] C.M.L.R. 674.

[48] Case 57/65 *Lütticke* [1966] E.C.R. 205; [1971] C.M.L.R. 674; Case 28/67 *Molkerei-Zentrale v. Hauptzollamt Paderborn* [1968] E.C.R. 143; [1968] C.M.L.R. 187; Case 45/75 *Rewe-Zentrale etc v. Hauptzollamt Landau/Pfalz* [1976] E.C.R. 181; [1976] 2 C.M.L.R. 1; Case 74/76 *Iannelli & Volpi v. Paolo Meroni* [1977] E.C.R. 557; [1977] 2 C.M.L.R. 688; Case C–119/89 *Commission v. Kingdom of Spain* [1991] E.C.R. I–641, para. 5; [1993] 1 C.M.L.R. 41.

[49] Case 54/72 *FOR v. VKS* [1973] E.C.R. 193; Case 20/76 *Schottle & Sohne v. Finanzampt Feudenstadt* [1977] E.C.R. 247; [1977] 2 C.M.L.R. 98; Case 74/76 *Iannelli & Volpi v. Paolo Meroni* [1977] E.C.R. 557; [1977] 2 C.M.L.R. 688; Case C–68/96 *Grundig Italiana SpA v. Ministero delle Finanze* [1998] E.C.R. I–3775; [1999] 2 C.M.L.R. 62.

[50] Case 169/78 *Commission v. Italy* [1980] E.C.R. 385; [1981] 2 C.M.L.R. 673; Case 55/79 *Commission v. Ireland* [1980] E.C.R. 481; [1980] 1 C.M.L.R. 734.

[51] Case C–375/95 [1997] E.C.R. I–5981.

[52] Case C–276/91 [1993] E.C.R. I–4413.

[53] Case 127/75 *Bobie-Getrankervertrieb v. Hauptzollamt aachen-Nord* [1976] E.C.R. 1079.

[54] Case 17/81 *Pabst & Richarz* [1982] E.C.R. 1331; [1983] 3 C.M.L.R. 11.

[55] Case C–90/94 *Haahr Petroleum Ltd v. Åbenrå Havn and Others* [1997] E.C.R. I–4085, para. 34; Case C–375/95 *Commission v. Greece* [1997] E.C.R. I–5981, [1998] 1 C.M.L.R. 771, para. 29.

In the *Hansen* case[56] the question arose whether an importer of spirits into Germany was entitled to take advantage of tax relief available, *inter alia*, in respect of spirits made from fruit by small businesses and collective farms. The Court acknowledged that advantages of this kind could serve legitimate economic or social purposes, such as the use of certain raw materials, the continued production of particular spirits of high quality, or the continuance of certain classes of undertakings such as agricultural distilleries. However, Article 90 (ex 95) required that such preferential systems must be extended without discrimination to spirits coming from other Member States.[57]

The above principle was applied to the Republic of Italy when that country charged lower taxes on regenerated oil than on ordinary oil, on ecological grounds, while refusing to extend this advantage to imported regenerated oil. Italy argued that it was impossible to distinguish whether oil was of primary distillation, or regenerated. The Court of Justice refused to accept this argument as a justification. It was for importers to establish that their oil qualified for the relief in question, while the Italian authorities were to set standards of proof no higher than was necessary to prevent tax evasion. The Court of Justice observed that certificates from the authorities of exporting Member States could provide one means of identifying oil which had been regenerated.[58] Similarly, in *Commission v. Greece*, the Greek government claimed that extending to imported cars the reduced rate of special consumer tax payable in respect of domestic cars using "anti-pollution technology" would require a technical test to be carried out on each import, which was not practical. The Court held that such considerations could not justify tax discrimination against imports, and held the tax contrary to Article 90 (ex 95).[59] In *Outokumpu Oy* the Court considered a Finnish tax regime whereby domestic electricity was subject to a rate varying with the method of production and energy sources used while imported electricity was subject to a flat-rate tariff which in certain cases exceeded the lowest rate applicable to domestic electricity. The Court noted that while the characteristics of electricity may indeed make it extremely difficult to determine precisely the method of production of imported electricity and hence the energy sources used for that purpose, "the Finnish legislation at issue does not even give the importer the opportunity of demonstrating that the electricity imported by him has been produced by a particular method in order to qualify for the rate applicable to electricity of domestic origin produced by the same method."[60] The Court concluded that the tax was contrary to Article 90 (ex 95).

---

[56] Case 148/77 *H. Hansen v. Hauptzollampt Flensburg* [1978] E.C.R. 1787; [1979] 1 C.M.L.R. 604. See also Case 26/80 *Schneider-Import* [1980] E.C.R. 3469; [1981] 3 C.M.L.R. 562; Case 277/83 *Commission v. Italy* [1985] E.C.R. 2049, para. 17; [1987] 3 C.M.L.R. 324; Case 196/85 *Commission v. France* [1987] E.C.R. 1597; [1988] 2 C.M.L.R. 851.

[57] *ibid.*

[58] Case 21/79 *Commission v. Italy* [1980] E.C.R. 1; [1980] 2 C.M.L.R. 613. See also Case 140/79 *Chemial Farmaceutici v. DAF* [1981] E.C.R. 1; Case 46/80 *Vinal v. Orbat* [1981] E.C.R. 77.

[59] Case C–375/95 [1997] E.C.R. I–5981, esp. para. 47.

[60] Case C–213/96 [1998] E.C.R. I–1777, at para. 39 for passage quoted.

Criteria for differentiating between products for tax purposes must not discriminate against similar imported products or products in partial or potential competition with imported products

Even if a Member State applies to similar imported products the same tax regime which applies to domestic products, the effect in practice may be that imported products fall into higher taxed categories, while domestic goods fall into lower taxed categories. In *Commission v. Greece* the Court considered Greek rules imposing the general VAT rate of 16 per cent on certain spirits (including ouzo, brandy, liqueurs), while imposing a higher rate of 36 per cent on others (including whisky, gin, vodka and rum). Spirits in the former category were produced in Greece, while those in the latter category were not, or to no significant extent. The Court proceeded on the basis that all the spirits in the former category were either similar products within the meaning of the first paragraph of Article 90 (ex 95), or were partly or potentially in competition with products in the second category, and considered that the tax regime in question contravened Article 90 (ex 95). The Court made the following observation:

"The tax system established by the Greek legislation displays undeniably discriminatory or protective features. Although it does not establish any formal distinction according to the origin of the products, it is arranged in such a way that all the national production of spirits falls within the most favoured tax category. Those features of the system cannot be cancelled out by the fact that a fraction of imported spirits benefits from the most favourable rate . ... It therefore appears that the tax system benefits national production and puts imported spirits at a disadvantage."[61]

It does not however follow automatically from the fact that all products falling within the most highly taxed category are imported products that the tax regime is contrary to Article 90 (ex 95) E.C., and the Court has emphasised on a number of occasions that "a system of taxation cannot be regarded as discriminatory solely because only imported products, in particular those from other Member States, come within the most highly taxed category".[62] The explanation for the apparent contradiction between the latter proposition and the quotation set out above from *Commission v. Greece* is that differentiating between products on objective grounds consistent with Community law may lead to imports rather than domestic products falling into the highest taxed categories simply because of the characteristics of the imports. As the Court stated in *Haahr Petroleum*:

". . . at its present stage of development Community law does not restrict the freedom of each Member State to lay down tax arrangements which differentiate between certain products, even products which are similar within the meaning of the first paragraph of Article 95 of the Treaty, on the basis of objective criteria, such as the nature of the raw materials used or the

---

[61] Case C–230/89 [1991] E.C.R. I–1909, at para. 10, [1993] 1 C.M.L.R. 869 for passage quoted.
[62] Case 140/79 *Chemial Farmaceutici v. DAF* [1981] E.C.R. 1, para. 18; Case C–132/88 *Commission v. Greece* [1990] E.C.R. I–1567, para. 18; [1991] 3 C.M.L.R. 1.

production processes employed. Such differentiation is compatible with Community law, however, only if it pursues objectives of economic policy which are themselves compatible with the requirements of the Treaty and its secondary legislation, and if the detailed rules are such as to avoid any form of discrimination, direct or indirect, in regard to imports from other Member States or any form of protection of competing domestic products."[63]

The Court has on a number of occasions considered progressive national taxes which at their higher level apply in practice exclusively to imports.

Humblot[64] arose from a challenge to a French special car tax payable by reference to "fiscal horsepower" or CV. Cars were subject in the first place to a tax which rose uniformly in proportion to increases in CV, and in the second place to a special tax levied at a single and considerably higher rate on cars rated at more than 16CV. No cars of more than 16CV were manufactured in France, all were imported. The Court emphasised that Member States were free to subject products such as cars to a system of tax which increases progressively in amount depending on an objective criterion, such as the power rating for tax purposes, which might be determined in various ways. Such a system of domestic taxation would only be compatible with Article 90 (ex 95) however if it were free of any discriminatory or protective effect. France denied any protective effect, arguing that there was no evidence that a consumer who might have been dissuaded from buying a vehicle of more than 16CV would purchase a car of French manufacture of 16CV or less. The Court of Justice rejected this argument, noting that cars on each side of the 16CV line were in competition with each other. The substantial additional increase in tax on cars of more than 16CV was liable to cancel out advantages which certain cars imported from other Member States might have in consumers' eyes over comparable cars of domestic manufacture. "In that respect," said the Court, "the special tax reduces the amount of competition to which cars of domestic manufacture are subject and hence is contrary to the principle of neutrality with which domestic taxation must comply."

It fell to the Court to consider the successor tax to the above in the *Feldain* case.[65] The successor tax was progressive, but not uniformly progressive in two respects. Firstly, it progressed less sharply at the level which applied to top of the range French cars. According to the Court, "It thus exhibits a discriminatory or protective effect . . . in favour of cars manufactured in France."[66] Secondly, it incorporated a factor in calculating the power rating which had the effect of placing in the higher tax bands only imported vehicles. The Court noted that the factor in question was not justified by considerations relating to fuel consumption which France has argued as the bases for the system. "It must therefore be held that that method of determining the power rating for tax purposes is not objective in character and favours cars manufactured in France."[67]

---

[63] Case C–90/94 *Haahr Petroleum Ltd v. Åbenrå Havn and Others* [1997] E.C.R. I–4085, [1998] 1 C.M.L.R. 771, para. 29, referring to a consistent case-law.
[64] Case 112/84 [1985] E.C.R. 1367; [1986] 2 C.M.L.R. 338.
[65] Case 433/85 [1987] E.C.R. 3521.
[66] *ibid.* at para. 14.
[67] *ibid.* at para. 16.

In *Commission v. Greece*[68] the Court considered another system of progressive taxation of cars, relating the tax payable to the cylinder capacity of the car. Greece argued that progression was justified by the fact that larger capacity cars were luxury products, and generated pollution. The progression was not uniform, increasing sharply at 1201 cc, and then at 1801 cc. Most cars produced in Greece were of 1300 cc; none were produced of more than 1600 cc capacity, and the tax rates which applied above that level applied exclusively to imports. The Court of Justice held that the system was compatible with Article 90 (ex 95) since a consumer deterred from buying a car of over 1800 cc would either buy one of 1600 to 1800 cc (all of which were of foreign manufacture), or one of below 1600 cc (which range included imports and cars of Greek manufacture). "Consequently," held the Court, "the Commission has not shown how the system of taxation at issue might have the effect of favouring the sale of cars of Greek manufacture."[69] This reasoning would be sustainable if the Court had found that cars of over 1800 cc were not in competition with cars below 1600 cc, though this is not self-evident, and the case referred to below, *Tarantik*, indicates that the reasoning is not so limited. In which case, in the words of the Court in *Humblot*, the tax in question "reduces the amount of competition to which cars of domestic manufacture are subject and hence is contrary to the principle of neutrality with which domestic taxation must comply".[70] To put the matter in a different way, the approach in *Commission v. Greece* appears to condone a higher tax rate being imposed on an imported car of over 1800 cc than on a domestically produced car below 1600 cc, because the competitive disadvantage of the 1800+ cc import may operate to the advantage of another import rather than a domestically produced car. Yet if the domestically produced car, and the 1800+ cc import, are "similar" within the meaning of Article 90(1), they should be subject to the same tax, and if they are not subject to the same tax, the tax discrimination in question cannot be justified on the ground that *other* imports are not subject to the same discrimination. In the *Greek Spirits* case[71] referred to above, it certainly does not appear that tax discrimination as between Greek brandy and Scotch and Irish whisky could be justified by an absence of discrimination against French and German brandy. As noted above, compliance with Article 90(1) requires a national tax regime to exclude any possibility of imported products being taxed more heavily than domestic products, so that it cannot in any circumstances have discriminatory effects.[72] The result in the case might be justified on the ground that, although the effect of the progressive tax was to indirectly discriminate against certain imports, this was objectively justified by the nature of the tax regime; but this was not the approach taken by the Court.

The French rules on fiscal horsepower, which were amended after the *Feldain* judgment, were considered by the Court in several further cases, including

---

[68] Case C–132/88 [1990] E.C.R. I–1567; [1991] 3 C.M.L.R. 1.
[69] *ibid.* at para. 20.
[70] Case 433/85 [1987] E.C.R. 3521, at para. 14.
[71] Note 59 and the main text to which it relates.
[72] n.55 and the text to which it relates.

Tarantik.[73] The fiscal horsepower arrangements referred to above in the context of the *Humblot* case by then included a 15-16 CV tax band, a 17-18 CV tax band, and a number of bands over 18 CV. The Court noted that, unlike the 15-16 CV band (which covered both imported and domestic cars), the tax bands above 18 CV covered exclusively imported vehicles. The Court also considered that certain vehicles in the 15-16 CV tax band could be considered similar to vehicles in the bands over 18 CV. The Court concluded *inter alia* that national rules such as those in issue would nevertheless be compatible with Article 90 (ex 95(1)) E.C. if consumers have a choice such that the increase in the progression co-efficient between the 15-16 CV band and the bands above 18 CV is not of a nature such as to favour the sale of vehicles of domestic manufacture. This reasoning is the same as that in *Commission v. Greece*,[74] and is open to criticism on the same ground.

While it is open to Member States to differentiate between like products on objective grounds consistent with the Treaty, they are not permitted to discriminate by conditioning tax concessions on requirements which can only be, or in fact only are, satisfied by national products.[75] Examples of such discrimination would be charging lower tax rates on those products which could be inspected on national territory at the manufacturing stage,[76] and charging lower rates on products without a designation of origin or provenance where no such protection was available for domestic products and the higher rate applied in practice only to imports.[77]

Article 90(1) (ex 95(1))—taxation in excess of that imposed "indirectly" on domestic products

It will be recalled that Article 90 first paragraph, prohibits internal taxation of any kind in excess of that imposed directly or indirectly on similar domestic products. In *Molkerei-Zentrale v. Hauptzollamt Paderborn*[78] the Court was asked for a definition of the "indirect" taxation in question. Advocate General Gand suggested that the charges in question must include all those imposed on raw materials and component goods and services. The Court agreed that the words "directly or indirectly" were to be construed broadly, and defined them as embracing all taxation which was actually and specifically imposed on the domestic product at earlier stages of the manufacturing and marketing process. This formulation might suggest that taxes on components, not being actually and specifically imposed on the product, might be excluded. This is not the case. As the Court's interpretation of the words "directly or indirectly" in Article 91 (ex

---

[73] Case C–421/97 *Yves Tarantik v. Direction des Services Fiscaux de Seine-et-Marne* [1999] E.C.R. I–3633; [1999] 2 C.M.L.R. 1083.

[74] Above, p. 301.

[75] Case C–90/94 *Haahr Petroleum Ltd v. Åbenrå Havn and Others* [1997] E.C.R. I–4085, [1998] 1 C.M.L.R. 771, at para. 30.

[76] Joined Cases 142–143/80 *Italian Finance Administration v. Essevi SpA* [1981] E.C.R. 1413; see also Case 277/83 *Commission v. Italy* [1983] E.C.R. 2049; [1987] 3 C.M.L.R. 324.

[77] Case 319/81 *Commission v. Italy* [1983] E.C.R. 601; [1984] 2 C.M.L.R. 517; see also Case 106/84 *Commission v. Denmark* [1986] E.C.R. 833; [1987] 2 C.M.L.R. 278.

[78] Case 28/67 [1968] E.C.R. 143; [1968] C.M.L.R. 187.

96) E.C. indicates,[79] "indirect" taxation indeed includes charges levied on raw materials and semi-finished products incorporated in the goods in question. Nevertheless, the Court entered a caveat in *Molkerei-Zentrale*: the effect of these charges diminished with the incidence of stages of production and distribution and tended rapidly to become negligible, and that fact ought to be taken into account by Member States when calculating the indirect charges applied to domestic products.

Although the taxation of undertakings manufacturing products will not in general be regarded as constituting taxation of the products themselves, the taxation of specific activities of an undertaking which has an "immediate effect" on the cost of the national imported product must by virtue of Article 90 be applied in a manner which is not discriminatory to imported products. Thus taxation imposed indirectly upon products within the meaning of Article 90 must be interpreted as including charges imposed on the international transport of goods by road according to the distance covered on the national territory and the weight of the goods in question.[80] Again, Article 90 applies to internal taxation which is imposed on the use of imported products were these products are intended for such use and have been imported solely for that purpose.[81]

Article 90 (ex 95) does not place imports in a privileged tax position

The object of Article 90 (ex 95) is to abolish direct or indirect discrimination against imported products, but not to place them in a privileged tax position.[82] Internal taxation may therefore be imposed on imported products, even in the absence of a domestically produced counterpart. In *Stier*,[83] the Court of Justice held that although Article 90 (ex 95) does not prohibit Member States from imposing taxation on imported products which lack a domestic counterpart, it would not be permissible to impose on such imports charges of such an amount that the free movement of goods would be impeded. In *Commission v. Denmark*[84] the Court held that such impediment to the free movement of goods would fall to be governed by Articles 28-30 E.C. (ex 30-36), rather than within the framework of Article 90 (ex 95) E.C.

Domestic products may not claim equality with imports

However, Article 90 (ex 95) does not prohibit the imposition on national products of internal taxation in excess of that on imported products.[85] It has been noted that Member States may differentiate for tax purposes between products, provided that discrimination against imports does not result. What if national law

---

[79] Case 45/64 *Commission v. Italy* [1965] E.C.R. 857; [1966] E.C.R. 97.
[80] Case 20/76 *Schottle & Sohne v. Finanzamt Freudenstadt* [1977] E.C.R. 247; [1977] 2 C.M.L.R. 98.
[81] Case 252/86 *Bergandi* [1988] E.C.R. 1343; [1989] 2 C.M.L.R. 933.
[82] Case 153/80 *Rumhaus Hansen* [1981] E.C.R. 1165; Case 253/83 *Kupferberg* [1985] E.C.R. 157.
[83] Case 31/67 [1968] E.C.R. 235; [1968] C.M.L.R. 187.
[84] Case C–47/88 [1990] E.C.R. I–4509.
[85] Case 86/78 *Grandes Distilleries Peureux v. Directeur des Services Fiscaux* [1979] E.C.R. 897; [1980] 3 C.M.L.R. 337.

imposes a higher rate of tax on product X than on competing product Y, where product X is largely, but not entirely, imported, and where the higher rate of tax contravenes Article 90 of the EEC Treaty? The position is that while importers of product X may claim the protection of Article 90, domestic producers may legitimately be taxed at the higher rate. In one example Danish revenue laws imposed a lower rate of tax on aquavit than on other spirits, which other spirits were mainly, but not entirely, imported. In proceedings instituted by the Commission under Article 226 (ex 169) E.C. the Court held that these rules were contrary to Article 90 (ex 95)[86] and in later proceedings the Court emphasised that only importers could rely on Article 90 (ex 95), and not domestic producers of those spirits subject to the "discriminatory" tax.[87]

Respective Scope of Article 90(1) and 90(2) (ex 95(1) and 95(2))

Whereas Article 90, first paragraph, prohibits internal taxation in excess of that imposed on similar domestic products, paragraph 2 adds that Member States shall furthermore impose no taxation of such a kind as to afford indirect protection to other products.

The respective scope of these two paragraphs is as follows. Under Article 90(1) it is necessary to consider as similar products those which have similar characteristics and which might meet the same needs from the point of view of consumers. The appropriate criterion is not the strictly identical nature of the products but their similar and comparable use.[88] The Court at one stage held that "similarity" within Article 90(1) (ex 95(1)) existed when the products were normally, for tax, tariff or statistical purposes, placed in the same classification.[89] In a later case the Court confirmed that classification under the same heading in the Common Customs Tariff was an important consideration in assessing similarity under Article 90 (ex 95).[90] But the Court has stressed that the fact that rum and whisky are given separate subdivisions under the CCT is not conclusive on the question of "similarity" under Article 90(1) (ex 95(1)),[91] and when asked by an Italian court whether it should apply the "tariff classification" test, or the broader economic approach referred to above, the Court reiterated the latter criterion, without adverting to the former.[92] Nevertheless, it would seem that CCT classification constitutes at least an indication one way or the other of "similarity" within the meaning of Article 90(1) (ex 95(1)).

---

[86] Case 171/78 *Commission v. Denmark* [1980] E.C.R. 447; [1981] 2 C.M.L.R. 688. And see Case 168/78 *Commission v. France* [1980] E.C.R. 347; [1981] 2 C.M.L.R. 631.

[87] Case 68/79 [1980] E.C.R. 501; [1981] 2 C.M.L.R. 714.

[88] Case 169/78 *Commission v. Italy* [1980] E.C.R. 385; [1981] 2 C.M.L.R. 673.

[89] Case 27/67 *Fink-Frucht v. Hauptzollamt Munchen-Landsbergstrasse* [1968] E.C.R. 223; [1968] C.M.L.R. 187; Case 28/69 *Commission v. Italy* [1976] E.C.R. 187; [1971] C.M.L.R. 448.

[90] Case 45/75 *Rewe-Zentrale etc. v. Hauptzollamt Landau/Pfalz* [1976] E.C.R. 181; [1976] 2 C.M.L.R. 1.

[91] Case 169/78 *Commission v. Italy*, n.88, *supra*; Case 168/78 *Commission v. France* [1980] E.C.R. 347; [1981] 2 C.M.L.R. 631; Case 106/84 *Commission v. Denmark* [1986] E.C.R. 833; [1987] 2 C.M.L.R. 278.

[92] Case 216/81 *Cogis SpA v. Italian Finance Ministry* [1982] E.C.R. 2701; [1983] 1 C.M.L.R. 685.

In *John Walker*,[93] the Court held that in order to determine whether the products in question (fruit liqueur wines and whisky) were "similar" within the meaning of Article 90(1) (ex 95(1)), it was first necessary to consider objective characteristics of the respective products, such as their origin, method of manufacture, and their organoleptic qualities, in particular taste and alcohol content, and secondly necessary to consider whether both categories of beverages were capable of meeting the same needs from the point of view of consumers. Applying the first test, it was not sufficient that the same raw material, alcohol, was to be found in both products. For the products to be regarded as similar that raw material would have to be present in more or less equal proportions in both products. Since whisky contained twice the alcoholic content of fruit liqueur wines, the products could not be regarded as "similar" within the meaning of Article 90(1) (ex 95(1)).

Once similarity is established and Article 90(1) applies, the tax rates on the domestic product and the similar imported product must be the same. Article 90(2), by way of contrast, covers all forms of indirect tax protection in the case of products which, without being similar within the meaning of Article 90(1), are nevertheless in competition, even partial, indirect or potential, with products of the importing country. It is sufficient for the imported product to be in competition with the protected domestic product by reason of one or several economic uses to which it may be put, even though the condition of similarity for the purposes of Article 90(1) are not fulfilled.[94]

While Article 90(1) prohibits a higher tax on imported products than similar domestic products, Article 90(2), because of the difficulty of making a sufficiently precise comparison between the products in question, employs a more general criterion, *i.e.* the indirect protection afforded by a domestic tax system. It follows that a tax on an imported product need not be identical with the tax imposed on a domestic product with which it is in partial or indirect competition, as it would have to be if the products were in a sufficiently close competitive relationship to be regarded as similar within the meaning of Article 90(1). In *Commission v. Belgium*[95] it was alleged that VAT on wine (imported) at 25 per cent afforded indirect protection to beer (a domestic product) which was subject to VAT at 19 per cent. The Court rejected this argument, in view of the insignificant impact of the difference in tax on the difference in price between the two products. The Commission had not shown that the difference in question gave rise to any protective effect favouring beer intended for domestic consumption. It seems that what the Court was looking for was not complex market analysis, but a price difference which on a common sense basis would suggest an advantage for beer over wine. Protective effect need not, however, be shown statistically. It is sufficient for the purposes of Article 90(2) for it to be shown that a given system of taxation is likely, in view of its inherent characteristics, to bring about the protective effect referred to by the Treaty.[96] Furthermore, statistics showing

---

[93] Case 243/84 [1986] E.C.R. 875; [1987] 2 C.M.L.R. 278.

[94] Case 169/78 *Commission v. Italy*, n.88, *supra*.

[95] Case 356/85 [1987] E.C.R. 3299; [1988] 3 C.M.L.R. 277. And for the *"de minimis"* effect see Case 27/67 *Fink-Frucht* [1968] E.C.R. 223 at 233; [1968] C.M.L.R. 187.

[96] Case 170/78 *Commission v. United Kingdom* [1980] E.C.R. 417; [1980] 1 C.M.L.R. 716.

import penetration by products allegedly discriminated against cannot rebut the inference of protective effect to be drawn from the inherent characteristics of a national tax system.[97] However, statistics are admissible to show that a tax system which is apparently neutral in fact burdens imports to a greater extent than domestic products.[98]

To illustrate the inter-relation between Article 90(1) and (2) (ex 95(1) and (2)), reference may be made to the great range of spirit drinks: aquavit, geneva, grappa, whisky, etc. While these drinks have common generic factors (distillation, high alcohol level), there are different types of spirits, characterised by the raw material used, their flavour and processes of manufacture.[99] Furthermore, spirits may be consumed in different forms: neat, diluted or in mixtures.[1] They may also be consumed on different occasions, as aperitifs or digestifs, at meal times or on other occasions.[2] The Court of Justice has held that among spirit drinks there exists an indeterminate number which can be regarded as similar products within the meaning of Article 90(1) (ex 95(1)), and that where it is impossible to identify a sufficient degree of similarity between the products concerned for the purposes of Article 90(1) (ex 95(1)), there exist nevertheless characteristics common to all spirits which are sufficiently marked for it to be said that they are all at least partly, indirectly or potentially in competition for the purposes of Article 90(2) (ex 90(2)).[3] The result is that in a case involving alleged discrimination between domestic spirits and imported spirits, it may not be necessary to distinguish between the application of Article 90(1) and that of Article 90(2), since it cannot reasonably be denied that the products are in at least partial, indirect or potential competition.[4] It will however be necessary to distinguish between the application of Article 90(1) and (2) if the tax on the import in question is greater than that on the domestic product without being sufficient to be shown to afford indirect protection to domestic products. In such a case, Article 90(1) would be infringed if the products were similar, but Article 90(2) would not be infringed if they were not.

The fact that Article 90(2) embraces potential as well as actual competition significantly widens its ambit. In *Commission v. United Kingdom*,[5] the United Kingdom argued that wine and beer could not be considered to be competing beverages, since beer was a popular drink consumed generally in public houses, while wine was generally consumed on special occasions. The Court of Justice stressed that it was necessary to examine not only the present state of the market in the United Kingdom but also possible developments in the free movement of goods within the Community and the further potential for the substitution of

---

[97] Case 168/78 *Commission v. France* [1980] E.C.R. 347; [1981] 2 C.M.L.R. 631; Case 319/81 *Commission v. Italy* [1983] E.C.R. 601; [1983] 2 C.M.L.R. 517.

[98] Case 319/81 *Commission v. Italy* [1983] E.C.R. 601; [1983] 2 C.M.L.R. 517.

[99] Case 168/78 *Commission v. France*, n.97, *supra;* Case 169/78 *Commission v. Italy* n.88, *supra.* Case 171/78 *Commission v. Denmark* [1980] E.C.R. 447; [1981] 2 C.M.L.R. 688.

[1] Case 169/78 *Commission v. Italy*, n.88, *supra.*

[2] Case 168/78 *Commission v. France*, n.97, *supra.*

[3] Case 319/81 *Commission v. Italy*, n.98, *supra*, referring to Case 168/78 *Commission v. France*, n.97, *supra;* Case 169/78 *Commission v. Italy*, n.88, *supra;* Case 171/78 *Commission v. Denmark* [1980] E.C.R. 447.

[4] Case 168/78 *Commission v. France*, n.97, *supra.*

[5] Case 170/78 [1980] E.C.R. 417; [1983] E.C.R. 2265.

products for one another which might result from an intensification of trade. Consumer habits varied in time and space, and the tax policy of a Member State must not crystallise given consumer habits so as to consolidate an advantage acquired by the national industries concerned to respond to them. The Court held that to a certain extent at least wine and beer were capable of meeting identical needs and that there was a degree of substitution one for another.

And it must be admitted that in the case of some products found to have a competitive relationship it may be extremely difficult to establish the appropriate basis for comparison of the tax applied to the respective products, and the appropriate rate to be applied to ensure fiscal neutrality. A striking illustration is afforded by the Court's decision in *Commission v. United Kingdom*,[6] in which the Court attempted to establish the degree of indirect protection afforded beer by the excessive taxation of wine. On the basis of tax per unit of volume, wine bore an overall tax burden of 400 per cent that on beer On the basis of alcoholic strength per unit of volume, wine was subject to a tax burden 100 per cent. in excess of that on beer. On the basis of tax as a proportion of the net price of the beverage free of tax, the court admitted that the evidence was difficult to assess, suggesting additional tax burdens of between 58 per cent and 286 per cent! The Court concluded that whichever criterion for comparison was used, the tax system offered indirect protection to national production, and that there was no need to express a preference for one or other of the criteria discussed! Though Article 90(2) (ex 90(2)) was long ago held to be directly effective,[7] in such a case one might well sympathise with an importer challenging a national tax claim who seeks to quantify the amount by which his national tax demand offends Article 90(2)!

Only true fiscal charges subject to Article 90 (ex 95)

It must be emphasised that while Article 90 permits the imposition of internal taxation on imports to the extent that domestic goods bear similar charges, it cannot justify any charges imposed with a view to assimilating the prices of imports to those of domestic goods. The point arose in *Commission v. Luxembourg and Belgium*,[8] a proceeding under Article 226 (ex 169) E.C. in which the Commission alleged infringement of Articles 23 and 25 (ex 9 and 12) E.C. in respect of charges levied on the issue of import licences for gingerbread. The defendants argued that the charges compensated for the effect of measures of price support for domestically produced rye, and were accordingly justified under Article 90 (ex 95). The purpose of the disputed charge, said the Court, was not to equalise charges which would otherwise unevenly burden domestic and imported products, but to equalise the very prices of such products.[9] A similar point arose in *Hauptzollamt Flensburg v. Hermann C. Andresen & Co. KG*.[10] A charge was imposed on spirits imported into Germany, being a charge also applicable to domestic spirits, and calculated to

---

[6] Case 170/78, n.5, *supra*.
[7] Case 27/67 *Fink-Frucht*, n.89. *supra*.
[8] Joined Cases 2–3/62 [1965] E.C.R. 425.
[9] See also Case 45/75 *Rewe-Zentrale* [1976] E.C.R. 181; [1976] 2 C.M.L.R. 1.
[10] Case 4/81 [1981] E.C.R. 2935; [1983] 1 C.M.L.R. 642.

defray (in the case of domestic spirits) the administrative and operating costs of the Federal Spirits Monopoly. The Court held that a charge such as this was not a true fiscal charge, and that Article 90 (ex 95) only permitted the imposition on imports of such elements of the price of domestic spirits which the monopoly was required by law to remit to the State Treasury.

PROHIBITION OF CUSTOMS DUTIES AND CHARGES HAVING EQUIVALENT EFFECT, AND PROHIBITION OF DISCRIMINATORY INTERNAL TAXATION, MUTUALLY EXCLUSIVE

The prohibitions of Articles 25 on the one hand, and Article 90 on the other, have often been contrasted by the Court. Article 25 applies to all charges exacted at the time of or by reason of importation which are imposed specifically on an imported product to the exclusion of the similar domestic product,[11] and it has also been held that pecuniary charges intended to finance the activities of an agency governed by public law can constitute charges having equivalent effect.[12] Article 90 applies to financial charges levied within a general system of internal taxation applying systematically to domestic and imported goods.[13] The application of these respective prohibitions has been held to be mutually exclusive, not only because one and the same charge could not have been both removed during the transitional period (as had originally been provided under Articles 13 and 14 of the EEC Treaty for customs duties and charges having equivalent effect), and by no later than the beginning of the second stage (as had originally provided for discriminatory internal taxation under Article 95 of the EEC Treaty),[14] but also because the requirement for customs duties and charges having equivalent effect is that they be abolished, while the requirement for discriminatory internal taxation is the elimination of any form of discrimination between domestic products and products originating in other Member States.[15] The Court has explicitly rejected the argument that an equalisation tax on an imported product which exceeds the charges applied to similar domestic products takes on the character of a "charge having equivalent effect" as to the difference.[16] It is thus

---

[11] Case 77/72 *Capolongo v. Azienda Agricola Maya* [1973] E.C.R. 611; [1983] 2 C.M.L.R. 381; Joined Cases C–149–150/91 *Sanders Adour SNC and Guyomarc'h Orthez Nutrition Animale SA v. Directeur des Services Fiscaux des Pyrénées-Atlantiques* [1992] E.C.R. I–3889, para. 15.

[12] Joined Cases C–149–150/91 *Sanders Adour SNC and Guyomarc'h Orthez Nutrition Animale SA v. Directeur des Services Fiscaux des Pyrénées-Atlantiques* [1992] E.C.R. I–3889, para. 15; Case C–114/91 *Criminal proceedings against Gérard Jerôme Claeys* [1992] E.C.R. I–6559, para. 13; Case C–144/91 *Gilbert Demoor en Zonen NV and others v. Belgian State* [1992] E.C.R. I–6613, para. 15; Case C–266/91 *Celulose Beira Industrial SA v. Fazenda Pública* [1993] E.C.R. I–4337, para. 10.

[13] Case 77/72 *Capolongo v. Azienda Agricola Maya* [1973] E.C.R. 611; [1974] 1 C.M.L.R. 230; Case C–347/95 *Fazenda Pública v. União das Cooperativas Abastecedoras de Leite de Lisboa, UCRL (UCAL)* [1997] E.C.R. I–4911.

[14] Case 10/65 *Deutschmann v. Federal Republic of Germany* [1965] E.C.R. 469; [1965] C.M.L.R. 259. And see Case 57/65 *Lutticke v. Hauptzollamt Saarlouis* [1966] E.C.R. 205; [1971] C.M.L.R. 674; Case 27/74 *Demag v. Finanzamt Duisburg-Sud* [1974] E.C.R. 1037.

[15] Case 94/74 *IGAV v. ENCC* [1975] E.C.R. 699; [1976] 2 C.M.L.R. 37.

[16] Case 25/67 *Milch- Fett- und Eierkontor v. Hauptzollamt Saarbrucken* [1968] E.C.R. 207; [1968] C.M.L.R. 187; Case 32/80 *Officier van Justitie v. Kortmann* [1981] E.C.R. 251; [1982] 3 C.M.L.R. 46.

established that "provisions relating to charges having equivalent effect and those relating to discriminatory internal taxation cannot be applied together, so that under the system of the Treaty the same imposition cannot belong to both categories at the same time".[17] Since the respective fields of application of the Treaty's prohibition on obstacles to the free movement of goods are to be distinguished, obstacles which are of a fiscal nature or have equivalent effect and are covered by Articles 25 or 90 E.C. cannot fall within the prohibition of Article 28, on quantitative restrictions and measures having equivalent effect.[18] Though an excessive tax impeding the free movement of goods which falls outside the scope of Article 25 because it lacks a domestically produced counterpart will fall to be governed by Articles 28–30 E.C.

A charge which is imposed both on imported products and on domestic products but in practice applies almost exclusively to imported products because domestic production is extremely small does not amount to a charge having equivalent effect if it is part of a general system of internal dues applied systematically to categories of products in accordance with objective criteria irrespective of the origin of the products. It therefore constitutes internal taxation within the meaning of Article 90.[19] Indeed, a charge comprises internal taxation even where there are no comparable domestic products at all, where the charge in question applies to whole classes of domestic or foreign products which are all in the same position irrespective of origin.[20] However, the Court has held that such a limited number of products as "groundnuts, groundnut products and Brazil nuts" cannot fall within the concept of such whole classes of products, a concept which implies a much larger number of products determined by general and objective criteria.[21]

But to fall within the scope of Article 90 a charge must be levied at the same marketing stage on both domestic goods and imports, and the chargeable event giving rise to the duty must be identical in each case,[22] and if there is an insufficiently close connection between the charges levied on domestic goods,

---

[17] Joined Cases C–78/90 etc. *Compagnie Commerciale de l'Ouest and others v. Receveur Principal des Douanes de La Pallice Port* [1992] E.C.R. I–1847, para, 22; [1994] 2 C.M.L.R. 425; Joined Cases C–149–150/91 *Sanders Adour SNC and Guyomarc'h Orthez Nutrition Animale SA v. Directeur des Services Fiscaux des Pyrenées-Atlantiques* [1992] E.C.R. I–3899, para. 14; Case C–114/91 *Criminal proceedings against Gérard Jerôme Claeys* [1992] E.C.R. I–6559, para. 12; Case C–144/91 *Gilbert Demoor en Zonen NV and others v. Belgian State* [1992] E.C.R. I–6613, para. 14; Case C–266/91 *Celulose Beira Industrial SA v. Fazenda Pública* [1993] E.C.R. I–4337, para. 9; Case C–347/95 *Fazenda Pública v. União das Cooperativas Abastecedoras de Leite de Lisboa, UCRL (UCAL)* [1997] E.C.R. I–4911, para. 17.

[18] Case 74/76 *Iannelli & Volpi v. Paolo Meroni* [1977] E.C.R. 557 at para. 9; [1977] 2 C.M.L.R. 688.

[19] Case 193/85 *Co-Frutta v. Amministrazione delle Finanze dello Stato* [1987] E.C.R. 2085, para. 14; Case C–343/90 *Manuel José Lourenço Dias v. Director da Alfândega do Porto* [1992] E.C.R. I–4673, para. 53.

[20] Joined Cases 2–3/69 *Chougol Diamond Co.* [1969] E.C.R. 211; [1969] C.M.L.R. 335.

[21] Case 27/67 *Fink-Frucht* n.89, *supra; Case 158/82 Commission v. Denmark* [1983] E.C.R. 3573; [1984] 3 C.M.L.R. 658.

[22] Case 132/78 *Denkavit Loire Sarl v. France* [1979] E.C.R. 1923; [1979] 3 C.M.L.R. 605; Joined Cases C–149–150/91 *Sanders Adour SNC and Guyomarc'h Orthez Nutrition Animale SA v. Directeur des Services Fiscaux des Pyrenées-Atlantiques* [1992] E.C.R. I–3889, para. 17. But VAT levied on imports does not amount to a charge having equivalent effect, Case 249/84 *Profant* [1986] E.C.R. 3237; [1986] 2 C.M.L.R. 378.

and those levied on imports, in that they are determined on the basis of different criteria, they will fall to be classified under Article 25, rather than Article 90.[23]

The Court added a qualification in *Wohrmann v. Hauptzollamt Bad Reichenhall*,[24] that *in the absence of any protective purpose*, an internal tax could not be regarded as a charge having equivalent effect to a customs duty. This seems at first sight surprising, since the Court has often emphasised that a charge may have an effect equivalent to a customs duty under Articles 12 and 13 (now Article 25) independently of either its purpose or the destination of its revenue.[25] The significance of protective purpose in this context is that a charge applicable equally to domestic and imported products—and therefore ostensibly "internal taxation" under Article 90—may nevertheless fall to be classified as a charge having equivalent effect, if the revenue from the charge is devoted exclusively to benefit domestic producers. In *Interzuccheri v. Ditta Rezzano e Cavassa*,[26] the Court considered a charge imposed on sales of sugar, whether home produced or imported, the proceeds of which were used for the exclusive benefit of national sugar refineries and sugar beet producers. The Court held that such a charge, on the face of it internal taxation, could only be considered a charge having equivalent effect if:

— it had the sole purpose of financing activities for the specific advantage of the taxed domestic product;
— the taxed product and the domestic product benefiting from it were the same;
— the charges imposed on the domestic product were made good in full.

Since the charge in issue in the national proceedings financed sugar beet producers, as well as sugar refiners, it would not seem to constitute a charge having equivalent effect, according to the Court's stringent criteria.

In the later case of *Commission v. Italy*,[27] the Commission challenged the same Italian charge in contentious proceedings, arguing that if the charge were entirely offset by reimbursements in the form of aid, it amounted to a charge having an equivalent effect to a customs duty, while if it were only partly offset, it infringed Article 90 (ex 95). Somewhat puzzlingly, the Court held that Italy had violated Article 90 (ex 95), and that internal taxation would be regarded as indirectly discriminatory within the meaning of that Article if its proceeds were used *exclusively* or principally to finance aids for the sole benefit of domestic products. Yet in the later case of *Officier van Justitie v. Kortmann*,[28] the Court confirmed the *Interzuccheri* proposition that an internal tax amounted to a charge having equivalent effect to a customs duty when in fact it was imposed solely on

---

[23] Case 132/80 *United Foods* [1981] E.C.R. 995; [1982] 1 C.M.L.R. 273.
[24] Case 7/67 [1967] E.C.R. 177; [1968] C.M.L.R. 187.
[25] *e.g.* 63/74 *Cadskey* [1975] E.C.R. 281; [1975] 2 C.M.L.R. 246; Joined Cases 2–3/69 *Chougol Diamond Co.* n.20, *supra.*
[26] Case 105/76 [1977] E.C.R. 1029; Case 77/72 *Capolongo* [1973] E.C.R. 611; [1974] 1 C.M.L.R. 230; Case 94/74 *IGAV* [1975] E.C.R. 699; [1976] 2 C.M.L.R. 37; Case 77/76 *Fratelli Cucchi v. Avez* [1977] E.C.R. 987; Case 222/78 *ICAP v. Walter Beneventi* [1979] E.C.R. 1163; [1979] 3 C.M.L.R. 475.
[27] Case 73/79 [1980] E.C.R. 1533; [1982] 1 C.M.L.R. 1.
[28] Case 32/80 [1981] E.C.R. 251.

imported products to the exclusion of domestic products. The explanation for the apparent inconsistency seems to be that *Commission v. Italy*[29] concerned a charge on one product (imported sugar) which was used to benefit sugar beet as well as sugar. Indeed, this was why it is clear from the Court's ruling in *Interzuccheri*[30] that the charge in question could not be regarded as a charge having equivalent effect. Thus the ruling in *Commission v. Italy* that an equal charge imposed on both imported and domestic products may amount to discriminatory internal taxation if used *exclusively* or principally to finance aids for the sole benefit of domestic products (which appears to be categorising as discriminatory internal taxation that which is a charge having equivalent effect to a customs duty) would seem to be confined to cases where the domestic products benefited are not identical to the imported products subject to the charge. The proposition is of course unexceptionable insofar as it refers to the proceeds of a charge used principally (or indeed at all) to benefit domestic products alone. Where the products are identical, and the *Interzuccheri*[31] criteria are satisfied, the ostensible internal tax is to be categorised as a charge having equivalent effect to a customs duty. It will be noted that these problems only arise if a Member State has resort to ear-marked taxes, as Italy pointed out to the Court during the proceedings in *Commission v. Italy*.[32]

The *Interzuccheri* formulation has been endorsed in a consistent subsequent case-law.[33] The Court explained the rationale underlying its case-law, and the manner in which an assessment is to be made of any advantages for domestic products which offset the burden of charges imposed upon such products, in *Celulose Beira Industrial SA (Celbi)*:

"The *ratio decidendi* of the above case-law on the intended use of the revenue from a charge applied without distinction as well as the offsetting of any burden from that charge rests on the finding that, in economic terms, the advantages financed by the revenue from such a charge constitute, for domestic products, the consideration for the amounts paid, the burden of which is thereby offset in full or in part. For imported products, on the other hand, which are excluded from those advantages, the charge represents a net additional financial burden.

In those circumstances, the criterion of whether the burden is offset, in order to be usefully and correctly applied, presupposes a check, during a reference period, on the financial equivalence of the total amounts levied on domestic products in connection with the charge and the advantages afforded exclusively to those products."[34]

---

[29] Case 73/79 [1980] E.C.R. 1533; [1982] 1 C.M.L.R. 1.

[30] Case 105/76 [1977] E.C.R. 1029.

[31] Case 105/76, n.30, *supra*.

[32] Case 73/79, n.29, *supra*.

[33] See, *e.g.* Joined Cases C–78/90 etc., *Compagnie Commerciale de l'Ouest and others v. Receveur Principal des Douanes de La Pallice Port* [1992] E.C.R. I–1847, paras, 24 and 26; [1994] 2 C.M.L.R. 425; Case C–266/91 *Celulose Beira Industrial SA v. Fazenda Pública* [1993] E.C.R. I–4337, paras 12–14; ; Case C–347/95 *Fazenda Pública v. União das Cooperativas Abastecedoras de Leite de Lisboa, UCRL (UCAL)* [1997] E.C.R. I–4911, paras 20–24.

[34] Case C–266/91 *Celulose Beira Industrial SA v. Fazenda Pública* [1993] E.C.R. I–4337, paras 17 and 18.

As is so often the case when national courts, or the Court of Justice, for that matter, are called upon to apply Community law, this may involve complex issues of economic fact.

DISCRIMINATORY TAX TREATMENT OF EXPORTS

The system adopted for taxing products in intra-Community trade is based on the "destination principle", *i.e.* goods exported from a Member State receive a rebate of internal taxation paid, and are in turn subjected to internal taxation in the country of destination.[35] The purpose of Article 90 is to prevent this process being used to place a heavier burden on imports than on domestic goods, but the system is vulnerable to another, equally damaging abuse: the repayment to exporters of an amount exceeding the internal taxation in fact paid, which would amount to an export subsidy for domestic production. It is to counteract this possibility that Article 91 provides that where products are exported to the territory of any Member State, any repayment of internal taxation shall not exceed the internal taxation imposed on them, whether directly or indirectly.

The Court laid down guidelines as to the extent of repayments permissible under this Article in *Commission v. Italy*,[36] a case arising from proceedings under Article 226 (ex 169) alleging excessive repayment of taxes levied on certain engineering products. The Commission claimed that the repayment of duties paid on licences, concessions, motor vehicles and advertising, in connection with the production and marketing of the products in question, were ineligible for repayment under Article 91 (ex 96). The Court ruled that the words "directly or indirectly" referred to the distinction between taxes which had been levied on the products themselves (directly), and taxes levied on the raw materials and semi-finished goods used in their manufacture (indirectly).[37] It followed that the charges referred to by the Commission could not be repaid consistently with Article 91 (ex 96), for the simple reason that they were not taxes imposed on the products at all, but "upon the producer undertaking in the very varied aspects of its general commercial and financial activity".[38] The Court has also held that when a Member State employs a flat-rate system for determining the amount of internal taxation which can be repaid on exportation to another Member State, it is for that former State to establish that such a system remains *in all cases* within the mandatory limits of Article 91 (ex 96).[39]

But whereas Article 25 applies to customs duties and charges having equivalent effect on both imports and exports, Article 90, on its face, applies only to tax discrimination against imports. Nevertheless, in *Staten Kontrol v. Larsen*,[40] the

---

[35] Case C–213/96 *Outokumpu Oy* [1998] E.C.R. I–1777, Opinion of Advocate General Jacobs, para. 46.

[36] Case 45/64 [1965] E.C.R. 857; [1966] E.C.R. 97. For infringements of Art. 96 (now Art. 91) see Case C–152/89 *Commission v. Luxembourg* [1991] E.C.R. I–3171; Case C–153/89 *Commission v. Belgium* [1991] E.C.R. I–3171.

[37] On the similar wording in Art. 90(1), see above at page 302, and Case 28/67 *Molkerei-Zentrale* [1968] E.C.R. 143 at 155.

[38] Case 45/64 [1965] E.C.R. 857 at 866.

[39] Case 152/89 *Commission v. Luxembourg* [1991] E.C.R. I–3141, para. 36.

[40] Case 142/77 [1978] E.C.R. 1543; [1979] 2 C.M.L.R. 680.

Court held that the rule against discrimination underlying Article 90 (ex 95) also applied when the export, rather than import, of a product constituted, within the context of a system of internal taxation, the chargeable event giving rise to a fiscal charge. It would be incompatible with the system of tax provisions laid down in the Treaty to acknowledge that a Member State, in the absence of an express prohibition laid down in the Treaty, were free to apply in a discriminatory manner a system of internal taxation to products intended for export to another Member State. Article 90, it seems, prohibits internal taxation which either discriminates against imports or exports, as compared to domestic products.[41]

Furthermore, in *Hulst v. Produktschap voor Siergewassen*,[42] the Court held that an internal levy applying to domestic sales and exports could have an effect equivalent to a customs duty when either its application fell more heavily on export sales than on sales within the country, or when the levy was intended to finance activities likely to give preferential treatment to the product intended for marketing within the country, to the detriment of that intended for export.

THE RELATIONSHIP BETWEEN ARTICLES 25 AND 90, AND OTHER PROVISIONS OF THE TREATY

Where national measures are financed by a discriminatory internal tax, Article 90 is applicable to the latter, despite the fact that it forms part of a national aid, subject to scrutiny under Articles 87 and 88 (ex 92 and 93) E.C.[43] Equally, Article 25 on the one hand, and Articles 87 and 88, on the other, are cumulatively applicable in such circumstances.[44] Articles 25 and 90 do not however overlap with Article 28 (ex 30). The Court held in *Ianelli & Volpi v. Paolo Meroni* that:

"However wide the field of application of Article 30 may be, it nevertheless does not include obstacles to trade covered by other provisions of the Treaty. Thus obstacles which are of a fiscal nature or have equivalent effect and are covered by Articles 9 to 16 and 95 of the Treaty do not fall within the prohibition of Article 30."[45]

---

[41] *cf.* Case 27/74 *Demag* [1974] E.C.R. 1037.

[42] Case 51/74 [1975] E.C.R. 79; [1975] 1 C.M.L.R. 236.

[43] Case 47/69 *France v. Commission* [1970] E.C.R. 487; [1970] C.M.L.R. 351; Case 73/79 *Commission v. Italy* [1980] E.C.R. 1533; Case 17/81 *Pabst and Richarz v. Hauptzollamt Oldenburg* [1982] E.C.R. 1331; [1983] 3 C.M.L.R. 11; Case 277/83 *Commission v. Italy* [1985] E.C.R. 2049; [1987] 3 C.M.L.R. 324; Case C–266/91 *Celulose Beira Industrial SA v. Fazenda Pública* [1993] E.C.R. I–4337, para. 21.

[44] Joined Cases C–78/90 etc. *Compagnie Commerciale de l'Ouest and others v. Receveur Principal des Douanes de La Pallice Port* [1992] E.C.R. I–1847, para. 32; [1994] 2 C.M.L.R. 425; Case C–144/91 *Gilbert Demoor en Zonen NV and others v. Belgian State* [1992] E.C.R. I–6613, para. 24; Case C–266/91 *Celulose Beira Industrial SA v. Fazenda Pública* [1993] E.C.R. I–4337, para. 21.

[45] Case 74/76, n.18, *supra.* Joined Cases C–78/90 etc. *Compagnie Commerciale de l'Ouest and others v. Receveur Principal des Douanes de La Pallice Port*, n.33, *supra.* para. 20; Case C–17/91 *Georges Lornoy en Zonen NV and others v. Belgian State* [1992] E.C.R. I–6523, para. 14. But if Art. 90 is inapplicable because an import lacks a domestic counterpart, Art. 28 may apply to the tax in question, see Case C–47/88 *Commission v. Denmark* E.C.R. I–4509.

The relationship between Article 31 on state monopolies (ex 37), and Article 90 (ex 95), was considered by the Court in *Grandes Distilleries Peureux*.[46] Whereas Article 31 (ex 37) was acknowledged to have provided an exception to certain rules of the Treaty—*in casu* Article 90 (ex 95)—during the transitional period, this was declared to be no longer the case. Where internal taxation is concerned, Article 90 apparently constitutes a *lex specialis*, even it seems in the case of activities which would otherwise qualify for scrutiny under Article 31.

In *Staten Kontrol v. Larsen*,[47] the Court held that, while a Member State was precluded under Article 90 (ex 95) from taxing exports more heavily than domestically traded goods, it was open to a Member State to tax exports in the same way as domestic goods, even if this led to taxes overlapping with those imposed in the country of destination: this latter problem would fall to be solved by harmonisation of national legislation under Articles 93 or 94 of the Treaty (ex 99 and 100). However, in *Gaston Schul*,[48] the Court held that a member State was required by Article 90 (ex 95) when imposing value added tax on imports, to take into account value added tax paid but not refunded (and not refundable under the applicable VAT Directive) in the country of export. So far from the harmonisation of national tax provisions ousting Article 90 (ex 95), the Court held that the applicable VAT Directive must be construed in accordance with the terms of Article 90 (ex 95), which were mandatory and binding upon the Community institutions in the enactment of such legislation.

THE
COMMON CUSTOMS TARIFF AND EXTERNAL RELATIONS

The preceding exposition has been concerned with the elimination of customs duties and other financial charges on trade between the Member States, but brief mention must be made of imports and exports between the Community and third countries.

Neither the relevant Articles of the Treaty, nor Regulation 950/68 on the Common Customs Tariff,[49] explicitly provided for the regulation of charges having an equivalent effect in trade relations between the Member States and third countries. Nevertheless, the Court held in *Sociaal Fonds voor de Dimantarbeiders v. Indiamex*[50] that the unilateral imposition of such charges after the adoption of the Common Customs Tariff was inconsistent with the aim of the Treaty that Member States adopt a common policy in their trade relations with the outside world. The Court has confirmed this position in a consistent case-

---

[46] Case 86/78 [1979] E.C.R. 897; [1980] 3 C.M.L.R. 337.

[47] Case 142/77, n.40, *supra*.

[48] Case 15/81 *Gaston Schul* [1982] E.C.R. 1409; [1982] 3 C.M.L.R. 229, and see Case 39/85 *Bergeres-Becque* [1986] E.C.R. 259; [1986] 2 C.M.L.R. 143; Case C–120/88 *Commission v. Italy* [1991] E.C.R. I–621; [1993] 1 C.M.L.R. 41; Case C–119/89 *Commission v. Spain* [1991] E.C.R. I–641; [1993] 1 C.M.L.R. 41; *Commission v. Greece* [1991] E.C.R. I–691; [1991] 1 C.M.L.R. 41.

[49] [1969] O.J. Sp.Ed. (1), p. 275. Repealed with effect from December 31, 1987 by Reg. 2658/87, [1987] O.J. L256/1.

[50] Joined Cases 37–38/73 [1973] E.C.R. 1609; [1976] 2 C.M.L.R. 222.

law,[51] but has indicated that the Treaty does not preclude the levying of a charge having equivalent effect to a customs duty on imports which, having regard to all its essential characteristics, must be regarded as a charge already in existence on July 1, 1968, provided that the level at which it is levied has not been raised, and where the level has been raised, only the amount by which it has been raised must be regarded as incompatible with the Treaty.[52]

The Treaty itself has no provision analogous to Article 90 E.C. applying to imports from non-member countries.[53] International agreements between the E.C. and third countries, and the provisions of agricultural regulations, may prohibit customs duties, charges having equivalent effect, and discriminatory internal taxation, on trade between the E.C. and third countries. It cannot be assumed without more that such provisions as these are to be construed as strictly as analogous provisions governing intra-Community trade, though a provision in an international agreement prohibiting charges having equivalent effect will be construed in the same way as the same term appearing in the E.C. Treaty if to give it more limited scope would deprive the agreement in question of much of its effectiveness.[54] But even where a provision of a regulation prohibits charges having equivalent effect on trade with third countries, and the Court takes the view that the concept is the same as that embodied in Article 25 E.C., the requirement may be subject to derogation authorised by the Community institutions in a way that would not be possible were intra-Community trade involved.[55] And where health inspections are permitted by Community regulations on imports from third countries, the inspections may be more strict, and the fees charged higher, than in intra-Community trade, since Community law does not require Member States to show the same degree of confidence towards non-member countries as they are required to show other Member States.[56]

Where an international agreement prohibits discriminatory internal taxation on imports from third countries, it will be a matter of interpretation whether or not the provision in question is intended to fulfil the same purpose in relations between the E.C. and third countries as Article 90 fulfils in respect of intra-Community trade. Thus the Court held in *Pabst & Richarz v. Hauptzollamt Oldenburg* that Article 53 of the Association Agreement between the EEC and Greece, which prohibited discriminatory internal taxation, fulfilled, within the framework of the Association between the Community and Greece, the same

---

[51] Case C–125/94 *Aprile Srl, in liquidation v. Amministrazione delle Finanze dello Stato* [1995] E.C.R. I–2919, paras 35–37; Case C–109/98 *CRT France International SA v. Directeur Régional des Impôts de Bourgogne* [1999] E.C.R. I–2237, para. 22.

[52] Case C–126/94 *Société Cadi Surgeléles etc. v. Ministre des Finances* [1996] E.C.R. I–5647; [1997] 1 C.M.L.R. 795.

[53] Case 148/77 *Hansen* [1978] E.C.R. 1787; [1979] 1 C.M.L.R. 604; Joined cases C–228–234, 339 and 353/90 *Simba SpA and others v. Ministero delle Finanze* [1992] E.C.R. I–3713, para. 14; Case C–130/92 *OTO SpA v. Ministero delle Finanze* [1994] E.C.R. I–3281, paras 18 and 19; [1995] 1 C.M.L.R. 84; Case C–284/96 *Didier Tabouillet v. Directeur des Services Fiscaux de Meurthe-et-Moselle* [1997] E.C.R. I–7471, para. 23.

[54] Case C–163/90 *Administration des Douanes et Droits Indirects v. Léopold Legros and others* [1992] E.C.R. I–4625, para. 26.

[55] Case 70/77 *Simmenthal* [1978] E.C.R. 1453; [1978] 3 C.M.L.R. 670.

[56] Case 30/79 *Land Berlin v. Wigei* [1980] E.C.R. 151; [1981] 3 C.M.L.R. 746.

function as that of Article 90 (ex 95), and should be interpreted in the same way. But in *Hauptzollamt Mainz v. Kupferberg*, which involved Article 21 of the EEC-Portugal free trade Agreement, also prohibiting discriminatory internal taxation, the Court observed that although Article 21 of the Agreement and Article 90 (ex 95) had the same object, they were nevertheless worded differently, and must be considered and interpreted in their own context. The Court concluded that the interpretation given to Article 90 (ex 95) of the Treaty could not be applied by way of simple analogy to the agreement on free trade. In *Metalsa Srl* the Court considered the interpretation to be given to Article 18 of the EEC-Austria Agreement, the wording of which was the same as that of Article 21 of the EEC-Portugal Agreement. It distinguished *Pabst and Richarz* and followed *Kupferberg*, and declined to extend to Article 18 the same interpretation as that applied to Article 90 (ex 95).[57] And in *Texaco A/S v. Middelfart Havn and others* the Court applied the same reasoning to the identical terms of Article 18 of the EEC-Sweden Agreement.[58]

Customs duties on trade with third countries are established by the Common Customs Tariff,[59] which the Court has held must be interpreted in such a way as to give effect to a single trading system with third countries, and not in such a way that products are treated differently according to the country by which they enter the Community.[60] But customs duties are only chargeable under the CCT upon goods capable of being lawfully traded within the Community, and not, for example, upon smuggled narcotic drugs,[61] or counterfeit currency.[62]

---

[57] Case C–312/91 [1993] E.C.R. I–3751; [1994] 2 C.M.L.R. 121.
[58] Joined Cases C–114–115/95 [1997] E.C.R. I–4263.
[59] n.49.
[60] Case 135/79 *Gedelfi* [1980] E.C.R. 1713.
[61] Case 50/80 *Horvath* [1981] E.C.R. 385; [1982] 2 C.M.L.R. 522; Case 221/81 *Wolf* [1982] E.C.R. 3681; [1983] 2 C.M.L.R. 170; Case 240/81 *Einberger* [1982] E.C.R. 3699; [1983] 2 C.M.L.R. 170.
[62] Case C–343/89 *Witzemann* [1990] E.C.R. I–4477.

CHAPTER 13

QUANTITATIVE RESTRICTIONS AND MEASURES HAVING EQUIVALENT EFFECT

INTRODUCTION

A quantitative restriction, or a quota, is a measure restricting the import of a given product by amount or by value. In order to obviate the risk of importers ordering goods, only to have them excluded at the frontier because the quota has been filled, a licensing system may be adopted, whereby a government agency formally authorises particular importers to import stated quantities, or money's worth, of goods.[1] Since quotas are capable of disturbing the flow of international trade to a greater extent than tariffs,[2] and indeed found favour during the 1930s as a means of restricting imports without infringing international agreements prohibiting the introduction of customs duties,[3] it is hardly surprising that the authors of the Spaak Report considered their elimination as a "fundamental element" in the creation of a common market.[4] Accordingly, the EEC Treaty in its original text provided for the abolition of quantitative restrictions and measures having equivalent effect on imports and exports,[5] in the former case by the end of the transitional period,[6] and in the case of exports by the end of the first stage.[7] "Standstill" provisions prevented Member States from introducing new quantitative restrictions or measures having equivalent effect,[8] or making more restrictive those measures already in existence when the Treaty entered into force.[9] The current provisions on quantitative restrictions and measures having equivalent effect are set out in Articles 28 and 29 (ex 30 and 34) E.C. Article 28 E.C. provides:

"Quantitative restrictions on imports and all measures having equivalent effect shall be prohibited between Member States."

Article 29 E.C. provides:

---

[1] Jackson, *World Trade and the Law of GATT* (1969), p. 305.

[2] The volume of imports cannot expand to meet increased demand, nor can the improvement of efficiency of manufacturers in exporting countries secure their access to the protected markets, Wilcox, *A Charter for World Trade* (1949), pp. 81 *et seq.*; K. Dam, *The GATT* (1970), p. 147; Jackson, *op. cit.*, pp. 309–310.

[3] Jackson, *op. cit.*, P. 306.

[4] *Rapport des Chefs de Délégation aux Ministres des Affaires Étrangères* (1956) p. 35.

[5] The Spaak Report points out that one result of the removal of restrictions on imports would be increased interdependence of the Member States. This would require, as a necessary corollary, that importing countries be able to rely on continuity of supplies from exporting countries, *Rapport*, p. 38.

[6] Arts 30, 32 and 33.

[7] Art. 34. For detailed treatment of Arts 30–36 (now Arts 28–30) see Oliver, *Free Movement of Goods in the EC*, (3rd ed., Sweet and Maxwell, 1996).

[8] Art. 31.

[9] Art. 32. There was no explicit standstill for quantitative restrictions and measures having equivalent effect on exports, but Art. 34(1) prohibited such measures outright.

"Quantitative restrictions on exports, and all measures having equivalent effect, shall be prohibited between Member States."

The Court has said that the principle of the free movement of goods is one of the fundamental principles of the Treaty, and that that principle is implemented by Article 28 et seq. (ex 30 et seq.) E.C.[10] Article 28 has direct effect and creates individual rights which national courts must protect.[11] The prohibition on quantitative restrictions and measures having equivalent effect is applicable without distinction to products originating in Member States and to those coming from non-member countries which are in free circulation.[12] Articles 28–30 (ex 30–36) E.C. apply to all trade in goods, subject only to the exceptions provided in the Treaty itself.[13] In *Campus Oil* the Irish Government argued unsuccessfully that oil, being of vital national importance, should be regarded as impliedly exempt from Article 28 (ex 30). The Court held that goods could not be considered to be exempt merely because they were of particular importance for the life or economy of the Member State.[14] Coins which constitute legal tender doe not fall within Articles 28–30; coins which no longer constitute legal tender do.[15] Electricity is a good for the purposes of Articles 28–30.[16] Waste, whether recyclable or not, falls within Articles 28–30.[17] But where the supply of goods is incidental to the provision of services Articles 28–30 do not apply.[18] The re-import of goods falls within Articles 28–30,[19] but not where the goods are exported for the sole purpose of re-importation in order to circumvent national legislation.[20] The provisions of Articles 28–30 also take effect within the framework of E.C. regulations on the common organisation of the markets for the various agricultural products.[21] Where national procedures are contrary to Articles 28–30, any charge made by the national authorities for completion of such procedures is likewise unlawful.[22]

While Articles 28 and 29 prohibit quantitative restrictions and measures having equivalent effect, Article 30 provide that these latter Articles shall nevertheless not preclude prohibitions or restrictions on imports exports or goods in transit

---

[10] Case C–265/95 *Commission v. France* [1997] E.C.R. I–6959, paras 24 and 27.
[11] Case 74/76 *Ianelli & Volpi v. Meroni* [1977] E.C.R. 557 at para. 13; [1977] 2 C.M.L.R. 688.
[12] Case Case 41/76 *Donckerwolcke* [1976] E.C.R. 1921; [1977] 2 C.M.L.R. 535; Case 288/83 *Commission v. Ireland* [1985] E.C.R. 1761; [1985] 3 C.M.L.R. 152; Case 212/88 *Levy* [1989] E.C.R. 3511; [1991] 1 C.M.L.R. 49.
[13] For exceptions under Art. 30 (ex Art. 36) and the so-called "mandatory requirements" see pp. 345–356 below. See also Art. 296 (ex Art. 223), dealing with trade in arms, munitions and war materials.
[14] Case 72/83 [1984] E.C.R. 2727, para 17; [1984] 3 C.M.L.R. 544.
[15] Case 7/78 *Thompson* [1978] E.C.R. 2247; [1979] 1 C.M.L.R. 47.
[16] Case C–393/92 *Almelo and Others v. Energiebedrijf IJsselmij* [1994] E.C.R. I–1477, para. 28; Case C–158/94 *Commission of the European Communities v. Italian Republic.* [1997] E.C.R. I–5789, para. 17.
[17] Case C–2/90 *Commission v. Belgium* [1992] E.C.R. I–4431; [1993] 1 C.M.L.R. 365.
[18] Case C–275/92 *Schindler* [1994] E.C.R. I–1039; Case C–55/93 *Johannes Gerrit Cornelis van Schaik* [1994] E.C.R. I–4837, para. 14.
[19] Case C–240/95 *Rémy Schmit* [1996] E.C.R. I–3179; [1996] 3 C.M.L.R. 549.
[20] Case 229/83 *Leclerc* [1985] E.C.R. 1; [1985] 2 C.M.L.R. 286.
[21] Joined Cases 3, 4 and 6/76 *Kramer and Others* [1976] E.C.R. 1279, paras 53 and 54; [1976] 2 C.M.L.R. 440; Case C–228/91 *Commission v. Italy* [1993] E.C.R. I–2701, para. 11; Case C–265/95 *Commission v. France* [1997] E.C.R. I–6959, para. 36.
[22] Case 50/85 *Schloh* [1986] E.C.R. 1855; [1987] 1 C.M.L.R. 450.

which are justified on such grounds as public policy, public security or public health. Furthermore, national measures which are on the face of it covered by Articles 28 and 29 may be held to fall outside the scope of those provisions where they are justified on such grounds as consumer protection, fiscal supervision or environmental protection. In this chapter consideration will first be given to national measures which in principle comprise quantitative restrictions and measures having equivalent effect, without reference to the question of possible justification,[23] while justification under Article 30, or otherwise, will be considered in later sections of this chapter.[24]

QUANTITATIVE RESTRICTIONS

The notion of a quantitative restriction is well understood, and definition poses little difficulty. As the Court explained in *Geddo v. Ente Nazionale Risi*, "The prohibition on quantitative restrictions covers measures which amount to a total or partial restraint of, according to the circumstances, imports, exports, or goods in transit."[25] Thus, when the Italian authorities suspended imports of pork into Italy from other Member States in June 1960, the Court ruled that such a measure amounted to an infringement of the "standstill" provision of Article 31, first paragraph, of the Treaty, as the text of the Treaty stood at the time.[26] In *Henn and Darby* a statutory prohibition in the United Kingdom on the import of pornographic material was held to amount to a quantitative restriction contrary to Article 28 (ex 30) E.C., subject to possible justification under Article 30 (ex 36),[27] and a restriction in the United Kingdom on imports of main crop potatoes was held to amount to a quantitative restriction.[28]

MEASURES HAVING EQUIVALENT EFFECT TO QUANTITATIVE RESTRICTIONS ON IMPORTS— DIRECTIVE 70/50

The concept of a measure having equivalent effect to a quantitative restriction is rather more complex than that of a quantitative restriction. Article 2(1) of Directive 70/50[29] prohibits measures, other than those applicable equally to domestic or imported products, which hinder imports which could otherwise take place, including those "which make importation more difficult or costly than the disposal of domestic production". This provision was relied upon by the Court in terms in *Ianelli & Volpi SpA v. Meroni*.[30] In other cases the Court has relied upon

---

[23] Pages 319–345.

[24] Pages 345–356.

[25] Case 2/73 [1973] E.C.R. 865 at 879; [1974] 1 C.M.L.R. 13.

[26] Case 7/61 *Commission v. Italy* [1961] E.C.R. 317; [1962] C.M.L.R. 39.

[27] Case 34/79 [1979] E.C.R. 3795; [1980] 1 C.M.L.R. 246.

[28] Case 118/78 *Meijer* [1979] E.C.R. 1387; [1979] 2 C.M.L.R. 398; Case 231/78 *Commission v. United Kingdom* [1979] E.C.R. 1447; [1979] 2 C.M.L.R. 427.

[29] [1970] O.J. Spec.Ed. (I), p. 17. While strictly this measure applies to measures in force at the end of the transitional period, it provides valuable guidance on the meaning of measures having equivalent effect.

[30] Case 74/76, n.11, *supra*.

the principle involved without reference to the Directive. Thus in *Commission v. Italy*[31] the Court held that an import deposit scheme was contrary to Article 28 (ex 30) because its effect was to render imports "more difficult or burdensome" than internal transactions, and thereby produced restrictive effects on the free movement of goods. With respect to imports, Article 2(2) of Directive 70/50 provides that measures having equivalent effect include those which "make imports or the disposal, at any marketing stage, of imported products subject to a condition—other than a formality—which is required in respect of imported products only, or a condition differing from that required from domestic products and more difficult to satisfy." This provision was cited with approval in *Rewe-Zentralfinanz v. Landwirtschaftskammer*,[32] in which the Court declared that health inspections of plant products at national frontiers constituted a measure having equivalent effect, where similar domestic products were not subject to a similar examination. Although the Article refers to measures other than formalities, the Court has held that national measures requiring import or export licences in intra-Community trade—even though such licences are granted automatically—infringe the prohibition of Articles 28 and 29 (ex 30 and 34).[33]

Article 2(3) lists examples of the national measures covered by the definitions contained in Articles 2(1) and 2(2). Thus Article 2(3)(g) refers to measures which make the access of imported products to the domestic market conditional upon having an agent or representative in the territory of the importing Member State. This provision was relied upon by the Commission in an action against the Federal Republic of Germany.[34] German legislation provided that pharmaceutical products could be placed on the market only by a pharmaceutical undertaking having its headquarters in the area in which that legislation was applicable. The Court held—without reference to the Directive—that the legislation in question was likely to involve additional costs for undertakings which found no good reason for having a representative of their own established in Germany, and which sold directly to customers. The legislation was therefore likely to hinder trade within the Community and amounted to a measure having equivalent effect. Again, Article 2(3)(s) refers to national measures which "confine names which are not indicative of origin or source to domestic products only."[35] However, even names which are indicative of origin or source may only be confined to domestic products if the geographical area of origin of a product confers upon it a specific quality and characteristic of such a nature as to distinguish it from all other products.[36] It follows that making the application of a

---

[31] Case 95/81 [1982] E.C.R. 2187.
[32] Case 4/75 [1975] E.C.R. 843; [1977] 1 C.M.L.R. 599.
[33] Cases 51–54/71 *International Fruit* [1971] E.C.R. 1107; Case 53/76 *Bouhelier* [1977] E.C.R. 197; [1977] 1 C.M.L.R. 436; Case 68/76 *Commission v. French Republic* [1977] E.C.R. 515; [1977] 2 C.M.L.R. 161; Case 124/81 *Commission v. United Kingdom* [1983] E.C.R. 203; [1983] 2 C.M.L.R. 1.
[34] Case 247/81 *Commission v. Germany* [1984] E.C.R. 1111. See also Case 87/85 *Laboratoires de Pharmacie Legia* [1986] E.C.R. 1707; [1987] 1 C.M.L.R. 646. Art. 2(3) contains a list of examples and cannot be pleaded to defeat the purpose of Art. 30; Case 103/84 *Commission v. Italy* [1986] E.C.R. 1759.
[35] Case 12/74 *Commission v. Germany* [1975] E.C.R. 181; [1975] 1 C.M.L.R. 340; Case 13/78 *Eggers* [1978] E.C.R. 1935; [1979] 1 C.M.L.R. 562; Joined Cases C–321–324/94 *Jacques Pistre* [1997] E.C.R. I–2343.
[36] Case 12/74 *Commission v. Germany*, n.35, *supra;* Case 13/78 *Eggers*, n.35, *supra.*

designation of quality which is neither an indication of origin nor source conditional upon one or more stages of the production process taking place on national territory, amounts to a measure having equivalent effect.[37]

Article 3 of Directive 70/50 covers measures governing the marketing of products which deal in particular with the presentation or identification of products and which apply equally to domestic and imported products, where the restrictive effects of such measures on the free movement of goods exceed the effects intrinsic to trade rules. This is stated to be the case, in particular, where the restrictive effects on the free movement of goods are out of proportion to their purpose, or where the same objective can be attained by other means which are less of a hindrance to trade. This provision has been cited by the Court of Justice.[38] It is to be noted that the tenth recital to the preamble of Directive 70/50 might suggest that Article 3, despite referring to measures which "are equally applicable" to domestic and imported products, only covers national measures which are indirectly discriminatory, since the recital refers to imports which are "either precluded or made more difficult or costly than the disposal of domestic production". The Court's so-called *Cassis* case-law[39] (developed without specific reference to Article 3) would suggest that Article 3 applies to obstacles to the free movement of goods where they are the consequence of national rules which lay down requirements to be met by goods (such as requirements as to composition, labelling, packaging etc.) even if those rules apply without distinction to all products, unless their application can be justified by a public-interest objective taking precedence over the free movement of goods.[40] And the Court appears to consider that such obstacles do not amount to discrimination, either direct or indirect, though in the view of the present writer the extension to imports of such national measures could indeed be said to be indirectly discriminatory.[41]

EVOLUTION OF THE COURT'S CASE-LAW

The *Dassonville* case

It was clear from the Court's early case-law that a national rule requiring import licences for the import of goods from other Member States would amount to a measure having equivalent effect to a quantitative restriction, even if the requirement was a formality.[42] This was consistent with the view that it was a characteristic of such measures that they applied specifically to imports and

---

[37] Case 13/78 *Eggers*, n.35, *supra.*
[38] Case 75/81 *Blesgen* [1982] E.C.R. 1211; [1983] 1 C.M.L.R. 431.
[39] See below at 323 *et seq.*
[40] See in particular Joined Cases C–267–268/91 *Bernard Keck and Daniel Mithouard* [1993] E.C.R. I–6097; [1995] 1 C.M.L.R. 101.
[41] In Joined Cases C–267–268/91 *Keck*, the Court's reference in para. 16 to "certain selling arrangements" not hindering trade in the absence of discrimination, in law or in fact, implies that the requirements as regards composition and labelling etc., referred to in para. 15 are not regarded as being directly or indirectly discriminatory. For the view that such latter measures might properly be regarded as indirectly discriminatory, see below, p. 329.
[42] Joined Cases 51–54/71 *International Fruit* [1971] E.C.R. 1107.

burdened them in some way. But it is in the judgment of the Court in *Procureur du Roi v. Dassonville* that one finds the first attempt to lay down a general definition of measures having equivalent effect to quantitative restrictions on imports. The defendants in the national proceedings imported into Belgium Scotch whisky which they had purchased from French distributors. Belgian legislation required such goods to be accompanied by a certificate of origin made out in the name of the Belgian importer, and the goods in question were without such certificates, which could have been obtained only with the greatest difficulty once the goods had been previously imported into France. On a reference for a preliminary ruling the Court of Justice stated:

"5. All trading rules enacted by Member States which are capable of hindering, directly or indirectly, actually or potentially, intra-Community trade are to be considered as measures having an effect equivalent to quantitative restrictions.

6. In the absence of a Community system guaranteeing for consumers the authenticity of a product's designation of origin, if a Member State takes measures to prevent unfair practices in this connexion, it is however subject to the condition that these measures should be reasonable and that the means of proof required should not act as a hindrance to trade between member states and should, in consequence, be accessible to all community nationals.

7. Even without having to examine whether or not such measures are covered by Article 36, they must not, in any case, by virtue of the principle expressed in the second sentence of that Article, constitute a means of arbitrary discrimination or a disguised restriction on trade between Member States.

8. That may be the case with formalities, required by a Member State for the purpose of proving the origin of a product, which only direct importers are really in a position to satisfy without facing serious difficulties."[43]

While the definition of measures having equivalent effect in paragraph 5 of the above judgment is stated in rather broad terms, it does not necessarily follow that it was intended to cover measures which reduce in one way or another the overall volume of trade, but without placing any particular burden on imports. Much depends on the notion of "hindering . . . intra-Community trade", and it is not self-evident that such trade can be regarded as being hindered by a national measure which is neutral as regards inter-State and intra-State trade and as between channels of inter-State trade. The national measure in issue in *Dassonville* was of course far from being trade-neutral. As the Court indicates in paragraphs 7 and 8 of its judgment set out above, the national measure in issue in that case imposed a considerably greater burden on one category of imports (imports from a Member State into which the goods had already been imported), than on another category of imports (imports directly from the country of origin). And since there is no indication that the latter category of imports were burdened less than domestic transactions as regards proof of origin, the national

---

[43] Case 8/74 [1974] E.C.R. 837, paras 5–8; [1974] 2 C.M.L.R. 436.

measure also placed a greater burden on the former category of imports than on comparable domestic transactions. In such circumstances it is not surprising that the measures were regarded as comprising "a means of arbitrary discrimination or a disguised restriction on trade" within the meaning of Article 30 (ex 36) E.C.

From *Cassis* to *Keck*

Prior to the judgment of the Court of Justice in the *Cassis* case[44] it was generally assumed—and the Court's case-law was consistent with this assumption—that Article 28 (ex 30) had no application to a national measure unless the measure in question discriminated in some way, formally or materially, between either imports and domestic products, or between channels of intra-Community trade.

The *Cassis* case involved the intended importation into Germany of a consignment of the alcoholic beverage "Cassis de Dijon". Under German legislation fruit liqueurs such as "Cassis" could only be marketed if they contained a minimum alcohol content of 25 per cent, whereas the alcohol content of the product in question was between 15 per cent and 20 per cent. A German court asked the Court of Justice whether legislation such as that in issue was consistent with Article 28 (ex 30) E.C. Before the Court of Justice the Federal Republic of Germany argued that the legislation in question was discriminatory in neither a formal nor a material sense; any obstacles to trade resulted simply from the fact that France and Germany contained different rules for the minimum alcohol contents of certain drinks. The Court's judgment makes no reference at all to the issue of discrimination. Rather it regards incompatibility with Article 28 (ex 30) as flowing from the very fact that the "Cassis" could not be placed lawfully on the German market, and addresses itself at once to the question whether there existed any justification for the restriction.

"In the absence of common rules relating to the production and marketing of alcohol . . . it is for the Member States to regulate all matters relating to the production and marketing of alcohol and alcoholic beverages on their own territory.

Obstacles to movement within the Community resulting from disparities between the national laws relating to the marketing of the products in question must be accepted in so far as those provisions may be recognised as being necessary in order to satisfy mandatory requirements relating in particular to the effectiveness of fiscal supervision, the protection of public health, the fairness of commercial transactions and the defence of the consumer."[45]

The Court rejected the arguments of the Federal Republic of Germany relating to the protection of public health and to the protection of the consumer against unfair commercial practices, and continued:

"It is clear from the foregoing that the requirements relating to the minimum alcohol content of alcoholic beverages do not serve a purpose which is in the

---

[44] Case 120/78 *Rewe-Zentral AG v. Bundesmonopolverwaltung für Branntwein* [1979] E.C.R. 649; [1979] 3 C.M.L.R. 494.
[45] Case 120/78 at paras 8, 9.

general interest and such as to take precedence over the requirements of the free movement of goods, which constitutes one of the fundamental rules of the Community."[46]

In the paragraphs which follow the Court describes the restrictive effect of national rules such as those in issue in terms which seem to make the existence of an element of discrimination irrelevant in establishing violation of Article 28 (ex 30), or to presume it to exist from the very fact of exclusion of products lawfully produced and marketed in one of the Member States.

"In practice, the principal effect of requirements of this nature is to promote alcoholic beverages having a high alcohol content by excluding from the national market products of other Member States which do not answer that description.

It therefore appears that the unilateral requirement imposed by the rules of a Member State of a minimum alcohol content for the purposes of the sale of alcoholic beverages constitutes an obstacle to trade which is incompatible with the provisions of Article 30 of the Treaty. There is therefore no valid reason why, provided that they have been lawfully produced and marketed in one of the Member States, alcoholic beverages should not be introduced into any other Member State; the sale of such products may not be subject to a legal prohibition on the marketing of beverages with an alcohol content lower than the limit set by the national rules."[47]

The judgment in this case was one of the great formative events in the establishment of the internal market. If the case had gone the other way, and the Court had held that rules such as those in issue were compatible with the Treaty, typical French liqueurs would have been largely excluded from the German market, while typical German liqueurs, which would seem to have complied with the French rules, would have enjoyed access to the French market. More generally, if the case had gone the other way, traders in the more highly regulated Member States would have enjoyed an advantage over traders in less heavily regulated Member States. Goods produced under the rules of the latter Member States would have been subject to numerous restrictions in the territories of the former, while goods produced under the rules of the former Member States would have enjoyed relatively free access to the markets of the latter. The obvious alternative solution to that offered by the Court's judgment—harmonisation of national product standards by Community legislation—would have promised a slow and tortuous solution, on a product by product basis, and a solution which would have risked the erosion of the distinct characteristics of national produce.[48] The *Cassis* judgment offered both free trade, and national diversity, while at the same time minimising the need for harmonisation of national rules.

---

[46] *ibid.*, para. 14.
[47] *ibid.*, para. 14.
[48] For harmonisation see Chap. 17 on completing the internal market.

The Court was soon to confirm the approach it had adopted in *Cassis* in *Gilli & Andres*,[49] a case concerning national legislation prohibiting the marketing of vinegar containing acetic acid derived otherwise than from the acetic fermentation of wine. The defendants in the national proceedings were prosecuted for being in possession of apple vinegar for sale for gain! In this case the Court slightly modified one of its observations in *Cassis*:

"In practice, the principal effect of provisions of this nature is to protect domestic production by prohibiting the putting on to the market of products from other Member States which do not answer the descriptions laid down by the national rules."

If discrimination was the distinguishing feature of national measures *prima facie* contrary to Article 28 (ex 30) before the *Cassis* judgment, emphasis after that case was placed upon the protective effect of national rules which excluded from the market of one Member State goods lawfully produced and marketed in the territory of another. As the Commission stated in its Communication of October 3, 1980 concerning the consequences of the *Cassis* case:

"Any product imported from another Member State must in principle be admitted to the territory of the importing Member State if it has been lawfully produced, that is, conforms to rules and processes of manufacture that are customarily and traditionally accepted in the exporting country, and is marketed in the territory of another."[50]

Examples of measures held by the Court to fall within the scope of the *Cassis* formulation (subject to justification in accordance with the Treaty)[51] are national rules imposing a labelling requirement[52]: national rules prohibiting use of the additive nisin in cheese[53]; national rules regulating the dry matter content, moisture content and salt content of bread[54]; national rules requiring silver products to be hall-marked[55]; national rules requiring margarine to be sold in cube-shaped packets[56]; national rules restricting or prohibiting certain forms of advertising[57]; national rules prohibiting the retail sale of certain products unless marked with their country of origin[58]; national rules prohibiting the marketing under the designation "beer" of beers manufactured in other Member States in accordance with rules different to those applicable in the Member State of import, and prohibiting the import of beers containing additives whose use is

---

[49] Case 788/79 [1980] E.C.R. 2071; [1981] 1 C.M.L.R. 146.
[50] [1980] O.J. C256/2.
[51] As to which, see below, p. 345 *et seq.*
[52] Case 27/80 *Fietje* [1980] E.C.R. 3839; [1981] 3 C.M.L.R. 722; Case 94/82 *De Kikvorsch* [1983] E.C.R. 947; [1984] 2 C.M.L.R. 323.
[53] Case 53/80 *Eyssen* [1981] E.C.R. 409.
[54] Case 30/80 *Kelderman* [1981] E.C.R. 517; Case C–358/95 *Tommaso Morellato v. USL No. 1 1, Prodenone* [1997] E.C.R. I–1431; Case C–17/93 *Van der Veldt* [1994] E.C.R. I–3537; [1995] 1 C.M.L.R. 621.
[55] Case 220/81 *Robertson* [1982] E.C.R. 2349; [1983] 1 C.M.L.R. 556; Case C–293/93 *Houtwipper* [1994] E.C.R. I–4249.
[56] Case 261/81 *Rau* [1982] E.C.R. 3961; [1983] 2 C.M.L.R. 496.
[57] Case 286/81 *Oosthoek's etc.* [1982] E.C.R. 4575; [1983] 3 C.M.L.R. 428.
[58] Case 207/83 *Commission v. United Kingdom* [1985] E.C.R. 1201; [1985] 2 C.M.L.R. 259.

authorised in the Member State of origin but forbidden in the Member State of import[59]; national rules prohibiting the use of common wheat flour in the production of pasta products[60]; national rules restricting the term "yoghurt" to fresh yoghurt and prohibiting its application to deep frozen yoghurt[61]; national rules restricting the name "Edam" to cheese having a minimum fat content of 40 per cent[62]; national rules providing that sales offers involving a temporary price reduction may not state the duration of the offer or refer to previous prices[63]; and advertisements relating to prices in which the new price is displayed so as to catch the eye and reference is made to a higher price shown in a previous catalogue or brochure.[64]

There can be no doubt that the *Cassis* formulation may cover national measures which the Court regards as discriminatory and at times the notions of protective effect and indirect discrimination appear to coalesce—indeed, it will be suggested below that the concepts should be treated as the same. Thus in *Prantl* the Court declared:

". . . even national legislation on the marketing of a product which applies to national and imported products alike falls under the prohibition laid down in Article 30 . . . if in practice it produces protective effects by favouring typical national products and, by the same token, operating to the detriment of certain types of products from other Member States."[65]

Nevertheless, the Court made it clear in the *Cinétheque* case[66] that the *Cassis* formulation was not limited in its application to national measures which are proved to have or are assumed to have some discriminatory purpose or effect. The case concerned French rules which provided that video-cassettes of films could not be distributed within one year of the release of the films in question at the cinema. The Court made the following observations:

". . . such a system, if it applies without distinction to both video-cassettes manufactured in the national territory and to imported video-cassettes, does not have the purpose of regulating trade patterns; its effect is not to favour national production as against the production of other Member States, but to encourage cinematograph production as such.

Nevertheless, the application of such a system may create barriers to intra-Community trade in video-cassettes because of the disparities between the systems operated in the different Member States and between the conditions for the release of cinematographic works in the cinemas of those States. In those circumstances a prohibition of exploitation laid down by such a system is not compatible with the principle of the free movement of goods provided for

[59] Case 178/84 *Commission v. Germany* [1987] E.C.R. 1227; [1988] 1 C.M.L.R. 780.
[60] Case 407/85 *Drei Glocken GmbH* [1988] E.C.R. 4233.
[61] Case 298/87 *SMANOR SA* [1988] E.C.R. 4489.
[62] Case 286/86 *Deserbais* [1988] E.C.R. 4907.
[63] Case C–362/88 *GB-INNO-BM* [1990] E.C.R. I–667; [1991] 2 C.M.L.R. 801.
[64] Case C–126/91 *Schutzverband gegen Unwesen in der Wirtschaft e.V. v. Yves Rocher GmbH* [1993] E.C.R. I–2361.
[65] Case 16/83 [1984] E.C.R. 1299, para. 21; [1985] 2 C.M.L.R. 238.
[66] Joined Cases 60–61/84 [1985] E.C.R. 2605; [1986] 1 C.M.L.R. 365.

in the Treaty unless any obstacle to intra-Community trade thereby created does not exceed what is necessary in order to ensure the attainment of the objective in view and unless that objective is justified with regard to Community law."[67]

The stage was reached where a wide range of commercial and marketing rules applied by national authorities in the Member States were potentially covered by the prohibition on measures having equivalent effect to quantitative restrictions, even if the national rules in question did not differentiate between domestic goods and imports, and were not intrinsically more difficult for imports to comply with than for domestic goods. Thus, for example, national rules on advertising and promotion were regarded as being capable of amounting to measures having equivalent effect if there was a possibility that they might affect the prospects of importing products from other Member States. As the Court explained in *Oosthoek's Uitqeversmaatschappij BV*:[68]

"Legislation which restricts or prohibits certain forms of advertising and certain means of sales promotions may, although it does not directly affect imports, be such as to restrict their volume because it affects marketing opportunities for the imported products. The possibility cannot be ruled out that to compel a producer either to adopt advertising or sales promotion schemes which differ from one Member State to another or to discontinue a scheme which he considers to be particularly effective may constitute an obstacle to imports even if the legislation in question applies to domestic products and imported products without distinction."[69]

Yet it must be said that the Court's case-law on the application of the abovementioned principles was not entirely consistent. In *Blesgen*[70] the Court considered that a legislative provision that concerned only the sale of strong spirits for consumption on the premises in all places open to the public and did not concern other forms of marketing the same drinks had in fact no connection with the import of the products and for that reason was not of such a nature as to impede trade between Member States. In *Quietlynn*[71] the Court referred to *Blesgen* in holding that national provisions prohibiting the sale of lawful sex articles from unlicensed sex establishments did not constitute a measure having equivalent effect. Yet it is difficult to reconcile the approach in these cases with the reasoning of the Court in the Sunday trading cases. In *Torfaen BC v. B & Q Plc*[72] the Court of Justice relied upon the *Cinétheque* case in support of the proposition that a prohibition on Sunday trading was not compatible with the principle of the free movement of goods provided for in the Treaty unless any obstacle to Community trade thereby created did not exceed what was necessary in order to ensure the attainment of the objective in view and unless that

---

[67] *ibid.*, paras 21–22.
[68] Case 286/81 [1981] E.C.R. 4575; [1983] 3 C.M.L.R. 428.
[69] *ibid.*, para. 15.
[70] Case 75/81 [1982] E.C.R. 1211 at para. 15; [1983] 1 C.M.L.R. 431.
[71] Case C–23/89 [1990] E.C.R. I–3059; [1990] 3 C.M.L.R. 55.
[72] Case 145/88 [1989] E.C.R. 3851; [1990] 1 C.M.L.R. 337.

objective was justified with regard to Community law.[73] Furthermore, the Court stated in *Marchandise*[74] that a prohibition on the employment of workers in retail shops on Sundays after 12 noon might have negative repercussions on the volume of sales and hence on the volume of imports (though the Court regarded any such restrictions as being justified). It is difficult to see the difference in principle, as regards potential effect on imports, between restrictions such as those in issue in *Blesgen* and *Quietlynn* on the one hand, and those in *Torfaen* and *Marchandise*, on the other, though differences in degree there may be.

Thus the concept of the non-discriminatory trade restriction developed by the Court covered (subject to justification) national measures defining not only the composition of products, and their labelling and packaging, but also methods of advertising and sales promotion, and indeed all manner of terms and conditions under which goods were marketed in Member States. As will be seen in the following section, the Court was to re-define the scope of the *Cassis* doctrine in the *Keck* case, in which the Court distinguished between national rules dealing with the composition, packaging and labelling of goods, etc., as regards which the *Cassis* case-law held good, and national rules prohibiting "certain selling arrangements", which the Court held would fall within the scope of Article 28 (ex 30) only if they discriminated in law or in fact between domestic goods and imports.[75]

This is perhaps an appropriate point at which to question whether the concept of the non-discriminatory trade restriction was ever necessary, or desirable. The concept might be said to be undesirable because it leads to national courts and the Court of Justice deciding whether national legislative bodies have excessively burdened trade by enacting and maintaining in force national rules, which, while they are trade-neutral, nevertheless tend simply to reduce the overall level of sales of domestic goods and imports alike (such as the Sunday trading rules), or to inconvenience producers or traders who might for example have chosen to adopt a sales promotion scheme under the law of one Member State and to seek to extend it to the territory of another Member State where such schemes are subject to restrictions not applicable in the first Member State (such as the rules referred to by the Court in the *Oosthoek's* case). Furthermore, the concept of the non-discriminatory trade restriction leads to courts judicially reviewing legislation decisions to ban totally the sales of a particular product in a Member State, whether it be on health grounds, moral grounds, environmental grounds, or whatever. Judicial resolution of the question whether any impact on imports caused by such measures is justified by the purpose of the measure in question (whether it be protection of shop-workers or consumer protection) involves making value judgments on broad policy questions, and places judges at the outer limits of their legitimate judicial role. It is one thing for a court to identify discrimination, whether direct or indirect, and determine whether that discrimination is justified or

---

[73] See also Case C–169/91 *Council of the City of Stoke-on-Trent and Norwich City Council v. B & Q plc* [1992] E.C.R. I–6635; [1993] 1 C.M.L.R. 426.

[74] Case C–332/89 [1991] E.C.R. 1027; [1993] 3 C.M.L.R. 746; see also Case C–312/89 *Union Départementale des Syndicats CGT de l'Aisne v. Conforama* [1991] E.C.R. I–997; [1993] 3 C.M.L.R. 746.

[75] See below at 331 *et seq.*

not; the question whether conduct amounts to discrimination (on grounds of sex or race) and if so the question whether that discrimination may be justified, arise not infrequently before national courts or tribunals, and such questions are generally held to raise justiciable issues. But the position is different where it is admitted that national rules are not discriminatory, and the sole question for the European or national judge is whether a national legislative body has extended "excessive" protection to consumers, employees or traders. Such broad policy questions are less obviously appropriate for judicial determination, at any rate as long as national courts and the Court of Justice substitute their own judgment for those of competent national legislative authorities on the proportionality of national measures, rather than confining judicial intervention to cases where such authorities have manifestly exceeded the bounds of their discretion.[76]

The basis for arguing that the concept of the non-discriminatory trade restriction was never necessary is that the extremely important case-law of the Court on access of imports to the markets of Member States notwithstanding non-compliance with national rules on product composition, labelling and packaging etc., deals with national measures which, in the view of the present writer, clearly discriminate, indirectly, against imports. It is of course well established that in the context of Article 28 (ex 30) the adoption of apparently neutral criteria will amount to indirect discrimination where the criteria in practice are satisfied entirely by domestic products rather than imports. In *Commission v. Ireland*[77] the Court considered the terms of a contract specification publicised for tender in connection with the augmentation of the Dundalk water supply. The specification referred to asbestos cement pressure pipes "certified as complying with Irish Standard Specification 188:1975 in accordance with the Irish Standards Mark Licensing Scheme of the Institute for Industrial Research and Standards". It appeared that only one undertaking—located in Ireland—had been certified to apply the Irish Standard Mark to pipes of the type required. Consequently, the inclusion of Clause 4.29 had the effect of restricting the supply of the pipes needed for the Dundalk scheme to Irish manufacturers alone. Since the contract specification did not allow for pipes of equivalent standard, the Court held that the inclusion of the specifications in question impeded imports contrary to Article 28 (ex 30) E.C. But criteria which do not in practice exlude all imports are nevertheless to be regarded as being indirectly discriminatory if they place importers at a particular disadvantage. This appears clearly from the cases on national price restrictions. Where a maximum selling price applies without distinction to domestic and imported products it does not of itself amount to a measure having equivalent effect. It will only do so when it is fixed at such a low level that the sale of imported products becomes, if not impossible, at any rate more difficult than that of domestic products.[78] This

---

[76] See also below at p. 354.
[77] Case 45/87 [1988] E.C.R. 4929.
[78] See, *e.g.* Case 65/75 *Tasca* [1976] E.C.R. 291, at para. 13; [1977] 2 C.M.L.R. 183; Cases 88–90/75 *SADAM* [1976] E.C.R. 323, at para. 15; [1977] 2 C.M.L.R. 183; Case 5/79 *Hans Buys* [1979] E.C.R. 3203, at para. 26; [1980] 2 C.M.L.R. 493; Cases 16–20/79 *Danis* [1979] E.C.R. 3327; [1980] 3 C.M.L.R. 492.

would be the case where imports could only be effected at a loss,[79] or where traders were impelled by the disparity between the lower cost of domestic goods and imports to give preference to the latter.[80] Imports would equally be impeded if the minimum prices which could be charged by traders were fixed at such a high level that the price advantage enjoyed by imports over domestic goods were cancelled out.[81] By way of analogy, in the context of the movement of workers, the Court has held that, unless it is objectively justified and proportionate to its aim, a provision of national law is indirectly discriminatory if it is intrinsically liable to affect migrant workers more than national workers and if there is a consequent risk that it will place the former at a particular disadvantage. A residence requirement is capable of comprising such a requirement.[82] It was noted above[83] that the Court appears to accept that extending national product requirements to imports may produce protective effects by favouring typical national products, and operating to the detriment of certain types of products from other Member States.[84] Applying such reasoning to the *Cassis* case would hold the 25 per cent alcohol requirement to be a product specification intrinsically likely to be satisfied by domestic products and placing at a particular disadvantage imports of products lawfully manufactured and placed on the market in a Member State where there was no 25 per cent minimum alcohol requirement and similar products were typically of between 15 per cent and 20 per cent alcohol content. The requirement, which has effects analogous to the national price restriction cases referred to above, should be regarded as indirectly discriminatory unless objectively justified (on such grounds as public health or consumer protection) and proportionate. While it is easy to be wise after the event, it is to be noted that if such an analysis had been adopted in *Cassis* and its progeny, that case-law would never have been applied in the *Cinétheque* case, nor would it have been applied in the cases on sales promotion and advertising, and Sunday trading, and the *Keck* re-appraisal of the *Cassis* case-law would have been unnecessary. From a slightly different perspective, it might be said that after *Keck*, the practical result is that the *Cassis* case-law is *almost* invariably to be applied *as if* it were based on the proposition that trade-neutral national rules do not fall within the scope of Article 28 (ex 30) E.C., which only covers national rules which differentiate between inter-State and intra-State trade, or between channels of inter-State trade.[85] It is appropriate at this point to consider the *Keck* case.

---

[79] Case 65/75 *Tasca* [1976] E.C.R. 291, at para. 13; [1977] 2 C.M.L.R. 183; Cases 88–90/75 *SADAM*, n.78, *supra*.

[80] Case 5/79 *Hans Buys* [1979] E.C.R. 3203, at para. 26; [1980] 2 C.M.L.R. 493; Cases 16–20/79 *Danis*, n.78, *supra*.

[81] Case 82/77 *Van Tiggele* [1978] E.C.R. 25; [1978] 2 C.M.L.R. 528.

[82] See, *e.g.* Case C–57/96 *H. Meints* [1997] E.C.R. I–6689; [1998] 1 C.M.L.R. 1159, paras 45–46.

[83] At p. 326.

[84] Case 16/83 *Prantl* [1984] E.C.R. 1299 at para. 21; [1985] 2 C.M.L.R. 238

[85] Almost invariably, but not always. The present writer accepts that the law is not precisely as he argues it should be. The Court has continued to identify measures which are not even indirectly discriminatory as falling within the scope of Art. 28 (ex 30), see, *e.g. Generics BV v. SmithKline and French Laboratories Ltd* [1997] E.C.R. I–7231; [1998] 1 C.M.L.R. 1 (right of proprietor of a patent to prevent third parties from using samples manufactured in accordance with patented process for the purpose of obtaining a market authorisation). See also Case C–473/98 *Toolex* judgment July 11, 2000 (national general prohibition on use of a product).

The *Keck and Mithouard* judgment

The facts giving rise to the national proceedings in *Bernard Keck and Daniel Mithouard*[86] were that Mr Keck and Mr Mithouard were prosecuted for reselling products in an unaltered state at prices lower than their actual purchase price contrary to French legislation. In their defence, they contended that a general prohibition on resale at a loss was incompatible with, *inter alia*, Article 28 (ex 30) E.C., and a reference, *inter alia*, on that question was made to the Court of Justice. In its judgment, the Court re-defined its *Cassis* case-law to date as follows:

"12. National legislation imposing a general prohibition on resale at a loss is not designed to regulate trade in goods between Member States.

13. Such legislation may, admittedly, restrict the volume of sales, and hence the volume of sales of products from other Member States, in so far as it deprives traders of a method of sales promotion. But the question remains whether such a possibility is sufficient to characterise the legislation in question as a measure having equivalent effect to a quantitative restriction on imports.

14. In view of the increasing tendency of traders to invoke Article 30 of the Treaty as a means of challenging any rules whose effect is to limit their commercial freedom even where such rules are not aimed at products from other Member States, the Court considers it necessary to re-examine and clarify its case-law on this matter.

15. It is established by the case-law beginning with "Cassis de Dijon" (Case 120/78 *Rewe-Zentral v. Bundesmonopolverwaltung für Branntwein* [1979] E.C.R. 649) that, in the absence of harmonisation of legislation, obstacles to free movement of goods which are the consequence of applying, to goods coming from other Member States where they are lawfully manufactured and marketed, rules that lay down requirements to be met by such goods (such as those relating to designation, form, size, weight, composition, presentation, labelling, packaging) constitute measures of equivalent effect prohibited by Article 30. This is so even if those rules apply without distinction to all products unless their application can be justified by a public-interest objective taking precedence over the free movement of goods.

16. By contrast, contrary to what has previously been decided, the application to products from other Member States of national provisions restricting or prohibiting certain selling arrangements is not such as to hinder directly or indirectly, actually or potentially, trade between Member States within the meaning of the *Dassonville* judgment (Case 8/74 [1974] E.C.R. 837), so long as those provisions apply to all relevant traders operating within the national territory and so long as they affect in the same manner, in law and in fact, the marketing of domestic products and of those from other Member States.

17. Provided that those conditions are fulfilled, the application of such rules to the sale of products from another Member State meeting the requirements laid down by that State is not by nature such as to prevent their

---

[86] Joined Cases C–267–268/91 [1993] E.C.R. I 6097; [1995] 1 C.M.L.R. 101.

access to the market or to impede access any more than it impedes the access of domestic products. Such rules therefore fall outside the scope of Article 30 of the Treaty."

The above passages from the judgment of the Court contrast on the one hand, national rules laying down requirements to be met by goods themselves, and on the other hand, rules which lay down "certain selling arrangements". The former continue to be governed by the *Cassis* case-law. The latter, notwithstanding the previous case-law of the Court, are no longer held to hinder trade and to require justification provided that they apply to all relevant traders operating within the national territory, and so long as they affect in the same manner, in law and in fact, the marketing of domestic products and of those from other Member States. Distinguishing between the former and latter categories is clearly of importance, and the Court gives some assistance in this regard. National measures in the latter category neither prevent the access of imports to the market nor impede the access of imports more than that of domestic products.[87] However, national measures of the kind under discussion only restrict imports to the extent that they restrict the overall volume of sales of both domestic goods and imports,[88] and it may be questioned whether such measures could ever be said to impede the *access* of products to the market at all. Rather, such measures deprive traders of a sales opportunity which affects equally all products which have secured access to the market and are the subject of transactions on that market. The Court also indicates, in the first of the paragraphs cited from its judgment above, that its reference to "certain selling arrangements" does not cover measures which are designed to regulate trade in goods between Member States.[89] The Court in *Keck* concluded that Article 28 (ex 30) did not apply to legislation of a Member State imposing a general prohibition on resale at a loss, which the Court clearly regarded as comprising "selling arrangements" of the type referred to above.[90]

In the view of the present writer, the former of the two categories referred to above in *Keck* comprises national measures which prevent or impede the access to the market of imports, and all national measures which are designed to regulate trade between Member States. As regards this category, it is not necessary to undertake an enquiry as to whether the measures in question are discriminatory or not. The latter of the two categories referred to above includes all national measures which regulate sales opportunities and the sales promotion of those products, domestic and imported alike, which have secured access to the market, and the restrictive effect of which measures on the sale of imports are incidental to the restrictive effects which they have on the overall sales of all products of that type, domestic and imported alike. Furthermore, the former and latter categories referred to above would seem to be applicable *mutatis mutandis* to national measures which neither prescribe composition or

---

[87] Para. 17 of judgment.
[88] Para. 13 of judgment.
[89] Case C–158/94 *Commission of the European Communities v. Italian Republic* [1997] E.C.R. I–5789, para. 31.
[90] For an analogous case concerning sales at low profit margins, see Case C–63/94 *Groupement National des Négociants en Pommes de Terre de Belgique* [1995] E.C.R. I–2467.

labelling rules, on the one hand, nor regulate sales or sales promotions, on the other, but which have effects analagous to measures of the former or latter type.

The case-law after the *Keck* judgment

The scale of the case-law caught by the words "contrary to what has previously been decided" became apparent as the Court applied the *Keck* reasoning in its subsequent cases. In *Punto Casa SpA* the Court considered Italian rules restricting the Sunday opening hours of shops; the Court held that Article 28 (ex 30) did not apply to national legislation on the closure of shops which applies to all traders operating within the national territory and which affects in the same manner, in law and in fact, the marketing of domestic products and of those from other Member States.[91] In *Lucien Ortscheit GmbH* the Court considered a national rule prohibiting advertisements containing an offer to obtain specified medicinal products by individual importation. This the Court held to fall within the scope of Article 28 (ex 30) because it applied solely to *foreign* medicinal products.[92] In *Hünermund* the Court considered a restriction imposed on advertising by pharmacists outside their pharmacy of quasi-pharmaceutical products which they were authorised to sell, and held that it did not fall within Article 28 (ex 30) because it did not affect the marketing of goods from other Member States differently from that of domestic products.[93] In *Société d'Importation Édouard Leclerc-Siplec* the Court held that legislation which prohibits television advertising in a particular sector concerns selling arrangements for products belonging to that sector in that it prohibits a particular form of promotion of a particular method of marketing products, and that a prohibition such as that in issue did not fall within the scope of Article 28 (ex 30), since it affected the marketing of imports and domestic goods in the same manner.[94] In *De Agostini*[95] the Court considered an outright ban on advertising aimed at children less than 12 years of age and of misleading advertising. The Court noted that the national measures in issue applied to all relevant traders operating within national territory, but added that it could not be excluded that an outright ban, applying in one Member State, of a type of promotion for a product which is lawfully sold there might have a greater impact on products from other Member States. It followed that such a ban was not covered by Article 28 (ex 30), unless it were shown that the ban did not affect in the same way, in fact and in law, the marketing of national products and of products from other Member States. In which case it would be necessary to consider the question of justification.[96]

---

[91] Joined Cases C–69 and 258/93 [1994] E.C.R. I–2355. See also Joined Cases C–401–402/92 *Tankstaton 't Heukske vof* [1994] E.C.R. I–2199.

[92] Case C–320/93 [1994] E.C.R. I–5243, para. 9; [1995] 2 C.M.L.R. 242.

[93] Case C–292/92 *Ruth Hünermund and others v. Landesapothekerkammer Baden-Württemberg* [1993] E.C.R. I–6787, para. 23.

[94] Case C–412/93 [1995] E.C.R. I–179, para. 23; [1995] 3 C.M.L.R. 422. For a thought provoking critique of the reasoning in *Keck* see the Opinion of Advocate General Jacobs at paras 38 *et. seq.*

[95] Joined Cases C–34–36/95 *Konsumentombudsmannen (KO) v. De Agostini (Svenska) Förlag AB* [1997] E.C.R. I–3843.

[96] *ibid.* paras 39–45.

The Court has applied the "selling arrangements" analysis to national rules which restrict the distribution of certain products to certain types of outlet. Thus in *Commission v. Greece*[97] the Court considered Greek rules which required processed milk for infants to be sold exclusively by pharmacies. The Court took the view that the legislation,

". . . the effect of which is to limit the commercial freedom of traders irrespective of the actual characteristics of the product referred to, concerns the selling arrangements of certain goods, inasmuch as it prohibits the sale, other than exclusively by pharmacies, of processed milk for infants and thus generally determines the points of sale where they may be distributed."

Since the legislation applied without distinction according to the origin of the products in question, to all of the traders operating within the national territory, and did not affect the sale of products originating in other Member States any differently from that of domestic products, the Court concluded that it did not fall within Article. The Court noted that this conclusion was not affected by the fact, pointed out by the Commission, that Greece did not itself produce processed milk for infants, and the Court added that the situation would be different "only if it was apparent that the legislation in issue protected domestic products which were similar to processed milk for infants from other Member States or which were in competition with milk of that type". But the Commission had not shown this to be the case.[98] Similar reasoning has been applied in the case of national rules confining tobacco sales to authorised retailers,[99] and national rules which require authorisation for the distribution of bovine semen.[1]

While not all national measures which might be said to impede trade will be capable of being classified as either rules relating to the goods themselves on the one hand, or selling arrangements, on the other, the above case-law indicates that a signficant number of restrictions can be so classified, and there can be no doubt that *Keck* has clarified the law, and has in practice focused Article 28's prohibition principally, if not quite exclusively, on national measures which discriminate, directly or indirectly, as between inter-State and intra-State trade, or between channels of inter-State trade. Where national measures do not fall neatly into one or other of the *Keck* categories, it is suggested above that those categories may be applied *mutatis mutandis* to measures having analogous effects, and reference may also be made to the various types of national measure, other than those which can obviously be so categorised, which have been held, in the Court's copious case-law, to amount to measures having equivalent effect, subject to justification.[2]

---

[97] Case C–391/92 [1995] E.C.R. I–1621; [1996] 1 C.M.L.R. 359; [1995] All E.R. (E.C.) 802.
[98] *ibid.*, paras 15–19.
[99] Case C–387/93 *Banchero* [1995] E.C.R. I–4663, paras 37 and 44; [1996] 1 C.M.L.R. 829.
[1] Case C–162/97 *Gunnar Nilsson* [1998] E.C.R. I–7477.
[2] For justification, see below p. 345.

OTHER CHARACTERISTICS OF THE PROHIBITION ON MEASURES HAVING EQUIVALENT EFFECT TO QUANTITATIVE RESTRICTIONS ON IMPORTS

Intra-State or regional restrictions

When a national measure has limited territorial scope because it applies only to a part of national territory, it cannot escape being characterised as discriminatory or protective for the purpose of the rules on the free movement of goods on the ground that it affects both the sale of products from other parts of the national territory and the sale of products imported from other Member States. For such a measure to be characterised as discriminatory or protective, it is not necessary for it to have the effect of favouring national products as a whole or of placing only imported products at a disadvantage.[3] Thus a Danish prohibition on keeping and importation into Laesø of any bee but the Laesø brown bee, for reasons of conservation, and having the effect of excluding bees both from other parts of Denmark and from other Member States, was held to amount to a measure having equivalent effect, though a measure justified on environmental grounds.[4]

Only conduct attributable to the state comprise measures having equivalent effect

The measures defined by the Court as amounting to measures having equivalent effect are invariably described as "national" measures, or trading rules "of the Member States" or measures "enacted by Member States". This would seem to exclude the conduct of private individuals and undertakings unsupported by State action of a legislative, executive or judicial character. The Court has condemned as a measure having equivalent effect a campaign funded by a Member State to promote the sale of domestic goods with a view to limiting imports, despite the fact that the campaign was conducted by a private company limited by guarantee. The management committee of the company was appointed by the national authorities, and the aims and outlines of the campaign were decided upon by those authorities. The Court held that the Member State in question could neither rely upon the fact that the campaign was conducted by a private company, nor upon the fact that the campaign was based upon decisions which were not binding upon undertakings, to avoid liability under Article 30 (now Article 28).[5] The Court observed in another case that a body

---

[3] Joined Cases C–1 and 176/90 *Aragonesa de Publicidad Exterior SA* [1991] E.C.R. I–4151 at para. 24; [1994] 1 C.M.L.R. 887. See also Joined Cases C–277/81, 318–319/91 *Ligur Carni Srl and Genova Carni Srl v. Unità Sanitaria Locale n. XV di Genova and Ponente SpA v. Unità Sanitaria Locale n. XIX di La Spezia and CO.GE.SE.MA Coop a r l.* [1993] E.C.R. I–6621.

[4] Case C–67/97 *Ditlev Bluhme* [1998] E.C.R. I–8033; [1999] 1 C.M.L.R. 612.

[5] Case 249/81 *Commission v. Ireland* [1982] E.C.R. 4005; [1983] 2 C.M.L.R. 104. In Joined Cases 266–267/87 *R. v. Pharmaceutical Society of Great Britain, ex p. Association of Pharmaceutical Importers* [1989] E.C.R. 1295, para. 15, [1989] 2 C.M.L.R. 751, the Court held that measures adopted by a professional body vested with statutory disciplinary powers might constitute "measures" within the scope of Art. 30 (now Art. 28). See also Case C–292/92 *Ruth Hünermund and others v. Landesapothekerkammer Baden-Württemberg* [1993] E.C.R. I–6787, para. 15

established and funded by Government with a view, *inter alia*, to promoting the sale of domestic products could not under Community law enjoy the same freedom as regards methods of advertising as that enjoyed by producers themselves or producer's associations of a voluntary character.[6] A Member State which abstains from taking action or fails to adopt adequate measures to prevent obstacles to the free movement of goods which are created, in particular, by actions of private individuals on its territory aimed at products originating in other Member State, will infringe Article 28 (ex 30), read in conjunction with Article 10 (ex 5).[7]

A measure having equivalent effect need not have an appreciable effect on trade

It is not necessary for a national measure to have an appreciable effect on trade for it to fall within the prohibition of Article 28 (ex 30). Indeed, in *Jan Van der Haar* the Court stressed that Article 28 (ex 30):

". . . does not distinguish between measures . . . according to the degree to which trade between Member States is affected. If a national measure is capable of hindering imports it must be regarded as a measure having an effect equivalent to a quantitative restriction, even though the hindrance is slight and even though it is possible for imported products to be marketed in other ways."[8]

In one case the Court referred to a "national measure which has, or may have, a restrictive effect on trade".[9] The position appears to be that even the possibility of a slight effect on intra-Community trade is sufficient to bring a national measure within the ambit of Article 28. Nevertheless, the Court held in *Kranz* that the possibility that nationals of one Member State might hesitate to sell goods on instalment terms to purchasers in another Member State because such goods would be liable to seizure in the latter Member State by the collector of taxes if the purchasers failed to discharge their tax debts is "too uncertain and indirect" to warrant the conclusion that a national provision authorising such seizure is liable to hinder trade between Member States.[10] In *CMC Motorradcenter GmbH* a national court asked whether it was compatible with Article 28 (ex 30) for a national rule to require an importer to be required to inform the purchaser of a motorcycle that dealers authorised by the manufacturer often refuse to carry out repairs under the guarantee for vehicles which are the subject of parallel imports. The Court held that the national rule of the law of contract applied without distinction, at least as regards products coming from the Community, to all contractual relationships covered by that law and that its purpose was not to regulate trade. As regards the question whether there was a risk of obstructing the free movement of goods, the Court noted that it was in

[6] Case 222/82 *Apple and Pear Development Council* [1983] E.C.R. 4083; [1984] 3 C.M.L.R. 733.
[7] Case C–265/95 *Commission v. France* [1997] E.C.R. I–6959.
[8] Joined Cases 177–178/82 [1984] E.C.R. 1797 at para. 13; [1985] 2 C.M.L.R. 57.
[9] Case 97/83 *Melkunie* [1984] E.C.R. 2367 at para. 12; [1986] 2 C.M.L.R. 318.
[10] Case C–69/88 *Kranz* [1990] E.C.R. I–583. The "too uncertain and indirect" formulation in *Kranz* has been applied by analogy in the context of the free movement of workers. See Case C–190/98 *Graf* judgment of January 27, 2000, para. 25.

any event not the obligation to provide information which would cause such a risk, but the fact that certain authorised dealers of the brand in question refuse to perform services under the guarantee on motorcycles which have been the subject of parallel imports. The Court concluded that the restrictive effects which the obligation to provide information might have on the free movement of goods were too uncertain and too indirect to warrant the conclusion that it is liable to hinder trade between Member States.[11] It is to be noted that *Krantz* and *CMC* pre-date *Keck*, and might well be decided today on the basis that they involve non-discriminatory selling arrangements and accordingly do not fall within the scope of Article 28 (ex 30). But not all national rules are being classified by the Court by reference to the *Keck* judgment, and in *Peralta* the Court applied the "too uncertain and too indirect" test, subsequently to *Keck*, citing *Krantz* and *CMC*.[12] In *DIP SpA* the Court considered national rules for the licensing of new shops. Citing *Peralta*, the Court noted that the rules made no distinction according to the origin of the goods distributed by the businesses concerned, that their purpose was not to regulate trade in goods with other Member States, and that the restrictive effects which they might have on the free movement of goods were too uncertain and indirect for the obligation which they impose to be regarded as being capable of hindering trade between Member States.[13] This comes close to applying the second category in *Keck* by analogy, since the Court's formulation suggests that if the measure *did* distinguish according to the origin of the goods the conclusion would be different. And the measure in issue in *DIP SpA* was certainly analogous to the measure actually in issue in *Keck*, inasmuch as in each case the only restrictive effect on imports would result from any overall reduction in sales of domestic goods and imports alike. Applying the *Keck* categories by analogy could only increase the consistency and predictability of the case-law of both national courts and the European Court.

The prohibition in Article 28 applies at the marketing stage rather than the production stage

The Court in the *Kramer* case contrasted the production stage of the economic process with the marketing stage, and indicated that Articles 28 *et seq.*, (ex 30 *et seq.*) applied to the latter but not to the former.[14]

A national restriction offering flexible exemptions may still amount to a measure having equivalent effect

A defence sometimes advanced by national authorities has been that although a particular measure is apparently contrary to Articles 28 *et seq.* (ex 30) it is in

---

[11] Case C–93/92 *CMC Motorradcenter GmbH v. Pelin Baskiciogullari* [1993] E.C.R. I–5009.
[12] Case C–379/92 *Matteo Peralta* [1994] E.C.R. I–3453, para. 3453, para. 24.
[13] Joined Cases C–140–142/94 [1995] E.C.R. I–3257 at para. 29; see also Case C–134/94 *Esso Española SA v. Comunidad Autónoma de Canarias* [1995] E.C.R. I–4223, para. 24; [1996] 5 C.M.L.R. 154.
[14] Joined Cases 3–4 and 6/76 *Kramer and Others* [1976] E.C.R. 1279, para 27; [1976] 2 C.M.L.R. 440.

fact administered with flexibility, and exceptions may be made. The Court has consistently rejected this argument.[15] As the Court explained in *Kelderman*:

". . . a measure caught by the prohibition provided for in Article 30 . . . does not escape that prohibition simply because the competent authority is empowered to grant exemptions, even if that power is freely applied to imported products. Freedom of movement is a right whose enjoyment may not be dependent upon a discretionary power or on a concession granted by the national administration."[16]

The application of Articles 28–30 may not be resisted on the ground that the national rules should have been harmonised

It is clear that many barriers to intra-Community trade are capable of elimination through the technique of harmonisation of national laws under Articles 94 or 95 (ex Articles 100 and 100a) E.C. The possibility of harmonisation however, cannot justify derogation from the requirements of Article 28 (ex 30). In *Commission v. Italy* the latter Member State argued that the Commission should have sought harmonisation before resorting to Articles 30 to 36 (now Articles 28–30) E.C. The Court rejected the argument as follows:

"The fundamental principle of a unified market and its corollary, the free movement of goods, must not under any circumstances be made subject to the condition that there should first be an approximation of national laws for if that condition had to be fulfilled the principle would be reduced to a mere cipher."[17]

Can the application of national rules to domestic products be called in question where the rules comprise measures having equivalent effect *vis-à-vis* imports?

It has been held that the inconsistency of national rules with Articles 28-30 (ex 30-36) is a point which can only be taken in respect of goods imported or to be imported from another Member State.[18] Where Article 28 (ex 30) precludes the application of national law to imports, the result may be that domestic products are placed at a disadvantage in comparison with imports. But this is consistent with Community law.[19] It is a consequence of, on the one hand, the choice of the national legislator, and, on the other hand, the fact that the prohibition of quantitative restrictions and measures having equivalent effect applies exclusively to imported products. The position is certainly different where Community rules

---

[15] Case 82/77 *Van Tiggele* [1978] E.C.R. 25; [1978] 2 C.M.L.R. 528; Case 251/78 *Denkavit* [1979] E.C.R. 3369; [1980] 3 C.M.L.R. 513; Case 27/80 *Fietje* [1980] E.C.R. 3839; [1981] 3 C.M.L.R. 722. It is of course otherwise if the restrictions are capable of being justified in accordance with the Treaty, as to which, see below, p. 345.

[16] Case 130/80 [1981] E.C.R. 527 at para. 14. See also Case 124/81 *Commission v. United Kingdom* [1983] E.C.R. 203, at para. 10; [1983] 2 C.M.L.R. 1.

[17] Case 193/80 [1981] E.C.R. 3019, at para. 17.

[18] See, *e.g.* Joined Cases 314–316/82 *Waterkeyn* [1982] E.C.R. 4337.

[19] Case 355/85 *Driancourt v. Cognet* [1986] E.C.R. 3231; Cases 80 and 159/85 *EDAH BV* [1986] E.C.R. 3359; [1988] 2 C.M.L.R. 113.

lay down the same conditions for the marketing of domestic products and imports alike.[20] But in *Pistre* the Court considered the compatibility with Article 28 (ex 30) of national rules restricting use of the description "mountain" to products having links with a specific region of national territory. The reference arose from national criminal proceedings against French nationals prosecuted for marketing French products wrongly bearing the designation in question. The Court rejected the argument that Article 28 (ex 30) could have no application since imports were not involved. It noted that nevertheless "the application of the national measure may also have effects on the free movement of goods between Member States, in particular when the measure in question facilitates the marketing of goods of domestic origin to the detriment of imported goods. In such circumstances, the application of the measure, even if restricted to domestic producers, in itself creates and maintains a difference of treatment between those two categories of goods, hindering, at least potentially, intra-Community trade." Since the legislation in issue in the national proceedings discriminated against goods from other Member States, Article 28 (ex 30) precluded the application of the rules in question.[21]

Article 28 applies to Community measures as well as to national measures

It is established that the prohibition of quantitative restrictions and of all measures having equivalent effect applies not only to national measures but also to measures adopted by the Community institutions.[22]

MEASURES HAVING EQUIVALENT EFFECT TO QUANTITATIVE RESRICTIONS ON EXPORTS

Article 29 (ex 34) E.C. provides that quantitative restrictions on exports, and all measures having equivalent effect, shall be prohibited between Member States. The notion of measures having equivalent effect clearly embraces measures which formally differentiate between domestic trade on the one hand, and the export trade on the other, as the *Bouhelier* case illustrates.[23] In order to ensure quality control, French legislation authorised a public authority to inspect pressed lever watches and watch movements made in France and destined for export to other Member States. If the watches of movements complied with the relevant quality standards, a certificate was issued to that effect. The export of such watches and movements was subject to the grant of a licence, except in the case of consignments in respect of which a standards certificate had been issued. The Court held that Article 29 (ex 34) precluded both export licensing and the imposition of quality

---

[20] Case 98/86 *Mathot* [1987] E.C.R. 809.
[21] Joined Cases C–321–324/94 *Jacques Pistre etc.*, [1997] E.C.R. I–2343. This reasoning is questionable.
[22] Case 15/83 *Denkavit Nederland v. Hoofdproduktschap voor akkerbouwprodukten* [1984] E.C.R. 2171, para. 15; Case C–51/93 *Meyhui NV v. Schott Zwiesel Glaswerke AG* [1994] E.C.R. I–3879, para. 11; Case C–114/96 *René Kieffer and Romain Thill* [1997] E.C.R. I–3629, [1997] 3 C.M.L.R. 1446, para. 27.
[23] Case 53/76 [1977] E.C.R. 197; [1977] 1 C.M.L.R. 436.

controls on exports. Since the latter controls were not required in the case of products for the domestic market, their imposition amounted to arbitrary discrimination and constituted an obstacle to intra-Community trade.

The evolution of the case-law on measures having equivalent effect to quantitative restrictions on exports has not mirrored that on imports. Notwithstanding developments in the *Cassis* doctrine the Court has consistently required a national measure to have discriminatory effects before it could be held to comprise a prohibited restriction on exports. As the Court explained in *Groenveld*:

"That provision [*i.e.* Art. 34(1), now Article 29] concerns the national measures which have as their specific object or effect the restriction of patterns of exports and thereby the establishment of a difference in treatment between the domestic trade of a Member State and its export trade in such a way as to provide a particular advantage for national production or for the domestic market of the State in question at the expense of the production or of the trade of other Member States. This is not so in the case of a prohibition like that in question which is applied objectively to the production of goods of a certain kind without drawing a distinction depending on whether such goods are intended for the national market or for export."[24]

The Court has repeated this formulation on numerous occasions.[25] An obligation on producers to deliver poultry offal to their local authority has been held to involve by implication a prohibition of exports and to fall accordingly within the scope of application of Article 29 (ex 34).[26] Similarly, an obligation to transport animals for short maximum periods and distances combined with an obligation for all such transport to end at the nearest suitable abattoir in national territory for slaughter was held to amount to a measure having equivalent effect to a quantitative restriction on both imports and exports.[27]

The prohibition in question binds the Community institutions as well as the Member States, and the requirements of Article 29 (ex 34) have been held to be satisfied where Community rules made equivalent but not identical provision for administrative supervision both for exports in bulk of compound feeding-stuffs and for the marketing thereof within the Community.[28]

CHARACTERISTICS OF NATIONAL MEASURES HELD TO HAVE EFFECTS EQUIVALENT TO QUANTITATIVE RESTRICTIONS

The general definitions of measures having equivalent effect advanced by the Court of Justice in *Dassonville*, *Cassis*, and *Keck*, are of course of enormous

---

[24] Case 15/79 [1979] E.C.R. 3409, at para. 7; [1981] 1 C.M.L.R. 207.
[25] See, *e.g.* Case 155/80 *Oebel* [1981] E.C.R. 1993, at para. 15; [1983] 1 C.M.L.R. 390; Case 286/81 *Oosthoek's* [1982] E.C.R. 4575, at para. 13; [1983] 3 C.M.L.R. 428; Case 172/82 *Inter-Huiles* [1983] E.C.R. 555, at para. 12; [1983] 3 C.M.L.R. 485; Case 237/82 *Jongeneel Kaas and Others v. Netherlands* [1984] E.C.R. 483; [1985] 2 C.M.L.R. 53; para. 22; [1985] 2 C.M.L.R. 649; Case C–412/97 *ED Srl v. Italo Fenocchio* [1999] E.C.R. I–3845, para. 10. But in the latter case the possible effects on exports were too uncertain and indirect to contravene Article 29 (ex 34); *ibid.*, para. 11.
[26] Case 118/86 *Nertsvoederfabriek Nederlandse* [1987] E.C.R. 3883; [1989] 2 C.M.L.R. 436.
[27] Case C–350/97 *Wilfried Monsees* [1999] E.C.R. I–2921.
[28] Case 15/83 *Denkavit* [1984] E.C.R. 2171.

importance.[29] But it is also the case that certain factual characteristics of national measures held to comprise measures having equivalent effect do seem to recur, and it may be of some assistance to consider some of the more common examples.

Frontier inspections

So far as health inspections carried out at frontiers are concerned, the Court has held that, as a result of the delays inherent in the inspections and the additional transport costs which the trader may incur thereby, the inspections in question are likely to make imports or exports more difficult or more costly and accordingly to amount to measures having equivalent effect, subject to justification.[30] The Court has also held that principle to be applicable to other types of frontier inspections, in particular national rules which provide for systematic inspections of goods when they cross a frontier.[31]

Import/export licences, declarations, etc.

Apart from the exceptions for which provision is made by Community law itself,[32]Articles 28 and 29 (ex 30 and 34) E.C. preclude the application to intra-Community trade of a national provision which requires, even purely as a formality, import or export licences or any other similar procedure.[33]

An obligation imposed by an importing Member State to produce a certificate of fitness issued by an exporting Member State in connexion with the import of a product amounts to a measure having equivalent effect.[34] Confining imports of alcohol to licensed traders who complied with conditions concerning their professional knowledge, financial capacity and possession of storage capacity has been held to amount to a measure having equivalent effect to a quantitative restriction.[35]

However, requiring declarations from importers concerning the origin of goods for the purpose of monitoring the movement of goods does not amount to a measure having equivalent effect provided that the importer is not required to declare more than he knows or can reasonably be expected to know, and provided that penalties for failure are not disproportionate.[36]

---

[29] See above, p. 323.

[30] Case 35/76 *Simmenthal v. Italian Minister for Finance* [1976] E.C.R. 1871, para. 7; [1977] 2 C.M.L.R. 1; Case C–272/95 *Bundesanstalt für Landwirtschaft und Ernährung v. Deutsches Milch-Kontor GmbH* [1997] E.C.R. I–1905, para. 27.

[31] Case 190/87 *Moormann* [1988] E.C.R. 4689, para. 8; [1990] 1 C.M.L.R. 656.

[32] Note that import licences may in principle be excused in appropriate cases under Art. 30 (ex Art. 36) (as to which see below at p. 345), see Case 124/81 *Commission v. United Kingdom* [1983] E.C.R. 203; [1983] 2 C.M.L.R. 1; Case 74/82 *Commission v. Ireland* [1984] E.C.R. 317; Case 40/82 *Commission v. United Kingdom* [1984] E.C.R. 283

[33] Note that import licences may in principle be excused in appropriate cases under Art. 30 (ex Art. 36) (as to which see below at p. 345), see Case 124/81 *Commission v. United Kingdom* [1983] E.C.R. 203; Case 74/82 *Commission v. Ireland* [1984] E.C.R. 317; Case 40/82 *Commission v. United Kingdom* [1984] E.C.R. 283

[34] Case 251/78 *Denkavit* [1979] E.C.R. 3369, at para. 11; [1980] 3 C.M.L.R. 513.

[35] Case C–189/95 *Harry Franzén* [1997] E.C.R. I–5909; [1998] 1 C.M.L.R. 1231.

[36] Case 41/76 *Donckerwolcke* [1976] E.C.R. 1921; [1977] 2 C.M.L.R. 535; Case 179/78 *Rivoira* [1979] E.C.R. 1147; [1979] 3 C.M.L.R. 456.

Preference for domestic or other products

National measures which express a preference for domestic products or confer some advantage on domestic products will amount to measures having equivalent effect to quantitative restrictions. The Court of Justice has so ruled in the case of a quality designation reserved for alcoholic drinks containing 85 per cent spirits distilled on national territory.[37] Similarly, in *Campus Oil* the Court held that Irish rules requiring importers of petroleum products to purchase a certain proportion of their requirements at prices fixed by the competent minister from a state-owned company operating a refinery in Ireland amounted to a measure having equivalent effect.[38] In *Commission v. Greece* it was conceded by the defendant Member State that requiring the Agricultural Bank of Greece not to finance purchases of imported agricultural machinery except upon proof that machinery of that kind was not manufactured in Greece amounted to a measure having equivalent effect. The Court held that the concession was rightly made.[39] In *Du Pont de Nemours Italiana* the Court held that Article 28 (ex 30) precluded national rules which reserved to undertakings established in particular regions of the national territory a proportion of public supply contracts.[40] In *Decker* the Court considered a national requirement of prior authorisation for reimbursement for spectacles purchased in another Member State, where no such requirement existed for purchase on national territory, and concluded that such a requirement encouraged insured persons to purchase those products on the home market rather than in other Member States, and to curb imports of spectacles assembled in those states.[41] A tender specifying a particular branded product and failing to indicate that equivalents will be considered has been held to amount to a measure having equivalent effect, though the product specified was not a domestic product.[42] It has even been held that state financed publicity campaigns promoting the purchase of national products on the grounds of national origin and disparaging products from other Member States infringe Article 28 (ex 30).[43]

---

[37] Case 13/78 *Eggers* [1978] E.C.R. 1935; [1979] 1 C.M.L.R. 562; Joined Cases C–321–324/94 *Jacques Pistre etc.*, [1997] E.C.R. I–2343 (designation "mountain" confined to products linked to region of national territory).

[38] Case 72/83 [1984] E.C.R. 2727; [1984] 3 C.M.L.R. 544. But the Court held that such a measure might in principle be excused under Art. 36 (now Art. 30) on grounds of national security.

[39] Case 192/84 [1985] E.C.R. 3967; [1988] 1 C.M.L.R. 420; Case 103/84 *Commission v. Italy* [1986] E.C.R. 1759 (subsidies for vehicles of national manufacture); Case C–137/91 *Commission v Greece* [1992] E.C.R. I–4023; [1992] 3 C.M.L.R. 117 (obligation to purchase cash machines comprising at least 35% added value in Greece).

[40] Case C–21/88 [1990] E.C.R. I–889; [1991] 3 C.M.L.R. 25; Case C–351/88 *Laboratori Bruneau Srl* [1991] E.C.R. I–3641; [1991] 1 C.M.L.R. 707.

[41] Case C–120/95 *Nicholas Decker v. Caisse de Maladie de Employés Privés* [1998] E.C.R. I–1831; [1998] 2 C.M.L.R. 879; see further below, p. 356.

[42] Case C–359/93 *Commission v. Netherlands* [1995] E.C.R. I–157; [1996] 1 C.M.L.R. 477 (specification of operating system "UNIX", a software system developed by Bell Laboratories of ITT (USA) for connecting several computers of different makes).

[43] Case 249/81 *Commission v. Ireland* [1982] E.C.R. 4005; [1983] 2 C.M.L.R. 104; Case 222/82 *Apple and Pear Development Council* [1983] E.C.R. 4083; [1984] 3 C.M.L.R. 733.

Conditions imposed in respect of imported products only

One of the most easily detected infringements of the Treaty's prohibition on measures having equivalent effect to quantitative restrictions is a national rule imposing conditions on imported products which are not imposed on their domestic counterparts. Thus phytosanitary inspections on imports of plant products where no compulsory examination is made of domestic products amounts to a measure having equivalent effect.[44] Again, a national requirement that imported drinks be at least of the alcohol content specified as the minimum in the country of origin, where no minimum alcoholic content was specified for similar domestic products, has been held to be contrary to Article 28 (ex 30).[45] In *Commission v. Italy* the Court condemned an Italian measure prohibiting the testing, for the purposes of registration, of buses which were more than seven years old and came from other Member States, where no such prohibition applied to Italian buses.[46]

Measures making imports more difficult or more costly

A ground advanced by the Court for holding frontier checks of imported products to amount to measures having equivalent effect is that such checks make imports more difficult or costly.[47] Examples of national measures which have been held to be contrary to Article 28 (ex 30) (subject to appropriate justification in accordance with the Treaty)[48] on this ground are an import deposit scheme for imports for which payment was made in advance[49]; the extension to imported products of national rules which prohibited the sales of silver goods without hall-marking[50]; the extension to imported products of a national rule which required that margarine be sold in cube-shaped packs[51]; the extension to imported products of a requirement that certain information not be provided on the packaging of certain products[52]; the extension to imported products of a national rule which prohibited the sale of goods by retail unless they bore an indication of their country of origin[53]; and the roadworthiness testing of imported vehicles.[54] It is often unclear whether the Court is referring to requirements which make the marketing of imports more difficult or costly than they would otherwise be, or more difficult or costly than imports. In truth, both propositions are usually corrrect, and in the view of the present writer it would be

---

[44] Case 4/75 *Rewe* [1975] E.C.R. 843; [1977] 1 C.M.L.R. 198. In this case the measures were justified under Art. 36.
[45] Case 59/82 *Schutzverband* [1983] E.C.R. 1217; [1984] 1 C.M.L.R. 319.
[46] Case 50/83 [1984] E.C.R. 1633.
[47] Case 4/75 *Rewe* [1975] E.C.R. 843, at para. 11; [1977] 1 C.M.L.R. 198; Case 42/82 *Commission v. France* [1983] E.C.R. 1013, at para. 50; [1984] 1 C.M.L.R. 160.
[48] As to which see below, pp. 345–356 *et seq.*
[49] Case 95/81 *Commission v. Italy* [1982] E.C.R. 2187
[50] Case 220/81 *Robertson* [1982] E.C.R. 2349; [1983] 1 C.M.L.R. 556.
[51] Case 261/81 *Rau* [1982] E.C.R. 3961; [1983] 2 C.M.L.R. 496.
[52] Case 94/82 *De Kikvorsch* [1983] E.C.R. 947; [1984] 2 C.M.L.R. 323.
[53] Case 207/83 *Commission v. United Kingdom* [1985] E.C.R. 1201; [1983] 2 C.M.L.R. 259.
[54] Case 50/85 *Schloh* [1986] E.C.R. 1855; [1987] 1 C.M.L.R. 450.

preferable for the Court to accept that measures such as those referred to are indirectly discriminatory.[55]

Impeding access to certain channels of distribution

The definition of measures having equivalent effect which the Court has adopted has led it to conclude that measures are forbidden which "favour, within the Community, particular trade channels or particular commercial operators in relation to others".[56] An example of such a measure is provided by the proceedings in *Procureur du Roi v. Dassonville*.[57] The Court reiterated its view that there must be no discrimination between channels of trade in *de Peijper*.[58] Dutch legislation laid down certain safety requirements in the case of imports of medicinal preparations. The importer was bound to present certain documentation, verified by the manufacturer, to the Dutch public health authorities. Centrafarm purchased quantities of Valium, manufactured by Hoffmann-La Roche in England, from a British wholesaler, packed the tablets in packages bearing the name Centrafarm and marked with the generic name of the product in question, and distributed them to pharmacies in the Netherlands. Centrafarm could not rely on Hoffmann-La Roche's co-operation with regard to the relevant documentation, and was charged under Dutch law. On a reference for a preliminary ruling, the Court ruled that national practices which resulted in imports being channelled in such a way that certain traders could effect these imports, while others could not, constituted measures having equivalent effect.

Price restrictions

The Court has considered on a number of occasions the compatibility with Article 28 (ex 30) of national measures fixing the selling prices of products. Selective price measures taken by national authorities to restrict importation of products from other Member States will clearly be incompatible with Article 28 (ex 30).[59] As has been explained, maximum selling prices which make the sale of imported products if not impossible, at any rate more difficult, comprise measures having equivalent effect, as do minimum prices fixed at such a high level that the price advantage enjoyed by imports over domestic goods is cancelled out.[60]

Even if national rules establish different criteria for fixing the selling prices of imports than are established for fixing the selling prices of domestic goods, there will only be a violation of Article 28 (ex 30) if imports are actually put at some disadvantage. This follows from the *Roussel* case, in which the Court held that:

"Legislation . . . which differentiates between the two groups of products, must be regarded as a measure having an effect equivalent to a quantitative

---

[55] See above, p. 330.
[56] Case 155/73 *Sacchi* [1974] E.C.R. 409, at para. 8; [1974] 2 C.M.L.R. 177.
[57] See above, p. 322.
[58] Case 16/74 [1974] E.C.R. 1183.
[59] Case 90/82 *Commission v. France* [1983] E.C.R. 2011, at para. 27; [1984] 2 C.M.L.R. 516.
[60] Above at p. 329.

restriction where it is capable of making more difficult, in any manner whatever, the sale of imported products."[61]

That separate rules for the price fixing of imports do not of themselves infringe Article 28 is confirmed in *Leclerc*, in which the Court condemned separate price fixing rules for imported books which were liable to impede trade between Member States.[62] Nevertheless, if price fixing rules applied exclusively to imported products, this would violate Article 28 without more since it would of itself place imported products at some disadvantage.

DEROGATION FROM ARTICLES 28–29

Article 30 (ex 36) E.C.

Article 30 (ex 36) E.C. provides:

"The provisions of Articles 28 and 29 shall not preclude prohibitions or restrictions on imports, exports or goods in transit justified on grounds of public morality, public policy or public security; the protection of health and life of humans, animals or plants; the protection of national treasures possessing artistic, historic or archaeological value; or the protection of industrial and commercial property. Such prohibitions or restrictions shall not however, constitute a means of arbitrary discrimination or a disguised restriction on trade between Member States."

Grounds of derogation

Article 30 E.C. constitutes an exception to the fundamental rule that all obstacles to the free movement of goods between Member States shall be abolished and the Article must be interpreted strictly.[63] It follows that the list of exceptions is exhaustive.[64] Thus the Court has held that Article 30 (ex 36) does not justify derogation from Article 28 (ex 30) on the grounds of the protection of consumers or the fairness of commercial transactions,[65] economic policy,[66] or the

---

[61] Case 181/82 [1983] E.C.R. 3849, at para. 19; [1985] 1 C.M.L.R. 834. If price controls are imposed, it may be necessary for any criteria set to take account of circumstances more likely to affect imports than domestic products.

[62] Case 229/83 [1985] E.C.R. 2; [1985] 2 C.M.L.R. 286.

[63] Case 46/76 *Bauhuis v. Netherlands* [1977] E.C.R. 5; Case 113/80 *Commission v. Ireland* [1981] E.C.R. 1625; [1982] 1 C.M.L.R. 706; Case 95/81 *Commission v. Italy* [1982] E.C.R. 2187.

[64] Case 95/81 *Commission v. Italy*, n.63, *supra*.

[65] Case 95/81 *Commission v. Italy*, n.63, *supra*. Case 220/81 *Robertson* [1982] E.C.R. 2349; [1983] 1 C.M.L.R. 556; Case 229/83 *Leclerc*, n.62, *supra*. Such considerations may however, in the case of non-discriminatory restrictions, amount to mandatory requirements justifying reasonable restrictions on the free movement of goods in the general interest, see below at p. 352.

[66] Case 7/61 *Commission v. Italy* [1961] E.C.R. 317; [1962] C.M.L.R. 39; Case 95/81 *Commission v. Italy* [1982] E.C.R. 2187; Case 238/82 Duphar [1984] E.C.R. 523; Case 72/83 *Campus Oil* [1984] E.C.R. 2727; [1984] 3 C.M.L.R. 544; Case 288/83 *Commission v. Ireland* [1985] E.C.R. 1761; [1985] 3 C.M.L.R. 152; Case C–324/93 *R. v. Home Secretary, ex p. Evans Medical Ltd and Macfarlan Smith Ltd* [1995] E.C.R. I–563, at para. 36; [1996] 1 C.M.L.R. 53; [1995] All E.R. (E.C.) 481. But non-discriminatory measures designed to limit the costs of a state health insurance scheme are compatible with Community law, see Case 238/82 *Duphar* at para. 17; see also Case

protection of creativity and cultural diversity,[67] since none of the foregoing are referred to in the Article. While the Court has accepted that the expression "public policy" is capable of embracing a national ban on the export of coins no longer constituting legal tender,[68] it has refused to accept that the expression includes the protection of consumers.[69]

In the absence of harmonised rules at the Community level, recourse to Article 30 (ex 36) may entail the application of different standards in different Member States, as a result of different national value-judgments, and different factual circumstances. Thus the Court has stated that:

> "In principle, it is for each Member State to determine in accordance with its own scale of values and in the form selected by it the requirements of public morality in its territory."[70]

Similarly, in the absence of harmonisation at Community level, it is for each Member State to determine the appropriate level of protection which they wish to accord to the protection of human health, whilst taking account of the free movement of goods within the Community.[71] As the Court explained in *Heijn*:

> "In so far as the relevant Community rules do not cover certain pesticides, Member States may regulate the presence of residues of those pesticides in a way which may vary from one country to another according to the climatic conditions, the normal diet of the population and their state of health."[72]

Nevertheless, while a public health risk to consumers is capable of justifying national rules under Article 30, "the risk must be measured, not according to the yardstick of general conjecture, but on the basis of relevant scientific research",[73] and the discretion of the Member States to decide, in the case of a food additive, on the degree of protection of the health and life of humans to be adopted, is one which is retained "in so far as there are uncertainties in the present state of scientific research with regard to the harmfulness" of the additive in question.[74]

While Article 30 (ex 36) leaves a margin of discretion in the national authorities as to the extent to which they wish to protect the interests listed therein, the discretion is limited by two important principles. First, that any discrimination between imports and domestic products must not be arbitrary. Secondly, that national measures must not restrict trade any more than is necessary to protect the interest in question.

C–120/95 *Nicholas Decker v. Caisse de Maladie des Employés Privés* [1998] E.C.R. I–1831, [1998] 2 C.M.L.R. 879, ". . . aims of a purely economic nature cannot justify a barrier to the fundamental principle of the free movement of goods. However, it cannot be excluded that the risk of seriously undermining the financial balance of the social security system may constitute an overriding reason in the general interest capable of justifying a barrier of that kind", at para. 39 (though it will be noted that in the latter case the measure was discriminatory, see below, p. 356).

[67] Case 229/83 *Leclerc*, n.62, *supra*.
[68] Case 7/78 *Thompson* [1978] E.C.R. 2247; [1979] 1 C.M.L.R. 47.
[69] Case 177/83 *Kohl* [1984] E.C.R. 3651; [1985] 3 C.M.L.R. 340.
[70] Case 34/79 *Henn & Darby* [1979] E.C.R. 3795; [1980] 1 C.M.L.R. 246.
[71] Case C–205/89 *Commission v. Greece* [1991] E.C.R. I–1361, para. 8.
[72] Case 94/83 [1984] E.C.R. 3263.
[73] Case C–17/93 *JJJ Van der Veldt* [1994] E.C.R. I–3537, para. 17; [1995] 1 C.M.L.R. 621; Case 178/84 *Commission v. Germany* [1987] E.C.R. 1227; [1988] 1 C.M.L.R. 780.
[74] Case C–113/91 *Criminal proceedings against Michel Debus* [1992] E.C.R. I–3617, para. 13.

Arbitrary discrimination or a disguised restriction on trade

Article 30 (ex 36) provides that prohibitions or restrictions permitted under that Article shall not however constitute a means of arbitrary discrimination or a disguised restriction on trade between Member States. The purpose of this proviso was described by the Court in *Henn & Darby* as being to:

". . . prevent restrictions on trade based on the grounds mentioned in the first sentence of Article 36 from being diverted from their proper purpose and used in such a way as either to create discrimination in respect of goods originating in other Member States or indirectly to protect certain national products."[75]

In determining whether or not discrimination against imported goods is arbitrary, an important yardstick will be a comparison with measures taken *vis-à-vis* domestic goods: *Rewe-Zentralfinanz v. Landwirtschaftskammer*.[76] As a precaution against transmission of the destructive San José Scale insect, German legislation provided for the phytosanitary examination of certain imported fruit and vegetables at point of entry. On a reference for a preliminary ruling, the Court held that such measures must be considered to be justified in principle under Art. 30 (ex 36), provided that they did not constitute a means of arbitrary discrimination. This would not be the case where effective measures were taken to prevent the distribution of contaminated domestic products, and where there was reason to believe that there would be a risk of the harmful organism spreading if no inspections were held on importation.

A measure which discriminates against imports and indeed excludes imports may however be justified if it is the only way to achieve the objective of protection for the health and life of humans. Thus in *R. v. Home Secretary, ex p. Evans Medical Ltd and Macfarlan Smith Ltd*, the Court of Justice held that a Member State was entitled to refuse a licence for importation of narcotic drugs from another Member State on the ground that such importation threatened the viability of the sole licensed manufacturer in the former State and jeopardised reliability of the supply of diamorphine for medical purposes, provided that the latter objective could not be achieved as effectively by measures less restrictive of intra-Community trade.[77] If a Member State seeks to preserve an indigenous animal population with distinct characteristics by banning imports of other species which might mate with the indigenous population and endanger its survival, this can be justified under Article 30 as a measure to protect the life of animals.[78]

National measures are only justified if they are no more restrictive than is strictly necessary

The Court has emphasised that Article 30 (ex 36) is not designed to reserve certain matters to the exclusive jurisdiction of Member States, but only permits

---

[75] Case 34/79 *Henn & Darby* [1979] E.C.R. 3795, at para. 21; [1980] 1 C.M.L.R. 246; Case 40/82 *Commission v. United Kingdom* [1984] E.C.R. 283, at para. 36.

[76] Case 4/75 [1975] E.C.R. 843.

[77] Case C–324/93 [1995] E.C.R. I–563, paras 35–39; [1996] 1 C.M.L.R. 53; [1995] All E.R. (E.C.) 481.

[78] Case C–67/97 *Ditlev Bluhme* [1998] E.C.R. I—8033; [1999] 1 C.M.L.R. 612.

national laws to derogate from the principle of the free movement of goods to the extent to which such derogation is and continues to be justified for the attainment of the objectives referred to in that Article.[79] The word "justified" is to be construed as meaning "necessary".[80] Application of the Article is thus to be conditioned upon compliance with the principle of proportionality.[81] As the Court explained in *Commission v. Belgium*:

> "However [public health] measures are justified only if it is established that they are necessary in order to attain the objective of protection referred to in Article 36 and that such protection cannot be achieved by means which place less of a restriction on the free movement of goods within the Community."[82]

Thus, in *de Peijper*,[83] the Court considered the argument that restrictive provisions of Netherlands legislation which favoured imports by dealers securing the co-operation of the manufacturer were justified on the basis that they were necessary for the protection of the health and life of humans. While the Court acknowledged that this interest ranked first among the interests protected by Article 30 (ex 36) of the Treaty, it emphasised that national measures did not fall within the exception if the health or life of humans could be as effectively protected by means less restrictive of intra-Community trade. In particular, Article 30 (ex 36) did not justify restrictions motivated primarily by a concern to facilitate the task of the authorities, or reduce public expenditure, unless alternative arrangements would impose unreasonable burdens on the administration.

Where a measure having equivalent effect has but a slight impact on trade, this will be relevant in assessing the proportionality of the national measures in question. As the Court explained in *Société Civile Agricole du Centre d'Insémination de la Crespelle*:

> "In order to ascertain that the restrictive effects on intra-Community trade of the rules at issue do not exceed what is necessary to achieve the aim in view, it must be considered whether those effects are direct, indirect or purely speculative and whether those effects do not impede the marketing of imported products more than the marketing of national products."[84]

Judicial assessment of the proportionality of a measure may well involve a review of possible alternative means of achieving the aim in question,[85] and determining the compatibility with Article 30 of, *e.g.* a national measure limiting the sulphur dioxide content of beer, can entail a detailed consideration of

---

[79] Case 5/77 *Tedeschi* [1977] E.C.R. 1556; [1978] 1 C.M.L.R. 1; Case 251/78 *Denkavit* [1979] E.C.R. 3369; [1980] 3 C.M.L.R. 513.

[80] Case 153/78 *Commission v. Germany* [1979] E.C.R. 2555, at para. 8; [1980] 1 C.M.L.R. 198; Case 251/78 *Denkavit* at para. 21.

[81] As to which, see above, p. 135.

[82] Case 155/82 [1983] E.C.R. 531; [1983] 2 C.M.L.R. 566. And a consistent case-law to this effect, see, *e.g.* Case 97/83 *Melkunie* [1984] E.C.R. 2367, at para. 12; Case C–189/95 *Harry Franzén*, [1997] E.C.R. I–5909; [1998] 1 C.M.L.R. 1231; at para. 75.

[83] Case 104/75 [1976] E.C.R. 613; [1976] 2 C.M.L.R. 271.

[84] Case C–323/93 [1994] E.C.R. I–5077, at para. 36.

[85] Case C–131/93 *Commission v. Germany* [1994] E.C.R. I–3303, para. 25; [1995] 2 C.M.L.R. 278.

available scientific evidence as regards the qualities and effects of the additive in question.[86] There can be no doubt that claims to restrict the free movement of goods on public health grounds are not beyond judicial scrutiny, and such matters as the burden of proof,[87] or, in cases on food additives, the tolerated levels of the additive in question in other beverages or foodstuffs, or other conduct of the relevant national authorities which suggests that alternative measures less restrictive of trade would be adequate to achieve the aims in question,[88] may play a large part in the outcome of a case.[89] In adversarial proceedings under Article 226 (ex 169) E.C. it will be for the Court of Justice to decide whether or not a national measure is proportional.[90] On a reference for a preliminary ruling the Court of Justice may consider it has enough information to allow it to determine itself whether the requirement of proportionality is satisfied, and do so, [91] or it may leave it to the national court to decide.[92]

As long as the rules relating to health protection in a particular sector have not been harmonised, it is open to the Member States to carry out any necessary inspections at national frontiers.[93] However, the free movement of goods is facilitated by the carrying out of health inspections in the country of production and the health authorities of the importing Member State should co-operate in order to avoid the repetition, in the importing country, of checks which have already been carried out in the country of production.[94] Similar considerations apply to approval by national authorities of products which have been approved on health grounds in other Member States. Whilst a Member State is free to require such products to undergo a fresh procedure of examination and approval, the authorities of that Member State are bound to assist in bringing about a relaxation of the controls applied in intra-Community trade,[95] and are not entitled unnecessarily to require technical or chemical analyses or tests where those analyses or tests have already been carried out in another Member State and their results are available to those authorities, or may at their request be placed at their disposal.[96] The same principles apply to

---

[86] Case C–113/91 *Criminal proceedings against Michel Debus* [1992] E.C.R. I–3617, paras 17–29.

[87] Case C–113/91 *Criminal proceedings against Michel Debus* [1992] E.C.R. I–3617, paras 18, 24; Case C–131/93 *Commission v. Germany* [1994] E.C.R. I–3303, para. 26; [1995] 2 C.M.L.R. 278; Case C–189/95 *Harry Franzén*, [1997] E.C.R. I–5909; [1998] 1 C.M.L.R. 1231; para. 76.

[88] Case C–131/93 *Commission v. Germany* [1994] E.C.R. I–3303, para. 27; [1995] 2 C.M.L.R. 270.

[89] Case C–113/91 *Criminal proceedings against Michel Debus* [1992] E.C.R. I–3617, para. 25.

[90] See, *e.g.* Case C–131/93 *Commission v. Germany* [1994] E.C.R. I–3303, paras 25–27; [1995] 2 C.M.L.R. 278.

[91] Case 315/92 *Verband Sozialer Wettbewerb EV v. Clinique Laboratories SNC* [1994] E.C.R. I–317, paras 20–23; though the Advocate General thought that the national court should decide the matter, Opinion of Mr Gulmann, esp. para. 26. In Case C–220/98 *Estée Lauder* judgment of January 13, 2000, the matter was left to the national court, para. 31.

[92] Case C–324/93 *R. v. Home Secretary,ex p. Evans Medical Ltd and Macfarlan Smith Ltd* [1995] E.C.R. I–563; [1996] 1 C.M.L.R. 53; [1995] All E.R. (E.C.) 481, where the Court left it to the referring court to determine whether it was necessary to refuse licences for the import of drugs from other Member States to ensure a reliable supply of drugs for essential medical purposes.

[93] Case 73/84 *Denkavit* [1985] E.C.R. 1013; [1986] 2 C.M.L.R. 482.

[94] Case 251/78 *Denkavit* [1979] E.C.R. 3369; [1980] 3 C.M.L.R. 513; Case 73/84 *Denkavit* [1985] E.C.R. 1013; [1986] 2 C.M.L.R. 482; Case C–228/91 *Commission v. Italy* [1993] E.C.R. I–2701.

[95] Case 104/75 *de Peijper* [1976] E.C.R. 613; [1976] 2 C.M.L.R. 271; Case 272/80 *Frans-Nederlandse* [1981] E.C.R. 3277; [1982] 2 C.M.L.R. 497.

[96] Case 272/80 *Frans-Nederlandse* [1981] E.C.R. 3277; [1982] 2 C.M.L.R. 497; Case C–373/92 *Commission v. Belgium* [1993] E.C.R. I–3107; Case C–228/91 *Commission v. Italy* [1993] E.C.R. I–2701.

checking for other purposes, for example to confirm the precious metal content of articles.[97]

Disguised restrictions, arbitrary discrimination and proportionality

The requirements that measures taken by Member States under Article 30 (ex 36) must not constitute a means of arbitrary discrimination, nor a disguised restriction on trade, and must comply with the principle of proportionality, overlap, and should not be considered in isolation. Thus, infringement of the principle of proportionality may lead to a measure being categorised as a disguised restriction on trade.[98] And discrimination between imports and domestic products as regards frequency of testing may lead to the conclusion that the level of scrutiny of imports is disproportionate. Thus in deciding in *Commission v. France*[99] whether or not the frequency of French frontier tests of Italian wine complied with the principle of proportionality, the Court of Justice took into account not only the fact that similar checks on Italian wine were carried out by the Italian authorities, but also the fact that the frequency of the French frontier inspections was distinctly higher than the occasional checks carried out on the transportation of French wine within France.

The effect of harmonisation directives and other Community measures on recourse to Article 30

Recourse to Article 30 is no longer justified if Community rules provide for the necessary measures to ensure protection of the interests set out in that Article.[1] This may be the case, *e.g.* when directives enacted under Articles 94 or 95 (ex Articles 100 or 100a) E.C. or otherwise provide for the full harmonisation of the measures necessary for the protection of animal and human health, and establish the procedures to check that they are observed.[2] Thus, if such a directive places the responsibility for public health inspections of a product upon the Member State of export, the national authorities of the importing Member State will no longer be entitled to subject the product to systematic inspection upon importation; only occasional inspections to check compliance with the Community standards will be permissible.[3] But procedures for checking imports authorised under Community law must not entail unreasonable cost or delay.[4] Where

---

[97] Case C–293/93 *Houtwipper* [1994] E.C.R. I–4249.

[98] Case 272/80 *Frans-Nederlandse* [1981] E.C.R. 3277, paras 13, 14; Joined Cases 2–4/82 *Le Lion* [1983] E.C.R. 2973, at para. 12

[99] Case 42/82 [1983] E.C.R. 1013, at paras 51–57.

[1] Case 72/83 *Campus Oil* [1984] E.C.R. 2727, at para. 27; [1984] 3 C.M.L.R. 544.

[2] Case 251/78 *Denkavit* [1979] E.C.R. 3369, at para. 14; Case 227/82 *Leendert* [1983] E.C.R. 3883, at para. 35; [1985] 2 C.M.L.R. 692; Case 29/87 *Denkavit* [1988] E.C.R. 2965; [1990] 1 C.M.L.R. 203; Case 190/87 *Moormann* BV [1988] E.C.R. 4689; [1990] 1 C.M.L.R. 656; Case C–304/88 *Commission v. Belgium* [1990] E.C.R. I–2801; *R. v. MAFF, ex p. Hedley Lomas* [1996] E.C.R. I–2553; [1996] 2 C.M.L.R. 391, para. 18; *R. v. MAFF, ex p. Compassion in World Farming Limited* [1998] E.C.R. I–1251, para. 47; [1998] 2 C.M.L.R. 661.

[3] Case 35/76 *Simmenthal* [1976] E.C.R. 1871; [1977] 2 C.M.L.R. 1; Cases 2–4/82 *Le Lion* [1983] E.C.R. 2973; [1985] 1 C.M.L.R. 561.

[4] Case 406/85 *Goffette* [1987] E.C.R. 2525.

however harmonisation is not complete, Member States may continue to rely upon Article 30.[5]

Burden of proof lies on the national authorities

It is for the national authorities of the Member States to prove that their restrictive trading rules may be justified under Article 30 (ex 36). As the Court stated in *Leendert van Bennekom*:

"it is for the national authorities to demonstrate in each case that their rules are necessary to give effective protection to the interests referred to in Article 36 of the Treaty."[6]

Thus in *Cullet* the French Government defended national rules fixing retail selling prices for fuel on grounds of public order and security represented by the violent reactions which would have to be anticipated on the part of retailers affected by unrestricted competition. The Court rejected this argument summarily:

"In that regard, it is sufficient to state that the French Government has not shown that it would be unable, using the means at its disposal, to deal with the consequences which an amendment of the rules in question . . . would have upon public order and security."[7]

The burden of proving that Article 30 (ex 36) applies accordingly entails:

(i) showing that the national measures in question fall within one of the categories (*e.g.* public health, public policy or public morality) referred to in Article 30[8];

(ii) establishing that the measure does not constitute a means of arbitrary discrimination, that is to say, that if it differentiates between domestic products and imports, it does so on objective and justifiable grounds[9];

(iii) establishing that the measure does not constitute a disguised restriction on trade, that is to say, that any restrictive effect on the free movement of goods is limited to what is necessary to protect the interest in question.[10]

The requirement that national authorities must prove the consistency of national legislation with Article 30 may be incapable of application if no national authorities are party to the proceedings in question.[11]

---

[5] Case C–323/93 *Société Civile Agricole du Centre d'Insémination de la Crespelle* [1994] E.C.R. I–5077, para. 35; Case C–39/90 *Denkavit* [1991] E.C.R. I–3069, para. 19; [1994] 1 C.M.L.R. 595.

[6] Case 227/82 [1983] E.C.R. 3883, at para. 40; [1985] 2 C.M.L.R. 692; see also Case 104/75 *de Peijper* [1976] E.C.R. 613; [1976] 2 C.M.L.R. 271; Case 251/78 *Denkavit* [1979] E.C.R. 3369, at para. 24; [1980] 3 C.M.L.R. 513; Case 174/82 *Sandoz* [1983] E.C.R. 2445, at para. 22; [1984] 3 C.M.L.R. 43; Joined Cases C–13 and 113/91 *Criminal proceedings against Michel Debus* [1992] E.C.R. I–3617, para. 18

[7] Case 231/83 [1985] E.C.R. 306, at paras 32–33; [1985] 2 C.M.L.R. 524.

[8] Above at p. 345.

[9] Above at p. 347.

[10] Above at p. 347.

[11] *cf.* Case C–368/95 *Vereinigte Familiapress Zeitungsverlags- und vertriebs GmbH v. Heinrich Bauer Verlag* [1997] E.C.R. I–3689; [1997] 3 C.M.L.R. 1329, a case involving mandatory requirements where it seems the national court was obliged to resolve the matter on the basis of a study of the market in question.

Mandatory requirements in the general interest

Although the Court has stated repeatedly that the exceptions listed in Article 30 (ex 36) are exhaustive,[12] it could be said that in effect it established further grounds upon which Member States may derogate from Article 28 (ex 30) in the *Cassis* case, in which it held that obstacles to the free movement of goods in the Community resulting from disparities between national marketing rules must be accepted in so far as they were necessary to satisfy mandatory requirements relating in particular to the effectiveness of fiscal supervision, the protection of public health, the fairness of commercial transactions, and the defence of the consumer.[13] One explanation for this apparent inconsistency is that the *Cassis* list does not so much provide grounds for derogating from Article 28 as define the circumstances in which national measures fall within Article 28 in the first place. Another explanation, favoured by the present writer, is that the indistinctly applicable measures described in the *Cassis* case and in subsequent case-law as amounting to measures having equivalent effect are in truth indirectly discriminatory, and the mandatory requirements amount to grounds which objectively justify the discrimination in question.[14]

The categories of justification under the *Cassis* formulation are not closed, as appears from the formulation itself, which refers to four categories "in particular". The categories of justification expanded during the period prior to the limitation imposed on the *Cassis* doctrine by *Keck and Mithouard.*[15] While some of the restrictions identified by the pre-*Keck* case-law would no longer be regarded as falling within the scope of Article 28 unless directly or indirectly discriminatory, the categories of justification upheld in such cases would seem to remain good law. The Court has added to the original *Cassis* list of mandatory requirements, *inter alia*, environmental protection,[16] and the encouragement of film-making, upholding on this latter ground national rules providing that video-cassettes of films could not be distributed until one year after the release of the films at the cinema.[17] In *Oebel* the Court stated that legitimate interests of economic and social policy, consistent with the Treaty, might similarly justify impediments to the free movement of goods.[18] And the Court has held that restrictions on imports which result from national rules governing the opening hours of retail premises, in particular as regards Sunday trading, may be justified by reference to national or regional socio-cultural characteristics.[19]

In *Oosthoek's Uitgeversmaatschaapij B.V.* the Court upheld national measures restricting the giving of gifts as a means of sales promotion, on the grounds of the

---

[12] Above, p. 345.

[13] Above, p. 323.

[14] See above, p. 329 for the view that the restrictions such as that involved in *Cassis* are indirectly discriminatory.

[15] Above, p. 331.

[16] Case 240/83 *Bruleurs d'Huiles Usagées* [1985] E.C.R. 532.

[17] Joined Cases 60 and 61/84 *Cinéthèque* [1985] E.C.R. 2605; [1986] 1 C.M.L.R. 365.

[18] Case 155/80 [1981] E.C.R. 1993, at para. 12; [1983] 1 C.M.L.R. 390.

[19] Case 145/88 *Torfaen BC v. B & Q Plc* [1989] E.C.R. 3851, para. 14; [1990] 1 C.M.L.R. 337; Case C–332/89 *Andrè Marchandise* [1991] E.C.R. I—1027, para. 12; [1993] 3 C.M.L.R. 746.

fairness of commercial transactions and the defence of the consumer, in the following terms:

"It is undeniable that the offering of free gifts as a means of sales promotion may mislead consumers as to the real prices of certain products and distort the conditions on which genuine competition is based. Legislation which restricts or even prohibits such commercial practices for that reason is therefore capable of contributing to consumer protection and fair trading."[20]

In *GB-INNO-BM* however, the Court took a different view of the need for state intervention in the interests of consumer protection. A Belgian company had distributed advertising leaflets in Luxembourg territory as well as on Belgian territory allegedly contrary to Luxembourg rules according to which sales offers involving a temporary price reduction may not state the duration of the offer or refer to previous prices. The Court held that under Community law concerning consumer protection the provision of information to the consumer is considered one of the principal requirements. It followed that Article 28 (ex 30) could not be interpreted as meaning that national legislation which denies the consumer access to certain kinds of information might be justified by mandatory requirements concerning consumer protection.[21]

Consumer protection and fair trading however, raise issues which extend beyond the market of the importing Member State. In *Prantl*[22] the Court considered trading rules reserving to national wine producers the use of the characteristically shaped "*Bocksbeutel*" bottle. Consumer protection and fair trading were pleaded in support of the national rules. The Court noted however that in the common market consumer protection and fair trading as regards the presentation of wines must be guaranteed "with regard on all sides for the fair and traditional practices observed in the various Member States".[23] It followed that an exclusive right to use a certain type of bottle granted by national legislation in a Member State could not be used to bar imports of wines originating in another Member State put up in bottles of the same or similar shape in accordance with a fair and traditional practice in that Member State.[24]

Recourse to mandatory requirements is subject to the principle of proportionality, as the Court made clear in the *Rau* case:

---

[20] Case 286/81 n.62, at para. 18. And in Cases C–1 and 176/90 *Aragonesa de Publicidad Exterior SA* [1991] E.C.R. I–4151; [1994] 1 C.M.L.R. 887, the Court upheld on public health grounds restrictions on advertising of certain alcoholic beverages. See also Case 382/87 *Buet* [1989] E.C.R. 1235; [1993] 3 C.M.L.R. 659 (prohibition of door to door canvassing of educational material justified).

[21] Case C–362/88 [1990] E.C.R. I–667; [1991] 2 C.M.L.R. 801.

[22] Case 16/83 [1984] E.C.R. 1299; [1985] 2 C.M.L.R. 238.

[23] Case 16/83 [1984] E.C.R. 1299; [1985] 2 C.M.L.R. 238, at para. 27.

[24] The principle may be confined to cases involving similar indirect indications of national provenenance, and the problem in *Prantl* is explained in Case C–3/91 *Exportur SA v. LOR SA and Confiserie du Tech SA* [1992] E.C.R. I–5529, para. 34, as being "how to reconcile user of an indirect indication of national provenance with concurrent user of an indirect indication of foreign provenance", which was "not comparable to the use of names of Spanish towns by French undertakings, which raises the problem of the protection in one State of the names of another State".

"It is also necessary for such rules to be proportionate to the aim in view. If a Member State has a choice between various measures to attain the same objective it should choose the means which least restrict the free movement of goods."[25]

While in principle the Court of Justice, or the competent national court must determine whether the least restrictive measure has in fact been selected by the national legislature there are occasions when less intensive review is appropriate. For example, the *Vereinigte Familiapress Zeitungsverlags- und vertriebs GmbH*[26] case concerned a national prohibition on the sale of periodicals containing prize puzzle competitions or games, which the Court of Justice regarded as impairing access of imported periodicals to the market of the Member State in question and as constituting in principle a measure having equivalent effect. Nevertheless, the Court held that "Maintenance of press diversity may constitute an overriding requirement justifying a restriction on the free movement of goods," noting that "Such diversity helps to safeguard freedom of expression as protected by Article 10 of the European Convention on Human Rights and Fundamental Freedoms, which is one of the fundamental rights guaranteed by the Community legal order." This part of the Court's reasoning is clearly unexceptionable. But the Court went on to examine in detail how the national court should go about assessing the proportionality of the matter in issue. This involved a detailed study by the national court of the economic conditions prevailing on the Austrian press market. The Court stated, *inter alia*,

"In carrying out that study, it will have to define the market for the product in question and to have regard to the market shares of individual publishers or press groups and the trend thereof.
      Moreover, the national court will also have to assess the extent to which, from the consumer's standpoint, the product concerned can be replaced by papers which do not offer prizes, taking into account all the circumstances which may influence the decision to purchase, such as the presence of advertising on the title page referring to the chance of winning a prize, the likelihood of winning, the value of the prize or the extent to which winning depends on a test calling for a measure of ingenuity, skill or knowledge."[27]

In other contexts, where a complex assessment is undertaken by a Community authority or a national authority, and is subject to review by a Community court or a national court, the latter courts are not required to substitute their assessment of the facts for the assessment made by the authority concerned, but must restrict themselves to examining the accuracy of the findings of fact and law made by the authority concerned and to verifying, in particular, that the action taken by the authority is not vitiated by a manifest error or a misuse of powers and that it did not clearly exceed the bounds of its discretion.[28] In the view of

---

[25] Case 261/81 [1982] E.C.R. 3961, at para. 12; [1983] 2 C.M.L.R. 496.
[26] Case C–368/95 [1997] E.C.R. I–3689.
[27] Case C–368/95 [1997] E.C.R. I–3689; [1997] 3 C.M.L.R. 1329, at paras 30–31.
[28] Case C–120/97 *Upjohn Ltd v. The Licensing Authority established by the Medicines Act 1968 and Others* [1999] E.C.R. I–223; [1999] 1 C.M.L.R. 825, at paras 33–34, and see cases cited at para. 34.

the present writer, it is the latter degree of judicial review which should apply in cases such as *Vereinigte Familiapress*, referred to above.

A further limitation on recourse to mandatory requirements is that they may only be invoked in the case of national rules which apply without discrimination to both domestic and imported products.[29] Thus in the case of national rules requiring certain imported products but not their domestically produced counterparts to bear an indication of country of origin, the Court held that considerations of consumer protection and the fairness of commercial transactions could have no application.[30] In the case of national rules requiring both domestic goods and imports to bear an indication of country of origin, the Court again refused to consider arguments based on considerations of consumer protection on the grounds that the national rules were in fact discriminatory:

"The requirements relating to the indication of origin of goods are applicable without distinction to domestic and imported products only in form because, by their very nature, they are intended to enable the consumer to distinguish between those two categories of products, which may thus prompt him to give his preference to national products."[31]

It seems that recourse to mandatory requirements is impermissible if national rules are either directly,[32] or indirectly[33] discriminatory, from the point of view of their effect on trade.[34] The foregoing principles are easier to state than to apply, since the distinction between an indistinctly applicable measure caught by the *Cassis* doctrine but not regarded as discriminatory, and an indistinctly applicable measure which is regarded as indirectly discriminatory, is difficult to draw, and, in the view of the present writer, wrong in principle.[35] Thus in *Denkavit Futtermittel GmbH* the Court considered a national requirement that all compound feedingstuffs intended for stock farming must bear an indication of all their ingredients in descending order of their proportion. The Court noted that such a requirement "has the effect of rendering more difficult the importation of compound feedingstuffs originating in other Member States which do not require such a declaration", yet regarded the measure as being indistinctly applicable to domestic goods and imports and eligible for justification in accordance with imperative requirements relating, *inter alia*, to fair trading and consumer transactions. The Court's language, principle and common sense suggest that this

---

[29] Case 113/80 *Commission v. Ireland* [1981] E.C.R. 1625, paras 8 and 11; [1982] 1 C.M.L.R. 706; Joined Cases C–321–324/94 *Jacques Pistre etc.*, [1997] E.C.R. I–2343, at para. 52.

[30] Case 113/80 *Commission v. Ireland* [1981] E.C.R. 1625; [1982] 1 C.M.L.R. 706.

[31] Case 270/83 *Commission v. United Kingdom* [1985] E.C.R. 1201.

[32] Direct discrimination involves drawing an express distinction between domestic goods and imports. Cases of direct discrimination excluding recourse to mandatory requirements include Case 113/80 *Commission v. Ireland* [1981] E.C.R. 1625; [1982] 1 C.M.L.R. 706; Case 59/82 *Schutzverband gegen Unwesen in der Wirtschaft v. Weinvertriebs-GmbH* [1983] E.C.R. 1217; [1984] 1 C.M.L.R. 319; Joined Cases C–321–324/94 *Jacques Pistre etc.*, [1997] E.C.R. I–2343.

[33] A measure is indirectly discriminatory if it applies both to domestic goods and imports but in practice burdens imports. Case C–177/83 *Th. Kohl KG v. Ringelhan & Rennett SA and Ringelhan Einrichtungs GmbH* [1984] E.C.R. 3651, at para. 14; [1985] 3 C.M.L.R. 340.

[34] Case C–177/83 *Th. Kohl KG v. Ringelhan & Rennett SA and Ringelhan Einrichtungs GmbH* [1984] E.C.R. 3651, at para. 14; [1985] 3 C.M.L.R. 340.

[35] See above, p. 329.

measure had indirectly discriminatory effects, and yet the Court considered jusification in accordance with mandatory requirements. In this respect the Court's case-law is not entirely consistent. In *Nicholas Decker* the Court considered a national measure which differentiated between reimbursement of costs of medical products purchased in the Member State in question, and the reimbursement of costs of medical products purchased in another Member State, which the Court held was liable to curb imports. The measure thus differentiated expressly between purchases on the home market and purchases in other Member States, yet the Court stated that "it cannot be excluded that the risk of seriously undermining the financial balance of the social security system may constitute an overriding reason in the general interest capable of justifying a barrier of that kind."[36] The Court appears to be countenancing the application of mandatory requirements to justify a directly discriminatory measure, contrary to what has previously been decided. In principle, mandatory requirements, being in substance analogous to grounds upon which indirect discrimination may be objectively justified, should be regarded as relevant to cases of *indirect* discrimination, and thus be applicable to a case such as *Denkavit* referred to above. This approach is supported by the Court's judgment in *Société Baxter*, in which the Court considers whether the effectiveness of fiscal supervision, a mandatory requirement, may justify unequal treatment as regards off-setting research expenditure against a charge to special tax levy.[37] But it would be correct to conclude that mandatory requirements are inapplicable to cases in which national rules specifically regulate frontier transactions, or otherwise directly discriminate between domestic goods and imports; in such cases Article 30 alone is applicable, and it would follow that the Court was wrong in *Decker* to suggest that the discriminatory measures in issue could be justified otherwise than by reference to that Article.

THE RELATIONSHIP BETWEEN ARTICLES 28 TO 30 AND OTHER PROVISIONS OF THE TREATY

However wide the field of application of Articles 28 and 29 (ex 30 and 34) may be, it does not include obstacles to trade covered by other provisions of the Treaty, such as Articles 23 to 25 (ex 9 to 16) (customs duties and charges having equivalent effect), Article 90 (ex 95) (discriminatory internal taxation), and Articles 87 and 88 (ex 92 and 93) (state aids).[38] Where national taxes are imposed on an import which lacks a domestic counterpart, the rate of tax must not be so high as to impede the free movement of goods. Such an impediment to free movement would fall to be governed by Articles 28–30 (ex 30–36), rather than within the framework of Article 90 (ex 95).[39] A national measure which

---

[36] Case C–120/95 *Nicholas Decker v. Caisse de Maladie de Employés Privés* [1998] E.C.R. I–1831, para. 39.

[37] Case C–254/97 *Société Baxter v. Premier Ministre* [1999] E.C.R. I–0000, at paras 15, 18.

[38] Case 74/76 *Iannelli & Volpi* [1977] E.C.R. 557; [1977] 2 C.M.L.R. 688; Case 222/82 *Apple and Pear Development Council* [1983] E.C.R. 4083, at para. 30; [1984] 3 C.M.L.R. 733.

[39] Case C–47/88 *Commission v. Denmark* [1990] E.C.R. I–4509.

facilitates an abuse of a dominant position will generally infringe Article 28, insofar as the measure restricts imports.[40]

National measures which fail to be scrutinised by the Commission under Articles 87 and 88 (ex 92 and 93) cannot be categorised as measures having equivalent effect simply by virtue of their effects upon trade, unless the aid in question produces "restrictive effects which exceed what is necessary to enable it to attain the objectives permitted by the Treaty".[41] This may be the case where aid is granted to traders who obtain supplies of imported products through a state agency but is withheld when the products are imported direct, if this distinction is not clearly necessary for the attainment of the objectives of the said aid or for its proper functioning.[42] Furthermore, the Court has held that the possibility that state subsidies to a campaign designed to favour domestic products might fall within Articles 87 and 88 (ex 92 and 93) does not mean that the campaign itself thereby escapes the prohibitions laid down in Article 28 (ex 30).[43] The fact that a public works contract relates to the provision of services cannot remove a clause in an invitation to tender restricting the material that may be used from the scope of the prohibitions set out in Article 28 (now 30).[44]

ARTICLE 31 (EX 37) E.C.—STATE MONOPOLIES OF A COMMERCIAL CHARACTER

Article 31 E.C., which comprises a slightly amended text of former Article 37, provides, in part:

"1. Member States shall adjust any State monopolies of a commercial character so as to ensure that no discrimination regarding the conditions under which goods are procured and marketed exists between nationals of Member States.

The provisions of this Article shall apply to any body through which a Member State, in law or in fact, either directly or indirectly supervises, determines or appreciably influences imports or exports between Member States. These provisions shall likewise apply to monopolies delegated by the State to others.

Member States shall refrain from introducing any new measure which is contrary to the principles laid down in paragraph 1 or which restricts the scope of the Articles dealing with the abolition of customs duties and quantitative restrictions between Member States."

The provisions of Article 37(2) (now Article 31(2)) were held to be directly applicable from the date of entry into force of the Treaty in *Costa v. ENEL*.[45] Article 37(1), which provided prior to its amendment on May 1, 1999 that

---

[40] Case C–179/90 *Merci convenzionali porto di Genova SpA v. Siderurgica Gabrielli SpA* [1991] E.C.R. I–5889, para. 21; [1994] 4 C.M.L.R. 422.
[41] Case 74/76 *Iannelli & Volpi* [1977] E.C.R. 557; [1977] 2 C.M.L.R. 688.
[42] n.41, *supra*.
[43] Case 249/81 *Commission v. Ireland* [1982] E.C.R. 4005, at para. 18; [1983] 2 C.M.L.R. 104.
[44] Case 45/87 *Commission v. Ireland* [1988] E.C.R. 4929.
[45] Case 6/64 [1964] E.C.R. 585; [1964] C.M.L.R. 425.

Member States were to "progressively adjust" state monopolies so as to ensure that no discrimination exists "when the transitional period has ended" was held to have similar effect from the end of the transitional period in *Pubblico Ministero v. Flavia Manghera* and *Rewe-Zentrale des Lebensmittel-Grosshandels v. Hauptzollamt Landau/Pfalz*.[46] The State monopolies in question are those enjoying exclusive rights in the procurement and distribution of goods, not services,[47] and Article 31 applies to monopolies over provision of services only in so far as such a monopoly contravenes the principle of the free movement of goods by discriminating against imported products to the advantage of products of domestic origin.[48] But the existence of national rules requiring the licensing of particular activities is not sufficient to amount to a State monopoly of a commercial character.[49] And Article 31 has no application to national legislation which reserves the retail sale of manufactured tobacco products to distributors authorised by the State, provided that the State does not intervene in the procurement choices of retailers.[50]

As from the end of the transitional period every national monopoly of a commercial character must have been adjusted so as to eliminate the exclusive right to import from other Member States.[51] Exclusive import rights give rise to discrimination prohibited by Article 31(1) against exporters established in other Member States, and such rights directly affect the conditions under which goods are marketed only as regards operators or sellers in other Member States.[52] But for the prohibition of all discrimination between nationals of Member States provided for in Article 31(1) to be applicable, it is not necessarily a requirement that the exclusive rights to import a given product relate to all imports; it is sufficient if those rights relate to a proportion such that they enable the monopoly to have an appreciable influence on imports.[53] However, the Court has repeatedly stated that Article 31 (ex 37) does not require national monopolies having a commercial character to be abolished but requires them to be adjusted in such a way as to ensure that no discrimination regarding the conditions under which goods are procured and marketed exists between nationals of Member States.[54] The purpose of Article 31 (ex 37) of the Treaty is to reconcile the possibility for Member States to maintain certain monopolies of a commercial character as instruments for the pursuit of public interest aims with the requirements of the establishment and functioning of the common market. It

---

[46] Case 45/75 [1976] E.C.R. 91.
[47] Case 155/73 *Sacch*i [1974] E.C.R. 409; [1974] 2 C.M.L.R. 177; Case 271/81 *Société d'Insemination Artificielle* [1983] E.C.R. 2057. In the latter case the Court recognised the possibility that a monopoly over the provision of services might have an indirect influence on trade in goods.
[48] Case 271/81 *Amélioration de l' Élevage v. Mialocq* [1983] E.C.R. 2057; Joined Cases C–46/90 and 93/91 *Procureur du Roi v. Jean-Marie Lagauche and others.* [1993] E.C.R. I–5267, para. 33.
[49] Case 118/86 *Nertsvoederfabriek Nederland BV* [1987] E.C.R. 3883; [1989] 2 C.M.L.R. 436.
[50] Case C–387/93 *Criminal proceedings against Giorgio Domingo Banchero* [1995] E.C.R. I–4663, para. 31; [1996] 1 C.M.L.R. 829.
[51] Case 59/75 *Manghera* [1976] E.C.R. 91; [1976] 1 C.M.L.R. 557.
[52] Case C–157/94 *Commission v. Netherlands* [1997] E.C.R. I–5699, para. 15.
[53] Case C–347/88 *Commission v. Greece* [1990] E.C.R. I–4747, para. 44; Case C–157/94 *Commission v. Netherlands* [1997] E.C.R. I–5699, para. 18.
[54] Case C–189/95 *Criminal proceedings against Harry Franzén.* [1997] E.C.R. I–5909, para. 38 and cases there cited.

aims at the elimination of obstacles to the free movement of goods, save, however, for restrictions on trade which are inherent in the existence of the monopolies in question.[55] Thus Article 31 only applies to activities intrinsically connected with the specific business of the monopoly and is irrelevant to national provisions which have no connection with such specific business.[56] While, during the transitional period, Article 31 (ex 37) suspended the operation of Article 90 (ex 95), prohibiting discriminatory internal taxation,[57] as of the end of the transitional period, the position of internal taxes has been subject exclusively to Article 90 (ex 95).[58] Furthermore, while Article 31 (ex 37) permits the continuation of the obligation to deliver goods to the monopoly, and a corresponding obligation upon the monopoly to purchase such goods, Article 28 (ex 30) applies so as to ensure equal treatment of domestic goods and imports.[59] It thus seems that Article 31 is cumulatively applicable with the earlier provisions of the chapter on the elimination of quantitative restrictions, and the provisions on customs duties and charges having equivalent effect.

In the second *Hansen* case,[60] arising from the operation of the German alcohol monopoly, the Court held:

(i) that after the end of the transitional period, Article 31(ex 37) remained applicable wherever the exercise by a state monopoly of its exclusive rights entailed a discrimination or restriction prohibited by that Article;

(ii) that Article 31 (ex 37) prohibited a monopoly's right to purchase and re-sell national alcohol from being exercised so as to undercut imported products with publicly subsidised domestic products; and

(iii) that Articles 31 (ex 37) and 87/88 (ex 92/93) were capable of cumulative application to one and the same fact situation.

In *Pigs and Bacon Commission v. McCarren*[61] the Court held that Article 32(1) (ex 38(2))[62] gave priority to the rules for the organisation of the agricultural markets over the application of Article 31 (ex 37). The better view is that this means merely that Article 31 (ex 37) cannot be pleaded by way of derogation from rules imposed by a common organisation: the positive obligations of the Article are surely to be implied into the framework of a common organisation and it is established that common organisations can derogate only in exceptional circumstances from the free movement provisions of the Treaty.[63]

Article 31(3) E.C. which contains the slightly amended text of that formerly found in Article 37(4), provides:

---

[55] Case C–189/95 *Criminal proceedings against Harry Franzén*. [1997] E.C.R. I–5909; [1998] 1 C.M.L.R. 1231, para. 39.
[56] Case 86/78 *Grandes Distilleries* [1979] E.C.R. 897; [1980] 3 C.M.L.R. 337.
[57] As to which, see above p. 296.
[58] Case 86/78 *Grandes Distilleries* [1979] E.C.R. 897; [1980] 3 C.M.L.R. 337.
[59] Case 119/78 *Grandes Distilleries* [1979] E.C.R. 975; [1980] 3 C.M.L.R. 337.
[60] Case 91/78 [1979] E.C.R. 935; [1980] 1 C.M.L.R. 162.
[61] Case 177/78 [1979] E.C.R. 2161; [1979] 3 C.M.L.R. 389.
[62] Art. 32(2) provides: "Save as otherwise provided in Arts 33 to 38, the rules laid down for the establishment of the common market shall apply to agricultural products."
[63] Cases 80–81/77 *Commissionaires Reunis* [1978] E.C.R. 927; Case 83/78 *Redmond* [1978] E.C.R. 2347; [1979] 1 C.M.L.R. 177.

"If a State monopoly of a commercial character has rules which are designed to make it easier to dispose of agricultural products or obtain for them the best return, steps should be taken in applying the rules contained in this Article to ensure equivalent safeguards for the employment and standard of living of the producers concerned."

In *Charmasson*[64] the Court held that Article 31(3) (ex 37(4)) had never allowed any derogation from Article 31 (ex 37), and that the "equivalent safeguards" referred to in Article 31(3) (ex 37(4)) must themselves be compatible with the provisions of Article 31(1) and (2) (ex 37(1) and (2)).

ARTICLES 28–30 AND INTELLECTUAL PROPERTY RIGHTS

Intellectual property and the common market

The co-existence of separate systems of protection for intellectual property rights in the different Member States is capable of conflicting with the objective of creating a single market. For example, if one hypothetically considers for a moment national law in isolation from E.C. law, and one supposes that a company holds a patent right protected under the law of two Member States, A and B, that company might be entitled to rely upon that patent in Member State B to oppose the import into that State of an article manufactured and placed on the market under the patent in Member State A, and *vice versa*, even though it was the company itself, or a licensee, which had itself placed that article on the market in the first place. Similarly, if a company held the rights to a trade mark in each Member State, it might oppose the import into Member State A of an article bearing the trade mark and placed on the market in Member State B, and *vice versa*, even though, once again, it was the company itself, or a licensee, which had placed that article on the market in the first place In fact, national patent and trade mark rights do not operate in isolation from Community law, and Community law has addressed the above problem from two perspectives. The first is that of the application of the free movement of goods provisions of the Treaty, which have been interpreted by the Court as preventing holders of patents, trade marks, or copyright or other intellectual property rights from using those rights to prevent the import of goods covered by those rights from being imported into a Member State where the holder of the rights in question has consented to their being placed on the market in another Member State. The second perspective has been the harmonisation of laws. Thus for example there has been harmonisation of national trade mark rules under Directive 89/104 to approximate the laws of the Member States relating to trade marks,[65] while under Regulation 40/94 on the Community Trade Mark,[66] trade mark owners have been able since April 1, 1996 to apply for a single registered trade mark for the whole of the European Community from the Office for Harmonisation of the

---

[64] Case 48/74 [1974] E.C.R. 1383; [1975] 2 C.M.L.R. 208.
[65] [1989] O.J. L40/1.
[66] [1994] O.J. L11/36.

Internal Market, which is located in Alicante, Spain. Such harmonisation does not however render the case-law of the Court of Justice on the free movement of goods provisions redundant, since E.C. secondary legislation must be interpreted in the light of the Treaty rules on the free movement of goods and in particular Article 30.[67] There are other examples of harmonisation of intellectual property rights.[68] In the field of patent law there has to date been co-ordination at the level of processing applications for patent protection in the various Member States, within the framework of the European Patent Convention,[69] but the Community Patent Convention, which provides for a unitary Community patent, has not come into force, because it has not been ratified by a sufficient number of Member States; nevertheless, the Court of Justice has been willing to take account of the Convention.[70] The following sections of this chapter deal with the relationship between intellectual property rights and the provisions of the Treaty on the free movement of goods, rather than with harmonising legislation relating to intellectual property, though reference to the latter is made where appropriate.

A distinction between the existence and exercise of intellectual property rights

A question which arose at the outset for the Court in the present context was how far it was bound to recognise rights conferred by national laws on holders of intellectual property ("industrial and commercial property" in the language of Article 30 (ex 36) E.C.), even if the exercise of those rights could lead in certain circumstances to impeding the movement of goods between Member States. The answer to this question, on a superficial reading of the relevant Treaty texts, appeared, and indeed appears, to be that effect must be given to intellectual property rights, even if the result is indeed to prevent imports in certain cases. A general Treaty provision of obvious relevance is Article 295 (ex 222) E.C., which provides:

"This Treaty shall in no way prejudice the rules in Member States governing the system of property ownership."

On the face of it, this might appear to uphold the rights of holders of intellectual property rights to exercise those rights, even if the result were some interference

---

[67] Joined Cases C–427, 429 and 436/93 *Bristol-Myers Squibb and Others v. Paranova* [1996] E.C.R. I–3457, para. 27.

[68] See, *e.g.* Dir. 92/100 on rental right and lending right and on certain rights related to copyright in the field of intellectual property, [1992] O.J. L346/61; Dir. 96/9 on the legal protection of databases, [1996] O.J. L77/20.

[69] The Convention on the Grant of European Patents, or European Patent Convention, came into force on October 7, 1977. The European Patent Office which processes patent applications has been established in Munich, with a branch in the Hague. An applicant for a European patent specifies the contracting States in which protection is sought. If granted, the patent will have the same effect as a national patent in each of those States. However, if the Community Patent Convention comes into force, subject to transitional arrangements, the only available form of European patent will be a unitary Community patent.

[70] Case C–316/95 *Generics BV v. SmithKline and French Laboratories Ltd* [1997] E.C.R. I–7231; [1998] 1 C.M.L.R. 1, at para. 38 of the Opinion of Advocate General Jacobs.

with the free movement of goods. Indeed, Article 30 (ex 36) E.C. provides, in relevant part:

> "The provisions of Articles 28 and 29 shall not preclude prohibitions or restrictions on imports, exports or goods in transit justified on grounds of . . . the protection of industrial and commercial property. Such prohibitions or restrictions shall not, however, constitute a means of arbitrary discrimination or a disguised restriction on trade between Member States."

While restrictions on imports that are necessary for the protection of industrial and commercial property are exempted from the prohibitions in Articles 28 and 29 (ex 30 and 34), it is made clear in the second sentence of the Article that there may be circumstances where, regardless of the rights existing under national law, the prohibition will apply. But where is this line to be drawn as regards intellectual property rights? The judicial answer to this question involves drawing a distinction between the *existence* of intellectual property rights, which remains intact, and the *exercise* of those rights, which must be modified in order to ensure the free movement of goods. This solution has been applied by analogy in the fields of competition and the provision of services. It is formulated as follows in *Terrapin v. Terranova*:

> ". . . whilst the Treaty does not affect the existence of rights recognised by the legislation of a Member State in matters of industrial and commercial property, yet the exercise of those rights may nevertheless, depending on the circumstances, be restricted by the prohibitions in the Treaty. Inasmuch as it provides an exception to one of the fundamental principles of the common market, Article 36 in fact admits exceptions to the free movement of goods only to the extent to which such exceptions are justified for the purposes of safeguarding the rights which constitute the specific subject matter of that property."[71]

The distinction drawn by the Court between the existence of rights and their exercise is evidently inspired by a wish to remain at least within the letter of Article 295 (ex 222). It invites the criticism that a form of property is the bundle of rights recognised by national law under a particular designation, and if Community law prevents any rights in the bundle from being exercised, the property is to that extent diminished. Yet such criticism taken to its logical conclusion would argue that, *e.g.*, the Treaty's prohibition of discrimination on grounds of nationality could have no application to the exercise of property rights, so that a municipal authority offering public housing to workers could charge nationals of other Member States a higher rent than nationals, or even exclude non-nationals altogether. What the Court has done, in reality, emerges from the second sentence in the quoted passage. The derogation in Article 30 (ex 36) E.C. has been confined to rights which, the Court considers, constitute the essential

---

[71] Case 119/75 [1976] E.C.R. 1039; [1976] 2 C.M.L.R. 482. The formulation is found, with minor variations, in a number of judgments.

core or "specific subject matter" of the property in question.[72] The exercise of the "specific subject matter" of such rights is permitted by Community law, even if it impedes trade or competition, because otherwise it would no longer be possible to say that the property was receiving protection. On the other hand, rights which the Court regards as merely incidental to the property are not allowed to be used to partition the market.

Free movement of goods—the exhaustion of rights principle

The exclusive right of an owner of intellectual property to put into circulation for the first time goods that are subject to the property is likely to be understood in the law of the Member State concerned (leaving aside Community law considerations) as applying to sale in that State's territory. Sales elsewhere will not count as an exercise of the right—in the jargon of the subject, they are not considered to "exhaust" that right. This means that, as a matter of national law alone, it would be open to the owner of the property to oppose the sale by other traders of imported products acquired in a Member State where they have been marketed by the owner himself, or by licensee of the owner. It is to be noted that there would be an incentive for such so-called "parallel" importing if, for some reason, the products in question were significantly cheaper in the State of initial distribution than in the one from which it was sought to exclude them.

On the other hand, the Court of Justice has repeatedly stated, as a general principle, that "the proprietor of an industrial or commercial property right protected by the legislation of a Member State may not rely on that legislation in order to oppose the importation of a product which has lawfully been marketed in another Member State by, or with the consent of, the proprietor of the right himself or a person legally or economically dependent on him."[73] Whatever the position in national law, the proprietor's exclusive right is deemed in Community law to be exhausted by putting products into circulation anywhere the common market. The rationale of the principle is to be found in the limitation of the exception in Article 30 (ex 36) by reference to the case-law derived notion of the specific subject-matter of the intellectual property in question. Where exhaustion occurs it is because the right to exclude imports originally marketed in another Member State is not seen as part of the specific subject-matter of the property in question. The exercise of the right would, therefore, not be "justified" within the meaning of Article 30 (ex 36) E.C. as being necessary for the protection of the industrial and commercial property right in question.[74] The principle of exhaustion has been applied by the Court of Justice to most of the important forms of intellectual property.

---

[72] The definitions the Court has given in its case-law of the "specific subject-matter" of various important forms of intellectual property are referred to below.

[73] See for one of many examples, Case 144/81 *Keurkoop v. Nancy Kean Gifts* [1982] E.C.R. 2853 at 2873; [1983] 2 C.M.L.R. 47.

[74] This analysis was applied by the Court for the first time in Case 78/70 *Deutsche Grammophon v. Metro* [1971] E.C.R. 487. It is more fully developed in Case 15/74 *Centrafarm v. Sterling Drug* [1974] E.C.R. 1147; [1974] 2 C.M.L.R. 480.

Free movement of goods and patents

The leading case on the application of the exhaustion of rights principle to patents is *Centrafarm v. Sterling Drug*.[75] Patents for a drug used in the treatment of urinary tract infections were held by Sterling Drug, an American company, in the United Kingdom and the Netherlands. The case originated in the proceedings brought for the infringement of the Dutch patent against Centrafarm, a company famous in the annals of European Court litigation as a parallel importer of pharmaceutical products.[76] Centrafarm's alleged infringement consisted of importing into the Netherlands and offering for sale there quantities of the patented product which had been lawfully marketed by licensees of Sterling Drug in the United Kingdom. This was commercially attractive for Centrafarm, because the price of the drug on the United Kingdom market was only about half the price on the Dutch market. The Court of Justice defined the specific subject-matter of a patent as:

"... the guarantee that the patentee, to reward the creative effort of the inventor, has the exclusive right to use an invention with a view to manufacturing industrial products and putting them into circulation for the first time, either directly or by the grant of licences to third parties as well as the right to oppose infringements."[77]

The essential function of a patent is here acknowledged to be the rewarding of (and hence encouragement of) creative effort. The reward comes from the patentee's ability to earn a monopoly profit through an exclusive right to manufacture the protected product and put it into circulation for the first time. That right may be exploited directly or by appointing licensees. It has, as a corollary, a right to oppose manufacturing or first marketing of the product by third parties.

In the light of that definition the Court went on to consider the circumstances in which the use of a patent to block the importation of protected products from another Member State might be justified. Two cases of possible justification were mentioned: where the product is not patentable in the Member State of origin and has been manufactured there by a third party without the consent of the patentee in the Member State of importation[78]; and where a patent exists in each of the Member States in question but the original proprietors of the patents are legally and economically independent. On the other hand, there could be no justification for opposing importation "where the product has been put onto the market in a legal manner, by the patentee himself or with his consent, in the Member State from which it has been imported, in particular in the case of parallel patents".[79] If a patent could be used in this way, the patentee would be

---

[75] Case 15/74 *Centrafarm v. Sterling Drug* [1974] E.C.R. 1147; [1974] 2 C.M.L.R. 480.

[76] There were parallel proceedings for the infringement of the Dutch trade mark: Case 16/74 *Centrafarm v. Winthrop* [1974] E.C.R. 1183; [1974] 2 C.M.L.R. 480.

[77] [1974] E.C.R. at 1162.

[78] This was the situation in Case 24/67 *Parke, Davis v. Centrafarm* [1968] E.C.R. 55; [1968] C.M.L.R. 47. The questions put to the Court were, however, formulated with reference to the competition rules.

[79] [1974] E.C.R. at 1163.

able to cordon off national markets, thereby restricting trade between Member States, "where no such restriction was necessary to guarantee the essence of the exclusive rights flowing from the parallel patents".[80] The objection that national patents were unlikely to be truly parallel, with the result that levels of protection would vary between Member State, was brushed aside. "It should be noted here," the Court said, "that, in spite of divergences which remain in the absence of any unification of national rules concerning industrial property the identity of the protected invention is clearly the essential element of the concept of parallel patents which it is for the courts to assess."[81] The Court concluded:

"... that the exercise, by a patentee, of the right which he enjoys under the legislation of a Member State to prohibit the sale, in that State, of a product protected by the patent which has been marketed in another Member State by the patentee or with his consent is incompatible with the rules of the EEC Treaty concerning the free movement of good within the common market."[82]

The basis of the ruling was not made altogether clear. On the one hand, it might be thought that the existence of parallel patents was a crucial factor: a right to oppose the importation of protected products could be regarded as superfluous, because the patentee would already have received the monopoly profit, which was his due, in the Member State where the products were first put on the market. On the other hand, the general terms in which the ruling was expressed, taken with other hints in the judgment,[83] strongly suggested the principle of exhaustion would apply, even where the initial marketing occurred without the benefit of patent protection. If that were so, then the explanation could only lie in the patentee's consent to the marketing. That such was indeed the Court's meaning was shown in the later case of *Merck v. Stephar*.[84]

The plaintiff in the national proceedings, Merck and Co. Inc., was the holder in the Netherlands of patents relating to a drug used mainly in the treatment of high blood pressure. The proceedings arose because Stephar BV had imported the drug into the Netherlands from Italy where, although it was not patentable, it had been put into circulation by Merck. On Merck's behalf it was argued that the function of rewarding an inventor's creative effort would not be fulfilled if, owing to the impossibility of patenting a product, its sale in the Member State in question did not take place under monopoly conditions. To this the Court replied:

"That right of first placing a product on the market enables the inventor, by allowing him a monopoly in exploiting his product, to obtain the reward for his creative effort, without, however, guaranteeing that he will obtain such a reward in all circumstances.

---

[80] *ibid.*
[81] *ibid.*
[82] *ibid.*
[83] See, in particular, the reference, *ibid.*, to non-patentable goods "manufactured by third parties without the consent of the patentee."
[84] Case 187/80 [1981] E.C.R. 2063; [1981] 3 C.M.L.R. 463.

It is for the proprietor of the patentee to decide, in the light of all the circumstances, under what conditions he will market his product, including the possibility of marketing it in a Member State where the law does not provide patent protection for the product in question. If he decides to do so he must accept the consequences of his choice as regards the free movement of the product within the Common Market, which is a fundamental principle forming part of the legal and economic circumstances which must be taken into account by the proprietor of the patent in determining the manner in which his exclusive right will be exercised."[85]

This approach seems wrong in principle. The justification for "exhaustion" of patent rights by first sale in a Member State is surely that the patent holder is entitled to exercise the specific subject matter of his right only once in the common market; but in the case of a sale in one Member State of a product not patented there, but entitled to patent protection in other Member States, there has been no exercise of the patent right at all, and the effect of holding that the right cannot be subsequently exercised to prevent parallel imports in the Member States where the product is covered by patent protection is to extinguish the right entirely. The conclusion that it is for the patent holder to make the choice whether or not to market patented products in a Member State where the product is not patentable, and must accept the consequences of that decision, rather begs the question as to whether this is an appropriate dilemma to impose upon patent holders in the first place.

It used to be debated whether an owner of parallel national patents was entitled to resist the importation into one of the Member States concerned of products manufactured under a compulsory licence issued in respect of his patent in another Member State.[86] The question received a clear affirmative answer in *Pharmon v. Hoechst*;[87] a case in which the Court's reasoning appeared to cast doubt some doubt on its approach in *Merck*. Parallel patents in a medicinal product were owned by Hoechst in Germany, the Netherlands and the United Kingdom. A compulsory licence for the manufacture of the product had been obtained in the United Kingdom, and Pharmon had purchased a consignment from the licensee with a view to selling it on the Dutch market. This Hoechst was anxious to prevent. Pharmon rested its case on the exhaustion of rights principle, arguing that Hoechst had entered the British market with its eyes open and must be taken to have accepted all the legal consequences flowing from the registration of a parallel patent. The passage quoted above from the judgment in *Merck* seemed to give force to that argument.[88] It was, however, rejected by the Court on the ground that the compulsory character of a licence meant the holder of the patent could not be regarded as having consented to the actions of the licensee. "Such a measure," the Court said, "deprives the patent proprietor of his right to determine freely the conditions under which he markets his products."[89] The

---

[85] [1981] E.C.R. at 2081–2082.
[86] Under a system of compulsory licensing a patentee may be deprived of his monopoly by an official decision to grant licences to third parties in return for a reasonable royalty.
[87] Case 19/84 [1985] E.C.R. 2281; [1985] 3 C.M.L.R. 775.
[88] [1981] E.C.R. at 2082.
[89] [1985] E.C.R. at para. 25.

provision of the Community Patent Convention excepting from the principle of exhaustion "the case of a product put on the market under a compulsory licence" was thus shown to reflect the law of the Treaty.[90] If *Pharmon*, apart from its intrinsic significance, also implied that the reasoning underlying *Merck* might at least be open to question, a later judgment on the law of copyright was to point strongly in the same direction.

In *Warner Bros v. Christiansen*,[91] the Court of Justice considered whether the marketing in the United Kingdom of a video-cassette of a film exhausted the right of the author to control the subsequent hiring out of the video-cassette in Denmark, where Danish law recognised such a right, but where under United Kingdom law the purchase of the video-cassette entitled the purchaser to hire it out without the need for the consent of the author. The Court held that:

"where national legislation confers on authors a specific right to hire out video-cassettes, that right would be rendered worthless if its owner were not in a position to authorise the operations for doing so. It cannot therefore be accepted that the marketing by a film-maker of a video-cassette containing one of his works, in a Member State which does not provide specific protection for the right to hire it out, should have repercussions on the right conferred on that same film-maker by the legislation of another Member State to restrain, in that State, the hiring out of that video-cassette."[92]

If the statement in the second sentence of the above paragraph were applied by analogy to patent rights in the context of circumstances such as those in *Merck*, the result would be that a patent holder could resist the import of products into a Member State where they were patented if they were marketed in a Member State where they could not be patented. The occasion for the Court to reconsider *Merck v. Stephar* arose in *Merck v. Primecrown*,[93] a case which arose in the context of the application of transitional arrangements in the Act of Accession of Spain and Portugal to parallel imports into the United Kingdom from the latter countries. Merck & Co. Inc. argued in reliance, *inter alia*, on *Pharmon* and *Warner Bros* that the Court should overrule *Merck v. Stephar*. Advocate General Fennelly agreed.[94] But the Court did not. As regards *Pharmon*, the Court distinguished the factual situation in *Merck* (patent holder's consent to marketing) with that in *Pharmon* (marketing under a compulsory licence to which the patent holder had not consented).[95] As regards *Warner Bros,* the Court briefly stated the facts, prefaced with the words "Unlike the cases now under consideration . . .". [96] In truth, the Court had already given what is perhaps the main reason for its judgment a few paragraphs earlier: the transitional measures provided for in the Act of Accession were adopted in light of the ruling

---

[90] Community Patent Convention, Art. 76(3) (formerly 81(3)).
[91] Case 158/86 [1988] E.C.R. 2605; [1990] 3 C.M.L.R. 684.
[92] Case 158/86 [1988] E.C.R. 2605, at para. 18; [1990] 3 C.M.L.R. 684. The case is also considered in the context of copyright at p. 375 below.
[93] Joined Cases C–267–268/95 [1996] E.C.R. I–6285.
[94] This lengthy Opinion is erudite and convincing
[95] Joined Cases C–267–268/95 [1996] E.C.R. I–6285, at para. 41.
[96] *ibid.*, para. 42.

in *Merck* and indicated the intention of the Member States that upon expiry of those transitional arrangements, the free movement of goods provisions of the Treaty, as interpreted in *Merck*, should apply in full to trade between Spain and Portugal. That is an entirely defensible ground for adhering to the result in *Merck* even if the reasoning underlying the original decision can no longer be defended.

Free movement of goods and trade marks

Exhaustion of rights

Centrafarm v. Sterling Drug[97] had a companion case, *Centrafarm v. Winthrop*,[98] relating to the infringement of the trade mark, Negram, under which the imported drug was sold. The conclusion of the Court of Justice was similar to that in the patent case and was reached by a similar process of reasoning. The specific subject-matter of a trade mark was said to be:

". . . the guarantee that the owner of the trade mark has the exclusive right to use that trade mark, for the purpose of putting products protected by the trade mark into circulation for the first time, and is therefore intended to protect him against competitors wishing to take advantage of the status and reputation of the trade mark by selling products illegally bearing that trade mark."[99]

The emphasis here is on what makes a trade mark valuable—the reservation to the owner, through his exclusive right to put trade marked products into circulation, of the goodwill associated with the mark. The Court did not on this occasion examine the reason why such a right should be given, the question of the "essential function" of a trade mark, but it did so in later cases, in which it described that essential function as being to guarantee the identity of the trade marked product to the consumer or ultimate user.[1] The exhaustion of rights conferred by a trade mark is now dealt with in Article 7 of the Trade Mark Directive,[2] which states in relevant part:

"1. The trade mark shall not entitle the proprietor to prohibit its use in relation to goods which have been put on the market in the Community under that trade mark by the proprietor or with his consent."

In *Bristol Myers-Squibb*[3] the Court held that Article 7 comprehensively regulates the question of the exhaustion of trade mark rights for products traded in the Community, and that national rules must be assessed in the light of that Article, but added that "the directive must be interpreted in the light of the

---

[97] Case 15/74 *Centrafarm v. Sterling Drug* [1974] E.C.R. 1147; [1974] 2 C.M.L.R. 480, see above, p. 364.
[98] Case 16/74 *Centrafarm v. Winthrop* [1974] E.C.R. 1183; [1974] 2 C.M.L.R. 480.
[99] [1974] E.C.R. at 1194.
[1] See Case 102/77 *Hoffmann-La Roche v. Centrafarm* [1978] E.C.R. 1139; [1978] 3 C.M.L.R. 217; Case 3/78 *Centrafarm v. American Home Products* [1978] E.C.R. 1823; Joined Cases C–427, 429 and 436/93 *Bristol-Myers Squibb and Others v. Paranova* [1996] E.C.R. I–3457; [1997] 1 C.M.L.R. 326; Case C–349/95 *Frits Loenderloot v. George Ballantine & Son Ltd and Others* [1997] E.C.R. I–6227; [1998] 1 C.M.L.R. 1015.
[2] Dir. 89/104 [1989] O.J. L40/1.
[3] Joined Cases C–427, 429 and 436/93 *Bristol-Myers Squibb and Others v. Paranova* [1996] E.C.R. I–3457.

Treaty rules on the free movement of goods and in particular Article 36."[4] Citing Article 7(1), the Court stated:

"That provision is framed in terms corresponding to those used by the Court in judgments which, in interpreting Articles 30 and 36 of the Treaty, have recognised in Community law the principle of the exhaustion of the rights conferred by a trade mark. It reiterates the case-law of the Court to the effect that the owner of a trade mark protected by the legislation of a Member State cannot rely on that legislation to prevent the importation or marketing of a product which was put on the market in another Member State by him or with his consent . . ."[5]

It follows from the foregoing that the concept of exhaustion of trade mark rights under Article 7(1) of the Directive and the concept of exhaustion under Articles 28 and 30 (ex 30 and 36) E.C. are one and the same concept.

The principle of exhaustion of trade mark rights referred to above is of course a concept applicable to the marketing of trade marked goods in a Member State of the Community. The issue which arose in *Silhouette International*[6] was whether national rules providing for exhaustion of trade-mark rights in respect of products put on the market outside the Community, indeed outside the EEA,[7] were contrary to Article 7(1) of the Directive. The Court concluded that Articles 5 to 7 of the Directive must be considered as embodying a complete harmonisation of the rules relating to the rights conferred by a trade mark, and that accordingly national rules providing for the exhaustion of trade mark rights put on the market outside the EEA under that mark by the proprietor or with his consent were contrary to Article 7(1) of the Directive.

Re-packaging

One of the boldest aspects of the case-law of the Court of Justice in the trade mark field has been the development of its jurisprudence on the extent to which a parallel importer may lawfully re-package a trade marked product and re-affix the mark to the re-packaged product. In *Hoffmann-La Roche v. Centrafarm*[8] the Court held that:

"The proprietor of a trade mark right which is protected in two Member States at the same time is justified pursuant to the first sentence of Article 36 of the EEC Treaty in preventing a product to which the trade mark has lawfully been applied in one of those States from being marketed in the other Member State after it has been repackaged in new packaging to which the trade mark has been affixed by a third party."[9]

---

[4] *ibid.*, paras 25–27.
[5] *ibid.*, para. 31.
[6] Case C–355/96 *Silhouette International Schmied GmbH & Co. KG v. Hatlauer Handelsgesellschaft mbH* [1998] E.C.R. I–4799; [1998] 2 C.M.L.R. 953. See also Case C–173/98 *Sebago Inc. and Ancienne Maison Dubois et Fils SA v. GB-Unic SA* [1999] E.C.R. I–4103; [1999] 2 C.M.L.R. 1317.
[7] The Directive applies to the European Economic Area, comprising the E.C., Iceland, Liechtenstein and Norway.
[8] Case 102/77 [1978] E.C.R. 1139; [1998] 3 C.M.L.R. 217. See also Case 3/78 *Centrafarm v. American Home Products* [1978] E.C.R. 1823; [1997] 1 C.M.L.R. 326.
[9] [1978] E.C.R. at 1164.

It reached that conclusion in the light of the "essential function of the trade mark", which, it said, was "to guarantee the identity of the trade marked product to the consumer or ultimate user, by enabling him without any possibility of confusion to distinguish that product from products which have another origin".[10] The Court took the view that the guarantee of origin meant "that the consumer or ultimate user can be certain that a trade marked product which is sold to him has not been subject at a previous stage of marketing to interference by a third person, without the authorisation of the proprietor of the trade mark, such as to affect the original condition of the product".[11] It followed that the right to prevent any dealing with the marked product which was likely to impair this guarantee formed part of the specific subject-matter of the trade mark right.

The Court concluded that Article 30 (ex 36) must be interpreted as meaning that a trade mark owner may rely on his rights as owner to prevent an importer from marketing a product put on the market in another Member State by the owner or with his consent, where that importer has repackaged the product in new packaging to which the trade mark has been affixed, unless:

— It is established that the use of the trademark right by the owner, having regard to the marketing system which he has adopted, will contribute to the artificial partitioning of the markets between Member States.
— It is shown that the repackaging cannot adversely affect the original condition of the product.
— The owner of the mark receives prior notice before the repackaged product is put on sale.
— It is stated on the new packaging by whom the product has been repackaged.[12]

In this way the Court sought to reconcile, on the one hand, the legitimate interests of consumers and the trade mark holder, and, on the other hand, the principle of the free movement of goods between Member States, requiring that the seller of the imported goods be given "a certain licence which in normal circumstances is reserved to the proprietor himself".[13]

Article 7(2) of the Trade Mark Directive[14] provides that the owner of a trade mark may oppose the further commercialisation of products where there is a legitimate reason for doing so, especially where the condition of the products has

---

[10] *ibid.*
[11] *ibid.*
[12] See Case 1/81 *Pfizer v. Eurim-Pharm* [1981] E.C.R. 2913; [1982] 1 C.M.L.R. 406 (outer wrapping removed from blister strips upon which strips the trade mark Vibramycin Pfizer was printed; each strip packed in a box with a transparent window through which the trade mark was clearly visible; names and addresses of manufacturer and importer on the boxes, with a statement that importer responsible for the packaging; advance warning given to the Pfizer—parallel importer could rely upon Art. 28 (ex 30)).
[13] [1978] E.C.R. at 1165–1166.
[14] Dir. 89/104 [1989] O.J. L40/1.

been changed or impaired since they were put on the market. In *Bristol-Myers Squibb*[15] the Court, after citing Article 7(2), observed that:

"Article 7 of the directive, like Article 36 of the Treaty, is intended to reconcile the fundamental interest in protecting trade mark rights with the fundamental interest in the free movement of goods within the common market, so that those two provisions, which pursue the same result, must be interpreted in the same way."[16]

The national proceedings which gave rise to the reference concerned the activities of a parallel importer company called Paranova, which purchased certain products in batches in Member States where prices were relatively low (Greece, the United Kingdom, Spain and Portugal) and imported them into Denmark, where it sold them below the manufacturers' official sale prices while still making a profit. For the purposes of sale in Denmark, Paranova repackaged all the medicines in new external packaging with a uniform appearance and its own style, namely white and coloured stripes corresponding to the colours of the manufacturers' original packaging. That packaging displayed, *inter alia*, the respective trade marks of the manufacturers and the statement that the product had been manufactured respectively by "Bristol Myers-Squibb" etc., together with the indication "imported and repackaged by Paranova". Certain other changes were made to the packaging of the products, including, for example, in the case of one product, replacing the spray in the original packaging with a spray from a source other than Bristol-Myers Squibb.

Referring to prior case-law, the Court stated that Article 7(2) of the Directive must therefore be interpreted as meaning that a trade mark owner may legitimately oppose the further marketing of a pharmaceutical product where the importer has repackaged it and re-affixed the trade mark, unless the conditions set out in the *Hoffmann-La Roche* judgment have been complied with. The Court went on to explain further the conditions laid down by the latter case.

As to "artificial partitioning of the markets between Member States", the Court said that this did not imply that a parallel importer must prove that the trade mark owner deliberately sought to partition the market between Member States, it simply meant that the owner may always rely on his rights as owner to oppose the marketing of repackaged products when such action was justified by the need to safeguard the essential function of the trade mark, in which case the resultant partitioning could not be regarded as artificial.[17] Reliance on trade mark rights by their owner in order to oppose marketing under that trade mark of products repackaged by a third party would contribute to the partitioning of markets between Member States in particular where the owner had placed an identical pharmaceutical product on the market in several Member States in various forms of packaging, and the product could not, in the condition in which

---

[15] Joined Cases C–427, 429 and 436/93 *Bristol-Myers Squibb and Others v. Paranova* [1996] E.C.R. I–3457; see also Joined Cases C–71–73/94 *Eurim-Pharm v. Beiersdorf and Others* [1996] E.C.R. I–3603; Case C–232/94 *MPA Pharma v. Rhône-Poulenc Pharma* [1996] E.C.R. I–3671; Case C–349/95 *Frits Loenderloot v. George Ballantine & Son Ltd and Others* [1997] E.C.R. I–6227; [1998] 1 C.M.L.R. 1015.
[16] *ibid.*, at para. 40.
[17] *ibid.*, para. 57.

it has been marketed by the trade mark owner in one Member State, be imported and put on the market in another Member State by a parallel importer.[18] The trade mark owner could not therefore oppose the repackaging of the product in new external packaging when the size of the packet used by the owner in the Member State where the importer purchased the product could not be marketed in the Member State of importation by reason, in particular, of a rule authorising packaging only of a certain size or a national practice to the same effect.[19] Where, in accordance with the rules and practices in force in the Member State of importation, the trade mark owner used many different sizes of packaging in that State, the finding that one of those sizes was also marketed in the Member State of exportation was not enough to justify the conclusion that repackaging was unnecessary. Partitioning of the markets would exist if the importer were able to sell the product in only part of his market.[20] The owner could however oppose the repackaging of the product in new external packaging where the importer was able to achieve packaging which could be marketed in the Member State of importation by, for example, affixing to the original external or inner packaging new labels in the language of the Member State of importation, or by replacing an additional article not capable of gaining approval in the Member State of importation with a similar article that has obtained such approval.[21] The power of the owner of trade mark rights protected in a Member State to oppose the marketing of repackaged products under the trade mark should be limited only in so far as the repackaging undertaken by the importer was necessary in order to market the product in the Member State of importation.[22]

The Court also explained that the concept of adverse effects on the original condition of the product referred to the condition of the product inside the packaging.[23] The trade mark owner could therefore oppose any repackaging involving a risk of the product inside the package being exposed to tampering or to influences affecting its original condition. To determine whether that applied, account had to be taken of the nature of the product and the method of repackaging.[24] As regards pharmaceutical products, repackaging was to be regarded as having been carried out in circumstances not capable of affecting the original condition of the product where, for example, the trade mark owner had placed the product on the market in double packaging and the repackaging affected only the external layer, leaving the inner packaging intact, or where the repackaging was carried out under the supervision of a public authority in order to ensure that the product remained intact.[25] The mere removal of blister packs, phials, ampoules or inhalers from their original external packaging and their replacement in new external packaging cannot affect the original condition of the product inside the packaging.[26] As regards operations consisting in the fixing of

---

[18] *ibid.*, para. 52.
[19] *ibid.*, para. 53.
[20] *ibid.*, para. 54.
[21] *ibid.*, para. 55.
[22] *ibid.*, para. 56.
[23] *ibid.*, para. 58.
[24] *ibid.*, para. 59.
[25] *ibid.*, para. 60.
[26] *ibid.*, para. 61.

self-stick labels to flasks, phials, ampoules or inhalers, the addition to the packaging of new user instructions or information in the language of the Member State of importation, or the insertion of an extra article, such as a spray, from a source other than the trade mark owner, there was nothing to suggest that the original condition of the product inside the packaging was directly affected thereby.[27] The Court however entered the caveat that the original condition of the product inside the packaging might be indirectly affected where, for example, the external or inner packaging of the repackaged product, or a new set of user instructions or information, omitted certain important information or gave inaccurate information concerning the nature, composition, effect, use or storage of the product. And the same would be the case if an extra article inserted into the packaging by the importer and designed for the ingestion and dosage of the product does not comply with the method of use and the doses envisaged by the manufacturer.[28]

The Court also commented on the other requirements to be met by the parallel importer, indicating, *inter alia*, that it was not necessary to require that it be stated on the packaging that the repackaging was carried out without the authorisation of the trade mark owner, but that a trade mark owner had a legitimate interest in being able to oppose the marketing of a product which had been poorly or untidily repackaged in a way which could damage the trade mark's reputation.[29]

The Court's case-law, particular the judgment in *Bristol-Myers Squibb*, amounts to a code on re-packaging rivalling in detail the terms of any conceivable harmonising legislation on the subject matter in question.

Whereas the judgments in *Hoffmann-La Roche* and *Bristol-Myers Squibb* concerned cases in which a parallel importer repackaged a trademarked product and reaffixed the original trade mark thereon, *Centrafarm BV v. American Home Products Corporation*,[30] concerned the case of a parallel importer replacing the original trade mark used by the proprietor in the Member State of export by the trade mark which the proprietor used in the Member State of import. In the latter case the Court held that prohibition by the proprietor of such unauthorised use of the mark by a third party would constitute a disguised restriction on trade between Member States within the meaning of the second sentence of Article 30 (ex 36) if it were established that the practice of using different trade marks for the same product had been adopted by the proprietor of those trade marks for the purpose of artificially partitioning the markets.[31] In *Pharmacia & Upjohn SA*[32] the Court of Justice considered the meaning of the latter expression, and concluded that the condition of artificial partitioning of the markets between Member States as defined by the Court in *Bristol-Myers Squibb* applied equally in a case where a parallel importer replaces the original trade mark by that used by the proprietor in the Member State of import.[33]

---

[27] *ibid.*, para. 64.
[28] *ibid.*, para. 65.
[29] *ibid.*, paras 72, 75 and 76.
[30] Case 3/78 [1978] E.C.R. 1823; [1979] 1 C.M.L.R. 326.
[31] Paras 22–23 of judgment.
[32] Case C–379/97 *Pharmacia & Upjohn SA, formerly Upjohn SA, v. Paranova A/S* [1999] E.C.R. I–6927.
[33] Para. 40 of judgment.

Common origin

A restriction on the exercise of trade mark rights derived from Article 28 (ex 30) which represented something of a wrong turning by the Court of Justice was the common origin principle. According to this principle, when trade marks held by different persons in different Member States had a common origin, the sale in a Member State of goods lawfully bearing one of the national marks could not be prevented merely because another of the marks was protected by the law of that State. The source of the common origin principle was the judgment of the Court of Justice in *Van Zuylen v. Hag*.[34] The case concerned trade marks for Hag decaffeinated coffee, one held by Hag AG in Germany, and the other held by a successor in title to a Belgian subsidiary of Hag AG in Luxembourg, the Belgian subsidiary having been sequestrated as enemy property at the end of the Second World War. The Court of Justice held that the Luxembourg holder of the Hag mark could not oppose imports bearing the German Hag mark, despite the fact that there were no longer any links whatsoever between the two companies. It was to be fifteen or so years before the Court reversed this decision, in *SA CNL-Sucal NV v. Hag GF AG*.[35] The Court observed that trade mark rights constituted an essential element in the system of undistorted competition which the Treaty seeks to establish and maintain. Under that system, an undertaking must be in a position to keep its customers by virtue of the quality of its products and services, something which was possible only if there were distinctive marks which enabled customers to identify those products and services. For the trade mark to be able to fulfil such a role, it had to offer a guarantee that all goods bearing it had been produced under the control of a single undertaking which was accountable for their quality.[36] In the circumstances of the case in point, the Court noted that:

> "From the date of expropriation and notwithstanding their common origin, each of the marks independently fulfilled its function, within its own territorial field of application, of guaranteeing that the marked products originated from one single source."[37]

It followed that each of the trade mark proprietors must be able to oppose the marketing, in the Member State in which the trade mark belonged to him, of goods originating from the other proprietor, in so far as they were similar products bearing an identical mark or one which is liable to lead to confusion.[38] Consistently with this approach, the Court described the principle of exhaustion of rights regarding trade marks as follows in *IHT Internationale Heiztechnik v. Ideal Standard*:

> "That principle, known as the exhaustion of rights, applies where the owner of the trade mark in the importing State and the owner of the trade mark in the exporting State are the same or where, even if they are separate persons, they

---

[34] Case 192/73 [1974] E.C.R. 731; [1974] 2 C.M.L.R. 127. The principle was foreshadowed in Case 40/70 *Sirena v. Eda* [1971] E.C.R. 69. In that case, however, the reference was made and dealt with by the Court on the basis of the rules of competition.

[35] Case C–10/89 [1990] E.C.R. I–3711; [1990] 3 C.M.L.R. 571.

[36] *ibid.*, at para. 13 of judgment.

[37] *ibid.*, at para. 18.

[38] *ibid.*, at para. 19.

are economically linked. A number of situations are covered: products put into circulation by the same undertaking, by a licensee, by a parent company, by a subsidiary of the same group, or by an exclusive distributor."[39]

Free movement of goods and copyright and related rights

The phrase "industrial and commercial property" in Article 30 (formerly Article 36), while it clearly applies to patents and trade marks, is less apt as a description of artistic property.[40] Nevertheless, after some initial hesitation by the Court of Justice[41] it is now beyond doubt that copyright and other rights protecting literary and artistic work are covered.

A right akin to copyright was the subject of the proceedings in *Deutsche Grammophon v. Metro*,[42] the earliest case in which the exhaustion of rights principle can be seen at work. Deutsche Grammophon (DG), the plaintiff in the national proceedings, supplied the records it manufactured to retailers in Germany under a retail price maintenance arrangement. It also exported records to France where they were marketed by its subsidiary, Polydor. Metro, the defendant, had succeeded in obtaining records originally sold in France by Polydor, which it then resold in Germany at prices well below the controlled price. DG sought to prevent these sales by invoking against Metro the exclusive right of distribution, akin to copyright, which manufacturers of sound recordings enjoy under German legislation. On a reference from the German court to which the case went on appeal, the Court of Justice held that:

". . . it would be in conflict with the provisions prescribing the free movement of products within the common market for a manufacturer of sound recordings to exercise the exclusive right to distribute the selected articles, conferred upon him by the legislation of a Member State, in such a way as to prohibit the sale in that State of products placed on the market by him or with his consent in another Member State solely because such distribution did not occur within the territory of the first Member State."[43]

The conclusion is clear but the steps by which it is reached are less so. The judgment contains the first mention of the limitation of the derogation in Article 30 (ex 36) to measures justified for the safeguarding of rights which constitute the specific subject-matter of a form of intellectual property. However, the Court did not go on to define the specific subject-matter of a record manufacturer's exclusive right of distribution; nor did it rule that a right to oppose the sale of records marketed by a manufacturer or with his consent in another Member State could not be included in such subject-matter. It simply reasoned that the purpose of unifying the market could not be attained "if, under the various legal

---

[39] Case C–9/93 [1994] E.C.R. I–2789, para. 34; [1994] 3 C.M.L.R. 857.

[40] See the remarks by Advocate General Warner in his Opinion in Case 62/79 *Coditel v. Ciné Vog Films* [1980] E.C.R. at 878–879, 881; [1981] 2 C.M.L.R. 362.

[41] In the *Deutsche Grammophon* case, cited in the following note, the Court left open the question whether a record manufacturer's right analogous to copyright came within the scope of Art. 30 (ex 36).

[42] Case 78/70 [1971] E.C.R. 487; [1971] C.M.L.R. 631.

[43] [1971] E.C.R. at 500.

systems of the Member States, nationals of those States were able to partition the market and bring about arbitrary discrimination or disguised restrictions on trade between Member States".[44]

A decade later the principle of exhaustion was applied by the Court in *Musik-Vertrieb Membran v. GEMA*.[45] The case concerned the importation of records and cassettes into Germany from other Member States, one being the United Kingdom, where they had been manufactured and put on the market with the consent of the copyright owners. The copyright management society, GEMA, claimed that the importation was in breach of the owners' rights in Germany. However, it did not seek to exclude the recordings from the German market but only to recover a sum representing the difference between the royalties payable in Germany and those paid in respect of the initial distribution. It was held that such recovery was contrary to Articles 28 and 30 (ex 30 and 36). The ground given by the Court for its ruling was that the exploitation of a copyright in a given market was a matter for the free choice of the owner. "He may", the Court said, "make that choice according to his best interests, which involve not only the level of remuneration provided in the Member State in question but other factors such as, for example, the opportunities for distributing his work and the marketing facilities which are further enhanced by virtue of the free movement of goods within the Community."[46] As a trader within the common market he must, in other words, abide by the consequences of his decisions.

GEMA has been distinguished in two subsequent cases. In *Warner Bros v. Christiansen*[47] the plaintiff in the national proceedings was the owner in the United Kingdom of the copyright in the film "Never Say Never Again". The defendant, who managed a video shop in Copenhagen, purchased a copy of the film in London with a view to hiring it out in Denmark and imported it into Denmark for that purpose. Under Danish law the hiring out of a video-cassette was subject to the consent of the author or producer, even after the video-cassette had been marketed, whereas under the law of the United Kingdom, the author had no right to control hiring out after the initial sale of the video-cassette. On a reference to the Court of Justice by a Danish court Warner Brothers claimed that reliance on Danish law to restrict the hiring out of the video-cassette was justified under Article 30 (ex 36) E.C. The defendant Christiansen relied upon *GEMA,* arguing that if an author chose to market a video-cassette in a country where national rules afforded no right to limit hiring out, he must accept the consequences of this choice and the exhaustion of his right to restrain the hiring out of that video-cassette in any other Member State. The Court rejected this latter view, on the ground that it would render "worthless" the specific right to authorise hiring out if that right were exhausted by sale in a Member State which afforded no specific protection for that right.[48]

---

[44] *ibid.*
[45] Joined Cases 55 and 57/80 [1981] E.C.R. 147.
[46] [1981] E.C.R. at 165.
[47] Case 158/86 [1988] E.C.R. 2605; [1990] 3 C.M.L.R. 684.
[48] *ibid.* at para. 18. The case is also considered in the context of patents, above at page 367.

In *EMI Electrola v. Patricia*[49] the plaintiff in the national proceedings was assignee of the production and distribution rights in Germany of the musical works of Cliff Richard. The defendant sold in Germany sound recordings originating in Denmark which incorporated some of Cliff Richard's works, and resisted the plaintiff's action for an injunction on the ground that the recordings had been lawfully marketed in Denmark after the expiry of the period during which exclusive rights were protected under Danish copyright law. The Court distinguished *GEMA* on the ground that the marketing in Denmark was due, not to an act or the consent of the copyright owner or his licensee, but to the expiry of the protection period under the law of that Member State.

Copyright and related forms of literary and artistic property[50] are complex forms of property, reflecting the diversity of the works to which they relate. *Deutsche Grammophon* and *GEMA* concerned the aspect of copyright which protects an owner's interest in the reproduction and sale of material objects incorporating creative work—sound recordings, in the cases in point. That kind of interest is adequately served by the control the copyright owner enjoys over the initial marketing of protected products. But literary and artistic works may be the subject of commercial exploitation by means other than the sale of the recordings made of them.[51] The release into circulation of a sound-recording cannot render lawful other forms of exploitation of the protected work, by such means as rental, and public performance, as the *Warner Bros* case indicated.[52]

Council Directive 92/100[53] was enacted in order to establish harmonised legal protection in the Community for the rental and lending rights and certain rights related to copyright in the field of intellectual property. Article 1(1) of the Directive requires the Member States to provide a right to authorise or prohibit the rental and lending of originals and copies of copyright works, and other subject-matter. Pursuant to Article 1(4), those rights are not to be exhausted by any sale or other act of distribution. Under Article 2(1) the exclusive right to authorise or prohibit rental and lending is to belong to the author in respect of the original and copies of his work, to the performer in respect of fixations of his performance, to the phonogram producer in respect of his phonograms and to the producer of the first fixation of a film in respect of the original and copies of his film. Under Article 9 of the Directive, without prejudice to the specific provisions concerning the lending and rental right, and those of Article 1(4) in particular, the distribution right, which is the exclusive right to make any of the above-mentioned objects available to the public by sale or otherwise, is not to be exhausted except where the first sale in the Community of that object is made by the rightholder or with his consent.

---

[49] Case 341/87 [1989] E.C.R. 79.

[50] The Court has held that the protection of industrial and commercial property within the meaning of Art. 30 (ex 36) includes literary and artistic property, see Case 262/81 *Coditel v. Ciné Vog* [1982] E.C.R. 3381; [1983] 1 C.M.L.R. 45, and in *Warner Bros*, n.38 above, the Court treated the rights in question as literary and artistic property, *ibid.*, at para. 13.

[51] Case C–200/96 *Metronome Musik Gmbh v. Musik Point Hokamp GmbH* [1998] E.C.R. I–1953; [1998] 3 C.M.L.R. 919, para. 15.

[52] *ibid.*, para. 18.

[53] [1992] O.J. L346/61.

In *Metronome Musik Gmbh v. Musik Point Hokamp GmbH* [54] the Court of Justice considered whether the introduction of an exclusive rental right pursuant to Directive 92/100 might infringe the principle of exhaustion of distribution rights in the event of the offering for sale, by the rightholder or with his consent, of copyright works. Referring to its previous case-law,[55] the Court noted that "like the right to present a work by means of public performance . . . the rental right remains one of the prerogatives of the author and producer notwithstanding sale of the physical recording",[56] and concluded:

> "Thus, the distinction drawn in the Directive between the effects of the specific rental and lending right, referred to in Article 1, and those of the distribution right, governed by Article 9 and defined as an exclusive right to make one of the objects in question available to the public, principally by sale, is justified. The former is not exhausted by the sale or any other act of distribution of the object, whereas the latter may be exhausted, but only and specifically upon the first sale in the Community by the rightholder or with his consent.
>
> The introduction by the Community legislation of an exclusive rental right cannot therefore constitute any breach of the principle of exhaustion of the distribution right, the purpose and scope of which are different."[57]

In *Foreningen af danske Videogramdistributører v. Laserdisken*,[58] a Danish court asked the Court of Justice whether it was contrary to Article 30 (ex 36) or to Directive 92/100 for the holder of an exclusive rental right to prohibit copies of a film from being offered for rental in a Member State even where offering those copies for rental has been authorised within another Member State. In other words, did offering copies of a film for rental in one Member State exhaust the exclusive rental right as regards those copies of the film? The plaintiffs in the national proceedings, the governments submitting observations, and the Commission, argued that it followed from the Court's case-law and the Directive that the right to authorise or prohibit the rental of a film is comparable to the right of public performance and, unlike the right of distribution, is not exhausted as soon as it has first been exercised.[59] The Court agreed, holding that just as a rental right remains one of the prerogatives of the author and producer notwithstanding sale of the physical recording, the same reasoning must be followed as regards the effect produced by the offer for rental. The exclusive right to hire out various copies of the work contained in a video film can, by its very nature, be exploited by repeated and potentially unlimited transactions, each of which involves the right to remuneration. "The specific right to authorise or prohibit rental would be rendered meaningless if it were held to be exhausted as soon as the object was first offered for rental."[60] The same result followed from Article 9 of Directive 92/100.[61]

---

[54] Case C–200/96 *Metronome Musik Gmbh v. Musik Point Hokamp GmbH* [1998] E.C.R. 1953.

[55] *Viz.*, Joined Cases 55 and 57/80 *Musik Vertrieb Membran and K-tel International v. GEMA* [1981] E.C.R. 147; Case 58/80 *Dansk Supermarked v. Imerco* [1981] E.C.R. 181; Case 158/86 *Warner Brothers and Metronome Video v. Christiansen* [1988] E.C.R. 2605; [1990] 3 C.M.L.R. 684.

[56] Case C–200/96, n.45; [1998] 3 C.M.L.R. 919, para. 18.

[57] Case C–200/96, n.45; [1998] 3 C.M.L.R. 919, paras 19 and 20.

[58] Case C–61/97 [1998] E.C.R. I–5171.

[59] *ibid.*, para. 11.

[60] *ibid.*, para. 18.

[61] *ibid.*, paras 20 and 21.

Free movement of goods and other intellectual property forms

In *Keurcoop v. Nancy Kean Gifts BV*[62] the Court of Justice considered the application of Article 30 (ex 36) to industrial designs. The case concerned the design of a ladies' handbag which had been registered under the Uniform Benelux Law on Designs by Nancy Kean Gifts BV. The registration had been effected without the consent of the American author of the design but this had no bearing on its validity in the Netherlands.[63] The reference to the Court was made in proceedings brought by Nancy Kean Gifts to prevent the sale on the Dutch market of handbags of the same design which has been imported by Keurcoop. It was held by the Court that industrial designs came within the protection afforded by Article 30 (ex 36) to "industrial and commercial property" since they had the aim of defining exclusive rights which was characteristic of such property. That protection enabled the owner of the right to a design in a Member State to prevent the sale of identical products imported from another Member State where they had been legally acquired by a third party—the situation described in the reference. However, the Court made it clear that the principle of the exhaustion of rights would apply if the products in question had been put on the market in the Member State of origin by or with the consent of the design owner in the Member State of importation or by a person legally or economically dependent on him.[64]

Analogous principles to those applicable to patents, trade marks, copyright and other artistic and literary property, and industrial designs, no doubt apply to other property rights falling within the term "industrial and commercial property" in Article 30 (ex 36) E.C. Rules on the protection of indications of provenance and designations of origin comprise "industrial and commercial property" within the meaning of the latter Article, providing that the protected names have not become generic in the country of origin.[65] And the Court has referred to the specific subject-matter of a trade mark as being applicable by analogy as regards the protection of trade names.[66]

---

[62] Case 144/81 [1982] E.C.R. 2853; [1983] 2 C.M.L.R. 47.

[63] One of the questions put by the referring court to the Court of Justice was whether a rule giving an exclusive right to the first person to register a design, irrespective of its authorship, was compatible with Art. 36. The Court's response was that, in the absence of standardisation or harmonisation of laws on industrial designs, it was for national law to lay down the necessary conditions and procedures. See also Case 53/87 *CICRA v. Maxicar* [1987] E.C.R. 6039.

[64] [1982] E.C.R. at 2871.

[65] Case C–3/91 *Exportur SA v. LOR SA and Confiserie du Tech SA.* [1992] E.C.R. I–5529, paras 37–39.

[66] Case C–255/97 *Pfeiffer Großhandel GmbH v. Löwa Warenhandel GmbH* [1999] E.C.R. I–2835, para. 22.

CHAPTER 14

FREEDOM OF MOVEMENT FOR WORKERS

General

The Treaties establishing the European Communities each contain provisions designed to facilitate the movement of workers between the Member States. The signatories to the Treaty establishing the European Coal and Steel Community undertook in Article 69 to remove any restrictions based on nationality upon the employment in the coal and steel industries of workers holding the nationality of one of the Member States and having recognised qualifications in coal-mining or steel-making, and a similar provision appears in Article 96 of the Treaty establishing the European Atomic Energy Community, declaring the right of nationals of the Member States to take skilled employment in the field of nuclear energy. Acting under this latter Article the Council issued a Directive in 1962[1] defining the scope of skilled employment and requiring that Member States adopt all necessary measures to ensure that any authorisation required for taking up employment in the field specified should be automatically granted.

As Treaties concerned only with limited economic integration, the ECSC and Euratom Treaties naturally only dealt with workers in their respective sectors. The E.C. Treaty, on the other hand, seeks to promote comprehensive economic integration, and its provisions requiring that "freedom of movement for workers shall be secured within the Community" are applicable to all "workers of the Member States" regardless of occupation.[2] It is with the provision of the E.C. Treaty, and the implementing legislation made thereunder, that we shall be hereafter concerned.

Since a common market requires the removal of all obstacles to the free movement of the factors of production, as well as of goods and services, the free movement of workers in the Community may be seen simply as a prerequisite to the achievement of an economic objective. Support for this view may be found in the Spaak Report,[3] and in the texts of Articles 39, 40 and 42 (ex 48, 49 and 51) E.C. Under Article 39 (ex 48) E.C., workers of the Member States are to be free to accept offers of employment actually made, and to remain in a Member State for the purposes of carrying on employment. Article 40 (ex 49) E.C. authorises legislation by the Council to eliminate administrative procedures likely to impede the movement of workers, and to set up machinery for matching offers of employment in one Member State with available candidates in another. The provisions of Article 42 (ex 51) E.C. empowering the Council to take legislative action in the field of social security appear to extend this authorisation only to

---

[1] [1962] O.J. 1650.

[2] Art. 39(1) E.C., amending and replacing Art. 48(1), by omitting reference to the transitional period, and Art. 39(2) (ex 48(2)). But the E.C. Treaty does not "affect" the provisions of the ECSC Treaty, nor "derogate" from those of the Euratom; see Art. 305 E.C. (ex 232).

[3] *Rapport des chefs de délégation aux ministres des affaires étrangères* (Brussels, April 21, 1956).

measures necessary for safeguarding the rights of the migrant worker *stricto sensu.*

Yet such a functional economic approach to the interpretation of the free movement provisions is likely to be inadequate for two reasons. First, in the graphic words of Article 6 of the Clayton Anti-Trust Act, because of the notion that "the labour of a human being is not a commodity or article of commerce", or as Advocate General Trabucchi has put it: "The migrant worker is not regarded by Community law—nor is he by the internal legal system—as a mere source of labour but is viewed as a human being."[4] A similar sentiment may be discerned in the fifth recital to the preamble to Regulation 1612/68 of the Council,[5] which speaks of the exercise of workers' rights in "freedom and dignity", and describes freedom of movement for workers as a "fundamental right" and "one of the means by which the worker is guaranteed the possibility of improving his living and working conditions and promoting his social advancement, while helping to satisfy the requirements of the economies of the Member States". As Advocate General Jacobs has observed, "The recital makes it clear that labour is not, in Community law, to be regarded as a commodity and notably gives precedence to the fundamental rights of workers over satisfying the requirements of the economies of the Member States."[6]

But for another reason a purely economic approach is likely to be deficient. The EEC was established after the failure of rather more ambitious attempts to institute a Western European military and political union, and it represented an attempt to achieve a similar political aim by means of economic integration. Thus the first recital to the preamble of the E.C. Treaty records the determination of the signatories to lay the foundation of an ever closer union among the peoples of Europe, and the eighth records their resolve to strengthen peace and liberty by a pooling of their respective resources. The closing words of Article 2 of the Treaty lay down as one of the Community's allotted tasks that of promoting economic and social cohesion and solidarity among the Member States. To this extent, there may be said to be a larger objective contained in the provisions relating to the free movement of persons. It is to be noted that the Declaration issued after the Summit Conference of October 1972 included the words: "The Member States re-affirm their resolve to base their Community's development on democracy, freedom of opinion, *free movement of men and ideas* and participation by the people through their elected representatives."[7]

The Court of Justice has sometimes interpreted the provisions of Articles 39–42 (ex 48 to 51) and the implementing legislation made thereunder, in a rather more liberal manner than would be dictated by a purely functional view of the Treaty based on its economic objectives. In *Hessische Knappschaft v. Maison*

---

[4] Case 7/75 *Mr and Mrs F. v. Belgian State* [1975] E.C.R. 679 at page 696; [1975] 2 C.M.L.R. 442.
[5] [1968] J.O. L257/2. The Court has referred to the fifth recital both as a guide to the interpretation of the Regulation, and as an indication of the scope of the application of the Treaty: Case 76/72 *Michel S.* [1973] E.C.R. 457, Case 9/74 *Casagrande* [1974] E.C.R. 773, [1974] 2 C.M.L.R. 423 (interpretation of Reg. 1612/68); Case 152/81 *Forcheri* [1983] E.C.R. 2323, [1984] 1 C.M.L.R. 334 (scope of application of the Treaty).
[6] Case 344/87 *Bettray* [1989] E.C.R. 1621 at 1637; [1991] 1 C.M.L.R. 459.
[7] Emphasis added. Bull. E.C. 10/72 at 15

Singer[8] a German national on holiday in France had been killed in a road accident. His dependants were paid benefit by a German social security institution, which then brought an action in France against the employer of the driver of the other vehicle, claiming that the French court was bound to recognise the subrogation that German law allowed, by virtue of Article 52 of Regulation 3.[9] In the course of the proceedings before the Court of Justice, it was argued that to apply Article 52 of the Regulation in circumstances such as those before the national court would be incompatible with Article 42 (ex 51) E.C., inasmuch as that provision only allowed the Council to adopt such measures as were necessary to provide freedom of movement for workers *qua* workers, not *qua* holidaymakers. The Court responded:

> "Since the establishment of as complete as possible a freedom of movement of labour is among the 'foundations' of the Community, it is the ultimate goal of Article 51 and, therefore, governs the exercise of the power it confers upon the Council. It would not be in keeping with such a concept to limit the idea of 'worker' to migrant workers strictly speaking or to travel connected with their employment. Nothing in Article 51 requires such a distinction; moreover, such a distinction would make the application of the contemplated rules unfeasible. On the other hand, the system adopted for Regulation No. 3, which consists in removing, as much as possible, the territorial limitations for applying the various social security systems, is quite in keeping with the objectives of Article 51 of the Treaty."[10]

It was in a similar spirit that the Court of Justice considered the purpose and effect of Regulation 1612/68[11] in *Commission v. Germany*[12] in the following terms:

> "It is apparent from the provisions of the regulation, taken as a whole, that in order to facilitate the movement of members of workers' families the Council took into account, first, the importance for the worker, from a human point of view, of having his entire family with him, and secondly, the importance, from all points of view, of the integration of the worker and his family into the host Member State without any difference in treatment in relation to nationals of that State."[13]

In Articles 17–22 (ex 8–8e) E.C. provision is made for citizenship of the Union, pursuant to which, any citizen of the Union shall, *inter alia*, have the right to move and reside freely within the territory of the Member States, subject to the limitations and conditions laid down in the Treaty and by measures adopted thereunder, to vote and to stand as a candidate in municipal and European Parliament elections in the Member State in which he resides, and to seek the

---

[8] Case 44/65 [1965] E.C.R. 965; [1966] C.M.L.R. 82.
[9] [1958] J.O. 561.
[10] [1965] E.C.R. 965 at 971.
[11] [1968] O.J. L257/2.
[12] Case 249/86 [1989] E.C.R. 1263; [1990] 3 C.M.L.R. 540.
[13] [1989] E.C.R. 1263 at para. 11.

protection of the diplomatic or consular authorities of any Member State in third countries in which his own country is not represented. The right to freedom of movement of individuals pursuant to, *inter alia*, Article 39 (ex 48) E.C. is thus linked to the concept of citizenship of the Union, and in the latter concept there is manifested a purpose which transcends the economic requirements of the common market.

The ambit of Article 39 (ex 48) E.C.

Article 39 (ex 48) E.C. aims to secure freedom of movement for workers. This provision, along with the other provisions of the Treaty relating to freedom of movement for persons, is intended to facilitate the pursuit of occupational activities of all kinds throughout the Community and preclude national legislation which might place Community nationals at a disadvantage when they extend their activities beyond a single Member State.[14] The fact that an individual invokes Article 39 in his own Member State against his own national authorities has no bearing on the application of the principle of freedom of movement for workers, since any Community national, irrespective of his place of residence and nationality, who has exercised the right to freedom of movement for workers and has been employed in another Member State falls within the scope of the provision in question.[15] While this provision may require Member States to amend their legislation, even with respect to their own nationals (*e.g.* to allow them to leave their own Member State to seek work in another),[16] it does not extend to situations wholly internal to a Member State,[17] for example the binding over of a person charged with theft on condition that she proceed to Northern Ireland and not return to England or Wales for three years.[18] A worker cannot rely upon Article 39 unless he or she has exercised the right to freedom of movement within the Community,[19] or is seeking to exercise that right, and the purely hypothetical possibility that an individual may at some time in the future seek work in another Member State is not sufficient.[20] But a national who has undertaken a course of study in another Member State and then returned to his or her Member State of origin may rely upon Article 39 (ex 48) E.C. against that

---

[14] Case C–443/93 *Ioannis Vougioukas v. IKA* [1995] E.C.R. I–4033, para. 39.

[15] Case C–419/92 *Scholz v. Opera Universitaria di Cagliari* [1994] E.C.R. I–505, para. 9, [1994] 1 C.M.L.R. 873; Case C–443/93 *Ioannis Vougioukas*, note 14, para. 38.

[16] See, *e.g.* Art. 2(1) of Dir. 68/360; see below, at p. 388.

[17] Case 175/78 *Saunders* [1979] E.C.R. 1129; [1979] 2 C.M.L.R. 216; Case 298/84 *Iorio* [1986] E.C.R. 247; [1986] 3 C.M.L.R. 665; Case C–332/90 *Steen* [1992] E.C.R. I–341, and Case C–132/93 *Steen* [1994] E.C.R. I–2715; [1992] 2 C.M.L.R. 406; Joined Cases C–64–65/96 *Land Nordrhein-Westfalen v. Kari Uecker* [1997] E.C.R. I–3171.

[18] Case 175/78 *Saunders* [1979] E.C.R. 1129; [1979] 2 C.M.L.R. 216. It is to be noted by way of contrast that in the context of the free movement of goods, charges on the intra-State movement of domestic goods are covered by Art. 25 E.C.; Joined Cases C–363/93 *etc., Lancry* [1994] E.C.R. I–3957, esp. paras 27–29, p. 291 above.

[19] Joined Cases 35–36/82 *Morson* [1982] E.C.R. 3723; [1983] 2 C.M.L.R. 221.

[20] Case 180/83 *Moser* [1984] E.C.R. 2539; [1984] 3 C.M.L.R. 720.

Member State to uphold his or her right to use the postgraduate academic title acquired in that other Member State.[21]

Article 39 E.C. not only applies to the action of public authorities, but also to rules of any other nature aimed at regulating gainful employment in a collective manner.[22] The application of the latter Article is not conditional upon all conduct pertaining to an economic relationship or activity occurring within the territory of the Member States: it applies in judging all legal relationships which can be localised within the Community, by reason either of the place where they were entered into, or the place where they take effect.[23] In *Boukhalfa* the Court held that the latter principle must be deemed to extend to cases in which there was a sufficiently close link between the employment relationship, on the one hand, and the law of a Member State and thus the relevant rules of Community law, on the other. The Court concluded that Article 48 (now Article 39) E.C. applied where a national of a Member State (a Belgian) permanently resident in a non-Member country (Algeria) was employed by another Member State (Germany) in its embassy in that non-Member country, where that person's contract of employment was entered into and permanently performed in that latter country, and where the plaintiff's situation was subject to the law of the employing State in several respects; the consequence was that the prohibition of discrimination laid down in the Treaty applied as regards all aspects of the employment relationship which were governed by the law of the employing Member State.[24] Article 39 E.C. is directly effective,[25] and it is to be noted that it may be relied upon not only by a worker, even in a case in which the adverse effects on a worker result from obligations imposed by national law upon the employer,[26] but also by an employer who wishes to employ, in a Member State in which he is established, a worker who is a national of another Member State.[27] As the Court said in *Clean Car Autoservice*, referring to Article 39(1) and (2) (ex 48(1) and (2)):

"While those rights are undoubtedly enjoyed by those directly referred to—namely, workers—there is nothing in the wording of Article 48 to indicate that they may not be relied upon by others, in particular employers."[28]

---

[21] Case C–19/92 *Dieter Kraus v. Land Baden-Württemberg.* [1993] E.C.R. I–1663; for further discussion of the latter case see below at p. 437.

[22] Case 36/74 *Walrave v. Union Cycliste Internationale* [1974] E.C.R. 1405, para. 17, [1975] 1 C.M.L.R. 320; Case C–415/93 *Union Royale Belge des Sociététes de Football Association ASBL v. Jean-Marc Bosman* [1995] E.C.R. I–4921, para. 82, [1996] 1 C.M.L.R. 645; [1996] All E.R. (E.C.) 97. The prohibition of discrimination "must be regarded as applying to private persons", see Case C–281/98 *Angonese* of June 1, 2000.

[23] Case 36/74 *Walrave* [1974] E.C.R. 1405; [1975] 1 C.M.L.R. 320; Case 237/83 *Prodest* [1984] E.C.R. 3153; Case 9/88 *Lopes da Veiga* [1989] E.C.R. 2989; [1991] 1 C.M.L.R. 217.

[24] *Ingrid Boukhalfa v. Bundesrepublik Deutschland* [1996] E.C.R. I–2253.

[25] Case 48/75 *Royer* [1977] E.C.R. 497, para. 23, [1976] 2 C.M.L.R. 619; Case 41/74 *Van Duyn v. Home Office* [1974] E.C.R. 1337; [1975] 1 C.M.L.R. 1; Case C–90/96 *David Petrie and Others v. Università degli Studi di Verona* [1997] E.C.R. I–6527, [1998] 1 C.M.L.R. 711, para. 28.

[26] Case C–27/91 *Union de Recouvrement des Cotisations de Sécurité Sociale et d'Allocations Familiales de la Savoie (URSSAF) v. Hostellerie Le Manoir SARL.* [1991] E.C.R. I–5531, para. 9.

[27] Case C–350/96 *Clean Car Autoservice GesmbH v. Landeshauptmann von Wien* [1998] E.C.R. I–2521; [1998] 2 C.M.L.R. 637.

[28] *ibid.*, para. 19.

The Court has held that national courts are under a duty to interpret national law, as far as is at all possible, to achieve the aims of Article 39 (ex 48);[29] this is in accordance with general principle, and it would follow that it would be for a national court, when interpreting and applying domestic law, to give to it, where possible, an interpretation which accords with Article 39, and, to the extent that this is not possible, to hold such domestic law inapplicable.[30]

The concept of "worker"

Article 39 refers to freedom of movement for "workers". Article 1 of Regulation 1612/68 (freedom of movement for workers within the Community) refers to the right to "take up an activity as an employed person". Neither term ("worker" or "employed person") is defined,[31] but the concepts must be interpreted according to their ordinary meaning, and in the light of the objectives of the Treaty.[32] The terms cannot be defined according to the national laws of the Member States,[33] but have a Community meaning.[34] The Court has in its case-law held that the essential characteristic of the employment relationship is that for a certain period a person performs services for and under the direction of another person in return for which he receives remuneration.[35] Since the concepts of worker and employed person define the field of application of one of the fundamental freedoms guaranteed by the Treaty, they must not be interpreted restrictively.[36] A person may be a "worker", or person pursuing an "activity as an employed person" even if engaged only in part-time work, and in receipt of pay below the minimum guaranteed wage in the sector in question.[37] However, the concepts cover only the pursuit of effective and genuine activities, and not activities on such a small scale as to regarded as "marginal and ancillary".[38] Work cannot be regarded as an effective and genuine economic activity if it constitutes merely a means of rehabilitation or reintegration for the persons concerned and

---

[29] Case C–165/91 *Simon J. M. van Munster v. Rijksdienst voor Pensioenen* [1994] E.C.R. I–4661, paras 34–35; [1995] 2 C.M.L.R. 513.

[30] Case 157/86 *Mary Murphy and others v. An Bord Telecom Eireann* [1988] E.C.R. 673, para. 11, [1998] 1 C.M.L.R. 879, for the general principle, see above at p. 71.

[31] Though the concept of "employed person" is defined for the purposes of co-ordination of the national social security systems pursuant to Arts 40 and 308 (ex 49 and 235), see Art. 1(a) of Council Reg. 118/97 amending and updating Reg. No. 1408/71 on the application of social security schemes to employed persons, to self-employed persons and to members of their families moving within the Community *etc.*, [1997] O.J. L28/1 (Part I of Annex A contains a consolidated text of Reg. 1408/71).

[32] Case 53/81 *Levin* [1982] E.C.R. 1035; [1982] 2 C.M.L.R. 454.

[33] Though to some extent they are defined by reference to coverage of the national social security systems in the context of the co-ordination of the national social security systems for employed and self-employed persons under Reg. 1408/71, see n.29.

[34] Case 75/63 *Hoekstra (neé Unger)* [1964] E.C.R. 177; [1964] C.M.L.R. 319; Case 53/81 *Levin* [1982] E.C.R. 1035; [1982] 2 C.M.L.R. 454.

[35] Case 66/85 *Lawrie-Blum v. Land Baden-Württemberg* [1986] E.C.R. 2121, paras 16 and 17; [1987] 3 C.M.L.R. 403; Case 85/96 *Martinez Sala v. Freistaat Bayern* [1998] E.C.R. I–2691, para. 32.

[36] Case 53/81 *Levin* [1982] E.C.R. 1035; [1982] 2 C.M.L.R. 454; Case 139/85 *Kempf* [1986] E.C.R. 1741; [1987] 1 C.M.L.R. 764; Joined Cases 389–390/87 *Echternach* [1989] E.C.R. 723; [1990] 2 C.M.L.R. 305.

[37] *ibid.*

[38] *ibid.*

the purpose of the paid employment, which is adapted to the physical and mental capabilities of each person, is to enable those persons sooner or later to recover their capacity to take ordinary employment or to lead as normal as possible a life.[39] But a person engaged in preparatory training in the course of occupational training must be regarded as a worker if the training period is completed under the conditions of genuine and effective activity as an employed person, even if the trainee's productivity is low, and he works only a small number of hours per week and consequently receives limited remuneration.[40] Furthermore, the motives which may have prompted a "worker" to seek employment in another Member State are of no account as regards his right to enter and reside in the territory of that State, provided that he pursues or wishes to pursue an effective and genuine activity.[41]

A person who has never been employed, and who goes to another Member State to study, is not to be regarded as a "worker", at any rate where he is not during his sojourn in the latter Member State subject to a social security scheme designed to benefit employed persons.[42] But a migrant worker who voluntarily ceases his employment in order to devote himself, after the lapse of a certain period of time, to full-time studies in another Member State, retains his status as a worker, provided that there is a relationship between his previous occupational activity, and the studies in question.[43]

The definition of "worker" in the Community sense rarely causes difficulty because if an economically active migrant is not a worker, he is as like as not self-employed, in which case either Article 43 (ex 52) E.C. or Article 49 (ex 59) E.C. will apply. The Court has held that Articles 39, 43 and 49 (ex 48, 52 and 59) are based on the same principles both as far as entry and residence and non-discrimination on grounds of nationality are concerned,[44] and so categorisation under Article 39 (ex 48) E.C., as opposed to Articles 43 or 49 (ex 52 or 59), will rarely be crucial. Thus, for example, Member States are obliged to issue a residence permit to a national of another Member State if it is not disputed that that person is engaged in economic activity, without its being necessary in that regard to classify the activity as that of an employed or self-employed person.[45] Nevertheless, the distinction may be significant in certain cases, and a person who has worked only in a self-employed capacity in the relevant Member State cannot be regarded as a "worker" within the meaning of Article 39 (ex 48) E.C. and therefore cannot rely upon that provision.[46]

---

[39] Case 344/87 *Battray v. Staatssecretaris van Justitie* [1989] E.C.R. 1621; [1991] 1 C.M.L.R. 459.

[40] Case 66/85 *Lawrie-Blum v. Land Baden-Württemberg* [1986] E.C.R. 2121, paras 19—21; [1987] 3 C.M.L.R. 403; Case 344/87 *Battray v. Staatssecretaris van Justitie* [1989] E.C.R. 1621, para. 15; [1991] 1 C.M.L.R. 459; Case C–3/90 *M.J.E. Bernini v. Minister van Onderwijs en Wetenshcappen* [1992] E.C.R. 1071, paras 15–16.

[41] Case 53/81 *Levin* [1982] E.C.R. 1035.

[42] Case 66/77 *Kuyken* [1977] E.C.R. 2311; Case 238/83 *Meade* [1984] E.C.R. 2631.

[43] Case C–3/90 *M.J.E. Bernini v. Minister van Onderwijs en Wetenshcappen* [1992] E.C.R. 1071, paras 20–21.

[44] Case 48/75 *Royer* [1976] E.C.R. 497; [1976] 2 C.M.L.R. 619, see below at p. 445.

[45] Case C–363/89 *Roux* [1991] E.C.R. I–273; [1993] 1 C.M.L.R. 3.

[46] Case C–15/90 *Middleburgh* [1991] E.C.R. I–4655; [1992] 1 C.M.L.R. 353.

REMOVAL OF RESTRICTIONS ON MOVEMENT AND RESIDENCE IN THE MEMBER STATES

The Treaty provides that freedom of movement for workers shall entail the right to move freely within the Member States for the purpose of accepting offers of employment actually made and empowers the Council to implement this object by legislation.[47] Acting under this authority the Council issued Directive 68/360 on the abolition of restrictions on movement and residence for workers of the Member States and their families.[48] The provisions of Article 39 (ex 48) E.C. are directly effective,[49] as are those of Directive 68/360.[50] As the Court explained in *Procureur du Roi v. Royer*,[51] "the directives concerned [including 68/360] determined the scope and detailed rules for the exercise of rights conferred directly by the Treaty."

Persons to whom Directive 68/360 is applicable

The Directive applies to nationals of the Member States and those members of their families to whom Regulation 1612/68 is applicable.[52] In Article 10(1) of the latter Regulation we find members of the worker's family defined as:

(a) his spouse and their descendants who are under the age of 21 years or are dependants[53];
(b) dependent[54] relatives in the ascending line of the worker and his spouse.

The Article declares that these members of the family, irrespective of nationality, have the right to "install" themselves with a worker who is a national of one Member State employed in the territory of another. In the *Morson* case[55] the Court held that Article 10(1) does not cover the relatives of a worker who is a national of the host State, and has never exercised the right of free movement. But it follows from the judgment in *Surinder Singh* that Article 10(1) applies to members of the family where a worker of one Member State who has been employed in another returns to his Member State of origin.[56] The members of the family referred to need not actually reside under the same roof as the worker, in order to claim the benefit of Article 10(1), and a spouse retains that status until the formal dissolution of the marriage.[57] In *Reed*, a case in which the Court considered the position of an unmarried partner of a migrant worker wishing to

---

[47] Art. 39(3)(a) and (b) E.C. and Art. 40 E.C. (ex 48(3)(a) and (b)) and Art. 49).
[48] [1968] J.O. L257/13; [1968] O.J. Spec.Ed. (II), 485.
[49] Case 167/73 *Commission v. France* [1974] E.C.R. 359; [1974] 2 C.M.L.R. 216; Case 41/74 *Van Duyn v. Home Office* [1974] E.C.R. 1337; [1975] 1 C.M.L.R. 1.
[50] Case 36/75 *Rutili v. French Minister of the Interior* [1975] E.C.R. 1219; [1976] 1 C.M.L.R. 140.
[51] Case 48/75 *Procureur du Roi v. Royer* [1976] E.C.R. 497; [1976] 2 C.M.L.R. 619.
[52] Art. 1.
[53] Dependency is a matter of fact and the reasons are immaterial, Case 316/85 *Lebon* [1987] E.C.R. 2811; [1989] 1 C.M.L.R. 337.
[54] *ibid.*
[55] Joined Cases 35–36/82 *Morson* [1982] E.C.R. 3723; [1983] 2 C.M.L.R. 221.
[56] *R. v. Immigration and Appeal Tribunal and Surinder Surinder Singh, ex p. Secretary of State for the Home Department* [1992] E.C.R. I–4265; [1992] 3 C.M.L.R. 358.
[57] Case 267/83 *Diatta* [1985] E.C.R. 567; [1986] 2 C.M.L.R. 164.

reside with that migrant in a Member State of which neither were nationals held that in referring to "spouse" Article 10(1) refers to a relationship based on marriage, but nevertheless upheld the right of residence of the unmarried partner because a right of residence would have been accorded by the Member State in question if she had been a partner of a national rather than of a non-national.[58]

Article 10(2) of the Regulation provides that Member States shall "facilitate the admission" of dependent members of a worker's family other than children or those in the ascending line, and any members of the family living under the worker's roof in the country whence he came.

The right of the worker and members of his family to leave their home country in order to pursue employment in another Member State

The Directive deals not only with the right to enter other Member States, it also grants the right to leave one's own.[59] Member States are obliged to grant workers the right to leave their territory for the purpose of taking up activities as employed persons and pursuing such activities in the territory of another Member State. The Court has held that nationals of a Member State have the right, which they derive directly from the Treaty, to leave their country of origin to enter the territory of another Member State and reside there to pursue an economic activity,[60] and that provisions which preclude or deter a national of a Member State from leaving his country of origin in order to exercise his right to freedom of movement therefore constitute an obstacle to that freedom even if they apply without regard to the nationality of the workers concerned.[61] Pursuant to Directive 68/360, members of their family enjoy the same right as the national on whom they are dependent.[62] The exercise of this right is conditioned simply on the production of a valid identity card or passport, which Member States are under a duty both to issue, and to renew. Passports must be valid for all Member States and for countries through which the holder must pass when travelling between Member States. Where a passport is the only document on which the holder may lawfully leave the country, its period of validity shall be at least five

---

[58] Case 59/85 *Reed* [1986] E.C.R. 1283; [1987] 2 C.M.L.R. 448. The Court based the right of residence on the right of the migrant to the same "social and tax advantages as national workers" within the meaning of Art. 7(2) of Reg. 1612/68. It is inappropriate to describe the right of residence of one person as a social and tax advantage of another and a preferable view is that Reg. 1612/68 makes no provision for a case such as that in issue in *Reed* but that the outcome in question can be justified on the basis of Art. 39 itself (since exclusion of an unmarried partner impedes freedom of movement), or Art. 12 E.C., which prohibits any discrimination on grounds of nationality within the sphere of operation of the Treaty (which would more closely parallel the reasoning of the Court in *Reed*).

[59] Art. 2.

[60] Case C–363/89 *Roux v. Belgium* [1991] E.C.R. I–273, para. 9; [1993] 1 C.M.L.R. 3; *R. v. Immigration and Appeal Tribunal and Surinder Surinder Singh, ex p. Secretary of State for the Home Department* [1992] E.C.R. I–4265, para. 17; Case C–415/93 *Union Royale Belge des Sociétés de Football Association ASBL v. Jean-Marc Bosman* [1995] E.C.R. I–4921, para. 95; [1996] 1 C.M.L.R. 645; [1996] All E.R. (E.C.) 97.

[61] Case C–10/90 *Masgio v. Bundesknappschaft* [1991] E.C.R. I–1119, paras 18–19; *Bosman*, n.260, para. 96.

[62] Art. 2.

years. Member States may not demand exit visas or equivalent documents from workers or members of their families.[63]

The right of a worker and members of his family to enter another Member State

Member States are required to allow the persons to whom Directive 68/360 applies to enter their territory simply on production of a valid identity card or passport.[64] No entry visas or equivalent documents may be demanded save from members of the family who are not EEC nationals.[65] Member States must accord to such persons every facility for obtaining the necessary visas.[66] The Court in the *Pieck* case construed "entry visa or equivalent document" as covering any formality for the purpose of granting leave to enter the territory of a Member State which is coupled with a passport check at the frontier, whatever the place or time at which leave is granted, and in whatever form it may be granted.[67]

Article 39(3)(b) (ex 48(3)(b)) E.C. envisages free movement of workers for the purpose of accepting offers of employment actually made, but makes no mention of a right to move freely in search of employment. It would seem to follow that Member States are only bound to apply Article 3 of the Directive in the case of workers who have already been offered a job, but the Court of Justice in *Procureur de Roi v. Royer* referred to the right of workers to enter the territory of a Member State and reside there for the purposes intended by the Treaty, in particular to look for or pursue an activity as an employed person. Such a construction of Article 39 (ex 48) E.C. is consistent with its purpose and wording. Freedom of movement entails the abolition of any discrimination based on nationality between workers of the Member States as regards, *inter alia*, employment. In Article 7 of Regulation 1612/68 the notion of equality in matters of employment is construed by the Council as involving reinstatement and re-employment. Preventing a national of a Member State who has lost his job from entering another Member State to seek re-employment could be said to amount to discrimination based on nationality, since he would be restricted to seeking employment in that Member State via the postal services and his own local labour exhange.[68] Article 69 of Regulation 1408/71[69] on the social security rights of migrant workers, in providing unemployment benefit to a national of one

---

[63] Art. 2(4).

[64] Art. 3(1).

[65] Art. 3(2).

[66] *ibid.*

[67] Case 157/79 *Pieck* [1980] E.C.R. 2171; [1980] 3 C.M.L.R. 220. But for the legality of non-discriminatory checks of identity documents, see Case 321/87 *Commission v. Belgium* [1989] E.C.R. 997; [1990] 2 C.M.L.R. 492. Case C–378/97 *Wijsenbeck* [1999] E.C.R. I–6207.

[68] Though the Court's judgment in Case 15/69 *Ugliola* [1969] E.C.R. 363; [1970] C.M.L.R. 194, to the effect that the public policy proviso applies only to the cases mentioned in Art. 39(3) implies that the right to enter a Member State in search of work must be founded upon Art. 39(3) rather than 39(2), see below at p. 415.

[69] See Council Reg. 118/97 amending and updating Reg. No. 1408/71 on the application of social security schemes to employed persons, to self-employed persons and to members of their families moving within the Community *etc.*, [1997] O.J. L28/1 (Part I of Annex A contains a consolidate text of Reg. 1408/71).

Member State seeking employment in another, certainly assumes that he will be admitted for such a purpose.

When the Council was adopting Directive 68/360, it was understood that a worker entering a Member State for employment could stay for three months to find a job and thus qualify for residence, but no specific provision was made.[70] Consistently with this view, Regulation 1408/71 Article 69(1)(c) provides that entitlement to unemployment benefit under that Article should continue for no more than three months.[71] In *Antonissen*[72] the Court considered whether national rules specifying a six-month period in which to find work were compatible with the right to enter and remain in a Member State in order to look for work. The Court held that in the absence of a Community provision prescribing the period during which Community nationals seeking employment in a Member State may stay there, a period of six months did not appear in principle to be insufficient to enable the persons concerned to apprise themselves, in the host Member State, of offers of employment corresponding to their occupational qualifications and to take, where appropriate, the necessary steps in order to be engaged and therefore, did not jeopardise the effectiveness of the principle of free movement. The Court added that if, after the expiry of the six-month period the person concerned provided evidence that he was continuing to seek work and that he had genuine chances of being engaged, he could not be required to leave the territory of the host Member State.

The right of residence

The worker, the worker's spouse, and children under the age of 21 years[73]

In accordance with Article 39(3)(c) (ex 48(3)(c)) E.C.,[74] Directive 68/360 provides that Member States shall grant the right of residence to workers able to produce:

(a) the document with which they entered the Member State's territory,[75] and

(b) a confirmation of engagement from an employer, or a certificate of employment.

In the case of a worker's spouse and children under the age of 21 years, the right of residence is acquired upon production of:

(a) the document with which they entered the territory,

---

[70] H. Ter Heide, 6 C.M.L. Rev. 466, 476.

[71] n.69.

[72] Case C–292/88 *Antonissen* [1991] E.C.R. I–745.

[73] Dir. 68/360, Art. 4(1) and (3)(c), (d). The right of residence of a spouse of a migrant worker is co-extensive with that of the migrant mother, see Case C–356/98 *Kaba* judgment of April 11, 2000, paras. 23–24.

[74] This provision refers to the right "to stay in a Member State for the purpose of employment in accordance with the provisions governing the employment of nationals of that State . . ."

[75] A Member State is required to recognise the right of residence of workers if they are in possession of a valid identity card, even if that card does not allow the holder to leave the territory of the Member State in which it was issued, Case C–376/89 *Panagiotis Giagounidis* [1991] E.C.R. I–1069; [1993] 1 C.M.L.R. 537.

and
(b) a document proving their relationship, issued either by their State of origin, or the State whence they came.

Dependent children over the age of 21 years, and other dependent relatives in the ascending line of the worker and the worker's spouse[76]

In the above-mentioned cases, there is required in addition to the document with which they entered the territory a document testifying to their dependence, issued either by the State of origin or the State whence they came.

Dependent relatives other than children or those in the ascending line, and relatives living under the worker's roof in the country whence they came

According to Article 10(2) of Regulation 1612/68, such members of the family do not have a right of entry, much less of residence, merely on account of their relationship to the worker, and Member States are simply under an obligation to "facilitate" their admission. Does Directive 68/360 indicate however that such members of the family must be accorded a right of residence? Directive 68/360 provides in Article 4(1) that Member States shall grant the right of residence to those persons:

(a) referred to in Article 1 of the Directive;
(b) who are able to produce the documents specified in Article 4(3).

As to (a), Article 1 of the Directive refers to members of the worker's family to whom Regulation 1612/68 is applicable. Article 10(2) of that Regulation, as has been pointed out, indeed makes provision for the relatives in question, albeit to a limited extent. As to (b), Article 4(3)(e), in specifying those documents production of which gives rise to a right of residence, provides in pertinent part: "in the cases referred to in Article 10(1) and (2) of Regulation (EEC) No. 1612/68, a document issued by the competent authority . . . testifying that they are dependent on the worker or that they live under his roof in such country." Just as Article 4 assumes that the members of the family in question may claim a right of residence, so Article 3 suggests that they are entitled to enter a Member State simply on production of a valid identity card or passport, as "persons referred to in Article 1 . . . " There is certainly some textual support for the proposition that such members of the family must indeed be accorded a right of residence.

The contrary, and better, argument, is that Article 4(1) of the Directive, in requiring Member States to grant a right of residence to members of worker's family to whom Regulation 1612/68 is applicable, contemplates that this right of residence will be co-extensive with the right of "installation" granted by Article 10(1) of Regulation 1612/68 to spouse, children under 21 years or over that age and dependent, and dependent relatives in the ascending line, but not to the other relatives in question. A legislative intent to ensure the conformity of the Directive with the Regulation may be discerned in the first recital to the

---

[76] Dir. 68/360, Art. 4(3)(e).

preamble to the former, which states: ". . . whereas, measures should be adopted . . . which conform to the rights and privileges accorded by the said Regulation to nationals of any Member States . . . and to members of their families."

However, it is doubtful whether a restrictive interpretation of Article 10 of Regulation 1612/68 would be consistent in all cases with the requirements of the Treaty itself. It would seem that dependent relatives in an analogous position to those specified in Article 10(1) of the Regulation could, at any rate in certain circumstances, enter and reside as of right, *e.g.* a dependent guardian, or a dependent brother or sister. A blanket refusal to allow residence to such persons would seem to constitute in practice a major obstacle to the free movement of workers. It is difficult to imagine a more potent disincentive to immigration than the inability to provide a home and personal support to a dependent relative for whom one has assumed responsibility, and it would seem to follow that a migrant worker would be entitled to invoke the direct effect of Article 39 E.C. in an appropriate case. This approach finds support in case-law of the Court to the effect that the right of a worker of one Member State to enter and reside in the territory of another, or indeed to return to his or her own Member State accompanied by family members, is derived directly from the Treaty, and that secondary legislation such as Regulation 1612/68 and 68/360 is declaratory rather than constitutive of the rights in question.[77] And if national rules allow such family members who are non-nationals to enter and reside if they can show dependency upon a national of the Member State in question, but exclude such family members where they can demonstrate the same relationship with a non-national migrant worker, the line of reasoning adopted in the *Reed* case would argue in favour of a right of residence.[78]

The residence permit

Article 4 of Directive 68/360 provides that a residence permit shall be issued to the worker and members of his family who are nationals of Member States of the E.C., as proof of the right of residence. This document must include a statement that it has been issued pursuant to Regulation 1612/68 and to the measures taken by the Member States for the implementation of the Directive. The text of the statement is given in the Annex to the Directive. A member of a worker's family who is not a national of a Member State must be issued with a residence document having the same validity as that issued to the worker on whom he or she is dependent.[79]

---

[77] In Case 48/75 *Procureur du Roi v. Royer* [1976] E.C.R. 497; [1976] 2 C.M.L.R. 619, the Court describes Art. 4(1) and (2) of Dir. 68/360 as being "intended to determine the practical details regulating the exercise of rights conferred directly by the treaty", at para. 35; In *R. v. Immigration and Appeal Tribunal and Surinder Surinder Singh, ex p. Secretary of State for the Home Department* [1992] E.C.R. I–4265, a spouse of a migrant worker is held to derive rights from Art. 48 on the return of the migrant to her own Member State, despite the fact that Art. 10 of Reg. 1612/68 only confers a right of installation where a national of one Member State is employed in the territory of another.

[78] See above, p. 388.

[79] Art. 4(4).

The drafting of the provisions of the Directive relating to the issue, validity, expiry and renewal of residence permits is not entirely satisfactory. Whereas Article 4(2) provides that a residence permit is issued as proof of the right of residence, subsequent provisions define the extent of the migrant's rights in terms of the validity of his or her permit. The conceptual confusion led the referring court in *Procureur du Roi v. Royer* to seek a preliminary ruling from the Court of Justice on the question, *inter alia*, whether a worker's right of residence was conferred directly by the Treaty and the terms of Directive 68/360, or was conditional on the issue of a document drawn up by national authorities. The Court held that Article 39 (ex 48) vested rights directly in all persons falling within its ambit. Implementing legislation gave rise to no new rights in favour of persons protected by Community law, but simply determined the scope and detailed rules for the exercise of rights conferred directly by the Treaty. The grant of a permit was to be regarded "not as a measure giving rise to rights but as a measure by a Member State serving to prove the individual position of a national of another Member State with regard to provisions of Community law".[80] It followed that Member States were under a duty to grant the right of residence to any person who was able to prove, by producing the documents specified in Article 4(3) of the Directive, that he or she fell within one of the categories referred to in Article 1.

The Directive provides that completion of the formalities for obtaining a residence permit shall not hinder the immediate commencement of employment under a concluded contract.[81] The residence documents granted to nationals of the Member States must be issued and renewed free of charge or on payment of an amount not exceeding the dues and taxes charged for the issue of identity cards to nationals. The visa which may be demanded of members of a worker's family who are not nationals of a Member State of the E.C. shall be free of charge.[82]

Community law does not prevent a Member State from carrying out checks on compliance with the obligation to produce a residence permit at all times, provided that it imposes the same obligation on its own nationals as regards their identification documents.[83] In the event of failure to comply with that obligation, the national authorities are entitled to impose penalties comparable[84] to those attaching to minor offences committed by their own nationals, such as those laid down in respect of failure to carry an identity card, provided that they do not impose a penalty so disproportionate that it becomes an obstacle to the free movement of workers.[85]

---

[80] Case 48/75 [1976] E.C.R. 497; [1976] 2 C.M.L.R. 619, esp. para. 28. No other permit may be required of worker of the Member States, Case 8/77 *Sagulo* [1977] E.C.R. 1495; [1977] 2 C.M.L.R. 585; Case 157/79 *Pieck* [1980] E.C.R. 2171; [1980] 3 C.M.L.R. 220. See Cases 389–390/87 *Echternach* [1989] E.C.R. 723, at para. 25, "The issue of such a permit does not create the rights guaranteed by Community law, and the loss of a permit cannot affect the exercise of those rights."

[81] Art. 5.

[82] Art. 9.

[83] Case 321/87 *Commission v. Belgium* [1989] E.C.R. 993, para, 12; [1990] 2 C.M.L.R. 492.

[84] This does not mean identical, see Case 8/77 *Sagulo* [1977] E.C.R. 1495; [1977] 2 C.M.L.R. 585, below at p. 398.

[85] Case C–265/88 *Messner* [1989] E.C.R. 4209; [1991] 2 C.M.L.R. 545, para. 14; Case C–24/97 *Commission v. Germany* [1998] E.C.R. I–2133, para. 14. In the latter case the Court stated at para.

Expiry and renewal of the residence permit

Although *Royer* and subsequent case-law[86] makes it clear that a right of residence arises independently of the issue of a residence permit, the Directive defines the substantive rights of migrants in terms of the validity of their permits. The transference of thought is a little confusing, but it is proposed to adopt it for the sake of consistency with the terms of the Directive.

A residence permit, issued when the worker or member of his family satisfies the conditions stated in Article 4 of the Directive, must be valid throughout the territory of the Member States which issued it for a period of at least five years from the date of issue, and be automatically renewable.[87] Although original acquisition of the residence permit requires a certification of employment, it must be noted that a valid residence permit may not be withdrawn from a worker solely on the grounds that he is involuntarily unemployed, this being duly confirmed by the competent unemployment office.[88] It would seem to follow that a worker who is voluntarily unemployed may have his permit withdrawn, *i.e.* lose his right of residence in the territory. This is certainly in accord with the scheme of Article 39 (ex 48) E.C. which guarantees residence for the purpose of seeking or engaging in activities as an employed person. An individual who is voluntarily unemployed can no longer be considered a "worker" within the meaning of Article 39 (ex 48),[89] though it is submitted that the concept of voluntary unemployment should not be interpreted to cover periods between employment with different employers taken by way of a holiday, where the financial arrangements, the activities in question, and the duration of the break from employment have characteristics typical of a holiday, and there is a genuine intention to resume employment afterwards.

If a Member State wishes to terminate a residence permit valid for five years for any other reason apart from voluntary unemployment or prolonged absence, it must have resort to the proviso contained in Article 39(3) (ex 48(3)) E.C., to the effect that the rights defined therein are subject to limitations justified on grounds of public policy, public security or public health.[90]

At the end of a five-year period, a Member State is obliged to renew the document automatically for a further five years. The only exception to this, apart from cases of voluntary unemployment, prolonged absence, or the public policy proviso, is on the occasion of renewal of a residence permit for the first time. In this case, the period of residence may be restricted to a period of not less than 12

---

15 that "it must be held that, by treating nationals of other Member States residing in Germany disproportionately differently, as regards the degree of fault and the scale of fines, from German nationals when they commit a comparable infringement of the obligation to carry a valid identity document, . . ." Germany had breached, *inter alia*, Art. 48 E.C. and Art. 4 of Directive 68/360. The formulation "disproportionately differently" reflects the fact that some differentiation between offences re residence permits by aliens and offences re identity documents by nationals is permissible, see Case 8/77 *Sagulo*, n.84.

[86] Joined Cases 389–390/87 *Echternach* [1989] E.C.R. 723; [1990] 2 C.M.L.R. 305, at para. 25, n.77 above.

[87] Art. 6.

[88] Art. 7(1).

[89] This follows from the reasoning in Case 53/81 *Levin* [1982] E.C.R. 1035; [1982] 2 C.M.L.R. 454.

[90] See below, p. 415.

months, if the worker has been involuntarily unemployed for more than 12 consecutive months.[91] When this second, curtailed period of residence expires, it would seem that the worker has no right to an automatic renewal of his permit, and must acquire his right of residence afresh, by producing the documents referred to in Article 4 of the Directive, *i.e.* an entry document and a declaration of employment.

The validity of a residence permit is stated to be unaffected by either breaks in residence not exceeding six consecutive months, or absence on military service.[92] It would seem to follow that breaks in residence lasting longer than six consecutive months may provide grounds for withdrawal of a residence permit, and loss of the right of residence, pending compliance once again with the provisions of Article 4 of the Directive.

Temporary residence permit

Workers employed for periods exceeding three months but not exceeding a year must be issued with a temporary residence permit, the validity of which may be limited to the expected period of their employment.[93] Such a permit is not stated to be automatically renewable, and on expiry the worker would be obliged to present anew the documents referred to in Article 4 of the Directive. Temporary residence permits are similarly issued to seasonal workers employed for more than three months. The period of employment must be indicated in the certificate of employment required, along with their entry document, for the acquisition of the residence permit.[94]

Recognition of the right of residence without the issue of permits

In three cases the Directive requires Member States to recognise the right of workers to reside in their territory without the issue of residence permits.[95] The first category comprises workers pursuing activities expected to last not more than three months. Presentation of the worker's entry document coupled with a certification from his employer stating the expected duration of his employment is sufficient to cover his stay.

The Directive makes similar provision for frontier workers, *i.e.* workers who, having their residence in one Member State to which they return in principle once a day or at least once a week, work in another Member State.[96] Although such a worker would *prima facie* be entitled to a full residence permit under Article 4 of the Directive (although, of course, he is not really "resident" at all), Article 8(1)(b) relieves the State where he is employed of any duty to provide such a permit, and provides that it may issue such a worker with a special permit valid for five years and automatically renewable.

---

[91] Art. 7(2).
[92] Art. 6(2).
[93] Art. 6(3).
[94] Art. 6(3).
[95] Art. 8.
[96] Dir. 68/360 does not use the term "frontier worker," but see Art. 1(b) of Reg. 1408/71, note 66 above. Does Art. 8(1)(b) intend to confer a right of "residence" in both the state of employment and the state of residence? The final sentence of the provision suggests only the former.

The final category of workers, seasonal workers, has already been considered in the context of workers who must be issued with temporary residence permits. Such workers holding contracts of employment stamped by the competent authority of the Member State in whose territory they have come to work need not be issued with residence permits, where they are employed for less than three months.[97]

In all the three cases referred to above the Member State may require the worker to report his presence in its territory. But anything going beyond having to report one's presence and having the character of an authorisation or a residence permit is not compatible with the Directive.[98]

The three "degrees" of residence

It will be appreciated that various workers falling within Article 4 of the Directive enjoy varying degrees of "security of tenure" in the State of employment.

The first group, those who find a job of an expected duration of more than 12 months, receive a permit entitling them to at least six years' residence in the host State, providing, of course, that they do not become voluntarily unemployed or conduct themselves in such a way as to fall within the scope of the "public policy" proviso of Article 39(3) (ex 48(3)).

The second group of workers comprises those who take up employment for a period of between three and 12 months, and seasonal workers who are employed for more than three months. Here security of residence is restricted by means of a temporary residence permit to the expected duration of the employment in question. Should such a worker become involuntarily unemployed, he would seem to retain his right of residence by virtue of Article 7(1) of the Directive until expiry of the temporary residence permit, providing he retained his status as a worker by seeking further employment.

The final group of workers contemplated by Directive 68/360 have the most precarious right of all —the right to reside in a Member State only for the actual duration of their employment. This group comprises workers who expect to pursue employment for less than three months, seasonal workers employed for less than three months holding stamped employment contracts, and frontier workers. As regards this last category, a "special residence permit" may be issued at the option of the host State. Such a permit must be valid for five years and be renewable automatically. On this occasion the context suggests that the Directive's reference to renewal of the permit is a reference to its formal validity rather than to the rights of its holder.

Rights bestowed directly by the Treaty

The rights of workers may be a little less clear than the text of Directive 68/360 suggests, since their rights stem directly from the Treaty, and it is the function of

---

[97] Art. 6(3), second para., and Art. 8(1)(c).
[98] Case C–344/95 *Commission v. Belgium* [1997] E.C.R. I–1035; [1997] 2 C.M.L.R. 187, at para. 31

secondary legislation merely to define their scope and provide the detailed rules for their employment. For instance, suppose a worker enters a Member State in search of a job. After three months he finds a job of an expected duration of six months. He is issued with a temporary residence permit for that period. After six months permit and employment expire. Is the worker entitled to remain in the Member State concerned for a reasonable time in order to seek further employment? The broad interpretation hitherto given to Article 39 (ex 48) suggest an affirmative answer; the text of the Directive the contrary. Other questions arise: for example, how often is a worker entitled to enter the same Member State in search of employment? The answer to such questions may turn less on the interpretation of the detailed provisions of Community secondary legislation, such as Directive 68/360, than on the general scheme and aim of that legislation, read in light of the Court's view of the ambit of Article 39 (ex 48) itself. It is to be noted that freedom of movement for workers forms one of the foundations of the Community and, consequently, the provisions laying down that freedom must be given a broad interpretation.[99] On the other hand, Article 39 does not preclude a Member State from drawing distinctions between workers on the basis of the length and continuity of their relationship with that State.[1] Thus a worker is entitled to remain in a Member State for a reasonable time seeking employment, but if it becomes apparent that he is unlikely to find a job, he may in effect be required to return to his country of origin, or to the Member State where he was last employed.[2] An extended period of employment in a Member State, however, entitles an unemployed worker to the same opportunities as a member of the indigenous workforce, *i.e.* indefinite equal access to the host State's employment exchanges and unemployment benefits—this is the first "degree" of residence, referred to above. The provisions of secondary legislation such as Directive 68/360 will be applicable to the extent that they regulate the modalities to the exercise of rights enjoyed directly under the Treaty, but ineffective to restrict their scope.

EQUALITY OF TREATMENT

General

Article 39(2) (ex 48(2)) E.C. provides that freedom of movement for workers shall entail the abolition of any discrimination based on nationality between workers of the Member States as regards employment, remuneration and other conditions of work and employment. Although, as we shall see later, this prohibition is not restricted to national measures which directly relate to the employment context, it may be restricted to discrimination which may, at least in principle, impede the free movement of persons. This could explain why Article 39 (ex 48) does not exclude the right of Member States to adopt reasonable

---

[99] Case C–292/89 *R. v. Immigration Appeal Tribunal, ex p. Gustaff Desiderius Antonissen* [1991] E.C.R. I–745; [1991] 2 C.M.L.R. 373, para. 11.
[1] See Case 20/75 *D'Amico v. Landesversicherunganstalt* [1975] E.C.R. 891; [1976] 2 C.M.L.R. 361.
[2] Case C–292/89 *R. v. Immigration Appeal Tribunal, ex p. Gustaff Desiderius Antonissen* [1991] E.C.R. I–745; [1991] 2 C.M.L.R. 373.

measures to keep track of the movement of aliens within their territory.[3] On the other hand, while Member States may impose penalties to compel compliance with the requirements of Community law relating to migrants, such penalties must be comparable to those attaching to the infringement of provisions of equal importance by nationals, and such punishment must be proportionate to the gravity of the offences involved.[4] However, where Community law permits differentiation between migrants and national workers, for instance in allowing Member States to require the possession of residence permits by aliens,[5] Member States may impose more serious penalties for infractions of such requirements than would be imposed in the case of the commission by nationals of comparable offences, for instance the failure to comply with the requirement that nationals possess identity cards.[6] But while such penalties may be more serious, they may not be disproportionately so.[7]

Whereas Directive 68/360 ensures entry and residence for Community workers, the right to equal treatment in respect of job opportunity and conditions of employment is governed by Regulation 1612/68 on freedom of movement for workers within the Community.[8] Part I of the Regulation is divided into three Titles:

— Eligibility for employment;
— Employment and equality of treatment; and
— Workers' families.

It is convenient to adopt the scheme of the Regulation for the purposes of exposition of its terms and discussion of the case-law of the Court.

Eligibility for employment

The Regulation guarantees to workers the right to take up employment in the territory of a Member State with the same priority as the nationals of the State in question.[9] Employees and employers are entitled to exchange their applications for and offers of employment, and to conclude and perform contracts in accordance with "the provisions in force laid down by law, regulation or administrative action, without any discrimination resulting therefrom".[10]

---

[3] Case 118/75 *The State v. Watson and Belmann* [1976] E.C.R. 1185; [1976] 2 C.M.L.R. 552, discussed (1975–76) 1 E.L. Rev. 556. But a requirement that nationals of other Member States make a declaration of residence within three days of arrival is unreasonable and contrary to Community law, Case 265/88 *Messner* [1989] E.C.R. 4209.

[4] Case 118/75 n.98, para. 21.

[5] As to which, see above, p. 392.

[6] Case 8/77 *The State v. Sagulo* [1977] E.C.R. 1495; [1977] 2 C.M.L.R. 585, discussed (1977) 2 E.L. Rev. 445. It may be that Case 118/75 *Watson and Belmann* [1976] E.C.R. 1185; [1976] 2 C.M.L.R. 552, may be explained on the basis that keeping track of aliens constitutes objective differentiation between nationals and non-nationals, but it is indirect rather than direct discrimination on grounds of nationality which is normally capable of objective justification.

[7] Case C–24/97 *Commission v. Germany* [1998] E.C.R. I–2133, n.85 above.

[8] [1968] J.O. L257/2, O.J. Spec.Ed. (II), 475.

[9] Art. 1(2).

[10] Art. 2.

National provisions, whether the result of legal regulation or administrative action, are stated to be inapplicable if they limit explicitly or implicitly the right of workers to take up and pursue employment.[11] An exception is made in the case of linguistic requirements necessitated by the nature of the post to be filled.[12] In the *Groener* case[13] the Court considered the compatibility with Regulation 1612/68 of national rules making appointment to a permanent full-time post as a lecturer in public vocational educational institutions conditional upon proof of an adequate knowledge of the Irish language. Knowledge of the Irish language was not required for the performance of the duties which teaching of the kind at issue specifically entailed. The Court held however that the post justified the requirement of linguistic knowledge, provided that the requirement in question was imposed as part of a policy for the promotion of the national language which was the first official language, and provided that the request was applied in a proportionate and non-disriminatory manner.

Article 3 of the Regulation itemises, as particular instances of the provisions declared inapplicable by the foregoing, those which:

"(a) prescribe a special recruitment procedure for foreign nationals;
(b) limit or restrict the advertising of vacancies in the press or through any other medium or subject it to conditions other than those applicable in respect of employers pursuing their activities in the territory of that Member State;
(c) subject eligibility for employment to conditions of registration with employment offices or impede recruitment of individual workers where persons who do not reside in the territory of that State are concerned."

Article 4 of the Regulation provides that national rules restricting by number or percentage the employment of foreign nationals are to be inapplicable to nationals of the Member States. Alleged infringement of this requirement by the Republic of France gave rise to proceedings before the Court of Justice at the suit of the Commission.[14] Article 3(2) of the Code du Travail Maritime of 1926 provided that such proportion of the crew of a ship as was laid down by order of the Minister for the Merchant Fleet must be French nationals. Ministerial Orders of November 1960 and June 1969 provided that certain employments on board ship were restricted exclusively to French nationals, and an overall ratio was imposed of three French to one non-French. The Commission took the view that such legislation contravened Article 39 (ex 48) E.C. and Article 4 of Regulation 1612/68. The French Government argued that Article 39 (ex 48) E.C. had no application to sea transport, but nevertheless proceeded to lay a draft amendment before the French Parliament. No legislation was in the event forthcoming, and the Commission referred the matter to the Court of Justice under Article 226 (ex 169) E.C., claiming a declaration that the failure of the French Republic to amend Article 3(2) of the Code insofar as it applied to nationals of the Member States amounted to a breach of Community law.

---

[11] Art. 3(1).
[12] Art. 3(1), last sub-para.
[13] Case 379/87 [1989] E.C.R. 3967; [1991] 1 C.M.L.R. 261.
[14] Case 167/73 *Commission v. France* [1974] E.C.R. 359; [1974] 2 C.M.L.R. 216.

In order to appreciate the significance of the Court's ruling, it must be noted that the French Government insisted that no discrimination had in fact taken place, since oral instructions had been given not to apply Article 3(2) of the Code to Community nationals, and that no finding was made on this issue. The Court (holding that Article 39 (ex 48) indeed applies to sea transport) acknowledged that the objective legal situation was clear—namely, that Article 39 (ex 48) E.C. and Regulation 1612/68 were directly applicable in France—yet found that by failing to amend Article 3(2) of the Code du Travail Maritime insofar as it appeared to nationals of the Member States, France was in breach of her legal obligations. In view of the position adopted by the French Government to the effect that the non-discriminatory application of the offending Article was a matter of grace, not of law, she had thereby brought about an ambiguous situation creating uncertainty for those subject to the law. Such an admittedly "secondary" obstacle to equal access to employment was nevertheless caught by the general prohibition of Article 39 (ex 48), and the specific provisions of Article 4 of Regulation 1612/68.

Regulation 1612/68 further provides that the engagement or recruitment of a national of one Member State for a post in another shall not depend on medical, vocational or other criteria which are discriminatory by comparison with those applied in the case of national workers.[15] Nevertheless, when an employer actually offers a job to a national of another Member State he may expressly condition this offer on the candidate undergoing a vocational test.[16]

A worker seeking employment in a Member State other than his own is entitled to receive from its employment services the same assistance as that afforded to national workers.[17]

Equality in the employment context and beyond

Article 39(2) (ex 48) provides for the abolition of discrimination based on nationality in terms and conditions of employment and this prohibition is reiterated and expanded in Article 7(1) of the Regulation, as follows:

"A worker who is a national of a Member State may not, in the territory of another Member State, be treated differently from national workers by reason of his nationality in respect of any conditions of employment and work, in particular as regards remuneration, dismissal, and should he become unemployed, re-instatement or re-employment."

Infringement of the principle of equality will occur where national legislation expressly attaches different terms to the conditions of employment of national workers and workers from other Community countries. In *Marsman v. Rosskamp*,[18] a Dutch national resident in the Netherlands was employed in Gronau, in the Federal Republic of Germany. After becoming incapacitated as a

---

[15] Art. 6(1).
[16] Art. 6(2).
[17] Art. 5.
[18] Case 44/72 [1972] E.C.R. 1243; [1973] C.M.L.R. 501.

result of an accident at work, he was dismissed by his employer. German legislation provided that seriously disabled workers could not be dismissed without the approval of the main public assistance office. While this protection extended to nationals resident outside Germany, it applied only to non-nationals within the jurisdiction. Mr Marsman challenged the legality of his dismissal before a German court, which sought a ruling from the Court of Justice as to whether a Community national in the position of Mr Marsmann was entitled to the same protection against dismissal as that afforded to German nationals. The Court replied in the affirmative, emphasising that the social law of the Community was based on the principle that the laws of every Member State were obliged to grant nationals of the other Member States employed in its territory all the legal advantages that it provided for its own citizens.

A slightly more complex situation arises when legislation conditions certain advantages on criteria which, although theoretically applicable to nationals and non-nationals alike, will in practice be fulfilled only by nationals. The point is illustrated in *Württembergische Milchverwertung-Shdmilch AG v. Ugliola*.[19] The respondent in the main suit was an Italian national employed by the appellant concern in the Federal Republic. He performed his military service in Italy between May 1965 and August 1966, and claimed the right to have this period taken into account in calculating his seniority with his employer. German legislation provided that military service in the German Army was to be taken into account for such purposes, but made no similar provision for services in the forces of other States. The German court seised of the dispute sought a preliminary ruling from the Court of Justice on the question whether Article 7 of Regulation 1612/68 entitled a Community national in the position of Mr Ugliola to have military service in his home country taken into account for the purposes of the German legislation in question. In its observation to the Court, the German Government argued that the Job Protection Law was not discriminatory, since (a) it did not apply to nationals who served in the forces of other States and (b) it did not apply to non-nationals who served in the German army. Advocate General Gand regarded such an argument as tempting, but was not convinced, since performance of military service in the Army of a Member State other than the one whose nationality one possessed was a hypothesis which the German Government agreed was quite theoretical. The Court agreed. The provisions of Community law in question prohibited Member States from "indirectly establishing discrimination"[20] in favour of their own nationals in such a way.[21]

The Court was faced with the problem of allegedly indirect discrimination once more in *Sotgiu v. Deutsche Bundespost*.[22] The plaintiff, an Italian whose family lived in Italy, was employed by the German postal service. He received a separation allowance of 7.50 DM per day, on the same basis as workers of German nationality. In accordance with a Government circular the allowance paid to workers residing within Germany at the time of their recruitment was

---

[19] Case 15/69 [1969] E.C.R. 363; [1970] C.M.L.R. 194.
[20] *ibid.*, para. 6.
[21] But see Case C–315/94 *Peter de Vos v. Stadr Bielefeld* [1996] E.C.R. I–1417.
[22] Case 152/73 [1974] E.C.R. 153.

increased to 10 DM per day, while those workers residing abroad at the time of their recruitment—German and foreign alike—continued to receive the allowance at the old rate. Sotgiu invoked Regulation 1612/68 before a German court, which sought a ruling, *inter alia,* on whether Article 7(1) of the Regulation could be interpreted as prohibiting discrimination on the basis of residence as well as on the basis of nationality. In the course of the arguments before the Court it became apparent that although workers residing within Germany at the time of the recruitment indeed received a larger allowance, it was conditional on their willingness to move to their place of work, and in any event was no longer paid after two years. No such conditions were attached to payment of the allowance to workers residing abroad at the time of the recruitment. The Court affirmed that Article 7 prohibited all covert forms of discrimination which, by the application of criteria other than nationality, nevertheless led to the same result.[23] Such an interpretation was consonant with the fifth recital to the Regulation, which required that equality of treatment for workers to be established in fact as well as in law. Application of criteria such as place of origin or residence, reasoned the Court, could, in appropriate circumstances, have a discriminatory effect in practice that would be prohibited by the Treaty and the Regulation. This would not, however, be the case where the payment of a separation allowance was made on conditions which took account of objective differences in the situation of workers, which differences could involve the place of residence of a worker when recruited. Similarly, the fact that in the case of one group of workers allowances were only temporary while in the case of another they were of unlimited duration, could be a valid reason for differentiating between the amounts paid.

In *Biehl*[24] the Court considered a national rule whereby overpaid tax deducted from salaries and wages was not repayable to taxpayers resident during only part of the year in the relevant Member State. The national tax administration argued that a difference in treatment between two distinct categories of taxpayers did not constitute discrimination if it was objectively justified, and that the rule prevented taxpayers from avoiding the effects of progressive taxation by spreading their tax liability between different States. The Court noted that there was a risk that the criterion of permanent residence in national territory would work in particular against taxpayers who were nationals of other Member States. The Court rejected the justification offered by the national tax authorities since a national rule such as that in issue was liable to infringe the principle of equal treatment in various situations; in particular where no income arose during the year of assessment to the temporarily resident taxpayer in the country which he had left or in which he had taken up residence. In such a situation, the taxpayer

---

[23] The Court has consistently held that Art. 48 of the Treaty (now Art. 39) prohibits not only overt discrimination by reason of nationality, but also all forms of discrimination which, by the application of other distinguishing criteria, lead in fact to the same result, see, *e.g.* Case 111/91 *Commission v. Luxembourg* [1993] E.C.R. I–817, para. 9; Case C–419/92 *Ingetraut Scholz v. Opera Universitaria di Cagliari* [1994] E.C.R. I–505; [1994] 1 C.M.L.R. 873, para. 7; Case 278/94 *Commission v. Belgium* [1996] E.C.R. I–4307, para. 27.

[24] Case C–175/88 *Klaus Biehl v. Administration des contributions du grand-duché de Luxembourg* [1990] E.C.R. I–1779; [1990] 3 C.M.L.R. 143.

would be treated less favourably than a resident taxpayer because he would lose the right to repayment of the over-deduction of tax which a resident taxpayer would always enjoy. It followed in the Court's view that such a measure was contrary to Article 39(2) (ex 48(2)). The *Biehl* case is not entirely satisfactory. Its ruling is based merely on the risk that non-nationals would be treated less favourably than nationals,[25] and the consequence of the ruling seems to be that such a national rule cannot be applied by the national court, even in a case in which the rule would produce neutrality as between residents and non-residents. Nevertheless, the Court has acknowledged that the coherence of the tax system may sometimes justify measures otherwise contrary to Article 39 (ex 48). Thus in *Bachmann*[26] the Court held that while a national rule making pension contributions tax deductible but confining this advantage to contributions made in national territory was in principle contrary to Article 39 (ex 48), it could be justified where the counterpart of making such contributions tax deductible was subjecting the resulting pensions to tax liability.

Unless it is objectively justified and proportionate to its aim, a provision of national law must be rgarded as *indirectly* discriminatory if it is intrinsically liable to affect migrant workers more than national workers and if there is a consequent risk that it will place the former at a particular disadvantage.[27] The Court has indicated that conditions imposed by national law are to be regarded as indirectly discriminatory where, although applicable irrespective of nationality, they affect essentially migrant workers, or the great majority of those affected are migrant workers, where they are indistinctly applicable but can more easily be satisfied by national workers than by migrant workers, or where there is a risk that they may operate to the particular detriment of migrant workers.[28] The Court seems willing to assume, on a common sense basis, that certain distinguishing criteria, such as a period of practical training administered by the authorities of the State in question, will in the vast majority of cases operate to the advantage of nationals rather than non-nationals.[29]

In order to ensure quality for Community workers in the employment context, Regulation 1612/68 provides that they shall have "by virtue of the same right and under the same conditions as national workers . . . access to training in vocational schools and retraining centres."[30] Freedom from discrimination for

---

[25] In Case 33/88 *Allué and Coonan* [1989] E.C.R. 1591; [1991] 1 C.M.L.R. 283, the Court found indirect discrimination where "only" 25% of persons affected were nationals of the host State, see para. 32 of judgment. But a numerical estimate is not a precondition to establishing indirect discrimination, see below.

[26] Case C–204/90 *Hanns-Martin Bachmann v. Belgian State* [1992] E.C.R. I–249; [1993] 1 C.M.L.R. 785.

[27] Case C–237/94 *John O'Flynn v. Adjudication Officer* [1996] E.C.R. I–2617; [1996] 3 C.M.L.R. 103, para. 20; Case 57/96 *H. Meints v. Minister van Landbouw* [1997] E.C.R. I–6689; [1998] 1 C.M.L.R. 1159, para. 45.

[28] Case C–237/94 *John O'Flynn v. Adjudication Officer* [1996] E.C.R. I–2617; [1996] 3 C.M.L.R. 103, para. 18.

[29] Case C–27/91 *Union de Recouvrement des Cotisations de Sécurité Sociale et d'Allocations Familiales de la Savoie (URSSAF) v. Hostellerie Le Manoir SARL* [1991] E.C.R. I–5531, para. 11. As indicated above, n.24, the Court will sometimes be in a position to make an assessment based on an actual numerical estimate of the relative numbers of nationals and non-nationals involved.

[30] Art. 7(3). For education and vocational training, see Chap. 28.

Community workers, although limited explicitly to the employment context in the Treaty, could not be achieved without requiring appropriate adjustments to all fields of national law and practice which might be likely to have an effect on the conditions under which migrants take up and pursue employment. Thus Article 7(2) of the Regulation provides that a national of one Member State employed in another "shall enjoy the same social and tax advantages as national workers". The wording and context of the Article suggest that it might be restricted to social and tax advantages conferred by national law on workers as such, but the Court of Justice has taken a more liberal view, as its judgment in *Fiorini v. SNCF* illustrates. French legislation provided that in families of three or more children under the age of 18 years, the father, mother, and each child under 18 years should receive a personal identity card entitling them to a reduction of between 30 and 75 per cent in the scheduled fare charged by French Railways, the SNCF. A French court sought a preliminary ruling from the Court of Justice on the question whether the reduction card issued by the SNCF to large families constituted for the workers of the Member States a "social advantage" within the meaning of Article 7(2) of the Regulation. The SNCF, in its observations to the Court, argued that Article 7(2) referred exclusively to advantages attaching to the nationals of Member States by virtue of their status as workers, and accordingly had no application to a benefit such as the reduction cared issued by the SNCF. The Court rejected this view, reasoning as follows:

> "Although it is true that certain provisions in this article refer to relationships deriving from the contract of employment, there are others, such as those concerning reinstatement and re-employment should a worker become unemployed, which have nothing to do with such relationships and even imply the termination of a previous employment.
>
> It therefore follows that, in view of the equality of treatment which the provision seeks to achieve, the substantive area of application must be delineated so as to include all social and tax advantages, whether or not attached to the contract of employment, such as reductions in fares for large families."[31]

The Court has subsequently held that Article 7(2) applies to any benefit payable by virtue of an individual's status as a worker, or residence on national territory, where the extension of the benefit to nationals of other Member States seems suitable to facilitate free movement of workers.[32] Applying this test, the Court has excluded from the ambit of Article 7(2) early retirement on full pension for those in receipt of an invalidity pension granted by an Allied Power in respect of war service,[33] and an advantage comprising partial compensation for those national workers called up for the consequences of the obligation to perform military service.[34] The above-mentioned formulation has on the other hand been held to cover seven-year interest-free means-tested loans to families in

---

[31] [1975] E.C.R. 1985 at 1094–1095.
[32] Case 207/78 *Even* [1979] E.C.R. 2019.
[33] *ibid.*
[34] Case C–315/94 *Peter de Vos v. Stadt Bielefeld* [1996] E.C.R. I–1417.

respect of newly-born children, even though the loans were of a discretionary nature.[35] Benefits held to fall within the ambit of the Article include an allowance to handicapped adults covered by Regulation 1408/71 on Social Security;[36] a guaranteed minimum subsistence allowance;[37] the possibility of using one's own language in court proceedings;[38] a special unemployment benefit for young persons falling outside the ambit of Regulation 1408/71;[39] an old age benefit for those lacking entitlement to a pension under the national social security system;[40] a guaranteed minimum income for old persons;[41] and a grant to cover funeral expenses.[42]

Article 8 of the Regulation provides that a worker who is a national of a Member State and who is employed in the territory of another Member State shall enjoy equality of treatment as regards membership of trade unions and the exercise of rights attaching thereto, including the right to vote and to be eligible for the administration and management posts of a trade union. He may however be excluded from taking part in the management of bodies governed by public law and from holding an office governed by public law. In *ASTI v. Chambre des employés privés*,[43] a case concerning "occupational guilds" from which non-nationals were excluded, it was denied that the bodies in question comprised trades unions for the purpose of the above-mentioned provision. The Court held that this Article constitutes a particular expression of the principle of non-discrimination in the specific field of workers' participation in trade union organisation and activities, and could not be limited by reference to the legal form of the body in question. "On the contrary", stated the Court, "the exercise of the trade-union rights referred to in that provision extends beyond the bounds of trade-union organisations in the strict sense and includes, in particular, the participation of workers in bodies which, while not being, in law, trade-union organisations, perform similar functions as regards the defence and representation of workers' interests."[44] Once more we are reminded of the inter-relation between the secondary legislation in this field and the fact that it is designed to facilitate the enjoyment of rights conferred directly by the Treaty, and is to be interpreted accordingly.

The Regulation recognises the importance of freely available housing to the migrant worker when it provides that he shall "enjoy all the rights and benefits accorded to national workers in matters of housing, including ownership of the housing he needs".[45] He may also, "with the same right as nationals, put his name down on the housing lists in the region in which he is employed, where

---

[35] Case 65/81 *Reina* [1982] E.C.R. 33; [1982] 1 C.M.L.R. 744.

[36] Case 63/76 *Inzirillo* [1976] E.C.R. 2057; [1978] 3 C.M.L.R. 596.

[37] Case 249/83 *Hoeckx* [1985] E.C.R. 973; [1987] 3 C.M.L.R. 638; Case 122/84 *Scrivner* [1985] E.C.R. 1027; [1987] 3 C.M.L.R. 638.

[38] Case 137/84 *Mutsch* [1985] E.C.R. 2681; [1986] 1 C.M.L.R. 648.

[39] Case 94/84 *Deak* [1985] E.C.R. 1873.

[40] Case 157/84 *Frascogna* [1985] E.C.R. 1739

[41] Case 261/83 *Castelli* [1984] E.C.R. 3199; [1987] 1 C.M.L.R. 465.

[42] Case C-237/94 *John O'Flynn v. Adjudication Officer* [1996] E.C.R. I-2617; [1996] 3 C.M.L.R. 103.

[43] Case C-213/90 [1991] E.C.R. 3507; [1993] 3 C.M.L.R. 621.

[44] *ibid.*, para. 16.

[45] Art. 9(1).

such lists exist; he shall enjoy the resultant benefits and priorities."[46] If the worker's family have remained in the country whence he came, they must be considered, for the purposes of priority on housing lists, as residing in the area where the worker is employed, where national workers benefit from a similar presumption.[47]

Workers' families

Under Article 10 of Regulation 1612/68, the following members of a worker's family are entitled to install themselves with the worker in the host state:

"(a) his spouse and their descendants who are under the age of 21 years or are dependants[48]'
(b) dependent[49] relatives in the ascending line of the worker and his spouse."

In the case of other members of the family who are dependent on the worker, or who were living under his roof in the country whence he came, Article 10(2) requires merely that Member States shall "facilitate" their admission.

The migrant is obliged to provide housing for his family that is considered normal for national workers in the region where he is employed. This requirement must not, however, give rise to discrimination between national workers and workers from other Member States.[50] Since discrimination must not occur in fact or in law, it is thought that housing must be "considered normal" when it attains a standard equivalent to that actually enjoyed by workers in the region, even though such a standard may not accord with officially recommended levels of occupancy, or even legal requirements. The discriminatory application of national rules in themselves non-discriminatory could clearly amount to a breach of the Treaty. The Court has held that once normal housing has been made available, and the family brought together, the fact that housing ceases to be normal, because, for example, of the birth of a child, cannot justify non-renewal of the residence permit.[51]

Although the Regulation's prohibition of discrimination is in terms limited to workers who are nationals of the Member States, their spouses and children under 21 years or dependent, regardless of nationality, are entitled to take up employment throughout the territory in which the worker is employed.[52] The Court held in the *Gül* case that this right entails the right of such persons to access to employment in the host State under the same conditions as nationals of that State.[53]

---

[46] Art. 9(2).

[47] Art. 9(2), second sub-para.

[48] The status of dependency is a result of a factual situation, namely the provision of support by the worker, without there being any need to determine the reasons for recourse to such support, see Case 316/85 *Lebon* [1987] E.C.R. 2811; [1989] 1 C.M.L.R. 337.

[49] *ibid.*

[50] Art. 10(3).

[51] Case 249/86 *Commission v. Germany* [1989] E.C.R. 1263; [1990] 3 C.M.L.R. 540.

[52] Art. 11.

[53] Case 131/85 *Emir Gül v. Regierungspräsident Düsseldorf* [1986] E.C.R. 1263; [1987] 1 C.M.L.R. 501.

The third recital of the preamble to Regulation 1612/68 describes freedom of movement as a fundamental right of workers and their families, and indeed, genuine equality for the worker could not be achieved if the members of his family could be deprived of social advantages in the host State on account of their nationality. Thus Article 12 provides that the children of a worker residing in the territory of a Member State shall be admitted to that State's general educational, apprenticeship and vocational training courses under the same conditions as nationals of that State. This provision clearly bestows rights directly upon such children, although the second paragraph of Article 12, to the effect that "Member States shall encourage all efforts to enable such children to attend courses under the best possible conditions", is not directly effective, and provides merely an admonition to Member States as to the spirit in which they should apply the first paragraph of that Article, and a guide to courts in its interpretation.

The Court of Justice has had cause to interpret Article 12 on several occasions. In *Michel S. v. Fonds national de reclassement social des handicapés*,[54] the plaintiff in the main suit was the mentally handicapped son of a deceased Italian national who had worked as a wage-earner in Belgium. He was refused benefit from a national fund established to assist persons of Belgian nationality whose chances of employment had been seriously diminished by physical or mental handicap. The Court, having declared that Article 7 of the Regulation protected workers, but not their families, went on to consider Article 12, drawing on the wording of the fifth recital of the preamble as an aid to its interpretation. According to the Court, the "integration" contemplated by the preamble presupposed that the handicapped child of a foreign worker would be entitled to take advantage of benefits provided by the law of the host country for rehabilitation of the handicapped on the same basis as nationals in a similar position. No conclusion to the contrary could be drawn from the failure of the Council explicitly to mention such benefits in the text of the Article; rather, this omission could be explained by the difficulty of including all possible hypotheses.

The Court's liberal approach to the text of Article 12 in *Michel S.* was followed in *Casagrande v. Landeshauptstadt München*,[55] in which the son of a deceased Italian national who had worked as a wage-earner in the Federal Republic was refused, on grounds of nationality, a means-tested educational grant under a Bavarian Statute. A German court sought a ruling from the Court of Justice on the consistency of such discriminatory provisions with Article 12. The Court resorted once again to the fifth recital of the Regulation's preamble. Read with the words of the second paragraph of Article 12, it became apparent that the Article guaranteed not simply access to educational courses, but all benefits intended to facilitate educational attendance. In *Echternach*[56] the Court held that Article 12 of Regulation 1612/68 refers to any form of education, including university courses in economics and advanced vocational studies at a technical

---

[54] Case 76/72 [1973] E.C.R. 457.
[55] Case 9/74 [1974] E.C.R. 773; [1974] 2 C.M.L.R. 423, and see Case 68/74 *Alaimo v. Prefect of the Rhone* [1975] E.C.R. 109; [1975] 1 C.M.L.R. 262.
[56] Case 389/87 [1989] E.C.R. 723; [1990] 2 C.M.L.R. 305.

college. The Court also accepted that a child of a worker of a Member State, which latter has been in employment in another Member State, retains the status of member of a worker's family within the meaning of the Regulation when that child's family returns to the Member State of origin and the child remains in order to continue his studies, which he could not pursue in the Member State of origin. In the *Lubor Gaal* case[57] the Court held that Article 12 also covers financial assistance for those students who are already at an advanced stage in their studies, even if they are already 21 years of age or older and are no longer dependants of their parents.[58]

The Court has retreated from its position in *Michel S.* that Article 7 of the Regulation protects workers but not their families. This will not be the case where the survivors of a worker living in the State where he was last employed claim a social advantage granted to the dependants of survivors of national workers in similar circumstances. In *Fiorini*, it will be recalled that the widow of a deceased Italian national applied for a reduced fare card on French national railways. The Court of Justice held that Article 7(2) must be interpreted as meaning "that the social advantages referred to by that provision include fares reduction cards issued by a national railway authority to large families and that this applies, even if the said advantage is only sought after the worker's death, to the benefit of his family remaining in the same Member State".[59] In *Inzirillo*,[60] the Court, dealing with a reference on the scope of Regulation 1408/71 on social security benefits for migrants, observed that the protection of Article 7(2) of Regulation 1612/68 extended to handicapped, dependent adult children of a worker who have installed themselves with the worker in accordance with Article 10 of Regulation 1612/68. And in *Castelli*,[61] and *Frascogna*,[62] the Court has held that Article 7(2) is intended to protect, as well as workers themselves, their dependent relatives in the ascending line who have installed themselves with the worker. It follows from the above cases that any member of a worker's family who is entitled to, and does, install himself with the worker, is also entitled to equal treatment with nationals of the host State in the grant of all social and tax advantages. The rationale of this proposition would seem to be the deterrent effect upon free movement for workers which would result from the possibility of discriminating against dependent members of his family.[63] In *Bernini*[64] the Court held that study finance granted by a Member State to the children of workers constitutes a social advantage within the meaning of Article 7(2) of Regulation 1612/68, where the worker continues to support the children, but that the child may himself or herself rely on that Article in order to obtain the financing if

---

[57] Case C-7/94 *Landesamt für Ausbildungförderung Nordrhein-Westfalen v. Lubor Gaal* [1995] E.C.R. I-1031.

[58] For education and vocational training, see Chap. 28.

[59] [1975] E.C.R. 1085 at 1095.

[60] Case 63/76 [1976] E.C.R. 2057; [1978] 3 C.M.L.R. 596.

[61] Case 261/83 [1984] E.C.R. 3199; [1987] 1 C.M.L.R. 465.

[62] Case 157/84 [1985] E.C.R. 1739.

[63] Case 63/76 *Inzirillo* [1976] E.C.R. 2057; [1978] 3 C.M.L.R. 596, at para. 17 of judgment. See Case 316/85 *Lebon* [1987] E.C.R. 2811; [1989] 1 C.M.L.R. 337, at para. 11 of judgment.

[64] Case C-3/90 *M.J.E. Bernini v. Minister van Onderwijs en Wetenschcappen* [1992] E.C.R. 1071, paras 25–26.

under national law it is granted directly to the student. A directly effective Treaty basis of this right to equality in the relatives (as opposed to rights vested in the workers) is to be found in Article 12 (ex 6) E.C., which prohibits any discrimination on grounds of nationality within the scope of application of the Treaty. Indeed, the Commission argued as much in *Fiorini*. Support for this view is to be found in the *Forcheri*[65] case, which held that discrimination against a national of one Member State lawfully established in another in the provision of vocational training, infringed the Article which is now Article 12 (ex 6) E.C. The plaintiffs in the national proceedings were a Commission official, and his wife (the latter being the victim of the alleged discrimination). The Court's reasoning appears to be based on Article 12 (ex 6) E.C., the Court being of the opinion that vocational training fell squarely within the "scope of application of the Treaty".

NON-DISCRIMINATORY RESTRICTIONS ON FREEDOM OF MOVEMENT FOR WORKERS

Article 39(1) (ex 48(1)) E.C. states that "freedom of movement shall be secured within the Community" and Article 39(2) E.C. states that such freedom "shall entail the abolition of any discrimination based on nationality" between workers of the Member States. While this formulation makes it clear that freedom of movement *includes* the abolition of discrimination based on nationality it also leaves room for the possibility that non-discriminatory restrictions which prevent freedom of movement being secured are also prohibited by the Treaty. The Community institutions and the Member States seem to have long proceeded on the basis that a worker of any Member State was in principle entitled to leave the territory of any Member State in order to take up activities as an employed person in the territory of another Member State.[66] This right seems to be derived directly from the right to freedom of movement, rather than the right to equality of treatment. Similarly the right of installation of those members of the family specified in Article 10 of Regulation 1612/68 does not appear to be a right which is conditional upon the same rights being enjoyed by nationals of the host State in question; it appears to be based on the proposition that without the right of installation in question workers would be prevented from exercising in practice the right to freedom of movement envisaged by the Treaty. An analysis which is consistent with the text of Article 39, and the terms of the secondary legislation referred to above, is that Article 39 prohibits all obstacles to freedom of movement, whether discriminatory or not, which impede the entry and residence of a migrant worker in a Member State, and the conditions of access to employment in that State, but that national rules which affect the migrant worker in the pursuit and exercise of activities as an employed person, and in the enjoyment of all the social, health, tax, educational and other advantages normally available for residents, are consistent with the latter Article if they do not discriminate either in law or in fact on grounds of nationality. The

---

[65] 152/82 [1983] E.C.R. 2323; [1984] 1 C.M.L.R. 334. See also Case 293/83 *Gravier* [1985] E.C.R. 593; [1985] 3 C.M.L.R. 1.

[66] Dir. 68/360, Arts 1 and 2.

case-law of the Court of Justice is consistent with the above statement of the law, and for a more complete picture of the place of the non-discriminatory restriction to freedom of movement for workers it is appropriate to turn to that case-law.

In *Kraus*[67] the Court of Justice considered a situation in which a German national who had passed the first State examination, went to the United Kingdom, where he took the LLM at Edinburgh University. After returning to Germany, he objected to a German legal requirement that as a precondition to using his Scottish academic title he must obtain authorisation from the competent German authority. The Court noted that a postgraduate academic title was not usually a prerequisite for access to a profession, either as an employee or on or on a self-employed basis, but that the possession of such a title nevertheless constituted, for the person entitled to make use of it, an advantage for the purpose both of gaining entry to such a profession and of prospering in it.[68] The Court held that Article 39 (ex 48) precluded any national measure governing the conditions under which an academic title obtained in another Member State might be used, where that measure, even though it was applicable without discrimination on grounds of nationality, was liable to hamper or to render less attractive the exercise by Community nationals, including those of the Member State which enacted the measure, of fundamental freedoms guaranteed by the Treaty. The situation would be different only if such a measure pursued a legitimate objective compatible with the Treaty and was justified by pressing reasons of public interest.[69] It is to be noted that the Court's recourse to a the very general test of whether a national measure was "liable to hamper or render less attractive" the exercise of free movement was in circumstances in which a national rule in effect governed the conditions of access (as regards the use of the title) of the worker concerned to the labour market of the Member State in question. It did not follow from *Kraus* that thereafter the above formulation would be applicable in all circumstances and that analysis of the question of discrimination would be rendered superfluous.

In *Bosman*[70] the Court considered the consistency with Article 39 (ex 48) E.C. of rules laid down by sporting associations under which a professional footballer who is a national of one Member State may not, on the expiry of his contract with a club, be employed by a club of another Member State unless the latter club has paid to the former a transfer, training or development fee. The Court held that the rules in question, although they did not discriminate on grounds of nationality, constituted an obstacle to freedom of movement for workers. The Court's reasoning was straightforward. It noted that nationals of Member States have in particular the right, which they derived directly from the Treaty, to leave their country of origin to enter the territory of another Member State and reside

---

[67] Case C–19/92 *Dieter Kraus v. Land Baden-Württemberg.* [1993] E.C.R. I–1663.
[68] *ibid.*, para. 18.
[69] *ibid.*, para.32. The Court of Justice in the event held that the national measure in question might be so justified.
[70] Case C–415/93 *Union Royale Belge des Sociététes de Football Association ASBL v. Jean-Marc Bosman* [1995] E.C.R. I–4921; [1996] 1 C.M.L.R. 645. See also Case C–176/96 *Jyri Lehtonen* judgment of April 13, 2000.

there in order to pursue an economic activity.[71] And it added that provisions which preclude or deter a national of a Member State from leaving his country of origin in order to exercise his freedom of movement constitute an obstacle to that freedom even if they apply without regard to the nationality of the workers concerned.[72] This was the effect of the rules in issue in the national proceedings in the cases in point, even if similar rules also governed transfers between clubs within a single Member State. The Court stated:

> "It is sufficient to note that, although the rules in issue in the main proceedings apply also to transfers between clubs belonging to different national associations within the same Member State and are similar to those governing transfers between clubs belonging to the same national association, they still directly affect players' *access to the employment market* in other Member States and are thus capable of impeding freedom of movement for workers (emphasis added)."[73]

The Court concluded that the transfer rules constituted an obstacle to freedom of movement for workers prohibited in principle by Article 48 (now Article 39). It could only be otherwise if the rules pursued a legitimate aim compatible with the Treaty and were justified by pressing reasons of public interest. In order to be so justified they would have to be appropriate to ensure achievement of the aim in question, and not go beyond what was necessary for that purpose.[74]

In *Terhoeve*[75] the Court considered the position of a migrant worker transferring his residence from one Member State to another who in the latter State is subject to a heavier social security burden than would be an employee who in otherwise identical circumstances had continued to reside throughout the whole year in the Member State in question. The Court, taking a very similar approach to that in *Bosman*, held that a national of a Member State could be deterred from leaving the Member State in which he resides in order to pursue an activity as an employed person, in the territory of another Member State if he were required to pay greater social security contributions than if he continued to reside in the same Member State throughout the year, without thereby being entitled to additional social benefits such as to compensate for that increase.[76] It followed, in the view of the Court, that national legislation of the kind in issue in the main proceedings constituted an obstacle to freedom of movement for workers, prohibited in principle by Article 39 (ex 48), and it was therefore unnecessary to consider whether there was indirect discrimination on grounds of nationality, liable to prohibited by the Treaty or by Article 7(2) of Regulation 1612/68.[77]

---

[71] *ibid.*, para. 95.

[72] *ibid.*, para. 96. In Case C–190/98 *Graf* judgment of January 27, 2000, the Court held that provisions could only constitute such an obstacle if they "affect access" of workers to the labour market, para. 23, and referred to events "too uncertain and indirect" to be capable of hindering freedom of movement, para. 25.

[73] *ibid.*, para. 103; the Court thus distinguishes the "selling arrangements" referred to in the context of the free movement of goods in Joined Cases C–267–268/91 *Keck and Mithouard* [1993] E.C.R. I–6097; [1995] 1 C.M.L.R. 101, as to which see above at p. 332.

[74] *ibid.*, para. 104.

[75] Case C–18/95 *F.C. Terhoeve v. Inspecteur van de Belastingdienst Particulieren/Ondermingen Buitenland* [1999] E.C.R. I–345.

[76] *ibid.*, para. 40.

[77] *ibid.*, para. 41.

The above case-law is consistent with the proposition that national measures which apply to the entry and residence of migrants, to their access to the employment market, or apply in any other way specifically to the transfer of the migrant from one Member State to another for the purposes of employment, will be prohibited by Article 39 if they restrict or impede freedom of movement for workers, even if they do not discriminate, directly or indirectly, on grounds of nationality. National measures which discriminate, not on grounds of nationality, but by placing at a disadvantage those who have exercised their right of free movement as compared to those who have not, will also be regarded as impeding the exercise of freedom of movement.[78] But once a migrant worker has secured entry and residence in a Member State, and gained access to the employment market of a Member State, and is pursuing employed activities in that State, it will not be possible to object to national rules concerning, *e.g.* the terms of conditions and employment, or the tax treatment of residents, solely on the ground that they might be described as excessively burdensome to those subject to them. Once integrated into the economic and social life of the host State, the migrant worker's fundamental right derived from Article 39 is the right to equality of treatment, in law and in fact.[79]

RESIDENCE AFTER RETIREMENT OR INCAPACITY

The preamble to Regulation 1251/70[80] describes the right of workers to remain in the territory of a Member State after having been employed there as a corollary to the freedom of movement secured by Regulation 1612/68 and Directive 68/360. The Regulation applies to nationals of one Member State who have worked in the territory of another, and to the members of their family referred to in Article 10 of Regulation 1612/68.

The right of workers to remain in a Member State after having been employed there

The Regulation grants a right of residence after termination of employment to two classes of workers—the retired and the incapacitated. A worker acquires a

---

[78] The Court has held that the provisions of the Treaty relating to the free movement of persons are thus intended to facilitate the pursuit by Community citizens of occupational activities of all kinds throughout the Community, and preclude national legislation which might place Community citizens at a disadvantage when they wish to extend their activities beyond the territory of a single Member State, see Case 143/87 *Christopher Stanton and SA belge d'assurances "L'Étoile 1905" v. Inasti (Institut national d'assurances sociales pour travailleurs indépendants)* [1988] E.C.R. 3877; [1989] 3 C.M.L.R. 761, para. 13

[79] If a restriction on access to the market is imposed on a migrant after his or her integration into the economic and social life of the host State, this does not of course preclude it being regarded as a restriction on access to the market, and it will required to be justified even if non-discriminatory. Thus if a restriction such as that in issue in Case C–19/92 *Dieter Kraus v. Land Baden-Württemberg.* [1993] E.C.R. I–1663 of its nature affects on access to the market, it is immaterial whether it is invoked against a new market entrant, or against a person already pursuing the relevant economic activity.

[80] [1970] J.O. L142/24. And see Dir. 90/365, [1990] O.J. L180/28, on the right of residence for employees and self-employed persons who have ceased their occupational activity, below, Chap. 16 (the Directive covers those who have not exercised the right of free movement).

right of residence on retirement provided: (i) that he has reached the age laid down by the law of the host State for entitlement an old age pension; (ii) that he has been employed in the host State for at least 12 months; and (iii) that he has resided continuously in the host State for more than three years.[81]

A worker who ceases employment as a result of permanent incapacity acquires a right to remain if he has resided in the host State for at least two years. If the permanent incapacity is the result of an accident at work, or an occupational disease entitling him to a pension for which an institution of the host State is entirely or partially responsible, he is entitled to remain regardless of the length of his previous residence.[82]

The above rules assume that a worker is employed and resident in the same Member State, but Regulation 1251/70 also makes limited provision for workers who live in one State while working in another. In the case of a worker who has completed three years' continuous employment and residence in the territory of one Member State, and then takes up employment in the territory of another, periods of employment completed in the latter are taken into account for the purposes of establishing a right to remain in the former State on retirement or in the event of incapacity, providing that the worker retains his residence in the former State, to which he returns, as a rule, each day, or at least once a week.[83] The preamble to the Regulation, after rehearsing the importance of guaranteeing to workers who have been resident and employed in a Member State the right to remain after ceasing work through retirement or incapacity, continues: "it is equally important to ensure that right for a worker who, after a period of employment or residence in the territory of a Member State, while still retaining his residence in the territory of the first State." It is difficult to see why this general consideration should be limited in its application to "frontier workers." Suppose a national of Member State X works and resides in Member State Y, and then takes up a job in Member State Z, returning to his home and family in Member State Y every two weeks. On retirement, Regulation 1251/70 apparently gives him no right of residence in Member State Y, where his home and family are located. Such differentiation between workers residing in a State other than that of employment would seem to be arbitrary, and unjustified by the object and purpose of Article 39 (ex 48) E.C.

In order to establish the requisite periods of residence, retiring or incapacitated workers are entitled to adduce any evidence normally accepted in the country of residence. Continuity is not affected by temporary absences totalling up to three months per year, nor by longer absences due to military service.[84] Periods of involuntary unemployment, duly recorded by the competent employment office, and absences due to illness or accident, are treated as equivalent to periods of employment.[85]

---

[81] Art. 2(1)(a).
[82] Art. 2(1)(b).
[83] Art. 2(1)(c). Workers who return daily or once a week are sometimes described as "frontier workers".
[84] Art. 4(1).
[85] Art. 4(2).

A retiring or incapacitated worker is not bound to fulfil the requisite periods of employment or residence if his spouse is a national of the Member State in question, or lost that nationality as a result of marriage to the worker.[86]

Once a worker has acquired a right to remain in a Member State under the terms of Regulation 1251/70, he has two years in which to decide whether or not to exercise it. During this period he is free to leave the territory of the State in question without prejudice to his right of permanent residence, which may be exercised without formality.[87]

Rights of workers' families

If a retiring or incapacitated worker has acquired a right of residence in a Member State, the members of his family to whom the Regulation applies are entitled to remain in the host State after his death.[88]

If however, a worker dies during his working life and before having acquired a right of residence, members of his family are nevertheless entitled to remain, provided that: (a) the worker, at the date of his death, has resided continuously in the territory of that Member State for at least two years; or (b) his death resulted from an accident at work or an occupational disease; or (c) the surviving spouse is a national of the State of residence or lost the nationality of that State by marriage to the worker.[89]

Equality of treatment

The right to equality of treatment provided by Regulation 1612/68 is also enjoyed by the beneficiaries of Regulation 1251/70.[90] Discrimination on grounds of nationality as regards registration by vessel owners of pleasure craft has been held to infringe this provision.[91]

Residence permits

Persons who have acquired a right to remain in the territory of a Member State are entitled to receive a residence permit which must be valid throughout the territory of the issuing State for a period of at least five years, and be automatically renewable. Any charge made must not exceed the amount charged to nationals for the issue or renewal of identity documents.[92]

Periods of non-residence not exceeding six consecutive months may not affect the validity of a residence permit, but it would seem to follow that periods exceeding six months may affect such validity.[93] Whether absence exceeding six

---

[86] Art. 2(2).
[87] Art. 5.
[88] Art. 3(1).
[89] Art. 3(2).
[90] Art. 7. For the application of Reg. 1612/68 to members of workers's families, see above at page 406.
[91] Case C–151/96 *Commission v. Ireland* [1997] E.C.R. I–3327; [1997] 3 C.M.L.R. 806, para. 15.
[92] Art. 6(1).
[93] Art. 6(2).

months is capable of prejudicing a person's substantive right to remain is unclear, since the function of the permit is not made explicit. It will be recalled that Article 4(2) of Directive 68/360 provides that the residence permit therein described be issued as proof of the right of residence,[94] but subsequent provisions, in particular Article 7, suggest that withdrawal of the residence permit has substantive implications. The better view would seem to be that Article 6 of Regulation 1251/70 provides for the possible forfeiture of the right to remain in a Member State in the event of non-residence exceeding six months. It is difficult to see any other purpose in the provision.

Derogation from national rules

The provisions of the Regulation in no way derogate from national rules more favourable to Community workers.[95] An express provision to this effect is probably unnecessary, since the Court has often expressed the view that the free movement provisions of the Treaty authorise legislative action only to improve the legal situation in which the worker would have found himself but for the Community rules.[96]

Admittance of workers without a strict right to residence

The Regulation places a duty on Member States to "facilitate readmission" to their territories of workers who have left after a long period of residence and employment and wish to return when they have reached retirement, or become incapacitated.[97] The legal effect of such a generalised provision is unclear. It can hardly be said to provide a right of re-entry; its terms are far too vague for that, nor can it be said to provide a principle in light of which related provisions must be interpreted.[98] At best it would seem to provide a principle account of which must be taken by national authorities when considering whether or not a person falling within the relevant category ought to be re-admitted to national territory.

LIMITATIONS JUSTIFIED ON GROUNDS OF PUBLIC POLICY, PUBLIC SECURITY OR PUBLIC HEALTH

General

Article 39(3) (ex 48(3)) E.C. rejects the free movement of workers to limitations justified on grounds of public policy, public security or public health. The text makes it clear that the exception limits the rights itemised in the third paragraph of the Article, but not the right to equality in terms and conditions of employment guaranteed in Article 39(2). As Advocate General Gand explained

---

[94] Above at p. 393.
[95] Art. 8(1).
[96] See, *e.g.* Case 191/73 *Niemann v. Bundesversicherungsanstalt für Angestellte* [1974] E.C.R. 571, Case 27/75 *Bonaffini v. INPS* [1975] E.C.R. 971.
[97] Art. 8(2).
[98] *cf. Casagrande,* in which the second para. of Art. 12 of Reg. 1612/68 was resorted to as an aid to interpretation of the first, *supra*, p. 407.

in *Ugliola*, "on grounds of public policy or public security a foreigner may not be permitted to enter a country and take up employment there, but those considerations have no bearing on conditions of work once employment has been taken up in an authorised manner."[99] The Court agreed; the proviso applied only to "the cases expressly referred to in paragraph 3".[1]

Since Article 39(3) (ex 48(3)) can be invoked to exclude a worker from the territory of a Member State, it would seem to follow that the exception could justify a partial restriction on residence, but this is not the case. In *Rutili v. French Minister of the Interior*,[2] an Italian national resident in France was issued with a residence permit subject to a prohibition on residence in certain French departments. The Court of Justice held that the reservation contained in Article 39(3) (ex 48(3)) had the same scope as the right subject to limitation. It followed that any prohibition on residence could be imposed only in respect of the whole of the national territory. In the case of partial prohibitions on residence. Article 12 (ex 6, formerly 7)) E.C. required that persons covered by Community law must be treated on a footing of equality with nationals of the host State.

The Court held in the *Pieck* case[3] that the public policy proviso in Article 39(3) (ex 48(3)) did not amount to a condition precedent to the acquisition of a right of entry and residence, but provided a possibility, in individual cases where there was sufficient justification, of imposing restrictions on the exercise of a right derived directly from the Treaty. It did not therefore justify general formalities at the frontier other than the simple production of a valid identity card or passport.

There is nothing to preclude individuals from relying on justifications on grounds of public policy, public security or public health. Neither the scope nor the content of those grounds of justification is in any way affected by the public or private nature of the rules in question.[4]

Directive 64/221

The scope of Article 39(3) may be clarified by reference to Directive 64/221 on the co-ordination of special measures concerning the movement and residence of foreign nationals which are justified on grounds of public policy, public security or public health.[5] The Directive *in toto* gives rise to rights in individuals which national courts are bound to safeguard.[6]

The Directive applies to workers of one Member State travelling to or residing in another for the purpose of employment, and to members of their families.[7] It declares that the proviso may not be invoked to serve economic ends.[8] All

---

[99] Case 15/69 [1969] E.C.R. 363; [1970] C.M.L.R. 194, at 365.

[1] [1969] E.C.R. 363 at 369. This suggests that the right to enter a Member State in search of work must be founded on Art. 48(3), rather than upon 48(2); see Case C–292/89 *Antonissen* [1991] E.C.R. I–745; [1991] 2 C.M.L.R. 373, at para. 13 of judgment.

[2] Case 36/75 [1975] E.C.R. 1219; [1976] 1 C.M.L.R. 140.

[3] Case 157/79 [1980] E.C.R. 2171; [1980] 3 C.M.L.R. 220.

[4] Case C–415/93 *Union Royale Belge des Sociététes de Football Association ASBL v. Jean-Marc Bosman* [1995] E.C.R. I–4921; [1996] 1 C.M.L.R. 645, para. 86.

[5] [1964] J.O. 859, [1963–1964] O.J. Spec.Ed. 117.

[6] Case 36/75 *Rutili* [1975] E.C.R. 1219; [1976] 1 C.M.L.R. 140.

[7] Art. 1.

[8] Art. 2(2).

measures relating to entry, the issue and renewal of residence permits, and expulsion, which are taken by Member States on grounds of public policy, public security or public health, are subject to its terms,[9] and must be based on the personal conduct of the individual concerned.[10] Previous criminal convictions, while no doubt relevant to the assessment of an individual's conduct, do not in themselves constitute grounds for applying the proviso.[11] These requirements are central to the protection afforded to individuals by Article 39(3) and Directive 64/221, as *Bonsignore v. Oberstadt-direktor Cologne*[12] illustrates. Carmelo Bonsignore, an Italian worker resident in the Federal Republic, unlawfully acquired a Beretta pistol, with which he accidentally shot his younger brother Angelo. He was fined for unlawful possession of a firearm, and deportation was ordered by the Chief Administrative Office of the City of Cologne. A reference to the Court of Justice sought a ruling on the question whether Article 3(1) and (2) of the Directive were to be interpreted as excluding deportation of a national of a Member State for the purpose of deterring other foreign nationals for such offences, or whether expulsion was only permissible when there were clear indications that an EEC national, who had been convicted of an offence, would himself commit further offences or in some other way disregard public security or public policy. "As departures from the rules concerning the free movement of persons constitute exceptions which must be strictly construed", declared the Court, "the concept of 'personal conduct' expresses the requirement that a deportation order may only be made for breaches of the peace and public security which might be committed by the individual affected."[13] In *R. v. Bouchereau*,[14] however, Advocate General Warner expressed agreement with the Government of the United Kingdom that "cases do arise, exceptionally, where the present conduct of an alien has been such that, whilst not necessarily evincing any clear propensity on his part [to indulge in future misbehaviour], it has caused such deep public revulsion that public policy requires his departure."[15] The Court apparently took a similar view. While emphasising that "The existence of a previous criminal conviction can therefore only be taken into account in so far as the circumstances which gave rise to that conviction are evidence of personal conduct constituting a present threat to the requirements of public policy", and admitting that, "in general, a finding that such a threat exists implies the existence in the individual concerned of a propensity to act in the same way in the future", the Court added that "it is possible that past conduct alone may constitute such a threat to the requirements of public policy."[16] It was for the national authorities, and, where appropriate, national courts, to consider each individual case in the light of the

---

[9] Art. 2(1).

[10] Art. 3(1). The proviso can only be applied to refuse access to individuals, not to exclude economic sectors, see Case C–355/98 *Commission v. Belgium* judgment March 9, 2000, para. 29.

[11] Art. 3(2). The word "measure" in Art. 3(1) and 3(2) includes a recommendation for deportation under the Immigration Act 1971; Case 30/77 *R. v. Bouchereau* [1977] E.C.R. 1999; [1977] 2 C.M.L.R. 800.

[12] Case 67/74 [1975] E.C.R. 297; [1975] 1 C.M.L.R. 472.

[13] [1975] E.C.R. 297 at 307.

[14] Case 30/77 [1977] E.C.R. 1999; [1977] 2 C.M.L.R. 800.

[15] [1977] E.C.R. 1999 at 2022.

[16] [1977] E.C.R. 1999 at 2012. For possible circumstances when past conduct may justify deportation, see Wyatt (1978) 15 C.M.L. Rev. 221 at pp. 224–225

legal position of persons subject to Community law and the fundamental nature of the principle of the free movement of persons. It seems clear, as Advocate General Warner notes, that it will only be in the most exceptional cases that past conduct will of itself be capable of justifying deportation.

The Directive provides that expiry of an identity card or passport used to enter the host country and obtain a residence permit shall not justify expulsion, and furthermore, that the State which issued such travel documents should allow the holder to re-enter its territory without formality even if the document is no longer valid, or the nationality of the holder is in dispute.[17]

Grounds of "public health" as well as "public policy" and "public security," justify recourse to the proviso. The fourth recital to the preamble of the Directive declares that it would be of little practical use to compile a list of diseases and disabilities which might endanger public health, public policy or public security, and that it is sufficient to classify such diseases and disabilities in groups. The result is an Annex to the Directive, comprising a Group A—diseases and disabilities which might threaten public health (infectious diseases), and a Group B—diseases and disabilities which might threaten public policy or public security (such as drug addiction or mental illness). Article 4 of the Directive provides that the only diseases or disabilities justifying refusal of entry into a territory or refusal to issue a first residence permit are those listed in the Annex. Diseases or disabilities occurring after a first residence permit has been issued do not justify refusal to renew the residence permit or expulsion from the territory.[18]

In addition to the substantive safeguards referred to above, the Directive also provides a number of procedural safeguards.

Decisions to grant or refuse a first residence permit must be taken as soon as possible and in any event not less than six months after the date of application for the permit, and the worker is entitled to remain in the territory of the host State pending a decision in his particular case.[19] Although a Member State may, if it thinks essential, request the Member State of origin of the applicant for details of any criminal record, and the latter State is obliged to respond within two months, such enquiries must not be made as a matter of routine.

The individual concerned must always be officially notified of any decision to refuse the issue of renewal of a residence permit, or to expel him from the territory, and of the time allowed him to leave.[20] Save in cases of urgency, this period must not be less than 15 days where the person has not yet been granted a residence permit, and not less than a month in all other cases.[21]

In order to allow workers an opportunity to safeguard their rights, Article 6 of the Directive provides that in all cases the individual concerned is entitled to be informed of the grounds of public policy, public security or public health upon which the decision taken in his case was based, unless to do so would be contrary to the interests of the security of the State involved.

---

[17] Art. 3(3), (4).
[18] Art. 4(2).
[19] Art. 5.
[20] Art. 7.
[21] *ibid.*

With respect to decisions relating to entry, the refusal to issue or renew a residence permit, or expulsion, the person concerned is entitled under Article 8 of the Directive to the same legal remedies as are available to nationals of the State concerned in respect of acts of the Administration.[22]

Under Article 9 of the Directive, there are three types of case in which a decision refusing renewal of a residence permit or ordering the expulsion of the holder of a residence permit must not be taken—save in cases or urgency—until an opinion has been obtained from a competent authority of the host country before which the person concerned enjoys such rights of defence and representation as are provided by domestic law.[23] These three types of case are: (i) where there is no right of appeal to a court of law; (ii) where such an appeal lies only in respect of the legal validity of the decision; (iii) where the appeal cannot have suspensory effect. The purpose of recourse to the "competent authority"[24] is, in the first case, to compensate for the absence of a right of appeal to the courts; in the second case to enable a detailed examination to be made of the situation of the person concerned, including the appropriateness of the measure contemplated, before the decision is finally taken; and in the third case to permit the person concerned to request and to obtain, if appropriate, a stay of the execution of the measure envisaged in such a way as to compensate for the absence of a right to obtain a stay of execution from the courts.

The "competent authority" referred to in Article 9 of Directive 64/221 must not be the same as that empowered to take the decision refusing renewal of the residence permit or ordering expulsion.[25] It must be independent of the administration, but Member States are given a margin of discretion as to the nature of the authority.[26] Thus it has been held that a recommendation for deportation made by a criminal court at the time of conviction may constitute an opinion of competent authority within the meaning of Article 9 of the Directive.[27] However, such an opinion must be sufficiently proximate in time to the decision ordering expulsion to ensure that there are no new factors to be taken into account occurring between the opinion and the decision, liable to deprive the opinion of its useful effect.[28]

Where a decision is taken refusing the issue of a first residence permit, or ordering expulsion of the person concerned before the issue of the permit, the worker must be entitled to refer the decision for reconsideration by the competent authority referred to above, where he can submit his defence in person.[29]

The Court of Justice considered Articles 6, 8 and 9 of the Directive in *Rutili v. French Minister of the Interior*,[30] and concluded that any person enjoying the protection of these provisions was entitled to a double safeguard comprising

---

[22] The Art. is directly effective: Case 131/79 *Santillo* [1980] E.C.R. 1585; [1980] 2 C.M.L.R. 308.

[23] Art. 9 is directly effective: Case 131/79 *Santillo* [1980] E.C.R. 1585; [1980] 2 C.M.L.R. 308.

[24] Case 98/79 *Pecastaing* [1980] E.C.R. 691; [1980] 3 C.M.L.R. 685.

[25] Art. 9(1).

[26] Case 131/79 *Santillo* [1980] E.C.R. 1585; [1980] 2 C.M.L.R. 308, para. 15 of judgment. Joined Cases 115–116/81 *Adoui* [1982] E.C.R. 1665; [1982] 3 C.M.L.R. 631; Case 175/94 *R. v. Secretary of State for the Home Department, ex p. John Gallagher* [1995] E.C.R. I–4523; [1996] 1 C.M.L.R. 543.

[27] *Santillo*, [1980] 2 C.M.L.R. 308, para. 17 of judgment

[28] *Santillo*, but see [1981] 2 All E.R. 897, C.A

[29] Art. 9(2).

[30] Case 36/75 [1975] E.C.R. 1219; [1976] 1 C.M.L.R. 140.

notification to him of the grounds on which any restrictive measure had been adopted and the availability of a right of appeal. The Court added that all steps should be taken by Member States to ensure that the double safeguard was in fact available to anyone against whom a restrictive measure had been adopted. "In particular," declared the Court, "this requirement means that the State concerned must, when notifying an individual of a restrictive measure adopted in his case, give him a precise and comprehensive statement of the grounds for the decision to enable him to take effective steps to prepare his defence."[31]

The question of the relationship between Articles 8 and 9 of the Directive arose in *Procureur du Roi v. Royer*,[32] in which the referring court sought a ruling from the Court of Justice on the question, *inter alia*, whether a decision ordering expulsion or a refusal to issue a residence permit could give rise to immediate measures of execution or whether such a decision could only take effect after the exhaustion of national remedies. The Court held that in the case of the remedies referred to in Article 8 of Directive 64/221, the person concerned must at least have the opportunity of lodging an appeal and thus obtaining a stay of execution before the expulsion order was carried out. If no remedy was available, or if it was available, but did not have suspensive effect, the decision could not be taken—save in cases of urgency which had been properly justified—until the party concerned had had the opportunity of appealing to the competent authority referred to in Article 9 of the Directive, and until this authority had reached a decision. Referring to the right of appeal provided for in Articles 8 and 9 of the Directive, the Court declared that "this guarantee would become illusory if the Member State could, by the immediate execution of a decision ordering expulsion, deprive the person concerned of the opportunity of effectively making use of the remedies which he is guaranteed by Directive No. 64/221."[33]

The Court returned to the relationship between Articles 8 and 9 in *Pecastaing*.[34] In its view Article 9 would be rendered nugatory unless expulsion were suspended pending the giving of the opinion of the competent authority (save that is, in cases of urgency). But there was no analogous requirement in the case of Article 8. While a decision ordering expulsion could not be executed (save in cases of urgency) before the party concerned was able to complete the formalities necessary to avail himself of the national remedy contemplated by Article 8, it could not be inferred from that provision that the person concerned was entitled to remain on the territory of the state concerned throughout the proceedings initiated by him.

In the case of decisions concerning entry, it will be noted that Article 8 is applicable, but that Article 9 is not, since the latter provision conspicuously omits such decisions. Article 8, it will be recalled, provides that the person concerned shall have the same legal remedies in respect of any decision concerning entry, or refusing the issue or renewal of a residence permit, or ordering expulsion from

---

[31] [1975] E.C.R. 1219 at 1233.
[32] Case 48/75 [1976] E.C.R. 497; [1976] 2 C.M.L.R. 619.
[33] [1976] E.C.R. 497 at 516. See also Case 175/94 *R. v. Secretary of State for the Home Department, ex p. John Gallagher* [1995] E.C.R. I–4523; [1996] 1 C.M.L.R. 543.
[34] Case 98/79 [1980] E.C.R. 691; [1980] 3 C.M.L.R. 685; See also Case 175/94 *R. v. Secretary of State for the Home Department, ex p. John Gallagher* [1995] E.C.R. I–4523; [1996] 1 C.M.L.R. 543.

the territory, as are available to nationals of the State concerned in respect of acts of the administration. In *Shingara*[35] the Court rejected the argument that Article 8 of the Directive requires the authorities in the Member States to accord Community nationals the same remedies as those available to nationals of the Member State concerned as regards the right of entry of such nationals. The Court noted that it had previously been held[36] that the reservations in Article 39(3) (ex 48(3)) permitted Member States to adopt, with respect to nationals of other Member States, measures which they could not apply to their own nationals, inasmuch as they had no authority to expel the latter from national territory or to deny them access thereto.[37] It followed that the remedies available to nationals of other Member States in the circumstances defined by the Directive—entry, expulsion, etc.,—could not be assessed by reference to the remedies available to nationals concerning the right of entry, and that on a proper construction of Article 8 of the Directive, where under the national legislation of a Member State remedies were available in respect of acts of the administration generally and different remedies were available in respect of decisions concerning entry by nationals into that Member State, the obligation imposed on the Member State by Article 8 of the Directive was satisfied if nationals of other Member States enjoyed the same remedies as those available against acts of the administration generally in that Member State.[38]

The area of discretion left to authorities under Article 39(3) (ex 48(3)) E.C.

The area of discretion left to national authorities in the application of Article 39(3) (ex 48(3)) has been clarified in a number of decisions of the court of Justice, in particular *Van Duyn*,[39] *Rutili*,[40] *Bouchereau*,[41] *Adoui and Cornuaille*,[42] and *Donatella Calfa*.[43]

Miss Yvonne van Duyn was a Dutch national who had been offered employment as a secretary with the Church of Scientology at its College at East Grinstead. Since the United Kingdom Government regarded Scientology as objectionable, socially harmful, and damaging to the health of its practitioners, it had announced its intention in 1968 of taking all steps within its power—short of legal prohibition—to curb its growth. Accordingly, Miss van Duyn was refused leave to enter the United Kingdom. Alleging violation of her rights as a

---

[35] Joined Cases C–65 and 111/95 *R. v. Secretary of State for the Home Department, ex p. Mann singh Shingara* [1997] E.C.R. I–3343; [1997] 3 C.M.L.R. 703.
[36] Joined Cases 115–116/81 *Adoui and Cornuaille v. Belgian State* [1982] E.C.R. 1665; [1982] 3 C.M.L.R. 631, para. 7.
[37] *Shingara*, n.32, para. 28.
[38] *ibid.*, paras 29 and 31.
[39] Case 41/74 *Van Duyn v. Home Office* [1974] E.C.R. 1337; [1975] 1 C.M.L.R. 1.
[40] Case 35/75 [1975] E.C.R. 1219.
[41] Case 30/77 [1977] E.C.R. 1999; [1977] 2 C.M.L.R. 800.
[42] Joined Cases 115–116/81 *Adoui and Cornuaille v. Belgian State* [1982] E.C.R. 1665; [1982] 3 C.M.L.R. 631.
[43] Case C–348/96 *Criminal Proceedings against Donatella Calfa* [1999] E.C.R. I–11; [1999] 2 C.M.L.R. 1138.

Community national under Article 4 of the Treaty, and Article 3 of Directive 64/221, she sought a declaration in the High Court to the effect that she was entitled to enter the United Kingdom to take up her employment at East Grinstead. The High Court posed the question, *inter alia*, whether

"a Member State, in the performance of its duty to base a measure taken on grounds of public policy exclusively on the personal conduct of the individual concerned is entitled to take into account as a matter of personal conduct:

(a) the fact that the individual is or has been associated with some body or organisation whose activities the Member State considers contrary to the public good but which are not lawful in that State;

(b) the fact that the individual intends to take employment in the Member State with such body or organisation, it being the case that no restrictions are placed upon nationals of the Member State who wish to take similar employment with such body or organisation."

On the first point the Court, acknowledging that a person's past association could not, in general, justify refusal of entry, declared that nevertheless present association, reflecting participation in the activities of the organisation as well as identification with its aims or designs, could be considered as a voluntary act of the person concerned and, consequently, as part of his personal conduct within the meaning of the Article cited. As to the fact that the United Kingdom authorities had not prohibited the practice of Scientology, the Court took the view that although Article 39(3) (ex 48(3)), as an exception to a fundamental freedom under the Treaty, must be interpreted strictly, nevertheless the Member States were allowed a margin of discretion, inasmuch as the particular circumstances justifying recourse to the concept of public policy might vary from one country to another and from one period to another. "It follows," the Court said, ". . . that where the competent authorities of a Member State have clearly defined their standpoint as regards the activities of a particular organisation and where, considering it to be socially harmful, they have taken administrative measures to counteract these activities, the Member State cannot be required, before it can rely on the concept of public policy, to make such activities unlawful, if recourse to such a measure is not thought appropriate in the circumstances."[44] The fact that the result of the policy of the United Kingdom authorities was to bar employment to non-national Community workers while allowing similar employment to United Kingdom nationals seemed to raise no further issue of principle for the Court. The very essence of the exception was that it enabled national authorities to treaty non-nationals in a discriminatory fashion. "It follows," declared the Court, "that a Member State . . . can, where it *deems necessary* [emphasis added], refuse a national of another Member State the benefit of the principle of freedom of movement for workers . . . where such a national proposes to take up a particular offer of employment even though the Member State does not place a similar restriction upon its own nationals."[45]

---

[44] [1974] E.C.R. 1337 at 1350.
[45] [1974] E.C.R. 1337 at 1351.

The Court's judgment in *van Duyn* introduces a subjective element into the application of Article 39(3) (ex 48(3)) that is apparently at odds with its statement that "its scope cannot be determined unilaterally by each Member State without being subject to control by the institutions of the Community".[46] But it must be remembered that the Court was faced with a very limited question—whether or not, in principle, a State was entitled to take into account the factors indicated. This question is answered in the affirmative. It did not have to examine the circumstances in which such factors could justify an exclusion in a particular case. Such a question was posed to the Court in *Rutili v. French Minister of the Interior.*

The plaintiff in the main suit was an Italian resident in France, who had incurred the displeasure of the French authorities as a result of political, and allegedly subversive activities. He was issued with a residence permit subject to a prohibition on residence in certain departments. Mr. Rutili brought proceedings before a French court for the annulment of the decision limiting the territorial validity of his residence permit. During the proceedings before that Court, the argument was advanced that Mr. Rutili's presence in the departments prohibited to him was "likely to disturb public policy." Two questions were referred to the Court for a preliminary ruling. The first asked whether the expression "subject to limitations justified on grounds of public policy" in Article 39(3) (ex 48(3)) E.C. concerned merely legislative decisions of the Member States, or whether it concerned also individual decisions taken in application of such legislative decisions. The second question sought the precise meaning to be attributed to the word "justified".

On the first question, the Court held that inasmuch as the object of the provisions of the Treaty and of secondary legislation was to regulate the situation of individuals and to ensure their protection, it was also for the national courts to examine whether individual decisions were compatible with the relevant provisions of Community Law.

The Court then considered the meaning to be given to the word "justified" in Article 39(3) (ex 48(3)). Since the exception was a derogation from a fundamental freedom granted by the Treaty, and must be interpreted strictly, it followed, argued the Court, that "restrictions cannot be imposed on the right of a national of any Member State to enter the territory of another Member State, to stay there and to move within it unless his presence or conduct constitutes *a genuine and sufficiently serious threat to public policy* (emphasis added)."[47] The Court concluded:

"Taken as a whole, these limitations placed on the powers of Member States in respect of control of aliens are a specific manifestation of the more general principle, enshrined in Articles 8, 9, 10 and 11 of the Convention for the Protection of Human Rights and Fundamental Freedoms, signed in Rome on November 4, 1950, and ratified by all the Member States, and in Article 2 of the Protocol No. 4 of the same Convention, signed in Strasbourg on September 16, 1963, which provide, in identical terms, that no restrictions in

---

[46] [1974] E.C.R. 1337 at 1350.
[47] [1975] E.C.R. 1219 at 1231.

the interests of national security or public safety shall be placed on the rights secured by the above-quoted articles other than such as are necessary for the protection of those interests in a democratic society."[48]

The Court thus makes explicit the test of "proportionality" in the judicial review of individual decision taken on the basis of Article 39(3) (ex 48(3)). The principle of "proportionality"—whereby legal authorisation of legislative or administrative action to a particular end extends only to those measures which, being apt to achieve the permitted end are, objectively speaking, least burdensome to those subject to the law—is well established in the jurisprudence of the Court of Justice. The principle may be invoked as a result of the express wording of the Treaty or implementing legislation, or as one of the basic principles of law which the Court of Justice is bound to safeguard.[49]

In *R. v. Bouchereau*, the Court added a gloss to its statement in *Rutili*. Not only must the threat to the requirements of public policy be "genuine and sufficiently serious," but the requirements invoked must affect "one of the fundamental interests of society."[50] The *van Duyn*[51] judgment seems in retrospect to have formulated somewhat generous criteria for the exercise of national discretion under Article 39(3). In *Adoui and Cornuaille*[52] the Court stressed that while Article 39(3) (ex 48(3)) allowed different treatment for aliens than for its own nationals (since Member States could not expel their own nationals), it did not authorise measures which discriminated against nationals of other Member States on arbitrary grounds. The Court amplified its reference in *Bouchereau* to "a genuine and sufficiently serious threat affecting one of the fundamental interests of society", as follows:

"Although Community law does not impose upon the Member States a uniform scale of values as regards the assessment of conduct which may be considered as contrary to public policy, it should nevertheless be stated that conduct may not be considered as being of a sufficiently serious nature to justify restrictions on the admission to or residence within the territory of a national of another Member State in a case where the former Member State does not adopt, with respect to the same conduct on the part of its own nationals, repressive measures or other genuine and effective measures to combat such conduct."[53]

It is clear that the national judge, in assessing the legality of action by national authorities under Article 39(3), must decide whether such action is "excessive" with regard to the threat to public policy posed by the individual concerned. In making such an assessment, he must take as his yardstick the view which the national authorities take of such conduct when engaged in by nationals, for although Article 39(3) by its nature permits discrimination, such discrimination must not be arbitrary.

---

[48] [1975] E.C.R. 1219 at 1232.
[49] For the principle of proportionality, see Chap. 6, pp. 135–137.
[50] Case 30/77 [1977] E.C.R. 1999; [1977] 2 C.M.L.R. 800, at para. 35.
[51] Case 41/74 [1974] E.C.R. 1337; [1975] 1 C.M.L.R. 1.
[52] Joined Cases 115–116/81 [1982] E.C.R. 1665; [1982] 3 C.M.L.R. 631.
[53] *ibid.*, para. 8.

In *Donatella Calfa*[54] the Court of Justice considered whether Article 39 (ex 48) and Directive 64/221 precluded national legislation which, with certain exceptions, in particular where there were family reasons, required a Member State's courts to order the expulsion for life from its territory of nationals of other Member States found guilty in that territory of the offences of obtaining and being in possession of drugs for their own personal use. The Court concluded that such automatic expulsion for life following such a criminal conviction, without any account being taken of the personal conduct of the offender, or of the danger which the person represents for the requirements of public policy, was incompatible with the requirements of Directive 64/221, and with the principle referred to in *Bouchereau*, to the effect that the concept of public policy could be relied upon in the event of a genuine and sufficiently serious threat to the requirements of public policy affecting one of the fundamental interests of society.

It is important to note that the Court refers in *Rutili* to the European Convention on Human Rights, ratified, as the Court points out, by all the Member States. The Court's judgment in *Rutili* was an early indication that Treaty provisions binding on the Member States, and in particular those permitting derogations from fundamental freedoms, will be interpreted by the Court in the light of the fundamental freedoms guaranteed by the European Convention.[55] If *van Duyn* supports the proposition that the "categories" of national interest which are eligible for protection under the proviso may vary in time and space[56] without prejudicing the uniform application of Community law, *Rutili* and subsequent cases emphasise that the extent to which such interests may be safeguarded will be subject to strict judicial control.

Naturally, each Member State has its own rules for controlling the entry of aliens and their residence in national territory. The judgment of the Court in *Royer*[57] makes it clear that failure to comply with national immigration formalities cannot of itself provide grounds for expulsion under Article 39(3) (ex 48(3)) E.C. Mr Royer, a Frenchman, had been expelled from Belgium for failing to comply with national formalities concerning the residence of aliens. He returned to Belgium, and was tried for the offence of illegal residence in the Kingdom. The referring court sought a ruling from the Court of Justice on the question, *inter alia*, whether the mere failure of a national of a Member State to comply with local entry formalities could provide a ground for expulsion under Article 39(3) (ex 48(3)). The Court replied in the negative. While Community law did not prevent Member States providing sanctions for breaches of national law relating to the control of aliens, such sanctions could not include expulsion. "Since it is a question of the exercise of a right acquired under the Treaty itself," said the Court, "such conduct cannot be regarded as constituting in itself a

---

[54] Case C–348/96 *Criminal Proceedings against Donatella Calfa* [1999] E.C.R. I–11; [1999] 2 C.M.L.R. 1138.
[55] See above, Chap. 6, at p. 148.
[56] Joined Cases 115–116/81 *Adoui and Cornuaille* [1982] E.C.R. 1665; [1982] 3 C.M.L.R. 631, confirm this proposition.
[57] Case 48/75 [1976] E.C.R. 497; [1976] 2 C.M.L.R. 619.

breach of public policy or public security."[58] The view of the Court accords with the principle enunciated in *Schluter & Maack v. Hauptzollamt Hamburg-Jonas*[59]— national requirements may be attached to rights arising under Community law, but not as a precondition to their exercise. Any other solution would prejudice the uniform application of Community law. From another perspective, it could simply be said that such minor infringements as those in issue could never amount to the genuinely and sufficiently serious threat to public policy required by the terms of Article 39(3) (ex 48(3)).

THE PUBLIC SERVICE PROVISO

Article 39(4) (ex 48(4)) E.C. declares that the "provisions of this Article shall not apply to employment in the public service". The provision does not apply to all employment in the public service, nor does it allow discrimination in the terms and conditions of employment once appointed. This much is clear from the Judgment of the Court in *Sotgiu v. Deutsche Bundespost*,[60] in which the referring court sought a ruling from the Court of Justice on the question whether or not Article 7 of Regulation 1612/68 was applicable to employees in the German postal service in view of this proviso. The Court replied that since the exception contained in Article 39(4) (ex 48(4)) could not be allowed a scope extending beyond the object for which it was included, the provision could be invoked to restrict the admission of foreign nationals to *certain activities* in the public service, but not to justify discrimination once they had been admitted.[61]

The Court further clarified the scope of Article 39(4) (ex 48(4)) in *Commission v. Belgium* (Case 149/79, No. 1), holding that that Article:

". . . removes from the ambit of Article 48(1)–(3) a series of posts which involve direct or indirect participation in the exercise of powers conferred by public law and duties designed to safeguard the general interests of the State or of other public authorities. Such posts in fact presume on the part of those occupying them the existence of a special relationship of allegiance to the State and reciprocity of rights and duties which form the foundation of the bond of nationality."[62]

Thus not all posts in the public service fall within the public service proviso. In the Court's view, to extend Article 39(4) (ex 48(4)) to posts which, while coming under the State or other organisations governed by public law, still do not involve

---

[58] [1976] E.C.R. 497 at 513.

[59] Case 94/71 [1972] E.C.R. 307; [1973] C.M.L.R. 113.

[60] Case 152/73 [1974] E.C.R. 153.

[61] On the point that Art. 39(4) cannot justify discrimination if non-nationals are admitted to the public service, see also Case 225/85 *Commission v. Italy* [1987] E.C.R. 2625; [1988] 3 C.M.L.R. 635, and Cases 389–390/87 *Echternach* [1987] E.C.R. 723; [1990] 2 C.M.L.R. 305. The Northern Ireland Court of Appeal has held that admission of non-nationals to a post in the public service within the meaning of Art. 39(4) (ex 48(4)) does not preclude subsequent reliance on the public service proviso as regards the post in question; *In the Matter of an Application by Edward Michael O'Boyle for Judicial Review; In the matter of an Applicaton by Suzanne Plunkett for Judicial Review*; Judgment of February 19, 1999, unreported.

[62] Case 149/79 [1980] E.C.R. 3881; [1981] 2 C.M.L.R. 413, para. 10.

any association with tasks belonging to the public service properly so called, would be to remove a considerable number of posts from the ambit of the principles set out in the Treaty and to create inequalities between the Member States according to the different ways in which the State and certain sectors of economic life are organised.

Nevertheless, classification of particular posts can cause difficulty. In *Commission v. Belgium* (Case 149/79, No. 2),[63] the Court approved the Commission's concession that the following posts fell within the ambit of Article 39(4) (ex 48(4)): head technical office supervisor, principal supervisor, works supervisor, stock controller, and nightwatchman, with the Municipalities of Brussels and Auderghem. The Court also upheld the Commission's view that a number of other jobs with Belgian National Railways, Belgian Local Railways, the City of Brussels, and the Commune of Auderghem, fell outside Article 39(4) (ex 48(4)). These jobs included railway shunters, drivers, platelayers, signalmen and nightwatchmen, and nurses, electricians, joiners and plumbers employed by the Auderghem.

Participation in the exercise of powers conferred by public law would clearly cover the exercise of police powers not exercisable by the ordinary citizen, and the exercise of other binding powers such as the grant or refusal or planning permission. A Commission notice has stated that:

". . . the derogation in Article 48(4) covers specific functions of the State and similar bodies such as the armed forces, the police and other forces for the maintenance of order, the judiciary, the tax authorities and the diplomatic corps . . . The derogation is also seen as covering posts in State Ministries, regional government authorities, local authorities and other similar bodies, central banks and other public bodies, where the duties of the post involve the exercise of State authority, such as the preparation of legal acts, the implementation of such acts, monitoring of their application and supervision of subordinate bodies."[64]

The nature of some of the posts held in *Commission v. Belgium* above to fall within the public service proviso seems to suggest that the reference to participation in the exercise of powers conferred by public law includes the exercise of senior managerial powers over state resources. This is confirmed by the judgment of the Court in *Commission v. Italy*,[65] in which the Court rejected the proposition that research posts at the national research centre (CNR) could be reserved to Italian nationals, and stated:

"Simply referring to the general tasks of the CNR and listing the duties of all its researchers is not sufficient to establish that the researchers are responsible for exercising powers conferred by public law or for safeguarding the general interests of the state. Only the duties *of management or of advising the state on*

---

[63] Case 149/79 [1982] E.C.R. 1845; [1982] 3 C.M.L.R. 539.
[64] [1988] O.J. C72/2.
[65] Case 225/85 [1987] E.C.R. 2625; [1988] 3 C.M.L.R. 635.

scientific and technical questions could be described as employment in the public service within the meaning of Article 48(4). However, it has not been established that these duties were carried out by researchers."[66] (emphasis added)

The italicised words in the above extract of the Court's judgment certainly suggest that managerial activities and advice to the state are regarded by the Court as falling within the scope of Article 39(4) (ex 48(4)), as interpreted by the Court in *Commission v. Belgium*.

Whereas access to the public service posts in question will often be direct, it might also be by promotion from other posts which could not be classified along with those "certain activities" to which access may be limited. It would seem to follow that Article 39(4) (ex 48(4)) E.C. should be read as permitting discrimination against Community nationals already holding posts in the public service, insofar as promotion to "sensitive" posts is concerned. This consideration was argued by the German Government in *Commission v. Belgium*[67] to militate against construing Article 39(4) (ex 48(4)) as only applying to certain posts within the public service, rather than to the public service at large. The Court's reply was that applying Article 39(4) (ex 48(4)) to all posts in the public service would impose a restriction on the rights of nationals of other Member States which went further than was necessary to achieve the aims of the proviso.

Applying the tests laid down by the Court of Justice, the Court of Appeal of Northern Ireland in the *O'Boyle* and *Plunkett* cases has found the post of Deputy Chief Fire Officer of Northern Ireland, and the post of Inland Revenue Claims Examiner, to be posts falling within the public service within the meaning of Article 39(4) (ex 48(4)).[68]

The Court of Justice has held that the following posts do not qualify for application of the public service proviso: a nurse in a public hospital,[69] a trainee teacher,[70] a foreign language assistant at a university,[71] researchers at a national research centre,[72] and numerous posts in the public sectors of teaching, research, inland transport, posts and telecommunications, and water gas and electricity, not being posts involving the direct or indirect participation in the exercise of powers conferred by public law and duties to safeguard the general interests of the State.[73] Article 39(4) cannot be relied upon by private security undertakings which do not as such comprise part of the public service.[74]

---

[66] *ibid.*, para. 9.
[67] Case 149/79 [1980] E.C.R. 3881; [1981] 2 C.M.L.R. 413.
[68] n.58.
[69] Case 307/84 *Commission v. France* [1986] E.C.R. 1725; [1987] 3 C.M.L.R. 555.
[70] Case 66/85 *Lawrie-Blum* [1986] E.C.R. 2121; [1987] 3 C.M.L.R. 403.
[71] Case 33/88 *Allué and Coonan* [1989] E.C.R. 1591; [1991] 1 C.M.L.R. 283.
[72] Case 225/85 *Commission v. Italy* [1987] E.C.R. 2625; [1988] 3 C.M.L.R. 635.
[73] Case C-473/93 *Commission v. Luxembourg* [1996] E.C.R. I-3207; [1996] 3 C.M.L.R. 981.
[74] Case C-114/97 *Commission v. Spain* [1998] E.C.R. I-6717; [1999] 2 C.M.L.R. 701, para. 33.

CHAPTER 15

THE RIGHT OF ESTABLISHMENT AND THE FREEDOM TO PROVIDE SERVICES

Introduction

As well as ensuring the free movement of workers, the Treaty guarantees the right of establishment, and the freedom to provide services between Member States: what Article 39 (ex 48) E.C. provides for the employee, Articles 43 and 49 (ex 52 and 59) E.C. provide for the employer, the entrepreneur and the professional. The employed and self-employed activities covered by the foregoing provisions include work done by members of a community based on religion or another form of philosophy, as part of the commercial activities of that community, and as a *quid pro quo* for services provided by it.[1]

The right of establishment is granted to natural and legal persons,[2] and subject to the exceptions and conditions laid down, it allows all types of self-employed activity to be taken up and pursued on the territory of any other Member State, undertakings to be formed and operated, and agencies, branches and subsidiaries to be set up.[3] It follows that a person may be established, within the meaning of the Treaty, in more than one Member State—in particular, in the case of companies, through the setting up of agencies, branches or subsidiaries, and in the case of the members of professions, by establishing a second professional base.[4] The concept of establishment within the meaning of the Treaty is a very broad one, allowing a Community national to participate, on a stable and continuous basis, in the economic life of a Member State other than his State of origin and to profit therefrom, so contributing to economic and social inter-penetration within the Community, in the sphere of activities of self-employed persons.[5]

The right of establishment is to be contrasted with the freedom to provide services. The former entails settlement in a Member State for economic purposes, and connotes permanent integration into the host State's economy, being generally exercised by a shift of a sole place of business, or by the setting up of agencies, branches or subsidiaries. The latter entails a person or undertaking established in one Member State providing services in another, as in the case of a doctor established in France visiting a patient in Belgium. The distinction may not always be clear-cut, because the provision of services may involve temporary residence in the host State, as in the case of a German firm of business consultants which advises undertakings in France, or a construction company which erects buildings in a neighbouring country. As long as such

---

[1] Case 196/87 *Udo Steymann v. Staatssecretaris van Justite* [1987] E.C.R. 6159, at paras 14 and 16.
[2] As defined in Art. 48 (ex 58) E.C.
[3] Case C–55/94 *Reinhard Gebhard v. Consiglio dell'Ordine degli Avvocati e Procuratori di Milano* [1995] E.C.R. I–4165; [1996] 1 C.M.L.R. 603, para. 23.
[4] *ibid.*, para. 24.
[5] *ibid.*, para. 25.

residence is temporary the activities in question will fall within the ambit of Articles 49–55 (ex 59–66), on freedom to provide services;[6] if the activities are carried out on a permanent basis, or, in any event, without a foreseeable limit to their duration, they will not fall within the provisions of the Treaty on the provision of services, but will be regulated by the provisions on the right of establishment.[7] But the fact that the provision of services is temporary does not mean that the provider of services within the meaning of the Treaty may not equip himself with some form of infrastructure in the host Member State, such as an office, chambers or consulting room.[8] The fact that both an established person and a person providing services may carry on business from such an office, consulting room or other place of business means that it may be in practice be difficult to distinguish activities subject to the Treaty provisions on establishment from those subject to the Treaty provisions on services, but as will be seen in subsequent sections of the present Chapter, the interpretation of the respective provisions of the Treaty on establishment and services by the Court of Justice has progressively reduced the significance of such a distinction being drawn. Be that as it may, whether the activities in question are to be regarded as temporary, and so subject to the Treaty provisions on services, rather than on establishment, has to be determined in the light, not only of the duration of the provision of the service, but of its regularity, periodicity or continuity.[9] It is evident that the provision of services from one Member State to another on a regular basis, accompanied by temporary residence and/or use of an office or similar facility in the host State, may shade imperceptibly into establishment.

THE RIGHT OF ESTABLISHMENT

Article 43 (ex 52) E.C. draws a distinction between the right of establishment of nationals of Member States *simpliciter*, and the right of establishment of nationals already established in the territory of a Member State. The former are entitled to establish themselves in any Member State, the latter are entitled to set up agencies and branches. The distinction between the right to establish oneself, and the right, once initially established in the territory of a Member State, to establish agencies, branches and subsidiaries, might be significant in relation to the establishment of companies, and will be considered later.[10] A Member State cannot refuse to accord rights under Article 43 (ex 52) to a national of another Member State on the ground that that national also holds the nationality of a third country.[11]

---

[6] Art. 50 (ex 60), E.C. third para. provides: "Without prejudice to the provisions of the Chap. relating to the right of establishment, the person providing a service may, in order to do so, temporarily pursue his activity in the State where the service is provided, under the same conditions as are imposed by that State on its own nationals."

[7] Case 196/87 *Udo Steymann v. Staatssecretaris van Justite* [1987] E.C.R. 6159, at para. 16.

[8] Case C–55/94 *Reinhard Gebhard v. Consiglio dell'Ordine degli Avvocati e Procuratori di Milano* [1995] E.C.R. I–4165; [1996] 1 C.M.L.R. 603, para. 27.

[9] *ibid.*

[10] Below at p. 466.

[11] Case C–369/90 *Mario Vicente Micheletti and Others v. Delegación del Gobierno en Cantabria* [1992] E.C.R. I–4239; see also Case C–122/96 *Stephen Austin Saldanha and MTS Securities Corporation v. Hiross Holding AG* [1997] E.C.R. I–5325.

Freedom of establishment includes a number of distinct rights. One is the right of a national or legal person to leave his or its Member State of origin or establishment in order to accomplish a shift in primary establishment, or to set up a secondary establishment, in another Member State.[12] Another is the right to have more than one place of business in the Community.[13] A third is the right to carry on business under the conditions laid down for its own nationals by the law of the host Member State.[14] The fourth is a much broader right. It is the right to resist the application of national measures which are liable to hinder or make less attractive the exercise of the right of establishment guaranteed by the Treaty;[15] though this broader right appears to be confined to situations where national measures comprise a restriction of one sort or another on *access to the relevant market* by nationals of Member States.[16] All the foregoing rights are of course subject to the exceptions and derogations recognised by Community law.[17] It must be noted, however, that Article 43 can have no application in a situation which is purely internal to a Member State.[18] The right of establishment guaranteed by Article 43 (ex 52) is directly applicable.[19]

ESTABLISHMENT OF NATURAL PERSONS

Evolution of the Court's case-law on the interpretation of Article 43 (ex 52) E.C.

The interpretation by the Court of Justice of Article 43 (ex 52) E.C. has been the subject of a quite significant evolution in two respects. The first respect concerns the extent to which the provision may be relied upon by a national of a Member State when returning to his Member State of origin and as against his own national authorities; the Court's early approach, relying upon a literal approach to the text, largely ruled out such reliance, but that approach has not been followed in later case-law. The second respect concerns the type of national rule regarded by the Court as comprising a restriction prohibited by Article 43 (ex 52). The Court's case-law until the 1990s was to the effect that only discriminatory restrictions could be so regarded, with the exception of measures preventing nationals from leaving their own Member States, and measures which

---

[12] Below at p. 435.
[13] *ibid.*
[14] Below at p. 446.
[15] Below at p.438.
[16] As to which, see below at p. 456–460.
[17] As to which see below at p. 487 *et seq.*, and 488 *et seq.*
[18] Case 204/87 *Bekaert* [1988] E.C.R. 2029; [1988] 2 C.M.L.R. 655; Cases C–54/88 *et al. Nino* [1990] E.C.R. I–3537; [1992] 1 C.M.L.R. 83; Case C–152/94 *Openbaar Ministerie v. Geert Van Buynder* [1995] E.C.R. I–3981. It appears that a person qualified in a Member State who carries on all his professional activity there may not rely upon Art. 43 (ex 52) solely because he resides in another Member State, Case C–112/91 *Hans Werner v. Finanzamt Aachen-Innenstadt* [1993] E.C.R. I–429, but the Court has treated a similar situation as being governed by Art. 49 (ex 59), see Case 39/75 *Coenen* [1975] E.C.R. 1555; [1976] 1 C.M.L.R. 30.
[19] Case 81/87 *R. v. HM Treasury and Commissioners of Inland Revenue, ex p. Daily Mail and General Trust plc* [1988] E.C.R. 3483, at para. 15; Case C–1/93 *Halliburton Services v Staatssecretaris van Financiën* [1994] E.C.R. I–1137; [1994] 3 C.M.L.R. 377, para. 16; Case C–254/97 *Société Baxter v. Premier Ministre* [1999] E.C.R. I–4809, para. 11.

prevented individuals from having a place of business in more than one Member State, or placed such individuals at a disadvantage. But more recently the Court has adopted a broader approach, which seems to have been inspired by its jurisprudence on the free movement of goods, and the provision of services, which holds that Article 43 E.C. covers all national measures which are liable to hinder or make less attractive the exercise of the right of establishment. It is appropriate to consider first the text of Article 43, and then to trace the major developments in the Court's interpretation of that text.

Article 43 (ex 52) E.C. provides that "Within the framework of the provisions set out below, restrictions on the freedom of establishment of *nationals of a Member State* in the territory of *another Member State* shall be prohibited." (emphasis added). It is to be noted that the words in italics indicate that the Article covers a national of one Member State exercising self-employed activities in the territory of another, but there is no indication that the scope of the Article extends to the case of a national of a Member State returning to his Member State of origin. The wording is however apt to cover restrictions imposed by a Member State of origin on the right of establishment of its own nationals in another Member State. Article 43 goes on to say that "freedom of establishment shall include the right to take up and pursue activities as self-employed persons . . ." etc., ". . . under the conditions laid down for its own nationals by the law of the country where such establishment is effected". The use of the word "include" in the latter formulation implies that the "restrictions" on freedom of establishment referred to in the first sentence of the Article, which are to be prohibited, are not confined to discriminatory restrictions. Beyond that, it is clear that the text leaves room for interpretation as regards the possible scope of the Article regarding discriminatory restrictions on the one hand, and non-discriminatory restrictions on the other. It is also to be noted that the "restrictions" referred to in the first sentence of the Article refer to the "framework of the provisions set out below", and the provisions in question authorise the issue of E.C. directives in order "to attain freedom of establishment as regards a particular activity",[20] and in order "to make it easier for persons to take up and pursue activities as self-employed persons" by providing for the "mutual recognition of diplomas, certificates and other evidence of formal qualifications".[21]

In *Reyners v. Belgian State* the Court of Justice held that the prohibition of discrimination contained in Article 43 (ex 52) was directly applicable, despite the reference in that Article to the prohibition of restrictions on the right of establishment "within the framework" of subsequent Articles of the Treaty providing for the adoption of Community secondary legislation. This judgment was of considerable significance, and it is referred to further below.[22] Other judgments on the applicability of the prohibition on discrimination followed.[23] But in the first *Auer* case,[24] the Court felt it necessary to address an important

---

[20] Art. 44 (ex 54) E.C.
[21] Art. 47 (ex 57) E.C.
[22] At p. 443.
[23] See below, p. 460.
[24] Case 136/78 *Ministère public v. Auer* [1979] E.C.R. 437; [1979] 2 C.M.L.R. 373; see also Case 271/82 *Auer v. Ministère public* [1983] E.C.R. 2727; [1985] 1 C.M.L.R. 123.

issue of principle as to the scope of Article 43 (ex 52). The national proceedings which gave rise to a reference to the Court of Justice involved a Mr Vincent Auer, originally of Austrian nationality, who studied veterinary medicine first in Austria, then in France, and then in Italy, at the University of Parma, where he was awarded in 1956 the degree of doctor of veterinary medicine, and in March 1957 a provisional certificate to practise as a veterinary surgeon. Mr Auer took up residence in France and in 1961 acquired French nationality by naturalisation. He then applied, pursuant to a provision of French law allowing veterinary surgeons who have acquired French nationality to be authorised to practise in France despite the absence of a French doctorate. The competent French authority refused to recognise the equivalence of Mr Auer's Italian qualification, but he practised in France nevertheless, and he was prosecuted on several occasions for doing so. One such prosecution led to a reference to the Court of Justice, asking whether the person concerned was in a position to claim in France the right to practise the profession of veterinary surgeon which he had acquired in Italy. The Court noted that the question referred to the situation as it existed at the time when Article 47(1) of the Treaty (ex 57(1)) relating to mutual recognition of diplomas, certificates and other qualifications had not yet been applied as regards the practice of the profession of veterinary medicine, though directives on mutual recognition and co-ordination of veterinary qualifications had been adopted subsequently. It remained to be considered whether, and if so to what extent, "nationals of the Member State in which they were established were entitled, at the time in question, to rely on the provisions of Articles 52 to 57 of the Treaty in situations such as that described above."[25] The Court might have proceeded on the basis that a person in the situation of Mr Auer could not rely upon the right of establishment because he had never, as a national of a Member State, exercised his right of free movement. But it did not, it proceeded instead on the basis that the only relevant right under Article 43 (ex 52) in such circumstances was the right of non-discrimination, and that right could only be invoked by a national of one Member State in the territory of another. The Court, citing the text of the Treaty, including the reference to "establishment of nationals of one Member State in the territory of another" stated:

"In so far as it is intended to ensure, within the transitional period, with direct effect, the benefit of national treatment, Article 52 concerns only—and can concern only—in each Member State the nationals of other Member States, those of the host Member State coming already, by definition, under the rules in question."[26]

The Court went on to explain that in order to ensure complete freedom of establishment, the Treaty provided for directives to be adopted on mutual recognition of qualifications, and that such directives could be invoked both by nationals of one Member State in the territory of another, and by the nationals of a Member State in that Member State.[27]

---

[25] *ibid.*, para. 14.
[26] *ibid.*, para. 20.
[27] *ibid.*, paras 22–26.

The above judgment supported three related propositions. The first was that the direct effect of Article 43 (ex 52) was confined to a guarantee of national treatment; the second was that that guarantee could only by definition be invoked by a national of one Member State in the territory of another; and the third was that any restrictions on freedom of movement caused to nationals of a Member State by national rules on qualifications could be removed by the adoption of directives on mutual recognition of qualifications. Only the last of these propositions was to be confirmed by subsequent case-law.

In a judgment given on the same day as *Auer*, in the *Knoors* case,[28] the Court explained the justification for allowing a national of a Member State, who had secured in another Member State a qualification which had been the subject of a directive issued under Article 44 (ex 54) E.C., to rely upon the terms of that directive. Referring to the free movement provisions of the Treaty, *viz.*, Articles 39, 43 and 49 (ex 48, 52 and 59), the Court stated:

"In fact, these liberties, which are fundamental in the Community system, could not be fully realised if the Member States were in a position to refuse to grant the benefit of the provisions of Community law to those of their nationals who have taken advantage of the facilities existing in the matter of freedom of movement and establishment and who have acquired, by virtue of such facilities, the trade qualifications referred to by the directive in a Member State other than that whose nationality they possess."[29]

This rationale was well-suited to the case in point; the plaintiff in the national proceedings was a Netherlands national who had resided in Belgium and there acquired the practical experience as a plumber which, pursuant to the directive, was to be accorded recognition by other Member States. The Court went on:

"Although it is true that the provisions of the Treaty relating to establishment and the provision of services cannot be applied to situations which are purely internal to a Member State, the position nevertheless remains that the reference in Article 52 to "nationals of a Member State" who wish to establish themselves "in the territory of another Member State" cannot be interpreted in such a way as to exclude from the benefit of Community law a given Member State's own nationals when the latter, owing to the fact that they have lawfully resided on the territory of another Member State and have there acquired a trade qualification which is recognised by the provisions of Community law, are, with regard to their State of origin, in a situation which may be assimilated to that of any other person enjoying the rights and liberties guaranteed by the Treaty."[30]

The effect of the judgment in *Knoors* is that nationals of a Member State may rely upon an "establishment" directive even in their own Member State, where they have acquired a qualification covered by that directive in the territory of

---

[28] Case 115/78 *Knoors v. Secretary of State for Economic Affairs* [1979] E.C.R. 399; [1979] 2 C.M.L.R. 357.

[29] *ibid.*, para. 20.

[30] *ibid.*, para. 24.

another Member State. The justification is that otherwise such nationals would be deprived of the advantages of the exercise of the right of establishment, in those cases where the qualification in question had in fact been secured by the exercise of the right of establishment in the first place.

In *Klopp*[31] the Court held that the right referred to in Article 43 (ex 52) to set up agencies and branches was a specific statement of a general principle, applicable equally to the liberal professions, according to which the right of establishment includes the freedom to set up and maintain, subject to observance of the professional rules of conduct, more than one place of work within the Community.[32] It was thus incompatible with freedom of establishment to deny to a national of another Member State the right to enter and to exercise the profession of advocate solely on the ground that he maintained chambers in another Member State, even if the national rules in question applied without discrimination on grounds of nationality This case provides a good example of a non-discriminatory restriction which falls within the ordinary meaning of the words used in the text of the Treaty. It is thus incompatible with the right of establishment if national rules place at a disadvantage a person who has a place of business in more than one Member State, as compared to a person whose business activities are located within a single Member State.[33]

In the *Daily Mail* case the Court made it clear that Article 43 (ex 52) prohibited restrictions imposed by a Member State on its own nationals seeking to establish themselves in the territory of another Member State. The Court stated:

"Even though those provisions are directed mainly to ensuring that foreign nationals and companies are treated in the host Member State in the same way as nationals of that State, they also prohibit the Member State of origin from hindering the establishment in another Member State of one of its nationals or of a company incorporated under its legislation which comes within the definition contained in Article 58."[34]

The foregoing case-law indicated that the right of establishment gave to the nationals of a Member State the right to leave that State in order to take up self-employed activities elsewhere, the right to set up a place of business in more than one Member State, and the right to carry on self-employed activities in another Member State under the same conditions as were laid down for nationals of that Member State. That the right to equality of treatment was the "core" guarantee of Article 43 (ex 52), and that that guarantee did not extend to a general prohibition on non-discriminatory measures which might be held to restrict the exercise of the right of establishment in some way, was made clear in *Commission*

---

[31] Case 107/83 *Ordre des Avocats au Barreau de Paris v. Klopp* [1984] E.C.R. 2971.

[32] The context makes it clear that it is contemplated that the Court is referring to a place of business in more than one Member State.

[33] For cases where national rules place at a disadvantage a person who has a place of business in more than one Member State, see Case 143/87 *Stanton* [1988] E.C.R. 3877; Cases 154–155/87 *Wolf* [1988] E.C.R. 3897; Case C–53/95 *Inasti v. Hans Kemmler* [1996] E.C.R. I–703.

[34] Case 81/87 *R. v. HM Treasury and Commissioners of Inland Revenue, ex p. Daily Mail and General Trust plc* [1988] E.C.R. 3483, at para. 16.

v. Belgium,[35] in which the Commission alleged that non-discriminatory Belgian rules governing the activities of clinical biology laboratories were incompatible with Article 43 (ex 52), on the ground that the rules in question were excessively restrictive, and that the latter Article prohibited not only discriminatory measures, but also "measures which apply to both nationals and foreigners without discrimination where they constitute an unjustified constraint for the latter".[36] The Court rejected this approach to the right of establishment, emphasising that the text of Article 43 (ex 52) guaranteed equality of treatment for nationals and non-nationals, and stating:

> ". . . provided that such equality of treatment is respected, each Member State is, in the absence of Community rules in this area, free to lay down rules for its own territory governing the activities of laboratories providing clinical biology services."[37]

It will be recalled that in *Knoors* the proposition that a national in his own Member State might rely upon the terms of a directive adopted to secure the implementation of the right of establishment was justified by the fact that such a person might have brought himself within the situation contemplated by the directive by prior exercise of the right of establishment. In this judgment we see what is perhaps the basis for the principle which later developed in the Court's jurisprudence, to the effect that the free movement provisions apply to the return of a national to his or her own Member State after he or she has exercised the right of free movement[38]; the legal basis for the proposition being that individuals would be deterred from exercising their right to take up activities in another Member State if on their return they would treated less favourably than a national of another Member State otherwise in the same position.[39] The Court took the proposition in *Knoors* a small step further in *Bouchoucha*, in that it described the scope of a case of a French national practising in France, while holding a professional diploma issued in another Member State, as "not purely national" and noted that "the applicability of the EEC Treaty provisions on freedom of establishment must be considered."[40]

It fell to the Court in *Surinder Singh*[41] to consider whether a spouse of a national of a Member State who had exercised her right of freedom of movement as an employed person in another Member State and then returned to her own Member State to carry on self-employed activities, was entitled to install himself in the latter Member State. If his wife has been taking up self-employed activities

---

[35] Case 221/85 [1987] E.C.R. 719.

[36] *ibid.*, para. 5.

[37] *ibid.*, para. 9. The Court confirmed this view of the scope of freedom of establishment in Case 198/86 *Erwin Conradi and others v. Direction de la Concurrence et des Prix des Hauts de Seine* [1987] E.C.R. 4469; [1989] 2 C.M.L.R. 155.

[38] Case C–419/92 *Scholz v. Opera Universitaria di Cagliari* [1994] E.C.R. I–505; [1994] 1 C.M.L.R. 873, para. 9; Case C–443/93 *Ioannis Vougioukas v. IKA* [1995] E.C.R. I–4033, para. 39.

[39] Case C–370/90 *R. v. Immigration and Appeal Tribunal and Surinder Singh, ex p. Secretary of State for the Home Department* [1992] E.C.R. I–4265, para. 23.

[40] Case C–61/89 *Criminal Proceedings against Marc Gaston Bouchoucha* [1990] E.C.R. I–3551; [1992] 1 C.M.L.R. 1033, para. 11.

[41] Case C–370/90 *R. v. Immigration and Appeal Tribunal and Surinder Singh, ex p. Secretary of State for the Home Department* [1992] E.C.R. I–4265.

in another Member State, it was clear that he would have derived that right from the applicable secondary legislation. It was argued however by the Member State of origin that the position was different where a national returned to her own Member State; such a situation was, it said, governed by national law. The Court replied as follows:

"However, this case is concerned not with a right under national law but with the rights of movement and establishment granted to a Community national by Articles 48 and 52 of the Treaty. These rights cannot be fully effective if such a person may be deterred from exercising them by obstacles raised in his or her country of origin to the entry and residence of his or her spouse. Accordingly, when a Community national who has availed himself or herself of those rights returns to his or her own country of origin, his or her spouse must enjoy at least the same rights of entry and residence as would be granted to him or her under Community law if his or her spouse chose to enter and reside in another Member State."[42]

This reasoning is worthy of remark. The Court appears disinclined to assert that the Treaty bestows directly on nationals of a Member State the right to enter that Member State—such a right is normally inherent in citizenship and arises under national law. So the Court asserts that an individual may be deterred from exercising his right to *leave* his own Member State in order to carry on economic activities in another Member State by the prospect of being treated less favourably on his return (as regards the right to be accompanied by his spouse) than he would be treated if he sought admission to another Member State instead. This might be plausible in a case in which a national of a Member State took up economic activities in another Member State, married there a national of a third country, and then found himself unable to return to his Member State of origin with his spouse. In such a case, the person in question would in a sense be disadvantaged as a consequence of having exercised his right of free movement. In *Surinder Singh*, however, no such disadvantage arose.

It is noted elsewhere in this work that in 1979 the Court in the *Cassis* case interpreted the free movement of goods provisions as covering non-discriminatory national measures which made the import of goods more difficult or costly,[43] and in 1991 in the *Säger* case the Court interpreted the provisions of the Treaty on the provision of services as applying to national rules which applied without distinction to nationals and non-nationals but nevertheless restricted the provision of services.[44] In 1993 the Court held in the *Kraus* case[45] that the right to freedom of movement for workers applied where a German national who had secured an academic title in the United Kingdom returned to his country of origin, it being the case that the possession of such a title constituted for the person entitled to make use of it, an advantage for the purpose both of gaining entry to such a profession, and of prospering within it. The Court held moreover

---

[42] *ibid.*. para. 23.
[43] Above at p. 323.
[44] Below at p. 477.
[45] Case C–19/92 *Dieter Kraus v. Land Baden-Württemberg.* [1993] E.C.R. I–1663.

that Article 39 (ex 48) precluded any national measure governing the conditions under which an academic title obtained in another Member State might be used, where that measure, even though it was applicable without discrimination on grounds of nationality, was liable to hamper or to render less attractive the exercise by Community nationals, including those of the Member State which enacted the measure, of fundamental freedoms guaranteed by the Treaty. The situation would be different only if such a measure pursued a legitimate objective compatible with the Treaty and was justified by pressing reasons of public interest.[46] That this latter principle was also applicable in the context of Article 43 was made clear in *Gebhard*:[47]

"... national measures liable to hinder or make less attractive the exercise of fundamental freedoms guaranteed by the Treaty must fulfill four conditions: they must be applied in a non-discriminatory manner; they must be justified by imperative requirements in the general interest; they must be suitable for securing the attainment of the objective which they pursue; and they must not go beyond what is necessary in order to attain it" (see Case C–19/92 *Kraus* . . ., para. 32).[48]

In *Aasscher* the Court considered whether a national of a Member State pursuing an activity as a self-employed person in another Member State, in which he resides, may rely on Article 43 (ex 52) as against his State of origin, on whose territory he pursues another activity as a self-employed person. The Court stated[49]:

"It is settled law that, although the provisions of the Treaty relating to freedom of establishment cannot be applied to situations which are purely internal to a Member State, Article 52 nevertheless cannot be interpreted in such a way as to exclude a given Member State's own nationals from the benefit of Community law where by reason of their conduct they are, with regard to their Member State of origin, in a situation which may be regarded as equivalent to that of any other person enjoying the rights and liberties guaranteed by the Treaty . . ."

It appears from the foregoing survey of the case-law that the Court's approach to the interpretation of the Treaty provisions on the right of establishment has been the subject of considerable development, as regards the right of a national

---

[46] *ibid.*, para.32. The Court of Justice in the event held that the national measure in question might be so justified. That a national of a Member State could rely upon the Treaty again his Member State of origin was justified in the terms referred to in *Knoors*, above, p. 434.

[47] Case C–55/94 *Reinhard Gebhard v. Consiglio dell'Ordine degli Avvocati e Procuratori di Milano* [1995] E.C.R. I–4165; [1996] 1 C.M.L.R. 603.

[48] *ibid.*, para. 37.

[49] Case C–107/94 *P.H. Asscher v. Staatssecretaris van Financiën* [1994] E.C.R. I–1137; [1996] 3 C.M.L.R. 61, para. 32, citing Case 115/78 *Knoors v. Secretary of State for Economic Affairs* [1979] E.C.R. 399; [1979] 2 C.M.L.R. 357; Case C–61/89 *Criminal Proceedings against Marc Gaston Bouchoucha* [1990] E.C.R. I–3551; [1992] 1 C.M.L.R. 1033; Case C–19/92 *Dieter Kraus v. Land Baden-Württemberg* [1993] E.C.R. I–1663; Case C–419/92 *Scholz v. Opera Universitaria di Cagliari* [1994] E.C.R. I–505; [1994] 1 C.M.L.R. 873. This formulation may also provide the true explanation of Case C–370/90 *R. v. Immigration and Appeal Tribunal and Surinder Singh, ex p. Secretary of State for the Home Department* [1992] E.C.R. I–4265.

of a Member State, and members of the family deriving rights through that person, to invoke the right of establishment against the authorities of that State, and as regards the application of Article 43 (ex 52) to non-discriminatory national measures capable of restricting the right of establishment. It will be examined in a subsequent section of this chapter to what extent the formulation of the Court set out in *Gebhard* above is helpful, since it implies that in all circumstances a non-discriminatory measure can be challenged simply on the grounds of its restrictive effects, when it seems that in a number of circumstances, *e.g.* the application of national tax legislation, it remains the case that Member States are free to lay down such rules as they think fit, providing that they do not discriminate in fact or in law.

Abolition of restrictions on the right of establishment—the General Programme and secondary legislation

The Treaty in its original text provided for the abolition of restrictions on freedom of establishment in progressive stages *during the transitional period.*[50] Such abolition was, and is to be facilitated by secondary legislation prohibiting discrimination on grounds of nationality,[51] ensuring the mutual recognition of "diplomas and certificates, and other evidence of formal qualifications",[52] and co-ordinating national requirements governing the pursuit of non-wage-earning activities.[53] Legislation on the abolition of restrictions was to be preceded by a General Programme, which was to be drawn up by the Council before the end of the first stage. The Programme[54] was adopted in December 1961,[55] and provided the basis for the Council's subsequent legislative activities in this area.

Entry and residence

Title II of the Council's General Programme sought the adjustment of the legislative and administrative requirements in the Member States governing entry and residence, to the extent that such requirements might impair the access of nationals of other Member States to non-wage-earning activities. Directive 64/220 followed,[56] providing for the abolition of restrictions on movement and residence within the Community, and applied, like many other instruments in this area, to the provision of services as well as to the right of establishment. It

---

[50] The words are omitted from Art. 43 since they are now superfluous.
[51] See Art. 44(2)(f) (ex 54(2)(f)) referring to "effecting the progressive abolition of restrictions on freedom of establishment in every branch of activity under consideration . . ."
[52] Art. 47(1) (ex 57(1)).
[53] Art. 47(2) (ex 57(2)).
[54] The General Programme constitutes neither a Regulation, Directive nor Decision within the meaning of Art. 189 of the Treaty. For the view that it bound the Community institutions, but not the Member States, see van Gerven (1966) 3 C.M.L. Rev. 344, at p. 354. There seems to be no reason why it could not bind the Member States, see Case 22/70 *ERTA* [1971] E.C.R. 263
[55] [1974] O.J. Spec.Ed. Second Series, IX, p. 7. The Court has referred to the General Programme in its case-law, see, *e.g.* Case 7/76 *Thieffry* [1977] E.C.R. 765; Case 136/78 *Auer* [1979] E.C.R. 452; [1979] 2 C.M.L.R. 373; Case 182/83 *Fearon* [1984] E.C.R. 3677; [1985] 2 C.M.L.R. 288; Case 107/83 *Klopp* [1984] E.C.R. 2971; [1985] 1 C.M.L.R. 99.
[56] [1964] J.O. 845.

was superseded by Directive 73/148,[57] which brought the law governing the entry and residence of the self-employed into line with that applying to employees, and indeed, it follows closely the pattern of Directive 68/360,[58] which has been considered in detail in the context of the free movement of workers.[59]

Directive 73/148, like its predecessor, applies to both the right of establishment and to the provision of services. Article 1(1) provides that the Member States shall, acting as provided in the Directive, abolish restrictions on the movement and residence of:

> "(a) nationals of a Member State who are established or who wish to establish themselves in another Member State in order to pursue activities as self-employed persons, or who wish to provide services in that State;
> (b) nationals of Member States wishing to go to another Member State as recipients of services;
> (c) the spouse and the children under 21 years of age of such nationals, irrespective of their nationality;
> (d) the relatives in the ascending and descending lines of such nationals and of the spouse of such nationals, which relatives are dependent on them, irrespective of their nationality."

Following the pattern of Directive 68/360, Directive 73/148 bestows the following rights on the above persons:

> — the right to be allowed to leave national territory, and to be issued with an identity card or passport (Art. 2);
> — the right to be allowed to enter the territory of the Member States merely on production of a valid identity card or passport (Art. 3).

A distinction is drawn between the right of residence of a person exercising the right of establishment, and the right of a person providing services. In the former case, Article 4(1) applies, requiring each Member State to "grant the right of permanent residence to nationals of other Member States who establish themselves within its territory in order to pursue activities as self-employed persons". This right is evidenced by a "residence Permit for a National of a Member State of the European Communities," which must be valid for not less than five years and be automatically renewable.[60] In the case of the provision of services, the Directive declares that "the right of residence for persons providing and receiving services shall be of equal duration with the period during which the services are provided."[61] Where such periods exceed three months, the Member State in whose territory the services are performed must issue a "right of abode" as proof of residence.[62] An applicant for a residence permit or right of abode is only required to produce: (a) the identity card or passport with which he or she

[57] [1973] O.J. L172/14.
[58] [1968] O.J. Spec.Ed. (II), 485.
[59] Above at p. 387.
[60] Art. 4(1), second sub-para.
[61] Art. 4(2), first sub-para.
[62] Art. 4(2), second sub-para.

entered the territory in question; and (b) proof that he or she comes within the protection of the Directive.[63]

Whereas Directive 68/360 is ambiguous as to the rights of entry and residence of dependent relatives other than children or those in the ascending line, and relatives living under the worker's roof in the country whence they came,[64] Directive 73/148 contains no such ambiguity in the case of the relatives of the self-employed. Article 1 of the Directive makes it clear that such persons do not enter and reside as of right, though Member States "shall favour" their admission. As indicated earlier,[65] it is believed that such differentiation between dependent relatives is capable in certain circumstances of constituting an obstacle to the free movement of persons, and could accordingly be contrary in such cases to Articles 43 or 49.

Where a national of one Member State who has worked in another returns to the first Member State to pursue self-employed activities there, the Court held in *Surinder Singh* that the latter Member State must grant entry and residence to the spouse of such person,[66] and the reasoning in the latter case indicates that this obligation extends to all the members of the family referred to in Article 1 of the Directive.

The right to remain in the territory of a Member State after having been self-employed there

The Court has on several occasions stressed the parallels between Articles 39, 43 and 49 (ex 48, 52 and 59).[67] Nevertheless, there are differences in the scheme and text of these various provisions, not least in the omission of any explicit authority in Articles 43-48 (ex 52-58): (i) to make provisions for the social security rights of the self-employed,[68] and (ii) to safeguard the position of self-employed persons who may wish to remain in the territory of the Member States after terminating their business activities. It is as a result of the latter omission that Directive 75/34[69] on the right of self-employed persons to remain in Member States, *inter alia*, after retirement is based on Article 308 (ex 235) E.C., the third recital to its preamble acknowledging the absence of authority in Article 44(2) (ex 54(2)). The rights of the self-employed enumerated in the Directive are identical to those bestowed upon workers in Regulation 1251/70,[70] and permit retired and incapacitated persons to remain in a Member State where they have previously been self-employed. For the details of these provisions, the reader is

---

[63] Art. 6. No other means of proof must be required by Member States in support of an application of a residence permit, see Case C–363/89 *Roux v. Belgian State* [1991] E.C.R. I–273; [1993] 1 C.M.L.R. 3.

[64] Above at p. 391.

[65] Above at p. 392.

[66] Case C–370/90 *R. v. Immigration and Appeal Tribunal and Surinder Singh, ex p. Secretary of State for the Home Department* [1992] E.C.R. I–4265, see above at p. 436.

[67] See below, p. 445.

[68] Reg. 1408/71 on the application of social security schemes to employed persons, was extended to self- empoyed persons by Reg. 1390/81, [1981] O.J. L143/32; the legal basis was Arts 2, 12, 41 and 308 (ex 2, 7, 51 and 235) E.C.

[69] [1975] O.J. L14/10.

[70] [1970] O.J. Spec.Ed. (II), 402.

referred to the treatment of Regulation 1251/70 in Chapter 14 on the free movement of workers.[71]

It will be noted that in the case of the self-employed, the Council proceeded by Directive, although a Regulation could have been adopted under Article 308 (ex 235) E.C., which authorises "appropriate measures." This is mildly curious, since the Council adopts an almost identical text to that of Regulation 1251/70. Workers may clearly rely on the latter instrument; its provisions are directly applicable and hence capable by their very nature of producing direct effects. Article 8(2) in both the Regulation and the Directive may lack the clarity and the precision characteristic of a directly effective provision (duty to "facilitate readmission" of certain persons), but this cannot be said of the principal rights enumerated in each instrument: they clearly give rise to rights in individuals which national courts are bound to safeguard.[72] This being the case, it would seem that both employed and self-employed persons may invoke in national courts the rights to remain in a Member State after having pursued economic activities therein.

Abolition of discriminatory restrictions by secondary legislation

Title III of the General Programme called for the abolition of discriminatory measures which might impair access to the non-wage-earning activities of nationals of the Member States, such as measures which:

— conditioned the access to or exercise of a non-wage earning activity on an authorisation or on the issuance of a document, such as a foreign merchant's card or a foreign professional's card;
— made the access to or exercise of a non-wage earning activity more costly through the imposition of taxes or other charges such as a deposit or surety bond paid to the receiving country;
— barred or limited membership in companies, particularly with regard to the activities of their members.

In addition to measures primarily likely to discriminate against nationals of the Member States with respect of access to non-wage-earning activities, the General Programme condemned specific national practices discriminating against such persons in the exercise of these activities, such as those limiting the opportunity:

— to enter into certain types of transactions, such as contracts for the hire of services or commercial and farm leases;
— to tender bids or to participate as a co-contractor or sub-contractor in public contracts or contracts with public bodies[73];
— to borrow and to have access to various forms of credit;
— to benefit from aids granted by the State.

---

[71] Above at p. 412 *et seq.*
[72] Above at p. 97.
[73] There has been substantial harmonisation in this field, see in particular Council Dir. 93/36 co-ordinating procedures for the award of public supply contracts, [1993] O.J. L199/1, and Council Dir. 93/37 concerning the co-ordination of procedures for the award of public works contracts, [1993] O.J. L199/54.

Subsequently, the Council issued a series of Directives implementing the General Programme, and dealing with the right of establishment in a wide variety of commercial callings, from the wholesale trade to the provision of electricity, gas, water and sanitary services.[74] Many such Directives are applicable to both establishment and the provision of services, emphasising again the close practical relationship between the two. Directive 64/223,[75] concerning the attainment of freedom of establishment and freedom to provide services in respect of activities in the wholesale trade, may be considered for illustrative purposes. Under the Directive Member States are required to abolish the restrictions itemised in Title III of the General Programmes with respect to the commercial activities concerned. Specific legislative provisions in effect in the Member States are singled out for prohibition, such as the obligation under French law to hold a *carte d'identité d'étrangère commerçant*,[76] while Member States are obliged to ensure that beneficiaries of the Directive have the right to join professional or trade organisations under the same conditions, and with the same rights and obligations as their own nationals.[77] Where a host State requires evidence of good character in respect of its own nationals taking up the commercial activities concerned, provision is made for accepting appropriate proof from other Member States, and for the taking of a solemn declaration by self-employed persons from such States, where the State in question does not issue the appropriate documentation.[78]

Prohibition of discrimination held directly applicable

Although Article 53 of the EEC Treaty,[79] which prohibited Member States from introducing any new restrictions on the right of establishment of nationals of other Member States, was held by the Court to be directly applicable in *Costa v. ENEL*,[80] the Council's extensive legislative scheme, based on the General Programme, appears to have been adopted on the basis that the prohibition of discrimination contained in Article 43 (ex 52) was ineffective in the absence of implementation. That this was not the case was made clear by the Court of Justice in *Reyners v. Belgian State*.[81] The plaintiff in the main suit was a Dutch national resident in Belgium. He had been born in Belgium, educated there, and taken his *docteur en droit belge*, only to be finally refused admission to the Belgian bar on the ground of his Dutch nationality. On a reference for a preliminary ruling, the Court held that the prohibition on discrimination

---

[74] The documents are too numerous to list.

[75] [1963–1964] O.J. Spec.Ed. (I), 123.

[76] Art. 3.

[77] Art. 4.

[78] Art. 6.

[79] This Art. appeared in the original text of the EEC Treaty, but was repealed as superfluous by the Amsterdam Treaty.

[80] Case 6/64 [1964] E.C.R. 585; [1964] C.M.L.R. 425.

[81] Case 2/74 [1974] E.C.R. 631; [1974] 2 C.M.L.R. 305. For a discriminatory provision remaining on the statute book contrary to Art. 43 (ex 52) see Case 159/78 *Commission v. Italy* [1979] E.C.R. 3247; [1980] 3 C.M.L.R. 446. And see Case 38/87 *Commission v. Greece* [1988] E.C.R. 4415. For discriminatory conditions of tender contrary to Art. 43 (ex 52), see Case 197/84 *Steinhauser* [1985] E.C.R. 1819; [1986] 1 C.M.L.R. 53.

contained in Article 43 (ex 52) was directly applicable as of the end of the transitional period, despite the opening words of the text of that Article, which referred to the abolition of restrictions "within the framework of the provisions set out below". These provisions—the General Programme and the Directives provided for in Article 44 (ex 54)—were of significance "only during the transitional period, since the freedom of establishment was fully attained at the end of it". According to the Court, the aim of Article 43 was intended to be facilitated by the Council's Legislative programme, but not made dependent upon it.

The Court's decision had immediate repercussions. The Commission undertook, at a meeting of the Permanent Representatives, to report to the Council its view of the implications of the *Reyners* case for the implementation of the right of establishment. In its promised memorandum,[82] the Commission expressed the view that all the rules and formalities cited in the Directives on the abolition of restriction were no longer applicable to nationals of the Member States, though, in the interests of legal certainty, the Member States should formally bring their legislation into line with the requirements of Article 43 (ex 52). In view of this, the Commission considered that it was no longer necessary to adopt Directives on the abolition of restrictions, and furthermore, since Directives were by their nature constitutive, that the adoption of such instruments having only declaratory effect would create confusion and protract the work of the Council unnecessarily. The latter view is open to question. Several Directives in the field of free movement of persons have been stated by the Court to give rise to no new rights, but merely to give closer articulation to rights bestowed directly by the Treaty.[83] This would also appear to be the case with Directive 75/117[84] on equal pay, which clarifies but does not add to the material scope of Article 119. It was on this ground that Advocate General Verloren van Themaat urged the Court to hold a Member State in breach of Article 141 (ex 119) E.C., rather than the Directive, in proceedings brought by the Commission under Article 226 (ex 169) E.C. The Court nonetheless held the Member State in default for failing to implement the Directive.[85] But as the Court commented in *Reyners* itself, Directives already issued under Article 44(2) (ex 54(2)) E.C. would not lose all interest, since they would "preserve an important scope in the field of measures intended to make easier the effective exercise of the right of freedom of establishment".[86] The Court was no doubt mindful of the value to the individual litigant before a national tribunal of some more precise formulation of his rights than the general prohibitions of the Treaty. In any event, the Commission formally withdrew a large number of proposed Directives on abolition of restrictions on freedom of establishment.

The prohibition in Article 43 (ex 52) of discrimination on grounds of nationality is not concerned solely with the specific rules on the pursuit of occupational activities but also with the rules relating to the various general

---

[82] Commission Communication, SEC (74) Final, Brussels.
[83] Case 48/75 *Royer* [1976] E.C.R. 497; [1976] 2 C.M.L.R. 619.
[84] [1975] O.J. L45/19.
[85] Case 58/81 *Commission v. Luxembourg* [1982] E.C.R. 2175.
[86] [1974] E.C.R. 631 at 652.

facilities which are of assistance in the pursuit of those activities, including access to housing, and to the facilities provided by national authorities to alleviate the financial burden of acquiring housing.[87]

Relationship between Article 12 (ex 6) and Articles 43 and 49 (ex 52 and 59) E.C.

Article 12 E.C. prohibits discrimination on grounds of nationality within the scope of operation of the Treaty. This general prohibition of discrimination has been implemented as regards freedom of establishment and the provision of services by Articles 43 and 49 (ex 52 and 59) E.C.[88] The Court has said that any rules incompatible with the latter articles are also incompatible with Article 12 (ex 6).[89] However, non-discriminatory rules which disadvantage a person by virtue of the fact that he has more than one place of business within the Community may be consistent with Article 12 but inconsistent with Article 43.[90] And non-discriminatory rules which amount to restrictions on the provision of services would be incompatible with Article 49 (ex 59), but consistent with Article 12 (ex.6).[91] Furthermore, Article 12 (ex 6) "applies independently only to situations governed by Community law in regard to which the Treaty lays down no specific prohibition of discrimination".[92]

Parallel interpretation of Articles 39, 43 and 49 (ex 48, 52 and 59) E.C.

Theoretically, problems may arise in differentiating between the employed and the self-employed, and between instances of establishment and provision of services, but it will in many cases be unnecessary to make any hard and fast classification, because the applicable principles will be the same in any event. Thus, in *Procureur du Roi v. Royer*,[93] the Court of Justice, considering a request for a preliminary ruling from a national court which was uncertain whether the subject of the proceedings before it was to be considered as falling within Article 39 (ex 48), Article 43 (ex 52) or Article 49 (ex 59), observed:

> ". . . comparison of these different provisions shows that they are based on the same principles both in so far as they concern the entry into and residence in the territory of Member States of persons covered by Community law

---

[87] Case 63/86 *Commission v. Italy* [1988] E.C.R. 129; [1989] 2 C.M.L.R. 601; Case 305/87 *Commission v. Greece* [1989] E.C.R. 1461; [1991] 1 C.M.L.R. 611.

[88] And as regards freedom of movement for workers, *ibid.*.

[89] Case 90/76 *Van Ameyde v. UCI* [1977] E.C.R. 1091; [1977] 2 C.M.L.R. 478 at 1126, para. 27; Case 305/87 *Commission v. Greece* [1989] E.C.R. 1461; [1991] 1 C.M.L.R. 611, para. 12.

[90] Case 143/87 *Stanton* [1988] E.C.R. 3877; [1989] 3 C.M.L.R. 761; Joined Cases 154–155/87 *Wolf* [1988] E.C.R. 3897.

[91] For the scope of Art. 49, see below p. 470 *et seq.*

[92] Case 305/87 *Commission v. Greece* [1989] E.C.R. 1461; [1991] 1 C.M.L.R. 611, at para. 13.

[93] Case 48/75 [1976] E.C.R. 497; [1976] 2 C.M.L.R. 619. And see Case 118/75 *Watson & Belmann* [1976] E.C.R. 1185; [1976] 2 C.M.L.R. 552.

and the prohibition of all discrimination between them on grounds of nationality."[94]

An important corollary is that Article 43 (ex 52), like Article 39 (ex 48), must be construed as prohibiting discrimination by private parties as well as by public authorities. In *Walrave v. Union cycliste internationale*,[95] the Court expressed the opinion that Article 39 (ex 48) E.C. extended to agreements and rules other than those emanating from public authorities, citing in support of its view the text of Article 7(4) of Regulation 1612/68, which nullifies discriminatory clauses in individual or collective employment agreements. A similar conclusion was justified in the case of Article 49 (ex 59), since the activities referred to therein were "not to be distinguished by their nature from those in Article 48 [now 39], but only by the fact that they are performed outside the ties of a contract of employment".[96] It follows that Article 43 (ex 52) has a similar ambit.

Direct and indirect discrimination

Article 43 (ex 52) prohibits both direct and indirect discrimination on grounds of nationality. Although the present section of this chapter is concerned with establishment of natural persons, for the purposes of examining direct and indirect discrimination it is appropriate to refer to examples involving both natural and legal persons. Direct discrimination takes place when individuals or undertakings are treated differently by reference to their nationality.

Examples of direct discrimination are:

— a requirement that nationals **of other Member States** set up a company incorporated in the host State before obtaining a licence to fish at sea[97];
— a requirement that in order for a ship to qualify for the nationality of a Member State, it must be **owned by nationals of that Member State**.[98]

In such cases the reference to nationality as a ground for differentiation is express, and such discrimination is described as "direct" or "overt".

The Court has held that Article 43 (ex 52) prohibits not only direct, or overt discrimination by reason of nationality but also all covert forms of discrimination which, by the application of other criteria of differentiation, lead in fact to the same result.[99] In *Commission v. Italy* a national measure providing that only companies in which all or a majority of the shares are either directly or indirectly in public or State ownership may conclude agreements for the development of data-processing systems for public authorities has been held to be contrary to

---

[94] [1976] E.C.R. 497 at 509. For parallel interpretation of Arts 39 (ex 48) and 43 (ex 52) see Case C–106/91 *Ramrath v. Ministre de la Justice* [1992] E.C.R. I–3351; [1992] 3 C.M.L.R. 173; [1995] 2 C.M.L.R. 187, para. 17; and Case C–107/94 *P.H. Asscher v. Staatssecretaris van Financiën* [1994] E.C.R. I–1137, para. 29.
[95] Case 36/74 [1974] E.C.R. 1405; [1975] 1 C.M.L.R. 320. For the application of Art. 39 to private parties see Case C–281/98 *Angonese* judgment of June 6, 2000, para. 36.
[96] [1974] E.C.R. 1405 at 1419.
[97] Case C–93/89 *Commission v. Ireland* [1991] E.C.R. I–4569; [1991] 3 C.M.L.R. 697.
[98] Case C–221/89 *Factortame* [1991] E.C.R. I–3905; [1991] 3 C.M.L.R. 589.
[99] Case C–3/88 *Commmission v. Italy* [1989] E.C.R. 4035; [1991] 2 C.M.L.R. 115.

Article 43 (ex 52).[1] The Court held that although the rules in issue applied without distinction to all companies, they *essentially favoured* domestic companies, and observed that no date-processing companies from other Member States qualified under the criteria in question at the material time.[2] In the *Asscher* case the Court identified as being potentially discriminatory legislation which was "liable to act mainly to the detriment of nationals of other Member States".[3] Criteria which have been identified as potential sources of indirect discrimination include the place of residence of self-employed persons or the principal place of establishment of companies.[4]

However, differentiation between situations on objective grounds consistent with the Treaty does not amount to prohibited discrimination. Although residence requirements may amount in certain cases to indirect discrimination,[5] the Court has held that a national law exempting rural land from compulsory acquisition if the owners have lived on or near the land for a specified period, is consistent with Article 43 (ex 52), where the purpose of the law is to ensure as far as possible that rural land belongs to those who work it, and where the law applies equally to its own nationals and to the nationals of other Member States.[6] Again, in *Commission v. France* the Court acknowledged the possibility that a distinction based on the location of the registered office of a company or the place of residence of a natural person might under certain conditions be justified in an area such as tax law.[7] Since the application of national tax rules are increasingly held to amount to restrictions on freedom of establishment, it is appropriate to give this particular matter further consideration.

National tax measures as restrictions on the right of establishment[8]

In *Commission v. France* the Court, *inter alia*, endorsed three propositions of considerable importance as regards the relationship between the right of establishment and the application of national tax legislation. The first proposition was that as regards the exercise of the right of establishment by companies, it was the location of their registered office, or central administration, or principal place of business, which served as the connecting factor with the legal system of a particular State, like nationality in the case of natural persons, and for a company seeking to establish itself in another Member State to be treated differently solely

---

[1] *ibid.*

[2] [1989] E.C.R. 4035 at paras 9–10.

[3] Case C–107/94 *P.H. Asscher v. Staatssecretaris van Financiën* [1994] E.C.R. I–1137; [1996] 3 C.M.L.R. 61, para. 38.

[4] Case C–1/93 *Halliburton Services v. Staatssecretaris van Financiën* [1994] E.C.R. I–1137; Case C–330/91 *R. v. Inland Revenue Commissioners, ex p. Commerzbank* [1993] E.C.R. I–4017; [1993] 3 C.M.L.R. 457; Case C–80/94 *Wielockx v. Inspecteur der Directe Belastingen* [1965] E.C.R. I–2493.

[5] Case C–80/94 *Wielockx v. Inspecteur der Directe Belastingen* [1995] E.C.R. I–2493; and see Case 152/73 *Sotgiu* and the discussion of indirect discrimination in the context of free movement of workers in Chap. 14 on p. 401.

[6] Case 182/83 *Fearon* [1984] E.C.R. 3677; [1985] 2 C.M.L.R. 228.

[7] Case 270/83 [1986] E.C.R. 273; [1987] 1 C.M.L.R. 401, at para. 19.

[8] The relevant case-law involves Art. 39 (ex 48), Art. 43 (ex 52) and Art. 49 (ex 59), and it is inappropriate to confine attention to the case-law on Art. 43, since the same principles apply as regards all the Treaty provisions mentioned.

by reason of the fact that its registered office etc., was situated in another Member State would deprive the right of establishment of all meaning.[9] The second proposition was that nevertheless the possibility could not "altogether be excluded" that a distinction based "on the location of the registered office of a company or the place of residence of a natural person may, under certain conditions, be justified in an area such as tax law".[10] The third proposition was that where national tax rules treat two forms of establishment in the same way for the purposes of taxing their profits (in the case in point, companies with a registered office in France on the one hand, and branches in France of companies with a registered office in another Member State on the other), that amounts to an admission that there is no objective difference between their positions as regards the detailed rules and conditions relating to that taxation which could justify different treatment.[11]

Even those with but the briefest familiarity with the intricacies of tax law will be aware that it frequently lays down different rules for residents and non-residents, whether they be individuals or companies. Yet it has been noted above that national rules which distinguish between individuals on the basis of their residence may amount to indirect discrimination on grounds of nationality, contrary to the free movement provisions of the Treaty.[12] And it will be noted that the criteria referred to in the second and third propositions derived from the judgment of the Court in *Commission v. France*, which allot to a company a status akin to that of the nationality, are also criteria used to determine the residence of a company. The result is that the application to individuals and companies of the residence criteria which are such a commonplace of the national tax regimes seem almost intrinsically to raise a question as to the application of Article 43 of the Treaty. The case-law certainly holds that the fact that a residence criterion is applied in the tax context is no guarantee of

---

[9] Case 270/83 [1986] E.C.R. 273; [1987] 1 C.M.L.R. 401, at para. 18. It seems from the context and from later case-law that what the Court means is that it is the registered office, central administration or principal place of business which determines the seat of the company, in accordance with relevant national rules, which comprises the relevant connecting factor, and that discrimination solely by reference to the fact that a company's seat is in another Member State is contrary to Art. 43 (ex 52), see Case C–311/97 *Royal Bank of Scotland plc v. Elliniko Dimosio (Greek State)* [1999] E.C.R. I–2651; [1999] 2 C.M.L.R. 973, para. 23.

[10] *ibid.*, para. 19. The better view is that this amounts to justification of indirect discrimination on grounds of nationality, rather than justification of direct discrimination, since the connecting factors referred to in Art. 48 (ex 58), *viz.*, registered office, *etc.*, not only comprise a link analogous to that of nationality, but may also be indicative of residence for tax purposes. Even if it is the case that direct discrimination on grounds of nationality cannot normally be justified, differentiation on grounds of residence may be so justified, perhaps particularly in the tax context, and it is to this latter possibility that the Court is referring in para. 19. Furthermore, the Court has accepted that it is consistent with Art. 39 (ex 48) for Member States to define nationality as one of the criteria for allocating their powers of taxation as between themselves, with a view to eliminating double taxation, see Case C–336/96 *Mr and Mrs Robert Gilly v. Directeur des Services Fiscaux du Bas-Rhin* [1998] E.C.R. I–2793; [1998] 3 C.M.L.R. 607, para. 30.

[11] Case 270/83 [1986] E.C.R. 273 at para. 20.

[12] See Chap. 14 at p. 402. For the proposition that differentiating between individuals on grounds of residence will amount to indirect discrimination on grounds of nationality unless justified, in the contest of freedom of movement for workers, see Case 152/73 *Sotgiu v. Deutsche Bundespost* [1974] E.C.R. 153; it is a case cited by the Court in support of the same proposition as regards companies in the context of Art. 43 (ex 52), see Case C–330/91 *R. v. Inland Revenue Commissioners, ex p. Commerzbank AG* [1993] E.C.R. I–4017; [1993] 3 C.M.L.R. 457, para. 14.

immunity from successful challenge under the Treaty. Thus in *Commerzbank* [13] the Court of Justice considered a national tax rule which restricted repayment supplement (a payment analogous to an interest payment) on overpaid tax to companies resident for tax purposes in the Member State in question. In the case in which the question arose a non-resident company had received a repayment of overpaid tax by virtue of non-residence, pursuant to a double tax convention, but been denied repayment supplement pursuant to the contested rule. The Court considered the rule was discriminatory, as follows:

"Although it applies independently of a company's seat, the use of the criterion of fiscal residence within national territory for the purpose of granting repayment supplement on overpaid tax is liable to work more particularly to the disadvantage of companies having their seat in other Member States. Indeed, it is most often those companies which are resident for tax purposes outside the territory of the Member State in question."[14]

The Member State in question argued that non-resident companies in the position of the claimant in the national proceedings, far from being discriminated against, enjoyed privileged treatment. They were exempt from tax normally payable by resident companies. In such circumstances there was no discrimination with respect to repayment supplement: resident companies and non-resident companies were treated differently because, for the purposes of corporation tax, there were in different situations.[15] The Court, however, did not accept that argument. The rule the benefit of which the non-resident company was denied was a rule allowing repayment supplement when tax was overpaid; the fact that the exemption from tax which gave rise to the refund was available only to non-resident companies could not justify a rule of a general nature withholding the benefit.[16]

In *Halliburton Services*[17] the Court considered the compatibility with Article 43 (ex 52) of an exemption from property transfer tax applicable in the case of an internal reorganisation of public limited companies and private limited companies, subject to the proviso that the companies party to the transfer were incorporated under the law of the Member State in question. The effect of the application of the Netherlands law in the national proceedings was that a transfer of property in the Netherlands from a German subsidiary of a U.S. company to a Netherlands subsidiary of the same U.S. company involved the liability of the latter subsidiary to the tax which would not have been payable if the transferor had also been a Netherlands company. The Netherlands Government argued that no discrimination was involved because the person liable to pay the tax was not the Germany company but the Netherlands company, which meant that the situation was purely internal to the Netherlands, and Community law was not involved. The Court rejected this argument, noting that "payment of a tax on the

---

[13] Case C–330/91 *R. v. Inland Revenue Commissioners, ex p. Commerzbank AG* [1993] E.C.R. I–4017; [1993] 3 C.M.L.R. 457.

[14] *ibid.*, para. 15.

[15] *ibid.*, para. 16.

[16] *ibid.*, paras 18–19.

[17] Case C–1/93 *Halliburton Services BV v. Staatssecretaris van Financiën* [1994] E.C.R. I–1137; [1994] 3 C.M.L.R. 377.

sale of immovable property constitutes a burden which renders the conditions of sale of the property more onerous and thus has repercussions on the position of the transferor".[18] The Court concluded that although "the difference in treatment has only an indirect effect on the position of companies constituted under the law of other Member States, it constitutes discrimination on grounds of nationality" prohibited by Article 43 (ex 52).[19] The Netherlands Government argued that the restriction of the exemption to companies constituted under national law was necessary because the competent tax administration was unable to check whether the legal forms of entities constituted in other Member States were equivalent to those of public and private limited companies within the meaning of the relevant national legislation. The Court rejected this argument because information relating to the characteristics of the forms in which companies can be constituted in other Member States could be obtained pursuant to Community legislation on mutual assistance by the competent authorities of the Member States in the field of direct taxation.[20]

It will be noted that in both *Commerzbank* and *Halliburton* the Court approached the question of indirect discrimination in the same way as it has approached that concept in other cases concerning the right of establishment, and in cases involving the free movement of workers. Thus, the Court showed itself willing, in principle, to examine whether the position of the non-resident was comparable to that of the resident, for the purpose of examining whether the national rule was discriminatory (*Commerzbank*), and to examine whether the difference in treatment could be justified (*Halliburton*). But in the *Bachmann* case[21] the Court introduced a new element, the concept of "the need to preserve the cohesion of the tax system". In the case in question a German national employed in Belgium, who made payments in respect of sickness invalidity and life insurance in Germany under arrangements made prior to his arrival in Belgium, challenged Belgian tax rules whereby contributions to sickness and invalidity and life insurance contracts were only tax deductible if paid to insurers based in Belgium. The Court noted that workers who have carried on an occupation in one Member State and who are subsequently employed in another Member State will normally have concluded their pension and life assurance contracts or invalidity and sickness insurance contracts with insurers established in the first State. It followed that there was "a risk that the provisions in question may operate to the particular detriment of those workers who are, as a general rule, nationals of other Member States". The Court however found that the restriction on freedom of movement involved could be justified, since there existed under Belgian law a connection between the deductibility of contributions and the liability to tax of sums payable by insurers under pension and life assurance contracts; under the tax system in question the loss of revenue resulting from the deduction of contributions was offset by the taxation of pensions, annuities or capital sums payable by the insurers. The Court stated:

---

[18] *ibid.*, para. 19.
[19] *ibid.*, para. 20.
[20] *ibid.*, para. 22.
[21] Case C–204/90 *Bachmann v. Belgian State* [1992] E.C.R. I–249; [1993] 1 C.M.L.R. 785; see also Case C–300/90 *Commission v. Belgium* [1992] E.C.R. I–305; [1993] 1 C.M.L.R. 785.

"The cohesion of such a tax system, the formulation of which is a matter for each Member State, therefore presupposes that, in the event of a State being obliged to allow the deduction of life assurance contributions paid in another Member State, it should be able to tax sums payable by insurers"[22]

Since it was not possible to guarantee that sums payable in other Member States could be subject to such tax to compensate for the tax deductibility of the contributions, the rules in question comprised the least restrictive rules possible, compatible with maintaining the cohesion of the tax system in question.

On the face of it, it is not easy to see how the introduction of the concept of the cohesion of the tax system was either necessary or appropriate in *Bachmann*. A more conventional analysis would have been to the effect that the situation of a migrant paying insurance contributions in Germany was not comparable with that of a non-migrant paying insurance contributions in Belgium because the resulting pension would in the latter case be taxable in Belgium and in the former case not. Alternatively, one could say that any difference in treatment between the two cases was objectively justifiable and proportionate.[23] In truth, the comparability test, and objective justification, are two sides of the same coin. The most plausible explanation of the "cohesion" formulation in *Bachmann* is that it simply represented a ground which objectively justified the difference in treatment to which objection was made. It appears from later case-law however that the formulation may be used as an additional test to that of comparability/objective justification, or as a yardstick to determine the outcome of arguments which are essentially arguments about comparability or objective justification. This would seem to be a matter of purely technical significance as long as the "cohesion" argument is applied to the same effect as arguments based on comparability/objective justification.

The second of the three propositions referred to above as having been endorsed by the Court of Justice in *Commission v. France*, to the effect that the possibility could not "altogether be excluded" that a distinction based "on the location of the registered office of a company or the place of residence of a natural person may, under certain conditions, be justified in an area such as tax law"[24] seemed to understate the significance of individual or corporate residence as a connecting factor with a State for tax purposes, and in later cases the Court allowed that "in relation to direct taxes, the situations of residents and of non-residents in a given State are not generally comparable, since there are objective differences between them from the point of view of the source of the income and the possibility of taking account of their ability to pay tax or their personal and family circumstances."[25] While the Court has acknowledged that "direct taxation

---

[22] *Bachmann*, para. 23.
[23] Unless it is objectively justified and proportionate to its aim, a provision of national law must be regarded as indirectly discriminatory if it is intrinsically liable to affect migrant workers and if there is a consequent risk that it will place the former at a disadvantage, Case C–237/94 *John O'Flynn v. Adjudication Officer* [1996] E.C.R. I–2617; [1996] 3 C.M.L.R. 103, para. 20; Case 57/96 *H. Meints v. Minister van Landbouw* [1997] E.C.R. I–6689; [1998] C.M.L.R. 1159, para. 45.
[24] Case 270/83 [1986] E.C.R. 273; [1987] 1 C.M.L.R. 401, para. 19.
[25] Case C–279/93 *Finanzamt Köln-Alstadt v. Schumacker* [1995] E.C.R. I–225; [1996] 2 C.M.L.R. 450, para. 31; Case C–80/94 *Wielockx v. Inspecteur der Directe Belastingen* [1995] E.C.R. I–2493, para. 18; Case C–107/94 *P.H. Asscher v. Staatssecretaris van Financiën* [1994] E.C.R. I–1137, para. 41.

does not as such fall within the purview of the Community", it has emphasised that "the powers retained by the Member States must nevertheless be exercised consistently with Community law",[26] and this in turn means examining in detail the distinctions drawn between resident and non-resident tax-payers to establish whether they are indeed compatible with Community law. While the situations of residents and of non-residents are not generally comparable, if they are comparable, and yet the non-resident is treated less favourably than the resident, this will amount to discrimination, and be contrary to Article 43 (ex 52).[27] Thus in *Schumacker* the Court held that it will not be discriminatory to deny to a non-resident certain tax benefits paid to a resident, where the major part of the income of the resident is concentrated in the State of residence, and the latter State has available all the information needed to assess the taxpayer's overall ability to pay, while this is not so in the case of the non-resident.[28] But the position will be different where the non-resident receives no significant income in the State of his residence and obtains the major part of his taxable income from an activity performed in the State of employment, with the result that the State of his residence is not in a position to grant him the benefits resulting from the taking into account of his personal and family circumstances.[29] The Court concluded that there was no objective difference between the situations of such a non-resident and a resident engaged in comparable employment, such as to justify different treatment as regards the taking into account for taxation purposes of the taxpayer's personal and family circumstances.[30] Such a finding is really the same as a finding that the difference in treatment effected by the national tax rules cannot be objectively justified, yet the Court goes on to deal with further arguments of Member States in the proceedings, which are also essentially to the effect that the position of such a non-resident is *not* comparable to that of a resident, on the basis that these arguments raise the question of the need for cohesion of the tax system. This is probably explicable on the basis that if that is the way the Member States argued the points in question before the Court, then that is the way the Court considered it appropriate to deal with them.

In *Asscher*,[31] the question arose before the referring court whether it was compatible with Article 43 (ex 52) for the Netherlands to tax a person resident in Belgium and carrying on business in its territory at a higher rate than a resident, in order to offset the fact that certain non-residents escape the progressive nature of the tax because their tax obligations are confined to income received in the Netherlands. The Court of Justice noted that it was open to Belgium, the state of

---

[26] See, *e.g.* Case C–279/93 *Finanzamt Köln-Alstadt v. Schumacker* [1995] E.C.R. I–225; [1996] 2 C.M.L.R. 450, para. 21, citing Case C–246/89 *Commission v. United Kingdom* [1991] E.C.R. I–4585; [1991] 3 C.M.L.R. 706, para. 12.

[27] See, *e.g.* Case C–279/93 *Finanzamt Köln-Alstadt v. Schumacker* [1995] E.C.R. I–225; [1996] 2 C.M.L.R. 450, (the case concerns Art. 39 (ex 48)); Case C–80/94 *Wielockx v. Inspecteur der Directe Belastingen* [1995] E.C.R. I–2493 (Art. 43 (ex 52)).

[28] Case C–279/93 *Finanzamt Köln-Alstadt v. Schumacker* [1995] E.C.R. I–225; [1996] 2 C.M.L.R. 450, paras 33–35.

[29] *ibid.*, para. 36. *Schumacker* is distinguished in Case C–391/97 *Frans Gschwind v. Finanzamt Aachen-Außenstadt* [1999] E.C.R. I–5451.

[30] *ibid.*, para. 37.

[31] Case C–107/94 *P.H. Asscher v. Staatssecretaris van Financiën* [1994] E.C.R. I–1137; [1996] All E.R. (E.C.) 757.

residence, pursuant to the relevant double taxation convention between Belgium and the Netherlands, to take account of income earned in the Netherlands in order to apply progressive rates of tax when taxing income arising in Belgium. The Court of Justice concluded that the fact that a taxpayer was a non-resident did not enable him to avoid, in the circumstances under consideration, the application of progressive rates of tax, and that resident and non-resident taxpayers in the Netherlands were thus in a comparable situation as regards the application of progressive rates of tax. It is to be noted that the Court treats as comparable to a Netherlands resident taxpayer who will have *Netherlands progressive tax rates* calculated by reference to the resident's entire income and applied to his Netherlands income, a Belgian resident taxpayer who works in the Netherlands and who will not have *Netherlands* progressive rates applied to take account of his income outside the Netherlands but will have *Belgian progressive tax rates* calculated by reference to his Netherlands income and imposed on his Belgian income. This is an analogous approach to that recognised as applicable where, pursuant to Article 39 (ex 48) an employer in one Member State is obliged to take account of military service, or public employment, in another Member State.[32] Having decided that the situation of the two are comparable, the Court goes on to examine whether the difference in tax rates can be *justified* because the non-resident is not subject to social security payments, and thereby enjoys a tax advantage over residents, and then to examine whether the difference can be justified *by the need to ensure cohesion of the tax system*, in view of the self-same fact—that the non-resident is exempt from social security contributions. Once again, however, there is no indication that application of the "cohesion" criterion makes any difference to the substance of the analysis which would be undertaken solely on the basis of comparability/objective justification.

In *Wielockx*[33] the Court considered a question which on the face of it raised essentially the same issue as that in *Bachmann*; whether it was compatible with Article 43 (ex 52) to allow residents to deduct from their taxable income business profits which they allocate to form a pension reserve, while denying that benefit to non-resident taxpayers who receive all or almost all of their income in the State in question. In this case however, there was a further issue—whether the difference in treatment could be justified by the fact that periodic pension payments subsequently drawn out of a pension reserve by the non-resident taxpayer would not be taxed in the State in which he worked but in the State of residence with which the first State had concluded a double tax convention. The Court regarded it as discriminatory to deny the advantage to non-residents in the circumstances identified by the referring court, since the non-resident receiving all or almost all his income in the State where he works was objectively in the same situation in so far as concerns income tax as a resident doing the same work there. The Court then turned to the question whether the non-deductibility could nevertheless be justified by the principle of social cohesion, as in *Bachmann*. But

---

[32] See Case 44/72 *Marsman v. Rosskamp* [1972] E.C.R. 1243; [1973] C.M.L.R. 501; Case C–419/92 *Scholz v. Opera Universitaria di Cagliari* [1994] E.C.R. I–505; [1994] 1 C.M.L.R. 873.
[33] Case C–80/94 *Wielockx v. Inspecteur der Directe Belastingen* [1995] E.C.R. I–2493; [1995] All E.R. (E.C.) 769.

the Court in effect distinguishes the latter case by reference to the terms of the double taxation convention mentioned by the referring court. The Court stated:

". . . the effect of double-taxation conventions which, like the one referred to above, follow the OECD model is that the State taxes all pensions received by residents in its territory, whatever the State in which the contributions were paid, but, conversely, waives the right to tax pensions received abroad even if they derive from contributions paid in its territory which it treated as deductible. Fiscal cohesion has not therefore been established in relation to one and the same person by a strict correlation between the deductibility of contributions and the taxation of pensions but is shifted to another level, that of the reciprocity of the rules applicable in the Contracting States."[34]

It is to be noted that the approaches in *Aascher* and *Wielockx* are in substance very similar. In the former case the national rule discriminates against non-residents because it fails to take account of the application of progressive tax rates in the country of residence based on earnings in both the State of residence and of work. In the latter case the national rule discriminates against non-residents because it refuses tax deductibility on pension contributions on the ground that it cannot tax the resulting pensions, without taking account of the fact that the pensions will be taxed in the country of residence. In each case the duty to take account of the application of the tax rules of the State of residence results from the terms of a double taxation convention. But whereas in the former case the terms of the double taxation convention establish comparability, in the latter case the double taxation convention establishes fiscal cohesion!

In *ICI v. Colmer (Her Majesty's Inspector of Taxes)*[35] the Court considered whether Article 43 (ex 52) precluded United Kingdom legislation which, in the case of companies established in that State belonging to a consortium through which they control a holding company, makes a particular form of tax relief ("consortium relief") subject to the requirement that the holding company's business consist wholly or mainly in the holding of shares in subsidiaries that have their seat in the Member State concerned. The Court considered that the requirement that the above-mentioned subsidiaries be wholly or mainly United Kingdom resident subsidiaries could inhibit exercise of the right of establishment by the holding company in a Member State other than the United Kingdom. One of the arguments put forward by the United Kingdom was that consortium relief was intended to place consortium companies in a comparable tax position to that which would apply if they had participated directly in the business undertaken by the joint venture comprised by the consortium, so as to permit those contemplating carrying on business through consortia to choose the appropriate organisational structure according to commercial rather than tax considerations,[36] and that this purpose could only be properly achieved if limitations were placed on participation by non-resident subsidiaries, since tax relief on losses incurred by

---

[34] *ibid.*, para. 24.
[35] Case C–264/96 [1998] E.C.R. I–4695; [1998] C.M.L.R. 293.
[36] Opinion of Advocate General Tesauro at para. 27; Noel Travers, "Residence Restraints on the transferability of corporate trading losses and the right of establishment in Community Law" (1999) 24 E.L. Rev. 403, at p. 406.

resident subsidiaries would be off-set by taxes on the profits of resident companies, but not be off-set by tax on the profits of *non*-resident subsidiaries (which would not be subject to tax). The Court said that the "argument that revenue lost through the granting of tax relief on losses incurred by resident subsidiaries cannot be offset by taxing the profits of non-resident subsidiaries" could not be regarded "as a matter of overriding general interest which could be relied upon to justify unequal treatment that is, in principle incompatible with Article 52".[37] The Court also rejected the argument that the principle of tax cohesion could justify the difference in treatment since in the *Bachmann* case there was a "direct link between the deductibility of contributions from taxable income and the taxation of sums payable by insurers" whereas in the instant case there was no such direct link between the consortium relief granted for losses incurred by a resident subsidiary and the taxation of profits made by non-resident subsidiaries.[38] This case seems somewhat satisfactory since it does not address as clearly as in former cases the question of comparability between the tax position of resident and non resident subsidiaries. It does not explain why the rationale of consortium relief does not provide a basis for distinguishing between holding companies whose business consisted wholly or mainly in the holding of shares in resident subsidiaries and those whose business did not. Nor does it explain why the rationale of consortium relief does not establish what it describes as the "direct link" between losses incurred by a resident subsidiary and the taxation of profits made by non-resident subsidiaries.

In *Futura Participations SA*[39] a non-resident taxpayer complained that Luxembourg rules allowing the carrying forward of tax losses limited this possibility to profits and losses arising from Luxembourg activities as regards non-residents, but imposed no such limitation in respect of residents. The Court held that this involved neither overt nor covert discrimination, since resident companies were chargeable to tax in respect of all their income, the basis of assessment not being limited to their Luxembourg activities, whereas for non-resident taxpayers the basis of assessment was comprised only profits and losses arising from their Luxembourg activities. This succinct formulation amounts to a conclusion that the position of non-resident and resident companies are not comparable, or— which amounts to the same thing—that any distinction drawn between the two is objectively justifiable.

It was noted above that the Court held in *Commission v. France* that differential tax treatment by a Member State of companies with their seat in that State, and the branches established in that State of companies with their seats in other Member States, might infringe Article 43 (ex 52).[40] In *Saint-Gobain*[41] the Court considered a situation in which German tax rules made provision for certain tax concessions to be enjoyed by companies having their seat in Germany,

---

[37] *ibid.*, para. 28.
[38] *ibid.*, para. 29.
[39] Case C–250/95 *Futura Participations SA v. Administrations des Contributions* [1997] E.C.R. I–2471; [1997] 3 C.M.L.R. 483. See also Case C–311/97 *Royal Bank of Scotland v. Elliniko Dimosio (Greek State)* [1999] E.C.R. I–2651; [1999] 2 C.M.L.R. 973.
[40] Case 270/83 see above, p. 448.
[41] Case C–307/97 *Compagnie de Saint-Gobain, Zweighniederlassung Deutschland v. Finanzamt Aachen-Innenstadt* [1999] E.C.R. I–6161.

but made no such provision for permanent establishments in Germany of companies their seats in other Member States. The German Government argued, *inter alia*, that the refusal to allow the tax concessions to the latter establishments was justified by the need to prevent a reduction in tax revenue given the impossibility for the German tax authorities to compensate for the reduction in revenue brought about by the grant of the tax concessions in question by taxing dividends distributed by non-resident companies, but the Court rejected this argument, referring to the *ICI* case.[42] The Court considered that the difference in treatment to which branches of non-resident companies were subject in comparison with resident companies, as well as the restriction of the freedom to choose the form of secondary establishment, were to be regarded as constituting a "single composite infringement" of Articles 43 (ex 52) and 48 (ex 58) E.C., which could not be justified by any matters of overriding general interest.

Non-discriminatory restrictions on the right of establishment

It has been noted in the section of this Chapter on the evolution of the Court's case-law on Article 43 (ex 52) that in *Kraus* and *Gebhard* the Court adopted the concept of the non-discriminatory restriction on establishment,[43] applicable in circumstances other than those in which an individual or company sought a right of "exit" from a Member State, or asserted the right to a place of business in more than one Member State. The question to be addressed is in *which* circumstances the non-discriminatory restriction will be prohibited, since despite the compendious formulation which appears in *Gebhard*,[44] which purports to prohibit discriminatory and non-discriminatory restrictions alike, the Court continues to apply the test of discrimination in numerous cases which come before it. Thus a number of the tax cases referred to in the previous section of this Chapter post-date *Gebhard*, yet they apply the test of discrimination to determine whether tax rates or tax reliefs applicable to natural or legal persons exercising their right of establishment are to be regarded as compatible with Article 43 (ex 52). Indeed, in *Royal Bank of Scotland*, a tax case, the Court states:

> "It is common ground that the essential aim of Article 52 of the Treaty is to implement, in the field of self-employment, the principle of equal treatment laid down in Article 6 of the Treaty."[45]

The present writer has already indicated, in Chapter 14, what is believed to be the scope of the prohibition on non-discriminatory restrictions laid down by Article 39 (ex 48) E.C.,[46] and it follows that Article 43 (ex 52) should have a similar scope, that is to say that that national measures which apply to the *entry and residence* of self-employed persons, and to their *access* to self-employed activities, or apply in any other way specifically to the transfer of the self-

---

[42] Judgment, para. 50.

[43] Above at p. 437 *et seq.*

[44] Above at p. 438.

[45] Case C–311/97 *Royal Bank of Scotland v. Elliniko Dimosio (Greek State)* [1999] E.C.R. I–2651; [1999] 2 C.M.L.R. 973, para. 21. Tax rules affecting access to the market might, however, be subject to scrutiny under Art. 43 even if not discriminatory.

[46] Above at p. 409.

employed person from one Member State to another for the purposes of self-employment, will be prohibited by Article 43 (ex 52) if they restrict or impede freedom of establishment, even if they do not discriminate, directly or indirectly, on grounds of nationality. Thus national measures which do not discriminate on grounds of nationality, but place at a disadvantage those who have exercised their right of freedom of establishment, as compared to those who have not, will be regarded as impeding the exercise of freedom of movement. But if a self-employed person is allowed entry and residence in a Member State, and is allowed access to self-employed activities in that Member State, it should not in principle be possible to object to national rules which relate to the conduct of his business activities rather than to access to the relevant market, solely on the ground that those rules might be described as excessively burdensome to those subject to them. *Gebhard* is consistent with this view, as is the indication in the *Royal Bank of Scotland* that the *essential aim* of Article 43 (ex 52) is the principle of equal treatment. It is however appropriate to consider other cases in which the Court has had recourse to the *Gebhard* formulation; it being borne in mind that the latter formulation covers both discriminatory and non-discriminatory restrictions, and that the purpose of the enquiry is to establish in what circumstances measures which are not discriminatory are nevertheless held to be restrictive of the right of establishment and to require justification.

It will be recalled that in *Futura Participations SA*[47] the Court considered Luxembourg rules which allowed the carrying forward of tax losses but limited this possibility to profits and losses arising from Luxembourg activities in the case of non-residents, while imposing no such limitation in respect of residents. The Court applied the test of discrimination to determine the compatibility of the rules in question with Article 43 (ex 52). But there was a second issue in *Futura*, namely, whether it was compatible with Article 43 (ex 52) to require non-residents, during the financial year in which the losses the taxpayer sought to carry forward were incurred, to have kept in Luxembourg accounts complying with the relevant national rules. As regards this issue the Court refers to the *Gebhard* test.[48] But the Court says of the national requirement in question that it

"may constitute a restriction, within the meaning of Article 52 of the Treaty, on the freedom of establishment of a company or firm . . . where that company or firm wishes to establish a branch in a Member State different from that in which it has its seat."[49]

This makes it clear that the Court regards the condition as one which specifically restricts the setting up by a company of a secondary establishment in another Member State. And the Court goes on to describe the imposition of such a condition as one which "specifically affects companies or firms having their seat in another Member State", which is in principle prohibited by Article 43 (ex 52), since it involves such a company or firm keeping, in addition to its own accounts

---

[47] Above at p. 455.
[48] Case C–250/95 *Futura Participations SA v. Administrations des Contributions* [1997] E.C.R. I–2471; [1997] 3 C.M.L.R. 483, at para. 26.
[49] *ibid.*, para. 24.

which comply with the tax accounting rules applicable in the Member State in which it has its seat, separate accounts for its branch's activities complying with the tax accounting rules applicable in the State in which the branch is established. This part of the Court's judgment, however seems to amount to a finding that the measure in question is indirectly *discriminatory,* since it imposes a requirement on companies or firms having a seat in another Member State which is in practice more burdensome than that imposed on domestic companies.[50] In truth, recourse to the *Gebhard/Kraus/Bosman* formulation as regards the restriction in question seems indistinguishable from asking whether the measure is indirectly discriminatory, and if so, whether it can be objectively justified.

But that is not to say that all the Court's case-law dealing with national restrictions which require to be justified in order to be regarded as compatible with Article 43 (ex 52) can be rationalised as case-law on indirect discrimination. Thus in *Sodemare* [51] the Court considered national rules which limited certain activities to non-profit-making organisations, and whether in particular such a rule amounted to a restriction on the right of establishment of a profit-making private company established in another Member State. In concluding that such a rule was compatible with the Treaty the Court referred to case-law which indicated that non-discriminatory restrictions on the free movement of goods could be justified on the basis that Member States retained the power to organise their social security systems and to adopt, in particular, provisions intended to govern the consumption of pharmaceutical preparations in order to promote the financial stability of their health-care insurance schemes.[52] It is true that the Court notes that a restriction such as that in issue does not place profit-making companies from other Member States in a less favourable factual or legal situation than similar domestic companies, but if this were in itself enough to condone the national measure the reference to national competence to organise their social security systems would have been unnecessary.[53] The national rule in *Sodemare* was of course one which restricted the *access* by a foreign company to the domestic market and it is on this basis that it was necessary to justify even a non-discriminatory restriction.

In *Pfeiffer Großhandel*[54] the Court considered whether a restraining order pursuant to national law which prevented an Austrian subsidiary of a German parent operating 139 discount stores in Austria from using the trade name "Plus"—a trade name which the subsidiary had begun to use to market its goods. The Court referred to the *Gebhard* test and stated:

"A restraining order of the type sought by the plaintiff in the main proceedings operates to the detriment of undertakings whose seat is in another Member

---

[50] On direct and indirect discrimination, see above at p. 446.

[51] Case C–70/95 *Sodemare SA, etc., v. regione Lombardia* [1997] E.C.R. I–3395; [1998] 4 C.M.L.R. 667.

[52] The Court refers to Case 238/82 *Duphar and Others v. Netherlands State* [1984] E.C.R. 523, para. 16; see *Sodemare*, para. 27.

[53] The same is true of the *Duphar* case; the absence of discrimination referred to in that case was significant since discriminatory national measures could only be justified under Art. 30 (ex 36); see Chap. 13 at p. 355.

[54] Case C–255/97 *Pfeiffer Großhandel Gmbh v. Löwa Warenahndel Gmbh* [1999] E.C.R. I–2835.

State where they lawfully use a trade name which they would like to use beyond the boundaries of that State. Such an order is liable to constitute an impediment to the realisation by those undertakings of a uniform advertising concept at Community level since it may force them to adjust the presentation of the businesses they operate according to the place of establishment."[55]

It is possible to see in this judgment the basis of a potentially far-reaching principle that any national measure which might constitute an impediment to the realisation by a company of a "uniform advertising concept at Community level" is to be treated as prima facie contrary to Article 43 (ex 52) and must accordingly be justified by imperative requirements in the public interest. This could be seen as indicating a rather different approach than that taken in the movement of goods context by the judgments in *Leclerc-Siplec* and *De Agostini*,[56] and to be vulnerable to the defects of the pre-*Keck* case-law on the movement of goods.[57] But a narrower analysis of the above case is possible and more plausible. It is that preventing a national of one Member State or a company with its seat in one Member State from carrying out economic activities in another Member State under a title or trade name which it is entitled to use in the first Member State is to be regarded as in principle a restriction on *access* to the market of that State. It has been suggested that this is an appropriate analysis of the *Kraus* judgment,[58] and this approach would allow at least a broad analogy to be drawn with case-law on the movement of goods concerning national rules preventing the marketing of goods under home country designation.[59]

Support for the view that Article 43 (ex 52) is to be given an interpretation which, while not necessarily precisely the same as that of Article 28 (ex 30), post *Keck*, is at any rate analogous, and will lead to a similar outcome in similar cases, is to be found in *Semeraro Casa Uno Srl*,[60] in which the Court considered whether national rules which (save for certain products) required retail shops to close on Sundays and public holidays, were contrary to Article 28 (ex 30) or Article 39 (ex 52). As regards Article 28 (ex 30) the Court referred to *Keck*, and concluded that such national rules amounted to non-discriminatory selling arrangements and were consistent with Article 28 (ex 30). As regards Article 43 (ex 52) the Court, referring to its reasoning concerning Article 28 (ex 30), stated:

"As far as Article 52 is concerned, suffice it to state that, as has been found above, the legislation in question is applicable to all traders exercising their activity on national territory; that its purpose is not to regulate the conditions concerning the establishment of the undertakings concerned; and that any restrictive effects which it might have on freedom of establishment are too uncertain and indirect for the obligation laid down to be regarded as being capable of hindering that freedom."[61]

---

[55] *ibid.*, at para. 20. Para. 19 refers to indirect discrimination, but the analysis in para. 20 does not disclose such discrimination.

[56] Chap. 13 at p. 333.

[57] For a discussion of the *Keck* case, see Chap. 13, at p. 331 *et seq.*

[58] Chap. 14 at p. 412.

[59] Chap. 13 at p. 326.

[60] Joined Cases C–418/93 *etc.*, *Semeraro Casa Uno Srl v. Sindaco de Comune di Erbusco etc.*, [1996] E.C.R. I–2975.

[61] *ibid.* at para. 32.

The above formulation is clearly akin to that applicable to "selling arrangements" pursuant to the *Keck* judgment. But while one would expect a similar outcome in similar cases, irrespective of whether a national measure fell to be assessed under Article 28 (ex 30) or Article 43 (ex 52), or indeed Article 39 (ex 48), cases which are superficially similar may raise essentially different issues. Thus reasoning essentially the same as that cited above has been used to justify the conclusion that national rules on the licensing of shops are consistent with Article 28 (ex 30);[62] but it would not automatically follow that such rules would escape scrutiny in all cases under Article 43 (ex 52), since licensing of a place of business might be said to affect access to self-employed activities.

Mutual recognition of diplomas and the co-ordination of national qualifications—direct applicability of Article 43 and secondary legislation

Article 47(1) (ex 57(1)) provides that the Council shall issue directives for the mutual recognition of diplomas, certificates, and other evidence of formal qualifications.

Even in the absence of directives under Article 47 (ex 57), recognition of foreign diplomas may be required under Article 43, prohibiting discrimination on grounds of nationality, as *Thieffry v. Paris Bar Council*[63] shows. A Belgian national held a Belgian law degree recognised by the University of Paris as equivalent to a French law degree. He acquired the qualifying certificate for the profession of advocate, but the Paris Bar Council refused to allow him to undergo practical training on the ground that he did not possess a French law degree. The Court of Justice held that such a refusal could amount to indirect discrimination prohibited by Article 43 (ex 52) E.C. As the General Programme for the abolition of restrictions on freedom of establishment made clear in Title III(B), the Council proposed to eliminate not only overt discrimination, but also any form of disguised discrimination, including "Any requirements imposed . . . in respect of the taking up or pursuit of an activity as a self-employed person where, although applicable irrespective of nationality, their effect is exclusively or principally to hinder the taking up or pursuit of such activity by foreign nationals".[64] It would be for the competent national authorities, taking account of the requirements of Community law, to judge whether a recognition granted by a university authority could, in addition to its academic effect, constitute valid evidence of a professional qualification. The Court has subsequently emphasised that a Member State, dealing with a request for authorisation to practise a profession access to which is under national legislation subject to the holding of a diploma or professional qualification, is obliged to take into account qualifications acquired in another Member State, by carrying out a comparison between the skills evidenced by those diplomas and the knowledge and qualifications

---

[62] Chap. 13, at p. 337.

[63] Case 71/76 [1977] E.C.R. 765; [1977] 2 C.M.L.R. 373. See Case 11/77 *Patrick* [1977] E.C.R. 119; [1977] 2 C.M.L.R. 523; and Case 65/77 *Razanatsimba* [1977] E.C.R. 2229; [1978] 1 C.M.L.R. 246 (Lomé Convention, Art. 62).

[64] [1974] O.J. Eng. Spec.Ed., Second Series, IX, p. 8.

required by national rules.[65] In the context of that review a Member State might take into consideration objective differences relating to the legal context of the profession concerned in the Member State of origin and it field of activity.[66] If such a comparison indicates the possession of a qualification equivalent to that required by the national law of the host State, the Member State is bound to accept the person concerned as being qualified. If the comparison shows only partial equivalence, the host State has the right to require that the person concerned should demonstrate that he has acquired the additional knowledge and qualifications needed.[67] Comparison of the national qualifications must be carried out according to a procedure complying with the requirements of Community law relating to the effective protection of fundamental rights conferred by the Treaty on nationals of Member States.[68] It follows that it must be possible for any decision to be made the subject of judicial proceedings in which its legality under Community law can be reviewed and it must be possible for the person concerned to ascertain the reasons for the decision.[69]

In addition to the right to claim recognition of equivalent qualifications as such pursuant to Article 43 (ex 52) it would seem to follow from *Kraus* and *Pfeiffer* that the latter Article also gives nationals of Member States the right, subject to relevant mandatory requirements in the public interest, to carry on economic activities under a title, or, in the case of an undertaking, a trade name, acquired in another Member State.[70] This right to practise under "home title" which is derived directly from the Treaty, provides the basis for the provisions of Directive 98/5 which deal with the right of a lawyer qualified in one Member State to practise under that title in the territory of another Member State.[71]

Paragraphs (1) and (2) of Article 47 (ex 57) provide, respectively, for the "mutual recognition of diplomas, certificates, and other evidence of formal qualifications," and for "the coordination of the provisions laid down by law, regulation or administrative action in Member States concerning the taking up and pursuit of activities as self-employed persons."

The General Programme contemplated transitional measures, whereby access to non-wage-earning activities might be allowed on proof of "actual and legitimate exercise of the activity in the country of origin".[72] An example of such a transitional regime is provided by Directive 75/369, dealing with the activities of itinerant tradespeople, such as fairground operators.[73] The Directive provides that where, in the case of its own nationals, a Member State requires documentary evidence of good repute, or of never having been declared bankrupt, it must

---

[65] Case 222/86 *UNECTEF v. Heylens* [1987] E.C.R. 4097; [1989] 1 C.M.L.R. 901; Case C–340/89 *Vlassopoulou v. Ministerium für Justiz, Bundes- und Europaangelegenheiten Baden-Württemberg* [1990] E.C.R. I–2327; [1993] 2 C.M.L.R. 221.

[66] Case C–340/89 *Vlassopoulou* [1990] E.C.R. I–2327; [1993] 2 C.M.L.R. 221, para. 18.

[67] *ibid.*, para. 19.

[68] *ibid.*, para. 22. See also Case C–234/97 *Teresa Fernández de Bobadilla v. Museo Nacional del Prado, Comité de Empresa del Museo Nacional del Prado and Ministerio Fiscal* [1999] E.C.R. I–4773; [1999] 3 C.M.L.R. 151.

[69] *ibid.*, para. 22.

[70] See above, p. 458.

[71] [1998] O.J. L77/36. See below, p. 463.

[72] [1974] O.J. Spec.Ed. Second Series, IX, p. 10.

[73] [1975] O.J. L167/29.

accept, in the case of nationals of other Member States, appropriate equivalent documentation issued in their country of origin.[74] Where no such documentation is issued, the host State must accept a declaration on oath, or a solemn declaration, made before, and duly certified by, a competent judicial or executive authority in the appropriate country of origin.[75] Where in a Member State the pursuit of the activities in question is subject to the possession of "general, commercial or professional knowledge and ability", that Member State must accept as sufficient evidence of such knowledge and ability the fact that the activity in question has been previously carried on in another Member State.[76] The period required is either two or three years, depending on whether it was completed in an employed or self-employed capacity, and on whether or not the relevant experience was preceded by a course of training.[77]

The Directive applies also to employees,[78] no doubt because differences in national vocational requirements are as capable of constituting an obstacle to the free movement of workers as they are of hindering that of the self-employed.

All in all, there has been considerable progress over the years in bringing about freedom of establishment for various professions. Directive 93/16 to facilitate the free movement of doctors and the mutual recognition of their diplomas, certificates and other evidence of formal qualifications, is worthy of mention.[79] It consolidates and repeals the original directives on the mutual recognition of medical diplomas and the co-ordination of national medical qualifications.[80] In the case of non-specialist medicine, the Directive requires that each Member State recognise diplomas awarded to nationals of the Member States by other Member States in accordance with the requirements specified in Article 23 of the Directive. This Article provides that diplomas awarded in the Member States must guarantee that a doctor, during his training period, has acquired:

"(a) adequate knowledge of the sciences on which medicine is based and a good understanding of the scientific methods including the principles of measuring biological functions, the evaluation of scientifically established facts and the analysis of data;
(b) sufficient understanding of the structure, functions and behaviour of healthy and sick persons, as well as relations between the state of health and the physical and social surroundings of the human being;
(c) adequate knowledge of clinical disciplines and practices, providing him with a coherent picture of mental and physical diseases, of medicine from the point of view of prophylaxis, diagnosis and therapy and of human reproduction;
(d) suitable clinical experience in hospital under appropriate supervision."

---

[74] Art. 3(1), (2).
[75] Art. 3(3).
[76] Art. 5(1).
[77] Art. 5(1).
[78] Art. 1(2).
[79] [1993] O.J. L165/24.
[80] Dirs 75/362–363, [1975] O.J. L167/1, as amended.

In addition, a course in medical training must comprise at least a six-year course or 5,500 hours of theoretical or practical instruction given in a university or under the supervision of a university.[81] In order to be accepted for this training, the candidate must have a diploma or a certificate which entitles him to be admitted to the universities of a Member State for the course of study concerned.[82] Provision is also made, *inter alia*, for recognition of qualifications in specialised medicine.[83] The directive applies to employed as well as self-employed persons.[84]

The Directive referred to above concerning the medical profession provides for mutual recognition on the basis of a certain degree of harmonisation of training requirements. Directive 89/48 on a general system for the recognition of higher education diplomas awarded on completion of professional education and training of at least three years' duration adopts a different approach—the mutual recognition of diplomas without harmonisation,[85] but accompanied by the safeguards of adaptation periods or aptitude tests in the host State, where the matters covered by the education and training he has received differ substantially from those covered by the diploma required in the host Member State[86] In principle the choice between adaptation period and aptitude test is left to the migrant, but an exception is made for legal qualifications, where an aptitude test may be required.[87] The latter Directive is limited to higher education, and Directive 92/51 was adopted as a complementary system to facilitate the pursuit all those professional activities which in a host Member State are dependent on the completion of a certain level of education and training.[88] It is based on the same system as Directive 89/48 and contains *mutatis mutandis* the same rules as the initial general system.

Perhaps the most interesting directive adopted under Article 47 (ex 57), in terms of the techniques which it uses to remove obstacles to freedom of movement of those engaged in a profession, and to secure "integration into the profession of lawyer in the host Member State", is European Parliament and Council Directive 98/5 to facilitate practice of the profession of lawyer on a permanent basis in a Member State other than that in which the qualification was obtained.[89] The Directive lists lawyers qualified under the laws of the Member States, and provides that any such lawyer shall be entitled to pursue on a permanent basis, in any other Member State under his home-country profes-sional title, the activities specified in the Directive.[90] These activities are described as the "same professional activities as a lawyer practising under the relevant professional title used in the host Member State and may, *inter alia,* give

---

[81] Art. 23(2).
[82] Art. 23(3).
[83] Chap. s II and III of the Directive.
[84] Art. 1.
[85] [1989] O.J. L19/16. See also Council Recommendation of 89/49 concerning nationals of Member States who hold a diploma conferred in a third State, [1989] O.J. L19/24.
[86] Art. 4(1)(b).
[87] See in particular Art. 4.
[88] [1992] O.J. L209/25.
[89] [1998] O.J. L77/36.
[90] Art. 1(2), 2.

advice on the law of his home Member State, on Community law, on international law and on the law of the host Member State."[91] There are two exceptions or qualifications to the foregoing. The first applies where a Member State authorises in its territory a prescribed category of lawyers to prepare deeds for obtaining title to administer estates of deceased persons and for creating or transferring interests in land which, in other Member States are reserved for professions other than that of lawyer. In such a case the Member State may exclude from such activities lawyers practising under a home-country professional title conferred in one of the latter Member States.[92] The second qualification to the right to practise under home-country title applies to the pursuit of activities relating to the representation or defence of a client in legal proceedings where the law of the host Member State reserves such activities to lawyers practising under the professional title of that State. In such circumstances the host Member State may require lawyers practising under their home-country professional title to work in conjunction with a lawyer who practises before the judicial authority in question and who would, where necessary, be answerable to that authority or with an "*avoué*" practising before it.[93]

Integration into the profession of lawyer in the host Member State is achieved *inter alia,* as follows. A lawyer practising under his home-country professional title who has "effectively and regularly pursued for at least three years an activity in the host Member State in the law of that State including Community law shall, with a view to gaining admission to the profession of lawyer in the host Member State, be exempted from the conditions set out in Article 4(1)(b) of Directive 89/48."[94]

ESTABLISHMENT OF COMPANIES

The right of establishment is enjoyed by companies and firms, as well as by natural persons. Article 48, first paragraph, (ex 58) provides:

"Companies or firms formed in accordance with the law of a Member State and having their registered office, central administration or principal place of business within the Community shall, for the purposes of this Chapter, be treated in the same way as natural persons who are nationals of Member States."

The Court has said that the "immediate consequence" of this latter provision is that "those companies are entitled to carry on their business in another Member State through an agency, branch of subsidiary", and that the location of their registered office, central administration or principal place of business "serves as the connecting factor with the legal system of a particular State in the same way as does nationality in the case of a natural person".[95]

---

[91] Art. 5(1).
[92] Art. 5(2).
[93] Art. 5(3). See the similar provisions of Dir. 77/249, below at p. 480.
[94] Art. 10.
[95] Case C–212/97 *Centros Ltd v. Erhvervs- og Selskabsstyrelsen* [1999] E.C.R. I–1459, para. 20, [1999] 2 C.M.L.R. 551, citing Case 79/85 *Segers v. Bedrijfsvereniging voor Bank- en Verzekeringswegen,*

While Article 1 of Directive 73/148[96] confirms the right of natural persons who are nationals of one Member State to leave that Member State in order to establish themselves in another, that provision does not apply by analogy to corporate persons.[97] However, the Court has said of Articles 43 (ex 52) and 48 (ex 58):

"Even though those provisions are directed mainly at ensuring that foreign nationals and companies are treated in the host Member State in the same way as nationals of that State, they also prohibit the Member State of origin from hindering the establishment in another Member State of one of its nationals or of a company incorporated under its legislation which comes within the definition contained in Article 58."[98]

As the Court has observed:

"In the case of a company, the right of establishment is generally exercised by the setting up of agencies, branches or subsidiaries, as is expressly provided for in the second sentence of the first paragraph of Article 52."[99]

An undertaking of one Member State which maintains a permanent presence in another "comes within the scope of the provisions of the Treaty on the right of establishment, even if that presence does not take the form of a branch or agency, but consists merely of an office managed by the undertaking's own staff or by a person who is independent but authorised to act on a permanent basis for the undertaking, as would be the case with an agency."[1]

The Court has held that to allow a Member State in which a company carried on its business to treat that company in a different manner solely because its registered office was in another Member State would deprive Article 48 (ex 58) of all meaning.[2] Furthermore, discriminatory tax treatment as between companies of the host Member State and branches of companies registered in other Member States is contrary to Article 43 (ex 52), and such discrimination cannot be justified on the ground that companies registered in other Member States are at liberty to establish themselves by setting up a subsidiary in order to have the benefit of the tax treatment in question.[3] As the Court has emphasised:

Groothandel en Vrije Beroepen [1986] E.C.R. 2375; [1987] 2 C.M.L.R. 247, para. 13; Case 270/83 *Commission v. France* [1986] E.C.R. 273; [1987] 1 C.M.L.R. 401, para. 18; Case C–330/91 *R. v. Inland Revenue Commissioners, ex p. Commerzbank AG* [1993] E.C.R. I–4017; [1993] 3 C.M.L.R. 457, para. 13; Case C–264/96 *ICI v. Colmer (Her Majesty's Inspector of Taxes)* [1998] E.C.R. I–4695; [1998] 3 C.M.L.R. 293, para. 20.

[96] As to which, see above p. 440.

[97] Case *R. v. HM Treasury and Commissioners of Inland Revenue, ex p. Daily Mail and General Trust plc* [1988] E.C.R. 5483, para. 28.

[98] *ibid.*, para. 16.

[99] *ibid.*, para. 17.

[1] Case 205/84 *Commission v. Germany* [1986] E.C.R. 3755; [1987] 2 C.M.L.R. 69, at para. 21.

[2] Case 79/85 *Segers v. Bedrijfsvereniging voor Bank- en Verzekeringswegen, Groothandel en Vrije Beroepen* [1986] E.C.R. 2375; [1987] 2 C.M.L.R. 247, para. 14, citing Case 270/83 *Commission v. France* [1986] E.C.R. 273; [1987] 1 C.M.L.R. 401, para. 18.

[3] Case 270/83 *Commission v. France* [1986] E.C.R. 273; [1987] 1 C.M.L.R. 401; and see Case C–307/97 *Compagnie de Saint-Gobain, Zweigniederlassung Deutschland v. Finanzamt Aachen--Innenstadt* [1999] E.C.R. I–6061.

"The second sentence of the first paragraph of Article 52 expressly leaves traders free to choose the appropriate legal form in which to pursue their activities in another Member State and that freedom of choice must not be limited by discriminatory tax provisions."[4]

The *Sodemare* case indicates that even non-discriminatory restrictions on the legal form in which a company incorporated in another Member State may carry on business in the host State will require justification if they are to be compatible with Article 43 (ex 52).[5]

Article 48 (ex 58) states that "'Companies or firms' means companies or firms constituted under civil or commercial law, including co-operative societies, and other legal persons governed by public or private law, save for those which are non-profit making." A company formed in accordance with the law of a Member State is entitled to exercise the right of establishment if it has either its registered office, its central administration, or its principal place of business within the Community. As indicated at the beginning of the present chapter, Article 43 (ex 52) draws a distinction between transferring a primary establishment to another Member State, and setting up a secondary establishment, in the form of a branch or a subsidiary. In the former case the only qualifying characteristic is the nationality of a Member State, while in the latter there must be an existing establishment in one of the Member States. The General Programme construed this qualification as requiring, in the case of companies having only the seat prescribed by their statutes in the Community, a "real and continuous link with the economy of a Member State".[6] In *Segers*[7] the Court of Justice regarded a company registered in one Member State and undertaking *all* its business through a branch in another Member State as entitled to exercise its right of establishment in the second Member State. Thus registration of a company in a Member State of itself amounts to establishment in that State, even if the company does no business in that Member State, and all its shareholders are nationals of the Member State in which it transacts all its business through an agency or branch (for such was the position in *Segers*). In *Centros*[8] the Court considered a situation in which Danish nationals resident in Denmark and carrying on business in Denmark set up a limited liability company in England whose only business activities would be carried out by a branch in Denmark. The share capital of the English company was £100, and the sole reason the Danish nationals set up a company in the United Kingdom rather than Denmark, was to secure the advantages of limited liability without having to meet the cost of the £20,000 minimum capital requirement then prevailing in Denmark. When the Danish nationals sought to register the Danish branch of the company, the Danish authorities refused to do so, since

---

[4] Case 270/83 *Commission v. France* [1986] E.C.R. 273; [1987] 1 C.M.L.R. 401, at para. 22.
[5] Case C–70/95 *Sodemare SA, etc., v. Regione Lombardia* [1997] E.C.R. I–3395; [1998] 4 C.M.L.R. 667. The proposition would seem to hold good even if the provisions were national tax rules.
[6] Title I, [1974] O.J. Spec.Ed., Second Series, IX, p. 7.
[7] Case 79/85 *Segers v. Bestuur van de Bedrijfsvereniging voor Bank- en Verzeleringswezen* [1986] E.C.R. 2375; [1987] 2 C.M.L.R. 247. The report refers to a "subsidiary" but the context indicates it was a branch.
[8] Case C–212/97 *Centros Ltd v. Erhvervs- og Selskabsstyrelsen* [1999] E.C.R. I–1459; [1999] 2 C.M.L.R. 551.

that branch would be the principal establishment of the English company, which would do no business in the United Kingdom, and since the sole purpose of setting up the English company was the avoidance of Danish minimum capital requirements. The Danish authorities regarded the situation as in reality being internal to Denmark, but made it clear that they would have registered the branch if the company had been also carrying on business in the United Kingdom. The Court of Justice referred to *Segers*, confirming that a company formed in one Member State, for the sole purpose of establishing itself in another, where its main or even sole business activities were to be carried on, could rely on the right of establishment, and added that the fact that the company was set up by nationals of the latter Member State resident in that State for the sole purpose of avoiding the minimum capital requirements of that State was immaterial.[9] The Court's judgment is most worthy of remark for its strong endorsement of the rights of individuals to choose the least restrictive corporate form of those available in the Member States as the vehicle of their entrepreneurial ambitions. The Court states:

"The provisions of the Treaty on freedom of establishment are intended specifically to enable companies formed in accordance with the law of a Member State and having their registered office, central administration or principal place of business within the Community to pursue activities in other Member States through an agency, branch or subsidiary.

That being so, the fact that a national of a Member State who wishes to set up a company chooses to form it in the Member State whose rules of company law seem to him the least restrictive and to set up branches in other Member States cannot, in itself, constitute an abuse of the right of establishment. The right to form a company in accordance with the law of a Member State and to set up branches in other Member States is inherent in the exercise, in a single market, of the freedom of establishment guaranteed by the Treaty."[10]

The Court held that the refusal in such circumstances of the national authorities of the State in which the branch was to be formed to register that branch amounted to an infringement of the right of establishment, which could not be justified by mandatory requirements in the public interest, or on the ground of improper circumvention of national rules.[11] But the enjoyment in practice of the right of establishment endorsed by the Court in this case would seem to be subject to limitation *vis-à-vis* those Member States which do not recognise that a company may be validly incorporated in a Member State other than that of its company headquarters or central administration.[12]

Article 44(2)(f) (ex 54(3)(f)) E.C. provides for the abolition of restrictions on the transfer of personnel from the main establishment to managerial or supervisory posts in its branches or subsidiaries. In the event of such personnel

---

[9] *ibid.*, paras 17–18.
[10] *ibid.*, paras 26–27.
[11] As to which see below, pp. 481 and 486.
[12] See below, p. 468.

holding the nationality of a Member State, they will, of course, be entitled to assert an independent right of entry and residence under the provisions of the Treaty guaranteeing freedom of movement for workers.[13] The implication is that certain senior personnel may be transferred under Article 44(2)(f) who would not otherwise be entitled to a right of residence under the Treaty. The principal reason for such lack of entitlement is likely to be that they are nationals of third countries. An undertaking providing services in another Member State may bring its workforce with it, irrespective of whether the employees concerned enjoy an independent right of free movement.[14] It seems that a national of a third country may be posted from the main establishment to a *senior* post in a branch or subsidiary in another Member State, and that workers employed by an undertaking established in a Member State may, *irrespective of status*, be posted on a temporary basis to another Member State under Article 49 (ex 59). This distinction between the scope of Article 43 and 49 as regards the status of employees who may be entitled to residence as a result of a posting would seem to reflect the permanent nature of establishment as against the temporary and sporadic nature ·of the provision of services, and the intent of the draftsman of the Treaty to place a clear limit on the duty of Member States to grant a right of residence to nationals of third countries.

A change of primary establishment involving a transfer of company head-quarters or central management may be hindered by national legal provisions to the effect: (a) that a company transferring its executive offices out of the jurisdiction loses it corporate personality; or (b) that a company wishing to establish its executive offices within the jurisdiction must be newly constituted there.[15] These requirements amount to a refusal to recognise the legal personality of a company incorporated in a Member State other than where its central administration is located. It might be said that to deny recognition to a company satisfying the requirements of the first paragraph of Article 48 (ex 58) amounts to a denial of that company's right of establishment.[16] However, in *Ex parte Daily Mail and General Trust Plc* the Court held that the differences in national legislation concerning the required connecting factor between a company and the Member State under which it is incorporated and the question whether—and if so how—the registered office or real head office of a company incorporated under national law may be transferred from one Member State to another were problems which were not resolved by the Treaty rules concerning the right of establishment but were to be dealt with by future legislation or conventions.[17] It followed that Articles 43 and 48 (ex 52 and 58) of the Treaty could not be interpreted as conferring on companies incorporated under the law of a Member State a right to transfer their central management and control and their central administration to another Member State while retaining their status as companies incorporated under the legislation of the

---

[13] See Chap. 14 above.
[14] Case C–113/89 *Rush Portuguesa Ldc* [1990] E.C.R. I–1417; [1991] 2 C.M.L.R. 818.
[15] See R.R. Drury, "Migrating Companies" (1999) 24 E.L. Rev. 354.
[16] Everling, *The Right of Establishment in the Common Market*, C.C.H. Chicago, 1964, p. 71.
[17] *R. v. HM Treasury and Commissioners of Inland Revenue, ex p. Daily Mail and General Trust Plc* [1988] E.C.R. 5483, para. 23.

first Member State.[18] While this result may be said to be reasonable (even if not on the face of it consistent with the text of the Treaty) where the national law of incorporation does not permit a transfer of central administration, it is less so where the law of incorporation does so allow and the host State recognises such a transfer. If a British company with a central administration located in a municipally owned office block in another Member State were charged a higher rent chargeable to foreign companies, does it follow from the *Daily Mail* decision that Article 43 could not be invoked by the company? If so, the result would seem anomalous. It might be that the *Daily Mail* ruling is strictly confined to claims to exercise the right of free movement by a shift of central administration, and that once the transfer of central administration is achieved in accordance with the applicable national law, Article 43 can be invoked to guarantee equal treatment in the host State.

The fact remains that a number of Member States will not recognise a company which is incorporated under the law of a State other than that in which its "real seat" (head office or central management and control) is located. The 1968 Convention on the Mutual Recognition of Companies and Legal Persons, seeks to resolve the difficulties which arise from the existence of different national rules relating to the recognition of foreign companies, but there seems no prospect of it being adopted.[19] The Commission has made a proposal for a Fourteenth Directive in the company law harmonisation series dealing with "The Transfer of the Registered Office of a Company from one Member State to Another with a Change of Applicable Law".[20]

The prospect of firms incorporated under the law of one Member State being free to establish themselves in another led those who drafted the Treaty to insert Article 44(2)(g) (ex 54(3)(g)), which requires the co-ordination of the provisions of national company law which safeguard the position of investors and "others". The rationale of such harmonisation is that in its absence the existence of different national rules could discourage the exercise of the right of establishment, and deter third parties from dealing with companies having their seats in other Member States. A number of directives have been adopted under this provision of the Treaty.[21] Article 47(2) (ex 57(2)) provides for the co-ordination of provisions concerning the pursuit of activities as self-employed persons,[22] and as regards undertakings and corporate persons, this provision has provided the basis for the harmonisation of national rules governing such matters as banking and insurance.[23]

---

[18] *ibid.*, at para. 24.

[19] R.R. Drury, *op.cit.*, n.8, p. 360.

[20] R.R. Drury, *op.cit.*, n.8, pp. 362 *et seq.* It is arguable that the *Centros* case, p. 466, n.8, overrules *Daily Mail* p. 468, n.17, and requires recognition of situations resulting from the exercise of the right of establishment.

[21] For a convenient and readable summary of the relevant directives, see the Company Law section of Chap. 20, Company, Banking and Insurance, by Stuart Isaacs Q.C., Neil Calver and Susan Belgrave, in *Practitioner's Handbook of E.C. Law*, edited by Gerlad Barling Q.C. and Mark Brealey, Trenton Publishing, Gosport, 1998.

[22] See above, p. 461.

[23] See the Banking and Insurance sections of Chap. 20 of the *Practitioner's Handbook of E.C. Law*, n.14.

PROVISION OF SERVICES

General Scope

Article 49 (ex 59) E.C. provides that "[w]ithin the framework of the provisions set out below, restrictions on freedom to provide services within the Community shall be prohibited in respect of nationals of Member States who are established in a State of the Community other than that of the person for whom the services are intended." It will be noted that in order to invoke this provision, nationals must be "established" in a Member State. In the case of companies whose registered office is situated inside the Community, but whose central management or principal place of business is not, this requirement is satisfied by their activities having "a real and continuous link with the economy of a Member State, excluding the possibility that this link might depend on nationality, particularly the nationality of the partners or the members of the managing or supervisory bodies, or of persons holding the capital stock".[24] It has already been noted that a company registered in a Member State may be established in that State even if it conducts all its business through an agency branch or subsidiary in another Member State.[25]

"Services" are defined in Article 50 (ex 60), and are considered as such when they are "normally provided for remuneration". One would expect the remuneration to be provided by the receiver of services, but this is not essential. In the *Debauve* and *Coditel* cases, Advocate General Warner expressed the opinion that the purpose of the definition of "services" in Article 50 (ex 60) was to exclude those that are normally provided gratuitously. Television broadcasting thus in his view fell within the definition whether it was financed by licence fee, or by advertising. The decision factor was that the broadcasting was remunerated in one way or another.[26] *Bond van Adverteerders v. Netherlands State*[27] concerned, *inter alia*, the provision of services by cable television operators in one Member State to broadcasters in another by relaying to network subscribers in the first Member State television programmes transmitted to them by the broadcasters. The Court held that these services were provided for remuneration. The cable network operators were paid, in the form of the fees which they charged their subscribers for the service which they provided to the broadcaster, and it was irrelevant that the broadcasters generally did not themselves pay the cable network operators for relaying their programmes.[28]

A non-exhaustive list of services in Article 50 (ex 60) specifies activities of an industrial character, activities of a commercial character, activities of craftsmen, and activities of the professions. Where a particular activity falls within the

---

[24] General Programme (Services), [1974] O.J. Spec.Ed., 2nd Series, IX, p. 3.

[25] Case 79/85 *Segers v. Bestuur van de Bedrijfsvereniging voor Bank- en Verzeleringswezen* [1986] E.C.R. 2375; [1987] 2 C.M.L.R. 247; Case C–212/97 *Centros Ltd v. Erhvervs- og Selskabsstyrelsen* [1999] E.C.R. I–1459, [1999] 2 C.M.L.R. 551, above at p. 466.

[26] Case 52/79 *Procureur du Roi v. Marc J.V.C. Debauve and others.* [1980] E.C.R. 833; [1981] 2 C.M.L.R. 362; Case 62/79 SA *Compagnie générale pour la diffusion de la télévision, Coditel, and others v. Ciné Vog Films and others* [1980] E.C.R. 881, [1981] 2 C.M.L.R. 362; Opinion at p. 876.

[27] Case 352/85 [1988] E.C.R. 2085; [1989] 3 C.M.L.R. 113.

[28] *ibid.* at para. 16.

provisions of the Treaty relating to the free movement of goods, capital or persons, however, these latter provisions govern. The Court has held that the broadcasting of television signals,[29] cable transmission,[30] tourism, medical treatment (including the termination of pregnancy[31]), education,[32] the importation of lottery advertisements and tickets into a Member State,[33] and unsolicited telephone calls to potential clients,[34] are covered by the provisions on the freedom to provide services.

Without prejudice to the right of establishment, a person providing a service may, in order to do so, "temporarily pursue his activity in the State where the service is provided, under the same conditions as are imposed by that State on its own nationals".[35] The Court of Justice in *Rush Portuguesa* concluded from these words that an undertaking could accordingly take with it its staff to the territory of another Member State to provide services there:

"Articles 59 and 60 of the Treaty therefore preclude a Member State from prohibiting a person providing services established in another Member State from moving freely in its territory with all his staff and preclude that Member State from making the movement of staff in question subject to restrictions such as a condition as to engagement *in situ* or an obligation to obtain a work permit."[36]

As observed above,[37] the pursuit of economic activities on a permanent basis in a host State, would amount to establishment, rather than to the provision of services. As the Court explained in *Steymann*:

"It is clear from the actual wording of Article 60 that an activity carried out on a permanent basis or, in any event, without a foreseeable limit to its duration does not fall within the Community provisions concerning the provision of services. On the other hand, such activities may fall within the scope of Articles 48 to 51 or Articles 52 to 58 of the Treaty, depending on the case."[38]

A literal interpretation of Articles 49 and 50 (ex 59 and 60) E.C. would guarantee freedom to provide cross-frontier services, in circumstances where provider and recipient remain in their respective Member States, as in the case of financial advice from United Kingdom advisers in the United Kingdom to French clients in France. It would similarly uphold the right of a person established in

---

[29] Case 155/73 *Sacchi* [1974] E.C.R. 490; [1974] 2 C.M.L.R. 177, para. 6.
[30] Case 52/79 *Procureur du Roi v. Marc J.V.C. Debauve and others.* [1980] E.C.R. 833; [1981] 2 C.M.L.R. 362, para. 8; Case C–23/93 *TV10 SA v. Commissariaat voor de Media* [1994] E.C.R. I–1963; [1995] 3 C.M.L.R. 284, para. 13.
[31] Case 159/90 *The Society for the protection of Unborn Children Ireland Ltd v. Stephen Grogan and Others* [1991] E.C.R. I– 4685; [1991] 3 C.M.L.R. 849, at para. 18.
[32] Joined Cases 286/82 and 26/83 *Graziana Luisi and Giuseppe Carbone v. Ministero del Tesoro* [1984] E.C.R. 377
[33] Case C–275/92 *Her Majesty's Customs and Excise v. Gerhart Schindler and Jörg Schindler* [1994] E.C.R. I–1039; [1995] 1 C.M.L.R. 4, at para. 37.
[34] Case C–384/93 *Alpine Investments BV v. Minister van Financiën* [1995] E.C.R. I–1141; [1995] 2 C.M.L.R. 209; [1995] All E.R. (E.C.) 543.
[35] Art. 50 (ex 60), third para.
[36] Case C–113/89 *Rush Portuguesa Ldc* [1990] E.C.R. I–1417; [1991] 2 C.M.L.R. 818, at para. 12.
[37] At p. 430.
[38] Case 196/87 *Udo Steymann v. Staatssecretaris van Justite* [1987] E.C.R. 6159, at para. 16.

one Member State to provide services *in situ* in the territory of another, as in the case of a French doctor practising in France making a house call on a patient in Luxembourg. The text also implies that a potential recipient of services would be entitled to visit another Member State so that those services could be provided there, as in the case of the hypothetical Luxembourg patient referred to above calling at the surgery in France of his French doctor. The Court has held that the right freely to provide services may be relied on by an undertaking as against the State in which it is established if the services are provided for persons established in another Member State,[39] and that the right includes the freedom for recipients of services to go to another Member State in order to receive a service there, without being obstructed by restrictions.[40] The Court has furthermore given a rather generous interpretation to the text, in holding that Article 49 of the Treaty "applies not only where a person providing services and the recipient thereof are established in different Member States, but also in cases where the person providing services offers those services in a Member State other than that in which he is established, wherever the recipients of those services may be established."[41] Thus Article 49 could be invoked, for example, by a German tourist guide alleging that Greek rules comprised an obstacle to his or her provision of services, in Greece, to German tourists.

Entry and residence

The entry and residence of self-employed persons under Article 49 (ex 59) E.C. is governed by the same secondary legislation as entry and residence under Article 43 (ex 52), on the right of establishment, and the reader is referred accordingly to the treatment of Directive 73/148 found earlier in this chapter.[42]

Like the original text of Article 44 (ex 54), the original text of Article 52 (ex 63) provided for the drawing up of a General Programme for the abolition of restrictions on freedom to provide services within the Community. The Programme was adopted in December 1961,[43] and closely resembles the General Programme for the abolition of restrictions on the right of establishment.[44] Thus, *e.g.* Title III calls for the abolition of restrictions such as those which "condition the provision of services on an authorisation or on the issuance of a document, such as a foreign merchant's card or a foreign professional's card".[45] As indicated

---

[39] Case C–70/95 *Sodemare and Others v. Regione Lombardia* [1997] E.C.R. I–3395; [1998] 4 C.M.L.R. 667, para. 37; Case C–224/97 *Erich Ciola v. Land Vorarlberg* [1999] E.C.R. I–4239; [1997] 3 C.M.L.R. 673, para. 11.

[40] Joined Cases 286/82 and 26/83 *Graziana Luisi and Giuseppe Carbone v. Ministero del Tesoro* [1984] E.C.R. 377, para. 16; Case 186/87 *Cowan v. Trésor Public* [1989] E.C.R. 195, para. 15.

[41] C–198/89 *Commission v. Greece* [1991] E.C.R. I–727, paras 8–10; Case C–398/95 *Syndesmos ton en Elladi Touristikon kai Taxidiotikon Grafeion v. Ypourgos Ergasias* [1997] E.C.R. I- 3091, para. 8.

[42] Above at p. 439.

[43] [1974] O.J. Spec.Ed., 2nd Series IX, p. 3. The programme has been referred to by the Court in a number of cases, see, *e.g.* Case 15/78 *Koestler* [1978] E.C.R. 1971; [1979] 1 C.M.L.R. 89; Case 136/78 *Auer* [1979] E.C.R. 452; [1979] 2 C.M.L.R. 373; Cases 286/82 and 26/83 *Luisi* [1984] E.C.R. 377; Case 63/86 *Commission v. Italy* [1988] E.C.R. 29; [1989] 2 C.M.L.R. 601; Case 305/87 *Commission v. Greece* [1989] E.C.R. 1461; [1991] 1 C.M.L.R. 611.

[44] See above, p. 439.

[45] [1974] O.J. Spec.Ed. 2nd Series IX, at p. 4.

earlier, most of the Directives issued to abolish restrictions on the right of establishment apply in addition to freedom to provide services. Thus Directive 64/223, used for illustrative purposes in the context of establishment,[46] also applies, in relation to the wholesale trade, to freedom to provide services. Furthermore, Article 47(2) (ex 57(2)) E.C., which provides for the harmonisation of national rules governing the pursuit of self-employed activities, is applied to the chapter on services by Article 55 (ex 66). Further reference is made to this below.[47]

Just as the Court's decision in *Reyners v. Belgian State* on the direct applicability of Article 43 (ex 52) reduced significantly the importance of Directives requiring the abolition of particular discriminatory restrictions, so its later decision in *Van Binsbergen v. Bedrijfsvereniging Metaalnijverheid*, upholding the direct effect of Articles 49 (ex 59), first paragraph and 50 (ex 60), third paragraph, entailed similar consequences for the provisions of Directives concerned with the abolition of restrictions on the supply of services.[48]

It is to be noted that Article 49 (ex 59), like Article 43 (ex 52), is concerned not only with the specific rules on the pursuit of occupational activities but also with the rules relating to the various general facilities which are of assistance in the pursuit of those activities, including the right to equal access to housing, and financial facilities to acquire housing.[49]

Prohibition of restrictions in respect of non-residence, nationality or otherwise—evolution of the Court's case-law

It has already been noted that the Court of Justice's interpretation of the Treaty provisions on the free movement of goods, on freedom of movement for workers, and on the right of establishment, have undergone a considerable evolution in the last decade or so, and that the Court has given increased prominence in its judgments to the concept of the non-discriminatory restriction on free movement in the latter contexts.[50] This phenomenon is also true of the case-law on freedom to provide services, and the significant stages in that evolution are indicated below. The survey which follows will concentrate principally on identifying restrictions on freedom to provide services which may conflict with the Treaty, referring only *en passant* to justifications for such restrictions, and possible justifications for such rules will be considered separately below.[51]

The starting point is the judgment in *Van Binsbergen*.[52] The case involved a Netherlands national who acted as a legal representative in proceedings in the

---

[46] See above, p. 443.

[47] See below, p. 479.

[48] Case 33/74 [1974] E.C.R. 1299; [1975] 1 C.M.L.R. 298; and see Case 36/74 *Walrave* [1974] E.C.R. 1405; [1975] 1 C.M.L.R. 320; Case 13/76 *Dona v. Mantero* [1976] E.C.R. 133; [1976] 2 C.M.L.R. 578; Joined Cases 110–111/78, *Van Wesemael* [1979] E.C.R. 35; [1979] 3 C.M.L.R. 87.

[49] Case 63/86 *Commission v. Italy* [1988] E.C.R. 29; [1989] 2 C.M.L.R. 601.

[50] See Chap. 13, at p. 326 *et seq.*, Chap. 14, at p. 409 *et seq.*, and this Chapter at p. 456 *et seq.*, above.

[51] See the section on the public policy proviso, at p. 485 *et seq.* and that on mandatory requirements in the general interest, at p. 486 *et seq.*

[52] Case 33/74 *Van Binsbergen v. Bedrijfsvereniging Metaalnijverheid* [1974] E.C.R. 1307; [1975] 1 C.M.L.R. 298.

Netherlands where representation by an *advocaat* was not obligatory. As a result of moving house to Belgium (he practised from home)[53] his right to practise before a Netherlands court was called in question by a provision of Netherlands law under which only persons established in the Netherlands could act as legal representatives before that court. The Court identified the national measures covered by the prohibition in these Articles as follows:

> "The restrictions to be abolished pursuant to articles 59 and 60 include all requirements imposed on the person providing the service by reason in particular of his nationality or of the fact that he does not habitually reside in the state where the service is provided, which do not apply to persons established within the national territory or which may prevent or otherwise obstruct the activities of the person providing the service.
>
> In particular, a requirement that the person providing the service must be habitually resident within the territory of the state where the service is to be provided may, according to the circumstances, have the result of depriving article 59 of all useful effect, in view of the fact that the precise object of that article is to abolish restrictions on freedom to provide services imposed on persons who are not established in the state where the service is to be provided."

The Court's judgment thus identifies discrimination on grounds of nationality and by reference to residence outside national territory as being characteristics of national measures prohibited by the Treaty. It appears from the text and context that the reference to the incompatibility with the Treaty of the residence requirement in issue was not based on the premise that such a requirement amounted to indirect discrimination *on grounds of nationality*. As regards the text, this follows from the terms of the Court's ruling on the direct effect of Articles 49 and 50 (ex 59 and 60), to the effect that those Articles "have direct effect . . . at least in so far as they seek to abolish any discrimination against a person providing a service by reason of his nationality *or of the fact that he resides in a Member State other than that in which the service is to be* provided."[54] As regards the context, it will be noted that the plaintiff in the national proceedings was a Netherlands national, and so no question of discrimination against him on grounds of nationality in the Netherlands arose. The statement by the Court that a residence requirement would deprive Article 49 of all useful effect has been endorsed in a consistent subsequent case-law. In *Commission v. Germany* the Court described the requirement of a permanent establishment as "the very negation" of freedom to provide services. "It has", said the Court, "the result of depriving Article 59 of the Treaty of all effectiveness, a provision whose very purpose is to abolish restrictions on the

---

[53] Advocate General Mayras at [1974] E.C.R. 1314.
[54] For further rulings on direct effect, see *e.g.*, Case 36/74 *Walrave v. Union Cycliste Internationale* [1974] E.C.R. 1405; [1975] 1 C.M.L.R. 320; Joined Cases 110–111/78 *Ministère public and "Chambre syndicale des agents artistiques et impresarii de Belgique" ASBL v. Willy van Wesemael and others* [1979] E.C.R. 35; [1979] 3 C.M.L.R. 87; Case 279/80. *Criminal proceedings against Alfred John Webb* [1981] E.C.R. 3305; [1982] 1 C.M.L.R. 719.

freedom to provide services of persons who are not established in the State in which the service is to be provided."[55]

In *van Wesemael*[56] the Court had to consider, *inter alia*, the extent to which national rules of one Member State could impose a licensing requirement on an employment agency established in another Member State placing employees in the first Member State. The Court repeated the proposition that Articles 49 and 50 (ex 59 and 60) "abolish all discrimination against the person providing the service by reason of his nationality or the fact that he is established in a Member State other than that in which the service is to be provided".[57] As regards the application of the licensing requirement, the Court held that it would be incompatible with the Treaty for a Member State to impose a licensing requirement on an employment agency established in another Member State, which was supervised and licensed in its home State, unless the requirement was objectively justified by the need to ensure observance of professional rules of conduct or the protection of the entertainers placed by the agency.[58] In the event, the Court held that such a requirement was not justified when the service was provided by an employment agency which was licensed in its home State under conditions comparable to those applicable in the host State and subject to the supervision of its home State authorities as regards all its activities in the Member State.[59] It follows from the reasoning in the latter case that it might be discriminatory to apply to a service provider established in another Member State all the requirements of host State law, and in the later case of *Webb*[60] (involving a "manpower" agency licensed in one Member State providing services in another) the Court, confirming that the Treaty provisions on provision of services prohibited all discrimination against the person providing the service by reason of his nationality or the fact that he is established in a Member State other than that in which the service is provided, added that the reference in Article 50 (ex 60), para. 3 to discrimination on grounds of nationality did not mean "that all national legislation applicable to nationals of that State and usually applied to the permanent activities of undertaking established therein may be similarly applied in its entirety to the temporary activities of undertakings which are established in another Member State".[61]

In *Commission v. Germany*[62] the Court considered the compatibility with Article 49 of German rules requiring *inter alia* that insurance companies

---

[55] Case 205/84 *Commission v. Germany* [1988] E.C.R. 3755; [1987] 2 C.M.L.R. 69, at para. 52, citing Case 39/75 *Coenen* [1975] E.C.R. 1547; [1976] 1 C.M.L.R. 30, and Case 76/81 *Transporoute* [1982] E.C.R. 417; [1982] 3 C.M.L.R. 382. See also Case C–101/94 *Commission v. Italy* [1996] E.C.R. I–2691; [1996] 3 C.M.L.R. 754, at para. 31; and Case C–222/95 *Société Civile Immobilière Paroldi v. Banque H. Albert de Bary et Die* [1997] E.C.R. I–3899; [1998] 1 C.M.L.R. 115, para. 31.

[56] Joined Cases 110–111/78. *Ministère public and "Chambre syndicale des agents artistiques et impresarii de Belgique" ASBL v. Willy van Wesemael and others.* [1979] E.C.R. 35; [1979] 3 C.M.L.R. 87.

[57] *ibid.*, at para. 27 of judgment.

[58] *Ibid.*, at para. 29.

[59] *ibid.*, at para. 30.

[60] Case 279/80. *Criminal proceedings against Alfred John Webb* [1981] E.C.R. 3305; [1982] 1 C.M.L.R. 719.

[61] *ibid.*, at para. 16.

[62] Case 205/84 *Commission v. Germany* [1988] E.C.R. 3755; [1987] 2 C.M.L.R. 69.

established in other Member States, and authorised and supervised in those Member States, obtain a separate German authorisation for their activities in Germany. The Court repeated its customary formulation to the effect that Article 49 (ex 59) covered discrimination on grounds of nationality or by reference to establishment in another Member State.[63] It reiterated the proposition that national rules could not necessarily be applied in their entirety to a service provider established in another Member State, but added that specific requirements could nevertheless be imposed on such a provider if the provisions in question were justified in the public interest, to the extent that the relevant public interest was not safeguarded by the provisions to which the provider was subject in the Member State of establishment. The Court says that *"In addition* such requirements must be objectively justified by the need to ensure that professional rules of conduct are complied with and that the interests which such rules are designed to safeguard are protected" (emphasis added).[64] The above formulation is significant, since it indicates that even national supervisory requirements which do not duplicate those applied in the Member State of establishment may only be applied to the out of State provider if they are objectively necessary. This is borne out by the Court's observation that the requirement of authorisation may not be justifiable on grounds relating to the protection of policy-holders and insured persons in all fields of insurance, and its suggestion that in the field of commercial insurance the policy-holders might simply not need the protection of mandatory rules of national law.[65] Whether the proposition can be said to emerge from the prior case-law or not, the proposition emerges from this case that to impose national supervisory requirements on service providers who are established in other Member States where they are authorised to provide the service in question will be regarded as discriminatory on grounds of nationality or by reference to establishment in another Member State if *the need for the supervisory requirements* of the host State cannot be objectively justified. This conclusion is borne out by the judgment in *Commission v. Greece*, in which the Court holds that it is discriminatory on grounds of nationality, or on the ground that the person providing the service is established in another Member State, for one Member State to insist that tourist guides established in another Member State possess the qualifications of the first Member State.[66]

It follows in particular from the last two cited cases that the Court had developed a broad concept of discrimination by reference to nationality, or by reference to establishment in another Member State, which was infringed if the host State, without objective justification, imposed the same qualification on a service provider established in another Member State as it imposed on services providers established in the host State. Thus an out-of-State service provider qualified in his home State must be allowed access to the host State market in the relevant services unless there are sound objective grounds to refuse him access. This is indistinguishable from the approach in the *Cassis* case in all but name; but

---

[63] *ibid.*, at para. 25.
[64] *ibid.*, at para. 27.
[65] *ibid.*, at para. 49.
[66] Case C–198/89 [1991] E.C.R. I–727, at paras 16 and 18. And see Case C–154/89 *Commission v. France* [1991] E.C.R. I–4221.

it is a legal development which took place—quite rightly—within the analytical framework of discrimination.[67] Yet a conceptual sea-change was about to take place.

Very shortly after *Commission v. Greece*, referred to above, the Court decided *Säger v. Dennemeyer & Co. Ltd*[68] The national proceedings arose from a legal action by a patent agent in Munich against a company incorporated in England and Wales. The plaintiff was a specialist in patent renewal services who claimed that the provision of such services by the defendant was contrary to German rules reserving such activities exclusively to persons possessing the relevant professional qualification. The provision of patent renewal services was not subject to regulation in the United Kingdom. The German court seised of the dispute asked the Court of Justice whether rules such as those in issue were compatible with Article 49 (ex 59). It is to be noted that the approach adopted by the Court of Justice in *Commission v. Germany* and *Commission v. Greece*, above, would have pointed towards the German rules in issue being treated as *discrimination* on grounds of nationality or on grounds that the service provider was established in another Member State, unless they could be justified by reference to the need to protect the interests asserted to be at stake. Instead, the Court adopted an analysis rather closer to that adopted in the *Cassis* case,[69] as follows:

"It should first be pointed out that Article 59 of the Treaty requires not only the elimination of all discrimination against a person providing services on the ground of his nationality but also the abolition of any restriction, even if it applies without distinction to national providers of services and to those of other Member States, when it is liable to prohibit or otherwise impede the activities of a provider of services established in another Member State where he lawfully provides similar services."[70]

The Court adopted the same approach to justification as it had adopted in *Commission v. Greece*, above.[71] In the view of the present writer the abandonment of the yard-stick of discrimination was unnecessary and unfortunate. Unnecessary because the Court's case-law on discrimination was adequate to cover cases such as this. And unfortunate because in principle it is not self-evident that genuinely non-discriminatory and therefore trade neutral measures should be subject to requirements of justification and proportionality.[72] If a particular service is prohibited outright in a particular Member State, a test based on discrimination will exempt the prohibition, applicable to in-State and out-of-State providers alike, from scrutiny. If Article 49 is read as laying down a general prohibition on non-discriminatory restrictions, then national rules prohibiting certain services outright will be subject to judicial scrutiny to determine whether

---

[67] Chap. 13, at p. 329.
[68] Case C–76/90 *Manfred Säger v. Dennemeyer & Co. Ltd* [1991] E.C.R. I–4221; [1993] 3 C.M.L.R. 639.
[69] Chap. 13, at p. 323.
[70] *ibid.*, at para. 12.
[71] Case C–198/89 [1991] E.C.R. I–727.
[72] The objections are made in connection with the development of the *Cassis* doctrine, see Chap. 13, at p. 329.

such a general ban can be upheld. Even in a case where most Member States banned a particular service, it seems that the final decision as to the sustainability of such a ban would lie in the hands of the judges, rather than national legislative authorities. In *Schindler*[73] the Court considered national rules which prohibited (with certain exceptions) lotteries in the United Kingdom, and prohibited the import of lottery tickets. If the pre-*Säger* case-law had been applied, the first question to be addressed would be whether the measure discriminated on grounds of nationality or on the ground that the service provider was established in another Member State. Since the Court regarded such national rules as non-discriminatory, that would have been the end of the matter.[74] But the Court applied the *Säger* formulation, which meant that it was necessary to address the issue of objective justification, and proportionality. The Court noted that the regulation of lotteries raised wide issues, including moral, religious and cultural issues, and the risk of crime and fraud.[75] Instead of applying an objective test, the Court adopted a subjective test, allowing Member States "to assess not only whether it is necessary to restrict the activities of lotteries but also whether they should be prohibited, providing that those restrictions are not discriminatory".[76] The Court referred to the "peculiar nature of lotteries, which has been stressed by many Member States".[77] It is tempting to draw the conclusion that the Court, having the developed the concept of the non-discriminatory restriction on the provision of services, found that its strict application could lead to a result which was rather obviously inappropriate, and that it found it necessary to adjust its reasoning accordingly. The question which inevitably arises is whether the concept of the non-discriminatory restriction on provision of services is applicable in principle in all contexts, or whether certain national rules will be regarded as consistent with Article 49 if they do not discriminate on grounds of nationality or on the ground that the service provider is established in another Member State.

Is the abolition of non-discriminatory restrictions a general requirement?

There is no doubt that the formulation in *Säger*, covering as it does both discriminatory and non-discriminatory restrictions, has been been applied on numerous occasions by the Court, and there is little sign that the Court acknowledges that a class of cases exists to which it has no application.

Yet it is nevertheless possible that the test is only applicable to national rules which restrict access to the market, or rather, that a category of cases exist in which national rules will not be regarded as restricting access to the market and will be compatible with Article 49 provided they do not discriminate on grounds of nationality or by reference to establishment in another Member State. In *Alpine Investments*[78] the Court of Justice considered whether rules of a Member

---

[73] Case C–275/92 *Her Majesty's Customs and Excise v. Gerhart Schindler and Jörg Schindler* [1994] E.C.R. I–1039; [1995] 1 C.M.L.R. 4. See also Case C–473/98 *Toulex* judgment of July 11, 2000, for a case involving Art. 28 and a national general prohibition on the use of a product.

[74] Para. 48.

[75] *Iibid.*, at para. 60.

[76] *ibid.*, at para. 61.

[77] *ibid.*, at para. 59; 11 governments intervened in the proceedings.

[78] Case C–384/93 *Alpine Investments BV v. Minister van Financiën* [1995] E.C.R. I–1141; [1995] 2 C.M.L.R. 209; [1995] All E.R. (E.C.) 543.

State prohibiting providers of services established in its territory from making unsolicited telephone calls to potential clients established in other Member States in order to offer their services constituted a restriction on freedom to provide services covered by Article 49 (ex 59). The Netherlands and the United Kingdom argued by analogy with *Keck*[79] that non-discriminatory rules such as those in issue should not be regarded as falling within Article 49 (ex 59) at all. The Court rejected this argument saying *inter alia*, that a prohibition such as that in issue "therefore directly affects *access to the market* in services in the other Member States and is thus capable of hindering intra-Community trade in services" (emphasis added).[80]

The compatibility of national tax provisions with Article 49 E.C. appears still to be governed by the concept of discrimination, rather than by the *Säger* formulation.[81] And the Court continues to rely on the principle that Article 49 (ex 59) precludes the application of any national rules which have the effect of making the provision of services between Member States more difficult than the provision of services purely within one Member State.[82] Equally, cases in which the *Säger* formulation is invoked more often than not concern national measures which are discriminatory, and/or amount to restrictions on access to the market.[83] Nevertheless, it is submitted that problems which have arisen in the context of the free movement of goods because of the indiscriminate development of the concept of the non-discriminatory trade restriction, are also capable of arising in the context of the provision of services, and principles analogous to those contained in the *Keck* judgment ought in principle to be applicable. It has been noted in that the Court has held that restrictions on Sunday trading are not caught by Article 28 (because of the application of *Keck*),[84] or Article 43 (because of application of analogous principles),[85] and it must surely follow that analogous principles also apply to ensure that such rules are not covered by Article 49.

Mutual Recognition of diplomas

The mutual recognition of professional qualifications and the co-ordination of national rules governing self-employed activities is as important a step to securing the free provision of services as it is to facilitating the right of establishment, and Directive 93/16 to facilitate the free movement of doctors and the mutual recognition of their diplomas, certificates, and other evidence of

---

[79] See Chap. 13, p. 331.
[80] Case C–384/93 *Alpine Investments BV v. Minister van Financiën* [1995] E.C.R. I–1141; [1995] 2 C.M.L.R. 209; [1995] All E.R. (E.C.) 543, at para. 38. Also see Joined Cases C–51/96 and C–191/97 *Deliège* judgment of April 11, 2000, para. 61.
[81] See, *e.g.* Case C–390/96 *Lease Plan Luxembourg SA v. Belgian State* [1998] E.C.R. I–2553; [1998] 2 C.M.L.R. 583.
[82] Case C–158/96 *Raymond Kohll v. Union des Caisses de Maladie* [1998] E.C.R. I–1931; [1998] 2 C.M.L.R. 928, para. 33.
[83] Case C–272/94 *Guiot* [1996] E.C.R. I–1905; Case C–3/95 *Broede* [1996] E.C.R. I–6511; [1997] 1 C.M.L.R. 224; Case C–398/95 *Syndesmos ton en Elladi Touristikon kai Taxidiotikon Grafeion v. Ypourgos Ergasias* [1997] E.C.R. I- 3091.
[84] Joined Cases C–418/93 *etc.*, *Semeraro Casa Uno Srl v. Sindaco di Comune di Erbusco etc.*, [1996] E.C.R. I–2975, see this Chapter, p. 459.
[85] *ibid.*

formal qualifications, considered in the context of the right of establishment,[86] is also applicable to the provision of services by doctors, as is Directive 89/48 on the recognition of higher education diplomas.[87] In order to facilitate the provision of services, medical practitioners established outside the host State are relieved of the obligation to register with professional organisations of bodies therein though they are subject to the applicable national rules of professional conduct.[88]

Surprisingly, in view of the differences between the laws and legal systems in the Member States, considerable progress has been made as regards both the right of establishment of lawyers,[89] and as regards the provision of services. Thus Directive 89/48 allows Member States to decide between an adaptation period and an aptitude test in the case of lawyers seeking recognition of their qualifications in another Member State.[90] However, Directive 98/5 allows lawyers to establish themselves under home-State title in other Member States, and to acquire a host State qualification on the basis of three-year period of practice in the host State, without complying with the adaptation period or aptitude test requirement of Directive 89/48.[91] Specific provision is made for the provision of services by lawyers in Directive 77/249.[92] Under the Directive, Member States must recognise designated legal practitioners[93] as "lawyers" for the purpose of pursuing "the activities of lawyers pursued by way of provision of services."[94] Since the substantive content of legal training differs in the Member States, and the Directive contains no provisions for the mutual recognition of diplomas, a designated legal practitioner must adopt the professional title used in the Member State from which he comes, expressed in the language of that State, and with an indication of the professional organisation by which he is authorised to practise.[95] When representing a client in legal proceedings, a lawyer must comply with the conditions laid down for lawyers in the host State, except for conditions requiring residence, or registration with a professional organisation in that State,[96] and the host State may further require him:

"— to be introduced, in accordance with local rules or customs, to the presiding judge and, where appropriate, to the President of the relevant Bar in the host Member State;
— to work in conjunction with a lawyer who practises before the judicial authority in question and who would, where necessary, be answerable to that authority . . ."[97]

---

[86] Above at p. 462.
[87] As to which see above at p. 463.
[88] Dir. 93/16, Art. 17(1); but see the third sub-para. of Art. 17(1), which allows a requirement of registration under certain conditions.
[89] As to which, see above at p. 463.
[90] See above, p. 463.
[91] See in particular Art. 10 of the Directive.
[92] [1977] O.J. L78/17.
[93] Art. 1(2).
[94] Art. 2.
[95] Art. 3.
[96] Art. 4(1).
[97] Art. 5.

The Court has held that the purpose of the requirement that a lawyer providing services "work in conjunction with" a local lawyer is intended to provide him with the support necessary to enable him to act within a judicial system different from that to which he is accustomed and to assure the judicial authority concerned that the lawyer providing services actually has that support and is thus in a position fully to comply with the procedural and ethical rules that apply.[98] But national implementing measures must not lay down disproportionate requirements in this regard, such as a requirement that a local lawyer be present throughout the oral proceedings, or a requirement that the local lawyer be the authorised representative or defending counsel.[99]

NATIONAL MEASURES TO PREVENT CIRCUMVENTION OF NATIONAL RULES IN THE CONTEXT OF THE RIGHT OF ESTABLISHMENT AND FREEDOM TO PROVIDE SERVICES

The Court of Justice has indicated in a number of cases that provisions of Community law should not be interpreted in such a way as to facilitate the wrongful avoidance of national rules.[1] It will be recalled that in the *Centros* case,[2] Danish nationals resident and carrying on business in Denmark incorporated a company to carry on that business and incorporated that company in England rather than Denmark in order to avoid the relatively high minimum capital requirement attendant upon incorporation in Denmark. The Danish authorities argued that those nationals could not rely upon the Treaty provisions on the right of establishment, since the sole purpose of the company formation in England was to circumvent the application of the Danish rules governing formation of private limited companies and therefore constituted abuse of the freedom of establishment.[3] The Court referred to its case-law on wrongful circumvention of national rules,[4] and explained it as follows: That case-law allowed national courts to take account, case by case, and on the basis of objective evidence, of abuse or fraudulent conduct on the part of the persons concerned in order, where appropriate, to deny them the benefit of provisions of Community law on which they relied. But it was nevertheless necessary to assess such conduct in the light of the objectives pursued by the provisions of Community law in question.[5] The Court noted that in the case in point, "the provisions of national law, application of which the parties concerned have sought to avoid, are rules governing the

---

[98] Case 427/85 *Commission v. Germany* [1988] E.C.R. 1123.

[99] *ibid.*, and see Case C–294/89 *Commission v. France* [1991] E.C.R. I–3591.

[1] Case 115/78 *Knoors* [1979] E.C.R. 399; [1979] 2 C.M.L.R. 357, para. 25; Case 61/89 *Bouchoucha* [1990] E.C.R. I—3557; [1992] 1 C.M.L.R. 1033, para. 14.

[2] Case C–212/97 *Centros Ltd v. Erhvervs- og Selskabsstyrelsen* [1999] E.C.R. I–1459; [1999] 2 C.M.L.R. 551, see above at p. 466.

[3] Case C–212/97 *Centros Ltd v. Erhvervs- og Selskabsstyrelsen* [1999] E.C.R. I–1459; [1999] 2 C.M.L.R. 551, para. 23.

[4] *ibid.*, at para. 24.

[5] *ibid.*, at para. 25.

formation of companies and not rules concerning the carrying on of certain trades, professions or businesses."[6] The Court went on to note that the provisions of the Treaty on freedom of establishment were intended specifically to enable companies of one Member State to pursue activities in other Member States through an agency branch or subsidiary, and held that that being so, the fact that a national of a Member State who wished to set up a company chose to form it in the Member State whose rules of company law seemed to him the least restrictive, and to set up branches in other Member States could not in itself constitute an abuse of the right of establishment.[7]

From the outset the case-law on freedom to provide services indicated that the Treaty did not prohibit Member States from taking appropriate steps to prevent the wrongful circumvention of national rules. The Court in *Van Binsbergen* stated:

"Likewise, a member state cannot be denied the right to take measures to prevent the exercise by a person providing services whose activity is entirely or principally directed towards its territory of the freedom guaranteed by article 59 for the purpose of avoiding the professional rules of conduct which would be applicable to him if he were established within that state; such a situation may be subject to judicial control under the provisions of the chapter relating to the right of establishment and not of that on the provision of services."[8]

It is to be noted that the Court clearly presupposed that control under the provisions of the Chapter relating to the right of establishment would involve a greater ability to impose requirements on economic operators than would be possible under the Chapter on the provision of services. While such a difference exists today in principle it seems that the extent of that difference has diminished almost to vanishing point,[9] and this perhaps explains why the Court's formulation of national anti-circumvention competence has evolved over the years. Thus in *Veronica*[10] the Court of Justice repeated the above formulation, but omitted the reference to the situation being subject to judicial control under the provisions of the Chapter relating to the right of establishment, and in *TV10 SA* the Court repeated the latter formulation, but added that it would therefore be compatible with the provisions of the Treaty on freedom to provide services to treat such organisations *as domestic organisations*.

---

[6] *ibid.*, at para. 26.

[7] *ibid.*, at paras 26–27; and see above, this Chapter, at p. 466.

[8] Case 33/74 *Van Binsbergen v. Bedrijfsvereniging Metaalnijverheid* [1974] E.C.R. 1307; [1975] 1 C.M.L.R. 298, at para. 13. This formulation was repeated *verbatim* by the Court in Case 205/84 *Commission v. Germany* [1986] E.C.R. 3755; [1987] 2 C.M.L.R. 69, at para. 22.

[9] For example, national rules on registration with professional bodies are presumptively applicable as regards those who are exercising the right of establishment, but not as regards those providing services. Thus, Art. 4 of Dir. 77/249 on provision of services by lawyers, exempts service providers from registration in the host State, while Art. 3 of Dir. 98/5 on the establishment of lawyers provides for such registration.

[10] Case C–148/91 *Vereniging Veronica Omroep Organisatie v. Commissariaat voor de Media.* [1991] E.C.R. I–487, para. 12

ARTICLES 45 AND 55—EXCEPTION IN THE CASE OF ACTIVITIES CONNECTED WITH THE EXERCISE OF OFFICIAL AUTHORITY

Article 45 (ex 55) provides that the provisions of the Chapter on establishment shall not apply, "so far as any given Member State is concerned, to activities which in that State are connected, even occasionally, with the exercise of official authority". Pursuant to Article 55 (ex 66) this latter provision also applies to the Chapter on freedom to provide services. This exception constitutes a derogation from a fundamental Treaty rule, and must be interpreted strictly, so as not to exceed the purpose for which it was inserted.[11]

In *Reyners v. Belgian State*,[12] it was argued that the profession of *avocat* was exempted from the chapter on establishment because it involved the exercise of official authority. The Court held that Article 45 (ex 55) applied only to those activities which, taken on their own, involved a direct and specific connection with the exercise of official authority,[13] and added that:

"Professional activities involving contacts, even regular and organic, with the courts, including even compulsory co-operation in their functioning, do not constitute, as such, connexion with the exercise of official authority. The most typical activities of the profession of *avocat*, in particular, such as consultation and legal assistance and also representation and the defence of parties in court, even when the intervention or assistance of the *avocat* is compulsory or is a legal monopoly, cannot be considered as connected with the exercise of official authority. The exercise of these activities leaves the discretion of judicial authority and the free exercise of judicial power intact."[14]

This latter observation certainly implies that the exercise of a judicial function by an advocate would amount to the exercise of official authority, which is in any event self-evident. Advocate General Mayras described official authority as "that which arises from the sovereignty and majesty of the State; for him who exercises it, it implies the power of enjoying the [sic] prerogatives outside the general law, privileges of official power and powers of coercion over citizens".[15] This is consistent with the approach of the Court of Justice in *Commission v. Belgium*, on the ambit of Article 39(4) (ex 48(4)).[16] In the latter case the Court held that Article 39(4) (ex 48(4)) covers posts which involve direct or indirect participation in the exercise of powers conferred by public law and duties designed to safeguard the general interests of the State.[17] Article 39(4) and Article 45 have essentially the same aim, and should be interpreted in an analogous way. As an exception to a fundamental principle, Article 45 (ex 55) is given a strict

---

[11] Case 2/74 *Reyners v. Belgian State* [1974] E.C.R. 631; [1974] 2 C.M.L.R. 305; Case 152/73 *Sotgiu v. Deutsche Bundespost* [1974] E.C.R. 153.
[12] Case 2/74 [1974] E.C.R. 631; [1974] 2 C.M.L.R. 305.
[13] *ibid.*, para. 45.
[14] *ibid.*, paras 51–53.
[15] [1974] E.C.R. 631 at 664.
[16] Case 149/79 [1980] E.C.R. 3881; [1981] 2 C.M.L.R. 413.
[17] *ibid.*, para. 10. See in general Chap. 14, at pp. 426 *et seq.*

construction.[18] Thus the Court has held that the activity of traffic accident expert does not involve the exercise of official authority where the reports of these experts are not binding on the courts, leaving the discretion of the judiciary and the exercise of judicial power intact.[19] Similarly, the Court has held that the "auxiliary and preparatory functions" of an "approved commissioner" *vis-à-vis* an "Insurance Inspectorate", which latter body was a body exercising official authority by taking the final relevant decision, could not be regarded as having a direct and specific connection with the exercise of official authority.[20] Security undertakings and security staff lacking legal powers of constraint cannot be described as exercising official authority because they make a contribution to the maintenance of public security, which any individual may be called upon to do.[21]

Article 45 (ex 55) refers to "activities" connected with the exercise of official authority, rather than to "professions". The Court of Justice in *Reyners* made it clear that while certain "activities" forming part of a particular profession might fall within Article 45 (ex 55), the profession as a whole might nevertheless be subject to the right of establishment. This would be the case wherever the activities could be "severed" from the profession concerned, as they could be so severed, it would seems, in the case of an advocate called upon to perform occasional judicial functions. The Court took the view that the exception allowed by Article 45 (ex 55) could only be extended to a whole profession where the activities in question "were linked with that profession in such a way that freedom of establishment would result in imposing on the Member State concerned the obligation to allow the exercise, even occasionally, by non-nationals of functions appertaining to official authority".[22]

In view of the Court's decision in *Sotgiu v. Deutsche Bundespost*, it would seem that Article 45 (ex 55) should be interpreted as applying only to *access* to activities connected with the exercise of official authority; not as authorising discriminatory conditions of work once a person had been allowed to take up such activities.[23]

The second paragraph of Article 45 (ex 55) provides that the Council may rule "that the provisions of this Chapter shall not apply to certain activities". It seems that these words must be construed subject to the text of the previous paragraph, *i.e.* as involving activities connected with exercise of official authority. The authority bestowed thereby upon the Council would thus seem to be rather limited, and has not, so far, been exercised. In applying Article 45 (ex 55) to a particular profession, it is necessary to establish the ambit of the "activities" which "taken on their own, constitute a direct and specific connection with the exercise of official authority."[24] While the "exercise of official authority" is a concept of Community law, the question of "direct and specific connection" with such exercise is one of fact which, unresolved, can lead to uncertainty on the part

---

[18] Case 2/74 *Reyners* [1974] E.C.R. 631; [1974] 2 C.M.L.R. 305, at para. 43.

[19] Case C–306/89 *Commission v. Greece* [1991] E.C.R. I–5863; [1994] 1 C.M.L.R. 803, para. 7.

[20] Case C–42/92 *Adrianus Thijssen v. Controledienst voor de verzekeringen*. [1993] E.C.R. I–4047, para. 22.

[21] Case C–114/97 *Commission v. Spain* [1998] E.C.R. I–6717, para. 37.

[22] Case 2/74 *Reyners* [1974] E.C.R. 631; [1974] 2 C.M.L.R. 305, at para. 46.

[23] Chap. 14, at p. 426.

[24] Case 2/74 *Reyners* [1974] E.C.R. 631; [1974] 2 C.M.L.R. 305, at para. 45.

of those subject to the law. It seems that the Council's function under this provision would be limited to establishing that certain activities do indeed have a "direct and specific connection" with the exercise of official authority.

ARTICLES 46 AND 55—THE PUBLIC POLICY PROVISO

Article 46 (ex 56) provides that the provisions of the Chapter on establishment and measures taken in pursuance thereof shall not prejudice the applicability of provisions providing for special treatment for foreign nationals on grounds of public policy, public security or public health. And Article 55 (ex 66) makes the same provision as regards the Chapter on provision of services. The scheme of Articles 39 to 55 (ex 48 to 66), and the parallel interpretation given to these provisions in relation to discrimination, entry and residence,[25] and the fact that the public policy provisos of Article 39(3) (ex 48(3)) and Article 46 (ex 56) are implemented by one and the same Directive—Directive 64/221—suggests that Article 46 (ex 56) is to be interpreted in an analogous manner to Article 39(3) (ex 48(3)).[26] Thus, for instance, it would seem to follow that Article 46 (ex 56) must be interpreted as permitting derogation from the Chapter on establishment only in respect of entry and residence—not in respect of the terms and conditions under which occupational activities are carried on.[27] For a detailed analysis of the terms of Directive 64/221, and an examination of the Court's jurisprudence on the public policy proviso in Article 39(3) (ex 48(3)), the reader is referred to the chapter on freedom of movement for workers.[28]

In the context of the right of establishment, the Court has said that while the need to combat fraud may justify a difference in treatment on grounds of nationality in certain circumstances, the mere risk of tax avoidance cannot justify discriminatory treatment.[29].Article 46 permits derogation from the right of establishment in the case of foreign nationals, but since this provision, by virtue of Article 55, also applies as an exception to the Treaty's prohibition on restrictions to provide services, and since the latter prohibition covers national measures which discriminate not only on grounds of nationality, but also by reference to the place of establishment of the provider,[30] or the place of residence of the recipient,[31] discrimination on these latter grounds also falls within the scope of this provision, and direct discrimination on any of these above grounds may be justified only by this provision or another express term of

---

[25] Above at p. 445.

[26] The provisions of Dir. 64/221 apply to any national of a Member State who resides in or travels to another Member State of the Community, either in order to pursue an activity as an employed or self-employed person, or as a recipient of services; see Art. 1.

[27] Case 152/73 *Sotgiu* [1974] E.C.R. 153; Case 15/69 *Ugliola* [1969] E.C.R. 363; [1970] C.M.L.R. 194; above at p. 415.

[28] Above at pp. 416 *et seq.*

[29] Case 79/85 *Segers v. Bestuur van de Bedrijfsvereniging voor Bank- en Verzeleringswezen* [1986] E.C.R. 2375; [1987] 2 C.M.L.R. 247, para. 17.

[30] Case C–484/93 *Svensson et Gustavsson v. Ministre du Logement et de l'Urbanisme* [1995] E.C.R. I–3955, para. 15;

[31] Case C–224/97 *Ciola v. Land Voralrberg* [1999] E.C.R. I–2517; [1999] 2 C.M.L.R. 1220, para. 16.

the Treaty.[32] In the context of the provision of services, in the *Kohll* case, the Court noted that the Treaty allowed Member States to limit freedom to provide services on grounds of public health, but added that that did not permit them to exclude the public health sector, as a sector of economic activity and from the point of view of the freedom to provide services, from the application of the fundamental principle of freedom of movement.[33] It did however permit Member States to restrict the freedom to provide medical and hospital services in so far as the maintenance of a treatment facility or medical service on national territory is essential for the public health and even the survival of the population.[34] It is established that economic aims do not constitute grounds of public policy within the meaning of Article 46 of the Treaty.[35] Nor do the aims of reinforcing the financial soundness of companies in order to protect public and private creditors.[36] In order to justify a national measure on the basis of the latter provision, it is necessary to demonstrate that it is indispensable for achieving one of the aims referred to.[37]

MANDATORY REQUIREMENTS IN THE GENERAL INTEREST

General

It has been noted in the last section that discriminatory restrictions on the right of establishment and the freedom to provide services may be justified on grounds of public policy, public security or public health. But that is not the only ground upon which measures which constitute or appear to constitute restrictions prohibited by the relevant provisions of the Treaty may be justified. The Court has interpreted the latter provisions in such a way that restrictions which arise from certain imperative requirements, which are imposed in the general interest, are not regarded as comprising prohibited obstacles to the right of establishment, and restrictions which arise for overriding reasons relating to the public interest, are not regarded as comprising prohibited obstacles to the freedom to provide services. It is appropriate to consider below, *inter alia*, the evolution of the Court's case-law in this regard, the categories of general interest, or public interest, which may justify restrictions, and the line of demarcation between the

---

[32] Case C–484/93 *Svensson et Gustavsson v. Ministre du Logement et de l'Urbanisme* [1995] E.C.R. I–3955, para. 15; Case C–224/97 *Ciola v. Land Voralrberg* [1999] E.C.R. I–2517; [1999] 2 C.M.L.R. 1220, para. 16; and see below p. 489.

[33] Case C–158/96 *Raymond Kohll v. Union des Caisses de Maladie* [1998] E.C.R. I–1931; [1998] 2 C.M.L.R. 928, para. 46.

[34] *ibid.*, para. 51; the Court refers by analogy to Case 72/83 *Campus Oil v. Minister for Industry and Energy* [1984] E.C.R. 2727; [1984] 3 C.M.L.R. 544, paras 33–36, which deals with public security within the meaning of Art. 30 (ex 36) E.C.

[35] Case C–288/89 *Stichting Collectieve Antennevoorziening Gouda and others v. Commissariaat voor de Media* [1991] E.C.R. I–4007, para. 11; Case C–484/93 *Svensson et Gustavsson v. Ministre du Logement et de l'Urbanisme* [1995] E.C.R. I–3955, para. 15.

[36] Case C–212/97 *Centros Ltd v. Erhvervs- og Selskabsstyrelsen* [1999] E.C.R. I–1459; [1999] 2 C.M.L.R. 551, paras 32–34.

[37] Case C–3/88 *Commission v. Italy* [1989] E.C.R. 4035; [1991] 2 C.M.L.R. 115, para. 15; Case C–101/94 *Commission v. Italy* [1996] E.C.R. I–2691; [1996] 3 C.M.L.R. 754, para. 26.

restrictions which may be so justified, and the discriminatory restrictions which the Court has stated on numerous occasion to be capable of justification exclusively by an express provision of the Treaty, and in particular by Articles 46 and 55 of the Treaty.

The Court's case-law on imperative requirements in the general interest in the context of the right of establishment

In the context of the right of establishment, it has only been with the development of the concept of the non-discriminatory restriction on this right, that recourse to mandatory requirements has become at all significant. That is not to say that the question of justification of restrictions has not arisen, but that the question tended in the context of alleged indirect discrimination on grounds of nationality, which would be prohibited by the provisions of the Treaty unless objectively justified.[38] The concept of objective justification, and the concept of mandatory requirements, are clearly close relations. The question of justification of indirect discrimination on grounds of nationality arising from national tax rules by reference to the "cohesion of the tax system", discussed above, is relevant in this regard.[39] Where national rules have been held to comprise a restriction on the right of establishment, not by discrimination on grounds of nationality, but by prohibiting or disadvantaging the setting up of a place of business in more than one Member State, the Court accepts that justification might in principle be possible.[40]

With the development of the concept of the non-discriminatory restriction on the right of establishment has come the "rolled up" formulation, in which the definition of the restriction and the possibilities for its justification are presented in a simple, apparently straightforward formulation, as the following statement of the Court in the *Gebhard* case indicates:

". . . national measures liable to hinder or make less attractive the exercise of fundamental freedoms guaranteed by the Treaty must fulfil four conditions: they must be applied in a non-discriminatory manner; they must be justified by imperative requirements in the general interest; they must be suitable for securing the attainment of the objective which they pursue; and they must not go beyond what is necessary in order to attain it . . ."[41]

In the *Centros* case[42] it was argued for the Danish authorities they were justified in refusing to register a branch of an English company in Denmark, where the English company carried on no business in the United Kingdom, and

---

[38] See Chap. 14, on indirect discrimination and jusification in the context of the free movement of workers, at pp. 402 *et seq.*, and this Chapter, p. 447 above.

[39] Above at p. 450 *et seq.*

[40] Case 107/83 *Ordre des avocats au Barreau de Paris v. Onno Klopp.* [1983] E.C.R. 2971; [1985] 1 C.M.L.R. 99, paras 20–21; Case 143/87 *Stanton v. Inasti* [1988] E.C.R. 3877; [1989] 3 C.M.L.R. 761, para. 15; Case C–53/95 *Inasti v. Kemmler* [1996] E.C.R. I–703, para. 13.

[41] Case C–55/94 *Gebhard v. Consiglio dell'Ordine degli Avvocati e Procuratori di Milano* [1995] E.C.R. I–4165; [1996] 1 C.M.L.R. 603; [1996] All E.R. (E.C.) 189, para. 37.

[42] Case C–212/97 *Centros Ltd v. Erhvervs- og Selskabsstyrelsen* [1999] E.C.R. I–1459; [1999] 2 C.M.L.R. 551.

where that latter company did not meet the minimum capital requirements laid down for Danish companies. The Danish companies argued that refusing to register the branch was the least restrictive means available of reinforcing the financial soundness of companies so as to protect the interests of public and private creditors, and in particular public creditors, who, unlike private creditors, were not in a position to secure their debts by obtaining personal guarantees from the directors of debtor companies.[43] The Court did not deny that interests such as those referred to might in principle justify measures such as those in issue, but rejected the argument on the ground that it was possible to adopt measures which were less restrictive, or which interfered less with fundamental freedoms, by, for example, making it possible in law for public creditors to obtain the necessary guarantees.[44] The Court has held that the effectiveness of fiscal supervision constitutes an "overriding requirement of general interest" capable of justifying a restriction on the exercise of fundamental freedoms guaranteed by the Treaty.[45] As regards the categories of mandatory requirement which may be invoked to justify national rules which might restrict the exercise of the right of establishment, reference by analogy may be made in particular to the case-law on the free movement of goods,[46] and on freedom to provide services.

The Court's case law on overriding reasons in the general interest in the context of freedom to provide services

In the *van Binsbergen* case the Court of Justice stated that restrictions on freedom to provide services would not be prohibited by the Treaty where they had the purpose of applying:

"professional rules justified by the general good—in particular rules relating to organisation, qualifications, professional ethics, supervision and liability— which are binding upon any person established in the state in which the service is provided, where the person providing the service would escape from the ambit of those rules by being established in another Member State."[47]

It is to be noted that the Court did not make any reference to Article 46 (ex 56) E.C., and seemed to countenance that, in principle, and in an appropriate case, a Member State might insist on establishment within national territory to ensure application of national rules such as those referred to. In *Ramrath* the Court held that a requirement that auditors maintain an establishment in national territory was justified in order to secure the application of national rules in the public interest designed to uphold the integrity and independence of those practising the profession in question.[48] In *van Binsbergen* the national rules

---

[43] *ibid.*, para. 32.
[44] *ibid.*, para. 37.
[45] Case C–254/97 *Société Baxter v. Premier Ministre and Others* [1999] E.C.R. I–4809, para. 18; this category of mandatory requirement was recognised as a justification for restricting the free movement of goods in the *Cassis* case, see Chap. 13, at p. 323.
[46] Chap. 13, pp. 352 *et seq.*
[47] Case 33/74 *Van Binsbergen v. Bedrijfsvereniging Metaalnijverheid* [1974] E.C.R. 1307; [1975] 1 C.M.L.R. 298, para. 12.
[48] Case C–106/91 *Ramrath v. Ministre de la Jusice, and L'Institut des réviseurs d'entreprises* [1992] E.C.R. I–3351; [1992] 3 C.M.L.R. 173; [1995] 2 C.M.L.R. 187.

identified as comprising restrictions on the freedom to provide services comprised those discriminating on grounds of nationality and those which discriminated by reference to the place of establishment of the service provider[49]—a formulation to be repeated in the Court's case law.[50] Yet in *van Binsbergen* and *Ramrath* the reference to national rules applicable to all persons pursuing the activities in the State in question suggests that the Court had in mind rules which, while they might differentiate between individuals by reference to their place of establishment, would nevertheless not discriminate on grounds of nationality, at any rate not directly.[51]

In *Seco* the Court considered an obligation imposed by national law on employers to pay social security contributions on behalf of their employees, which was also applicable to employers who were established in other Member States and temporarily providing services in the host State, and who were already liable to make similar contributions under the legislation of the Member States where they were established. The Court held that this amounted to indirect discrimination on grounds of nationality, which could not be justified on account of the general interest in providing workers with social security, since no benefits were payable to the employees in such circumstances. It will be noted that in this case the examination of justification in the general interest is in fact an assessment of whether or not the indirect discrimination can be objectively justified.[52]

In *Bond van Adverteerders* the Court stated that national rules which "are not applicable to services without distinction as regards their origin and which are therefore discriminatory are compatible with Community law only if they can be brought within the scope of an express derogation, such as Articles 45 and 55 (ex 56 and 66).[53] In *Stichting Collectieve Antennevoorziening Gouda* repeated and expanded upon this earlier statement. While national rules which were not applicable to services without discrimination as regards their origin could only be justified if brought within an express provision of the Treaty, and in particular Articles 46 and 55,[54] the Court contrasted restrictions on the freedom to provide services which may arise as a result of the application of national rules which may affect any person established in national territory to persons providing services established in the territory of another Member State who already have to satisfy the requirements of that State's legislation.[55] As regards restrictions in this latter category, the Court indicates that they are not prohibited if they are justified by "overriding reasons relating to the public interest or if the requirements

---

[49] See above, p. 474.
[50] Above at p. 475.
[51] Case 33/74 *Van Binsbergen v. Bedrijfsvereniging Metaalnijverheid* [1974] E.C.R. 1307; [1975] 1 C.M.L.R. 298, para. 12; Case C–106/91 *Ramrath v. Ministre de la Justice, and L'Institut des réviseurs d'entreprises* [1992] E.C.R. I–3351; [1992] 3 C.M.L.R. 173; [1995] 2 C.M.L.R. 187, para. 29.
[52] Joined Cases 62–63/81 *Société anonyme de droit français Seco et Société anonyme de droit français Desquenne & Giral v. Etablissement d'assurance v. la vieillesse et l'invalidité* [1982] E.C.R. 223, paras 8 to 10.
[53] Case 352/85 *Bond van Adverteerders and others v. The Netherlands State.* [1988] E.C.R. 2085; [1989] 3 C.M.L.R. 113, para. 32.
[54] Case C–288/89 *Stichting Collectieve Antennevoorziening Gouda and others v. Commissariaat voor de Media* [1991] E.C.R. I–4007, para. 11.
[55] *ibid.*, para. 12.

embodied in that legislation are already satisfied by the rules imposed on those persons in the Member State in which they are established".[56] The Court goes on to list overriding reasons relating to the public interest which the Court had recognised to date.[57] It appears from that list that the Court regards the second category to which it has referred, which covers restrictions which need not be justified by reference to Articles 46 and 55, as covering national rules which discriminate indirectly on grounds of nationality (where the overriding reasons in the general interest in effect amount to objective justification),[58] and national rules which discriminate indirectly on the ground that the service provider is established in another Member State. The Court of Justice has held that national rules which are not applicable to services without distinction as regards the place of residence *of the recipient* are discriminatory and can be justified only by an express derogation such as Article 46.[59]

It would appear from the foregoing judgment of the Court in *Gouda* that prohibiting a service provider from providing services in the host state because he is established in another Member State could only be justified on the basis of Article 46. Yet *Van Binsbergen* and *Ramrath* indicate that overriding reasons in the general interest can be relied upon in such circumstances.

The Court in *Gouda*, after listing the categories of public interest referred to above, added with a reference to the need for national measures being appropriate and proportionate in order to be justified:

"Lastly, as the Court has consistently held, the application of national provisions to providers of services established in other Member States must be such as to guarantee the achievement of the intended aim and must not go beyond what is necessary in order to achieve that objective. In other words, it must not be possible to obtain the same result by less restrictive rules . . ."[60]

While the above test for the proportionality of national measures is almost invariably an objective one, it seems that in exceptional cases the importance and sensitivity of the issues of public interest involved allow Member States a wide

---

[56] *ibid.*, para. 13.

[57] The Court listed professional rules intended to protect recipients of the service (Joined Cases 110–111/78 *Van Wesemael* [1979] E.C.R. 35; [1979] 3 C.M.L.R. 87, para. 28); protection of intellectual property (Case 62/79 *Coditel* [1980] E.C.R. 881; [1981] 2 C.M.L.R. 362); the protection of workers (Case 279/80 *Webb* [1981] E.C.R. 3305; [1982] 1 C.M.L.R. 719, para. 19); Joined Cases 62–63/81 *Seco v. EVI* [1982] E.C.R. 223, para. 14; Case C–113/89 *Rush Portuguesa* [1990] E.C.R. I–1417; [1991] 2 C.M.L.R. 818, para. 18); consumer protection (Case 220/83 *Commission v. France* [1986] E.C.R. 3663, para. 20; Case 252/83 *Commission v. Denmark* [1986] E.C.R. 3713; [1987] 2 C.M.L.R. 169, para. 20; Case 205/84 *Commission v. Germany* [1986] E.C.R. 3755; [1987] 2 C.M.L.R. 69, para. 30; Case 206/84 *Commission v. Ireland* [1986] E.C.R. 3817; [1987] 2 C.M.L.R. 150, para. 20; Case C–180/89 *Commission v. Italy* [1991] E.C.R. I–709, para. 20; and Case C–198/89 *Commission v. Greece*, [1991] E.C.R. I–727, para. 21), the conservation of the national historic and artistic heritage (*Commission v. Italy*, cited above, para. 20); turning to account the archaeological, historical and artistic heritage of a country and the widest possible dissemination of knowledge of the artistic and cultural heritage of a country (*Commission v. France*, cited above, para. 17, and *Commission v. Greece*, cited above, para. 21).

[58] Note that the Court refers to the *Seco* case, which, as shown above, concerns in reality the question of objective justification for indirect discrimination.

[59] Case C–224/97 *Ciola v. Land Vorarlberg* [1999] E.C.R. I–2517; [1999] 2 C.M.L.R. 1220, para. 16.

[60] Case C–288/89 *Stichting Collectieve Antennevoorziening Gouda and others v. Commissariaat voor de Media* [1991] E.C.R. I–4007, para. 15.

discretion to judge whether it is necessary to restrict and/or prohibit certain activities.[61]

Consistently with the approach in *Gouda* whereby national rules which *indirectly* discriminate as regards the State of establishment of a service provider may in principle be justified, the Court has undertaken such an analysis of justification in a number of cases involving such indirect discrimination.[62] The Court's analysis of "overriding reasons in the general interest" has continued to follow the pattern established prior to the development of the concept of the non-discriminatory restriction in the *Säger* case.[63] The Court has upheld national rules which prohibit lotteries on grounds of consumer protection and the maintenance of order in society,[64] and national rules which confine the judicial recovery of debts to members of the legal profession on the grounds of consumer protection and safeguarding the proper administration of justice,[65] and the Court has acknowledged that the risk of seriously undermining the financial balance of the social security system may constitute an overriding reason in the general interest capable of justifying an indirectly discriminatory measure.[66]

---

[61] Case C–275/92 *Her Majesty's Customs and Excise v. Gerhart Schindler and Jörg Schindler.* [1994] E.C.R. I–1039; [1995] 1 C.M.L.R. 4, para. 61. Also see Case C–124/97 *Läärä* [1999] E.C.R. I–6007 and Case C–67/98 *Zenatti* [1999] E.C.R. I–7289.

[62] Case C–158/96 *Raymond Kohll v. Union des Caisses de Maladie* [1998] E.C.R. I–1931; [1998] 2 C.M.L.R. 928, paras 34 and 41. Case C–410/96 *André Ambry* [1998] E.C.R. I–7875, paras 28–31. In Case C–484/93 *Svensson et Gustavsson v. Ministre du Logement et de l'Urbanisme* [1995] E.C.R. I–3955, the Court repeated the proposition that a national rule which discriminates by reference to place of establishment can only be justified by reference to Art. 46 (ex 56), but then goes on to examine whether the measure may nevertheless be justified by the need to maintain cohesion of the tax system; paras 15 and 16. The Court's case law is not entirely consistent.

[63] Case C–76/90 *Manfred Säger v. Dennemeyer & Co. Ltd* [1991] E.C.R. I–4221; [1993] 3 C.M.L.R. 639.

[64] Case C–275/92 *Her Majesty's Customs and Excise v. Gerhart Schindler and Jörg Schindler* [1994] E.C.R. I–1039; [1995] 1 C.M.L.R. 4, para. 61.

[65] Case C–3/95 *Broede v. Sandker* [1996] E.C.R. I–6511; [1997] 1 C.M.L.R. 224.

[66] Case C–158/96 *Raymond Kohll v. Union des Caisses de Maladie* [1998] E.C.R. I–1931; [1998] 2 C.M.L.R. 928, para. 41

CHAPTER 16

RESIDUARY RIGHTS OF RESIDENCE AND CITIZENSHIP OF THE UNION

Residuary rights of residence

The fundamental freedoms include the right of the employed and self-employed to carry on economic activities in other Member States, and to exercise rights of free movement and of residence in the territory of other Member States.[1] As has been noted the rights of movement and of residence have been extended by secondary legislation to members of the family of employed and self-employed persons, and to certain of those no longer economically active.[2] Similarly, the Treaty bestowed the right to equal access to vocational training courses, and the right to reside in the territory of a Member State for that purpose.[3] In 1990 the Council adopted three directives designed to vest rights of residence in those who did not at the time derive such rights from the terms of the Treaty or secondary legislation in force. These directives dealt with the rights of residence of (1) employees and self-employed persons who have ceased their occupational activity; (2) students; and (3) those who do not enjoy a right of residence under Community law.

Directive 90/365—right of residence for employees and self-employed persons who have ceased their occupational activity

Council Directive 90/365[4] provides that Member States shall grant the right of residence to nationals of Member States who have pursued an activity as an employee or self-employed person and to members of their families as defined in the Directive, provided that they are recipients of an invalidity or early retirement pension, or old age benefits, or of a pension in respect of an industrial accident or disease of an amount sufficient to avoid becoming a burden on the social security system of the host Member State during their period of residence, and provided they are covered by sickness insurance in respect of all risks in the host Member State.[5] The resources of the applicant shall be deemed sufficient where they are higher than the level of resources below which the host Member State may grant social assistance to its nationals, taking into account the personal circumstances of persons comprising the members of the family referred to in the

---

[1] See in particular Chaps 14 and 15 of this book.

[2] For Reg. 1251/70 on the right of workers to remain in the territory of a Member State after having been employed in that State, see Chap. 14 at p. 412; for Dir. 75/34 concerning the right of nationals of a Member State to remain in the territory of another Member State having pursued therein an activity in a self-employed capacity, see Chap. 15 at p. 441.

[3] Chap. 28, at p. 786, and see in particular Case C–295/90 *European Parliament v. Council* [1992] E.C.R. I–4193; [1991] E.C.R. I–5299.

[4] [1990] O.J. L180/28. See Case C–96/95 *Commission v. Germany* [1997] E.C.R. I–1653; and Case C–424/98 *Commission v. Italy* judgment of May 25, 2000.

[5] *ibid.*, Art. 1(1), first para.

Directive.[6] The members of the family who, irrespective of their nationality, have the right to "install themselves" in another Member State with the holder of the right of residence referred to above, are (a) his or her spouse and their descendants who are dependants; (b) dependent relatives in the ascending line of the holder of the right of residence and his or her spouse.[7] The right of residence of beneficiaries is to be enjoyed for as long as they fulfil the conditions laid down by the Directive.[8]

Exercise of the right of residence shall be evidenced by means of the issue of a document known as a "Residence permit for a national of a Member State of the E.C.", whose validity may be limited to five years on a renewable basis. However, the Member States may, when they deem it necessary, require revalidation of the permit at the end of the first two years of residence. Where a member of the family does not hold the nationality of a Member State, he or she shall be issued with a residence document of the same validity as that issued to the national on whom he or she depends.[9] For the purposes of issuing the residence permit of document, the Member State may require only that the applicant present a valid identity card or passport and provide proof that he or she meets the conditions laid down by the Directive.[10]

Certain Articles of Directive 68/360 on the abolition of restrictions on movement and residence within the Community for workers of Member States and their families apply *mutatis mutandis* to beneficiaries of Directive 90/365.[11] The Articles of Directive 68/360 referred to are Article 2 (right to leave national territory on production of a valid passport or identity card); Article 3 (right to enter territory of a Member State on production of a valid passport or identity card); Article 6(1)(a) (residence permit must be valid throughout territory of the Member State which issued it); Article 6(2) (breaks in residence not exceeding six consecutive months shall not affect the validity of a residence permit); and Article 9 (residence documents shall be issued and renewed free of charge, etc.).

Directive 90/365 provides that the spouse and dependent children of a national of a Member State entitled to the right of residence within the territory of a Member State shall be entitled to take up any employed or self-employed activity anywhere within the territory of that Member State even if they are not nationals of a Member State.[12] Member States may not derogate from the provisions of the Directive save on grounds of public policy, public security or public health, in which event, Directive 64/221[13] shall apply.[14]

---

[6] *ibid.*, Art. 1(1), second para.
[7] *ibid.*, Art. 1(2).
[8] *ibid.*, Art. 3.
[9] *ibid.*, Art. 2(1), first para.
[10] *ibid.*, Art. 2(1), second para.
[11] *ibid.*, Art. 2(2). first para. For Dir. 68/360, see Chap. 14, p. 387.
[12] *ibid.*, Art. 2(2). second para.
[13] Chap. 14, at p. 416.
[14] *ibid.*, Art. 2(2). third para.

Directive 93/96—right of residence for students pursuing vocational training course

Council Directive 93/96 deals with the right of residence for students pursuing vocational training courses.[15] Further reference to this directive is made in Chapter 28 of this book.[16]

Directive 90/364—right of residence for those who do not have such a right under other provisions of community law

Directive 90/364[17] provides that Member States shall grant the right of residence to nationals of Member States who do not enjoy this right under the provisions of Community law and to the members of their families referred to in the directive, provided that they themselves and the members of their families are covered by sickness insurance in respect of all risks in the host Member State and have sufficient resources to avoid becoming a burden on the social assistance system of the host Member State during their period of residence.[18] The provisions regarding sufficiency of resources are the same as in Directive 90/365,[19] as are the members of the family accorded a right of residence.[20] The Directive also contains identical provisions to Directive 90/365 on the residence permit,[21] on the application *mutatis mutandis* of certain articles of Directive 68/360,[22] on the right of the spouse and dependent children to take up employed or self-employed activity,[23] and on derogation pursuant to Directive 64/221.[24]

Citizenship of the Union

It was against the background of the three directives referred to above[25] that the Maastricht Treaty introduced the concept of citizenship of the Union; that is to say, in circumstances in which it had been established that all nationals of one Member State enjoyed in the territory of another Member State at least the rights of residence contained in Directive 90/365. Article 17(1) (ex 8) E.C. provides that Citizenship of the Union is hereby established.[26] Every person

---

[15] [1993] O.J. L317/59. The Directive superseded Council Dir. 90/366 which had the same subject matter, but which was annulled, while its effects were maintained until the entry into force of a directive adopted on the appropriate legal basis, see Case C–295/90 *European Parliament v. Council* n.3, *supra*. See Case C–424/98 *Commission v. Italy* judgment May 25, 2000.

[16] Page 786.

[17] [1990] O.J. L180/26. See Case C–96/95 *Commission v. Germany* [1997] E.C.R. I–1653. And Case C–424/98 n.15.

[18] *ibid.*, Art. 1(1), first para.

[19] Dir. 90/364/EEC, Art. 1(1), second para.

[20] *ibid.*, Art. 1(2).

[21] *ibid.*, Art. 2(1).

[22] *ibid.*, Art. 2(2), first para.

[23] *ibid.*, Art. 2(2), second para.

[24] *ibid.*, Art. 2(2), third para.

[25] Dirs 90/364, 90/365, and 90/366, as to the last of which see n.15 above.

[26] See O'Keeffe, "Reflections on European Union Citizenship", 49 Current Legal Problems (1996), p. 347; Shaw, "European Union Citizenship: the IGC and beyond", (1997) EPL 413; Shaw, "The Many Pasts and Futures of Citizenship in the European Union", (1997) 22 E.L. Rev. 554.

holding the nationality of a Member State shall be a citizen of the Union. Citizenship of the Union "shall complement and not replace national citizenship". Article 18(1) (ex 8a) E.C. states:

"Every citizen of the Union shall have the right to move and reside freely within the territory of the Member States, subject to the limitations and conditions laid down in this Treaty and by the measures adopted to give it effect."

It is tempting to conclude that this provision is simply declaratory of the rights of movement and residence contained elsewhere in the Treaty and in secondary legislation made thereunder.[27] It follows directly after another provision which is surely declaratory—Article 17(2) (ex 8) E.C. provides that citizens of the Union "shall enjoy the rights conferred by this Treaty and shall be subject to the duties imposed thereby". It is nevertheless arguable that Article 18(1) has a "standstill" effect, precluding erosion of rights of residence derived from secondary legislation in force at the time Article 8a originally came into force. Consistently with the declaratory view, the Court of Justice has held that citizenship of the Union was not intended to extend the scope *rationae materiae* of the Treaty to internal situations which have no link with Community law.[28]

But the concept of citizenship of the Union did herald the introduction of new rights for nationals of the Member States, in particular as regards standing and voting in municipal elections and elections to the European Parliament. Every citizen of the Union residing in a Member State of which he is not a national must be given the right to vote and to stand as a candidate at municipal elections in the Member State in which he resides, under the same conditions as nationals of that State. This right is to be exercised subject to detailed arrangements adopted by the Council, and these arrangements may provide for derogations where warranted by problems specific to a Member State.[29] Council Directive 94/80 lays down such arrangements for the exercise of the right to vote and to stand as a candidate in municipal elections.[30] The municipal elections concern representative councils and the local government units listed in the Annex to the Directive. As regards England the local government units listed are parishes, districts, counties, London Boroughs, and the City of London in relation to ward elections for common councilmen. As regards Wales, the relevant local government units are county boroughs and communities. As regards Scotland, the relevant local government units are districts, regions and Islands. As regards Northern Ireland, the relevant local government units are districts. Article 5(3), first paragraph, of the Directive provides:

"Member States may provide that only their own nationals may hold the office of elected head, deputy or member of the governing college of the executive of

---

[27] The declaratory view is not endorsed by Advocate General Cosmas in Case C–378/97 *Criminal proceedings against Florus Ariël Wijsenbeek* [1999] E.C.R. I–6207, paras 78–87 of his Opinion.

[28] Joined Cases C–64–65/96 *Land Nordrhein-Westfalen v. Kari Uecker* and *Vera Jacquet v. Land Nordrhein-Westfalen.* [1997] E.C.R. I–3171, para. 23. But the treaty attaches to the status of citizen of the Union the right not to suffer discrimination on grounds of nationality within the scope of application *ratione materiae* of the treaty, C–85/96 *Martinez Sala* [1998] E.C.R. I–2691, para. 62.

[29] Art. 19(1) (ex 8b).

[30] [1994] O.J. L368/38. See Case C–323/97 *Commission v. Belgium* [1998] E.C.R. I–4281. Amended by Council Dir. 96/30/EC, [1996] O.J. L122/14.

a basic local government unit if elected to hold office for the duration of his mandate."

This provision is worthy of remark. The right of a citizen of the Union to "stand as a candidate . . . under the same conditions as nationals of that State" would be worthless if he or she were not entitled, if elected, to carry out all the functions and exercise all the prerogatives of an elected member of the nationality of the State in question. It is true that Article 19(1) E.C. permits derogations, but these must be "warranted by problems specific to a Member State", and the issue addressed by Article 5(3) could not be so described. It appears from the preamble to the Directive that the justification for Article 5(3) is to be found by analogy with Article 55 E.C., which provides that the right of establishment for self-employed persons does not apply to activities connected, even occasionally, with the exercise of official authority.[31] This latter provision is the counterpart of Article 39(4), which provides that the right of freedom of movement of workers does not apply to "employment in the public service".[32] It is true that the directives described in this chapter as bestowing "residuary rights of residence" on nationals of Member States incorporate by reference the "public policy proviso" applicable by way of derogation from Articles 39 and 43 under Article 39(3) E.C. and 46(1) E.C., and refer to Directive 64/221.[33] The "public policy proviso" thus comprises one of the "limitations and conditions laid down in this Treaty and by the measures adopted to give it effect" within the meaning of Article 18(1) E.C. which defines the right of movement and residence referred to in that Article. But it does not follow that a principle based on the official authority/public service proviso may be invoked to limit the right to vote in municipal elections which is laid down in Article 19(1) E.C. The official authority/public service proviso is concerned with access to certain remunerated posts in the public service, and seeks to distinguish economic activity from the exercise of powers of governance. But the right to hold elected office in a local government authority intrinsically involves the right to exercise official authority, by way of participation in the exercise of powers conferred by public law (*e.g.* decisions on licensing, planning permission). Even an allegedly limited and proportionate application of the official authority/public service proviso in the context in question appears to take back by secondary legislation some part of the very right which the Treaty has bestowed. The application of the official authority/ public service proviso by way of Article 5(3) of Directive 94/80 appears to be as much an exercise in second thoughts on the part of the Council as regards the implications of bestowing the right to stand for office in the first place as a laying down of detailed arrangements for the exercise of the right in question.

As regards elections to the European Parliament, every citizen of the Union residing in a Member State of which he is not a national must be given the right

---

[31] See Chap. 15, p. 483. The preamble of the Directive states in relevant part: "Whereas, since the duties of the leadership of basic local government units may involve taking part in the exercise of official authority and in the safeguarding of the general interest, Member States should be able to reserve these offices for their nationals; whereas Member States should also be able to take appropriate measures for that purpose; whereas such measures may not restrict more than is necessary for the achievement of that objective the possibility for other Member States' nationals to be elected . . ."

[32] Chap. 14, at p. 426.

[33] This Chapter, above, p. 493. For Dir. 64/221 see Chap. 14, at p. 416.

to vote and to stand as a candidate in elections to the European Parliament in which he resides, under the same conditions as nationals of that State. Council Directive 93/109 lays down detailed arrangements for the exercise of this right.[34] It is to be noted that the Directive provides that Community voters shall exercise their right to vote either in the Member State of residence or in their home Member State.[35] No person may vote more than once at the same election, and no person may stand as a candidate in more than one Member State at the same election.[36]

Citizenship of the Union also bestows advantages for individuals as regards diplomatic and consular protection in the territory of third countries. Every citizen of the Union shall, in the territory of a third country in which the Member State of which he is a national is not represented, be entitled to protection by the diplomatic or consular authorities of any Member State, on the same conditions as the nationals of that State. Member States are obliged to establish the necessary rules among themselves and start the international negotiations required to secure this protection. In accordance with this obligation, the Representatives of the Governments of the Member States meeting within the Council adopted a Decision regarding protection for citizens of the European Union by diplomatic and consular representations.[37] The Decision, *inter alia*, defines the diplomatic protection to be extended to citizens of the Union, as follows:

"(a) assistance in cases of death;
(b) assistance in cases of serious accident or serious illness;
(c) assistance in cases of arrest or detention;
(d) assistance to victims of violent crime;
(e) the relief and repatriation of distressed citizens of the Union.

In addition, Member States' diplomatic representations or consular agents serving in a non-member State may, in so far as it is within their powers, also come to the assistance of any citizen of the Union who so requests in other circumstances."[38]

Further rights enjoyed by citizens of the Union are the right to petition the European Parliament,[39] the right to apply to the Ombudsman established under Article 195 (ex 138e) E.C.,[40] and the right to write to the Community institutions or the Ombudsman in any of the E.C.'s official languages and to have an answer in the same language.[41]

---

[34] [1993] O.J. L329/34.
[35] *ibid.*, Art. 4.
[36] *ibid.*, Art. 4.
[37] Decision 95/553, [1995] O.J. L314/73.
[38] *ibid.*, Art. 5.
[39] Art. 21 (ex 8d), first para. , and Art. 194 (ex 138d).
[40] Art. 21 (ex 8d), second para.
[41] Art. 21 (ex 8d), third para.

CHAPTER 17

THE COMPLETION OF THE INTERNAL MARKET[1]

Background

As previous chapters will have made clear, when the 12-year transitional period for the establishment of the common market ended on December 31, 1969, "the elimination of all obstacles to intra-Community trade in order to merge the national markets into a single market bringing about conditions as close as possible to those of a genuine internal market"[2] was still far from having been achieved. The rapid development of the case-law of the Court of Justice on the scope and the direct effect of the prohibitions contained in such provisions of the E.C. Treaty as Articles 28, 29, 43 and 49 (ex Articles 30, 48, 52 and 59) allowed a great variety of discriminatory or otherwise unjustifiable interferences with freedom of movement to be challenged successfully, but the completion of the internal market could not be achieved by judicial action alone. A major legislative effort was needed, and this was finally set in train by the Commission which took office in January 1985 under the Presidency of Mr Jacques Delors.

Responding to an invitation issued at the Brussels meeting of the European Council in March 1985, the Commission prepared a White Paper[3] on completing the internal market, which it presented at the Milan meeting in June of that year. The White Paper set out a detailed legislative programme for the unification of the market, focusing on the removal of the remaining physical, technical and fiscal barriers to freedom of movement for goods, persons, services and capital. Annexed to the programme was a timetable for the adoption of the specific measures the Commission considered necessary to achieve the desired unification. The deadline fixed for the final establishment of the internal market was December 31, 1992, which gave a period of some eight years (corresponding to two Commission terms of office), for the enactment of the necessary measures.

The European Council welcomed the Commission's White Paper and instructed the Council to initiate a precise programme of action based upon it, which was to give high priority to the following:

(i) the removal of physical barriers to the free movement of goods within the Community;

(ii) the removal of technical barriers to the free movement of goods within the Community (in particular the adoption of common or compatible

---

[1] The present chapter was, in its original version, largely a reworking of a report by Alan Dashwood on research carried out within the Centre for Studies and Research of The Hague Academy of International Law at its 1991 session: see *The Legal Implications of 1993 for Member and Non-Member Countries of the EEC* (1992, Martinus Nijhoff), pp. 91 *et seq.* The authors express their thanks to the Curatorium of the Academy for their kind permission to draw on that report.

[2] Case 15/81 *Schul v. Inspecteur de Invoerrechten en Accijnzen* [1982] E.C.R. 1409 at 1431–1432; [1982] 3 C.M.L.R. 11.

[3] COM (85) 310.

standards for major new technologies in order to open up public purchasing and satisfy the needs of the economy);

(iii) the creation of a free market in the financial services and transport sectors;

(iv) the creation of full freedom of establishment for the professions;

(v} the liberalisation of capital movements.[4]

New legal machinery for the attainment of the political objectives stated in the White Paper and endorsed by the European Council was included in the SEA which represented the outcome of inter-governmental negotiations undertaken in the light of the conclusions reached at the Milan meeting. The SEA was signed on February 17, 1986, and entered into force, after ratification by the Member States, on July 1, 1987. The provisions relating to the internal market which the SEA added to the E.C. Treaty were broadly of two kinds: general principles defining the project to be implemented by the end of 1992, which are to be found, notably, in Article 14 (ex 7a); and new or modified legal bases for the enactment of internal market legislation by the co-operation procedure, notably Article 95 (ex 100a) which applies where measures are needed for the approximation of provisions laid down by law, regulation or administrative action in Member States.[5]

Progress in the implementation of the legislative programme contained in the White Paper of 1985 was the subject of annual reports submitted by the Commission to the Council and the European Parliament. The seventh, and last, such report,[6] which the Commission presented in September 1992, noted that, of the 282 measures proposed in the White Paper, 32 remained to be adopted by the Council; nine of these were of low priority, not being linked to the removal of frontier controls, so that there were only 23 measures which, in the Commission's view, the Council needed to tackle as a matter of urgency, if necessary by holding special meetings.[7] As for the rate of transposition of directives by the Member States, this was estimated by the Commission as 75 per cent (89 per cent in the case of directives that were in force in June 1991).[8] The Commission's overall assessment was that "in view of the decisions already in force, the economic framework for the single market is now in place, with people, goods, capital and services able to move around freely either on the basis of harmonised or common rules or on the basis of mutual recognition."[9] In similar vein, the 27th General Report spoke of the White Paper programme's "having been all but completed".[10]

There is nothing in the wording of Article 95, or of the other legal bases for internal market measures, to suggest it was intended that their force should be

---

[4] Conclusion on the completion of the internation market, point 1.

[5] For a full analysis of the background to the SEA and of its provisions, see J. De Ruyt, *L'Acte unique européen* (1987, Editions de l'Université de Bruxelles). On the internal market aspects of the SEA, see A. Mattera, *Le marché unique européen* (2nd ed., 1990, Jupiter).

[6] COM (92) 383 final.

[7] At points 17–19.

[8] *ibid.*, point 11.

[9] *ibid.*, point 1.

[10] 27th Gen. Rep. E.C., p. 36, point 70.

spent once the deadline of December 31, 1992 was reached: indeed, the reference in Article 95(1) to "the establishment *and functioning* of the internal market"[11] indicates the opposite. Since 1992, legislation has continued to be enacted on the basis of Article 95, though at a lower level of intensity. Reacting to the recommendations of a study group, which was set up under one of its former Members, Mr Sutherland, and which reported in October 1992,[12] the Commission has sought ways of ensuring that the internal market operates so as to produce the expected benefits. An attempt has been made to organise legislative activity in a series of framework programmes, setting strategic targets and identifying the specific measures needed to achieve them: the current programme, covering the years 2000 to 2004 and entitled "The Strategy for Europe's Internal Market", was set out in a Commission Communication of November 24, 1999, which received the endorsement of the Helsinki European Council in December 1999.[13] Another important Commission initiative has been the project aiming to simplify internal market legislation, which is known by its acronym "SLIM".[14] The project, which has been encouraged by successive European Councils, operates through the establishment of small teams composed of representatives of national administrations and of "users" of the legislation in question, with a mandate to produce reform proposals in a short time. The Commission also publishes periodically a "single market scoreboard", providing an overall view of the progress made and the difficulties encountered in the various sectors of the internal market.[15]

Article 14: the internal market project

Article 14 E.C., as amended by the T.A., provides as follows:

"1. The Community shall adopt measures with the aim of progressively establishing the internal market over a period expiring on December 31, 1992, in accordance with the provisions of this Article and of Articles 15, 26, 47(2), 49, 80, 93 and 95 and without prejudice to the other provisions of this Treaty.

2. The internal market shall comprise of an area without internal frontiers in which the free movement of goods, persons, services and capital is ensured in accordance with the provisions of this Treaty.

3. The Council, acting by a qualified majority on a proposal from the Commission, shall determine the guidelines and conditions necessary to ensure balanced progress in all the sectors concerned."[16]

Paragraph (1) of the Article creates an obligation for "the Community" to achieve a specified object (the establishment of the internal market) within a

---

[11] Emphasis added.

[12] 26th Gen. Rep. E.C., p. 37, point 70.

[13] COM (1999) 624 final. See also Gen. Rep. E.U. 1999, point 127. This was the successor to the 1997 "Action plan for the single market", designed to improve the functioning of the latter during the period leading up to the introduction of the euro: see Gen. Rep. E.U. 1997, point 180.

[14] Gen. Rep. E.U. 1996, point 106.

[15] Gen. Rep. E.U. 1998, point 149.

[16] Art. 14 was originally numbered Art. 8. This was changed to Art. 7a by the TEU. Para. (3) was added to the Article by the T.A.

specified time limit (December 31, 1992) and by specified means (the adoption of "measures" in accordance with certain Articles of the E.C. Treaty but without prejudice to its other provisions). Paragraph (2) defines the notion "internal market". Although, for convenience in presentation, we examine the two paragraphs separately, it is important to stress that the Article must be read as a whole, the second paragraph merely clarifying the object to be achieved within the deadline, and by the means, laid down in the first paragraph. The provisions of paragraph (3) were previously contained in the second paragraph of Article 7b, which was repealed by the T.A.

The obligation in the first paragraph

The obligation imposed on "the Community" was for its institutions to use their respective powers under the Treaty to adopt the measures necessary for the completion of the internal market before 1993. Article 14 does not directly address the Member States but they are bound, pursuant to Article 10 (ex 5) E.C., to co-operate fully in the internal market project.[17] The nature and scope of the obligation falling on the Market States will be examined below.

The provisions referred to in Article 14(1) are, besides that Article itself: Article 15 (ex 7c) requiring allowance to be made, in the drafting of internal market proposals, for the effort demanded of "certain economies showing differences in development"; Article 26 (ex 28) on the fixing of Common Customs Tariff duties; Article 47(2) (ex 57(2)) on the co-ordination of provisions concerning the taking up and pursuit of self-employed activities; Article 49 (ex 59) on the abolition of restrictions on the freedom to provide servies; Article 80 (ex 84) on sea and air transport; Article 93 (ex 99) on harmonisation of indirect taxation; and Article 95 (ex 100a), as to which, see below.

However, it is expressly stipulated that the list of provisions in Article 14(1) is without prejudice to the other provisions of the Treaty. This is important for two reasons.

First, by no means all of the legal bases central to the internal market project are mentioned in the list. For example, veterinary and plant health measures, necessary for the removal of obstacles to trade in live animals and plants and in the whole range of animal and plant products, fall within the purview of Article 37 (ex 43) E.C., the general basis of legislation for the purposes of the common agricultural policy.[18] Similarly, the liberalisation of transport services by rail, road or inland waterway has been pursued on the basis of Article 71 (ex 75) E.C.

Secondly, Article 14 does not derogate from Article 30, or from other similar provisions of the Treaty allowing freedom of movement to be restricted for certain narrowly-defined, non-economic reasons.[19] Nor does it modify the rule,

---

[17] On the principle of loyal co-operation in Art. 5 EEC, see de Cockborne *et al.*, *Commentaire Mégret* (2nd ed., 1992, Éditions de l'Université de Bruxells), Vol. 1, Chap. II.

[18] See the discussion of Art. 37 as a basis for internal market legislation, *infra*.

[19] *Cf.* proviso to Art. 39(3) (ex 48(3)), and para. (4) of the same Article (workers); Art. 46(1) (ex 56(1)) (establishment and services). Such exceptions to fundamental Community principles are very narrowly construed. As to goods, see Case 46/76 [1977] E.C.R. 5; Case 251/78 *Denkavit Futtermittel* [1979] E.C.R. 3369; [1980] 3 C.M.L.R. 513. As to persons, see Case 30/77 *Bouchereau* [1977] E.C.R. 1999; [1977] 2 C.M.L.R. 800.

which was confirmed by the *Cassis de Dijon* line of authority, that the Treaty does not prohibit the non-discriminatory application of national provisions that are necessary to serve important purposes of public interest, even where, owing to disparities between the legal solutions adopted by different Member States, such application may result in impediments to free movement.[20] Thus a major part of the task for the Community institutions consisted of removing the justification hitherto available to Member States under the Treaty for maintaining restrictive national provisions, through the enactment of harmonised rules or of measures for the mutual recognition of standards and qualifications that would adequately protect the interests in question.

The definition in the second paragraph

The definition of the internal market in the second paragraph of Article 14 comprises two elements—absence of internal frontiers and the free movement of goods, persons, services and capital. Those elements may be contrasted in terms of their relative precision and scope.

The first element, a space without internal frontiers, sets the Community institutions the measureable objective of securing the abolition of all frontier controls on goods or persons moving between the Member States. As long as any such controls remain in place, it will be clear that the objective has not been achieved. The second element, consisting of the realisation of the four freedoms, is more elusive: there is simply no way of identifying the exact moment at which the requisite degree of liberalisation will have been attained.

On the other hand, for all its psychological importance, the complete removal of physical frontiers will not, in itself, ensure freedom of movement. For instance, divergent national rules on such things as maximum levels of food additives or the labelling of foodstuffs, could be enforced, even in the absence of frontier controls, by inspection at the retail stage of distribution. Similarly, immigration controls are not the only way of restricting the entry and residence of non-nationals (although perhaps a uniquely effective one in the case of the insular Member States). Controls can be exercised, for example, through hotels or lodging houses, through employers or by spot checks in public places.

Indeed, for certain kinds of restriction on freedom of movement, the abolition of physical frontiers would have little or no impact. An example, of the greatest importance for the internal market in goods and, to some extent, in services, is the protection of intellectual property rights, still largely organised at the level of individual Member States[21]: such protection is achieved not by checks on imports

---

[20] The abundant case-law on the limits of the directly effective prohibitions imposed by the relevant Treaty Articles has been analysed in previous chapters in this book. As to Art. 28 (goods), leading cases are Case 8/74 *Procureur du Roi v. Dassonville* [1974] E.C.R. 837; [1974] 2 C.M.L.R. 436. Case 120/78 *Rewe-Zentral v. Bundesmonopolverwaltung für Branntwein ("Cassis de Dijon")* [1979] E.C.R. 649; [1979] 3 C.M.L.R. 494. As to establishment and services (Arts. 43 and 59), leading cases are Case 2/74 E.C.R. 1299; Case 39/75, *Coenen* [1975] E.C.R. 1547; [1976] 1 C.M.L.R. 30. As to capital, the original requirement was only to liberalise "to the extent necessary to ensure the proper functioning of the common market". However, Art. 56 (ex 73(6)) E.C. contains a prohibition against *all* restrictions on capital movements between Member States and between Member States and third countries.

[21] See Chap. 26, *infra*.

but by infringement proceedings brought by interested parties in national courts. Another, very obvious, example, affecting the free movement of persons, is that of differences between Member States as to professional qualifications or the conditions of access to business activities, where impediments can only be removed by harmonisation or mutual recognition.[22]

A question that arises is whether the unqualified reference in the second paragraph of Article 14 to the free movement of *persons* can be taken at face value, or whether it must be interpreted in the sense of Title III, Chapters 1 to 3 of Part Three of the Treaty, as relating only to Community nationals who travel to another Member States to carry on employed or self-employed activities, or as providers or recipients of services, *i.e.* as market actors. It is submitted that the wider interpretation is the correct one. Not only does it correspond to the letter of Article 14 (as well as to that of Article 3(c)) but it is also necessary to ensure the *effet utile* of the removal of internal frontiers since, if controls are retained for any categories of travellers, they are liable to be applied to all.

The four freedoms are to be ensured "in accordance with the provisions of this Treaty". This confirms the point made in relation to the first paragraph that Article 14 does not derogate from the provisions under which certain justified restrictions are tolerated by the Treaty, despite their incompatibility with a single market. The strategy of the Article is to implement a legislative programme removing any such justification, thereby enabling the basic Treaty provisions on freedom of movement to apply with full effect.[23]

A final question is how the notion of the internal market, as defined by Article 14, relates to that of the common market with which it has co-existed in the E.C. Treaty since the SEA. It would be confusing if, as is sometimes said, the two notions were simply interchangeable. "Common market" is nowhere defined in the Treaty but its primary meaning can be gathered from Article 2 where it is juxtaposed with economic and monetary union as one of the two principal mechanisms by which the Community is to carry out its task of pursuing the objectives specified in that Article. Here "common market" seems to be used as a term of art, covering the whole range of Community activities other than those connected with EMU; and legislative practice over the years suggests that a similarly broad meaning has been given to the term in Article 94 and Article 308. The internal market should, therefore, be regarded as the more specific notion, introduced to provide a sharper focus for the project that was set in motion by the 1985 White Paper.

---

[22] The report of the *ad hoc* Committee for a People's Europe ("Adonnimo Report"), which was admitted to the European Council in March 1985, recommended a new approach to the implementation of the Treaty provisions on freedom of establishment, based on mutual trust and the assumption that qualifications awarded in different Member States are broadly equal. That was the approach adopted by the White Paper, which led to the enactment of a general system for the mutual recognition of higher education diplomas awarded on completion of professional education and training of at least three years' duration: see Council Dir. 89/48 of December 31, 1988, O.J. 1989 L19/16. For a full analysis of the background to the Directive and its provisions, see J. M. Laslett, *Legal Issues of European Integration*, 1990/91, p. 1; A. Carnelutti, *Revue du Marché unique*, No. 1–1991, p. 1.

[23] On the same lines, see de Cockborne *et al.*, *op. cit.* n.17, *supra*, pp. 20 *et seq.*

The legal effects of Article 14

Effects for the Community institutions

Does Article 14 impose on the Community institutions involved in the legislative process a *legally* binding obligation? Or is the commitment expressed in the Article to the task of establishing the internal market before the deadline of December 31, 1991 purely political?

The Declaration on Article 14 annexed to the Final Act of the SEA might seem to indicate the latter, since it states:

> "The Conference wishes by means of the provisions in Article 8a to express its firm political will to take before January 1, 1993 the decisions necessary to complete the internal market defined in those provisions, and more particularly the decisions necessary to implement the Commission's programme described in the White Paper on the Internal Market.
>
> Setting the date of December 31, 1992 does not create an automatic legal effect."

However, it is thought the Declaration does not express any view as to the nature of the obligation resulting from the Article *for the Community institutions*. The reference in the final sentence to the date of December 31, 1992 as not creating "an automatic legal effect" suggests that the issue the Conference intended to address was that of the possible effect of the Article, if the necessary legislation had not been enacted by that date. This is an altogether different issue, to which we return when we examine the effects for the Member States. It is, therefore, submitted that the mandatory language of Article 14(1) ("The Community *shall* adopt . . .") must be given its plain meaning.

It does not necessarily follow that the admitted failure to ensure, before December 31, 1992, the complete realisation of the internal market as envisaged by Article 14, exposed the Commission (or the Council, in matters in respect of which proposals were lying unadopted on its table) to an adverse finding pursuant to Article 232 (ex 175) E.C. Whether an infringement of the Treaty, through the inaction of the institution concerned, could be established, would depend on the test that was formulated by the Court of Justice in Case 13/83, where proceedings under Article 175 were brought against the Council by the European Parliament in respect of the failure to introduce a common transport policy before the end of the transitional period.[24] According to that test, the measures which are the subject of the allegation of a failure to act must be defined with sufficient precision for them to be identified individually, and adopted in compliance with the Court's judgment, pursuant to Article 233 (ex 176). This cannot be the case where discretionary power is given to the institution concerned, allowing it to make policy choices the content of which is not specified by the Treaty.

---

[24] Case 13/83 *European Parliament v. Council* [1985] E.C.R. 1513. See, more particularly, 1592–1593 and 1596–1597; [1986] 1 C.M.L.R. 138.

In applying the test laid down in the *Transport* case to Article 14, it is useful to recall what was said in the previous section about the two elements of the definition of the internal market in paragraph (2) of the Article.

Ensuring the free movement of goods, persons, services and capital, with all that implies in terms of the harmonisation or mutual recognition of standards, qualifications and control procedures, is too general an objective, and its attainment too fraught with policy choices, to be the subject of proceedings under Article 232: it would not be possible, if the Court found there had been a failure to act, to specify the legislative steps that would have to be taken to comply with the judgment.

Turning to the other element of the definition, the absence of internal frontiers, a further distinction needs to be drawn—between controls on goods and controls on persons. On the one hand, the Commission was able to spell out with reasonable precision the measures necessary to allow the removal of internal physical frontiers in respect of goods[25] (which is not the same as saying that the adoption of such measures proved to be politically a straightforward matter). The measures in question related essentially to the administration of systems of indirect taxation, commercial policy matters affecting Member States individually, human, animal and plant health, the requirements of transport policy and the collection of statistics. In the event, the Commission could declare in its 27th General Report that "border checks on goods are now a thing of the past".[26] On the other hand, the abolition of controls on persons can finally be achieved only when a whole range of matters relating to the entry and residence of third country nationals—among other things, the crossing of external borders, immigration policy, visa policy and the right of asylum—have been regulated.[27] Decisions on these matters, whether adopted by the Community institutions under powers conferred by the Treaty or by way of conventions between the Member States, clearly involve discretionary choices.

In summary, there is a fundamental difference between the legal position in respect of persons and that in respect of goods: namely that, for persons, Community law has no equivalent to the Common Customs Tariff, nor any principle corresponding to that of the free circulation of third country products once these have cleared customs. We conclude that, whereas proceedings under Article 232 might well have been brought successfully against the Commission or the Council, if the legislative steps necessary for the removal of border controls on goods had not been taken in time, the failure thus far to secure the complete abolition of border controls persons would be unlikely to pass the test of justiciability in the *Transport* case.[28]

---

[25] White Paper, points 24–26.

[26] At p. 37, para. 70. On the final legislative steps in the process, see 26th Gen. Rep. E.C., p. 38, para. 70.

[27] The T.A. has pointed the way forward, through the incorporation of the Schengen *acquis* into the legal order of the E.U. and through the creation, in Title IV of Part Three of the E.C. Treaty, of a series of new legal bases. In particular, Art. 61 places a duty on the Council to adopt, within five years after the entry into force of the T.A. "measures aimed at ensuring the free movement of persons in accordance with Article 14 . . .".

[28] The opposite view has been taken by the European Parliament. After calling upon the Commission to put forward proposals for the abolition of border controls on persons, and having received what

Effects for the Member States

Here the main question is whether, or to what extent, Article 14 may be directly effective. Is it still possible for a Member State to apply its national rules in areas where internal market legislation is not yet in place or where it has not yet been fully implemented, despite the tendency of such rules to restrict the free movement of goods, persons, services or capital? Or would individuals affected by such rules have the right, pursuant to Article 14, to resist their continued application, and would national courts be required to recognise and give effect to that right?

The conditions under which provisions of the E.C. Treaty and of acts of the institutions produce direct effects for the subjects of the Community legal order, as established in the case-law of the Court of Justice, were discussed in Chapter 4, above. To summarise: the provision in question must be clear and unconditional; and it must also be complete, in the sense of being immediately usable by the Court of Justice or by national courts in determining the rights and obligations of individuals, without any need for further definition of those rights and obligations by the legislator.

Article 14 would not seem to fulfil those conditions since, as we have seen, the creation of an area without internal frontiers in which the four freedoms are ensured *in accordance with the provisions of the Treaty* requires the enactment of Community measures making recourse to restrictive national provisions, in the cases allowed by the Treaty, no longer justifiable. Given the need for such legislation, until this is fully in place certain impediments to freedom of movement, resulting from the application of national provisions, will continue.

That analysis would seem to be consistent with the Declaration to Article 14, cited above, in which it was stated that the setting of the end of 1992 deadline "does not create an automatic legal effect". While the case-law of the Court of Justice casts doubt on the interpretative value of statements entered in the minutes of the Council,[29] a published declaration of a negotiating conference is in a quite different category. The Declaration in question made manifest the intention of the Conference of the Representatives of the Government of the Member States, at the time of signing the SEA, to avoid the result that, independently of the state of implementation of the White Paper, complete freedom of movement might be legally a *fait accompli* after December 31, 1992.[30]

---

it regarded as an unsatisfactory reply, the Parliament brought proceedings under Art. 232 against the Commission in November 1993: see Case C–445/93 [1994] O.J. C1/12. In July 1995, the Commission submitted to the Council proposals for three measures, founded on provisions of the E.C. Treaty, with a view to securing the free movement of persons, including third country nationals, across internal Community frontiers: see Editorial Comments in 33 C.M.L.Rev. (1996), 1. These made no headway within the Council. The proceedings in Case C–445/93 were terminated in July 1996.

[29] Case 38/69 *Commission v. Italy* [1970] E.C.R. 47; [1970] C.M.L.R. 77; Case 237/84, *Commission v. Belgium* [1986] E.C.R. 1247. More recently in Case C–292/89 *Antonissen* [1991] E.C.R. 745 at 778; [1991] 2 C.M.L.R. 373, the Court said: ". . . a declaration cannot be used for the purpose of interpreting a provision of secondary legislation where, as in this case, no reference is made to the content of the declaration in the wording of the provision in question."

[30] On the effect of the Declaration, see the article by Judge F. Schokweiler, R.M.C. 1991, p. 882. As to the effect in international law of such interpretative declarations, see Art. 31(3) of the Vienna Convention of 1969 on the law of Treaties. In Case C–378/97, *Criminal proceedings against Florus Arieël Wijsenbeek* (not yet published), Advocate General Cosmas expressed the opinion that the rule

It has sometimes been claimed that the maintenance of controls at the internal frontiers of the Community has been absolutely prohibited since December 31, 1992. The Commission seemed, at one time to believe that Article 14, taken together with Article 10, imposed such a prohibition.[31] If that were correct, any Member State which had not dismantled internal frontier controls by the end of 1992 would have been in breach of the Treaty and liable to be condemned in enforcement proceedings under Article 226 (ex 169) or Article 227 (ex 170), and it would also run the risk of having to pay compensation to undertakings or individuals suffering loss as a result of the failure to abolish controls.[32]

However, as the foregoing analysis will have made clear, the matter is more complicated. Frontier controls on movement between Member States become illegal if, but only if, they are no longer necessary to safeguard interests recognised as legitimate by the Treaty. That will obviously be the case where harmonised rules, standards or qualifications are *fully* in place. It is further submitted that, even where the legislative framework remains incomplete, the combined effect of Article 14 and the obligation of loyal co-operation in Article 10 will prevent Member States from having recourse to frontier controls, if the interests in question could be protected by some other means. The principle of proportionality, too, would seem to require, in the conditions of the internal market, that frontier controls be retained only where they are truly indispensable.[33] So, while there was no automatic obligation to abolish all controls at the Community's internal frontiers before January 1, 1993, as from that date there has been a heavy burden of proof on Member States to justify the retention of such controls.

The continuing justification for Member States' requiring persons crossing one of the Community's internal borders to produce a passport or other proof of nationality, was at issue in the *Wijsenbeek* case.[34] The proceedings arose out of the prosecution of a Dutch national for refusing to show his passport or to prove his nationality by other means, on re-entry into the Netherlands. His claim that, since January 1, 1993, there has been a directly effective prohibition against internal border controls, was rejected by the Court. Article 14, the Court said, "cannot be interpreted as meaning that, in the absence of measures adopted by the Council before December 31, 1992 requiring the Member States to abolish controls of persons at the internal frontiers of the Community, that obligation automatically arises from expiry of that period".[35] Such an obligation

---

of international law could not be transposed into Community law: once amending provisions become part of the E.C. Treaty, they acquire a legal force independent of their authors' wishes. See his Opinion, paras 51 to 54. We respectfully disagree. It must be possible for the supreme constitutional authority of the European Union as determined by Art. 48 (ex Art. N) TEU, to decide the scope and legal effect of amending provisions, and to make its intentions clear in a published text.

[31] See the Commission's Communication of May 18, 1992 (SEC(92) 877 final). See also the remarks by Vice-President Bangemann reported in *Agence Europe*, February 26, 1992, pp. 9 and 10. However, the Commission now takes a different view: see Case C–378/97, considered below.

[32] On the doctrine of State liability, see Chap. 5, above.

[33] See the discussion of the proportionality principle in Chap. 6.

[34] Case C–378/97 (n.y.r.). See also, in the field of social security, Case C–297/92 *Baglieri* [1993] E.C.R. I–5211, paras 16–17.

[35] At para. 40 of the *Wijsenbeek* judgment. See also the Opinion of Advocate General Cosmas, para. 77.

presupposed harmonisation of national laws on the crossing of external borders, immigration, the granting of visas and asylum, and the exchange of information on those matters. Mr Wijsenbeek also invoked his right of free movement as a citizen of the Union, pursuant to Article 18(1) (ex 8a(1)) E.C.; but here, again, the Court held that it remained justifiable for the authorities to insist upon proof of nationality.

The Court referred in its judgment both to the Declaration on Article 14 E.C., and to another Declaration adopted on the occasion of the signing of the Final Act of the SEA and relating to Articles 13 to 19 of that Treaty, which states: "Nothing in these provisions shall affect the right of Member States to take such measures as they consider necessary for the purpose of controlling immigration from third countries, and to combat terrorism, crime, the traffic in drugs and illicit trading in works of art and antiques." However, there is no discussion in the judgment as to the legal effect of the two Declarations.

It is important to be clear that, in *Wijsenbeek*, the Court was not saying that Articles 14 and 18 are incapable, in princple, of conferring rights on individuals. Without specifically addressing the issue of the direct effect of those Articles, the Court observed that, even if they did confer on nationals of the Member States an "unconditional right" of internal free movement, it was still open to the authorities to carry out identity checks "in order to be able to establish whether the person concerned is a national of a Member State, thus having the right to move freely within the territory of the Member States, or a national of a non-member country, not having that right".[36]

The *Wijsenbeek* judgment confirms the foregoing analysis of Article 14. The passing of the deadline set by the Article did not have the "automatic legal effect" of prohibiting the imposition of internal border controls. These may be retained, however, only as long as they can be justified in accordance with the provisions of the Treaty.

Pursuant to a Protocol annexed to the TEU and the E.C. Treaty by the T.A.,[37] the United Kingdom and Ireland have been authorised, notwithstanding Article 14 or any other provision of the Treaties or measures adopted under them, to go on applying border controls, for the purpose of verifying the right of entry of Union citizens (or the citizens of non-Union EEA countries, who have similar rights) or of controlling the entry of other persons.[38] Those two Member States are, therefore, protected against the legal consequences of the interaction between Article 14 and future Community measures, which may render such controls unlawful. As long as the special arrangements of the Protocol apply, other Member States will be entitled, notwithstanding Article 14, to exercise similar controls on person (of whatever nationality) arriving from the United Kingdom and Ireland.[39]

---

[36] At para. 43.
[37] Protocol No. 3 on the application of certain aspects of Art. 14 of the Treaty establishing the European Community to the United Kingdom and to Ireland. Art. 2 of the Protocol provides for the continuance of the Common Travel Area between the two countries (which explains why Ireland wished to be covered by the special arrangements).
[38] See Art. 1 of the Protocol.
[39] See Art. 3 of the Protocol.

Article 95: approximation by qualified majority

It has been said that the central idea which dominated the inter-governmental negotiations leading to the signature of the SEA was that wider recourse to the qualified majority was essential for the attainment of the objective of completing the internal market before January 1, 1993.[40] The most significant of the amendments to the EEC Treaty giving effect to that idea was the introduction of Article 95 (ex 100a) as a general legal basis for the adoption of "measures for the approximation of the provisions laid down by law, regulation or administrative action in Member States which have as their object the establishment and functioning of the internal market". After being left intact by the TEU, Article 95 was amended by the T.A. in several respects, including through the substitution of co-decision for co-operation as the procedure for enacting the measures provided for.

Article 95 operates by way of derogation from Article 94 which enables the Council, acting *unanimously*, to issue directives for the approximation of national provisions directly affecting the establishment or functioning of the common market.[41] Article 94 has thus been reduced to a residual role. It is available, for example, in the cases expressly excluded by paragraph (2) of Article 95 from the scope of that Article (see below), as well as in respect of matters not linked with the establishment or functioning of the internal market but covered by the broader notion of the common market.

In its turn, Article 95 is a residual provision, since it applies "save where otherwise provided in this Treaty". This means that the specific legal bases provided by the Treaty in areas such as the common agricultural policy, the right of establishment, freedom to provide services and the common transport policy,[42] should be used, in preference to Article 95, for the adoption, in those areas, of legislation having as its object the establishment and functioning of the internal market. Some problems of choosing between Article 95 and other available legal bases are discussed in the next section of this chapter.

The reference to "measures" in Article 95(1) leaves the institutions the choice as to the particular form of act appropriate in a given case, in contrast to Article 94 which only allows the adoption of directives. In practice, however, the Council has shown a clear preference for using directives for the enactment of approximation measures under Article 95, even in cases where an act in the form of a regulation has been proposed by the Commission.

The prospect of having approximation measures adopted by majority decision prompted concerns among the different Member States, which could only be assuaged by subjecting the power created by Article 95(1) to a number of

---

[40] See J.-L. Dewost in Capotorti *et al.* (eds), *Du droit international au droit communautaire, Liber amicorum Pierre Pescatore* (1988, Nomos), pp. 167 *et seq.*

[41] On the approximation of laws pursuant to Art. 100, see Mégret *et al.*, *Le droit de la CEE* (1973, Éditions de l'Université de Bruxelles), Vol. 5, pp. 152 *et seq.*; A Dashwood in Wallace, Wallace and Webb (eds), *Policy-making in the European Community* (2nd ed., 1983, John Wiley & Sons), Chap. 6.

[42] See, respectively, Art. 37 (ex 43), Art. 44 (ex 54), Art. 47 (ex 57) and Arts 71 and 80(2) (ex 75 and 84(2)) E.C.

qualifications. Thus it is expressly provided by paragraph (2) of the Article that paragraph (1) does not apply to fiscal provisions[43] or to provisions relating to the free movement of persons[44] or to the rights and interests of employed persons.[45] By paragraph (3) the Commission is required, in the proposals it makes concerning health, safety, environmental protection and consumer protection, to take as a base a high level of protection: account must be taken, in particular, of any new development based on scientific facts. The European Parliament and the Council have been placed under a similar obligation, when carrying out their respective roles in the legislative process. In paragraph (10) it is recalled that harmonisation measures may include safeguard clauses authorising Member States "to take, for one or more of the non-economic reasons referred to in Article 30, provisional measures subject to a Community control procedure".

It is, however, paragraphs (4) to (9) of Article 95 that require special attention, because of the exception created to the fundamental principles of the uniform application of Community law and the unity of the market.[46] Those six paragraphs were inserted into Article 95 by the T.A., replacing the original paragraph (4), which dated from the SEA. They provide as follows:

"4. If, after the adoption by the Council or by the Commission of a harmonisation measure, a Member State deems it necessary to maintain national provisions on grounds of major needs referred to in Article 30, or relating to the protection of the environment or the working environment, it shall notify the Commission of these provisions as well as the grounds for maintaining them.

5. Moreover, without prejudice to paragraph 4, if, after the adoption by the Council or by the Commission of a harmonisation measure, a Member State deems it necessary to introduce national provisions based on new scientific evidence relating to the protection of the environment or the working environment on grounds of a problem specific to that Member State arising after the harmonising measure, it shall notify the Commission of the envisaged provisions as well as the grounds for introducing them.

6. The Commission shall, within six months of the notifications as referred to in paragraphs 4 and 5, approve or reject the national provisions involved after having verified whether or not they are a means of arbitrary discrimination or a disguised restriction on trade between Member States and whether or not they shall constitute an obstacle to the functioning of the internal market.

---

[43] The legal basis for the harmonising of indirect taxation is Art. 93, which requires the Council to act unanimously on a proposal from the Commission and after consulting the European Parliament and the Economic and Social Committee. There is no specific legal basis provided for the harmonisation of direct taxation, so it is necessary to fall back on the general power of approximation in Art. 94.

[44] As we have seen, the legal bases for legislating on the free movement of persons are now to be found in Title IV of Part Three. The procedure prescribed by Art. 87 E.C. during a transitional period of five years, is a variant of the consultation procedure, with the Council acting by unanimity. At the end of the transitional period, the Council has power to substitute co-decision for consultation. See Chap. 3, above.

[45] See the extensive powers provided for by Art. 137(2) E.C. which are exercisable by co-decision.

[46] See Opinion of Advocate-General Tesauro in Case C–41/93 France v. Commission [1994] E.C.R. I–1829, at I–1833, para. 4.

In the absence of a decision by the Commission within this period the national provisions referred to in paragraphs 4 and 5 shall be deemed to have been approved.

When justified by the complexity of the matter and in the absence of danger for human health, the Commission may notify the Member State concerned that the period referred to in this paragraph may be extended for a further period of up to six months.

7. When, pursuant to paragraph 6, a Member State is authorised to maintain or introduce national provisions derogating from a harmonisation measure, the Commission shall immediatly examine whether to propose an adaptation to that measure.

8. When a Member State raises a specific problem on public health in a field which has been the subject of prior harmonisation measures, it shall bring it to the attention of the Commission which shall immediately examine whether to propose appropriate measures to the Council.

9. By way of derogation from the procedure laid down in Articles 226 and 227, the Commission and any Member State may bring the matter directly before the Court of Justice if it considers that another Member State is making improper use of the powers provided for in this Article."

Essentially, this allows an escape route for a Member State which considers that harmonised rules, adopted under Article 95, do not constitute a sufficient guarantee of attaining certain important public interest objectives. In effect, the fulfilment of the prescribed substantive and procedural condition prevents the operation, in respect of the Member State concerned, of the general rules of Community law that, once the standards protecting the interests in question have been fully harmonised, recourse to national provisions previously allowed under the Treaty despite potential interference with freedom of movement, can no longer be justified.[47]

According to paragraph (4), after a "harmonisation measure" has been adopted by the Council or the Commission, a Member State which "deems it necessary to *maintain* national provisions on grounds of major needs referred to in Article 30, or relating to the protection of the environment or the working environment"[48] should notify those provisions to the Commission, specifying the grounds on which it relies. The paragraph, as amended by the T.A., thus caters for the situation where a Member State wishes to continue applying provisions already in force at the time of the enactment of the Community measure in question.

A first comment on the paragraph relates to the term "harmonisation measure", which is also found in paragraph (5). The reference is manifestly to measures of the kind provided for by paragraph (1) of the Article, there described as "measures for the *approximation* of the provisions laid down by law, etc." (emphasis added). That "harmonisation" and "approximation" should be treated, within the same Article, as interchangeable terms, is strong evidence that

---

[47] See Case 251/78 *Denkavit Futtermittel*, n.19, *supra*. On the background to the inclusion of original para. (4) in Art. 100a, see De Ruyt, *op. cit.* n.5, *supra*, pp. 170 *et seq.*
[48] Emphasis added.

no difference of substance is indicated by the draftsman's choice of one term or the other, elsewhere in the Treaty.[49]

Secondly, the harmonisation measure from which derogation is sought may be one which has been adopted by either the Council or the Commission. Of course, only the Council is empowered (with the European Parliament) to act directly on the basis of Article 95. The mention of the Commission, added by the T.A., is presumably to make clear that derogation obtained in respect of primary legislation will also cover any implementing measures adopted under powers which have been created pursuant to Article 202 (ex 145), third indent E.C.[50]

Thirdly, the justification for maintaining national provisions has to be found among the "major needs" (*exigences importantes*) mentioned in Article 30 E.C. to which are added the protection of the environment and the working environment. Consistently with the requirement of strict interpretation,[51] the catalogue of possible justifications must be taken to be exhaustive, unlike the open-ended list of "mandatory requirements" which, according to the *Cassis de Dijon* line of authority, may justify the application of disparate national provisions until harmonisation rules are in place.[52] The onus is on the Member State invoking the safeguard to prove that its national provisions, which give a higher standard of protection of the interests expressly indicated by Article 95(4), than the relevant Community measure, are necessary and proportionate.[53]

A fourth comment concerns the former limitation of the safeguard clause to cases where a harmonisation measure had been adopted by the Council acting by a qualified majority, so that it was not available where a compromise solution commanding unanimity had been arrived at. Some writers drew the conclusion that the clauses could only be relied on by Member States which had voted against the measure in question.[54] In the previous edition of this work, we pointed out that the benefit of paragraph (4), as then drafted, was not expressly confined to those forming part of the outvoted minority; and such a restriction would have detracted from the *effet utile* of a provision designed to facilitate the formation of qualified majorities, since a Member State, wanting to have the right to apply its national rules but otherwise willing for a given measure to be passed, would have been forced to join with those irreconcilably opposed to the measure, in voting it down.[55] The controversy has been laid to rest by the T.A., which deleted the reference to a qualified majority decision from paragraph (4). It is now clear that the escape clause can be resorted to, regardless of whether a given harmonisation measure was adopted unanimously or by a qualified majority; and, in the latter event, whether the Member State concerned voted for or against the measure.

---

[49] See, *e.g.* Art. 93 (ex 99), which refers to "harmonisation", and Art. 94 (ex 100), which refers, like Art. 95, to "approximation".

[50] See, *e.g.* Case C–359/92 *Germany v. Council* [1994] E.C.R. I–3681; [1995] 1 C.M.L.R. 413.

[51] See p. 507, above.

[52] See Chap. 13, above.

[53] See the Opinion of Advocate General Tesauro in Case C–41/93 *France v. Commission* [1994] E.C.R. at I–1834, para. 7.

[54] *cf.* De Ruyt, *op. cit.* n.5, above, pp. 171 and 174.

[55] Third edition, at p. 365.

Paragraph (5) of Article 95 disposes of another old controversy from the period prior to the T.A.: whether national provisions introduced subsequently to a Community harmonisation measure may be saved by the escape clause. The paragraph recognises this possibility, but subject to conditions more restrictive than those applicable to pre-existing national provisions. The provisions it is sought to introduce must be "based on new scientific evidence relating to the protection of the environment or the working environment" (so that the justifications in Article 30 are not available); and their introduction must be considered necessary "on grounds of a problem specific to that Member State arising after the adoption of the harmonisation measure".

The procedure under which the Commission is required to deal with notifications pursuant to paragraphs (4) and (5) is laid down by paragraph (6). The Commission has six months in which to approve or reject the national provisions involved "after having verified whether or not they are a means of arbitrary discrimination or a disguised restriction on trade between Member States and whether or not they shall constitute an obstacle to the functioning of the internal market". The last-mentioned element, added by the T.A., gives scope for a denial of authorisation, even where a genuine need for the provisions, on one of the specified public interest grounds, has been made out to the satisfaction of the Commission, if the well functioning of the internal market is put at risk.

Commission decisions pursuant to Article 95(6) are constitutive, and not merely declaratory, in their effects. Unless and until approval is obtained, either by a decision or through the expiry of the six-month time limit, the continued application (or the introduction) of the national provisions in question is unlawful: their notification to the Commission does not give provisional exemption, and the Community harmonisation measure, if it satisfies the criteria of direct effect, may be relied on by individuals in the courts of the Member State concerned.[56]

The point may be illustrated by the *Kortas* case from Sweden, which arose out of the prosecution of a shopkeeper, for selling imported confectionery products containing the colorant E124 (or cochineal red). Use of the latter in foodstuffs was authorised by Directive 94/36,[57] but banned under the relevant Swedish legislation. The case fell to be decided on the basis of the pre-Amsterdam version of Article 95, which fixed no time limit for the Commission to decide on notifications: the Swedish authorities had notified their national provisions to the Commission, with a request for a derogation, in November 1995, but had still received no reply in July 1998. Even in those circumstances, however, the Court refused to countenance the unilateral disapplication of the Directive. If the Commission was in breach of its obligation to act with all due diligence in discharging its responsibilities, then the proper remedy would have been an action under Article 232 (ex 175); such action, the Court noted, could be accompanied, where appropriate, by an application for interim relief. However, the failure of the Commission to act with due diligence could not affect the full application of the Directive concerned.[58]

---

[56] Case C–319/97 *Criminal proceedings against Antoine Kortus*, judgment of June 1, 1999 (n.y.r.).
[57] European Parliament and Council Dir. 94/36 on colours for use in foodstuffs, [1994] O.J. 237/13.
[58] Case C–319/97, at para. 36.

The strict attitude of the Court is explained by the logic of the internal market, where the emphasis is on the removal of impediments to free movement and of elements liable to distort the play of competition, through harmonisation measures. Article 95(6) effectively empowers the Commission to grant individual Member States *ad hoc* derogations from common standards which have been judged by the Community legislator adequately to protect the interests referred to in Article 30 (and, in matters of health, safety, the environment and consumer protection, to do so at the "high level" prescribed by Article 95(3)). In *Kortas*, Advocate General Saggio drew a contrast between a safeguard clause of that kind, which cuts across the objective of harmonised legislation and must, therefore, be kept severely within bounds; and Article 176 (ex 130t) E.C., where the more stringent measures the Member States are authorised to maintain or introduce, would be serving the same purpose (of protecting the environment) as the corresponding Community measures, so that a lighter control regime is justified.[59]

The Commission must satisfy itself that all the conditions which allow a Member State to invoke the safeguard clause are fulfilled. In particular, it must establish whether the national provisions in question are justified on the grounds specified, respectively, by paragraphs (4) and (5) of Article 95, and also that they do not constitute a means of arbitrary discrimination or a disguised restriction on trade between Member States, or an obstacle to the functioning of the internal market.[60]

If authorisation is given, the reasons of fact and law explaining why all of the prescribed conditions are to be regarded as fulfilled in the case in point, must be set out by the Commission in its decision. The very first Commission Decision granting a derogation under Article 95 was annulled by the Court of Justice for not being adequately reasoned.[61] It concerned German provisions prohibiting the substance pentachlorophenol (PCP), which were significantly more restrictive than the rules applicable under the relevant Community Directive.[62] According to Advocate General Tesauro, the Commission failed to mention any factors justifying the application in Germany of national rules assuring a higher degree of protection than that provided by the Community.[63] On the issue of the proportionality of the German rules, the Advocate General said: ". . . I think it would have been appropriate for the decision to have specified to what extent the additional protection of health and the environment guaranteed by the Germany rules justifies the possibility of greater barriers to intra-Community trade; or, again, for it to have examined the consequences of the need to use other products instead of PCP."[64] As to the verification the Commission was required to undertake, in order to establish that the German rules did not result in

---

[59] At para. 26 of his Opinion. Under Art. 176 E.C. the Member State concerned must notify to the Commission any measures it wishes to maintain or introduce, but there is no special vetting procedure.

[60] Case C–41/93 *France v. Commission* [1994] E.C.R. I–1829, at para. 27 of judgment.

[61] *ibid.*

[62] Council Dir. 91/173 amending for the ninth time Council Dir. 76/769 concerning PCP [1991] O.J. L85/34.

[63] Case C–41/93 [1994] E.C.R. at I–1838, para. 14.

[64] *ibid.*, at I–1839.

arbitrary discrimination or a disguised restriction on trade between Member States, the decision was criticised by the Advocate General for confining itself to repeating slavishly the relevant wording of Article 95, "without the statements made being in any way supported by any consideration which might justify the Commission's conclusions".[65] The judgment of the Court, though expressed less concretely and trenchantly, was in the same sense.[66]

The case on the PCP Decision was specifically concerned with the inadequacy of the statement of reasons furnished by the Commission, which was in contravention of Article 253 (ex 190) E.C. However, the analysis undertaken by Advocate General Tesauro provides valuable insight into the delicately nuanced judgment the Commission is called upon to make, when acting under the safeguard clause of Article 95. The interests of the Member State wishing to maintain or introduce provisions giving a higher level of protection, are not to be considered paramount. They have to be carefully weighed against the possibly adverse consequences for the well functioning of the internal market.[67]

Paragraphs (7) and (8) of Article 95 are designed to activate the legislative process of the Community, where appropriate, in the light of concerns brought forward by a particular Member State. Under paragraph (7), the Commission, if it authorises a Member State to maintain or introduce provisions derogating from a harmonisation measure, must immediately examine whether it should propose that the measure be amended. Under paragraph (8), a Member State seised of a public health problem in a field which has been the subject of prior harmonisation measures, must bring this immediately to the attention of the Commission, which must examine whether it should make a proposal to the Council.

Should a Member State be suspected of making improper use of the safeguard clause in Article 95, an enforcement action can be brought against it by the Commission or another Member State, using the accelerated procedure provided for by paragraph (9).[68] In such circumstances, the Court of Justice might also be persuaded to issue an interim order prohibiting the application of the provision pending the outcome of the proceedings.

At the time of the signature of the SEA, it was feared by some critics of the new Treaty that the then paragraph (4) of Article 100a would undermine the case

---

[65] *ibid.*

[66] Case C–41/93 [1994] E.C.R. at I–1850, paras 35–37.

[67] The Danish Government made a unilateral Declaration to the Final Act of the SEA, in these terms:

> "The Danish Government notes that in cases where a Member State is of the opinion that measures adopted under Article 100a do not satisfy higher requirements concerning the working environment, the protection of the environment or the needs referred to in Article 36, the provisions of Article 100a(4) *guarantee* that the Member State in question can apply national provisions. Such national provisions are to be taken to fulfil the above-mentioned aim and may not entail hidden protectionism" (emphasis added).

If the Danish Government's interpretation of the provisions now contained in paras. (4) to (6) of Art. 95 were correct, the vetting of notifications by the Commission would have been a pure formality. We contested that interpretation in the third edition of this work, and the case-law has now confirmed that it is untenable.

[68] *cf.* the accelerated procedure under Art. 88(2) (ex 93(2)).

law of the Court of Justice on Article 30.[69] There would, indeed, be a danger, if the safeguard clause in Article 95 were very frequently resorted to, that the effectiveness of the Article as an instrument for achieving the single market objectives of Article 14 might be compromised. However, in practice (so far, at least) this has not happened. It remains to be seen whether the sensitivities, to issues of public health and environmental protection, of the Member States which acceded to the European Union in 1995, may result in greater use being made of the safeguard clause.

Why should the dire predictions of eminent commentators have proved so wrong? Three reasons may be hazarded. First, the common political will to complete the internal market within the time limit set by Article 14(1) must have helped to overcome inhibitions. Secondly, Member States which may have hoped to use the safeguard clause to protect the high health status of their livestock industries have been prevented from doing so by the evolution of the case-law on Article 43 which has shown that Article to be the appropriate legal basis for internal market legislation in the veterinary field.[70] Thirdly, the obligation imposed by Article 95(3) to propose high common standards of consumer and environmental protection may have helped to deter Member States from having recourse to the safeguard clause, as it was clearly intended to do.

A final question is how the mechanism relates to the practice known as "minimal harmonisation". The latter occurs when Community legislation lays down certain minimum standards which must be observed in all the Member States, while authorising any Member State that so wishes to apply stricter standards in respect of the same matters.[71] The answer to the question is that paragraphs (4) and following only come into play once the rules relating to the matters in question have been fully harmonised: minimal harmonisation represents a step in a process which remains incomplete, leaving it open for Member States to invoke, as the case may be, Article 30 or one of the "mandatory requirements" recognised under the *Cassis de Dijon* doctrine. Step by step harmonisation is, in principle, a legitimate strategy for the Community legislator to adopt,[72] bearing in mind, however, the time limit that was fixed by Article 14(1) for the completion of the internal market.

Prior to its amendment by the T.A., the E.C. Treaty include an Article 100b creating a mechanism under which steps could have been taken, in the last year of the programme for the completion of the internal market (1992), to compel the mutual recognition by the Member States of national laws, regulations and administrative provisions falling within the scope of Article 95 (Article 100a, as it then was), but which had not been harmonised. The mechanism remained unused and Article 100b was one of the provisions repealed by the T.A.

---

[69] Notably P. Pescatore in J.-V. Lous (ed.), *L'acte unique européen* (Journée d'études, Bruxelles, March 1, 1986), pp. 39 *et seq.*; *contra*, H.-L. Glaesner, R.M.C. 1986, p. 321.

[70] See the cases cited in n.77, *infra*.

[71] An example of a minimal harmonisation measure adopted on the basis of Art. 100a is Council Dir. 90/31 on package holidays [1990] O.J. L158/59. See also Council Dir. 91/477 of June 18, 1991 on the acquisition and detention of weapons, [1991] O.J. L256/51.

[72] See Case 215/87 *Heinz Schumacher v. HZA Frankfurt-am-Main* [1989] E.C.R. 638; [1990] 2 C.M.L.R. 465; Case C–42/90 *Bellon* [1990] E.C.R. 4863.

Legal bases for internal market legislation

Choice of legal bases

The issue addressed in this section is that of the selection of the correct legal basis for a given piece of internal market legislation. In practice, disputed choices are generally between Article 95 and some other provision of the E.C. Treaty. Preferences are liable to be influenced by the perception of political advantage (or disadvantage) in the procedure for the adoption of harmonisation measures by the Council acting by a qualified majority by way of co-decision with the European Parliament, on the one hand, or in the escape route the Article may offer from the consequences of such measures, on the other. Disputes may arise between different Community institutions, especially where the Council has amended by unanimity the legal basis proposed by the Commission, or between the Council and one or more of the Member States, when a proposal has been adopted in the face of minority opposition.

General principles governing the choice of the legal basis of Community acts have been laid down by the Court of Justice. According to those principles, the choice must be made in the light of objective factors capable of being the subject of judicial review,[73] in particular the aim and content of the act.[74] Where examination of the relevant factors shows that the act is concerned with two or more distinct matters which are dealth with in separate provisions of the E.C. Treaty, a dual or multiple legal basis may be required.[75] However, legal bases must not be combined if the procedures which they prescribe are incompatible. Thus the Court has held that it is impossible for an act to be based on Treaty Articles one of which provided for the co-operation procedure, while the other required the Council to act unanimously after simple consultation of the European Parliament.[76] In such cases, it seems, preference should be given to the former legal basis, as providing a reinforced role for the European Parliament on the legislative process, so long as the different objectives of the proposal are capable of being furthered by legislation based on the Article in question.

The choice between Article 95 and Article 37

The leading cases concern legislation pre-dating the SEA, when the disputed demarcation was between Article 37 (ex 43) and Article 94 (ex 100). However, the lessons to be drawn from those cases are equally applicable to the demarcation between Article 37 and Article 95.

Article 37 does not prescribe the co-decision procedure but only consultation of the European Parliament. The Council acts by a qualified majority, so the choice of legal basis does not affect the voting rule but does limit the degree of the Parliament's involvement. There is also the possibility of invoking the safeguard clause of Article 95, which has no equivalent in Article 37. Delegations wishing to maintain national rules guaranteeing, as they claim, a higher health status for their countries than harmonised rules which it is proposed to adopt on

---

[73] Case 45/86, *Commission v. Council* [1987] E.C.R. 1493; [1988] 2 C.M.L.R. 131.
[74] Case C–300/89, *Commission v. Council* (*Titanium Dioxide Waste*) [1990] E.C.R. 2867.
[75] Case 165/87, *Commission v. Council* [1988] E.C.R. 5545; [1990] 1 C.M.L.R. 457.
[76] Case C–300/89, note 74, *supra*.

veterinary or plant health matters, may accordingly press for the proposal to be based on Article 95.

The cases establish that Article 37 is the correct legal basis for legislation satisfying two conditions: it must relate to the production or marketing of the agricultural products listed in Annex II to the EEC Treaty; and it must contribute to the attainment of one or more of the objectives of the common agricultural policy set out in Article 33 (ex 39) of the Treaty.[77] It has further been held that, where the bulk of the products to which legislation applies are Annex II products, the fact that the legislation may also apply, in an accessory way, to certain non-Annex II products does not take it outside the scope of the common agricultural policy[78]; nor does the fact that the legislation pursues, at the same time, certain general aims, such as the protection of health.[79]

Applying those principles, the Court has found that Article 37 was the correct legal basis for a ban on the administration of growth hormones to livestock,[80] a directive laying down conditions for the treatment of battery hens,[81] a directive relating to the importation of animal glands and organs for use by the pharmaceutical industry,[82] and a directive on undesirable substances in animal feedingstuffs.[83]

On the other hand, where internal market measures apply equally to certain agricultural and non-agricultural products, a dual legal basis, Article 37 together with Article 95, seems both desirable and possible, since there is no difference of Council voting rule liable to distort the operation of the co-decision procedure (see the discussion of the *Titanium Dioxyde Waste* case below).

The choice between Article 95 and Article 175

A Title on the Environment, comprising Articles 174 to 176 (ex 130r to 130t) was added to Part Three of the E.C. Treaty by Article 25 of the SEA. Article 174 defines the objectives and the general principles of action by the Community relating to the environment. The legislative procedure originally laid down by Article 175 was for the Council to act by unanimity after consulting the European Parliament and the Economic and Social Committee. The TEU substituted the co-operation procedure for simple consultation, except in respect of a few matters considered especially sensitive politically; and the T.A. replaced co-operation with co-decision. So under the E.C. Treaty, as amended, the choice between Article 95 and Article 175 will no longer make any difference, in most cases, as to the procedure to be used for adopting measures. The difference that remains—and it is significant—relates to the ability of Member States to

---

[77] See, in particular, Case 68/86, *United Kingdom v. Council* [1988] E.C.R. 855; [1988] 2 C.M.L.R. 543; Case 131/86 *United Kingdom v. Council* [1988] E.C.R. 905; [1988] 2 C.M.L.R. 364; Case 13/87 *Commission v. Council* [1989] E.C.R. 3743; Case 11/88 *Commission v. Council* [1989] E.C.R. 3799.

[78] Case 11/88, *loc. cit.* n.77, *supra*.

[79] See cases cited in n.77, *supra*.

[80] Council Dir. 87/519 of October 19, 1987, [1987] O.J. L304/38.

[81] Council Dir. 86/113 of March 25, 1986, [1986] O.J. L95/45.

[82] Council Dir. 87/64 of December 30, 1986, [1987] O.J. L34/52.

[83] Council Dir. 87/519 of October 19, 1987, [1987] O.J. L304/38. See also Joined Cases C–164 and 165/97, judgment of February 25, 1999, [1999] E.C.R. I–1139, where the choice of legal basis was between Art. 37 and Art. 175.

maintain or introduce higher protective standards than those provided for by the Community. As we have seen, the conditions of the safeguard clause under Article 95 are much stricter than those imposed by Article 176.

Articles 174 to 176 were clearly intended to provide a coherent framework for organising a Community environmental policy. Like regional policy or social policy, this is a Community policy applying in an area where the Member States enjoy concurrent competence ("Community policy on the environment still contribute . . .", as Article 174(1) puts it). It is to be contrasted with the common policies in the fields of agriculture and transport, where Community competence is potentially exclusive, and actually so, once it has been exercised.

However, it is equally clear that Article 95 was intended to serve as the legal basis of measures for the approximation of national provisions on the protection of the environment, where such measures have as their object the establishment or functioning of the internal market. This follows from the reference in Article 95(3) to Commission proposals "concerning . . . environmental protection". There is a fine dividing line between such harmonisation measures and the specific Community action in relation to the environment which is the province of Article 175.

An uncontroversial example of the use of Article 95 would be the harmonisation of legislation laying down technical specifications, with a view to the protection of the environment, for certain manufactured products which are traded within the internal market. By removing disparities between national provisions, while guaranteeing a high level of environmental protection throughout the Community, the harmonising measure would obviously contribute towards ensuring the free movement of the products in question. Article 95 was thus correctly chosen as the legal basis for Community measures in relation to the control of emissions from motor vehicles.

A more difficult case is that of Community measures designed to protect the environment against the harmful consequences of industrial processes, such as legislation on the disposal of industrial waste. Such measures cannot be regarded as removing impediments to the free movement of goods within the internal market. However, since pollution control is expensive for the undertakings concerned, disparities between the levels of protection prescribed by the legislation of different Member States may result in distortions of competition, which the harmonisation of national provisions would help to remedy. The Court of Justice has said that action by the Community for the approximation of national rules relating to conditions of production in a given industrial sector, with a view to eliminating distortions of competition in that sector, is capable of contributing to the attainment of the internal market and, accordingly falls within the purview of Article 95.[84] On the other hand, if that logic is pressed too far, it would completely exclude Article 175 as a basis for legislation on such matters as the control of industrial pollution, which lie at the very heart of any policy on the protection of the environment. This seems inconsistent with the letter and spirit of the Treaty Title on the Environment.

---

[84] Case C–300/89, n.74, *supra*, at point 23.

The choice between Article 95 and Article 175 (in their previous versions) was the subject of the litigation in Case C–300/89 concerning the Council Directive of June 21, 1989, on the harmonisation of national programmes for the reduction, with a view to its elimination, of pollution caused by the titanium dioxyde waste industry.[85] The Directive was annulled by the Court on the ground that Article 95, as proposed by the Commission, and not Article 175, substituted by the Council, was the correct legal basis. Analysis of the aim and content of the Directive led the Court to conclude that it was a measure with the dual object of protecting the environment and removing distortions of competition, which seemed to point to the requirement of a dual legal basis. However, that solution had to be rejected since, in the Court's view, the unanimity rule then applicable to all legislation adopted under the Title on the Environment was incompatible with the co-operation procedure prescribed by Article 95. A choice had, therefore, to be made, and the Court opted for Article 95, apparently because it considered both the objects of the Directive could effectively be pursued on that legal basis, although the judgment does not explain why they could not be pursued, as effectively and appropriately, on the basis of Article 175.

The judgment in *Titanium Dioxide Waste* is explained by the drafting of the Directive in question. This emphasised the dual object of the measure; while the normal expedient of providing a dual legal basis could not be adopted, because, as the Court saw it, the respective decision-making procedures of Articles 95 and 175, in their original versions, were mutually incompatable. In subsequent cases, relating to measures the aim and content of which showed that their essential object was the protection of the environment, Article 175 has been confirmed as the correct legal basis.[86] The mere fact, the Court of Justice has said, that the establishment or functioning of the market is affected, is not sufficient for Article 95 to apply. Recourse to that Article is not justified where the measure to be adopted has only the *incidental* effect of harmonising market conditions within the Community.[87]

Other cases

The exclusions in paragraph (2) of Article 95 may sometimes give rise to difficult borderline cases.

For instance, it was a question whether the Regulation on the elimination of controls and formalities applicable to the cabin and hold baggage of persons taking an intra-Community flight and the baggage of persons making an intra-Community sea crossing should have been based on Article 95, as a measure facilitating the movement of goods, or on Article 94, as a measure facilitating the movement of persons[88] The choice of Article 95 seems correct, since the provisions of the Regulation apply specifically to controls on baggage. The fact that baggage is accompanied by its owner when frontiers are crossed does not

---

[85] [1989] O.J. L201/6.

[86] Case C–155/91 *Commission v. Council* [1993] E.C.R. I–939; Case C–187/93, *European Parliament v. Council* [1994] E.C.R. I–2857; [1995] 2 C.M.L.R. 309.

[87] See *ibid.* and Case C–70/88 *European Parliament v. Council* [1991] E.C.R. I–2041; [1991] E.C.R. I–4529; [1992] 1 C.M.L.R. 91.

[88] See Council Reg. 3925/91 of December 19, 1991, [1991] O.J. L374/4. This has been supplemented by Commission Reg. 1823/92 of July 3, 1992 laying down detailed rules.

prevent it from being regarded as "goods" within the meaning of the Treaty. Similar reasoning justified the choice of Article 95 as the legal basis for the Directive on the acquisition and detention of weapons.[89]

A different position was taken by the Council in the case of the Regulation on co-operation between tax authorities, the aim of which was to ensure the effective collection of revenue, while avoiding interference with the free movement of goods.[90] Since the administrative arrangements in question were ancillary to the objective of levying taxation, the right legal basis for the measure was thought to be Article 93 (ex 99) E.C.

A limitation on the scope of Article 95 that must not be forgotten is that it only applies to measures for the approximation of national provisions. The Article cannot, therefore, be used for doing things which are beyond the capability of individual Member States. For instance, national rules on the protection of intellectual property rights may be the subject of harmonisation measures adopted pursuant to Article 95; but for the creation of entirely new property forms, protected by Community law independently of the law of the Member States, recourse must be had to Article 308 (ex 235) E.C.

---

[89] Council Dir. 91/477 of June 18, 1991 L256/51.
[90] Council Reg. 218/92 of January 27, 1992, [1992] O.J. L24/1.

CHAPTER 18

ECONOMIC AND MONETARY UNION

From the Werner Plan to the Delors Plan

The idea of going on from the completion of the internal market to the establishment of an economic and monetary union (or EMU) is not a new one. The wish to see such a development was expressed in the final communiqué of the Conference of Heads of State of Government held in December 1969 in The Hague, and the following year a working group was set up under the chairmanship of Luxembourg's Prime Minister and Minister of Finance. Mr Pierre Werner, to study ways and means of achieving EMU. The Werner Committee presented an interim report in May 1970 and its final report in October of that year,[1] and in March 1971 a first Resolution on the attainment by stages of EMU in the Community was adopted by the Council and the representatives of the government of the Member States.[2] The Resolution looked forward to the establishment of EMU before the end of the decade and set out a number of measures to be taken with that in view, including the strengthening of the co-ordination of short term economic policies, the reduction of the margin of fluctuation between Member States' currencies and the organisation of a European Monetary Co-operation Fund. Those provisions were supplemented by a second Resolution, adopted in March 1972.[3]

Although steps that were taken to implement the Resolutions of 1971 and 1972 helped to prepare the way for later developments, little headway could be made in the economic and political circumstances of the early and mid-1970s. Fresh impetus was given to EMU, however, by the introduction in March 1979 of the European Monetary System (or EMS).[4] This was based on guidelines laid down at the meeting of the European Council in Bremen in July 1978 and further elaborated in a Resolution at the Brussels meeting in December of the same year.[5] The main objective of the EMS was "the creation of closer monetary co-operation leading to a zone of monetary stability in Europe". This was to be achieved, notably, by an exchange rate mechanism (ERM) under which fluctuations in exchange rates were limited to 2.5 per cent above or below a "central rate" fixed for each pair of participating currencies. It was possible to opt for a wider margin of fluctuation of up to 10 per cent; and if margins became too difficult to defend, the central rates of the national currencies concerned could be adjusted, although this required the agreement of all participants in the mechanisms. To help finance interventions by monetary authorities in currency markets in order to prevent margins from being exceeded, various credit

---

[1] Bull. E.C. Suppl. 11/70.

[2] O.J. Eng.Sp.Ed. (Second Ser.) IX, p. 40.

[3] O.J. Eng.Sp.Ed. (Second Ser.) IX, p. 65.

[4] The EMS replaced an earlier, less successful, system of monetary co-operation which had been set up in 1972, the so-called "snake in a tunnel".

[5] The text of the Resolution and other relevant documents were published by the Committee of Governors of the Central Banks. See *Texts concerning the European Monetary System*, 1979.

mechanisms were available. Last but not least, a European Currency Unit (the ECU), defined as a weighted basket of European Community currencies, served as the denominator for different operations under the EMS, although its uses were extended much more widely: for instance, the statements of revenue and expenditure in the Community budget were expressed in ECU, as also were Community loans and aid to third countries.[6]

Participation in the ERM was optional for the Member States of the Communities. In 1979 all the then Member States except for the United Kingdom decided to take part, and they were joined by Spain in 1989, by the United Kingdom in 1990 and by Portugal in 1992. In September 1992 Italy and the United Kingdom were forced to suspend their participation because of turbulence in the money markets; though Italy came back into the ERM in November 1996, after the margin of fluctuation had been increased to 15 per cent.[7] Non-participants in the ERM were not excluded from other aspects of co-operation within the EMS and their currencies were included in the ECU basket.

The Brussels Resolution on the EMS refrained (no doubt wisely) from defining the steps whereby the system might evolve towards a fully fledged monetary union in which exchange rates would be fixed irrevocably and the national currencies would ultimately be replaced by a single currency. Nor, on this point, were matters taken much further by the SEA.[8]

It was at the European Council in Hanover in June 1988, in the light of progress made towards the completion of the internal market, and of the successful adoption of the financial package necessary to implement the policies introduced or developed by the SEA,[9] that the decisive step was taken of inviting a committee chaired by the President of the Commission, Mr Jacques Delors, to study and put forward proposals for concrete stages leading to economic and monetary union.[10] The plan formulated by the Delors Committee for the attainment of EMU in three stages was put to the European Council in Madrid in June 1989, where it was decided that the first stage, which did not require any Treaty amendments, would begin on July 1, 1990. Preparations were to be made for an inter-governmental conference that would meet, once the first stage had begun, to lay down the subsequent stages. As we have seen, that conference came to be held in parallel with another relating to "political union," and the final outcome of the two conferences was the TEU.

---

[6] For a fuller exposition of the EMS, see J.-J. Rey, (1980) C.M.L.Rev. 78. See, in particular, the explanation of a "basket-type" unit of account at pp. 14 *et seq.*

[7] In the light of the financial turbulence experienced in September 1992, the Birmingham European Council called for "reflection and analysis" to be undertaken. This was to cover recent economic and financial developments within Europe and in the major industrialised countries as well as the implications of changes in the general economic and financial environment, notably the impact of the increasing size and sophistication of financial markets and greater capital liberatisation.

[8] The Article on EMU which the SEA inserted into the E.C. Treaty was replaced by the provision of the present Title, introduced by the TEU.

[9] Known as "Delors I", to differentiate it from the "Delors II" package of financial measures to allow implementation of the TEU.

[10] See Committee for the Study of Economic and Monetary Union, *Report on economic and monetary union in the European Community* (the "Delors Committee Report").

Scope and strategy

The provisions of the E.C. Treaty relating to EMU are found among the Principles in Part One, as well as in Title VII (ex Title VI) of Part Three, and in various Protocols, notably the Protocol (No. 3) on the Statute of the European System of Central Banks and of the European Central Bank (hereinafter "the Statute"). Those provisions were added to the Treaty by the TEU and left intact by the T.A.

The two aspects of EMU are defined by Article 4 (ex 3a). According to that Article, the activities of the Member States and the Community shall include, in accordance with the timetable laid down by the Treaty:

— the adoption of an economic policy which is based on the close co-ordination of Member States' economic policies, on the internal market and on the definition of common objectives, and conducted in accordance with the principle of an open market economy with free competition;
— concurrently with such a policy, the irrevocable fixing of exchange rates leading to the introduction of a single currency, the ECU, and the definition and conduct of a single monetary policy and exchange-rate policy the primary objective of both of which shall be to maintain price stability and, without prejudice to this objective, to support the general economic policies in the Community, in accordance with the principle of an open market economy with free competition.

It is added that the activities of the Member States and the Community in economic and monetary matters shall comply with the guiding principles of stable prices, sound public finances and monetary conditions and a sustainable balance of payments.

There is a striking contrast between the rather general terms in which the economic aspect of EMU is defined and the more specific and coercive terms used in defining its monetary aspect. This difference of approach comes out even more clearly in the detailed provisions contained in the Title of the Treaty devoted to Economic and Monetary Policy. As we shall see, economic policy remains the province of the Member States.[11] The emphasis in Chapter 1 of the Title is on effective co-ordination and "peer group" pressure on Member States to manage their economies responsibly, though the somewhat loose arrangements of the Treaty have been reinforced by the so-called "Stability and Growth Pact". In contrast, on monetary and exchange-rate matters, there was to be a virtually complete transfer of powers, in the third stage of EMU, from the Member States to the European System of Central Banks (ESCB) or, as the case may be, to the Community.

. The TEU established a strict timetable for the attainment of EMU in three stages. No date was mentioned for the beginning of the first stage, since this was

---

[11] Thus it was stated, in the Resolution of the Luxembourg European Council of December 1997 on economic policy co-ordination in stage 3 of EMU, that economic policy and wage determination remain "a national responsibility", subject to the Treaty provisions prohibiting excessive government deficits and to the Stability and Growth Pact (as to which, see below): [1998] O.J. C35/1, at point I.(1).

assumed to be under way, in accordance with the decision of the European Council in Madrid in June 1989. The second stage was to begin on January 1, 1994.[12] A controversial issue in the negotiations was the transition to the third stage which, it was eventually agreed, would take place in one of two ways. Up to the end of 1997, the decision whether to move to the third stage would be for the Council, meeting in the formation of Heads of State or Government, which was to consider the matter not later than December 31, 1996.[13] A positive decision could only be taken if the Council were satisfied that a majority of the Member States fulfilled the conditions for the adoption of a single currency to be judged on the basis of certain economic criteria indicating the attainment of a high level of economic convergence (as to which, see below). If by the end of 1977 the Council had not yet fixed a date for the transition to the third stage, this would take place automatically on January 1, 1999.[14]

The timetable was, therefore, ineluctable. Entry into the third stage of EMU could not have been delayed beyond January 1, 1999, even if only a few of the Member States had fulfilled the conditions for the adoption of a single currency on that date.

The corollary of establishing such a timetable was that special arrangements had to be made to allow certain Member States to escape, or at least to defer, submission to the full rigours of participation in the third stage. There are two cases to condider.

The first is that of Member States which, at the relevant time, did not fulfil the conditions prescribed by the Treaty for the adoption of a single currency. For those Member States to be let into the single currency would not only have been damaging to their own economies: it would have threatened the stability of the monetary union. Provision was, therefore, made under Article 122 (ex 109k) E.C. for the Member States concerned to have, for as long as they might need it, a derogation from the relevant provisions of the E.C. Treaty and of the Statute. Member States with a derogation, and their Central Banks, are excluded from rights and duties within the European System of Central Banks and are authorised to continue managing their monetary policy in accordance with national law.[15] On the other hand, provisions belonging to the third stage but which are not closely linked to the adoption of a single currency, will apply to such Member States.[16] Article 122(2) (ex 109k(2)) lays down a procedure for the abrogation of a Member State's derogation, once it is found to fulfil the necessary conditions.

The other case is that of two Member States, Denmark and the United Kingdom, which were unwilling to accept, from the entry into force of the TEU, a firm commitment in principle to full participation in the third stage of EMU. Solutions to the problems of these two Member States was provided by separate Protocols.

According to Protocol (No. 12 to the Final Act of the TEU) "the Danish Constitution contains provisions which may imply a referendum in Denmark

---

[12] Art. 116(1) (ex 109e(1)) E.C.
[13] Art. 121(3) (ex 109j(3)) E.C.
[14] Art. 121(4) (ex 109j(4)) E.C.
[15] Art. 122(3) (ex 109l(3)) and Statute Chap. IX.
[16] *e.g.* the obligation under Art. 104(1) (ex 104c(1)).

prior to Danish participation in the third stage. . . ." To allow for the holding of a referendum and a possibly negative outcome, Denmark was given a right, if it notified the Council that it would not be taking part in the third stage, to treatment corresponding, for most purposes, to that of Member States with a derogation pursuant to Article 122.

Protocol (No. 11) goes somewhat further, by "Recognising that the United Kingdom shall not be obliged or committed to move to the third stage of economic and monetary union without a separate decision to do so by its government and Parliament". The effect of the Protocol is to entitle the United Kingdom, as long as it has not opted into the third stage, to the treatment *mutatis mutandis,* of a Member State in the second stage. This means that, unlike Member States with a derogation, the United Kingdom is not subject to obligations which are applicable in the third stage but not closely linked to the adoption of a single currency.

The transition to the third stage

Two important decisions relating to EMU were taken at the meeting of the European Council held in Madrid in December 1995.

In the first place, it was confirmed by the European Council that the third stage of EMU would begin on January 1, 1999, the latest date allowed by Article 121(4) E.C.[17] An earlier start would have been impracticable, owing to the delay in the ratification of the TEU, which meant that the Treaty only entered into force on Novbember 1, 993.

Secondly, the future single currency was given the name "euro" in all the official languages of the European Union. Each euro was to be made up of one hundred "cent". The naming of the euro required a considerable effort of interpretation, since the E.C. Treaty uses the term "ECU", standing for "European currency unit". The expedient was adopted of declaring "ECU" to be a "generic term", and that "the Governments of the 15 Member States have achieved the common agreement that this decision is the agreed and definitive interpretation of the relevant Treaty provisions"[18] The legal value of such *ex post facto* interpretative statements is, to say the least, dubious. However, unsurprisingly in view of the political consensus, the change of name has not been the subject of legal challenge.

During the second stage of EMU, which began, as required by the Treaty, on January 1, 1994, the formulation and implementation of monetary policy remained a matter for the Member States (as it still does for those not participating in the single currency). However, the task of co-ordinating the different monetary policies, and of developing co-operation between the National Central Banks ("NCBs"), which had previously been carried out by a Committee of Central Bank Governors, was entrusted to a new, transitional body, the

---

[17] See Council Reg. 1103/97 on certain provisions relating to the introduction of the euro, [1997] O.J. L12/1, first recital.

[18] *Ibid.,* second recital and Arts 1 and 2.

European Monetary Institute ("EMI").[19] The Statute of the EMI was contained in Protocol (No. 4) annexed to the E.C. Treaty by the TEU. By Article 4(2) of its Statute, the EMI was charged with specifying "the regulatory, organisational and logistical framework necessary for the ESCB to perform its tasks in the third stage". A duty for the EMI to address an annual report to the Council was imposed by Article 7(1). The reports must "include an assessment of the progress towards convergence in the Community, and cover in particular the adoption of monetary policy instruments and the preparation of the procedures necessary for carrying out a single monetary policy in the third stage, as well as the statutory requirements to be fulfilled for national central banks to become an integral part of the ESCB". The most important of the latter requirements was that NCBs (like the future ECB) be made entirely independent, as provided for by Article 108 (ex 107) to which we return below.

The procedure for determining the Member States qualified to participate in the single currency from the outset, was laid down by Article 121 (ex 109j) E.C. As noted in Chapter 2, the procedure had the unusual feature of requiring Council action at two levels. There had, first, to be an assessment, and the formulation of a recommendation, by the Council in its usual composition (*in casu*, the Ecofin Council of Ministers of Finance),[20] as to whether each Member State fulfilled the necessary conditions for participation; the assessment was to be based on reports received from the Commission and the EMI, and the European Parliament had to be consulted. The final decision, to be taken in the light of the two reports and the Opinion of the European Parliament, and on the basis of Ecofin's recommendation, was reserved for the Council meeting in the composition of Heads of State or Government.

To qualify for participation, Member States were required to have brought their national legislation, including the statutes of their NCBs, into line with the Treaty. They must also satisfy the "convergence cnteria" fixed by Article 121(1), *viz*:

"— the achievement of a high degree of price stability, evidenced by a rate of inflation of not more than $1\frac{1}{2}$ per cent above that of, at most, the three best performing Member States;

— the sustainability of the government financial position, evidenced by the fact that the Member State in question was not the subject of a Council decision that it was running an excessive deficit;[21]

— the observance of the normal fluctuation margins under the exchange-rate mechanism of the EMS, for at least two years, without devaluing against the currency of any other Member State;

---

[19] In the third stage of EMU, the co-ordinating task of the EMU, so far as concerns the relationship between the euro and the currencies of non-participating Member States, has been assigned to the General Council, which brings together the Governors of all the NCBs. For an assessment of the achievement of the EMI, see J.-V. Louis, "A Legal and Institutional Approach for Building a Monetary Union", 35 E.L.Rev. (1998), p. 33, at pp. 35–50.

[20] Declaration (No. 3) to the Final Act of the TEU affirmed that, for the purposes of the Title on Economic and Monetary Policy, among other things, "the usual practice, according to which the Council meets in the composition of Economic and Finance Ministers, shall be continued . . .".

[21] Pursuant to Protocol (No. 6), the indicators of a sustainable financial position are, in principle, an annual budget deficit not exceeding 3 per cent of gross domestic product (GDP), and total government debt not exceeding 60 per cent of GDP.

— convergence of interest rates, evidenced by an average nominal long term rate not more than 2 per cent above that of, at most, the three best performing Member States".[22]

By a Decision of May 3, 1998, the Council, meeting in the composition of Heads of State or Government, found that the necessary conditions for the adoption of the single currency had been fulfilled by 11 out of the 15 Member States.[23] Greece and Sweden, it was stated, did not yet fulfil the conditions, and they would accordingly have a derogation, as provided for by Article 122(1).[24] Notice that they did not wish to join in had been given by the United Kingdom and by Denmark, under their respective Protocols.[25] The "Euro-11" are referred to collectively hereinafter in this Chapter as "participating Member States", to distinguish them from the four "non-participating Member States". This is the terminology used in implementing Council instruments.[26]

The same day, the Council enacted Regulation 974/98 on the introduction of the euro.[27] This was based on Article 123(4) (ex 109(4)), as constituting a measure "necessary for the rapid introduction of the [euro] as the single currency of [the participating] Member States".[28] The Regulation provides for the substitution, as from January 1, 1999, of the euro for those Member States' currencies, at the rate to be irrevocably fixed pursuant to the first sentence of Article 123(4) ("the conversion rate").[29] During a transitional period, from the beginning of 1999 to the end of 2001, the euro can be used only as a unit of account and in non-cash transactions: banknotes and coins denominated in the national currencies continue to be available for cash transactions, at the conversion rate.[30] Euro banknotes, and coins denominated in euro or cent, will be put into circulation from January 1, 2002,[31] and from July 1, 2002, at the

---

[22] Detailed provisions on the convergence criteria are contained in Protocol (No. 6) to the E.C. Treaty.

[23] Dec. 98/317 E.C. [1998] O.J. L139/30.

[24] The Swedish Government had taken a political decision against joing the single currency. The technical reason given in the Decision for the non-fulfilment of the necessary conditions was that "the currency of Sweden has never participated in the ERM; in the two years under review, the Swedish crown (SEK) fluctuated against the ERM currencies reflecting among others (sic) the absence of an exchange rate target". No evidence is offered in the Decision that the margin of fluctuation exceeded the 15% limit. Participation in the ERM is not expressly referred to as an element of the convergence criterion defined in the third indent of Art. 121(1). It remains to be seen whether such participation, at least for part of the prescribed two-year period, will in future be regarded as a necessary condition.

[25] Indeed, Denmark had already given notice even before the entry into force of the TEU: see the Decision taken by the Heads of State or Government in Edinburgh in December 1992, Section B, point 1: [1992] O.J. C348/1.

[26] See Reg. 1103/97, loc. cit., n.17, above, Art. 1, second indent; Council Reg. 974/98 on the introduction of the euro, [1998] O.J. L139/1, Arts 1, first indent. Cf. Art. 122 E.C., which refers, respectively, to "Member States without a derogation" and "Member States with a derogation". The terminology used in the Regulations is preferable, not only on stylistic grounds but also because the phrase "Member States with a derogation" does not, strictly speaking, cover the United Kingdom and Denmark. There is a somewhat tendentious practice in certain institutions of referring to "Ins" and "Pre-ins".

[27] Loc. cit., n.26, above.

[28] See the third sentence of Art. 121(4) E.C.

[29] ibid., Arts 2 and 3.

[30] See the transitional provisions in Part III of Reg. 974/98, esp. Art. 6.

[31] ibid., Arts 10 and 11.

latest, banknotes and coins denominated in the national currencies of participating Member States will cease to be legal tender.[32] The participating Member States must ensure adequate sanctions against counterfeiting or falsification of euro banknotes and coins.[33]

After a fierce political wrangle, the governments of the 11 participating Member States appointed the President, the Vice-President and the other four members of the Executive Board of the ECB on May 25, 1998.[34] Their appointment took effect on June 1, marking the establishment of the ECB, and also the beginning of the liquidation of the EMI after the successful accomplishment of its preparatory mission.[35]

It remained for the Council, acting with the unanimity of the participating Member States, formally to take the decisive step of adopting the conversion rates at which their currencies would thenceforward be irrevocably fixed. That was done by Regulation 2866/98,[36] and the euro was launched as the single currency of those 11 countries on January 1, 1999.

Surveillance and co-ordination of economic policies

Although, as we have seen, the Member States retain responsibility for conducting their general economic policies, they are now required to regard these as a matter of common concern, and to co-ordinate them within the Council.[37] In the relatively open conditions of the internal market, the need for such co-ordination is clear as between all 15 Member States; and it is especially so in the case of the participating Member States, since they share a single monetary policy and a single exchange rate. Economic decisions taken purely in the light of national political considerations could have an adverse impact on the prospects for inflation, and hence on the monetary situation, in the euro area. The forum of co-ordination is the Ecofin Council, which meets before its regular sessions as "the Euro-11 Group" to consider matters of specific concern to those participating in the single currency.[38]

---

[32] *ibid.*, Art. 15.

[33] *ibid.*, Art. 12.

[34] Art. 123(1), second indent.

[35] EMI Statute, Art. 23.

[36] Council Reg. 2866/98 on the conversion rates between the euro and the currencies of the Member States adopting the euro. According to Art. 1 of the Regulation, the rates are as follows:

```
1 euro = 40,3399 Belgian francs
       = 1,95583 German marks
       = 166,386 Spanish pesetas
       = 6,55957 French francs
       = 0,787564 Irish pounds
       = 1936,27 Italian lire
       = 40,3399 Luxembourg francs
       = 2,20371 Dutch guilders
       = 13,7603 Austrian schillings
       = 200,482 Portuguese escudos
       = 5,94573 Finnish marks
```

[37] Art. 99(1) (ex 103) E.C.

[38] See the report of the Council on economic policy co-ordination, which was endorsed by the Vienna European Council in December 1998, points 1, 2 and 6.

To ensure that Member States pursue economic policies compatible with the objectives of the Community, and more particularly with the principles of Article 4 E.C. two main mechanisms have been made available by the Treaty: the "multilateral surveillance" procedure of Article 99 (ex 103), under which the Ecofin Council monitors economic developments in each of the Member States, against broad policy guidelines adopted in the form of a recommendation; and the excessive deficit procedure laid down by Article 104 (ex 104c), to deal with serious lapses of budgetary discipline. As set out in the Treaty, both mechanisms are somewhat loose and cumbersome. Their effectiveness has, however, been enhanced by the combination of political and legal instruments comprising the Stability and Growth Pact, which was adopted in 1997.[39]

Article 99 fixes no timetable for the forwarding by the Member States to the Community institutions, of information about their economic policies, nor does it specify the information that should be provided.[40] Moreover, where it is established that a Member State's policies are not consistent with the broad guidelines laid down pursuant to paragraph (2) of the Article, or that they risk jeopardising the proper functioning of EMU, the Council may only act on a recommendation from the Commission, and its power is discretionary.[41]

On all of those matters, a tighter procedure was introduced by Regulation 1466/97. Participating Member States were put under an obligation to submit to the Council and the Commission "stability programmes", and non-participating Member States to submit "convergence programmes", with a specified content (largely identical for the two groups). Essentially, such programmes are required to explain how the Member State concerned proposes to achieve, and maintain, "the medium term objective for the budgetary position of close to balance or in surplus".[42] The initial submissions were to be made before March 1, 1999, and thereafter updated programmes must be submitted annually.[43] The Council is legally bound, as part of multilateral surveillance in accordance with Article 99(3), to monitor the implementation of programmes, "in particular with a view to identifying actual or expected significant divergence of a budgetary position from the medium-term budgetary objective, or the adjustment path towards it . . .".[44] If such divergence is detected, the Council must, without waiting for the Commission to take the initiative, address a recommendation to the Member State concerned, by way of an early warning to prevent the occurrence of an excessive deficit; and, should subsequent monitoring indicate that the divergence is persisting or worsening, the Council is required to issue a recommendation

---

[39] The ingredients of the Stability and Growth Pact are: the Resolution of the Amsterdam European Council on the Pact, [1997] O.J. C236/1; Council Reg. 1466/97 on the strengthening of the surveillance of budgetary positions and the surveillance and co-ordination of economic policies, [1997] O.J. L209/1; and Council Reg. 1467/97 on speeding up and clarifying the implementation of the excessive deficit procedure, [1997] O.J. L209/6. As to the nature of these intruments as a package, see the second recital of Reg. 1466/97 and the third recital of Reg. 1467/97. For a full analysis, see Hahn, "The Stability Pact for European Monetary Union: Compliance with deficit limit as a constant legal duty", 35 C.M.L.Rev. (1998), p. 77.

[40] Art. 99(3) E.C.

[41] Art. 99(4) E.C..

[42] See respectively, Reg. 1466/97, Arts 3 and 7.

[43] *ibid.*, Art. 4(1) and Art. 8(1).

[44] *ibid.*, Art. 6(1) and Art. 10(1).

that the Member State take "prompt corrective measures", and may, as provided for by Article 199(4), make this public.[45]

Pursuant to Article 104 (ex 104c), the Member States have been under a duty, since the beginning of the second stage of EMU, to endeavour to avoid excessive deficits. Quantitative criteria for judging whether a Member State is observing budgetary discipline are provided for by Article 104(2), supplemented by Protocol No. 5, namely:

— a ratio of the planned or actual government deficit to gross domestic product not exceeding 3 per cent;
— a ratio of total government debt to gross domestic product not exceeding 60 per cent.

"Government" is defined as including central and local government and social security funds.[46] The criteria are to be applied "dynamically": thus the appreciation may be positive if, in the case of an excess over the 3 per cent deficit ratio, this is found to be "only exceptional and temporary" and it is not very great; or, in the case of an excess over the 60 per cent debt ratio, if the ratio has been moving steadily downwards and is approaching the reference value. The Commission has responsibility for monitoring the development of the budgetary situation and of the stock of government debt in the Member States and where necessary, for setting the excessive deficit procedure in motion.[47] The procedure may lead to a decision by the Council, "after an overall assessment" (implying a political judgment, not the mechanical application of the quantitative criteria), that an excessive deficit exists in the Member State concerned.[48] In that event, recommendations must be made to the Member State, with a view to bringing the excessive deficit situation to an end within a specified period.[49] When it is established that no effective action has been taken in response to its recommendations, the Council may proceed to make them public.[50]

Reinforcement of the excessive deficit procedure came with the third stage of EMU. Member States have been placed under a positive duty to avoid excessive government deficits,[51] and the Council has additional powers to force deficit reductions. If recommendations made with a view to bringing an excessive deficit situation to an end are not complied with, it is empowered to give notice to the Member State concerned to take, within a specified time, measures to achieve the reduction which it judges necessary[52]; and, in case of non-compliance with such a notice, there is provision for the imposition by the Council of sanctions of various kinds, including fines of an appropriate size.[53]

Regulation 1467/97 seeks in different ways to bring greater force and precision to the provisions of Article 104 E.C. For instance, criteria are supplied by Article

---

[45] *ibid.*, Art. 6(2) and (3) and Art. 10(2) and (3).
[46] Protocol No. 5, Art. 2.
[47] Art. 104(2) and (3).
[48] Art. 104(6).
[49] Art. 104(7).
[50] Art. 104(8).
[51] Art. 104(1), read with Art. 1, second sub-para.
[52] Art. 104(9).
[53] Art. 104(11).

2 of the Regulation to guide the judgment of the Commission in deciding whether a government deficit in excess of 3 per cent of GDP may be considered "exceptional and temporary", so as not to constitute a breach of budgetary discipline requiring action at Community level. The excess must be the result of "an unusual event outside the control of the Member State concerned and which has a major impact on the financial position of the general government", or it must be caused by "a severe economic downturn"; and budget forecasts provided by the Commission must indicate that the deficit will fall below the 3 per cent ratio once the unusual event or economic downturn comes to an end. To provide an excuse, an economic downturn should, as a rule, entail an annual fall in real GDP of at least 2 per cent. In addition, the Regulation imposes time limits at certain points in the procedure. Finally, the sanctions regime is strengthened. Article 11 provides that, where a decision is taken by the Council to apply a sanction to a participating Member State, this should normally be in the form of a non-interest bearing deposit; while Article 12 contains rules on the calculation of such deposits. Article 13 establishes the general rule that a deposit shall be converted into a fine, if the excessive deficit has still not been corrected two years later.

Besides the main mechanisms of multilateral surveillance and the excessive deficit procedure, various rules intended to enforce budgetary discipline by public bodies at all levels in the Community have been applicable since the beginning of the second stage of EMU. Thus it is forbidden for Community institutions and for central or local government or public undertakings in the Member States to be granted credit facilities by central banks[54] or, generally, to enjoy privileged access to financial institutions.[55] It is also forbidden for the Community or a Member State to be liable for, or to assume, the commitments of, central or local government or public undertakings (the so-called "no bailing out" rule).[56]

The ESCB and the ECB[57]

Article 8 (ex. 4(a)) EC establishes a European System of Central Banks (ESCB) and a European Central Bank (ECB). The ESCB is composed of the ECB and the NCBs of the participating Member States.[58]

The primary objective of the ESCB is stated by Article 105(1) to be the maintenance of price stability. While the ESCB is required also to support the general economic policies of the Community, this is without prejudice to the overriding price stability objective.

Four "basic tasks" have been entrusted to the ESCB[59]:

---

[54] Art. 101 (ex 104) E.C.

[55] Art. 102 (ex 104a) E.C.

[56] Art. 103 (ex 104b) E.C.

[57] There is a large literature on the ECB. Particularly illuminating are: R. Smits, *The European Central Bank* (Kluwer, 1997); M. Andenas *et al.* (eds), *European Economic and Monetary Union: The Institutional Framework* (Kluwer, 1997); C. Zilioli and M. Selmayr, "The European Central Bank, its system and its law", EUREDIA, 1999/2, 187 and 1999/3, 305.

[58] Art. 107(1) (ex 106) E.C.

[59] Art. 105(2) E.C.; Statute, Art. 3(1)

— defining and implementing the monetary policy of the Community (which includes the fixing of interest rates and, pursuant to Article 16 of the statute, the exclusive right to authorise the issue of banknotes);
— conducting foreign exchange operations;
— holding and managing the official foreign reserves of the Member States;
— Promoting the smooth operation of payment systems (which has entailed the establishment of the system known as "TARGET").[60]

The ESCB is governed by the decision-making bodies of the ECB, namely the Governing Council and the Executive Board.[61] The Governing Council comprises the members of the ECB's Executive Board and the Governors of the NCBs of participating Member States.[62] The Executive Board consists of a President, a Vice-President and four other members.[63] These must be "persons of recognised standing and professional experience in monetary or banking matters". Their method of appointment is by common accord of the governments of the Member States at the level of Heads of State or Government, on a recommendation from the Council, which must consult the European Parliament and the Governing Council of the ECB. The specific legal requirement of a decision taken at the highest political level of the Member States is unique among the institutional provisions of the Treaty, and is one of several indicators of the *sui generis* position of the ECB in the legal order of the E.C.[64]

Other such indicators may be mentioned. Like the E.C. itself, the ECB has legal personality.[65] It has, moreover, been endowed with quite extensive law-making powers. Regulations may be made by the ECB for implementing the monetary policy of the Community, and for some more specific purposes.[66] The ECB may also take decisions necessary for carrying out the tasks of the ESCB, make recommendations and deliver opinions. Those different forms of instrument are defined by Article 110(2) (ex 108a(2)) E.C. in similar terms to Article 249 (ex 189) E.C. In addition, the ECB may issue guidelines and instructions, which are binding acts internal to the ESCB. Thus Article 14(3) of the Statute provides that the NCBs "are an integral part of the ESCB and shall act in accordance with the guidelines and instructions of the ECB", and charges the Governing Council with ensuring that they do so.

The ECB has also been given a right, under Article 105(4) E.C. to be consulted by other legislative authorities, both at the Community and the national level, on any draft measure in its fields of competence. Such consultations have in practice been quite frequent. The direct link with the national

---

[60] The initials stand for "Trans-European Automated Real-time Gross-settlement Express Transfer" system. This was organised on the basis of an internal Guideline and an Intra-ESCB Agreement.
[61] Art. 107(3) (ex 106(3)) E.C.
[62] Art. 112(1) (ex 109a(1)) E.C.; Statute, Art. 10(1).
[63] Art. 112(2) E.C.; Statute, Art. 11.
[64] On the constitutional position of the ECB, see C. Zilioli and M. Salmayr, "The European Central Bank: an Independent Specialised Organisation of Community Law", 37 C.M.L. Rev. (2000), 591.
[65] Art. 107(2) (ex 106(2)) E.C.
[66] Art. 110(1) (ex 108a(1), first indent. The power has been used sparingly. See Reg. 2818/98 on the application of minimum reserves, [1998] O.J. L356/1; Reg. 2819/98 concerning the consolidated balance sheet of the monetary financial institutions sector, [1998] O.J. L365/7; Reg. 2157/1999 on the power of the ECB to impose sanctions, [1999] O.J. L264/21. One might have expected TARGET to be established by regulation.

legislator is another highly individual feature of the ECB's constitutional position.

The ECB has adopted a decentralised mode of operation. It is authorised, indeed encouraged, to do so by Article 12(1), third subparagraph of the Statute, which says: "To the extent deemed possible and appropriate . . . the ECB shall have recourse to the national central banks to carry out operations which form part of the tasks of the ESCB". For instance, there is an ECB Guideline on ESCB monetary policy instruments and procedures under which, among other things, the NCBs carry out open market operations. Similarly, as regards the management of the reserves which have been transferred to the ECB pursuant to Article 30 of the Statute, the NCBs operate under a series of Guidelines and Instructions established by the ECB, and subject to its monitoring. Also, the production of euro banknotes and coins is carried out by the NCBs, under ECB supervision.

A fundamental principle of the ESCB is the independence of the ECB and of national central banks, in performing the tasks and duties conferred on them by the Treaty and the ESCB Statute, both from the Community institutions and from national governments.[67] There is an explicit Treaty undertaking by the Community institutions and by governments to respect that principle and not to seek to influence the members of the decision-making bodies of the ECB or of national central banks. A duty is placed on the Member States to take the legislative steps necessary to ensure the complete independence of their national central banks, not later than the date of the establishment of the ESCB.[68]

The institutional independence of the ECB is reinforced by the guarantees of the personal independence of members of the Executive Board and of the Governing Council, which are found in both the Treaty and the Statute. Executive Board members serve for a term of eight years, which is not renewable, thus avoiding a possible source of pressure.[69] They can be removed from office only under the compulsory retirement procedure laid down by Article 11(4) of the Statute, which entails an application to the Court of Justice by the Governing Council or the Executive Board. The members of the Governing Council, apart from the Executive Board, are all Governors of NCBs and must therefore, pursuant to Article 14(2) of the Statute, have terms of appointment of at least five years. Under the same provision, an NCB Governor may only be removed from office if he no longer fulfils the conditions required for the performance of his duties or if he has been guilty of serious misconduct; and such a decision may be referred to the Court of Justice by the Governing Council or by the Governor concerned, on grounds of infringement of the Treaty or any rule of law relating to its application — the only example of an act of national authorities that can be directly challenged by an individual before the Court.

In addition, the ECB is entirely independent of the General Budget of the European Communities. Its financial situation is exclusively governed by Chapter VI of the Statute. The ECB's assets come either from the NCBs, in the form of its paid capital and transferred foreign reserve assets, or from the profits of its

[67] Art. 108 (ex 106) E.C.; Statute, Art. 7.
[68] Art. 109 (ex 108) E.C.
[69] Art. 112(2)(b) (ex 109a(2)(b)) E.C.

operations.[70] Any losses the ECB might sustain, would have to be covered by the NCBs, pursuant to Article 33(2) of the Statute.

The separation of the ECB from the political process of the European Union is not complete. The President of the Council and a member of the Commission may participate, without having the right to vote, in meetings of the Governing Council,[71] and the ECB's President must be invited to Council meetings when matters relating to the objectives and tasks of the ECB are being discussed.[72] Moreover, the ECB is required by Article 113(3) (ex 109b(3)) to address an annual report on its activities, and on the monetary policy of both the previous and the current year, to the European Parliament, the Council and the Commission, as well as to the European Council. The President of the ECB presents the report to the Council and the Parliament. He, and other members of the Executive Board, may, at the Parliament's request or on their own initiative, be heard by the competent Parliamentary committees. Nevertheless, it is broadly true that the formulation and management of monetary policy in the euro area has been taken out of the hands of politicians and entrusted to the technocrats of the ECB and the NCBs. That may be seen as compounding the democratic deficit in the constitutional order of the European Union; or alternatively, as a sensible (indeed, an unavoidable) strategy, to shield monetary policy against the contending winds of national politics.[73]

---

[70] See Statute, Arts 28–30.
[71] Art. 113(1) (ex 109b(1)) E.C.
[72] Art. 113(2) (ex 109b(2)) E.C.
[73] See, e.g. the balanced commentary of M. Herdegen, "Price stability and budgetary restraints in the Economic and Monetary Union: The law as guardian of economic wisdon", 35 C.M.L. Rev. (1998), 9.

PART VI: COMPETITION POLICY

CHAPTER 19

INTRODUCTION TO THE RULES ON COMPETITION

Competition and the common market

The list of "activities of the Community" in Article 3 E.C. includes "the institution of a system ensuring that competition in the common market is not distorted."[1] This seemingly mild reference belies the importance attached to competition law and policy in securing the broad objectives laid down for the Community in Article 2.

In the first place, some distinctions should be drawn between *competition, competition policies* and *competition law.*[2] Competition, at least in a commercial context, describes a struggle for superiority in the market place. It is an essential aspect of the market mechanism because the availability of choice between goods and services establishes a link between the success of an undertaking and its ability to satisfy consumers' wishes. However, this idea is not the perfect competition model of neo-classical economics, in which efficiency is maximised by equilibrium between consumer demand and producer supply.[3] Instead, the development of E.C. law has adapted this theoretical paradigm and concentrated upon the pursuit of *workable* competition. As explained by the European Court, this is the "degree of competition necessary to ensure the observance of the basic requirements and attainment of the objectives of the Treaty, in particular the creation of a single market achieving conditions similar to those of a domestic market."[4]

This approach reveals that competition law is an instrument to serve particular competition policies. In the introduction to its *First Report on Competition Policy* the Commission wrote:

"Competition is the best stimulant of economic activity since it guarantees the widest possible freedom of action to all. An active competition policy pursued in accordance with the provisions of the Treaties establishing the Communities makes it easier for the supply and demand structure continually to adjust to technological development. Through the interplay of decentralized decision-making machinery, competition enables enterprises continuously to improve their efficiency, which is the sine qua non for a steady improvement in living standards and employment prospects within the countries of the Community. From this point of view, competition policy is an essential means for satisfying to a great extent the individual and collective needs of our society."[5]

---

[1] For a discussion of the inter-relationship of competition policy and industrial policy, see W. Sauter, *Competition Law and Industrial Policy in the EU* (Oxford, 1997).
[2] See M. Cini and L. McGowan, *Competition Policy in the European Union* (Macmillan, 1998).
[3] See R. Whish, *Competition Law* (Butterworths, 3rd ed, 1993), Chap. 1.
[4] Case 26/76 *Metro v. Commission (No. 1)* [1977] E.C.R. 1875 at 1904; [1978] 2 C.M.L.R. 1.
[5] Comp. Rep. 1971, p. 11.

This early statement clearly portrayed competition policy as ensuring that the common market envisaged by the Treaty functioned as a genuine *market*. Moreover, as the first sentence of the quoted passage implies, competition policy goals will reflect political value judgments as well as economic desiderata. Political benefits of competition may include the dilution of power away from the State and large businesses or the increased freedom of opportunity for consumers or business.

Thus, the role of competition regulation will vary in the light of how Community objectives are perceived and prioritised. Among the disparate areas which competition policies might address are the following:[6] consumer welfare, the redistribution of wealth, the protection of small and medium-sized enterprises,[7] regional, social or industrial considerations and the integration of the single market. These concerns are not necessarily mutually compatible or easily reconciled in any given situation. Questions as to how they are to be balanced or, indeed, whether they are legitimate elements in competition policy at all, remain controversial for lawyers and economists alike.[8] The Court's notion of "workable competition" is, in effect, a compromise aimed at achieving pragmatic solutions to these complex issues.

Many factors affecting competition and competition policy, such as industrial or social policy, are not peculiar to the European context. The exception, of course, is the influence wrought by the drive to create a single internal market.[9] Here competition policy reinforces the provisions of the Treaty aiming at the removal of barriers between the economies of the Member States. Dismantling those public obstacles to trade will hardly be effective if they are simply replaced by private ones. It would be futile to attempt to create a single market without internal frontiers in goods, persons, services and capital, as required by Article 14 E.C., if the isolation of national markets could effectively be maintained by restrictive practices on the part of undertakings, or by State aid policies giving competitive advantages to national industries. As will be seen in the discussion of Articles 81 and 82 in succeeding chapters, market partitioning is a particularly serious infringement of the rules on competition.

As the instrument to give effect to competition policies, competition law is hardly neutral. Its attempts to de-regulate may substitute re-regulation of particular markets or sectors. In this sense it is different from the negative integration which flows from the implementation of the fundamental freedoms. By curtailing or accepting the freedom of action of particular parties, competition law makes judgments about the content of notions of consumer welfare and other objectives, and the best means of promoting them. Market regulation by law in this way raises in turn much wider issues about the scope for and extent of

---

[6] See M. Cini and L. McGowan, *op. cit, supra*, n.2., p. 4.

[7] Specifically mentioned in the E.C. Treaty as part of Art. 157 in Title XVI Industry.

[8] See, *inter alia*, the discussion of so-called Harvard and Chicago School economic theories by Burton, "Competition over competition analysis: a guide to some contemporary economics disputes" in Lonbay (ed.), *Frontiers of Competition Law* (Wiley Chancery Law, 1994), Chap. 1. Also Bork, *The Antitrust Paradox: A Policy at War with Itself* (Basic Books, 1978).

[9] See Ehlermann, "The contribution of E.C. competition policy to the Single Market" (1992) 29 C.M.L.Rev. 257.

any "economic constitution" in the E.C.[10] In particular, the idea of a market without a State raises issues about how E.C. competition law should cope with the role of States themselves. As Micklitz and Weatherill note,[11] the policies of market integration and competition have to find a *modus vivendi* with the role of the state in the market—and, more broadly still, with the role of the state in society. Additional problems are posed by the increasing interface between E.C. competition law on the one hand and the forces of globalisation and pressures for international legal regulation[12] on the other. Faced with this mix of economic, regulatory and governance issues, there can be little doubt as to the complexity of the theoretical and practical framework in which the E.C. rules must operate.

The E.C. Treaty provisions on competition

The preamble to the Treaty and the general provisions of Articles 2 and 3 have played a significant part in the development of the case-law on competition.[13] However, the primary Treaty provisions in which the substantive law on the topic is to be found are Articles 81 to 89.

So far as the behaviour of undertakings is concerned, the Treaty adopts a distinction which is familiar in competition law (or, to use the American term, "antitrust law")[14] between two types of problem that may arise. The first concerns restrictive agreements or practices involving a degree of collusion between undertakings that are economically independent of each other. Such combinations in restraint of trade are sometimes referred to as "cartels". Examples can be found in agreements between A and B to keep out of each other's markets or to fix prices. Article 81 of the Treaty is designed to deal with such situations. It is considered in Chapter 20, *infra*. The second type of problem arises where a single undertaking or a group of undertakings has reached a position of such strength on a given market that the normal constraints of the competitive process no longer apply to it. This is known in Community law as a "dominant position". Dominant undertakings represent a danger to other operators on the same market and to their customers or suppliers. They may, for example, drive the remaining participants in the same market out of business or charge unreasonably high prices for their products. One way of averting this danger is to attack the fact of dominance itself, by seeking to prevent the growth of undertakings beyond a certain point, and by taking power to break up any that

---

[10] This idea is not pursued in detail in this book. However, for a flavour of the arguments, see Micklitz and Weatherill, *European Economic Law* (Ashgate, Dartmouth, 1997); also Joerges, "European Economic Law, the Nation-State and the Maastricht Treaty" in Dehousse (ed.), *Europe after Maastricht—an Ever Closer Union?* (Munich, 1994), Chap. 3.

[11] *op. cit.*, n.10 *supra*, p. 175.

[12] See generally, Doern and Wilks (eds), *Comparative Competition Policy: National Institutions in a Global Market* (Clarendon Press, Oxford, 1996); Ehlermann and Laudati (eds), *European Competition Law Annual 1997: Objectives of Competition Policy* (Robert Schuman Centre at the European University Institute, Hart Publishing, 1998).

[13] See, *e.g.* Case 32/65 *Italy v. Council and Commission* [1966] E.C.R. 389 at 405; [1969] C.M.L.R. 39; Case 6/72 *Europemballage and Continental Can v. Commission* [1973] E.C.R. 215 at 243–244; [1973] C.M.L.R. 199.

[14] In the nineteenth century anti-competitive arrangements were often carried out in the USA through trusts, hence this term.

may succeed in doing so. An alternative approach is to attempt to regulate the behaviour of dominant undertakings. Here regulatory power is used as a constraining influence, to compensate for the absence of effective competition. Initially the latter approach was adopted by the E.C. Treaty in its focus upon the "abuse" of dominance. Subsequently, the European Court held that, in certain circumstances, a further accretion of market power to a dominant undertaking may, in itself, constitute an abuse. Now, the former approach has been adopted in the Merger Regulation which is considered in Chapter 23, *infra*.

Provision for the application of the substantive rules in Articles 81 and 82 is made by Articles 83 to 85 of the Treaty. Article 83 empowers the Council, acting by a qualified majority on a proposal from the Commission and after consulting the European Parliament, to adopt implementing regulations or directives. This power has been used for the enactment of, *inter alia*, Regulation 17, which established the basic machinery for the execution of E.C. competition policy, giving primary responsibility to the Commission.[15] Regulation 17 covers all sectors of the economy except where other provisions have been made. Particularly significant special regimes include: merger control[16]; rail, road and inland waterway transport[17]; maritime transport[18]; and air transport.[19]

Problems arising from the relationships between governments, on the one hand, and public undertakings or undertakings which have been entrusted with the performance of certain tasks in the public interest, on the other, are the subject of Article 86. This relationship, although clearly liable to affect the conditions of competition, has a wider significance for the operation of the common market. It is discussed in Chapter 25, *infra*.

Under Articles 87 to 89 the Community institutions, and in particular the Commission, have supervisory powers over the granting of aids to industry in the various Member States. The general principle is that aid must not be granted if it distorts or threatens to distort competition by favouring certain undertakings or forms of production, in so far as trade between Member States may be affected. However, exceptions are permitted in relation to a number of economic, regional, social and cultural concerns, enabling the Commission to take account of the various pressures to which the Member States are subject. These provisions are discussed in Chapter 24, *infra*.

Other sources of E.C. competition law

Besides the E.C. Treaty itself, the principal sources of E.C. competition law are regulations pursuant to Article 83, the case-law of the Court of Justice and the Court of First Instance, and the administrative practice of the Commission.

Regulations on competition have been adopted by both the Council and the Commission, the latter acting under delegated powers. Regulation 17,[20] the general

---

[15] [1962] J.O. 204; [1959–1962] O.J. 87.
[16] Reg. 4064/89, for which see Chap. 23, *infra*.
[17] Reg. 1017/68 [1968] O.J. L175/1.
[18] Reg. 4056/86 [1986] O.J. L378/4; Reg. 479/92 [1992] O.J. L55/3; Reg. 870/95 [1995] O.J. L89/7.
[19] Regulations 3975/87 [1987] O.J. L374/1, 1617/93 [1993] O.J. L155/18.
[20] n.15, *supra*.

implementing measure, has already been mentioned. This is supplemented by various measures governing more detailed measures, such as limitation periods,[21] notification forms and procedures,[22] and the hearing of parties.[23] Regulations were also used expansively in respect of "block" exemptions under Article 81(3) concerning categories of agreements (for example exclusive distribution agreements, franchising agreements, technology transfer agreements) which would otherwise be liable to prohibition under Article 81(1). However, the reform of the system of enforcement and application of Article 81 (discussed in Chapter 22, *infra*) will restrict the proliferation of this particular line of legislative activity.[24]

The Court of Justice has played a vital part in the development of the rules on competition, as of other areas of Community law. Competition matters normally come to the courts by way of proceedings under Article 230 E.C. for the review of decisions of the Commission applying the rules, or of references under Article 234 from national courts before which the rules have been invoked. In addition, Regulation 17 has conferred on the Court unlimited jurisdiction as provided by Article 229 E.C., to hear appeals against the imposition by the Commission of fines for infringements of the rules.[25] Since its establishment[26] proceedings under Article 230 relating to the implementation of the competition rules of the E.C. must be brought before the Court of First Instance.[27] Appeal lies to the Court of Justice from the Court of First Instance only on points of law.[28]

As a result of this realignment of responsibilities, the Court of Justice no longer has the same opportunities to influence the development of competition law.[29] After the early heady days in which the Commission's desire to secure an effective regulatory regime gained judicial endorsement, the Court of Justice has been instrumental in ensuring that the Commission is itself subject to rule of law considerations, requiring it to provide more detailed economic evidence in support of its conclusions and establishing procedural rights for undertakings.[30] The Court of First Instance has in turn taken a robust approach to factual issues in competition cases.

The Commission is the authority charged with the administration of the competition system at Community level. For this purpose it has been empowered to take decisions, *inter alia,* ordering the termination of infringements,[31] granting exemptions under Article 81(3)[32] and imposing fines[33] or periodic penalty payments.[34] In addition to its decisions in individual cases, the Commission's

---

[21] Reg. 2988/74 [1974] O.J. L319/1.
[22] Reg. 3385/94 [1994] O.J. L377/28.
[23] Reg. 2842/98 [1998] O.J. L354/18.
[24] See the Commission's *White Paper on Modernisation of the Rules Implementing Arts 85 and 86 of the E.C. Treaty*, Brussels, April 28, 1999.
[25] See Reg. 17, Art.17.
[26] Council Dec. 88/591 Establishing an E.C. Court of First Instance [1988] O.J. L319/1.
[27] *ibid.*, Art. 3(1)(c).
[28] Art. 51 Statute of Court of Justice as amended by Art. 7, Council Dec. 88/591, *loc. cit.*
[29] See generally Gerber, *Law and Competition in Twentieth Century Europe* (1998).
[30] Arnull, *The European Union and its Court of Justice* (Oxford, 1999), p. 397.
[31] Reg. 17, Art. 3(1).
[32] Reg. 17, Art. 9(1).
[33] Reg. 17, Art. 15.
[34] Reg. 17, Art. 16.

policy and practice can also be discerned from its Annual Reports on Competition Policy. Moreover, in recent years the Commission has increasingly made greater use of "soft law" mechanisms such as Notices. These have covered a variety of topics, including market definition, *de minimis* rules, and the Commission's own relationship with national courts in the disposal of individual cases. Notices are technically not binding but will be influential in the areas they cover, offering guidance and some element of certainty for the business community.

Finally, it may be noted, the directly effective provisions of Articles 81 and 82 invite recourse to national courts for the application of E.C. competition law. The resulting case-law is an additional source of persuasive authority on the interpretation of those provisions. It may be anticipated that some increased role for national courts will follow in the wake of the enforcement reforms discussed further in Chapter 22 *infra*. In particular, the envisaged switch from a system of notification and exemption built around Commission approval to reliance upon *ex post facto* control of anti-competitive activity at the behest of complainants will trigger litigation in national courts.[35]

The scope of the E.C. rules on competition

Personal scope

The rules in Articles 81 and 82 apply to "undertakings". No definition of this concept for the purposes of competition law is provided by the E.C. Treaty. However, the Court has taken an expansive view of the notion, holding that it encompasses every entity engaged in an economic activity, regardless of the legal status of the entity and the way in which it is financed.[36] The requirement of participation in economic activities must be understood in a wide sense. It covers not only the production and distribution of goods but also the provision of services.[37] A body that exists for a non-economic purpose but engages in certain operations of a commercial nature will be, to that extent, an undertaking[38]: for example a public service broadcasting establishment when it licenses the manufacture of toys based on a popular children's series.[39] Nor is there any need for the body in question to be motivated by the pursuit of profits. Thus societies that manage the rights of authors and performing artists on a non-profit making basis qualify as undertakings because they provide a commercial service.[40]

The entities accepted as undertakings by the Court of Justice and the Commission exhibit a wide range of legal forms. They include companies, partnerships,[41] co-operatives[42] and even the mutual marine insurance associations

---

[35] Commission's *White Paper on Modernisation of the Rules Implementing Arts 85 and 86 of the E.C. Treaty, supra*, n.24.
[36] Case C–41/90 *Höfner v. Macrotron* [1991] E.C.R. I–1979, at para. 21; [1993] 4 C.M.L.R. 306.
[37] Case 155/73 *Sacchi* [1974] E.C.R. 409; [1974] 2 C.M.L.R. 177.
[38] *ibid.*
[39] *Re BBC* [1976] 1 C.M.L.R. D89.
[40] Case 127/73 *BRT v. SABAM* [1974] E.C.R. 51 and 313; [1974] 2 C.M.L.R. 238; Case 7/82 *GVL v. Commission* [1983] E.C.R. 483; [1983] 3 C.M.L.R. 645.
[41] *e.g. Re William Prym-Werke* [1973] J.O. L296/24; [1973] C.M.L.R. D250.
[42] *e.g. Re Rennet* [1980] O.J. L51/19; [1980] 2 C.M.L.R. 402. The decision was upheld by the Court in Case 61/80 *Co-operatieve Stremsel-en-Kleurselfabriek v. Commission* [1981] E.C.R. 851; [1982] 1 C.M.L.R. 240.

known as "P and I Clubs".[43] Individuals may be undertakings, for example, an inventor who grants licences for the use of patents he has taken out[44] or opera stars who contract to perform for a television company.[45] However, individuals who are "workers" within the meaning of Article 39 E.C. will not be undertakings. Thus in *Becu*[46] "recognised dockers" were found to perform their work for and under the direction of undertakings, thus satisfying the definition of "worker".[47] Since they were, for the duration of that relationship, incorporated into the undertakings concerned and formed an economic unit with each of them, the dockers did not in themselves constitute undertakings within the meaning of Community competition law.[48] Nor could the recognised dockers viewed collectively in a port area be regarded as an undertaking.[49]

At the opposite end of the spectrum are nationalised industries and the other kinds of public corporation.[50] The Commission regards as undertakings the foreign trade organisations of countries, even if under their domestic law they have no identity separate from the state.[51] Within the Community, actions of a Member State or some sub-division of it such as a local authority or municipality must be examined to see if they are carried out *qua* public authority or as a commercial activity. Thus in *Bodson*,[52] no agreement "between undertakings" existed for the purposes of the Treaty in relation to the exclusive concessions granted by French communes to local providers of funeral services. The nuances of the meaning of "undertaking" and the scope of "commercial activity" in the context of the State are discussed in greater detail in Chapter 25, *infra*.

In applying the rules on competition to groups of companies the Court of Justice does not hesitate to go behind the facade of separate corporate personality. This pragmatic approach is illustrated by the *Hydrotherm* case[53] which concerned the block exemption granted by Regulation 67/67[54] to certain categories of exclusive dealing agreements. The exemption was expressly limited to agreements "to which only two undertakings are party."[55] That condition was held to be fulfilled where the parties to a contract were, on the distribution side, a German company, and on the manufacturing side, the Italian developer of a product and two legally independent firms controlled by him. The Court explained that "[i]n competition law, the term 'undertaking' must be understood as designating an economic unit

---

[43] See, *Re P and I Clubs* [1985] O.J. C9/11; also *Re P & I Clubs IGA and P & I Clubs Pooling Agreement* [1999] O.J. L125/12, [1999] 5 C.M.L.R. 646. The Clubs are groupings of shipowners, charterers and operators who agree to share certain liabilities, in particular contractual and third party liabilities, on a non-profit making basis. Risks in excess of certain agreed thresholds are often shared between "pools" of P and I Clubs.

[44] See, *e.g. Re AOIP/Beyrard* [1976] O.J. L6/8; [1976] 1 C.M.L.R. D14.

[45] *Re Unitel* [1978] O.J. L157/39; [1978] 3 C.M.L.R. 306.

[46] Case C–22/98 *Becu and others* [1999] E.C.R. I–5665.

[47] See Case C–170/90 *Merci Convenzionali v. Porto di Genova* [1991] E.C.R. I–5889.

[48] Case C–22/98 *Becu, supra*, n.46, at para. 26.

[49] *ibid.*, para. 27.

[50] *e.g. Re British Telecom* [1982] O.J. L360/36 [1983] 1 C.M.L.R. 457. The decision was upheld by the Court in Case 41/83 *Italy v. Commission* [1985] E.C.R. 873; [1985] 2 C.M.L.R. 368.

[51] *Re Aluminium Imports from Eastern Europe* [1985] O.J. L92/1; [1987] 3 C.M.L.R. 813.

[52] Case 30/87 *Bodson v. Pompes Funèbres des Regions Libérées SA* [1988] E.C.R. 2479; [1989] 4 C.M.L.R. 984.

[53] Case 170/83 *Hydrotherm* [1984] E.C.R. 2999; [1985] 3 C.M.L.R. 244.

[54] [1967] J.O. 849. [1967] O.J. 1967, 10.

[55] *ibid.*, Art. 1(1).

for the purpose of the subject-matter of the agreement in question even if in law that economic unit consists of several persons, natural or legal."[56] In practice, the main impact of the "enterprise entity" doctrine has been on two issues: the assertion of jurisdiction against a parent company established in a third country which has subsidiaries within the common market; and the application of Article 81 to agreements and practices between parent companies and subsidiaries. These issues are examined further below.

Material scope

The E.C. rules on competition apply generally, to all sectors of the economy, except where express derogations are provided in other Articles of the Treaty.[57]

The main sectors falling outside the rules are coal and steel, which are governed by the ECSC Treaty.[58] However, where an ECSC undertaking deals in goods other than those defined in Annex I to the ECSC Treaty, the E.C. rules will apply to it.[59] The Commission has adopted a communication[60] setting out plans for the alignment of coal and steel regulation with other industrial sectors when the ECSC Treaty comes to an end in July 2002.

The approach taken by the E.C. Treaty to agriculture reflects the potential tension between the objectives of the common agricultural policy established by Title II and the notion of undistorted competition envisaged by Article 3(g). The extent to which the competition rules apply was made a matter for the discretion of the Council in what is now Article 36. In exercising that discretion the Council differentiated between the rules applicable to undertakings and the rules on state aids. The former were extended to agricultural products by Regulation 26,[61] subject to an exemption from the prohibition in Article 81(1) for the benefit of agreements that form an integral part of a national market organisation or that are necessary for the attainment of the objectives of the E.C.'s common agricultural policy set out in Article 33 E.C. The exception has been narrowly interpreted and is of limited practical significance.[62] In the case of state aids, effect has been given to the relevant provisions of the E.C. Treaty by the basic regulations of the various common organisations of national markets.

Special mention should also be made of the transport sector. Whilst the Treaty provisions on competition apply,[63] separate arrangements have been made for their implementation in this sector.[64]

---

[56] [1984] E.C.R. 3016.

[57] Joined Cases 209–213/84 *Ministère Public v. Asjes and others* [1986] E.C.R. 1425; [1986] 3 C.M.L.R. 173.

[58] See Art. 305 E.C.

[59] Case 1/59 *Macchiorlatti Dalmas v. High Authority* [1959] E.C.R. 199.

[60] *The Global and Sustainable Competitiveness of the Steel Industry in the EU.*

[61] [1962] J.O. 993; [1959–1962] O.J. 129.

[62] The first limb of the exception ceased to be available once a common organisation of the market had been established in respect of the product in question: Case 83/78 *Pigs Marketing Board v. Redmond* [1978] E.C.R. 2347 at 2369–2370; [1979] 1 C.M.L.R. 177. To satisfy the second limb of the exception, an agreement must be shown to be necessary for the attainment of all five of the objectives in Art. 33 E.C.: Case 71/74 *FRUBO v. Commission* [1975] E.C.R. 563 at 582–583; [1975] 2 C.M.L.R. 123. For the role of national courts, see Case C–399/93 *Oude Luttikuis* [1995] E.C.R. I–4515; [1996] 5 C.M.L.R. 178.

[63] Joined Cases 209–213/84 *Ministère Public v. Asjes and others, supra*, n.57.

[64] See nn.17–19, *supra*.

Territorial scope

The prohibition in Article 81 applies to arrangements between undertakings "which may affect trade between Member States and which have as their object or effect the prevention, restriction or distortion of competition within the common market", and that in Article 82 to any abuse of a dominant position "within the common market or in a substantial part of it . . . in so far as it may affect trade between Member States." This wording makes it clear that the target of the prohibitions is behaviour having an actual or intended impact on the conditions of competition in the territory over which the common market extends, *i.e.* the territory of the Community as defined by Article 299 E.C.

It follows that undertakings carrying on business in the Community are free under the E.C. rules on competition to participate in agreements or practices that may interfere with the functioning of the market mechanism in third countries, so long as the consequences are unlikely to spill back into the common market.[65] Thus, in its *VVVF* Decision[66] the Commission allowed a Dutch association of paint and varnish manufacturers to continue a system of minimum prices and uniform conditions of sale in respect of exports by its members outside the common market, after securing the abolition of the system in respect of intra-Community trade.

The converse case is where undertakings not physically present on Community territory behave in ways that are liable to affect competition on the common market. How far does the Community claim extraterritorial jurisdiction in competition matters? In addressing this question it is useful to bear in mind the distinction drawn by international lawyers between "prescriptive jurisdiction" (the power to make rules and to take decisions under them) and "enforcement jurisdiction" (the power to give effect to such rules or decisions through executive action).[67] The assertion of either form of jurisdiction, but especially the latter, against an undertaking located in another state's territory raises legal and political issues of some delicacy. Three possible bases for the application of the E.C. rules in such cases fall to be considered.

First, it is generally accepted in international law that a state is entitled to jurisdiction where activity which was commenced abroad is brought to consummation in its territory. This is known as the "objective territorial principle." It would, for example, allow the Commission to apply Article 81 to a contract made in a third country but substantially performed, at least on one side, within the Community.

Secondly, and more controversially, the Court of Justice has developed a doctrine of enterprise entity as a basis of jurisdiction against a parent company which has subsidiaries inside the Community, though situated itself on the outside. Under the doctrine, where material aspects of the subsidiary's commercial policy are controlled by the parent company, behaviour of the former in

---

[65] Community law is not alone in tolerating anti-competitive behaviour when its effects are limited to export markets. *cf.* the Webb-Pomerene Act in the United States. However, the application of bilateral and multilateral agreements containing rules analogous to E.C. law may of course reduce the scope of such freedom.

[66] [1969] J.O. L168/22; [1970] C.M.L.R. D1.

[67] See Shaw, *International Law* (4th ed, CUP, 1997), Chap. 12.

contravention of the rules on competition may be imputed to the latter. The leading case is *Dyestuffs*,[68] which concerned a decision by the Commission that a group of major manufacturers of aniline dyes had been guilty on three separate occasions of concerted price fixing. The addressees of the decision included ICI (at that time the UK was not a Member State) and certain Swiss companies. Objections by these companies to the jurisdiction of the Commission were dismissed by the Court on the ground that all of them had subsidiaries within the common market for whose decisions on pricing they could be held responsible.

This approach to parent-subsidiary relationships has received regular judicial affirmation. In the context of fines, for example, the Court of First Instance recently observed,[69] quoting *Dyestuffs*, that:

"It is well established that the fact that a subsidiary has separate legal personality is not sufficient to exclude the imputation of its conduct to the parent company, especially where the subsidiary does not determine its conduct independently but in all material respects carries out the instructions given to it by the parent company."

Whilst there may still be some room for doubt in individual cases about the point at which autonomy exists in the subsidiary, the main indicators will be the size of the parent's shareholding, its control of the subsidiary's board of directors and other organs and the parent's general ability to influence decisions.[70] In the *PVC Cartel II* case,[71] the Court of First Instance ruled that since the subsidiary was wholly owned by the parent it was superfluous to inquire whether the latter was able to exercise a decisive influence on the former's commercial behaviour.

The enterprise entity doctrine has been used by the Court and the Commission to found not only prescriptive but also enforcement jurisdiction. Thus competition proceedings may be validly initiated against the foreign parent of a Community subsidiary by sending it a statement of objections through the post,[72] and the final decision finding the company guilty of an infringement of the rules may be similarly served.[73] Fines may be imposed on the parent company for the infringement, and it may be ordered to take remedial action. In *Commercial Solvents*,[74] for example, an American multinational corporation was found to have abused its dominant position under Article 82 by refusing, through its Italian subsidiary, to supply a customer with a product in which it held the world monopoly. The Court did not question the power of the Commission, besides fining Commercial Solvents, to require it to make an immediate delivery of a specified quantity of the product in question to the customer and to submit proposals for longer term supply arrangements. Of course, if fines are not paid,

---

[68] There was, in fact, a group of cases brought by different addressees of the decision in question, to which this collective designation is given. See, in particular, Case 48/69 *ICI v. Commission* [1972] E.C.R. 619; [1972] C.M.L.R. 557.

[69] Joined Cases T–305–307, 313–316, 318, 325, 328–329 and 335/94 *Re the PVC Cartel II: Limburgse Vinyl Maatschappij NV and others v. Commission* [1999] 5 C.M.L.R. 303.

[70] *cf.* the notions of "control" set out in the Merger Regulation, discussed in Chap. 23, *infra*.

[71] *supra*, n.69, para. 984 of judgment.

[72] See, *e.g.* Case 52/69 *Geigy v. Commission* [1972] E.C.R. 787; [1972] C.M.L.R. 557.

[73] Case 6/72 *Europemballage and Continental Can v. Commission*, *supra*, n.13.

[74] Joined Cases 6 and 7/73 *Commercial Solvents Corporation v. Commission* [1974] E.C.R. 223.

they can only be enforced by levying execution on property of the parent or subsidiary which is in the territory of a Member State.[75]

A third, and still more controversial, basis for the extraterritorial application of competition law is the so-called "effects doctrine". Broadly, the doctrine holds that a state is entitled to assert jurisdiction in respect of non-nationals abroad, where these produce effects felt within the state's own territory. In E.C. law, the question is whether the Court of Justice has followed the approach of American courts in constructing a principle of jurisdiction based on direct, substantial and foreseeable effects.[76] The leading case is *Wood Pulp*,[77] where the Commission imposed fines on various American and Scandinavian producers of wood pulp for concertation on the fixing of prices at which they supplied the paper industry in the common market. The activities regarded by the Commission as constituting the concertation took place in the producers' home countries, and several of those involved had no establishment and no subsidiaries within the Community.

When the applicants challenged the Commission's decision before the Court, Advocate General Darmon proposed the adoption of a qualified effects doctrine of the type used in American competition law. However, the Court did not grasp this particular nettle, instead expressing its view in terms of an 'implementation' test as follows:

"If the applicability of prohibitions laid down under competition law were made to depend on the place where the agreement, decision or concerted practice was formed, the result would obviously be to give undertakings an easy means of evading those prohibitions. The decisive factor is therefore the place where it is implemented. The producers in this case implemented their pricing agreement within the common market. It is immaterial in that respect whether or not they had recourse to subsidiaries, agents, sub-agents or branches within the Community in order to make their contacts with purchasers within the Community. Accordingly the Community's jurisdiction to apply its competition rules to such conduct is covered by the territoriality principle as universally recognised in public international law."[78]

The scope of this concept of implementation, and its relationship to any effects doctrine, remains subject to debate.[79] In particular, it may be asked whether it applies to situations where the distortion to intra-Community trade is caused by the parties diverting their goods away from the Community as distinct from, say, fixing the prices at which those goods will eventually be sold on Community

---

[75] See Art. 256 E.C.
[76] The classic U.S. statement can be found in *US v. Aluminium Co. of America* 148 F.2d 416 (1945) where it was said that "any state may impose liabilities, even upon persons not within its allegiance, for conduct outside its borders that has consequences within its borders which the state reprehends." This was modified in later cases such as *Timberlane Lumber Co. v. Bank of America* 549 F.2d 597 (1976).
[77] Joined Cases 89, 104, 114, 116, 117 and 125–129/85 *Åhlström v. Commission* [1988] E.C.R. 5193; [1988] 4 C.M.L.R. 901; [1993] E.C.R. I–1307; [1994] E.C.R. I–99; [1993] 4 C.M.L.R. 407.
[78] *ibid.*, [1988] E.C.R. 5193, paras 16–18 of judgment.
[79] See Lange & Sandage, "The *Woodpulp* decision and its implications . . ." (1989) 26 C.M.L.Rev. 137. *cf.* Mann, "The public international law of restrictive trade practices in the ECJ" (1989) 38 I.C.L.Q. 375.

territory. It might be hard to see how refraining from trade would amount to an "implemented" agreement although it might equally well be said that this would also produce insufficiently direct consequences to be caught by an effects doctrine. Thus there may be little difference in real outcomes, despite the different language used by the Court. In the later *Gencor* case,[80] decided in relation to the Merger Regulation, the Court of First Instance took the view that the *Wood Pulp* test was satisfied by mere sale within the Community, irrespective of the sources of supply and the production plant.

Ultimately, the delicate issues raised in cases with extraterritorial dimensions are perhaps best solved by international co-operation over the allocation of jurisdiction, rather than unilateral assertions of extensive jurisdiction. Concerns about regulatory co-operation and the interdependence of competition policies across states are expressed in a variety of legal forms. These range from political decisions about whether jurisdiction should be exercised in particular cases to bilateral and multilateral enforcement agreements and the creation of regional and global frameworks for the development of competition policy principles. Each of these responses is mentioned briefly below.

It is one thing to claim jurisdiction over particular activities, but quite another to exercise it. That decision may be influenced by considerations relating to the impact it would have on the relationship with authorities of another jurisdiction. Vigorous pursuit of an effects doctrine, for example, might provoke harmful retaliatory action by the home state of a parent company. Self-restraint may therefore be a preferable course in the light of these factors of comity. The Commission has recognised the presence of such influences, although it has on occasions been highly reluctant to concede them. In *Re Aluminium*,[81] for example, it dismissed the arguments for not applying the E.C.'s anti-cartel rules to the state trading entities of eastern Europe, noting:

"Moreover, there are no reasons of comity which militate in favour of self restraint in the exercise of jurisdiction by the Commission. The exercise of jurisdiction by the Commission does not require any of the undertakings concerned to act in any way contrary to the requirements of their domestic laws, nor would the application of Community law adversely affect important interests of a non-member State. Such an interest would have to be so important as to prevail over the fundamental interest of the Community that competition within the common market is not distorted . . ., for that is an essential means under the Treaty for achieving the objectives of the Community."

Community considerations can be given a more formal status by the adoption of agreements between the E.C. and individual states. A prime example is the E.C.-U.S. Agreement,[82] further elaborated by the E.U.-USA Positive Comity

---

[80] Case T–102/96 *Gencor v. Commission* [1999] 4 C.M.L.R. 971.

[81] *Aluminium Imports from Eastern Europe* [1985] O.J. L92/1; [1987] 3 C.M.L.R. 813.

[82] First made in 1991 but struck down by the Court of Justice in Case C–327/91 *France v. Commission* [1994] E.C.R. I–3641; [1994] 5 C.M.L.R. 517. It was then re-adopted with proper ratification by the Council as Dec. 95/145, [1995] O.J. L95/45, corrected by [1995] O.J. L131/38, and taking effect from its original date.

Agreement 1998.[83] The 1991 Agreement provides for the competition authorities of the parties to notify each other where enforcement activities affect important interests of the other. It also seeks to avoid conflicts over enforcement by adoption of a so-called "negative comity" clause.[84] This states that "each party shall consider important interests of the other party in decisions as to whether or not to initiate an investigation or proceeding, the scope of an investigation or proceeding, the nature of the remedies or penalties sought, and in other ways, as appropriate". Use of this provision was made in the controversy surrounding the *Boeing/McDonnell Douglas* merger.[85] The concentration in question reduced the number for manufacturers of large commercial aircraft from three to two, leaving Airbus Industrie (the European producer) up against a single dominant American competitor. The merger was cleared by the American authorities, but authorisation was only given by the European Commission after last-minute assurances as to Boeing's future conduct.

According to the 1998 E.U.-USA Positive Comity Agreement,[86] the competition authorities of one party may request the competition authorities of the other to investigate and, if warranted, to remedy anti-competitive activities in accordance with the requested party's competition laws. Such a request may be made regardless of whether the activities also violate the requesting party's competition laws, and regardless of whether the competition authorities of the requesting party have commenced or contemplate taking enforcement activities under their own competition laws. Article IV sets out the conditions on which the competition authorities of the requesting party will normally defer or suspend their own enforcement activities in favour of those of the requested party. *Inter alia,* these require that the adverse effects on the interests of the requesting party can be and are likely to be fully and adequately investigated and, as appropriate, eliminated or adequately remedied. The competition authorities of the requested party must devote adequate resources to the investigation, carry it out promptly and use their best efforts to pursue all reasonably available sources of information, including such sources of information as may be suggested by the competition authorities of the requesting party.

As well as bilateral agreements of this type,[87] multilateral arrangements also provide for the application of competition rules akin to E.C. provisions in other territories. The European Economic Area ("EEA") Agreement was concluded[88] between the E.C. and the EFTA states, with the exception of Switzerland. It applies the fundamental freedoms and some of the horizontal policies of the

---

[83] [1998] O.J. L173/28; [1999] 4 C.M.L.R. 502. It does not apply to mergers.
[84] 1991 Agreement, Art. VI.
[85] [1997] O.J. L336/16.
[86] *Supra*, n.83, Art. III.
[87] See also the Competition Laws Co-operation Agreement 1999 between the E.C., ECSC and Canada [1999] O.J. L175, [1999] 5 C.M.L.R. 713. There is also the important series of so-called Europe Agreements entered into by the E.C. with Eastern European States as a precursor to further co-operation and ultimate membership of the EU. Agreements exist with Hungary, Poland, Romania, Bulgaria, the Slovak Republic, the Czech Republic, Estonia, Latvia, Lithuania and Slovenia.
[88] [1994] O.J. L1/3.

E.C., such as competition and social policies, to the EEA. As a number of former members of EFTA have since become full members of the E.C., the importance of the EEA agreement has declined. Only Iceland, Norway and Liechtenstein remain as contracting states outside membership of the E.C. Articles 53 and 54 EEA replicate for practical purposes Articles 81 and 82 E.C., whilst Article 57, 59 and 61–64 EEA essentially incorporate the E.C. Merger Regulation and the rules on public undertakings and state aids. It is also provided that in the application of the rules the principles of the European Commission's notices must be taken into account.

Finally, it should be noted that competition policy has been moving up the agenda of the World Trade Organisation (WTO).[89] Although competition policy was not included in the original remit of the organisation, a Working Group on the interaction between trade and competition policy was established at the Singapore Ministerial Conference in December 1996, producing a report in December 1998.[90] Approximately 80 WTO Member countries, including 50 developing and transition countries, have adopted competition laws. Unsurprisingly, the negotiations about a possible WTO framework for competition policy have encountered disputes as to which (if any) existing local or regional model could form a useful basis for wider WTO regulation. Whatever the eventual outcome, the boundaries of E.C. competition law and the methods of dispute settlement in competition cases clearly face future challenges.[91]

Temporal scope

The rules on competition came into force under the EEC Treaty with effect from January 1, 1958. Each time the Community has been enlarged, a new range of agreements and practices has been brought within the purview of the competition rules from the date of accession. It must, however, be remembered that undertakings established in the territory of a new Member State may have been subject to the rules even prior to accession, for example as parties to an agreement to be performed in the E.C. or because they had subsidiaries there.[92]

The prohibitions in Article 81(1) and Article 82 began to have direct effect for the general class of agreements and practices from the date when Regulation 17 with its implementing machinery came into force, viz. March 13, 1962.[93]

---

[89] See generally, van Dijck and Faber (eds), *Challenges to the New World Trade Organisation* (Kluwer, 1996). For documentation on developments in relation to trade and competition policy see the WTO's website on http://www.wto.org

[90] Including matters such as the impact of anti-competitive practices of enterprises and associations on international trade; the impact of state monopolies and exclusive rights; the relationship between the trade-related aspects of intellectual property rights and competition policy; the relationship between investment and competition policy and the impact of trade policy on competition.

[91] See Trebilcock, "Reconciling competition laws and trade policies: a new challenge to international co-operation" in Doern and Wilks (eds), *Comparative Competition Policy: National Institutions in a Global Market* (Clarendon Press, Oxford, 1996) at p. 268. Also, Iacobucci, "The interdependence of trade and competition policies" (1997) 21 W.Comp. 5; Ní Chatháin, "The European Community and the Member States in the Dispute Settlement Understanding of the WTO: united or divided?" (1999) E.L.J. 461.

[92] See the discussion of the enterprise entity doctrine, *supra*.

[93] Case 13/61 *Bosch v. de Geus* [1962] E.C.R. 45; [1962] C.M.L.R. 1.

CHAPTER 20

RESTRICTIVE PRACTICES

Article 81 E.C.

Article 81 addresses the problem of interference with the play of competition on the common market resulting from collusion between market participants over their business decisions. The strategy of the Article is to prohibit such interference subject to the possibility of exemption for arrangements, which, on balance, are seen to be economically beneficial.

The Article provides:

"1. The following shall be prohibited as incompatible with the common market: all agreements between undertakings, decisions by associations of undertakings and concerted practices which may affect trade between Member States and which have as their object or effect the prevention, restriction or distortion of competition within the common market, and in particular those which:

(a) directly or indirectly fix purchase or selling prices or any other trading conditions;

(b) limit or control production, markets, technical development, or investment;

(c) share markets or sources of supply;

(d) apply dissimilar conditions to equivalent transactions with other trading parties, thereby placing them at a competitive disadvantage;

(e) make the conclusion of contracts subject to acceptance by the other parties of supplementary obligations which, by their nature or according to commercial usage, have no connection with the subject of such contracts.

2. Any agreements or decisions prohibited pursuant to this Article shall be automatically void.

3. The provisions of paragraph 1 may, however, be declared inapplicable in the case of:

— any agreement or category of agreements between undertakings;

— any decision or category of decisions by associations of undertakings;

— any concerted practice or category of concerted practices;

which contributes to improving the production or distribution of goods or to promoting technical or economic progress, while allowing consumers a fair share of the resulting benefit, and which does not:

(a) impose on the undertakings concerned restrictions which are not indispensable to the attainment of these objectives;

(b) afford such undertakings the possibility of eliminating competition in respect of a substantial part of the products in question."

553

The scope of paragraph (1) is potentially wide indeed. Its list of examples of prohibited arrangements is non-exhaustive and there is no attempt to distinguish between so-called horizontal and vertical arrangements. However, as we shall see, a more lenient view has generally been taken of vertical restrictions between, for example, producer and retailer, and this stance is now embodied in legislative changes. Paragraph (1) is also silent on the meaning of its primary elements, allowing controversy to develop as to the degree of distortion of competition required and the scope for weighing the pros and cons of particular arrangements. Paragraph (2) withdraws the support of national law from arrangements intended to have binding effect which are caught by the prohibition. Paragraph (3) sets out the criteria that must be met by arrangements prima facie within paragraph (1), in order to benefit from a declaration of the inapplicability of the paragraph. The power to exempt, hitherto reserved exclusively by Regulation 17 to the Commission,[1] has undergone thorough review as part of modernisation proposals[2] designed to promote the decentralised enforcement of E.C. competition law.

Overall, as Article 81 has evolved, what was once perhaps a sweeping prohibition subject to narrow and tightly controlled exceptions has become a more sophisticated instrument which permits pragmatic assessments of collusive arrangements to be made in the light of their effects in the relevant market. As noted in Chapter 19, *supra*, the Commission and Court of Justice have adopted the notion of "workable competition"[3] as the touchstone for regulating the behaviour of undertakings and the structures of markets. This approach inherently encourages some flexibility in the application of a provision such as Article 81, so that, for example, it recognises that effective competition is not to be measured simply against prices and that certain restrictions may be necessary to secure the legitimate purposes of particular arrangements. In short, there is a discernible movement towards decisions based on greater economic analysis instead of formulaic legal appraisal. However, this is not to say that Article 81 lacks shape or coherence; the presence of the single market imperative has meant that those practices which are the very antithesis of that goal, such as market compartmentalisation, will be unhesitatingly characterised as anti-competitive.

Collusive market behaviour between undertakings

The target of the prohibition in Article 81(1) is co-operative or collusive market behaviour between undertakings. As was seen in Chapter 19, the notion of "undertakings" as independent economic entities limits the scope of Article 81 in relation to parent-subsidiary relationships[4] and to some acts of public

---

[1] The machinery for the implementation of Art. 81 is discussed in Chap. 22 *infra*.

[2] *White Paper on Modernisation of the Rules Implementing Arts 85 and 86 of the E.C. Treaty*, April 28, 1999.

[3] Case 26/76 *Metro v. Commission* [1977] E.C.R. 1875; [1978] 2 C.M.L.R. 1.

[4] There will be no agreement between undertakings for the purposes of Art. 81 where the subsidiary enjoys no real freedom to determine its course of action on the market: Case 22/71 *Béguelin Import Co. v. SA GL Import Export* [1971] E.C.R. 949; [1972] C.M.L.R. 81. See also Case C–73/95P *Viho Europe BV v. Commission* [1996] E.C.R. I–5457; [1997] 4 C.M.L.R. 419.

authorities.[5] Similarly, agreements within a pure agency relationship may fall outside the provision where the agent acts in the name and for the account of his principal, taking none of the risks of a transaction upon himself.[6] Such an agent, the Court of Justice has said, when working for his principal can be regarded "as an auxiliary organ forming an integral part of the latter's undertaking bound to carry out the principal's instructions and thus, like a commercial employee, forms an economic unit with this undertaking".[7] An agreement by the agent not to trade in goods competing with the products of his principal would not in these circumstances fall within Article 81(1).[8]

A question which has arisen more recently has been the extent to which ostensibly unilateral conduct might be caught by the Article. At first sight, the obvious source available to combat anti-competitive acts by single undertakings is Article 82. However, this is limited to firms occupying dominant positions, implying that unilateral conduct by non-dominant individual firms was not seen as a threat to competition by the drafters of the Treaty. But this does not mean that acts in furtherance of a contract escape prohibition under Article 81(1) merely because they are performed by a single party. In the *AEG* case[9] the Court of Justice was called upon to assess the compatibility with that Article of a system of selective distribution. Under such a system the resale of goods is limited to a network of "approved" dealers. One of the arguments put forward by AEG was that refusal to admit prospective dealers to its network was a unilateral act and therefore not within the scope of the prohibition. The argument was rejected by the Court on the ground that refusals of approval were acts performed in the context of AEG's contractual relations with approved dealers.[10]

The limits to the notion of consensus have certainly been stretched on occasion. In *Bayer v. Commission*[11] an agreement was found by the Commission in the system operated by Bayer's subsidiaries in Spain and France in relation to supplies of the heart drug Adalat. In order to prevent the high prices which could be charged in the United Kingdom from being threatened by quantities of parallel imports through wholesalers located in Spain and France, Bayer's subsidiaries restricted supplies of Adalat to the latter to the amounts needed to satisfy domestic demand. There was evidence that the wholesalers had tried different tactics to obtain extra supplies, but that these were detected and countered by Bayer. The Commission took the view that the monitoring and supply restrictions constituted an agreement between Bayer's subsidiaries and the wholesalers to restrict exports. According to the Commission, an agreement for the purposes of Article 81(1) requires an interest of two parties in concluding an

---

[5] The key question being whether such a body is acting as a public authority at the time: see Case 30/87 *Bodson v. Pompes Funèbres* [1988] E.C.R. 2479; [1989] 4 C.M.L.R. 984.
[6] Joined Cases 40–48, 50, 54–56, 111, 113 and 114/73 *Suiker Unie and others v. Commission (Sugar)* [1975] E.C.R. 1663; [1976] 1 C.M.L.R. 295.
[7] *ibid.*, [1975] E.C.R. at 2007.
[8] *ibid.* In the instant case the relationship between a German sugar producer and its trade representatives was found not to be such as to escape the prohibition.
[9] Case 107/82 *AEG v. Commission* [1983] E.C.R. 3151; [1984] 3 C.M.L.R. 325.
[10] See also Joined Cases 25–26/84 *Ford v. Commission* [1985] E.C.R. 2725; [1985] 3 C.M.L.R. 528.
[11] Case T–41/96R *Bayer* [1996] E.C.R. II-381; [1996] 5 C.M.L.R. 290, seeking interim suspension of the order made in Dec. 96/478 *Bayer/Adalat* [1996] 5 C.M.L.R. 416, noted (1996) 16 Y.E.L. 474.

agreement, without there being any need for that interest to be held in common. In this case Bayer's interest was in preventing, or at least reducing, parallel imports. The wholesalers' interest was to avoid a reduction in supplies of Adalat. The Commission adopted a decision which included a provision that Bayer should issue a circular to the wholesalers stating that exports were permitted and would not cause any penalty to be incurred. The Court of First Instance suspended this decision on application by Bayer, noting that its claim that there was no agreement was not manifestly without foundation and that compliance with the Commission's order would risk major and irreparable loss of profit for Bayer in its U.K. sales.

The Commission's approach met with criticism.[12] It certainly appears to go further than the established case-law which accepts that consent may arise implicitly from clear and unequivocal conduct by undertakings in the context of continuing commercial relations.[13] As the Court of First Instance noted, it appeared that any agreement between Bayer and the wholesalers concerned only the volume of orders that the latter placed. Such an agreement could not in principle be interpreted as implicitly comprising an export prohibition.[14] It is perhaps also striking that the Commission in its original decision fined only Bayer, observing that the wholesalers had already suffered enough by losing business, customers and commercial credibility as a result of not being able to supply their British customers under normal conditions.

Forms of co-operation

Article 81(1) refers to three forms of co-operation on which the prohibition may bite—agreements between undertakings, decisions of associations of undertakings and concerted practices. Something will be said about each of these forms, although the lines of demarcation between them are mainly of theoretical interest.

Agreements between undertakings

There is no need for an arrangement to be legally binding for it to be treated as an agreement for the purposes of Article 81(1). In the *Quinine* cases,[15] for instance, the Court had to consider the application of the rules to arrangements between European producers of quinine and quinidine contained in an "export agreement" and a "gentlemen's agreement": the former, which was signed and made public, purported to apply only to trade with third countries but its provisions were extended by the latter, which remained unsigned and secret, to trade within the then EEC. In view of its clandestine character, let alone its name, the gentlemen's agreement cannot have been intended to be legally enforceable. The parties had, however, made clear that it faithfully expressed

---

[12] See Lidgard, "Unilateral refusal to supply: an agreement in disguise?" [1997] E.C.L.R. 352.
[13] Case C–277/87 *Sandoz v. Commission* [1990] E.C.R. I–45; [1990] 4 C.M.L.R. 242, a case in which the company's invoices had the words "Exports prohibited" stamped on them. See also Dec. 80/1283 *Johnson and Johnson* [1980] O.J. L377/16; [1981] 2 C.M.L.R. 287 where an export prohibition accompanying price lists was backed up by threats to suspend or delay supplies.
[14] [1996] E.C.R. II-381, at para. 50.
[15] See Joined Cases 41, 44–45/69 *ACF Chemiefarma and others v. Commission* [1970] E.C.R. 661.

their joint intention as to their conduct and that they considered themselves no less bound by it than by the export agreement. The Court accepted it as an agreement. The decisive test, that there has been an expression by the participating undertakings of their joint intention to conduct themselves on the market in a specific way, has been consistently relied upon by the Court in subsequent cases.[16]

Decisions of associations of undertakings

A typical example would be a resolution of a trade association laying down standard terms on which its members are required to do business. An express reference to "decisions of associations of undertakings" in Article 81(1) may not have been strictly necessary.[17] Such decisions, if they fulfil the other criteria in the paragraph, are likely to be caught by the prohibition, either as representing the consequence of an agreement (the association's constitution) or as providing the basis for a concerted practice between the members. The reference, however, enhances legal certainty and makes it possible, in an appropriate case, for the Commission to impose a fine on the trade association itself.[18]

The Court of Justice is inclined to brush aside technical arguments about the precise legal character of acts of trade associations. Its attitude is summed up by the remark in the *FRUBO* judgment[19] that Article 81(1) "applies to associations in so far as their own activities or those of the undertakings belonging to them are calculated to produce the results to which it refers".[20] For example, the constitution of an association has sometimes been treated as a decision[21] and sometimes as an agreement.[22]

There is no more need for "decisions" than for "agreements" to be legally binding. In *Re Fire Insurance*[23] the Commission applied Article 85 (as it was then) to a "recommendation" by an association of insurers in Germany that premiums for various classes of policy be raised by a stipulated percentage. Although described in its title as "non-binding" the recommendation was found to constitute a decision within the meaning of the first paragraph. "It is sufficient for this purpose", the Commission said, " that the recommendation was brought to the notice of members as a statement of the association's policy provided for, and issued in accordance with, its rules."[24] In other cases a pattern of past compliance with recommendations has been emphasised.[25] The conclusive factor, it is submitted, is the ability of the association, in fact if not in law, to influence its members' conduct. But where an association plays no distinguishable role in the implementation of an anti-competitive arrangement, or where its acts are not

---

[16] *e.g.* Case C–49/92P *Commission v. Anic Partecipazioni SpA* (1999) E.C.R. I–4125, para. 130.
[17] Whish, *Competition Law* (3rd ed., Butterworths, 1993,), discusses this at pp. 193–194.
[18] See, *e.g.* *Re AROW/BNIC* [1982] O.J. L379/1; [1983] 2 C.M.L.R. 240.
[19] Case 71/74 *FRUBO v. Commission* [1975] E.C.R. 563; [1975] 2 C.M.L.R. 123.
[20] [1975] E.C.R. at 583.
[21] *Re ASPA* [1970] J.O. L148/9; [1970] C.M.L.R. D25.
[22] *Re Nuovo CEGAM* [1984] O.J. L99/29; [1984] 2 C.M.L.R. 484.
[23] [1985] O.J. L35/20. The Decision was upheld by the Court of Justice in Case 45/85 *Verband der Sachversicherer* [1987] E.C.R. 405; [1988] 4 C.M.L.R. 264.
[24] [1985] O.J. at L35/24.
[25] See, in particular, Joined Cases 209–215 and 218/78 *Van Landewyck v. Commission (FEDETAB)* [1980] E.C.R. 3125; [1981] 3 C.M.L.R. 134; Joined Cases 96–102, 104, 105, 108 and 110/82 *IAZ v. Commission* [1983] E.C.R. 3369; [1984] 3 C.M.L.R. 276.

severable from those of its members, it may escape liability or the imposition of fines.[26]

Concerted practices

The concept of a concerted practice represents the outer limits of the prohibition imposed by Article 81(1). It has provoked considerable controversy and uncertainty in the case-law, both as regards the elusiveness of its boundaries and in respect of the evidence necessary to establish it. However, a rigid categorisation of particular circumstances as either agreements or concerted practices is not demanded. Indeed, where a number of firms are engaged to varying degrees in complex infringements, it is possible to treat those patterns of conduct as manifestations of a single infringement, made up partly of agreements and partly of concerted practices without having to specify exact borderlines between them.[27] According to the Court, agreements and concerted practices "are intended to catch forms of collusion having the same nature and are only distinguishable from each other by their intensity and the forms in which they manifest themselves".[28]

The Court's first attempts at defining a concerted practice treated it as "a form of coordination between undertakings which, without having been taken to a stage where an agreement properly so called has been concluded, knowingly substitutes practical co-operation between them for the risks of competition".[29] These criteria of coordination and co-operation are to be understood in the light of the concept inherent in the provisions of the Treaty relating to competition, according to which each economic operator must determine independently the policy which he intends to adopt on the market.[30] According to the Court:

"although that requirement of independence does not deprive economic operators of the right to adapt themselves intelligently to the existing and anticipated conduct of their competitors, it does however strictly preclude any direct or indirect contact between such operators, the object or effect whereof is either to influence the conduct on the market of an actual or potential competitor or to disclose to such a competitor the course of conduct which they themselves have decided to adopt or contemplate adopting on the market, where the object or effect of such contact is to create conditions of competition which do not correspond to the normal conditions of the market in question, regard being had to the nature of the products or services offered, the size and number of the undertakings and the volume of the said market."[31]

---

[26] Joined Cases 89, 104, 114, 116, 117 and 125–128/85 *A. Åhlström Oy v. Commission* ("*Wood Pulp*") [1988] E.C.R. 5193; [1988] 4 C.M.L.R. 901 at para. 27.

[27] Case C–49/92P *Commission v. Anic Partecipazioni SpA*, n.16, *supra*.

[28] *ibid.*, para. 131

[29] Case 48/69 *ICI v. Commission* [1972] E.C.R. 619 at 655; [1972] C.M.L.R. 557; reiterated in Joined Cases 40–48, 50, 54–56, 111, 113 and 114/73 *Suiker Unie and others v. Commission* ("*Re Sugar*") n.6, *supra*; Joined Cases 89, 104, 114, 116, 117 and 125–128/85 *A. Åhlström Oy v. Commission* ("*Wood Pulp*"), [1993] E.C.R. I–1307; [1993] 4 C.M.L.R. 407 para. 63; Case C–49/92P *Commission v. Anic Partecipazioni SpA*, n.16, *supra*.

[30] *Re Sugar*, n.6, *supra*, para. 173; Case 172/80 *Züchner* [1981] E.C.R. 2021; [1982] 1 C.M.L.R. 313 para. 13; Case C–7/95P *John Deere v. Commission* [1998] E.C.R. I–3111; [1998] 5 C.M.L.R. 311, para. 86.

[31] Case C–49/92P *Commission v. Anic Partecipazioni SpA*, n.16, *supra*, para. 117, citing the cases listed in n.30, *supra*.

This approach makes the question of "contact", whether direct or indirect, central to the idea of a concerted practice. An example of how such contact may be established can be seen from the various infringements known collectively as the *Polypropylene* cases.[32] Following its investigations into the relevant market, the Commission had concluded that between 1977 and 1983 producers had regularly set target prices by way of a series of price initiatives and brought about a system of annual volume control to share out the available market between them according to agreed percentage or tonnage targets. The Commission cited the following evidence to support its allegations of agreements and concerted practices: contact through regular meetings in secret to discuss and determine commercial policies; the setting of target or minimum prices for sales in each Member State; the exchange of detailed information on deliveries, a system of "account management" designed to implement price rises to individual customers; simultaneous price increases implementing the said targets; and a limitation on monthly sales by reference to some previous period. The ensuing protracted litigation focused, *inter alia,* upon whether the Commission had been entitled to characterise the infringements as agreements *and* concerted practices, the requisite levels of intention and market effect for each and the extent to which each party could be responsible for the acts of others.

The Court of First Instance[33] held that if a company participated in meetings of the type in question then it and the other undertakings could not fail to take into account, directly or indirectly, the information obtained during the course of those meetings. However, this was an erroneous approach according to the Court of Justice. In its view, "a concerted practice implies, besides undertakings' concerting together, conduct on the market pursuant to those collusive practices, and a relationship of cause and effect between the two".[34] But there is no need for that resulting conduct to have concrete anti-competitive effects if the *object* of concertation is anti-competitive. In this regard concerted practices are governed by the same considerations as agreements.[35]

Proof and responsibility

Proving that a concerted practice exists may be a delicate task. It will be especially difficult in those cases that tread the borderline between co-ordinated market behaviour prohibited by Article 81(1) and parallel behaviour resulting from decisions by traders which have been independently arrived at. Such innocent

---

[32] For the Commission's original Decision, see [1986] O.J. L230/1; [1988] 4 C.M.L.R. 347.

[33] *e.g.* Case T–6/89 *Enichem Anic v. Commission* [1991] E.C.R. II-1623. By the time of the appeal to the Court of Justice as Case C–49/92P, n.16, *supra,* the company was known as Anic.

[34] Case C–49/92P, n.16, *supra,* para. 118. The Court of Justice went on to find that, despite faulty reasoning on this point, the operative part of the judgment of the Court of First Instance was well founded on other legal grounds.

[35] Case 56/65 *Société Technique Minière v. Maschinenbau Ulm* [1966] E.C.R. 235; [1966] 1 C.M.L.R. 357.

parallelism may, in particular, entail the exercise of the right, acknowledged by the Court, to "adapt intelligently" to the decisions of competitors, of which a trader has become aware in the ordinary course of his business.

Direct evidence of relevant contact between the parties may be available in the form of letters, faxes, emails, or records of telephone conversations or meetings. For instance, the concerted practice between the Belgian and Dutch sugar producers examined in the *Sugar* judgment was proved by a wealth of documentation discovered during the Commission's investigation.[36] This consisted in the main of correspondence between a major Belgian producer and a Belgian sugar dealer, and the Dutch producers contested its admissibility as evidence against them. The Court, however, agreed with Advocate General Mayras that such evidence must be treated on its merits. In case any misgivings may be felt about the use of hearsay evidence in competition proceedings, it is worth pointing out that the fines that may be imposed are expressly declared by Regulation 17 "not to be of criminal law nature".[37]

Where direct evidence of concertation is lacking or inconclusive, the Commission has to rely on circumstantial evidence, *i.e.* on the inferences that can be drawn from the behaviour of the alleged parties, in the light of an analysis of conditions on the market in question.[38] In such cases the Commission, and ultimately the Court, must be satisfied that there can be no reasonable explanation of the parties' behaviour other than the existence of a concerted practice between them.

The point is well illustrated by the *Zinc Products* case.[39] The concerted practice in issue was allegedly designed to protect the German market for rolled zinc products, where prices were higher than elsewhere in the Community, against parallel imports. A French producer, CRAM, and a German producer, Rheinzink, had delivered quantities of zinc products to a Belgian dealer, Schiltz, under contracts which stipulated that the products be exported to Egypt. Schiltz, however, relabelled them and sent them back to Germany, where they were sold below the normal price. It was common ground that employees of Rheinzink found out about the reimports towards the end of October 1976 and that CRAM and Rheinzink discontinued their deliveries to Schiltz on, respectively, 21st and 29th of that month. In its Decision[40] the Commission had taken the view that the cessation of deliveries by CRAM and Rheinzink could only be explained as the result of an exchange of information for the purpose of preventing imports into Germany. "Faced with such an argument", the Court said, "it is sufficient for the applicants to prove circumstances which cast the facts established by the Commission in a different light and which thus allow another explanation of the facts to be substituted for the one adopted by the contested decision".[41] In the event, CRAM was able to point to two such circumstances: the fact that, when it ceased deliveries on October 21, it had completed a particular order from Schiltz;

---

[36] n.29, *supra*, [1975] E.C.R. at 1924 *et seq.*

[37] [1962] J.O. 204; [1959–1969] O.J. 87. See Art. 15(3).

[38] Case 48/69 *ICI v. Commission*, n.29, *supra*, at 655.

[39] Joined Cases 29 and 35/83 *CRAM and Rheinzink v. Commission* [1984] E.C.R. 1679; [1985] 1 C.M.L.R. 688.

[40] *Re Rolled Zinc Products and Zinc Alloys* [1982] O.J. L362/40 [1983] 2 C.M.L.R. 285.

[41] [1984] E.C.R. at 1704.

and the fact that there had been difficulties over obtaining payment for products supplied to Schiltz in September (and there were similar difficulties in respect of the October delivery). The Court concluded that the Commission had failed to provide "sufficiently precise and coherent proof" of a concerted practice.[42]

Oligopolistic markets present particular difficulties for the application of the prohibition in Article 81(1). Such markets[43] are typically characterised by small numbers of participants with roughly equal shares and, crucially, a mutual dependence that invites parallel conduct. There is likely to be transparency in market information and little incentive to compete on price. Changes in market strength are likely to arise from either investment in advertising or acquisition of competitors. In the absence of collusive agreements between the parties, any application of Article 81(1) will require proof that they have gone beyond independently acting in parallel to a point where concertation has been reached.

The *Wood Pulp* saga[44] indicates the problems in policing this particular line. At the heart of this epic[45] was an alleged concertation on prices between woodpulp producers mainly located in Finland, Sweden, Canada and the United States. In the Commission's view, concertation could be found in the virtually simultaneous and identical quarterly price announcements made by the producers. These announcements, though made to customers, circulated quickly through the trade press and agents who acted for more than one producer. Having ruled out the Commission's documentary evidence,[46] the Court of Justice considered the nature of the market in the light of the evidence provided by experts it had appointed.

According to the Court, the Commission had failed to establish a "firm, precise and consistent body of evidence".[47] In particular, it had not excluded other plausible explanations for the parallel conduct of the producers. Pulp buyers tended to spread their sources and habitually disclosed to producers the prices of competitors. Market transparency was further enhanced by rapid communication and a dynamic trade press. The net result was that the Court relied on the experts' evidence that the features of the market were at least as likely an explanation of price movements as any alleged concertation. Contrary to the inferences drawn by the Commission, the system of price announcements was a rational response to the fact that the pulp market constituted a long-term market and to the need felt by both buyers and sellers to limit commercial risks. The coincidence of timing in announcements could be attributed to market

---

[42] *ibid.*

[43] See Whish and Sufrin, "Oligopolistic markets and E.C. competition law" (1992) 12 Y.E.L. 59; Stevens, "Covert collusion and conscious parallelism in oligopolistic markets: a comparison of E.C. and U.S. competition law" (1995) 15 Y.E.L. 47.

[44] Joined Cases C–89, 104, 114, 116, 117 and 125–128/85 *A. Åhlström Oy v. Commission*, n.29, *supra*.

[45] The Commission's original contested Decision was issued in 1984 but the Court's judgment on the merits was only given in 1993, having made a separate ruling on jurisdictional matters in 1988: see n.26, *supra*.

[46] Inadmissible on several grounds, including the Commission's failure to identify all the parties adequately.

[47] Para. 127 of judgment.

transparency and the parallelism of the prices could be satisfactorily explained by the oligopolistic tendencies of the market.[48] Article 1(1) of the Commission's decision in relation to collusion was therefore annulled by the Court.

The Court's approach in *Wood Pulp* reflects the position suggested by Advocate General Cosmas that parallelism of conduct is an evidential issue, not an element of the concept of concerted practice.[49] As expressed subsequently by the Court of First Instance, where the Commission relies upon bare parallelism it is sufficient for the parties to prove circumstances which cast the facts established by the Commission in a different light, allowing another explanation of the facts to be substituted for the one adopted by the Commission.[50] The burden is different in cases where other documented evidence of concertation is available. In those circumstances, the onus is on the parties not merely to submit an alternative explanation for the facts found by the Commission but to challenge the existence of those facts established on the basis of the documents produced by the Commission.[51] Once the Commission establishes that undertakings have participated in regular meetings exchanging information with other producers, a presumption is created that the undertakings participating in those sessions and remaining active on the market take account of the information exchanged with their competitors when determining their conduct, especially when the concertation has taken place on a regular basis over a long period.[52] It is therefore for the economic operators to adduce evidence to rebut that presumption.

Almost inevitably, cases which arouse suspicions of concerted practices are likely to involve multiple parties and thus give rise to questions as to the extent of collective responsibility. Not every party will always have attended every meeting or received every circular or fax. In one of the appeals arising from the *Polypropylene* cases, the Court of Justice noted the contradiction in the Court of First Instance's judgment, whereby the latter had accepted the Commission's claim that Anic had been a participant to a single extended infringement made up of several agreements and practices with the same economic objective in common, but at the same time had condemned the Commission's failure to prove the extent of Anic's participation in particular meetings or conduct. The Court of Justice set out the relevant test as follows:

"the Commission must, in particular, show that the undertaking intended to contribute by its own conduct to the common objectives pursued by all the participants and that it was aware of the actual conduct planned or put into

---

[48] But *cf.* the outcome in Case C–7/95P *John Deere v. Commission*, n.30, *supra*. Here the information exchanged was between only the main suppliers on the relevant market instead of to purchasers. The information went beyond price announcements and amounted to business secrets enabling traders to know the market positions and strategies of their competitors. Unlike the situation in *Wood Pulp*, such exchanges lessened each undertaking's uncertainty as to the future attitude of its competitors.

[49] Para 188 of Opinion.

[50] Joined Cases T–305–307, 313–316, 318, 325, 328–329 and 335/94 *Re PVC Cartel II: Limburgse Vinyl Maatschapij NV and others v. Commission* [1999] 5 C.M.L.R. 303, para. 725.

[51] *ibid.*, para. 728.

[52] Case C–49/92P *Commission v. Anic Partecipazioni SpA*, n.16, *supra*, para. 121. To the same effect, see Case C–199/92P *Hüls v. Commission* [1999] E.C.R. I–4287; [1999] 5 C.M.L.R. 1016, para. 162. The parties in these cases failed to provide the necessary rebuttal.

effect by other undertakings in pursuit of the same objectives or that it could reasonably have foreseen it and that it was prepared to take the risk."[53]

In the Court's view, the findings of fact made by the Court of First Instance supported the fixing of responsibility upon Anic for conduct followed by other undertakings in the period after it had stopped participating in meetings mid-1982. Anic was perfectly aware of all the elements of the single infringement by virtue of its participation in regular meetings over a period of years and must have assumed that they would continue after mid-1982.[54]

The problems associated with applying Article 81(1) to oligopolistic markets and, in particular, drawing a line between collusion and parallelism, reflect the fact that a behavioural control is being applied to an essentially structural issue. It may not be surprising that the European Courts have insisted on considerable evidential restraints to prevent unwarranted regulation.

Restricting competition

Article 81(1) refers to agreements, etc.[55] "which have as their object or effect the prevention, restriction or distortion of competition within the common market". This phrase has proved to be the very nub of the provision, its deceptive simplicity conflating a bundle of fundamental issues relating not just to the scope of the prohibition but also the methodology of investigation. These questions include whether the same test should be applied to all types of agreements, the nature and extent of economic market analysis required, the thresholds of scale and foreseeability to determine anti-competitive effects and the relevance of any offsetting benefits. Interpretative approaches to these problems have evolved over time in response to changes in the economic and political context in which Article 81 must operate. On the one hand, the advancing process of market integration and economic re-appraisal of certain types of activity have led to some of the strictest applications of the prohibition being relaxed. On the other, recurring pressures for decentralisation and subsidiarity in decision-making and enforcement, as well as the workload problems of the Commission, have created an environment which seeks to devolve judgments about the efficacy and effect of agreements down to national courts and competition authorities.

The phrase "object or effect" must be read disjunctively.[56] The precise purpose of the agreement must first be ascertained by examining its terms in the particular context in which they will have to be performed. Where it can be seen

---

[53] Case C–49/92P *Commission v. Anic Partecipazioni SpA*, n.16, *supra*, para. 87. See also the views of the Court of First Instance in Case T–334/94 *Sarrió v. Commission* [1998] E.C.R. II-1439; [1998] 5 C.M.L.R. 195 arising from a cartonboard cartel, paras 164–171.

[54] *ibid.*, para. 206. However, it is clear that the Court of Justice sees marginal participation as relevant to a reduction in any fine. See further, Chap. 22 on enforcement of competition law, *infra*.

[55] References hereinafter to "agreements" should be understood as applying also to decisions and concerted practices unless the context indicates otherwise.

[56] Case 56/65 *Société Technique Minière v. Maschinenbau Ulm*, n.35, *supra*, and confirmed in Case C–219/95P *Ferrière Nord SpA v. Commission* [1997] E.C.R. I–4411, [1997] 5 C.M.L.R. 575. In the latter case the Court held that the Italian version of the Treaty, referring to object *and* effect, could not prevail over the unambiguous and express use of the disjunctive in all the other language versions.

that the purpose, if achieved, will entail the prevention, restriction or distortion of competition to an appreciable degree,[57] there will be no need to go on and show that such has in fact been the outcome. Where, however, the implications an agreement may have for competition are less clear-cut, it will be necessary to undertake an analysis of economic conditions on the relevant market to assess the extent of any adverse impact.[58] This, however, is not a matter of measuring actual effects on trade between Member States but a question of whether the agreement is capable of such effects.[59]

Nothing turns on the distinction between "prevention", "restriction" and "distortion" of competition. The *Consten and Grundig* judgment,[60] for instance, describes the agreement in question as being "such as to *distort* competition in the common market", while a few lines later it refers to "the above-mentioned *restrictions*"[61] (emphasis added). The three terms express, with varying emphasis, the basic idea of a change in the state of competition.

The starting point for an inquiry into the implications of an agreement for competition is the situation as it would have been if the agreement did not exist.[62] Without some competition capable of being restricted by the agreement, there can be no infringement of Article 81. In *Re Cement Makers Agreement*,[63] for example, the Commission gave negative clearance to an agreement between an association of manufacturers of Portland cement in Belgium and a number of lime-burning companies which produced "natural" cement. In consideration of the payment to them of an indemnity the lime burners had undertaken, *inter alia*, to refrain from manufacturing Portland cement; but the Commission found they would not have been able, anyway, to finance a change in their production. Lack of competition in a market may also be the result of government intervention.[64] In the *Sugar* judgment[65] the Court of Justice held that measures taken to regulate the market in Italy had fundamentally restricted the scope for competition between sugar producers. The Commission's finding of an infringement of Article 81 was, therefore, quashed, although it was manifest that concertation had taken place between the Italian producers and exporters from other Member States.

Where, however, despite intervention by the public authorities, some room remains for competitive pressures to influence the decisions of market participants, further restriction of competition through an agreement between undertakings is liable to fall foul of Article 81(1). Indeed, the Commission contends that in such circumstances the anti-competitive effects of private arrangements

---

[57] On the *de minimis* rule, see *infra*, pp. 571–572.
[58] [1966] E.C.R. at 249.
[59] Case 19/77 *Miller Schallplatten v. Commission* [1978] E.C.R. 131; [1978] 2 C.M.L.R. 334.
[60] Joined Cases 56 and 58/64 *Consten and Grundig v. Commission* [1966] E.C.R. 299; [1966] C.M.L.R. 418.
[61] [1966] E.C.R. at 343.
[62] Case 56/65 *Société Technique Minière v. Maschinenbau Ulm*, *supra*, n.35, at 250. See also Case C–7/95P *John Deere v. Commission*, n.30, *supra*, para. 76.
[63] [1969] C.M.L.R. D15.
[64] The extent to which Art. 81, in combination with Art. 10 of the Treaty, may give rise to State responsibility is discussed further at the end of this Chapter.
[65] n.6, *supra*.

are all the more significant.[66] A central issue in the *Van Landewyck* case was whether competition had effectively been banished from the Belgian market for tobacco products as a result of the system of levying excise duties on those products, combined with legislation imposing price controls.[67] The Court of Justice accepted that in the circumstances it was practically impossible for manufacturers and importers to compete in such a way as to affect the level of retail selling prices. However, there did still appear to be a possibility of competition in respect of the profit margins allowed to wholesalers, which could have provided an incentive for the latter to pursue a sales policy beneficial to the producers or importers willing to treat them more generously. That kind of competition had been prevented from developing because of the agreement between the tobacco manufacturers and importers relating to the size of the margins and bonuses allowed to traders, which accordingly amounted to a restriction within the meaning of Article 81(1).

The economic context

As summarised by the Court of First Instance, in assessing an agreement under Article 81(1),

> "account should be taken of the actual conditions in which it functions, in particular the economic context in which the undertakings operate, the products or services covered by the agreement and the actual structure of the markets concerned, unless it is an agreement containing obvious restrictions of competition such as price-fixing, market-sharing or the control of outlets. In the latter case, such restrictions may be weighed against their claimed pro-competitive effects only in the context of [Article 81(3)] of the Treaty, with a view to granting an exemption . . .

> It must also be stressed that the examination of conditions of competition is based not only on existing competition between undertakings already present on the relevant market but also on potential competition, in order to ascertain whether, in the light of the structure of the market and the economic and legal context within which it functions, there are real concrete possibilities for the undertakings concerned to compete among themselves or for a new competitor to penetrate the relevant market and compete with the undertakings already established . . ."[68]

The nature and purpose of this inquiry is sometimes characterised in terms of a "rule of reason". However, great care must be taken in using this label, especially

---

[66] See, *e.g. Re Stichting Sigarettenindustrie Agreements* [1982] O.J. L232/1; [1982] 3 C.M.L.R. 702. The point is mentioned in Joined Cases 209–215 and 218/78 *Van Landewyck v. Commission*, n.25, *supra*, at 3261.

[67] *loc. cit.* n.25, *supra*, at 3251–3265.

[68] Joined Cases T–374–375, 384 and 388/94 *European Night Services and others v. Commission* [1998] E.C.R. II–3141; [1998] 5 C.M.L.R. 718, paras 136–137, citing Case C–234/89 *Delimitis v. Henninger Bräu* [1991] E.C.R. I–935; [1992] 5 C.M.L.R. 210, Case C–250/92 *Göttrup-Klim v. Dansk Landbrugs Grovvareselskab* [1994] E.C.R. I–5641; [1996] 4 C.M.L.R. 191, Case C–399/93 *Oude Luttikhuis and others v. Verenigde Coöperatieve Melkindustrie* [1995] E.C.R. I–4515; [1996] 5 C.M.L.R. 178, Case T–77/94 *VGB and others v. Commission* [1997] E.C.R. II–759, Case T–148/89 *Trefilunion v. Commission* [1995] E.C.R. II–1063.

since any meaning it might have in E.C. law is not necessarily the same as that developed in US antitrust law.[69]

In the United States this idea arose to mitigate the rigour of the prohibition in section 1 of the Sherman Act against contracts in restraint of trade.[70] The rule of reason applies to agreements other than those, such as horizontal price-fixing agreements, which are treated by the American courts as illegal *per se*. Essentially, a court is required under the rule to consider the overall impact of the agreement in question on competition within the relevant market. This involves, in particular, identifying any pro-competitive effects the agreement may have and weighing them against its anti-competitive effects. A straightforward example would be a promise by the seller of a business not to compete with the buyer for a reasonable period. Without protection of this kind for the buyer, the goodwill of the business might have been worth a great deal less, or have been unsaleable. The pro-competitive effect of permitting the disposal of a going concern may be regarded as outweighing the temporary restriction of competition between the buyer and the seller.[71] However, it must be emphasised that the rule of reason cannot be used to *justify* behaviour that restricts competition.[72] Its importance in American antitrust law is, indeed, explained by the absence of any "gateway" through which a restrictive agreement which is felt, nevertheless, to be economically beneficial may escape prohibition. Where application of the rule leads to a favourable assessment of an agreement under the Sherman Act, that will be because the agreement is judged, on balance, not to be restrictive of competition.

In E.C. law, on the other hand, an agreement that restricts competition within the meaning of Article 81(1) may still qualify for exemption under Article 81(3). Where pro-competitive aspects of an agreement are not regarded as tipping the scales against a finding that it is restrictive, they may be taken into account in assessing the economic benefits that may justify a grant of exemption. This has institutional implications for the enforcement of the competition rules, at least until such time as implementation of the Commission's modernisation proposals eventually removes exemptions from its exclusive preserve.[73] Champions of a rule of reason for E.C. law have often advocated its merits in terms of the empowerment of national courts as well as its promotion of economic analysis.

It may, therefore, be preferable to consider the approach taken by the European Courts as marking a growing insistence that investigations are founded upon adequate reasoning informed by market contexts rather than the adoption of any rigid evaluative technique derived from other jurisdictions. In this sense, the history of the controversy about a rule of reason in E.C. competition law

---

[69] See Peeters, "The rule of reason revisited: prohibition on restraints of competition in the Sherman Act and EEC Treaty" (1989) A.J. Comp. Law 521; Forrester and Norall, "The laïcization of Community law: self-help and the rule of reason: how competition law is and could be applied" (1984) 21 C.M.L.Rev. 11.

[70] The rule is summarised by Whish and Sufrin (1987) 7 Y.E.L. 1, at 4–12. See also Black, "Per se rules and rules of reason: what are they?" [1997] 3 E.C.L.R. 145.

[71] See *National Society of Professional Engineers v. United States* 435 U.S. 679 at 689. The example is cited by Steindorff (1984) 21 C.M.L.Rev. 639. On the position in E.C. law, see *infra*.

[72] See Steindorff, *op. cit.* n.71, *supra*, at pp. 640–641.

[73] n.2, *supra*.

mirrors the evolution of its counterpart in relation to the fundamental free-doms.[74] Moreover, the *leitmotif* of market integration may further explain the particular orientation of E.C. competition law analysis as well as making analogies with U.S. law less exact. The Court's view that E.C. law is concerned with "workable competition"[75] further underlines the likelihood of a pragmatic and adaptable framework to delimit the prohibition of Article 81(1). Three strands of case-law illustrate the tendencies of the Court.

First, in a number of cases the Court has held that contractual provisions giving a measure of protection against competition do not fall within Article 81(1) if they are genuinely necessary to enable a partner to be found in a business transaction.[76] The earliest reference to this "indispensable inducement" rationale is in *Société Technique Minière v. Maschinenbau Ulm*[77] which concerned an exclusive distribution agreement. Under the agreement the supplier promised not to appoint another distributor in the concession territory or to sell the goods there himself, but no protection was provided against parallel imports. The Court said that "it may be doubted whether there is an interference with competition if the said agreement seems really necessary for the penetration of a new area by an undertaking".[78] The case is distinguishable from *Consten and Grundig*,[79] where the absolute territorial protection sought by the parties could not be regarded as "really necessary" to secure access for Grundig products to the French market. In the *Maize Seeds* case[80] the analysis was applied to a licensing agreement for the exploitation of plant breeders' rights. An "open" exclusive licence, which would not impede parallel imports, was held compatible with Article 81(1), since without some protection against competition no one might have been willing to take the risk of introducing previously unknown crop varieties on to the market in question.[81] In *Pronuptia*,[82] on the other hand, exclusivity provisions in a franchising agreement were found to be within Article 81(1) because the franchisor's trademark was already widely known.[83] The novelty of the product, or at least of the brand, may thus be of crucial significance where the territorial

---

[74] Case 120/78 *Rewe-Zentrale Advocate General v Bundesmonopolverwaltung für Branntwein* ("Cassis de Dijon") [1979] E.C.R. 649; [1979] 3 C.M.L.R. 494. Here, too, the conceptual classification of the rule of reason has been inconsistent; its role variously seen as either a limitation on the scope of the Treaty prohibitions or as a list of additional justifications beyond those found in the Treaty derogations.

[75] Case 26/76 *Metro v. Commission* [1977] E.C.R. 1875; [1978] 2 C.M.L.R. 1; see Chap. 19 *supra*.

[76] See Steindorff, *op.cit.* n.71, *supra*, at p. 646.

[77] Case 56/65 n.35, *supra*.

[78] [1966] E.C.R. at 250. The lack of further authority on "indispensable inducement" in respect of exclusive distribution agreements is due, presumably, to the enactment of a block exemption regulation soon afterwards.

[79] Note 60, *supra*.

[80] Case 258/78 *Nungesser v. Commission* [1982] E.C.R. 2105; [1983] 1 C.M.L.R. 278.

[81] See also Case 262/81 *Coditel v. Cine Vog Films* [1982] E.C.R. 3381; [1983] 1 C.M.L.R. 49. The case concerned an exclusive licence of the performing rights in a film.

[82] Case 161/84 *Pronuptia de Paris v. Schillgalis* [1986] E.C.R. 353; [1986] 1 C.M.L.R. 414.

[83] The relevant passage of the judgment is far from clear. However, the Court appears to have contemplated that absolute territorial protection of the members of the network might have been acceptable if the franchisor had been a new market entrant. On this, see Venit, (1986) 11 E.L.Rev. 213 at 218.

protection of distributors is in issue. A last example to mention is *Remia*[84] where the Court accepted that the seller of a business could be put under an obligation not to compete with the buyer, while emphasising that "such clauses must be necessary to the transfer of the undertaking concerned and their duration and scope must be strictly limited to that purpose".[85] The Court refused to interfere with the Commission's finding that four years' protection for the buyer of a sauce-manufacturing business would have been enough to cover the introduction of a new trademark and to win customer loyalty, instead of the 10-year period which had been agreed.

Secondly, in its *Pronuptia*[86] judgment the Court held that various provisions in an agreement forming part of a distribution franchise system did not restrict competition within the meaning of Article 81(1) because they were necessary to the successful functioning of the system. Its approach has been described as amounting to the application of a doctrine of "ancillary restraints" similar to that developed in American antitrust law. This goes beyond the simple "but for" analysis of the cases referred to in the previous paragraph: the issue is not whether, apart from the provisions in question, a bargain could have been struck but whether the essential aims of the transaction (considered to be one that competition law ought not to disfavour) could have been realised. As applied by the Court the analysis comprises four logical steps: (i) definition of the salient features of the transaction; (ii) finding that the transaction is not in itself restrictive of competition; (iii) identification of the conditions that have to be met to enable such a transaction to be satisfactorily performed; (iv) identification of the contractual terms indispensable to the fulfilment of those conditions. Distribution franchising, the Court explained, is a marketing system under which an established distributor whose success is associated with a certain trademark and certain commercial methods (the franchisor) puts his mark and methods at the disposal of independent traders (the franchisees) in return for the payment of a royalty. This has the advantage to the franchisor of enabling him to exploit his know-how without having to commit his own capital; and to the franchisees of giving them access to methods they could otherwise only have acquired through prolonged effort and research, while also allowing them to profit from the reputation of the mark. The success of such a system depends on two things: the franchisor must be able to communicate his know-how to the franchisees and help them in putting his methods into practice without running the risk that his competitors might benefit, even directly; and he must be able to take appropriate measures to preserve the identity and reputation of the network symbolised by the mark. Under the agreement in question the franchisee had undertaken not to open a shop selling competing goods and not to dispose of the franchise premises except with the prior consent of the franchisor. These terms imposed quite severe restraints on the running of the franchisee's business but they were found to be indispensable to the fulfilment of the first condition and so outwith Article 81(1). Among the terms excluded from Article 81(1) by the second condition was the

---

[84] Case 42/84 *Remia v. Commission* [1985] E.C.R. 2545; [1987] 1 C.M.L.R. 1.
[85] See para. 20 of judgment.
[86] n.82, *supra*.

franchisee's obligation to obtain stock only from the franchisor or from suppliers chosen by him. This helped to protect the reputation of the network by ensuring that the public would find goods of uniform quality in all Pronuptia shops. Given the character of the franchise products (wedding dresses and formal wear) it would, in the Court's view, have been impossible to achieve that result by formulating a set of objective quality specifications. The Court has been criticised, however, for holding that terms in the agreement giving members of the network a measure of territorial protection were contrary to Article 81(1).[87] In a system of uniform business-format franchising like that of Pronuptia a particular area may, in practice, be able to support no more than one outlet. Depending on the size of territories, exclusivity could, it is argued, be an indispensable element in a well-functioning franchise system.

Thirdly, it is well established that a system of selective distribution based on objective quality criteria which are applied in a non-discriminatory way may be compatible with Article 81(1).[88] Under such a system, for example, a manufacturer may limit the outlets for a product which is expensive and technically complex to dealers able and willing to promote it effectively and to provide pre-sales advice, and an after-sales maintenance and repair service, for customers.[89] Selectivity is likely, on the one hand, to result in higher prices. On the other, opportunities are created for competition between manufacturers in respect of the customer services associated with their brands. The rationale of the Court's approach to selective distribution can be seen from the *AEG* case[90], where it said:

"... there are legitimate requirements, such as the maintenance of a specialist trade capable of providing specific services as regards high-quality and high-technology products, which may justify a reduction of price competition in favour of competition relating to factors other than price. Systems of selective distribution, in so far as they aim at the attainment of a legitimate goal capable of improving competition in relation to factors other than price, therefore constitute an element of competition which is in conformity with Article 85(1)."[91]

The analytical method in such cases consists of weighing the pros and cons of different forms of competition against each other. This rather sophisticated application of the rule of reason has not been extended to other terms that may be found in selective distribution agreements, for example the limitation of

---

[87] See Venit, *op. cit.* n.83, *supra* at pp. 220–221. The relevant provisions were given exemption under Art. 81(3).

[88] See, in particular, Case 26/76 *Metro*, n.75, *supra*; Joined Cases 253/78 and 1–3/79 *Guerlain, Rochas, Lanvin and Nina Ricci (Perfumes)* [1980] E.C.R. 2327; [1981] 2 C.M.L.R. 99; Case 86/82 *Hasselblad v. Commission* [1984] E.C.R. 883; [1984] C.M.L.R. 559; Case 75/84 *Metro v. Commission (no 2)* [1986] E.C.R. 3021; [1987] 1 C.M.L.R. 118; Case C–376/92 *Metro v. Cartier* [1994] E.C.R. I–15; [1994] 5 C.M.L.R. 331; Case T–19/92 *Groupement D'Achat Edouard Leclerc v. Commission* [1996] E.C.R. II-1961; [1997] 4 C.M.L.R. 995.

[89] The *Perfumes* cases, n.88, *supra*, illustrate selective distribution of another kind of product thought to require special handling, *viz.* luxury items.

[90] Case 107/82 *AEG v. Commission*, n.9, *supra*.

[91] [1983] E.C.R. 3151, at 3194.

outlets on a *quantitative* basis,[92] resale price maintenance[93] and export bans.[94] The unwillingness of the Court and the Commission to recognise such terms as being "capable of improving competition", thus eluding Article 81(1), brought accusations of inconsistency, since the purpose of their inclusion in the agreement may be to ensure a sufficient turnover for the dealer to support the desired range of customer services.[95] They might, in other words, constitute "ancillary restraints", indispensable to the selective method of marketing judged appropriate for goods of the kind in question.

However, implementation of the modernisation reforms contemplated by the Commission relating to both vertical restraints and competition law more generally[96] will have implications for the development of this last-mentioned line of case-law. Although the Commission wishes to see a more economic approach taken, the legal framework it advocates for this purpose does not embrace an expanded role for the rule of reason in relation to Article 81(1). Instead, the adoption of secondary legislation creating a block exemption under Article 81(3)[97] is designed to provide a "safe harbour" in the form of a presumption of legality for vertical agreements concerning the sale of goods and services which are concluded by firms with less than 30 per cent market share and which do not include any of the "black" clauses identified in the Regulation.[98] For the purposes of the block exemption, which applies to vertical restraints generally, a selective distribution system means "a distribution system where the supplier undertakes to sell the contract goods or services, either directly or indirectly, only to distributors selected on the basis of specified criteria and where these distributors undertake not to sell such goods or services to unauthorised distributors".[99] Instead of applying *Metro*-style analysis to weigh the effects of selective distribution agreements, national courts will more likely be called upon, as with any block exemption,[1] to patrol the boundaries of the block exemption by determining whether its conditions, especially the market share ceilings, are satisfied.

The upshot of this approach, curiously perhaps, is to exempt agreements which might otherwise escape Article 81(1) anyway by recourse to the cases discussed earlier. Similarly, as far as the general modernisation proposals are concerned,[2]

---

[92] See Case 243/83 *Binon v. Agence et Messageries de la Presse* [1985] E.C.R. 2015; [1985] 3 C.M.L.R. 800.

[93] See Case 107/82 *AEG v. Commission*, n.9, *supra*.

[94] See, *Perfumes* cases, n.88, *supra*.

[95] See Chard, (1982) 7 E.L.Rev. 83.

[96] For the background, see *Commission Green Paper on Vertical Restraints in E.C. Competition Policy* COM (96) 721 Final [1997] 4 C.M.L.R. 519; *Commission Communication on Vertical Restraints 1998 (follow up to Green Paper)* [1998] O.J. C265/3; [1999] 4 C.M.L.R. 281, Commission White Paper on Modernisation, n.2, *supra*. Also, Hawk, "System failure: vertical restraints and E.C. competition law" (1995) 32 C.M.L. Rev. 973.

[97] Commission Reg. 2790/1999 on the application of Art. 81(3) of the Treaty to categories of vertical agreements and concerted practices, [1999] O.J. L336/21. Its main provisions came into force June 1, 2000; the Regulation expires on May 31, 2010. See also Reg. 1215/1999; [1999] O.J. L148/1.

[98] The "hardcore" restrictions for which exemption is not possible are set out in Art. 4 of Reg. 2790/1999.

[99] Art. 1 (d) of Reg. 2790/1999.

[1] Case 170/83 *Hydrotherm* [1984] E.C.R. 2999; [1985] 3 C.M.L.R. 224.

[2] Discussed further in Chap. 22 on enforcement.

there is a tension between the Commission's stated preferences and the developments in the existing case-law. In short, the Commission argues against further systematic expansion of a rule of reason for the purposes of Article 81(1) since this would result in the exemption provisions of Article 81(3) being "cast aside".[3] However, it has been noted[4] that such claims conflate the concept of a rule of reason and the concerns of the exemption process in a way that is not reflected in the case-law. The Court's approach as described in the previous pages, it is submitted, utilises what might be called a rule of reason in the context of Article 81(1) to establish whether there is, on balance, a restriction of competition, whereas the exemption process offers the chance to defend a restrictive agreement on grounds that extend to non-competition criteria.[5] The Commission's White Paper, by apparently treating this *economic* rule of reason in Article 81(1) as coterminous with the *policy* rule of reason offered by Article 81(3) may be proposing changes which effectively restrict the scope of the latter.

The de minimis rule

For Article 81(1) to apply, the agreement must affect trade between Member States and the free play of competition to an appreciable extent. This *de minimis* rule is a further illustration that the prohibition contained in the Article must be adapted to practical contexts. It was first laid down by the Court of Justice in *Völk v. Vervaecke*,[6] where the manufacturer in question held only around 0.2 per cent of the market. Thus even agreements conferring absolute territorial protection, which would otherwise normally be considered to be restrictive in their object,[7] may be treated as insignificant, regard being had to the weak position of the parties concerned on the market in the products in question.[8]

Following the Court's lead, the Commission adopted, and has periodically revised, a Notice on Minor Agreements to offer guidance to business on when agreements will be deemed to lack the appreciable effect necessary for the purposes of Article 81(1). The 1997 Notice[9] is built upon market share criteria,[10] the relevant figures being 5 per cent for horizontal agreements and 10 per cent for vertical ones. However, not too much store should be set by the Notice. The Commission itself is careful to indicate that particular types of restriction may render the Notice inapplicable.[11] Moreover, as a piece of "soft" law the Notice is

---

[3] *White Paper on Modernisation*, n.2, *supra*, para. 57.

[4] Wesseling, "The Commission White Paper on Modernisation of E.C. Antitrust Law: unspoken consequences and incomplete treatment of alternative options" [1999] E.C.L.R. 420.

[5] See the discussion of exemptions more generally, *infra*.

[6] Case 5/69 *Völk v. Vervaecke* [1969] E.C.R. 295; [1969] C.M.L.R. 273.

[7] Joined Cases 56 and 58/64 *Consten and Grundig*, n.60, *supra*.

[8] See Joined Cases 100–103/80 *Musique Diffusion Française v. Commission* [1983] E.C.R. 1825; [1983] 3 C.M.L.R. 221, para. 85; affirmed in Case C–306/96 *Javico International and Javico A.-G. v. Yves Saint Laurent Parfums SA* [1998] E.C.R. I–1983, [1998] 5 C.M.L.R. 172, para. 17.

[9] [1997] O.J. C372/13; [1998] 4 C.M.L.R. 192.

[10] The previous Notice, of 1986, additionally used turnover criteria. For the assessment of market shares, see paras 13–17 of the 1997 Notice.

[11] Para. 11 of the 1997 Notice, referring, *e.g.* to fixing prices or sharing markets in horizontal agreements.

not legally binding and, in particular, is subject to the jurisprudence of the Court. This, however, can cut both ways. A market share of 3 per cent, for example, might be appreciable where it exceeds that of most competitors.[12] Conversely, market shares above the 5 per cent threshold of the Notice will not inevitably mean an appreciable effect is established.[13] As the Notice itself concedes, the quantitative definition of appreciability serves only as a guideline.[14] Moreover, in a passage that betrays a belief in some kind of rule of reason, the Notice observes that even agreements which are not of minor importance can escape the prohibition in Article 81(1) "on account of their exclusively favourable impact on competition".[15]

The guiding principle must therefore be the paramount need to set a particular agreement in its legal and economic context. This is particularly pertinent in circumstances where there may be networks of parallel agreements. In the *Delimitis* case[16] a German court sought a preliminary ruling on the question of the applicability of Article 81(1) to the terms of a contract between publican and brewery. According to the Court of Justice, the national court must inquire into whether the contract would restrict access to the market and "the extent to which the agreements entered into by the brewery in question contribute to the cumulative effect produced in that respect by the totality of similar contracts found on that market".[17] However, this may be a particularly onerous task for the national court to perform, even with the assistance and resources available to it from the Commission by use of the Co-Operation Notice.[18]

The Commission's own application of the *Delimitis* ruling can be seen in *Van den Bergh Foods*[19] in relation to the exclusivity clause imposed by the Unilever group company on retail outlets to which freezer cabinets were made available by Van den Bergh for stocking ice-cream products, on terms whereby such freezer cabinets could only be used to hold Unilever ice-cream products. Most other ice-cream suppliers also had networks using exclusive freezer cabinet agreements, resulting in over 80 per cent of retail outlets being party to such agreements. It was established that retailers were unlikely to install more than one cabinet. Unilever sales accounted for between 40–55 per cent of retail outlets and over 40 per cent of all impulse ice cream sales in Ireland. The Commission rejected Van den Bergh's argument that if its agreements infringed Article 81(1) then on the principle of equal treatment all the other networks did so too.

---

[12] Joined Cases 100–103/80 *Musique Diffusion Française v. Commission*, n.8, *supra*.

[13] Case T–7/93 *Langnese-Iglo v. Commission* [1995] E.C.R. II–611; [1995] 5 C.M.L.R. 602. See also Joined Cases T–374, 375, 384 and 388/94 *European Night Services and others v. Commission*, n.68, *supra*, where the Commission disputed the claims of the parties that their market shares fell below 5%. The Court of First Instance ruled that the Commission had failed to provide adequate reasoning, but that in any event a slight excess over the 5% Notice threshold would not in itself indicate an appreciable effect.

[14] 1997 Notice, para. 3.

[15] *ibid.*

[16] Case C–234/89 *Delimitis v. Henninger Bräu*, n.68, *supra*.

[17] *ibid.*, para. 24.

[18] *Notice on Co-operation between National Courts and the Commission in Applying Arts 85 and 86 of the EEC Treaty*, [1993] O.J. C39/6; [1993] 4 C.M.L.R. 12. Discussed further in Chap. 22 on enforcement.

[19] [1998] O.J. L246/1.

Effect on trade between Member States

The purpose of the condition in Article 81(1) relating to the effect of an agreement on trade between Member States is, in the words of the Court of Justice, "to define, in the context of the law governing competition, the boundary between the areas respectively covered by Community law and the law of the Member States".[20] Where behaviour may have implications for competition in more than one of the Member States, the E.C. rules apply: where its effects are confined to a single Member State, the matter is one exclusively for national law. The line of demarcation is the same under both Articles 81 and 82.[21]

The approach normally adopted by the Court and the Commission is to examine the effect of an agreement on the flow of goods and services between Member States. The test, first formulated in *Société Technique Minière,* is that "it must be possible to foresee with a sufficient degree of probability on the basis of a set of objective factors of law or of fact that the agreement in question may have an influence, direct or indirect, actual or potential, on the pattern of trade between Member States".[22] The crucial element is the diversion of trade flows from the pattern they would naturally follow in a unified market. Where trade has been so diverted, it is immaterial that the agreement may have led to an increase in the volume of goods or services reaching the market in other Member States. Thus in *Consten and Grundig,*[23] trade was held to be affected in the necessary sense, regardless of any increase in imports of Grundig products into France, because not only were all such imports to be channelled through Consten but their re-exportation to the Member States was prohibited.

In practice, the requirement of a direct or indirect, actual or potential influence on the pattern of trade does not usually present a serious obstacle to establishing an infringement of Article 81(1). The necessary effect is normally the result of a combination of several factors which, taken separately, are not necessarily decisive.[24] Trade is liable to be affected directly by, for instance, the grant of an exclusive distributorship or an exclusive patent licence in respect of a Member State's territory. An example of indirect effect would be where the product covered by an agreement is not itself exported to other Member States but a product derived from it is exported. Thus in *BNIC v. Clair*[25] it was pointed out that the product in question, potable spirits used in the manufacture of cognac, was not normally sent outside the Cognac region of France. The Court responded that "any agreement whose object or effect is to restrict competition by fixing minimum prices for an intermediate product is capable of affecting intra-Community trade, even if there is no trade in that intermediate product between the Member States, where the product constitutes the raw material for another product marketed elsewhere in the Community".[26] An agreement between parties in the same Member State and relating to sales of domestic

---

[20] Case 22/78 *Hugin v. Commission* [1979] E.C.R. 1869, at 1899; [1979] 3 C.M.L.R. 345.
[21] [1979] E.C.R. at 1899.
[22] Case 56/65 *Société Technique Minière v. Maschinenbau Ulm,* n.35, *supra,* [1966] E.C.R. at 249.
[23] Joined Cases 56 and 58/64, n.60, *supra.*
[24] Case C–250/92 *Gottrup-Klim v. Dansk Landbrugs Grovvareselskab,* n.68, *supra,* para. 54.
[25] Case 123/83 *BNIC v. Clair* [1985] E.C.R. 402; [1985] 2 C.M.L.R. 430.
[26] [1985] E.C.R. at 425.

products within that State may affect trade indirectly, for example by making it harder for imports to penetrate the market, especially where it extends over the whole national territory.[27] Since a potential effect on trade will suffice, there is no need for the Commission to produce statistical evidence showing that, as a result of the agreement, trade has actually begun to flow through different channels.[28]

This is not to say that all agreements will be treated as capable of affecting inter-State trade. In *Bagnasco*[29] the Tribunale di Genova sought a ruling from the Court of Justice on the compatibility of certain clauses in the standard banking conditions (the NBU) of the Italian Banking Association (ABI) relating to contracts for the opening of current-account credit facilities, and general guarantee agreements linked to them, with Article 81. Advocate General Colomer concluded that the NBU conditions were both restrictive of competition and capable of affecting inter-State trade. In his view, they affected the ability of banks belonging to the ABI to determine the conditions which they would like to apply to their customers on the basis of their internal profitability, their specialisation and their commercial policy. Since the vast majority of Italian banks belonged to the ABI, the scope for choice available to customers seeking to open a current-account credit facility was drastically reduced. Furthermore the provisions of the NBU relating to the opening of credit facilities and general guarantees had an appreciably restrictive effect on competition since the margin of manoeuvre available to a bank when first negotiating the interest rate and other conditions governing the opening of a credit facility with a customer is reduced because the rate is mainly determined by interest rates on the capital markets.[30] As far as the question of affecting inter-State trade was concerned the Advocate General offered five reasons why this was substantiated. First, the globalisation of banking and the use of new technologies enabled banking to be conducted as a cross-border activity, making any reference to national financial services untenable. Secondly, the NBU rules held up the establishment of a single market in all Member States by compartmentalising the Italian market. Thirdly, many Italian banking institutions were subsidiaries or branches of banks in other Member States which were "forced" to apply the provisions of the NBU because of the other advantages in belonging to the ABI. Fourthly, by applying across the whole of a State territory, the NBU conditions were presumed to affect inter-State trade on the case-law as understood by the Advocate General.[31] Finally, the opening of a current-account credit facility was the most important loan facility concluded by banks and of great importance to businesses.

However, the Court of Justice rejected this view, relying principally on evidence from the Commission that the banking service in question involved economic activities with a very limited impact on trade between Member States and that the participation of subsidiaries or branches of non-Italian financial establishments was limited. Moreover, the Commission had also indicated that

---

[27] Case 8/72 *Cementhandelaren v. Commission* [1972] E.C.R. 977; [1973] C.M.L.R. 7.
[28] Case C–219/95P *Ferrière Nord v. Commission*, n.56, *supra*.
[29] Joined Cases C–215–216/96 *Bagnasco and others v. Banco Popolare di Novara Soc. Coop. Arl and Cassa di Risparmio di Genova e Imperia SpA* [1999] E.C.R. I–135; [1999] 4 C.M.L.R. 624.
[30] *ibid.*, para. 38 of Opinion.
[31] Citing, in particular, Case 42/84 *Remia*, n.84, *supra*.

the potential recourse to the services in question by the main customers of foreign banks, *i.e.* large undertakings and foreign economic operators, was not great. In any event, contracts of the kind in issue were not decisive factors for foreign banks when deciding whether or not to establish in Italy. The Court accordingly concluded that there was nothing else in the documents before it to justify finding, with a sufficient degree of probability, an appreciable effect on intra-Community trade brought about by the reservations entertained by customers concerning their choice of bank in the light of the NBU conditions when wishing to conclude a current-account credit facility.[32]

The different approaches taken by the Advocate General and the Court in *Bagnasco* present a stark contrast. The former's stance was overtly normative, stating that the criteria adopted by the Commission to determine whether trade between Member States was affected in the banking sector "must be thoroughly revised"[33] in the light of technological change, a globalised competitive environment and the introduction of the single currency in accordance with Article 121(4) E.C. The Court, on the other hand, confined itself to the evidence of the parties and, in particular, the uncontested submissions of the Commission as to the actual state of the market in banking services at the time. Although Advocate General Colomer's arguments were policy-oriented and highly purposive in nature, it is submitted that they were hardly the stuff of pure fantasy. The Court's circumspection appears all the more striking since it chose to answer the national court's questions about the effect on trade directly itself, instead of treating the assessment of complex economic issues as a matter for the national court to decide.

An alternative to the *Société Technique Minière* test has been adopted by the Court of Justice in some cases under Article 82. Attention is focused not on any change in the pattern of imports or exports but on the consequences of the behaviour in question for the structure of competition within the common market. The leading case is *Commercial Solvents*.[34] The abuse of a dominant position was committed by Commercial Solvents in refusing to supply an Italian company (Zoja) with a raw material used in the manufacture of a medicinal drug. The argument that trade between Member States could not be affected, since Zoja sold almost all of its production outside the common market, was rejected by the Court. The requirement of an effect on trade would, it was held, be satisfied by the impairment of the competitive structure caused by the elimination of a major E.C. producer. This structural test is less likely to be relevant in cases under Article 81, where the starting point is not, as it is under Article 82, the existence of a dominant position. However, the Court considers the test to be available is such cases,[35] and it has occasionally been applied by the Commission.[36]

---

[32] [1999] 4 C.M.L.R. 624, at paras 51–52.

[33] Opinion, para. 26.

[34] Joined Cases 6–7/73 *Commercial Solvents Corporation v. Commission* [1974] E.C.R. 223; [1974] 1 C.M.L.R. 309.

[35] This is clear from the reference to Arts 85 and 86 (as they were) in the passage in the *Hugin* judgment concerning the purpose of the requirements of an effect on inter-Member State trade: Case 22/78 [1979] E.C.R. at 1899.

[36] Although ultimately there was no breach of Art. 81(1) on other grounds, the Commission had argued in the *Wood Pulp* case, n.29, *supra*, that trade between Member States was affected by the impairment of competition throughout the E.C. by the creation of an artificially uniform price level.

Exemptions under Article 81(3)

Agreements that appreciably affect competition may nevertheless bring significant economic advantages. Accordingly, the prohibition of Article 81(1) is tempered by the possibility of exemption under Article 81(3). The function of the latter is to enable a balance to be struck between the maintenance of effective competition and other aspects of the Community's task as defined in Article 2 E.C.

Pursuant to Article 81(3) the provisions of Article 81(1) may be declared inapplicable to "any agreement or category of agreements". The power to grant individual exemptions is reserved by Regulation 17 to the Commission,[37] although the proposals contained in the *White Paper on Modernisation*[38] would bring about radical change in this area.[39] "Block" exemption of categories of agreements is given by regulations of the Commission which are adopted under powers delegated by the Council in accordance with Article 83 E.C. Block exemptions have been adopted in relation to a range of agreements, including: franchising, motor vehicle distribution and servicing, specialisation, research and development and technology transfer. A general block exemption applicable to vertical restraints was enacted in 1999.[40] The detailed contents of these block exemptions are not examined in this work, although their principles are discussed further below.

In principle, any agreement, no matter how restrictive of competition, is capable of being justified under Article 81(3).[41] There are two positive criteria and two negative ones. An exemption must satisfy all the criteria, so that if it fails on one there is no need for the Commission to go on and examine the others.[42] The benefits required do not necessarily have to occur within the territory of the Member State or States in which the undertakings party to the agreement are established.[43] The four criteria for exemption under Article 81(3) are discussed in turn below.

Economic benefits

The first of the positive criteria identifies in broad terms a number of economic benefits that provide the rationale for refraining from applying Article 81(1). The agreement must contribute "to improving the production or distribution of goods or to promoting technical or economic progress". It may be found

---

[37] Notifications for individual exemption are discussed further in Chap. 22 on enforcement.

[38] Note 2, *supra*.

[39] *Viz*, enabling national courts and national authorities to dispense exemptions on an *ex post facto* basis in cases coming before them. The envisaged timetable would implement such changes by 2003.

[40] Reg. 2790/1999, n.97, *supra*.

[41] Case T–17/93 *Matra Hachette v. Commission* [1994] E.C.R. II-595

[42] Case C–137/95P *Vereniging van Samenwerkende Prijsregelende Organisaties in de Bouwnijverheid (SPO) v. Commission* [1996] E.C.R. I-1611.

[43] Case C–360/92P *Publishers Association v. Commission* [1995] E.C.R. I–25; [1995] 5 C.M.L.R. 33.

that a given agreement helps to further more than one, or even all, of these objects.

The basic target of the Commission in applying the criterion of economic benefit is that the gain to welfare must exceed what could have been achieved without any restriction of competition. As the Commission has stated:

"For the agreements to contribute to the improvement of production or distribution, or to promote technical or economic progress, they must objectively constitute an improvement on the situation that would otherwise exist. The fundamental principle in this respect, established at the time the Common Market was formed, lays down that fair and undistorted competition is the best guarantee of regular supply on the best terms. Thus the question of a contribution to economic progress within the meaning of Article [81(3)] can only arise in those exceptional cases where the free play of competition is unable to produce the best result economically speaking."[44]

The matter is to be judged in the light of the general interest in a well-functioning market. It is not sufficient merely that the parties themselves may secure advantages in their production and distribution activities.[45]

The balance of advantage and disadvantage may go against an agreement because of the way in which it is applied in practice. In *Re Ford Werke*[46] the Commission considered the compatibility with Article 81 of the standard form agreement concluded between Ford Germany and its main dealers. Essentially, a dealer would be given an exclusive right to distribute and service Ford vehicles within an allotted territory, while undertaking not to sell vehicles of other makes. The agreement was caught by Article 81(1), since it affected the intensity of competition within the distribution network, as well as limiting the outlets available to other car manufacturers, but might have been expected, on its terms, to qualify for exemption under Article 81(3). Exemption was, however, refused by the Commission on the ground that Ford Germany had cut off supplies of right hand drive vehicles to its dealers. The purpose of this action was to staunch the flow of parallel imports into the United Kingdom where local Ford prices were significantly higher than in Germany. Ford's arguments that it had acted purely unilaterally, and therefore outside Article 81, was rejected by the Commission and subsequently by the Court of Justice.[47] The Court held that the refusal to supply formed part of the contractual relationship between Ford and its dealers, whose admission to the network implied acceptance of the company's policy regarding the models to be delivered to the German market. It could, therefore, properly be taken into account in assessing the eligibility of the agreement for exemption.

In preserving the delicate balance between the benefits claimed to flow from an agreement and the need to maintain effective competition, an important part is played by the time limits and conditions imposed pursuant to Article 8(1) of

---

[44] *Re Bayer/Gist-Brocades* [1976] O.J. L30/13; [1976] 1 C.M.L.R. D98. See para. 57 of the Decision.
[45] Joined Cases 56 and 58/64 *Consten and Grundig v. Commission*, n.60, *supra*. See also *VNP/Cobelpa* [1977] 2 C.M.L.R. D28.
[46] [1983] O.J. L327/31; [1984] 1 C.M.L.R. 596.
[47] Joined Cases 25–26/84 *Ford v. Commission* [1985] E.C.R. 2725; [1985] 3 C.M.L.R. 528.

Regulation 17. Time limits are at the discretion of the Commission. Agreements are generally given a period of five to ten years to produce the hoped-for result but, in the case of research and development agreements and manufacturing joint ventures not yet established on the market, 15 years may be judged appropriate.[48] Despite their limited period of validity, many exemptions will produce permanent changes in the structure of the market concerned: thus specialisation agreements by their very nature entail a decisive shift in the business activities of the parties. In addition, where a period of exemption has elapsed the Commission may renew it, though not necessarily on the same terms.[49] The conditions attached to a grant of exemption will be designed to ensure that benefits really are obtained and competition is not unduly prejudiced. An example would be an obligation to report from time to time on the progress made in implementing the agreement,[50] although more far-reaching changes of substance may also provide necessary pre-conditions to obtaining approval from the Commission.[51] Exemption decisions will be interpreted restrictively, so as to ensure that their effects are not extended to situations which they are not intended to cover.[52]

Cases involving exemptions are highly fact-specific, making generalisation a fruitless exercise. However, typical of improvements in production are those likely to be derived from specialisation agreements[53] or collaboration in research and development,[54] such as: a reduction in costs or an increase in productivity, thanks to economies of scale; enhancement of output or the quality and range of goods, through the modernisation of plant or the centralisation of production and planning; and avoidance of duplication in research and development projects, giving a better chance of obtaining a useful result and reducing the time needed to do so. Benefits in distribution are likely to consist of, *inter alia*, better market penetration, continuity of supply, more effective promotion of the goods or services and increased inter-brand competition. Production and distribution elements may well be linked, as for example in the *Fiat/Hitachi* decision.[55] Here a joint venture for the manufacture, distribution and sale of hydraulic excavators offered benefits for production in the form of technically better components and

---

[48] See, *e.g. Re United Reprocesors* [1976] O.J. L51/7; [1976] 2 C.M.L.R. D1. In *De Laval/Stork* [1988] O.J. L59/32 an initial nine-year exemption was renewed for a further 20 years.

[49] See, *e.g. Re Transocean Marine Paint Association (No. 2)* [1974] O.J. L19/18; [1974] 1 C.M.L.R. D11; *Re Vacuum Interrupters (No. 2)* [1980] O.J. L383/1; [1981] 2 C.M.L.R. 217.

[50] *e.g. Ford/Volkswagen* [1993] O.J. L20/14; [1993] 5 C.M.L.R. 617. This was a joint venture bitterly opposed by competitors to the parties, who argued that it would reduce rather than increase competition. A 10 year exemption was only granted after several amendments to the agreement, including an obligation to report on progress.

[51] See, *e.g. Phoenix/Atlas* [1996] O.J. L239/57; [1997] 4 C.M.L.R. 147.

[52] Case C–70/93 *BMW v. Ald Auto Leasing* [1995] E.C.R. I–3439; [1996] 4 C.M.L.R. 478. See also Case C–306/96 *Javico International and Javico A.-G. v. Yves Saint Laurent Parfums*, n.8, *supra*. In the latter case, the Court of Justice held that provisions intended to prevent a distributor from selling directly in the Community and re-exporting to the Community contractual products which the distributor has undertaken to sell in non-member countries do not escape prohibition under Art. 81(1) on the ground that the Community supplier of the products concerned distributes those products within the Community through a selective distribution network covered by an exemption under Art. 81(3).

[53] *e.g. Re Prym/Beka* [1973] O.J. L296/24; [1973] C.M.L.R. D250.

[54] *e.g. Re BP/Kellogg* [1986] O.J. L369/6; [1986] 2 C.M.L.R. 619.

[55] Dec. 93/48 [1993] O.J. L20/10, [1994] 4 C.M.L.R. 571.

improved distribution as a result of the parties' separate and complementary distribution systems being merged.

"Technical progress" is often linked by the Commission with improvements in production, and the range of agreements it may be invoked to justify is similar. Examples include the development of new technology, new or improved products, better standards of safety and the saving of energy. In *Re X/Open Group*[56] exemption was granted in respect of an agreement between a number of substantial computer manufacturers having as its object the establishment of a standard interface for an operating system which it was possible to use on a wide variety of machines. An "open industry standard" would extend the availability of software and increase the opportunities for users to switch between hardware and software from different sources. This, it was found, would contribute to promoting technical progress by enabling software houses, and conceivably members of the Group as well, to develop application programmes for which there might not otherwise have been a market.

"Economic progress" seems at first sight to be the widest of the criteria identified in the first positive condition of Article 81(3). Its boundaries still remain somewhat fluid and there have been controversies in relation to its application, notably[57] with regard to crisis cartels, formed to enable an industry to adapt in an orderly way to adverse economic conditions such as a decline in the overall market for its products. In *Re Synthetic Fibres*[58] an agreement providing for joint measures to cut capacity, in an industry where the trend in demand had not kept pace with increased output resulting from rapid technical advances, was considered eligible for exemption. The advantages identified by the Commission included the shedding of the financial burden of keeping under-utilised capacity open, the achievement of optimum plant size and specialisation in the development of products adapted to user's requirements. "The eventual result", the Commission said, " should be to raise the profitability and restore the competitiveness of each party".[59]

Social factors may also be legitimately included within the heading of "economic progress".[60] Among the elements mentioned in support of the *Synthetic Fibres* exemption was the possibility of cushioning the social effects of restructuring by making suitable arrangements for the retraining and redeployment of redundant workers. Public interest concerns, of the sort arising under Article 86(2), may be taken into account by the Commission in the context of an exemption under Article 81(3) but not without examining the specific criteria of the latter.[61]Environmental concerns might also seem arguable as economic benefits, especially since the Treaty of Amsterdam,[62] but the Commission's

---

[56] [1987] O.J. L35/36
[57] See Weatherill & Beaumont, *EU Law* (3rd ed, Penguin, 1999) pp. 829–830.
[58] [1984] O.J. L207/17; [1985] 1 C.M.L.R. 787.
[59] *ibid.* at para. 36.
[60] The creation of employment is mentioned by the Court in Case 26/76 *Metro*, n.3, *supra*, para. 43.
[61] Joined Cases T–528, T–542–543 and 546/93 *Métropole Télévision and others v. Commission* [1996] E.C.R. II–649; [1996] 5 C.M.L.R. 386.
[62] Inserting into the E.C. Treaty (Art. 6) that environmental protection requirements must be integrated into the definition and implementation of Community policies referred to in Art. 3 E.C.; thereby including competition policy.

practice appears to place them within the second positive criterion, benefit to consumers. As it noted in *Philips/Osram*,[63] "The use of cleaner facilities will result in less air pollution, and consequently in direct and indirect benefits for consumers from reduced negative externalities. This positive effect will be substantially reinforced when R&D in the field produces lead-free materials".

Benefit to consumers

The second positive benefit is that consumers must receive a fair share of the benefit resulting from the restriction of competition. At first sight, the use of the term "consumer" suggests that only the consuming public, or end consumer, is meant. Such a construction, however, would have the effect of severely limiting the scope of possible exemptions, because in many cases the parties to the agreement cannot by themselves do anything to ensure that the condition is met. For instance, manufacturers often, and if small usually, sell through intermediaries; they could not guarantee that these intermediaries will pass on the benefits of the agreement, even if they themselves do. It is not therefore surprising that the Commission has taken the view that consumers include persons at intermediate stages in the marketing process. Moreover, the term "consumer" in English may have a narrower connotation than the term used in other language texts: the French text uses the term *utilisateur*.

The requirement of a "fair share of the resulting benefit" involves two considerations: what is a benefit, so far as the consumer is concerned; and how can the Commission be sure that the consumer will receive it? Considerable criticism has been levelled at the Commission in this area for what may seem to be less than rigorous application of the distributional element of the test.[64] A general assumption in the cases seems to be that if an economic benefit is made out under the first criterion of Article 81(3) then the consumer benefit will naturally "trickle down" thereafter.[65] Thus improvements in production or technical progress should entail a cheaper and/or better product, while improvements in distribution or economic progress should engender better supply and greater choice of product.

It is also widely suggested that the Commission gives undue emphasis to price reductions rather than other forms of consumer benefit. Although there are certainly examples of better service or a broader product range being relevant,[66] price considerations often take priority. *Re VBBB/VBVB*[67] concerned an agreement between associations of booksellers and publishers in the Netherlands and Belgium which established a system of collective resale price maintenance for trade between the two countries in books in the Dutch language. The main grounds relied on to justify this system were that it made possible the cross-

---

[63] Dec. 94/986, at para. 27. See also Dec. 91/38 *KSB/Goulds/Lowara/ITT* [1991] O.J. L19/25.

[64] See Weatherill & Beaumont, *op. cit.*, n.57, *supra*, at pp. 831–833, asserting that "little more than lip-service is paid to any independent notion of consumer interest". A rather milder reproach is administered in Goyder, *EC Competition Law* (3rd ed., Oxford, 1998) p. 141.

[65] See, *e.g. Rockwell/Iveco* [1983] O.J. L224/19; *Carbon Gas Technologie* [1983] O.J. L376/17.

[66] See, *e.g. Ford/Volkswagen*, n.50, *supra*.

[67] [1982] O.J. L54/36; [1982] 2 C.M.L.R. 344.

subsidisation of less popular titles by more popular ones and also helped to ensure the survival of small bookshops. The Commission did not deny the worthiness of these objectives but took the view that their dependence on the disputed system had not been demonstrated. Cross-subsidisation could have been achieved by individual publishers' decisions on pricing, while the number of specialised booksellers had declined sharply, despite retail price maintenance, owing in part to the rise of self-service shops and the activities of book clubs. By excluding price competition in respect of a given title, the agreement removed an important means of rationalising and improving the system of book distribution.[68]

No restrictions that are not indispensable

The first negative criterion is that exemption cannot be given to restrictions of competition going beyond what is absolutely necessary to achieve the objectives regarded as beneficial. In other words, the adverse effects on competition must be proportionate to the benefits made out for the agreement.[69] A robust approach to this particular requirement allows the Commission to extract modifications to agreements before granting authorisation. For example, under the joint venture arrangements in *Re Optical Fibres*,[70] as they were originally conceived, the technology provider (the American firm, Corning) had a share of the equity giving it effective control over production and marketing policies. This, it was feared, might enable Corning to prevent the joint ventures from competing actively with each other. The Commission, therefore, persuaded the parties to reduce Corning's voting rights to below the level that could give it a veto over decisions at shareholders' meetings, while also curbing its influence over day-to-day management.[71]

A useful guide to the Commission's views as to the indispensable extent of restrictions pertaining to particular types of agreement can be gleaned from the permitted and prohibited clauses indicated by block exemptions. Any refusal of an exemption by the Commission without countering the evidence put forward by the parties in respect of indispensability will, of course, provide grounds for review of the decision.[72]

No possibility of eliminating competition

The final criterion is that the agreement must not afford the parties the possibility of eliminating competition in respect of a substantial part of the product in question. There is thus, in principle, a limit beyond which considerations of general economic policy cannot be allowed to prevail over the maintenance of effective competition in the common market.

---

[68] The Decision was upheld by the Court of Justice in Joined Cases 43 and 63/82 [1984] E.C.R. 19; [1985] 1 C.M.L.R. 87.

[69] Case T–17/93 *Matra Hachette*, n.41, *supra*, at para. 135.

[70] [1986] O.J. L236/30.

[71] See also *Bayer/Gist-Brocades*, n.43, *supra*, where the result of the Commission's pressure was that the proposed joint subsidiaries were replaced by reciprocal supply arrangements.

[72] See, *e.g.* Case C–360/92P *Publishers Association v. Commission*, n.43, *supra*. In the Court's view the Commission (and indeed the Court of First Instance) had failed to address properly the parties' claim that a collective system of fixed prices for books was indispensable.

Market definition is an essential element to this criterion.[73] In *Kali and Salz*[74] a Decision of the Commission refusing exemption to an agreement for the exclusive sale of "straight" potash fertilizer was annulled by the Court on the ground, *inter alia*, that the relevant product market had been wrongly defined. The Commission had taken the view that the agreement was liable to result in the substantial elimination of competition because between them the parties accounted for the whole production of "straight" potash fertilizer in the Federal Republic of Germany. However, the Commission's own reasoning showed there was competition between the product and "compound" potash fertilizer, which ought therefore to have been regarded as belonging to the same market.

Experience suggests that an agreement which clearly satisfies the other criteria in Article 81(3) is unlikely to fail under this one.

Block exemptions

An agreement that would otherwise be liable to prohibition under Article 81(1) will automatically escape this fate if it fulfils the terms of a block exemption regulation. The parties to qualifying agreements are saved the uncertainty and delay of seeking individual exemption, although that route would remain open where none of the regulations applied. The price to be paid for these advantages is that the regulations impose a degree of *dirigisme*, since the parties to a prospective agreement are inevitably under pressure to conduct their affairs so as to secure block exemption, if it should be available.

In relation to the exemptions enacted before the regulation applicable to vertical restraints, a certain standard approach is discernible. The category of agreements to which the regulation applies is identified in broad terms and lists are then given of specific obligations which may or may not be included without forfeiting the benefit of the block exemption. These are sometimes referred to as, respectively, the "white" and "black" lists. Provision will be made for the withdrawal of the exemption by the Commission if it finds that, despite compliance with the regulation, an agreement has certain effects that do not satisfy the criteria in Article 81(3). There will also be transitional provisions, and the duration of the regulation will be specified. Some of the regulations[75] include an "opposition" procedure to expedite the process of obtaining exemption on an individual basis. An agreement not covered by the regulation may be notified to the Commission which is given a period (normally six months) to express its opposition. If the agreement is not opposed by the Commission within the prescribed period, it is brought within the scope of the block exemption.

The approach taken by the 1999 block exemption for vertical restraints[76] is somewhat different. It relies upon a "black" list only, relating to unacceptable hardcore restraints, coupled with a market share cap. The absence of a "white"

---

[73] See Chap. 21 for discussion of the tests of product substitution and geographical markets under the Market Definition Notice and cases under Art. 82.

[74] Joined Cases 19–20/74 *Kali und Salz v. Commission* [1975] E.C.R. 499; [1975] 2 C.M.L.R. 154.

[75] *e.g.* Reg. 417/85 on specialisation agreements [1985] O.J. L53/1; Reg. 418/85 on research and development agreements [1985] O.J. L53/5; Reg. 4087/88 on franchising agreements [1988] O.J. L359/46; Reg. 240/96 on technology transfer agreements [1996] O.J. L31/2.

[76] Reg. 2790/1999, n.97, *supra*. For comments in relation to selective distribution, see n.97 *et seq.*, *supra*, and accompanying text.

list is intended to avoid some of the more prescriptive side-effects of previous block exemptions. However, the point might be made that the inclusion of a "black" list, applicable to firms without market power, signifies a concern about threats to market integration rather than workable competition. The regulation adopts a broad umbrella approach, removing the need for the earlier more specialised regulations, and includes selective distribution agreements for the first time.[77] This structure reflects the lenient approach to vertical restraints adopted in the Commission's original Green Paper[78] and modified in the light of later consultation. Apart from the prohibited restraints, the other bar to enjoyment of the vertical agreements exemption is through the operation of rules relating to market shares. Having canvassed the possibilities of a two-tier market share rule, the Commission finally adopted a single figure of 30 per cent as the threshold below which vertical agreements are protected.

National legislation and Article 81

Although the discussion of Article 81 in this chapter has focused on the collusive behaviour of undertakings, there is also a well-established strand of case-law dealing with situations in which restrictive practices and distortions of competition are linked in some way to specific legislation or the general legal framework of a Member State.[79] The Court of Justice has consistently maintained that although Article 81 is concerned solely with the conduct of undertakings, that provision, in conjunction with Article 10 of the Treaty, requires the Member States not to introduce or maintain in force measures, even of a legislative nature, which may render ineffective the competition rules applicable to undertakings.[80] It is clear from the case-law that a Member State will not be made liable for every anti-competitive consequence of legislation, however tenuous or remote. Instead, the Court has indicated that liability can only attach to the Member State if it requires or favours the adoption of agreements, decisions or concerted practices contrary to Article 81, or reinforces their effects, or deprives its own rules of the character of legislation by delegating to private economic operators responsibility for taking decisions affecting the economic sphere. Each of these three tests is discussed further below.

Requiring or favouring anti-competitive agreements

Although the Court repeatedly refers to this scenario,[81] examples of such direct influence are unusual. However, an enforcement action brought by the

---

[77] *i.e.* Reg. 1983/83 on exclusive distribution, Reg. 1984/83 on exclusive purchasing and Reg. 4087/88 on franchising. However, Reg. 1475/95 on selective distribution agreements for motor vehicles is left in place: [1995] O.J. L145/25.

[78] n.96, *supra*.

[79] For the liability of Member States under Art. 86 and discussion of situations involving public undertakings and undertakings entrusted with services of general economic interest, see Chap. 25.

[80] Case 267/86 *Van Eycke* [1988] E.C.R. 4769; [1990] 4 C.M.L.R. 330, para. 16; Case C–185/91 *Reiff* [1993] E.C.R. I–5801, para. 14; Case C–153/93 *Delta Schiffahrts- und Speditionsgesellschaft* [1994] E.C.R. I–2517, para. 15; Case C–35/96 *Commission v. Italy (Re CNSD)* [1998] E.C.R. I–3851; [1998] 5 C.M.L.R. 889.

[81] *e.g.* Case 229/83 *Leclerc v. Sarl "Au Blé Vert"* [1985] E.C.R. 1; [1985] 2 C.M.L.R. 286, para. 15; Joined Cases 209–213/84 *Ministère Public v. Asjes* [1986] E.C.R. 1425; [1986] 3 C.M.L.R. 173, para.

Commission against Italy in relation to its rules governing customs agents provides a case in point.[82] According to Italian Act No. 1612/1960 the National Council of Customs Agents (CNSD) was made responsible for setting the tariff for services provided by customs agents. This tariff was compulsory and anyone contravening it was liable to disciplinary action, including suspension or removal from the register of customs agents. The Commission took action against Italy on the basis that the tariff-fixing was a decision of an association of undertakings, for which the Member State was responsible. The Court agreed. Having found that in adopting the tariff, the CNSD infringed Article 81,[83] it went on to condemn Italy's direct participation, observing:

> "By adopting the national legislation in question, the Italian republic clearly not only required the conclusion of an agreement contrary to [Article 81] and declined to influence its terms, but also assists in ensuring compliance with that agreement."[84]

Reinforcing anti-competitive effects

This is a particularly important aspect of the Court's formulation, since it could embrace looser forms of influence than those where the State directly requires anti-competitive conduct. However, it appears that the Court only entertains its application in relation to legislation that adopts or reinforces previous private arrangements. In *Van Eycke*,[85] for example, holders of certain Belgian savings accounts could get tax exemptions provided that the bank kept interest rates to below maximum levels specified in a Royal Decree. This Decree was alleged to reinforce a previous arrangement between banks and financial institutions restricting interest rates. However, the Court of Justice left it to the national court to decide whether this was indeed the case.[86]

In later cases it has proved difficult to persuade the Court of the reinforcing effects of national legislation. Thus, in *Meng*[87] the relevant German rules forbade insurance agents from sharing their commission with customers. Faced with the argument that this legislation restricted the competitiveness of agents, the Court declined to accept that it fell within the reach of Article 81 in combination with Article 10. In its view, the measure was no more than regulation by the State of the insurance market. This reluctance on the part of the Court coincided with its drawing of lines in the sand in relation to other areas of market regulation under E.C. law.[88]

72; Case 311/85 *VZW Vereniging van Vlaamse Reisbureaus v. VZW Sociale Dienst* [1987] E.C.R. 3801; [1989] 4 C.M.L.R. para. 10; Case 254/87 *Syndicat des Libraires de Normandie v. L'Aigle Distribution* [1988] E.C.R. 4457.

[82] Case C–35/96 *Commission v. Italy (Re CNSD)*, n.80, *supra*.

[83] The Court had no difficulty treating the activity of customs agent as economic and finding that the CNSD was an association of undertakings regardless of its national public law categorisation.

[84] [1998] E.C.R. I–3851, at para. 55.

[85] Case 267/86 n.80, *supra*.

[86] The evidence of direct reinforcement was much clearer in Case 311/85 *Van Vlaamse*, n.81, *supra*.

[87] Case C–2/91 *Meng* [1993] E.C.R. I–5751; see also Case C–245/91 *Ohra* [1993] E.C.R. 5851.

[88] Notably Cases C–267–268/91 *Keck and Mithouard* [1993] E.C.R. I–6097; [1995] 1 C.M.L.R. 101. See Reich, "The 'November Revolution' of the European Court of Justice: Keck, Meng and Audi revisited" (1994) 31 C.M.L.Rev. 459.

Legislation deprived of its State character

Member States cannot absolve themselves from responsibility by simply delegating or transferring decision-making powers to private bodies. The question is whether the legislation is deprived of its state character, a conclusion that the Court again appears reluctant to draw. In *Reiff*,[89] for example, it was called upon to consider German legislation under which the rates for the carriage of goods by road were set by tariff boards made up of industry representatives appointed by the relevant Minister. The Court noted that the industry representatives were not bound by instructions from the undertakings from which they were drawn and as such were not representatives of those undertakings. Moreover, the Minister was able to take part in meetings of the tariff boards and held powers to substitute his own tariffs in substitution for those of the boards. These features, the Court concluded, meant that the system was not a delegation of the State's powers.[90]

The objection to States delegating their powers to private bodies is, presumably, the scope thereby conferred for those bodies to take anti-competitive decisions in their own favour. Consequently, it seems there will be no breach by the State if the transfer includes requirements to take public interest considerations into account. In the Italian customs agents case,[91] for example, the Court noted that Italian Act 1612/90 neither obliged nor even encouraged the members of the CNSD to take into account not only the interests of the undertakings which appointed them but also the general interest and the interests of undertakings in other sectors or users of the services in question.[92] Instead, the legislation "wholly relinquished"[93] to private economic operators the powers of the public authorities as regards the setting of tariffs. The Italian Republic had accordingly failed to fulfil its obligations under Articles 10 and 81 of the Treaty.

---

[89] Case C–185/91, n.80, *supra*.
[90] See also Joined Cases C–140, 141, 142/94 *DIP v. Commune di Bassano del Grappa* [1995] E.C.R. I–3257.
[91] Case C–35/96, n.80, *supra*.
[92] *ibid.*, para. 44.
[93] *ibid.*, para. 57.

CHAPTER 21

ABUSE OF A DOMINANT POSITION

Introduction

The Court of Justice has said that Articles 81 and 82 "seek to achieve the same aim on different levels, *viz,* the maintenance of effective competition within the common market".[1] The "level" at which Article 82 operates is that of seeking to neutralise the adverse consequences of an absence of effective competition. In short, it is about restraining market power.

Dominant undertakings may conduct their business efficiently, keeping down prices and maintaining or improving the quality of their product; indeed, the existence of a dominant position may have positive economic advantages, for example enabling the undertaking in question to pursue an adventurous research and development policy. On the other hand, insulation from competitive pressure is liable to encourage bad habits: for example an undertaking may choose to limit its output and charge higher prices. The function of Article 82 is to ensure that the market conduct of dominant undertakings remains consistent with the objectives of the E.C. Treaty. As the Court explained in the *Michelin* case:

"A finding that an undertaking has a dominant position is not in itself a recrimination but simply means that, irrespective of the reasons for which it has such a dominant position, the undertaking concerned has a special responsibility not to allow its conduct to impair genuine undistorted competition on the common market."[2]

Moreover, whilst the fact that an undertaking is in a dominant position cannot deprive it of its entitlement to protect its own commercial interests when they are attacked, and whilst such an undertaking must be allowed the right to take such reasonable steps as it deems appropriate to protect those interests, such behaviour will not be allowed if its purpose is to strengthen that dominant position and thereby abuse it.[3] Dominant undertakings are thus subject to legal obligations which are not incumbent on those with less economic power.

Article 82 provides:

"Any abuse by one or more undertakings of a dominant position within the common market or in a substantial part of it shall be prohibited as incompatible with the common market in so far as it may affect trade between Member States. Such abuse may, in particular, consist in:

---

[1] Case 6/72 *Europemballage and Continental Can v. Commission* [1973] E.C.R. 215 at 244; [1973] C.M.L.R. 199.

[2] Case 322/81 *NV Nederlandsche Banden-Industrie Michelin v. Commission* [1983] E.C.R. 3461 at 3511; [1985] 1 C.M.L.R. 282.

[3] Case 27/76 *The United Brands Company v. Commission* [1978] E.C.R. 207. para. 189; [1978] 1 C.M.L.R. 429.

(a) directly or indirectly imposing unfair purchase or selling prices or other unfair trading conditions;

(b) limiting production, markets or technical development to the prejudice of consumers;

(c) applying dissimilar conditions to equivalent transactions with other trading parties, thereby placing them at a competitive disadvantage;

(d) making the conclusion of contracts subject to acceptance by the other parties of supplementary obligations which, by their nature or according to commercial usage, have no connection with the subject of such contracts."

The concept of a dominant position

The E.C. Treaty does not define a dominant position,[4] but the meaning and scope of the concept have been clarified by the approach of the Commission and the case-law of the Court of Justice. Although the latter is, of course, the sole arbiter of the meaning of E.C. law concepts the Commission has adopted a Market Definition Notice[5] which provides a fruitful source of day-to-day practice.

The definition of a dominant position which has become the standard one was first put forward by the European Court in *United Brands*.[6] According to this definition, as formulated in the Court's *Michelin* judgment, a dominant position consists of:

"a position of economic strength enjoyed by an undertaking which enables it to hinder the maintenance of effective competition on the relevant market by allowing it to behave to an appreciable extent independently of its competitors and customers and ultimately of consumers."[7]

The concept, therefore, refers to the economic power of the undertaking concerned, which frees it from the constraints normally imposed by dealing at arm's length on a competitive market. This liberation is qualified, since the Court speaks of the "power to behave *to an appreciable extent* independently" (emphasis added). So understood, a dominant position is compatible with the survival of some competition.[8] It will be sufficient if the undertaking in question is able "at least to have an appreciable influence on the conditions under which that competition will develop, and in any case to act largely in disregard of it so long as such conduct does not operate to its detriment".[9]

Thus in the *United Brands* case it was admitted that UBC encountered very lively competition in Denmark and Germany during 1973 when other banana suppliers had mounted advertising and promotional campaigns and had cut their

---

[4] *cf.* Art. 66(7) ECSC which spoke of undertakings holding or acquiring "a dominant position shielding them against effective competition in a substantial part of the common market".

[5] [1997] O.J. C372/5; [1998] 1 C.M.L.R. 177.

[6] n.3, *supra*, at p. 277.

[7] [1984] E.C.R. at 3503, and reiterated on numerous occasions. See Case 85/76 *Hoffmann-La Roche v. Commission* [1979] E.C.R. 461 at 520; [1979] 3 C.M.L.R. 211; Case 31/80 *L'Oréal v. PVBA De Nieuwe AMCK* [1980] E.C.R. 3775 at 3793; [1981] 2 C.M.L.R. 235.

[8] Case 85/76 n.7, *supra*.

[9] *ibid.*, at 520.

prices; while in the Netherlands competition had pushed banana prices below those in Germany, which was traditionally a lower priced market. Indeed, the European Court seems to have accepted, for the sake of argument, UBC's claim that its banana division had made a loss over several years. However, not only was the competition limited in its duration and its geographical scope, it was also finally ineffective: UBC had suffered no significant reduction of its market share, while remaining the highest priced supplier. Of course, if UBC had been forced by the tactics of its competitors to sustain continuing losses over a long period, at some point its "overall independence of behaviour"[10] would have been put in question.[11]

Although dominant positions more often relate to the supply of goods or services, it must not be forgotten that they may also exist on the demand side. For instance Eurofima,[12] an agency set up by a number of national railway administrations to supply them with rolling stock of standard design, was regarded by the Commission as a dominant customer for a new form of passenger carriage for which tenders had been invited. The terms offered by Eurofima, which appeared to the Commission to be extremely harsh, were amended without a formal decision being necessary. Another example of dominance as a purchaser would be that of companies with the exclusive right to provide television services in a Member State, in respect of the market for materials for broadcasting.[13]

The existence of a dominant position

It is well-established in Community law that the process of determining the existence of a dominant position in a particular case should normally comprise two distinct stages: first the definition of the relevant market; and secondly, the assessment of the strength of the undertaking in question on that market. The Court has emphasised that for the purposes of examining a dominant position it is of "fundamental importance" to define the market in question and to define the substantial part of the common market in which the undertaking may be able to engage in abuses which hinder effective competition.[14]

The relevant market

This expression is used to designate the field of competitive forces within which the undertaking operates in either satisfying, or obtaining satisfaction of a certain demand. The aim of defining the relevant market is to differentiate

---

[10] A phrase used by the Commission in its Decision in the *Continental Can* case: [1972] J.O. L7/25 at L/35.

[11] In the *Michelin* case the Court similarly brushed aside the argument that NBIM had been incurring losses, remarking that "*temporary* unprofitability or even losses are not inconsistent with the existence of a dominant position" (emphasis added): [1983] E.C.R. at 3511.

[12] [1973] C.M.L.R. D217.

[13] See, *e.g.* the complaint that was the subject of the proceedings in Case 298/83 *C.I.C.C.E. v. Commission* [1985] E.C.R. 1105; [1986] 1 C.M.L.R. 486.

[14] Case C-242/95 *GT-Link v. DSB* [1997] E.C.R. I-4449, para. 36; [1997] 5 C.M.L.R. 601; affirmed in Case C-7/97 *Oscar Bronner v. Mediaprint* [1998] E.C.R. I-7791, para. 32.); [1999] 4 C.M.L.R. 112.

between those performances of other undertakings which must be taken into account in evaluating the position of the undertaking subject to the investigation, and those which can safely be left out of account for this purpose. The two main questions to be answered are how wide a range of products, and what geographical distribution of offers, should be covered by the evaluation. The timing of the offers is also likely to be significant. These three criteria of relevance—material, geographic and temporal—will be examined separately.

(i) The material product market

The definition of the product market is not always an easy matter because, on the one hand, things which are physically dissimilar may be in competition with regard to a particular application (for example, oil and gas domestic heating systems) while on the other hand, things which are physically similar may not be in competition (for example, tyres for heavy vehicles and tyres for vans or motor cars).[15] It will usually be an advantage for the undertaking in question to have the product market defined as widely as possible, since the greater the variety of products involved, the more difficult it will be to make out the existence of a dominant position.

Tests for delineating product markets and dominance have always provoked criticism and debate among economists.[16] The fundamental test for product differentiation is that of the interchangeability of product X and product Y as to their end uses. In the words of the European Court,

> ". . . the possibilities of competition must be judged in the context of the market comprising the totality of the products which, with respect to their characteristics, are particularly suitable for satisfying constant needs and are only to a limited extent interchangeable with other products."[17]

The Court has stressed, however, that examination should not be limited to the objective characteristics of the products in question: "the competitive conditions and the structure of supply and demand on the market must also be taken into consideration".[18] A test which sometimes proves useful, since it focuses on the real reactions of consumers, is "cross-elasticity of demand". By this is meant the degree to which sales of X increase in response to an increase in the price of Y; high elasticity, i.e. a substantial increase in the quantity of X sold when the price of Y rises only slightly, provides a clear indication of competition between the two products. There is also the narrower test in the case-law of "peculiar characteristics and uses", which makes the common sense point that highly specialised products are likely to be found on a separate market.[19]

The Commission's Market Definition Notice of 1997[20] specifically takes up the cross-elasticity approach, treating demand substitution as the most immediate

---

[15] See Case 322/81 *Michelin*, n.2, *supra* and the discussion, *infra*, of the issue of the relevant product market in that case.

[16] See Gyselen and Kyriazis, "Art. 86: Monopoly power measurement issue revisited" (1986) 11 E.L.Rev. 134.

[17] Case 31/80 *L'Oréal* , n.7, *supra*, at 3793.

[18] Case 322/81 *Michelin*, n.2, *supra*, at 3505.

[19] *e.g.* the different groups of vitamins in Case 85/76 *Hoffman-La Roche v. Commission*, n.7, *supra*.

[20] n.5, *supra*.

and effective disciplinary force on the suppliers of a given product, in particular in relation to their pricing decisions.[21] In an attempt to provide firms with transparency and certainty of guidance, the Commission's test[22] is whether the parties' customers would switch to readily available substitutes or to suppliers located elsewhere in response to a hypothetical small (in the range 5 to 10 per cent), permanent relative price increase in the products and areas being considered. Although this test does not as such contradict the Court's case-law it relies upon a statistical inquiry absent from the latter's more flexible approach.

The Court's position may be illustrated by its attitude to interchangeability in the *United Brands*[23] case on the supply of bananas to certain of the Member States. The proceedings arose out of the condemnation of the supplier concerned, the United Brands Company (UBC), by the Commission on four counts of abusive conduct contrary to what was then Article 86. According to the Commission, the product market consisted of "bananas of all varieties, where branded or unbranded". On the other hand, UBC argued that bananas formed part of the general market for fresh fruit: in other words, customers make their choice freely between bananas and other varieties of fruit on the basis of availability and relative prices. If this were so, even a very large supplier of bananas like UBC would not be at liberty to set prices within a wide range, since allowance would have to be made for the risk of potential customers altering their preferences (assuming of course that the same company did not control the supply of other fruits). The Court said that:

> "For the banana to be regarded as forming a market which is sufficiently differentiated from other fruit markets it must be possible for it to be singled out by such special features distinguishing it from other fruits that it is only to a limited extent interchangeable with them and it is only exposed to their competition in a way that is hardly perceptible."[24]

In the Court's view, the test was satisfied. It noted, in particular, the year-round excess of banana supplies over demand, which enabled marketing to be adapted to the seasonal fluctuations of other fruits. There was no evidence of "significant long term cross-elasticity", nor of "seasonal substitutability in general between the banana and all the seasonal fruits", the latter occurring only in Germany in respect of peaches and table grapes. Bananas, also, had characteristics enabling them to play an important part in the diet of a large section of the population comprising the very old, the very young and the sick. The constant needs of such consumers, and the limited and sporadic nature of the competition, justified recognition of the separate entity of the banana market.

The question arises whether, perhaps, the relevant market in this case ought to have been defined still more narrowly, in terms of a separate market for the "Chiquita" brand of UBC. Such fragmentation of the market might be the result of building up consumer preferences for the branded fruit by advertising and by maintaining a consistently high quality. That some development of this kind had

---

[21] *ibid.*, para. 13.
[22] *ibid.*, para. 17.
[23] n.3, *supra*.
[24] [1978] E.C.R. at 272.

taken place is suggested by the difference of 30 to 40 per cent between the prices of UBC's branded and unbranded bananas.[25] The Commission, however, did not examine this possibility in its Decision (so that there was no call for the Court to do so), presumably because it felt sufficiently confident of proving the dominance of UBC on the general banana market; had there been any doubt on the matter it might have seemed worthwhile to establish the independence of the narrower market.

Interchangeability must also be considered on the supply side of the market as well as on the demand side, although it is clear from the Market Definition Notice that the Commission treats this as a secondary consideration for use where demand substitution would be inappropriate. It will be relevant, for example,[26] in situations where companies market a wide range of qualities or grades of one product; even if for a given final customer or group of consumers, the different qualities are not substitutable, the different qualities will be grouped into one product market, provided that most of the suppliers are able to offer and sell the various qualities immediately and without incurring significant additional costs or risks. The Commission cites paper as a practical example, so that standard writing paper and high quality artwork paper might not be interchangeable in terms of demand yet would still fall within the same product group on the basis that paper plants are prepared to switch swiftly, with negligible costs and no particular difficulties of distribution, between the different qualities.

Supply-side considerations were responsible for the Court's quashing of the Commission's Decision in *Continental Can*.[27] The Commission had found that the acquisition of a Dutch packaging firm, TDV, by the Continental Can subsidiary, Europemballage Corporation, amounted to an abuse of the dominant position which the American firm enjoyed, through its German subsidiary, SLW, on the market in Germany for meat tins, fish tins and metal closures for glass jars; the abuse consisting of an unacceptable strengthening of SLW's position on the markets concerned since, in the Commission's view, TDV had been a potential competitor of SLW. The main ground for the annulment of the Decision was that the Commission had not shown convincingly why manufacturers, for example of tins for vegetables, condensed milk, olive oil or fruit juice could not, by making some adaptation to their product, enter the field as serious competitors to SLW, if the latter raised its prices unduly. The Commission was also criticised for not dealing adequately with the possibility that SLW's major customers might begin to manufacture the relevant types of container themselves. The essence of these objections was that potential competition from new products or new producers ("elasticity of supply") had not been ruled out.

On occasions it may be necessary to combine demand and supply substitution tests in order to define the relevant market. This was the case in *Michelin*,[28] concerning a Decision of the Commission that NBIM, the Dutch subsidiary of the Michelin tyre group, was guilty of infringing the predecessor of Article 82

---

[25] See the note by Korah on the Decision of the Commission (1975–76) 1 E.L. Rev. 322 at p. 324.
[26] Market Definition Notice, n.5, *supra*, para. 21.
[27] n.1, *supra*.
[28] n.2, *supra*.

because of certain terms included in the contracts under which it supplied
dealers. The Court of Justice approved the Commission's definition of the
market as that in new "replacement" tyres for heavy vehicles. This market was
distinguishable from: (a) the market in "original equipment" tyres; (b) the
market in tyres for cars and light vans; and (c) the market in retreads. As to (a),
it was common ground that the structure of demand for replacements was
entirely different from that for original equipment tyres, although they were
identical products: while the former were supplied to dealers for retail sale, the
latter were supplied to manufacturers to be fitted to new vehicles. As to (b),
besides the lack of interchangeability at user level between car and van tyres and
heavy vehicle tyres, there was again a difference of demand structures. For car
and van drivers the purchase of tyres was an occasional event; whereas buyers of
heavy vehicle tyres were normally haulage undertakings for which tyres represented an important business cost and which expected specialised advice and
services from dealers. Nor was there elasticity of supply between tyres for light
and heavy vehicles: the time and expenditure needed to switch production from
one to the other made this impracticable as a way of responding to fluctuations
in demand.[29] As to (c), the Court acknowledged that retreads were to some
extent interchangeable, and hence in competition, with new tyres, but not
sufficiently to undermine a dominant position on the market for the latter. Some
consumers had reservations, whether rightly or wrongly, about the safety and
reliability of retreads. In addition, a significant proportion of retreads used by
transport undertakings were made to order from their own tyre carcasses. These
would not compete with new tyres, since their production involved the provision
of a service directly by retreading firms to the tyre owners. A further consideration was the dependence of the market for retreads, with respect to price and
supply, on the market for new tyres. Every retread must have started life as a new
tyre; and there was a limit to the number of times retreading could be done. So a
dominant supplier of new tyres would have a privileged position *vis-à-vis*
retreading undertakings. On an opposite tack, NBIM had suggested that the
various types and sizes of tyres for heavy vehicles could be regarded as belonging
to separate markets, because from a user's point of view they were not
interchangeable. That suggestion was rejected by the Court on the ground that
dealers had to be ready to meet demand from their customers for the whole
range of such tyres. Also, in the absence of specialisation on the part of the
undertakings concerned, the similarity between heavy vehicle tyres of different
types and sizes and the way in which they complemented one another at the
technical level meant they were subject to the same conditions of competition on
the market.

When acquiring evidence of the interchangeability of products, the conditions
of competition and/or structure of supply and demand on the market in question

---

[29] The Court noted that in 1977, when there was a shortfall in the supply of heavy vehicle tyres,
NBIM chose to grant an extra bonus rather than use surplus car tyre capacity to meet demand;
[1983] E.C.R. at 3506. *cf.* the *Continental Can* case, n.1, *supra*, where the Decision of the
Commission adverted to the barriers to market entry confronting possible competitors, notably the
size of the necessary investments, but the Court did not think the burden of proof had been
discharged.

must be examined.[30] Thus in answering a request for a preliminary ruling in Oscar Bronner,[31] the Court replied that it was for the national court to determine whether home-delivery schemes for daily newspapers constituted a separate market, or whether other methods of distribution, such as sale in shops or at kiosks or delivery by post, were sufficiently interchangeable to have to be taken into account as well. Furthermore, the possibility of regional delivery schemes being interchangeable with Mediaprint's nationwide network would also need to be examined.

The complexity of the task involved in measuring interchangeability can be seen from the case of Tiercé Ladbroke.[32] Central to the dispute was the question whether there was a general market in the transmission of horse races in sound and pictures or whether there was a distinct market in coverage by French sound and pictures. Tiercé Ladbroke ("Ladbroke") ran a bookmaking business taking bets in Belgium on races run abroad. In Belgium the only sound and pictures available in betting shops were of British races, but 60 per cent of bets placed were on French races. The companies holding the rights to televised coverage of French races in France and Germany had refused to allow Ladbroke to retransmit the races in its Belgian shops. Ladbroke unsuccessfully complained to the Commission that this refusal was an abuse of a dominant position. The Commission took the view that the relevant product market was for retransmission of horse races in sound and pictures generally, basing this on an examination of the German market, where French races were already transmitted in parallel with other races. It had done this because in Belgium the only foreign races were British, so that it was impossible to verify the substitutability of French races in a Belgian context. The evidence from the German market was that although 40 per cent of the bets placed there were on French races, 40 per cent on German races and 20 per cent on British races, 67 per cent of bookmakers chose to receive the French sound and pictures, 23 per cent opted for British race transmissions and 10 per cent chose both networks. According to the Commission, and upheld by the Court of First Instance, these features of the German market showed that sound and picture coverage of French races was not unique. Moreover, the fact that in Belgium 60 per cent of bets were on (unseen) French races despite the presence of televised coverage of British races further indicated that a betting outlet's purchase of retransmitted sound and pictures could not be based solely on the bettors' wish to see only races on which they have placed bets.

Prior economic choices by a consumer may narrow the range of offers from which future demands have to be met. This phenomenon is sometimes referred to as "lock-in".[33] It operates where the opportunity cost of reversing a choice is felt to outweigh the advantages in the longer term of doing so. For instance, oil, gas and other domestic fuels may form a single market from the point of view of a person contemplating the installation of a new central heating system, but not after one or other system has been installed. Similar reasoning may apply where

---

[30] A more detailed list of factors examined by the Commission can be found in Part III of its Market Definition Notice, n.5, supra.

[31] Case C–7/97, n.14, supra.

[32] Case T–504/93 Tiercé Ladbroke v. Commission [1997] E.C.R. II-923.

[33] See the discussion of lock-in by Gyselen and Kyriazis, op. cit. n.16, supra, at pp. 143–144.

spare parts for a consumer durable are available only from the manufacturer. In such situations the spare parts from another product may be wholly useless for the durable in question. Moreover, supply-side substitution may be impossible because of the existence of intellectual property rights. In *Hugin*,[34] the Court found that most of the spare parts for Hugin cash registers were not interchangeable with parts made to fit any other type of machine, so that the operator of an independent maintenance, repair or reconditioning business, was entirely dependent on Hugin for supplies. The relevant market was, accordingly, that for Hugin spare parts required by such businesses. This was a crucial issue in the case, since the share held by Hugin of the market for cash registers as such was very modest.[35] A similarly restricted view of the relevant market was taken in *Hilti*,[36] where nails and cartridges were seen as distinct markets from the nail guns in which they were to be used as fastenings in the construction industry. This finding was based not on classes of user, as in *Hugin*, but primarily on the existence of independent suppliers of nails and cartridges for use in Hilti nail guns, together with the fact that nails and nail guns are not necessarily purchased together.

Another way of limiting the relevant market adopted by the Commission has been to identify targetable submarkets. Thus in *Napier Brown/British Sugar*[37] the Commission was able to distinguish retail and industrial customers as submarkets for granulated sugar. The *Magill*[38] litigation over TV programme listings (see below) also accepted the notion of submarkets, treating markets for weekly programme listings of television broadcasts and the magazines in which they were published as distinct submarkets within the market for television programme information in general.

A different issue in *Commercial Solvents*[39] was whether the market for a raw material (or base or intermediate product) may be considered separately from the market for the end product. The case arose from a complaint to the Commission by the Italian pharmaceutical firm, Zoja, that CSC, through its Italian subsidiary, Istituto, had refused to supply it with aminobutanol, the base product for the manufacture of the drug ethambutol, which was used in the treatment of tuberculosis. CSC contended, *inter alia*, that the relevant market could not be that for aminobutanol, on which its dominance was relatively easy to prove, since the derivative, ethambutol, formed part of a wider market for antitubercular drugs. With this the Court disagreed:

---

[34] Case 22/78 *Hugin Kassaregister AB v. Commission* [1979] E.C.R. 1869; [1979] 3 C.M.L.R. 345. For criticism, see Baden Fuller (1979) 4 E.L.Rev. 423, at 426–427.

[35] Hugin had a market share of 12%. in the common market as a whole and 13% in the U.K. Its largest competitor, the American company, National Cash Register had shares of 36% and 40% respectively.

[36] Case C–53/92 P *Hilti A.-G. v. Commission* [1994] E.C.R. I–667; [1994] 4 C.M.L.R. 614, upholding the findings of the Court of First Instance in Case T–30/89 [1991] E.C.R. II–1439; [1992] 4 C.M.L.R. 16.

[37] [1988] O.J. L284/41; [1990] 4 C.M.L.R. 196.

[38] Joined Cases C–241–242/91 P *RTE and ITP v. Commission* [1995] E.C.R. I–743; [1995] 4 C.M.L.R. 718. However, it may be noted that the Court also referred to the analogy of raw materials discussed in *Commercial Solvents*, n.39, *infra*.

[39] Cases 6–7/73 *Istituto Chemioterapico Italiano and Commercial Solvents Corporation v. Commission* [1974] E.C.R. 223; [1974] 1 C.M.L.R. 309.

"Contrary to the arguments of the applicants it is in fact possible to distinguish the market in raw material necessary for the manufacture of a product from the market on which the product is sold. An abuse of a dominant position on the market in raw materials may thus have effects restricting competition in the market on which the derivatives of the raw material are sold and these effects must be taken into account when considering the effects of an infringement, even if the market for the derivative does not constitute a self-contained market."[40]

Thus, according to the Court, the raw material may constitute a relevant market in its own right; but it may still be valid, in determining whether a dominant position on that market has been abused, to take into account any anti-competitive effects which may have been felt on the market for the derivative. This problem of the relevance of potentially separate markets is especially acute in the context of vertically integrated organisations, whose behaviour in one market may produce or be directed towards effects in others. In *AKZO*[41] the abuse in the benzoyl oxide market occurred as a result of predatory pricing in the flour additives market.

(ii) The geographic criterion

The geographic distribution of producers and consumers may prevent effective competition taking place between goods or services which in other circumstances would be readily interchangeable. For instance, a motorway café may be able to set its prices within a very wide range, because travellers are unwilling to make a detour in search of equivalent services offered by other establishments in the neighbourhood. It is, therefore, necessary in defining a relevant market for the purpose of Article 82 to identify the specific territory within which the interplay of supply and demand is to be considered. The starting point will normally be the sales area of the undertaking concerned, and the question will be whether the geographic market is co-terminous with that area, or wider or narrower in extent. Once the relevant geographic unit has been established, a further question arises as to whether it constitutes a sufficiently substantial part of the common market.

The area must first be identified as one "where the conditions of competition are sufficiently homogeneous for the effect of the economic power of the undertaking to be able to be evaluated".[42] In *United Brands* it was held that the Commission had been right to exclude France, Italy and the United Kingdom from the relevant market because, for historical reasons, each of these Member States applied a different preferential system in respect of banana imports (for example, Commonwealth preference in the United Kingdom). On the other hand, a system of free competition was common to the six Member States included in the market. It is possible for there to be a Community-wide market even though there is varying demand within different Member States.[43]

---

[40] *ibid.*, 249–250.
[41] Case C–62/86 *AKZO v. Commission* [1991] E.C.R. I–3359; [1993] 5 C.M.L.R. 215.
[42] Case 27/76 *United Brands*, n.3, *supra*.
[43] *Tetra Pak I* [1988] O.J. L272/77; [1990] 4 C.M.L.R. 47.

In its Market Definition Notice[44] the Commission lists the type of evidence relevant to determine a geographic market as follows: past evidence of diversion of orders to other areas, basic demand characteristics (such as preferences for national brands, language, culture and life style), views of customers and competitors, current geographic pattern of purchases, trade flows/patterns of shipments (where statistics are sufficiently detailed for the relevant products) and barriers and costs connected with switching orders to companies in other areas. The impact of transportation costs is particularly relevant for the last-mentioned consideration, especially in relation to bulky, low-value products.

It might be expected that the significance of distinct national geographic markets will diminish as integration continues in the context of an evolving single Community-wide market. Certainly, the Commission has indicated[45] that it will use caution in assessing past evidence which only reflects national markets artificially isolated by legislative obstacles since removed. Nevertheless, numerous examples can still be found of geographic markets which present sufficiently distinctive national conditions. In *Tiercé Ladbroke*[46] the Court of First Instance found that the conditions existing on the market in sound and pictures had to be considered in relation to betting outlets. This was because the latter constituted the demand-side for sound and pictures for retransmission to final consumers (the punters), with the result that the conditions in which the downstream market in sound and pictures operated were determined by the conditions under which the main betting market was conducted.[47] The conditions in which the main betting market operated were characterised by close geographical links between punters and betting outlets, insofar as the mobility of punters is necessarily limited and marginal. The effect of that proximity was that competition between betting outlets developed within geographical areas which, considered as a whole, could not in any event extend beyond national boundaries. Since the geographic betting market was national, this also had to be the case for the ancillary market in sound and pictures.[48]

Having identified the appropriate geographic area, it must then be considered whether it amounts to a "substantial part" of the common market. The test to be applied is not the geographic extent of the territory in question but the economic importance of the market situated there. This was made clear in the *Sugar* judgment where the Court said:

"For the purpose of determining whether a specific territory is large enough to amount to 'a substantial part of the common market' . . . the pattern and volume of the production and consumption of the said product as well as the habits and economic opportunities of vendors and purchasers must be considered."[49]

---

[44] n.5, *supra*, paras 44–52.

[45] *ibid.*, para. 32.

[46] n.32, *supra*.

[47] *ibid.*, para. 103 of judgment.

[48] *ibid.*, paras 106–107. The relevant *product* market, as discussed earlier, was not confined to national limits.

[49] Joined Cases 40–48, 50, 54–56, 11, 113 and 114/73 *Suiker Unie and others v. Commission* [1975] E.C.R. 1663, at 1977; [1976] 1 C.M.L.R. 295.

On this basis the Belgo-Luxembourg market and the southern part of Germany were considered a substantial part of the common market.

A market amounting to a substantial part of the common market may cover a number of Member States or a single Member State[50] or parts of one or more Member States. In a number of cases single ports or other economic hubs have been held to satisfy the "substantial" criterion. Thus, in *Merci Convenzionali Porto di Genova*[51] the Court held that regard must be had to the volume of traffic in the port in question and its importance in relation to maritime import and export operations as a whole in the Member State concerned.

(iii) The temporal criterion
Market power will only give a dominant position if it is capable of enduring for a considerable time. The prospect of substitutes becoming available in the short run limits freedom of action because of the risk of future defections by customers.[52] The market on which an undertaking operates may fluctuate from time to time with respect both to the range of products and the geographical area covered. For example, if the view had been taken in *United Brands* that the demand for bananas was seriously affected by the availability of various seasonal fruits, it might have concluded that bananas formed part of a series of different markets at different times of the year; and it would have followed that the position of UBC must be examined in relation to each of these markets. Another example is provided by *Commercial Solvents*. It had been argued by CSC that the manufacture of ethambutol was possible by processes other than that involving aminobutanol. However, the Court held that the processes in questions were still of an experimental nature and incapable at the material time of being used for production on an industrial scale. They, therefore, did not constitute a realistic alternative for the customer, Zoja.[53]

The criteria of dominance
The existence of a dominant position may derive from several factors which, taken separately, are not necessarily decisive. The most frequently used indicators are discussed below.

(i) Market share
The most important factor is the size of the undertaking's share of the relevant market. According to the Court, extremely large market shares are in themselves, save in exceptional circumstances, evidence of the existence of a dominant

---

[50] Case 322/81 *Michelin*, n.2, *supra*; Case C–323/93 *Centre d'Insémination de la Crespelle* [1994] E.C.R. I–5077; Case C–7/97 *Oscar Bronner*, n.14, *supra*. In Case 77/77 *BP v. Commission* [1978] E.C.R. 1511; [1978] 3 C.M.L.R. 174 Advocate General Warner observed, at 1537, that he would "shrink from" saying that a monopoly held in Luxembourg would be insubstantial, even though the population of that State was 0.23% of the whole Community.

[51] Case C–179/90 [1991] E.C.R. I–5889, at para. 15; [1994] 4 C.M.L.R. 422; reiterated in Case C–242/95 *GT-Link*, n.14, *supra*, para. 37. See also Case C–163/96 *Raso and others* [1998] E.C.R. I–533; [1998] 4 C.M.L.R 737 where the port of La Spezia was also held to a substantial part of the common market, being the leading Mediterranean port for container traffic.

[52] Gyeselen and Kyriazis, *op. cit.* n.16, *supra* stress that market power only gives cause for concern if it is a long-run phenomenon.

[53] [1973] E.C.R. at 248.

position.[54] Not surprisingly, monopolies will constitute dominance even where that position is the result of statute or other legal means.[55] A market share of over 50 per cent will also in itself give rise to dominance.[56] Where the share of the market held by the undertaking is smaller, other factors take on increased significance. Thus, in *United Brands*, the European Court cited as a consideration affording evidence of "preponderant strength" the fact that UBC's percentage of the market was several times greater than that of Castle and Cooke (16 per cent.) which was its nearest competitor, with the remaining market participants well behind.[57]

(ii) Barriers to market entry

Even a very large market share can be rapidly eroded when the market is penetrated by lively new competitors. A careful analysis of a dominant position should, therefore, refer to any advantages enjoyed by the undertaking in question, or to any difficulties in the way of potential market entrants, making it unlikely that the structure of the market will change radically in the shorter run.

This might be the case, for example, because the undertaking controls essential patents or know-how; or because, like UBC, it is vertically integrated, with privileged access to supplies, means of transport and distribution outlets;[58] or because, like Michelin, it has a well-developed network of commercial representatives providing continuous contact with customers;[59] or because of its technical superiority[60], its range of products[61] or a strong brand image resulting from advertising.[62] Established consumer preferences may also act as barriers, as in *British Midland/Aer Lingus*[63] where the Commission noted that Irish nationals preferred to use the national airline.

From the point of view of a potential competitor the chief difficulty in overcoming such advantages would be that of cost. Very large resources may be needed, for example, to finance independent research or countervailing advertising. The crucial consideration will be the range within which the undertaking is free to fix its prices without making it commercially attractive for others to risk the investment required in order to mount a challenge. Also in the present

---

[54] Case 85/76 *Hoffmann-La Roche*, n.7, *supra*; Case C–62/86 *AKZO*, n.41, *supra*; Joined Cases T–24–26 and 28/93 *Compagnie Maritime Belge Transports v. Commission* [1996] E.C.R. II-1201; [1997] 4 C.M.L.R. 273; Case T–228/97 *Irish Sugar plc v. Commission* [1999] 5 C.M.L.R. 1300.

[55] Case 26/75 *General Motors Continental v. Commission* [1975] E.C.R. 1367; [1976] 1 C.M.L.R. 95; Case 13/77 *INNO v. ATAB* [1977] E.C.R. 2115; [1978] 1 C.M.L.R. 283; Case 41/83 *Italy v. Commission (British Telecom)* [1985] E.C.R. 873; [1985] 2 C.M.L.R. 368; Case C–163/96 *Raso and others*, n.51, *supra*.

[56] Case C–62/86 *AKZO*, n.41, *supra*, at para. 60.

[57] [1978] E.C.R. at 282–283. See also Case 85/76 *Hoffmann-La Roche v. Commission*, n.7, *supra*, where the smallness of its competitors' market shares helped to establish the dominance of Roche on the markets for Vitamins A, C and E.

[58] Case 27/76 [1978] E.C.R. at 278–280.

[59] Case 322/81 [1983] E.C.R. at 3511. See also the reference to "a highly developed sales network" in Case 85/76 *Hoffmann-La Roche* [1979] E.C.R. at 524.

[60] Case C–53/92 P *Hilti*, n.36, *supra*.

[61] Case 322/81 *Michelin*, n.2, *supra*, at para. 55.

[62] Case 27/76 *United Brands*, n.3, *supra*, at para. 91.

[63] Dec. 92/213 [1992] O.J. L96/34; [1993] 4 C.M.L.R. 596. Aer Lingus' market share was also high, being 75% of the London Heathrow—Dublin route.

context it is important to bear in mind the time factor. The possibility that, at the end of a very long period of development, another undertaking may succeed in establishing itself as a serious competitor would not normally be sufficient to impair an existing dominant position.[64]

(iii) Financial resources

The ability of an undertaking to command finance is bound to enhance its freedom of action. In particular, it will allow the undertaking to keep abreast of the latest developments in technology, to adapt rapidly to changes in the pattern of demand and to expand its operation, either vertically or horizontally. Thus, in *Continental Can*[65] the Commission drew attention to the fact that Continental Can, because of its large size, was able to resort to the international capital market and had done so to finance the acquisition which constituted the alleged abuse. The concept of parent companies and their subsidiaries all forming part of the same undertaking is important in the present context.[66] Its consequences may be particularly striking where the undertaking concerned is a conglomerate, *i.e.* a business group having interests in a wide variety of separate economic sectors.

(iv) Conduct and performance of the undertaking

The criteria examined so far have related to the structure of the market,[67] *i.e.* the reasonably stable features of the competitive environment within which the undertaking operates and to which accordingly its decisions must be adjusted, and of the undertaking itself, *i.e.* its general organisation and resources both for the purposes of the particular line of business in question and for any other purpose having a bearing on that business. It remains to say something about the behavioural criteria of dominance, consisting of the conduct and performance of the undertaking on the relevant market. Roughly speaking, by "conduct" is meant the activities pursued by the undertaking in the course of its business, for example, its policies on pricing, output and sales promotion[68]; and by "performance" is meant the result of these activities, for example, the level of profits, the efficiency of production of the quality and range of the goods produced.[69]

Writers have warned of the dangers of inferring dominance from such considerations.[70] Given that in practice the competitive process works more or less imperfectly, it may be possible for an undertaking to make very large profits, to limit its output or to impose discriminatory prices, although it does not enjoy market power amounting to dominance. On the other hand, a monopolist wishing to safeguard his long-term position may treat his customers relatively benignly. Predatory practices such as local price cutting may be an indication of a wish to acquire a dominant position, rather than of dominance already achieved.

---

[64] See the very full analysis of those features of UBC's banana operation which the European Court regarded as contributing to its retention of a large market share: [1978] E.C.R. at 278–281.

[65] [1972] J.O. L7/25.

[66] See the discussion, *supra*, Chap. 19.

[67] This definition is taken from the discussion in Joliet in *Monopolization and Abuse of Dominant Position* (Nijhoff, 1970), pp. 25–26.

[68] See *ibid.*, pp. 27–28.

[69] See *ibid.*, pp. 29–30.

[70] See *ibid.*, pp. 96 *et seq.* and references. See also Gyselen and Kyriazis, n.16, *supra*, at pp. 135–137.

The better view is, therefore, that behavioural evidence should not normally be treated as sufficient in itself to establish the existence of a dominant position. Otherwise there is the real risk that the fact that particular behaviour, alleged to be abusive, could occur at all becomes the rationalisation for the existence of dominance. However, behavioural considerations may be invoked to corroborate the evidence resulting from a structural analysis. It will be more persuasive, the longer the conduct or performance in question is found to have continued.

In *United Brands*, the European Court was faced with a choice between two performance criteria: the loss which UBC claimed that its banana division had suffered from 1951 to 1976; and the success of UBC in retaining its share of the banana market against vigorous competition. Because it accorded with the impression of overall strength gained from a structural analysis of the relevant market, the Court gave greater weight to the latter.[71]

The concept of joint or collective dominance

The concept of an undertaking was examined in Chapter 19. It will be remembered that legally distinct companies may be regarded as forming a single undertaking, if in practice they are subject to common control. The importance of this principle in the context of Article 82 is that, in determining whether the conduct of one member of a group constitutes an abuse of a dominant position on a relevant market within the common market, it may be possible to take into account the economic strength of other members of the group, some or all of them established in third countries. For example, in *Commercial Solvents*[72] it was CSC's control over world supplies of aminobutanol that gave Istituto a dominant position on the common market; CSC was legally answerable for Istituto's refusal to supply Zoja.

A more controversial use of the phrase "one or more undertakings" in Article 82 involves its attachment to so-called joint or collective dominance by non-connected firms. The Commission tried on a number of occasions in the 1970s to use the concept as a way of strengthening its enforcement armoury and avoiding any gap in the regulatory scheme resulting from Articles 81 and 82. In markets where a limited number of undertakings have comparable market shares and exhibit closely parallel conduct there could be no investigation under Article 81 without evidence of collusion. Yet no undertaking, individually, would be dominant either, so Article 82 would also be inapplicable unless some notion of collective or joint dominance could be invoked. After early resistance by the European Court to the idea,[73] it is now clear that collective dominance is embraced by Article 82. However, the exact scope of the doctrine is still evolving.

The first real judicial endorsement of the idea came from the Court of First Instance in *Italian Flat Glass*,[74] where it stated:

---

[71] [1978] E.C.R. at 284–285.

[72] Cases 6–7/73, n.39, *supra*.

[73] See Case 85/76 *Hoffmann-La Roche*, n.7, *supra*; also Case 247/86 *Alsatel* [1988] E.C.R. 5987; [1990] 4 C.M.L.R. 434, where the Court did not take up the Commission's arguments.

[74] Joined Cases T–68, 77 and 78/89 *SIV and others v. Commission* [1992] E.C.R. II-1403; [1992] 5 C.M.L.R. 302.

"There is nothing, in principle, to prevent two or more independent economic entities from being, on a specific market, united by such economic links that, by virtue of that fact, together they hold a dominant position *vis-à-vis* the other operators on the same market. This could be the case, for example, where two or more independent undertakings jointly have, through agreements or licences, a technological lead affording them the power to behave to an appreciable extent independently of their competitors, their customers and ultimately of their consumers."[75]

This approach was still limited, being based on the need for links between the undertakings rather than on market structure *simpliciter*. On the facts, the Commission had failed to adduce sufficient evidence to make out its claim. Nevertheless, the principle of collective dominance was subsequently developed by the Court of Justice in the context both of Article 82 and the Merger Regulation.[76]

These cases confirm that a joint dominant position consists in a number of undertakings being able together, in particular because of factors giving rise to a connection between them, to adopt a common policy on the market.[77] In *Almelo*, for example, the issue left to be determined by the national court was whether the requisite links between the regional electricity suppliers in question were "sufficiently strong". One such factor was that the contracts between the regional distributors and local purchasers had common exclusive purchasing conditions. The links allegedly present in the *Flat Glass* case included structural ties relating to production in the form of systematic exchange of products between the three producers. In *Irish Sugar*[78] the Court of First Instance did not disturb the Commission's findings that Irish Sugar occupied a joint dominant position on the Irish granulated sugar market with Sugar Distribution Holdings (SDH), the latter being the parent company of the principal distributor (SDL) in that market. The factors relied upon by the Commission were Irish Sugar's 51 per cent shareholding in SDH, its representation on the boards of SDH and SDL, the policy-making structure of the companies and the communication process established to facilitate it, and the direct economic ties constituted by SDL's commitment to obtain its supplies exclusively from Irish Sugar and the latter's financing of all consumer promotions and rebates offered by SDL to its customers.

In the same case, the Court of First Instance specifically ruled out the applicant's contention that the concept of joint dominance is inapplicable to two or more undertakings in a vertical relationship.[79] To have accepted that proposition would have left a lacuna in the application of Article 82 in relation to

---

[75] *ibid.*, para. 358.

[76] Reg. 4064/89 on the control of concentrations between undertakings; [1990] O.J. L257/13, amended by Reg. 1310/97; [1997] O.J. L180/1, see Chap. 23.

[77] Case C–393/92 *Almelo* [1994] E.C.R. I–1477, at para. 42; Case C–96/94 *Centro Servizi Spediporto v. Spedizioni Marittima del Golfo* [1995] E.C.R. I–2883, paras 32–33; [1996] 4 C.M.L.R. 613; Joined Cases C–140–142/94 *DIP and others* [1995] E.C.R. I–3257, para. 26; [1996] 4 C.M.L.R. 157; Case C–70/95 *Sodemare and others v. Regione Lombardia* [1997] E.C.R. I–3395, paras 45–46; [1998] 4 C.M.L.R. 667.

[78] Case T–228/97, n.54, *supra*.

[79] *ibid.*, para. 63.

firms which, though not integrated into a single undertaking, abusively exploited a position of joint power. The Court of First Instance also emphasised that in cases of joint dominance the abuse does not necessarily have to be the action of all the undertakings in question. It only has to be capable of being identified as one of the manifestations of such a joint dominant position being held. Therefore, undertakings occupying a joint dominant position may engage in joint or individual abusive conduct.[80]

One issue which remains difficult is whether the notion of collective dominance applicable under Article 82 is affected by the tests used under the Merger Regulation. The essential difference between the provisions in this context is that whereas the former is concerned only with abuses of market power, the rationale of the Regulation is based on the curbing of prospective changes which would undermine an effective market structure. This might explain any apparent divergence in the language used in the case-law from the two areas. In *France and others v. Commission*,[81] the first case to uphold the application of joint dominance to the Merger Regulation, the Court of Justice referred to the need to establish an impediment to effective competition arising in particular from "correlative factors" existing between the undertakings involved in the concentration. The Court of First Instance, in the subsequent case of *Gencor*,[82] observed that it had referred to structural links in *Flat Glass* only by way of example and had not laid down that such links must exist for a finding of collective dominance to be made.[83] Crucially, it went on to state:

". . . there is no reason whatsoever in legal or economic terms to exclude from the notion of economic links the relationship of interdependence existing between the parties to a tight oligopoly within which, in a market with the appropriate characteristics, in particular in terms of market concentration, transparency and product homogeneity, those parties are in a position to anticipate one another's behaviour and are therefore strongly encouraged to align their conduct in the market, in particular in such a way as to maximise their joint profits by restricting production with a view to increasing prices . . ."[84]

If this stance is not confined to the Merger Regulation context in which it was adopted, it would seem to redefine and enlarge the scope of Article 82 by indicating that the structure of the market can itself be the "links" necessary to satisfy the *Almelo* and *Flat Glass* tests. Support for this view can be found in the subsequent paragraph in *Gencor*, where the Court of First Instance referred to its conclusion being "all the more pertinent" for mergers, thereby suggesting that the principle was not confined to that arena.

---

[80] *ibid.*, para. 66.
[81] Joined Cases C–68/94 and C–30/95 [1998] E.C.R. I–1375, at para. 221; [1998] 4 C.M.L.R. 829.
[82] Case T–102/96 *Gencor Ltd v. Commission* [1999] 4 C.M.L.R. 971. See Porter Elliott, "The Gencor judgment: collective dominance, remedies and extraterritoriality under the Merger Regulation" (1999) 24 E.L.Rev. 638.
[83] Para. 273 of judgment in *Gencor*, n.82, *supra*.
[84] *ibid.*, para. 276.

The concept of an abuse

The wording of Article 82 indicates that the existence of a dominant position does not in itself attract the prohibition contained in the Article.[85] But whilst not unlawful, it is clear that dominance creates special obligations for the undertakings concerned,[86] so that they must not abuse their power. There is no definition of abuse in the E.C. Treaty, and the instances listed in Article 82 itself (such as unfair pricing or limiting production) are only non-exhaustive examples.[87] However, the Court of Justice gave what has become a benchmark test of abuse in *Hoffmann-La Roche*:

> "The concept of abuse is an objective concept relating to the behaviour of an undertaking in a dominant position which is such as to influence the structure of a market where, as a result of the very presence of the undertaking in question, the degree of competition is weakened and which, through recourse to methods different from those which condition normal competition in products or services on the basis of the transactions of commercial operators, has the effect of hindering the maintenance of the degree of competition still existing in the market or the growth of that competition."[88]

A number of general observations may be made from this starting point and its later applications.

First, there is a potential tension in the notion of abuse in so far as it is not expressly directed at the protection of one particular set of interests.[89] So-called exploitative abuses, such as excessive pricing, tend to harm consumers. On the other hand, anti-competitive conduct, such as predatory pricing or tying contracts, may more directly affect other actual or potential firms in the market. Both types of abuse are caught by Article 82. In addition, it was made clear at an early stage in the case-law that the provision was not confined to behavioural abuses but could also cover the strengthening of dominance by structural means such as the acquisition of competitors.[90]

Secondly, abuse is an objective concept, requiring neither an intention to harm nor any morally reprehensible dimension. However, it is also immensely flexible. There is no formal exemption system in Article 82 corresponding to Article 81(3), but conduct may escape condemnation as abuse if it can be objectively justified. Examples can be found in the cases relating to refusals to deal, discussed further below. As the above extract from the Court also shows, the test

---

[85] However, as discussed in the context of Art. 86 (Chap. 25, *infra*), the Court has developed an "inevitable abuse" doctrine in relation to certain situations involving the creation and exercise of exclusive rights; see principally Case C–41/90 *Höfner v. Macrotron* [1991] E.C.R. I–1979; [1993] 4 C.M.L.R. 306; also Case C–55/96 *Job Centre Coop* [1997] E.C.R. I–7119, paras 34–35; [1998] 4 C.M.L.R. 708.

[86] See the passage quoted from the *Michelin* judgment, text accompanying n.2, *supra*.

[87] Case 6/72 *Continental Can*, n.1, *supra*.

[88] Case 85/76 n.7, *supra* at 541.

[89] Although in Case C–7–97 *Oscar Bronner*, n.14, *supra*, Advocate General Jacobs observed that the "primary" purpose of Art. 82 was to protect consumers, rather than safeguarding the position of particular competitors.

[90] Case 6/72 *Continental Can*, n.1, *supra*. Discussion of the (now residual) relevance of Art. 82 to merger control is postponed to Chap. 23.

of abuse invites a judgment as to what is "abnormal" without very clear guidance as to what might be normal. There is thus considerable room for debate whether particular conduct is a firm's rational response to meet the challenge of competition or if it is abusive. This problem is highlighted in developments concerning discriminatory pricing,[91] discussed below.

Thirdly, there is the question of causation. Must the undertaking have used its power as the means of achieving the result which is regarded as objectionable? Ever since *Continental Can* it has been clear that the Court does not require a causal relationship of this type. As a result, an allegation of abuse cannot be negated by evidence that the same conduct is pursued by non-dominant firms or is a normal practice in the market concerned. Moreover, the abuse does not necessarily have to be committed in the same market as the one in which the firm is dominant. It may affect downstream or neighbouring markets, as in the *CBEM* case,[92] where action by an undertaking dominant on the television broadcasting market had abusive effects in the telemarketing services market. Conversely, conduct on a different market which strengthens the undertaking's position in the dominated market will also be caught.[93] In some situations the reach of Article 82 may go even further, so long as there are some "associative" links between the markets in which the dominance and abuse are found.

The extent of this more controversial notion[94] was tested in *Tetra Pak*.[95] The Court of First Instance[96] had upheld a Commission decision fining Tetra Pak 75 million ecus for abusing its dominant position in the markets for aseptic liquid repackaging machinery and aseptic cartons. The abusive conduct included predatory pricing and tying contracts undertaken on the non-aseptic machinery and carton markets in which Tetra Pak had not been established as dominant. According to the Court of First Instance, application of Article 82 was justified by the situation on the different markets and the close associative links between them, noting that Tetra Pak occupied a "leading position" in the non-aseptic market whilst holding a quasi-monopolistic 90 per cent share of the aseptic sector, and that its customers in one sector were also potential customers in the other. On appeal, the Court of Justice observed:

"It is true that application of Article 86 presupposes a link between the dominant position and the alleged abusive conduct, which is not normally present where conduct on a market distinct from the dominated market produces effects on that distinct market. In the case of distinct, but associated, markets, as in the present case, application of Article 86 to conduct found on the associated, non-dominated, market and having effects on that associated market can only be justified by special circumstances."[97]

---

[91] *e.g.* Case T–228/97 *Irish Sugar*, n.54, *supra*.

[92] Case 311/84 *Centre Belge d'Etudes de Marché Télémarketing v. CLT* [1985] E.C.R. 3261; [1986] 2 C.M.L.R. 558.

[93] Case C–310/93 P *BPB Industries and British Gypsum v. Commission* [1995] E.C.R. I–865; [1997] 4 C.M.L.R. 238.

[94] See Art and Van Liderkerke (1997) 34 C.M.L.Rev. 895 at 929–934.

[95] Case C–333/94 P *Tetra Pak International SA v. Commission* [1996] E.C.R. I–5951; [1997] 4 C.M.L.R. 662.

[96] Case T–83/91 [1994] E.C.R. II-755; [1997] 4 C.M.L.R. 726.

[97] [1996] E.C.R. I–5951, at para. 27.

However, it then adopted the "associative" approach of the Court of First Instance to find that such special circumstances existed, concluding that Tetra Pak was placed in a situation "comparable to that of holding a dominant position on the markets in question as a whole".[98]

Finally, the fact that an abuse of a dominant position may have been encouraged by national legislative provisions does not provide any justification for the undertaking concerned.[99] However, some element of free will on the part of the undertaking is required. If it acts under legal constraint there will be no direct infringement of Article 82, but the Member State responsible will be in breach of its general duty under the second paragraph of Article 10 E.C. to abstain from any measure capable of jeopardising the attainment of the objectives of the Treaty.[1]

Examples of abuses

The following, non-exhaustive, examples represent the most frequent or important manifestations of abuses in the case-law.

(i) Unfair prices

(a) **Excessively high prices.** This is probably the first example of an abuse of a dominant position which would occur to most people, because of the direct impact felt by consumers. However, it is not easy to formulate theoretically adequate and practically useful criteria for determining where the line between fair and unfair prices should be drawn in a given case.[2]

The European Court in its *United Brands* judgment, echoing its earlier judgment in *General Motors Continental*,[3] spoke of a price being excessive "because it has no reasonable relation to the economic value of the product supplied".[4] It went on to approve as one test of excess over economic value, a comparison between the selling price of a product and its cost of production, which would disclose the size of the profit margin. As the Court said, the question was "whether the difference between the costs actually incurred and the price actually charged is excessive" and if so, "whether a price has been imposed which is either unfair in itself or when compared to competing products".

Such a test may attract criticism. High profits may be the result of a firm's efficiency which deserves to be rewarded (although it is reasonable to require some element of cost saving to be handed on to consumers); while low profits may be the result of inefficiency, in which case prices may still be excessive. The task of assessing how efficiently a dominant undertaking employs its resources is likely to be a formidable one. There is also the question of the proportion of indirect costs

---

[98] *ibid.*, para. 31.
[99] Case 13/77 *INNO v. ATAB* [1977] E.C.R. at p. 2144; [1978] 1 C.M.L.R. 283.
[1] *ibid.* If a public or privileged undertaking is concerned, there will be an infringement of Art. 86(1): see Chap. 25, *infra*.
[2] See Sharpe, "Pricing by an undertaking in a dominant position" in Maitland-Walker, (ed.), *Towards 1992—The Development of International Antitrust* (Oxford, ESC, 1989).
[3] Case 26/75 n.55, *supra*.
[4] [1978] E.C.R. at p. 301.

and general expenditure which should be allocated to the cost of putting a particular product on the market. The structure of the undertaking, the number of subsidiaries and their relationship with each other and with their parent company, may cause further complications. However, it is clear that the Court was aware of these problems and intended the test to be applied sensitively, with due regard to its limitaitons. In the case of the banana market, the Court was of the opinion that a satisfactory estimate could have been arrived at.

The Commission in its *United Brands* Decision[5] sought to avoid the pitfalls of comparing production costs and prices by offering indirect evidence of unfair pricing. This took the form of comparisons between the prices charged by UBC for "Chiquitas" destined, respectively, for the Irish and Continental markets, between UBC's prices for "Chiquitas" and the prices of other branded bananas of similar quality and between the prices of "Chiquitas" and UBC's unbranded bananas. The Court took the Commission to task for not having at least required UBC to give particulars of its production costs, but did not dispute the relevance of the indicators actually referred to in the Decision: it was the lack of supporting evidence which led to the annulment of this head of abuse.[6]

From *United Brands* it seems that, in seeking to establish an abuse in the form of unfairly high prices, the Commission should normally proceed by way of an analysis of the cost structure of the undertaking concerned. However, other methods of proving unfairness will continue to be acceptable, if the Court is satisfied of their appropriateness in the specific circumstances of the case. For example, in *Bodson*[7] the Court noted that since in more than 30,000 communes in France the provision of the relevant funeral services was unregulated or operated by the communes themselves, there would be comparisons available to provide a basis for assessing whether the prices charged by the holders of exclusive concessions for those services were indeed excessive.[8] Legislation may also on occasion lend assistance to the evaluative task.[9]

(b) **Predatory prices.** A dominant seller may adopt a tactic of pricing his goods very low, or even below cost, in order to drive out of business competitors with more limited resources who cannot for long sustain the losses occasioned by matching the terms he is offering. Consumers, of course, benefit from price reductions in the short run but risk finding themselves even more at the mercy of the dominant undertaking after it has captured a larger share of the market.

The application of Article 82 to predatory price cutting was first clearly established in the *AKZO* case.[10] AKZO was the E.C.'s major supplier of a

---

[5] *Chiquita*; [1976] O.J. L95/1.

[6] See the reasoning of the Court at [1978] E.C.R. at 299–303.

[7] Case 30/87 *Bodson v. SA Pompes funèbres des regions liberées* [1988] E.C.R. 2479; [1989] 4 C.M.L.R. 984.

[8] See also Case 395/87 *Ministère Public v. Tournier* [1989] E.C.R. 2521; [1991] 4 C.M.L.R. 248 and Cases 110 and 241–242/88 *Lucazeau v. SACEM* [1989] E.C.R. 2811 at paras 38 and 25 respectively of the Court's judgments; [1991] 4 C.M.L.R. 248.

[9] Case 66/86 *Ahmed Saeed* [1989] E.C.R. 803; [1990] 4 C.M.L.R. 102, in which a Directive on air fares was used as a reference point, albeit with criteria not unlike the judicial approach in *United Brands*.

[10] Case C–62/86, n.41, *supra*.

chemical substance, benzoyle peroxide, which is used in the manufacture of plastics and in the blanching of flour.[11] The Commission found that, in order to deter ECS, a small competitor in the market in flour additives, from expanding its business into the market in organic peroxides for plastics, AKZO had first threatened and later implemented a campaign of price cuts aimed at important customers of ECS in the former market. If successful, the campaign would not only have eliminated ECS as a competitor in the supply of organic peroxides; it would also have discouraged other potential challenges to AKZO's established position. AKZO's appeal against the decision was dismissed.[12]

Having indicated that not all forms of price competition were legitimate, the Court proceeded to set out a twofold test for determining whether an undertaking has practised predatory pricing, stating:

"Prices below average variable costs (that is to say, those which vary depending on the quantities produced) by means of which a dominant undertaking seeks to eliminate a competitor must be regarded as abusive. A dominant undertaking has no interest in applying such prices except that of eliminating competitors so as to enable it subsequently to raise its prices by taking advantage of its monopolistic position, since each sale generates a loss, namely the total amount of the fixed costs (that is to say, those which remain constant regardless of the quantities produced) and, at least, part of the variable costs relating to the unit produced. Moreover, prices below average total costs, that is to say, fixed costs plus variable costs, but above average variable costs, must be regarded as abusive if they are determined as part of a plan for eliminating a competitor."[13]

This approach was affirmed by the Court in *Tetra Pak*,[14] together with the additional observation that it was not necessary for the purposes of establishing predatory pricing to prove that the company had a realistic chance of subsequently recouping its losses. According to the Court, it must be possible to penalise predatory pricing whenever there is a risk that competitors will be eliminated. The aim pursued, which is to maintain undistorted competition, rules out waiting until such a strategy leads to the actual elimination of competitors.[15]

These principles have been criticised, especially the need for a plan to eliminate competition before predatory pricing can be established under the second limb of the *AKZO* test. The requisite element of intention can only be inferred from the surrounding evidence, such as the duration, continuity and scale of the losses made.[16] Commentators[17] have argued that the emphasis on

---

[11] AKZO estimated its share of the relevant market as 50% or more. It was equivalent to those of all the remaining producers together.
[12] After considerable delay, the Commission's Decision being in 1985 and the Court's judgment in 1991. The fine was reduced for several reasons, and allegations of discrimination were held to be unfounded.
[13] At paras 71–72 of judgment.
[14] Case C–333/94P, n.95, *supra*.
[15] *ibid.*, para. 44.
[16] Not all companies will be so obliging as AKZO, which had committed its plans to paper.
[17] *e.g.* Mastromanolis, "Predatory pricing strategies in the European Union: a case for legal reform" [1998] E.C.L.R. 211.

intention is arbitrary, and fails to take account of a firm's rational economic behaviour. Instead, contrary to the Court's position in *Tetra Pak*, it is argued that any assessment should first entail a structural analysis with a view to establishing whether market conditions favour the undertaking being able to recoup its losses, since it is only the latter prospect which would rationally induce the undertaking to engage in predatory activity. Only if this attracts a positive answer need the inquiry then move on to a costs analysis.[18] Over-extensive reliance by the Commission on AKZO's intention and plan to destroy ECS, it is claimed, could not have provided hints as to the rationality of AKZO's behaviour, or the adverse impact it had on competition, on efficiency, or on market integration.[19]

(ii) Discriminatory prices

A dominant undertaking may fall foul of Article 82 by charging different prices in respect of equivalent transactions without objective justification. If the customers concerned are "trading parties", *i.e.* the purchase is made for the purposes of an economic activity in which they are engaged, the objectionable feature of such a pricing policy is found in the competitive disadvantage suffered by those called upon to pay the higher prices, and the case falls precisely within Article 82(c). However, even in transactions with ultimate consumers, discriminatory pricing may be abusive, if incompatible with any aims of the Treaty.

An abuse may take the form of discriminating between customers within the same market or of following different pricing policies on different markets, although in the latter case objective justification may be more readily available. It should be noted that the customers concerned need not be in competition with each other: the one paying the higher price suffers a "competitive disadvantage" simply because he is, to that extent, less well equipped to meet competition, whatever quarter it may come from.

The *United Brands* case highlighted the particular problem of how far it is permissible for dominant undertakings to adapt their pricing policies to take account of the diversity of marketing conditions in the various Member States.[20] For instance, there may be significant disparities in rates of taxation, freight charges or the wages paid to workers for assembling or finishing the product, which may influence costs; or in other factors relevant to a marketing strategy, such as consumer preferences or the intensity of competition. In addition, price differences may result from government action over which a supplier has no control, for example, the imposition of a price freeze on certain products. Some convergence of these conditions may be expected as progress to the single market and economic and monetary union develops, but markets within the Community are bound to retain a degree of territorial specificity (although not necessarily along national lines) due, for example, to climate, geography and cultural differences.

---

[18] A position adopted in the American cases discussed in Mastromanolis, *loc. cit.* n.17, *supra*.

[19] Mastromanolis, *loc. cit.*, n.17, *supra*, at p. 224.

[20] Case 27/76 n.3, *supra*, at 294 *et seq.* The Commission found that UBC's differential pricing policy amounted to a separate head of abuse, and this part of the Decision was upheld by the Court of Justice.

UBC had put forward, as objective justification for its policy of charging different prices for its bananas, depending on the Member State where the ripened fruit was to be sold, the continuing division of the market for bananas along national lines. Each of the national markets had its own internal characteristics, and accordingly different price levels; and the prices to the ripener/distributors in a given week were intended to reflect as accurately as possible the prices which ripened bananas were expected to fetch on the individual markets during the following week. The defect which the European Court found in this argument was that UBC did not operate directly on the retail markets. It was not, therefore, entitled to take account of market pressures which only made themselves felt at the retail stage. However, not all commentators find this convincing,[21] resisting in particular the suggestion that a producer can be immune from the risks of demand conditions at the retail level.

Attempts have been made to justify discriminatory pricing on the basis of the need to meet competition. Thus, in *Irish Sugar*,[22] the dominant party granted discounts to customers situated near the boundary with Northern Ireland in order to counter the effects of cheap imports into the Republic of Ireland from across that border. Irish Sugar accused the Commission of failing properly to take account of the fact that price competition in the United Kingdom had widened the gap in prices between Northern Ireland and the Republic, that part of the border trade was illegal and that, at that time, Irish Sugar was incurring considerable losses. Irish Sugar also asserted that it had the right to defend its market position by meeting competition through selective, but non-predatory, pricing tactics.

The Court of First Instance gave short shrift to these arguments. First, the influence of the pricing differential in the United Kingdom was "of the very essence"[23] of a common market, so that obstacles to its enjoyment raised by a dominant firm were abusive. This was all the more so since the lower prices outside Ireland were not themselves below cost. Secondly, Irish Sugar could not use its financial situation in the way it claimed without making a "dead letter"[24] of the Treaty rule. Thirdly, on the question of defensive pricing, the Court of First Instance noted that Irish Sugar was defeated by its own arguments. By claiming that it did not have the financial resources to offer discounts and rebates throughout the Irish territory, the undertaking was in effect admitting that it was subsidising the discounts for border customers from the high prices being charged in the rest of the country. This practice was preventing the development of free competition on the market and distorting its structures, in relation to both purchasers and consumers.[25] If "meeting competition" was available as an argument to a dominant firm in Irish Sugar's position at all then, at the very least, it would have to satisfy criteria of economic efficiency and be consistent with the interests of consumers.[26] The position adopted by the Court of First

---

[21] See Bishop, "Price discrimination under Art. 86:political economy in the European Court" (1981) 44 M.L.R. 282.
[22] Case T–228/97, n.54, *supra*.
[23] *ibid.*, para. 185.
[24] *ibid.*, para. 186.
[25] *ibid.*, para. 188.
[26] *ibid.*, para. 189.

Instance is a further example of how difficult it is to mount a defence to discriminatory pricing where the core values of market integration are threatened by that policy, in particular the inhibition of parallel imports.

(iii) Refusals to deal

There is a well-developed case-law on the circumstances in which a refusal by a dominant undertaking to deal, in the ordinary course of its business, with another undertaking—especially to supply goods or services or to supply them in the desired quantity—may amount to an abuse. Such conduct is liable to conflict with the objective of undistorted competition in Article 3(g), and more particularly to fall within the terms of Article 82 (b) and (c), involving the limitation of markets and discrimination. Whether it does so may require a nuanced decision, taking account of, *inter alia*, the relationship between the parties, the nature of the order which has been refused, the effect of the refusal and the reasons for the refusal. At one time, the underlying influence when assessing refusals seemed to be the preservation of some broad notion of commercial fair dealing between dominant firm and established customer. However, the increasing focus upon the single market imperative provided additional interests to be considered concerning access to markets and the avoidance of foreclosure. As a result, the central problem now to be addressed is the nature and extent of any duty owed by the holders of market power to facilitate and maintain effective competition in the market. The commercial freedom of an undertaking to determine its own policies will give way at some point to the protectable interests of actual and potential competitors. In order to explore where this line may be drawn, the discussion below begins with a review of the established case-law on refusals to supply goods and services before considering analogous situations in intellectual property and the so-called essential facilities doctrine.

(a) **Goods and services.**   The earliest case on refusal to deal was *Commercial Solvents* [27] The refusal from the end of 1970 to supply Zoja with aminobutanol required for the manufacture of the derivative, ethambutol, was the result of a policy decision by the CS group to manufacture and sell the derivative on its own account. The Court said:

> ". . . an undertaking being in a dominant position as regards the production of raw material and therefore able to supply to manufacturers of derivatives, cannot, just because it decides to start manufacturing these derivatives (in competition with its former customers) act in such a way as to eliminate their competition which in the case in question, would amount to eliminating one of the principal manufacturers of ethambutol in the common market."[28]

Three main points emerge from this passage. In the first place, Zoja was an established customer of CSC. Admittedly, at the beginning of 1970 Zoja had cancelled its orders under the current supply contract, but the Court regarded this as irrelevant because CSC had anyway decided to cut off the supplies once

---

[27] Cases 6–7/73, n.39, *supra*.
[28] *ibid.*, at 250–251.

deliveries under the contract had been completed. Secondly, the effect of withholding supplies of the raw material was likely to be serious, namely the elimination of a major producer from the market for the derivative. Thirdly, the reason for driving Zoja out of the market was to smooth CSC's own entry. The Court made it clear that the conduct in question could not be justified as a legitimate competitive tactic.

The *United Brands* judgment contains an even more forthright condemnation of refusal to supply:

". . . it is advisable to assert positively from the outset that an undertaking in a dominant position for the purpose of marketing a product—which cashes in on the reputation of a brand name known to and valued by the consumers— cannot stop supplying a long standing customer who abides by regular commercial practice, if the orders placed by that customer are in no way out of the ordinary."[29]

The victim was the Danish ripener/distributor, Olesen, which UBC had refused to supply with "Chiquitas" after it had taken part in a sales campaign mounted by the rival supplier, Castle and Cooke. That collaboration was not regarded by the Court as justifying the refusal. Even a dominant undertaking may act in defence of its commercial interests, but such action must be reasonable and proportional to the threat, which that taken against Olesen had not been.

Refusal to supply a service may be illustrated by the *Tele-marketing* case.[30] "Tele-sales" or "tele-marketing" is a technique whereby an advertisement in the media includes a telephone number which the public are invited to call in order to obtain further information or to respond in some other way. The proceedings arose from the fact that the company which operated the RTL television station in Luxembourg would only sell advertising time for telephone marketing if the number used was that of an agency, Information Publicité, which belonged to the same group. Such behaviour, it was held, was tantamount to a refusal to provide the services of a broadcasting station to other tele-marketing undertakings. If the purpose of the refusal were to reserve the downstream market in tele-sales operations for an affiliated agency, and the other conditions of Article 82 were satisfied, there would be an infringement of the Article analogous to that in *Commercial Solvents*.

The apparent importance of distinguishing carefully between different categories of customer was highlighted by the *BP*[31] judgment, in which the Court annulled the Decision of the Commission that BP had abused the dominant position which it enjoyed in relation to its Dutch customers during the oil supply crisis of 1973–74 by reducing deliveries of motor spirit to a particular customer, ABG, more drastically than to others. The Court found that BP had given notice of the termination of its supply contract with ABG in November 1972, and that at the time when the crisis broke, ABG's relationship with BP, so far as concerned supplies of motor spirit, was that of a casual customer. BP could not,

---

[29] [1978] E.C.R. at 292.
[30] Case 311/84 n.92, *supra*.
[31] Case 77/77 n.50, *supra*.

therefore, be blamed for treating ABG less favourably than its regular customers, since the latter would have received a substantially smaller quantity than they were entitled to expect, if a standard rate reduction had been applied.[32] However, not all prioritising of customers will be objectively justified. In *BPB Industries*,[33] the Court of First Instance found that BG was abusing its dominance in the plasterboard market by favouring customers who were not importers of plasterboard from other sources. It accordingly dismissed BG's argument that this was justified prioritisation for the benefit of regular customers in times of shortage. Whilst selection criteria can be adopted in such circumstances, they must be objectively justified and observe the rules governing fair competition between economic operators.

(b) **Analogous applications.** From the above cases it might appear that a pre-existing relationship between the parties is required before a later refusal to deal can constitute an abuse.[34] However, no such pre-existing arrangement was present in cases concerning refusals to allow access to rights protected by copyright in the *Magill*[35] saga. The three television companies involved had hitherto reproduced advance weekly listings of their programmes in separate magazines. Magill, which wanted to launch a single publication containing all the listings, was refused access to this information by the various copyright-holding companies. The Commission treated this refusal as an abuse, a view upheld by the Court of First Instance on the basis that preventing the emergence of a new product for which there was potential consumer demand went further than was necessary for protection of the essential function of copyright. The Court of Justice endorsed this conclusion, adding a direct reference to *Commercial Solvents*[36] and treating the programme scheduling as the indispensable raw material for the compilation of a new final magazine product.

Critics of the Court's judgment claimed that it took insufficient account of the rights and interests of holders of intellectual property rights, to the point of undermining the Court's own often-stated position that a refusal to license such rights was not itself an abuse.[37] However, fears that the scope of the *Magill* cases might be unbounded seem to have been misplaced. First, the Court of First Instance in *Tiercé Ladbroke*[38] expressly rejected the application of the *Magill* judgment on the footing that the copyright holders who were refusing to license their television rights for transmission in Belgium were not themselves already

---

[32] As Advocate General Warner pointed out, a legal and moral right to security of supplies is the counterpart, for a contractual customer, of his loss of freedom to seek the best available bargain at a given moment, and the loyalty of regular, though non-contractual, customers also merits special consideration: [1978] E.C.R. at 538.

[33] Case T–65/89 *BPB Industries and British Gypsum v. Commission* [1993] E.C.R. II-389; [1993] 5 C.M.L.R. 32; this aspect of the case was not dealt with on appeal in Case C–310/93P, n.93, *supra*.

[34] See also the application of these principles by a national court in *Garden Cottage v. Milk Marketing Board* [1983] 3 C.M.L.R. 43 (House of Lords).

[35] Joined Cases C–241–242/91 P *RTE and ITP v. Commission*, n.38, *supra*.

[36] Cases 6–7/73, n.39, *supra*.

[37] Case 238/87 *Volvo v. Erik Veng* (UK) [1988] E.C.R. 6211; [1989] 4 C.M.L.R. 122; Case 53/87 *Maxicar v. Renault* [1988] E.C.R. 6039.

[38] Case T–504/93, n.32, *supra*.

exploiting them on the Belgian market. The Court of First Instance added that Article 82 could not apply

"unless it concerned a product or service which was either essential for the exercise of the activity in question, in that there was no real or potential substitute, or was a new product whose introduction might be prevented, despite specific, constant and regular potential demand on the part of consumers."[39]

Secondly, in *Oscar Bronner*[40] the *Magill* judgment was described by Advocate General Jacobs as having special circumstances. In particular, the existing weekly guides were inadequate, the provision of copyright protection for television listings was hard to justify in any event, and, since the shelf-life of listings was short, any refusal to supply the information was bound to act as a permanent barrier to a new product.

(c) **Essential facilities.** As with some other developments in E.C. competition law, such as the rule of reason,[41] the concept of essential facilities has a counterpart originating in the USA. Put shortly, the idea requires that dominance over key facilities, such as transport or other infrastructure, requires access to be opened up to other users in particular circumstances. The American case-law, as discussed by Advocate General Jacobs in *Oscar Bronner*, contains five conditions. First, an essential facility is under the control of a monopolist. Secondly, a competitor is unable practically or reasonably to duplicate the essential facility. Thirdly, the use of the facility is denied to a competitor. Fourthly, it is feasible for the facility to be provided and, fifthly, there is no legitimate business reason for refusing access to the facility.

The term essential facilities has been expressly adopted in Community law by the Commission, although the Court's position is less clear. In *Sea Containers v. Stena Sealink*[42] the Commission decided that Sealink's refusal, as operator of the port of Holyhead, to allow access on reasonable and non-discriminatory terms to a potential competitor on the market for ferry services was an abuse of a dominant position. A facility will be essential if the handicap to a new entrant resulting from denial of access is one that can reasonably be expected to make competitors' activities in the market in question either impossible or permanently, seriously and unavoidably uneconomic.[43] This test is to be applied objectively, so that the special vulnerability of a particular competitor is irrelevant.

In his Opinion in *Oscar Bronner*, Advocate General Jacobs suggested that legal intervention, whether understood as an application of the essential facilities doctrine or, more traditionally, as a response to a refusal to supply goods or services, can only be justified in cases where the dominant undertaking has a

---

[39] *ibid.*, para. 131.
[40] Case 7/97 n.14, *supra*.
[41] See Chap. 20, *supra*.
[42] Dec. 94/19 of December 21, 1993; [1994] O.J. L15/8.
[43] Temple Lang, "Defining legitimate competition: companies duties' to supply competitors, and access to essential facilities" (1994) 18 Fordham International Law Journal 245, quoted by Advocate General Jacobs in *Oscar Bronner*, n.14, *supra*.

"genuine stranglehold" on the related market. This could be the case, for example, where duplication of the facility is impossible or extremely difficult because of physical, geographical or legal constraints or is highly undesirable for reasons of public policy.[44] Applying these criteria to the claim by Oscar Bronner to have access to the national home-delivery network for newspapers established by Mediaprint, the Advocate General noted that although the applicant might be unable to duplicate that network it still had a variety of other distribution options open to it. The case thus fell "well short" of the type of situation in which it might be appropriate to impose an obligation on a dominant undertaking to allow access to a facility which it has developed for its own use.

The Court of Justice, notably, reformulated the question referred to it in *Oscar Bronner* in terms of a refusal to supply and did not expressly articulate an essential facilities doctrine. However, it took a narrow view of the requirements necessary to make out a breach of Article 82, observing that not only would the refusal of access have to be likely to eliminate all competition in the daily newspaper market on the part of the person requesting the service and that such refusal be incapable of being objectively justified, but that the service must also be indispensable to carrying on that person's business. The last requirement was not satisfied in the particular case since Oscar Bronner could choose other methods of distributing its newspapers besides home delivery. The Court also emphasised that in order to demonstrate that it had no realistic alternatives, the applicant could not just assert that it would not be economically viable to set up its own distribution network for the small circulation of its newspapers. This view acknowledges criticisms prior to the judgment expressing fears about the rising tide of essential facilities doctrine.[45]

It thus appears[46] that Community law is reluctant to establish a distinct essential facilities doctrine but, instead, treats it as a particular species of refusal to supply. Such a conclusion casts doubt on the Commission's previous approach in cases such as *London European v. Sabena*,[47] where the refusal to allow access to a computer reservation system was condemned without a particularly rigorous assessment of Sabena's market position. Whilst a case may still be made by an applicant that a particular facility is indispensable, it will also have to show the clear exclusionary effects of any refusal to grant access.

Taking the developments in relation to refusals to supply as a whole, it can be seen that the modern difficulty is how to balance intervention in the name of more effective competition against the rights of firms to conduct their own policies and protect their own commercial interests. The case of *Oscar Bronner* is significant for the Court's own refusal to extend the obligations already incumbent upon dominant firms. As the Advocate General pointed out, the right to choose one's trading partners and freely to dispose of one's property are generally recognised principles in the laws of the Member States, in some cases with constitutional status. In addition, from the point of view of competition, the

---

[44] Note 14, *supra*, para. 65 of Opinion.
[45] *e.g.* Ridyard, "Essential facilities and the obligation to supply competitors under U.K. and E.C. competition law" [1996] E.C.L.R. 438.
[46] See Hancher, (1999) 36 C.M.L.Rev. 1289.
[47] Dec. 88/589; [1988] O.J. L317/47.

long-term interests of consumers may be better served by allowing the undertaking to keep its facilities. Otherwise, automatic rights for new entrants would act as a disincentive to those parties to develop competing facilities. Short-term gains by opening access might well thus be offset by longer-term disadvantages.

(iv) Tying, discounts and other conditions

Dominant firms may use their market power to insist that customers are bound by a variety of contractual conditions which, depending on their context, may constitute abuses. Only a few selective examples are covered here.

The illustration in Article 82(d) covers all kinds of "tying" arrangements, where a person is required to accept, as a condition of entering into a contract, "supplementary obligations which, by their nature or according to commercial usage, have no connection with the subject of such contracts". In simple terms this can mean that to order X goods the customer must also take quantities of Y as well. Similarly, services may be tied so that the purchase of a heating system may include an obligation to sign up for a five-year service contract. The main objection to tying in this way is that it enables a dominant position on one market to be used in order to gain a competitive advantage on another. It may also be directly oppressive to consumers in the first market. Thus, in *Hilti*[48] it was held to be an abuse for Hilti to supply cartridge strips to certain end-users or distributors on terms that the requisite complement of nails was purchased as well. Hilti claimed as an objective justification that its policy was based on safety grounds, alleging that other manufacturers' nails were dangerous when used in the Hilti system. This argument was forcefully rejected by the Court of First Instance, noting that it was not for Hilti to take unilateral action in that way; safety issues could be referred to the relevant public authorities. Even in relation to products where tied sales are part of commercial usage, the possibility of such practice being an abuse cannot be ruled out.[49]

A loyalty discount[50] consists of a reduction in the price of a product which is granted on condition that the purchaser obtain a specified proportion (normally very high) of his requirements of the product from the supplier granting the discount. The usual arrangement will be for the discount to be paid as a rebate at the end of, say, a year, and entitlement will be lost in respect of the whole period, if the limit agreed for procurements from third parties is exceeded. This means that a competing supplier will have to pitch his offer at a level that takes into account not only the rebate on the particular quantity ordered but also the higher price the customer will have to pay for the remainder of the goods purchased from the first supplier.[51]

In the case of a target discount the price reduction is conditional on the purchasing of an agreed quantity of products from the supplier in question during the reference period. The target is not linked to any specific proportion of the customer's requirements but is likely in practice to be set at a level that will

---

[48] Case C–53/92P, n.36, *supra*.
[49] Case C–333/94 P *Tetra Pak*, n.95, *supra*, at para. 37.
[50] Also known as a "fidelity" discount.
[51] See the analysis of loyalty discounts in Case 85/76 *Hoffmann-la Roche v. Commission* [1979] E.C.R. at pp. 539–541. Also Case T–228/97 *Irish Sugar*, n.54, *supra*.

lead to the loss of the discount if substantial purchases are made from third parties. To win orders from the customer, therefore, competing suppliers must, again, be prepared to cover that loss.[52]

Loyalty and target discounts are to be distinguished from "quantity" discounts, where the reduction in price is determined by the actual volume of goods purchased from the supplier. Quantity discounts are not considered anti-competitive, because of the correlation between cost savings to the supplier and the lower price paid by the purchaser.[53]

On the other hand, an exclusive or preferential right of supply, whether it operates directly or through a discount system, is very likely to infringe Article 82 if the supplier occupies a dominant position on the market in question. Such arrangements, according to the European Court,[54] are incompatible with the objective of undistorted competition because, except in circumstances of the kind that might lead to a grant of exemption under Article 81(3), they have no economic justification but are designed to deprive the customer of any choice of his sources of supply, or at least to restrict his choice, and to deny other producers access to the market. The effect will be further to strengthen the position of the dominant supplier. Another possible objection, when loyalty or target discounts are involved, is that charging two customers different net prices for the same quantity of goods, because of purchases made or not made on other occasions, amounts to discrimination contrary to Article 82(c).

(v) Non-contractual abuses

In addition to terms and conditions on which dominant firms supply their goods or services, other actions may also amount to abuses within the scope of Article 82. For example, putting direct pressure upon traders not to use a competitor's rival machines was accepted as an abuse by the Court of First Instance in *Tetra Pak*.[55]

It appears from *ITT Promedia*[56] that vexatious litigation may be abusive. In rejecting a complaint that Belgacom, the Belgian telecommunications operator, had infringed Article 82 by initiating legal action against ITT Promedia, the Commission stated that vexatious litigation could be abusive subject to two conditions. First, the action must not reasonably be considered as an attempt to establish the undertaking's rights and must instead be viewed as harassment. Secondly, the litigation must be conceived in the framework of a plan whose goal is to eliminate competition. The Court of First Instance confined itself to considering whether the Commission had applied its own criteria correctly. It noted that as access to court is a fundamental right and a general principle ensuring the rule of law, it is only in wholly exceptional circumstances that the fact that legal proceedings are brought is capable of constituting an abuse of a dominant position. The Commission's twofold criteria therefore had to be

---

[52] See analysis of target discounts in Case 322/81 *Michelin* [1983] E.C.R. at 3514–1515; [1985] 1 C.M.L.R. 282.

[53] Case 85/76 *Hoffmann-La Roche* [1979] E.C.R. at p. 540; [1979] 3 C.M.L.R. 211.

[54] *ibid.*

[55] Case T–83/91 [1994] E.C.R. II–755, at para. 212.

[56] Case T–111/96 *ITT Promedia v. Commission* [1998] 5 C.M.L.R. 491

construed strictly. Nevertheless, the judgment appears to accept the possibility in principle that litigation might be abusive. The difficulty of the test adopted by the Commission is its reliance upon intention. This seems to be at odds with the objective nature of abuse as laid down generally in the case-law.

Effect on trade between Member States

An abuse of a dominant position only attracts the prohibition in Article 82 if it is capable of affecting trade between Member States.

As we have seen, the same condition applies under Article 81, and the general principles relating to its operation were discussed in Chapter 20, *supra*, including those established in cases which have arisen under Article 82.[57] It was noted, in particular, that the Court of Justice considers the purpose of the condition to be that of defining the boundary between the E.C. rules on competition and the competition laws of Member States. The Court has made it clear that the condition may be satisfied in different ways: through the diversion of the flow of goods or services from its normal channels; or through the modification of the structure of competition within the common market.

The application of the condition in the context of Article 82 was substantially developed in *Hugin*. The abuse found by the Commission against the Swedish manufacturer of cash registers, Hugin, was that it had refused to supply spare parts for its machines to a London firm, Liptons, and had prohibited its subsidiaries and distributors in the common market from selling spare parts outside its distribution network. The business of Liptons was the maintenance and repair of cash registers and the renting-out or sale of reconditioned machines. The supply of spare parts from Sweden to the United Kingdom would not entail trade between Member States (Sweden not being a member of the Community at that time), but there were two ways in which the condition might have been satisfied. One was that the withholding of the parts might have interfered with the commercial activities of Liptons in other Member States. However, the Court of Justice was satisfied that the firm had never extended its activities outside the United Kingdom; indeed, its business was of a kind that could only be carried on profitably within a local area. The second possibility was that Hugin's policy of not supplying spare parts outside its distribution network restricted intra-Community trade in the parts. This, too, was rejected. The Court pointed out that the value of the articles was small and that anyone needing a part which the local Hugin subsidiary could not supply would normally address its request directly to the parent company. Hugin had not, therefore, been guilty of diverting trade from channels it would otherwise have followed. The Court regarded cases like that of Liptons, which had attempted to obtain Hugin spare parts in other Member States, as exceptional and, therefore, it seems, covered by the *de minimis* principle.[58]

---

[57] See, in particular, Joined Cases 6–7/73 *Commercial Solvents*, n.39, *supra*; Case 22/78 *Hugin*, n.34, *supra*.

[58] See Chap. 20, *supra*.

The effect on trade was also important in the *Bodson* case.[59] Both the French Government and the Commission took the view that the concessions relating to the provision of local funeral services did not affect trade between Member States. The only goods involved were coffins and a monopoly only existed in 14 per cent of the communes in France. In two-thirds of these the concession was held by a single group of undertakings. This same group provided funeral services in a number of other Member States. The Court observed that the inter-State requirement demanded account to be taken of the consequences for the effective competitive structure in the common market. It was thus for the national court to consider whether the conduct of the concessionaires affected the importation of goods from other Member States or the possibility of competing undertakings established in other Member States to provide services in the original State.

---

[59] Case 30/87 n.7, *supra*.

CHAPTER 22

APPLICATION OF ARTICLES 81 AND 82

Introduction

The national delegations meeting at the Messina Conference prior to the establishment of the EEC Treaty agreed on the need for a prohibition against anti-competitive practices. However, they were less sure about the appropriate path to take regarding the conditions under which that prohibition could be lifted. Two choices presented themselves: a system based on authorisation or one in which the prohibition was simply directly applicable. The first would require an authorising agency to deal with applications and would deem any practices void until such time as they were approved. In the second option, practices would be valid until such time as they were challenged and defeated. The EEC Treaty eventually incorporated a compromise solution whereby the prohibition against restrictive practices could be declared inapplicable[1] but the task of implementing the principles of Articles 81 and 82 was given to the Community legislator.[2] When the Council first exercised this power,[3] it created a system of authorisation in which agreements could only obtain exemption by notification to the Commission, which was given exclusive competence in the matter.

However, after nearly 40 years of application this regime is undergoing radical overhaul in the light of many factors, including changes in the competitive environment, administrative workload considerations, political pressures for decentralisation and concern for a more prioritised investigative approach. The Commission's preferred model in proposals published in 1999[4] adopts the second of the choices identified by the Treaty framers, namely a system of *ex post facto* control in which agreements would be valid until challenged in front of national courts, national competition authorities or the Commission, any of which would be empowered to consider the compatibility of a restrictive practice with the provision of Article 81 as a whole. This Chapter accordingly considers both the existing rules for the administration of the E.C. competition rules, developed on the basis of Regulation 17, and the reforms anticipated in the modernisation proposals.

Under the system established by Regulation 17,[5] the Commission wields real executive powers, subject to judicial control by the Court of Justice and the Court of First Instance. As we shall see, the European Courts have played a significant role in the elaboration of Regulation 17, subjecting the extensive powers of the Commission to rule of law considerations. The centrality of the Commission's role under the legislation has also constrained the nature and scope of the part

---

[1] As Art. 85(3), now Art. 81(3) E.C.
[2] As Art. 87, now Art. 83 E.C.
[3] Reg. 17/62; [1962] J.O. 204; [1959–1962] O.J. 87, which came into force on March 13, 1962.
[4] *White Paper on Modernisation of the Rules Implementing Arts 85 and 86 of the E.C. Treaty*, April 28, 1999.
[5] See generally, Kerse, *EC Antitrust Procedure* (4th ed., 1998).

played by national courts in competition law enforcement, leading to a number of developments in both case-law and the Commission's own practice that have endeavoured to develop a workable level of participation in the adjudication process for national bodies.

The following discussion begins by examining the application of Articles 81 and 82 by the Commission under Regulation 17 before going on to explain the role of national courts and authorities under the existing arrangements. The Chapter ends with consideration of the *White Paper on Modernisation*.

The Commission's application of Regulation 17

First steps

Proceedings for the application of Article 81 or 82 may be started by the Commission on its own initiative[6] or in response to an application for negative clearance[7] and/or the notification of an agreement[8] or to a complaint.[9]

(i) Action by the Commission

Where the Commission itself takes the initiative in a competition matter it is said to act *ex officio*. It may be prompted to do so by various factors for example, newspaper reports, the results of studies or unofficial representations.

(ii) Action by the parties to a possible infringement

A feature of Regulation 17 is the encouragement given to the parties to a possible infringement of the competition rules to bring the matter themselves to the attention of the Commission, through the negative clearance and notification procedures.[10]

The purpose of an application for negative clearance is to enable undertakings to ascertain whether the Commission considers any aspects of an agreement to which they are party, or of their business conduct, to fall within Article 81(1) or Article 82. A formal grant of clearance consists of a decision by the Commission certifying that, on the basis of the facts in its possession, there are no grounds under those provisions for action to be taken in respect of the agreement or conduct in question. An application will only have point where infringement of Article 81 or Article 82 seems a genuine possibility. Undertakings that feel any doubts about an agreement should consider, in particular, whether it may be covered by a block exemption regulation or by one of the Commission's Notices.

With the adoption of Regulation 17 the national competition authorities lost their transitional power under Article 84 to declare the prohibition in Article

---

[6] Reg. 17, Art. 3(1).

[7] Reg. 17, Art. 2. See, *infra*.

[8] Reg. 17, Arts 4(1) and 5(1). See, *infra*.

[9] Reg. 17, Art. 3(1) and (2).

[10] Although the efficacy of this facility may be doubted. According to the *White Paper on Modernisation*, n.4, *supra*, in more than 35 years of Reg. 17's application there were only nine decisions in which a notified agreement was prohibited without a complaint having been lodged against it. Measured in another way, Commissioner Monti has said that in the five years preceding the 1999 *Annual Competition Report* only 0.5% of notifications resulted in the adoption of a prohibition decision: see Foreword to 1999 *Annual Competition Report*.

81(1) inapplicable to agreements which fulfil the criteria of Article 81(3). Article 9(1) of the Regulation confers that power exclusively upon the Commission. Notification of an agreement to the Commission is made for the purpose of seeking exemption, either by an individual grant or under the opposition procedure of a block exemption regulation.[11] Where there are grounds for believing that an agreement may be caught by Article 81(1), Regulation 17 provides a number of incentives for the parties to notify punctually.

In the first place, Article 4(1) of the Regulation lays down the general rule that, until agreements have been notified to the Commission, they cannot be the subject of a decision in application of Article 81(3). Thus, although there is no general duty on the parties to notify agreements, no exemption can be forthcoming without so doing. This is so, even if the agreement in question manifestly satisfies the criteria of exemption in the paragraph. Certain categories of agreements are, however, excused notification, as a matter of administrative convenience and legal certainty, because they pose no serious threat to competition. The list, which is to be found in Article 4(2),[12] has been significantly expanded as part of the reform process in relation to vertical restraints. As a result of amendments introduced by Regulation 1216/99,[13] notification is not required for agreements entered into by two or more undertakings, each operating, for the purpose of the agreement, at a different level of the production or distribution chain, which relate to the conditions under which the parties may purchase, sell or resell certain goods or services.[14]

Secondly, the date of notification determines how far a grant of exemption may be made retrospective. For this purpose Regulation 17 draws a distinction between agreements which have been entered into since the date when it came into force, known as "new agreements", and agreements then already in existence, known as "old agreements". Under Article 6(1) in the case of new agreements exemption cannot be granted from a date earlier than that of notification. In respect of any period which may have elapsed between its making and notification, a new agreement caught by Article 81(1) is irretrievably void pursuant to Article 81(2). Old agreements, on the other hand, benefit from transitional arrangements. If notified by the dates specified in Article 5(1) of Regulation 17,[15] or in accordance with the accession agreements applicable to

---

[11] For exemption considerations and the opposition procedure, see Chap. 20, *supra*.

[12] In addition to the vertical restraints discussed in the text, other agreements which escape notification as a requirement for exemption eligibility include: intellectual property licences involving only two parties which only impose restrictions on the exercise of the rights of the assignee or user of industrial property rights; and agreements which have as their sole object: a) the development or uniform application of standards or types; b) joint research and development; c) specialisation in the manufacture of products, provided that the products subject to specialisation do not amount to more than 15% of market share and that the parties' combined annual turnover does not exceed 200 million euros. In relation to both intellectual property licensing and specialisation agreements, parties should also check relevant block exemptions to maximise the security of their protection.

[13] [1999] O.J. L148/5.

[14] Inserted in Reg. 17 as part of an amended Art. 2(2).

[15] February 1, 1963 for bilateral agreements, otherwise November 1, 1962. For an example of longevity, see Case C–39/96 *Koninklijke Vereeniging ter Bevordering van de Belangen des Boekhandels v. Free Record Shop* [1997] E.C.R. I–2303; [1997] 5 C.M.L.R. 521, where an agreement

successive enlargements of the Community,[16] they are eligible for exemption extending back to the date when Article 81(1) first applied to them.

Thirdly, where activity takes place under an agreement which has been notified, the parties are protected by Article 15(5) of Regulation 17 against the imposition of fines for the infringement of Article 81. However, the Commission may put an end to that immunity by informing the parties that, in the light of a preliminary examination, it has formed the view that Article 81(1) applies to the agreement and exemption under Article 81(3) is not justified. The intimation of such an assessment is an act reviewable under Article 230, since it alters the legal position of the parties to the agreement.[17]

A final incentive to notify, which applies only to old agreements, is found in the doctrine of provisional validity. The Court of Justice held in *Brasserie de Haecht (No. 2)*[18] that the general principle of contractual certainty requires that a notified "old" agreement can only be declared void after the Commission has taken a decision upon it.

For Article 82 there is, of course, no equivalent to the procedure for notifying agreements with a view to obtaining exemption under Article 81(3).

A special form, known as Form A/B, has been provided for applications for negative clearance in respect of Articles 81(1) and for notifications,[19] and its use is compulsory.[20] The form may also be used in relation to negative clearances sought in relation to Article 82. In all cases the relevant information sent to the Commission must be correct and complete.[21] A decision granting negative clearance on the basis of incomplete or incorrect information could be without effect, and one granting exemption could be revoked. The Commission also has power under Article 15(1)(a) of Regulation 17 to impose fines on undertakings that intentionally or negligently supply incorrect or misleading information.[22]

(iii) Complaints

Article 3(2) of Regulation 17 provides that those entitled to make application to the Commission to set infringement proceedings in motion are Member States and "natural or legal persons who claim a legitimate interest". Formal complaints account for almost 30 per cent of new cases dealt with by the Commission,[23] and most own-initiative procedures begin with information sent to it informally. There is a form for the submission of complaints (Form C), but its use is optional.

---

duly notified on October 30, 1962 was contested 34 years later. As there had been no decision by the Commission in the interim, the question of whether the agreement had been modified during that period to a degree sufficient to deprive it of its provisional validity was sent back by the Court of Justice to the national court for resolution.

[16] Reg. 17, Art. 25

[17] Joined Cases 8–11/66 *Cimenteries v. Commission* [1967] E.C.R. 75; [1967] C.M.L.R. 77.

[18] Case 48/72 [1973] E.C.R. 77; [1973] C.M.L.R. 287.

[19] Reg. 3385/94, O.J. 1994 L337/28.

[20] *ibid.*, Art. 2(1).

[21] *ibid.*, Art. 3(1).

[22] Although the permissible amounts are low: from 100 to 5,000 euros. The Commission has indicated its wish to multiply them tenfold to achieve alignment with the corresponding fines available to it under the Merger Reg. 4064/89: see the *White Paper on Modernisation*, n.4, *supra*, para. 124.

[23] *White Paper on Modernisation*, n.4, *supra*, para. 117.

A complainant has no right to insist that the Commission adopt a final decision as to the existence or otherwise of the alleged infringement.[24] However, this is not to say complainants are without protection. The Commission must take a complaint seriously, otherwise it will be exposed to allegations of failure to act under Article 232.[25] It must consider attentively all the matters of fact and law which the complainants bring to its attention.[26] Moreover, according to Article 6 of Regulation 2842/98[27], if the Commission considers that on the basis of the information in its possession there are insufficient grounds for acting on the complaint it shall inform the complainant of its reasons and set a date by which the complainant may make known its views in writing. The rights of the complainant and the duties of the Commission in this process have repeatedly come up for examination by the European Courts.

Three stages can be identified in the administrative procedure arising from complaints.[28] The first consists of clarification of the issues, and may include an informal exchange of views and information between the complainant and the Commission. The second stage comprises a notification under Article 6, described above, and the third culminates in a final decision by the Commission in the light of the complainant's reactions to the Article 6 notification. A letter sent by the Commission under Article 6 will constitute a definition of its position for the purposes of fending off an action for failure to act. As a preliminary measure paving the way for a final decision, such a letter will not be susceptible to an action for annulment.[29] Once the second stage is complete, the Commission is bound either to initiate a procedure against the subject of the complaint or to adopt a definitive decision rejecting the complaint, which may be the subject-matter of an annulment action under Article 230.[30] That definitive decision must be adopted by the Commission in a reasonable time from receiving the complainant's observations, in accordance with the principles of good administration.[31] In the absence of such a decision, the complainant will be able to bring an action for failure to act.[32]

An example of these principles being applied can be seen in *UPS Europe*,[33] a case where the applicant had originally lodged a complaint with the Commission

---

[24] Case 125/78 *GEMA v. Commission* [1979] E.C.R. 3173; [1980] 2 C.M.L.R. 177, para. 18; Case T–387/94 *Asia Motor France and others v. Commission ("Asia Motor III")* [1996] E.C.R. II–961, [1996] 5 C.M.L.R. 537, para. 46.

[25] Case 210/81 *Demi-Studio Schmidt v. Commission* [1983] E.C.R. 3045; [1984] 1 C.M.L.R. 63.

[26] Case 298/83 *CICCE v. Commission* [1985] E.C.R. 1105; [1986] 1 C.M.L.R. 486; Joined Cases 142 and 156/84 *BAT and Reynolds v. Commission* [1987] E.C.R. 4487; [1987] 2 C.M.L.R. 551; Case C–119/97P *Union Française de l'Express (Ufex) and others v. Commission and May Courier* [1999] E.C.R. I–1341, [2000] 4 C.M.L.R. 268, para. 86.

[27] Reg. 2842/98 [1998] O.J. L354/18 on the hearing of parties in certain proceedings under Arts 81 and 82 E.C. This provision replaced the similarly worded Art. 6 of Reg. 99/63; [1963–1964] O.J. Spec.Ed. p. 47 with effect from February 1, 1999.

[28] Case T–64/89 *Automec v. Commission ('Automec I')* [1990] E.C.R. II–367; [1991] 4 C.M.L.R. 177, paras 45–47.

[29] Case C–282/95P *Guérin Automobiles v. Commission* [1997] E.C.R. I–1503; [1997] 5 C.M.L.R. 447, paras 33–34, following Case 60/81 *IBM v. Commission* [1981] E.C.R. 2639; [1981] 3 C.M.L.R. 635.

[30] Case C–282/95P *Guérin Automobiles v. Commission*, n.29, *supra*, para. 36.

[31] *ibid.*, para. 37.

[32] *ibid.*, para. 38. Such an action will lie even though the complainant may already have brought an action under Art. 232 to obtain a notification from the Commission under Art. 6 of Reg. 2842/98.

[33] Case T–127/98 *UPS Europe v. Commission* [1999] E.C.R. II–000, [2000] 4 C.M.L.R. 94.

in July 1994, alleging that Deutsche Post had infringed Articles 82 and 87 by using its income from the letter market to cross-subsidise its parcel services. The Commission had sent the applicant an Article 6 notification on December 19, 1997 to the effect that it did not intend to pursue the Article 82 elements of the complaint but that the state aid procedures would be initiated. The applicant submitted its observations on that notification on February 2, 1998, objecting to the Commission's intention to abandon the Article 82 inquiry and asking it to reject its complaint, if it was still minded to do so, by a formal decision within a reasonable time. On June 2, 1998 the applicant sent a formal request to the Commission to act within the meaning of Article 232 of the Treaty, asking it to take a position on its complaint. In the absence of any decision being forthcoming, the applicant duly opened proceedings before the Court of First Instance. The Commission claimed that when it received the applicant's observations on the Article 6 notification in February 1998 it had re-opened investigation of the Article 82 aspects of the complaint, and that it was therefore unreasonable to have completed that task by June. However, the Court of First Instance flatly rejected this position, noting that when measuring whether the period between the applicant's observations on the Article 6 notification and its sending of the formal request to act was reasonable, it was appropriate to "take account of the years already spent on the investigation, the present state of the investigation of the case and the attitudes of the parties considered as a whole". Applying the *Guérin*[34] tests, explained above, the Court observed that instead of re-opening its inquiries in February 1998 the Commission should have either adopted a definitive decision rejecting the complaint or initiated a procedure under Article 82 against Deutsche Post. The applicant was therefore entitled to a declaration that the Commission had failed to act,[35] although its request that the Court of First Instance impose a time-limit of one month on the Commission to act was ruled inadmissible.[36]

The upshot of the cases in this area is that the Court of Justice and the Court of First Instance have ensured that complainants are entitled to have the fate of their complaint settled by a decision of the Commission against which an action may be brought,[37] even though this is not explicit in the secondary legislation.[38] Although complainants cannot insist on an investigation, they must, if none is forthcoming, be given reasons why not.[39] Rejection by the Commission of a complaint does not constitute a definitive ruling upon the legal status of the practice or conduct in question. There is accordingly nothing to prevent a

---

[34] Case C–282/95P *Guérin Automobiles v. Commission*, n.29, *supra.*

[35] The Commission itself conceded it was "probably guilty of a technical infringement" of Art. 232, and that it had not acted "in an impressive manner" in the case.

[36] The Court of First Instance has no jurisdiction to issue directions to Community institutions: Order of the Court of First Instance in Case T–47/96 *SDDA v. Commission* [1996] E.C.R. II–1559, para. 45.

[37] Case C–119/97P *Union Française de l'Express (Ufex) and others v. Commission and May Courier*, n.26, *supra*, para. 86.

[38] A point acknowledged by the Court of First Instance in *UPS Europe*, n.33, *supra*, para. 40.

[39] In its *White Paper on Modernisation*, n.4, *supra*, the Commission describes the Art. 6 procedures as "cumbersome" (para. 121), taking up a considerable proportion of the Commission's resources. Decisions rejecting complaints accounted for over half the Commission's formal decisions in recent years. It calls, perhaps optimistically, for simpler and more flexible arrangements.

national court from finding, for example, that a restrictive agreement is void under Article 81(2).[40]

It has been clear since the early 1990s that the Commission is entitled to prioritise its selection of cases to investigate in relation to private complainants.[41] Its wish to do so is hardly surprising, given the pressure on its resources as a result of its many functions under the Treaty, the rising number of complaints in the competition arena and the availability, in particular, of national courts to provide alternative protection. The Court of First Instance and, later, the Court of Justice have upheld the Commission's policy of giving priority to cases involving a "Community interest". In the first such judgment, the Court of First Instance stated:

". . . unlike the civil courts, whose task is to safeguard the subjective rights of private persons in their mutual relations, an administrative authority must act in the public interest. Consequently it is legitimate for the Commission to refer to the Community interest in order to determine the degree of priority to be accorded to the different matters before it. This does not mean removing the Commission's acts from judicial review: as [Article 253 E.C.] requires the reasons on which decisions are based to be stated, the Commission cannot merely refer to the Community interest in isolation. It must set out the legal and factual considerations which lead it to conclude that there is not a sufficient Community interest which would justify the adoption of measures of investigation. Thus by reviewing the legality of those reasons the Court can review the Commission's acts.

To assess the Community interest in pursuing the examination of a matter, the Commission must take account of the circumstances of the particular case, particularly the factual and legal aspects set out in the complaint referred to it. It is for the Commission in particular to weigh up the importance of the alleged infringement for the functioning of the Common Market, the probability of being able to establish the existence of the infringement and the extent of the investigation measures necessary in order to fulfil successfully its task of securing compliance with [Articles 81 and 82]."[42]

Having received this boost for its approach, the Commission set out further elaboration in its Co-Operation Notice,[43] stating its intention to concentrate on those cases having "particular political, economic or legal significance for the Community".[44] It pointed out, in particular, that "there is not normally a sufficient Community interest in examining a case when the plaintiff is able to secure adequate protection of his rights before the national courts".[45]

---

[40] Case C–59/96P *Koelman v. Commission* [1997] E.C.R. I–4809, paras 42–44. See also Case C–282/95P *Guérin Automobiles v. Commission*, n.29, *supra*, para. 39.

[41] The Commission must investigate a complaint from a Member State: Art. 85(1) E.C. and Case T–24/90 *Automec v. Commission ("Automec II")* [1992] E.C.R. II–2223; [1992] 5 C.M.L.R. 431, para. 76.

[42] Case T–24/90 *Automec v. Commission ('Automec II')*, n.41, *supra*, paras 85–86.

[43] *Notice on Co-operation between National Courts and the Commission*; [1993] O.J. C39/6.

[44] *ibid.*, para. 14.

[45] *ibid.*, para. 15.

The Commission thus enjoys a significant breadth of discretion in rejecting complaints on the ground of insufficient Community interest, subject to adequate reasoning. It will be difficult, for example, to make a successful challenge against a refusal to handle a case concerned with a situation confined to the territory of one Member State.[46] Moreover, the Court of Justice has underlined the need for flexibility in relation to the concept of "Community interest", pointing out in the *Ufex* case[47] that

"In view of the fact that the assessment of the Community interest raised by a complaint depends on the circumstances of each cases, the number of criteria of assessment the Commission may refer to should not be limited, nor conversely should it be required to have recourse exclusively to certain criteria.

In a field such as competition law, the factual and legal circumstances may differ considerably from case to case, so that it is permissible for the Court of First Instance to apply criteria which have not hitherto been considered."[48]

However, in the same case the Court emphasised that when deciding the order of priority for dealing with the complaints brought before it, the Commission may not regard as excluded in principle from its purview certain situations which come under the task entrusted to it by the Treaty.[49] With regard to the facts of the instant case, the Commission was not entitled to rely solely on the fact that practices alleged to be contrary to the Treaty had ceased, without having ascertained that their anti-competitive effects no longer continued and that the seriousness of the alleged interferences with competition or the persistence of such consequences had not been such as to give the complaint a Community interest.[50]

Fact finding

Where fact-finding is necessary, the Commission has important powers under Article 11 and Article 14 of Regulation 17.

Article 11 enables the Commission to obtain "all necessary information from the Governments and competent authorities of all the Member States and from undertakings and associations of undertakings". A two-stage procedure is involved. The first consists of an informal request for specified information to be given by a certain date.[51] If the information requested is not forthcoming, the procedure enters its second, formal, stage with the adoption by the Commission

---

[46] *e.g.* Case T–114/92 *BEMIM v. Commission* [1995] E.C.R. II–147; [1996] 4 C.M.L.R. 305. See also Case T–5/93 *Tremblay and others v. Commission* [1995] E.C.R. II–185, para. 65; [1996] 4 C.M.L.R. 305; appeal dismissed by the Court of Justice in Case C–91/95 *Tremblay and others v. Commission* [1996] E.C.R. I–5574; [1997] 4 C.M.L.R. 211. It may be noted that in *Tremblay* the Court of First Instance referred to the Commission being able to reject a complaint "provided that the rights of the complainant . . . can be adequately safeguarded, in particular, by the national courts."

[47] Case C–119/97P *Union Française de l'Express (Ufex) and others v. Commission and May Courier,* n.26, *supra.*

[48] *ibid.,* paras 79–80.

[49] *ibid.,* para. 92.

[50] *ibid.,* para. 95

[51] Reg. 17, Art. 11(3). An incorrect response will attract a fine under Art. 15(1)(b) of the Reg. See, *e.g. Re Telos* [1982] O.J. L58/19; [1982] 1 C.M.L.R. 267.

of a decision ordering that it be supplied.[52] Failure to comply with such a decision may result in the imposition of a fine under Article 15(1)(b) or of a periodic penalty payment under Article 16(1)(c). For information to be "necessary" within the meaning of Article 11 the Commission must reasonably suppose that it would assist it in establishing that the alleged infringement had occurred.[53] Moreover, the information to be supplied must not be disproportionate to the requirements of the investigation.[54] As with other areas of the Commission's investigative powers, the Court of Justice has insisted on certain constraints which do not expressly appear in the legislation. Thus, in *Orkem*[55] the undertaking claimed that it had been forced into giving answers of a self-incriminating nature pursuant to an order under Article 11. The Court of Justice, whilst apparently denying the existence of any rule against self-incrimination as such in E.C. law,[56] nevertheless held that the Commission could not compel an undertaking "to provide it with answers which might involve an admission on its part of the existence of an infringement [of the E.C. competition rules] which it is incumbent upon the Commission to prove".[57]

Under Article 14 the Commission is empowered to enter the premises of undertakings,[58] to examine and take copies of, or extracts from, books and business records and to ask for oral explanations on the spot. Inspections may take place on the basis of an authorisation in writing pursuant to paragraph (2) of the Article or of a Commission decision pursuant to paragraph (3). In neither case need any advance warning be given.[59] Where the Commission's inspectors are armed merely with a written authorisation, the undertaking concerned may refuse to submit to investigation; but once it has agreed, there is an obligation to co-operate fully. Refusal of an investigation ordered by a decision may attract a fine under Article 15(1)(c) or a periodic penalty payment under Article 16(1)(d). In *National Panasonic*[60] the Court rejected the argument that Article 14 envisages a two-stage procedure, like that of Article 11, under which a binding decision may be adopted only after an attempt to carry out an investigation on

---

[52] Reg. 17, Art. 11(5).

[53] Case C–36/92P *Samenwerkende Electriciteits-produktiebedrijven (SEP) v. Commission* [1994] E.C.R. I–1911.

[54] Case T–39/90 *Samenwerkende Electriciteits-produktiebedrijven (SEP) v. Commission* [1991] E.C.R. II–1497; [1992] 5 C.M.L.R. 33; the point was not commented upon by the Court of Justice on appeal, n.53, *supra*.

[55] Case 374/87 *Orkem v. Commission* [1989] E.C.R. 3283; [1991] 4 C.M.L.R. 502.

[56] But *cf.* Art. 6(1) of the European Convention on Human Rights and the right to silence as part of the right to a fair trial. See Van Overbeek, "The right to remain silent in competition investigations: the *Funke* decision of the Court of Human Rights makes revision of the ECJ's case law necessary" [1994] 15 E.C.L.R. 127. Also, Arnull, *The European Union and its Court of Justice*, pp. 443–444.

[57] [1989] E.C.R. 3283, para. 35. See also Case 27/88 *Solvay v. Commission* [1989] E.C.R. 3255 (summary publication).

[58] The Commission may not, however, investigate at an individual's private home: Joined Cases 46/87 and 227/88 *Hoechst v. Commission* [1989] E.C.R. 2859; [1991] 4 C.M.L.R. 410. The Court's rejection of the application of Art. 8(1) of the European Convention on Human Rights to business premises is at odds with the subsequent judgment of the European Court of Human Rights in *Niemietz v. Germany*, (1993) 16 E.H.R.R. 97; see Tridimas, *The General Principles of E.C. Law*, pp. 237–238.

[59] Case 136/79 *National Panasonic v. Commission* [1980] E.C.R. 2033; [1980] 3 C.M.L.R. 169.

[60] *ibid.*

the basis of a written authorisation has proved unsuccessful. The Court took the view that, on a true construction of the Article, the Commission has a choice between two possible methods of proceeding.

The decision authorising an investigation under Article 14(3) must set out the subject-matter and the purpose of an investigation, this being held by the Court of Justice in *Hoechst*[61] to be essential so that the undertakings concerned are informed about the matters being investigated. In this case, the Court observed that the statement of reasons, although it could have been more precise, contained sufficient detail in that it specified the products (PVC and low density polyethylene) in which there was a suspected cartel contrary to Article 81 and that the cartel was suspected to concern prices, quantities or sales targets for those products.

The Commission may be denied access to documents protected by the principle of the confidentiality of communications between lawyer and client. The principle, which is narrower in scope than the legal professional privilege of English law, was recognised by the Court of Justice in the *AM & S* case.[62] Protection of confidentiality was held to be subject, in effect, to three conditions. First, the communication must be "made for the purposes and in the interests of the client's rights of defence". That extended, in particular, to "all written communications exchanged after the initiation of the administrative procedure under Regulation No. 17 which may lead to a decision on the application of Articles 85 and 86 [now 81 and 82] or to a decision imposing a pecuniary sanction on the undertaking",[63] as well as to "earlier written communications which have a relationship to the subject-matter of that procedure".[64] Secondly, the communication must "emanate from independent lawyers, that is to say, lawyers who are not bound to the client by a relationship of employment".[65] Thirdly, the lawyers in question must be entitled to practise their profession in one of the Member States. Communications with two classes of lawyers are accordingly outside the privilege, viz. in-house lawyers, even in those Member States where they are subject to professional ethics and discipline, and lawyers from non-EU countries in the absence of any reciprocal arrangements with the EU. Where the status of a document is disputed, the Commission may adopt a decision ordering its disclosure, which may then be challenged in proceedings under Article 230. Such proceedings would not automatically have suspensory effect, although suspension of the application of the decision, or any other interim measure, could be ordered in an appropriate case.[66]

Positive outcomes

(i) General
Once the relevant facts have been found, the Commission will consider the legal position and, if its seems likely that an infringement of Article 81 and/or Article

---

[61] Joined Cases 46/87 and 227/88 *Hoechst v. Commission*, n.58, *supra.*
[62] Case 155/79 *AM & S v. Commission* [1982] E.C.R. 1575; [1982] 2 C.M.L.R. 264.
[63] [1982] E.C.R. at 1611.
[64] *ibid.*
[65] *ibid.*
[66] See Arts 242 and 243 E.C.

82 has occurred, proceedings may be initiated by sending the undertaking or undertakings concerned a statement of objections. Infringement proceedings are discussed in the next section of this Chapter. Where, on the other hand, Article 81 or Article 82 are thought not to apply, or exemption under Article 81(3) is available, a positive reaction will be prepared. In some cases a decision of the Commission formally granting negative clearance or exemption may be considered necessary. Most proceedings, however, are brought to an end by a letter signed by a director of the Directorate General IV informing the parties that the file in the case is to be closed. Developed in the early 1970s as a response to an increasing backlog of cases, these are known as "comfort letters".[67]

(ii) Negative clearance

We have seen that negative clearance is a certification by the Commission that the facts in its possession provide no grounds under Article 81 or Article 82 for intervention.[68] The value of the assurance given is proportional to the completeness of the disclosure made to the Commission. A decision granting negative clearance is probably not binding on national courts which derive jurisdiction to apply Article 81(1) and Article 82 from the direct effect of those provisions though it is likely to have considerable persuasive authority. Where the Commission intends to grant negative clearance, it is required by Article 19(3) of Regulation 17 to publish in the Official Journal a summary of the relevant application and invite all interested third parties to submit their observations within a specified time limit, which may not be less than a month. The final decision must also be published.[69]

(iii) Individual exemption

A decision of the Commission granting individual exemption pursuant to Article 81(3) declares the prohibition in Article 81(1) inapplicable to the agreement in question. The extent to which exemption may be made retrospective was considered above. Under Article 8 of Regulation 17 exemption is granted for a fixed period and may be subject to conditions. Before imposing an onerous condition the Commission must inform the parties of what it has in mind and give them an opportunity of making representations.[70] This right is derived from general principle rather than the text of secondary legislation.[71] Exemption may be revoked pursuant to Article 8(3) where there has been a material change in the facts, where an obligation attached to the grant has been breached, where the decision was based upon incorrect information or induced by deceit or where the parties have abused the exemption. In the last three cases, the revocation may be made retroactive. As with negative clearance, the Commission must publish an Article 19(3) notice before adopting a final decision; the latter must similarly also be published.

---

[67] According to the *White Paper on Modernisation*, n.4, *supra*, the Commission issues about 150–200 comfort letters a year. Over 90% of notifications are closed informally, either by comfort letter or simply filed without further action.

[68] Reg. 17, Art. 2.

[69] Reg. 17, Art. 21(1).

[70] Case 17/74 *Transocean Marine Paint v. Commission* [1974] E.C.R. 1063; [1974] 2 C.M.L.R. 459.

[71] *ibid.*, para. 15.

(iv) Block exemption

(a) **Conformity.**   Where a notified agreement is found to be in conformity with a block exemption regulation, the parties will be so informed by letter. Such letters merely state a view as to the applicability of directly effective provisions of Community law, there being no need to notify an agreement to secure the benefit of a block exemption.

(b) **"No opposition" or "withdrawal of opposition".**   Where the Commission expresses no opposition to a notified agreement within the period (normally six months) stipulated in a block exemption containing an opposition procedure, or withdraws its opposition, the effect is to trigger the Regulation in respect of the agreement.[72] Since it alters the legal situation, the decision not to oppose or to withdraw opposition must, it is submitted, be susceptible of review under Article 230.

(v) Comfort letters
These are, in the phrase used by the Court of Justice in the *Perfumes* cases,[73] "merely administrative letters", signed by an official of DG IV. Comfort letters may be used to indicate either that there are no grounds for applying Article 81(1) or Article 82 (in other words, as an informal negative clearance) or that an agreement falling within Article 81(1) is considered eligible for exemption under Article 81(3). They state that the file will be closed, with the proviso that it may be re-opened if material legal or factual circumstances change. Dealing with a case in this way has the great advantage of simplifying and shortening the proceedings by eliminating the publication requirement provided for in Articles 19 and 21 of Regulation 17 and the formal consultation of the Advisory Committee, as well as reducing the amount of translation required.[74] However, such letters establish an uneasy comfort zone for the reasons explained below.

First, it is clear that the Commission will be able to depart from the indications of a comfort letter in the light of changed circumstances. In *Langnese-Iglo*,[75] for example, the Commission had issued a comfort letter to Schöller in response to its request for negative clearance in relation to the ice cream supply agreements it concluded with retail distributors. Langnese-Iglo operated parallel contracts in relation to its ice cream products. However, six years later a competitor lodged a complaint with the Commission, in the light of which the Commission proceeded to take action against the two ice cream suppliers. The latter claimed before the Court of First Instance that the Commission had infringed their legitimate expectations by re-opening scrutiny of the agreements. The Court of First Instance ruled that the Commission had signalled its reservations about the

---

[72] See Waelbroeck, (1986) 11 E.L.Rev. 268. *cf.* Venit, (1985) 22 C.M.L.Rev. 167.
[73] Joined Cases 253/78 and 1–3/79 *Procureur de la République v. Giry and Guerlain* [1980] E.C.R. 2327; [1981] 2 C.M.L.R. 94; Case 99/79 *Lancôme v. Etos* [1980] E.C.R. 2511; [1981] 2 C.M.L.R. 164; Case 31/80 *L'Oréal v. De Nieuwe AMCK* [1980] E.C.R. 3775; [1981] 2 C.M.L.R 235.
[74] *White Paper on Modernisaton*, n.4, *supra*, paras 34–35.
[75] Case C–279/95P *Langnese-Iglo v. Commission* [1998] E.C.R. I–5609; [1998] 5 C.M.L.R. 933, on appeal from Case T–7/93 *Langnese-Iglo v. Commission* [1995] E.C.R. II–1533; [1995] C.M.L.R. 602. There was no appeal from the case involving the original recipient of the comfort letter: Case T–9/93 *Schöller Lebensmittel v. Commission* [1995] E.C.R. II–1611; [1995] 5 C.M.L.R. 602.

future in the original letter and was entitled to review its position in the light of new circumstances. Moreover, this approach was in conformity with the Commission's duties to examine complaints carefully.[76] On appeal by Langnese-Iglo, the Court of Justice refused to disturb the findings of the Court of First Instance, confining itself to the observation that the fact that the Commission has issued a comfort letter cannot mean that it is no longer entitled to take account of a factual situation which existed before the letter was sent but was brought to its notice only later, particularly in connection with a complaint lodged at a later stage.[77] It may be noted that the Advocate General expressly stated that the protection of legitimate expectations is available only, if at all, to the undertaking receiving the comfort letter. In his view, since such letters do not affect third parties and are not binding on national courts, it is logical that they likewise cannot be invoked by third parties—here Langnese-Iglo—in support of their claims.[78] The reference to "if at all" in this comment appears over-strict in the light of the comments of the Community judicature.[79]

The second caveat about comfort letters concerns the fact that they are not binding upon national courts. They lack the status of a decision, and the Court of Justice treats the existence of a comfort letter as no more than a fact which a national court may properly take into account.[80] Although informal steps have been taken to assist national courts in the discharge of their functions and powers under the E.C. competition rules,[81] there are still awkward scenarios. In particular, the presence of a comfort letter indicating a positive view by the Commission about the exemption prospects of an agreement poses a problem for national courts currently still disenfranchised from granting exemptions under Article 81(3). The Notice on Co-Operation offers little guidance on the point[82] other than to reiterate the position of the Court of Justice indicated above. For the national court to say that such an agreement does not constitute a restriction within the meaning of Article 81(1) would clearly fly in the face of the premise that exemption is needed at all, whilst to hold it void as a restriction would contradict the express views of the Commission as to the merits of the agreement in the comfort letter.

Thirdly, comfort letters still lack transparency. Although some are published, there is no requirement to do so. The steps taken in this direction by the Commission,[83] thus enabling representations from third parties to be made, might increase the persuasiveness of comfort letters. Of course, if the proposals contained in the *White Paper on Modernisation*[84] for *ex post facto* scrutiny of

---

[76] See, *supra*, text accompanying notes 24–39.

[77] Case C–279/95P *Langnese-Iglo v. Commission*, n.75, *supra*, para. 30.

[78] *ibid.*, Opinion para. 18.

[79] Presciently captured much earlier by Advocate General Reischl in Case 31/80 *L'Oréal v. De Nieuw AMCK*, n.73, *supra*, when he observed: "... having regard to the principle that legitimate expectations must be upheld, the Commission may depart from the judgment arrived at by its officers only if the factual circumstances change or if its finding was reached on the basis of incorrect information": [1980] E.C.R. at 3803.

[80] See, *Perfumes* cases, n.73, *supra*.

[81] Notably in the *Notice on Co-Operation*, n.43, *supra*.

[82] *ibid.*, para. 25.

[83] See [1982] O.J. C343/4, O.J. C295/6.

[84] n.4, *supra*.

restrictive agreements were implemented then the particular problems of comfort letters would disappear on the basis that notifications of fresh agreements would no longer be necessary.[85]

Finally, it should be noted that comfort letters bring to an end the provisional validity enjoyed by duly notified old agreements.[86]

Infringement proceedings

(i) The right to a hearing

(a) **Legal basis.** Before it adopts a decision applying Article 81 or Article 82 the Commission is required, pursuant to Article 19 of Regulation 17, to give the undertakings concerned the opportunity of being heard on the matters to which the Commission has taken objection. Other natural or legal persons, if they can show a sufficient interest, will also be entitled to a hearing. Detailed provisions on hearings were first laid down by the Commission in Regulation 99/63, subsequently replaced by Regulation 2842/98.[87]

Those provisions implement in the sphere of competition the general principle of law that a person whose interests are liable to be adversely affected by an individual decision of a public authority has a right to make his views known to the authority before the decision is taken. As the ensuing discussion shows, the European Courts have been vigilant to ensure that the Commission does not abuse its very wide enforcement powers.

(b) **The statement of objections.** In order for a person effectively to exercise his right to a hearing, he must be informed of the facts and considerations on the basis of which the responsible authority is minded to act.[88] Article 3 of Regulation 2842/98 places the Commission under a duty to inform the parties in writing of the objections raised against them. The issuing of a "statement of objections" marks the formal initiation of proceedings that may culminate in a finding that Article 81 or Article 82 has been infringed. Under Article 3(3) of the Regulation a fine or periodic penalty payment may only be imposed on an undertaking where objections have been notified in the requisite manner. Article 2(1) lays down that the Commission shall in its decisions deal only with objections in respect of which the parties have been afforded an opportunity of making their views known.[89]

The statement of objections thus provides the boundaries of the case. The Court of Justice has repeatedly affirmed that it must set forth clearly all the

---

[85] However, the Commission still sees a need in the proposed regime for so-called "positive decisions" (*ibid.*, paras 88–89) which would have a declaratory value in relation to transactions raising new points. Such positive decisions are envisaged to be of a declaratory nature and would have the same legal effect as negative clearances under the existing rules.

[86] See, *Perfumes* cases, n.73, *supra*.

[87] n.27, *supra*.

[88] Case 17/74 *Transocean Marine Paint v. Commission*, n.70, *supra*.

[89] The undertakings may waive their right to a hearing: Joined Cases T–213/95 and 18/96 *SCK and FNK v. Commission* [1997] E.C.R. II–1739; [1998] 4 C.M.L.R. 259. However, this must be unambiguously done if the Commission is to be able to omit to communicate documents: Case T–30/91 *Solvay v. Commission* [1995] E.C.R. II–1775, para. 57; [1996] 5 C.M.L.R. 57; [1995] All E.R. (E.C.) 600.

essential facts upon which the Commission relies against the respondent under-takings.[90] A fairly succinct summary may be judged adequate for this purpose,[91] although the Commission must identify in the objections each of the infringe-ments which it alleges to have occurred.[92] The final decision need not be an exact replica of the statement of objections, since the Commission must take into account factors which emerge during the administrative proceedings: some objections may be abandoned altogether, and different arguments may be put forward in support of those which are maintained.[93] Where, however, the Commission wishes to introduce fresh objections, a supplementary statement should be sent to the respondents.[94]

(c) **Access to the file.**   One of the most frequently contested aspects of the rights of defence in competition cases down the years has concerned access to the Commission's file. The evolution of principle in this area displays the tensions between efficient and effective enforcement on the one hand, and fundamental rights and due process on the other.[95] Establishing clear rules is not made any easier by the confidential and commercially-sensitive nature of many documents in competition cases. The legislative framework contained in Regulation 2842/98[96] does not resolve all the issues and the more generalised principles of the case-law have made a significant contribution to the present position.

According to Article 13(1) of Regulation 2842, the Commission "shall make appropriate arrangements for allowing access to the file, taking due account of the need to protect business secrets, internal Commission documents and other confidential information". This statement appears to encapsulate the case-law which preceded its enactment.[97] In particular, the Court of First Instance had held in *Hercules*[98] that the Commission was not able to depart from the standards it had voluntarily set for itself in its *Twelfth Report on Competition Policy*. As a result, the Commission was obliged to make available to the undertakings involved in proceedings under Article 81(1) proceedings all documents, whether in their favour or otherwise, which it had obtained during the course of the investigation, save where the business secrets of other undertakings, the internal documents of the Commission or other confidential information were involved.[99]

---

[90] See, *e.g.* Case 45/69 *Boehringer v. Commission* [1970] E.C.R. 769; Case 85/76 *Hoffmann-La Roche v. Commission* [1979] E.C.R. 461; [1979] 3 C.M.L.R. 211; Joined Cases 43 and 63/82 *VBVB and VBBB v. Commission* [1984] E.C.R. 19; [1985] 1 C.M.L.R. 27.

[91] Case 48/69 *ICI v. Commission* [1972] E.C.R. 619 at 650–651; [1972] C.M.L.R. 557; Joined Cases 100–103/80 *Musique Diffusion Française v. Commission* [1983] E.C.R. 1825; [1983] 3 C.M.L.R. 221.

[92] Joined Cases C–89/85 etc *Åhlström Oy and others v. Commission ("Wood Pulp")* [1993] E.C.R. I–1307. [1993] 4 C.M.L.R. 407.

[93] Joined Cases 209–215 and 218/78 *Van Landewyck v. Commission* [1980] E.C.R. 3125; [1981] 3 C.M.L.R. 134, paras 68–70. See also Joined Cases T 305–307, 313–316, 318, 325, 328–329 and 335/94 *Re the PVC Cartel II: Limburgse Vinyl Maatschappij and others v. Commission* [1999] E.C.R. II–000; [1999] 5 C.M.L.R. 303.

[94] Case 54/69 *Francolor v. Commission* [1972] E.C.R. 851; [1972] C.M.L.R. 557.

[95] See Levitt, "Access to the file: the Commission's administrative procedures in cases under Arts 85 and 86" (1997) 34 C.M.L.Rev. 1413; Joshua, "Balancing the public interests: confidentiality, trade secrets and disclosure of evidence in E.C. competition procedures" [1994] 2 E.C.L.R. 68.

[96] n.27, *supra.*

[97] Reg. 99/63, the predecessor to Reg. 2842, had been silent on the matter of access to the file.

[98] Case T–7/89 *Hercules Chemicals v. Commission* [1991] E.C.R. II–1711; [1992] 4 C.M.L.R. 84, para. 53, relying on Case 81/72 *Commission v. Council* [1973] E.C.R. 575; [1973] C.M.L.R. 639.

[99] [1991] E.C.R. II–1711, at para. 54.

The Court of Justice has always refrained from holding the right of access to the file to be absolute. Instead, it has concentrated on the need for effective defence. In the appeal in the *Hercules*[1] case it reiterated its previous case-law, stating:

"access to the file in competition cases is intended in particular to enable the addressees of statements of objections to acquaint themselves with the evidence in the Commission's file so that on the basis of that evidence they can express their views effectively on the conclusions reached by the Commission in its statement of objections.

Thus the general principles of Community law governing the right of access to the Commission's file are designed to ensure effective exercise of the rights of the defence . . ."[2]

To ensure that effectiveness, it is clear that it cannot be for the Commission alone to decide which documents are of use for the defence. Having regard to the general principle of equality of arms, the Commission cannot be permitted to decide on its own whether or not to use documents against the undertakings, where the latter have no access to them and are therefore unable to take the relevant decision whether or not to use them in their defence.[3]

The Commission first clarified its practice in a Notice in 1997,[4] largely in response to the *Hercules* judgment in the Court of First Instance. The Notice enlarges upon the meaning of the three categories of "non-communicable documents",[5] and makes clear that the remaining field of communicable documents is not limited to those which the Commission sees as "relevant". However, only the evidence or documentation relied upon by the Commission will be attached to the statement of objections. Thereafter parties may request access to the file. Decisions on whether to grant such requests rest with the Hearing Officer.[6] Any refusal must be in the form of a decision susceptible to judicial review.[7] This particular route may provide the path for further clarification of the boundaries of the non-communicable categories of documentation, especially

---

[1] Case C–51/92P *Hercules Chemicals v. Commission* [1999] E.C.R. I–4235; [1999] 5 C.M.L.R. 976.

[2] *ibid.*, paras 75–76, citing Case 322/81 *Michelin v. Commission* [1983] E.C.R. 3461; [1985] 1 C.M.L.R. 282, para. 7; Case 85/76 *Hoffmann-La Roche*, n.90, *supra*, paras 9 and 11; Case C–310/93P *BPB Industries and British Gypsum v. Commission* [1995] E.C.R. I–865; [1997] 4 C.M.L.R. 238, para. 21; Case C–185/95P *Baustahlgewebe v. Commission* [1998] E.C.R. I–8417, [1999] 4 C.M.L.R. 1203.

[3] Case T–30/91 *Solvay v. Commission* [1995] E.C.R. II–1775; [1996] 5 C.M.L.R. 57; T–36/91 *ICI v. Commission* [1995] E.C.R. II–1847, Joined Cases T 305–307, 313–316, 318, 325, 328–329 and 335/94 *Re the PVC Cartel II: Limburgse Vinyl Maatschappij and others v. Commission*, n.93, *supra*.

[4] Notice on the internal rules of procedure for processing requests for access to the file in cases pursuant to Arts 81 and 82 E.C., Arts 65 and 66 of the ECSC Treaty and Council Reg. 4064/89, [1977] O.J. C23/3; [1997] 4 C.M.L.R. 490. The guidelines relate essentially to undertakings which are the subject of investigations, not to third parties (especially complainants).

[5] *viz.*, business secrets, confidential documents and internal documents.

[6] See further, Dec. 94/810 on the terms of reference of hearing officers in competition procedures before the Commission; [1994] O.J. L330/67. By Art. 2(1) of this Decision, the Hearing Officer "shall ensure that the hearing is properly conducted and thus contribute to the objectivity of the hearing itself and of any decision taken subsequently." Art. 2(2) adds that "the Hearing Officer shall see to it that the rights of the defence are respected, while taking account of the need for effective application of the competition rules . . ."

[7] *ibid.*, Art. 5.

business secrets and confidentiality.[8] Third parties and complainants seeking to defend their legitimate interests have less extensive rights of access than the objects of a Commission investigation.[9] However, they may receive edited non-confidential forms of documentation.[10]

Developments in relation to confidentiality, as with others in the general field of procedural safeguards discussed above, have extended beyond the particular textual confines of secondary legislation. The case of *Samenwerkende*[11] provides a good example. Article 20(2) of Regulation 17 requires that the Commission and the competent authorities of the Member States do not disclose information of the kind covered by professional secrecy obtained under the Regulation.[12] The applicant's business in the case was electricity generation sourced from natural gas. It had previously obtained gas supplies from the Dutch state supplier, Gasunie, but was engaged in buying from a Norwegian alternative, Statoil. Exercising its powers to request information, the Commission sought documents concerning the terms of business with Statoil. The applicant refused, claiming that the confidentiality of that information would be jeopardised as it would eventually fall into Gasunie's hands via the liaison between the Commission and Member State authorities envisaged by Article 10(1) of Regulation 17.

Following a different line of reasoning from the Court of First Instance,[13] the Court of Justice chose to rely on a "general principle of the right of undertakings to the protection of their business secrets", of which Article 20(2) was just one expression. The consequence was that the party claiming confidentiality was entitled to receive from the Commission a decision on whether to release the information to national authorities under Article 10, with enough opportunity to subject that decision to judicial review before it was implemented. In creating this additional procedural step the Court was replicating the approach it had adopted much earlier in *AKZO*[14] in relation to the disclosure of confidential information by the Commission to third parties.

---

[8] In Case C–310/93P *BPB Industries and British Gypsum v. Commission*, n.2, *supra*, the Court of Justice observed, at para. 26, that it must be recognised that a firm in a dominant position might adopt retaliatory measures against competitors, suppliers or customers who might have supplied the Commission with information against it. In such circumstances, the Court said, such undertakings would only co-operate if they knew that account would be taken of their requests for confidentiality. For procedural safeguards in respect of releasing confidential information, see Reg. 2842/98, especially Arts 3, 12 and 13.

[9] Joined Cases 142 and 156/84 *BAT and Reynolds v. Commission* [1987] E.C.R. 4487; [1988] 4 C.M.L.R. 24. See also Case 53/85 *AKZO v. Commission* [1986] E.C.R. 1965; [1987] 1 C.M.L.R. 231.

[10] Reg 2842/98, Art. 13(2) provides: "Any party which makes known its views under the provisions of this Regulation shall clearly identify any material which it considers to be confidential, giving reasons, and provide a separate non-confidential version by the date set by the Commission. If it does not do so by the set date, the Commission may assume that the submission does not contain such material."

[11] Case C–36/92P *SEP v. Commission*, n.53, *supra*.

[12] See Case C–67/91 *Dirección General de Defensa de la Competencia v. Asociación Española de Banca Privada ("Spanish Banks")* [1992] E.C.R. I–4785.

[13] Which had found sufficient protection in Art. 20 of Reg. 17.

[14] Case 53/85 n.9, *supra*.

The Court's reasoning in *Samenwerkende* may be compared with that of the Court of First Instance in *Postbank*.[15] The Commission was investigating the practices of Postbank and other Dutch banks, and had supplied bank customers who had complained to it with copies of the statement of objections, despite opposition from the banks. The complainant customers had then secured Commission authorisation to use the documents in proceedings which had been initiated in the Dutch courts on the basis of the E.C. rules. Postbank only received notification of this happening after the material had been adduced before the Dutch court, and sought to challenge the validity of the release by the Commission. The Court of First Instance distinguished *Samenwerkende* on the basis that it concerned national administrative authorities, not courts. It went on to say that Article 287 of the Treaty, containing a broad principle of confidentiality, did not prevent disclosure to national courts. But, in offering its cooperation to national courts the Commission could not undermine the guarantees given to individuals by Article 20(2) of Regulation 17. It was therefore under a duty to take precautions when releasing material, such as alerting the national court to its sensitive nature and leaving the court to take over the mantle of responsibility for ensuring confidentiality. However, the Court of First Instance recognised that in some cases it would not be possible for the Commission to enable the parties to be protected despite those precautions. In such situations, which the Court of First Instance did not elaborate upon,[16] the Commission could refuse to disclose documents to national courts.

The relationship between national courts and the Commission is one that the latter increasingly places centre-stage in the evolving decentralisation of competition law enforcement.[17] By allowing for the complete withholding of information by the Commission in some circumstances the *Postbank* ruling does not perhaps give the greatest vote of confidence to that link. Yet, on the other hand, there is equally a case for saying that the passing down to national courts of responsibility for maintaining confidentiality could actually result in information indirectly becoming available to litigants at national level which would not be accessible directly by complainants under the rules discussed earlier. Much will depend on future practice and the challenges it provokes.

(ii) Final decision

(a) **Termination of infringement.** The Commission has a number of powers at its disposal once it has concluded that there has been an infringement of Article 81 or Article 82. Informal resolution is possible if the parties accept the Commission's recommendations,[18] but this is rare. If a formal outcome is to be adopted, Article 3(1) of Regulation 17 provides that the Commission may by

---

[15] Case T–353/94 *Postbank NV v. Commission* [1996] E.C.R. II–921; [1996] All E.R. 817.

[16] Weatherill & Beaumont, *EU Law* (3rd ed.) suggest, p. 901, n.87, that third-party "whistleblowers" may be a suitable case for such protection. See Case 145/83 *Adams v. Commission* [1985] E.C.R. 3539; [1986] 1 C.M.L.R. 506 for a particularly distressing example.

[17] See the discussion, *infra*, of the *Co-operation Notice*, n.43, *supra*. *The White Paper on Modernisation*, n.4, *supra*, envisages an even greater responsibility for national courts.

[18] Art. 3(3) of Reg. 17. On the basis of acceptance of the recommendations the Commission could adopt a negative clearance, exemption or comfort letter.

decision order an infringement to be brought to an end. Termination may involve positive action on the part of the addressee or addressees, and the decision may specify the steps to be taken. Thus in *Commercial Solvents*,[19] a case involving an abuse of a dominant position, the Commission imposed on CSC and Instituto an obligation to deliver an initial quantity of aminobutanol to Zoja within 30 days and to submit within two months a plan for making supplies available in the longer term. The order was upheld by the Court of Justice which said of Article 3:

> "This provision must be applied in relation to the infringement which has been established and may include an order to do certain acts or provide certain advantages which have been wrongly withheld as well as prohibiting the continuation of certain action, practices or situations which are contrary to the Treaty."[20]

A periodic penalty payment may be attached to the order to ensure that it is complied with.

However, in *Automec II*[21] the Commission claimed that it had no power in the circumstances of the case to require the positive action sought from the applicant in order to remedy an infringement of Article 81(1). In particular, it claimed it lacked the competence to order BMW to resume deliveries to its distributor and that this could only be done on the basis of national law. The Commission expressly distinguished between cases under Article 82, where specific acts of abuse could be remedied, and Article 81, where the infringing element must be the agreement. Therefore, it argued, its only power available under Article 3 of Regulation 17 with regard to the latter was to compel the parties to bring the agreement to an end. But in the case in question Automec wanted to be included in the agreement (*ie* the selective distribution network), not to see it terminated. This step, the Commission also argued, would be too great an incursion into freedom of contract. The Court of First Instance endorsed the Commission's position, stressing that "the Commission undoubtedly has power to find the existence of the infringement and order the parties concerned to end it, but it is not for the Commission to impose upon the parties its own choice among the different potential courses of action which all conform to the Treaty".[22]

In the *GVL* case[23] it was argued that the Commission had no power to adopt a decision recording an infringement which had already been brought to an end. The Court of Justice held that the Commission might well have a legitimate interest in taking such a decision, where it was necessary to clarify the legal position in order to prevent a repetition of the infringement.[24]

---

[19] Joined Cases 6 and 7/73 *Commercial Solvents Corporation v. Commission* [1974] E.C.R. 223, [1974] 1 C.M.L.R. 309. The abuse consisted of a refusal to supply.

[20] [1974] E.C.R. at 255.

[21] Case T–24/90, n.41, *supra*.

[22] *ibid.*, para. 52.

[23] Case 7/82 *GVL v. Commission* [1983] E.C.R. 483; [1983] 3 C.M.L.R. 645.

[24] No decision is necessary to bring the prohibition in Art. 81(1) or Art. 82 into force. See Reg. 17, Art. 1.

Any decisions adopted by the Commission must comply with its own procedural formalities.[25] In the *PVC Cartel* cases,[26] a failure to comply with the collegiate principle and other aspects of the proper authentication of decisions led the Court of First Instance to treat the decision in question as "non-existent". However, this approach was overturned by the Court of Justice,[27] who held that acts of Community institutions were presumed lawful and produced legal effects, even when tainted by irregularities. Although some of these might be so grave as to require acts to be considered non-existent, this position should be reserved for quite extreme cases.[28] Accordingly, the Court treated the particular failures as insufficiently grave to warrant a finding of non-existence, but still found sufficient procedural infringements to declare the decision void.[29]

(b) **Fines.** A key weapon in the Commission's armoury is the power conferred on it by Article 15 of Regulation 17 to fine undertakings for negligent or intentional infringements in relation to the competition rules. Relatively minor fines[30] may be imposed under paragraph (1) for supplying incorrect or misleading information or not complying with an investigation under Article 14. Of more significance is the power under paragraph (2) to impose fines for infringements of Article 81(1) or Article 82. These may range from 1,000 euros to 1 million euros, or a sum in excess of that but not exceeding 10 per cent of turnover of each of the undertakings participating in the infringement.

Regulation 17 has little to say about the status and calculation of fines. However, according to Article 15(4) decisions taken pursuant to paragraphs (1) and (2) "shall not be of a criminal nature". This statement, made in 1962, is not surprising, especially given that the E.C. has no general legislative criminal jurisdiction.[31] But it is difficult to sustain in the light of subsequent developments influenced by Article 6(1) of the European Convention on Human Rights (ECHR). This provides that "in the determination of his civil rights and obligations or of any criminal charge against him, everyone is entitled to a fair and public hearing within a reasonable time by an independent and impartial tribunal established by law". In a case heard by the European Commission on Human Rights, domestic rules which provided for extensive penalties to be applied for breaches of competition law were said to be criminal in nature for the purposes of the Convention.[32] Advocate General Vesterdorf made similar observations in relation to fines imposed under the E.C. rules in the *PVC Cartel*

---

[25] Commission's Rules of Procedure; [1993] O.J. L230/16.

[26] See Joined Cases T-79/89 etc. *BASF and others v. Commission* [1992] E.C.R. II-315; [1992] 4 C.M.L.R. 357.

[27] Case C-137/92P *Commission v. BASF and others* [1994] E.C.R. I-2555.

[28] *ibid.*, para. 50.

[29] The Commission subsequently adopted a new decision reiterating its finding of an infringement of Art. 81 by the 12 undertakings and imposing fines. These decisions were again challenged by the undertakings, but (with some reductions in fines for some parties) their claims were rejected by the Court of First Instance in Joined Cases T-305-307/94 etc. *PVC Cartel II*, n.93, *supra*.

[30] From 100 to 5,000 euros, but the Commission wishes to increase these figures: see *White Paper on Modernisation*, n.4, *supra*, para. 124.

[31] Although national criminal laws and procedures may well be undermined or rendered inapplicable by virtue of the impact of E.C. law: see Baker, "Taking European criminal law seriously" [1998] Crim.L.R. 361.

[32] *Société Stenuit v. France* (1992) Series A no 232-A, (1992) 14 E.H.R.R. 509.

cases.[33] Later, in the *Baustahlgewebe* case,[34] Advocate General Léger une-quivocally asserted that "It cannot be disputed—and the Commission does not dispute—that, in the light of the case-law of the European Court of Human Rights and the opinions of the European Commission of Human Rights, the present case involves a 'criminal charge'".[35]

The Court of Justice, however, has proceeded cautiously on the question. It established in early case-law that competition law proceedings before the Commission are administrative in nature, even where they can lead to the imposition of fines.[36] Furthermore, it has said that the Commission is not a "tribunal" for the purposes of Article 6(1) of the Convention.[37] Nevertheless, as discussed elsewhere,[38] the Court of Justice adopts a well-established practice of using the Convention as an inspiration from which to derive principles of Community law. In addition, the presence of Article 6(2) TEU[39] has led Advocate General Léger to conclude that "it is now accepted that it is within the Court's remit to secure respect for the rights recognised by the Convention".[40] The furthest commitment offered so far by the Court of Justice can be seen in the *Baustahlgewebe* case, where it referred directly to Article 6(1) of the Convention and then observed:

" The general principle of Community law that everyone is entitled to fair legal process, which is inspired by those fundamental rights [of the Convention], and in particular the right to legal process within a reasonable period, is applicable in the context of proceedings brought against a Commission decision imposing fines on an undertaking for infringement of competition law."[41]

This passage does not address whether the Commission is a tribunal for the purposes of Article 6(1) since *Baustahlgewebe* concerned whether the proceedings before the Court of First Instance were susceptible to the requirements of a "reasonable period".[42] However, the Court of Justice appears to concede that a "criminal charge" must be present by virtue of the fines attached to competition law enforcement. If this is indeed the case, then further challenges may ensue to

---

[33] Case T–7/89 *Hercules v. Commission*, n.98, *supra*, observing also that it was "vitally important" to bring about a state of legal affairs not susceptible of any justified criticism with reference to the ECHR.

[34] Case C–185/95P *Baustahlgewebe v. Commission*, n.2, *supra*. The case concerned, *inter alia*, the question whether the proceedings of the Court of First Instance in relation to the undertaking's challenge to the Commission's adverse decision had taken an excessively long time. The Commission had imposed fines in August 1989 and the undertaking lodged its appeal in October 1989. Judgment was not given by the Court of First Instance until April 1995.

[35] *ibid.*, para. 31 of the Opinion.

[36] Case 45/69 *Boehringer Mannheim v. Commission*, n.90, *supra*.

[37] Joined Cases 209–215 and 218/78 *Van Landewyck v. Commission*, n.93, *supra*; Joined Cases 100–103/80 *Musique Diffusion Française v. Commission*, n.91, *supra*.

[38] See Chap. 6, *supra*.

[39] "The Union shall respect fundamental rights, as guaranteed by the [ECHR] . . . and as they result from the constitutional traditions common to the Member States, as general principles of Community law." This provision is made justiciable before the Court of Justice in relation to acts of Community institutions by virtue of Art. 46 TEU.

[40] Case C–185/95P *Baustahlgewebe v. Commission*, n.2, *supra*, para. 25 of Opinion.

[41] *ibid.*, para. 21 of judgment.

[42] The Court of Justice reduced the original fine of 3 million ecus by 50,000 ecus as "reasonable satisfaction" for the excessive duration of the proceedings.

establish whether the Commission's multiple roles to investigate facts, decide on infringements of the rules and impose fines satisfy Convention and Community law rules about fair hearing and due process.

With regard to the amounts and calculation of fines, Article 15(2) of Regulation 17 stipulates only that "regard shall be had both to the gravity and to the duration of the infringement". The Commission has adopted Notices that seek to establish some transparency and certainty in the calculation of fines as well as offering incentives to undertakings to co-operate with it. At the heart of the guidelines[43] is the idea that gravity and duration of the infringement are used to determine a basic amount for the fine, which can then be increased or reduced in the light of the aggravating or attenuating circumstances of the particular case. The guidelines divide both gravity and duration into three categories. Thus, in relation to gravity, infringements may be "minor", "serious" or "very serious", examples respectively being vertical restraints with limited market impact, vertical or horizontal restrictions with more extensive effects and horizontal cartels engaging in price-fixing or market-sharing. The basic element of the fine for these three types of gravity is likely to comprise up to 1 million euros for minor infringements, up to 20 million euros for serious ones, and above that for the very serious category. The three categories which make up duration are "short", "medium" and "long", representing periods of, respectively, up to one year, five years or longer. Nothing is to be added to the gravity sum for short infringements, but medium term breaches may increase it by up to 50 per cent and long violations may add on 10 per cent of the gravity amount per year of the duration.

The guidelines Notice also sets out examples of aggravating and attenuating circumstances to apply to the basic amount.[44] Among the former are: repeated infringements of the same type, acting as leader in or instigator of the infringement, retaliatory measures to enforce practices and attempts to obstruct the Commission's investigations. The following factors are included in the list of attenuating circumstances: a purely "follow-my-leader" role in the infringement, prompt termination of the violation as soon as the Commission intervenes, reasonable doubt on the part of the undertaking as to whether its conduct constitutes an infringement and negligent or unintentional breaches. However, these lists are non-exhaustive and the Commission will undoubtedly articulate further factors in the exercise of the discretion which the European Courts recognise that it holds in the field of fining policy.[45]

The Commission claims in its guidelines Notice that it seeks a "coherent and non-discriminatory" approach to fines. Its main priorities appear to be deterrence and encouragement of the discovery of long-term deeply embedded cartels. The efficacy of the former is open to criticism,[46] with contested views on the

---

[43] Guidelines on the method of setting fines imposed pursuant to Art. 15(2) of Reg. 17 and Art. 65(5) of the ECSC Treaty; [1998] O.J. C9/3. See Wils, "The Commission's new method for calculating fines in antitrust cases" (1998) 23 E.L.Rev. 252.

[44] For applications by the Commission of its criteria, see Decision 98/273 *Volkswagen* [1998] O.J. L124/93 in which it set a then record fine of 102 million ecus.

[45] Case C-137/95P *SPO v. Commission* [1996] E.C.R. I-1611, acknowledging that gravity is to be determined by the particular circumstances of the case, its context and the dissuasive effect of fines.

[46] See Wils, "EC competition fines: to deter or not to deter" (1995) 15 Y.E.L. 17.

empirical evidence for the gains and costs of anti-competitive conduct, the advantages of alternative enforcement strategies and the question of who really ends up paying the fine. Moreover, even though dissuasiveness might demand hefty fines to be imposed, there are constraints imposed in any event by the maximum figure in Article 15(2)[47] and the general Community law of proportionality. The Court of Justice has indicated in this respect that it is permissible, for the purpose of determining the fine, "to have regard both to the total turnover of the undertaking, which constitutes an indication, albeit approximate and imperfect, of the size of the undertaking and its economic power, and to the proportion of that turnover accounted for by the goods in respect of which the infringement was committed, which gives an indication of the scale of the infringement".[48]

The Commission's desire to detect as well as deter can be seen from its so-called Leniency Notice,[49] which sets out some incentives for information in relation to the most pernicious forms of horizontal cartels. A reduction of at least 75 per cent in the fine on an undertaking will be forthcoming if it supplies particular information about secret agreements aimed at fixing prices, production or sales quotas, sharing markets or banning imports or exports. However, a number of fairly stringent conditions apply in order to obtain the benefits of this co-operation. First, the information must relate to a secret cartel which the Commission has not investigated by decision and about which the Commission does not have enough material to establish its existence. Secondly, the informing undertaking must be the first to adduce decisive evidence. Thirdly, the undertaking must put an end to its own involvement in the cartel by the time of providing the information. Fourthly, it must provide all the evidence at its disposal and maintain co-operation with the Commission throughout the investigation. Finally, an undertaking will be deprived of the potential reduction if it has been the instigator of the cartel or compelled another enterprise to participate in it.

The Commission's power to adopt interim measures

Regulation 17 does not expressly empower the Commission to adopt interim measures in respect of behaviour which is the subject of proceedings for the infringement of Article 81 or Article 82. The drafting of Article 3 of the Regulation in particular, seems to assume that, before a binding order is made, the Commission must have found that an infringement exists. However, in the *Camera Care* case[50] the Court of Justice held that a power to adopt interim measures is impliedly conferred on the Commission "to avoid the exercise of the power to make decisions given by Article 3 from becoming ineffectual or even illusory because of the action of certain undertakings".[51] According to the

---

[47] *i.e.* up to 1 million euros or 10% of turnover.

[48] Case C–185/95P *Baustahlgewebe v. Commission*, n.2, *supra*, para. 139, citing Joined Cases 100–103/80 *Musique Diffusion Française v. Commission*, n.91, *supra*.

[49] Notice on the non-imposition of fines in cartel cases [1996] O.J. C207/4. It is also sometimes referred to as a "whistleblower's charter". For an example of applying the Notice by analogy, see Dec. 99/210 *British Sugar plc, Tate & Lyle plc, Napier Brown & Co. Ltd, James Budgett Sugars Ltd*.

[50] Case 792/79R *Camera Care v. Commission* [1980] E.C.R. 119; [1980] 1 C.M.L.R. 334.

[51] [1980] E.C.R. at 131.

Camera Care judgment, the adoption of interim measures is subject to four conditions: that the case is urgent and the measures are needed to avoid a situation likely to cause serious and irreparable damage to the party seeking them, or one which is intolerable for the public interest; that the measures are of a temporary and conservatory nature and are restricted to what is necessary in the situation; that in adopting the measures the Commission maintains the essential safeguards guaranteed under Regulation 17, in particular by Article 19[52]; and that the decision is made in a form that would enable it to be challenged before the Court.

Any party requesting the Commission to take interim measures is only required to demonstrate that there is a prima facie breach of the competition rules and need not also show that the breach is clear and flagrant. Thus, in *La Cinq*,[53] the Court of First Instance annulled a refusal by the Commission to order interim measures requiring the European Broadcasting Union to allow the French broadcasting company La Cinq access to Eurovision film (such as coverage of sporting events). The Commission had also argued that the requirement that the damage be serious and irreparable meant that it could only use its powers if the damage could not be remedied by a final decision. This was held to be too limited a view. In this case, La Cinq held a licence to broadcast in France for a limited period only, and failure to secure access to Eurovision film might prejudice its chances of obtaining renewal. In effect, if required to wait until the Commission reached a final decision, La Cinq would run the risk of being refused the grant of a new licence and so going out of business in the interim, hence suffering serious and irreparable damage, whatever the outcome of the final decision.

Action in the form of interim measures is designed to preserve the *status quo ante* in the market place. However, the Co-operation Notice indicates that national courts can usually adopt interim measures and order the ending of infringements more quickly than the Commission is able to do.[54]

Review by the European Courts

Decisions of the Commission in the exercise of its powers in connection with the application of Articles 81 and 82 are subject to review by the Court of First Instance under Article 230. By virtue of Article 225 and the first paragraph of Article 51 of the E.C. Statute of the Court of Justice, an appeal to the Court of Justice may be based only on grounds relating to the infringement of rules of law, to the exclusion of any appraisal of the facts.[55] As the Court tartly pointed out in *John Deere*,[56] "that requirement is not satisfied by an appeal confined to repeating or reproducing word for word the pleas in law and arguments

---

[52] Hearing of parties and third persons.
[53] Case T–44/90 *La Cinq v. Commission* [1992] E.C.R. II–1; [1992] 4 C.M.L.R. 449.
[54] Notice on Co-Operation between national courts and the Commission, n.43, *supra*, para. 16.
[55] Case C–283/90P *Vidrányi v. Commission* [1991] E.C.R. I–4339, Case C–19/95P *San Marco v. Commission* [1996] E.C.R. I–4435; Case C–7/95 *John Deere v. Commission* [1998] E.C.R. I–3111; [1998] 5 C.M.L.R. 311; Case C–279/95P *Langnese-Iglo v. Commission*, n.75, *supra*.
[56] Case C–7/95 *John Deere v. Commission*, n.55, *supra*, para. 20.

previously submitted to the Court of First Instance, including those based on facts expressly rejected by that court". It is for the Court of First Instance alone to assess the value which should be attached to the evidence adduced before it, save where the sense of that evidence has been distorted.[57] The Court of First Instance has on a number of occasions demonstrated its willingness to subject the Commission's evidence to robust scrutiny.[58]

With regard to fines, the Court of First Instance alone has jurisdiction to examine how in each particular case the Commission appraised the gravity of unlawful conduct. In the *Baustahlgewebe* case the Court of Justice stated that the purpose of an appeal on fines is:

"first, to examine to what extent the Court of First Instance took into consideration, in a legally correct manner, all the essential factors to assess the gravity of particular conduct in the light of Article [81] of the Treaty and Article 15 of Regulation 17 and, second, to consider whether the Court of First Instance responded to a sufficient legal standard to all the arguments raised by the appellant with a view of having the fine cancelled or reduced."[59]

In carrying out these tasks, it is not for the Court of Justice to substitute, on grounds of fairness, its own assessment of a fine for that of the Court of First Instance exercising its unlimited jurisdiction to rule on the appropriate amount.[60]

The E.C. rules on competition and national courts

In *BRT v. SABAM* the Court of Justice said: "As the provisions of Articles 85(1) and 86 tend by their very nature to produce direct effects in relations between individuals, these Articles create direct rights in respect of the individuals concerned which the national courts must safeguard".[61] However, matters are not quite so straightforward as this statement might suggest. First, there are some situations outside the purview of national courts. For example, they cannot rule on the validity of "old" agreements protected by the doctrine of provisional validity.[62] Moreover, the fact that the power to grant exemptions under Article 81(3) is for the moment still reserved to the Commission means that national courts have an incomplete function in relation to restrictive practices. Secondly, the dual system whereby the Commission may also be considering the same set of facts as those before a national court may give rise to risks of inconsistent treatment. The difficulties here are heightened by the Commission's use of non-binding instruments such as comfort letters. Thirdly, the greater responsibilities

---

[57] Case C–19/95P *San Marco v. Commission*, n.55, *supra*; Case C–53/92P *Hilti v. Commission* [1994] E.C.R. I–667; [1994] 4 C.M.L.R. 614.

[58] See, *e.g.* Joined Cases T-68, 77 and 78/89 *Società Italiano Vetro (SIV) v. Commission ("Flat Glass")* [1992] E.C.R. II–1403; [1992] 5 C.M.L.R. 302, para. 205, where the Court of First Instance condemned the Commission for "cutting and pasting" pieces of evidence to reconstruct classification of customers.

[59] Case C–185/95P *Baustahlgewebe v. Commission*, n.2, *supra*, para. 128.

[60] Case C–219/95P *Ferriere Nord v. Commission* [1997] E.C.R. I–4411; [1997] 5 C.M.L.R. 575.

[61] Case 127/73 [1974] E.C.R. at 62.

[62] See, *Perfumes* cases, n.73, *supra*.

that are increasingly being placed upon national courts require them to develop and deliver effective protection to the parties involved. Problems may be foreseen in relation both to expertise, especially in relation to the economic analysis demanded by Articles 81 and 82, and to the remedies available in national law for breaches of the E.C. competition rules. As will be seen from the discussion below, a number of measures have already been put in place to empower national courts and improve dialogue with the Commission. The *White Paper on Modernisation* envisages an even more enhanced role for national agencies, both courts and competition authorities.

The Notice on Co-operation[63]

Adopted in the wake of the *Delimitis*[64] ruling by the Court of Justice on the powers of national courts under Article 81(1) and the *Automec II* [65] judgment by the Court of First Instance approving the Commission's claims to pursue prioritisation of its workload, the Co-operation Notice provides a guide to the respective positions of the Commission and national courts in the competition law enforcement process. It sets out the advantages for individuals and companies in resorting to national courts instead of the Commission.[66] In particular, the Notice points out that the Commission cannot award compensation for loss suffered as a result of an infringement of Article 81 or Article 82. Moreover, national courts can entertain claims combining E.C. law and national law. They may also award legal costs to the successful applicant, something not available in the Commission's administrative procedure.

The Notice goes on to explain how national courts might deal with particular scenarios of difficulty. For example,[67] it suggests that if the court is faced with a notified agreement that is not covered by block exemption and which has not received an individual exemption or comfort letter it should assess the likelihood of an exemption being granted. If it comes to the view that the agreement or concerted practice cannot be the subject of an individual exemption, having regard to the case-law of the European Courts and the practice of the Commission, then the national court should apply Article 81(1) and (2). On the other hand, if the national court concludes that individual exemption is possible it should stay proceedings to await the Commission's decision. In such a situation the national court remains free to adopt any appropriate interim measures pursuant to national law.

Increased transparency and clarity are essential underpinnings to the co-operation envisaged in the Notice. Block exemptions, guidance notices and annual reports on competition policy are all instruments from which national courts can glean pointers to the Commission's policy and practice. As a further device, the Notice indicates three areas in which national courts may, within the limits of their national procedural law, ask the Commission for information. First, they may seek to elicit procedural details, for example whether a case is

---

[63] n.43, *supra*.
[64] Case C–234/89 *Delimitis v. Henninger Bräu* [1991] E.C.R. I–935; [1992] 5 C.M.L.R. 210.
[65] Case T–24/90, n.41, *supra*.
[66] Notice, para. 16.
[67] *ibid.*, paras 29–30.

pending before the Commission, whether a comfort letter has been issued or how long it will take for the Commission to grant or refuse an exemption. Secondly, national courts may consult the Commission on points of law of a general nature, such as its practice on the meaning of "inter-State trade" or other concepts within Article 81 or Article 82. Any replies cannot, of course, be binding or authoritative and will not be concerned with the merits of the particular case. Thirdly, national courts may request factual data, such as market studies, statistics and economic analyses as long as they are not confidential. However, the Commission does not appear to have been deluged with requests from national courts under the Co-Operation Notice.[68]

Nullity of prohibited agreements

So-called "Euro-defences", based on the alleged infringement of Article 81 or Article 82, may be invoked in proceedings before national courts to cast doubt on the validity of transactions of which the enforcement is being sought. In the case of Article 81 the civil consequences of infringement are spelt out by the second paragraph, which provides: "Any agreements or decisions prohibited pursuant to this Article shall be automatically void". The Court of Justice has stated that Article 81(2) is directly effective.[69] Article 82 contains no equivalent provision but it is clear from general principle that a national court would be required to refrain from giving effect to an agreement caught by the prohibition in the Article, for example one binding a purchaser to obtain all or most of his requirements of goods of a certain description from a dominant supplier.

The automatic nullity in Article 81(2) "applies to those parts of the agreement affected by the prohibition, or to the agreement as a whole if it appears that those parts are not severable from the agreement itself".[70] Whether any offending clauses can be severed, leaving the main part of the agreement intact, falls to be determined under the law of the Member State concerned.[71]

Civil remedies for infringements

It is clear in principle that the directly effective rights conferred upon individuals by Articles 81 and 82 should be exercisable offensively as well as defensively. However, there is no Community law remedy in damages equivalent to that provided by *Francovich*[72] for individuals in respect of serious breaches of Community law by the State. The case in favour of a Community right to damages against individuals who infringe Treaty rules was forcefully presented by Advocate General van Gerven in *H. Banks & Co Ltd v. British Coal Corporation,*[73] pointing

---

[68] The XXIXth Competition Report notes five requests during 1999.

[69] Case 48/72 *Brasserie de Haecht v. Wilkin (no.2)*, n.18, *supra.*

[70] Case 56/65 *Société Technique Minière v. Maschinenbau Ulm* [1966] E.C.R. 235; [1966] C.M.L.R. 357.

[71] Case C–230/96 *Cabour SA and Nord Distribution Automobile SA v. Automobiles Peugeot SA and Automobiles Citroen SA* [1998] E.C.R. I–2055; [1988] 5 C.M.L.R. 679. See also Joined Cases T–185 and 190/96 *Riviera Auto Service Etablissements Dalmasso and others v. Commission* [1999] E.C.R. II–93; [1999] 5 C.M.L.R. 31.

[72] Joined Cases C–6 and 9/90 *Francovich and Bonifaci v. Italy* [1991] E.C.R. I–5357; [1993] 2 C.M.L.R. 66. See Chap. 5, *supra.*

[73] Case C–128/92 [1994] E.C.R. I–1209; [1994] 5 C.M.L.R. 30.

to the remedy as both the logical consequence of horizontal direct effect and an important step in the more effective enforcement of decentralised competition law. However, the Court of Justice avoided the need to discuss these questions by finding that the rules of the ECSC at issue in that case were not directly effective in the first place.

The matter of civil remedies for breach of Articles 81 or 82 is therefore a question of national law, subject to the general Community law principles of effectiveness and equivalence developed elsewhere in the Court's jurisprudence with regard to national procedural autonomy.[74] There is certainly authority in English law for the granting in appropriate cases of remedies by way of an injunction or damages to the victims of infringements of the E.C. competition rules.[75] It was suggested by Lord Denning M.R. many years ago that special new torts had been created by Articles 81 and 82 entitled, respectively "undue restriction of competition within the common market" and "abuse of dominant position within the common market",[76] but this suggestion won little support.[77] The preferred approach of English courts appears to be to treat claims in such cases as arising out of a breach of statutory duty. As far as Article 81 is concerned there has been little enthusiasm to grant damages to a party to a restrictive agreement, the view being taken that the agreement is void for illegality.[78]

The role of national competition authorities

(i) application of the E.C. rules on competition
The leading role given to national authorities under the transitional regime of Article 84[79] was lost to the Commission with the coming into force of Regulation 17. The authorities referred to in Article 84 are those responsible in the Member States for the application of domestic competition law, including courts specifically entrusted with this function, but not the ordinary courts before which directly effective Community provisions may be invoked.[80] Under Article 9 of Regulation 17 the national authorities have no power to apply Article 81(3); and their power to apply Article 81(1) and Article 82 is lost as soon as the Commission initiates any procedure under Article 2 (negative clearance), Article 3 (termination of infringements) or Article 6 (exemption). One of the questions

---

[74] See Chap. 5. For the Court's reiteration of these principles in a competition context, see Case C–60/92 *Otto v. Postbank* [1993] E.C.R. I–5683; Case C–242/95 *GT-Link v. De Dansk Statsbaner* [1997] E.C.R. I–4449; [1997] 5 C.M.L.R. 601.

[75] Especially *Garden Cottage Foods v. Milk Marketing Board* [1984] A.C. 130, a case concerned with an abuse of a dominant position under Art. 82. This was a majority ruling in the House of Lords, Lord Wilberforce dissenting on the basis that an award of damages would go further than was required to protect Community law rights.

[76] *Applications des Gaz SA v. Falks Veritas Ltd* [1974] 3 All.E.R. 51 at 58.

[77] See the reservations expressed by Roskill L.J. in *Valor International Ltd v. Applications des Gaz and EPI Leisure Ltd* [1978] 3 C.M.L.R. 87.

[78] *Parkes v. Esso* [1999] 1 C.M.L.R. 455 (English High Court). See also Kon & Maxwell, "Enforcement in national courts of the E.C. and new U.K. competition rules: obstacles to effective enforcement?" [1998] E.C.L.R. 443.

[79] *ex* Art. 88.

[80] Case 127/73 *BRT v. SABAM*, n.61, *supra*.

put to the Court of Justice in *Brasserie de Haecht (No. 2)*[81] was whether acknowledgment of the receipt of an application for negative clearance or of a notification amounted to the initiation of a procedure for this purpose. The Court held that it did not. The reference in Article 9(3) concerned "an authoritative act of the Commission, evidencing its intention of taking a decision under the said Articles".[82]

A Co-Operation Notice in relation to national authorities was issued in 1997,[83] heavily influenced by the corresponding guidance previously given to national courts. It represents an attempt to draw national authorities into a widening decentralised model of competition law surveillance and enforcement. However, not all Member States have the procedural machinery to apply Articles 81 and 82,[84] despite the exhortation in the Notice for them to take the appropriate facilitative steps.[85] The particular role for national authorities is seen as the safeguarding of the public interest in cases where the effects of an infringement are felt primarily or exclusively within the territory of the Member State.

Many provisions of the 1997 Notice, such as those relevant to the best course of conduct for an authority faced with an undertaking in receipt of a comfort letter, mirror the solutions advocated in the 1993 Notice. Requests for economic and legal information may likewise be made to the Commission by national authorities.[86] The Commission also asserts its power to reject complaints that lack the necessary "Community interest", reinforcing its view that national authorities are best placed to detect and take action against local problems. So far the 1997 Notice appears to be making more impact than its 1993 counterpart, with 50 cases being handled on the basis of the Notice in 1999.[87]

(ii) Application of national competition law

There is scope for conflict between the E.C. rules of competition and the competition law of Member States but in practice this has not proved to be a serious problem. The general principle was laid down by the Court of Justice in *Wilhelm v. Bundeskartellamt*[88] which arose out of action by the German authorities overlapping that of the Commission in respect of the famous dyestuffs cartel. The principle is that, since their objectives are different, the national rules may be applied in parallel with those of the E.C.; but not so as to prejudice the uniform application of the latter throughout the common market. The implications of the principle are not free from doubt but they may be summarised as follows. First, if behaviour is contrary to both sets of rules, it may be dealt with under both, though to avoid double jeopardy there should be a set-off of any

---

[81] Case 48/72 n.69, *supra*.
[82] [1973] E.C.R. at 88.
[83] [1997] O.J. C313/3.
[84] At the end of 1999 the Commission identified eight States with enforcement machinery for administrative authorities directly to apply Arts 81 and 82: Belgium, France, Germany, Greece, Italy, Netherlands, Portugal and Spain. See Commission's web site, http://europa.eu.int/comm/
[85] 1997 Notice, para. 15.
[86] *ibid.*, para. 52.
[87] See XXIXth Competition Report, pp. 16–17.
[88] Case 14/68 [1969] E.C.R. 1; [1969] C.M.L.R. 100.

pecuniary sanctions that may be imposed.[89] Secondly, behaviour prohibited by Article 81 or Article 82 but permissible under the competition rules of a given Member State, cannot be treated as lawful in that one State. Thirdly, behaviour which does not satisfy the criteria in Article 81(1) or Article 82, for example, because trade between Member States is not appreciably affected, may nevertheless be prohibited under national law.[90] Fourthly, a grant of exemption pursuant to Article 81(3) or a block exemption probably overrides any conflicting rules of national competition law, since it represents a positive choice of policy by the Community authorities.[91] To come to any other conclusion, the Commission argues,[92] would impair the effectiveness of the Treaty as manifested by an exemption pursuant to Article 81(3).

The scope for conflict between national competition laws and those of the E.C. is reduced further by the tendency among Member States to enact or adapt legislation to match or mirror E.C. approaches. In the United Kingdom, for example, the Competition Act 1998 provides for a regime of cartel and monopoly control closely modelled on the system of Articles 81 and 82. Moreover, section 60 expressly provides that questions arising under the Act are to be dealt with so far as is possible in a manner consistent with the treatment of corresponding questions arising in Community law in relation to competition within the Community.

The Commission's White Paper on Modernisation

The political changes in the developing European Union in the 1990s inevitably affected competition law. Calls for subsidiarity and further decentralisation led the Commission and commentators[93] to question the prevailing system of enforcement and demarcation of responsibilities between the various actors on the competition law stage. The Commission launched a White Paper in 1999[94] calling for radical reform based on two principal objectives: releasing the Commission from tasks which are not contributing sufficiently to the efficient enforcement of the competition rules, and bringing the decision-making process closer to citizens.[95]

The essential change suggested in the White Paper is to move away from prior authorisation to a system based on subsequent suppression of possible infringements. This, it is argued,[96] will allow the Commission to concentrate on those

---

[89] *ibid.*

[90] The Court of Justice so held in the *Perfumes* cases, n.73, *supra.*

[91] This was the view argued by the Commission in Case C–266/93 *Bundeskartellamt v. Volkswagen and VAG Leasing* [1995] E.C.R. I–3477; [1996] 4 C.M.L.R. 505, but not decided on this point by the Court.

[92] 1997 Notice, para. 19.

[93] See, *inter alia*, Walz, "Rethinking Walt Wilhelm, or the supremacy of Community competition law over national law" (1996) 21 E.L.Rev. 449; Rodger & Wylie, "Taking the Community interest line: decentralisation and subsidiarity in competition law enforcement" [1997] E.C.L.R. 485; Waller, "Decentralisation of the enforcement process of E.C. competition law—the greater role of national courts" L.I.E.I. 1996/2 p. 1.

[94] n.4, *supra.*

[95] See also Commissioner Monti's Foreword to the XXIXth Competition Report.

[96] *ibid.*

breaches which are never notified and which are the most harmful for European consumers and the European economy. In turn, citizens should have greater recourse to their local courts and competition authorities to obtain redress for infringements. The Commission would relinquish its exclusive powers of exemption under Article 81(3) and it would be open to any court or competition authority to pronounce on the justifications for alleged violations of the competition rules.

The Commission is at pains to indicate that decentralisation is not the only driving force behind its proposals. A well established *acquis* of Community law principles has been built up in the cases and other sources. The needs of the single market no longer justify a hostile view of vertical restraints. But there is an enhanced risk in a globalised environment of artificial barriers being erected to compartmentalise a world market, presenting a spectre of complex international cartels warranting greater investment of surveillance and regulatory resources.

There has already been a favourable reception to the White Paper in several quarters.[97] The Commission itself insists that the proposals do not constitute a threat to consistent application of Community competition law. It acknowledges that decentralised enforcement requires a clear framework of legislative and other texts to enable the local agencies to undertake their tasks properly. However, it may be noted that the sparse take-up of E.C. competition rights by individuals before national courts to date does not perhaps augur that well for the new regime. It may be a little too sanguine to assume that the proposed ability of national courts and authorities to grant exemptions will automatically enhance effective enjoyment of competition law rights.

---

[97] The European Parliament adopted a resolution on the paper on January 18, 2000 welcoming it as a means of bolstering the European "culture of competition."

CHAPTER 23

MERGERS

A merger takes place when two or more undertakings which were formerly independent are brought under common control.[1] There are many ways in which this may come about, most obviously where undertaking A acquires a controlling percentage of shares in undertaking B. A merger between undertakings operating on totally unrelated markets may result in an accretion of economic power, through improved access to finance, entailing either the creation or the enhancement of a dominant position on one of the markets. However, the type of merger which is most likely to have an adverse effect on competition is one between undertakings which are actually or potentially competitors, or between an undertaking and its major supplier or consumer. Mergers thus affect the structure of the market place, through the concentration of economic power in fewer units, and may arouse fears of anti-competitive behaviour being exercisable as a result. In this sense, merger control is a "pre-emptive strike" by the regulatory authorities seeking to prevent market structures being created which might facilitate anti-competitive conduct. Engaging in a predictive exercise of this sort is controversial, and economists have been divided over time as to the varying merits of whether "small is beautiful" or the extent of efficiency gains to be achieved by concentration. Similar tensions can be discerned in the case-law under the Merger Regulation, discussed further *infra*.

The E.C. Treaty does not contain any explicit merger control provision equivalent to Article 66 ECSC, which requires the prior authorisation of the Commission for mergers involving coal or steel undertakings. Only since the adoption of Regulation 4064/89 ("the Merger Regulation")[2] has there been a specific Community law regime directed at significant mergers. However, during the prolonged gestation period of this secondary legislation the Commission took steps to apply the general provisions of competition law under the Treaty to the mergers context. First, Article 82 was successfully invoked to challenge mergers that constituted abuses of existing dominance.[3] Then Article 81 was held to be capable of applying to acquisition agreements in some circumstances.[4] Nevertheless, it was always acknowledged that both these Treaty provisions had significant limitations and weaknesses as methods of merger supervision.[5]

The impact of the Merger Regulation upon the continued scope of Articles 81 and 82 for merger control still awaits definitive judicial resolution, although the

---

[1] This test forms the basis of the Merger Regulation, discussed below.

[2] [1989] O.J. L395/1 came into force September 21, 1990. Subsequently amended by Reg. 1310/97 [1997] O.J. L180/1. For consolidated text see [1997] 5 C.M.L.R. 387.

[3] Case 6/72 *Europemballage and Continental Can v. Commission* [1973] E.C.R. 215; [1973] C.M.L.R. 199.

[4] Cases 142 and 156/84 *BAT Ltd and R.J. Reynolds Inc. v. Commission and Philip Morris* [1987] E.C.R. 4487; [1987] 2 C.M.L.R. 551.

[5] Recital 6 to the Merger Regulation states that the Treaty provisions "are not . . . sufficient to control all operations which may prove to be incompatible with the system of undistorted competition envisaged in the Treaty."

Commission itself relies solely upon the Regulation. In the discussion that now follows, the original application of the Treaty rules is outlined first before analysing the scope and effects of the Regulation.

Article 82[6]

The leading case on the application of this provision is *Continental Can*,[7] involving the acquisition by a dominant firm of a potential competitor in the packaging markets. Although the Commission's decision was annulled by the Court for lack of adequate analysis of the markets, the Court agreed that, in principle, Article 82 could apply to such acquisitions. This judgment was a landmark because it showed that an adverse effect on the competitive structure of a market could be sufficient in itself to attract the prohibition in Article 82. The Court rejected the claim that the provision could only govern market behaviour rather than structural measures, observing that "any structural measure may influence market conditions, if it increases the size and the economic power of the undertaking".[8]

However, as an instrument of merger control, Article 82 has serious drawbacks. Most importantly, it only applies to mergers which abuse existing dominance. The creation of a serious restriction or distortion of competition is not of itself enough to infringe Article 82. Moreover, this provision contains neither any advance notification procedure nor any system for exemption and supervision. Evaluation of the competitive merits or disadvantages of a proposed merger is thus not an integral part of the machinery of Article 82. In the light of these difficulties, it is not surprising that the Commission made only modest use[9] of Article 82 in the wake of *Continental Can*.

Article 81[10]

In the early years of the Community, the Commission concluded that Article 81 did not apply to agreements whose purpose was the acquisition of total or partial ownership of enterprises or the reorganisation of the ownership of enterprises.[11] However, failure by the Member States to conclude specific legislation about mergers led to further litigation testing the available Treaty tools. In the *BAT* case[12] complainants challenged the Commission's view that a particular acquisition agreement did not infringe Article 81(1). The Court observed[13]:

---

[6] See Chap. 21, *supra*.
[7] n.3, *supra*.
[8] [1973] E.C.R. at 243.
[9] See further Downes and Ellison, *The Legal Control of Mergers in the European Communities* (1991), Chap 1, esp. pp. 7–13.
[10] See Chap. 20, *supra*.
[11] *Memorandum on the problem of concentration in the common market*, Competition Series, No. 3, 1966, para. 58.
[12] n.4, *supra*.
[13] Paras 37–39.

"Although the acquisition by one company of an equity interest in a competitor does not in itself constitute conduct restricting competition, such an acquisition may nevertheless serve as an instrument for influencing the commercial conduct of the companies in question so as to restrict or distort competition on the market on which they carry on business.

That will be true in particular where, by the acquisition of a shareholding or through subsidiary clauses in the agreement, the investing company obtains legal or *de facto* control of the commercial conduct of the other company or where the agreement provides for commercial co-operation between the companies or creates a structure likely to be used for such co-operation. That may also be the case where the agreement gives the investing company the possibility of reinforcing its position at a later stage and taking effective control of the other company. Account must be taken not only of the immediate effects of the agreement but also of its potential effects and of the possibility that the agreement may be part of a long-term plan."

But, having established these wide-ranging points of principle, the Court took the view in *BAT* that sufficient safeguards had been provided in relation to revised voting rights and management representation to mean that the acquiring company would not be in a position to restrict competition. The complainants' claim against the Commission was therefore dismissed.

A small flurry of Commission activity followed this judicial signal as to the possibilities of using Article 81.[14] But, despite the rather flexible nature of the Court's tests, the provision was hardly an appropriate tool for merger control. In particular, the need for an agreement within Article 81(1), the nullity consequences of Article 81(2) and the repercussions of the revocability of exemptions under Article 81(3) all cast doubt on the suitability of the Article as a long-term measure in the area.

However, the presence of the possibilities of intervention using the Treaty may have been partly responsible for giving impetus to concluding negotiations over the Merger Regulation. In December 1989 the Member States finally reached agreement on the legislation, which took effect from September 21, 1990.[15]

THE MERGER REGULATION

In broad terms, the Merger Regulation[16] represents an attempt to provide a system of unitary control for mergers with a significant Community impact, based on pre-notification to the Commission for evaluation and sanction. In other words, it seeks to provide business with a "one-stop" shop for clearance of large mergers, thereby avoiding the need to go through multiple authorisations from different national authorities as well as establishing the Commission's pivotal role in supervising the evaluative process. As will be seen below, there are some departures from this "one-stop" principle as well as ongoing controversies about

---

[14] *e.g. Carnaud/Schmalbach* [1988] 4 C.M.L.R. 262, although the Commission ultimately approved the acquisition.

[15] The antecedents of the Regulation go back to 1973; see the first proposal published in [1973] O.J. C92/1

[16] See generally, Cook and Kerse, *E.C. Merger Control* (2nd ed. 1996).

the impact of the Regulation on the scope for action under Articles 81 and 82. The Regulation has generated considerable case-law in terms of Commission decisions, but it is an area where the Court has had only limited opportunities to contribute to the jurisprudence.[17] As Arnull has noted,[18] parties to a merger are unlikely to challenge a Commission ruling blocking it or imposing unacceptable conditions because the consequent delay renders such a path commercially unrealistic. This is not to say that the Regulation is unattractive to the business community; indeed, its streamlined procedures and definitive outcomes are benefits worth paying some price for. Nevertheless, some unease may be felt at a system which *de facto* is not easily susceptible to active judicial review.

Qualifying conditions

To trigger the application of the Merger Regulation there must be a concentration having a Community dimension. The former requirement is concerned with the structural alteration that is being achieved, whilst the latter is directed towards the economic significance and international character of the parties' activities.

Concentration

This is defined in Article 3 of the Regulation and is deemed to arise under paragraph (1) where:

"(a) two or more previously independent undertakings merge; or
(b) one or more persons already controlling at least one undertaking, by one or more undertakings acquire, whether by purchase of securities or assets, by contract or by any other means, direct or indirect control of the whole or parts of one or more other undertakings."

The key concept of control is then further explained in Article 3(3) as constituted by rights, contracts or any other means which confer the possibility of exercising decisive influence on an undertaking.

A flexible approach to the notion of control can be seen in the Commission's case-law. In *Arjomari-Prioux/Wiggins Teape*,[19] for example, it considered that the acquisition of a 39 per cent stake gave the purchaser the ability to exercise decisive influence because the remaining shares were widely dispersed among over 100,000 shareholders with no single member holding more than 4 per cent. The Commission has also examined the historical exercise of a block of votes to see if it has previously been associated with control.[20] Moreover, acquisition of minority holdings may confer important rights of veto which will be sufficient to

---

[17] Although these have proved significant; see, *e.g.* the discussion of the Regulation's application to oligopolies, *infra*.
[18] *The European Union and its Court of Justice* (Oxford, 1999), p. 449.
[19] IV/M025 [1990] O.J. C321/16; [1991] 4 C.M.L.R. 8.
[20] See IV/M613 *Jefferson Smurfit Group plc/Munksjo AB*, 1995, where a shareholding of 29.04% gave control as it had historically represented more than 70% of the votes actually cast at general meetings.

have the transaction classified as the creation of joint control. This has occurred in relation to the approval of annual budgets, strategic plans and financially important contracts.[21]

However, the Commission found in *Renault/Volvo*[22] that the proposed share swap of up to 25 per cent in their car subsidiaries did not give rise to the parties enjoying joint control over them. With no contractual provisions in place requiring co-decisions, the Commission pursued the circumstances of the deal to establish whether sufficient "commonality of interests" was present. It decided this question in the negative for several reasons, principally that a "standstill" clause preventing either party from exceeding the 25 per cent stake "secured the majority position of each party". The Commission was also of the view that it remained commercially feasible for each party to proceed independently in its car business, despite the co-operation agreement. For example, a Joint Car Committee had been established which could take decisions binding on both parties, so long as both parties agreed with those decisions. The practicality of this arrangement, according to the Commission, was that this provision formed a device to deny the Committee control over the car business of either party.

Further guidance on the meaning of "concentration" can be found in the Commission's Notice on the subject.[23] This emphasises that purely economic relationships may be decisive in determining whether control has been acquired. In exceptional circumstances a situation of dependence may lead to control, as in the case of very important long-term supply agreements or credits provided by suppliers or customers, coupled with structural links.[24] It is the possibility of decisive influence, not its actual exercise, that is important. The Notice also sets out a number of indicators with which to establish joint control, stressing that veto rights which do not relate either to commercial policy and strategy or to the budget or business plan cannot be regarded as giving joint control to their owner.[25] A change from joint control to sole control will be deemed to be a concentration since decisive influence exercised alone is substantially different from that exercised jointly.[26]

A special problem concerns the treatment to be given to joint ventures. Indeed, this issue proved so vexing that the approach adopted in the original Merger Regulation was amended by Regulation 1310/97 with effect from March 1, 1998. The reason for the difficulty is that the Merger Regulation seeks to embrace "only operations bringing about a lasting change in the structure of the undertakings concerned".[27] On the other hand, joint ventures, as commercial activities, take a number of forms with varying degrees of co-operation and permanence. They may be almost merger-like to the extent of a new subsidiary jointly owned by A and B, but may also be more loosely constructed as particular

---

[21] See IV/M010 *Conagra/Idea*; [1991] O.J. C175/18, IV/M097 *Péchiney/Usinor-Sacilor* [1991] O.J. C175/18 and IV/M076 *Lyonnaise des Eaux Dumez/Brochier* [1991] O.J. C188/20. But *cf.* IV/M062 *Eridiania/ISI* 1991 O.J. C204/12.

[22] IV/M004 [1990] O.J. C281/2; [1990] 4 C.M.L.R. 906.

[23] [1998] O.J. C66/5; [1998] 4 C.M.L.R. 586.

[24] *e.g.* IV/M258 *CCIE/UTE*, 1992.

[25] IV/M295 *SITA-RPC/SCORI*, 1993.

[26] See also the Notice on Undertakings [1998] O.J. C66/14; [1998] 4 C.M.L.R. 599, paras 30–32.

[27] Merger Regulation, Recital 23.

co-operation agreements in relation to a specialised area of activity such as research, production or distribution. The regulatory challenge is therefore how to find a satisfactory regime which does not create artificial or counter-productive boundaries between the application of the Merger Regulation and Article 81 of the Treaty.

The solution originally adopted was to establish a sharp boundary between concentrative joint ventures falling under the Merger Regulation and co-operative joint ventures governed by Article 81. However, this line proved hard to hold and was also seen to be distorting commercial arrangements to the extent that the speedier processes of the Regulation provided an incentive for joint ventures to be presented as concentrative. As a result the Merger Regulation was amended by Regulation 1310/97 to facilitate greater procedural harmony in the assessment of different types of arrangement. On the one hand, the amended Article 3(2) now states that "the creation of a joint venture performing on a lasting basis all the functions of an autonomous economic entity, shall constitute a concentration". On the other, a new Article 2(4) provides that "to the extent that the creation of a joint venture constituting a concentration pursuant to Article 3 has as its object or effect the co-ordination of the competitive behaviour of undertakings that remain independent, such co-ordination shall be appraised in accordance with the criteria of Article 81(1) and (3) of the Treaty, with a view to establishing whether or not the operation is compatible with the common market". In other words, where there is a concentrative joint venture which has co-operative elements the Merger Task Force will conduct the evaluation of the latter through the lens of Article 81 but in accordance with the framework of the Merger Regulation. Prior to the amendment such a scheme would have had to have been classified as either concentrative or co-operative and, if the latter, would have been handed over to the general competition directorate of the Commission for consideration under Article 81.

The key to application of the Merger Regulation to joint ventures is thus whether they have the full-function characteristics necessary to satisfy Article 3(2). A further guidance Notice[28] develops the Commission's thinking and draws upon the case-law of the previous legal regime.[29] According to paragraph 12 of the Notice, a "full-function" joint venture essentially means that, in addition to the basic requirement of being jointly controlled, it must "operate on a market, performing the functions normally carried out by undertakings operating on the same market. In order to do so the joint venture must have a management dedicated to its day-to-day operations and access to sufficient resources including finance, staff, and assets (tangible and intangible) in order to conduct on a lasting basis its business activities within the area provided for in the joint venture agreement". A joint venture will not be full-function if it only takes over one specific function within the parent companies' business activities without access to the market. Such a joint venture, as might be the case with research and development, would be merely auxiliary to the parents' activities. Furthermore,

---

[28] [1998] O.J. C66/1; [1998] 4 C.M.L.R. 581.
[29] The earlier decisions on the autonomy necessary to make out a concentrative joint venture are still relevant to determining a full-function joint venture under the amended Art. 3(2).

the joint venture must be intended to operate on a lasting basis to be considered full-function. This does not rule out ventures of a fixed duration where the period is sufficiently long.[30]

Article 2(4) provides for the appraisal of the co-operative elements of a full-function joint venture against the criteria of Article 81(1) and (3) but in the procedural framework of the Merger Regulation. The Commission is required to take into account in particular two things: first, whether two or more parent companies retain to a significant extent activities in the same market as the joint venture or in a market which is downstream or upstream from that of the joint venture or in a neighbouring market closely related to this market; and secondly, whether the co-ordination which is the direct consequence of the creation of the joint venture affords the undertakings concerned the possibility of eliminating competition in respect of a substantial part of the products or services in question. In 1998[31] 13 of the 76 joint venture cases decided under the amended Regulation required analysis under Article 2(4), with the most detailed examination being made of activities in the telecommunications and Internet areas.

The case of *Telia/Telenor/Schibsted*[32] demonstrates some of the issues in an Article 2(4) assessment. Telia and Telenor were the incumbent telecoms operators in Sweden and Norway respectively, whilst Schibsted was a Norwegian publishing and broadcasting company. The joint venture in question was to provide Internet gateway services and offer website production services. The former enable users to access content more easily, either offering access to content free of charge (financed by advertising) or as "paid-for content". In its analysis of the case, the Commission decided that the supply of gateway services was not in itself a market, but that advertising on web pages and paid-for content could be considered relevant for the purposes of considering dominance.[33] The production of websites was also treated as a candidate market for the analysis of co-ordination under Article 2(4) since the joint venture and two of the parent companies (Telia and Telenor) were present on it. The other candidate market was the provision of dial-up Internet access where again both Telia and Telenor were present.

The Commission concluded that there was no likelihood of co-ordination contrary to Article 2(4) after assessing two distinct situations for this purpose. As regards website production, where the joint venture and two of the parents were involved, their combined market share was less than 10 per cent even if the market definition least favourable to the parties was adopted. Secondly, in relation to the dial-up Internet access market in Sweden, the Commission found that it was characterised by high growth, relatively low barriers to entry and low switching costs. Although market shares were bigger here, Telia and Telenordia (in which Telenor had a stake) holding 25–40 per cent and 10–25 per cent respectively, the Commission took the view that they were still of limited significance in such a growing market. The likelihood of co-ordination was

---

[30] *e.g.* IV/M791 *British Gas Trading Ltd/Group 4 Utility Services Ltd* 1996; *cf.* IV/M722 *Teneo/Merrill Lynch/Bankers Trust*, 1996.
[31] See Comp. Rep. 1998, p. 60.
[32] *ibid.*
[33] Dominance under the Merger Regulation is discussed further, *infra*.

further reduced by the relative size of the dial-up Internet access market compared with the size of the other markets on which the joint venture would be active.

It thus appears that the Commission's approach to Article 2(4) concerns is to pay particular attention to the relative size of the Article 2(4) market and the joint venture's market. The commercial incentives, and hence the risk of co-ordination, are smaller if the joint venture's market is significantly smaller than the Article 2(4) market, although the Commission has made it clear[34] that this is not to be taken as a sufficient condition to eliminate co-ordination between the parent companies.

The Community dimension

The Merger Regulation only applies to concentrations having "a Community dimension". Article 1(2) sets out the basic rules for qualification, although these are supplemented by the even more laborious provisions of Article 1(3).[35] The terms of Article 1(2) are met where:

> "(a) the combined aggregate worldwide turnover of all the undertakings concerned is more than ECU 5,000 million; and
>
> (b) the aggregate Community-wide turnover of each of at least two of the undertakings concerned is more than ECU 250 million, unless each of the undertakings concerned achieves more than two-thirds of its aggregate Community-wide turnover within one and the same member state."

It is thus size and the Community impact of activity which combine to form the requisite significance of a concentration. However, failure among Member States to agree generally lowered threshold limits when the Regulation came up for review led to a compromise in the form of Article 1(3), the construction of which reinforces the concern to establish a "one-stop" principle in the context of mergers which cut across several national regimes. According to Article 1(3), a concentration which does not meet the thresholds laid down in paragraph (2) will still have a Community dimension where:

> "(a) the combined aggregate world-wide turnover of all the undertakings concerned is more than ECU 2,500 million;
>
> (b) in each of at least three member states, the combined aggregate turnover of all the undertakings concerned is more than ECU 100 million;
>
> (c) in each of at least three member states included for the purpose of point (b), the aggregate turnover of each of at least two of the undertakings concerned is more than ECU 25 million; and
>
> (d) the aggregate Community-wide turnover of each of at least two of the undertakings concerned is more than ECU 100 million;
>
> unless each of the undertakings concerned achieves more than two-thirds of its aggregate Community-wide turnover within one and the same member state."

---

[34] Comp. Rep. 1998, p. 61.
[35] Introduced by Reg. 1310/97.

It is provided[36] that the Commission shall report to the Council on the operation of all thresholds by July 1, 2000. Revisions to the criteria of paragraph (3) are possible by a qualified majority of the Council acting on a proposal from the Commission.[37] However, the thresholds remain politically sensitive as they form the jurisdictional boundary between E.C. and national laws for the control of mergers. Following the revisions to the thresholds, 14 cases falling under the rule in Article 1(3) were notified in 1998, amounting to 6 per cent of all cases notified.[38]

Calculation of turnover is set out in detail in the Regulation[39] and in a Commission Notice.[40] Essentially, it comprises the amounts derived by the undertakings concerned in the preceding financial year from the sale of products and the provision of services falling within the undertakings' ordinary activities and after deductions of sales rebates and of value added tax and other taxes directly related to turnover, without taking into account intra-group transactions entered into by companies within the meaning of Article 5(4) of the Regulation. Special considerations apply to credit and financial institutions and insurance undertakings.[41] The proviso to the turnover thresholds, amounting to the "two-thirds" rule, is designed to prevent the Regulation from applying to concentrations in national markets.[42] It seems to be the Commission's position that the proviso requires all undertakings to be assessed, not just the major players. This could mean that a concentration between two very big companies both of whose turnover was mainly achieved in the same Member State could still be caught by the Merger Regulation if a small undertaking was also involved which did not satisfy the two-thirds rule in that State.[43]

The focus upon turnover and international activity to establish the requisite Community dimension also means that an undertaking need not be domiciled in the EEA for it to be subject to the Merger Regulation, provided the necessary figures are achieved. Thus a concentration between two giant American producers of commercial aircraft was held to be subject to Commission supervision.[44] The extraterritoriality tests established in the context of Article 81 E.C. by the Court of Justice in *Woodpulp*[45] have been applied by the Court of First Instance in relation to the Merger Regulation. Thus in *Gencor*[46] the concentration at issue related to mining operations and platinum metals in South Africa, and had not met with objections from the South African competition authorities.

---

[36] Art. 1(4), Merger Regulation.

[37] Art. 1(5).

[38] 1998 Comp. Rep. p. 49; the Commission stated that this figure was broadly in line with its previous estimates.

[39] Art. 5.

[40] *Calculation of Turnover*; [1998] O.J. C66/25; [1998] 4 C.M.L.R. 613.

[41] Art. 5(3), Merger Regulation.

[42] Used, *e.g.* in IV/M777 *AGF/Camat*, 1996.

[43] It is possible that such a situation could be referred back by the Commission to the authorities of the State in question under Art. 9, discussed *infra*, but this would not dispose of the need for notification of the concentration to the Commission in the first place.

[44] IV/M877 *Boeing/McDonnell Douglas* [1997] O.J. L336/16; see further the discussion of extraterritoriality and principles of comity in Chap. 19 *supra*.

[45] Joined Cases C–89, 104, 114, 116–117, 125–129/85 *Åhlström Oy v. Commission* [1988] E.C.R. 5193; [1988] 4 C.M.L.R. 901.

[46] Case T–102/96 *Gencor Ltd v. Commission* [1999] 4 C.M.L.R. 971.

However, according to the Court of First Instance, the implementation criterion laid down in *Woodpulp* was satisfied by mere sale within the Community, irrespective of the location of the sources of supply and the production plant.[47] Moreover, the Court of First Instance did not accept the arguments of the parties that they could rely on Recital 11 of the Regulation to require the presence of production facilities in the Community. That paragraph states:

"a concentration with a Community dimension exists . . . where the concentrations are effected by undertakings which do not have their principal fields of activities in the Community but which have substantial operations there."

The Court of First Instance observed that this did not indicate that production took priority over sales as an indicator of operations, and noted that it was common ground that Gencor and Lonrho each carried out significant sales in the E.C. (valued in excess of 250 million ECUs). Finally, the Court of First Instance reinforced the scope of the Merger Regulation by stating that its application was justified in public international law when it was foreseeable that a proposed concentration would have an immediate and substantial effect in the Community.[48]

Substantive appraisal of concentrations

The relevant criteria

The purpose of requiring notification of qualifying concentrations is to enable the Commission to establish whether they are compatible with the common market. According to Article 2(2) of the Regulation:

"A concentration which does not create or strengthen a dominant position as a result of which effective competition would be significantly impeded in the common market or in a substantial part of it shall be declared compatible with the common market".

Conversely, a concentration which does have such effects must be held incompatible with the common market.[49] It may be noted immediately that this test goes further than the limits of *Continental Can*[50] relating to the application of Article 82 E.C. by contemplating that the *creation* of dominance is susceptible to control.

The substance of the appraisal exercise is contained in Article 2 of the Regulation, together with guidance from its Recitals. Article 2(1) provides:

"In making this appraisal, the Commission shall take into account:
(a) the need to maintain and develop effective competition within the common market in view of, among other things, the structure of all the markets concerned and the actual or potential competition from undertakings located either within or outwith the Community;

---

[47] *ibid.*, para. 87 of judgment.
[48] *ibid.*, para. 90.
[49] Merger Regulation, Art. 2(3).
[50] Case 6/72 n.3, *supra*.

(b) the market position of the undertakings concerned and their economic and financial power, the alternatives available to suppliers and users, their access to supplies or markets, any legal or other barriers to entry, supply and demand trends for the relevant goods and services, the interests of the intermediate and ultimate consumers, and the development of technical and economic progress provided that it is to consumers' advantage and does not form an obstacle to competition."

This competition-oriented evaluation must be set alongside the wider obligation of Recital 13, which states that the Commission "must place its appraisal within the general framework of the achievement of the fundamental objectives referred to in Article 2 of the Treaty, including that of strengthening the Community's economic and social cohesion . . .".

As the case-law applying the Merger Regulation has developed,[51] a number of recurring themes can be detected. Not surprisingly, some of these have also arisen in the context of Article 82, such as the type of market analysis to be conducted and the extent to which collective dominance is subject to the Regulation. Others are more specifically connected to the mergers context, including the degree to which non-competition criteria can be taken into account in the appraisal of a concentration, and the scope for firms to defend mergers on grounds of efficiency or other arguments. These issues are each discussed further below.

Market analysis

Despite the different wording of the Merger Regulation, many of the issues relating to market analysis rehearse arguments familiar from the Article 82 case-law.[52] The Commission's Market Definition Notice[53] is equally relevant to the Merger Regulation, though with the caveat that the general approach may require adaptation when dealing with concentrations. For example, the prospective inquiry demanded by the Merger Regulation might prompt a view of the geographic market and time horizons different from those appropriate to an investigation into past behaviour alleged to constitute an abuse under Article 82.[54] Nonetheless, the need to establish relevant product and geographic markets remains. The Commission's approach to the former favours a demand-based inquiry. According to Form CO, "A relevant product market comprises all those products and/or services which are regarded as interchangeable or substitutable by the consumer, by reason of the products' characteristics, their prices and their intended use".[55] However, this does not rule out supply-side measurement of the relevant market in appropriate circumstances.[56]

---

[51] The early years are analysed in Downes and MacDougall, "Significantly impeding effective competition: substantive appraisal under the Merger Regulation" (1994) 19 E.L.Rev. 286.
[52] See Chap. 21, *supra*.
[53] [1997] O.J. C372/5, discussed in Chap 21, *supra*.
[54] *ibid.*, para. 12.
[55] Form CO, relating to the notification of a concentration pursuant to Reg. 4064/89; [1998] O.J. L61/1, s.6.
[56] See, *e.g.*, IV/M222 *Mannesmann/Hoesch* [1993] O.J. L114/34.

Two points in particular may be made about the Commission's approach to markets in its evolving application of the Merger Regulation. First, the prospective nature of the appraisal invites concern as to the rigour and reliability of the market assessment. The risks of exaggerating or understating the likely market consequences of a concentration are reinforced where the industry may be newly emerging. These tensions may be seen in the case of *WorldCom Inc./MCI*,[57] arising from the merger of two large Internet service providers (ISPs). Faced with a lack of publicly available reliable and comprehensive information on market shares, the Commission (aided by the Department of Justice in the U.S.) set about acquiring views and information from businesses active in the sector as well as from the parties to the concentration. A hierarchical market emerged in which at the lower levels there were generally a range of suppliers and few barriers to entry. However, the Commission concluded that a vital element in any package of Internet services was "universal connectivity"—the ability to offer access to all points on the Internet, worldwide and at appropriate standards of quality, speed and reliability, without having to pay others to complete the connection. For these, so-called "top-level", services there were significant barriers to entry. Each connectivity service was unique, offering a blend of connections to the ISP's own customers and to the networks of other ISPs and their customers. It was the Commission's view that the combined networks of the parties to the concentration would be significantly larger in these top-level activities than the size of their nearest competitor measured in terms of revenue and traffic flows.[58] The Commission concluded:

> "Because of the specific features of network competition and the existence of network externalities which make it valuable for customers to have access to the largest network, MCI WorldCom's position can hardly be challenged once it has obtained a dominant position. The more its network grows, the less need it has to interconnect with competitors and the more need they have to interconnect with the merged entity . . . Indeed, it could be argued that, as a result of the merger, the MCI WorldCom network would constitute, either immediately or in a relatively short time thereafter, an essential facility, to which all other ISPs would have no choice but to interconnect (directly or indirectly) in order to offer a credible Internet access service."[59]

Despite these findings, the Commission still cleared the merger on the strength of undertakings given by the parties promising the divestment of MCI's Internet business to a subsidiary for sale to a new entrant.

The approach taken in the appraisal of *WorldCom/MCI* attracted criticism, especially on the basis that it was economic theory without sufficient evidential foundation.[60] Certainly, if unsurprisingly, the parties had contested the

---

[57] Case IV/M1069, 1998; [1999] O.J. L116/1; [1999] 5 C.M.L.R. 876.
[58] For the methodology of these calculations, see paras 107–113 of the Commission's Decision. The concentration brought together WorldCom's 50–60% market share and MCI's 15–25%. The Commission maintained that its methodology had been designed on a conservative basis, to be as generous as possible to the parties within reasonable limits, and was likely to understate market share.
[59] Para. 126.
[60] See Art, "Developments in E.C. Competition Law in 1998: an overview" (1999) 36 C.M.L.Rev. 971, at pp. 998–999.

Commission's methodology and findings, especially in relation to traffic flows and their significance. Moreover, it has been argued[61] that the network externalities theory applied in the decision is based on unverified assumptions by presupposing the ability to degrade the quality of interconnections selectively with individual competitors, while maintaining the quality of interconnection with other competitors at the same interconnection point. As such, it is said, the Commission's analysis falls short of the standards demanded by the Court of First Instance in the context of Article 81 agreements that any hypothesis should be a "real, concrete possibility".[62]

The second observation to make about market analysis under the Merger Regulation concerns the relevance of global considerations. Article 2(1)(a) expressly refers to the need to examine: "the structure of all the markets concerned and the actual or potential competition from undertakings located either within or outwith the Community". This not only allows for the evaluation of concentrations against worldwide geographic markets, but also raises the spectre of "Euro-champions" being given clearance under the Regulation in order to challenge American, Japanese or other rivals. Informally, at least, the latter is not seen as an appropriate use of the Regulation. A former Commissioner for competition has observed:

> "our only concern is for competition within the Community and I reject the argument that a competitive world market may justify a dominant position in the Community . . . There can be no trade-off between competition in the Community and competitiveness elsewhere. This would be economic nonsense and bad law . . ."[63]

Nevertheless, the evaluation of concentrations in global markets is likely to raise sensitive political issues.

An example of the Commission's approach can be seen from its decision in *Aérospatiale/Messerschmitt-Bölkow-Blohm*.[64] The concentration arose from a joint venture between AS and MBB, respectively French and German helicopter manufacturers. The initial question as to the product market concerned the differences between civil and military markets. Although there was considerable interdependency between them, the Commission found that there were essential distinctions with regard to product characteristics, the structure of demand and the conditions of competition. In particular, the markets for military helicopters were in reality firmly drawn along national lines for those Member States who had their own helicopter industries (France, Germany, Italy and the United Kingdom). Given that AS and MBB held national monopolies, the Commission took the view that there would be no strengthening of dominance since there was no international competition between these States anyway. Moreover, competition in those Member States without national industries only amounted to 7 per cent of the Community market in military helicopters. Therefore, according to

---

[61] *ibid.*
[62] Joined Cases T–374/94, T–375/94, T–384/94 and T–388/94 *European Night Services Ltd (ENS) and others v. Commission* [1998] E.C.R. II–3141.
[63] Sir Leon Brittan, (1990) 15 E.L.Rev. 351.
[64] IV/M017 [1992] 4 C.M.L.R. M70.

the Commission, the concentration raised no problems of compatibility for this part of the market.

With regard to civil helicopters, the Commission concluded that the absence of barriers to entry and the mutual penetration of markets between the E.C., the USA and the rest of the world meant that competition was worldwide. The proposed concentration would have given AS and MBB a combined share of just over 50 per cent in the E.C. geographical market. The Commission cleared the proposal on the basis that the American competition potential was a sufficient guarantee to prevent the AS/MBB entity from being able to behave to an appreciable extent independently of its competitors and customers.[65] This was particularly likely given that American manufacturers were being faced with cuts in military budgets which would turn their attention to the civil market. In addition, AS and MBB had indicated that there would be no foreclosure of access by other manufacturers to technical co-operation and European development programmes as a result of the concentration. Finally, the Commission accepted that there would be little change in national civil markets apart from Germany, where AS had 40 per cent and MBB 22 per cent. Here the Commission was satisfied that the total volume of trade was small and that the US presence amounting to 33 per cent was sufficient counterweight.

In other cases, the Commission's conclusions on the importance to be attached to world influences have not been free from criticism. Its findings in *Aérospatiale/ Alenia-Aeritalia/de Havilland*,[66] for example, provoked considerable argument.[67] This was the first concentration to be rejected by the Commission under the Regulation. The proposed takeover of a Canadian manufacturer of turboprop aircraft by a Franco-Italian joint venture would have given the French and Italian parties concerned around 50 per cent of the world market and over 65 per cent of the European market in commuter aircraft. Such a position would have far outstripped the market shares of other European rivals such as Fokker and British Aerospace. The Commission identified three separate product markets based on seat capacity, and went on to find a worldwide geographical market with the exception of China and Eastern Europe. Despite pressure from governments and from within DG-III of the Commission,[68] the merger was prohibited. The decision was criticised in a minority opinion expressed within the Advisory Committee on Concentrations,[69] who did not accept the description or analysis of the market. In a strongly worded statement, the minority observed:

"The Commission has chosen a methodology that gives the highest market shares possible to the parties . . . not only is the Commission's approach to statistical analysis of the market flawed but . . . the Commission has underestimated the strength of competitors and customers in the market, exaggerated

---

[65] This, of course, borrows the language of dominance embraced by the case law under Art. 82, especially Case 322/81, *Michelin* [1983] E.C.R. 3461; see Chap. 21, *supra*.

[66] IV/M053 [1991] O.J. L334/2; [1992] 4 C.M.L.R. M2.

[67] See the background to the case, discussed in Cini and McGowan, *Competition Policy in the European Union* (Macmillan, 1998), p. 129.

[68] Concerned with industrial policy.

[69] This must be consulted under Art. 19 of the Merger Regulation (see procedures, *infra*); it consists of representatives of the authorities of the Member States.

the real strength of [de Havilland], ignored the history of competition in the market and the potential for new entrants. Further, this minority considers that the Commission is not so much protecting competition but rather protecting the competitors of the parties to this proposed concentration".

This particular line of attack has since surfaced in other contexts, especially in relation to the Commission's appraisal of collective dominance and the general evaluation of the strength of potential competition. These matters are dealt with in the following section.

Finding dominance

Dominance is the key concept of the Merger Regulation. A concentration cannot be held incompatible with the common market unless it is likely significantly to impede competition as a result of the creation or strengthening of a dominant position. For this reason the concept of dominance perhaps demands more rigorous elucidation than under Article 82, where it performs more of a gatekeeping role as the precursor to investigating abuse. The case-law under the Regulation provides strong echoes of the Article 82 case-law, whilst developing some particular nuances for the treatment of mergers.

First, as with Article 82, it is certainly true that market share is not the sole determinant of dominance.[70] Indeed, and perhaps unlike Article 82 in this respect, it is even possible for a concentration between holders of high market shares to be unremarkable.[71] The presence of preponderant buyers,[72] the maturity or otherwise of the market,[73] the relative market shares of other players[74] and the dynamics of the market[75] may all speak against dominance.

Secondly, a factor of considerable importance for the Commission when assessing whether there is sufficient dominance to act as a significant impediment to competition is the presence of actual or likelihood of potential competition. In this way the Commission can take account of the dynamics of the particular market and focus on the extent to which the merged entity will be able to act independently. For example, in *ITS/Signode/Titan*[76] the investigation concerned the supply of steel and plastic strapping in Western Europe. The Commission's inquiries revealed that although the parties had a significant combined market share in steel strapping, plastic strapping could be used as a substitute effectively in many applications. Entry into steel strapping was seen as difficult, but the plastic version was thought to be relatively easy to produce and market, and

---

[70] See Chap. 21, and the discussion in Case 85/76 *Hoffmann-La Roche* [1979] E.C.R. 461; [1979] 3 C.M.L.R. 211. The Court of First Instance directly quoted the latter with approval for the context of the Merger Regulation in Case T–221/95 *Endemol Entertainment Holding BV v. Commission* [1999] E.C.R. II–1299; [1999] 5 C.M.L.R. 611.

[71] IV/M18 *Alcatel/Telettra* [1991] O.J. L122/48; there was no creation or strengthening of dominance.

[72] *ibid.*; also *Renault/Volvo*, n.22, *supra*. See also IV/M1225 *Enso/Stora*, Comp.Rep. 1998, para. 151 where the Commission found "exceptionally, a situation of mutual dependence between buyers and sellers, which the merger was unlikely to disturb".

[73] Expressly considered in IV/M024 *Mitsubishi/Union Carbide* [1992] 4 C.M.L.R. M50, para. 14 of the Commission's decision.

[74] See IV/M043 *Magneti Marelli/CEAc* [1992] 4 C.M.L.R. M61. Also Case T–221/95 *Endemol Entertainment Holding BV v. Commission*, n.70, *supra*.

[75] *Aérospatiale/Alenia-Aeritalia/de Havilland*, n.66, *supra*.

[76] IV/M970; see Comp. Rep. 1998, para. 158.

demand for it (unlike that for steel strapping) was growing. Therefore, in the Commission's view, new entry into the plastic strapping sector was an adequate safeguard against any risk of the parties using their steel strapping position to try to raise prices.

The complex interaction of the various factors which may affect an appraisal can be seen from *Mercedes-Benz/Kässbohrer*,[77] a case involving a merger between two major bus manufacturers. In determining the product market the Commission had first considered there to be three markets comprising city buses, intercity buses and touring coaches but then subsequently took the view that there was sufficient supply-side substitutability to treat the market as one. Customer loyalty and lack of import penetration led the Commission to conclude that the geographic market was Germany. However, it still cleared the merger on the basis of the potential competition that was foreseeable. In particular, E.C. public procurement directives, requiring Europe-wide tendering, were seen as likely to have an impact on bus purchasing patterns. Furthermore, the Commission also concluded that the merger could in fact have a "shrinkage" effect. Since most German bus operators worked on the basis of "dual sourcing", the result of the merger would be that some switching would occur in favour of third parties by customers who had previously used the two merging parties as their alternative sources. Thus, even though the merged entity would acquire over 50 per cent of the market as defined by the Commission, the potential competition was such that clearance could be given. Of course, in any such case there must be a realistic time frame for that competition to materialise. In *Mercedes-Benz/Kässbohrer* other suppliers were judged to be able to compete effectively within two or three years.

Thirdly, the case-law under the Merger Regulation has endured a phase of uncertain development in relation to collective dominance similar, if not quite so protracted, to that seen in the context of Article 82. Whereas the latter conceivably had a textual base for its application to collective dominance,[78] the Merger Regulation is silent on the point. On the other hand, it might be said that the teleological or contextual arguments for using the Merger Regulation are stronger since its very rationale is the supervision of structural change and market power. The Commission, from a comparatively early point,[79] applied the Regulation to oligopolistic and duopolistic situations and has been vindicated in its approach by both the Court of Justice and the Court of First Instance.

The Court of Justice dealt with the issue in *France and others v. Commission*.[80] The Commission had approved a concentration between two German potash undertakings but had attached conditions to prevent the emergence of a duopolistic dominance between Kali und Salz (K & S) and SCPA, a French potash producer. According to the conditions, K & S was required to remove itself from two joint ventures in which it was involved. The French Government,

[77] IV/M477; [1995] O.J. L211/1.
[78] *i.e.* in the use of the phrase "one or more undertakings"; see Chap. 21, *supra*.
[79] IV/M190 *Nestlé/Perrier*, Dec. 92/553 [1993] 4 C.M.L.R. M17.
[80] Joined Cases C–68 and 30/95 *France and SCPA v. Commission* [1988] E.C.R. I–1375; [1998] 5 C.M.L.R. 136. See Venit, "Two steps forward and no steps back: economic analysis and oligopolistic dominance after *Kali & Salz*" (1998) 35 C.M.L.Rev. 1101.

which indirectly owned SCPA, sought to challenge the Commission's decision on the basis that the Merger Regulation had no application to collective dominance. Departing from the views of the Advocate General, the Court held that Article 2 of the Regulation did not in itself exclude the possibility of applying the Regulation to cases where concentrations lead to the creation or a strengthening of a collective dominant position, that is, a dominant position held by the parties to the concentration together with an entity not a party thereto.[81] To find otherwise would be to frustrate part of the purpose of the Regulation, depriving it of a not insignificant aspect of its effectiveness, without that being necessary from the perspective of the general structure of the Community system of control of concentrations.[82]

According to the Court, in cases of alleged collective dominance the Commission is obliged to assess, using a prospective analysis of the reference market, "whether the concentration which has been referred to it leads to a situation in which effective competition in the relevant market is significantly impeded by the undertakings involved in the concentration and one or more other undertakings which together, in particular because of correlative factors which exist between them, are able to adopt a common policy on the market and to act to a considerable extent independently of their competitors, their customers, and also of consumers".[83] Having established this test the Court then rejected the Commission's assessment of the case, noting that the cluster of structural links which formed the core of the contested decision was not as tight or as conclusive as the Commission sought to make out. Moreover, the Court expressly reserved its position on the question whether, had the links been properly evidenced, the relevant requirements for a collective dominant position would have been satisfied.[84]

The approach demanded in cases of concentrations may be compared with the tests developed earlier in the context of Article 82.[85] Are the "economic links" discussed in that case-law to be seen as synonymous with the "correlative factors" demanded by the Court for the purposes of the Merger Regulation? On one view, the prospective nature of the latter inquiry might justify a broader interpretation of the necessary element since the essence of a concentration is the bringing together in closer form of previously more loosely connected or wholly separate entities. The need to guard against significant threats to competition might arguably justify intervention at a stage before firm structural links between firms are in existence.

Certainly, the Commission believes[86] that correlative factors need not include structural links in the strict sense of cross-holdings or contracts between the alleged dominant firms. The key issue is whether such factors provide convincing evidence of a common interest among the firms concerned in not competing actively against each other. That common interest might be derived from the

---

[81] *ibid.*, para. 166.
[82] *ibid.*, para. 171.
[83] *ibid.*, para. 221.
[84] *ibid.*, para. 249.
[85] See Chap. 21, *supra*.
[86] Comp. Rep. 1998, para. 147.

symmetry of market shares, production capacities and cost structures of the alleged dominant firms. This argument is consistent with the position adopted by the Court of First Instance in *Gencor*.[87] Having noted that the economic links necessary to support a finding of collective dominance under Article 82 were not limited to structural links, it went on to state:

> " there is no reason whatsoever in legal or economic terms to exclude from the notion of economic links the relationship of interdependence existing between the parties to a tight oligopoly within which, in a market with the appropriate characteristics, in particular in terms of market concentration, transparency and product homogeneity, those parties are in a position to anticipate one another's behaviour and are therefore strongly encouraged to align their conduct in the market, in particular in such a way as to maximise their joint profits by restricting production with a view to increasing prices."[88]

The Court of First Instance further explained that the control of concentrations sought to prevent anti-competitive market structures arising from either economic links in the strict sense *or* from structures of an oligopolistic kind where each undertaking may become aware of common interests and, in particular, cause prices to increase without having to enter into an agreement or resort to a concerted practice.[89]

The Commission undoubtedly enjoys a margin of discretion in exercising its powers in relation to the provisions of an economic nature which form part of the rules on concentrations.[90] However, it is equally clear that it must adduce convincing evidence that the oligopolistic characteristics of the market in question will produce or strengthen the dominant position liable to impede significantly effective competition. Some of the considerations to be taken into account can be seen from the investigation into the market for auditing and accountancy services to large firms in *Price Waterhouse/Coopers & Lybrand*.[91] The post-merger market share would have been below 40 per cent in any Member State and four other competitors would still remain. In its assessment of the incentives for the firms to engage in parallel pricing and similar behaviour, the Commission found that demand was static, innovation unlikely and prices relatively transparent.[92] However, it concluded that the number of surviving competitors would make it difficult to sustain a coherent oligopoly. There was, for example, evidence from customers that they were willing and able to switch business between firms notwithstanding the long-term nature of most auditing relationships. In addition, the market shares of the non-merged survivors varied considerably between the different (national) geographic markets. The Commission inferred from this that the merged entity would find it difficult to ensure

---

[87] Case T–102/96 *Gencor v. Commission*, n.46, *supra*.
[88] *ibid.*, para. 276.
[89] *ibid.*, para. 277.
[90] Joined Cases C–68/94 and C–30/95 *France and SCPA v. Commission*, n.80, *supra*.
[91] IV/M 1016, 1998.
[92] In some countries audit fees had to be published in the audited company's accounts.

parallel behaviour among enough of those competitors to secure coherence across a large part of the market. The merger was accordingly cleared.[93]

This may be compared with the outcome in *Airtours/First Choice*,[94] a case in which the Commission appears to have used the possibilities offered by the Court of First Instance in *Gencor* to full advantage. The market for the supply of foreign package tour holidays to U.K. residents consisted of four large vertically integrated operators, Airtours, First Choice, Thomson and Thomas Cook, holding between them about 80 per cent. The remainder of the market was split among a number of much smaller non-integrated operators who found it difficult to get their holidays distributed through the agencies of the large operators because of their practice of giving preference to their own products. Airtours had announced its intention to acquire First Choice by public bid but allowed its bid to lapse on the launch of the Commission's investigation.

In analysing the market, the Commission found that package tours are a high volume low margin product, which is specially characterised by the fact that numbers of holidays are fixed before sales begin with few adaptations being possible later. As a result the overall supply/demand balance is crucial to profitability, with an incentive for operators to keep the market tight. Links existed between the major operators since they supplied each other with airline seats and distributed each other's products. Furthermore, the Commission identified similar cost structures, high barriers to entry and a lack of countervailing buying power. The proposed concentration would have eliminated First Choice as a competitor in itself, in turn isolating the minor players still further by cutting off a source of airline seats and travel agency outlets. Consequently, the Commission prohibited the acquisition on the basis that it would lead to a collective dominant position among the remaining three big operators with extra incentives to restrict capacity.[95]

In its 1998 Competition Report, the Commission remarked that one notable consequence of the trend towards globalisation and specialisation in merger activity is the increased occurrence of mergers in oligopolistic markets. It is therefore likely that opportunities for further refinement of the tests and evidence needed to support the use of the Merger Regulation to control them will not be long in coming before the Community Courts.

Non-competition criteria and defences to mergers

Analysis of the relevant markets and the degree of dominance resulting from the notified concentration will provide a competition-based view of its effects. But, as noted earlier, the overall compatibility of the concentration with the common market permits consideration of other factors. In addition to the economic and social cohesion reference made by Recital 13, there is the Commission's

---

[93] See also *Enso/Stora*, n.72, *supra*. Some familiar oligopolistic characteristics were established: low demand growth, concentrated supply side, homogeneous products, mature technology, high entry barriers, similar cost structures. However, some features were missing: no market transparency (in fact there were secret discounts) and a measure of countervailing buying power. As a result the Commission cleared the merger.

[94] IV/M 1524, September 22, 1999.

[95] Airtours has appealed against the Commission's decision: Case T–342/99.

observation[96] that account should be taken in particular of the competitiveness of undertakings located in regions which are greatly in need of restructuring owing, *inter alia* to slow development.

Moreover, the criteria expressly set out in Article 2(1)(b) of the Regulation are not limited to matters of competition. The references to "economic and technical progress" and to the "interests of the intermediate and ultimate consumers" are reminiscent of the grounds for exemption under Article 81(3). The former, especially, could be construed as an invitation to examine matters of industrial policy.[97] However, the proviso that technical and economic progress must not form an obstacle to competition appears to minimise any such possibility. Indeed, it may be difficult to see what function is left for this consideration since any concentration must satisfy the competition criteria to achieve compatibility.

Nevertheless, an argument still rumbles on as to the extent to which the Regulation acknowledges any so-called "efficiency" defence. Some commentators have denied that the Regulation affords any legal basis to such a defence altogether.[98] Others have suggested[99] that the Commission has softened its previous rejection of the possibility and is willing to look at efficiency gains in a more positive light but not at the expense of competition. The most robust presentation of the argument in favour of endorsing efficiency considerations[1] is built upon the premise that the notions of dominance and impediment to competition are separate elements within the appraisal analysis envisaged by the Regulation. Using this distinction, it is claimed that a transparent articulation of policy and competition concerns alongside each other in assessing the degree of acceptable impediment serves the rationale behind the Regulation without disturbing its textual integrity.

Apart from the general notion of an efficiency defence, there is the more specific question of whether mergers involving "failing firms" should be accorded special treatment on the basis that acquisition is preferable to exit when the social costs which result from a firm's failure are taken into account. Such a defence exists in American antitrust law,[2] though not expressly in the Merger Regulation.[3] To date the response of the Court of Justice[4] has been to construct the issue as one of causation. Where a merger is not the *cause* of dominance or a strengthened dominant position then it must be cleared. So if, without the merger, the firm would fail and the putative acquirer would become dominant anyway no incompatibility with the Regulation can arise. Whilst this may be an

---

[96] *Accompanying statements entered in the minutes of the E.C. Council* [1990] 4 C.M.L.R. 314.

[97] Understood as the promotion of structural adjustment; see Sauter, *Competition Law and Industrial Policy in the EU* (Oxford, 1997), especially pp. 137–140.

[98] Jones and González-Díaz, *The EEC Merger Regulation* (Sweet & Maxwell, 1992). Apart from textual objections to using the Regulation in this way, there is also the pragmatic claim that measuring the efficiency gains from a merger is an unworkable exercise.

[99] Banks, "Non-competition factors and their future relevance under European merger law" [1997] 3 E.C.L.R. 182.

[1] Monti and Rousseva, "Failing firms in the framework of the E.C. Merger Control Regulation" (1999) 24 E.L.Rev. 38.

[2] Discussed further, *ibid.*

[3] However, the Commission appears to recognise it in its *Green Paper on the Review of the Merger Regulation* COM (96) 19, para. 91.

[4] Joined Cases C–68 and 30/95 *France and SCPA v. Commission,* n.80, *supra.*

elegant way of avoiding a difficult question,[5] it does not amount to an unequivocal acceptance of a "failing firm" defence. In particular, this narrowly legalistic approach[6] does not resolve the larger question about the proper weight to be attached to economic and social policy concerns in carrying out an appraisal under the Regulation.

One-stop shopping under the Merger Regulation

The appeal of the Regulation to the business community comes from its speedy and definitive assessment of the concentrations falling within its scope. However, the political compromises which shaped the final version of the legislation created holes in the blanket coverage which was once intended. The discussion below considers three aspects of the Regulation, none of which appears to have been as disruptive or threatening to the integrity of the Regulation as was first feared in some quarters. These provisions govern requests to refer cases back to national authorities (the so-called German clause), referrals to the Commission by Member States (the so-called Dutch clause) and reliance upon notified legitimate interests.

Article 9: referrals back to national authorities

According to Article 9(2) of the Merger Regulation, within three weeks of receiving its copy of a concentration notification, a Member State

"may inform the Commission, which shall inform the undertakings concerned, that:
  (a) a concentration threatens to create or to strengthen a dominant position as a result of which effective competition will be significantly impeded on a market within that member state, which presents all the characteristics of a distinct market, or
  (b) a concentration affects competition on a market within that member state, which presents all the characteristics of a distinct market and which does not constitute a substantial part of the common market."

If the Commission decides that such a distinct market and threat exist, it may either itself deal with the case or refer it to the competent authorities of the Member State concerned with a view to the application of that State's national competition law.[7] In the latter event, the Member State may take only the measures strictly necessary to safeguard or restore effective competition on the

---

[5] Monti and Rousseva, *op. cit.*, n.1, *supra*, p. 54.

[6] *Cf.* the approach of the Court of First Instance when confronted by claims that the Commission's clearance of the *Nestlé/Perrier* merger had led to adverse social consequences, particularly job losses. When works councils and employee representatives challenged the Commission's decision, the Court of First Instance took the view that any losses were the result of the policy of the merged entity, not the Commission: Case T–96/92 *CCE de la Société Générale des Grandes Sources et al v. Commission* [1995] E.C.R. II-1213; Case T–12/93 *CCE de Vittel et al v. Commission* [1995] E.C.R. II-1247.

[7] Art. 9(3). The Commission does not always accede to requests made by Member States: see IV/M165 *Alcatel/AEG Kabel*, 1991; IV/M238 *Siemens/Philips*, 1992.

market concerned.[8] National authorities must decide the case within four months after referral by the Commission.[9]

In a joint statement[10] concerning the use of Article 9, the Council and Commission indicated that the referral procedure should only be applied in exceptional cases where the interests in respect of competition of the Member State concerned could not be adequately protected in any other way. The first occasion on which the procedure was used concerned the notification in relation to bricks and clay tiles made by *Steetley/Tarmac*.[11] With regard to bricks, there were two local markets within the United Kingdom, the North-East and the South-West, where there was a threat of the creation of a dominant position if the proposed joint venture between the two companies went ahead. The position regarding clay tiles was different in so far as the relevant market was Great Britain as a whole. However, the key point was that the venture would give the new company a clear lead in what had hitherto been a highly concentrated market between three principal companies. This, together with significant entry barriers and little impact on any other part of the Community, led to the decision to send the matter back to the national authorities. A final consideration was that one of the parties was the target of a bid by a third party, although the transaction would not have crossed the turnover thresholds to trigger the Regulation.[12] The Commission accordingly concluded that it was better for related cases to be dealt with by one regulatory authority if at all possible.[13]

Despite the expansion and hardening of the single market, distinct markets do exist in particular sectors. For example, the Commission accepted in *Vendex/KBB*[14] that in retailing markets consumer habits and tastes were important factors which might display national, regional or even local characteristics. Non-food retailing was thus capable of being a distinct market for the purposes of Article 9, all the more so since the two parties to the concentration were the only retailers in the Netherlands who owned department stores there. Similarly, pharmaceutical wholesaling has been found to be essentially regional or local in scope, justifying a referral back to national authorities in order for the precise boundaries in a given case to be established.[15]

The number of cases referred back by the Commission under Article 9 has remained consistently modest down the years.[16] In part this may be attributable

---

[8] Art. 9(8).

[9] Art. 9(6), (*i.e.* the same as the comparable E.C. level machinery: see Art. 10(3)).

[10] n.96, *supra*.

[11] IV/M180; [1992] O.J. C50/25.

[12] Once the concentration was sent back under Art. 9, the Secretary of State announced the referral of the joint venture to the (then) Monopolies and Mergers Commission. On the same day it was announced that the separate bid for Steetley would also be referred unless adequate undertakings were given. These were in fact obtained and the latter reference abandoned.

[13] [1992] 4 C.M.L.R. 343. The Commission does not always take this view; in IV/M213 *Hong Kong and Shanghai Bank/Midland*, 1992, it indicated it would not make any Art. 9 referral even though there was a parallel bid for Midland in progress which would not have been within the jurisdiction of the Regulation.

[14] IV/M1060, 1998, Comp. Rep. 1998, para. 168.

[15] *e.g.* IV/M1220 *Alliance Unichem/Unifarma*,1998, a case concerning the north-west of Italy.

[16] The pace in seeking referrals under Art. 9 was set by the U.K. and German regulatory authorities, but a number of successful requests have also been made by the French, Dutch and Italian

to the fact that the threshold figures governing the general application of the Merger Regulation remain high, and therefore Member States have little incentive to wrest cases back from the Commission by the Article 9 procedure. In any event, it seems clear that the mechanism for referral back has not driven a coach and horses through the one-stop philosophy of the Regulation.

Article 22(3) and requests for the Commission to deal

The converse of the "German" clause may be seen in the "Dutch" clause contained in Article 22(3) whereby a Member State or two or more Member States jointly may request the Commission to apply the Regulation to a concentration which does not have a Community dimension in relation to the territory of that State or States. This provision was intended to prevent lacunae arising where concentrations which fall beneath the Regulation's thresholds occur in Member States without merger controls. The need for some Community impact is nevertheless maintained by the requirement that the Commission's intervention is only possible at the request of the Member State concerned and if trade between Member States is affected. The appraisal under the Article 22(3) procedure seeks to examine whether effective competition will be significantly impeded within the territory of the Member State concerned. Exercising powers under Article 22(3) authorises the Commission to investigate the entire con-centration, even though the request may have come from a Member State concerned about a particular market.[17] The Court of First Instance has confirmed that Article 22 grants no power to the Member State either to control the Commission's conduct of the investigation once it has referred the concentration in question to it or to define the scope of the Commission's investigation.[18]

Strictly speaking, Article 22(3) is hardly an exception to one-stop shopping in so far as it actually extends the jurisdiction of the Merger Regulation, although that very fact may undermine the hope or expectation of the parties that their arrangements escape the reach of Community law. Since the amendments to the Regulation, the powers available to enforce Article 22(3) have been assimilated to the general merger rules to a greater extent, so that the Commission may use Article 7[19] to suspend the putting into effect of a concentration. The value of Article 22(3), in particular to smaller States, can perhaps be seen from the fact that a number of such requests have led to the prohibition of the concentration in question by the Commission.[20]

The protection of legitimate interests under Article 21(3)

Article 21(2) of the Regulation baldly states that "No Member State shall apply its national legislation on competition to any concentration that has a

---

authorities. The first ever Spanish request was made in 1999 in relation to IV/M1555 *Cruzcampo/Heineken* [1999] 5 C.M.L.R. 771. Here the special features were possible collective dominance within the Spanish territory and possible single dominance in several regional Spanish beer markets.

[17] IV/M553, *RTL/Veronica/Endemol*, Dec. 96/346; [1996] O.J. L134/32.

[18] Case T–221/95 *Endemol Entertainment Holding BV v. Commission* [1999] E.C.R. II–1299; [1999] 5 C.M.L.R. 611, at para. 42, the case being an appeal from Dec. 96/346, n.17, *supra*.

[19] Discussed further, *infra*.

[20] *e.g.* IV/M 784 *Kesko/Tuko*; [1996] O.J. C193/4; IV/M 890 *Blokker/Toys'R'Us*; [1997] O.J. C32/6.

Community dimension". However, this is qualified by paragraph (3), which provides that:

"Member States may take appropriate measures to protect legitimate interests other than those taken into consideration by this Regulation and compatible with the general principles and other provisions of Community law.

Public security, plurality of the media and prudential rules shall be regarded as legitimate interests within the meaning of the first sub-paragraph.

Any other public interest must be communicated to the Commission by the Member State concerned and shall be recognised by the Commission after an assessment of its compatibility with the general principles and other provisions of Community law before the measures referred to above may be taken. The Commission shall inform the Member State concerned of its decision within one month of that communication."

This provision, inserted at the request of several States as the price to be paid for giving up national control over concentrations, is likely to receive the strict interpretation that the European Court has always applied to derogations in Community measures. In its interpretative statement[21] on Article 21, the Commission has observed that it does not create any new rights for Member States, nor does it imply the attribution to them of any power to authorise concentrations which the Commission may have prohibited under the Regulation.

In the three specified cases, public security, plurality of the media and prudential rules, Member States may intervene as of right. The first of these concepts covers defence interests as interpreted in other areas of the Treaty by the Court.[22] Plurality of the media recognises the legitimate concern to maintain diversified sources of information for the sake of plurality of opinion and multiplicity of ownership.[23] The prudential rules which form the third concrete interest relate to the surveillance of financial bodies and usually take the form of requirements as to the honesty of transactions, the good repute of individuals and rules governing solvency.

Any other interest which a Member State may wish to plead must be notified in advance. Three limitations operate to prevent this becoming an open-ended escape route from the Community's jurisdiction. First, the terms of the provision make it clear that any legitimate interest must be beyond the matters already contained in the Regulation. The reference to technical and economic progress in Article 2 may play an important role in excluding any further arguments by Member States on these grounds. Secondly, any pleaded interest must satisfy the general principles and other provisions of Community law. Thus well-established doctrines recognised by the Court, such as proportionality, may defeat overly extensive claims. Finally, although strictly no more than a specific allusion to one of the "other provisions" to be applied, the Commission has stated that it is

---

[21] n.96, *supra*.
[22] Thus embracing the approach taken in Case 72/83 *Campus Oil* [1984] E.C.R. 2727, taking a wider view of "law and order" than simply national security interests.
[23] See IV/M423 *Newspaper Publishing*, 1994.

essential that prohibitions or restrictions placed on the forming of concentrations should constitute neither a form of arbitrary discrimination nor a disguised restriction on trade between Member States.[24]

The first use of this power to make a notification was by the United Kingdom in *Lyonnaise des Eaux/Northumbrian Water*.[25] It successfully asked the Commission to authorise use of domestic rules concerning the water industry, which required mergers of undertakings above a certain threshold to be automatically referred to the national competition authorities for an investigation into whether sufficient companies remained independent for comparisons to be made regarding industrial and private prices. In recognising the U.K.'s interest, the Commission specified that the national authorities should confine themselves to analysing the factors envisaged by the particular national regulations.

Procedural considerations under the Merger Regulation

This chapter is not an appropriate place for detailed explanation of the forms, time-limits, investigative powers and follow-up procedures which are essential to the practical application of the Regulation.[26] However, the following indicates the key stages in the notification and enforcement process. The relevant sources primarily comprise the Merger Regulation itself and the Regulation on notifications, time-limits and hearings.[27]

Generally speaking, the Merger Regulation envisages a two-stage process. The first, which must normally be settled within one month, consists of notification by the parties and preliminary examination by the Commission. The second phase, which need not take place depending on the outcome of the first stage, consists of a full investigation into whether the concentration is compatible with the common market and will normally be limited to a further four-month period.

Notifications must be submitted on Form CO[28] and will normally be subject to pre-notification discussion between the parties and the Merger Task Force of the Commission. Once notification has occurred, the Commission must come to one of three conclusions under Article 6(1) of the Merger Regulation: (a) to issue a decision stating that the concentration does not fall within the scope of the Regulation; (b) a non-opposition decision clearing the concentration on the basis that there are no serious doubts as to its compatibility with the common market, extending to any restrictions directly related and necessary to the implementation of the concentration; or (c) the initiation of a full second phase investigation. In relation to a decision by the Commission to proceed with the latter, the parties may be able to get the Commission to change its mind by offering modifications to the concentration, in which case the Commission is able[29] to

---

[24] *Accompanying Statements*, n.96, *supra*. The formula is taken from the proviso to Art. 30 E.C., allowing derogations from the free movement of goods rules.

[25] IV/M567; [1995] O.J. C94/2.

[26] See Cook and Kerse, *op.cit.*, n.16, *supra*.

[27] Reg. 447/98; [1998] O.J. L61/1; [1998] 4 C.M.L.R. 542.

[28] Set out as an Annex to Reg. 447/98.

[29] Using Art. 6(1A) of the Merger Regulation.

attach conditions and obligations to secure compliance by the parties with their commitments.

Most concentrations are dealt with by the first phase machinery, a feature which is hardly surprising given the close liaison inherent in the pre-notification process. The likelihood of termination during the first phase has been increased by the amendments to the Merger Regulation introduced by Regulation 1310/97 allowing the Commission to accept commitments from the parties without moving to a phase two inquiry. Any such commitments must be offered within three weeks of receipt of the notification. The Commission is not obliged to accept such undertakings, and it has made it clear that the facility is not to be abused by parties holding back from offering a fully effective remedy until the last moment in the hope that something less might prove sufficient.[30] The first full year of the operation of the new rules confirmed the Commission's expectations, namely that such commitments would often comprise relatively simple and straightforward divestments of overlapping businesses.[31]

If the Commission moves to a second phase inquiry the outcome will either be a clearance (subject to conditions or not, as the case may be) or a prohibition. Any closure of a full investigation initiated under Article 6(1)(c), whether resulting in clearance or prohibition, must take the form of a decision complying with Article 8 of the Regulation. The Advisory Committee on Concentrations, consisting of representatives of the authorities of the Member States, must be consulted on any draft decision of this type.[32] The Commission is obliged to "take the utmost account" of the Committee's opinion and has to inform it of the manner in which this has been done.[33] The Committee may recommend publication of the opinion, in which case the decision to publish must take account of the undertakings' legitimate interests.

Mergers may not be put into effect either before notification or until it has been declared compatible with the common market by one of the specified decision-making routes.[34] The Commission may, however, grant derogations on a reasoned request. Such derogations must take account of the effects of the suspension on the parties or on a third party and the threat to competition posed by the concentration.[35]

The Commission also has general powers under the Merger Regulation to obtain all necessary information from Governments and competent authorities of Member States, from persons in control within the meaning of Article 3(1)(b) and from undertakings and associations of undertakings.[36] Article 13 allows the Commission to undertake all necessary investigations, including rights of entry and examination of books and records.[37]

---

[30] Comp. Rep. 1998, para. 160.

[31] *e.g. Owens-Illinois/BTR Packaging*, IV/M1109, 1998.

[32] Art. 19(3) of the Merger Regulation.

[33] Art. 19(6).

[34] Art. 7(1).

[35] The Commission will not be likely to grant a derogation if it only amounts in effect to a partial implementation of the operation: see IV/M 1517 *Rhodia/Donau Chemie/Albright & Wilson*, a provisional decision under Art. 7(4), June 15, 1999.

[36] Art. 11(1).

[37] *cf.* its powers under Reg. 17.

Breaches of the notification rules are enforceable by fines. This is a different regime from the rules laid down in Regulation 17 for competition policy generally.[38] Under Article 14 of the Merger Regulation, fines ranging from 1,000 to 50,000 EUR may be levied for failing to notify or for submitting inaccurate or misleading information. Fines representing up to 10 per cent of aggregate turnover of the undertakings may be imposed for failing to comply with decisions or going ahead with incompatible concentrations. Decisions to impose fines must go before the Advisory Committee. The Commission exercised its fining powers for the first time in relation to failure to notify in 1998[39] and in regard to inaccurate information in 1999.[40]

As with any other decision-making by E.C. institutions, the Commission's decisions under the Merger Regulation are susceptible to judicial review. Rights of challenge will be governed by Articles 230 and 232 E.C. in the usual way. This means that in some cases there may be obstacles to satisfying the requisite *locus standi* conditions for direct and individual concern.[41]

The relationship of the Merger Regulation to the Treaty rules

The objective of one-stop shopping assumes that the only regime for control of relevant concentrations should be at Community level through the Commission as adjudicator. However, the effect of the Merger Regulation on the application of Articles 81 and 82 is not entirely conclusive, despite its textual claims and the evidence of the intention behind its drafting. One reason for the difficulty is that one of the principal tools used to establish one-stop shopping, the disapplication of Regulation 17, may not be capable of achieving all the desired results. In discussing the possible residual value of the Treaty provisions in the mergers context, regard must be paid to the respective positions of the Commission, national competition authorities and individuals.

For the Commission, disapplying Regulation 17 from concentrations means it has given up its rights to utilise Articles 81 and 82 of the Treaty. However, this still leaves intact Article 85, which provides that the Commission may conduct investigations, either on its own initiative or at the request of a Member State, and propose appropriate measures in circumstances constituting infringement of the principles of Articles 81 and 82. Indeed, at the time the Merger Regulation was adopted, the Commission expressly reserved[42] its right to take action under Article 85 in respect of concentrations not having a Community dimension.

---

[38] See Chap. 22, *supra*.

[39] IV/M 920 *Samsung/AST*, 1998, the fine being 33,000 EUR, with the Commission recognising in mitigation that no damage to competition had resulted, that the infringement had not been intentional, the parties had eventually notified the concentration and they had co-operated with the Commission in its investigations. In the later case IV/M 969 *A.P. Møller*, 1999, the Commission imposed a fine of 219,000 EUR to take account of the significant duration of the infringements and the fact that the company should have been aware of its notification obligations.

[40] IV/M 1543 *Sanofi/Synthélabo*, 1999.

[41] Case C–480/93 P *Zunis Holdings and others v. Commission* [1996] E.C.R. I–1; [1996] 5 C.M.L.R. 219.

[42] See n.96, *supra*.

However, the real prospects of such intervention occurring are limited, given that the Commission also indicated *de minimis* thresholds before it would act.

As far as national competition authorities are concerned, the position depends on the view taken of the Merger Regulation as an instrument for achieving the principles of Articles 81 and 82. This is because Article 84 E.C. only empowers national authorities to rule on the application of Articles 81 and 82 in the absence of measures to give effect to the latter adopted under Article 83. The Merger Regulation was based on *both* Article 83 and Article 308, so there is some conceivable mileage in the argument that it does not qualify as a measure for the purposes of Article 83, leaving the national authorities free to act under Article 84. However, this view seems to run counter to the spirit and purposes of the Regulation.

Finally, the area where there is most scope to claim the surviving application of Treaty rules is in relation to individual rights, although the consequences under Articles 81 and 82 seem distinguishable. In relation to the former, the effect of the disapplication of Regulation 17 is to remove the sanction of nullity available under Article 81(2). In a different context, the Court has held[43] that in the absence of implementing legislation adopted under Article 83, agreements alleged before national courts to fall foul of Article 81 are deemed to be provisionally valid until such time as the Commission, acting under Article 85 or the Member State, invoking Article 84, has established their illegality. It would therefore seem that if the disapplication of Regulation 17 is effective, the rights of individuals to use Article 81 with regard to any concentration as defined in the Merger Regulation have been removed.

Recourse to Article 82, however, would seem to remain available for individuals. The Court's judgment in *Ahmed Saeed*[44] affirmed the direct effect of this provision, and held it to be fully applicable to the air transport sector even without the presence of implementing rules. Whereas the absence of such legislation under Article 81 gave rise to the possibility of national authorities or the Commission intervening to give exemptions under Articles 84 or 85, no such exemption considerations existed within Article 82. Its prohibition could therefore be applied by national courts. Translating this into the context of the Merger Regulation, the effect is that its disapplication of Regulation 17 has no impact on the applicability of Article 82 for individuals. This may not necessarily be of great practical value, however, in so far as the weaknesses of Article 82 as a tool for regulating mergers have already been explained at the start of this Chapter. Where a concentration has a Community dimension, the Regulation will, of course, be applicable.

After a decade of its operation, it is hard to escape the conclusion that the Merger Regulation has come close to its goal of being a paradigm of subsidiarity in the competition law field. However, the continued growth in cases coming up

---

[43] Cases 209–213/84 *Ministère Public v. Asjes and others* [1986] E.C.R. 1425; [1986] 3 C.M.L.R. 173.
[44] Case 66/86 *Ahmed Saeed* [1989] E.C.R. 838; [1990] 4 C.M.L.R. 102.

for scrutiny[45] will put a premium on consistent and transparent decision-making by the Commission to offset the fears that it holds too many of the trump cards in securing particular outcomes from parties to concentrations.

---

[45] The Commission explains this trend in terms of the effects of the single currency, creating the possibility of synergies from simplified financial and commercial operations within groups of companies, and in a fall in oil prices worldwide, prompting major restructuring operations aimed at maintaining profitability in the face of lower margins: see Comp. Rep. 1998, para 137.

CHAPTER 24

STATE AIDS

State aids and the single market

The provision out of public funds of subsidies or other forms of aid to undertakings is generally considered a necessary instrument of government policy even in countries like the Member States of the E.U. where free competition and the market mechanism continue to occupy a central place in the economic system. The purpose of such aid may be, for example, to attract investment into areas that are economically underdeveloped or where the existing industries are declining; or to enable the undertakings in a given industrial sector to improve their efficiency; or to encourage the development of new, high-technology industries requiring heavy expenditure on research and development. In particular, during periods of economic difficulty, there are strong social and political pressures for State aids to be used to preserve jobs, even where there is no real prospect of the undertakings in question returning to profitability.[1]

By curtailing the freedom of Member States to pursue unilateral industrial strategies, State aid policy has been described as "clearly the most original of the EU's competition policies".[2] Granting State aid is liable to cause serious difficulties in a system which has as a primary objective the creation and maintenance of a single internal market. As the Court of Justice has observed,

"The aim of Article 92 [now 87] of the Treaty is to prevent trade between Member States from being affected by advantages granted by public authorities . . ."[3]

In the first place, by giving particular firms in a Member State an unearned competitive advantage over other providers of the goods or services in question, aid may interfere with the functioning of the market mechanism at the Community level. This may be so, whether the aided product is sold on the domestic market or exported to another Member State. In the former case, the aid may constitute an indirect barrier to trade by protecting the less efficient home industry against competition from imports. In the latter case, the aid may make it possible to penetrate an export market, threatening an industry in the State of importation which would otherwise be perfectly viable. Either situation is likely to give rise to pressure from the disadvantaged industry for its own government to provide compensatory aid, which makes no economic sense. There will also be temptation, when the threat comes from aided imports, for a government to take steps to keep them out, even at the risk of infringing Article 28 E.C.[4]

---

[1] An idea of the vast range of aids applied by the Member States can be obtained from the annual *Report on Competition Policy* produced by the Commission.
[2] Cini & McGowan, *Competition Policy in the European Union*, p. 135.
[3] Case C–39/94 *SFEI v. La Poste* [1996] E.C.R. I–3547, para. 58; [1996] All E.R. (E.C.) 685.
[4] *e.g.* Case 40/82 *Commission v. United Kingdom* [1982] E.C.R. 2793; [1982] 3 C.M.L.R. 497.

Secondly, the dismantling of barriers between the national economies means that the aid policies of one Member State react on those of another, affecting both their cost and their prospects of success. Job creation by state aid in one Member State may drive unemployment figures up in another. Similarly, competition to attract investment funds may lead Member States to fix regional aids at higher levels than are warranted to compensate for the disadvantage of a given region; and resources may be diverted from those parts of the Community where they are needed most.

The express adoption of a policy of economic and social cohesion,[5] directed towards reduction in the disparities between the levels of development of the various regions and the backwardness of the least favoured regions, creates additional pressure upon the system of State aids supervision. Despite claims by the Commission[6] that it is alert to the role of aids in promoting cohesion, the operation of the supervisory regime has attracted criticism for its continued heavy emphasis upon aid to large companies in central regions.[7]

State aids have thus always played a pivotal role in the creation and maintenance of the single internal market, and will be controversial in the expansion of more concrete Community policies in industrial, social and environmental fields. Their original inclusion in the EEC Treaty might have been as an element in a common industrial policy to be formulated at Community level. However, the only option that was politically feasible was to allow the Member States to continue granting aids but to establish a system of supervision by the Community institutions.

The relevant provisions of the Treaty are Articles 87 to 89.

The structure of Article 87 E.C.

Article 87 E.C. sets out the principles on the basis of which the compatibility of State aids with the common market is to be judged.[8]

Paragraph (1) of the Article lays down the general principle that State aids fulfilling certain broadly defined criteria are incompatible with the common market. The paragraph does not expressly declare incompatible aids to be prohibited (*cf.* the drafting of Articles 81 and 82 E.C.) but the European Court has accepted that it contains an implied prohibition, though neither absolute nor unconditional.[9]

The general principle in Article 87(1) is qualified by "exceptions *ipso jure*" listed in paragraph (2) and "discretionary exceptions" listed in paragraph (3). If

---

[5] See Art.2 E.C., amplified in Title XVII, Arts 158–162 E.C.

[6] See, *7th Survey on State Aid in the European Union in the manufacturing and certain other sectors*, March 30, 1999.

[7] See, *Opinion of the Economic and Social Committee on the XXIVth Report of the Commission on Competition Policy 1994*; [1996] O.J. C39/79, at para 6.2.

[8] For further comment, see Evans, *EC Law of State Aid*; Keppenne, *Guide des aides d'État en droit communautaire*; D'Sa, *European Community Law on State Aid*; Hancher, Slot and Ottervanger, *EC State Aids*.

[9] See the references to "an aid which is prohibited" in Case 6/69 *Commission v. France* [1969] E.C.R. 523; [1970] C.M.L.R. 43 and "the prohibition in Art. 92(1)" in Case 78/76 *Firma Steinike und Weinlig v. Germany* [1977] E.C.R. 595; [1977] 2 C.M.L.R. 688.

an aid is found to be within one of the categories in paragraph (2), it must, as a matter of law, be regarded as compatible with the common market. On the other hand, the compatibility of aids falling within the categories in paragraph (3) is a discretionary matter, requiring an assessment of the positive and negative effects of the aid form the point of view of the Community as a whole. Under the machinery of Article 88 (see below) that discretion is exercised by the Commission, subject to reserve powers of the Council and the usual control by the European Court. The latter's case-law has also significantly enhanced the responsibilities of national courts in relation to the protection of individuals against failure by Member States to observe their duties under Article 88(3). Enabling legislation agreed by the Council in 1998[10] permits the Commission to adopt Regulations setting out block exemptions for certain types of aid.

Article 87(1): aids incompatible with the common market

Article 87(1) provides:

"Save as otherwise provided in this Treaty, any aid granted by a Member State or through State resources in any form whatsoever which distorts or threatens to distort competition by favouring certain undertakings or the production of certain goods shall, in so far as it affects trade between Member States, be incompatible with the common market."

A general definition of State aid for the purposes of the E.C. Treaty was offered by the European Court in Case 61/79 *Amministrazione delle finanze dello stato v. Denkavit*,[11] where it said that paragraph (1) of the Article:

"refers to the decisions of Member States by which the latter, in pursuit of their own economic and social objectives give, by unilateral and autonomous decisions, undertakings or other persons resources or procure for them advantages intended to encourage the attainment of the economic or social objectives sought."[12]

State aid is thus to be understood in terms of its function as an instrument of national economic and social policy involving the provision of some kind of tangible benefit for specific undertakings or individuals.

It is immaterial what form the benefit may take or what particular goal of policy it may be designed to serve. The European Court has repeatedly held that the prohibition in paragraph (1) does not distinguish between measures of State intervention by reference to their causes or aims but defines them in relation to their effects.[13] A useful list of forms of aid was given by the Commission in reply

---

[10] Council Reg. 994/98; [1998] O.J. L142/1.

[11] [1980] E.C.R. 1205; [1981] 3 C.M.L.R. 694.

[12] [1980] E.C.R. at 1228; *cf.* the position under the ECSC Treaty, Case 30/59 *Steenkolenmijnen v. High Authority* [1961] E.C.R. 1 at 19; "An aid is a very similar concept [to a subsidy], which, however, places emphasis on its purpose and seems especially devised for a particular objective which cannot normally be achieved without outside help."

[13] Case 173/73 *Italy v. Commission* [1974] E.C.R. 709; [1974] 2 C.M.L.R. 593; Case C–241/94 *France v. Commission* [1996] E.C.R. 4551; [1997] 1 C.M.L.R. 983.

to a Written Question in 1963,[14] comprising: direct subsidies; exemption from duties and taxes; exemption from parafiscal charges; preferential interest rates; guarantees of loans on especially favourable terms; making land or buildings available either gratuitously or on especially favourable terms; provision of goods or services on preferential terms; indemnities against operating losses; or any other measure of equivalent effect. Further examples may be added, such as deferred collection of fiscal or social contributions, direct and indirect State participation in share capital and logistical or commercial assistance granted in return for unusually low consideration. The catalogue should not, of course, be regarded as exhaustive, although it covers the forms of aid most frequently granted by the Member States.[15]

Central to the notion of aid is the requirement that it must "favour" certain undertakings or the production of certain goods. As Advocate General Cosmas has pointed out,[16] there is an elliptical quality to this formulation, since it impliedly requires some comparison to be made between the treatment accorded to the alleged beneficiary and the position of other undertakings. Put another way, "the prohibition of State aid appears as the result of the general principle of equality and the rule derived from it that a like rule should apply to like situations".[17]

The Commission's view, supported now by ample case-law from the European Courts, is that the necessary element of advantage is to be determined by use of a hypothetical market investor test. This approach had its origins in the cases of the 1980s which established that equity participation by the State in corporate financing could in principle amount to aid within the meaning of Article 87(1). Thus, in *Re Boch*[18] the Court observed:

"In the case of an undertaking whose capital is almost entirely held by the public authorities, the test is, in particular, whether in similar circumstances a private shareholder, having regard to the foreseeability of obtaining a return and leaving aside all social, regional policy and sectoral considerations, would have subscribed the capital in question."

In the wake of this judicial support, the market investor principle has been refined and elaborated by both Commission guidance[19] and application in the case-law beyond the context of capital investment. The key question has essentially become whether the recipient undertaking receives an economic advantage which it would not have obtained under normal market conditions.[20] Expressions of the principle can be found, for example, in relation to loans and

[14] [1963] J.O. 2235.
[15] See further, 7th Survey, n.6, *supra*.
[16] Case C–353/95P *Tiercé Ladbroke v. Commission* [1997] E.C.R. I–7007.
[17] *ibid.*, at 7021.
[18] Case 40/85 *Re Boch: Belgium v. Commission* [1986] E.C.R. 2321; [1998] 2 C.M.L.R. 301. See also Joined Cases 296 and 318/82 *The Netherlands and Leeuwarder Papierwaren fabriek BV v. Commission* [1985] E.C.R. 809; [1985] 3 C.M.L.R. 380; Joined Cases C–278–280/92 *Spain v. Commission* [1994] E.C.R. I–4103.
[19] Communication to Member States concerning the application of Arts 92 and 93 and the Transparency Dir. 80/723 to public undertakings in the manufacturing sector, 1991 O.J. C273/2.
[20] Case C–39/94 *SFEI v. La Poste* [1996] E.C.R. I–3547, para. 60; [1996] All E.R. (E.C.) 685.

interest rates thereon,[21] guarantees[22] and the renegotiation of credit terms.[23] Put shortly, the Court will only find that an aid exists if the State has been acting other than as an "ordinary economic agent".[24]

Attempts to question the appropriateness of the comparison with private investors have so far failed, although the principle is not without its critics.[25] It was suggested by the applicant in *Italy v. Commission*[26] that a private holding company might provide money to ailing subsidiaries for reasons other than profitability, such as the desire to maintain the group's image or to redirect its activities. The Court replied that capital provided by a public investor who is not interested in profitability, even in the long term, must be regarded as an aid for the purposes of the E.C. rules. In another judgment on the same day,[27] the Court went further and held that the concept of the private investor, whilst not limited to one placing capital for a short- or medium-term profit, must at least relate to a private holding company or private group of undertakings carrying out a global structural policy or one limited to a particular sector which is guided by the prospects of profit in the longer term. On this test, therefore, the Commission was entitled to find that the capital contributions in question which had been made to car companies were beyond the contemplation of private investors and should be seen as solely designed to absorb the debts of the recipient undertaking in order to ensure that it survived.

Application of the market investor principle demands selection of the appropriate comparator. This may not always be easy, as can be seen from *Spain v. Commission*[28], a case concerning credit rather than capital. Tubacex, a company in provisional insolvency, restructured its wage bills with Fogasa, a State-controlled organisation charged with paying employees in the event of their employer's insolvency. Tubacex also made arrangements with the Social Security Fund, whereby debts on social security payments were to be repaid over extended instalments at 9 per cent interest, the legal rate for default interest at the time. The Commission treated the interest rate as an aid, deeming it preferential when compared to the rates charged by banks on private loans. However, the Spanish Government claimed that neither Fogasa nor the Social Security Fund were acting as loan providers but were instead renegotiating the terms of existing debts. This view was accepted by the Court in annulling the Commission's decision. In contrast, Advocate General La Pergola had analysed the arrangements as containing an aid element, not because of the rate of interest but because of the fact that the debt rescheduling had occurred at all at a time when

---

[21] Case T–214/95 *Vlaams Gewest v. Commission* [1998] E.C.R. II-717; Case T–16/96 *Cityflyer Express v. Commission* [1998] E.C.R. II-757; [1998] 2 C.M.L.R. 537.

[22] Joined Cases C–329/93 and C–62–63/95 *Germany v. Commission, Hanseatische Industrie-Beteiligungen GmbH v. Commission, Bremer Vulkan Verbund A.-G. v. Commission* [1996] E.C.R. I–5151, noted by Ross (1997) 34 C.M.L.Rev. 1293. See also the Commission's *Notice on the application of Arts 87 and 88 E.C. to State aid in the form of guarantees*, November 24, 1999.

[23] Case C–256/97 *Déménagements-Manutention Transport SA (DMT)* [1999] E.C.R. I–3913.

[24] Case C–56/93 *Belgium v. Commission* [1996] E.C.R. I–723.

[25] Abbamonte, "Market economy investor principle: a legal analysis of an economic problem" [1996] 4 E.C.L.R. 258.

[26] Case C–303/88 *Italy v. Commission* [1991] E.C.R. I–1433; [1993] 2 C.M.L.R. 1.

[27] Case C–305/89 *Italy v. Commission* [1991] E.C.R. I–1603.

[28] Case C–342/96 *Spain v. Commission* [1999] E.C.R. I–2459.

Tubacex was deeply in crisis. According to the Advocate General, the "normal" response of creditors to such a grave economic situation would be to prevent the opening of fresh credit.

The question clearly highlighted by the difference between Opinion and judgment in this case is how to analyse the function of the State when drawing up and applying rules authorising debt rescheduling of insolvent enterprises. If the Court's ruling is generally applicable, it suggests that the State will never be treated as more than a private creditor seeking to enhance its chances of eventually recovering its debt by granting extended or revised terms. This seems to ignore the reality of many such schemes, where their operation is guided by the desire to maintain jobs for as long as possible. A stricter view, and one closer to the operation of the market investor principle in capital cases, would demand individual assessment of the revised terms taking into account more than just the interest rate.[29] The Court has certainly adopted this approach in other cases, notably *DMT*[30], where it concluded."

> "It is for the national court to determine whether the payment facilities granted . . . are manifestly more generous than those which a private creditor would have granted. To that end the ONSS [Belgian national social security office] must be compared with a hypothetical private creditor which, so far as possible, is in the same position *vis-à-vis* its debtor as the ONSS and is seeking to recover the sums owed to it."[31]

Ultimately it should be remembered that the presence of favour or advantage is not always to be determined by the market investor/creditor tests despite their increasing predominance. Certain activities are especially problematic to assess in this way, an example being the funding of services entrusted with services of general economic interest where the very rationale for state intervention will often be the inability of private investment to guarantee the quality or universal provision of such services.[32] It has also been noted[33] that State support for the activities of voluntary groups providing care for parts of the community may be non-commercial but also capable of alleviating the economic burden that would otherwise fall on the State.

It seems clear that conferring a benefit as such does not constitute an aid. It must additionally be without any real counterpart on the side of the recipient. However, the Court has said that a measure does not lose the quality of a "gratuitous advantage" merely because it is wholly or partially financed out of contributions levied on the undertakings concerned.[34] But no aid will exist where the benefit corresponds to burdens imposed on the undertaking by the State.

---

[29] See Criscuolo, "The State in a liberal market economy: a private investor and creditor or a public authority?" (1999) 24 E.L.Rev. 531.

[30] *supra*, n.23.

[31] *ibid.* para. 25.

[32] See also Chap. 25.

[33] Waddington, "The application of the Community state aid rules to voluntary organisations" LIEI 1998/1, 59, at 67.

[34] Case 78/76 *Firma Steinike und Weinlig v. Germany*, n.9, *supra*.

This might be the case, for example, where grants made to public television companies are intended to compensate them for specific public-service obligations imposed on them by national legislation.[35]

To fall within the scope of Article 87(1) the aid must be granted "by a Member State or through State resources". That must be taken to include grants by regional or local authorities as well as by central government.[36] Nor is it material whether the authorities choose to act directly or through the agency of some public or private body. Community law does not permit the rules on State aid to be circumvented merely through the creation of autonomous institutions charged with allocating aid.[37] In the *Air France* case,[38] the Court of First Instance was called upon to analyse the status of the Caisse, a body established in France by the Finance Law of 1816 under the supervision and guarantee of the legislature and having tasks which included the administration of public and private funds composed of compulsory deposits. However, such deposits were not non-repayable, so unlike revenue from taxation or compulsory contributions those sums were not permanently at the disposal of the public sector. Nevertheless, the Court of First Instance held that it was necessary to consider the extent to which the legal status of the funds managed by the Caisse was reflected by economic reality. On this approach, the deposits and withdrawals produced a constant balance at the disposal of the Caisse and the investments it made could distort competition in the same way as funding resourced by taxation or compulsory contributions. Investment by the Caisse therefore amounted to an aid within the meaning of the Treaty.

The reference in Article 87(1) to aid "by a Member State or through State resources" has been given a restrictive interpretation by the Court. It is clear that measures adopted by a State conferring benefits on undertakings which are not attributable to a charge on the public account will not fall within the provision. Thus, in *Sloman Neptun*,[39] German legislation created a shipping register which allowed ships flying under the German flag but employing non-E.C. crew to escape the full rigours of German labour law. This was claimed to be in effect an aid to such shipowners as they could employ cheap labour. However, the Court stated:

"advantages granted from resources other than those of the State do not fall within the scope of the provisions in question. The distinction between aid granted by the State and aid granted through State resources serves to bring within the definition of aid not only aid granted directly by the State, but also aid granted by public or private bodies designated or established by the State."[40]

---

[35] Case T–95/96 *Gestevisión Telecinco v. Commission* [1998] E.C.R. II-3407; [1998] 3 C.M.L.R. 1112.

[36] *cf.* the terms of the Transparency Dir. 80/723, discussed further in Chap. 25, *infra*.

[37] Case T–358/94 *Air France v. Commission* [1996] E.C.R. II-2109, para. 62; [1997] 1 C.M.L.R. 492.

[38] *ibid.*

[39] Joined Cases C–72–73/91 *Firma Sloman Neptun Schiffahrts A.-G. v. Seebetriebsrat Bodo Ziesmer, Sloman Neptun Schiffahrts AG* [1993] E.C.R. I–887; [1995] 2 C.M.L.R. 97. A similar approach was taken in Case C–189/91 *Kirsammer-Hack v. Sidal* [1993] E.C.R. I–6185. See Davies, "Market integration and social policy in the Court of Justice" (1995) 24 I.L.J. 49.

[40] *Sloman Neptun, supra*, n.39, para. 19.

This approach was confirmed in *Epifanio Viscido v. Ente Poste Italiane*,[41] in relation to a provision giving relief to Poste Italiane from the normal rule of Italian law that employment contracts are of indefinite duration. The flexibility of fixed-term contracts, whilst arguably conferring benefits or saved costs for the undertaking, did not involve any direct or indirect transfer of State resources to it. Advocate General Jacobs, whilst reaching the same conclusion, acknowledged the difficulties of line-drawing in this area by noting:

"It might be asked why, given their potential effect on competition, Article 92(1) does not cover all labour and other social measures which by virtue of being selective in their impact might distort competition and thereby have an equivalent effect to State aid. The answer is perhaps an essentially pragmatic one: to investigate all such regimes would entail an enquiry on the basis of the Treaty alone into the entire social and economic life of a Member State."[42]

However, the social character of assistance is not sufficient to exclude it outright from being categorised as an aid for the purposes of Article 87(1).[43] The Commission has published guidance on whether certain types of measures reducing labour costs constitute State aid.[44]

Article 87(1) only covers aid which is selective "by favouring certain undertakings or the production of certain goods". A distinction is, therefore, drawn between general measures of economic policy, such as the easing of credit controls or a specific tax regime for the self-employed, which may very well improve the position of undertakings in the country concerned *vis-à-vis* their competitors elsewhere in the Community, and measures giving a competitive advantage to particular undertakings or industrial sectors. In Cases 6 and 11/69 *Commission v. France*[45] the European Court held that a preferential discount rate for exports must be regarded as an aid falling within the Treaty supervisory regime, despite the fact that it applied to all national products without distinction. The explanation seems to be[46] that some undertakings would be producing solely for the domestic market so that not all undertakings would in fact be claiming the preferential entitlement.

This distinction between aids and general measures is sometimes slippery. Where the scope of rules is defined by regional location, industrial sector or size of undertaking selectivity is clearly present, but problems may arise where criteria for the provision of resources appear to be universal. The key indication in such cases is whether the application of the measure rests upon discretion. According to the Court in the *DMT* case:

"where the body granting financial assistance enjoys a degree of latitude which enables it to choose the beneficiaries or the conditions under which the

---

[41] Joined Cases C–52–54/97 *Epifanio Viscido and others v. Ente Poste Italiane* [1998] E.C.R. I–2629; [1998] 3 C.M.L.R. 184.

[42] *ibid.*, Opinion para. 16.

[43] Case C–241/94 *France v. Commission* [1996] E.C.R. I–4551, at para. 21; [1997] 1 C.M.L.R. 983.

[44] Commission letter to the Member States, SG(96)D/8034, Notice on monitoring of State aid and reduction of labour costs.

[45] [1969] E.C.R. 523; [1970] C.M.L.R. 43.

[46] Following the Opinion of Advocate General Roemer, at 552.

financial assistance is provided, that assistance cannot be considered to be general in nature."[47]

The Court then left to the national court the question of whether the practices of the national social security office, which had included allowing payments from the undertaking to be postponed for eight years, were indeed part of a discretionary system.

Examples of the interaction of selectivity criteria can be seen in cases involving the special insolvency procedure of Italian law. By Act No. 95/79 large companies in difficulties could continue trading subject to Ministerial supervision. Certain thresholds had to be satisfied for the law to apply, including a minimum number of employees and a minimum level of debt owed to particular types of creditor, including the State. One of the consequences of applying the law was that the undertaking had exemption from fines and penalties which would otherwise arise from failure to meet social security contributions. In a case arising under the ECSC Treaty[48] selectivity was held to exist in both the conditions dictating whether an undertaking qualified to take advantage of the law at all and in the discretionary nature of the dispensation to continue trading which was vested in the relevant Minister.[49] This approach was confirmed in the *Piaggio*[50] case, where the Court added that:

"even if the decisions of the Minister ... to place the undertaking in difficulties under special administration and to allow it to continue trading are taken with regard, as far as possible, to the interests of the creditors and, in particular, to the prospects for increasing the value of the undertaking's assets, they are also influenced ... by the concern to maintain the undertaking's economic activity in the light of national industrial policy considerations."[51]

One effect of using the operation of discretionary rules as a measure of selectivity is to invite a closer scrutiny of national decision-making processes than is the case in relation to other, more self-evident, criteria such as those based upon membership of a particular industrial sector.

Finally, the prohibition in Article 87(1) requires that the aid distorts or threatens to distort competition in so far as it affects trade between Member States. These tests, whilst integral to satisfying the need to reason decisions under Article 253 E.C., do not demand precise, quantified analysis. In *Philip Morris Holland v. Commission*[52] the Court came close to enunciating a *per se* rule as to the effect on inter-State trade which would result from aids designed to enable a cigarette manufacturer to close one of of its two factories in the Netherlands and to expand production at the other. The Court said that:

---

[47] *DMT* case, n.23 *supra*, para. 27.
[48] Case C–200/97 *Ecotrade v. AFS*, judgment December 1, [1998] E.C.R. I–7907; [1999] 2 C.M.L.R. 833.
[49] See also the observations of Advocate General La Pergola in Case C–342/96 *Spain v. Commission* [1999] E.C.R. I–2459.
[50] Case C–295/97 *Industrie Aeronautiche e Meccaniche Rinaldo Piaggio v. Ifitalia, Dornier, Ministero della Difesa* [1999] E.C.R. I–3735. Although the wording of the ECSC Treaty is different, the notion of selectivity was treated as being the same as that for an aid under the E.C. Treaty.
[51] *ibid.* para. 38.
[52] Case 730/79 [1980] E.C.R. 2671; [1981] 2 C.M.L.R. 321.

"When financial aid strengthens the position of an undertaking as compared with other undertakings competing in intra-Community trade the latter must be regarded as affected by that aid."[53]

Consequently, the amount of aid can be very little, yet still be held to distort competition.[54] For example, in *Vlaams Gewest*[55] the Court of First Instance swiftly dismissed a claim by the beneficiary airline that the measly amount of aid it had received, described as a few Belgian francs per passenger, could scarcely have enabled it to avoid increasing its fares or ward off insolvency. Nor can a beneficiary use the fact that other undertakings are receiving aids (even illegal ones) from their States to argue that its own aid is only neutralising other distortions.[56]

For some years it was doubtful whether the State aids regime of control included a *de minimis* rule comparable to that used for the purposes of Articles 81–82. The European Courts were certainly reticent to embrace such a prospect in relation the size of either the undertaking or the aid.[57] However, the Commission has been operating a limited form of the principle for some time.[58] The ceiling for aid covered by its *De Minimis* Notice is 100,000 euros over a three-year period beginning when the first de minimis aid is granted. Such aid does not need to be notified in advance to the Commission.[59] This informal "soft law" approach has been placed on a firmer legal footing by a Council Regulation of 1998[60] which authorises the Commission to adopt group exemptions in relation to State aids incorporating *de minimis* limits.[61]

Article 87(2): exceptions *ipso jure*

Article 87(2) provides that the following categories of aid shall be compatible with the common market:

"*(a) aid having a social character, granted to individual consumers, provided that such aid is granted without discrimination related to the origin of the products concerned.*"

The scope of this exception is limited, especially by the requirement that the aid must be for final consumers. Intervention by the State to buy wheat and then resell it at a discount to enable cheaper bread to be available for consumers

---

[53] *ibid.*, at para. 11.
[54] Joined Cases C–278–280/92 *Spain v. Commission* [1994] E.C.R. I–4103, para. 42.
[55] Case T–214/95 *Vlaams Gewest v. Commission* [1998] E.C.R. II-717.
[56] *ibid.*
[57] Case 142/87 *Belgium v. Commission (Re Tubemeuse)* [1990] E.C.R. I–959; [1991] 3 C.M.L.R. 213 at para. 43, where the Court expressly rejected the contention put forward by the Belgian Government that the 5% threshold then used by the Commission in general competition matters should also apply to State aids.
[58] Notice on the *de minimis* rule for state aid; [1996] O.J. C68/9.
[59] Export aid is excluded from the scope of the Notice.
[60] Council Reg. 994/98 on the application of Arts 92 and 93 to certain categories of horizontal state aid; [1998] O.J. L142/1.
[61] *ibid.*, Art. 2.

might conceivably qualify.[62] The Commission cites the possible application of the exception where an air route concerns an underprivileged region, such as an island. Aid to transport facilities for the island's population could fall within paragraph (a).[63]

> *"(b) aid to make good the damage caused by natural disasters or exceptional occurrences."*

Aid to make good the damage caused by natural disasters is an obvious candidate for automatic exemption from the general principle in Article 87(1). Italian measures which the Commission has treated as falling under this heading were the assistance given in Liguria to repairs and reconstruction required as a result of the floods in 1977, and the provision in Friuli-Venezia Giulia of low interest loans and subsidies for the reconstruction of industrial plant destroyed by the earthquake in 1976.[64] The aid must be to make good the damage, rather than just promote the industrial development of the area. However, the latter could still qualify for exemption under the discretionary provisions of Article 87(3)(a) or (c).

The notion of "exceptional circumstances" is very vague, but is taken to extend the scope of Article 87(2)(b) to "man-made" damage such as that caused by war, serious political disturbances[65], terrorism or catastrophic transport accidents. On the other hand, its applicability in the case of difficulties of an economic nature is more doubtful. The exceptional aid measures adopted by the Member States in the face of the serious recession which began to affect the Community from the second half of 1974 onwards were dealt with by the Commission under the predecessor to Article 87(3)(b).

> *"(c) aid granted to the economy of certain areas of the Federal Republic of Germany affected by the division of Germany, in so far as such aid is required in order to compensate for the economic disadvantage caused by that division".*

Following the unification of Germany in 1990[66] the State aids rules apply with full effect throughout the State. The Commission has consistently taken the view that the exemption must now be applied restrictively[67] and that the provisions of the discretionary exemptions of Article 87(3) are adequate to deal with remaining problems.[68] However, this point was contested in the *Saxony* and *Volkswagen*

---

[62] Case 52/76 *Benedetti v. Munari* [1977] E.C.R. 163. However, as pointed out by Advocate General Reischl at 190, the problem in this case was that the benefit appeared to go to the flour mills, not just the final consumers.

[63] Application of Arts 92 and 93 E.C. and Art. 61 EEA to state aids in the aviation sector; [1994] O.J. C350/5, para. 24.

[64] Comp. Rep. 1978, point 164.

[65] See Communication 3/94 concerning aids for fruit growers affected by a road blockade in France during the summer of 1992, cited in Evans, *op. cit, supra*, n.8, p. 7.

[66] Monetary union came into effect on July 1 and political union on October 3.

[67] *e.g.* in relation to investment aids for Volkswagen, Commission Dec. 94/1068, 1994 O.J. L385/1.

[68] *Aid to Buna;* [1996] O.J. L239/1; the Commission did not regard the difficulties facing companies of the former GDR in meeting the challenges of EU competitors as disadvantages caused by the division of Germany.

cases.[69] It was submitted by the company and Government that as sub-paragraph (c) had been left intact by the Maastricht and Amsterdam Treaties, its modern purpose must extend to use in compensating disadvantages experienced by the East in its exposure to a market economy. The Court of First Instance rejected this argument, noting that the difficulties of economic transition were caused not by the division of Germany as such but, in particular, by the nature of the politico-economic regime which then applied. The Commission, accordingly, had not erred in law in taking the view that new aid by investment in the car industry was to be assessed against the criteria of Article 87(3) rather than Article 87(2)(c).

Article 87(3): exceptions at the discretion of the Commission

The discretion given to the Commission under Article 87(3) is a wide one. Advocate General Capotorti described it in *Philip Morris Holland* as "implying an assessment of an economic, technical and policy nature".[70] The Court said that the exercise of the discretion "involves economic and social assessments which must be made in a Community context".[71]

When applying the discretionary exceptions, the Commission seeks to ensure that aid measures are approved only if they both promote recognised Community objectives and do not frustrate the maintenance of the internal market. The Commission only has power to authorise aids which are necessary for the furtherance of one of the objectives listed in paragraph (3). Since 1980 it has adopted the principle of compensatory justification; to gain approval, any aid proposal

> "must contain a compensatory justification which takes the form of a contribution by the beneficiary of aid over and above the effects of normal play of market forces to the achievement of Community objectives . . ."[72]

The Court upheld this principle in *Philip Morris Holland*, ruling that an aid purporting to be an incentive for investment that would have been made in any event was ineligible, on that ground alone, for exemption.[73]

The categories of aid that the Commission may determine to be compatible with the common market are as follows:

> "(a) *aid to promote the economic development of areas where the standard of living is abnormally low or where there is serious under-employment*".

The economic problem of the region in question must be more serious to fall for consideration under this exception than to attract the general exception relating

---

[69] Joined Cases T–132 and 143/96 *Freistaat Sachsen and Volkswagen v. Commission* (judgment of Court of First Instance December 15, 1999, n.y.r.)

[70] [1980] E.C.R. at 2701.

[71] *ibid.*, at 2691.

[72] Comp. Rep. 1980, point 213.

[73] For further discussion of compensatory justification, see Evans, op. cit, *supra*, n.8, Chap. 3. However, Ottervanger, Hancher and Slot, *op. cit, supra*, n.8, point out that Commission decisions do not always systematically show why the normal play of market forces would not achieve the stated goals.

to sectoral and regional aids in paragraph (c) (see below). The use of the words "abnormally" and "serious" restricts the scope for invoking paragraph (a) by requiring assessment of socio-economic problems to be made in a Community, not a national, context.[74] Using the Commission's Guidelines[75], the conditions are fulfilled if the region, being a NUTS[76] level II geographical unit, has a per capita gross domestic product, measured in purchasing power standards, of less than 75 per cent of the Community average.

> *"(b) aid to promote the execution of an important project of common European interest or to remedy a serious disturbance in the economy of a Member State."*

The exception applies to two completely different types of aid. Originally seen as covering infrastructure or technological advancement,[77] it is now clear that there will be no common European interest in a scheme "unless it forms part of a transnational European programme supported jointly by a number of governments of the Member States, or arises from concerted action by a number of Member States to combat a common threat such as environmental pollution".[78] The Court has indicated that research and development projects do not *per se* qualify.[79]

As for the second category under Article 87(3)(b), serious disturbances, the Commission used it as a safety valve in the economic troubles besetting Member States which followed the energy crisis of 1974.[80] It would appear that disturbances must relate to the whole of a national economy, not just one region or sector.[81] In the latter case the appropriate tool is Article 87(3)(c).

> *"(c) aid to facilitate the development of certain economic activities or of certain economic areas, where such aid does not adversely affect trading conditions to an extent contrary to the common interest."*

This is the most important of the exceptions to the general principle in Article 87(1). It enables the Commission to authorise aids to particular industrial sectors, aids which promote certain "horizontal" policies, and aids to particular regions of a Member State. Sectors to attract attention have been those in difficulties (such as textiles, shipbuilding, motor vehicles, coal and steel), those for which the Community has established policies (agriculture, fisheries and transport) and sectors which merit particular promotion (such as energy).

"Horizontal" policies address common themes and problems which may arise in any industry. The areas for which frameworks and guidelines have been

---

[74] Case 248/84 *Germany v. Commission* [1987] E.C.R. 4013, at para. 19; [1989] 1 C.M.L.R. 591.
[75] Guidelines on National Regional Aid; [1998] O.J. C74/9.
[76] Nomenclature of Statistical Territorial Units.
[77] *e.g.* a common standard for the development of high-definition colour television: see Comp. Rep. 1989, point 151.
[78] Joined Cases 62/87 and 72/87 *Executif Regional Wallon and Glaverbel v. Commission* [1988] E.C.R. 1573; [1989] 2 C.M.L.R. 771.
[79] *ibid.*
[80] See Comp. Rep. 1975, point 133.
[81] See measures authorised in Greece, Comp. Rep. 1987, points 185–187.

developed[82] include the following: small and medium-sized enterprises (SMEs)[83]; research and development (R&D)[84]; environmental protection[85]; employment[86]; training[87]; rescue and restructuring.[88] Aid schemes which might otherwise be deemed incompatible with the common market may be justified against these horizontal considerations.

The legal limits of the Commission's discretion under paragraph (c) are defined by the notion of facilitating the development of the activities or areas concerned and by the proviso that aid must not have an adverse effect on trading conditions "to an extent contrary to the common interest".

"Development" presupposes some improvement in economic performance or prospects. Thus aids of a purely conservatory nature, designed to prevent undertakings in a given industry or area from going out of business, thereby creating unemployment, do not fall within the exception.[89] Recipients of aid must be at least potentially competitive. It seems to follow that financial assistance to an undertaking should normally be temporary and given on a declining scale. The purpose of the aid must be the development of the sector or region in question and not of particular undertakings within it. In the *Belgian Textile Aid* case the Advocate General was of the opinion that the Commission ought not to have authorised grants to certain weak undertakings, given the relative strength of the market sector as a whole.[90]

A crucial distinction between Article 87(3)(a) and (c) when applied to regional aid is that the latter allows for aid to develop areas which are disadvantaged in relation to the national, as distinct from Community, average.[91] As the Commission's Guidelines indicate:

"In contrast to [paragraph] (a), where the situation in view is identified precisely and formally, [paragraph] (c) allows greater latitude when it comes to defining the difficulties of a region that can be alleviated with the help of aid measures. The relevant indicators do not therefore necessarily boil down in this case to standards of living and underemployment. In any case, the appropriate framework for evaluating these difficulties may be provided not only by the Community as a whole but also by the relevant Member State in particular."[92]

Nevertheless, regional aid under paragraph (c) must still form part of a coherent regional policy of the Member State. Since it is for areas less disadvantaged than

---

[82] For a more detailed approach to these policies, see one of the more specific works listed in n.8, *supra*.

[83] See [1996] O.J. C213/4

[84] See [1996] O.J. C45/5.

[85] See [1994] O.J. C72/3.

[86] See [1995] O.J. C334/4.

[87] See [1998] O.J. C343

[88] See [1997] O.J. C283/2. Aid for rescuing and restructuring firms in dificulty accounts for a high proportion of the aid given to individual recipients on an ad hoc basis; see Comp. Rep. 1998, para. 223.

[89] See the remarks of Advocate General Slynn in Case 84/82 *Germany v. Commission (Belgian Textile Aid)* [1984] E.C.R. 1451; [1985] 1 C.M.L.R. 153.

[90] *ibid.* at 1504.

[91] Case 248/84 *Commission v. Germany* [1987] E.C.R. 4013; [1989] 1 C.M.L.R. 591.

[92] Guidelines on National Regional Aid; [1998] O.J. C74/9, para. 3.6.

ones falling within the scope of paragraph (a), aid granted under (c) is exceptional and permissible only to a limited degree. The 1998 Guidelines therefore indicate that only a small part of the national territory of a Member State may prima facie qualify for such aid. Thus the population coverage of regions falling within paragraph (c) must not exceed 50 per cent of the national population not covered by the derogation under paragraph (a).[93]

The proviso in paragraph (c) imposes a limit, albeit a flexible one, on the extent to which the disruption of the market mechanism may be tolerated for the sake of the socio-economic benefit sectoral or regional aids may bring. Its operation can be illustrated by Case 47/69 *France v. Commission*.[94] The aid in question took the form of contributions towards research and the restructuring of French textile undertakings, and seemed prima facie to be exactly the type of sectoral aid to which paragraph (c) was intended to apply. However, the Commission objected to the fact that the aid was financed out of a parafiscal charge imposed both on textile products manufactured in France and on imports. The European Court agreed with the Commission that the method of financing an aid system was one of the factors to be taken into account in assessing its compatibility with the common market. It was capable of adding to the disturbance of trading conditions, thus rendering the system as a whole contrary to the common interest. That was the case here, because of the protective effect of applying the charge to imports. The amount of aid available increased automatically in proportion to any increase in revenue, so that the more undertakings from other Member States succeeded in making sales in France, the more they would have to contribute for the benefit of their French competitors, who might not have made similar efforts.

In that case, the Court seems to have assessed the extent to which trading conditions were liable to be adversely affected independently of the benefits expected to flow from the aid. Its approach was that, however worthwhile the objective being pursued, disruption of the market beyond a certain point must be judged contrary to the common interest. In applying the proviso, account must be taken of any factors that may moderate the anti-competitive impact of an aid. In its *Intermills* judgment the Court said that "the settlement of an undertaking's existing debts in order to ensure its survival does not necessarily affect trading conditions to an extent contrary to the common interest, as provided in Article 92(3), where such an operation is, for example, accompanied by a restructuring plan".[95] Failure to show that the possibly mitigating effects of restructuring had been adequately considered was one of the reasons for the annulment of the decisions of the Commission in the *Intermills* and *Leeuwarder*[96] cases.

> *"(d) aid to promote culture and heritage conservation where such aid does not affect trading conditions and competition in the Community to an extent that is contrary to the common interest."*

---

[93] *ibid.*, para. 3.7.
[94] [1970] E.C.R. 487.
[95] [1984] E.C.R. at p. 3832.
[96] *loc. cit., supra*, n.18.

This exception was inserted into the E.C. Treaty by the Treaty on European Union with effect from November 1, 1993, although aids to support culture had previously been capable of consideration under paragraph (c).[97] It has been used by the Commission on a number of occasions, especially in relation to films and books. For example, in 1998 it authorised[98] aid to support the export of books in the French language to non-French-speaking countries, provided it was intended to offset the extra cost involved in handling small orders. In other words, approval was given on the basis that the aid pursued a cultural objective and was not to support the other, commercial, activities of the beneficiary. This expressly used the derogation of paragraph (d), having had a previous authorisation made in the context of paragraph (c) annulled by the Court of First Instance on grounds of inadequate market assessment.[99]

The proviso attached to paragraph (d) is the same as for paragraph (c), with the express addition of competition as a consideration pertinent to the common interest, presumably to take account of the particular impact that aids in the fields of broadcasting, media and other conduits of cultural expression might have. Where, for example, broadcasting undertakings are given support in return for carrying out specific public service obligations, other considerations may also apply (in particular Article 86(2), dealt with in Chapter 25).

Authorisation of aid by the Council

The Council's powers to authorise state aids are limited, being confined to Article 87(3)(e) and Article 88(2) third sub-paragraph. The former represents the last in the list of express discretionary exceptions, namely: "(e) such other categories of aid as may be specified by decision of the Council acting by a qualified majority on a proposal from the Commission". A series of directives on aids to shipbuilding in the Member States was adopted under this provision.[1] It was not possible to rely on paragraph (c) because the measures included "production aids" which could not be regarded as facilitating "development".

Authorisation by the Council under Article 88(2) third sub-paragraph is expressly reserved for exceptional circumstances, and has been described as one of the safety valves of the Treaty.[2] The third and fourth sub-paragraphs provide:

"On application by a Member State, the Council may, acting unanimously, decide that aid which that State is granting or intends to grant shall be considered to be compatible with the common market, in derogation from the provisions of Article 87 or from the regulations provided for in Article 89, if such a decision is justified by exceptional circumstances. If, as regards the aid in question, the Commission has already initiated the procedure provided for in the first sub-paragraph of this paragraph, the fact that the State concerned

---

[97] e.g. Dec. 89/441, 1989 O.J. L208/3 in relation to Greek aid to the film industry for the production of Greek films.

[98] See Comp. Rep. 1998, para. 275 and Dec. 1999/133; [1999] O.J. L44/37.

[99] Case T–49/93 SIDE v. Commission [1995] E.C.R. II–2501

[1] See Reg. 1540/98; [1998] O.J. L202/1, valid until December 31, 2003. This replaced the long-standing Seventh Dir. 90/684; [1990] O.J. L380/27.

[2] Advocate General Cosmas in Case C–122/94 Commission v. Council [1996] E.C.R. 881, at para. 62.

has made its application to the Council shall have the effect of suspending that procedure until the Council has made its attitude known.

If, however, the Council has not made its attitude known within three months of the said application being made, the Commission shall give its decision on the case."

The case-law interpreting this provision is limited, but most examples are to be found in the agricultural sector.[3] The wording suggests that Member States can only take advantage of the special Council procedure if the Commission has not already taken a final decision on the aid.[4]

By their very nature, "exceptional circumstances" are hardly susceptible to definition. Advocate General Cosmas has suggested[5] that the idea means "something extraordinary and unforeseen, or at least something not permanent or continuous and of course something other than normal". In other words, taking a regime subject to common organisation as an example, the Council's intervention must be needed for the adoption of measures to deal with a short-term dysfunction that might more particularly affect one Member State against others. The Court of Justice will not interfere with the Council's finding of exceptional circumstances unless there has been a manifest error of assessment. Thus, in a case arising from the common organisation in wine,[6] the Court accepted the Council's view that the aids in question were necessary to avoid the risk in Italy of serious economic and social repercussions, in particular for small producers and co-operative wine cellars, and, in France, the risk of engendering a critical situation.

The application of Article 87

We have seen that State aids meeting the criteria in Article 87(1) are not automatically to be regarded as incompatible with the common market, since they may fall within one of the excepted categories in paragraphs (2) and (3) of the Article, or be exempted using the special powers of the Council. Moreover, the application, in particular, of Article 87(3) entails a complex appreciation of economic and social factors in the light of the overall Community interest. The approach adopted by the Treaty is, accordingly, to make the Community institutions responsible in the first instance for giving concrete effect to the principles of Article 87, and machinery for this purpose has been provided in Articles 88 and 89.

The corollary of the provision of special machinery at Community level is that courts in the Member States may not apply Article 87 independently of that machinery. In the words of the European Court, the parties concerned cannot:

---

[3] For figures on the increasing use of the provision, see the Opinion, *ibid.*

[4] Otherwise, this would conflict with the Commission's ability to take a Member State directly to the Court of Justice following an adverse decision on the aid; see Advocate General Mayras in Case 70/72 *Commission v. Germany* [1973] E.C.R. 813, at 835; [1973] C.M.L.R. 741.

[5] Case C–122/94 *Commission v. Council* loc. cit. *supra*, n.2. See Ross, (1997) 34 C.M.L.Rev. 135.

[6] *ibid.*

". . . simply, on the basis of Article 92 alone, challenge the compatibility of an aid with Community law before national courts or ask them to decide as to any compatibility which may be the main issue in actions before them or may arise as a subsidiary issue. There is this right however where the provisions of Article 92 have been applied by the general provisions provided for in Article 94 or by specific decisions under Article 93(2)."[7]

In that sense, Article 87 is not directly effective. However, it does not follow that national courts may not sometimes have to interpret Article 87, for example to decide whether a measure introduced by a Member State without obtaining clearance under Article 88(3) constitutes "aid". Such scrutiny forms part of the general obligation upon national courts to provide effective protection of individuals' rights conferred by these procedural requirements.[8] In such cases the national court may seek the assistance of the Commission[9] as well as having recourse to the mechanism of Article 234 to seek a preliminary ruling from the European Court.

The machinery in Articles 88 and 89 E.C.

Procedural legislation in the state aids field akin to the scheme applied to competition law generally by Regulation 17/62[10] took years to materialise. However, in March 1999 the Council finally used its powers under Article 89 to adopt Regulation 659/1999.[11] This Regulation, aimed at codifying case-law practices and making the procedural rules more transparent and accessible, came into force on April 16, 1999. It distinguishes four different situations for procedural purposes: notified aid, unlawful aid, misuse of aid and existing aid schemes, each governed by a different chapter.

Notified aid

Article 88(3) of the Treaty provides:

"The Commission shall be informed, in sufficient time to enable it to submit its comments, of any plans to grant or alter aid. If it considers that any such plan is not compatible with the common market having regard to Article 87, it shall without delay initiate the procedure provided for in paragraph 2. The Member State concerned shall not put its proposed measures into effect until this procedure has resulted in a final decision."

The paragraph establishes a system of prior control which is designed to prevent any aid incompatible with the common market from being introduced. Member States are required to notify the Commission of plans to grant or alter aid sufficiently in advance of the date set for their implementation to enable it to

---

[7] Case 78/76 *Firma Steinike und Weinlig v. Germany* [1977] E.C.R. at p. 609; [1977] 2 C.M.L.R. 688.
[8] Case C–39/94 *SFEI v. La Poste* [1996] E.C.R. I–3547; [1996] All E.R. (E.C.) 685.
[9] Notice on Cooperation between national courts and the Commission in the field of state aid; [1995] O.J. C312/8.
[10] [1962] O.J. 13/204.
[11] [1999] O.J. L83/1. See Sinnaeve and Slot, "The new regulation on State aid procedures" (1999) 36 C.M.L.Rev 1153.

examine the plans and form a view as to whether the procedure under Article 88(2) should be initiated against them. According to Article 2 of Regulation 659/1999, the notification requirement relates to "any plans to grant new aid", aid being defined in Article 1 as any measure fulfilling all the criteria laid down in Article 87(1) of the Treaty. This means that notification is not required for all measures which might constitute aid, but only for those which embrace each of the elements of Article 87(1). There is thus the capacity for "existential" uncertainty[12] because of the potential gap between a Member State's view as to whether a measure, for example, affects inter-State trade or represents a sufficiently significant distortion of competition, compared to the Commission's *ex post facto* assessment of the situation. Aid falling within group exemptions need not be notified, nor in principle is notification required for individual applications of an approved aid scheme.[13]

The last sentence of Article 88(3) imposes a "standstill" obligation upon the Member State proposing to introduce an aid.[14] This applies during the period of preliminary review by the Commission and, if the procedure under Article 88(2) is initiated, continues until a final decision is reached. *A fortiori*, a Member State is prohibited from putting an aid into effect without notifying it at all.

Where aid is notified, Article 4 of Regulation 659 provides for three outcomes to be determined in the form of a decision by the Commission after conducting a preliminary examination. First, it may record that the notified measure does not constitute aid at all. Secondly, it may decide not to raise objections, specifying which exception of the Treaty has been applied. It does not appear that the Commission could attach conditions to such a finding, as these would imply incompatibility with the common market requiring a formal investigation.[15] Thirdly, if doubts are raised as to the compatibility of the aid with the common market the Commission shall take a decision to initiate the formal investigation procedure of Article 88(2). One of these decisions must be taken within two months commencing the day following a complete notification.[16] Following the expiry of that period without a decision by the Commission the aid shall be deemed to have been authorised and the Member State may implement the measures after giving the Commission prior notice.[17]

Where an aid proposal is altered after having been notified to the Commission, the latter must be informed of the amendment, although this may be done in the course of consultations arising from the original notification.[18] Failure to bring amendments to the attention of the Commission will cause the standstill under Article 88(3) to remain in force against a scheme which has otherwise been found compatible with the common market. Regulation 659 is notably silent on the question of what amounts to an alteration. However, the Court recognises

---

[12] *ibid.*, p. 1165.
[13] Under Reg. 659, such an individual application constitutes "existing aid".
[14] Case 84/82 *Germany v. Commission* [1984] E.C.R. at p. 1488; [1985] 1 C.M.L.R. 153. This is now also stated in Art. 3 of Reg. 659.
[15] *cf.* Reg. 659, Art. 7(3) and closure of the formal investigation procedure.
[16] Reg. 659, Art. 4(5). Case-law had established a two month period as early as 1973 in Case 120/73 *Lorenz* [1973] E.C.R. 1471.
[17] Reg. 659, Art. 4(6).
[18] Joined Cases 91 and 127/83 *Heineken Brouwerijen* [1984] E.C.R. 2435; [1985] 1 C.M.L.R. 389.

that not every technical modification to an existing aid must be notified. Thus in the *Namur* case,[19] Belgian legislation endowed OND with particular advantages such as State guarantees and State bonds, to carry out its function of assisting exports through reduction of credit risks. OND's actual market conduct was restricted as a result of agreement between it and COBAC, a private credit-insurance undertaking, as to the type of risk each would undertake to cover. That agreement was then terminated by instructions given to OND by its supervising ministers, thereby for practical purposes enlarging OND's areas of activity although the legislation itself remained intact. The Commission unsuccessfully contended that this practical change constituted aid.

Detailed rules for the operation of the formal investigation procedure are set out in Article 6 of Regulation 659. A decision to open this procedure must summarise the relevant issues of fact and law, include a preliminary assessment of the Commission as to the aid character of the proposed measure and set out the doubts as to its compatibility with the common market. Member States and interested parties must be invited to submit comments within a prescribed period, normally not exceeding one month. Comments received are to be communicated to the Member State concerned, although a third party may request its identity to be withheld on grounds of potential damage.

Closure of the formal investigation procedure must follow the paths indicated by Article 7 of Regulation 659. Thus, as with the ending of the preliminary stage, the Commission may decide that no aid is involved. However, unlike the position under Article 4, closure of the formal investigation in this way may follow modification of the measure by the Member State concerned. This provision emphasises that negotiations between State and Commission should be confined to the formal, and not the preliminary, stage of investigation.[20] A second possibility is a positive decision confirming the aid and specifying which Treaty exception[21] is being relied upon. The Commission has the power[21] to attach conditions to a positive decision. Finally, the Commission may adopt a negative decision ruling that the notified aid is not compatible with the common market.

Decisions taken under Article 7 are, as far as possible, to be taken by the Commission within a period of 18 months from the opening of the formal investigation procedure. After the expiry of this period, the Member State may request the Commission to take a decision within two months. The overall length of the investigation period has been criticised,[22] not least because the necessity might be questioned of any aid project which takes almost two years to be approved.[23]

Unlawful aid

According to Article 1(f) of Regulation 659, unlawful aid is new aid put into effect in contravention of Article 88(3) of the Treaty. Thus it covers not only aid

---

[19] Case C–44/93 *Namur-Les Assurances du Crédit SA v. Office National du Ducroire and Belgium* [1994] E.C.R. I–3829.

[20] Confirming Case 84/82 *Germany v. Commission* [1984] E.C.R. 1451; [1985] 1 C.M.L.R. 153.

[21] Art. 7(4) of the Regulation.

[22] See Sinnaeve and Slot, *loc. cit, supra*, n.11.

[23] At least two months for the preliminary stage, 18 months under Art. 7(6) and the additional two months afterwards.

which has not been notified at all, but also aid which is notified but implemented prior to authorisation and aid implemented in breach of the terms of authorisation. Where the Commission has in its possession information from whatever source regarding alleged unlawful aid it shall examine that information without delay.[24] Although the time-limits for the preliminary assessment of a properly notified aid do not apply, the Commission must still act within a reasonable time.[25]

Regulation 659 authorises three types of injunction for the Commission to use in the context of possible unlawful aid. First,[26] it can issue an injunction requiring a Member State to submit information, failure to comply giving the Commission the right to take a decision on the basis of the information it already has. Secondly,[27] the Commission may, after giving the Member State concerned the opportunity to submit its comments, adopt a decision requiring the Member State to suspend any unlawful aid until the Commission has taken a decision on the compatibility of the aid with the common market. Thirdly,[28] the Commission has the power to issue a decision requiring the Member State provisionally to recover any unlawful aid until the Commission has taken a decision on the compatibility of the aid. Such an injunction can only be used, however, where according to established practice there are no doubts as to the aid character of the measure, there is an urgency to act and there is a serious risk of substantial and irreparable damage to a competitor. Non-compliance with either a suspensory or provisional recovery injunction will entitle the Commission to refer the matter to the European Court direct and apply for a declaration that the failure constitutes an infringement of the Treaty.

Where the Commission adopts a negative decision in cases of unlawful aid, it is obliged to issue a recovery decision requiring the Member State concerned to take all necessary measures to recover the aid from the beneficiary.[29] Whilst the power of the Commission to order recovery is well established in earlier case-law,[30] the obligation to do so is a new feature established in Regulation 659. Article 14(2) provides that recovery shall not be required if this would be contrary to a general principle of Community law. However, this restriction is likely to apply only in exceptional situations. It is clear from the Court's previous case-law that beneficiaries will not normally be able to invoke the protection of legitimate expectations as a reason for resisting recovery. The reason for this is that a diligent business person should normally be able to determine whether the procedural requirements of Article 88 of the Treaty have been observed.[31] Unjustified delays by the Commission in reaching decisions might give rise to legitimate expectations that the aid was not objectionable,[32] although the

---

[24] Art. 10(1) of Reg. 659.
[25] Case T–95/96 *Gestevisión Telecinco v. Commission* [1998] E.C.R. II-3407; [1998] 3 C.M.L.R. 1112.
[26] Art. 10(3) of Reg. 659.
[27] Art. 11(1).
[28] Art. 11(2).
[29] Art. 14(1).
[30] Case 70/72 *Commission v. Germany* [1973] E.C.R. 813; [1973] C.M.L.R. 741.
[31] Case 301/87 *France v. Commission (Boussac)* [1990] E.C.R. I–307, para. 14.
[32] Case 223/85 *Rijn-Schelde-Verolme (RSV) Maschinefabrieken en Scheepswerven NV v. Commission* [1987] E.C.R. 4617; [1989] 2 C.M.L.R. 259, where the Commission delayed proceedings by 26 months.

timetables introduced by the Regulation will usually pre-empt recourse to this route.

Any use by the Commission of its powers to order recovery is subject to a limitation period of ten years.[33] This runs from the day on which the unlawful aid is awarded to the beneficiary either as individual aid or as aid under an aid scheme. Any interruption, such as the result of the Commission making a request for information, starts the time period running afresh. It may therefore be assumed that the operation of the rule is hardly likely to circumscibe the Commission's position unduly. In any event the distortive effects of an aid which has operated undetected and without complaint for ten years must be open to doubt.

Once the Commission has made an order against a Member State seeking recovery, it is for the State to execute it using national laws and procedures. By Article 14(3) of Regulation 659 "recovery shall by effected without delay and in accordance with the procedures under the national law of the Member State concerned, provided that they allow the immediate and effective execution of the Commission's decision". This provision, described as a "real innovation",[34] allows the Commission to act against delaying procedures in Member States so that measures by national judges merely ordering suspensive effects of an aid could be seen as contrary to Regulation 659.

Prior to enactment of the Regulation, the Court had taken a strict view as to the nature of the obligation to repay in a line of cases following *Commission v. Belgium*[35] where it emphasised the need to consider whether it was *impossible* for the Member State to comply with the Commission's decision. The mere fact that beneficiaries of the aid might suffer financial hardship from its revocation is not sufficient to thwart recovery.[36] Nor is conflict with national rules of company law in cases where undoing aid in the form of equity participation may run counter to standard principles about priorities between creditors and shareholders.[37] Apart from satisfying orthodox doctrines concerning the supremacy of Community law and the need to achieve effectiveness of enforcement, this position also makes clear that repayment is not a matter of countering improper benefits but is an absolute consequence of infringement of the obligations under the aids super-visory regime. Thus in *Re Tubemeuse*,[38] the beneficiary was in liquidation, so that it was no longer able to take advantage of the unlawfully paid aid. Any repayment would in effect come from the company's other creditors, who would be disadvantaged *pro tanto* by the State's claim. The Court, citing previous authority,[39] ruled that:

"recovery of unlawful aid is the logical consequence of finding that it is unlawful. Consequently, the recovery of State aid unlawfully granted for the

---

[33] Art. 15(1) of Reg. 659. This rule was inserted into the Regulation by the Council and did not form part of the Commission's original proposal.
[34] Sinnaeve and Slot, *loc. cit*, n.11, *supra*.
[35] Case 52/84 *Commission v. Belgium* [1986] E.C.R. 89; [1987] 1 C.M.L.R. 710.
[36] Case 63/87 *Commission v. Greece* [1988] E.C.R. 2875; [1989] 3 C.M.L.R. 677.
[37] See Case C–142/87 *Re Tubemeuse: Belgium v. Commission*, n.57, *supra*.
[38] *ibid.*
[39] Case 310/85 *Deufil v. Commission* [1987] E.C.R. 901; [1988] 1 C.M.L.R. 553.

purpose of re-establishing the previously existing situation cannot in principle be regarded as disproportionate to the objectives of the Treaty in regard to State aids."

One situation where it would seem impossible to recover aid is illustrated by the *Boussac* case.[40] The aid had consisted of capital injections, loans and reductions in employers' social security contributions. However, the Commission ruled out of account the sums paid out by Boussac to meet the cost of transferring certain production sites and employees to independent companies which had subsequently ceased production. These amounts were treated as lost and impossible to recover. The Court accepted this view and, moreover, cited the pursuit by the Commission of only partial repayment as an answer to the French Government's claim that the recovery of aid was disproportionate to the effect on competition. It is submitted that the statement of principle made in *Re Tubemeuse*, above, is better preserved if the *Boussac* observation is seen as a statement that the test of impossibility was satisfied, rather than one applying proportionality criteria. Impossibility is not for the State merely to assert; it must be demonstrated after an active search for a solution in the context of a dialogue between the Commission and the State concerned.[41]

Misuse of aid

The notion of misuse appears in the Treaty itself in Article 88(2):

"If, after giving notice to the parties concerned to submit their comments, the Commission finds that aid granted by a State or through State resources is not compatible with the common market having regard to Article 87, *or that such aid is being misused*, it shall decide that the State concerned shall abolish or alter such aid within a period of time to be determined by the Commission." (emphasis added).

Misuse is further defined in Article 1(g) of Regulation 659 as aid used by the beneficiary in contravention of a decision taken under the Regulation not to raise objections at the preliminary stage or a decision closing a formal investigation on the basis of either a positive or conditional approval. The key difference between misuse and unlawful aid is that in the former case it the beneficiary who has brought about the infringement whereas the Member State is responsible for unlawful aid. Procedurally, the reference in Article 88(2) means that misuse cannot be addressed without opening a formal investigation. Subject to this important limitation, Regulation 659 adopts the same principles *mutatis mutandis* for enforcement against misuse as for unlawful aid. The only exception is that a provisional recovery injunction under Article 11(2) is not available to the Commission.

---

[40] n.31, *supra*.
[41] Case C–349/93 *Commission v. Italy* [1995] E.C.R. I–343. See also Case C–6/97 *Commission v. Italy* [1999] E.C.R. I–2981 where the fact that Italy had taken no steps to recover the tax credit in question meant that implementation of the recovery decision could not be shown to be impossible.

Existing aids

Article 88(1) of the Treaty provides:

"The Commission shall, in co-operation with Member States, keep under constant review all systems of aid existing in those States. It shall propose to the latter any appropriate measures required by the progressive development or by the functioning of the common market."

The notion of existing aid is dealt with at length in Article 1(b) of Regulation 659, and comprises the following five categories:

(i) all aid which existed prior to the entry into force of the Treaty in the respective Member States, with the exception of Austria, Finland and Sweden for whom the relevant date is the entry into force of the EEA-Agreement[42];

(ii) aid schemes or individual aids authorised by the Commission or Council;

(iii) aid authorised by default[43];

(iv) aid deemed to be existing by operation of the 10 year limitation period for recovery;

(v) aid which is deemed to be an existing aid because it can be established that at the time when it was put into effect it did not constitute an aid, and subsequently became an aid due to the evolution of the common market and without having been altered by the Member State.[44]

It would clearly make no sense for the maintenance of the single market if aids were only subject to controls at the time of their proposal. Article 88(1) thus provides for ongoing supervision and review of existing measures. Under Article 17(1) of Regulation 659 the Commission shall obtain all necessary information for this purpose and, if it forms a preliminary view that existing aid is not, or is no longer, compatible with the common market, it shall inform the Member State of that view and give it one month to submit comments. If it remains of its adverse opinion, the Commission shall then address recommendations to the Member State.[45] Ultimately, if the Member State does not accept those recommendations, the Commission must initiate the formal investigation procedure. However, because of the existing status of the aid, it is not open to the Commission to use the enforcement mechanisms appropriate for unlawful aid. Instead, once a negative decision is finally adopted at the end of a formal investigation, the existing aid scheme is at that point rendered unlawful for the future if it remains in force.

---

[42] January 1, 1994.

[43] *e.g.* using Art. 4(6) of Reg. 659 where the Commission fails to comply with the two-month time limit to make a decision.

[44] Sinnaeve and Slot, *loc. cit, supra* n.11, suggest that this might apply to an activity or product for which the State provides support and for which there is at the time no Community market or trade.

[45] Art. 18 of Reg. 659.

Rights of interested parties

The supervisory regime established for state aids does not replicate the system for competition law enforcement generally. It is instead characterised by dialogue between Member States and the Commission and use of a two-stage procedure of preliminary and formal investigation. These features have affected the scope and content of rights of interested parties as developed by the European Court and incorporated into Chapter VI of Regulation 659.

Adherence to the distinction between the preliminary stage and formal investigation led the Court in *Sytraval*[46] to find that there was no obligation on the Commission to conduct an exchange of views with a complainant during the preliminary stage. Similarly, it has no duty to examine of its own motion objections which the complainant would certainly have raised had it been consulted. Nevertheless, the Court added:

"However, this finding does not mean that the Commission is not obliged, where necessary, to extend its investigation of a complaint beyond a mere examination of the facts and points of law brought to its notice by the complainant. The Commission is required, in the interests of sound administration of the fundamental rules of the Treaty relating to State aid, to conduct a diligent and impartial examination of the complaint, which may make it necessary for it to examine matters not expressly raised by the complainant."[47]

Where the Commission acts on a complaint but decides not to move to a formal investigation, either because it thinks there is no aid at all or that there is an aid which is compatible with the common market, its decision is treated as being one addressed to the Member State only, even though it may send a letter to the complainant setting out that position. However, that decision is challengeable by any persons intended to benefit from the procedural guarantees set out in Article 88(2) since by definition they are now precluded from having the opportunity to enjoy those protections. "Parties concerned" within the meaning of Article 88(2) are those persons, undertakings or associations whose interests might be affected by the grant of the aid, in particular competing undertakings and trade associations.[48] The Court of First Instance has refused to entertain the admissibility of claims brought by parties not in competition with the beneficiaries of the aid in question.[49]

Formal decisions adopted by the Commission at the end of a full investigation under Article 88(2) are challengeable under Article 230 using the normal criteria for such actions. Satisfying the conditions of admissibility should present no

---

[46] Case C–367/95P *Commission v. Chambre Syndicale Nationale des Enterprises de Transport de Fonds et Valeurs (Sytraval) and Brink's France SARL* [1998] E.C.R. I–1719, noted by Slot, (1999) 36 C.M.L.Rev. 1335.

[47] *ibid.*, para. 62.

[48] *ibid.*, para. 41.

[49] Case T–398/94 *Kahn Scheepvaart v. Commission* [1996] E.C.R. II-477. See also Case T–188/95 *Waterleiding Maatschappij 'Noord-West Brabant' NV v. Commission* [1998] E.C.R. II–3713.

problem to a direct recipient of the aid[50] or to an undertaking which responded to the Commission's invitation to submit comments and which is able to produce prima facie evidence of substantial harm to its interests resulting from the granting of the aid to a competitor.[51] However, the mere fact that a competitor would be an "interested party" for the purposes of an invitation to comment under Article 88(2) does not make it necessarily directly and individually concerned under Article 230 for the purposes of a subsequent challenge to a final decision by the Commission. Submission of comments during the formal investigative stage is seen as a procedural guarantee in its own right, so that it cannot be used as the sole reason for subsequently claiming sufficient locus standi to challenge the final outcome.[52]

An example of these various rules in operation can be seen in *BP Chemicals v. Commission*[53] where Italy made aid available to Enichem, the leading ethylene producer, in the form of three capital injections. The first two contributions were not notified in accordance with Treaty requirements and the Commission opened the procedure of Article 88(2) in relation to them. During the course of those proceedings the third capital injection was raised by the Italian Government. The original injections were discussed in the United Kingdom by a working party which included BP, one of Enichem's main competitors in the ethylene market. Taking account of the working party's comments, the United Kingdom made observations to the Commission and also noted the reports about a proposed third injection. The Commission subsequently decided to close procedures relating to the first two injections and further decided that the third capital contribution did not constitute aid at all since it satisfied the market investor test.

It was held by the Court of First Instance that BP could challenge the Commission's implied refusal to open proceedings on the third injection, following the argument that such a step precluded BP from exercising its rights as an interested party for the purposes of submitting comments under Article 88(2). However, in relation to the first two capital contributions BP could not show individual concern. It had not complained to the Commission nor had it approached the Commission under its own name with a view to submitting comments as an interested party. Being a member of the working party which had influenced the United Kingdom's submissions was also insufficient to distinguish BP. According to the Court of First Instance, the Commission had no knowledge at the time of the administrative procedure of either BP's specific objections or of any role which it had played in the preparation of the United Kingdom's comments. Nor were there any other specific circumstances to make BP individually concerned. In particular, it was not enough that BP's competitive position might be affected by the Commission's decision.

---

[50] Case 730/79 *Philip Morris Holland v. Commission*, loc. cit, *supra* n.52.
[51] Case 169/84 *COFAZ and others v. Commission* [1986] E.C.R. 391; [1986] 3 C.M.L.R. 385.
[52] Case T–86/96 *Arbeitsgemeinschaft Deutscher Luftfahrt-Unternehmen and Hapag-Lloyd Fluggesellschaft mbH v. Commission* [1999] E.C.R. II–179.
[53] Case T–11/95 [1998] E.C.R. II–3235.

The role of national courts

Although national courts are unable to rule on the compatibility of aid with the common market, their role in the supervisory regime is highly significant because of the responsibilities placed upon them in relation to safeguarding the rights of individuals against non-observance by Member States of the procedural rules. That the standstill clause of Article 88(3) could create directly effective rights was established as early as 1973 in the *Lorenz* case.[54] This was elaborated upon by the Court in its so-called *French Salmon* ruling,[55] stressing the fundamental difference between the central executive role performed by the Commission and the task of national courts. Whilst the Commission was required to examine the compatibility of the planned aid with the common market, even in cases where the Member State infringed the prohibition of implementing aid measures, national courts merely safeguarded, pending a final decision by the Commission, the rights of individuals against any disregard by the State authorities of the prohibition contained in the last sentence of Article 88(3). A decision in that regard by a national court did not amount to an adjudication on the compatibility of the aid with the common market. Nevertheless, the national court had to ensure that individuals were in a position to enforce rights of action in respect of any disregard of Article 88(3), from which all the proper consequences would follow, in accordance with their national law, both regarding the validity of acts involving the implementation of aid measures and the recovery of financial support granted in breach of that provision or of any provisional measures.

It is clear that a finding by a national court that an aid has been granted in breach of Article 88(3) "must in principle lead to its repayment in accordance with the procedural rules of domestic law".[56] Nevertheless, as Advocate General Jacobs pointed out,[57] there might exceptionally be situations in which a repayment order might be inappropriate. These might arise where there was considerable delay in any simultaneous Commission investigation or where the aid character of the measures at stake was not self-evident. Even if the Commission subsequently declares the aid compatible with the common market, this does not regularise a previous violation by the State of its notification obligations so that a national court's power to order repayment of aid already paid out is unaffected. Recovery of the aid alone may not be sufficient to give effective protection for individuals. Since the rights of individuals flow from the Member State's breach of the duty to notify under Article 88(3), claims for liability in damages may apply if the principles of *Francovich*[58] and *Brasserie du Pêcheur/Factortame*[59] are satisfied.[60]

---

[54] Case 120/73 *Lorenz* [1973] E.C.R. 1471.
[55] Case C–354/90 *Fédération Nationale du Commerce Extérieur des Produits Alimentaires v. France* [1991] E.C.R. I–5505
[56] Case C–39/94 *SFEI v. La Poste* [1996] E.C.R. I–3547; [1996] All E.R. (E.C.) 685.
[57] *ibid.*
[58] Joined Cases C–6, 9/90 *Francovich and another v. Italy* [1991] E.C.R. I–5357; [1993] 2 C.M.L.R. 66.
[59] Joined Cases C–46 and 48/93 *Brasserie du Pêcheur v. Germany, R. v. Secretary of State for Transport, ex p. Factortame* [1996] E.C.R. I–1029; [1996] 1 C.M.L.R. 889; [1996] All E.R. (E.C.) 301.
[60] See Hernandez, "The principle of non-contractual State liability for breaches of E.C. law and its application to State aids" [1996] 6 E.C.L.R. 355.

Although the Commission has been keen to involve national courts in the state aids supervisory process, it is arguable how far this aim has actually been realised. A Union-wide investigation[61] carried out by local experts for the Commission identified a low number of actions brought by competitors in national courts, and an even lower number of successful ones. In a total of 116 cases seen as involving the application of the state aids rules, only 28 were brought by competitors and a mere three of these were successful. According to the authors of the report, these figures result from "lack of transparency of substantive and procedural rules at E.C. level and the limited knowledge of these rules at lower and mid-level courts in the Member States".[62] It remains to be seen what impact the various Regulations of 1998 and 1999 will make upon such transparency and knowledge problems, although it may be noted that the *Co-operation Notice on State Aids*[63] had already been applicable for some time during the period of the experts' investigatory study.

As noted in Chapter 25, national courts may also incur responsibilities in the context of the application of the derogation set out in Article 86(2). Undertakings entrusted with services of general economic interest may invoke this provision to justify state aids in their favour.[64] A scenario which seemingly might thus arise[65] is where a privatised utility is challenged by customers or competitors on the basis that it is being aided in some form and that a breach of Article 88(3) has occurred by non-notification. On the authorities discussed above, this question undoubtedly falls within a national court's purview. But the undertaking might respond that there is either no aid or that the application of Article 86(2) would justify it. Indeed, it might even try to claim there is no duty to notify at all on the basis that Article 86(2) excludes the *application* of the Treaty's competition rules (thus including Article 88(3)). National courts placed in such a situation would be exercising evaluative judgments about the aid itself and its relationship to the interests of the Community if they applied the proviso in Article 86(2). This, it is submitted, sits oddly with the division of responsibilities between national courts and the Commission identifed and upheld by the regime of Articles 87–89.

Finally, national courts cannot be used by disgruntled competitors where the real nature of the claim is one which should have been protected by recourse to Article 230. In a case where the beneficiary of an aid had not used its undoubted position as an individually concerned undertaking to challenge an adverse decision addressed to the granting Member State,[66] the Court refused to allow the validity of the Commission's decision to be challenged via Article 234 in national proceedings arising from the recovery procedure.

---

[61] *Application of E.C. State Aid Law by the Member State Courts* (Commission, 1999), detailing the experiences in all 15 Member States.

[62] *ibid.*, p. 244.

[63] Notice on Co-operation between national courts and the Commission in the field of State aid, [1995] O.J. C312/8.

[64] Case C–174/97P *FFSA v. Commission* [1998] E.C.R. I–1303, extending Case C–387/92 *Banco Exterior de España* [1994] E.C.R. I–877; [1994] 3 C.M.L.R. 473. See Hancher and Buendia Sierra, "Cross-subsidization and E.C. law" (1998) 35 C.M.L.Rev. 901, esp. 938–942.

[65] see further Ross, "State aids and national courts: definitions and other problems—a case of premature emancipation?" (2000) 37 C.M.L.Rev. 401.

[66] Case C–188/92 *TWD Textilwerke Deggendorf GmbH v. Germany* [1994] E.C.R. I–833; [1995] 2 C.M.L.R. 145.

Article 89

Article 89 provides:

"The Council, acting by a qualified majority on a proposal from the Commission and after consulting the European Parliament, may make any appropriate regulations for the application of Articles 87 and 88 and may in particular determine the conditions in which Article 88(3) shall apply and the categories of aid exempted from this procedure."

For a long time the Commission preferred to use guidelines and frameworks to build up a system of State aid control. Indeed, it specifically rejected a call that it should bring forward a proposal in 1990.[67] However, by the mid-1990s it had reversed its position and had adopted the view that minor aids were causing unnecessary work without any real significance for competition policy.[68] Legislation so far has concentrated upon facilitating group exemptions in some areas of State aid[69] and in codifying and strengthening the procedural rules for applying Article 88.[70]

The relationship between Articles 87–89 and other provisions of Community law

By virtue of Article 32(2) E.C. the agricultural provisions of the Treaty contained in Articles 33–38 take precedence over Articles 87–89, as they do over the other rules laid down for the establishment of the common market.[71] In particular, the rules on State aids are among those the application of which Article 36 puts at the discretion of the Council. Provision was made in Article 4 of Regulation 26 for their application in the agricultural sphere, but only to a very limited extent. However, it has become customary for the basic regulations of the various common organisations of agricultural markets established under Article 34 E.C. to lay down that, "save as otherwise provided" in the regulation, Articles 87–89 are to apply *in toto* to the production of and trade in the products in question. Thus, in the case of goods covered by a common organisation of the market, Member States are required to observe the State aid provisions of the Treaty in the normal way, except where such observance would be incompatible with the rules of the common organisation.[72]

The European Court has had to deal with the question whether Articles 87–89 may have a similar pre-emptive effect to the Treaty provisions on agriculture

---

[67] See Slot, "Procedural law of State aids" in Harden (ed.), *State Aid: Community Law and Policy* (1993) 36.

[68] Comp. Rep. 1994, point 395.

[69] Reg. 994/98; [1998] O.J. L142/1 is the enabling measure.

[70] Reg. 659/99; [1999] O.J. L83/1.

[71] See Case 83/78 *Pigs Marketing Board v. Redmond* [1978] E.C.R. 2347; [1979] 1 C.M.L.R. 177; Case 177/78 *Pigs & Bacon Commission v. McCarren Ltd* [1979] E.C.R. 3409; [1979] 3 C.M.L.R. 389.

[72] Case 169/82 *Commission v. Italy* [1984] E.C.R. 1603; [1985] 3 C.M.L.R. 30. See also the discussion of the relevance of the aids rules to the wine sector in Case C–122/94 *Commission v. Council*, *supra* n.2.

(except, of course, in relation to those provisions). In other words, if a measure can be regarded as forming part of an aid system, does its compatibility with Community law fall to be determined exclusively on the basis of the State aid provisions?

The answer that emerges from the case-law is definitely negative. Thus it was made clear in Case 73/79[73] that a measure of discriminatory taxation, which may be considered at the same time as forming part of an aid system covered by Article 87, remains nonetheless subject to the prohibition in Article 90.[74] A similar approach was taken in *Hansen v. Hauptzollamt Flensburg*[75] where one of the questions raised concerned the relationship between the State aid rules and those governing State monopolies. The Court said:

> ". . . Article 37 [now 31] of the Treaty constitutes in relation to Articles 92 and 93 a *lex specialis* in the sense that State measures, inherent in the exercise by a State monopoly of the commercial character of its exclusive right must, even where they are linked to grant of an aid to producers subject to the monopoly, be considered in the light of the requirements of Article 37."[76]

The relationship between the State aids rules and Article 28 has also posed difficulties for the Court. It has adopted a severability test whereby some aspects of aid contravening specific Treaty provisions other than Articles 87–89 may be so indissolubly linked to the object of the aid that it would be impossible to evaluate them separately; but where a particular part of an aid system could be seen as not necessary for the attainment of its object or for its proper functioning, severance would be possible to enable directly effective provisions of the Treaty to operate.

Such a demarcation line is not always easy to draw. In *Commission v. Ireland ("Buy Irish")*[77] an advertising campaign inspired and financed by the Irish Government through the medium of a private company was held by the Court to fall within the then Article 30, contrary to the views of Advocate General Capotorti. The fact that the State aids rules might apply to the method of financing the operation did not mean that the campaign itself could escape the prohibition of Article 30. In *Du Pont de Namours Italiana*[78] the Court went further and classified the entire arrangement for minimum public tendering as falling within the free movement of goods provisions. This was despite arguments that the rule requiring bodies to take at least 30 per cent of their purchases from companies operating in the Mezzogiorno region was a regional aid.

---

[73] *Commission v. Italy* [1980] E.C.R. 1411

[74] For a general discussion of fiscal issues, see Schön, "Taxation and State aid law in the European Union" (1999) 36 C.M.L.Rev. 911.

[75] Case 91/78 [1979] E.C.R. 935; [1980] 1 C.M.L.R. 162.

[76] *ibid.*, at 953.

[77] Case 249/81 [1982] E.C.R. 4005; [1983] 2 C.M.L.R. 99.

[78] Case 21/88 *Du Pont de Namours Italiana v. Unita Sanitaria Locale No. 2 di Carrara* [1990] E.C.R. 889; [1991] 3 C.M.L.R. 25.

The Court's approach is not without its critics,[79] who argue that only the discretions and supervisory functions embodied in the Commission under Article 87 are appropriate to balance issues of social and economic cohesion against the creation and maintenance of the single market.

---

[79] See Fernandez Martin & Stehmann, "Product market integration versus regional cohesion in the Community" (1991) 16 E.L.Rev. 216; Wishlade, "Competition policy, cohesion and the co-ordination of regional aids in the European Community" [1993] 4 E.C.L.R. 143.

CHAPTER 25

PUBLIC AND ENTRUSTED UNDERTAKINGS

The present chapter is primarily concerned with Article 86 E.C. There is another provision of the Treaty, Article 31, which relates to a particular category of public undertakings, namely state monopolies of a commercial character.[1] However, since Article 31 constitutes a specialised regime for the removal of obstacles to the free movement of goods which may be associated with the arrangements under which such monopolies operate, it has been dealt with in Chapter 13.

The influence of the State in the economic life of the Community may appear in a variety of forms, whether as regulator,[2] participant or provider of resources.[3] This chapter concentrates upon the Community rules which apply in relation to undertakings which are State controlled or which enjoy a privileged legal status, normally in return for carrying out certain tasks deemed to be of public importance. Activities which are undertaken in this way to varying degrees in the Member States include the public utilities, railway and other transport services, broadcasting and some key industrial sectors such as the motor industry. The organisation of Member State participation may be at national, regional or local level.

The extent to which the competition rules of the Treaty are applied to public or privileged undertakings inevitably has fundamental implications for the relationship between State and market. A number of approaches can be envisaged for the treatment of legal monopolies.[4] At one end of the spectrum, for example, the State might be said to have absolute sovereignty to grant exclusive rights. At the other, a paradigm of absolute competition could hold such exclusivity to be an infringement *per se* of the competition rules by creating a dominance in which abuses could be pursued. The case-law of the Court indicates a middle ground, sometimes favouring a limited form of sovereignty and intervening only when abuses necessarily flow from the grant of exclusivity, but on other occasions adopting a limited competition model in which the existence of a monopoly requires justification against higher interests recognised in Community law. Certainly, the Court recognises that the full force of the competition rules cannot always be applied. In the specific context of undertakings falling within the scope of Article 86(2) (see below), the Court has observed that Member States

"cannot be precluded, when defining the services of general economic interest which they entrust to certain undertakings, from taking account of objectives

---

[1] Arts 86 and 31 belong to a wider group of "provisions relating to infringements of the normal functioning of the competition system by actions on the part of the States": see Case 94/74 *IGAV v. ENCC* [1975] E.C.R. 699; [1976] 2 C.M.L.R. 37. The Court also mentioned in this connection what are now Arts 87–89 and Arts 96 and 97.

[2] Subject to Treaty regulation by, for example, Art. 28.

[3] *e.g.* in the form of state aids; see Chap. 24. *supra*.

[4] Edward and Hoskins, "Art. 90: Deregulation and E.C. law, reflections arising from the XVI FIDE conference" (1995) 32 C.M.L.Rev. 157.

pertaining to their national policy or from endeavouring to attain them by means of obligations and constraints which they impose on such undertakings."[5]

Taking the Treaty at face value, the approach taken by Community law to public and privileged undertakings would seem that, while there can be no objection in principle to their special relationship with the State,[6] whatever legal form this may take, their behaviour as market participants is governed by the same rules as those applicable to purely private undertakings, except where the Treaty itself specifically permits some derogation. The first limb of this proposition depends in part upon Article 295 E.C., preserving intact the systems of property ownership in the Member States, which are therefore free to determine the extent and internal organisation of their public sectors; and in part upon the clear inference to be drawn from Article 86(1) E.C. that the conferment of special or exclusive rights upon an undertaking does not, in itself, constitute an infringement of any Treaty rule.[7] Support for the second limb of the general proposition can be found in the unqualified reference to "undertakings" in Articles 81 and 82, and in the limited exemption contained in Article 86(2) for the benefit of entrusted undertakings and fiscal monopolies which would have been formulated differently if the rules of the Treaty did not normally apply to public undertakings.

However, this general proposition does not wholly encapsulate the case-law developments, particularly those of the 1990s in which the tension between market concerns and national policy goals repeatedly came before the Court. On the one hand, it was willing to recognise that the impact of Article 295 is diminished where its strict application would prejudice more fundamental principles of Community law. Even though that Article presupposes the existence of undertakings which have special or exclusive rights, it does not follow that all special or exclusive rights are necessarily compatible with the Treaty.[8] On the other hand, by an increasingly lenient interpretation of the Article 86(2) derogation, the Court acknowledged that ejection of the State from the market completely would deny the legitimate concerns of Member States in pursuit of certain policy and public service objectives. Finding the appropriate balance between these competing factors continues to dominate the evolution of Article 86. In addition, the Treaty of Amsterdam inserted a new Article 16 (see below) into the E.C. Treaty to highlight the particular position occupied by services of general economic interest.

---

[5] Case C–157/94 *Commission v. Netherlands* [1997] E.C.R. I–5699, para. 40.

[6] But see Deringer in *Equal Treatment of Public and Private Enterprises*, FIDE (1978), para. 36 to the effect that expansion of the public sector might be inconsistent with the mixed economy foundations of the Community. See now the reference in Art. 4(1) E.C. to "an open market economy with free competition".

[7] So held by the Court in Case 155/73 *Sacchi* [1974] E.C.R. 409; [1974] 2 C.M.L.R. 177, and affirmed on numerous occasions since. See, for example, Case C–266/96 *Corsica Ferries France* [1998] E.C.R. I–3949; [1998] 5 C.M.L.R. 402.

[8] Case C–202/88 *France v. Commission* [1991] E.C.R. I–1223; [1992] 5 C.M.L.R. 552, para. 22.

Article 86 E.C.

The Article provides as follows:

"1. In the case of public undertakings and undertakings to which Member States grant exclusive or special rights, Member States shall neither enact nor maintain in force any measure contrary to the rules contained in this Treaty, in particular to those rules provided for in Article 12 and Articles 81 to 89.

2. Undertakings entrusted with the operation of services of general economic interest or having the character of a revenue producing monopoly shall be subject to the rules contained in this Treaty, in particular to the rules on competition, insofar as the application of such rules does not obstruct the performance, in law or in fact, of the particular tasks assigned to them. The development of trade must not be affected to such an extent as would be contrary to the interests of the Community.

3. The Commission shall ensure the application of the provisions of this Article and shall, where necessary, address appropriate directives or decisions to Member States."

The scheme of the Article contemplates State responsibility in the situations embraced by paragraph (1), relief from the obligations of the Treaty for the undertakings satisfying the criteria of paragraph (2) and a mechanism for enforcement using the machinery provided by paragraph (3). As summarised by the Court of Justice, the provision:

". . . concerns only undertakings for whose actions States must take special responsibility by reason of the influence which they may exert over such actions. It emphasises that such undertakings are subject to all the rules laid down in the Treaty, subject to the provisions contained in paragraph (2); it requires the Member States to respect those rules in their relations with those undertakings and in that regard imposes on the Commission a duty of surveillance which may, where necessary, be performed by the adoption of directives and decisions addressed to Member States."[9]

As the case-law demonstrates, the use of Article 86 has changed drastically over time. Starting from a prolonged period in which the provision was hardly invoked at all, the influence of the single market imperative gave rise to a vigorous application of State responsibility and a flurry of legislative liberalisation activity. The position has now been reached where the rigour of paragraph (1) is seemingly tempered by a more generous use of the paragraph (2) exception.

Article 86(1): the responsibility of Member States for the conduct of public or privileged undertakings

Article 86(1) constitutes a particular application of the general principle contained in the second paragraph of Article 10 E.C. that Member States are

---

[9] Joined Cases 188–190/80 *France, Italy and the United Kingdom v. Commission* [1982] E.C.R. 2545; [1982] 3 C.M.L.R. 144.

required to abstain from measures which are liable to jeopardise the attainment of the objectives of the Treaty.[10] The inclusion of a specific provision concerning the relationship between the State and public and privileged undertakings served both to highlight the particular seriousness of the problems which may arise, and to clarify the extensive nature of the responsibility imposed upon Member States in this situation. It also enabled provision to be made in Article 86(3) (see below) for a more flexible and effective procedure than that of Article 226 in dealing with such cases.

The categories of undertaking in Article 86(1)

The concept of an undertaking as a body having legal capacity and carrying on economic (not necessarily profit-making) activities was discussed in relation to Articles 81 and 82, but some nuances may be added in the context of Article 86. In the *Sacchi* case,[11] it was held by the European Court that, even where the primary objects of a body are non-economic, it will have the status of an undertaking to the extent that it engages in economic activity. Thus a broadcasting organisation may be entrusted with tasks of a cultural or informative nature; but it behaves as an undertaking, for example, when purchasing programmes or selling advertising time. Questions are likely to arise, therefore, in relation to whether a body is acting as a public authority or as an undertaking. In *SAT v. Eurocontrol*[12] the body involved was an international organisation charged with supervising air traffic control services within the air space of the States party to the Convention under which it was established, and to collect the charges levied for those services. In the Court's view, Eurocontrol was carrying out, on behalf of the Contracting States, tasks in the public interest aimed at contributing to the maintenance and improvement of air navigation safety. Collection of route charges, the subject of the dispute in the case, could not be separated from the organisation's other activities as they were merely the consideration, payable by users, for the obligatory and exclusive use of air navigation control facilities and services. Thus, taken as a whole, Eurocontrol's activities were connected with the exercise of powers relating to the control and supervision of air space which are typically those of a public authority. They were not of an economic nature justifying the application of the Treaty rules of competition.[13] Similarly, charges levied by a body made responsible by the State for anti-pollution surveillance at a particular port were held to be integral to its general surveillance activities and outside the scope of Article 82.[14]

Difficulties may arise in the classification of pension schemes, since these may take a variety of forms ranging from State social security arrangements to private individual schemes operated by commercial insurers. The Court held in *Poucet and Pistre*[15] that the concept of undertaking did not encompass organisations charged with the management of certain compulsory social security schemes,

---

[10] Case 13/77 *INNO v. ATAB* [1977] E.C.R. 2115 at 2144–2145; [1978] 1 C.M.L.R. 283.
[11] Case 155/73 *Sacchi*, n.7, *supra*.
[12] Case C–364/92 *SAT Fluggesellschaft v. Eurocontrol* [1994] E.C.R. I–43; [1994] 5 C.M.L.R. 208.
[13] *ibid.*, para 30.
[14] Case C–343/95 *Calì & Figli v. SEPG* [1997] E.C.R. I–1547; [1997] 5 C.M.L.R. 484.
[15] Case C–160/91 *Poucet and Pistre* [1993] E.C.R. I–637

based on the principle of solidarity. Indicators were provided by the fact that the sickness and maternity benefits involved were the same for all beneficiaries, regardless of contributions. The retirement pensions also operated on the basis that entitlements were not proportional to contributions paid into the scheme. Finally, schemes with a surplus contributed to the financing of those with structural financial difficulties.

In contrast, a non-profit-making organisation which managed a pension scheme intended to supplement a basic compulsory scheme, established by law as an optional scheme and operating according to the principles of capitalisation, was held to be an undertaking.[16] Benefits depended solely on the amount of the contributions paid by the beneficiaries and on the financial results of the investments made by the managing organisation, thus implying that the organisation carried on an economic activity in competition with life assurance companies. A similar result was reached in *Albany International*,[17] even though affiliation in that case was compulsory for workers in the relevant industrial sector. The Court, however, acknowledged that the pursuit of a social objective, the presence of solidarity features in the scheme and various restrictions on investments made by the sectoral fund might make its service less competitive than comparable services rendered by insurance companies. Although these considerations did not prevent the fund being an undertaking, they could be taken into account in applying the derogation of Article 86(2).[18]

Community law must provide its own test of what constitutes a *public* undertaking, specifically adapted to the aims of Article 86(1). There would be no consistency in its application if it were necessary to rely upon the widely varying classifications of undertakings as "public" or "private" in the national legal systems. Although the Court of Justice has yet to define the concept exhaustively, in the Transparency Directive case[19] it approved the Commission's definition set out in the measure in question.[20] According to Article 2 of the Directive, a public undertaking is:

"any undertaking over which the public authorities may exercise directly or indirectly a dominant influence by virtue of their ownership of it, their financial participation therein, or the rules which govern it."

The provision also establishes certain presumptions, so that a "dominant influence" will be taken to exist where the public authorities: hold the major part of the undertaking's subscribed capital; or control the majority of the votes attaching to shares issued by the undertaking; or can appoint more than half of the members of the undertaking's administrative, managerial or supervisory body.

The Court held that this definition of a public undertaking did not amount to an abuse by the Commission of its powers under Article 86(3), since the financial

---

[16] Case C–244/94 *Fédération Française des Sociétés d'Assurance and others v. Ministère de l'Agriculture et de la Pêche* [1995] E.C.R. I–4013; [1996] 4 C.M.L.R. 536.

[17] Case C–67/96 *Albany International BV v. Stichting Bedrijfspensioenfonds Textielindustrie* [1999] E.C.R. I–5751.

[18] *ibid.*, para. 86.

[19] Joined Cases 188–190/80 *France, Italy and the United Kingdom v. Commission*, n.9 *supra*.

[20] Dir 80/723 [1980] O.J. L195/35.

criteria which the Directive adopted reflected the substantial forms of influence exerted by public authorities over the commercial decisions of public undertakings and were thus compatible with the Court's view of Article 86(1).

The category of undertakings to which Member States grant special or exclusive rights partially overlaps that of public undertakings. Such rights may be granted to public or private undertakings. The rationale behind the category is the fact that the State has deliberately intervened to relieve the undertaking concerned either wholly or partially from the discipline of competition, and must bear responsibility for the consequences. A right conferred by national legislation upon those carrying on an economic activity which is open to anyone, who thus form an indefinite class, is unlikely to be regarded as "exclusive".[21] Similarly, undertakings which are licensed to engage in an activity on the basis of their fulfilment of certain objective conditions (for example the financial safeguards imposed in the public interest upon insurance businesses) would be excluded from the category. The mode of granting the right (whether by an act under public law, for example a statute, regulation or administrative order, or by a private contract) is immaterial, again because formal differences between the legal systems of the various Member States cannot be allowed to interfere with the operation of Article 86(1).

There is nothing in the wording of Article 86(1) to explain the notion of "special or exclusive" rights. Early legislation adopted by the Commission failed to define such rights to the satisfaction of the Court.[22] However, in an amended version of the directive on competition in the markets for telecommunications services[23] the following definitions are used:

" 'exclusive rights' means the rights that are granted by a Member State to one undertaking through any legislative, regulatory or administrative instrument, reserving it the right to provide a telecommunication service or undertake an activity within a given geographical area.

'special rights' means the rights that are granted by a Member State to a limited number of undertakings through any legislative, regulatory or administrative instrument which, within a given geographical area,

— limits to two or more the number of such undertakings authorised to provide a service or undertake an activity, otherwise than according to objective, proportional and non-discriminatory criteria, or

— designates, otherwise than according to such criteria, several competing undertakings as being authorised to provide a service or undertake an activity, or

— confers on any undertaking or undertakings, otherwise than according to such criteria, legal or regulatory advantages which substantially affect the ability of any other undertaking to provide the same telecommunications service or to undertake the same activity in the same geographical area under substantially equivalent conditions."

---

[21] See Case 13/77 *INNO v. ATAB*, n.10, *supra* at 2146.

[22] See proceedings arising from the Telecommunications Terminal Equipment Dir. 88/301 [1988] O.J. L131/73: Case C–202/88 *France v. Commission*. n.8 *supra*. Also Joined Cases C–271, 281 and 289/90 *Spain and others v. Commission* [1992] E.C.R. I–5833 in relation to Dir. 90/388 on the markets for telecommunications services.

[23] Dir. 94/96; [1994] O.J. L268/15.

Examples of exclusive rights include exclusive concessions to funeral enterprises in French communes,[24] statutory monopolies in the field of broadcasting[25] and the exclusive right of insemination centres authorised to serve defined areas.[26] Special right holders would include the commercial television companies in the United Kingdom.

The scope of the obligation imposed on Member States under Article 86(1)

The phrase "shall neither enact nor maintain in force any measure" is wide enough to cover any forms of positive action taken by a Member State, or the failure to remedy such action previously taken. There is no reason to exclude from the category of "measures" general legislative acts, such as statutes or regulations. However, a distinction must be drawn between legislation specifically relating to public or privileged undertakings, and legislation relating to such undertakings only among others, for example an aid for nationalised industries, as opposed to a general regional aid system: the latter would not in itself constitute a measure for the purposes of Article 86(1), but its application in a particular case might do so. At the other end of the scale would be the exercise by the State of its rights as a shareholder, and the application to management of wholly informal pressures.

The first decision under Article 86(3) (see below) to challenge specific legislation of the type prohibited by Article 86(1) was issued by the Commission in 1985.[27] This related to a measure requiring all public property in Greece to be insured with a Greek State-owned insurance company, and also obliging State banks to recommend customers seeking a loan to take out associated insurance with a State-owned company. In the Commission's view, the preferential treatment accorded to domestic State-owned companies had the effect of excluding from large sections of the Greek insurance market not only Greek private insurers but also insurance companies from other Member States with subsidiaries or branches in the country. The legislation thus amounted to a restriction on freedom of establishment, enacted by Greece in contravention of Article 86(1).[28]

A literal view of Article 86(1) clearly embraces a standstill obligation upon Member States and the need to take positive action to undo prohibited measures. Additionally, the paragraph impliedly makes Member States accountable for the behaviour of public and privileged undertakings. In other words, responsibility under Article 86(1) does not presuppose positive action by the Member State itself: it suffices merely that a public undertaking or an undertaking granted special or exclusive rights has been guilty of conduct which, on the part of the State, would have involved a Treaty violation. In such a situation the

---

[24] Case 30/87 *Bodson v. Pompes Funèbres des Régions Libérées SA* [1988] E.C.R. 2479; [1989] 4 C.M.L.R. 984.

[25] Case 155/73 *Sacchi*, n.7 *supra*.

[26] Case C–323/93 *Société Civile Agricole du Centre d'Insémination de la Crespelle v. Coopérative d'Elevage et d'Insémination Artificielle du Département de la Mayenne* [1994] E.C.R. I–5077.

[27] Dec. 85/726 [1985] O.J. L152/25.

[28] Greece did not comply with the Decision, giving rise to enforcement proceedings: Case 226/87 *Commission v. Greece* [1988] E.C.R. 3611

Member State is under an obligation to take any remedial steps which may be necessary; and if its existing legal powers are inadequate, it may be required by the Commission to equip itself with additional powers.

Interpreting the notion of maintaining a measure in force in this way is consistent with the obligation to take general and particular measures imposed on Member States by Article 10 and with the policy of Article 86(1). If State responsibility under this paragraph is derived, respectively, from the ability to influence public undertakings and from the assumption of the risk inherent in the deliberate distortion of competition by a grant of special or exclusive rights, it ought to make no difference whether the role of the State has been active, in imposing or encouraging certain behaviour, or passive, in failing to correct it.[29] As the Court has put it, the purpose of Article 86(1) is to prevent Member States from adopting or maintaining in force measures which deprive the Community's competition rules of their effectiveness.[30]

The responsibility of a Member State under Article 86(1) is entirely independent of any violation of Community law by the undertaking in question: it is not based upon a theory of imputation, like the joint liability of a parent company for infringements of the competition rules by a subsidiary which it controls.[31] The undertaking's own conduct may be unimpeachable, for example where it has been compelled by the State to enter a cartel, so that the element of agreement required by Article 81 is missing. However, there must be a causal link between a Member State's legislative or administrative intervention on the one hand and anti-competitive behaviour of undertakings on the other.[32] The Court has held that in the context of Article 86(1) alleged abuses must be the "direct consequence" of the national legal framework.[33]

One of the most difficult questions pertaining to the scope of the obligation in Article 86(1) is whether the mere grant of exclusive or special rights can itself constitute a "measure" susceptible to challenge. In *Höfner v. Macrotron*[34] the Court was asked whether a national law conferring exclusive rights over the placement of business executives constituted an abuse under Article 82. It was acknowledged that in practice some competition in the market for business placements was tolerated despite the legal monopoly. The Court observed in relation to Articles 82 and 86(1) that:

"A Member State is in breach of the prohibition contained in those two provisions only if the undertaking in question, merely by exercising the exclusive rights granted to it, cannot avoid abusing its dominant position."[35]

---

[29] *cf.* the position in relation to State measures and Art. 81; discussed in Chap. 20. *supra*. See Bacon, "State regulation of the market and E.C. competition rules: Arts 85 and 86 compared" [1997] 5 E.C.L.R. 283.

[30] Case C–260/89 *ERT* [1991] E.C.R. I–2925, at para. 35; [1994] 4 C.M.L.R. 540.

[31] See the discussion in Chap. 19, *supra*.

[32] Advocate General Jacobs in Case C–67/96 *Albany International BV*, n.17 *supra*, para. 388 of Opinion.

[33] Case C–323/93 *Société Civile Agricole du Centre d'Insémination de la Crespelle v. Coopérative d'Elevage et d'Insémination Artificielle du Département de la Mayenne*, n.26, *supra*.

[34] Case C–41/90 *Höfner and Elser v. Macrotron* [1991] E.C.R. I–1979; [1993] 4 C.M.L.R. 306.

[35] *ibid.*, para. 29.

Such a situation is created by a Member State

"when the undertaking to which it grants an exclusive right . . . is manifestly not in a position to satisfy the demand prevailing on the market for activities of that kind and when the effective pursuit of such activities by private companies is rendered impossible . . ."[36]

Subsequent judgments have not always expressed the test in quite the same terms. In *Corsica Ferries France*[37] the Court noted that a Member State will be in breach if the undertaking in question, "merely by exercising the exclusive rights granted to it, is led to abuse its dominant position or if such rights are liable to create a situation in which that undertaking is led to commit such abuses".[38] A potentially still wider formulation can be found in *Chemische Afvalstoffen Dusseldorp BV*,[39] where the Court held that Articles 86(1) and 82 will be infringed by a Member State "if it adopts any law, regulation or administrative provision which enables an undertaking on which it has conferred exclusive rights to abuse its dominant position". Advocate General Jacobs in that case had suggested that although the exclusive rights over waste management granted by the Netherlands Government to a particular undertaking ("AVR") might facilitate the charging of unfair prices by the latter for its services, there was no inevitability about that outcome sufficient to satisfy the *Höfner* test. However, the expression adopted by the Court could be said to embrace the facilitative element rejected by the Advocate General as well as the direct causal requirement. But because the Court seized upon the restriction of outlets as the abuse, rather than unfair pricing, the prima facie breach by the Netherlands would in fact have satisfied even the narrower versions of the test. As a result of the exclusive responsibility entrusted to AVR, businesses in effect had to deliver their waste to AVR even though the quality of processing available in another Member State was comparable to that provided by AVR. The Court ultimately left it to the national court to ascertain whether the national rules did indeed have the effect of favouring the national undertaking and increasing its dominant position. The Court also indicated that it was for the national court to decide whether the derogation of Article 86(2), discussed further below, might apply.

The scope of the notion of "inevitable abuse" thus remains problematic, at least as regards the shades of difference between State measures which enable, induce or unavoidably lead to anti-competitive results. Given the repeated declarations by the Court that the existence of exclusive rights is not *per se* unlawful it may be expected that the closer a claim comes to challenging a bare right the greater will be the causal connection to be demanded before State responsibility arises. Hence the emphasis in *Höfner* upon the "manifest failure" of the monopoly to meet demand; any insistence by it upon the enforcement of its exclusive rights in the face of such market realities would have been

---

[36] *ibid.*, para. 31. To similar effect, see Case C–55/96 *Job Centre Coop* [1997] E.C.R. I–7119; [1998] 5 C.M.L.R. 167, paras 34–35.

[37] Case C–266/96, n.7, *supra*.

[38] *ibid.* para. 40. The same formula was repeated by the Court in Case C–67/96 *Albany International BV*, n.17, *supra*, at para. 93.

[39] Case C–203/96 *Chemische Afvalstoffen Dusseldorp BV v. Minister van Volkhuisvesting, Ruimtelijke Ordening en Milieubeheer* [1998] E.C.R. I–4075, at para. 61; [1998] 3 C.M.L.R. 873.

inescapably abusive.[40] Advocate General Fennelly has accordingly suggested that it is not sufficient for a breach of Article 86(1) in conjunction with Article 82 to occur in the context of exclusive rights which facilitate opportunities for abuse "unless the monopoly system itself compels or strongly encourages the abuse by being directly linked to and largely responsible for it".[41]

Such an approach seems to explain the strands of the case-law. For example, the grant of exclusive rights to French insemination centres was not seen as necessarily leading them to charge excessive prices for their services.[42] However, on the other hand, it is clear that an extension of a monopoly by granting special or exclusive rights in an adjacent or ancillary market will be prohibited where there is no objective justification.[43] In such cases, a conflict of interest is certain to arise between the existing monopolist and the competitive situation in the allied market. Thus, in *ERT*,[44] the monopolist was a broadcasting undertaking which not only held the exclusive right to broadcast its own programmes but also to retransmit foreign broadcasts. In the Court's view this created a situation in which the undertaking would be liable to infringe Article 82 by virtue of a discriminatory policy favouring its own programmes. Quite clearly, if a Member State actually directly imposes abusive behaviour on an undertaking there will be a breach of Article 86(1) by that State.[45]

Article 86(2): the exception relating to entrusted undertakings and fiscal monopolies

Article 86(2) is drafted in terms which first emphasise that "undertakings entrusted with the operation of services of general economic interest or having the character of a revenue-producing monopoly" are normally subject to the rules of the Treaty and then goes on to exclude the application of the rules where the performance of the particular tasks assigned to the undertakings is liable to be obstructed. The exception is subject to a proviso which states that "the development of trade must not be affected to such extent as would be contrary to the interests of the Community." The case-law of the Commission and Court initially showed a marked disinclination to accept the application of the derogation. However, the greater use of the competition rules to curb monopolies and public undertakings in the 1990s saw a corresponding development of arguments justifying the activities of such bodies by reference to Article 86(2). The position today is that obtaining the benefit of the derogation is no longer the impossible task it once was, at least for undertakings charged with providing universal services of public interest.

---

[40] per Advocate General Fennelly in Case C–163/96 *Raso and others* [1998] E.C.R. I–533; [1998] 5 C.M.L.R. 737 at para. 62 of his Opinion.

[41] *ibid.*, para. 66.

[42] Case C–323/93 *Société Civile Agricole du Centre d'Insémination de la Crespelle v. Coopérative d'Elevage et d'Insémination Artificielle du Département de la Mayenne*, n.26, *supra*.

[43] Case C–18/88 *RTT v. GB-Inno-BM* [1991] E.C.R. I–5941.

[44] Case C–260/89, n.30, *supra*. See also Case C–179/90 *Merci Convenzionali Porto di Genova* [1991] E.C.R. I–5889; [1994] 4 C.M.L.R. 422; Case C–163/96 *Raso and others*, n.40, *supra*.

[45] *e.g.* the discriminatory tariffs applied as a result of a State administrative act by an airport authority holding exclusive rights in *Re Discount on Landing Fees at Zaventem*: Dec. 95/364 1995 O.J. L216/8.

The categories of undertaking in Article 86(2)

There is nothing in the text of the Article that would restrict the categories of undertaking in the second paragraph to those covered by the first. However, undertakings called upon to perform services of the type envisaged by Article 86(2) are often either State controlled or given a *quid pro quo* in the form of special or exclusive rights. The more important of the two categories in Article 86(2) is that of entrusted undertakings. Because of the possible derogation which may be involved, the European Court has said that the category must be strictly defined.[46]

It is immaterial whether the undertaking concerned is public or private, provided that the service has been entrusted to it "by an act of the public authority".[47] This does not imply that the act need be in any particular form, and references by Advocate General Mayras in *SABAM* to a "legislative" or "unilateral" act seem unduly restrictive.[48] The essential point is that the State must have taken legal steps to secure the provision of the service by the undertaking in question. Thus an undertaking created as a result of private initiative and managing the intellectual property rights of its members on an ordinary contractual basis, could not be an entrusted undertaking, even if it happened to serve public purposes.[49] The same is true where legislation only *authorises* an undertaking to act, even though some supervision of those activities may be exercised by a public agency. Thus, in *GVL v. Commission*,[50] the Court held that the relevant German legislation did not confer the management of copyright and related rights on specific undertakings but defined in a general manner the rules applying to the activities of companies which intended to undertake the collective exploitation of such rights.

The phrase "operation of services" seems to have been chosen advisedly to indicate the organisation of some kind of regular performance, for example a public utility.[51] It is generally agreed that the definition of "services" in Article 50 E.C., as a residual concept relating to types of performance not governed by the provisions on the free movement of goods, persons or capital, does not apply in the context of Article 86(2). The Commission, in a document forming the background to the eventual adoption of Article 16 E.C.,[52] expressly distinguished between services of general economic interest and those (such as compulsory education, diplomacy or the register of births, deaths and marriages) which are non-economic or prerogatives of the State and for which any Community action can be at most complementary. As Advocate General Jacobs has pointed out,[53] the reason for the assignment of particular tasks to undertakings is often that the tasks need to be undertaken in the public interest

---

[46] Case 127/73 *BRT v. SABAM* [1974] E.C.R. 313; [1974] 2 C.M.L.R. 238.
[47] [1974] E.C.R. at 318.
[48] *ibid.*, at 327. See also Case C–159/94 *Commission v. France* [1997] E.C.R. I–5815 at para. 66.
[49] SABAM was such an undertaking.
[50] Case 7/82 [1983] E.C.R. 483; [1983] 3 C.M.L.R. 645.
[51] The relevant phrase in the other official versions of the Treaty has been chosen with equal care to denote the conduct of a service rather than the provision of services.
[52] *Services of General Interest in Europe* [1996] O.J. C281/03.
[53] Case C–203/96 *Chemische Afvalstoffen Dusseldorp BV v. Minister van Volkhuisvesting, Ruimtelijke Ordening en Milieubeheer*, n.39 *supra*.

but might not be undertaken, usually for economic reasons, if the service were to be left to the private sector.

A service will be "of general economic interest" where it involves economic activity (although its aims may, for example, be social) and is furnished in what the Member State believes[54] to be the interest of the general public (although the ultimate benefit of the service may be enjoyed by specific recipients).[55] Not surprisingly, telecommunications undertakings,[56] water supply companies,[57] electricity suppliers[58] and postal services[59] have all been treated as serving the general economic interest, although the derogation was not always applicable in each case. Waste management functions may also qualify.[60] In *Ahmed Saeed*[61] the Court noted that Article 86(2) may be applied to airline carriers who may be obliged, by the public authorities, to operate on routes which are not commercially viable but which it is necessary to operate for reasons of the general interest. This was also the view of the Court of First Instance in *Air Inter*[62] in the context of an airline running unprofitable routes to open up French cities and regions as part of regional development. In *Campus Oil Ltd v. Minister for Industry and Energy*[63] the Court of Justice apparently did not dispute the Greek Government's contention that a State-owned oil refinery could be an undertaking operating a service of general economic interest.[64]

On the other hand, a bank will not perform such a service when transferring customers' funds from one Member State to another.[65] Nor, it seems,[66] would the management company in the *GVL* case have fulfilled the criterion, since the collecting society was only engaged in the furtherance of the interests of private

---

[54] The arguments are summarised by Page, "Member States, Public Undertakings and Art. 90" (1982) 7 E.L.Rev. 19.

[55] In Case 90/76 *Van Ameyde v. UCI* [1977] E.C.R. 1091; [1977] 2 C.M.L.R. 478 the Commission argued that the national insurers' bureau responsible for the settlement of claims in relation to damage caused by foreign vehicles in Italy did not qualify as an entrusted undertaking "since its activities do not benefit the whole of the national economy," but this view seems too restrictive. The Court seems to have taken for granted that the bureau would so qualify: *ibid.*, at 1126.

[56] *Telespeed Services v. United Kingdom Post Office* [1982] O.J. L360/36; [1983] 1 C.M.L.R. 457. The Commission's Decision was unsuccessfully challenged in Case 41/83 *Italy v. Commission (British Telecom)* [1985] E.C.R. 873; [1985] 2 C.M.L.R. 368. See also Case C–18/88 *RTT v. GB-Inno-BM* [1991] E.C.R. I–5941.

[57] *The Community v. ANSEAU-NAVEWA* [1982] 2 C.M.L.R. 193; challenged on other issues in Joined Cases 96–102, 104–105, 108 and 110/82 *IAZ International Belgium and others v. Commission* [1983] E.C.R. 3369; [1984] 3 C.M.L.R. 276.

[58] Case C–393/92 *Almelo* [1994] E.C.R. I–1477; Case C–19/93 P *Rendo NV and others v. Commission* [1995] E.C.R. I–3319.

[59] Case C–320/91 *Re Corbeau* [1993] E.C.R. I–2533; [1995] 4 C.M.L.R. 621.

[60] Per Advocate General Jacobs in Case C–203/96 *Chemische Afvalstoffen Dusseldorp BV v. Minister van Volkhuisvesting, Ruimtelijke Ordening en Milieubeheer*, n.39, *supra*, although the Court did not rule on the point.

[61] Case 66/86 *Ahmed Saeed Flugreisen v. Zentrale zur Bekampfung unlauterer Wettbewerbs* [1989] E.C.R. 803; [1990] 4 C.M.L.R. 102.

[62] Case T–260/94 *Air Inter v. Commission* [1997] E.C.R. II–997; [1997] 5 C.M.L.R. 851, although the other conditions of the derogation were not actually made out.

[63] Case 72/83 [1984] E.C.R. 2727; [1984] 3 C.M.L.R. 544.

[64] *ibid.*, paras 18–19 of judgment.

[65] Case 172/80 *Zuchner v. Bayerische Vereinsbank (Bank Charges)* [1981] E.C.R. 2021; [1982] 1 C.M.L.R. 313. Nor was the bank "entrusted".

[66] Per Advocate General Reischl.

artistes. In *Merci Convenzionali Porto di Genova v. Siderurgica Gabriella*[67] the Court held that on the evidence submitted, dock work consisting of the loading, unloading, transhipment and storage of goods was not necessarily of general economic interest. However, in *Corsica Ferries France*[68] the Court accepted that the provision of mooring services had special characteristics sufficient to bring them within the scope of Article 86(2). In particular, the grantees of the exclusive rights in question were obliged to provide at any time and to any user a universal mooring service, for reasons of safety in port waters.

Undertakings "having the character of a revenue-producing monopoly", the second category in Article 86(2), are distinguished by the overriding purpose of raising revenue for the national exchequer through the exploitation of their exclusive right. They are normally combined with commercial monopolies, so that (as noted elsewhere) they must also satisfy the requirements of Article 31 E.C. In an important series of energy cases[69] decided in 1997 the Court ruled that the derogation of Article 86(2) could be applied to the grant of exclusive rights to Article 31 monopolies.

In the discussion that follows references to entrusted undertakings should be understood to include fiscal monopolies, unless the context indicates otherwise.

The scope of the exception

The exception is capable of restricting the application of any Community provision, including Article 86(1). It makes no difference whether the rule in question is one designed primarily to influence the conduct of undertakings, for example Articles 81 or 82, or that of States, for example Articles 28 or 87.[70] To benefit from the exception, an undertaking must show that application of the Treaty rules would obstruct the performance of the tasks assigned to it. This standard has been expressed in a variety of ways in the case-law, although the strictest formulations tied to the impact upon the undertaking's economic viability appear to have been mitigated more recently, at least in the context of undertakings entrusted with the provision of universal services for the public benefit.

Early examples of interpretation include the Commission's declaration in its *ANSEAU-NAVEWA* Decision that:

"It is not sufficient . . . that compliance with the provisions of the Treaty makes the performance of the particular task more complicated. A possible limitation of the application of the rules on competition can be envisaged only in the event that the undertaking concerned has no other technically and economically feasible means of performing its particular task."[71]

---

[67] Case C–179/90, n.44, *supra*. The Court reiterated this view in Case C–242/95 *GT-Link A/S v. De Danske Statsbaner* [1997] E.C.R. I–4449; [1997] 5 C.M.L.R. 601.

[68] Case C–266/96, n.7, *supra*.

[69] Case C–157/94 *Commission v. Netherlands* [1997] E.C.R. I–5699; Case C–158/94 *Commission v. Italy* [1997] E.C.R. I–5789; Case C–159/94 *Commission v. France* [1997] E.C.R. I–5815; Case C–160/94 *Commission v. Spain* [1997] E.C.R. I–5851; [1998] 2 C.M.L.R. 373.

[70] The application of Art. 86(2) to the state aids rules was expressly recognised in Case C–174/97P *FFSA v. Commission* [1998] E.C.R. I–1303, extending Case C–387/92 *Banco Exterior de Espana* [1994] E.C.R. I–877; [1994] 3 C.M.L.R. 473.

[71] *supra*, n.57.

In similar vein, Advocate General Rozès argued in the *Tobacco Margins* case[72] that the undertaking must have no choice but to infringe Treaty rules before the conditions for the exception would be satisfied. The Court's original position[73] was that rules of the Treaty continued to apply so long as it was not shown that their prohibitions were "incompatible" with the performance of the undertaking's tasks.

However, these approaches must now be read in the light of the Court's subsequent analysis of the scope of the exception in numerous cases involving the tension between the granting of exclusive rights by States and the Community's drive towards liberalisation of sectors in pursuit of the single market. The flurry of cases expanding the scope of Article 86(1) (see above) brought in turn a re-appraisal of the conditions needed to satisfy paragraph (2). Cases such as *Corbeau*[74] indicated that in principle there could be a "core" monopoly activity worthy of relief from the full force of the competition rules, even though in that particular case the core provision of basic postal services was not actually threatened by the peripheral competition posed by Corbeau's specialised premium-rate services. Significantly, the Court recognised that the obligation to perform the relevant services in conditions of economic equilibrium presupposed that it would be possible to offset less profitable sectors against the profitable ones. This approach was extended in *Almelo*,[75] concerning the terms on which electricity was supplied in the Netherlands. The Court noted that in applying the derogation of Article 86(2) it was necessary to take into consideration "the economic conditions in which the undertaking operates, in particular the costs which it has to bear, and the legislation, particularly concerning the environment, to which it is subject".[76] On this basis the Court indicated to the national court that an exclusive purchasing clause effectively prohibiting local distributors from importing electricity might be justified in the light of the regional distributor's obligations to ensure uninterrupted supplies to meet demand at all times, on the basis of uniform tariffs and non-discriminatory terms.

Explicit confirmation that the derogation is not solely concerned with the economic viability of the undertaking was given by the Court in the 1997 energy cases[77] and applied subsequently in a non-utility context. Thus, dealing with the pension fund arrangements in *Albany International*,[78] the Court summarised its position regarding the conditions for Article 86(2) as follows:

". . . it is not necessary . . . that the financial balance or economic viability of the undertaking entrusted with the operation of a service of general economic interest should be threatened. It is sufficient that, in the absence of the rights at issue, it would not be possible for the undertaking to perform the particular

---

[72] Case 78/82 *Commission v. Italy* [1983] E.C.R. 1955. The Court found no breach of the former Art. 37 (now 31) and accordingly did not discuss the exception.

[73] Case 155/73 *Sacchi*, n.7, *supra*, and repeated in Case 311/84 *CBEM Télé-Marketing v. Compagnie Luxembourgeoise de Télédiffusion and Information Publicité Benelux* [1985] E.C.R. 3261; [1986] 2 C.M.L.R. 558

[74] n.59, *supra*.

[75] n.58, *supra*.

[76] *ibid.*, para 49 of judgment.

[77] n.69, *supra*.

[78] n.17, *supra*.

tasks entrusted to it, defined by reference to the obligations and constraints to which it is subject . . . or that maintenance of those rights is necessary to enable the holder of them to perform tasks of general economic interest which have been assigned to it under economically acceptable conditions . . ."[79]

Taken as a whole, the evolving case-law suggests that determination of whether an undertaking will be "obstructed" is not to be confined to assessing the severity of the financial detriment which would ensue by requiring it to comply with the rules of the Treaty. Instead, the focus of the Court's approach is directed towards ensuring that the disturbances to the market and competitive conditions resulting from granting the exception of Article 86(2) are restricted to those necessary for performance of the legitimate service by the undertaking.

Where, in particular, the entrusted task involves the provision of a universal service on a regular basis such distortions may be more readily accepted. Thus, in *Corsica Ferries France*[80] the Court held that in calculating its prices the provider of mooring services could include a component designed to cover the cost of maintaining their universal nature and to lay down different tariffs for mooring services on the basis of the particular characteristics of individual ports. In contrast, in the *Dusseldorp* case,[81] the Court was not persuaded that the exclusive rights over waste management granted by the Netherlands to AVR were justified. Undertakings were required to deliver waste to AVR unless processing in another Member State would be of higher quality. In the Court's view, Article 86(2) could only be invoked if the Netherlands Government could show to the satisfaction of the national court that the entrusted objectives could not be achieved equally well by other means. However, it seems unlikely that this would be the case as the only argument advanced by the Netherlands was that exclusivity would reduce AVR's costs and make it economically viable.

Despite the greater scope for application of the Article 86(2) exception as a result of the recent case-law, the burden of proof remains on the undertaking (or State) to show that compliance with the Treaty would "obstruct" the performance of the entrusted tasks. Thus, in *Air Inter*,[82] the applicant merely asserted that cross-subsidy between its profitable and unprofitable routes was justified without putting a figure on the probable loss of revenue if other air carriers were allowed to compete with it on its exclusive routes. Nor had it shown that any such loss of income would be so great as to force it to abandon certain routes within its network. On the other hand, in the 1997 energy cases[83] the Court made it clear that the burden of proof did not extend so far as to require the State to prove positively that no other conceivable measure, which by definition would be hypothetical, could enable the entrusted tasks to be performed under the same conditions.

The proviso in the second sentence of Article 86(2) states that the development of trade must not be affected to such an extent as would be contrary to the interests of the Community. It thus identifies the point at which it still becomes

---

[79] *ibid.*, para. 107 of judgment.
[80] Case C–266/96, n.7, *supra*.
[81] Case C–203/96, n.39, *supra*.
[82] Case T–260/94, n.62, *supra*.
[83] n.69, *supra*.

necessary to apply the relevant provisions of Community law, even at the cost of preventing an entrusted undertaking or a fiscal monopoly from performing its allotted task. However, the proviso has received remarkably little discrete interpretation, mainly because for many years attempts to rely on Article 86(2) were consistently rejected on other grounds. Advocate General Cosmas in the 1997 energy cases suggested that the draftsmen of the Treaty inserted the proviso to exclude use of the derogation of Article 86(2) in relation to measures which, in addition to *potentially* restricting trade in the Community, have *in practice* done so, the restrictive effects being so great that intra-Community trade in the sector in question is practically non-existent.[84] The Court in the same cases ruled that the Commission had failed to explain why the Community interest was adversely affected by the exclusive import and export rights which formed the subject-matter of the infringement proceedings. Evidence presented to the Court indicated that there had been increasing inter-State trade in electricity and natural gas despite the existence of the exclusive rights. Accordingly, the Commission was obliged to define the Community interest against which the development of trade was said to be affected. However, it had not done so; in particular, it had not shown why, in the absence of a common policy in the area concerned, development of direct trade between producers and consumers, in parallel with the development of trade between major networks, would have been possible having regard in particular to the existing capacity and arrangements for transmission and distribution.

Direct effect of the exception

It must be kept firmly in mind that we are here concerned with a provision under which the scope of obligations imposed by the E.C. Treaty is restricted in relation to certain categories of undertakings. The question is how far a claim that a matter falls within the exception of Article 86(2) will interfere with the application by a national court of Community provisions on which individuals would normally be entitled to rely.

It has long been clear that a national court may decide whether an undertaking qualifies as "entrusted" within the meaning of Article 86(2).[85] Any lingering doubts[86] as to the powers of national courts in relation to whether undertakings are "obstructed" in the performance of their tasks were removed by the Court's judgment in *ERT*.[87] National courts are accordingly competent to apply the first sentence of the exception either in favour of or against an undertaking. This does not, of course, diminish the complexity of the task involved in deciding the point at which relief from the full force of the competition rules is no longer necessary to secure the undertaking's entrusted aims. Article 86(2) requires a proportionality assessment,[88] a task which has notoriously posed problems for national courts in other contexts.[89]

---

[84] *ibid.*, para. 126 of Opinion.
[85] Case 127/73 *BRT v. SABAM*, n.46, *supra*.
[86] Discussed in detail in the 3rd edition of this work, at pp. 563–565.
[87] Case C–260/89, n.30, *supra*.
[88] Advocate General Darmon in Case C–393/92, n.58, *supra*, at para. 142 of Opinion.
[89] *e.g.* the question of whether the old Art. 30 (now 28) applied to measures banning Sunday trading; see Chap. 13 *supra*.

Strictly speaking, the applicability of the proviso contained in the second sentence of the exception still awaits definitive resolution by the Court. The point was sidestepped in *Rendo*,[90] where part of the challenge to the ruling by the Court of First Instance was on the basis that it had erroneously distinguished between the two sentences of the derogation. The Court of Justice merely observed[91] that the second sentence had not arisen before the Court of First Instance and so there was no reason to treat the latter's judgment as having impliedly given exclusive competence over the proviso to the Commission. Advocate General Tesauro had argued that the derogation was "commonly" applied in its entirety[92] and that the Court had never drawn a distinction between the first and second sentences. On this view, a national court can only consider if particular conduct is necessary for the performance of an undertaking's task by taking an holistic approach to Article 86(2). It has also been claimed[93] that the very scheme of Article 86 invites the direct effect of paragraph (2), citing in evidence the Court's own statements elsewhere that Article 86 "confers powers on the Commission only in relation to State measures"[94] leaving the regulation of acts by undertakings on their own initiative for decisions under Articles 81 and 82.

Although it is increasingly difficult to resist the conclusion that a national court is empowered in respect of all aspects of Article 86(2), the arguments against that outcome remain cogent. First, it is odd that the Court has never expressly taken the opportunities given to it to clarify the matter. Its own pronouncements on the meaning of the proviso are mainly confined to infringement proceedings brought by the Commission (see above). Although it refers to the presence of the proviso in many instances, the language of the Court's preliminary rulings consistently maintain[95] that it is for the national court to establish that the undertaking has indeed been entrusted and that its conduct is necessary to perform its tasks. If the proviso is merely an integral part of that overall assessment, it might be expected that the Court would offer more guidance to the national court regarding the relevant criteria. Secondly, the very nature of the proviso may in any event be unsuitable for determination by national courts insofar as they will neither possess the information on which to take an overview of the Community's interests nor have the political legitimacy to determine the place at which the balance should be drawn. The advent of the Co-Operation Notice[96] in theory assists on the first point, establishing a channel of communication between national court and the Commission. It may well be appropriate, therefore, for a national court confronted by an undertaking pleading the derogation of Article 86(2) as a defence to what would otherwise be Treaty infringements to stay the proceedings and ask the Commission for its opinion before making any decision

---

[90] Case C–19/93P, n.58, *supra*.

[91] *ibid.*, para. 19 of judgment.

[92] *ibid.*, para. 38 of Opinion.

[93] Advocate General Darmon in Case C–393/92, n.58, *supra*, at paras 132–134 of Opinion.

[94] Case C–202/88 *France v. Commission*, n.8, *supra*, at para. 55 of judgment; also Joined Cases C–271, 281 and 289/90 *Spain and others v. Commission* [1992] E.C.R. I–5833 at para. 24 of judgment.

[95] See, for example, Case C–242/95 *GT-Link*, n.67, *supra*.

[96] [1993] O.J. C39/6; [1993] 4 C.M.L.R. 12. See Waller, "Decentralization of the enforcement process of E.C. competition law" [1996/2] L.I.E.I. 1.

on whether to apply the derogation. It will also be open to the Commission to adopt a decision under Article 86(3) (see below) in relation to the application of the derogation to the undertaking.

Article 86(3): the supervisory and legislative competence of the Commission

By Article 86(3) the Commission is both placed under an obligation to ensure the application of the Article and equipped with a special power to issue directives or decisions for this purpose. Directives or decisions under Article 86(3) can only be addressed to Member States. However, where appropriate the Commission may have recourse to other powers, for example under Regulation 17, against the undertaking concerned. There is, of course, nothing in Article 86 to prevent the Commission, if it so chooses, from issuing non-binding recommendations.

By conferring, unusually, a specific legislative competence on the Commission Article 86(3) became a subject of controversy when it was eventually brought into play. In the first of the challenges[97] to directives adopted under the provision, the Court was called upon to examine the validity of the so-called Transparency Directive.[98] This legislation seeks to ensure the transparency of financial relations between Member States and public undertakings, and requires Member States to keep available for five years relevant information and to supply it on request to the Commission. The preamble to the Directive stresses the Commission's duty to ensure that Member States do not grant undertakings, public or private, aids incompatible with the common market, and the need for equal treatment of public and private enterprises. The complexity of financial relations between Member States and public undertakings hinders the achievement of that equality, and provides the rationale for the measure. The Court upheld the Commission's power to adopt the Directive in the face of arguments that it could only have been adopted by the Council using its legislative powers in relation to state aids. According to the Court, the Commission's power depended on the needs inherent in its duty of surveillance provided for in Article 86.

A challenge was also mounted, this time by France and supported by Italy, Belgium, Germany and Greece,[99] against the next principal Directive issued under the then Article 90(3), relating to telecommunications terminal equipment.[1] This measure provided, *inter alia*, that Member States which had granted special or exclusive rights for the importation, marketing, connection, bringing into service of telecommunications terminal equipment and/or the maintenance of such equipment were to ensure that those rights were withdrawn. One argument advanced to challenge the Commission's competence was that the provision constituted a normative act which could only properly belong under the rules concerning competition or the single market (thereby requiring Council

---

[97] Joined Cases 188–190/80 *France, Italy and the United Kingdom v. Commission* [1982] E.C.R. 2545; [1982] 3 C.M.L.R. 144.
[98] n.20, *supra*.
[99] Case C–202/88, n.8, *supra*.
[1] 1 Dir. 88/301; [1988] O.J. L131/73.

action). Following its earlier reasoning in the *Transparency Directive* case, the Court ruled that the duty imposed upon the Commission under the then Article 90 was more specific than the other general competences conferred on the Council.

A further argument raised in the *Telecommunications Directive* case was the relationship between the Commission's specific powers and general enforcement actions under what is now Article 226. According to the Court, the specific legislative powers of Article 86 allow the Commission to define in a general way the obligations which the Treaty imposes upon Member States. The directive in question satisfied these normative criteria. However, if a Member State does not comply, the default can then only be pursued by recourse to normal infringement proceedings.[2]

Directives and decisions are to be distinguished when considering the Commission's powers under Article 86(3). In an appeal from a case involving Netherlands express delivery services,[3] the Court explained that a decision necessarily involves an assessment of a particular situation in one or more Member States from the point of view of Community law and determines the resulting consequences for the Member State concerned. The Court added that in order not to deprive of all useful purpose the power to adopt decisions under Article 86(3) it must be recognised that the Commission has power to find that a particular State measure is incompatible with the rules of the Treaty and to specify the measures which the addressee State must adopt in order to comply with its obligations under Community law. However, the Court then annulled the particular decision on the basis that the Commission had given neither the Netherlands Government nor the PTT a fair hearing.

Strengthened by judicial support, the Commission proceeded to seek liberalisation of particular sectors by legislation adopted under Article 86(3).[4] However, and perhaps because of the Commission's successful use of its specialist powers, legislation has also been enacted by the Council. Thus the Directive on developing the internal market for postal services[5] was eventually enacted on the basis of the Treaty rules applicable to establishment, services and the single market. It may be claimed that this approach[6] enjoys greater democratic credibility as well as permitting a more broadly-based regulatory regime than would be authorised by Article 86 legislation. However, it may well be the case that no such progress would have been made in the Council if the antecedents of Article 86(3) had not been present to focus minds.

---

[2] As happened in the context of the Transparency Directive when Italy refused to supply requested information. See Case 118/85 *Re AAMS: Commission v. Italy* [1987] E.C.R. 2599; [1988] 3 C.M.L.R. 255.

[3] Joined Cases C–48 and 66/90, *Netherlands, Koninklijke PTT Nederland NV and PTT Post BV v. Commission* [1992] E.C.R. I–565; [1993] 5 C.M.L.R. 316.

[4] For example, Dir. 90/388 on telecommunications services; [1990] O.J. L192/10; Dir. 95/51 on the use of cable television networks; [1995] O.J. L256/49; Dir. 96/2 on mobile and personal communications; [1996] O.J. L20/59.

[5] Dir. 97/67 [1998] O.J. L15/14.

[6] The Commission has also taken this path for measures in the energy sector (electricity and natural gas).

Article 16 E.C. and services of general economic interest

The case-law of the 1990s and the different views among Member States as to the role of public service obligations led to discussion of possible reforms.[7] For the Commission,[8] services of general interest form a key element in the European model of society:

"European societies are committed to the general interest services they have created which meet basic needs. These services play an important role as social cement over and above practical considerations. They also have a symbolic value, reflecting a sense of community that people can identify with. They form part of the cultural identity of everyday life in all European countries."[9]

Rather modestly, the Commission sought to amend Article 3 E.C. to add "a contribution to the promotion of services of general economic interest" to the list of Community activities. The Reflection Group Report on the 1996 Inter-Governmental Conference referred to the "majority" view in favour of reinforcement of the concept of public service utilities (*services publics d'intérêt général*) as a principle supplementing market criteria. In its final form, the Treaty of Amsterdam inserted a new provision into the E.C. Treaty as Article 16:

"Without prejudice to Articles 73, 86 and 87, and given the place occupied by services of general economic interest in the shared values of the Union as well as their role in promoting social and territorial cohesion, the Community and the Member States, each within their respective powers and within the scope of application of this Treaty, shall take care that such services operate on the basis of principles and conditions which enable them to fulfil their missions."

The scope of this Article, which might be seen as a triumph for ambiguous drafting,[10] has yet to receive judicial scrutiny.

It therefore remains to be seen whether Article 16 satisfies the wish of some Member States to provide further security for public services against the full impact of the competition rules of the Treaty. Certainly, the reference to being without prejudice to Article 86 must mean that Article 16 cannot be used to make it more difficult for providers of universal services to escape the rigours of Community competition law. As discussed above, the case-law under Article 86(2) already exhibits an increasingly benign view of entrusted undertakings.

Perhaps the greatest interest in the legal development of Article 16 is to be found in its latent acknowledgment of a Community notion of general interest services, and the extent to which this may prove different from national concepts. Whilst it does not confer a specific legislative power on the Community for further action, Article 16's position in the part of the Treaty headed "Principles" might suggest an importance going beyond mere rhetoric. Indeed, the fact that it

---

[7] France, for example, initially wanted the Treaty competition rules to be disapplied in their entirety from public services provision.

[8] *Services of General Interest in Europe*, n.52, *supra*.

[9] *ibid.*, para. 6.

[10] See Ross, "Art. 16 E.C. and services of general interest: from derogation to obligation?" (2000) 25 E.L.Rev. 22.

is not tied to the derogation of Article 86(2) and the competition rules indicates that it is capable of being relevant to all aspects of Community activity. The express references to shared Union values and to the particular objectives of social and territorial cohesion upgrade regard for general interest services into a positive horizontal policy-shaping consideration for both Member States and the Community institutions. In other words, Article 16 captures the tension at the heart of the Union's current process of development: the balancing or prioritising of market-based considerations and those more concerned with cohesion and social solidarity.[11]

---

[11] See Freedland and Sciarra (eds), *Public Services and Citizenship in European Law* (Oxford, 1998).

CHAPTER 26

INTELLECTUAL PROPERTY AND COMPETITION

Introduction

The explicit reference to the protection of industrial and commercial property in Article 30 E.C.[1] has no counterpart in the Treaty rules relating to competition. Finding a balance between the needs of effective and workable competition and the essential rationale behind intellectual property such as patents, copyrights and trademarks has therefore been the task of the Community institutions. At first sight, the exclusive and potentially monopolistic character of intellectual property rights inevitably puts them on a collision path with some of the fundamental tenets of Articles 81 and 82. For example, the terms on which a licence may be granted to exploit a right may impose conditions which in any other context would be condemned as restrictive. Similarly, exploitative terms or refusals to grant licences arouse comparisons with the general case-law based on abuse of a dominant position. However, as this Chapter shows, these issues have largely received a more delicate and tailored approach that seeks to temper the blunt application of raw principle by an awareness of the role and merits of intellectual property.

In essence, this position acknowledges that intellectual property rights must be allowed to carry certain restrictions in order to further competition. The particular rationales for different rights may vary. Patents, for example, encourage innovation and technological advance, whilst trademarks purport to give their holders the goodwill attached to the brand name and assure customers of the quality of the branded goods. Copyright may attach to a vast range of activities, but in essence recognises authorship and artistic creativity. Despite these different characteristics, such rights share a common interest in seeking protection. Put simply, no company will invest the necessary research money to discover new therapeutic drugs if the result can simply be pocketed by a rival without any effort. By the same token, having one's trademark appropriated and stuck on inferior goods harms both the holder's reputation and bank balance. Similar arguments apply to unauthorised performances of artistic work.

The more difficult question is how to strike a balance between the benefits of intellectual property and the detriment to competition in a conceptually satisfying manner. As with the cases under Article 30, the theoretical basis for the application of the rules on competition in respect of national rights of intellectual property is the purported but sometimes tricky distinction between the existence of such rights and their exercise. Indeed, the distinction was first developed by

---

[1] For discussion of the impact of the free movement of goods rules on intellectual property, see Chap. 13, p. 360 *et seq. supra*. This chapter uses the term "intellectual property" throughout rather than the Art. 30 nomenclature.

the Court of Justice in competition cases.[2] Later attempts to place plant breeders' rights beyond the scope of this compromise solution were decisively rejected in the *Maize Seeds* case.[3]

The Court has stressed that an intellectual property right, as a legal entity, does not in itself possess the elements that activate the prohibitions in Article 81(1) or Article 82 E.C.[4] The grant of protection by the authorities of a Member State is not the kind of collusive arrangement (agreement between undertakings, decision of an association of undertakings or concerted practice) to which Article 81(1) refers; nor does it automatically entail the existence of a dominant position within a substantial part of the common market.

The early case of *Parke, Davis v. Centrafarm*[5] provides an illustration. The background to the case was the absence of patent protection in Italy for medicinal drugs. At issue was the importation, in contravention of patents held in the Netherlands, of a drug manufactured in Italy not by the patent owner himself but by a third party. Two questions were put by the referring court. The first asked, in effect, whether the holder of a national patent was prevented by Articles 85 and 86 (now 81 and 82) "possibly considered in conjunction with the provisions of Articles 36[6] and 222"[7] from using it to block imports from a country where they could lawfully be produced without a patent; the second whether it was significant that the price of the patented product which was manufactured locally was higher than the price of the imported product. The Court replied:

"1. The existence of rights granted by a Member State to the holder of a patent is not affected by the prohibitions contained in Articles 85(1) and 86 of the Treaty.

2. The exercise of such rights cannot of itself fall either under Article 85(1), in the absence of any agreement, decision or concerted practice prohibited by this provision, or under Article 86, in the absence of any abuse of a dominant position.

3. A higher sale price for the patented product as compared with that of the unpatented product coming from another Member State does not necessarily constitute an abuse."[8]

The reply acknowledges that Article 81 or Article 82 may, in principle, be invoked to prevent the exercise of intellectual property rights, but only where additional factors, satisfying the criteria of prohibition in those provisions, are present; and of such factors there was no evidence before the Court.

In principle, therefore, the application of the rules on competition to an agreement respecting intellectual property rights should take place in two stages.

---

[2] See Joined Cases 56 and 58/64 *Consten and Grundig v. Commission* [1966] E.C.R. 299; [1966] C.M.L.R. 418; Case 24/67 *Parke, Davis v. Centrafarm* [1968] E.C.R. 55; [1968] C.M.L.R. 47; Case 40/70 *Sirena v. Eda* [1971] E.C.R. 69; [1971] C.M.L.R. 260.

[3] Case 258/78 *Nungesser v. Commission* [1982] E.C.R. 2015; [1983] 1 C.M.L.R. 278.

[4] Case 40/70 *Sirena v. Eda*, n.2, *supra*; Case 51/75 *EMI v. CBS United Kingdom* [1976] E.C.R. 811, at 848; [1976] 2 C.M.L.R. 235.

[5] Case 24/67 n.2, *supra*.

[6] Now Art. 30.

[7] Now Art. 295: "This Treaty shall in no way prejudice national systems of property ownership."

[8] [1968] E.C.R. at 73–74.

The first stage involves considering whether particular provisions of the agreement go to the very existence of the property form in question[9] or merely regulate its exercise. If the former, the competition rules cannot normally be applied at all. If the latter, then the second stage—consideration of whether the contested provision or act infringes Articles 81 or 82—commences. In practice, however, the distinction between these two stages is not always marked in the reasoning of the Commission, or even of the Court.[10]

The principal developments in the relationship between intellectual property and the rules on competition are discussed below. First, issues arising in respect of Article 81 are examined. Here the central plank in regulation has been the enactment of block exemptions under Article 81(3) for certain types of licensing agreement. Secondly, the case-law applying Article 82 is discussed. The principal controversy in this area has been whether the Court's judgment in the so-called *Magill*[11] cases has improperly or unjustifiably eroded the rightholder's interests.

Developments in relation to Article 81

Assignments of intellectual property
Where rights of intellectual property are assigned outright, as opposed to being licensed, the contract between the assignor and the assignee will be discharged by completion of performance. In such a case, will there be any consensual relationship to which the prohibition in Article 81 may attach? This question was first addressed by the Court of Justice in *Sirena v. Eda*.[12] Under a contract concluded in 1937 the Italian rights to the trademark PREP had been assigned to Sirena by an American company, Mark Allen. Sirena subsequently re-registered the mark in its own name, together with two other marks incorporating the word PREP. The right to use the mark in Germany had been granted by Mark Allen at some unspecified date to a German company and marked products manufactured by the latter were imported into Italy, where they were sold at much lower prices than Sirena's products. The national proceedings were brought by Sirena to prevent the infringement of its rights by the importer, a company called Novimpex.

The Italian Court referred the compatibility of the assignment with the competition rules to the European Court. It was stated by the Court that the exercise of a trademark right "might fall within the ambit of the prohibitions contained in the Treaty each time it manifests itself as the subject, the means or the result of a restrictive practice".[13] The suggestion has been made, and it was evidently the view taken by the national court, that in fact, a concerted practice existed between Mark Allen and its assignees in the common market countries

---

[9] *cf.* the notion of "specific subject matter", visible in the cases decided under Art. 30; see Chap. 13, *supra*.

[10] Case 40/70 *Sirena v. Eda*, n.2, *supra*.

[11] Joined Cases C–241–242/91P *Radio Telefis Eireann (RTE) and Independent Television Publications Ltd (ITP) v. Commission* [1995] E.C.R. I–743; [1995] 4 C.M.L.R. 718.

[12] Case 40/70 n.2, *supra*.

[13] [1971] E.C.R. at 82.

under which each respected the territorial rights of the others.[14] The Court contented itself with the statement that:

"If the restrictive practices arose before the Treaty entered into force, it is both necessary and sufficient that they continue to produce their effects after that date".[15]

This indicates, mysteriously,[16] that Article 81(1) can somehow be "applied" to a practice which ceased before the Article came into force.

The statement was qualified in *EMI v. CBS*.[17] CBS' second main line of defence in the infringement proceedings brought by EMI was that the agreements for the assignment of the COLUMBIA trademark were caught by the prohibition in Article 81(1) because they formed part of a complex of agreements the object of which had been to partition the world market. The agreements themselves had been terminated before the EEC Treaty (as it was) came into force but CBS argued, with the support of the Commission, that the prohibition would apply so long as they continued to produce effects which were felt within the common market.

The Court observed:

"An agreement is only regarded as continuing to produce its effects if from the behaviour of the persons concerned there may be inferred the existence of elements of concerted practice and of coordination peculiar to the agreements and producing the same result as that envisaged by the agreement.

This is not so when the said effects do not exceed those flowing from the mere exercise of the national trademark rights."[18]

This statement is not entirely convincing, since if a concerted practice can be shown to exist, why bother going back to the original agreement? However, we have seen[19] that mere parallelism will not suffice as evidence of a concerted practice, so the presence of the earlier agreement may have evidential value for the ongoing concertation. The later case of *IHT*[20] confirms that not every assignment agreement will be taken to constitute an infringement of Article 81(1). Before it can be so treated, it is "necessary to analyse the context, the

---

[14] In his Opinion in *Van Zuylen v. Hag* Advocate General Mayras suggested that the European Court may have acted on this assumption: see [1974] E.C.R. 731 at 750. For the view of the Tribunale di Milano, see [1975] 1 C.M.L.R. 409 at 430–431.

[15] [1971] E.C.R. at 83.

[16] Craig & de Búrca in *EU Law Text, Cases and Materials* (2nd ed., Oxford, 1998) describe the Court's response on this point as "somewhat cavalier" (p. 1049, n.40).

[17] Case 51/75 n.4, *supra*. Other proceedings flowing from the same history arose in Case 86/75 *EMI v. CBS Grammofon* [1976] E.C.R. 871; [1976] 2 C.M.L.R. 235; Case 96/75 *EMI v. CBS Schallplatten* [1976] E.C.R. 913; [1976] 2 C.M.L.R. 235. In each case the European Court was invited to consider whether EMI's use of its E.C. trademark rights in the name COLUMBIA to restrain the importation and sale of records made in the USA by CBS, who owned the COLUMBIA mark in the United States, was compatible with E.C. rules on free movement of goods and on competition.

[18] [1976] E.C.R. at 848–849.

[19] See Chap. 20 on restrictive practices, *supra*.

[20] Case C–9/93 *IHT International Heiztechnik v. Ideal Standard* [1994] E.C.R. I–2789; [1994] 3 C.M.L.R. 857.

commitments underlying the assignment, the intention of the parties and the consideration for the assignment".[21]

Licensing intellectual property

In the field of intellectual property the greatest practical impact of Article 81 and associated secondary legislation has been upon the terms of licensing agreements. In its enforcement activity the Commission has been concerned mainly with patent licensing[22]; but many of the principles it has developed are capable of being applied to other property forms. There have also been important judicial decisions on the licensing of trademarks,[23] copyright[24] and plant breeders' rights.[25]

A licensing transaction consists essentially of the granting by the owner of an intellectual property right of permission for a third party to exploit the right, in consideration of the payment of a royalty. The possibility of exploitation through licences was explicitly recognised by the Court in *Centrafarm v. Sterling Drug*[26] as an element in the specific subject-matter of a patent; and the same is true, it is submitted, of all intellectual property. It would follow that any terms in a licensing agreement that may be recognised as indispensable to this indirect method of exploitation would enjoy immunity from the competition rules. At the other end of the spectrum there are some licensing terms that will be viewed as so inimical to the principles of competition and the proper functioning of the single market that the parties' freedom of contract will be overridden. The best way to predict how particular clauses will be received is by examination of block exemptions. However, before looking at the principal example of these, mention should be made of the more general guidance discernible from the case-law principles established by the Court of Justice.

In particular, the Court has been influential in determining the extent to which grants of exclusivity may fall outside the scope of Article 81(1) altogether. Indeed, the final version of the original patent licensing block exemption[27] was

---

[21] *ibid.*, para. 59. This was again a trademark assignment. The Court disposed of the case on the basis of the derogation provided by Art. 30.

[22] The Commission's preoccupation with patent licensing goes back to the earliest days of competition policy. A Notice on Patent Licensing Agreements ("the Christmas message"), setting forth its views on the application of the competition rules to such agreements, was issued on December 24, 1962. Over the years those views came to be modified in important respects and the Notice ceased to be a reliable guide. It was withdrawn, following the adoption of the block exemption regulation on patent licensing agreements: [1984] O.J. C220/14. This in turn was replaced by the Reg. 240/96 on technology transfer agreements: [1996] O.J. L31/2, discussed further *infra*.

[23] Joined Cases 56 and 58/64 *Consten and Grundig v. Commission*, n.2, *supra*; Case 28/77 *Tepea v. Commission* [1978] E.C.R. 1391; [1978] 3 C.M.L.R. 392; Case 10/89 *CNL-SUCAL v. Hag ("Hag II")* [1990] E.C.R. I–3711; [1990] 3 C.M.L.R. 571.

[24] Case 262/81 *Coditel v. Ciné Vog Films (No. 2)* [1982] E.C.R. 3381; [1983] 1 C.M.L.R. 49; Case 53/87 *CICRA and Maxicar v. Renault* [1988] E.C.R. 6067; Case 238/87 *Volvo v. Erik Veng (UK) Ltd* [1988] E.C.R. 6211; [1989] 4 C.M.L.R. 122; Joined Cases C–241–242/91 *RTE and ITP v. Commission*, n.11, *supra*; Case T–504/93 *Tiercé Ladbroke v. Commission* [1997] E.C.R. II-923, [1997] 5 C.M.L.R. 309.

[25] Case 258/78 *Nungesser v. Commission*, n.3, *supra*; Case 27/87 *Erauw-Jacquery v. Hesbignonne* [1988] E.C.R. 1919.

[26] Case 15/74 [1974] E.C.R. 1147, at 1162; [1974] 2 C.M.L.R. 480.

[27] Reg. 2349/84; [1984] O.J. L219/15. For a detailed examination of the legislative history, see Goyder, *EC Competition Law* (3rd ed., Oxford, 1998,), pp. 269–278.

delayed by the Commission to take account of the Court's judgment in *Maize Seeds*.[28] This case concerned a contract between INRA, a French research institute engaged in the development of seeds, and Eisele, a German supplier of seeds. Under its terms, INRA would not sell the relevant seeds to anyone else in Germany and would prevent third parties from doing so. In turn, Eisele could use his rights to preclude all imports into Germany of the seeds. The combined effect of these terms was to confer absolute territorial protection upon the licensee.[29]

In its judgment, the Court of Justice distinguished between two kinds of licensing arrangement—"open exclusive licences" and "absolute territorial protection". Under the former, the licensor agrees not to allow any other undertaking to exploit the relevant property within the contract territory; and also not to manufacture or market the protected product itself within that territory. Here the exclusivity is a matter between the contracting parties: the market in the contract territory remains open to parallel imports by third parties, including licensees for other territories. Such an arrangement, the Court held, would not infringe Article 81(1) in the circumstances of the *Maize Seeds* case. Those circumstances involved "the cultivation and marketing of hybrid maize seeds which were developed by INRA after years of research and experimentation and were unknown to German farmers at the time when the co-operation between INRA and the applicants was taking shape".[30] The Court concluded that, unless it were able to obtain an open exclusive licence, an undertaking might be deterred from running the risk of introducing the product onto the German market, a result which, it said, "would be damaging to the dissemination of a new technology and would prejudice competition in the Community between the new product and similar existing products".[31] On the other hand, the Court condemned the absolute territorial protection which had been undertaken in the particular case, repeating its view that such protection "granted to a licensee in order to enable parallel imports to be controlled and prevented results in the artificial maintenance of separate national markets, contrary to the Treaty".[32]

The Court's judgment did not receive unreserved acclaim, criticism especially being directed at the caveats that seemed to be attached to the conditions whereby an "open exclusive licence" would indeed be sufficiently open to competition to enable it to escape the prohibition of Article 81(1) without recourse to exemption.[33] What, for example, would qualify as a "new technology" and was the reference to competition based on intra- or inter-brand considerations? The thrust of the *Maize Seeds* judgment seemed to suggest that it would take the presence of some special features to save an open exclusive licence from being restrictive for the purposes of Article 81(1). Certainly, on the facts in question, greater marketing risks would attach to the licence because the product

---

[28] Case 258/78 *Nungesser v. Commission*, n.3, *supra*.

[29] Nungesser, an undertaking controlled by Eisele, was the assignee of his exclusive rights.

[30] [1982] E.C.R. at 2069.

[31] *ibid.*.

[32] See Case 27/87 *Erauw-Jacquery v. Hesbignonne*, n.25, *supra*.

[33] See Hoffmann and O'Farrell, "The 'open exclusive licence'—scope and consequences" [1984] 4 E.I.P.R. 104.

was "unknown" in the licensed territory.[34] As far as competition is concerned, it has been clear from the very early days of the *Consten and Grundig*[35] judgment that distribution arrangements which might enhance inter-brand competition will not be allowed to nullify cross-border intra-brand flows. In the case of a patent licence, it might be the case that a particular "new technology" product would not have serious rivals among other producers. With little or no inter-brand competition around, the case for defending the licensee against intra-brand competition is made even weaker.

Despite the rather ambivalent ruling given by the Court in *Maize Seeds*, its recognition that certain open licences could escape prohibition prompted a more lenient approach by the Commission in the eventual 1984 patent licensing block exemption[36] to the types of restriction that could lawfully be imposed by licensing agreements. The current expanded form of the block exemption[37], discussed further *infra*, still adheres to the Court's approach. Recital 10 states:

> "Exclusive licensing agreements, *i.e.* agreements in which the licensor undertakes not to exploit the licensed technology in the licensed territory himself or to grant further licences there, may not be in themselves incompatible with [Article 81(1)] where they are concerned with the introduction and protection of a new technology in the licensed territory, by reason of the scale of the research which has been undertaken, of the increase in the level of competition, in particular inter-brand competition, and of the competitiveness of the undertakings concerned resulting from the dissemination of innovation within the Community. In so far as agreements of this kind fall, in other circumstances, within the scope of [Article 81(1)], it is appropriate to include them in [this block exemption] . . ."

The reduction in notifications of individual agreements brought about by the introduction of block exemptions diminished the opportunities for the Court to confirm or initiate principles with respect to licensing. However, its judgment in *Windsurfing International*[38] provides an illustration of its attitude to other types of restriction besides exclusivity.

The case concerned an American company, Windsurfing International (WI), which held a patent for the rig used on a windsurfer. The licensed product was stated to be the complete sailboard, even though the patent only covered the rig.[39]

---

34 *cf.* Case 262/81 *Coditel v. Ciné Vog Films (No. 2)*, n.24, *supra*, where it was held that a contract under which the owner of the copyright in a film grants an exclusive right to exhibit the film for a specific period in a Member State is not, as such, subject to the prohibition in Art. 81(1). The Court said that the exercise of the exclusive right may fall within the prohibition "where there are economic or legal circumstances the effect of which is to restrict film distribution to an appreciable degree or to distort competition on the cinematographic market, regard being had to the specific characteristics of that market." [1982] E.C.R. at 3402. Here the risk, arguably, attached to the licensee's capital investment, not marketing.

35 Joined Cases 56 and 58/64 *Consten and Grundig v. Commission*, n.2, *supra*.

36 n.27, *supra*.

37 Reg. 240/96, n.22, *supra*.

38 Case 198/83 *Windsurfing International v. Commission* [1986] E.C.R. 611; [1986] 3 C.M.L.R. 489. This was the first case following the introduction of the block exemption in which the Court was able to consider the position of an individual patent licence. No exemption was possible, leaving aside any question of the merits of the licence, for lack of notification.

39 *i.e.* "an assemblage consisting essentially of a mast, a joint for the mast, a sail and spars".

WI licensed certain undertakings in the E.C. but with particular conditions attached. Among these were: 1) the licensor's approval was required for any type of board on which the licensee intended to place the rig; 2) the licensee was obliged to sell only complete sailboards, *i.e.* the patented rig plus an approved board; 3) royalties were payable on the entire selling price of the complete sailboard; 4) the licensee was required to indicate on the board that it was "licensed" by the licensor; 5) a no-challenge clause in respect of the licensor's trademark and patent; and 6) the licensee was prevented from manufacturing the sailboard other than at particular factories in Germany. WI claimed that these restrictions were needed to ensure quality control over the licensed product.

The Court, however, approached the agreement from the perspective of what was needed to preserve the specific subject matter of the patent. The fact that several of the restrictions extended beyond the rig to the whole sailboard meant that the case for them being essential collapsed. In the Court's view, restrictions designed to ensure quality control must be agreed in advance and be objectively verifiable.[40] Thus, even if the whole sailboard had been covered in the instant case, the controls in question would still have been outside the specific subject matter of the patent, owing to their discretionary character, which made it possible for WI to impose its own selection of models on the licensees. Similarly, the production restrictions were unconnected to the patent in so far as WI would have no say in the quality control of manufacturers anyway. The no-challenge clauses did not come within the specific subject matter of the patent either, "in view of the fact that it is in the public interest to eliminate any obstacle to economic activity which may arise where a patent was granted in error".[41] Because of his privileged access to information and experience of working the patent, a licensee is particularly well placed to detect any possible flaws in the patentee's title.[42] The "licensed-by" restriction only served to encourage uncertainty as to the scope of the patent, thereby diminishing the consumer's confidence in the licensees so as to gain a competitive advantage for WI itself.[43] Finally, the provisions concerning royalties were restrictive in principle by being linked to the extended product rather than the subject of the patent. However, the Court found that in fact the amounts charged were no higher than they would have been had they been based solely on the price of the rigs.[44]

Probably as important as the treatment of these particular clauses was the Court's insistence that the agreement as a whole should be considered in order to examine the effect on inter-State trade. The Commission was not obliged to establish that each individual clause had such an effect.[45]

---

[40] [1986] E.C.R. 611, para. 46.

[41] *ibid.*, para. 92.

[42] However, in Case 65/86 *Bayer v. Süllhöfer* [1988] E.C.R. 5249; [1990] 4 C.M.L.R. 182, the Court held that no-challenge clauses which cannot affect the licensee's economic activity may escape Art. 81(1); for example, if no royalties are payable by the licensee or the licensee does not use the patented process because it is technically outdated. This seems to take a narrower view of the public interest, which previously was equated with the desirability of not maintaining the registration of invalid patents as a deterrent to the use by anyone of such technology.

[43] [1986] E.C.R. 611, para. 73.

[44] The fine imposed by the Commission was accordingly reduced slightly.

[45] Maher draws attention to the contrast between the Court's approach in *Windsurfing International*

Block exemptions: the Technology Transfer Regulation

In 1996 the previously separate block exemptions for patent licensing and know-how[46] agreements were brought together and replaced by a single revised and expanded Regulation.[47] This change had been on the Commission's agenda for some time, partly because the previous patent licensing regulation was due to expire in 1994 and also as recognition that the practical overlap between patents and know-how invited a simplified regulatory framework. However, the new Technology Transfer Regulation[48] was implemented rather later than the Commission had envisaged since draft versions provoked hostile reactions in the commercial world. In particular, there was resistance to the Commission's plan to make the block exemption subject to limitations determined by market shares. The Commission backed down, and the final form of the Regulation only contains one reference to market shares.[49] It took effect on April 1, 1996 and expires on March 31, 2006. The principal features of the Regulation are outlined below,[50] although the discussion is not intended as an exhaustive treatment of detail but as a guide to how the Regulation reflects the development of a less formalistic and more accommodating approach to licensing agreements.

According to Article 1(1) of Regulation 240/96, pursuant to Article 81(3) the prohibition of Article 81(1) shall not apply to:

"pure patent licensing or know-how licensing agreements and to mixed patent and know-how licensing agreements, including those agreements containing ancillary provisions relating to intellectual property rights other than patents, to which only two undertakings are party and which include one or more of the following obligations:

(1) an obligation on the licensor not to license other undertakings to exploit the licensed technology in the licensed territory;

(2) an obligation on the licensor not to exploit the licensed technology in the licensed territory himself;

(3) an obligation on the licensee not to exploit the licensed technology in the territory of the licensor within the common market;

(4) an obligation on the licensee not to manufacture or use the licensed product, or use the licensed process, in territories within the common market which are licensed to other licensees;

(5) an obligation on the licensee not to pursue an active policy of putting the licensed product on the market in the territories within the common market which are licensed to other licensees, and in particular not to

---

and the line-by-line formalism of the first patent licensing block exemption: see "Competition law and intellectual property rights: evolving formalism" in Craig & de Búrca, *The Evolution of EU Law* (Oxford, 1999), p. 597, at p. 612.

[46] Reg. 556/89.

[47] For a more detailed exposition of the legislative history, see Goyder, *op. cit.*, n.27, *supra*, pp. 269–290 and Maher, *op.cit.*, n.45, *supra*.

[48] Reg. 240/96, n.22, *supra*.

[49] *ibid.*, Art. 7(1), dealing with the circumstances in which the Commission would be prepared to withdraw the benefit of the block exemption.

[50] See Robertson, "Technology transfer agreements: an overview of how Reg. 240/96 changes the law" [1996] 3 E.C.L.R. 157.

engage in advertising specifically aimed at those territories or to establish any branch or maintain a distribution depot there;

(6) an obligation on the licensee not to put the licensed product on the market in the territories licensed to other licensees within the common market in response to unsolicited orders;

(7) an obligation on the licensee to use only the licensor's trademark or get-up to distinguish the licensed product during the term of the agreement, provided that the licensee is not prevented from identifying himself as the manufacturer of the licensed products;

(8) an obligation on the licensee to limit his production of the licensed product to the quantities he requires in manufacturing his own products and to sell the licensed product only as an integral part of or a replacement part for his own products or otherwise in connection with the sale of his own products, provided that such quantities are freely determined by the licensee."

Patent and know-how licensing agreements are defined for this purpose as agreements whereby one undertaking which holds a patent or know-how[51] permits another undertaking to exploit the patent thereby licensed, or communicates the know-how to it, in particular for the purposes of manufacture, use or putting on the market.[52] The patents may be national, Community or European[53] and include certain other rights deemed to be patents for the purpose of the Regulation.[54] In recognition of the mixed nature of many licences in practice, the Regulation applies to mixed agreements containing the licensing of intellectual property rights other than patents (in particular, trademarks, design rights and copyright, especially software protection) when such additional licensing contributes to the achievement of the objects of the licensed technology and contains only ancillary provisions. For this purpose "ancillary" provisions are those non-patent rights containing no obligations restrictive of competition other than those also attached to the licensed patents or know-how and exempted under the Regulation.[55]

The duration of the territorial protection allowed by Article 1(1) is dependent on the type of licence in question. Article 1(2) spells out the permutations for pure patent licences, pure know-how licences and mixed patent and know-how agreements. For example, in relation to obligations (1)—(5) listed in Article 1(1) above, the duration of exemption for pure patent licensing agreements is to the extent that and for so long as the licensed product is protected by parallel patents in the relevant territories. In the case of pure know-how agreements the period is ten years from the date when the licensed product is first put on the market in the common market by one of the licensees, or until the know-how ceases to be secret and substantial if that

---

[51] Defined in Art. 10 as "a body of technical information that is secret, substantial and identified in any appropriate form".

[52] Recital 5.

[53] Recital 4.

[54] Art. 8(1). The list includes patent applications, utility models and plant breeders' certificates.

[55] Art. 5(1)(4).

happens during the ten-year period. For mixed patent and know-how licences, the exemption concerning obligations (1)—(5) applies in Member States in which the licensed technology is protected by necessary patents for as long as the licensed product is protected if this exceeds the periods specified for know-how agreements. The key term here is "necessary patents", an idea newly established by this Regulation. It is defined in Article 10(5) as "patents where a licence under the patent is necessary for the putting into effect of the licensed technology in so far as, in the absence of such a licence, the realisation of the licensed technology would not be possible or would be possible only to a lesser extent or in more difficult or costly conditions. Such patents must therefore be of technical, legal or economic interest to the licensee".[56] This requirement appears[57] to be directed against attempts to lengthen the duration of protection artificially by repeated improvement patents.

Of particular interest for appreciating the way the Regulation seeks to balance contractual freedom and competition goals is the attitude adopted towards "passive" sales. An obligation of the kind envisaged in Article 1(6), *supra*, prevents the licensee from responding to unsolicited orders from the territories of other licensees. This makes commercial sense in so far as some licensees could fail to recover any of the costs put into the venture if they were exposed to such competition, with a resulting disincentive to enter into agreements without protection. However, the restriction on passive sales is clearly capable of inhibiting market integration. Therefore, such restraints may only last for up to five years from the date when the licensed product is first put on the market in the common market by one of the licensees.[58] This applies regardless of the type of agreement. The need to ensure that restrictions on passive sales do not grow into absolute territorial protection is reflected in Article 3(3)(a) of the Regulation, which provides that the exemption will not apply if one or both of the parties are required without any objectively justified reason to refuse to meet orders from users or resellers in their respective territories who would market products in other territories within the common market. This concern to maintain a flow of parallel trade is entirely in keeping with the approach taken by the Court of Justice in *Maize Seeds*.[59]

In addition to the obligations which are to be exempted in Article 1(1), Regulation 240/96 goes on to specify those obligations which will not generally be considered restrictive of competition at all (the "white list" in Article 2) and those which are prohibited (the "black list" in Article 3). As a further indication of the more tolerant approach taken by the Regulation, the white list is longer and the black list shorter than in the legislation it replaces. It also retains the device of an opposition procedure used in its predecessors, so that it is possible

---

[56] For an example of the Commission considering the question of necessary patents in the context of a mixed agreement prior to the enactment of Reg. 240/96, see *Boussois/Interpane*, Dec. 87/123 [1987] O.J. L50/30.

[57] See Robertson, *op. cit.*, n.50, *supra*. There is no Recital in the Regulation which explicitly addresses the rationale for the "necessary patents" test.

[58] Art. 1(2), (3), (4). *cf.* the longer period of exemption conferred upon restrictions against active selling pursuant to Art. 1(1)(5).

[59] See discussion in text accompanying nn.28–32, *supra*.

to put restrictions not falling within white or black lists to the Commission for approval.[60]

The white list, which is not exhaustive,[61] runs to eighteen examples of clauses which will not generally be restrictive of competition. These include obligations on the *licensee*: to maintain the confidentiality of know-how, to observe minimum quality specifications; to pay royalties; to grant, subject to conditions, the licensor a licence in respect of improvements made by the licensee to the licensed technology and to produce minimum quantities of the licensed product. The white-listed clauses also allow the *licensor* to enter reservations such as: the right to exercise the rights conferred by a patent to oppose the exploitation of the technology by the licensee outside the licensed territory; the right to terminate the agreement if the licensee contests the secret or substantial nature of the licensed know-how or challenges the validity of licensed patents within the common market belonging to the licensor or undertakings connected with him; and to terminate the licence agreement of a patent if the licensee raises the claim that such a patent is not necessary.

The last-mentioned rights of the licensor in relation to termination of the agreement reveal an interesting approach to no-challenge clauses. In previous block exemptions clauses prohibiting a licensee from mounting a challenge to the validity of a patent or the secrecy of know-how were black-listed outright. However, Regulation 240/96 does not include them in its Article 3 list.[62] Instead, Article 4(2) expressly mentions no-challenge clauses as a particular instance of obligations capable of exemption via the opposition procedure. However, licensees will remain discouraged from trying to challenge validity in cases where the licence includes a white-listed reservation of a right on the part of the licensor to terminate the agreement.

Among the clauses black-listed in Article 3 are price restrictions on any party, any obligation on the licensee to assign in whole or in part to the licensor rights to improvements to or new applications of the licensed technology; restrictions relating to customers where the parties were competing manufacturers before the grant of the licence[63]; and any obligations requiring one or both parties in effect to impede parallel imports or exports. Tying clauses, such as a requirement on the licensee to procure goods or services which are not necessary for a technically satisfactory exploitation of the licensed technology, were black-listed in previous block exemptions but no longer appear in Article 3 of Regulation 240/96. Instead, they are another example specifically mentioned in Article 4(2) as open to approval through the opposition procedure.

The opposition procedure machinery had in fact been omitted by the Commission in its first draft of Regulation 240/96, but was reinstated in the face

---

[60] The Commission has only four months within which to raise objection, the time-limit being six months in previous block exemptions.

[61] Recital 18.

[62] Mindful, perhaps, of the position taken by the Court of Justice in Case 65/86 *Bayer v. Süllhöfer*, n.42, *supra*.

[63] Since the Regulation is silent in relation to the position where the parties were not previously competing manufacturers, restrictions as to customers need to be notified in accordance with the opposition procedure.

of commercial reaction.[64] However, it may be noted that few applications are in fact made by this route and its real utility may be in doubt.[65] The Commission's own scepticism is discernible in Article 12(1), whereby it is obliged to undertake regular assessments of the application of the Regulation, and in particular of the opposition procedure.

Finally, it should be noted that the Commission is empowered, as was the case in predecessor regulations, to withdraw the benefit of the exemption in accordance with Article 7. In addition to those situations previously mentioned where attempts are made to impose absolute territorial protection by various means, withdrawal is specifically mentioned as a possibility where the licensee's market share in the licensed territory exceeds 40 per cent of the market in identical products or services, or services considered equivalent by users, or where the licensee refuses, without objectively justified reasons, to meet unsolicited demand from users or resellers in the territory of other licensees.

The Commission's attitude to the impact of Article 81 on the licensing of intellectual property has undergone significant phases of reconstruction and revision.[66] The Technology Transfer Regulation represents a far greater recognition of the pro-competitive features of intellectual property than was the case, say, in the 1970s. Whilst not strictly applicable to other forms of intellectual property licensing, its approach has been expressly taken into account by the Commission when determining cases in other fields.[67]

The application of Article 82

It has been seen that assignments and licences of intellectual property rights can be subject to Article 81. Article 82 may impose limits on the unilateral exercise of such rights.

The issue of the extent to which an intellectual property right itself is evidence of the existence of a dominant position has already been referred to in the introduction to this chapter.[68] Two principal questions arise once the existence of a dominant position is established: is the existence of rights granted under national intellectual property laws capable of constituting an abuse, and can exercise of those rights constitute an abuse?

The answer to the first question was considered in two references to the Court of Justice, from Italy in *CICRA v. Renault*[69] and from the United Kingdom High Court in *Volvo v. Veng*,[70] in answer to which the Court handed down its judgments on the same day. Renault and Volvo had the benefit of design copyright in the respective Member States for motor vehicle spare parts, as well as for complete motor vehicles. Both manufacturers sought to rely on their rights

---

[64] See Saltzman, "The new Technology Transfer block exemption regulation" (1996) 9 E.I.P.R. 506.
[65] See Robertson, *op. cit.*, n.50, *supra*. The block exemption on vertical restraints 1999 discards the procedure: see Chap. 20, *supra*.
[66] See Maher, *op. cit.*, n.45, *supra*.
[67] *e.g. Re SICASOV*; [1999] O.J. L4/27; [1999] 4 C.M.L.R. 192, a decision made by the Commission in respect of plant breeders' rights.
[68] See text accompanying notes 4–8, *supra*.
[69] Case 53/87 *CICRA and Maxicar v. Renault*, n.24, *supra*.
[70] Case 238/87 *Volvo v. Erik Veng (UK) Ltd*, n.24, *supra*.

to prevent other automotive component manufacturers from copying their spare parts. The effect of this, given the nature of car spare parts which demands that, except for the most standard components, a spare part must be an exact copy of the manufacturer's original design, was to exclude any competition for the manufacturer's own spare parts. The spare part manufacturers argued in both cases that this constituted an abuse of a dominant position.

The Court ruled, citing *Keurkoop v. Nancy Kean Gifts*,[71] that in the absence of Community standardisation or harmonisation of laws, it was solely a matter for national law to determine what protection to grant to designs, even for such functional items as car spare parts. Moreover, it was part of the subject-matter of such rights that the owner be allowed to prevent others from manufacturing, selling or importing spare parts which copied such designs. Accordingly, taking action to protect the existence of the intellectual property right could not constitute an abuse of a dominant position.[72]

The Court then turned to deal with the second question, namely the effect of Article 82 on the exercise of intellectual property rights. It held that exercise of a right could be an abuse, for example arbitrary refusal to supply spare parts to an independent repairer, unfair pricing of spare parts or refusal to continue supplying spare parts for a model of motor vehicle of which many were still in circulation.[73] As there was no evidence of such conduct in either of the cases referred to the Court, no finding of abuse was made.

These cases must, however, be read in the light of the Court's subsequent judgment in the *Magill* cases,[74] without doubt the most significant of the developments in relation to the possible application of Article 82 to the exercise of intellectual property rights. It will be recalled[75] that this saga involved an attempt by an Irish magazine publisher (Magill) to introduce a weekly advance TV listings magazine to cover all TV programmes capable of being received in both the Republic of Ireland and Northern Ireland. This involved programmes of three authorities: the Irish State broadcaster RTE, the BBC which is the United Kingdom equivalent and the Independent Broadcasting Authority which was responsible for the output from independent television in the United Kingdom. Each of these authorities owned copyright in the advance listings of their programmes[76] and produced their own separate weekly advance guide. In response to advance listings being published in the Magill guide, each obtained an interim injunction in the Irish High Court preventing its future publication in breach of their respective copyrights. The Commission launched an investigation on receiving a complaint from Magill and concluded that the exercise of

---

[71] Case 144/81 *Keurkoop v. Nancy Kean Gifts* [1982] E.C.R. 2853.

[72] Case 53/87 *CICRA and Maxicar v. Renault*, n.24, *supra*, paras 10, 11 and 15 of judgment; Case 238/87 *Volvo v. Erik Veng (UK) Ltd*, n.24, *supra*, paras 7 and 8 of judgment.

[73] Case 53/87 *CICRA and Maxicar v. Renault*, n.24, *supra*, para. 18 of judgment; Case 238/87 *Volvo v. Erik Veng (UK) Ltd*, n.24, *supra*, para. 9 of judgment.

[74] Cases C–241–242/91P *Radio Telefis Eireann (RTE) and Independent Television Publications Ltd (ITP) v. Commission*, n.11, *supra*.

[75] These cases are also discussed in the wider context of abusive refusals to supply under Art. 82 in Chap. 21, *supra*.

[76] In the case of the IBA, through its subsidiary Independent Television Publications Ltd

copyright in this way constituted a breach of Article 82, as it exceeded the scope of the specific subject matter of that right.[77]

On appeal by the broadcasting authorities, the Court of First Instance[78] upheld the Commission's finding of an abuse of a dominant position. Noting the Court of Justice's decisions in *CICRA v. Renault* and *Volvo v. Veng*, the Court of First Instance agreed that ". . . in principle the protection of the specific subject-matter of a copyright entitles the copyright holder to reserve the exclusive right to reproduce the protected work".[79] However, the Court continued, the exclusive right to reproduce could constitute an abuse ". . . when, in the light of the details of each individual case, it is apparent that the right is exercised in such ways and circumstances as in fact to pursue an aim manifestly contrary to the objectives of [Article 82]. In that event, the copyright is no longer exercised in a manner which corresponds to its essential function, within the meaning of [Article 30], which is to protect the moral rights in the work and ensure a reward for the creative effort . . ."[80]

In this case, because each of the broadcasters allowed publication of their programme listings in other publications, such as newspapers, on a day-by-day basis and allowed their publications in other Member States on a weekly basis, it appeared to the Court of First Instance that they were using their respective copyrights to exclude the competition in their own Member States for their own weekly programmes listings magazines. It was held that this went beyond what was necessary to fulfil the essential function of the copyright in question.

The perceived threat to intellectual property protection from this judgment led to a further appeal to the Court of Justice by RTE and ITP. Despite a lengthy and closely argued Opinion to the contrary from Advocate General Gulmann, the Court of Justice confirmed the finding of abuse. However, the reasoning of the Court does not establish any clear doctrinal position. Indeed, it said very little beyond concurrence with the decision of the Court of First Instance and made no response to the detailed critique presented by the Advocate General. Citing its earlier judgment in *Volvo v. Veng*, the Court noted that the exercise of an exclusive right by the proprietor may, "in exceptional circumstances", involve abusive conduct.[81] Turning to the particular circumstances of the *Magill* case, the Court found that

"the appellants' refusal to provide basic information by relying on national copyright provisions thus prevented the appearance of a new product, a comprehensive weekly guide to television programmes, which the appellants did not offer and for which there was a potential consumer demand. Such refusal constitutes an abuse . . ."[82]

---

[77] *Re Magill TV Guide* [1989] O.J. L78/43; the Commission's decision only devoted the most cursory attention to the copyright issue however, see p. 50.

[78] Case T–69/89 *RTE v. Commission* [1991] E.C.R. II-485; [1991] 4 C.M.L.R. 586; Case T–70/89 *BBC v. Commission* [1991] E.C.R. II-535; [1991] 4 C.M.L.R. 669; Case T–76/89 *ITP v. Commission* [1991] E.C.R. II-575; [1991] 4 C.M.L.R. 745.

[79] Case T–69/89 *RTE v. Commission*, n.78, *supra*, para. 70 of judgment; the same statement is made at para. 57 of Case T–70/89 and para. 55 of Case T–76/89.

[80] Case T–69/89 *RTE v. Commission*, n.78, *supra*, para. 71 of judgment; the same statement is made at para. 58 of Case T–70/89 and para. 56 of Case T–76/89.

[81] Cases C–241–242/91P *RTE and ITP v. Commission*, n.11, *supra*, para. 50.

[82] *ibid.*, para. 54.

No justification for such refusal could be found in either the activity of television broadcasting or in that of publishing television magazines. The conduct of the appellants reserved to themselves the secondary market of weekly television guides by excluding all competition on that market as a result of denying access to the basic information which was the raw material indispensable for the compilation of such a guide.[83]

Questions still remain as to the scope of this ruling. The Court of Justice, by adhering to an ad hoc "exceptional circumstances" approach, sidestepped a number of issues of concern to intellectual property owners and commentators.[84] In particular, it expressly made no comment on the relevance of the tests arising under Article 30 in relation to the specific subject-matter of property rights. Nor was there any elaboration upon the possible justifications that might be available to an owner.[85]

Nevertheless, it appears that the *Magill* judgment is not as radical as defenders of intellectual property rights might at first have feared. It is not easily extrapolated to support claims that proprietors must justify any refusals to grant licences or that there is any principle of "compulsory licensing" being introduced by the back door. To begin with, the Court's formulation of the abuse in terms of the consequences of a monopoly over *information*, rather than the copyright in the *listings*, avoids a full-frontal assault on the underpinning property rights. Moreover, the reference to the effects in a secondary market (the magazine) is closer to the example of refusing spare parts cited as an abuse in *Volvo v. Veng* than it is to a requirement of a compulsory licence in the copyright itself.[86]

Cases since *Magill* also indicate only limited scope for its application. In *Tiercé Ladbroke*[87] the Court of First Instance considered a claim by Ladbroke in Belgium that it was the victim of an unlawful refusal of a licence to broadcast the sound and pictures of French horse races in its Belgian betting shops. The holders of the rights had granted licences for transmission of French races in Germany and Austria but had granted no licences for exploitation in Belgium. The Court of First Instance disposed of Ladbroke's claim as follows:

"In contrast to the position in *Magill*, where the refusal to grant a licence to the applicant prevented it from entering the market in comprehensive television guides, in this case the applicant is not only present in, but has the largest share of, the main betting market on which the product in question, namely sound and pictures, is offered to consumers whilst the *sociétés de courses*, the owners of the intellectual property rights, are not present on that market. Accordingly, in the absence of direct or indirect exploitation by the *sociétés de courses* of their intellectual property rights on the Belgian market,

---

[83] *ibid.*, paras 55–56, citing Cases 6 and 7/73 *Commercial Solvents v. Commission* [1974] E.C.R. 223; [1974] 1 C.M.L.R. 309.

[84] See Greaves, "Magill est arrivé . . . RTE and ITP v. Commission of the European Communities" [1995] 4 E.C.L.R. 244.

[85] For the general rules about objective justification in relation to abuse of a dominant position, see Chap. 21, *supra*.

[86] But *cf*. Advocate General Gulmann who rejected this comparison: see paras 99–102 of his Opinion.

[87] Case T–504/93 *Tiercé Ladbroke v. Commission*, n.24, *supra*. The facts of this case and the problems of market definition it raised under Art. 82 were discussed in Chap. 21, *supra*.

their refusal to supply cannot be regarded as involving any restriction of competition on the Belgian market.

Even if it were assumed that the presence of the *sociétés de courses* on the Belgian market in sound and pictures were not, in this case, a decisive factor for the purposes of applying [Article 82] of the Treaty, that provision would not be applicable in this case. The refusal to supply the applicant could not fall within the prohibition laid down by [Article 82] unless it concerned a product or service which was either essential for the exercise of the activity in question, in that there was no real or potential substitute, or was a new product whose introduction might be prevented, despite specific, constant and regular potential demand on the part of consumers."[88]

Magill is thus kept firmly within the confines of its own factual situation. Indeed, the Court of Justice has taken a similarly restrictive view itself, albeit in a case not involving intellectual property at all.[89]

An unresolved issue concerns the relevance, if any, of the nature of the copyrighted material in *Magill* to its outcome. In his Opinion in *Oscar Bronner*,[90] Advocate General Jacobs remarked that the provision of copyright protection for television listings was difficult to justify in terms of rewarding or providing an incentive for creative effort. Even Advocate General Gulmann in *Magill* had conceded that it could reasonably be claimed that the effort involved in drawing up programme listings did not consist of anything more than the setting out on paper of certain information.[91] However, he carefully balanced this by observing that if there is a need under Community law to restrict the copyright protection of specific products, that must be done by rules adopted by the Community legislature.[92] The text of the Court's judgment in *Magill* eschews any reference to the merits of copyright protection, repeating only the customary statement that in the absence of harmonisation such matters are for national laws to decide. However, the suspicion that the lack of creativity in the listings may have made the associated information a "softer" target for the application of Article 82 has implications for other developing areas of technology in which works may be essentially functional and utilitarian in nature.[93]

---

[88] [1997] E.C.R. II-923, paras 130–131.

[89] Case C–7/97 *Oscar Bronner v. Mediaprint* [1998] E.C.R. I–7791; [1999] 4 C.M.L.R. 112. The Court listed the "exceptional" circumstances in *Magill* as: a product (information) indispensable to the carrying on of a person's business (TV guides), refusal of which made it impossible to publish the guide as a new product with potential consumer demand, the refusal having no justification and being likely to exclude all competition in the market for guides. (para. 40). The Court, at para. 41, also reserves its position on whether the case-law on intellectual property is applicable to the exercise of any property right whatever.

[90] *ibid.*, para. 63 of Opinion.

[91] [1995] E.C.R. I–743, para. 123 of Opinion.

[92] *ibid.*, para. 125.

[93] See Stamatoudi, "The hidden agenda in Magill and its impact on new technologies" (1998) 1 Journal of World Intellectual Property, 153. She cites multimedia products and services, Internet, virtual reality and interactive television as examples: p. 171.

Intellectual property and the interplay between Articles 28–30, 81 and 82

There are two issues relevant to intellectual property rights to be dealt with here: first, what is the relationship between Articles 81 and 82, and, second, what is the relationship between these two Articles and the provisions on the free movement of goods?

The first issue was dealt with by the Court of First Instance in *Tetra Pak*.[94] The case arose out of the takeover by Tetra Pak, which occupied a dominant position in the Community liquid food packaging market, of one of its competitors, Liquipak. Liquipak was exclusively licensed under an agreement which complied with the provisions of the extant patent licensing block exemption to use a new process for sterilising milk cartons prior to filling. The effect of the takeover was that Tetra Pak also acquired exclusive rights to use the new process, to the exclusion of its other competitors. One of these complained to the Commission which, after investigation, held that the acquisition of exclusive patent rights was an abuse of Tetra Pak's dominant position.[95] It also indicated that had Tetra Pak not renounced exclusivity under the patent licence, thus allowing the patent owner to license its competitors under the patent as well, it would have withdrawn the benefit of the patent licensing block exemption using its powers under that Regulation.[96]

This decision was challenged by Tetra Pak which argued that as Articles 81 and 82 pursue the same objective, it was not open to the Commission to apply Article 82 to an agreement exempted under the provisions of the block exemption. The Court of First Instance rejected this argument holding that Articles 81 and 82 "constitute, in the scheme of the Treaty, two independent legal instruments addressing different situations".[97] It ruled that although the acquisition of an exclusive patent licence by a dominant business could not constitute an abuse *per se*,[98] in the specific circumstances of this case it did, given that the effect would have been to deprive other businesses of the means of competing with Tetra Pak.[99] To have held otherwise, the Court observed,[1] would have been in effect to incorporate into Article 82 a means of obtaining an exemption from liability for an abuse of a dominant position.

Turning to the second issue, it will be apparent that reliance on intellectual property rights to exclude imports coming from other Member States may fall foul of the E.C. Treaty provisions on both freedom of movement[2] and competition. In the *Maize Seeds* case,[3] the Government of the United Kingdom argued, *inter alia*, that the licensing agreement in question could not be regarded as

---

[94] Case T–51/89 *Tetra Pak Rausing v. Commission* [1990] E.C.R. II-309; [1991] 4 C.M.L.R. 334.
[95] *Elopak/Tetra Pak* [1988] O.J. L272/77; [1990] 4 C.M.L.R. 47.
[96] A similar power of withdrawal can be found in Art. 7 of the current Technology Transfer Regulation.
[97] [1990] E.C.R. II–309, at para. 22.
[98] *ibid.*, para. 23.
[99] *ibid.*
[1] *ibid.*, para. 25.
[2] See Chap. 13, *supra*.
[3] Case 258/78 n.3, *supra*.

incompatible with Article 85 (now 81) because it would be possible for third parties to invoke Article 30 (now 28) in order to prevent the enforcement of the terms designed to achieve absolute territorial protection. In other words, even if the parties had anti-competitive intentions, these would inevitably have been frustrated through the operation of the exhaustion of rights principle. Rejecting that argument, the Court of Justice said it failed to take into account:

". . . the fact that one of the powers of the Commission is to ensure, pursuant to Article 85 of the Treaty and the regulations adopted in implementation thereof, that agreements and concerted practices between undertakings do not have the object or the effect of restricting or distorting competition, and that that power of the Commission is not affected by the fact that persons or undertakings subject to such restrictions are in a position to rely upon the provisions of the Treaty relating to the free movement of goods in order to escape such restrictions".[4]

The prohibitions in Article 28 and in Articles 81 and 82, therefore, apply cumulatively.

What if the application of the two sets of rules to the exercise of an intellectual property right leads to conflicting results? This ought to be unlikely in the case of attempts to exclude parallel imports, since the exhaustion of rights principle seems to equate with the authorities on absolute territorial protection. Moreover, the idea of the specific subject-matter of rights has been applied to the scrutiny of licensing agreements for the purposes of Article 81.[5] Its explicit application in the conceptualisation of abuse in the context of Article 82 is less consistent.[6] However, in drawing a line between objectively justified conduct on the one hand and abuse on the other it would be remarkable if the notion of abuse as something abnormal did not draw upon the concept of the specific subject matter of an intellectual property right in order to establish what is normal and acceptable. But given that the dispute in a case involving an Article 82 case is likely to focus on one party's behaviour, there is less room for overt discussion by the Court of the legislation upon which intellectual property rights are based. This opportunity is much more directly available in cases where a "Euro-defence" is argued on the footing of Article 30.[7]

Practical matters also affect the interplay between the Treaty provisions. As the Court pointed out in the passage quoted from *Maize Seeds* above, it is a feature of the competition regime that the Commission enjoys executive powers which can be used against individual undertakings. Anti-competitive exploitation of intellectual property may, for example, be the subject of an order under Article 3(1) of Regulation 17 to terminate an infringement of Article 81 or Article 82; or it may provide grounds for the imposition of a fine under Article

---

[4] [1982] E.C.R. at 2070.
[5] See Case 193/83 *Windsurfing International*, n.38, *supra*, and accompanying text.
[6] Advocate General Gulmann argued that the concept of essential function is an *auxiliary* concept which enables the Court of Justice to carry out the assessment of where to draw the balance between protecting intellectual property or protecting free movement or competition. He went on to say that the balance must always be in favour of the intellectual property rights. See Cases C–241–242/91P *RTE and ITP v. Commission*, n.11, *supra*, paras 79–80 of Opinion.
[7] See also Stamatoudi, *op.cit.*, n.93, *supra*.

15(2) of the Regulation.[8] No such powers exist in relation to Article 28 (or Article 49 in relation to services). The only action open to the Commission, if national legislation or intellectual property represents an unjustifiable barrier to intra-Community trade, is to bring proceedings under Article 226 against the Member State concerned. Where complaints are lodged with the Commission, it may invoke the *Automec II* doctrine[9] and refuse to handle the case on the basis of a lack of Community interest.[10]

Both the rules on freedom of movement and the rules on competition are directly effective. However, to make out a case under the competition rules, an individual resisting the exercise of an intellectual property right must be able to show that the right is the "subject, the means or the consequence of"[11] an agreement or concerted practice or that its owner is abusing a dominant position in a substantial part of the common market. Where a choice exists, therefore, the absence of the additional ingredients needed for the other actions may still lead Article 28 to strike importers as providing a simpler and surer route to success in national proceedings.[12]

---

[8] For a fuller discussion of the enforcement of competition law, see Chap. 22, *supra*.

[9] Case T–24/90 *Automec v. Commission* [1992] E.C.R. II-2223; [1992] 5 C.M.L.R. 431, discussed more fully in Chap. 22, *supra*.

[10] A series of cases involving collecting societies was spawned in this area, including Case T–5/93 *Roger Tremblay and others v. Commission* [1995] E.C.R. II-185; [1996] 4 C.M.L.R. 305; on appeal as Case C–91/95P [1996] E.C.R. I–5547; [1997] 4 C.M.L.R. 211; Case C–59/96P *Koelman v. Commission* [1997] E.C.R. I–4809. For a sceptical view of the reasons for the Commission's approach see Torremans and Stamatoudi, "Collecting societies: sorry, the Community is no longer interested!" (1997) 22 E.L.Rev. 352.

[11] Case 40/70 *Sirena v. Eda*, n.2, *supra*.

[12] The point was first brought home in the *Deutsche Grammophon* judgment: Case 78/70 [1971] E.C.R. 487; [1971] C.M.L.R. 631.

PART VII: ASPECTS OF SOCIAL LAW AND POLICY

CHAPTER 27

SEX DISCRIMINATION

THE DEVELOPMENT OF THE COMMUNITY RULES

When the EEC Treaty was drawn up, there was a widely held belief among the Member States that the common market would produce better living and working conditions and that a developed set of rules on social policy was unnecessary.[1] Although the Treaty contained a title headed "Social Policy",[2] it was largely programmatic in character, laying down few substantive rules and conferring only limited powers on the Community institutions. One of the provisions of the title on social policy, however, was more adventurous. Article 119 said that "[e]ach Member State shall during the first stage ensure and subsequently maintain the application of the principle that men and women should receive equal pay for equal work". The Court would in due course emphasise that the elimination of discrimination based on sex formed part of the fundamental rights it had a duty to uphold.[3]

Notwithstanding the apparently mandatory terms of Article 119, however, it was not initially taken very seriously and by the expiry of the deadline laid down in it[4] the equal pay principle had not been implemented in some Member States. In 1961, the Member States adopted a resolution on harmonising the pay of men and women which purported to require the complete elimination of discrimination by the end of 1964. Several Member States failed to observe the terms of that resolution and in due course the Commission threatened to institute proceedings under Article 226, although no such proceedings were in fact brought. Following a decision by the Heads of State and Government of the Member States in 1972 to give greater prominence to action in the social field, Article 119 of the Treaty was supplemented in February 1975 by Council Directive 75/117 on the approximation of the laws of the Member States relating to the application of the principle of equal pay for men and women.[5] That Directive gave the Member States a period of one year to take the necessary steps. Shortly after it was adopted, however, the Cour du Travail, Brussels, made a reference to the Court of Justice which was to transform the situation. Gabrielle Defrenne, an air hostess formerly employed by the airline Sabena, had sued her ex-employer in the Belgian courts, claiming compensation for the discrimination she claimed to have suffered as a result of not having been paid as much as male "cabin stewards" doing the same work as her. The national court wanted to know whether Article 119 of the Treaty had direct effect and, if so, from what date.

---

[1] See Shanks, "The social policy of the European Communities" (1977) 14 C.M.L.Rev 375; Nielsen and Szyszczak, *The Social Dimension of the European Union* (3rd ed., 1997), p. 19.

[2] Arts 117–128 EEC.

[3] See Case 149/77 *Defrenne v. Sabena* [1978] E.C.R. 1365, para. 27; [1978] 3 C.M.L.R. 312. For a detailed analysis of this area, see Ellis, *EC Sex Equality Law* (2nd ed., 1998).

[4] January 1, 1962.

[5] [1975] O.J. L45/19.

The Court began its judgment in the second *Defrenne* case[6] by emphasising that Article 119 pursued a double aim. First, it sought to avoid employers in States which had implemented the equal pay principle from being placed at a competitive disadvantage by comparison with employers in States which had not.[7] Secondly, the Court said, Article 119 "forms part of the social objectives of the Community, which is not merely an economic union, but is at the same time intended, by common action, to ensure social progress and seek the constant improvement of the living and working conditions of their peoples, as is emphasized by the Preamble to the Treaty".[8] The economic and social aim of the article showed that the principle of equal pay formed part of the foundations of the Community. On the question of direct effect, the Court drew a distinction between "first, direct and overt discrimination which may be identified solely with the aid of the criteria based on equal work and equal pay referred to by the article in question and, secondly, indirect and disguised discrimination which can only be identified by reference to more explicit implementing provisions of a Community and national character".[9] Although Article 119 could not have direct effect in cases involving discrimination of the second type, the Court held that it did have that effect in cases involving discrimination of the first type, which could be "detected on the basis of a purely legal analysis of the situation".[10] The Court added that the question whether the employer was in the public or the private sector was irrelevant. In other words, Article 119 was capable of producing direct effect in both the vertical and the horizontal senses.[11]

As Advocate General Warner was subsequently to point out,[12] the use of the adjectives "direct and overt" to describe the type of discrimination in respect of which Article 119 produced direct effect was unfortunate. Although the distinction between the two types of discrimination is an important one, it is not normally treated as relevant to the question whether a rule prohibiting discrimination has direct effect. The crucial question for that purpose is whether the discrimination can be detected by a court through legal analysis. Thus, in *Worringham and Humphreys v. Lloyds Bank*,[13] the Court modified the language it had used in *Defrenne*, ruling that Article 119 applied directly "to all forms of discrimination which may be identified solely with the aid of the criteria of equal work and equal pay referred to by the article in question, without national or Community measures being required to define them with greater precision in order to permit of their application".[14]

---

[6] Case 43/75 *Defrenne v. Sabena* [1976] E.C.R. 455; [1976] 2 C.M.L.R. 98.

[7] This concern, felt especially keenly by France, was the reason for the inclusion of Art. 119 in the Treaty: see Ellis, *op. cit.,* pp. 59–60.

[8] Para. 10. The Court was later to rule that the economic aim of Art. 119 was secondary to its social aim: see Joined Cases C–270/97 and C–271/97 *Deutsche Post A.G. v. Sievers and Schrage,* judgment of February 10, 2000, para. 57; Case C–50/96 *Deutsche Telekom v. Schröder,* judgment of February 10, 2000, para. 57.

[9] Para. 18.

[10] Para. 21.

[11] See also Case C–333/97 *Lewen v. Denda*, judgment of October 21, 1999, para. 26.

[12] See Case 69/80 *Worringham and Humphreys v. Lloyds Bank* [1981] E.C.R. 767; [1981] 2 C.M.L.R. 1; Case 96/80 *Jenkins v. Kingsgate* [1981] E.C.R. 911; [1981] 2 C.M.L.R. 24.

[13] *supra.*

[14] Para. 23.

As for the date from which Article 119 produced direct effect, the Court pointed out in *Defrenne* that the express terms of the article required the equal pay principle to be secured by the original Member States by the end of the first stage of the transitional period. Being laid down in the Treaty itself, that deadline could not be affected by the Member States' 1961 resolution. For the Member States which joined the Community on January 1, 1973, the equal pay principle should have been fully effective since that date since no transitional provisions had been laid down in the Accession Treaty. Neither deadline was affected by Directive 75/117. However, Ireland and the United Kingdom underlined the serious economic repercussions, including the bankruptcy of many employers, which might result from such a ruling. The Court accepted that the behaviour of several of the Member States and of the Commission might have led employers to believe that they did not have to comply with Article 119 until it had been implemented in national law. The Court therefore ruled that, for reasons of legal certainty, the direct effect of Article 119 could not be invoked in support of claims concerning pay periods prior to the date of the judgment (April 8, 1976), except in the case of those who had already brought proceedings. The *Defrenne* case represented the first occasion on which the Court limited what is sometimes called the temporal effect of a judgment in this way.[15]

The Court's decision in the *Defrenne* case made Directive 75/117 largely redundant. Admittedly, the directive required men and women to be paid equal pay not just for equal work but also for work of equal value. However, in *Jenkins v. Kingsgate*,[16] the Court stated that the equal pay principle laid down in the directive "in no way alters the content or scope of that principle as defined in the Treaty". In *Murphy v. Bord Telecom Eireann*,[17] the Court was asked whether Article 119 entitled a worker to claim equal pay with someone whose work was of lower value but who was nevertheless paid more than the complainant. In answering that question in the affirmative, the Court made it clear that Article 119 required men and women to be paid equal pay, not just for equal work, but also "in the case of work of equal value". There are, however, at least two respects in which the directive may be regarded as facilitating the application of the equal pay principle. One is that it protects an employee who seeks to enforce that principle from dismissal.[18] The other is that it entitles employees who claim that they are not being paid as much as other employees performing work of equal value to ask an independent authority to assess the value of their respective jobs.[19] This is a task which national courts might be unable to carry out. In the absence of such an assessment, the equal pay principle might therefore be deprived of direct effect.

---

[15] The device is employed by the Court in exceptional cases only, where pressing considerations of legal certainty call for a restriction on the effect which a judgment of a court of law would normally be expected to have. Another example of its use is provided by the notorious *Barber* case, discussed below. See further Chap. 4.

[16] *supra,* para. 22.

[17] Case 157/86 [1988] E.C.R. 673, para. 9; [1988] 1 C.M.L.R. 879.

[18] Art. 5.

[19] See Case 61/81 *Commission v. United Kingdom* [1982] E.C.R. 2601.

THE EQUAL TREATMENT DIRECTIVES AND CHANGES TO THE TREATY

Directive 75/117 was the first in a series of directives on equal treatment for men and women. It was followed by Directive 76/207 on the implementation of the principle of equal treatment for men and women as regards access to employment, vocational training and promotion and working conditions.[20] As its title suggests, Directive 76/207 laid down a principle of equal treatment extending beyond pay to a range of other matters connected with employment. In principle, however, it did not cover matters of social security,[21] contemplating instead further action by the Council to ensure equal treatment in that field. The Council accordingly adopted Directive 79/7,[22] providing protection to the working population and to retired or invalided workers and self-employed persons[23] against discrimination on the ground of sex in statutory schemes offering protection against certain specified risks.[24] Article 7(1) contained a lengthy list of matters which Member States were permitted to exclude from the scope of the directive. Particularly noteworthy was the first item on the list, "the determination of pensionable age for the purposes of granting old-age and retirement pensions and the possible consequences thereof for other benefits". A similar exclusion[25] was included in Directive 86/378 on the implementation of the principle of equal treatment for men and women in occupational social security schemes.[26] These were defined as "schemes not governed by Directive 79/7 whose purpose is to provide workers, whether employees or self-employed, in an undertaking or group of undertakings, area of economic activity, occupational sector or group of sectors with benefits intended to supplement the benefits provided by statutory social security schemes or to replace them, whether membership of such schemes is compulsory or optional".[27] Developments in the Court's case-law on the scope of Article 119 (now, after amendment, Article 141) of the Treaty would subsequently require Directive 86/378 to be modified.[28] Some of the directives referred to in this paragraph are discussed in more detail below.

The Single European Act inserted into the EEC Treaty (as it then was) a new Article 118a (now 138) giving the Council specific authority to act in the field of the health and safety of workers.[29] No changes were made to Article 119. By the

---

[20] [1976] O.J. L39/40.

[21] In Case C–116/94 *Meyers v. Adjudication Officer* [1995] E.C.R. I–2131, para. 13; [1996] 1 C.M.L.R. 461; [1995] All E.R. (E.C.) 705, the Court held that a benefit scheme "may come within the scope of the directive if its subject-matter is access to employment, including vocational training and promotion, or working conditions".

[22] [1979] O.J. L6/24.

[23] See Art. 2.

[24] See Art. 3.

[25] See Art. 9(1)(a).

[26] [1986] O.J. L225/40. On the application of the principle of equal treatment to the self-employed, see further Dir. 86/613; [1986] O.J. L359/56.

[27] Art. 2(1).

[28] See Dir. 96/97; [1997] O.J. L46/20. The relevant case-law is considered below.

[29] The Court gave a broad interpretation to the scope of Art. 118a in Case C–84/94 *United Kingdom v. Council* [1996] E.C.R. I–5755; [1996] 3 C.M.L.R. 671, where the validity of Dir. 93/104 concerning certain aspects of the organisation of working time [1993] O.J. L307/18, was largely upheld.

time of the negotiations which led to the Treaty on European Union, many Member States had formed the view that the Treaty provisions on social policy, including Article 119, needed a much more thorough overhaul. The United Kingdom was strongly opposed to any strengthening of the Treaty in this area, so instead a Protocol on Social Policy was annexed at Maastricht to the E.C. Treaty. In that protocol, the United Kingdom agreed with the other Member States that they could make use of the institutions and mechanisms of the Treaty in order to give effect to the provisions of an Agreement on Social Policy annexed to the protocol. Those provisions concerned matters such as working conditions and the labour market and they included a slightly amended version of Article 119, although the original version of that article remained in force. Neither the Agreement itself nor any measures taken under it were to apply in the United Kingdom, which would not take part in the adoption of such measures.

Although the Protocol and Agreement on Social Policy gave rise to a good deal of controversy, the Agreement resulted in little new legislation.[30] Following a change of government in the United Kingdom, the Protocol and Agreement were repealed by the Treaty of Amsterdam and new versions of Articles 117 to 120 (now renumbered Articles 136 to 143) were inserted in the E.C. Treaty.[31] In addition, the statement of the Community's task in Article 2 E.C. was amended to include a reference to promoting equality between men and women. A new second paragraph was also added to Article 3 E.C. stating: "In all the activities referred to in this Article, the Community shall aim to eliminate inequalities, and to promote equality, between men and women".

The new version of Article 119, now Article 141, agreed at Amsterdam contains some significant alterations to the original text and goes further in some respects than the corresponding provision of the Agreement on Social Policy. It provides as follows:

"1. Each Member State shall ensure that the principle of equal pay for male and female workers for equal work or work of equal value is applied.

2. For the purpose of this Article, 'pay' means the ordinary basic or minimum wage or salary and any other consideration, whether in cash or in kind, which the worker receives directly or indirectly, in respect of his employment, from his employer.

Equal pay without discrimination based on sex means:

(a) that pay for the same work at piece rates shall be calculated on the basis of the same unit of measurement;

(b) that pay for work at time rates shall be the same for the same job.

3. The Council, acting in accordance with the procedure referred to in Article 251, and after consulting the Economic and Social Committee, shall adopt measures to ensure the application of the principle of equal opportunities and equal treatment of men and women in matters of employment and

---

[30] For a catalogue, see Weatherill and Beaumont, *EU Law* (3rd ed., 1999), pp. 753–754. One significant measure adopted under the Agreement was Dir. 97/80 on the burden of proof in cases of discrimination based on sex; [1998] O.J. L14/6. That Directive is considered below.

[31] The directives made under the agreement were amended and extended to the United Kingdom on the basis of Art. 100 (now 94) E.C. For the amendments to Dir. 97/80, see Dir. 98/52; [1998] O.J. L205/66.

occupation, including the principle of equal pay for equal work or work of equal value.

4. With a view to ensuring full equality in practice between men and women in working life, the principle of equal treatment shall not prevent any Member State from maintaining or adopting measures providing for specific advantages in order to make it easier for the under-represented sex to pursue a vocational activity or to prevent or compensate for disadvantages in professional careers."

By making it clear that the Treaty requires equal pay not only for equal work but also for work of equal value, Article 141(1) endorses the decision of the Court in *Murphy*, referred to above. Article 141(3) provides a specific legal basis for the adoption by the Council of legislation on equal treatment for men and women. To that extent it overlaps with another provision introduced at Amsterdam, Article 13 E.C., which authorises the Council, within the limits of the powers conferred by the Treaty on the Community, to "take appropriate action to combat discrimination based on sex, racial or ethnic origin, religion or belief, disability, age or sexual orientation". Before the Treaty of Amsterdam, Council legislation on equal treatment for men and women had been based on the general powers contained in Articles 100 (now 94) or 235 (now 308). Article 141(4) allows the Member States to pursue a policy of positive or affirmative action in favour of "the under-represented sex". Notwithstanding the gender-neutral language of that provision, a declaration agreed at Amsterdam stated that "Member States should, in the first instance, aim at improving the situation of women in working life". Article 141(4) seems to represent a response to a controversial decision of the Court of Justice, discussed below.

THE MEANING OF "PAY"

Article 141 prohibits discrimination between men and women in relation to "pay", a term defined remarkably broadly by the first paragraph of the article. The Court's case-law has been equally expansive. In *R. v. Secretary of State for Employment, ex parte Seymour-Smith and Perez*,[32] the Court reaffirmed that "the concept of pay . . . comprises any other consideration, whether in cash or in kind, whether immediate or future, provided that the worker receives it, albeit indirectly, in respect of his employment from his employer".[33] Thus, in *Garland v. British Rail Engineering*,[34] the Court held that the concept encompassed special travel facilities granted by an employer to its former employees on their retirement, even though it was not under any contractual obligation to do so. It has been held to extend to a redundancy payment,[35] maternity pay[36] and compensation for unfair dismissal.[37]

---

[32] Case C–167/97 [1999] E.C.R. I–623.

[33] Para. 23.

[34] Case 12/81 [1982] E.C.R. 359; [1982] 1 C.M.L.R. 696.

[35] Case C–262/88 *Barber* [1990] E.C.R. I–1889; [1990] 2 C.M.L.R. 513.

[36] Case C–342/93 *Gillespie and Others v. Northern Health and Social Services Board and Others* [1996] E.C.R. I–475; [1996] 2 C.M.L.R. 969; [1996] All E.R. (E.C.) 284. The Court held that this did not mean that women could claim full pay during maternity leave, only an amount which was enough to ensure that the purpose of the leave was not undermined.

[37] *Seymour-Smith, supra.*

A question which has confronted the Court with particularly complex issues is whether Article 141 covers pensions.[38] In the first *Defrenne* case,[39] the Court held that Article 141 did not cover social security schemes, including pensions, which were governed by legislation and which were determined "less by the employment relationship between the employer and the worker than by considerations of social policy". However, in *Bilka v. Weber von Hartz*,[40] the Court concluded that an occupational pension scheme set up by agreement between an employer and its employees did fall within the scope of Article 141 where it supplemented the benefits paid under a statutory scheme with additional benefits financed exclusively by the employer. The supplementary nature of the scheme at issue in *Bilka* left unclear the status of occupational schemes which took the place of a legislative scheme. That was the question the Court was asked to resolve in *Barber*.[41] Mr Barber had been made redundant by his employer at the age of 52. Had he been a woman, he would have received an immediate pension. However, under the rules of the scheme he was not entitled to a pension until he reached 62, the normal pensionable age for male employees like Mr Barber under his employer's pension scheme. The Court ruled that this was inconsistent with Article 141. Occupational pension schemes of the type in question[42] were, it pointed out, "the result either of an agreement between workers and employers or of a unilateral decision taken by the employer. They are wholly financed by the employer or by both the employer and the workers without any contribution being made by the public authorities in any circumstances". Article 141 therefore prevented the payment of pensions under such schemes at ages which varied according to the sex of the employee.[43]

The pensionable ages laid down by the disputed scheme had been fixed by reference to those laid down by the State scheme which it was designed to replace. As noted above, the maintenance of different pensionable ages for men and women, in both statutory and occupational social security schemes, appeared to have been sanctioned by the Community legislature.[44] The Court recognised that it might therefore legitimately have been thought that schemes such as the one at issue in *Barber* were not in this respect subject to the principle of equal treatment. To avoid upsetting the financial balance of such schemes, the Court ruled that Article 141 "may not be relied upon in order to claim entitlement to a pension with effect from a date prior to that of this judgment", except in the case of those who had already made a claim.

---

[38] See Whiteford, "Lost in the mists of time. The ECJ and occupational pensions" (1995) 32 C.M.L. Rev. 801; Fredman, "The poverty of equality: pensions and the ECJ" (1996) 25 I.L.J. 91.

[39] Case 80/70 [1971] E.C.R. 445, para. 8; [1974] 1 C.M.L.R. 494.

[40] Case 170/84 [1986] E.C.R. 1607; [1986] 2 C.M.L.R. 701.

[41] Case C–262/88 [1990] E.C.R. I–1889; [1990] 2 C.M.L.R. 513.

[42] *i.e.* so-called "contracted-out" schemes. For an explanation of this term, see Advocate General van Gerven in *Barber* at I–1918–1919.

[43] The Court subsequently held that the funding arrangements made to secure the payment of a pension did not constitute pay for the purposes of Art. 141. It was therefore permissible for those arrangements to be based on actuarial factors which differed according to sex, in particular assumptions about the average life expectancy of men and women: see Case C–152/91 *Neath* v. *Steeper* [1993] E.C.R. I–6935; [1995] 2 C.M.L.R. 357; Case C–200/91 *Coloroll* [1994] E.C.R. I–4389; [1995] 2 C.M.L.R. 357.

[44] See Dir. 79/7, Art. 7(1)(a); Dir. 86/378, Art. 9(1)(a).

In view of the serious financial implications of the judgment, the Court was undoubtedly justified in limiting its temporal effect, but the way in which it chose to do so caused serious confusion. The problem was that the judgment did not make it clear whether equality was henceforward required in relation to *all benefits paid* or only in relation to those paid in respect of *periods of employment completed after the date of the judgment.* Several further references were made to the Court in order to clarify this issue, but, before any of them could be decided, the Member States decided at Maastricht to take the unusual step of annexing a protocol to the E.C. Treaty to resolve the matter. That protocol, which became an integral part of the E.C. Treaty[45] on the entry into force of the Treaty on European Union, provides: "For the purposes of Article 119 [now 141] of this Treaty, benefits under occupational social security schemes shall not be considered as remuneration if and in so far as they are attributable to periods of employment prior to May 17, 1990, except in the case of workers or those claiming under them who have before that date initiated legal proceedings or introduced an equivalent claim under the applicable national law". The Court adopted the same solution in *Ten Oever*,[46] the facts of which took place before the TEU had entered into force, and in several subsequent cases.[47] The result was to reduce the financial implications of the *Barber* judgment to the bare minimum compatible with the terms in which it had been expressed.

The Court later ruled, however, that *Ten Oever* and the *Barber* protocol were concerned only with the benefits paid under an occupational pension scheme, not with the right to belong to such a scheme. It had been clear since the *Bilka* ruling in 1986 that the latter right was also covered by Article 141 because the pay of employees who were not permitted to join would be less than that of members. The temporal effect of *Bilka* had not been limited, so the right to join an occupational pension scheme without discrimination on grounds of sex could be invoked with effect from the date of the judgment in *Defrenne v. Sabena*, when Article 141 began to produce direct effect.[48] The result was not, however, as favourable to employees excluded from membership as might have been hoped. The Court held in *Fisscher*[49] that "the fact that a worker can claim retroactively to join an occupational pension scheme does not allow the worker to avoid paying the contributions relating to the period of membership concerned".

Another issue addressed by the Court in the aftermath of *Barber* was whether an employer could reduce the cost of complying with Article 141 by lowering the benefits paid to existing members of a pension scheme, or whether it had to grant members of the previously disdvantaged sex the same benefits as existing members. The ruling in *Defrenne v. Sabena* suggested that the former approach

---

[45] See Art. 311(ex 239) E.C.
[46] Case C–109/91 [1993] E.C.R. I–4879; [1995] 2 C.M.L.R. 357.
[47] See, *e.g.* Case C–110/91 *Moroni* [1993] E.C.R. I–6591; [1995] 2 C.M.L.R. 357; *Neath v. Steeper, Coloroll, supra.*
[48] See Case C–57/93 *Vroege* [1994] E.C.R. I–4541; [1995] 1 C.M.L.R. 881; Case C–7/93 *Beune* [1994] E.C.R. I–4471; [1995] 3 C.M.L.R. 300; Case C–78/98 *Preston and Others v. Wolverhampton Healthcare NHS Trust and Others,* judgment of May 16, 2000. Member States are not precluded from laying down rules on equal treatment for men and women which are more generous than those contained in the Treaty: *Deutsche Telekom v. Schröder, supra; Deutsche Post AG v. Sievers and Schrage, supra.*
[49] Case C–128/93 [1994] E.C.R. I–4583, para. 37; [1994] 1 C.M.L.R. 881.

(so-called "levelling down") was not an acceptable way of complying with the Treaty. There the Court observed: "since Article 119 [now 141] appears in the context of the harmonisation of working conditions while the improvement is being maintained, the objection that the terms of this article may be observed in other ways than by raising the lowest salaries may be set aside".[50] In *Coloroll*,[51] however, the Court moderated that strict view. It held that, while the scheme had not been changed to eliminate discrimination, the benefits enjoyed by the advantaged sex had to be extended to the disadvantaged one. However, in making the scheme gender-neutral, it was acceptable to reduce the benefits paid to those who were previously in a privileged position. In *Avdel Systems*,[52] the employer had attempted to cushion through transitional arrangements the adverse consequences for its female employees of the introduction of a non-discriminatory scheme, but the Court said that this was not permitted: Article 141 required unlawful discrimination to be eliminated forthwith and in full.

The equal pay principle laid down in Article 141 is a specific expression of the general principle of non-discrimination recognised by the Court. For the purposes of that general principle, discrimination involves the application, without objective justification, of different rules to comparable situations or of the same rule to different situations.[53] In cases involving the effect of Article 141, the question may therefore arise whether the situation of men and women is comparable. An example is *Boyle and Others v. Equal Opportunities Commission*,[54] where the applicants challenged a clause in their employment contract requiring a female employee on maternity leave to refund some of the pay she had received from her employer during that period if she did not return to work after the birth of her child. The point was that workers on other forms of paid leave, such as sick leave, were entitled to the agreed salary without having to undertake to return to work when their leave came to an end. The Court held that this did not involve an infringement of Article 141 because the situation of workers who were pregnant or who had recently given birth could not be compared with that of workers on sick leave.[55]

In *Macarthys v. Smith*,[56] the applicant, a woman, sought to rely on a comparison with a so-called hypothetical male worker. In other words, she argued that Article 141 entitled her to the salary she would have received had she been a man and that it was irrelevant whether there was a man doing the same work. The Court rejected that view, ruling that Article 141 applied only where it

---

[50] [1976] E.C.R. 455, para. 15.

[51] Case C–200/91 [1994] E.C.R. I–4389; [1995] 2 C.M.L.R. 357. See also Case C–28/93 *van den Akker* [1994] E.C.R. I–4527.

[52] Case C–408/92 [1994] E.C.R. I–4435.

[53] See further Chap. 6.

[54] Case C–411/96 [1998] E.C.R. I–6401; [1998] 3 C.M.L.R. 1133. See also Case C–249/97 *Gruber v. Silhouette International Schmied*, judgment of September 14, 1999; Case C–218/98 *Abdoulaye and Others* v. *Régie Nationale des Usines Renault*, judgment of September 16, 1999; Case C–333/97, *Lewen v. Denda*, judgment of October 21, 1999. *cf.* Case C–342/93 *Gillespie and Others v. Northern Health and Social Services Board and Others* [1996] E.C.R. I–475; [1996] 2 C.M.L.R. 969.

[55] The case-law reflects a general reluctance on the part of the Court to compare pregnant women with men: see, *e.g.* Case C–177/88 *Dekker* [1990] E.C.R. I–3941; Case C–32/93 *Webb v. EMO Air Cargo* [1994] E.C.R. I–3567; [1994] 2 C.M.L.R. 729. The protection accorded to pregnant women by Community law is discussed in more detail below.

[56] Case 129/79 [1980] E.C.R. 1275; [1980] 2 C.M.L.R. 205.

was possible to make "concrete appraisals of the work actually performed by employees of different sex in the same establishment or service".[57] The Court did make it clear, however, that it did not matter whether or not the man and woman being compared were employed by the undertaking concerned at the same time. In *Levez v. T H Jennings (Harlow Pools) Ltd*,[58] a woman discovered, on leaving her job, that for part of the time she had been employed she had been paid less than her male predecessor, whose salary had been falsely declared to her by her then employer. She brought proceedings before the Industrial Tribunal in an attempt to recover the arrears. However, under the applicable national legislation a claimant could not claim arrears in respect of a period earlier than two years before the start of the proceedings. The rule was an inflexible one, industrial tribunals having no discretion to extend the two-year period. It would have prevented the applicant from recovering part of the arrears she was seeking. The Court was asked whether a rule of that type was compatible with Article 141 and the Equal Pay Directive. The Court said that such a rule was not in principle open to criticism, but that it could not be applied "where the delay in bringing a claim is attributable to the fact that the employer deliberately misrepresented to the employee the level of remuneration received by persons of the opposite sex performing like work".[59] Otherwise the effect of the rule "would be to facilitate the breach of Community law by an employer whose deceit caused the employee's delay in bringing proceedings for enforcement of the principle of equal pay".[60]

DIRECTIVE 76/207

Notwithstanding the breadth of the definition of "pay" within the meaning of Article 141, that article does not apply to discrimination on grounds of sex concerning other aspects of the working relationship. Thus, in the third *Defrenne* case[61] it was held that Article 141 could not be used to challenge a clause in the employment contract of an air hostess bringing it to an end when she reached the age of 40, even though there was no equivalent clause in the contracts of male cabin attendants doing the same work. Cases of this type are now covered by Directive 76/207, which provides that "there shall be no discrimination what-soever on grounds of sex either directly or indirectly by reference in particular to marital or family status"[62] as regards access to employment, including promotion, and to vocational training and as regards working conditions.[63] There is to be no discrimination on grounds of sex in the conditions for access to jobs,[64] vocational guidance and vocational training[65] or with regard to working conditions,

---

[57] Para. 15.
[58] Case C–326/96 [1999] 2 C.M.L.R. 363. *cf. Preston and Others v. Wolverhampton Healthcare NHS Trust and Others, supra.*
[59] Para. 34.
[60] Para. 32. The Court referred to its case-law to the effect that national procedural rules must not treat claims based on Community law less favourably than similar domestic actions or make Community rights excessively difficult to exercise. See further Chap. 5.
[61] Case 149/77 *Defrenne v. Sabena* [1978] E.C.R. 1365; [1978] 3 C.M.L.R. 312.
[62] Art. 2(1).
[63] Art. 1(1).
[64] Art. 3(1).
[65] Art. 4.

including the conditions governing dismissal.[66] The Court has made it clear that the directive does not make the liability of a person guilty of discrimination conditional on proof of fault.[67]

The material scope of Directive 76/207

The material scope of Directive 76/207 has been interpreted broadly. In the first *Marshall* case,[68] for example, the Court was asked whether the directive permitted an employer to dismiss a female employee when she became entitled to a social security pension, even though she would not have been dismissed at the same age had she been a man because male employees were not entitled to social security pensions until later. It will be remembered that Directive 79/7[69] entitles the Member States to exclude from the equal treatment principle laid down in that directive "the determination of pensionable age for the purposes of granting old-age and retirement pensions . . ." Nevertheless, the Court regarded the *Marshall* case as concerned not with pensions but with dismissal and as falling for that reason within the scope of Directive 76/207. Since the employer's retirement policy treated men and women differently, it involved an infringement of that directive.

Even more dramatic was *P v. S and Cornwall County Council*,[70] where the Court was asked whether Directive 76/207 prohibited discrimination against transsexuals. The applicant, who was born with the physical attributes of a male, was dismissed after a series of operations intended to change his gender. Although Directive 76/207 seems confined to cases of discrimination between men and women, the Court ruled that it prohibited the dismissal of a transsexual for a reason related to a gender reassignment. The Court emphasised that the right not to be discriminated against *on the ground of* one's sex was one of the fundamental rights it a duty to uphold. The directive could not therefore be confined "simply to discrimination based on the fact that a person is of one or other sex".[71] Discrimination arising from a gender reassignment was to be regarded as based essentially on the sex of the person concerned. "To tolerate such discrimination would be tantamount, as regards such a person, to a failure to respect the dignity and freedom to which he or she is entitled, and which the Court has a duty to safeguard".[72]

It was widely thought that the ruling in *P v. S* would lead to discrimination on the ground of sexual orientation being found incompatible with the Community rules on equal treatment. The issue came before the Court in *Grant v. South-West*

---

[66] Art. 5(1).
[67] Case C–177/88 *Dekker* [1990] E.C.R. I–3941; Case C–180/95 *Draehmpaehl v. Urania Immobilienservice* [1997] E.C.R. I–2195; [1997] 3 C.M.L.R. 1107.
[68] Case 152/84 *Marshall v. Southampton and South-West Hampshire Area Health Authority* [1986] E.C.R. 723; [1986] 1 C.M.L.R. 688.
[69] Art. 7(1)(a).
[70] Case C–13/94 [1996] E.C.R. I–2143; [1996] 2 C.M.L.R. 247; [1996] All E.R. (E.C.) 397.
[71] Para. 20.
[72] Para. 22.

Trains,[73] an equal pay case. The respondent was a railway company which granted travel concessions to its employees, their spouses and dependents and to "common law opposite sex" spouses. The applicant was a lesbian who applied for travel concessions for her female cohabitee. Her application was turned down on the basis that concessions were not granted to same-sex cohabitees. On a reference for a preliminary ruling, the Court decided to draw a line in the sand, pointing out that "travel concessions are refused to a male worker if he is living with a person of the same sex, just as they are to a female worker if she is living with a person of the same sex".[74] The Court concluded that, "in the present state of the law within the Community, stable relationships between two persons of the same sex are not regarded as equivalent to marriages or stable relationships outside marriage between persons of opposite sex. Consequently, an employer is not required by Community law to treat the situation of a person who has a stable relationship with a partner of the same sex as equivalent to that of a person who is married to or has a stable relationship outside marriage with a partner of the opposite sex".[75] Although it was not yet in force, the Court found support for that conclusion in Article 13 E.C., introduced at Amsterdam. The Court saw the new provision as confirming that discrimination on the basis of sexual orientation was not caught by the existing rules on equal treatment for men and women. It might be thought desirable, if only in the interests of the coherence of the law, that the Council should make early use of its powers under Article 13 of the Treaty. It is hard to see what grounds of policy could justify prohibiting discrimination against transsexuals but not discrimination against homosexuals.[76]

The Court has also held that Directive 76/207 may in some circumstances protect women against adverse treatment on the ground that they are pregnant. In *Dekker*,[77] the Court ruled that, since only women could become pregnant, to refuse to employ a woman on that ground constituted direct discrimination[78] on the grounds of sex, contrary to the principle of equal treatment laid down in the directive. It later became clear that to dismiss a female employee for a reason connected with pregnancy (such as illness) was also incompatible with the directive if the dismissal took place while the employee concerned was actually

---

[73] Case C–249/96 [1998] E.C.R. I–621; [1998] 1 C.M.L.R. 993. See Barnard, "Some are more equal than others: the decision of the Court of Justice in *Grant v. South-West Trains*" (1998) 1 C.Y.E.L.S. 147; Case T–264/97 *D v. Council*, judgment of January 28, 1999.

[74] Para. 27.

[75] Para. 35.

[76] It may be noted that the European Court of Human Rights has been more receptive to claims by homosexuals than transsexuals, although under the European Convention the issue is predominantly one of privacy rather than discrimination. See *Lustig-Prean and Beckett v. United Kingdom* and *Smith and Grady v. United Kingdom*, judgments of September 27, 1999 (homosexuals); *Sheffield and Horsham v. United Kingdom* (1999) 27 E.H.R.R. 163 (transsexuals).

[77] Case C–177/88 [1990] E.C.R. I–3941.

[78] The significance of the finding of direct discrimination is that the Court has never accepted that such discrimination may be justified on grounds other than those expressly laid down. By contrast, indirect discrimination is permissible if objectively justified: see further below. The case-law does not, however, exclude the possibility that direct discrimination on grounds of sex may also be capable of justification: see Advocate General van Gerven in Case C–132/92 *Birds Eye Walls v. Roberts* [1993] E.C.R. I–5579, 5592–5594; [1993] 3 C.M.L.R. 822; Arnull *The European Union and its Court of Justice* (1999), pp. 499–500; Ellis, *op. cit.*, pp. 134–136.

pregnant[79] or while she was on maternity leave.[80] Once the employee's maternity leave came to an end, however, no distinction was to be drawn between illnesses attributable to pregnancy or confinement and other illnesses. A female employee would only enjoy protection under the directive in those circumstances if she had been subjected to adverse treatment which would not have been accorded to a sick man. The Court has also indicated that a woman employed for a fixed term, or who applies for such employment, might not be protected by the directive if she is or would be prevented by pregnancy from working during a significant part of the term of the contract.[81] In addition, a woman who conceals from a prospective employer the fact that she is pregnant is unlikely to be viewed favourably by the Court.[82]

This case-law has to some extent been overtaken by Directive 92/85 on the safety and health at work of pregnant workers and workers who have recently given birth or are breastfeeding.[83] The directive contains provisions designed to: (a) avoid the exposure of such workers to hazardous agents, processes or working conditions[84]; (b) ensure that such workers are not obliged to perform night work[85]; (c) ensure that such workers are entitled to a continuous period of maternity leave of at least 14 weeks[86] and time off without loss of pay for ante-natal examinations.[87] Provision is also made for the maintenance of rights linked to the employment contract.[88] In particular, a worker on maternity leave is entitled to receive payment and/or an allowance which "guarantees income at least equivalent to that which the worker concerned would receive in the event of a break in her activities on grounds connected with her state of health, subject to any ceiling laid down under national legislation".[89] Article 10 requires the Member States to prohibit the dismissal of workers covered by the directive "during the period from the beginning of their pregnancy to the end of the maternity leave referred to in Article 8(1), save in exceptional cases not connected with their condition which are permitted under national legislation and/or practice and, where applicable, provided that the competent authority has given its consent". The directive does not distinguish between workers employed on fixed-term contracts and those employed for an unlimited term. In laying down a special code to protect pregnant women in the workplace, Directive 92/85 avoids some of the logical difficulties which arise from dealing with such women under the principle of equal treatment. Directive 92/85 is not, however, comprehensive in its coverage. In particular, it does not extend to job applicants or to

---

[79] See Case C–394/96 *Brown v. Rentokil* [1998] E.C.R. I–4185; [1998] 2 C.M.L.R. 1049, overruling Case C–400/95 *Larsson v. Føtex Supermarked* [1997] E.C.R. I–2757; [1997] 2 C.M.L.R. 915.

[80] Case C–179/88 *Handels- og Kontorfunktionærernes Forbund* [1990] E.C.R. I–3979.

[81] See Case C–421/92 *Habermann-Beltermann* [1994] E.C.R. I–1657; [1994] 2 C.M.L.R. 681; Case C–32/93 *Webb v. EMO Air Cargo* [1994] E.C.R. I–3567; [1994] 2 C.M.L.R. 729; Case C–207/98 *Mahlburg v. Land Mecklenburg-Vorpommern* judgment of February 3, 2000.

[82] See *Habermann-Beltermann, supra.*

[83] [1992] O.J. L348/1. The directive is based on Art. 118a (now 138) E.C.

[84] Arts 3–6.

[85] Art. 7.

[86] Art. 8.

[87] Art. 9.

[88] Art. 11. See Case C–333/97 *Lewen v. Denda*, judgment of October 21, 1999.

[89] Art. 11(3).

women refused access to vocational training or promotion[90] on the ground of pregnancy. In cases such as these, Directive 76/207 remains the only Community instrument applicable.

Derogations from the principle of equal treatment

Article 2 of Directive 76/207 contains three derogations from the principle of equal treatment. According to Article 2(2), the directive does not prejudice "the right of Member States to exclude from its field of application those occupational activities and, where appropriate, the training leading thereto, for which, by reason of their nature or the context in which they are carried out, the sex of the worker constitutes a determining factor". By virtue of Article 9(2), Member States must "periodically assess the occupational activities referred to in Article 2(2) in order to decide, in the light of social developments, whether there is justification for maintaining the exclusions concerned. They shall notify the Commission of the results of this assessment".

An attempt to rely on Article 2(2) was made in *Johnston v. Chief Constable of the Royal Ulster Constabulary*,[91] which concerned the legality of the Chief Constable's refusal to renew a female officer's contract as a member of the RUC full-time reserve or to permit her to be trained in the use of firearms. The Court said that, as a derogation from an individual right, Article 2(2) had to be interpreted strictly. None the less, it concluded that, in deciding whether the sex of a police officer was relevant, a Member State was entitled to take into consideration "requirements of public safety in order to restrict general policing duties, in an internal situation characterized by frequent assassinations, to men equipped with fire-arms".[92] The Court emphasised that reliance on Article 2(2) was permitted only where the principle of proportionality had been respected. It was the responsibility of the national court to determine whether that was so here and in particular whether the refusal to renew the applicant's contract could have been avoided "by allocating to women duties which, without jeopardising the aims pursued, can be performed without fire-arms".[93]

It had been suggested, on the basis of safeguard clauses applicable under the Treaty in other contexts, that the directive simply did not apply to measures taken for the purpose of protecting public safety. That suggestion was rejected by the Court, which stated that "the application of the principle of equal treatment for men and women is not subject to any general reservation as regards measures taken on grounds of the protection of public safety, apart from the possible application of Article 224 [now 297] of the Treaty which concerns a wholly exceptional situation . . ."[94] Article 297 applies to measures taken by a Member State "in the event of serious internal disturbances affecting the maintenance of

---

[90] See, *e.g.* Case C–136/95 *CNAVTS v. Thibault* [1998] E.C.R. I–2011; [1998] 2 C.M.L.R. 516.

[91] Case 222/84 [1986] E.C.R. 1651; [1986] 3 C.M.L.R. 240. See also Case 165/82 *Commission v. United Kingdom* [1983] E.C.R. 3431; [1984] 1 C.M.L.R. 44; Case 318/86 *Commission v. France* [1988] E.C.R. 3559; Case C–273/97 *Sirdar v. The Army Board* [1999] 3 C.M.L.R. 559; Case C–285/98 *Kreil v. Bundesrepublik Deutschland,* judgment of January 11, 2000.

[92] Para. 40.

[93] Para. 39.

[94] Para. 27. See also *Sirdar, supra,* para. 19; *Kreil, supra,* paras 16–18.

law and order, in the event of war, serious international tension constituting a threat of war, or in order to carry out obligations it has accepted for the purpose of maintaining peace and international security". Because of the view it had taken of the effect in the circumstances of Directive 76/207, the Court said that Article 297 did not need to be considered.

Article 2(3) of Directive 76/207 provides: "This Directive shall be without prejudice to provisions concerning the protection of women, particularly as regards pregnancy and maternity". In *Johnston*, the Court made it clear that, like Article 2(2), Article 2(3) was also to be interpreted strictly. It was "intended to protect a woman's biological condition and the special relationship which exists between a woman and her child".[95] It could not justify the complete exclusion of women from an occupational activity on the basis of risks which affected men and women in the same way.[96]

In *Hofmann v. Barmer Ersatzkasse*,[97] a father challenged the refusal of the competent German authorities to extend to him the benefit of national rules on maternity leave and the payment of an allowance to mothers who took such leave. The Court found that rules of that nature were covered by Article 2(3) of Directive 76/207, which constituted recognition of the legitimacy of respecting women's needs in two respects. "First, it is legitimate to ensure the protection of a woman's biological condition during pregnancy and thereafter until such time as her physiological and mental functions have returned to normal after childbirth; secondly, it is legitimate to protect the special relationship between a woman and her child over the period which follows pregnancy and childbirth, by preventing that relationship from being disturbed by the multiple burdens which would result from the simultaneous pursuit of employment".[98]

Article 2(4) is the third of the derogations from the principle of equal treatment laid down in Directive 76/207. It provides: "This Directive shall be without prejudice to measures to promote equal opportunity for men and women, in particular by removing existing inequalities which affect women's opportunities in the areas referred to in Article 1(1)". The scope of that provision was considered by the Court in one of its most controversial recent decisions, *Kalanke v. Bremen*.[99] The applicant was a man who had been shortlisted for a job in the Bremen Parks Department. The other candidate was a woman with equally good qualifications. A Bremen statute provided that female candidates for a job or for promotion were to be given priority over male candidates with the same qualifications in sectors where women were under-represented. This was the case in the Bremen Parks Department, so the female candidate was given the job. The Court of Justice was asked for guidance on the scope of Article 2(4) of Directive 76/207. The Court ruled that, as a derogation from an individual right, Article 2(4) was to be interpreted strictly. It permitted "national measures relating to access to employment, including promotion, which

---

[95] Para. 44.
[96] *cf.* Case 312/86 *Commission v. France* [1988] E.C.R. 6315.
[97] Case 184/83 [1984] E.C.R. 3047; [1986] 1 C.M.L.R. 242.
[98] Para. 25.
[99] Case C–450/93 [1995] E.C.R. I–3051; [1996] 1 C.M.L.R. 175; [1996] All E.R. (E.C.) 66. See generally Fredman, "Reversing discrimination" (1997) 113 L.Q.R. 575.

give a specific advantage to women with a view to improving their ability to compete on the labour market and to pursue a career on an equal footing with men".[1] However, national rules guaranteeing women "absolute and unconditional priority for appointment or promotion" were not confined to promoting equal opportunities: "such a system substitutes for equality of opportunity as envisaged in Article 2(4) the result which is only to be arrived at by providing equality of opportunity".[2]

The Court's judgment was greeted with dismay in several Member States and the Commission, whose own staffing policy seemed now to be open to question,[3] issued a communication[4] suggesting that the judgment did not affect quota systems "which fall short of the degree of rigidity and automaticity provided for by the Bremen law". That view was endorsed by the Court itself in *Marschall v. Land Nordrhein-Westfalen*.[5] The Law on Civil Servants of the Land of North Rhine-Westphalia provided: "Where, in the sector of the authority responsible for promotion, there are fewer women than men in the particular higher grade post in the career bracket, women are to be given priority for promotion in the event of equal suitability, competence and professional performance, unless reasons specific to an individual [male] candidate tilt the balance in his favour". Apparently chastened by the chorus of criticism provoked by its ruling in *Kalanke*,[6] the Court held that the proviso to that rule brought it within the scope of Article 2(4) because it meant that female candidates were not given absolute and unconditional priority. Male candidates with equivalent qualifications had a guarantee that their applications would be the subject of an objective assessment and that any priority accorded to female candidates would be overridden where criteria specific to a male candidate tilted the balance in his favour.

The *Kalanke* and *Marschall* cases served to underline the potential weaknesses of Article 2(4) in authorising so-called positive or affirmative action. That this outcome was unacceptable to the Member States is clear from the insertion in Article 141 at Amsterdam of a new fourth paragraph, quoted above. Although based on Article 6(3) of the Agreement on Social Policy, Article 141(4) is broader in scope and is clearly intended to permit a wider range of positive action than Article 2(4) of Directive 76/207. However, it cannot be used to justify national rules which the Court consider disproportionate.[6a]

Enforcing the principle of equal treatment

Article 6 of Directive 76/207 requires Member States to "introduce into their national legal systems such measures as are necessary to enable all persons who consider themselves wronged by failure to apply to them the principle of equal

---

[1] Para, 19.

[2] Para. 23.

[3] See Ellis, *op. cit.*, pp. 257–258.

[4] COM(96) 88 final.

[5] Case C–409/95 [1997] E.C.R. I–6363. See also Case C–158/97 *Badeck*, judgment of March 28, 2000; Fredman, "After *Kalanke* and *Marschall*: affirming affirmative action" (1998) 1 C.Y.E.L.S. 199.

[6] See the Opinion of Advocate General Jacobs in *Marschall*.

[6a] See Case C–407/98 *Abrahamsson and Anderson v. Fogelvist*, judgment of July 6, 2000.

treatment within the meaning of Articles 3, 4 and 5 to pursue their claims by judicial process after possible recourse to other competent authorities". This provision has led to the development by the Court of a principle of effective protection with implications stretching beyond the field of equal treatment for men and women.[7] It was in *Von Colson and Kamann v. Land Nordrhein-Westfalen*[8] that the significance of Article 6 started to become clear. That case arose out of a difficulty encountered by a German court in deciding what sanction to impose on an employer found to have discriminated on the grounds of sex against two female job applicants. The national court took the view that German law only permitted it to order the reimbursement of expenses incurred by the applicants, likely to be a fairly small sum. The Court of Justice was asked whether such an outcome would be compatible with Directive 76/207. The Court declared: "Although . . . full implementation of the directive does not require any specific form of sanction for unlawful discrimination, it does entail that that sanction be such as to guarantee real and effective judicial protection. Moreover it must also have a real deterrent effect on the employer. It follows that where a Member State chooses to penalise the breach of the prohibition of discrimination by the award of compensation, that compensation must in any event be adequate in relation to the damage sustained".[9] National provisions which limited the right to compensation to a purely nominal amount were not enough to satisfy the requirements of the directive.[10]

In the second *Marshall* case,[11] the Court was asked whether Directive 76/207 allowed the Member States to set an upper limit to the amount of compensation payable to those who had suffered discrimination on the grounds of sex and whether any compensation awarded had to include interest. The Court ruled that Article 6 of the directive precluded an upper limit on the amount of compensation, "since it limits the amount of compensation *a priori* which is not necessarily consistent with the requirement of ensuring real equality of opportunity through adequate reparation for the loss and damage sustained as a result of discriminatory dismissal".[12] Interest was an essential part of any compensation awarded, because "full compensation for the loss and damage sustained as a result of discriminatory dismissal cannot leave out of account factors, such as the effluxion of time, which may in fact reduce its value".[13] The Court added, notwithstanding indications to the contrary in *Von Colson*,[14] that, although the Member States were free to decide how to ensure that the objectives of the directive were achieved, individuals had a directly effective right to ensure that the means chosen satisfied the requirements of effectiveness and deterrence.

---

[7] See Chap. 5.
[8] Case 14/83 [1984] E.C.R. 1891; [1986] 2 C.M.L.R. 430. See also Case 222/84 *Johnston v. Chief Constable of the Royal Ulster Constabulary* [1986] E.C.R. 1651; [1986] 3 C.M.L.R. 240.
[9] Para. 23.
[10] The Court went on to rule that the national court was required to interpret its national law on the matter in the light of the requirements of the directive. See further Chap. 4.
[11] Case C–271/91 *Marshall v. Southampton and South-West Hampshire AHA* [1993] E.C.R. I–4367; [1993] 3 C.M.L.R. 293.
[12] Para. 30.
[13] Para. 31.
[14] See Advocate General van Gerven in the second *Marshall* case at I–4386–4387.

The decision in the second *Marshall* case seems in retrospect to represent the high-water mark of the Court's case-law on Article 6 of Directive 76/207. In *Draehmpaehl v. Urania Immobilienservice*,[15] the Court was slightly more guarded. At issue in that case were provisions of German law which placed a ceiling of three months' salary on the amount of compensation which might be claimed by unsuccessful job applicants who said they had suffered discrimination on the grounds of their sex. The Court ruled that it was incompatible with the directive for a Member State to fix an upper limit to the amount of compensation payable to an applicant who would have obtained the position in the absence of discrimination in the selection process. However, the directive did not preclude national provisions limiting the amount of compensation payable to an applicant who would not in any event have obtained the vacant position because his or her qualifications were inferior to those of the successful candidate. The Court was also asked whether it was compatible with the directive for national law to limit the aggregate amount of the compensation which could be awarded where several applicants showed that they had been discriminated against on the basis of their sex in the making of an appointment. On this question the Court took a stronger line, ruling that such a rule of national law was precluded by the directive, since it "may have the effect of dissuading applicants . . . from asserting their rights. Such a consequence would not represent real and effective judicial protection and would have no really dissuasive effect on the employer, as required by the Directive".[16]

Article 7 of Directive 76/207 requires Member States to "take the necessary measures to protect employees against dismissal by the employer as a reaction to a complaint within the undertaking or to any legal proceedings aimed at enforcing compliance with the principle of equal treatment". The question whether the directive conferred protection against adverse treatment by a *former* employer as a reaction to an attempt to enforce the principle of equal treatment before the employment relationship came to an end was considered by the Court in *Coote v. Granada Hospitality*.[17] The Court said that it could not be inferred from Article 7 that the legislature had intended to limit the protection of workers against retaliation by an employer solely to cases of dismissal. The principle of effective judicial control laid down in Article 6 of the directive would be deprived of an essential part of its effectiveness if it did not cover measures taken by an employer (such as refusal to supply a reference) as a response to steps taken by an employee to enforce the principle of equal treatment: "Fear of such measures, where no legal remedy is available against them, might deter workers who considered themselves the victims of discrimination from pursuing their claims by judicial process, and would consequently be liable seriously to jeopardise implementation of the aim pursued by the Directive".

---

[15] Case C–180/95 [1997] E.C.R. I–2195; [1997] 3 C.M.L.R. 1107. See also Case C–66/95 *The Queen v. Secretary of State for Social Security, ex p. Sutton* [1997] E.C.R. I–2163; [1997] 2 C.M.L.R. 382, discussed below.

[16] Para. 40. The Court attached significance to the fact that no such ceiling on compensation was laid down by other provisions of domestic civil or labour law: see paras 41–43. This suggests that, if it had been, the outcome might have been different, although the comparison seems irrelevant in the light of *von Colson* and the second *Marshall* case.

[17] Case C–185/97 [1998] E.C.R. I–5199; [1998] 3 C.M.L.R. 958.

THE SOCIAL SECURITY DIRECTIVE

Directive 79/7[18] is designed to give effect to the principle of equal treatment for men and women in statutory social security schemes providing protection against the following risks: sickness, invalidity, old age, accidents at work and occupational diseases, unemployment.[19] The directive does not apply to survivors' benefits or family benefits[20] and is stated to be "without prejudice to the provisions relating to the protection of women on the grounds of maternity".[21] The Court has held that, in order to fall within the scope of the directive, a benefit must be "directly and effectively linked to the protection provided against one of the risks specified in Article 3(1) of the directive". In *R. v. Secretary of State for Health, ex parte Richardson*,[22] that test was found to have been satisfied by a national rule exempting certain groups of people, in particular the elderly, from prescription charges. The exemption afforded "direct and effective protection against the risk of sickness referred to in Article 3(1) of Directive 79/7 in so far as grant of the benefit to any of the categories of people referred to is always conditional on materialization of the risk in question".[23] By contrast, in *Atkins v. Wrekin District Council and Department of Transport*,[24] the Court found that a national provision under which concessionary fares on public transport were granted to certain groups of people, notably the elderly, fell outside the scope of the directive. Old age and invalidity, which were included among the risks listed in Article 3(1)(a), were only two of the criteria used to define the beneficiaries of the disputed provision. The Court rejected the Commission's argument that the directive extended to social protection as a whole.

By virtue of Article 2, Directive 79/7 applies to "the working population—including self-employed persons, workers and self-employed persons whose activity is interrupted by illness, accident or involuntary unemployment and persons seeking employment—and to retired or invalided workers and self-employed persons". In *Drake v. Chief Adjudication Officer*,[25] the Court held that a person who was not herself ill but who had given up work in order to care for her invalid mother was to be regarded as having done so solely because of one of the risks listed in Article 3 of the directive. Such a person therefore constituted a member of the working population for the purposes of Article 2. However, the term "activity" in that article means "an economic activity, that is to say an activity undertaken in return for remuneration in the broad sense".[26] A person

---

[18] See Sohrab, "Women and social security: the limits of EEC equality law" [1994] J.S.W.F.L. 5.

[19] See Art. 3(1)(a). The Directive also applies to social assistance (where entitlement to benefit depends on the exercise of a discretionary power in the claimant's favour) to the extent that it is intended to supplement or replace such schemes: Art. 3(1)(b).

[20] Except in the case of family benefits granted by way of increases of benefits due in respect of the risks mentioned in Art. 3(1)(a).

[21] Art. 4(2).

[22] Case C–137/94 [1995] E.C.R. I–3407; [1995] 3 C.M.L.R. 376.

[23] Para. 12. See also Case C–382/98 *The Queen v. Secretary of State for Social Security, ex p. Taylor*, judgment of December 16, 1999.

[24] Case C–228/94 [1996] E.C.R. I–3633; [1996] All E.R. (E.C.) 719.

[25] Case 150/85 [1986] E.C.R. 1995; [1986] 3 C.M.L.R. 42.

[26] Case C–77/95 *Züchner v. Handelskrankenkasse (Ersatzkasse) Bremen* [1996] E.C.R. I–5689, para. 13.

who takes on responsibility for looking after a handicapped relative without abandoning an occupational activity or interrupting efforts to find employment in order to do so is not therefore a member of the "working population" within the meaning of Article 2.[27]

The principle of equal treatment is laid down in Article 4(1) of Directive 79/7, according to which:

"there shall be no discrimination whatsoever on ground of sex either directly, or indirectly by reference in particular to marital or family status, in particular as concerns:
— the scope of the schemes and the conditions of access thereto,
— the obligation to contribute and the calculation of contributions,
— the calculation of benefits including increases due in respect of a spouse and for dependants and the conditions governing the duration and retention of entitlement to benefits."

Article 4(1) has direct effect.[28] Moreover, in the absence of appropriate implementing measures, members of the disadvantaged sex are entitled to have the same rules applied to them as members of the opposite sex who are in the same situation. As the Court has explained, those rules represent the only valid point of reference where the directive has not been implemented correctly.[29]

Article 7 of Directive 79/7 sets out a number of matters which Member States are entitled to exclude from the scope of the principle of equal treatment. As noted above, the list includes, in Article 7(1)(a), "the determination of pensionable age for the purposes of granting old-age and retirement pensions and the possible consequences thereof for other benefits". In *Secretary of State for Social Security v. Thomas and Others*,[30] the Court held that Article 7(1)(a) could be used to justify discrimination under benefit schemes other than old-age and retirement pension schemes "only if such discrimination is objectively necessary in order to avoid disrupting the complex financial equilibrium of the social security system or to ensure consistency between retirement pension schemes and other benefit schemes".[31] That decision was applied in the *Richardson* case,[32] which concerned the compatibility with the principle of equal treatment of national legislation exempting from prescription charges women who had reached the age of 60 and men who had reached the age of 65. Those were the ages at which old-age and retirement pensions became payable, but there was no evidence that exempting men at the same age as women would undermine the financial equilibrium of the social security system or that it was necessary to treat men and women differently in order to ensure consistency between the retirement pension scheme and the disputed legislation. The Court concluded that such legislation was inconsistent with the requirements of the directive.

---

[27] *Züchner, supra.*
[28] See Case 71/85 *Netherlands v. Federatie Nederlandse Vakbeweging* [1986] E.C.R. 3855.
[29] See *e.g.* Case 384/85 *Borrie Clarke v. Chief Adjudication Officer* [1987] E.C.R. 2865.
[30] Case C–328/91 [1993] E.C.R. I–1247; [1993] 3 C.M.L.R. 880.
[31] Para. 12.
[32] *Supra.* See also *The Queen v. Secretary of State for Social Security, ex p. Taylor, supra. cf.* Case C–9/91 *Equal Opportunities Commission* [1992] E.C.R. I–4297; Case C–196/98 *Hepple v. Adjudication Officer*, judgment of May 23, 2000.

Article 6 of Directive 79/7 is substantially identical to Article 6 of Directive 76/207, which is set out above. However, the different contexts in which they apply has led the Court to adopt a different approach to their interpretation. In *The Queen v. Secretary of State for Social Security, ex p. Sutton*,[33] the Court was called upon to decide whether Article 6 of Directive 79/7 entitled a claimant to interest on arrears of benefit which had been withheld in breach of the principle of equal treatment. It will be recalled that, in the second *Marshall* case,[34] the Court had ruled that Article 6 of Directive 76/207 required interest to be paid on compensation awarded for discriminatory dismissal. However, in *Sutton* the Court distinguished *Marshall* on the basis that the latter case had been concerned with interest on a sum intended as compensation for loss suffered as a result of discrimination on grounds of sex. By contrast, the *Sutton* case was concerned with interest on amounts payable by way of social security benefits. Such amounts did not in any way constitute reparation for loss or damage sustained. The payment of interest on arrears of benefits could not therefore be regarded as an essential component of the right to non-discriminatory treatment under Directive 79/7.[35] The distinction drawn by the Court between benefits and compensation is not entirely convincing and may in part have been prompted by growing caution on the part of the Court about the desirability of interfering with the procedural autonomy of the Member States and the financing of their social security systems. However, the Court sugared the pill as far as the claimant was concerned by reminding the national court of its responsibility to assess whether she was entitled to reparation under the principle of State liability[36] for any loss she had suffered by reason of the failure of the competent authority to pay the contested benefits on time.

INDIRECT DISCRIMINATION

It is well established that the general principle of non-discrimination, of which the Community rules on equal treatment for men and women are a particular expression,[37] prohibits not just direct discrimination but also indirect discrimination. Indirect discrimination is in fact prohibited expressly by a number of the equal treatment directives.[38] According to Article 2(2) of Directive 97/80 on the burden of proof, indirect discrimination for the purposes of the principle of equal treatment between men and women exists "where an apparently neutral provision, criterion or practice disadvantages a substantially higher proportion of the members of one sex unless that provision, criterion or practice is appropriate and

---

[33] Case C–66/95 [1997] E.C.R. I–2163; [1997] 2 C.M.L.R. 382.
[34] *Supra.*
[35] *cf.* Case C–338/91 *Steenhorst-Neerings* [1993] E.C.R. I–5475; [1994] 1 C.M.L.R. 773; [1995] 3 C.M.L.R. 323 and Case C–410/92 *Johnson* [1994] E.C.R. I–5483; [1994] 1 C.M.L.R. 725, where the Court accepted that it was compatible with the Directive for a Member State to limit the period prior to a claim in respect of which arrears of benefit could be recovered. For further discussion, see Chap. 5.
[36] See Chap. 5.
[37] See *P v. S and Cornwall County Council, supra,* para. 18 (Dir. 76/207); *Abdoulaye v. Renault, supra,* para. 16 (equal pay).
[38] See Dir. 76/207, Art. 2(1); Dir. 79/7, Art. 4(1); Dir. 86/378, Art. 5(1); Dir. 86/613, Art. 3.

necessary and can be justified by objective factors unrelated to sex". That provision represents a synthesis of the substantial body of case-law on the issue. The directive applies to situations covered by Article 141 of the Treaty and Directive 75/117, by Directive 76/207, and (in so far as discrimination based on sex is concerned) by Directives 92/85 and 96/34.[39] The core provision of Directive 97/80 is Article 4(1), which requires the Member States to ensure "that, when persons who consider themselves wronged because the principle of equal treatment has not been applied to them establish, before a court or other competent authority, facts from which it may be presumed that there has been direct or indirect discrimination, it shall be for the respondent to prove that there has been no breach of the principle of equal treatment". In cases of indirect discrimination, this means that it is for the employer to prove that the contested provision or practice is objectively justified. Article 4(1) gives legislative expression to the decision of the Court in *Danfoss*,[40] an equal pay case. Although the directive does not expressly apply to situations covered by Directive 79/7, the Court seems to apply essentially the same approach to the burden of proof in that context too.[41]

One of the leading cases on the concept of indirect discrimination is *Bilka v. Weber von Hartz*,[42] which concerned the legality of the refusal of a department store called Bilka to allow part-time employees, most of whom were women, to join its occupational pension scheme. The store sought to justify its policy by reference to the need to ensure adequate staff cover whenever it was open. Part-timers, it said, generally refused to work in the late afternoons and on Saturdays and excluding them from the pension scheme was meant to make full-time work more attractive. The Court said that it was the task of the national court to establish to what extent the store's practice could be regarded as objectively justified on economic grounds: "If the national court finds that the measures chosen by Bilka correspond to a real need on the part of the undertaking, are appropriate with a view to achieving the objectives pursued and are necessary to that end, the fact that the measures affect a far greater number of women than men is not sufficient to show that they constitute an infringement of Article 119 [now 141]".

Although the approach of the Court has not been entirely consistent, it has on the whole insisted that national courts should scrutinise closely claims that discrimination concerning pay is objectively justified. In *Rinner-Kühn v. FWW Spezial-Gebäudereinigung*,[43] the Court was asked to consider the effect of Article 141 on German legislation which allowed employers to refuse sick pay to employees whose working hours fell below a certain threshold. The effect was to exclude a lot more women than men from the right to sick pay. The German

---

[39] On the framework agreement on parental leave concluded by UNICE, CEEP and the ETUC, [1996] O.J. L145/9 (extended to the U.K. by Dir. 97/75; [1998] O.J. L10/24).

[40] Case 109/88 *Handels- og Kontorfunktionærernes Forbund i Danmark v. Dansk Arbejdsverforening, acting on behalf of Danfoss* [1989] E.C.R. 3199; [1991] 1 C.M.L.R. 8. See also Case C–127/92 *Enderby* [1993] E.C.R. I–5535; [1994] 1 C.M.L.R. 80.

[41] See below.

[42] Case 170/84 [1986] E.C.R. 1607; [1986] 2 C.M.L.R. 701. See also Case 96/80 *Jenkins v. Kingsgate* [1981] E.C.R. 911; [1981] 2 C.M.L.R. 24.

[43] Case 171/88 [1989] E.C.R. 2743; [1993] 2 C.M.L.R. 932.

Government maintained that the disputed legislation was objectively justified because the workers adversely affected by it were less integrated in or dependent on their employer. The Court's response was that "those considerations, in so far as they are only generalizations about certain categories of workers, do not enable criteria which are both objective and unrelated to any discimination on grounds of sex to be identified".[44] In *Nimz*,[45] the issue was the compatibility with Article 141 of a provision in a collective agreement reducing the promotion chances of employees who worked less than three-quarters of normal working hours. Most such employees were women. It was said that employees whose hours exceeded the threshold had more experience and acquired the skills they needed more quickly than other employees. The Court said that generalisations of this kind were not sufficient to establish objective justification: "Although experience goes hand in hand with length of service, and experience enables the worker in principle to improve performance of the tasks allotted to him, the objectivity of such a criterion depends on all the circumstances in a particular case, and in particular on the relationship between the nature of the work performed and the experience gained from the performance of that work upon completion of a certain number of working hours".[46]

In *R. v. Secretary of State for Employment, ex p. Seymour-Smith and Perez*,[47] the House of Lords referred various questions to the Court in the context of a challenge to the legality of a national rule excluding from protection against unfair dismissal any employee who had not been employed for a continuous period of at least two years. One of the questions asked for guidance on the extent of the disparity between a measure's effect on women and its effect on men which was required to establish indirect discrimination for the purposes of Article 141. The Court said that the necessary degree of disparity would be present if the available statistics indicated that a considerably smaller percentage of women than men could satisfy the disputed rule. Alternatively, "a lesser but persistent and relatively constant disparity over a long period between men and women"[48] might also constitute evidence of discrimination. According to the order for reference, in the year in which the requirement of two years' employment was introduced, it was satisfied by 77.4 per cent of men and 68.9 per cent of women. The Court observed that "[s]uch statistics do not appear, on the

---

[44] Para. 14.
[45] Case C–184/89 [1991] E.C.R. I–297. *cf. Enderby, supra*; Case C–360/90 *Bötel* [1992] E.C.R. I–3589; Case C–457/93 *Kuratorium für Dialyse und Nierentransplantation v. Lewark* [1996] E.C.R. I–243; Case C–278/93 *Freers and Speckmann v. Deutsche Bundespost* [1996] E.C.R. I–1165.
[46] Para. 14. The decision marked a departure from *Danfoss, supra*, where the Court said that an employer was free to reward length of service without having to demonstrate its importance to the performance of an employee's tasks.
[47] Case C–167/97, [1999] E.C.R. I–623. For a critical commentary on the case, see Barnard and Hepple, "Indirect discrimination: interpreting *Seymour-Smith*" (1999) 58 C.L.J. 399. *cf.* the decision of the House of Lords in *R v. Secretary of State for Employment, ex p. EOC* [1994] 2 W.L.R. 409.
[48] Para. 61.

face of it, to show that a considerably smaller percentage of women than men is able to fulfil the requirement imposed by the disputed rule".[49]

In the social security context, the basic test is the same[50] but Court has taken a less exacting approach to attempts to show that indirectly discriminatory rules are objectively justified. In *Nolte v. Landesversicherungsanstalt Hannover*,[51] for example, the Court was asked to consider the compatibility with Directive 79/7 of a national provision excluding from eligibility for an invalidity pension those employed in work classified as minor and which was not subject to compulsory insurance. Work was considered minor if it took less than 15 hours a week and the wages were below a certain level. Substantially more women than men were engaged in such work, for which there was social demand. The Court stated that indirectly discriminatory measures were not caught by the directive where they "reflect a legitimate social policy aim of the Member State whose legislation is at issue, are appropriate to achieve that aim and are necessary in order to do so".[52] The Member States had a "broad margin of discretion"[53] in deciding how to achieve the aims of their social and employment policy. The national legislature was reasonably entitled to consider the contested legislation necessary to meet demand for minor employment. This was "a social policy aim unrelated to any discrimination on grounds of sex".[54] The legislation in question could not therefore be described as indirectly discriminatory for the purposes of Article 4(1) of the directive. The Court's unwillingness to subject the justification advanced to closer examination, or to encourage the national court to do so, may be due to a reluctance to interfere too closely in the social security systems of the Member States, which are under increasing pressure.[55]

The divergence between this test and the test applied in equal pay cases was underlined in *Seymour-Smith*,[56] where the House of Lords asked what criteria were to be applied in establishing whether a measure adopted by a Member State in pursuance of its social policy was objectively justified for the purposes of Article 141. The United Kingdom Government argued that allowing recently recruited employees to bring proceedings for unfair dismissal would deter recruitment. Referring, *inter alia*, to *Megner and Scheffel* and *Nolte*, the Court accepted that encouraging recruitment was a legitimate aim of social policy. However, it emphasised the importance of establishing whether that aim was unrelated to any discrimination based on sex, whether the disputed rule was capable of advancing it and whether it could be achieved by other means. The

---

[49] Para. 64. See also Case C–226/98 *Jørgensen v. FAS*, judgment of April 6, 2000, para. 34. *cf.* Case C–243/95 *Hill and Stapleton v. Revenue Commissioners and Department of Finance* [1998] E.C.R. I–3739, para. 25; [1998] 3 C.M.L.R. 81, where the Court unsurprisingly found that a rule which adversely affected a group 98% of whose members were women had discriminatory effects based on sex.

[50] See, *e.g.* Case C–343/92, *De Weerd and Others* [1994] E.C.R. I–571, para. 33; [1994] 2 C.M.L.R. 325. See also *Jørgensen*, *supra*.

[51] Case C–317/93 [1995] E.C.R. I–4625; [1996] All E.R. (E.C.) 212. See also Case C–444/93 *Megner and Scheffel v. Innungskrankenkasse Rheinhessen Pfalz* [1995] E.C.R. I–4741.

[52] Para. 28.

[53] Para. 33.

[54] Para. 34.

[55] *cf.* Case C–9/91 *Equal Opportunities Commission* [1992] E.C.R. I–4297.

[56] See also Case C–281/97 *Krüger v. Kreiskrankenhaus Ebersberg*, judgment of September 9, 1999.

Court observed that the discretion enjoyed by Member States in determining their social policy could not "have the effect of frustrating the implementation of a fundamental principle of Community law such as that of equal pay for men and women".[57] It declared: "Mere generalisations concerning the capacity of a specific measure to encourage recruitment are not enough to show that the aim of the disputed rule is unrelated to any discrimination based on sex nor to provide evidence on the basis of which it could reasonably be considered that the means chosen were suitable for achieving that aim".[58]

AN ASSESSMENT

The extensive body of Community rules on equal treatment for men and women has on the whole been applied with great vigour by the Court. However, the persistent disparities between the pay and career opportunities of men and women have led some feminist commentators to call for a more radical approach to eradicating disadvantage among women[59] and to criticise the part played by the Court.[60] The Court's role, in this area as in others, is to give effect to the policy laid down by the Community legislature. Thus, when the Court remarked in the *Hofmann* case[61] that Directive 76/207 was not intended "to settle questions concerned with the organisation of the family, or to alter the division of responsibility between parents",[62] it was not expressing any view about whether the position was satisfactory, nor would it have been appropriate for it to do so. Indeed, by the time *Hill and Stapleton*[63] fell to be decided almost 14 years later, the Court felt able to say that "Community policy in this area is to encourage and, if possible, adapt working conditions to family responsibilities".[64] Whether the Community legislature will be prepared to take the kind of far-reaching steps to eliminate structural disadvantage advocated by some commentators remains to be seen.[65]

---

[57] Para. 75.
[58] Para. 76.
[59] See, *e.g.* Fredman, "European Community discrimination law: a critique" (1992) 21 I.L.J. 119, 134, and, by the same author, "Reversing discrimination" (1997) 113 L.Q.R. 575, 600.
[60] See, *e.g.* Fenwick and Hervey, "Sex equality in the Single Market: new directions for the European Court of Justice" (1995) 32 C.M.L.Rev 443.
[61] *Supra.*
[62] [1984] E.C.R. 3047, para. 24.
[63] *Supra.*
[64] [1998] E.C.R. I–3739, para. 42. For intervening developments, see point 16 of the Community Charter of the Fundamental Social Rights or Workers adopted in 1989; Dir. 96/34 on the framework agreement on parental leave concluded by UNICE, CEEP and the ETUC; [1996] O.J. L145/9 (extended to the U.K. by Dir. 97/75; [1998] O.J. L10/24).
[65] See further Mancini and O'Leary, "The new frontiers of sex equality law in the European Union" (1999) 24 E.L.Rev. 331; Arnull, *op. cit.,* Chap. 13.

CHAPTER 28

EDUCATION AND VOCATIONAL TRAINING

INTRODUCTION

Over the 40 or so years of the Community's development, education has moved from the periphery to occupy a central place in its activities.[1] The term "education" did not appear in the original text of the EEC Treaty, although some of the Treaty's provisions had implications for education construed in a broad sense. Thus, in order to make it easier for persons to take up and pursue activities as self-employed persons, the Council was required by Article 57(1) EEC (now, after amendment, Article 47(1) E.C.) to "issue directives for the mutual recognition of diplomas, certificates and other evidence of formal qualifications".[2] The Treaty provisions on the free movement of workers did not deal expressly with the question of education and training, but the Court explained in *Casagrande v. Landeshauptstadt München*[3] that "[a]lthough educational and training policy is not as such included in the spheres which the Treaty has entrusted to the Community institutions, it does not follow that the exercise of powers transferred to the Community is in some way limited if it is of such a nature as to affect the measures taken in the execution of a policy such as that of education and training". The suggestion, implicit in these provisions, that the Treaty only applied to education to the extent necessary to ensure the proper functioning of the common market was reinforced by Article 128 EEC, which required the Council, acting on a proposal from the Commission and after consulting the Economic and Social Committee, to "lay down general principles for implementing a common vocational training policy capable of contributing to the harmonious development both of the national economies and of the common market".

These apparently meagre provisions were to form the basis for the development of a body of case-law which would interfere to a startling extent with the freedom of the Member States to organise their systems of education as they saw fit. Regulation 1612/68 (which was at issue in the *Casagrande* case) contains several provisions affecting the right of a migrant worker and certain members of his family to education in the host State. In addition, the Court treated Article 128 EEC as bringing "vocational training" within the scope of application of the Treaty for the purposes of the prohibition against discrimination on the grounds of nationality laid down in the first paragraph Article 7 EEC (subsequently Article 6, now Article 12, E.C.). The implications of that conclusion were far-reaching, as we shall see. Moreover, in *Commission v. Council*,[4] the Court

---

[1] See Shaw, "From the margins to the centre: education and training law and policy" in Craig and de Búrca (eds), *The Evolution of EU Law* (1999), Chap. 15.
[2] See further Chap. 15.
[3] Case 9/74 [1974] E.C.R. 773, para. 12; [1974] 2 C.M.L.R. 423.
[4] Case 242/87 [1989] E.C.R. 1425; [1991] 1 C.M.L.R. 478. See also Joined Cases C–51, 90 and 94/89, *United Kingdom and Others v. Council* [1991] E.C.R. I–2757; [1992] 1 C.M.L.R. 40.

endorsed the view of the Commission that the fact that Article 128 EEC provided for the implementation of a common vocational training policy precluded "any interpretation of that provision which would mean denying the Community the means of action needed to carry out that common policy effectively".[5] It followed that the Council was entitled under Article 128 "to adopt legal measures providing for Community action in the sphere of vocational training and imposing corresponding obligations of co-operation on the Member States".[6]

These decisions, however adventurous they might have been, were not enough to keep pace with the political importance which the Member States began to attach to action at the Community level in the educational field.[7] Accordingly at Maastricht the list of the Community's activities in Article 3 (now 3(1)) E.C. was amended to include "a contribution to education and training of quality and to the flowering of the cultures of the Member States". Article 128 EEC was replaced by new and considerably expanded articles dealing separately with education (Article 126) and vocational training (Article 127). Since the two articles originally laid down different decision-making procedures (co-decision in the case of the former, co-operation in the case of the latter), the distinction between education and vocational training, which had become somewhat blurred by the case-law on Article 128,[8] seemed certain to assume major importance.[9] However, the Treaty of Amsterdam aligned the relevant decision-making processes, co-decision now applying under both provisions (which were renumbered Articles 149 and 150 respectively).

The limits to the Community's powers to act under these provisions should, however, be noted. Article 149(1) provides: "The Community shall contribute to the development of quality education by encouraging co-operation between Member States and, if necessary, by supporting and supplementing their action, while fully respecting the responsibility of the Member States for the content of teaching and the organisation of education systems and their cultural and linguistic diversity". By virtue of Article 149(4), the Council may adopt "incentive measures",[10] but these may not entail "any harmonisation of the laws and regulations of the Member States". Article 150 is less restrictive, but only slightly. Article 150(1) states that the Community "shall implement a vocational training policy which shall support and supplement the action of the Member States, while fully respecting the responsibility of the Member States for the content and organisation of vocational training". The Council is empowered by Article 150(4)

---

[5] Para. 9.

[6] Para. 11.

[7] Shaw identifies the mid-1970s as "the beginning of the slow process whereby *educational* concerns generally have moved from the margins to the centre of the Community's policy preoccupations": *op. cit.,* p. 561 (emphasis in the original).

[8] See below.

[9] See Lenaerts, "Education in European Community law after 'Maastricht' " (1994) 31 C.M.L.Rev. 7, 24–37. He observes, at p. 26, that "[t]he article dealing with education is the *lex generalis* . . . and the article dealing with vocational training is the *lex specialis*."

[10] "Incentive measures" may take the form of any of the acts described in Art. 249(ex 189) E.C. or of acts *sui generis* (Beschlüsse): see Lenaerts, *op. cit.,* p. 31, who observes (at p. 32): "What is involved is incentive and supplementary actions with a view to pushing the policies of the Member States in a particular direction."

to "adopt measures to contribute to the achievement of the objectives referred to in this Article", but again such measures must not involve "any harmonisation of the laws and regulations of the Member States". These provisions reflect a careful balance between a desire to protect the sovereignty of the Member States and a recognition of the contribution which the Community can make towards the achievement of "education and training of quality".[11] The principle of subsidiarity will help to determine when the Community should act and the principle of proportionality how intense any such action should be.[12]

At Amsterdam, the importance of education policy in its own right was emphasised by the addition of a new recital to the preamble to the E.C. Treaty recording the Member States' determination "to promote the development of the highest possible level of knowledge for their peoples through a wide access to education and through its continuous updating . . . " The thinking behind that recital was also reflected in *Agenda 2000*, a communication issued by the Commission in 1997 outlining "the broad perspectives for the development of the Union and its policies beyond the turn of the century . . ."[13] There the Commission emphasised the need to derive maximum benefit in terms of growth, competitiveness and employment from the shift towards globalisation and the development of information and communication technologies. It declared: "Knowledge policies—research, innovation, education and training—are therefore of decisive importance for the future of the Union".[14]

The rest of this chapter is divided into two parts. The first part examines the right of students to move freely throughout the Community, to take up residence and to pursue a course of study in any Member State. It also discusses the entitlement of workers, the self-employed and members of their families to education and training in Member States other than their own. The second part looks at the use which has been made by the Community institutions of their legislative powers in the field of education and vocational training.

THE RIGHT TO EDUCATION IN ANOTHER MEMBER STATE

Access to courses and tuition fees

The right of students to move freely throughout the Community in order to take up and pursue vocational training studies in any Member State was affirmed by the Court of Justice in a complex body of case-law beginning in 1983 with *Forcheri v. Belgium*.[15] That case concerned an Italian national resident in Belgium who wished to pursue, in that country, a three-year course which would qualify her to practise as a social worker. Mrs Forcheri was married to a Commission official, also of Italian nationality. When she applied to the Institut Supérieur de

---

[11] Art. 3(1)(q) E.C.
[12] See Art. 5(ex 3b) E.C.; Chap. 7, above.
[13] Bull. E.C., Supplement 5/97, p. 11.
[14] *op. cit.,* p. 19. See also the Millennium Declaration adopted by the European Council at its meeting in Helsinki on December 10 and 11, 1999.
[15] Case 152/82 [1983] E.C.R. 2323; [1984] 1 C.M.L.R. 334.

Sciences Humaines Appliquées she was required to pay an enrolment fee described as a "fee for foreign students", commonly known in Belgium as the "minerval." The fee was not charged to Belgian students. Mrs Forcheri contested the right of the Belgian authorities to charge this fee in the light of Articles 7, 48 and 49 of the EEC Treaty (now Articles 12, 39 and 40 E.C. respectively) The Court ruled that, ". . . although educational and vocational training policy is not as such part of the areas which the Treaty has allotted to the competence of the Community institutions . . .", the Treaty did, in Article 128, empower the Council to "lay down general principles for implementing a common vocational training policy." The Court therefore held:

> "Consequently if a Member State organises educational courses relating in particular to vocational training, to require of a national of another Member State lawfully established in the first Member State an enrolment fee which is not required of its own nationals in order to take part in such courses constitutes discrimination by reason of nationality, which is prohibited by Article 7 of the Treaty."[16]

Subsequent case-law clarified the precise scope of the concept of vocational training. In *Gravier v. City of Liège*,[17] a case involving a French national who wished to study the art of strip cartoon design in Liège, the Court said that ". . . any form of education which prepares for a qualification for a particular profession, trade or employment or which provides the necessary skills for such a profession, trade or employment is vocational training whatever the age and level of the pupil or student."

In *Blaizot v. University of Liège and Others,*[18] the Court was confronted with the question whether a course of studies, the first part of which was general in nature and therefore did not in itself lead to any qualification for a particular trade, profession or employment, and the second part of which did lead to such a qualification, was to be classified as vocational as a whole or whether only the second part could be so classified. The course in question was that of veterinary medicine. Blaizot and 16 other students, all of French nationality, were studying veterinary medicine in four Belgian universities. In the wake of the *Gravier* judgment, they brought an action against the refusal of their respective universities to repay them the supplementary enrolment fee, the "minerval," which they had paid prior to February 13, 1985, the date of the judgment in *Gravier.* The question arose as to whether university studies in veterinary medicine fell within the meaning of the term "vocational training".

It appeared that a course of studies leading to a qualification in veterinary medicine in Belgium consisted initially of three years of study leading to the award of a preliminary diploma entitled a "candidature" and a further three years leading to the award of a doctorate. The Belgian universities in question and the Belgian Government argued that the "candidature" and the doctorate represented two separate types of studies, one academic, the other vocational. Studies leading to the "candidature" could not be regarded as vocational training

---

[16] Para. 18.
[17] Case 293/83 [1985] E.C.R. 606; [1985] 3 C.M.L.R. 1.
[18] Case 24/86 [1988] E.C.R. 355; [1989] 1 C.M.L.R. 57.

since, in order to take up and pursue the profession of veterinary medicine, a student had to complete the further period of study leading to the doctorate, his final degree. The Court did not accept this argument. It held that vocational training included studies ". . . not only where the final examination directly provided the required qualification for a particular profession, trade or employment but also in so far as the studies in question provide specific training and skills, that is where a student needs the knowledge so acquired for the pursuit of a profession, trade or employment . . ." University studies in general, the Court held, fulfilled these criteria. The only exception would be certain courses of study which, because of their general nature, were intended for persons wishing to improve their general knowledge rather than prepare themselves for an occupation. The fact that university studies were divided into two stages could not be taken into account in deciding whether they were of a vocational training nature or not. Access to the second stages leading to the final diploma or degree, was conditional on completion of the first stage so that the two stages together had to be regarded as a single unit. It was not possible to make a distinction between one stage which did not consitute vocational training and a second which did.

The Court's ruling in *Blaizot* thus brought most university studies within the scope of the concept of vocational training and so required access to university education to be made available on the same terms to nationals and non-nationals alike. For the purposes of Article 12 E.C., however, the inclusion in the E.C. Treaty since Maastricht of provisions dealing with not only vocational training but also education would seem to deprive any remaining distinction between the two of its significance. Both are now within the scope of application of the Treaty and are therefore equally subject to the prohibition against discrimination on the grounds of nationality.

Grants and scholarships

Financial assistance for the purpose of meeting the cost of registration and other fees charged for access to a course must be granted to non-nationals on the same terms as nationals: such grants form part of the conditions of access to education and therefore discrimination on the grounds of nationality is prohibited by virtue of Article 12 of the E.C. Treaty.[19]

The determination of rights to maintenance and training grants is a more complex issue. In *Brown v. Secretary of State for Scotland*,[20] the Court held that maintenance grants paid to students fell outside the scope of Article 12 of the Treaty because they constituted an aspect of educational and social policy which, in general, fell within the competence of the Member States. However, a migrant worker may claim such a grant from the host Member State on the basis of Article 7(2) of Regulation 1612/68, which, it will be recalled, gives him the right to the same social and tax advantages as nationals of the host Member State. However, this right is subject to two conditions: first, the Court held in *Lair*[21] that

---

[19] See Case 39/86, *Lair v. Universität Hannover* [1988] E.C.R. 3161; [1989] 3 C.M.L.R. 545.
[20] Case 197/86 [1988] E.C.R. 3205; [1988] 3 C.M.L.R. 403 See also *Lair v. Universität Hannover*, *supra*.
[21] *supra*.

there must, in general, be "some continuity between the previous occupation and the course of study". Secondly, in *Brown*[22] the Court held that where a person becomes employed in a Member State with a view to undertaking studies there, the employment being "merely ancillary to the studies to be financed by the grant", he cannot rely on Article 7(2) to claim a maintenance grant payable to students who are nationals of the host State.

In so far as *Lair* and *Brown* excluded students in some circumstances from protection against discrimination on grounds of nationality, there are two reasons for doubting whether they remain good law. First, as we have seen, educational policy is no longer excluded *per se* from the Community's competence. Secondly, the Court held in *Martínez Sala v. Freistaat Bayern*[23] that a citizen of the European Union lawfully resident in a Member State other than his own could rely on Article 12 E.C. in all situations falling within the substantive scope of Community law. It is strongly arguable that a national of a Member State who is lawfully resident[24] in another Member State may therefore now rely on Article 12 to claim maintenance grants under the same conditions as students who are nationals of the host State.

It is in any event clear that, where a worker wishes to pursue a course of study which is linked with his previous employment and that employment was more than "merely ancillary" to the course, the right under Article 7(2) of Regulation 1612/68 to assistance with the costs of maintenance and education may not be made conditional upon the completion of a minimum period of employment in the host Member State. In *Bernini*[25] the Court ruled that an Italian national who had worked for 10 weeks in a factory in the Netherlands as a trainee could be considered a worker and retained that status even when she left that employment in order to take up, after a certain lapse of time, a course of full-time study, provided there was a link between that employment and the studies in question.

The right to grants for vocational training under Article 7(2) includes the right to grants for study abroad. In *Matteucci,*[26] an Italian national, herself the child of an Italian migrant worker, who had been born and brought up in Belgium where she subsequently worked as a teacher of rhythmics, was refused a scholarship to study singing and voice production in Berlin. The scholarship in question was provided under a bilateral cultural agreement between Belgium and Germany and was expressed to be confined to nationals of those countries. The Court held that Article 7(2) of Regulation 1612/68 laid down a general rule of equality of treatment under the law of the host Member State with regard to social benefits with respect to every worker who is a national of another Member State and who is working in that State. Consequently, where a Member State gives its national workers the opportunity of pursuing training provided in another Member State, that opportunity must be extended to Community workers established in its territory. The Court stated:

---

[22] *supra.*
[23] Case C–85/96 [1998] E.C.R. I–2691. See Chap. 16.
[24] The right of residence of students is discussed below.
[25] Case C–3/90 [1992] E.C.R. I–1071.
[26] Case 235/87 [1988] E.C.R. 5589; [1989] 1 C.M.L.R. 357.

"... a bilateral agreement which reserves the scholarships in question for nationals of the two Member States which are parties to the agreement cannot prevent the application of the principle of equality of treatment between national and Community workers established in the territory of one of those two Member States."

Article 7(3) of Regulation 1612/68 entitles a worker who is a national of a Member State to access, under the same conditions as national workers, "to training in vocational schools and retraining centres".[27] The scope of Article 7(3) is fairly limited. In *Brown*,[28] the Court said that "the fact that a teaching establishment provides a measure of vocational training is not sufficient to enable it to be regarded as a vocational school within the meaning of that provision. The term vocational school has a narrower meaning and refers solely to establishments which provide only instruction interposed between periods of employment or else closely connected with employment, particularly during apprenticeship. That is not the case as far as universities are concerned".

The rights of the children of such a worker to take advantage of educational opportunities available in the host State are the subject of Article 12 of Regulation 1612/68,[29] which provides:

"The children of a national of a Member State who is or has been employed in the territory of another Member State shall be admitted to that State's general educational, apprenticeship and vocational training courses under the same conditions as nationals of that State, if such children are residing in its territory.

Member States shall encourage all efforts to enable such children to attend these courses under the best possible conditions."

In *Gaal*, the Court stated that "to make the application of Article 12 subject to an age-limit or to the status of dependent child would conflict not only with the letter of that provision, but also with its spirit".[30] The concept of education for these purposes is broad, embracing "any form of education, including university courses in economics and advanced vocational training at a technical college".[31] Article 12 gives the children of migrant workers the same rights to all types of educational grant as nationals of the host State. In *Casagrande*[32] and *Alaimo*[33] the Court held that Article 12 referred not only to rules governing admission to courses but also to other educational facilities such as grants. To this could be added other benefits given to students, such as cheap travel between home and school or college. Article 12 is not confined to education or training provided within the host State. In *di Leo*,[34] the Court made it clear that, where a Member

---

[27] It may also be noted that discrimination between men and women in connection with access to vocational training is incompatible with Art. 4 of Dir. 76/207. That directive is discussed in more detail in Chap. 27.

[28] *supra,* para. 12.

[29] See also Dir. 77/486 on the education of the children of migrant workers, [1977] O.J. L199/32.

[30] Case C–7/94 [1995] E.C.R. I–1031, para. 25. *cf.* Arts 10(1) and 11 of Reg. 1612/68.

[31] Joined Cases 389 and 390/87, *Echternach and Another v. Minister for Education and Science* [1989] E.C.R. 723, para. 30; [1990] 2 C.M.L.R. 305.

[32] Case 9/74 [1974] E.C.R. 773; [1974] 2 C.M.L.R. 423.

[33] Case 68/74 [1975] E.C.R. 109; [1975] 1 C.M.L.R. 262.

[34] Case C–308/89 [1990] E.C.R. I–4185. See also Case C–3/90 *Bernini* [1992] E.C.R. I–1071.

State gives its nationals the opportunity to obtain a grant for education or training provided abroad, Article 12 required the child of a Community worker to be accorded the same advantage if he decides to pursue his studies in another country, even if it is the country of which the child is a national.

Although the benefit of Article 12 of Regulation 1612/68 is expressly confined to the children of migrant workers who are resident in the host State,[35] Article 7(2) of the regulation is not limited in that way. In *Meeusen v. Hoofddirectie van de Informatie Beheer Groep*,[36] a Belgian student applied to the Netherlands authorities for a grant when she began a course at a college of higher education in Antwerp in Belgium. The student was resident in Belgium, as were her parents, who were also of Belgian nationality. A connection with the Netherlands arose because the student's father was the director and sole shareholder of a company established there, by which her mother was employed. The relevant Netherlands legislation did not impose a residence requirement on the children of national workers and the Court ruled that such a requirement was to be considered discriminatory if imposed on the children of workers who were nationals of other Member States. It therefore held that "the dependent child of a national of one Member State who pursues an activity as an employed person in another Member State while maintaining his residence in the State of which he is a national can rely on Article 7(2) of Regulation No 1612/68 in order to obtain study finance under the same conditions as are applicable to children of nationals of the State of employment, and in particular without any further requirement as to the child's place of residence".[37]

The Court's judgment made it clear that the student's mother might well constitute a worker within the meaning of Article 39 (ex 48) of the Treaty, although the final decision on that question was for the national court. Had the national court concluded that she did not, that would have prevented the student from invoking Article 7(2) of Regulation 1612/68, but it would not have been fatal to her claim for a grant. This is because the Court went on to hold that the prohibition against discrimination based on nationality laid down in Article 43 (ex 52) of the Treaty (relevant because of the self-employed status of the student's father) produced the same result. As the Court put it, "the dependent child of a national of one Member State who pursues an activity as a self-employed person in another Member State while maintaining his residence in the State of which he is a national can obtain study finance under the same conditions as are applicable to children of nationals of the State of establishment, and in particular without any further requirement as to the child's place of residence".[38]

Entry and residence

The Court's case-law establishing that Community nationals had the right of access to vocational training courses (broadly defined) on equal terms with

---

[35] See Case 263/86 *Belgian State v. Humbel* [1988] E.C.R. 5365; [1989] 1 C.M.L.R. 393.
[36] Case C–337/97, judgment of June 8, 1999.
[37] Para. 25.
[38] Para. 30.

nationals of the Member State in which the course was to be provided did not make it clear whether they had a concomitant right to enter and take up residence in that State. Accordingly the Council adopted Directive 90/366 on the right of residence for students.[39] To facilitate access to vocational training, the Directive required Member States to grant a right of residence to any student who was a national of another Member State and to his or her dependent children, provided three conditions were met. First, the student had to have sufficient resources to avoid becoming a burden on the social assistance system of the host State. Secondly, the student had to be enrolled on a vocational training course at a recognised educational establishment. Thirdly, the student and his or her family had to be covered by comprehensive sickness insurance. The right of residence was limited to the duration of the course in question and the Directive did not give rise to a right to the payment of maintenance grants by the host State. Member States were permitted to derogate from its requirements only on grounds of public policy, public security or public health.

Before the deadline for giving effect to Directive 90/366 had expired, the Court held in *Raulin*[40] that "a student admitted to a course of vocational training might be unable to attend the course if he did not have a right of residence in the Member State where the course takes place. It follows that the principle of non-discrimination with regard to conditions of access to vocational training deriving from Articles 7 and 128 of the EEC Treaty implies that a national of a Member State who has been admitted to a vocational training course in another Member State enjoys, in this respect, a right of residence for the duration of the course". It seemed to follow from that ruling that Directive 90/366 could have been adopted under the second paragraph of Article 7 EEC, as the Commission had originally proposed. That provision (in the version then in force) required the Council to act in co-operation with the European Parliament.[41] The Council had in fact based the directive on Article 235 (now 308), under which it was required to act unanimously after consulting the European Parliament. In *Parliament v. Council*,[42] a challenge to the validity of the Directive on the ground that its legal basis was defective was upheld. However, for reasons of legal certainty the Court decided to maintain the effects of the directive until it had been replaced with a new directive adopted on the correct legal basis. On October 29, 1993, the Council accordingly adopted Directive 93/96 on the right of residence for students.[43] The deadline for giving effect to that Directive expired on December 31, 1993,[44] on which date Directive 90/366 ceased to produce any effects. Directive 93/96 is in substantially the same terms as its predecessor, but it may be doubtful, in the light of *Martínez Sala*,[45] whether some of the limitations it seeks to impose on the rights of students who are nationals of a Member State are compatible with their status as citizens of the Union.

---

[39] [1990] O.J. L180/30.
[40] Case C–357/89 [1992] E.C.R. I–1027, para. 34; [1994] 1 C.M.L.R. 227.
[41] The second para. of Art. 12 E.C. now requires the co-decision procedure to be followed.
[42] Case C–295/90 [1992] E.C.R. I–4193.
[43] [1993] O.J. L317/59.
[44] See Art. 6.
[45] *supra.*

According to its preamble, Directive 93/96 "does not apply to students who enjoy the right of residence by virtue of the fact that they are or have been effectively engaged in economic activities or are members of the family of a migrant worker". The rights of students in this position are governed by the rules on freedom of movement for workers and the self-employed. The migrant worker has the right to enter and take up residence in a Member State in order to enter into employment there. Once in employment he has the right, under the same conditions as a national of the Member State, to vocational training. In addition, we have seen that his right to social and tax advantages accords him the right to financial assistance from the host Member State on the same terms as nationals of that Member State. Retired workers who have been employed in the host Member State for a certain period of time have the right to continue to reside on the territory of that State and continue to enjoy the right to equality of treatment prescribed in Regulation 1612/68.[46]

If a migrant worker decides to give up his employment in order to pursue studies on a full-time basis either in the host Member State or any other Member State (for example his Member State of origin), this does not mean that he loses his status as such. As long as a worker has been in genuine employment, that is if he has pursued ". . . an activity which is effective and genuine, to the exclusion of other activities on such a small scale as to be regarded as purely marginal and ancillary" in respect of which he had received remuneration, he retains his status as a migrant worker. Thus in *Lawrie-Blum*,[47] a trainee teacher who gave lessons for which she was paid a salary below the starting level of a qualified teacher was held to be a worker and remained so when she began the second part of her studies leading to appointment as a secondary school teacher. Similarly, employment as a bank clerk for two and a half years followed by intermittent periods of other employment qualified a person to be considered a "worker" and to retain that status during a subsequent university course in languages and literature. The Court observed:

> "Persons who have previously pursued in the host Member State an effective and genuine activity as an employed person ... but who are no longer employed are nevertheless to be considered to be workers ... it is therefore clear that migrant workers are guaranteed certain rights linked to the status of worker even when they are longer in an employment relationship."[48]

In *Brown v. Secretary of State for Scotland*,[49] the Court held that a student who enters a Member State and works there for a short period with a view to subsequently undertaking studies in the host State in the same field of activity and who would not have been employed by his employer if he had not already been accepted for admission to university was nonetheless to be regarded as a worker. Steven Brown had dual French and British nationality. For eight months prior to commencing studies leading to a degree in electrical engineering at the University of Cambridge he was employed as a trainee engineer with Ferranti Plc

---

[46] See Art. 7, Reg. 1251/70; Chap. 14.
[47] Case 66/85 [1986] E.C.R. 2121; [1987] 3 C.M.L.R. 398.
[48] *Lair, supra,* paras. 33 and 36. See also *Bernini, supra.*
[49] *supra.*

in Edinburgh. His employment was described as "pre-industrial training". It was a pre-condition for such training that he should have been awarded a university place. The Court held that Mr Brown was a worker.

The members of the family of a migrant worker all have the right to enter and reside in the host Member State with him. As we have seen, under Article 12 of Regulation 1612/68, they are granted the right to be admitted to ". . . general, educational, apprenticeship and vocational training courses under the same conditions as nationals of that State." But what of the child whose parent leaves the host Member State whilst he is still pursuing his studies there? Must he leave with the parent from whom he derives the right to be in that Member State? This question arose in the *Echternach* case[50] where the Court held that education in the host Member State was to be regarded as a continuous process, so granting the child of a migrant worker the right to continue to reside and to pursue studies in the host Member State even after the return of his parents to their Member State of origin. In coming to this conclusion the Court was influenced by the fundamental aim of Article 12 of Regulation 1612/68, which is to ensure "as complete an integration as possible of workers and members of their families" in the host Member State. Such integration requires that the children of migrant workers should be able to complete their education in the host Member State.

LEGISLATIVE INITIATIVES IN THE FIELD OF EDUCATION AND VOCATIONAL TRAINING

The first concrete application of Article 128 EEC was Council Decision 63/266 laying down general principles for implementing a common vocational training policy.[51] The preamble to that Decision stated that implementation of an effective common vocational training policy would help to bring about freedom of movement for workers and that everyone should, during his working life, be able to receive adequate basic and advanced training and any necessary vocational re-training. While the scope of Decision 63/266 may have been limited, it played an important part in the reasoning which led the Court to conclude, in *Forcheri* and *Gravier*, that the conditions of access to vocational training fell within the scope of the Treaty.

The Court's case-law provided the impetus for a series of more ambitious legislative measures. In 1987, the Council introduced what is perhaps the best known of the Community's initiatives in this area, the Erasmus programme, which was designed to promote the mobility of university students.[52] Two years later, the Council adopted the Lingua programme to promote foreign language competence in the Community.[53] In 1994, after the entry into force of the Treaty on European Union, further steps to secure the implementation of a European Community vocational training policy were taken in the form of the Leonardo da Vinci programme.[54]

---

[50] *supra.*
[51] [1963–64] O.J. Eng. Spec.Ed., p. 25.
[52] See Dec. 87/327, [1987] O.J. L166/20. The validity of that decision was upheld in Case 242/87 *Commission v. Council* [1989] E.C.R. 1425; [1991] 1 C.M.L.R. 478, discussed above.
[53] Dec. 89/489, [1989] O.J. L239/24.
[54] See Dec. 94/819, [1994] O.J. L340/8.

The following year, the Erasmus and Lingua programmes were brought together by Decision 95/819[55] under the umbrella of the Socrates programme, which added several additional elements. Based on Articles 149 and 150 E.C., Decision 95/819 entered into force on January 1, 1995 and expired on December 31, 1999. According to Article 1, the Socrates programme was intended "to contribute to the development of quality education and training and the creation of an open European area for co-operation in education". The programme comprised three areas of action, two of which may be described as vertical and the third as horizontal. The first of the vertical areas of action represented a continuation of the Erasmus programme (a title it retained). It had two main objectives: to encourage transnational co-operation between universities "with the aim of gradually reinforcing the European dimension in higher education"[56] and to encourage student mobility by providing them with an opportunity to undertake a period of study in another Member State. The second of the vertical actions, known as Comenius, concerned school education. It was intended to encourage: (a) partnerships between schools in different Member States; (b) the education of the children of migrant workers as well as the children of occupational travellers, travellers and gypsies; (c) intercultural education; and (d) the updating and improvement of the skills of educational staff. The horizontal measures envisaged by Decision 95/819 applied at all levels of education and comprised steps to promote language skills (Lingua), open and distance learning and the exchange of information and experience on educational matters. Article 6(1) of Decision 95/819 required the Commission, in partnership with the Member States, to "ensure overall consistency" between the Socrates programme and other Community actions, notably the Leonardo da Vinci programme. The Socrates programme was open to the participation of associated countries of central and eastern Europe, Cyprus, Malta and the EFTA/EEA States. Expenditure of ECU 850 million over the period January 1, 1995 to December 31, 1999 was envisaged to support the programme.[57]

The Socrates programme was considered highly successful in boosting European co-operation in education at all levels and providing for structured transnational collaboration. In early 1999, the European Parliament and the Council accordingly adopted Decision 253/2000 establishing the second phase of the programme.[58] According to Article 1(3) of that decision, "[t]his programme shall contribute to the promotion of a Europe of knowledge through the development of the European dimension in education and training by promoting life-long learning, based on formal and informal education and training. It shall support the building up of the knowledge, skills and competences likely to foster active citizenship and employability." The emphasis on life-long learning is reflected in an "action" known as Grundtvig, which is designed to support adult education of both a formal and a non-formal kind.

---

[55] See Dec. 95/819, [1995] O.J. L87/10.
[56] Dec. 95/819, Annex, Chap. I, Action 1.
[57] See Art. 7(1) of Dec. 95/819.
[58] See [2000] O.J. L28/1.

The second phase of the Socrates programme runs from January 1, 2000 until December 31 2006.[59] A budget of Euro 1,850 million has been allocated to it over that period. However, Decision 253/2000 was not adopted until January 24, 2000 and did not enter into force until February 3, 2000, the date of its publication in the Official Journal.[60] In order to preserve the continuity of the programme, it was therefore decided that it should run on similar lines to the first phase during 2000. The more substantial changes contemplated by Decision 253/2000 took effect in 2001 in order to give potential participants and the competent authorities at both Community and national level more time to prepare for them.

---

[59] See Art. 1(2) of Dec. 253/2000.
[60] See Art. 15.

INDEX